OXFORD MEDICAL PUBLICATIONS

The Oxford textbook of clinical pharmacology and drug therapy

The Oxford textbook of clinical pharmacology and drug therapy

D. G. Grahame-Smith, MBBS, PhD, FRCP

Rhodes Professor of Clinical Pharmacology, University of Oxford
Honorary Director, Medical Research Council Unit of Clinical Pharmacology
Honorary Consultant Physician to the Oxfordshire Health Authority

and

J. K. Aronson, MBChB, DPhil, FRCP

Clinical Reader in Clinical Pharmacology (Wellcome Lecturer)
University of Oxford
Honorary Consultant in Clinical Pharmacology to the
Oxfordshire Health Authority

Oxford New York Toronto
OXFORD UNIVERSITY PRESS

Oxford University Press, Walton Street, Oxford OX2 6DP

Oxford New York Toronto
Delhi Bombay Calcutta Madras Karachi
Petaling Jaya Singapore Hong Kong Tokyo
Nairobi Dar es Salaam Cape Town
Melbourne Auckland

and associated companies in
Berlin Ibadan

Oxford is a trademark of Oxford University Press

First published 1984
Reprinted 1985
Reprinted 1987 (with corrections), 1990, 1991

British Library Cataloguing in Publication Data
Grahame-Smith, D. G.
The Oxford textbook of clinical pharmacology and drug therapy.
1. Pharmacology   2. Therapeutics
I. Title   II. Aronson, J. K.
615   RM21
ISBN 0-19-261172-0 (paperback)
ISBN 0-19-261492-4 (cased)

Library of Congress Cataloging in Publication Data
Grahame-Smith, David Grahame.
The Oxford textbook of clinical pharmacology and drug therapy.
(Oxford medical publications)
Bibliography: p.
Includes index.
1. Pharmacology.   2. Chemotherapy.   I. Aronson, J. K.   II. Title.   III. Series.   [DNLM:
1. Pharmacology, Clinical.   2. Drug therapy. WB 330 G7420]
RM300. G715   1984   615.5'8   83–27517
ISBN 0-19-261172-0 (paperback)
ISBN 0-19-261492-4 (cased)

Printed and bound in Great Britain
by Biddles Ltd, Guildford and King's Lynn

Preface

We have written this book with the needs of medical students in their clinical years paramount in our minds. Nevertheless, medical education is not restricted to the pre-qualification years, and we hope that the text may also prove of interest to those with more experience.

The book is composed of four sections. In Section I we have dealt with the general aspects of clinical pharmacology, our aim being to provide a scientific basis upon which a knowledge and understanding of drug therapy can be built.

Section II is brief and deals mainly with practical aspects of prescribing.

Section III is the drug therapy section, in which we have described the role of drugs in the treatment of disease. We have restricted ourselves to discussing drugs, and have not generally dealt with other matters concerned with the management of illness.

Section IV is a Pharmacopoeia. In this we have tried to bring together essential information about the majority of drugs mentioned elsewhere in the text. We felt that it was important to have this information in a separate section, but complementing the information about the use of drugs in disease. Too often the sciences of basic and clinical pharmacology are divorced from the practice of medicine, and one of our particular aims in writing this book has been to try to marry the scientific disciplines with the practical approach to drug therapy. The Pharmacopoeia will enable the student to recall those aspects of the basic and clinical pharmacology of individual drugs strictly relevant to the use of the drug in treatment, while the complementary drug therapy section will provide the means for understanding the role that each drug plays in the overall drug therapy of disease, interpreted in the light of the basic principles outlined in Section I.

We hope that this method of organization of the book, in addition to the information it contains, will enable the student to gain both the knowledge which is essential to the practice of safe and effective drug therapy and the understanding of how to effect that practice.

Some may be surprised that we have not included references. We did not feel this to be necessary. Instead we have included in Section II a chapter on sources of information, which for the interested student will lead to further reading.

We are conscious that in our approach to the subject we may not have hit on the ideal format first time round, and that there will be room for improvements. We shall welcome constructive criticism and suggestions.

There is a great deal of detailed information about drugs in this book, and we have tried very hard to make it accurate. However, it is always possible that errors have been missed, particularly in regard to the important matter of dosages. Furthermore, dosage schedules are constantly being revised and new adverse effects and drug interactions being described. For these reasons we urge all who use this book to consult pharmaceutical manufacturers' Data Sheets or other sources of information before prescribing or administering the drugs described in this book, or indeed any drugs. One cannot be too careful.

Oxford   D. G. G.-S.
June 1984   J. K. A.

Acknowledgements

We should like to thank Christine Causby for typing the manuscript so beautifully and accurately. Our thanks are due too to the staff of the Oxford University Press for their very great patience with us over the several years during which this book was taking shape, and for ever so gently keeping us at it.

Contents

SECTION III The drug therapy of disease

SECTION IV Pharmacopoeia

GENERAL INDEX

Drug dosages and availability

We have made every effort to check that the drug dosages listed in this book are correct. Nevertheless it is possible that mistakes may have occurred and have been missed in the checking. Furthermore new dosage regimens are constantly being devised and previously unrecognized adverse effects and interactions being described.

We therefore urge all who use this book to consult pharmaceutical manufacturers' data sheets, or other sources of information, before prescribing or administering the drugs described in this book, or indeed any drugs.

All the drugs mentioned in this book in the context of drug therapy were available for prescription in the UK at the time of going to press. However, the availability of drugs varies considerably both worldwide and from time to time, and national availability of drugs may have to be checked and may influence prescribing.

SECTION I
Clinical pharmacology: the
scientific basis of drug therapy

1 The four processes of drug therapy

The processes of drug therapy are very complex, although not more complex than those processes which underlie the illness for which therapy is being given. Historically modern drug therapy has developed from the herbal and folklore medicine of the past with its mixture of magic, empirical pharmacology, and faith of the patient in the doctor. Some cynics might hold that not much has changed! However there *have* been changes, even though the magic of drug therapy is still a potent force in its success. The changes which have occurred are in the understanding of the modes of action of the drugs we use and in the optimal application of those drugs to the treatment of disease. Underlying all this is an immense amount of work in the sciences of basic and clinical pharmacology.

The rationalization of drug therapy has lagged behind the understanding of disease processes for obvious reasons. The rational man obviously wants to be able to understand a pathological process and to make a precise diagnosis before instituting treatment. Until quite recently few specific and effective therapies were available and it is not, therefore, surprising that medical education and training has concentrated upon the art and science of diagnosis and the minute understanding of disease processes, neglecting, to a great extent, their treatment with drugs. The art and science of surgical treatment was not so neglected because manifestly it is profoundly effective in appropriate cases and demonstrates in a most dramatic way the doctor's concern and masterly activity on behalf of his patients.

In recent years, however, drug therapy has been undergoing a process of increasing rationalization. Advances in the understanding of the detailed events underlying the pathology of disease have allowed their manipulation with drugs. Conversely the empirical development of drugs useful in specific diseases has led to improvements in our understanding of those diseases. For example, the discovery of the precise biochemical abnormality in Parkinson's disease has led to the introduction of specific therapy with levodopa, while the study of the mode of action of psychotropic drugs has been one of the major factors in promoting the biochemical and pharmacological investigation of brain function in relation to mental disease.

One of the main aims of the approach to therapeutics outlined here is to analyse drug therapy within a discipline as strict as that by which a diagnosis is reached. It does not matter that in the course of this analysis there may arise questions to which there are at present no answers, for only by asking such questions can we begin to understand the depths of our understanding or ignorance.

The approach which we shall describe is one in which drug therapy is analysed step by step by various processes. The scheme as outlined can be applied to any type of drug therapy and, more attractively, can be applied to optimize any individual patient's drug therapy.

There are four main processes involved in drug therapy (see Fig. 1.1). They are:

1. The pharmaceutical process.
2. The pharmacokinetic process.
3. The pharmacodynamic process.
4. The therapeutic process.

These four processes can be more simply formulated as simple questions, one for each process:

1. Is the drug getting into the patient?
2. Is the drug getting to its site of action?
3. Is the drug producing the required pharmacological effect?
4. Is the pharmacological effect being translated into a therapeutic effect?

1.1. PHARMACEUTICAL PROCESS: Is the drug getting into the patient?

The pharmaceutical process is concerned with all those factors inherent in the pharmaceutical formulation and presentation of a drug preparation which determine whether or not it is absorbed (in the case of oral, rectal, or parenteral administration) or reaches the appropriate site of action for an appropriate time in the desired form (for topical preparations). Strictly speaking we are not here concerned with the process of absorption itself but with the properties of the drug preparation, e.g. tablet content of drug, drug crystal size, tablet compression, excipients, and predictability of tablet properties such as rates of disintegration and dissolution.

Although it is not strictly relevant to the pharmaceutical process it is convenient here to remember to consider the question of patient compliance since that is an important factor in determining whether or not the drug gets into the patient.

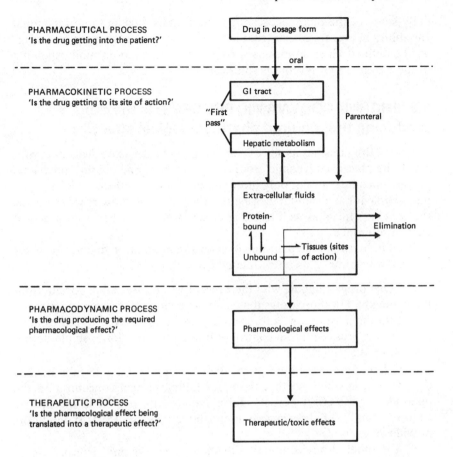

Fig. 1.1. The four main processes involved in drug therapy. Compare this figure with Fig. 6.1 in which more detail is given.

1.2. PHARMACOKINETIC PROCESS: Is the drug getting to its site of action?

The pharmacokinetic process is concerned with the absorption, distribution, and elimination (by metabolism and excretion) of drugs. It can be studied in the patient by measurement of drug and metabolite concentrations in blood and/or urine over periods of time after dosing. It is evident that, however many structural and metabolic barriers drug molecules have to pass, the concentration of a drug at its site of action must have the blood concentration as one of its major determinants. Thus, proper mathematical description of the pharmacokinetic characteristics of a drug can provide a great deal of information of relevance to both the pharmacological and the therapeutic or toxic effect.

By study of the pharmacokinetic process individual and interindividual variability in absorption, distribution, metabolism, and excretion of drugs can be defined. Such studies have contributed much to our understanding of the variability of responses to drugs.

1.3. PHARMACODYNAMIC PROCESS: Is the drug producing the required pharmacological effect?

When the drug reaches its site of action it has a pharmacological effect with which the pharmacodynamic process is concerned. The pharmacodynamic process encompasses not only those pharmacological effects which may be responsible for an eventual therapeutic effect but also those responsible for the adverse effects as well as some effects which may be of no practical clinical relevance.

The link between the pharmacokinetic and pharmacodynamic processes is not always simple, as a few related examples will show.

1. Some drugs combine with their receptors quickly and dissociate from them quickly. For those drugs the pharmacological effects wax and wane in time with the plasma concentration. An example is the use of intravenous sodium nitroprusside in the control of blood pressure, for example during neurosurgery.

2. Other drugs combine with their receptors but do not readily dissociate from them so that despite a falling plasma concentration the pharmacological effect persists and is not directly related to the plasma concentration. The irreversible monoamine oxidase (MAO) inhibitors provide an example.

3. Yet other drugs combine with their receptors and, irrespective of their rates of association or dissociation, set in train a sequence of events which runs on despite a falling plasma concentration. An example is that of the anti-inflammatory effects of corticosteroids.

It can be very difficult to sort out the relationships between plasma concentrations and the pharmacological effects with drugs of types 2 and 3 above.

1.4. THERAPEUTIC PROCESS: Is the pharmacological effect being translated into a therapeutic effect?

If the patient is to benefit from drug therapy the pharmacological effect of the drug must result in clinical benefit. Of course this part of the exercise presumes that the detailed nature of the pharmacological effect responsible for the therapeutic action of the drug is known and this is not always so, as in the case of tricyclic antidepressants in depression. One of the problems here is that the question: Is the pharmacological effect translated into a therapeutic effect? can be countered by two further questions.

(a) What do you consider to be the pharmacological effect of a drug?
(b) What do you mean by the therapeutic effect?

In case the reader thinks that this is unnecessary obscurantism, an example will illustrate the point.

Consider the treatment of asymptomatic hypertension with, say, propranolol, a non-selective β-adrenoceptor antagonist. There is no doubt that propranolol lowers the blood pressure. But how does it do it? Presumably β-blockade in the heart is involved, but is the hypotensive effect exerted through the fall in cardiac output, or through subsequent adaptive changes, such as alterations in ventricular muscle performance, baroreceptor reflex arcs, or the renin-angiotensin system via renal β-adrenoceptor blockade? The practical man will deal only with the observed hypotensive effect and consider that to be the pharmacodynamic action of the drug. In the management of the hypertensive patient plainly this is the correct attitude. However, the clinical scientist will be forgiven for pondering upon the exact mechanism by which propranolol produces its effects, because hidden in the responses to the drug are the mechanisms causing the hypertension, the answers to why some patients respond better than others, and the details from which the relationships amongst the pharmacokinetic, pharmacodynamic, and therapeutic processes can be elucidated.

The question: What is the therapeutic effect? may appear even more stupid, but in fact there are several possible answers. One might for example consider a lowering of the blood pressure to be the therapeutic effect but this does not make the patient feel any better since he is asymptomatic and may indeed make him feel worse. In any case the lowering of the blood pressure is the first stage toward the ultimate aim which is to try to reduce the incidence of myocardial infarction, stroke, heart failure, and renal failure. So the lowering of blood pressure produced by the treatment is probably closer to the pharmacodynamic action than to the therapeutic action, which in an individual patient is going to be virtually impossible to calculate. Assessment of the therapeutic action in this case is going to depend upon the results of large-scale clinical trials of the efficacy of antihypertensive drugs in the prevention of the complications of hypertension, evaluated by statistical methods. It will probably never be possible for any one practitioner to know from his personal experience whether the treatment of asymptomatic hypertension produces any real benefit.

Consideration of this example of very common therapy reveals many problems. It is the very analysis of drug therapy in this way which brings these sorts of problems to light. In the following four chapters we shall consider this approach of analysing drug therapy through the pharmaceutical, pharmacokinetic, pharmacodynamic, and therapeutic processes to impose upon drug therapy the same kind of academic discipline as exists for the process of diagnosis with its component processes of history-taking, examination, and investigation. That in its application in the clinical setting unanswerable questions may be raised is all to the good. The only word of caution is that one should not allow one's ignorance of the answers to such questions to interfere with the treatment of a patient with a drug therapy which has been shown, however empirically, to be definitely effective.

2 The pharmaceutical process
Is the drug getting into the patient?

The two important factors which determine whether a drug gets into the patient or not are:

1. Patient compliance.
2. Bioavailability (systemic availability).

2.1. PATIENT COMPLIANCE

A prescription is a complicated, often rather imprecise set of instructions. Consider the following prescription for a woman of 60 with atrial fibrillation, heart failure, hypertension, diabetes mellitus, osteo-arthritis, depression, and insomnia, who has an acute urinary infection:

propranolol 80 mg t.d.s.
bendrofluazide 10 mg daily
digoxin 0·25 mg daily
ibuprofen 400 mg t.d.s.
chlorpropamide 250 mg daily
cotrimoxazole tabs 2 twice daily
amitriptyline 25 mg t.d.s.
nitrazepam 5 mg o.n.

There may be every medical justification for the prescription of each of these drugs, but to organize oneself to remember to take correctly 18 tablets a day, three drugs to be taken three times a day, one drug twice daily, three drugs once daily in the morning, and one (nitrazepam) at bedtime, is a formidable task.

It is not surprising, therefore, as numerous studies have shown, that patient compliance with complicated prescriptions is poor. However, poor compliance extends to simple prescriptions as well. It is not easy to put a precise figure on the frequency of non-compliance because the problem is difficult to study and this is reflected in the results of various studies which show the incidence of non-compliance to vary between about 10 per cent and 90 per cent of patients. Non-compliance is so common that it should be the first matter to check when drug therapy appears ineffective. Similarly mistakes in medicine-taking should be checked in the event of unexpected drug toxicity. Simple therapeutic regimens, patient education, manipulation of drug formulation, and avoidance of adverse effects, are all measures which might be expected to improve drug compliance. These matters are discussed in more detail in Chapter 12.

2.2. BIOAVAILABILITY (systemic availability)

Bioavailability (or systemic availability) is a term used to describe the proportion of administered drug which reaches the site of action. It is usually applied to oral preparations, although the pharmaceutical formulation has an important influence on the access of the contained drug to the site of action, whatever the route of administration. The precise meaning of the term is best explained by reference to Fig. 2.1 in which the several steps involved are defined.

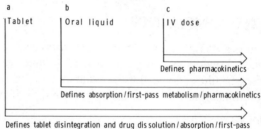

Fig. 2.1. A diagrammatic definition of bioavailability (or systemic availability). The bioavailability of a drug formulation can be defined as the amount of the administered drug which reaches the systemic circulation, and hence the site of action, as a proportion of the dose. This definition should also incorporate some notion of the *rate* at which that happens.

1. When an intravenous dose of the drug is given it all enters the systemic circulation, producing 100 per cent bioavailability. From the plot of plasma concentration of the drug versus time with or without urinary drug concentration analyses, the way the body handles the drug can be defined, i.e. Fig. 2.1(c).

2. When an oral liquid solution of the drug is given all the drug is theoretically available to the gastrointestinal mucosa for absorption. The plasma concentration versus time plot and urinary analyses of drug and metabolites compared with the intravenous data give an index of the degree of absorption and the effect of the first passage through the liver of a dose of the drug, i.e. Fig.2.1(b), (c).

3. When a tablet or capsule is given, by following the plasma concentration versus time plot and cumulative urinary drug and metabolite excretion, and by comparing these data with those collected after dosage with an oral liquid form, one can define those factors intrinsic to the tablet or capsule form which affect the ultimate bioavailability. These factors include the rate of disintegration of the tablet, and the rate of dissolution of the drug particles in the intestinal fluid. This may be termed 'pharmaceutical availability', i.e. Fig. 2.1(a), (b), (c).

Generally, prescribing doctors depend upon the skills of the pharmacist and pharmaceutical chemist to provide preparations of drugs of high stability and predictable pharmaceutical availability which should reach the standards set by national pharmacopoeias. The physical factors which have to be taken into account and controlled are:

(a) Particle size. Smaller drug particles dissolve more quickly.

(b) The drug form. Whether the drug is in crystalline form, a salt, or complexed with a tablet constituent will affect the rate of dissolution.

(c) Tablet compression and excipients. These factors affect the rate of tablet disintegration.

(d) Other tablet excipients. These affect the interaction of the drug with aqueous intestinal juices and therefore the rate of dissolution.

If two formulations are of equal bioavailability they are said to be bioequivalent. If formulations differ in their bioavailability they are said to be bioinequivalent. There have been cases in which problems of bioinequivalence caused by manufacturing factors have had serious clinical effects. In Australia in 1968 an outbreak of phenytoin toxicity occurred because of the switch from calcium sulphate to lactose as an apparently inert tablet excipient. This change rendered the phenytoin more soluble and increased its bioavailability with a consequent increase in plasma concentration and an increased incidence of toxicity. Variability in the bioavailability of digoxin led, in 1975, to the imposition of new pharmacopoeial standards for digoxin tablets in both the USA and the UK. This problem came to light because of the application of plasma digoxin concentration measurements following their introduction in 1968, when variable bioavailability of digoxin from different preparations was discovered.

Alterations in pharmaceutical availability are of particular importance in the case of drugs with a low therapeutic index (i.e. drugs for which the dose which will result in a toxic effect is very little more than the dose which will result in a therapeutic effect). Digoxin and phenytoin are examples of such drugs and if a patient is on effective therapy with a preparation of low availability, then switching to a preparation of high availability can tip the patient into toxicity.

The definition of bioavailability given at the beginning of this section incorporates the process of absorption, which is dealt with further in Chapter 3. The pharmaceutical and chemical skills in drug development are aimed not only at providing formulations which will deliver the drug in a soluble form to the site of absorption, but even before that stage is reached the pharmaceutical chemist will have had to produce a molecule which, in the case of an oral medication, is stable in the gastro-intestinal juices, and capable of absorption.

The process of drug absorption from oral formulations involves passage of the drug across the gastro-intestinal mucosa, into the mesenteric circulation. For the sake of our discussion here (and it is merely a matter of arbitrary definition and not some absolute truth) absorption will be taken to mean only the process of passage across the gastro-intestinal mucosa into the capillary blood of the mesenteric circulation, and not to include the appearance of the drug in the systemic circulation (Fig. 6.1). This distinction is made because between the gut and the systemic circulation lies the liver, the great 'poison trap', protecting the systemic circulation from numerous potential toxins which enter the gastro-intestinal tract. Evolutionary experience of environmental toxins has provided the liver with an extraordinary range of detoxicating mechanisms for natural toxins which are active in detoxicating many drugs. The very presence of the trap, however, means that for many drugs all that is absorbed does not enter the systemic circulation intact. This is known as the 'first-pass effect' (the second and subsequent passes being as the drug comes round in the hepatic artery as part of the systemic circulation and therefore in much lower concentrations).

As far as therapeutics is concerned the most practical definition of bioavailability is that which incorporates some guide to the rate and extent of appearance of the drug in the systemic circulation but it is most important to understand the various component parts of the process which enables them to be analysed separately. The scheme outlined above will help to understand those component parts.

2.3. SPECIAL DRUG FORMULATIONS

Before leaving the subject of bioavailability it is worthwhile considering some special pharmaceutical factors involved in the bioavailability of certain preparations.

2.3.1. Injections

The absorption of drugs from parenteral sites may be retarded by the use of thick oils, which slow down diffusion of the drug from the site of injection, e.g. vasopressin tannate in oil in the treatment of diabetes insipidus; fluphenazine decanoate in oil in the treatment of schizophrenia.

Control of absorption of insulin from the site of injection is afforded by differences in the physical state of the insulin, e.g. crystalline or non-crystalline, differences in the zinc or protein content, and in the nature and pH of the buffer in which it is suspended. At one end of the scale is insulin injection BP, which is non-crystalline or amorphous, soluble insulin with a rapid onset and short duration of action (about 6h); at the other end is ultralente insulin with large crystals of insulin and a high zinc content, suspended in a solution of sodium acetate–sodium chloride (pH 7·1–7·5), with an onset of action at about 7h and a duration of action of about 36h.

Superficially one might think that intramuscular administration would always provide better bioavailability than oral administration. This is not so, a prime example being phenytoin. Intramuscular phenytoin results in about half the plasma concentration produced by an equal oral dose, because of precipitation at the site of injection. This should be borne in mind when changing the patient from oral to intramuscular phenytoin or vice versa, or when using intramuscular phenytoin as routine prophylaxis against epilepsy after intracranial operations.

Local anaesthetic preparations are available containing adrenaline which by causing vasoconstriction prevents the local anaesthetic, say lignocaine, from being carried away from the site of injection by the circulation. This prolongs the effect of the local anaesthetic but incidentally provides a potential interaction with tricyclic antidepressants and MAO inhibitors.

2.3.2. Inhalations

Inhaled formulations are of several forms with different intentions. Sodium cromoglycate is formulated as a powder for inhalation designed to have a local stabilizing effect upon mast cells in the bronchial mucosa in the treatment of bronchial asthma. Salbutamol aerosol, on the other hand, is designed to produce bronchodilatation by a metered dose (100 μg) of droplets of a size 2–5 μm down the bronchial tree to bronchiolar level. Just how much actual drug reaches the bronchial mucosa and affects either mast cell function or bronchiolar muscle contraction directly is uncertain. Plainly it will depend upon how the patient uses the inhaler, the depth of inspiration, and so on, but it has been reckoned that only about 10 per cent of any drug in an aerosol or other form for inhalation reaches the bronchial tree, the rest being lost in the air, absorbed from the oropharynx, or swallowed.

An ergotamine aerosol is available for the treatment of migraine. The metered dose is 360 μg, which is close to the usual dose for intramuscular or oral administration. However in migraine, the nausea and vomiting associated with the illness may impair the absorption of oral therapy and ergotamine tends to be most effective when given very early following the onset of an attack. The aerosol is designed to produce rapid absorption from the tracheobronchial mucosa thus avoiding the absorption problems posed by other routes of administration.

The semi-synthetic glucocorticoids, beclomethasone and betamethasone have been formulated in aerosol preparations for the treatment of bronchial asthma, and since they undoubtedly have a steroid-sparing effect (i.e. it is possible to switch from *oral* glucocorticoids to one of the *aerosol* preparations), they avoid the adverse systemic effects of corticosteroid therapy, and yet control the asthma. It may be assumed that the glucocorticoid is having an anti-inflammatory effect locally in the bronchial tree.

2.3.3. Combination products in oral therapy

Combination products for oral use are widely available but only under certain circumstances may they be acceptable and even, for reasons of convenience, preferable. These circumstances arise when the following criteria are met:

(a) When the frequency of administration of the two drugs is the same.

(b) When the *fixed doses* in the combination product are therapeutically and optimally effective in the majority of cases (i.e. it is not necessary to alter the dose of one drug independently of the other).

Good examples of well tried combination products are:

(a) Combination products of aspirin or paracetamol with codeine, in which two agents achieve their analgesic effects through different mechanisms and summate therapeutically but not with regard to adverse reactions.

(b) Levodopa together with a peripheral decarboxylase inhibitor, either benserazide or carbidopa. Here the peripheral action of the decarboxylase inhibitor blocks the peripheral metabolism of L-dopa which is 'spared' and which enters the brain, where its conversion to the pharmacologically active product dopamine produces the therapeutic effect in Parkinson's disease.

(c) The combined oral contraceptive containing ethinyloestradiol and a progestogen such as norethisterone.

(d) Triple vaccine containing a combination of vaccines against diphtheria, tetanus, and pertussis.

(e) Ferrous sulphate and folic acid tablets for the prophylaxis of anaemia in pregnancy.

There are many other examples of valuable combinations (see Table 2.1), but it is also necessary to give some examples of what might be considered bad combinations which are presently on the market:

(a) A combination of phenylbutazone 50 mg and prednisone 1·25 mg with the therapeutic indications of rheumatoid arthritis, osteoarthritis, and ankylosing spondylitis. This combination offends both criteria above, i.e. the factors of frequency of administration and of independent dosage schedules.

Table 2.1 *Potential advantages of combination products*

Potential advantages	Examples
Improved compliance	Antituberculous drugs (rifampicin + isoniazid)
	Ferrous sulphate + folic acid (pregnancy)
Ease of administration	Triple vaccine (diphtheria, tetanus, pertussis)
Synergistic or additive effects	Trimethoprim + sulphonamides (e.g. co-trimoxazole)
	Aspirin + codeine (simple analgesia)
	Paracetamol + metoclopramide (migraine)
	Combined oral contraceptive
	(oestrogen + progestogen)
	Pyrimethamine + dapsone (malaria prophylaxis)
Decreased adverse effects	L-dopa + decarboxylase inhibitor (Parkinson's disease)
	Diuretics (potassium-wasting + potassium-sparing)
	Antacids (aluminium salts + magnesium salts)

(b) The combination of methyldopa 250 mg and hydrochlorothiazide 15 mg with the indication of hypertension. It is difficult to see how one can possibly employ these two constituent drugs optimally in the treatment of hypertension, and both criteria are again offended.

(c) The combination of amitriptyline 12·5 mg and chlordiazepoxide 5 mg for the treatment of mixed anxiety and depression with a recommended dosage of one capsule three times daily. Again there is no flexibility of dosage and probably different optimal dosage frequencies of the two components.

2.3.4. Slow-release preparations

Slow-release and controlled-release preparations are being increasingly used through the development of advanced pharmaceutical technology which allows the formulation of preparations from which drugs may be slowly absorbed. Some of these preparations are useful for particular reasons and good examples are those of enteric-coated aspirin, the use of which leads to a lower incidence of gastro-intestinal erosion, and slow-release preparations of anti-arrhythmic drugs such as quinidine and procainamide, which allow less frequent administration through the day than would be possible with ordinary formulations. It is difficult to know whether the production of some so-called slow-release preparations is a real contribution to therapeutics or not. Take for instance the slow-release β-adrenoceptor antagonists propranolol and oxprenolol. There is increasing evidence that once a day therapy of the ordinary tablets of these compounds is as effective in the treatment of hypertension and that slow-release preparations may therefore be unnecessary.

2.3.5. Sublingual and rectal preparations

Drugs absorbed through the buccal or rectal mucosa enter the venous circulation and pass into the systemic circulation intact, avoiding first-pass metabolism in the liver. Glyceryl trinitrate is administered sublingually when it is effective in doses about ten times less than those required by the oral route. In addition, its administration in this fashion results in a very rapid therapeutic effect. Aminophylline and indomethacin are frequently given by suppository though here the object is not so much to avoid metabolism as to avoid gastric irritation.

These, and many other examples, illustrate the several ways in which pharmaceutical chemists can manipulate drug formulations in order to meet a particular therapeutic objective.

3   The pharmacokinetic process
Is the drug getting to its site of action?

The pharmacokinetic process comprises:

1. Drug absorption and bioavailability.
2. Drug distribution.
3. Drug metabolism.
4. Drug excretion.

3.1. DRUG ABSORPTION AND BIOAVAILABILITY

After oral administration a drug will reach the systemic circulation intact only if it is absorbed from the gastro-intestinal tract and if it escapes metabolism both in the gastro-intestinal tract and in the liver.

In practice, however, it can be difficult to characterize the separate contributions of absorption and metabolism to the changes in plasma drug concentrations with time after an oral dose. The concept of bioavailability or systemic availability has therefore been developed (see Fig. 2.1).

The bioavailability of a drug is defined in terms of (a) the *amount* of administered drug which reaches the systemic circulation intact, and (b) the *rate* at which that happens. The *rate* of bioavailability depends upon pharmaceutical factors (see Chapter 2) and gastro-intestinal absorption, metabolism being relatively unimportant. On the other hand the *extent* of bioavailability depends on both the extent of absorption *and* the extent of metabolism.

These two components of bioavailability may be assessed by considering Fig. 3.1. The three curves shown represent the theoretical plasma concentrations resulting over a period of time following the oral administration of three different preparations of the same dose of the same drug. Each curve contains three features of interest:

1. The peak height.
2. The time taken to reach the peak ($t_{\max}$).
3. The total area under the curve (AUC).

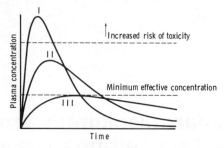

Fig. 3.1. The theoretical plasma concentrations resulting over a period of time following the oral administration of three different preparations of the same dose of the same drug. The profile in each case depends on the rate and extent of systemic availability.

The peak height and t_{max} are measures of the *rate* of availability and the total AUC is a measure of its *extent* (i.e. the proportion of administered drug which reaches the systemic circulation intact). In the three hypothetical cases the *rates* of bioavailability are clearly different. In the case of preparation I bioavailability is fast, perhaps too fast, leading to potentially toxic plasma concentrations. Preparation II is not so quickly bioavailable, but plasma concentrations are never in the potentially toxic range. Preparation III is slowly bioavailable and plasma concentrations are always subtherapeutic. However, the *extent* of bioavailability, as assessed by the total AUC, is the same in each case.

For drugs whose action may depend on the threshold plasma concentration achieved after a single dose (e.g. analgesics) such differences may be important. Thus a soluble aspirin preparation which gives a curve like preparation II would be preferable for the rapid relief of pain to an enteric-coated preparation giving a curve like preparation III. The latter would be more useful in the long-term treatment of rheumatoid arthritis, since accumulation could occur to therapeutic concentrations during long-term therapy. Sometimes a curve of type I can be therapeutically useful, for example if a very fast rate of absorption is needed in order to produce a quick therapeutic effect, e.g. sublingual glyceryl trinitrate in the treatment of angina pectoris. With glyceryl trinitrate the fast rate of absorption of a large amount of drug leads to the rapid relief of symptoms but also to the adverse effect of headache caused by vasodilatation of extracranial blood vessels. For drugs whose action is related to a steady-state concentration after multiple dosing the differences in rate of bioavailability become less important and the chief consideration is the extent.

3.1.1. Factors affecting rate of absorption

(a) Gastro-intestinal motility

Since drug absorption occurs mainly in the upper part of the small intestine, alterations in the rate of gastric emptying will result in corresponding alterations in the rate of absorption. In migraine the rate of absorption of analgesics may be reduced because of reduced gastric motility and the response to oral analgesics may be delayed. This delay can be reduced by using metoclopramide, a drug which increases gastric emptying rate.

These changes in rate of absorption depend on the rapid dissolution of the drug before it reaches the site of absorption. When the rate of dissolution is much longer than gastric emptying time then enhanced gastro-intestinal motility may reduce both the rate and extent of absorption, as in the case of enteric-coated preparations which may on occasions pass through the gut intact.

(b) Malabsorptive states

Although one would expect drug absorption to be impaired in patients with malabsorptive states, such is not always the case. For example, the absorption of propranolol, co-trimoxazole, and cephalexin are *increased* in patients with coeliac disease, as is the absorption of propranolol in Crohn's disease. Digoxin, however, is less well absorbed in patients with coeliac disease, radiation-induced enteritis, and other forms of gastro-intestinal disease, and thyroxine absorption is impaired in coeliac disease.

(c) Food

Food may either enhance or impair the rate and may also affect the extent of absorption. For example, eggs impair iron absorption, and milk (and indeed any calcium, aluminium, magnesium, or ferrous salt) impairs tetracycline absorption by the formation of an insoluble chelate. The rate, but not the extent, of absorption of most penicillin antibiotics is impaired by food while that of hydralazine, propranolol, metoprolol and nitrofurantoin is increased. Fat specifically improves the absorption of griseofulvin. The mechanisms of these effects are mostly unknown. They are generally of little clinical importance.

3.1.2. First-pass metabolism

An important factor separate from absorption across the gut wall which is often a determinant of bioavailability is the extent of metabolism occurring before the drug enters the systemic circulation. The organs which may be involved in this first-pass metabolism are the gut, the liver, and the lungs (the last being relatively unimportant).

The sites of first-pass metabolism are as follows:

(a) The gut lumen. For example, benzylpenicillin and insulin are both almost completely inactivated by gastric acid and proteolytic enzymes respectively.

(b) The gut wall. For example, chlorpromazine and isoprenaline both of which are sulphated. Metabolism of tyramine by gut wall monoamine oxidase (MAO) forms the basis of the interaction between amine-containing foods and MAO inhibitors (see Chapter 10).

(c) The liver. The liver is a much more important site of first-pass metabolism. For example, lignocaine is metabolized to two active compounds which have less anti-arrhythmic activity than lignocaine itself, but which are more toxic. Propranolol is metabolized to 4-hydroxypropranolol, which is pharmacologically active.

When first-pass metabolism results in the formation of compounds with less pharmacological activity than the parent compound then there is a decrease in efficacy of the drug by comparison with the effect that would be achieved following, say, intravenous administration. In some cases this may be surmountable by using an oral dose greater than that which is effective by the intravenous route. For example, by the i.v. route, propranolol produces a β-blocking effect in a single dose of about 5 mg but a dose of about 100 mg as a single dose would be needed to produce a similar effect after oral administration. In some cases metabolism renders oral therapy impossible with conventional pharmaceutical formulations (e.g. lignocaine, insulin). In such cases the drug must be given by another route, usually intravenously, intramuscularly, or subcutaneously, but in some cases it may be possible to administer the drug via the gastro-intestinal tract. For example, the sublingual route may be used for the administration of glyceryl trinitrate, since absorption will be directly into the systemic circulation. The rectal route, with drainage via the inferior rectal veins directly into the systemic circulation, offers a comparable alternative, but is more commonly used to achieve a topical effect on the rectum and colon (e.g. prednisolone enemas in the treatment of ulcerative colitis) or to minimize adverse effects occurring in the upper gut (e.g. indomethacin, which may cause gastric ulceration).

Hepatic drug metabolism is discussed in more detail below.

3.2. DRUG DISTRIBUTION

Many drugs are bound to circulating proteins, usually albumin, but also globulins, lipoproteins, and acid glycoproteins. Only that fraction of drug which is non-protein-bound can bind to cellular receptors, pass across tissue membranes, and gain access to cellular enzymes, thus being distributed to other body tissues, being metabolized, and being excreted (e.g. by the kidney). Thus changes in protein binding may sometimes cause changes in drug distribution. For such changes to be important, however, the following criteria must be met:

(a) The bound drug must constitute more than 90 per cent of the total drug in the plasma

This is because changes in protein binding are usually of the order of a few per cent. Thus a decrease of 5 per cent binding for a drug which is only 20 per cent bound (e.g. digoxin) results in a change from 80 to 85 per cent of free drug, a negligible effect. A similar change in binding of a drug which is 95 per cent bound (e.g. phenytoin) results in a change from 5 to 10 per cent of unbound drug, a relatively large, and therefore important effect.

(b) The extent of distribution of the drug to tissues must be small

If the drug is widely distributed then even large increases in the amount of unbound drug in the plasma will be unimportant since the increment of unbound drug, small in comparison with total body content, will be readily redistributed in body tissues and the unbound concentration in the plasma will rise by a negligible amount.

Protein binding, therefore, is only important in practice for a few drugs, principally phenytoin, warfarin, and tolbutamide. The extent of protein binding of some commonly used drugs is given in Table 3.1.

Table 3.1 *Values of percentage protein binding for some commonly used drugs*

>99% bound	95–99% bound	90–95% bound	50–90% bound	<50% bound
Phenylbutazone*†	Amitriptyline	Diazoxide	Aspirin*†	Alcohol
Thyroxine	Chlorpromazine	Disopyramide*	Carbamazepine	Aminoglycosides
Tri-iodothyronine	Clofibrate*	Glibenclamide	Chloramphenicol	Chlorpropamide
Warfarin‡	Diazepam	Phenytoin‡	Chloroquine	Digoxin
	Digitoxin	Propranolol	Disopyramide*	Disopyramide*
	Frusemide	Tolbutamide‡	Lignocaine	Insulin
	Gold salts	Valproate	Quinidine	Paracetamol
	Heparin		Sulphonamides†	Phenobarbitone
	Imipramine		Theophylline	Procainamide
				Trichloroethanol†
				(chloral
				metabolite)

* Protein-binding saturable. Disopyramide binding varies between 35 per cent at high therapeutic doses and 95 per cent at low doses.
† May be precipitant drug in protein-binding displacement interactions (see Chapter 10).
‡ May be object drug in protein-binding displacement interactions (see Chapter 10).

The factors which may cause an increase in the fraction of circulating unbound drug are:

1. Renal impairment in which the binding characteristics of drugs for albumin are altered by unknown mechanisms.

2. Severe hypoalbuminaemia (plasma albumin concentration less than 20–25 g/l).

3. The last trimester of pregnancy, due in part to hypoalbuminaemia, but also to other as yet unidentified factors.

4. Displacement by other drugs (see Chapter 10).

5. Saturability of protein binding at increasing plasma drug concentrations within the therapeutic range.

The second aspect of drug distribution is that of distribution to the tissues of the body, the extent of which varies widely from drug to drug. Some drugs are limited in distribution to body fluids while others are bound extensively in body tissues. The apparent volume of distribution (see the later sections in this chapter on pharmacokinetic calculations) gives a mathematical measure of the *extent* of tissue distribution, but does not give any *anatomical* or *physiological* information about that distribution.

The following factors may influence the distribution of drugs to different tissues.

(a) Plasma protein binding.

See above.

(b) Specific receptor sites in tissues

For example, the binding of cardiac glycosides to Na^+, K^+-ATPase in cell membranes throughout the body.

(c) Regional blood flow

For drugs which are highly extracted (have a high 'extraction ratio') from the blood by a particular tissue, small changes in tissue blood flow lead to large changes in the distribution of drug to that tissue. Well-perfused organs such as the heart, kidneys, and liver tend to accumulate drugs to a greater extent that poorly perfused organs such as fat and bone.

(d) Lipid solubility

Since cell membranes are composed mostly of lipoproteins, non-polar drugs, which are relatively lipid soluble, will distribute more readily to tissues than polar compounds (e.g. compare digoxin with digitoxin, Table 3.4).

(e) Active transport

A few drugs are actively transported across cell membranes, for example, the adrenergic neurone blocking drugs [see also (g) below].

(f) Disease

Some diseases are associated with altered distribution characteristics of some drugs, the underlying mechanisms often being obscure. The effects of disease on plasma protein binding have been mentioned above. Renal failure, apart from its effect on protein binding, may also be associated with a decreased distribution of some drugs (e.g. insulin, digoxin), as is hyperthyroidism (cardiac glycosides). This change in distribution results, for example, in higher plasma digitalis concentrations than expected but the interpretation of plasma digitalis concentrations in these circumstances is not clear (see Chapter 7). In cardiac failure the distribution of some anti-arrhythmic drugs is decreased (e.g. disopyramide, lignocaine). Obesity influences the distribution of drugs which are highly fat soluble (e.g. anaesthetics).

(g) The effects of other drugs (see Chapter 10)

Tricyclic antidepressants inhibit the active transport of the adrenergic neurone blockers, reducing their access to the site of action in the brain and thus reducing their efficacy. Quinidine decreases the distribution of digoxin by an unknown mechanism.

(h) Miscellaneous examples

These include the binding of tetracyclines to growing bones and teeth (because of the formation of a calcium chelate, resulting in mottling of the teeth and increased bone fragility in children), and the binding of chloroquine to retinal melanin with consequent retinopathy.

3.3. DRUG METABOLISM

Most drug metabolism occurs in the liver, although some occurs elsewhere (e.g. suxamethonium in the plasma, insulin and vitamin D in the kidneys, cytosine arabinoside, cyclophosphamide and other cytotoxic drugs in many cells, acetylcholine and other neurotransmitters at synapses and within nerves).

The end result of drug metabolism is of inactivation, although during the process compounds with pharmacological activity may be formed. There are three classes of metabolic events.

3.3.1. Metabolism of a pharmacologically inactive compound to one with pharmacological activity

Inactive drugs, administered for the known effects of their active metabolites are called 'pro-drugs' and the reasons for their use are numerous.

(a) Improved absorption

For example, carfecillin and talampicillin are better absorbed than their active counterparts carbenicillin and ampicillin.

(b) Prevention of an adverse effect on the gastro-intestinal tract

For example, the incidence of diarrhoea is less with talampicillin than with ampicillin; the incidence of gastro-intestinal bleeding is less with benorylate than with aspirin.

(c) Improved distribution

Dopamine, for example, is of no value in treating Parkinson's disease since it does not enter the brain. Its precursor, L-dopa, does enter the brain where it is metabolized to dopamine.

(d) Chance

Carbimazole, for example, whose therapeutic activity depends on its conversion to methimazole. There is no rational reason for preferring carbimazole in routine therapy.

3.3.2. Metabolism of a pharmacologically active compound to other active compounds

In some cases the active metabolites have equal or greater pharmacological activity than the parent compound, for example diamorphine (which is rapidly metabolized to morphine but which enters the brain more rapidly than morphine and therefore has a faster onset of action), phenacetin (which, because of its adverse effects on the kidneys has been supplanted by its active metabolite paracetamol), and some benzodiazepines (such as diazepam and chlordiazepoxide which are metabolized to temazepam and oxazepam, which have the advantage of shorter durations of action). Some active compounds may be metabolized to toxic compounds, for example, lignocaine, phenytoin (whose main metabolite may inhibit the further metabolism of phenytoin), and isoniazid (whose acetylated metabolite is hepatotoxic resulting in liver damage more often in fast acetylators; but see p. 385).

3.3.3. Metabolism to pharmacologically inactive compounds

This is the most common process and it takes part in two phases, that of chemical alteration of the basic structure of the drug (e.g. by oxidation, reduction, or hydrolysis) and that of conjugation (e.g. by sulphatation, glucuronidation, methylation, or acetylation). Some drugs undergo one or other phase and some both. The end products are compounds which are more water-soluble and therefore more rapidly eliminated from the body.

The following factors affect hepatic (and other) drug metabolism:

(a) Genetic

See Chapter 8.

(b) Other drugs

See Chapter 10.

(c) Hepatic blood flow

For drugs with a high extraction ratio small changes in hepatic blood flow result in large changes in hepatic clearance rates. Such effects are generally of little clinical importance.

(d) Liver disease

The capacity of the liver is so great that liver disease must be extensive before effects on drug metabolism become important. Arteriovenous shunting in the absence of much hepatocellular damage may, however, impair drug metabolism.

(e) Age

Elderly patients are less capable of metabolizing drugs than younger patients, as are children under the age of about 6 months, particularly premature babies. In both cases the impairment is due to diminished hepatic microsomal enzyme activity. An example of the clinical importance of this effect is the effect, in neonates, of chloramphenicol which causes peripheral circulatory collapse (the 'grey syndrome') when given in weight-related doses which are non-toxic to adults.

3.4. DRUG EXCRETION

The kidney is the main route whereby drugs are excreted from the body. Other routes include the lungs (important for paraldehyde), breast milk (see Chapter 9), sweat, tears, and genital secretions (alarming if the patient is not expecting the orange-red discolouration caused by rifampicin), bile (leading to recirculation of some compounds, e.g. chloramphenicol—whose inactive metabolites are reactivated by hydrolysis in the gut—morphine, rifampicin, tetracyclines, and digitoxin), and saliva (sometimes used in monitoring drug concentrations in body fluids; see chapter 7).

Renal excretion of drugs occurs chiefly by three processes (Fig. 3.2):

1. Glomerular filtration.
2. Passive tubular reabsorption.
3. Active tubular secretion.

If a drug is mainly metabolized to inactive compounds then renal function will not affect elimination of the active compound. If, however, the drug or an active metabolite, is excreted unchanged via the kidneys, then changes in renal function *will* influence its elimination.

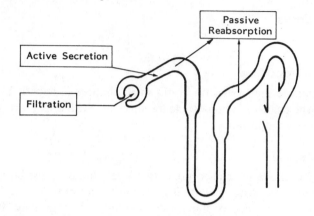

Fig. 3.2. A diagrammatic representation of a nephron, showing the sites of the three major processes whereby drugs are excreted via the kidney.

3.4.1. Glomerular filtration

All drugs are filtered at the glomerulus. The extent of filtration is directly proportional to the glomerular filtration rate (GFR = 120 ml/min) and the fraction of unbound drug in the plasma (f_u). Thus:

Rate of clearance by filtration = $f_u \times$ GFR.

If the *total* renal clearance of a drug is equal to $f_u \times$ GFR then it is *principally* cleared by filtration. It may, of course, also be affected by the other two mechanisms but in that case those effects must balance each other. Examples of drugs principally cleared by filtration are digoxin, gentamicin, procainamide, methotrexate, and ethambutol. Since creatinine is cleared principally by filtration, measurement of the rate of renal creatinine clearance is useful in estimating the clearance rates of these drugs.

3.4.2. Passive tubular reabsorption

If the value of renal clearance of a drug is *less* than $f_u \times$ GFR then its clearance after filtration is being restricted by passive reabsorption by the renal tubules. The renal clearance of drugs with very low rates of renal clearance (i.e. approaching urine flow rate) will be affected by changes in urine flow rate but the principal factor affecting the passive reabsorption of many drugs is the pH of the renal tubular fluid in relation to the type of drug and its pK_a. For example, weak acids with a pK_a below 7·5, such as aspirin, are less well reabsorbed and therefore more rapidly cleared in an alkaline urine, while the reverse is true for weak bases with a pK_a greater than 7·5, such as amphetamine, whose clearance is enhanced by an acid urine. These principles are sometimes put to use in the treatment of drug overdose (see Chapter 32). Renal failure alters passive reabsorption indirectly, by alterations in urine flow rate and pH.

3.4.3. Active tubular secretion

If the value of renal clearance of a drug is *greater* than $f_u \times$ GFR then as well as being filtered it is also being cleared by active tubular secretion in the proximal tubule. Penicillin is an example of such a drug. Some drugs inhibit active tubular secretion, forming the basis of drug interactions (see Chapter 10). For example, probenecid inhibits the active secretion of penicillin, prolonging its duration of action. Quinine and quinidine both inhibit the active secretion of digoxin leading to reduction in dosage requirements of digoxin by 50 per cent. Other examples of the effects of drugs on active tubular secretory processes are the effects of diuretics, aspirin, sulphinpyrazone, and probenecid on the secretion of uric acid. Some diuretics (e.g. frusemide, bumetanide, thiazides) and low doses of aspirin, sulphinpyrazone, and probenecid inhibit the secretion of uric acid leading to its retention. Higher doses of sulphinpyrazone, probenecid, and aspirin also inhibit *active reabsorption* of uric acid in the proximal tubule and the net result is increased excretion of uric acid.

In renal failure active tubular secretion of drugs is impaired.

The two following parts of this chapter deal with pharmacokinetic calculations, the first descriptively, the second mathematically. If you want to retain the thread of the four phases of drug therapy you should skip these two parts for the time being and go on to Chapter 4.

3.5. SIMPLE PHARMACOKINETIC CALCULATIONS

Although a full description of the pharmacokinetic properties of a drug requires complex mathematical analysis of appropriately collected data, it is possible to grasp the principles of pharmacokinetics using a simple approach and to use those principles in tackling practical problems.

Pharmacokinetics is the science of interpreting data on changing concentrations or amounts of a drug and its metabolites in blood, plasma, urine, and other body tissues and fluids. Before considering how such interpretations are made, we must consider the meaning of 'order' in kinetics.

3.5.1. Kinetic 'order'

Kinetic processes are defined according to their 'order' (a term which simply means that the various processes are ranked in order of increasing complexity). The important kinetic processes which concern us here are those governing the entry of the drug into the blood, its distribution in body tissues, and its elimination from the blood by metabolism and excretion. Such processes are generally of 'zero-order' or 'first-order'.

(a) Zero-order kinetics

A zero-order process is one whose rate is independent of the amount of drug undergoing the process. For such a process the plot of drug plasma concentration against time is linear (see the example of ethyl alcohol in Fig. 3.3).

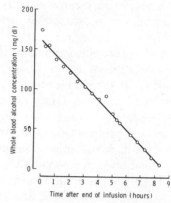

Fig. 3.3. Whole blood concentrations of alcohol (ethanol) following the i.v. infusion of 15 per cent alcohol in 5 per cent dextrose. Note the *linear* scale of alcohol concentration on the vertical axis. For most of the time after administration the relationship between whole blood concentration and time is linear. [Adapted from Korsten *et al.* (1975) *New Engl. J. Med.* **192**, 386–389 with permission.]

The following are examples of zero-order processes:

(i) Entry of a drug into the circulation during intravenous infusion

Given a fixed concentration of drug in an infusion solution its rate of administration can be controlled independent of that concentration.

(ii) The absorption of many depot forms of administration

For example, fluphenazine decanoate in oil in the treatment of schizophrenia, and oestrogen pellet implants in the treatment of the menopausal syndrome.

(iii) Saturable metabolism

When the concentration of a drug approaches a value at which its metabolizing enzymes are saturated its rate of metabolism becomes predominantly zero-order (Fig. 3.4). Examples of importance are those of ethyl alcohol, whose metabolism is zero-order at virtually all plasma concentrations (Fig. 3.3), and both phenytoin and acetylsalicylic acid (aspirin), whose metabolism becomes predominantly zero-order within the therapeutic range of plasma concentrations.

The consequences of this peculiarity of metabolism on changes in plasma concentrations with changing dose in the therapeutic range of doses is illustrated in the case of phenytoin in Fig. 3.5. For a relatively small change in dose there may be a large change in plasma concentration if metabolism is saturated.

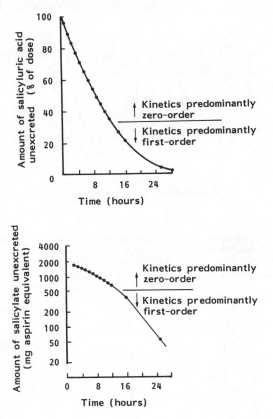

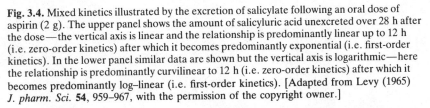

Fig. 3.4. Mixed kinetics illustrated by the excretion of salicylate following an oral dose of aspirin (2 g). The upper panel shows the amount of salicyluric acid unexcreted over 28 h after the dose—the vertical axis is linear and the relationship is predominantly linear up to 12 h (i.e. zero-order kinetics) after which it becomes predominantly exponential (i.e. first-order kinetics). In the lower panel similar data are shown but the vertical axis is logarithmic—here the relationship is predominantly curvilinear to 12 h (i.e. zero-order kinetics) after which it becomes predominantly log–linear (i.e. first-order kinetics). [Adapted from Levy (1965) *J. pharm. Sci.* **54**, 959–967, with the permission of the copyright owner.]

(b) First-order kinetics

Most kinetic processes affecting drug disposition in therapeutic practice are first-order. A first-order process is one whose rate is directly proportional to the amount of drug undergoing the process—the greater the amount, the faster it changes. For such a process the plot of, for example, drug plasma concentration against time, is curvilinear; however, the plot of the *logarithm* of the plasma concentration against time is linear. This is

illustrated below for the case of ampicillin (Fig. 3.6). When semilogarithmic plots of this kind are linear the kinetics are first-order. That this is so is
proved in the section outlining the mathematics of these processes (see
p.50).

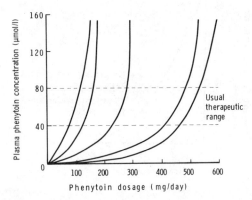

Fig. 3.5. The relationship between steady-state plasma concentrations of phenytoin and daily
phenytoin dosage in five different patients. Each curve was constructed by making discrete
measurements of steady-state concentrations at several different daily dosages. Note two
important features: first, the large variability in steady-state phenytoin concentrations from
patient to patient at any one dosage; and second, the non-linearity of the
relationship—within the therapeutic dosage range small changes in dosage can cause large
changes in plasma concentration. [Adapted from Richens and Dunlop (1975) *Lancet* **ii**,
247–248, with permission.]

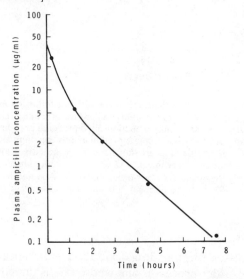

Fig. 3.6. Plasma ampicillin concentrations during the 8 h following an i.v. dose of ampicillin
(570 mg). Note that the vertical scale is logarithmic and that the relationship between plasma
concentration and time is log–linear for most of the time (i.e. first-order kinetics). [Adapted
from Jusko and Lewis (1973) *J. pharm. Sci.* **62**, 69–76, with the permission of the copyright
owner.]

3.5.2. Interpretation of plots of plasma drug concentrations against time

Consider what happens when we give a drug in a single intravenous bolus. We will assume that we give the injection very rapidly and that the drug distributes in the circulating plasma and throughout the tissues of the body within a few minutes and is not metabolized. We shall also assume that first-order kinetics apply. If we take repeated small samples of blood at various times after injection and measure the concentration of the drug in the plasma, and if we then plot the plasma drug concentrations against time we will find something like the result shown in Fig. 3.7(a).

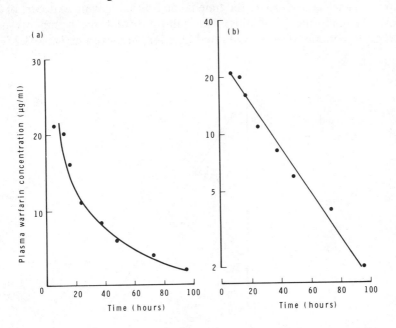

Fig. 3.7. Plasma warfarin concentrations during the 100 h following an i.v. dose of warfarin (200 mg). In the left hand panel the data are plotted in linear scale, in the right hand panel the same data are plotted in semilogarithmic scale (i.e. first-order kinetics). [Adapted from O'Reilly *et al.* (1971) *Thrombosis diathesis haemorr.* **25**, 178–186, with permission.] (Same data as in Figs. 3.8 and 3.14.)

At first the plasma concentration falls rapidly, later on more slowly, the *rate* of fall at any time being proportional to the concentration at that time. If instead of using a linear scale for plasma concentration we use a logarithmic scale, we find that the curve becomes a straight line [Fig. 3.7(b)] and because straight lines are easier to handle mathematically than curves, that is a useful observation. We can now define certain pharmacokinetic variables—half-time, apparent volume of distribution, and clearance rate.

(a) Half-time (or half-life) ($t_{1/2}$)

Because the plot on a semilogarithmic scale of plasma drug concentration against time is linear the rate of decline of plasma concentration is logarithmically constant. Linear constancy would imply the *subtraction* of a constant amount in unit time. Because logarithmic subtraction is equivalent to linear division the concentration will be *divided* by a constant amount in unit time. If we choose, arbitrarily, to make two the factor of division in unit time, then that time is the time taken for the concentration to halve, no matter what the starting concentration. This is illustrated in Fig. 3.8. Each downstroke represents a halving of the plasma concentration and each across-stroke the time taken for that halving to occur. In this case the half-time is 26 mins. The half-times of some commonly used drugs, in patients with normal renal function, are given in Table 3.2.

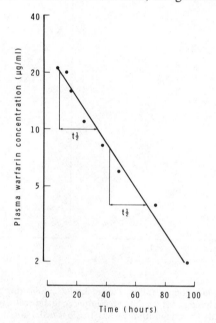

Fig. 3.8. The principle of the half-time ($t_{1/2}$). When plasma concentration versus time data are linear in a semilogarithmic plot then the time taken for the plasma concentration to fall from *any* value to half that value is a constant, the half-time. (Same data as in Figs. 3.7 and 3.14.)

The following are the uses of the half-time:

(i) As a guide to the time taken for drug to be eliminated from the body

The percentages of total drug in the body eliminated after one or more half-times without further administration of the drug are given in Table 3.3.

Table 3.2 *Mean half-times of some drugs in patients with normal renal function*

<1 h	1–4 h	4–12 h	12–24 h	1–2 days	>2 days	Dose-dependent
Dobutamine	Aminoglycosides*	β-adrenoceptor antagonists (most)	Carbenoxolone	Allopurinol†	Amiodarone	Phenobarbitone (in overdose)
Dopamine	Bumetanide	Glibenclamide	Chlorpromazine	Carbamazepine	Chloroquine	Phenytoin
Insulin	Cephalosporins	Hydralazine	Clonidine	Chlorpropamide	Diazepam	Salicylates
Naloxone	Chloramphenicol	Quinidine	Doxycycline	Clonazepam	Digitoxin	
Nitroprusside	Colchicine	Sulphonamides (many)	Haloperidol	Diazoxide	Phenobarbitone	
Penicillins (most)	Diamorphine†	Tetracyclines (most)	Lithium	Digoxin	Thyroxine	
	Erythromycin	Theophylline	Minocycline	Triiodothyronine		
	Ethambutol	Tolbutamide	Ouabain	Warfarin		
	Frusemide	Trimethoprim	Spironolactone†			
	Heparin	Valproate				
	Isoprenaline					
	L-dopa					
	Lignocaine					
	Morphine					
	Paracetamol					
	Procainamide					

* But see Pharmacopoeia.
† These drugs have shorter half-times than shown, but are listed under the half-times of their active metabolites.

It can be seen that over 90 per cent of the drug originally present will be eliminated by the time four half-times have elapsed.

Table 3.3. *The percentages of any amount of drug eliminated by first-order elimination after different numbers of half-times*

No. of half times	Percent eliminated	
1	50	= 50%
2	50 + 25	= 75%
3	50 + 25 + 12.5	= 87.5%
4	50 + 25 + 12.5 + 6.25	= 93.75%
5	50 + 25 + 12.5 + 6.25 + 3.125	= 96.9%

(ii) As a guide to the rate of accumulation of drug in the body during multiple dosing

The half-time is the *only* variable which determines the rate at which drug accumulates in the body during regular multiple dosing. Consider the regular oral administration of a drug which is rapidly absorbed (Fig. 3.9). After the first dose the concentration of drug in the plasma rises sharply as the drug is absorbed; it reaches a peak, and then starts to decline as the

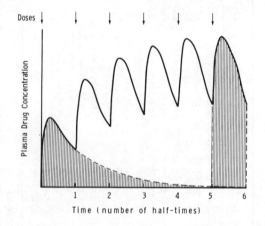

Fig. 3.9. The theoretical plasma concentrations of a drug over a period of time following repeated oral doses of the drug. Following the administration of the drug (at the times indicated by the arrows—in this case once every half-time) the plasma concentration rises as the drug is absorbed and then, because of subsequent drug distribution and elimination, reaches a peak and starts to fall. Note that with repeated administration there is accumulation to steady state (97 per cent after five half-times), and that the area under the plasma concentration versus time curve during a single dosage interval at steady state is equal to the area under the curve extrapolated to infinite time following a single dose (hatched areas).

drug is distributed throughout the body and eliminated. Following the second dose the rise in concentration to the next peak is the same as after the first dose, but because the new peak is higher than the first the rate of decline is faster (first-order kinetics) and there is a greater absolute fall in plasma concentration before the third dose is given than there was before the second. After each successive dose the increase in plasma concentration is the same but the size of the fall after the peak is progressively greater as the height of the peak increases. Eventually the size of fall after the peak is as great as the size of the preceding rise, and a 'steady state' is reached in which the amount eliminated from the body in a single dosage interval is the same as the amount being administered.

Strictly speaking this is not a true steady state since plasma concentrations are fluctuating all the time but the mean concentrations during consecutive dosage intervals are similar. Of course even those concentrations do not reach a true steady value until infinite time but for practical purposes a steady state can be considered to have occurred after three to five half-times, when 88–97 per cent of the steady-state value will have been reached.

If you substitute 'accumulated' for 'eliminated' in the legend to Table 3.3 the same percentage figures apply. This means that the time taken to reach steady state depends neither on the size of the dose nor on the frequency of administration but only on the *half-time* of the drug. The effects of varying the *dose* are shown in Fig. 3.10. Curves a and b show the plasma concentrations of a drug given once every half-time where the dose in case a is twice that in case b. The time taken to reach steady state is the same in each case and the final plasma concentration is proportional to the dose.

The effect of varying the *frequency of administration* of the drug without altering the total daily dose is also shown in Fig. 3.10. Curve a shows the plasma concentrations of a drug given once every half-time and curve c shows the concentrations of the drug when *half* the dose is given *twice* every half-time. Thus the total dose given is the same in both cases. In this instance both the time to steady state and the final mean plasma concentration are the same for the two cases, but the degree of fluctuation is less when the drug is administered more frequently.

The extreme case of repeated administration is that of continuous intravenous infusion (Fig. 3.11). In this instance there is no fluctuation in plasma drug concentration—it is as if infinitely small doses of the drug were being given at infinitely small dosage intervals. However, it still takes five half-times to reach 97 per cent of steady state.

Finally, consider what happens when the half-time of a drug is prolonged because its clearance is reduced (Fig. 3.12). Because the half-time is prolonged it takes proportionately longer for a steady state to be reached. However, because less drug is being eliminated during a dosage interval the eventual steady-state plasma concentration is proportionately higher.

This is what happens, for example, when renal digoxin elimination is decreased in renal failure—it takes longer to reach steady state and for a given dosage regimen the eventual steady-state plasma concentration is higher. In such cases dosages must be reduced and a delay in onset of effect must be expected if no loading dose is given (see below).

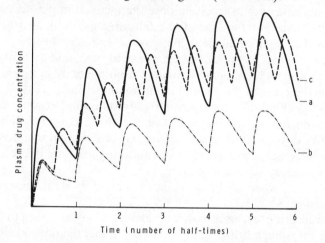

Fig. 3.10. The effects of varying dose and frequency of administration on the time taken to reach steady state and the eventual steady-state plasma concentration.

   1. *Effect of varying the dose.* Curve a represents the standard dose given once every half-time (compare Fig. 3.9). Curve b represents half the standard dose given at the same frequency—the time to reach steady state is unaffected but the eventual steady-state plasma concentration is proportional to the dose.

   2. *Effect of varying the frequency of administration.* Curve a represents the standard dose given once every half-time. Curve c represents half the standard dose given twice as frequently (i.e. the *total* dose is unchanged). Neither the time taken to reach steady state nor the eventual *mean* steady-state plasma concentration is affected, but the fluctuations in plasma concentration during a dosage interval are reduced in case c (compare Fig. 3.11).

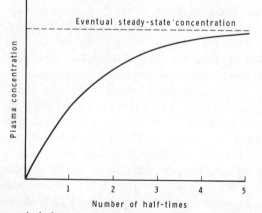

Fig. 3.11. The theoretical plasma concentrations of a drug over a period of time during continuous i.v. infusion. The plasma concentration rises steadily during infusion but does not reach steady state any sooner than in the various cases of oral administration (compare Fig. 3.10).

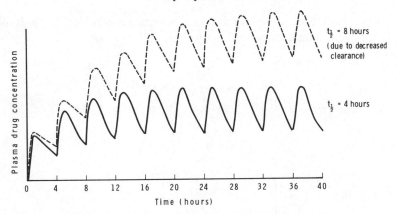

Fig. 3.12. The effect of reduced body clearance of a drug on the time taken to reach steady state and the eventual steady-state plasma concentration. Reducing the clearance has two effects.

1. *Prolongation of the half-time.* The time taken to reach steady state is prolonged proportionately.

2. *Increased accumulation of the drug.* The eventual steady-state plasma concentration is increased proportionately.

(iii) As a guide to the relationship between the loading dose and the maintenance dose

When the drug has a half-time greater than 24 h (e.g. digoxin, 40 h; digitoxin, 7 days; $S(-)$ warfarin, 32 h) it takes several days or weeks of regular administration of the same dose before the steady-state plasma concentration or amount of drug in the body is reached. Such a delay may be unacceptable if the eventual steady-state plasma concentration is that associated with therapeutic effect. In such cases a loading dose may be given to boost the amount of drug in the body to the required level. This is followed by administration of the regular maintenance dose to maintain the steady state (Fig. 3.13).

If one has decided on a particular loading dose then the maintenance dose calculation is simple. Since half the total body load will be lost in one half-time the maintenance dose should be half the loading dose given once every half-time. Take as an example the administration of digoxin (half-time about 40 h if renal function is normal). If the loading dose is 15 micrograms/kg the loading dose for a 60 kg patient will be 0·9 mg (in practice one would give 1 mg). The maintenance dose will be 0·45 mg every 40 h; if one scales this dose down to 24 h by simple proportion one calculates a daily maintenance dose of

$$\frac{(0\cdot45 \times 24)}{40} = 0\cdot27 \, \text{mg}.$$

In practice one would give 0·25 mg once daily . This proportionality calculation yields a slightly inaccurate answer since it assumes that the dose–time relationship is arithmetic whereas it is in fact logarithmic. The error is so small, however, as to be negligible in practice.

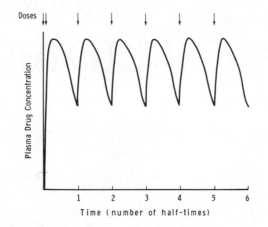

Fig. 3.13. The effect of an initial loading dose. If the correct loading dose is given a steady state can be achieved rapidly and then maintained by giving a smaller maintenance dose. In this example because the drug is being given once every half-time the maintenance dose is half the loading dose. Compare this figure with Fig. 3.9.

The process can, of course, be carried out in reverse. Having decided on a particular maintenance dose which you think will be suitable you can back-calculate the total body load. Take the example of digoxin again. You decide to give a daily maintenance dose of 5 micrograms/kg to a 70 kg patient, i.e. 0·35 mg once daily (in practice you would give 0·375 mg, i.e. 0·25 mg + 0·125 mg). This daily maintenance dose is roughly equivalent (by arithmetical proportionality) to 0·6 mg every 40 h and the total body load is therefore 1·2 mg (given as 1·25 mg). Use of these simple relationships will allow you to calculate the total body load for a given maintenance dose and thus to calculate any alterations in dose which may be necessary if, for example, there is a change in renal function. To know how to do this we shall have to wait until we have discussed the concept of clearance (below).

Even when the half-time of a drug is short it may be necessary to give a loading dose when a very rapid effect is required. Take the example of the use of lignocaine in the treatment of cardiac arrhythmias. The half-time of lignocaine is about 1 h. Because it would take about 4 h before a steady state was reached during continuous intravenous infusion a loading dose is usually given because the treatment of arrhythmias is an urgent matter. Here in making the calculation we cannot assume arithmetic proportionality because the error is much too large. The formula used is:

$$\text{Loading dose (mg)} = \frac{\text{intended infusion rate (mg/h)} \times t_{1/2}\text{ (h)}}{0·7}$$

Thus if it is intended to use an hourly infusion rate of 2 mg/kg in a 70 kg patient the loading dose would be

$$\frac{(2 \times 70 \times 1)}{0\cdot7} = 200 \text{ mg}.$$

(b) Apparent volume of distribution (V_d)

In Fig. 3.7 we saw how, with first-order kinetics, the plasma drug concentration falls linearly with time when plotted in semilogarithmic scale. Let us assume that after intravenous administration there is *instantaneous* distribution of drug throughout the body. If we now extrapolate the line back to the time of administration, the point at which it crosses the vertical axis represents the theoretical plasma concentration which would have occurred at a time when all the drug given was still in the body and uniformly distributed throughout it (Fig. 3.14).

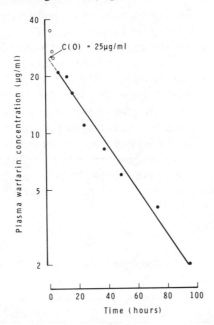

Fig. 3.14. Calculation of the apparent volume of distribution (same data as in Figs. 3.7 and 3.8). Extrapolation of the linear plasma concentration versus time curve to the vertical axis yields a value for the *theoretical* plasma concentration, $C(0)$, which would have occurred at the time of administration had there been uniform distribution of the drug throughout the body at that time. The apparent volume of distribution (V) is given by the expression $V = $ dose/$C(0)$.

Note that the assumption of uniform distribution leads to an overestimate of the volume, since the warfarin concentrations measured during the relatively short time before the linear phase (open circles) were actually higher than $C(0)$. However in this case the extent of the overestimate is small enough to ignore. A better estimate would be given by the expression shown as eqn (3.13) (p.51).

In the illustrated case for warfarin the theoretical plasma concentration at zero time, the time of administration, $C(0)$, is 25 micrograms/ml. The dose given was 200 mg. We can therefore calculate the theoretical volume of body fluid, equivalent to a theoretical amount of plasma, in which the drug is distributed—it is the ratio of the dose to the zero-time concentration:

$$V_d = \text{dose}/C(0) = \frac{200 \text{ mg}}{25 \text{ } \mu g/\text{ml}}$$
$$= 8 \cdot 0 \text{ l of plasma.}$$

In this case the apparent volume of distribution of the drug is similar to that of the extracellular fluid. One might, therefore, postulate that the drug is distributed evenly throughout the extracellular fluid volume in which its concentration would be the same as that in the plasma. Although it is sometimes the case that the apparent volume of distribution can be related to a known identifiable fluid volume in the body, more often the apparent volume of distribution is greater than even that of total body water (about 0·6 l/kg). For example, the apparent volume of distribution of propranolol is about 3 litres of plasma per kg body weight. This theoretical volume simply gives an index of how widely or extensively the drug is distributed to the *tissues* of the body compared with the plasma. Incidentally, we attribute this volume to the plasma because the drug concentration was measured in plasma—if the concentration were measured in, for example, serum or whole blood the volume would be expressed in litres of serum or whole blood. The higher the apparent volume of distribution of a drug the more extensively is it distributed in the body tissues. In Table 3.4 are listed the values of the apparent volume of distribution of various commonly used drugs.

Table 3.4   *Values of the apparent volume of distribution of some commonly used drugs*

<12 l	12–40 l	40–100 l	100–200 l	>200 l
Frusemide	Acetazolamide	Carbamazepine	Procainamide	Chlorpromazine
Phenylbutazone	Alcohol	Lignocaine	Propranolol	Digoxin
Sulphonylureas	Aminoglycosides	Lithium		Haloperidol
(e.g. tolbutamide)	(e.g. gentamicin)	Paracetamol		Tricyclics
Warfarin	Digitoxin			(e.g.
	Insulin			amitriptyline)
	Penicillin G			
	Phenytoin			
	Quinidine			
	Theophylline			
	Valproate			

Intuitively, we can see that the more highly protein bound a drug is in the circulation the less readily will it distribute to the body tissues and the lower will be its apparent volume of distribution. It should be remembered in this discussion that the *protein bound* drug is not reckoned as being *tissue bound*, since what is generally measured as plasma drug concentration includes both bound and unbound drug. Thus the apparent volume of distribution of total drug must be roughly proportional to the circulating non-protein-bound fraction.

In the tissues drug may or may not be bound to tissue proteins and the apparent volume of distribution will obviously also be inversely proportional to the non-tissue-protein-bound fraction.

The relationship between the extent of a drug's apparent volume of distribution and its protein binding (a) in the plasma and (b) in the tissues is expressed by the following equation:

$$V_d = V_p + V_T \left(\frac{f_u}{f_{uT}}\right)$$

where V_d = apparent volume of distribution; V_p = volume of plasma (i.e. about 3 l); V_T = volume of total body 'tissue' fluid (i.e. about 39 l); f_u = fraction unbound in plasma; and f_{uT} = fraction unbound in tissues.

This expression is useful in assigning possible mechanisms to observed changes in the apparent volume of distribution. For example, if one finds that the apparent volume of distribution of a drug is altered in some particular circumstances then by measuring the extent of any change in plasma protein binding one can assess to what extent the change in apparent volume of distribution is due to the change in plasma protein binding and determine whether one needs to invoke changes in tissue binding as an alternative mechanism.

The following are the uses of the apparent volume of distribution:

(i) In planning dosage regimens
The apparent volume of distribution (expressed in volume of plasma) relates the amount of drug in the body to the plasma drug concentration thus:

V_d = amount in body/concentration in plasma.

This relationship allows one, in theory, to calculate the loading dose of drug required to produce a given steady-state plasma drug concentration. In some cases, however, one does not know what plasma concentration is appropriate to produce a therapeutic effect or to avoid toxicity, and in such cases one relies upon collective practical experience for guidance to dosage. In contrast, in those cases for which a target plasma drug concentration *is* known from clinical studies (e.g. digoxin, gentamicin) and the apparent volume of distribution from pharmacokinetic studies, one uses these factors in designing dosage regimens and thus improves the precision of one's drug therapy. Although this may sound a little highfalut-ing, in practice it is implicit in one's use of doses recommended in textbooks, manufacturers' literature, etc., and in particular of dosages based on body weight, since the variability of the apparent volume of distribution is less when that volume is expressed in litres per kilogram of body weight than when expressed without such correction.

It may also be useful to know that in some circumstances the apparent volume of distribution may be altered and that in those cases the loading dose may have to be altered accordingly. For example, the apparent volume of distribution of digoxin may be lowered in renal failure and loading doses should be reduced by about a third.

(ii) In relating half-time to total clearance

The half-time of a drug is related to the apparent volume of distribution and the total body clearance by the following expression:

$$\text{Total body clearance} = \frac{\text{volume of distribution} \times 0.7}{\text{half-time}}$$

Clearance and apparent volume of distribution are independent of each other. For example, the clearance of drug from the plasma by glomerular filtration is obviously not dependent on the concentration of the drug in the tissues. Since clearance and apparent volume of distribution are independent variables, it follows that the half-time must depend on the values of those variables. Thus a change in half-time implies a change in either clearance, or apparent volume of distribution, or both. Further-more if one notes that the half-time of a drug is unchanged during an interaction or in the presence of some disease, that does not necessarily imply that the pharmacokinetic properties of the drug are unaffected since proportionately equal, independent changes in clearance and apparent volume of distribution will result in no change in half-time.

(iii) In interpretation of drug interactions

When a new interaction between two drugs is described the question of its mechanism always arises. One can confidently rule out protein-binding displacement interactions if one knows that the object drug (see Chapter 10) has a high apparent volume of distribution (greater than about 30 l of plasma). This is because any rise in free concentration of the object drug in the plasma due to displacement from protein binding sites will only be clinically obvious if the drug does not have to distribute through a large volume of distribution which will literally dilute out the effects of the increase in free drug concentration.

(c) Clearance (CL)

The clearance of a drug is defined as that fraction of the apparent volume of distribution from which drug is removed in unit time. It is expressed in units of amount per time (e.g. ml/min), sometimes corrected for body weight (e.g. ml/min/kg).

Total body clearance is equal to the sum of the clearances by all routes of elimination and is usually divided into renal and non-renal clearances. The relationship relating total body clearance to apparent volume of distribution and half-time has been given above.

(i) Renal clearance (CL_R)

Adapting the above definition of total clearance we can define renal clearance as that fraction of the apparent volume of distribution from which drug is removed by renal excretion in unit time.
Thus:

CL_R = fraction of amount of drug in body excreted in urine in unit time
$\times V_d$

$$\therefore CL_R = \frac{A_e}{A_{TOT}} \times V_d$$

where A_e = amount excreted in unit time and A_{TOT} = total amount in body.
But:

$$V_d = A_{TOT}/C \text{ (see above)}$$

$$\therefore CL_R = A_e/C$$

i.e. $CL_R = \dfrac{\text{total amount of drug excreted in the urine in unit time}}{\text{mean plasma drug concentration during unit time}}$

You will note that this expression is precisely the same as that commonly used in renal physiology for the expression of renal clearance:

$$\text{renal clearance} = \frac{UV}{P}$$

where U = urinary concentration of compound; V = volume of urine excreted per unit time; and P = mean plasma concentration of compound.

Non-renal clearance is usually calculated as the difference between total and renal clearances.

The mechanisms whereby drugs are cleared from the body have been discussed in the earlier part of this chapter.

(ii) Hepatic clearance (CL_H)

Adapting the definition of clearance we can define hepatic clearance as that fraction of the apparent volume of distribution from which drug is removed by metabolism and biliary excretion in unit time. As in the case of renal clearance we can derive the following expression for hepatic clearance:

$$CL_H = \frac{\text{total amount of drug excreted in the bile + total amount of}}{\text{metabolite appearing in hepatic venous blood in unit time}}{\text{mean drug concentration in the plasma entering the liver}}{\text{during unit time}}$$

It is clear, however, that while we could measure separately the components of the corresponding equation for renal clearance, we cannot for practical purposes measure the variables in the equation for hepatic clearance. However, for drugs whose non-renal clearance is entirely by the hepatic route (and that is the case for most drugs), the problem can be solved by measured total clearance and renal clearance. Hepatic clearance will be the difference between the two:

$CL_{NR} = CL_{TOT} - C_R$

(assumption $CL_H = CL_{NR}$).

Two factors influence hepatic clearance—the rate of hepatic blood flow, and the extent of protein binding in the circulation—and the extent to which either or both of these factors affects hepatic clearance depends on how well the liver is capable of removing drug from incoming blood.

If we think of the liver as a reservoir (Fig. 3.15) into which drug in solution flows and from which drug may either flow out unchanged or after metabolism, we can judge how these factors affect hepatic clearance.

Case 1. The ability of the liver to clear drug by metabolism or by excretion into the bile is high

In this case there is virtually no restriction to flow through either outlet from the reservoir, and clearance will only depend on the rate of flow *into* the reservoir (i.e. total hepatic blood flow). The higher the rate of flow the higher the rate of clearance.

Case 2. The ability of the liver to clear drug by metabolism or by excretion into the bile is low

In this case outflow via hepatic clearance is restricted and will not be affected by the rate of inflow. Instead the extent of protein binding becomes important since it will determine how much drug is available for transport to the sites of clearance. The higher the fraction of unbound drug in the blood, the higher the rate of clearance.

Case 3. The ability of the liver to clear drug by metabolism or by excretion into the bile is intermediate

In this case both hepatic blood flow *and* protein binding will influence hepatic clearance.

The proof of these relationships is given in the mathematical section of this chapter, along with a list of drugs which are subject to high, low, or intermediate degrees of extraction by the liver (see Table 3.6).

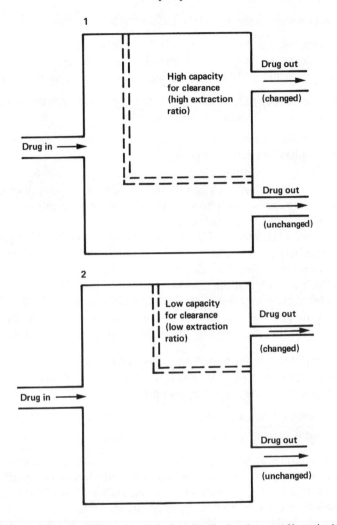

Fig. 3.15. A diagrammatic representation of the factors affecting the rate of hepatic clearance of a drug. The liver is represented as a reservoir into which drug flows (i.e. 'drug in') in the portal venous and hepatic arterial blood. It leaves the reservoir (i.e. 'drug out') either 'changed' (e.g. metabolized or via the bile) or 'unchanged' (i.e. via the hepatic veins).

Case 1. If the ability of the liver for clearance of the drug is high (i.e. if the extraction ratio is high) then the rate-limiting factor is the *speed* with which it is presented to the sites of clearance, which in turn is equal to the rate of blood flow through the organ [i.e. for $E \to 1$, $CL_H \approx Q_H$, see eqn (3.26)].

Case 2. If the ability of the liver for the clearance of the drug is low (i.e. if the extraction ratio is low) then the rate-limiting factor is the *quantity* of drug which is presented to the sites of clearance, and since only non-protein-bound drug can be metabolized this is dependent on the fraction of unbound drug in the plasma [i.e. for $E \to 0$, $CL_H \approx CL_{int}$ and $CL_H \, \alpha \, f_u$, eqns (3.27) and (3.29)].

Case 3 (not illustrated). For drugs for which the liver has an intermediate capacity for clearance (i.e. $E \approx 0.5$) both hepatic blood flow and the unbound fraction of drug in the plasma affect the rate of hepatic clearance.

The following are the uses of the clearance:

(i) In assessing the mechanism of renal excretion

The magnitude of the renal clearance rate of a drug is related to its principal mechanism of renal excretion. This arises from the relationship:

Renal clearance = $(f_u \times GFR)$ − (rate of passive reabsorption) + (rate of active secretion)

where f_u = the fraction of drug unbound in the plasma and GFR = glomerular filtration rate (see p.26).

If a drug has a renal clearance equal to $f_u \times GFR$ its *principal* mechanism of excretion is by filtration. That does not mean that the drug is not subject to passive reabsorption and tubular secretion—it may be subject to both but in equal measure.

If the renal clearance of a drug is *less* than $f_u \times GFR$ it is both filtered and reabsorbed (and perhaps secreted, but only to a small extent). Its excretion may therefore be influenced by alterations in the pH of the urine (if it is both a weak acid or a weak base, and lipophilic).

If the renal clearance is *greater* than $f_u \times GFR$ then it is both filtered and secreted (and perhaps reabsorbed, but only to a small extent). Its excretion may therefore be influenced by other drugs which alter tubular secretion.

(ii) In calculating dosage regimens (see also p.416)

Total body clearance of a drug and its steady-state plasma concentration (C_{ss}) are related in the following manner:

$$C_{ss} = \frac{\text{dose} \times \text{fraction of dose absorbed}}{\text{total clearance} \times \text{dosing interval}}$$

Thus in circumstances in which total body clearance is changing one may maintain the same mean steady-state plasma concentration by altering the dose or dosing interval proportional to the change in total body clearance (assuming that there is no concomitant change in the fraction of the dose that is absorbed). If the drug is cleared entirely by the kidneys (e.g. gentamicin) then dosage should be changed in proportion to *renal* clearance. Furthermore if, as happens to be the case for gentamicin, renal clearance is principally by glomerular filtration then measurement of the creatinine clearance will give an estimate of total body clearance of the drug on which to base dosage changes. In the case of gentamicin a halving of the creatinine clearance would require a halving of the dose or a doubling of the dosing interval. In the case of a drug (such as digoxin) which is eliminated by glomerular filtration and by metabolism the calculation is only slightly more difficult. The relationship involved is:

percentage eliminated in one dosing interval
= percentage eliminated by non-renal routes +
(constant × creatinine clearance).

The percentage eliminated in one dosing interval by non-renal routes is usually constant and known from published data. The constant by which the creatinine clearance must be multiplied to give the percentage excreted in one dosing interval by renal routes will be known from published experiments in patients with different degrees of renal impairment or can be calculated from the half-time and non-renal clearance. For digoxin the equation reads:

percentage of total body load eliminated in one day =
14 per cent + (0·2 × creatinine clearance).

From this relationship one can calculate the daily elimination rate of drug for different values of creatinine clearance.

In Table 3.5 is a list of drugs for which such calculations may be useful in altering dosage regimens in conditions of changing renal function. Also listed are the percentages eliminated in unit time by non-renal mechanisms and the constant by which creatinine clearance must be multiplied to assess the contribution to clearance by the kidneys. This enables the calculations necessary to adjust dosage regimens to be made as illustrated here for digoxin:

Creatinine clearance in ml/min	Daily elimination rate in per cent (fraction) of total body load	Ratio $\dfrac{\text{Renal failure dose}}{\text{Usual dose}}$
100	34 (⅓)	34:34 = 1
50	25 (¼)	25:34 ≈ 3:4
25	19 (⅕)	19:34 ≈ 3:5
10	16 (⅙)	16:34 ≈ 3:6
0	14 (⅐)	14:34 ≈ 3:7

3.5.3. Non-linear kinetics

In section 3.5.2. we have been making the assumption that the pharmaco-kinetics of the drugs we were discussing were linear, i.e. obeyed first-order kinetics at all therapeutic (or even toxic) doses. However such is not always the case. In some instances a pharmacokinetic process (e.g. metabolism, protein binding) may be saturated at doses within the therapeutic range, and then a mixture of first-order and zero-order kinetics occurs (see Fig. 3.4). The most important examples involve saturable *metabolism* and include phenytoin, alcohol, and acetylsalicylic acid. The example of pheny-toin is illustrated in Fig. 3.5. For some drugs (e.g. clofibrate, disopyr-amide) there is saturable protein binding and the kinetics of those drugs become non-linear at high doses or if there is hypoalbuminaemia.

There are several tests for non-linearity of pharmacokinetics but the simplest is that of measuring steady-state plasma concentrations at diffe-rent doses. For most drugs steady-state concentrations vary proportionate-ly with the dose. If there are non-linearities this proportionality does not occur (see Fig. 3.5). Other methods include measuring half-times or clearance rates at different doses. If the kinetics are linear these values should be constant. If there are non-linearities then half-time may be prolonged and clearance rate slowed at increasing doses.

Table 3.5   *Renal and non-renal contributions to the clearance of some drugs whose dosages should be reduced in renal impairment (see also p. 417)*

Instructions: to calculate the per cent of total body drug which is eliminated in one hour, or one day (P) calculate:

$$P = NR + (R.CL_{creat}).$$

Compare the value of P obtained with the patient's creatinine clearance (ml/min) with that obtained with a normal CL_{creat} (100 ml/min) and adjust the dose proportionately.

Drug	NR (%/h)	R (per hour)
Ampicillin	10	0.6
Carbenicillin	6	0.6
Cephalexin	3	0.7
*Gentamicin	2	0.3
*Kanamycin	1	0.25
*Lincomycin	6	0.1
*Methyldopa	3	0.2
Penicillin G	3	1.4
*Procainamide	0.7	0.2
*Streptomycin	1	0.25
Trimethoprim	2	0.04

Drug	NR (%/day)	R (per day)
*Digoxin	14	0.2
*Ouabain (G-strophanthin)	30	0.9

Other drugs whose dosages should be reduced in renal failure include allopurinol, amphotericin, disopyramide, ethambutol, lithium, methotrexate, quinine, and most other penicillins, cephalosporins, and aminoglycosides besides those listed here. For drugs which should be avoided in patients with renal failure see Table 24.7.
* Drugs marked thus have a low toxic:therapeutic ratio (low therapeutic index).

The details of this phenomenon of non-linear kinetics are discussed later in this chapter (p.56), but it should be apparent that the change from predominantly first-order to predominantly zero-order kinetics with increasing dose produces an unstable pharmacokinetic state. In such unstable pharmacokinetic circumstances drug half-time and clearance change with dosage. It may be important, therefore, to measure plasma drug concentrations to monitor drug therapy when such drugs are used (see Chapter 7 for reference to phenytoin).

3.6. THE MATHEMATICS OF PHARMACOKINETICS

In this section we shall describe the mathematical derivations of the principles outlined in the foregoing section.

3.6.1. Zero-order kinetics

A zero-order process is one whose rate is *independent* of the amount of drug undergoing the process. Thus:

$$\frac{dA}{dt} = -k_0 \tag{3.1}$$

where A = amount of drug, t = time, and k_0 = zero-order rate constant. In this equation the rate of change of amount is expressed as a constant and the negative sign is used for the zero-order rate constant because drug amounts are taken to be falling with time.

Integration of eqn (3.1) yields:

$$A(t) = -k_0 t + \text{constant} \tag{3.2}$$

where $A(t)$ is the amount of drug yet to undergo the process at time t, and 'constant' is the constant of integration.

When $t = 0$, $A(t) = A(0)$ (the amount at zero time).

$$\therefore A(t) = A(0) - k_0 t. \tag{3.3}$$

Equation (3.3) is the equation of a straight line relating to $A(t)$ to t.

The slope of the line is $-k_0$ (i.e. the rate of change, or the rate of elimination, e.g. 5 mg/min) and the intercept on the vertical axis is $A(0)$ (Fig. 3.16).

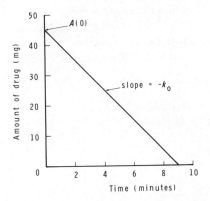

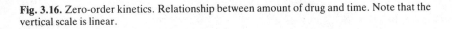

Fig. 3.16. Zero-order kinetics. Relationship between amount of drug and time. Note that the vertical scale is linear.

3.6.2. First-order kinetics

A first-order process is one whose rate is *directly proportional* to the amount of drug undergoing the process. Thus:

$$\frac{\mathrm{d}A}{\mathrm{d}t} = -kA. \tag{3.4}$$

(Note that this equation can also be written thus:

$$\frac{\mathrm{d}A}{\mathrm{d}t} = -kA^1$$

and that eqn (3.1) can be written thus:

$$\frac{\mathrm{d}A}{\mathrm{d}t} = -k_0A^0, \text{ since } A^0 = 1.$$

In these forms these two equations indicate the origin of the terms 'first-order' and 'zero-order'.)

Integration of eqn (3.4) yields:

$$\ln A(t) = -kt + \text{constant}. \tag{3.5}$$

When $t = 0$, $A(t) = A(0)$

$$\therefore \ln A(t) = \ln A(0) - kt \tag{3.6}$$

$$\text{or } A(t) = A(0)\mathrm{e}^{-kt}. \tag{3.7}$$

In these equations $A(t)$ and $A(0)$ represent the amount of drug yet to undergo the process at times t and zero respectively.

Equation (3.6) is the equation of the straight line relating $\ln A(t)$ to t. The slope of the line is $-k$ and the intercept on the vertical axis is $\ln A(0)$. Therefore, if one plots $\log_{10} A(t)$ against t (Fig. 3.17) then the intercept on the vertical axis is $A(0)$ and the slope is $-k/2 \cdot 3$ (since $2 \cdot 3 = \ln 10$).

Here k is the first-order rate constant and has units of reciprocal time (e.g. 'per hour'). This is to be contrasted with the zero-order rate constant [eqn (3.1)], k_0, which has units of amount per time (e.g. 'mg/min').

3.6.3. Half-time ($t_{1/2}$)

When $t = t_{1/2}$, $A(t) = A(0)/2$.
Substituting in eqn (3.7) yields:

$$\frac{A(0)}{2} = A(0)\mathrm{e}^{-kt_{1/2}} \tag{3.8}$$

$$\mathrm{e}^{-kt_{1/2}} = 1/2 \tag{3.9}$$

$$kt_{1/2} = \ln 2 \tag{3.10}$$

$$t_{1/2} = \ln 2/k \approx 0 \cdot 7/k. \tag{3.11}$$

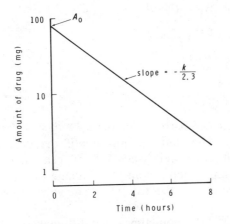

Fig. 3.17. First-order kinetics. Relationship between amount of drug and time. Note that the vertical scale is logarithmic.

3.6.4. Apparent volume of distribution (V_d)

$$V_d = A(0)/C(0) = \text{dose}/C(0) \tag{3.12}$$

where $C(0)$ = the theoretical concentration at zero time (cf. Fig. 3.16). This is the so-called extrapolated V_d (V_d^{extrap}).

In all the discussion so far we have assumed that the drug is equally distributed throughout the body (i.e. that the body behaves as if it were a single 'compartment'). A glance at Fig. 3.14 will show that in the case of warfarin such an assumption is wrong—measurements of plasma warfarin concentrations, if taken early enough after a single i.v. dose, show concentrations higher than those predicted by instantaneous distribution. In the case of warfarin the error involved in our assumption is quite small. For other drugs, however, the error is large and for such cases other models of drug distribution, both multicompartmental and physiological, have been evolved. Discussion of their complexities, however, is beyond the scope of this book. It is, in any case, often simpler to derive the values of pharmacokinetic variables without recourse to any formal theoretical model, single-compartment or otherwise. The apparent volume of distribution so calculated is usually known as V_d^{area} since it is derived from the following relationship:

$$V_d^{\text{area}} = \frac{\text{dose}}{\text{area} \times k} \tag{3.13}$$

where 'area' is the area under the plasma concentration versus time curve extrapolated to infinite time and 'dose' is the fraction of the dose that reaches the systemic circulation intact. Apply this equation to the case of single-compartment distribution after intravenous administration discussed above:

$$\text{area} = \int_{\infty}^{0} C(0)e^{-kt}dt = C(0)/k. \tag{3.14}$$

Substituting in eqn (3.13) yields:

$$V_d^{\text{area}} = \frac{\text{dose}}{C(0)/k \times k} \tag{3.15}$$

$$\therefore V_d^{\text{area}} = \text{dose}/C(0). \tag{3.16}$$

Thus for the single-compartment model $V_d^{\text{extrap}} = V_d^{\text{area}}$ [compare eqns (3.12) and (3.16)]. The same is not true if the data do not fit the single-compartment model well, when V_d^{extrap}, calculated on the assumption of a single compartment, is an *over*estimate of V_d^{area}. V_d^{area} is the more accurate measure of the true apparent volume of distribution at steady state.

In calculating V_d^{area} it is sometimes useful to make use of the observation (see Fig. 3.9) that the area under the curve of plasma concentration versus time, measured to infinity after a single dose, is the same as that measured during a single dosage interval at steady state.

3.6.5. Clearance (CL)

$$CL = V_d^{\text{area}} \times k = V_d^{\text{area}} \times \ln 2/t_{1/2}. \tag{3.17}$$

But

$$V_d^{\text{area}} = \frac{\text{dose}}{\text{area} \times k} \text{ [eqn (3.13)]}$$

$$\therefore CL = \frac{\text{dose}}{\text{area}} \tag{3.18}$$

After oral administration one must allow for the possibility of incomplete absorption and first-pass metabolism and adjust the dose accordingly. The fraction of orally administered drug which reaches the systemic circulation is usually designated F. Thus

$$CL = \frac{F \times \text{dose}}{\text{area}}$$

and

$$V_d = \frac{F \times \text{dose}}{\text{area} \times k}$$

Renal clearance

$$CL_R = \frac{C_{\text{urine}} \times V_{\text{urine}}}{C_p \times t} \tag{3.19}$$

where C_{urine} is the concentration of drug in the urine, the volume of which is V_{urine}, collected over a period of time, and C_p is the mean concentration of drug in the plasma over the collection period (t). For drugs with a long half-time relative to the collection period, and for which therefore the plasma concentration does not change much during the period of measurement, this equation gives a good approximation of the value of renal clearance when C_p is measured at the mid-point of the collection period. It is not so accurate for drugs with short half-times when alternative methods must be used. One such method is based on repeated plasma drug concentration measurements during the collection period:

$$CL_R = \frac{C_{urine} \times V_{urine}}{area} \qquad (3.20)$$

where 'area' is the area under the plasma concentration versus time curve during the urine collection period.

Hepatic clearance

(i) Extraction ratio

The extraction ratio (E) of a drug is a measure of the extent to which the drug is removed by the liver (to metabolism or biliary excretion) from incoming blood (i.e. portal venous and hepatic arterial blood). It is the difference in drug concentration between incoming and outgoing blood ($C_{IN} - C_{OUT}$), expressed as a fraction of the incoming concentration:

$$E = \frac{C_{IN} - C_{OUT}}{C_{IN}} \qquad (3.21)$$

If a drug is subject to a high degree of removal by the liver then the concentration in the outflowing blood (C_{OUT}) will be low and E will approach the value of one ($E{\to}1$). If there is poor extraction, on the other hand, then C_{OUT} will be close in value to C_{IN} and $E{\to}0$.

(ii) The effect of hepatic blood flow

If the *extent* to which a drug is extracted by the liver is given by ($C_{IN} - C_{OUT}$) then the *rate* at which it is removed must be the product of this extent and hepatic blood flow, i.e. $Q_H(C_{IN} - C_{OUT})$. Therefore the hepatic clearance rate will be the rate of extraction expressed as a fraction of the incoming concentration:

$$CL_H = \frac{Q_H(C_{IN} - C_{OUT})}{C_{IN}} \qquad (3.22)$$

$$CL_H = Q_H \times E. \qquad (3.23)$$

However this relationship is only strictly true at high degrees of extraction, i.e. high values of E (see Fig. 3.15). At low values of E the relationship between hepatic clearance becomes more complex and we must introduce another concept.

(iii) Intrinsic clearance

The intrinsic clearance of a drug is a measure of the maximal ability of the liver to remove drug from the incoming blood, *independent of the rate of hepatic blood flow*. Intrinsic clearance is a complicated function which depends partly on the activity of hepatic drug metabolizing enzymes, the rate of biliary excretion, the partition coefficient of drug between the liver and outflowing blood, and the apparent volume of distribution of the drug in the liver (i.e. the extent of tissue protein binding). It can be shown (although the derivation is too complicated to give here) that hepatic blood flow, E, and intrinsic clearance (CL_{int}) are related as follows:

$$E = \frac{CL_{int}}{Q_H + CL_{int}} \tag{3.24}$$

$$\therefore CL_H = Q_H \left(\frac{CL_{int}}{Q_H + CL_{int}} \right). \tag{3.25}$$

Case 1 (see p.44)
When $E \rightarrow 1$, $CL_{int} \gg Q_H$

$$\therefore CL_H \approx Q_H. \tag{3.26}$$

Case 2 (see p.44)
When $E \rightarrow 0$, $Q_H \gg CL_{int}$

$$\therefore CL_H \approx CL_{int}. \tag{3.27}$$

Thus for drugs with a high extraction ratio hepatic clearance is proportional to hepatic blood flow [eqn (3.26)]. For drugs with a low extraction ratio hepatic clearance is proportional to intrinsic clearance [eqn (3.27)]. For drugs with an intermediate extraction ratio both factors influence hepatic clearance. A list of commonly used drugs, categorized by extraction ratio, is given in Table 3.6.

Intrinsic clearance can be measured by comparing the clearance of an i.v. dose of drug with the clearance of an oral dose of drug, but only for low extraction ratio drugs which are completely absorbed intact from the gut.

(iv) Relationship between CL_H and protein binding

$$CL_{TOT} \times C_{TOT} = CL_u \times C_u \tag{3.28}$$

$$CL_{TOT} = CL_u \times \frac{C_u}{C_{TOT}} = CL_u \times f_u \tag{3.29}$$

where u indicates unbound drug.

Thus at low values of E, hepatic clearance is directly proportional to the fraction of drug which is unbound to plasma proteins in the circulation.

This is an important result when we come to consider the course of events during displacement of drugs from protein binding sites (see, for example, Chapter 10, p.161).

Table 3.6 *Drugs of low, intermediate, and high hepatic extraction ratio*

Low	Intermediate	High
Chloramphenicol	Aspirin	Chlormethiazole
Diazepam	Codeine	Ergotamine*
Digitoxin	Quinidine	Labetalol
Isoniazid	Nortriptyline	Lignocaine
Paracetamol		Pethidine
Phenobarbitone		Morphine
Phenylbutazone		Nitroglycerine
Phenytoin		Propranolol
Procainamide		
Theophylline		
Tolbutamide		
Warfarin		

* May reduce its own clearance by reducing hepatic blood flow.

3.6.6. Relationship of loading dose to maintenance dose during intermittent dosage at steady state

Let D_L = the maximum amount of drug in the body at steady state (i.e. the loading dose).

Let D_M = the difference between the maximum amount of drug in the body at steady state and the amount of drug left in the body at the end of a dosage interval (i.e. the maintenance dose).

$$\therefore D_M = D_L - D_L e^{-kt} \tag{3.30}$$

$$\therefore D_M = D_L (1 - e^{-kt}). \tag{3.31}$$

3.6.7. Relationship of loading dose to maintenance dose during continuous intravenous infusion

At steady state, input = output.

$\therefore$ Rate of infusion (R_0) = rate of elimination

$$\therefore R_0 = CL \times C_{ss}. \tag{3.32}$$

But

$$CL = V_d^{area} \times k \text{ [eqn (3.17)]}$$

$$\therefore R_0 = V_d^{area} \times k \times C_{ss}. \tag{3.33}$$

But

$$D_L = V_d{}^{area} \times C_{ss}$$

$$\therefore R_0 = D_L \times k \tag{3.34}$$

$$\therefore R_0 = \frac{D_L \times 0.7}{t_{1/2}}. \tag{3.35}$$

3.6.8. Non-linear kinetics

From the characteristics of the plot of steady-state plasma concentration against dose as shown in Fig. 3.18 one can define two features.

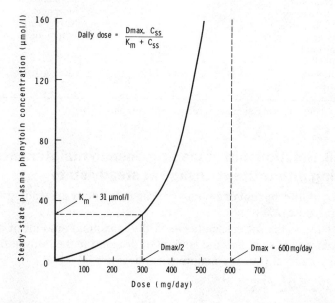

Fig. 3.18. Non-linear kinetics. The curve was constructed by measuring the steady-state plasma concentrations found at different daily maintenance dosages of phenytoin in the same individual. Analysis of the curve (see Fig. 3.19) yielded values for D_{max} and K_m as shown. D_{max} is the asymptote of the curve and K_m is the steady-state plasma concentration found when the daily maintenance dosage is half D_{max}.

1. The D_{max}—that dose at which the curve becomes perpendicular (i.e. the asymptote).
2. The K_m—the steady-state plasma concentration which results from half the D_{max}.

These two parameters, which are constant in an individual, are related to the rate of dosing and the resultant steady-state plasma concentration (C_{ss}), as follows:

$$\text{Rate of dosing } \left(\frac{dD}{dt}\right) = \frac{D_{max} \times C_{ss}}{K_m + C_{ss}} \tag{3.36}$$

This equation is comparable with the Michaelis–Menten equation of enzyme kinetics and with the equation of the dose–response curve [eqn (4.10)]. The shape of the curve which it defines is shown in Fig. 3.18.

At low doses, and therefore low values of C_{ss}, $K_m \gg C_{ss}$, and thus $K_m + C_{ss} \approx K_m$.

Now eqn (3.36) becomes:

$$\frac{dD}{dt} \approx \frac{D_{max} \times C_{ss}}{K_m} = \text{constant} \times C_{ss}. \tag{3.37}$$

Equation (3.37) is recognizable as a *first-order equation* [compare eqn (3.4)].

At high doses, and therefore high values of C_{ss}, $C_{ss} \gg K_m$, and thus $K_m + C_{ss} \approx C_{ss}$.

Now eqn (3.36) becomes:

$$\frac{dD}{dt} \approx D_{max} = \text{constant}. \tag{3.38}$$

Equation (3.38) is recognizable as a *zero-order equation* [compare eqn (3.1)].

Thus, at high doses, the pharmacokinetic properties are predominantly zero-order, at low doses predominantly first-order, and at intermediate doses mixed.

Since eqn (3.36) describes the curve in Fig. 3.18 it will be apparent that K_m and D_{max} cannot be calculated properly on the basis of one measurement of a steady-state concentration during maintenance therapy with one dose of drug. To define the characteristics of the curve with a reasonable degree of accuracy several measurements need to be made at steady state during dosage with different doses. In practice, however one can approximately calculate K_m and D_{max} on the basis of two such measurements. This can be done using any one of the classical linearizations used in enzyme kinetics (e.g. the plot of

$$\frac{1}{\text{dose}} \text{ versus } \frac{1}{C_{ss}},$$

comparable with the Lineweaver–Burke plot). However, it is much simpler to use a plot known as the 'direct linear plot' as illustrated in Fig. 3.19. In this plot, instead of plotting each value of C_{ss} and its corresponding daily dose as a single point, as on conventional plots, each pair of values (C_{ss} and dose) is plotted as a straight line joining the two values—C_{ss} on the x-axis, conventionally to the left, and daily dose on the y-axis. The point at which two such lines cross indicates the value of K_m (on the x-axis to the right) and D_{max} (on the y-axis).

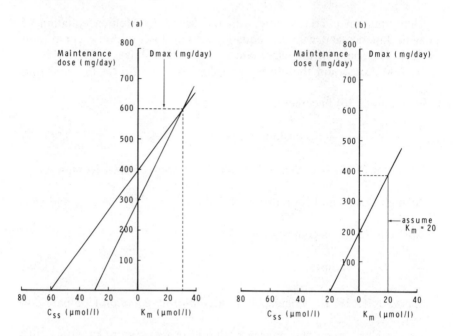

Fig. 3.19. The direct linear plot for analysis of non-linear kinetics.

(a) *Calculation of phenytoin D_{max} and K_m using two separate steady-state measurements (same data as in Fig. 3.18).* Each line is formed by joining the points indicating the steady-state plasma concentration (horizontal axis to the left) and the corresponding daily maintenance dosage (vertical axis). The point where these extrapolated lines cross shows the K_m (horizontal axis to the right) and the D_{max} (vertical axis).

(b) *Prediction (first approximation) of steady-state plasma phenytoin concentrations at any daily maintenance dosage from a single measurement.* The line joining the daily dosage of 200 mg to the measured steady-state plasma phenytoin concentration has been constructed. Assume, for the first approximation, that the patient's K_m is 20 μmol/l. To calculate the approximate steady-state phenytoin concentration likely to be encountered at a different dosage construct the line joining the new dose to the 20 μmol/l K_m point on the first line and extrapolate it to the horizontal axis on the left. This method can also be used to calculate the approximate dose required to produce a desired steady-state plasma concentration (see text).

In the example shown in Fig. 3.19(a) two doses of phenytoin were administered to steady state, 300 mg and 400 mg, and the corresponding steady-state plasma concentrations were 30 μmol/l and 60 μmol/l. The two lines formed cross at the point of K_m = 31 μmol/l and D_{max} = 600 mg/day.

Although accurate measurement of K_m and D_{max} depends on at least two (preferably more) measurements of C_{ss} at different maintenance doses, one can use a single measurement in combination with the mean K_m calculated from studies on large numbers of individuals, to assess D_{max} and hence to assess appropriate daily dosage. That is because, while the values of D_{max} in individuals are very variable, the values of K_m are much less so (see Fig. 3.5). The method for the calculation is illustrated in Fig. 3.19(b).

In the example illustrated, for phenytoin, a steady-state plasma concentration of 20 μmol/l was achieved at a daily maintenance dose of 200 mg. If we assume that this patient's K_m for phenytoin is 20 μmol/l the D_{max} can be estimated at 385 mg/day. If one wanted to know the daily dose required to produce a steady-state plasma concentration of 60 μmol/l one would draw a line joining the point of (K_m, D_{max}) to 60 μmol/l on the x-axis. The point where the line crosses the y-axis shows the daily maintenance dose required. Try it yourself. The answer is 300 mg.

4 The pharmacodynamic process
Is the drug producing the required pharmacological effect?

The pharmacodynamic process describes all those matters concerned with the pharmacological action of a drug, whether they be determinants of the therapeutic effect or of the toxic effect.

4.1. TYPES OF PHARMACOLOGICAL EFFECT

One of the most difficult problems in clinical pharmacology and therapeutics is the understanding of the relationships linking the pharmacokinetic, pharmacodynamic, and therapeutic phases, i.e. the links in quantitative terms in time between the concentration of the drug at an active site (usually rising and falling with intermittent dosage), drug association with and dissociation from receptors at the active site, activation or inhibition of those receptors, the ensuing sequence of events in the tissue leading to the pharmacological response, and the link between the pharmacological response and the therapeutic response. Many drug–receptor interactions have been worked out in pharmacological terms at a stable state of equilibrium which frequently does not apply during clinical drug therapy.

Three examples will serve to illustrate these links.

4.1.1. Drug–receptor interaction easily reversible: pharmacological effect easily reversible

In these circumstances the plasma drug concentration is closely related quantitatively, and in time, to the pharmacological effect.

Examples are the acute effects of propranolol in blocking β-adrenoceptors, the effect of insulin in lowering the blood glucose concentration, and the effect of naloxone in reversing opiate toxicity. In these cases the drugs associate with and dissociate from their receptors easily and quickly and the response follows accordingly. It is in such circumstances that plasma drug concentration measurements would be expected to reflect the pharmacological action of the drug well. If, however, the pharmacological effect itself, or the response to that effect, whether it be a therapeutic or toxic response, is clear-cut and easily measured, then plasma drug concentration measurements may not be necessary.

4.1.2. Drug–receptor interaction not easily reversible: pharmacological effect prolonged

Drugs which do not readily dissociate from receptors despite a falling concentration in the immediate environment of the receptor lead to a prolonged pharmacological effect.

Digoxin, for example, binds to cell membrane Na^+, K^+-ATPase and dissociates rather slowly. Its effect is not closely related to its plasma concentration in time. Irreversible monoamine oxidase (MAO) inhibitors, such as phenelzine and isocarboxazid, have such a prolonged effect that new enzyme needs to be synthesized before MAO activity can be restored. Aspirin acetylates a serine moiety at the active site of the enzyme cyclo-oxygenase. In platelets this leads to inhibition of prostaglandin synthesis for the life of the platelet. Thus although aspirin is cleared from the body within hours, its effects on platelets last for days and can be detected by diminution of platelet aggregation responses.

4.1.3. Drug–receptor interaction easily reversible: pharmacological effect prolonged

In these circumstances although the drug–receptor association is easily reversible, the association of drug with receptor puts into train a sequence of events which takes time to run through.

For example, corticosteroids react with receptor protein in the cytoplasm of certain sensitive cells to form a steroid–receptor complex. This complex enters the cell nucleus where it binds to chromatin and directs the genetic apparatus to transcribe RNA. This leads, for instance in liver cells, to the *de novo* production of several enzymes involved in gluconeogenesis and amino acid metabolism. One action of steroid hormones is to stimulate RNA transcription and ultimately the synthesis of specific proteins. The induction of these proteins takes some hours and each protein will have its own biological lifespan. Once the steroid has bound to the intracellular protein it sets off a sequence of reactions, which then has its own time scale independent of the quantity of steroid either in the blood or combined with the receptor.

The problem with examples of this type is that portions of the drug molecule may remain bound to tissue components even though the drug is undetectable in the blood, and such binding might be an integral part of the drug's action.

A clearer example is that of the biological agents used in immunization and vaccination. For example, immunization with tetanus toxoid provokes the production of protective antibodies and not only will the antibody titre remain high after the toxoid has been eliminated from the body but an immunological memory remains, so that if tetanus toxoid (or toxin) is reintroduced a secondary response, with high antibody titres, occurs.

A drug or agent which switches on or turns off the synthesis of a protein which is involved in the sequence of events leading to a therapeutic effect will potentially show a dissociation in time between its presence in the blood and its pharmacological effect because of the biological lifespan of the protein which is coupling the drug/agent receptor stimulation to the eventual pharmacological effect.

4.2. DISTINCTION BETWEEN THE PHARMACOLOGICAL EFFECTS OF A DRUG AND ITS THERAPEUTIC EFFECTS

The pharmacodynamic effect of a drug is not to be confused with its therapeutic effect. An example will illustrate this point (Fig. 4.1).

Consider the use of frusemide in the treatment of cardiac failure. Frusemide is a 'high-ceiling' diuretic acting mainly to inhibit sodium and chloride reabsorption in the ascending limb of the loop of Henle. The precise molecular mechanism involved is not yet understood, but presumably frusemide interferes reversibly with a tubular cellular process either at the membrane or intracellularly, such that the inward flux of sodium and chloride from the luminal surface of the cell is inhibited. If there is a good intraluminal flow of glomerular filtrate containing sodium and chloride then inhibition of their reabsorption will produce a diuresis. If the heart failure is very severe and causing serious underperfusion of the kidneys, resulting in diminished glomerular filtration, then the tubular flow of filtrate may be poor, and insufficient sodium and chloride may reach the ascending limb of the loop of Henle for the inhibition of their reabsorption to produce much of a diuresis. Improvement of renal perfusion in cardiac failure by drugs which increase the force of myocardial contraction, and therefore cardiac output (e.g. digoxin, dobutamine, or dopamine), and in the case of dopamine the production of renal vasodilatation, may overcome the apparent resistance to the diuretic effect of frusemide. Another factor in severe heart failure which might interfere with the diuretic effect of frusemide is the sodium-retaining effect of secondary hyperaldosteronism.

The fact that the link between the pharmacodynamic effect of frusemide on the renal tubular cell, and the production of a therapeutic effect (diuresis) is a highly variable one is a fundamental point to understand if the oedema of a patient with cardiac failure is resistant to the diuretic effect.

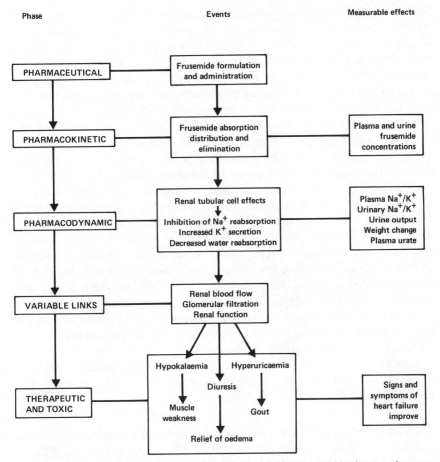

Fig. 4.1. The chain of events linking the administration of frusemide and its therapeutic or toxic effects. Note the variables which link the pharmacodynamic effects of frusemide to its therapeutic or toxic effects.

4.3. THERAPEUTIC OR TOXIC EFFECTS DUE TO MORE THAN ONE PHARMACOLOGICAL EFFECT

There is a tendency to consider only that pharmacological effect which results directly in the therapeutic effect. This narrow viewpoint is wrong. Some drugs have more than one molecular mechanism of action. For example aspirin, which in therapeutic doses inhibits prostaglandin synthesis, in toxic doses uncouples oxidative phosphorylation, an effect not dependent on prostaglandins. D-tubocurarine not only acts as a competitive neuromuscular blocking agent but also releases histamine from mast cells, thus lowering the blood pressure, and these are quite different pharmacological actions.

Commonly, various *different pharmacological effects* may be produced by the actions of a single drug on a *similar molecular mechanism* in different tissues. Non-selective ($\beta_1 + \beta_2$), β-adrenoceptor antagonists not only slow the pulse rate and decrease cardiac work, reducing myocardial oxygen requirements, and preventing anginal pain, but also, through their β_2 antagonistic effects, lead to increased airways resistance, particularly in patients with bronchial asthma. Non-selective β-adrenoceptor antagonists may also cause decreased hepatic glycogenolysis by inhibition of the β_2-agonist activity of circulating adrenaline, and therefore potentiate hypoglycaemic reactions to insulin and oral hypoglycaemic drugs in a diabetic patient. The antihypertensive action of α-methyldopa may be mediated by an agonist effect of its chief metabolite, α-methylnoradrenaline acting on α-adrenoceptors in areas of the brain controlling sympathetic nervous system activity, and therefore peripheral resistance; α-methyldopa probably has α-adrenergic activity elsewhere in the brain, resulting in drowsiness, lethargy, and depression, central adverse effects which are not all that uncommon. This drug also competitively inhibits aromatic amino acid decarboxylation, but in the patient this effect generally has no physiologically detectable end point, probably because the overall inhibition of this prolific enzyme is rather small and relatively unimportant in terms of its function in converting L-dopa to dopamine, which is part of the pathway leading to the synthesis of catecholamines.

It is as well to remember 'peripheral' or 'non-therapeutic' effects of drugs, since they can be of clinical importance in several ways. For example:

1. The effect of phenobarbitone in inducing hepatic microsomal enzyme activity is peripheral to its anticonvulsant effect, but can cause difficult problems with drug interactions by causing, for instance, increased metabolism of warfarin (see Chapter 10).

2. Neuroleptic drugs, such as phenothiazines (e.g. chlorpromazine) and butyrophenones (e.g. haloperidol) are used in the treatment of psychoses, and are thought to act by inhibition of dopamine function. An inevitable pharmacological adverse effect of this action is drug-induced Parkinsonism, a serious clinical problem in the treatment of patients with the neuroleptic drugs.

3. Aminoglycoside antibiotics (e.g. gentamicin, amikacin), if given in high dosage, will all produce cochlear and vestibular damage leading to impairment or loss of hearing, and disordered balance. These effects are quite apart from the antibiotic activity of these substances but profoundly influence their therapeutic index, and have to be taken into account when deciding the therapeutic regimen for an individual patient. This leads to the requirement of plasma concentration monitoring (see Chapter 7).

4.4. HIERARCHIES IN THE THERAPEUTIC PROCESS

In Fig. 4.2 is shown the build up from the level of molecular pharmacology to the clinical level of the therapeutic response. The aim of this analysis is to link the pharmacodynamic phase with the therapeutic phase more coherently. Eventually one can use this synthesis in analysing the results of certain drug therapies. Each of the following examples illustrates some facet of the relationships linking the pharmacodynamic phase with the therapeutic phase.

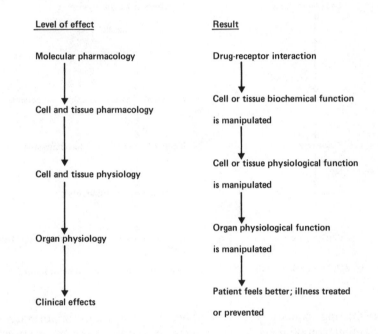

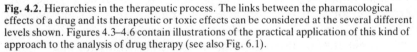

Fig. 4.2. Hierarchies in the therapeutic process. The links between the pharmacological effects of a drug and its therapeutic or toxic effects can be considered at the several different levels shown. Figures 4.3–4.6 contain illustrations of the practical application of this kind of approach to the analysis of drug therapy (see also Fig. 6.1).

4.4.1. Digoxin therapy in heart failure in sinus rhythm (Fig.4.3)

Digoxin binds to and inhibits membrane-bound Na^+, K^+-ATPase and by so doing inhibits active transport of sodium out of cells and of potassium into cells. As a result the intracellular concentration of sodium rises. It is thought that this leads to an alteration in intracellular calcium disposition, which in turn leads to an increased rate of myocardial contractility. That causes an increase in cardiac output and other haemodynamic changes, and the end result is the relief of the signs and symptoms of heart failure. The biggest assumption in this analysis is that it is by the inhibition of Na^+, K^+-ATPase that digoxin exerts its therapeutic effects.

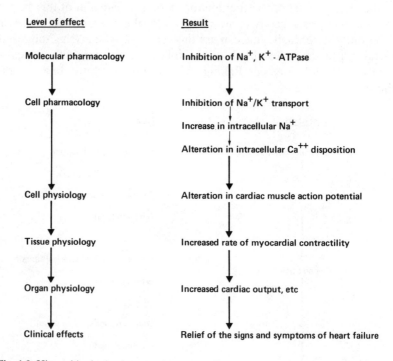

Fig. 4.3. Hierarchies in the therapeutic process: digoxin therapy in heart failure in sinus rhythm.

In making an analysis of this kind one begins to see the importance of the individual components of the effects of a drug in producing the final therapeutic effect. It is conceivable, for example, that in some patients digoxin might inhibit ATPase and increase intracellular sodium concentrations without altering the rate of myocardial contractility (as may happen in chronic cor pulmonale); or that the rate of myocardial contractility might be increased but without a consequent increase in cardiac output (as in hypertrophic obstructive cardiomyopathy, in which the positive inotropic effect of digoxin is deleterious because of the fixed obstruction); or even that there may be changes in the haemodynamic function of the heart without subsequent clinical improvement (as in patients who may have a poor diuresis for some reason unrelated to the heart, e.g. due to fluid-retaining drugs).

It is well to remember that simply because one can demonstrate effects of drugs at these different levels, one cannot automatically assume that consequent effects will occur at the other levels.

4.4.2. Neuroleptic drug therapy in schizophrenia (Fig. 4.4)

When neuroleptic drugs, such as chlorpromazine and haloperidol, block dopamine receptors in the brain this leads to inhibition of dopamine neurotransmission, and this manifests itself in at least three ways.

First, it is believed that somehow or other inhibition of dopamine neurotransmission produces an improvement in psychosis. Second, inhibition of dopamine neurotransmission interferes with extrapyramidal function leading to Parkinsonism. Third, inhibition of dopamine function in the pituitary causes a prolactin release and may lead in some women to galactorrhoea and in men to painful breasts.

The understanding of the actions of neuroleptic drugs in blocking central dopamine receptor function has led to the dopamine hypothesis in schizophrenia. This proposes that there is a primary dysfunction in the brain which, in some unknown way, is responsible for the psychiatric state. This, however, is a dangerous argument because drug actions may not indicate primary pathology. Inhibition of dopamine function could produce an improvement in schizophrenia anywhere down the line of the number of events, one of which might be an involvement of dopamine at quite a secondary level in the production of certain symptoms in the whole illness of schizophrenia.

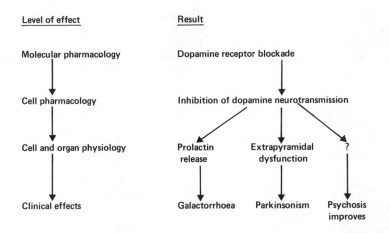

Fig. 4.4. Hierarchies in the therapeutic process: neuroleptic drug therapy in schizophrenia.

4.4.3. Salbutamol and theophylline in bronchial asthma (Fig. 4.5)

There has been a lot of discussion about whether theophylline adds anything to β_2-adrenoceptor agonist therapy in asthma and vice versa. At the molecular pharmacological level salbutamol acts as a β_2-agonist, stimulating adenylate cyclase and increasing intracellular concentrations of cyclic AMP. Whether this increase in cyclic AMP is of importance in bronchial mast cells decreasing inflammatory mediator release (which would produce bronchodilatation), or in smooth muscle (producing relaxation) is unknown, but it is probably one or the other of these. Theophylline is a phosphodiesterase inhibitor which blocks the metabolism of cyclic AMP to its inactive metabolite 5′AMP (Fig. 4.5). One would therefore expect salbutamol to enhance the bronchodilator effect of theophylline. At the clinical level some studies have shown that salbutamol *can* improve on the maximum bronchodilator theophylline response produced in bronchitic patients with reversible airways obstruction. It is not known yet whether theophylline at maximal effective doses can add to the maximal effect of stable background salbutamol therapy but that would be a reasonable presumption.

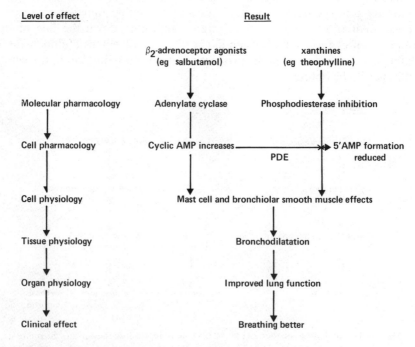

Fig. 4.5. Hierarchies in the therapeutic process: β_2-adrenoceptor agonists (e.g. salbutamol) and xanthines (e.g. theophylline) in bronchial asthma.

4.4.4. Myasthenia gravis—disease and treatment (Fig. 4.6)

For myasthenia one can analyse both the disease and its treatment simultaneously.

In many cases, myasthenia is associated with a circulating antibody to the acetylcholine receptor. Acetylcholine activity is therefore blocked at nerve endings, leading to defective neurotransmission and neuromuscular fatigue. At the clinical level this leads to muscle weakness. In considering treatment with anticholinesterases, such as neostigmine and pyridostigmine, a great deal is understood about the mechanisms by which the anticholinesterases inhibit the enzyme cholinesterase, which normally breaks down released acetylcholine. If cholinesterase is inhibited then the concentration of acetylcholine levels at the motor end-plate rises, and its action is potentiated. This overcomes the defect in neuromuscular transmission, neuromuscular fatigue improves, and muscle weakness is relieved.

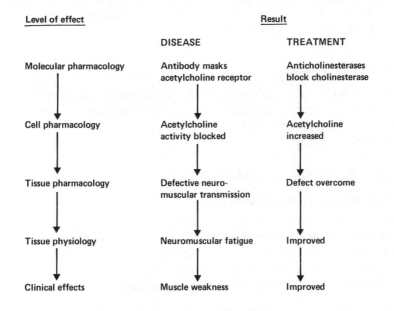

Fig. 4.6. Hierarchies in the therapeutic process: myasthenia gravis—disease and treatment.

It is in the nature of pyridostigmine as an anticholinesterase inhibitor that one would expect a drug–receptor interaction of type 1 (see p.5), i.e. as the inhibitor goes on and off the enzyme with changing plasma concentrations there is increased cholinergic function, which rapidly reverses as the inhibition of the enzyme ceases. It has been shown that although the plasma concentration of pyridostigmine required to restore transmission to normal varies over a five-fold range in different patients, perhaps reflecting the variable severity of the disease, there is a good relationship between the concentration of pyridostigmine in the plasma and the effect on neuromuscular transmission.

4.5. TYPES OF PHARMACOLOGICAL ACTIONS PRODUCED BY DRUGS IN THERAPY

4.5.1. Receptor stimulation

(a) β_2-adrenoceptor agonists

Salbutamol is a β_2 agonist and produces bronchial dilatation in bronchial asthma.

(b) Succinylcholine

Succinylcholine is used as a muscle relaxant accompanying general anaesthesia during major surgery. It acts, like acetylcholine, at cholinergic receptors at the muscle motor end-plate but produces a depolarization block so that naturally released acetylcholine can no longer cause muscle contraction.

(c) Bromocriptine

Bromocriptine acts as a direct agonist stimulating dopamine receptors. It therefore mimics the action of dopamine on the pituitary, inhibits prolactin release, and suppresses lactation. It is also useful as a dopamine agonist in some patients with Parkinson's disease.

4.5.2. Receptor antagonism

(a) β_1-adrenoceptor antagonists

Absolute specificity of β-adrenoceptor antagonists has not been achieved but there is some degree of selectivity towards β_1 receptors by practolol, atenolol, and metoprolol. These drugs block the β_1 actions of noradrenaline released from cardiac sympathetic nerves and of circulating adrenaline, and are used in the treatment of angina pectoris and hypertension.

(b) H_1 histamine receptor antagonists

H_1 histamine receptor antagonists, such as diphenhydramine, promethazine, and mepyramine, are used mainly to block the actions of histamine released during hypersensitivity reactions. They are most useful in controlling the effects of histamine on mucous membranes and skin.

(c) Neuroleptic drugs

Neuroleptic drugs such as the phenothiazines (e.g. chlorpromazine, fluphenazine, thioridazine) and butyrophenones (e.g. haloperidol) inhibit the action of dopamine on post-synaptic dopamine receptor sites in various areas of the brain. They are used in the treatment of schizophrenia and mania and their pharmacological action also results in the adverse effect of Parkinsonism.

4.5.3. Drugs affecting transport processes

(a) Probenecid

Probenecid is an organic acid, a benzoic acid derivative, which was developed to depress tubular secretion of penicillin. It inhibits the transport of organic acids across epithelial barriers and not only blocks the active *secretion* of penicillin into the renal tubular lumen but also blocks the active *reabsorption* of uric acid. It is now mainly used as a uricosuric agent in the treatment of gout, and occasionally to decrease the renal clearance of penicillin from the blood, thereby raising blood penicillin concentrations in, for example, the treatment of bacterial endocarditis. Usually, however, this is achieved without probenecid, simply by increasing the dose.

(b) Thiazide diuretics

The thiazide diuretics decrease sodium reabsorption in the cortical diluting segment of the renal tubule (distal tubule) thereby producing an increased excretion of sodium and water.

(c) Insulin

One of the many actions of insulin is to increase the inward flux of glucose into cells. The exact mechanism of this action is unknown. In the treatment of hyperglycaemic diabetic coma the rapid fall in blood glucose produced by insulin is undoubtedly largely due to this action. In addition insulin causes an inward flux of potassium into cells and in the treatment of hyperglycaemic diabetic coma with insulin this may result in hypokalaemia. For this reason the fluids infused intravenously during the treatment of diabetic coma with insulin should usually contain potassium.

4.5.4. Enzyme inhibitors

(a) Neostigmine

Neostigmine is a reversible cholinesterase inhibitor. It is used in the treatment of myasthenia gravis because of its effect in increasing the concentration of acetylcholine at the muscle motor end-plate, thereby alleviating the block in neuromuscular transmission occurring in this condition.

(b) Allopurinol

Xanthine and hypoxanthine are oxidized to uric acid by the enzyme xanthine oxidase, which is inhibited by allopurinol. Allopurinol therefore decreases the synthesis of uric acid. The drug has this effect mainly through its metabolite alloxanthine, a potent noncompetitive inhibitor of xanthine oxidase, which persists for a long time in tissues. The decrease in uric acid production may prevent the occurrence of attacks of acute gouty arthritis, decreases the incidence of chronic gouty arthritis, and prevents the occurrence of uric acid stones (gouty nephropathy). Xanthine and hypoxanthine are considerably more water soluble than uric acid, and their renal clearance is rapid.

(c) Mono-amine oxidase (MAO) inhibitors

Isocarboxazid and phenelzine bind irreversibly to MAO and new enzyme molecules must be synthesized to restore the metabolism of monoamines to normal, which takes about two weeks. The inhibition of MAO by tranylcypromine is reversible. MAO inhibitors are used in the treatment of depression, and although the sequence of events by which they exert their antidepressant activity is largely unknown, it is presumably associated with their inhibitory effects on the metabolism of 5-hydroxytryptamine, noradrenaline, or dopamine in the brain.

4.5.5. Replacement drugs

This is a slightly artificial subheading pharmacologically, but useful from the clinical point of view. It includes those drugs which are used to replace some missing endogenous component of the body.

(a) Hydroxocobalamin (vitamin B_{12})

Hydroxocobalamin is used intramuscularly in the treatment of pernicious anaemia, in which the absorption of dietary vitamin B_{12} is impaired due to lack of production of a glycoprotein, intrinsic factor, by gastric parietal cells. It is also used in the treatment of other conditions associated with vitamin B_{12} deficiency.

(b) Thyroxine

L-thyroxine, orally, is used to replace natural thyroid hormone secretion in hypothyroidism, whether primary, or secondary to the treatment of hyperthyroidism.

(c) Ferrous iron salts

Ferrous sulphate, gluconate, or fumarate are used in the treatment of anaemia due to iron deficiency.

4.5.6. Non-receptor–mediated drug actions

This group consists of a miscellany of drug actions.

(a) Chelating agents

Calcium sodium edetate ($CaNa_2EDTA$) chelates many divalent and trivalent metals and is used in the treatment of poisoning, particularly with lead. Dimercaprol chelates certain heavy metals and is used in the treatment of mercury poisoning. Penicillamine chelates copper and is used in the treatment of hepatolenticular degeneration (Wilson's disease).

(b) Osmotic diuretics

Mannitol is a hexahydric alcohol related to mannose, and an isomer of sorbitol. It is freely filtered at the glomerulus but is only slightly reabsorbed by the renal tubules. Its action within the kidney depends primarily upon the concentration of osmotically active particles in the tubular fluid which take water with them, thus increasing urine volume. It has no other pharmacological effects. It is used to produce a diuresis in the treatment of some acute poisonings and cerebral oedema. On occasions it has been used to restore renal tubular function and urinary output in shock.

(c) Volatile general anaesthetics

These agents lack any obvious molecular feature in common. Diverse agents, such as the halogenated hydrocarbons (halothane, methoxyflurane, trichloroethylene) and non-halogenated agents, such as nitrous oxide, ether, and cyclopropane, produce very similar effects on the brain. The usual drug–receptor model for drug action does not readily accommodate this group of drugs. It is generally thought that the primary action of volatile general anaesthetics is on the lipid matrix of the biological membrane, that the biophysical properties of the membrane are thereby changed, and that this results in changes in the fluxes of ions or in other functions of the membranes that are crucial for the normal operation of neuronal excitability.

(d) Cytotoxic agents and the 'counterfeit incorporation mechanism'

It was previously thought that purine antimetabolites, such as 6-mercaptopurine, and pyrimidine antimetabolites, such as cytosine arabinoside and 5-fluorouracil, might act by being incorporated into nucleic acids, the so-called 'counterfeit incorporation mechanism', which would then cause structural abnormalities in either DNA or RNA, and prevent the transfer of normal genetic information, resulting in actual codings. However, with increased understanding of the mode of action of these drugs, it appears that they are converted to intermediate metabolites which act as inhibitors of the various enzymes involved in the synthesis of DNA and RNA.

4.5.7. Chemotherapeutic agents in infective disease

This is an important group of drugs, but it consists of such a large number of compounds with different effects on bacteria and other micro-organisms that a separate but brief consideration of some of their mechanisms of action must suffice. Several mechanisms of action of antimicrobial agents have been proposed.

(a) Inhibition of synthesis of bacterial cell walls or activation of enzymes that disrupt bacterial cell walls

Penicillins and cephalosporins belong to this group.

(b) Increased permeability of bacterial cell membranes with leakage of essential intracellular components

The antifungals, nystatin and amphotericin B, act in this way.

(c) Inhibition of bacterial protein synthesis by inhibition of ribosomal function

Chloramphenicol, the tetracyclines, erythromycin, lincomycin, and clindamycin belong to this group.

(d) Interference with the transcription of mRNA

The aminoglycoside antibiotics (e.g. gentamicin, kanamycin, streptomycin, neomycin, amikacin) bind to the 30s ribosomal sub-unit and cause the production of abnormal polypeptides through misreading of the mRNA code.

(e) Interference with bacterial nucleic acid metabolism

Rifampicin, which inhibits DNA-dependent RNA polymerase belongs to this group.

(f) Antimetabolites

This group includes trimethoprim and the sulphonamides. These interfere with metabolic reactions essential for the viability of the organism.

4.6. PHARMACOLOGICAL ASPECTS OF LONG-TERM DRUG THERAPY: ADAPTATION, WITHDRAWAL, AND REBOUND

Some drugs are used in single doses to deal with an acute problem, for example subcutaneous adrenaline in the treatment of an anaphylactic response to a bee sting. In contrast, other drugs may be taken by patients for many years, for example β-adrenoceptor antagonists in the treatment of hypertension. Between these extremes lie drug courses which vary in duration, for example antibiotics are taken for days or weeks, anticoagulants for weeks or months after a deep venous thrombosis, antidepressant drug therapy lasts months, and anti-asthmatic drugs are taken intermittently over years. There are many different patterns of drug use to fit individual clinical problems.

Prolonged drug therapy, however, brings with it the phenomenon of adaptation to the acute pharmacological effects of the drug. The clinical results of adaptation are several (see Table 4.1).

Table 4.1   *The different ways in which adaptation to drug effects may become apparent clinically*

1. *Tolerance—increasing ineffectiveness of therapy*
   (a) Metabolic 'auto-induction', e.g. barbiturates, alcohol.
   (b) Physiological homoeostatic mechanisms, e.g. hydralazine (reflex tachycardia).
   (c) Target cell tolerance, e.g. depletion of noradrenaline by ephedrine; changes in sulphydryl structures by nitrates; opiate tolerance, mechanism unknown; digitalis tolerance by an increase in receptor numbers.
2. *Withdrawal syndromes*
   e.g. opiates, alcohol, benzodiazepines, clonidine, corticosteroids, enzyme inducers, β-adrenoceptor antagonists.
3. *Adverse reactions directly due to adaptation*
   e.g. tardive dyskinesia due to dopamine antagonists.
4. *Therapeutic effects through adaptation*
   e.g. immunization and vaccination; tricyclic antidepressants.

4.6.1. Tolerance—increasing ineffectiveness of therapy

Drug tolerance is a state of decreased responsiveness to a drug, brought about by previous exposure to that drug, or to a drug with similar acute effects. It may occur in several ways.

(a) Metabolic tolerance

Metabolic tolerance results from an increased rate of metabolism. Although in the cases of barbiturates and alcohol there is undoubtedly some cellular adaptation to their effects, nevertheless it has been shown that the hepatic inactivation of barbiturates and alcohol is increased after chronic exposure, so that a given dose produces a reduced effect. Induction of hepatic microsomal drug-metabolizing enzymes is the commonest cause of metabolic drug tolerance—so-called 'auto-induction' (see also Chapter 10, p.163).

(b) Physiological homoeostatic mechanisms

Hydralazine was introduced in the 1950s for the treatment of hypertension. When used alone its efficacy was not impressive because the short-term fall in blood pressure, which it causes by peripheral vasodilatation, causes reflex activation of the sympathetic nervous system resulting in a reflex tachycardia and increased cardiac output. Thus the homoeostatic 'adaptive' mechanism caused long-term ineffectiveness of therapy. This problem has been overcome by the use of β-adrenoceptor antagonists which prevent the reflex tacycardia and which increase the effectiveness of hydralazine as an antihypertensive agent. This also allows the use of fairly low doses of hydralazine, thus reducing the risk of hydralazine-induced lupus.

(c) Tolerance at the level of the target cell

Tolerance may develop to the vasoconstricting effects of ephedrine nose-drops, used in the treatment of vasomotor rhinitis. This is because ephedrine acts by releasing noradrenaline from sympathetic nerve endings and when the noradrenaline is depleted ephedrine can no longer be effective.

Tolerance to organic nitrates has been described in workers handling nitroglycerin (glyceryl trinitrate) in munitions factories. When they first handle nitroglycerin they develop headaches due to the vasodilatory effects of nitroglycerin on the extra-cranial arteries. As exposure continues the headaches wear off. At the weekend, when they are away from work, the tolerance disappears and on returning to work on the Monday morning they once more experience headaches which wear off again as the week progresses. Patients taking penta-erythritol tetranitrate (PETN) chronically for angina pectoris may develop tolerance to its effects and may not respond to the acute effects of glyceryl trinitrate.

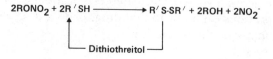

Fig. 4.7. Tolerance to the effects of nitrates — a proposed mechanism.

A mechanism for this effect has been proposed (see Fig. 4.7). Normally organic nitrates ($RONO_2$) would interact with 'receptors' containing sulphydryl groups ($R'SH$). Nitrite ions would be formed and the sulphydryl groups oxidized to disulphide groups ($R'S-SR'$). This effect renders the tissue unresponsive to nitrates. It can be shown *in vitro* that responsiveness is restored by dithiothreitol, which regenerates sulphydryl groups.

Workers handling nitroglycerin have been reported in some cases to have developed acute episodes of angina pectoris and myocardial infarction on Sundays and on Monday mornings before work. Eight out of nine such cases were in women, and in one coronary artery spasm in normal coronary arteries occurred during coronary angiography and was relieved by glyceryl trinitrate. Some of the other patients had coronary angiography and were shown to have normal coronary arteries. Thus long-term exposure to organic nitrates may result in rebound coronary artery spasm following withdrawal. The mechanism of this effect is unknown.

In the treatment of severe chronic pain, for example in malignant disease, tolerance to the analgesic effect of morphine, and other narcotic analgesics, may occur, and increasing doses may be required to alleviate the pain. This tolerance is not so marked to other effects of morphine (e.g. miosis of the pupils and decreased gastro-intestinal motility) and it is not of metabolic origin. Despite the discovery of opiate receptors, of endogenous opioid peptides (enkephalins and endorphins) and of the interrelationship of endogenous opiate functions with neurotransmitters such as acetylcholine, 5-hydroxytryptamine, noradrenaline, and dopamine, the precise mechanism of morphine tolerance (and addiction withdrawal) is still not understood. It is generally agreed, however, that the effect is at the neuronal level.

Tolerance to the long-term effects of cardiac glycosides may occur during long-term therapy because of an adaptive increase in the numbers of cardiac glycoside receptor sites on cells. The clinical relevance of this effect is as yet uncertain.

4.6.2. Withdrawal syndromes

A common, although not inevitable, accompaniment of an adaptive response to chronic drug usage is the occurrence of a withdrawal response when the drug is withdrawn. The withdrawal response usually takes the form of some sort of adverse reaction.

(a) Opiates

A withdrawal syndrome occurs in opiate addicts when the opiate is withdrawn or naloxone is administered. The symptoms consist of yawning, rhinorrhoea, and sweating, followed by the so-called 'cold turkey' in which there is shivering and goose-flesh. Later nausea, vomiting, diarrhoea, and hypertension may occur. The acute syndrome subsides within a week but the addict may have anxiety and sleep disturbances for several weeks or months after. This syndrome can be avoided by introducing increasing doses of methadone as the opiate is withdrawn, since withdrawal of methadone at a later date does not result in this syndrome.

(b) Alcohol

Delirium tremens may occur on withdrawal of alcohol from chronic alcoholics. The syndrome consists of disorientation and visual hallucinations.

(c) Benzodiazepines

Withdrawal of benzodiazepines after long-term therapy may result in a disturbance of sleep pattern (rebound insomnia associated with abnormal EEG sleep patterns), agitation, restlessness, and occasionally epileptic convulsions.

(d) Clonidine

Sudden withdrawal of clonidine after long-term therapy results in a severe and acute rise in blood pressure, accompanied by nervousness, headache, abdominal pain, sweating, and tachycardia, occurring 8–12 h after the last dose. This syndrome should be treated with α and β-adrenoceptor antagonists (e.g. phentolamine and propranolol). The mechanism is not yet understood.

(e) Corticosteroids

Long-term therapy with corticosteroids suppresses pituitary ACTH secretion leading to 'wasting' of the adrenal cortex and a diminution in the degree of its immediate steroidogenic response to ACTH. When long-term steroid therapy is suddenly withdrawn, ACTH secretion by the pituitary may take several weeks or months to pick up. Since the adrenal cortex has to hypertrophy in order to become normally responsive to ACTH the patient is at great risk of an Addisonian crisis, if stressed. As shown in Fig. 4.8 it may take several months for the pituitary–adrenal axis to become normal.

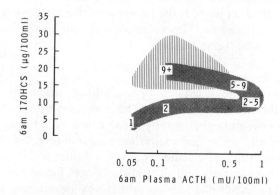

Fig. 4.8. Recovery of adrenal function after suppression by long-term corticosteroid therapy. The numbers in the cross-hatched area indicate the numbers of months after withdrawing corticosteroids. The vertically hatched region contains the normal values. During long-term corticosteroid therapy plasma endogenous corticosteroids and ACTH are both reduced. Following withdrawal there is a gradual increase in the secretion of ACTH by the pituitary over the succeeding weeks and months. However, only much later does the adrenal gland become responsive to the increase in ACTH. As plasma endogenous corticosteroid concentrations then increase, ACTH secretion by the pituitary gradually returns to normal. [Adapted from data of Gruber *et al.* (1965) *J. Clin. Endocrinol.* **25**, 11–16, with permission.]

(f) Barbiturates and other enzyme inducers

A metabolic withdrawal syndrome (see section 4.6.1.(a), metabolic tolerance, above) may occur when a barbiturate or other enzyme inducer is withdrawn from a patient taking warfarin. The sequence of events is as follows:

(i) warfarin clearance is increased by hepatic enzyme induction caused by phenobarbitone or another enzyme-inducing drug;

(ii) warfarin dose is increased to produce a measurable pharmacological effect on clotting;

(iii) withdrawal of the inducing agent leads to decreased clearance of warfarin, which then accumulates;

(iv) bleeding occurs.

(g) β-adrenoceptor antagonists

There is an increased risk of angina pectoris and myocardial infarction in patients with ischaemic heart disease on withdrawal of β-blockers after long-term therapy. This may be because of an increase in the numbers of β-receptors in tissues (as has been shown in lymphocytes). If there is an increased number of β-receptors in the heart, then when the β-blocker is withdrawn the heart might be supersensitive to the β-adrenergic effects of sympathetic nervous activity.

4.6.3. Adverse effects directly due to adaptation

(a) Drug-induced dyskinesias

Patients taking neuroleptic drugs such as chlorpromazine, fluphenazine, and haloperidol continuously for long periods of time commonly develop abnormal movements. Because the abnormal movements come on late during drug use they are known collectively as *tardive dyskinesia*. The face, mouth, and tongue are most commonly affected, causing stereotyped sucking and smacking of the lips, lateral jaw movements, and fly-catching-like darting movements of the tongue. Occasionally the dyskinesia may be more widespread, and resemble choreoathetosis. It is thought that the continuous long-term blockade of brain dopamine function with neuroleptic drugs leads to increased sensitivity to the effects of dopamine in certain areas of the brain (perhaps by an increase in dopamine receptor numbers) and that tardive dyskinesia is an expression of that increased sensitivity in extrapyramidal areas of the brain.

4.6.4. Therapeutic effects through adaptation

(a) Immunization and vaccination

By adaptation to an initial immunological challenge the immune system develops the ability to respond to a subsequent similar challenge (for example tetanus immunization, discussed above, p.61).

(b) Tricyclic antidepressants

Although tricyclic antidepressants very quickly produce inhibition of re-uptake of noradrenaline and 5-hydroxytryptamine in the brain, the therapeutic effect of these drugs takes 1–2 weeks to become evident. Gradually it has become obvious that the brain adapts to the increased concentrations of noradrenaline and 5-hydroxytryptamine in the synaptic clefts in certain areas, where the sensitivity of certain responses to the neurotransmitters is decreased (so-called 'down-regulation'). It could be that some part of this adaptive effect is the pharmacological action through which the antidepressant drugs produce their therapeutic effects.

It is not known to what extent other therapeutic responses to drugs may be mediated through adaptive responses but questions can be raised in regard to the therapeutic effectiveness of β-adrenoceptor antagonists and thiazide diuretics in hypertension.

4.7. GRADED RESPONSES TO DRUGS—THE DOSE–RESPONSE CURVE

The pharmacological effects of drugs are related to the concentration of drug at its site of action—within certain limits the higher the concentration, the greater the pharmacological effect. The relationship between the concentration of a drug at its site of action and the intensity of its

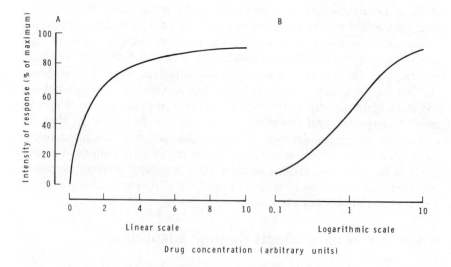

Fig. 4.9. Dose–response curves. When the intensity of the response to a drug is plotted against the drug concentration the curve takes the form of a rectangular hyperbola (left-hand panel). When it is plotted against the logarithm of the drug concentration the shape is sigmoid (right-hand panel—the log dose–response curve).

pharmacological effect is called its *dose–response curve* and often takes the shape illustrated in Fig. 4.9. Note that when the intensity of response is plotted against drug concentration on a linear scale (left-hand panel) the shape of the curve is that of a rectangular hyperbola, and when it is plotted against the logarithm of the drug concentration (right-hand panel) the shape is sigmoid. The latter is sometimes known as the *log dose–response curve*.

4.7.1. Mathematics of the dose–response curve

Let us suppose that a drug molecule combines with a corresponding tissue molecule (its 'receptor') to produce its pharmacological effect. We shall assume that one drug molecule (D) combines with one receptor molecule (R) to produce a drug–receptor complex (DR); that the association of the two molecules is reversible; and that the pharmacological effect on the tissue depends on the presence of the drug on the receptor.

We can write the relationship between drug and receptor as follows:

$$D + R \underset{k_{diss}}{\overset{k_{ass}}{\rightleftharpoons}} DR \tag{4.1}$$

where k_{ass} and k_{diss} are rate constants, expressions of the speed of association and speed of dissociation of drug and receptor respectively.

[DR] is the number of receptors occupied by drug and [R] the number unoccupied. Then at equilibrium, by the law of mass action,

$$\frac{[D]\,[R]}{[DR]} = \frac{k_{diss}}{k_{ass}} \tag{4.2}$$

where square brackets indicate concentrations. The ratio of the two rate constants is called the dissociation constant of the reaction between drug and receptor, abbreviated to K_D. The lower the value of K_D the less readily reversible is the reaction (i.e. the value of K_D will be very low in a slowly-reversible drug–receptor interaction). We shall shortly see what the K_D represents in terms of the drug concentration/effect relationship.

If the total number of receptors available to the drug is $[R_{tot}]$, then

$$[R_{tot}] = [R] + [DR]. \tag{4.3}$$

Substituting for [R] in eqn (4.2) we find that

$$\frac{[D]\,[R_{tot} - DR]}{[DR]} = \frac{k_{diss}}{k_{ass}} = K_D \tag{4.4}$$

and that therefore

$$\frac{[DR]}{[R_{tot}]} = \frac{[D]}{K_D + [D]} \tag{4.5}$$

Let us assume that the intensity of response (I) is proportional to the number of receptors occupied by the drug (DR) (the so-called receptor-occupancy theory). Then

$$I = k[DR].\tag{4.6}$$

The maximum possible effect, I_{max}, will occur when all the receptors are occupied, and so

$$I_{max} = k[R_{tot}].\tag{4.7}$$

Dividing eqn (4.6) by eqn (4.7) we find that

$$\frac{I}{I_{max}} = \frac{[DR]}{[R_{tot}]}\tag{4.8}$$

If we now substitute eqn (4.8) in eqn (4.5) we find that

$$\frac{I}{I_{max}} = \frac{[D]}{K_D + [D]}\tag{4.9}$$

or

$$I = \frac{I_{max}[D]}{K_D + [D]}\tag{4.10}$$

Equation (4.10) is identical in form to the equation we have already seen in relation to the non-linear kinetics of drugs such as phenytoin and alcohol [Chapter 3, eqn (3.36), p.57] and also to the Michaelis–Menten equation for rates of enzyme reactions.

4.7.2. Properties of the dose–response curve

Equation (4.10) defines the shape of the dose–response curve (Fig. 4.9) as we shall see if we examine its properties:

1. When $I = I_{max}/2$, $K_D = [D]$. In other words, K_D is the concentration of drug required to produce a half-maximal effect.
2. When $[D] = 0$, $I = 0$ (i.e. there is no effect when there is no drug!).
3. When $[D]$ is low, $[D] < K_D$ and thus

$$I \approx \frac{I_{max}}{K_D} \times [D].\tag{4.11}$$

In other words at low concentrations of D the response is directly proportional to the drug concentration.

4. When $[D]$ is high, $[D] > K_D$ and thus

$$I \to I_{max}.\tag{4.12}$$

In other words at high drug concentrations and large effects, only small further increases in effect can be achieved by increasing the drug concentration.

We can now see why the relationship between drug concentration and the intensity of its pharmacological effect has the shape it has (Fig. 4.9)—at drug concentrations below the K_D the relationship is approximately linear, while at concentrations above the K_D the increase in effect becomes progressively smaller and smaller until a plateau is reached at the maximum effect.

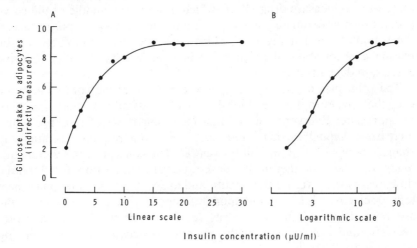

Fig. 4.10. The relationship between the concentration of insulin and its effect on glucose uptake by human adipocytes *in vitro*. [Adapted from Cuatrecasas (1969) *Proc. Nat. Acad. Sci.* **63**, 450–457, with permission.]

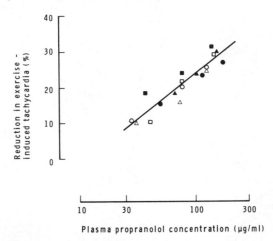

Fig. 4.11. The relationship between plasma propranolol concentrations in man and the effect of propranolol in reducing exercise-induced tachycardia. [Adapted from McDevitt and Shand (1975) *Clin. Pharmacol. Ther.* **18**, 708–713, with permission.]

Dose–response curves of the kind shown in Fig. 4.9 are often found in experiments using human tissues *in vitro* or in animals. An example is given in Fig. 4.10, which shows the relationship between the concentration of insulin and its effect on glucose uptake by human adipocytes *in vitro*.

In man it is not usual to be able to define the full dose–response curve in this way—it is usually too difficult to measure the small effects produced by *low* doses or concentrations of drugs, and measurements cannot be made at *high* doses or concentrations because of toxicity. It is more usual, therefore, to measure drug effects which occur in the middle of the curve (i.e. on the approximately linear portion of the log dose–response curve). An example is given in Fig. 4.11, which shows the relationship between the plasma concentration of propranolol in man and its effect in reducing exercise-induced tachycardia.

The principles of the dose–response curve are at the core of accurate drug therapy, even if at the clinical level all the details are sometimes hard to appreciate. Everyone can see that increasing doses of insulin produce increasing hypoglycaemia, and that the dose–response relationship changes with so-called 'insulin resistance'. The concept of the therapeutic index, i.e. the toxic:therapeutic dose ratio relies in part upon differential dose–response curves for therapeutic and toxic effects. At times pharmacological selectivity is dependent upon different dose–response curves for the different actions of the same drug (e.g. the effects of β-adrenoceptor agonists and antagonists with relative selectivity for β_1- or β_2-adrenoceptors).

These examples illustrate only a few of the areas in which dose-responsiveness can be seen to be of clinical relevance.

5 The therapeutic process
Is the pharmacological effect being translated into a therapeutic effect?

5.1. PATHOPHYSIOLOGY OF DISEASE

We have seen how *the pharmaceutical process* involving the formulation or 'delivery' of the drug substance, can affect the availability of the drug, how *the pharmacokinetic process* determines the concentrations of the drug over a period of time at the active site, and how in *the pharmacodynamic process* a pharmacological effect occurs. Now we must examine how this pharmacological effect is translated into a therapeutic effect.

To do this it is necessary to understand something of the pharmacological effects of the drug, and the way in which those effects interact with the processes underlying the pathology of the disease, described in a way allowing interpretation of drug action. Unfortunately, in our present state of knowledge that is not always possible. However, we may still try to understand the underlying processes of the disease (its 'pathophysiology') and base our questions about the role of specific drugs on our understanding of the pathophysiology of the disease and the relevant pharmacological effects of the drugs used in its treatment.

The pathophysiological processes involved are illustrated in Fig. 5.1 and can be considered in the light of an example. Consider pneumococcal pneumonia.

The *'cause'* is infection with the pneumococcus (*Streptococcus pneumoniae*) and there may be *contributory factors*, such as impairment of host defence mechanisms.

The *primary pathology* is the inflammatory response which results in the pneumonic change. This results in abnormalities in lung function which result in *secondary pathology* (in this case hypoxia as a direct result of the primary pathological change).

Whether one calls pleurisy and pleural effusion *secondary pathology* or *complications* is a matter of choice. Metastatic pneumococcal infection (e.g. cerebral abscess) would be regarded as a *complication*.

Each of these, the primary pathology, the secondary pathology, and complications, produces its own *signs* and *symptoms*.

The point of this type of analysis of the pathophysiology of disease is that it enables one to analyse as far as possible those processes one hopes to manipulate with drug therapy, and to define the scope of individual modes of treatment and their overall therapeutic impact. We shall now take this approach one step further with two detailed examples.

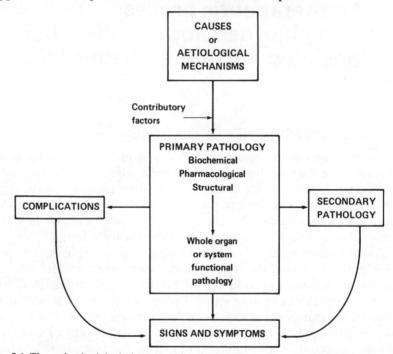

Fig. 5.1. The pathophysiological processes involved in disease. Drug treatment may be aimed at any or all of the different processes.

5.1.1. The pathophysiology and treatment of bronchial asthma (see Fig. 5.2)

The 'causes' of bronchial asthma are often several since the bronchi may be hyper-reactive to a number of different stimuli. Hypersensitivity reactions due to external allergens in the inspired air are responsible for so-called 'extrinsic' asthma. These allergens may be pollens, house-dust containing mite protein, feathers, fungal spores, or animal dander. The hypersensitivity reactions are usually of Type I and are IgE mediated, the antigen–antibody reaction occurring on the cell membrane of the bronchial mast cell. Occasionally a Type III, IgG-mediated reaction may occur. Allergic aspergillosis is of this type. These reactions cause the release of pharmacologically active substances such as histamine, leukotrienes (e.g. SRS-A), 5-hydroxytryptamine, bradykinin, and perhaps other peptides which promote contraction of bronchial smooth muscle leading to broncho-constriction and an inflammatory reaction in the bronchial mucosa. In certain sensitive individuals *bronchial infections* may lead to a similar set of reactions. *Irritants*, such as tobacco smoke, cold air, and acid fumes may trigger bronchoconstriction. Certain *drugs* may be responsible—aspirin is now recognized as a cause of asthma in certain sensitive individuals in whom nasal polyps also occur frequently. Such individuals are often also sensitive to tartrazine, a yellow dyestuff used as a colouring agent in some foods and drug formulations. In patients with a history of bronchial asthma β-adrenoceptor antagonists may precipitate an acute attack. *Emotional stress* may trigger attacks of bronchial asthma.

PATHOPHYSIOLOGY	THERAPEUTIC MEASURES
1 Aetiological mechanisms	
Hypersensitivity reactions (Types I and III)	Avoidance of provocative factors; corticosteroids; ? desensitization
Bronchial infection	Antibiotics (early treatment)
Irritants	Identification and avoidance
Exercise	(Cromoglycate, β_2-adrenoceptor agonists)
Drugs	Recognition and avoidance
Psychological stress	Psychosocial management
2 Primary pathology	
Release of inflammatory mediators	Cromoglycate; β_2-adrenoceptor agonists; corticosteroids
Increased vagal tone ↓	Ipratropium
Bronchoconstriction	β_2-adrenoceptor agonists; theophylline
Oedema of bronchial mucosa	Corticosteroids
Mucus obstruction of bronchi ↓	
Airways obstruction	
3 Secondary pathology	
Hypoxia	Oxygen
Emphysema	
4 Complications	
Pneumothorax	Drainage
Bronchial infection	Antibiotics
Status asthmaticus	

Fig. 5.2. The pathophysiology of bronchial asthma and the corresponding therapeutic measures available.

The release of inflammatory mediators results in the primary pathology, consisting of bronchoconstriction, oedema of the bronchial mucosa, and the production of bronchial mucus. All these result in *airway obstruction* which causes the signs and symptoms of breathlessness, wheezing, coughing, fatigue, and anxiety.

Airway obstruction leads to the secondary functional pathology of hypoxia, and if alveolar ventilation is very poor and the residual volume greatly increased, hypercapnia (increased $p_A CO_2$) may result. Emphysema may also occur because of hyperinflation, though in the irreversible chronic obstructive airways disease associated with chronic bronchitis, emphysema may occur because of direct structural damage. Emphysema is not reversible and this is a very important point to remember in assessing the possible results of therapy by tests of lung function [e.g. forced expiratory volume in one second (FEV_1), forced vital capacity (FVC), peak flow rate].

Complications of airway obstruction are pneumothorax, bronchial infection, and status asthmaticus in which there is severe, continuous, prolonged, and unremitting airway obstruction.

As shown in Fig. 5.2 therapy can be aimed at various points in the sequence of pathological events.

Hypersensitivity reactions may theoretically be prevented by avoidance of provocative factors and this requires the identification of allergens. Only occasionally is desensitization to an identified allergen successful in preventing asthma because individuals may be sensitive to a wide range of allergens. It is possible that one of the mechanisms of action of corticosteroids in very severe bronchial asthma, particularly systemically administered steroids such as oral prednisolone, is by immune suppression.

For patients in whom bronchial infections trigger asthmatic attacks early treatment of upper and lower respiratory tract infections may be effective.

Irritants should obviously be avoided and every effort made to dissuade the patient from smoking. Exercise-induced asthma can be prevented in many patients by the prophylactic use of sodium cromoglycate or a β_2-adrenoceptor agonist, such as salbutamol, by inhalation. Obviously precipitant drugs should be avoided. Where emotional stress seems to be involved psychotherapy and appropriate psychosocial management may seem indicated but in practice is very difficult to carry out.

Many of the therapeutic alternatives are aimed at the primary pathology. Sodium cromoglycate and corticosteroids (e.g. beclomethasone) are used in inhalers to prevent attacks. They both probably act by preventing the release of inflammatory mediators. In addition corticosteroids have direct anti-inflammatory effects and prevent or reduce oedema of the bronchial mucosa and the degree of mucus secretion. β_2-adrenoceptor agonists, such as salbutamol, are not generally used in prophylaxis, but a pharmacological case (rather than a proven therapeutic case) can be made for their use as such since they stimulate mast cell adenylate cyclase, raise intracellular cyclic AMP concentrations, and thus inhibit the release of inflammatory mediators.

Whether there is increased vagal tone in patients with chronic bronchitis accompanied by bronchial asthma is uncertain but it does seem that the anticholinergic drug, ipratropium bromide, by aerosol, might be particularly effective in these patients.

Bronchoconstriction may be relieved by β_2-adrenoceptor agonists, such as salbutamol, which relax bronchial smooth muscle, possibly by a mechanism involving stimulation of bronchial smooth muscle adenylate cyclase with a consequent rise in intracellular cyclic AMP concentrations. Theophylline, which inhibits phosphodiesterase, which metabolizes cyclic AMP, also acts as a bronchodilator. The combination of these two forms of therapy may be more effective in producing bronchodilatation than either alone, although there is also the theoretical risk of an increased incidence of cardiac arrhythmias with combined therapy.

Corticosteroids act by decreasing the inflammatory reaction and by diminishing mucosal oedema and mucus production. Breathing exercises and coughing during aerosol bronchodilator administration may be effective in removing mucus obstruction and thus allowing easier access to the site of action of inhaled corticosteroids.

For hypoxia, the secondary pathology, oxygen should be administered, although if the airway obstruction is severe and the p_ACO_2 raised, the danger of reducing the hypoxic drive to ventilation by the administration of oxygen, and the induction of CO_2 narcosis because of decreased ventilation, must be borne in mind.

The treatment of status asthmaticus is carried out with similar principles in mind (see p.357). Bronchial infection should be treated with antibiotics.

Although the scheme in Fig. 5.2 shows the principles of treatment and the pharmacological aims, it gives no feeling for the therapeutic practices required for the management of the different clinical presentations of asthma (chronic asthma with or without acute episodic exacerbations, acute episodes with relatively normal airways between attacks, and status asthmaticus). Furthermore the scheme does not indicate the different ways in which the drugs may be administered to achieve their particular effects. For example cromoglycate may be administered through a 'spinhaler' which delivers a spray of power from a pierced capsule. Corticosteroids such as beclomethasone are now taken by inhalation and undoubtedly use of this method of administration avoids most of the serious adverse effects of long-term systemic corticosteroid therapy. Nevertheless in very severe cases of chronic asthma oral corticosteroid therapy may still be required occasionally. In status asthmaticus corticosteroids are given initially intravenously as hydrocortisone and then as improvement occurs oral prednisolone is substituted and gradually tailed off and usually withdrawn within a week or two.

Salbutamol can be administered orally, or by pressurized inhaler, or in severe cases intravenously. In hospital during a severe acute attack it can be administered as a 0.5 per cent aerosol in 40 per cent oxygen delivered by intermittent positive pressure ventilation via a face-mask or mouth-tube.

Ipratropium bromide is given by aerosol. Theophylline can be given orally as slow-release tablets, rectally as aminophylline suppositories, by intravenous bolus of aminophylline, or by continuous infusion of aminophylline (as in the treatment of status asthmaticus).

This illustrates the potential complexity of drug therapy. The combination of drugs used and the most suitable route of administration depends on the type and severity of the case. It also illustrates how drug therapy can be rationally analysed.

5.1.2. The pharmacodynamic actions of the drugs used in the treatment of hypertension

Although the main sites of action of most of the drugs used to lower blood pressure are known with some confidence, the fine details of their effects and the precise ways in which their actions are translated into a hypotensive effect during long-term treatment are only partly understood.

There are many factors involved in the maintenance of high blood pressure and the principal cause (if indeed there is only one such) of essential hypertension is still unknown. Fig. 5.3 shows the inter-relationships of some of the factors involved, and the ways in which most of the drugs used in the treatment of hypertension may act. There are two general matters of importance here:

(i) some drugs may act in more than one place upon more than one process;

(ii) the acute effect of a drug may produce a 'knock-on' effect, secondarily altering other factors relating to blood pressure.

(a) Diuretics

The initial effect of diuretics is to increase sodium and water excretion, thus decreasing plasma and extracellular fluid (ECF) volumes. After a few weeks plasma and ECF volumes return to normal, and after an initial fall the cardiac output also returns to normal. By that stage, however, there is a decrease in peripheral resistance. This may be due to a loss of sodium from smooth muscle cells leading to a decreased sensitivity to vasoconstrictor substances (e.g. noradrenaline released from sympathetic nerve-endings, or angiotensin). There is also a possibility that thiazide diuretics have a direct relaxant effect on arteriolar smooth muscle causing arteriolar vasodilatation and decreasing peripheral resistance.

(b) β-adrenoceptor antagonists

β-adrenoceptor antagonists ('β-blockers') probably act primarily on the heart, decreasing cardiac output. Through autoregulatory mechanisms this results in arteriolar vasodilatation and decreased peripheral resistance. The details of these changes in autoregulation are not yet known. β-blockers may also have an effect on the kidney, decreasing renin secretion by blocking renal β-adrenoceptors but that is not thought to be a

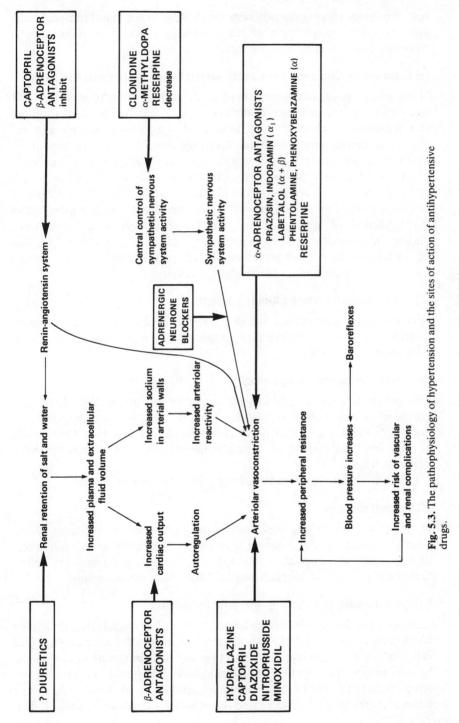

Fig. 5.3. The pathophysiology of hypertension and the sites of action of antihypertensive drugs.

very important mechanism whereby these drugs lower blood pressure. It is unlikely that a major part of the hypotensive action of β-blockers is mediated through effects on the brain.

(c) Drugs affecting blood pressure control mechanisms in the brain

Clonidine is an α_2-adrenoceptor agonist, and is thought to act in the mid-brain by stimulating α_2-adrenoceptors, leading to activation of vasodepressor mechanisms, i.e. decreased sympathetic activity and increased parasympathetic activity. Although there is still some confusion about the exact details of these actions, a central effect is generally agreed.

α-methyldopa is converted in the brain to α-methylnoradrenaline, which is thought to act by a mechanism similar to clonidine. One of the actions of reserpine in lowering blood pressure might be through its general effect of the depletion of noradrenaline and 5-hydroxytryptamine from nerve endings in vasomotor regulatory areas of the brain. It also causes depletion of noradrenaline from sympathetic nerve endings, and that too would interfere with sympathetic vasoconstrictor activity.

(d) Adrenergic neurone blocking agents

Guanethidine, bethanidine, and debrisoquine act by blocking the release, on stimulation of sympathetic post-ganglionic fibres, of noradrenaline from sympathetic nerve endings.

(e) α-adrenoceptor antagonists

Prazosin is a fairly selective α_1-adrenoceptor antagonist and blocks the action of noradrenaline at vascular smooth muscle α-adrenoceptors. It does not affect the presynaptic α_2-adrenoceptors and therefore allows normal feedback control of noradrenaline release from the sympathetic nerve endings.

Labetalol has both α- and β-adrenoceptor antagonist activity.

(f) Vasodilatation

Hydralazine, minoxidil, and sodium nitroprusside all act directly on arterial smooth muscle, causing it to relax. The resultant vasodilatation causes a fall in peripheral resistance: If there is a consequent reflex tachycardia, it can be blocked with a β-adrenoceptor antagonist.

(g) Angiotensin converting–enzyme inhibitors

Captopril blocks the conversion of angiotensin I to angiotensin II. It also blocks certain aminopeptidases and therefore prevents the metabolism and inactivation of bradykinin. The effect on angiotensin results in a decrease in any vasoconstricting effect angiotensin may be having. It will also lead to a reduction in the angiotensin-stimulated production of aldosterone by the adrenal cortex leading to decreased retention of sodium by the kidney. The importance of these mechanisms in the lowering of blood pressure produced by captopril is not clear, but its therapeutic effects are probably mainly due to its action in inhibiting the angiotensin-converting enzyme.

The practical management of hypertension is discussed in Chapter 21. This analysis of mechanisms of disease and corresponding mechanisms of drug action is designed to illustrate how the pharmacology of therapy can be rationalized. We shall emphasize this approach in the therapeutics section of this text.

6 Practical applications of the analysis of drug therapy

6.1. APPARENT FAILURE TO RESPOND TO TREATMENT ANALYSED

Having considered separately each of the four phases involved in drug therapy (Chapters 2, 3, 4, and 5) and the principal questions with which each is concerned, we can now consider how those questions may be used in tackling therapeutic problems. The previously simplified scheme (Fig. 1.1) has been elaborated upon in Fig. 6.1.

The main categories of therapeutic problem are:

1. apparent failure to respond to treatment;
2. adverse drug effects;
3. drug interactions.

Besides these 'operational' problems there is also the question of the benefit:risk ratio which we have discussed elsewhere (see p. 236). However, this is not specifically a problem involving the analytical approach we have been discussing.

We shall deal here with the first problem. Adverse effects of drugs and drug interactions are discussed separately in Chapters 9 and 10 respectively and similar principles apply.

If a patient appears not to be responding to treatment with a particular drug we must examine the possible reasons.

6.1.1. The pharmaceutical process (Is the drug getting into the patient?)

(a) Compliance

Is the patient taking the drug? This problem is discussed in Chapter 12.

(b) Is the formulation ideal?

It has been suggested that the absorption of iron from slow-release iron preparations may be erratic. If a patient is being treated, for convenience,

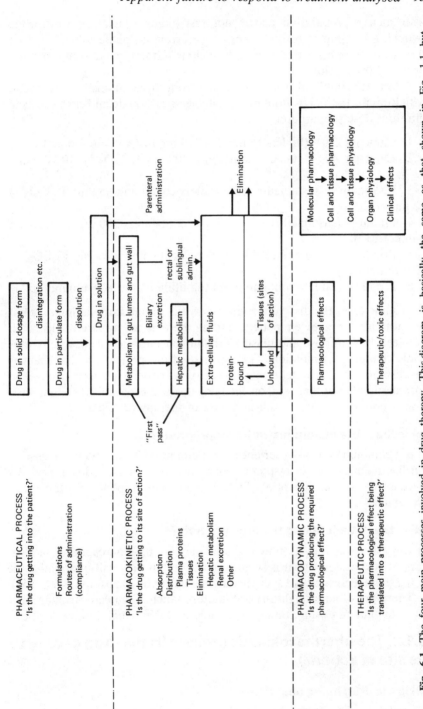

Fig. 6.1. The four main processes involved in drug therapy. This diagram is basically the same as that shown in Fig. 1.1 but more detail is given. In addition it shows the hierarchies in the therapeutic process (compare Fig. 4.2).

with such a preparation and is not responding it may be worthwhile switching to simpler formulations (e.g. ferrous sulphate tablets) before trying more sophisticated measures such as intramuscular administration or blood transfusion.

Another example of problems arising from formulations is to be found with lithium. In the UK lithium is available as carbonate and citrate salts in different dose preparations:

1. Camcolit 250® (tablets containing 250 mg Li_2CO_3 = 6.7 mmol Li^+).
2. Camcolit 400® (tablets containing 400 mg Li_2CO_3 = 10.77 mmol Li^+).
3. Liskonum® (sustained-release tablets containing 450 mg Li_2CO_3 = 12 mmol Li^+).
4. Phasal® (sustained-release tablets containing 300 mg Li_2CO_3 = 8 mmol Li^+).
5. Priadel® (sustained-release tablets containing 400 mg Li_2CO_3 = 10.7 mmol Li^+).
6. Litarex® (tablets containing 564 mg lithium citrate = 6 mmol Li^+).

In some cases the dissolution characteristics of one formulation may not be suitable for a given patient and if there is an apparent mismatch between lithium dose and plasma lithium concentration it may be worthwhile changing formulation. The converse of this principle is that changes in response to treatment may occur if a patient changes from one formulation to another (e.g. on changing doctors, especially if communication is poor). This may result in failure of therapy or toxicity.

(c) Is the route of administration appropriate?

It is a common clinical experience that patients with oedema in congestive cardiac failure may not respond to *oral* frusemide in usual doses, perhaps because of erratic absorption. Such patients may respond to intravenous frusemide.

(d) Is the patient taking the drug properly?

If you ask asthmatics to show you how they use their aerosol bronchodilators or corticosteroids, it is surprising how often they will be found to be using them incorrectly (e.g. activating the puffer on expiration, see p.356).

There are other straightforward matters which may need checking such as frequency of dosing, timing of dosing, and the actual dose prescribed.

6.1.2. The pharmacokinetic process (Is the drug getting to its site of action?)

(a) Is the drug being absorbed?

In malabsorption states, or in patients with intestinal resections, absorption of some drugs may be impaired (e.g. digoxin, thyroxine). In patients with gastro-intestinal hurry the absorption of drugs from slow-release preparations may be impaired. In such cases an alternative (e.g. effervescent potassium salts rather than slow-release preparations; see Pharmacopoeia) should be used.

(b) Is there altered protein binding?

This question is discussed in Chapters 3 and 10. The common drugs for which it may be important are warfarin and phenytoin.

(c) Is there altered tissue distribution?

There are only a few instances in which the apparent volume of distribution of a drug is so increased as to decrease plasma concentrations and significantly reduce the amount of drug reaching its site of action. One example is the use of digoxin in the treatment of atrial fibrillation caused by hyperthyroidism, in which the apparent volume of distribution of digoxin is increased by about 50 per cent. In this case, however, the poor response to digoxin is also caused by a decreased pharmacodynamic response.

(d) Is there an increase in metabolic or renal clearance?

Theophylline clearance is increased in patients who smoke cigarettes and their dosage requirements may be increased.

Patients with septicaemic shock and poor renal function may be treated with gentamicin. As their condition improves and renal function returns to normal the dosage of gentamicin may need to be increased to maintain therapeutic efficacy.

In hyperthyroidism the clearance of some drugs may be increased and higher doses required (see p.437).

6.1.3. The pharmacodynamic process (Is the drug producing the required pharmacological effect?)

Sometimes there are factors which affect drug effects at the site of action, even when the concentration reaching the site of action is that which one would usually expect to have an appropriate pharmacodynamic effect.

For example, lignocaine and other Class I anti-arrhythmic drugs have reduced efficacy if there is potassium depletion. Bacterial resistance may be the cause of therapeutic failure with antibiotics. There is resistance to the effects of cardiac glycosides in hyperthyroidism (see also above, section 6.1.2(c)).

Progressive tolerance to drugs may reduce their efficacy, as in the case of narcotic analgesics. The subject of drug tolerance is discussed in Chapter 4, and the related topic of drug dependence in Chapter 31.

Insulin resistance is common in certain obese diabetics who are also taking glucocorticoids, and in diabetic ketoacidosis. In these circumstances the need for increased insulin dosages is readily appreciated because of the ease with which therapy may be monitored by measuring blood glucose concentrations.

Some drugs used in the treatment of hypertension may cause fluid retention (e.g. captopril, minoxidil), and that in turn diminishes their hypotensive effects. Such drugs are more effective, therefore, when used in combination with a diuretic.

6.1.4. The therapeutic process (Is the pharmacological effect being translated into a therapeutic effect?)

If a drug treatment does not produce therapeutic benefit in a patient, and if pharmaceutical, pharmacokinetic, and pharmacodynamic factors can be excluded as a cause, then clearly the pharmacological effect of the drug is *not* being translated to a therapeutic effect. There may be a number of causes for this.

(a) Inappropriate therapy

Some patients with endogenous depression do not respond to antidepressant drug therapy, despite faultless compliance and 'adequate' plasma drug concentrations. There is no way at present of being sure in such circumstances that the drugs are producing an appropriate pharmacodynamic effect because the precise mechanism by which tricyclic antidepressants produce their therapeutic effect is unknown. However, considering the occurrence of adverse effects of these drugs it would be surprising if they were not having their expected and usually therapeutic pharmacological effects even in many cases in which the desired therapeutic response is not seen, i.e. relief of depression. It is interesting, therefore, that some of those patients who do not respond to tricyclic antidepressants *do* benefit from electroconvulsive therapy, which may produce its therapeutic effect in depression by mechanisms different from those of the tricyclic antidepressants.

Not infrequently patients with supraventricular and ventricular arrhythmias are unresponsive to anti-arrhythmic drug therapy, even when there is every reason to believe that the drug is exerting the pharmacological effect which normally stops or prevents such arrhythmias. For instance quinidine causes a widening of the QRS complex of the ECG and prolongs the QT_c interval, and these effects are concentration-related. In circumstances where ECG changes of this kind are seen but no therapeutic benefit is obtained, it may be beneficial to try a drug with a different pharmacological effect on the cardiac conducting system, e.g. amiodarone.

(b) Variable links between the pharmacodynamic effect and the therapeutic effect

Consider the use of the diuretic frusemide in the treatment of cardiac failure. Frusemide inhibits sodium and chloride reabsorption by the renal tubules. The precise molecular mechanism by which frusemide produces this effect is still not fully understood, but there is good evidence to suppose that frusemide affects some process in the renal tubular cell so that the inward flux of sodium and chloride from the luminal surface of the tubular cell is inhibited. If there is a good intraluminar flow of glomerular filtrate containing sodium chloride, then a diuresis will result. If glomerular filtration is poor, and if secondary hyperaldosteronism is increasing sodium reabsorption, then frusemide may be less effective. In these circumstances the effect of frusemide is dependent on:

(i) renal blood flow (heart failure; hypovolaemia);
(ii) glomerular filtration;
(iii) humoral factors modulating tubular sodium reabsorption (hyperaldosteronism), e.g. in heart failure, hepatic cirrhosis, or the nephrotic syndrome).

These are the links between the molecular action of frusemide at the renal tubular cell and its eventual diuretic effect. If frusemide is ineffective in severe cardiac failure a diuresis may sometimes be produced by the administration of dopamine (causing renal vasodilatation and an increase in cardiac output with a consequent increase in renal blood flow), or of spironolactone (inhibiting the effects of aldosterone).

(c) Problems with the time-course of the therapeutic effect

Many drug treatments now in use are intended to return a physiological variable to normal on the basis that a therapeutic effect will result in the future.

For example, in mild to moderate asymptomatic hypertension treatment of the increased blood pressure and its return to more normal values reduces the incidence in the population of stroke, heart failure, and renal failure. Over the short term, however, it is very difficult to define the link between the lowering of the blood pressure and its prophylactic effect in the individual. The older the patient, therefore, the more difficult it is to decide on the value of long-term treatment.

In diabetes of mature onset, diet, with or without oral hypoglycaemic drugs, is intended to keep the blood glucose within more normal limits in the hope that the complications of diabetes (peripheral vascular disease, retinopathy, neuropathy, nephropathy) will be prevented. Of course one is also aiming to prevent the more acute complications of diabetes such as ketoacidotic and hyperosmolar hyperglycaemia, but as far as the long-term therapeutic effects of treatment are concerned it is not possible to determine in the individual patient, over a short span of time, whether one is producing a therapeutic effect, i.e. preventing the progression of neurovascular disease.

(d) The disease or symptom may be too severe for the drug therapy to be effective

One has to be realistic in drug therapy and understand the limitations of what may be achieved. For instance oral hypoglycaemic agents often do not and cannot produce adequate control of blood glucose in maturity-onset diabetics, and insulin must be given. The degree of hypoglycaemia produced by the maximum effect of, say, chlorpropamide is generally less than that produced by insulin. This difference in dose-responsiveness is illustrated schematically in Fig. 6.2.

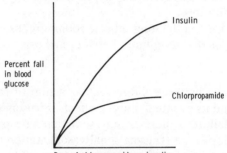

Fig. 6.2. Theoretical dose–response curves for the hypoglycaemic effects of insulin and chlorpropamide. The maximum possible effect of chlorpropamide (and other oral hypoglycaemic drugs) is limited to a level considerably below that of insulin.

(e) Toxicity limits the maximum tolerable dose

Two examples of this are firstly the emetic action of morphine which increases in incidence at a dose of about 10 mg, a dose at which the analgesic effect has not reached maximum, and secondly gentamicin whose toxicity to the ears and kidneys prevents one's using doses associated with high plasma concentrations (see Chapter 7). Other examples include the limited positive inotropic effect of digoxin in severe heart failure, and the limited anti-inflammatory effects of non-steroidal anti-inflammatory drugs in severe rheumatoid arthritis.

(f) The therapeutic effect is annulled by incidental adverse effects

For a treatment to be valuable its benefit must outweigh its risk. Take, for example, the large World Health Organization (WHO) study of the effect of long-term clofibrate therapy on the incidence of ischaemic heart disease. Clofibrate reduced the incidence of major ischaemic heart disease but there was an overall *increase* in mortality from all causes in clofibrate-treated patients. The causes of death included diseases of the liver, gall bladder, and small and large intestine. In this case the risks outweighed the potential benefit in the population as a whole. The study was not designed to examine benefit versus risk in high-risk patients with hyperlipidaemias.

All these examples should give an idea of how the unified scheme outlined in Chapters 2–5 and illustrated in Figs. 1.1 and 6.1 can be used in assessing the results of treatment in both an individual and a population. Sometimes the answers to one's questions will not be known, but one should not be inhibited from asking the questions nonetheless, for it is only by questioning that one can improve one's understanding of the therapeutic process.

7 Monitoring drug therapy

7.1. INDIVIDUAL MONITORING AND POPULATION MONITORING

In previous chapters we have discussed the way in which drug therapy can be analysed through its constituent parts, typified by four questions:

1. Is the drug getting into the patient? (The pharmaceutical process.)
2. Is the drug getting to its site of action? (The pharmacokinetic process.)
3. Is the drug producing the required pharmacological effect? (The pharmacodynamic process.)
4. Is the pharmacological effect being translated into a therapeutic effect? (The therapeutic process.)

In this chapter we shall examine the ways in which we can obtain information to help us answer these questions in clinical practice and to assist us in rationalizing drug therapy.

Questions 1 and 2 can sometimes be answered by measuring drug and metabolite concentrations in body fluids.

Question 3 can sometimes be answered by direct measurement of some pharmacological effect of the drug.

Question 4 can sometimes be answered by direct measurement of the therapeutic outcome.

Not infrequently the answers to questions 3 and 4 may be imprecise, but that should not discourage us from asking the questions. Future research may yield techniques for improving the precision.

Normally one would try to measure the clinical response directly. If that is difficult to measure, or is not related directly in time to a dose of the drug, then some measure of the pharmacological action of the drug may be necessary. If measurement of the pharmacological action of the drug is difficult we may have to resort to measurement of plasma concentration of the drug.

Because this is the desirable sequence of priorities we shall deal with our questions in reverse order, starting with therapeutic monitoring, and continuing with pharmacodynamic and pharmacokinetic monitoring.

7.2. THERAPEUTIC MONITORING

Here we must distinguish between those events which can be monitored in the individual patient, and those events which can be monitored in a population under study, and which can only be applied statistically to the individual.

7.2.1. Monitoring therapeutic events in the individual

(a) Anticonvulsant drug therapy—seizure frequency

As mentioned below in the section on pharmacokinetic monitoring, knowledge of the concentrations of anticonvulsant drugs present in the plasma of patients taking them can be very useful in the management of epilepsy. However, the end-point of therapy is a decreased frequency of seizures, and patients should be encouraged to keep a diary documenting the occurrence of seizures so that the success of one's treatment or of changes in treatment may be more readily assessed.

(b)Anticholinesterases in myasthenia gravis—improvement in muscle power

The efficacy of anticholinesterases, such as neostigmine, in myasthenia gravis can be measured by the patients' own assessment of their muscle power and by simple quantitative tests of that power. In cases in which respiratory paralysis might be a problem, tests of pulmonary function, e.g. vital capacity, may be required.

(c) Drugs for angina pectoris—frequency of attacks

Patients with angina are readily able to tell whether sublingual glyceryl trinitrate prevents an anticipated attack of angina or shortens the duration of pain when an attack occurs. In trials of drugs designed to prevent angina, such as β-adrenoceptor antagonists or nifedipine, the fall in the number of glyceryl trinitrate tablets a patient has to take is often used as a measure of efficacy.

(d) Diuretics in the treatment of oedema

Various measures can be made of the efficacy of diuretic therapy in oedema. Urine volume is commonly used, but can be unreliable because of errors in recording or because of incontinence. Much more reliable is body weight, daily measurement of which gives an accurate assessment of the trend of response to therapy. Assessment of the degree of swelling of the legs in patients with leg oedema gives a more subjective assessment but should not be neglected. One should also try to make sure that dehydration does not occur by examining the tongue and skin.

(e) Glucocorticoids and sulphasalazine in the treatment of ulcerative colitis

Besides systemic improvement, for example lessening of fever and general malaise, increased appetite and vigour, there should be a reduction in the number and severity of attacks of diarrhoea with a reduction in the amount of blood, mucus, and pus in the stools. These effects are easily measured. Sigmoidoscopy with mucosal biopsy may also allow objective assessment of therapeutic effect.

These examples serve to show how therapy can be objectively assessed. Some effects of therapy are obvious, such as the clearing of psoriatic skin lesions with the use of topical corticosteroids or tar preparations, while others are more difficult to assess. For example, in no area of medicine is it more difficult to assess the therapeutic effect of treatment than in mental illness, where one has to assess how patients feel and behave. In clinical trials mental symptoms and behavioural signs can be scored and the patient's state quantified. Such an approach is useful in a collective study, but is rarely used in routine individual psychiatric care. Here the assessment is a subjective one for both patient and doctor and precision in psychotropic drug therapy is therefore currently something of an illusion.

7.2.2. Monitoring the effects of drug therapy at the population level

With the introduction of public health measures, immunization and vaccination procedures, and 'population therapy', we need to consider what evidence is required to monitor these widely used treatments. The following are examples:

(a) Immunization procedures

Obviously the effects of immunizing the population against diphtheria, tetanus, whooping cough, poliomyelitis, and other infectious disease can be monitored by surveying the incidence of those infections in the population.

(b) Currently recommended 'preventive medicine' procedures

By encouraging members of the general population to make changes in their life–style it is hoped that the incidence of certain diseases will fall:

Stopping smoking—coronary heart disease, peripheral vascular disease, chronic bronchitis, bronchial carcinoma.
Losing weight—diabetes mellitus, coronary heart disease, hypertension, osteoarthritis.
High-fibre diet—diverticular disease, irritable colon syndrome.
Reducing cholesterol and saturated fat in diet—coronary heart disease.

(c) Some long-term prophylactic drug therapies widely prescribed

Prevention of pregnancy—oral contraceptives, intra-uterine devices.

Secondary prevention of myocardial infarction—aspirin, sulphin-pyrazone, β-adrenoceptor antagonists.

Hypertension and its complications—antihypertensive drug therapy.

Diabetes mellitus and its complications—insulin and oral hypogly-caemics.

To discover the efficacy of such measures and treatments it is necessary to carry out large-scale studies of comparable groups taking or not taking the treatment (i.e. to carry out a clinical trial). Thereafter one has to rely on the findings of such a trial to yield a *probability* that the treatment will work in an individual, but one will often not know for sure whether or not one's aim was fulfilled in that individual.

Assessment of the efficacy of such measures is a public health matter no better exemplified that in the assessment of the efficacy of immunization procedures through the agency of the systems whereby the occurrence of communicable diseases is notified to government authorities. In the UK the collection of records of births and deaths by the Office of Population Censuses and Surveys can be used to study changes in the patterns of causes of deaths at a national level and this can be used as a method of monitoring the efficacy of immunization programmes, as can the system for notifying particular communicable diseases, such as diphtheria.

7.3. PHARMACODYNAMIC MONITORING

In some circumstances the pharmacological effects of a drug can be carefully measured, followed sequentially, and used as precise guides to the therapeutic process. These effects may or may not be correlated precisely with the therapeutic effect. A number of important examples of commonly used pharmacodynamic measurements used in monitoring therapy follows.

7.3.1. Insulin therapy in diabetes mellitus—effect on blood glucose

There is a tendency to forget how serious a disease diabetes mellitus would be were it not for insulin therapy. Between the years 1897 and 1914 the death rate for young diabetics was 614 per 1000 and from 1914 to 1922 411 per 1000. Insulin was isolated in 1922 and in 1922–26 there was a dramatic fall in the death rate to 89 per 1000. Since then the mortality rate has continued to fall.

The management of severe diabetic ketoacidosis using low-dose con-tinuous i.v. infusion of insulin with frequent monitoring of blood glucose concentrations by simple colorimetric techniques is now accepted practice.

Although there are biochemical abnormalities to correct besides the increased blood glucose, lowering of the blood glucose is of prime importance since the entry of glucose into cells is accompanied by resolution of the other abnormalities to a great extent. In this acute situation the blood glucose is a good guide to the patient's clinical state. Of course, other measurements must be made, and it is particularly important to ensure that the plasma potassium concentration is kept within normal limits, and that the patient is well hydrated.

However, one cannot be so confident about the relationship between the degree of blood glucose control during long-term treatment and the occurrence of complications such as diabetic retinopathy and cataract, neuropathy, nephropathy, and peripheral vascular disease. Nevertheless, it is generally assumed that good control of the blood glucose concentration is a desirable long-term aim, so much so that patients are now encouraged to measure their own blood glucose concentrations using simple equipment at home. Such measurement has the objective of allowing patients to alter their doses of insulin as required in order to maintain the blood glucose concentration within reasonable limits— 10 mmol/l is usually regarded as the maximum and about 4 mmol/l the minimum—in order to avoid hyperglycaemia. For those patients who cannot measure their own blood glucose, or for whom such measurement is considered unnecessary, measurements of the concentration of glucose in the urine give a guide to therapy, the aim being to reduce glycosuria to about 0.25–0.5 per cent (i.e. 2.5–5 g/l, 14–28 mmol/l). Whether patients measure blood glucose or urine glucose it is important that they make measurements regularly so that a careful assessment may be made of their day-to-day requirements.

7.3.2. Anticoagulant therapy with warfarin—effect on prothrombin time

The use of the prothrombin time in monitoring warfarin therapy is discussed in detail in the Pharmacopoeia. The extent to which the prothrombin time should be prolonged during warfarin therapy has been chosen on the basis of avoiding spontaneous bleeding and bruising rather than on the basis of any evidence that it is at such levels that therapeutic benefit is likely to accrue. When one measures the prothrombin time in a patient taking warfarin one is measuring the effect of warfarin on the ability of the patient's blood to clot, not, for example, on the likelihood of a pulmonary embolus in a patient with a deep venous thrombosis. However, the accumulated evidence suggests that if one keeps the prothrombin time within the generally accepted therapeutic limits one increases the chance of effective treatment.

7.3.3. Bronchodilator therapy in reversible airway obstruction (e.g. bronchial asthma)—effect on FEV₁ and peak flow rate

In asthma, particularly chronic asthma, it can be very difficult to assess the effectiveness of therapy over short periods of time on the basis of symptoms and ordinary physical signs. The effects of bronchodilators, such as salbutamol by inhalation or slow-release aminophylline tablets, can be objectively assessed by measuring their effects on the forced expiratory volume in one second (FEV_1), normally 70 per cent or more of the forced vital capacity (FVC), or more simply by measuring peak flow rate recorded during maximal forced expiration. This is such a simple measurement that a patient can monitor his or her own progress at home using simple, cheap equipment.

It is very important to know *when* after dosing to assess the effectiveness of the bronchodilator. The usual peak effect of a single inhalation of salbutamol from an aerosol occurs 10–15 min after inhalation, and the effect persists for up to an hour; the peak effect of ipratropium is at 45–60 min. If at these times there is little effect, however, it would be as well to test later to see if there is a delayed response.

7.3.4. Allopurinol in gout—effect on blood uric acid

Allopurinol reduces blood uric acid concentrations by inhibiting the conversion of hypoxanthine to uric acid, and the fall in blood uric acid concentration is used to monitor this pharmacological effect. In this case there is no doubt that the fall in blood uric acid is accompanied by a decreased incidence of acute gouty arthritis and prevention of gouty renal disease.

7.3.5. Carbimazole in hyperthyroidism—effect on thyroid hormones

In patients with hyperthyroidism physical signs may be difficult to interpret both in assessing the response to treatment and in preventing overtreatment with resultant hypothyroidism. As an aid to therapy, therefore, one measures the serum concentrations of triiodothyronine (T_3) and thyroid stimulating hormone (TSH). The therapeutic effects of carbimazole can be detected by a fall in serum T_3 concentrations (normal range 1.5–3.0 nmol/1) and overtreatment will cause a fall below normal in serum T_3 and an increase above normal of serum TSH (normal range 0–6 mi.u./l).

7.3.6. Cancer chemotherapy—effect on tumour markers

The effectiveness of cytotoxic drug therapy using methotrexate in uterine choriocarcinoma can be monitored by measuring serum concentrations of human chorionic gonadotrophin. Undoubtedly this is a field which will advance as techniques for detecting markers of cancers improve.

Other obvious examples of pharmacodynamic monitoring are: the measurement of reticulocyte response and haemoglobin in the treatment of anaemias (e.g. with ferrous sulphate, vitamin B_{12}, or folic acid); the lowering of the blood pressure by antihypertensive drugs (see Chapter 21); the measurement of intra-ocular pressure in patients with glaucoma.

7.4. PHARMACOKINETIC MONITORING (PLASMA CONCENTRATION MEASUREMENT)

It is obvious that the more information one can gather about drug concentrations in various body tissues, particularly at the site of action, the more likely it is that one will be able to relate those concentrations to the clinical therapeutic response. But one cannot measure the concentration of digoxin in the heart, or of phenytoin in the brain, and therefore a great deal of research has been and is being carried out to try to relate *plasma* drug concentrations to drug effects. In only a few cases has this approach proved itself of value in the practice of clinical medicine.

Occasionally the *qualitative* detection of drugs in urine is useful in screening for drug abuse (e.g. cannabis), in drug overdose (e.g. paraquat), or for assessing patient compliance (e.g. salicylates).

It is very important to know for which drugs plasma concentration monitoring has been shown to be useful and in what circumstances measurements should be made. It is also important to be able to evaluate the potential usefulness of measurements of newer drugs. The uncritical use of plasma drug concentration monitoring can lead to the collection of useless data at the expense of a great deal of money, time, and manpower.

There is a combination of criteria which determine whether measuring the plasma concentration of a particular drug will be useful in practice. Drugs which fulfil those criteria are listed below.

7.4.1. Drugs with a low toxic: therapeutic ratio (i.e. therapeutic dose close to toxic dose)

There are many drugs for which the margin between their therapeutic effects and toxic effects is very narrow, and in the following discussion we shall see why measurement of their plasma concentrations may be useful in monitoring therapy. These drugs contrast with drugs such as penicillin, for which generally (in the absence of hypersensitivity) there is a large margin between the therapeutic and toxic doses. With those drugs one can, with reasonable safety, make large changes in dose, ensuring that the amount of drug in the body is sufficient, or more than sufficient, to produce a therapeutic effect, without running into problems of toxicity. Generally measurement of plasma concentrations is unnecessary in these cases.

7.4.2. Drugs for which the relationship between dose and plasma concentration is unpredictable

If the absorption, clearance rate, and apparent volume of distribution of a drug varies widely between individuals then the relationship between dose and plasma concentration will be unpredictable. Measurement of the plasma drug concentration will then give a better assessment of the effect of the drug than the dose. An important example of this is in the treatment of epilepsy with phenytoin. In Fig. 3.5 is shown the range of steady-state plasma phenytoin concentrations resulting from the administration of phenytoin to five different individuals.

7.4.3. Drugs which are not metabolized to active metabolites

Some drugs have one or more metabolites which themselves have pharmacological activity producing either toxic or therapeutic effects. To obtain a comprehensive picture of the relationships between total plasma concentrations of pharmacologically active compounds and clinical effects it would be necessary to measure each active compound separately, or to use an assay which measured the total biological activity of those compounds.

For example, procainamide is metabolized to N-acetylprocainamide which has equipotent anti-arrhythmic activity. This metabolism varies according to N-acetylator status (see Chapter 8), and between 10 and 40 per cent of the procainamide administered may be metabolized to N-acetylprocainamide. Measurement of plasma procainamide concentrations alone, therefore, gives an imprecise guide to therapy.

Chlorpromazine, a neuroleptic drug used in the treatment of psychoses such as schizophrenia, is metabolized to several active metabolites, each of which has different pharmacological degrees of neuroleptic activity. It has proved very difficult to relate plasma chlorpromazine concentrations to its therapeutic effects in psychiatric conditions, and the confounding effects of metabolites may be the reason. An interesting development is the possibility of measuring 'all' the active neuroleptic moieties by using a radioreceptor assay. In this type of assay active compounds in plasma are made to compete for a specific receptor with an appropriate radioligand. In the case of chlorpromazine and its metabolites the receptor used is a dopamine receptor present in membranes prepared from the caudate nucleus of calf brain and the radioligand is ^{3}H-haloperidol.

7.4.4. Drugs for which there is difficulty in measuring or interpreting the clinical evidence of therapeutic or toxic effects

Some chronic diseases vary naturally in the intensity of their effects from time to time, for example, the frequency of depressive episodes in manic–depressive psychosis or of fits in epilepsy. If in careful clinical trials one can demonstrate a relationship between the plasma concentration of a drug and its effects in reducing episodes of illness then this relationship can be a helpful guide with that drug therapy in patients at large. For example, the measurement of lithium plasma concentrations helps in two respects: (a) to guide dosage into a therapeutic range within which one may expect therapeutic benefit in the prevention of manic or depressive episodes and (b) to avoid plasma concentrations with which short- and long-term adverse effects are associated (see Pharmacopoeia).

Toxic symptoms often mimic disease. For example, nausea and vomiting occur with both digitalis toxicity and in congestive cardiac failure; sometimes phenytoin toxicity can result in an increased rather than a decreased frequency of epileptic seizures; renal failure may occur in a patient with Gram-negative septicaemia because of the disease or because of an adverse effect of the gentamicin used to treat it. If one can demonstrate a relationship between plasma concentrations of a drug and its toxic effects then one can use such measurements to distinguish between drug-induced and disease-induced effects; or, as in the case of gentamicin, to prevent the drug-induced effect.

7.4.5. Drugs for which there is a good relationship between plasma concentrations of the drug and either its therapeutic or toxic effects

This is obvious and has been alluded to in section 7.4.4 above. In some cases it has proved difficult to demonstrate conclusively the usefulness of plasma concentration measurements for drugs which would otherwise fulfil the necessary criteria. These drugs comprise the category forming part B of Table 7.1.

7.4.6. Which drugs fulfil these criteria?

The drugs which fulfil some or all of these criteria, and which are measured in everyday practice are listed in part A of Table 7.1. In addition to the measurement of these drugs, measurement of salicylate and paracetamol plasma concentrations is of value in overdose cases (see Chapter 32).

Some drugs which fulfil some or all of the criteria of sections 7.4.1–7.4.4, but which have not been shown conclusively to fulfil criterion 7.4.5, are listed in part B of Table 7.1. These drugs warrant some extra discussion.

There has been, and in some centres still is, enthusiasm for monitoring anti-arrhythmic drug therapy by plasma concentration measurements. While, in our view, 'routine' monitoring of this group of drugs has not been proven to be very useful there are undoubtedly occasional patients with chronic symptomatic arrhythmias which prove to be very difficult to manage with anti-arrhythmic drugs, and in whom it can be very useful to know whether the plasma drug concentration is within an empirical 'therapeutic' range. If in such a case the plasma concentration is 'inadequate' and the arrhythmia uncontrolled then one would be justified in increasing the dose; if when an 'adequate' concentration had been reached the arrhythmia was still uncontrolled one would be justified in changing to another drug.

Table 7.1 *Measuring plasma drug concentrations*

A. *Measurement of proven value—should be considered*

Aminoglycoside antibiotics
   Gentamicin
   Kanamycin
Anticonvulsants
   Carbamazepine
   Phenytoin
Digitoxin and digoxin
Lithium
Theophylline

B. *Case not proven*

Anti-arrhythmic drugs
   Disopyramide
   Lignocaine
   Procainamide
   Quinidine
Anticonvulsants other than phenytoin and carbamazepine
Methotrexate
Tricyclic antidepressants

Despite interest in the relationship between the plasma concentrations of antidepressant drugs and their therapeutic effects, particularly in endogenous depression, there is at present little case for adopting plasma concentration measurement as a routine method for monitoring anti-depressant drug therapy. One aspect of this subject, however, is particularly interesting. In patients treated with nortriptyline there appears to be what is called an 'inverted U' effect relating plasma concentrations to thera-peutic effects (see Fig. 7.1). This phenomenon is explained on the basis that above a certain plasma concentration (about 110 ng/ml) nortriptyline somehow negates its own therapeutic effect. This is not seen with other tricyclic antidepressants, e.g. imipramine.

7.4.7. Indications for measuring plasma drug concentrations

We have seen that there are certain criteria which must be fulfilled before a drug becomes 'eligible' as a drug whose plasma concentration measure-ment may prove useful in clinical practice. We must now consider when in

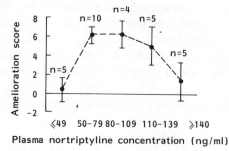

Fig. 7.1. Relationship between plasma concentrations of nortriptyline and its antidepressant effect ('inverted U'). Improvement is seen when plasma concentrations increase to between 50 and 110 ng/ml but above 110 ng/ml the clinical response is less good. [Adapted from Åsberg *et al.* (1971) *Br. med. J.* **iii**, 331–334, with permission.]

practice such measurement is likely to contribute significantly to patient care.

(a) Individualizing therapy

For reasons discussed above it may be desirable to aim for a particular range of plasma drug concentrations within which a therapeutic effect is likely to occur and toxic effects are likely to be minimized. This may be particularly useful:

(a) at the very start of therapy when the relationship between dose and plasma concentration in the individual is uncertain;

(b) when rapid changes in renal function alter the relationship between dose and plasma concentration—this is of particular importance in the cases of digoxin, lithium, and aminoglycoside antibiotics;

(c) when an interacting drug is introduced altering the relationship between dose and plasma concentration—for example, plasma concentrations of lithium are increased by thiazide diuretics, those of digoxin by quinidine, and those of phenytoin by phenylbutazone.

(b) In the diagnosis of suspected toxicity

One difficulty in practice is the measuring of the 'therapeutic' range, which is a statistical concept based on observations of populations of patients. However, in an individual a plasma concentration below the lower end or above the upper end of the range may merely represent a value at the extremes of the distribution and may be associated with therapeutic efficacy. In a patient who has definitely responded to treatment but who nonetheless has a plasma concentration below the 'therapeutic' range it might be wrong to adjust the dose simply to engineer a plasma concentration within the 'therapeutic' range, and in some cases the finding of a plasma concentration below the therapeutic range may be an indication for *withdrawal* of therapy.

In addition to the problem of interpretation of a statistical range there are for some drugs factors which actually alter the 'therapeutic' range. For example, hypokalaemia increases the response to digoxin and lowers the upper end of the range; alterations in protein binding lower the 'therapeutic' range for phenytoin because of a fall in total phenytoin concentrations but no change in free concentrations (see below under phenytoin for a full discussion). Factors of this kind are discussed under the individual drugs below.

If, however, one has a clinical suspicion of drug toxicity then a plasma concentration above the 'therapeutic' range will undoubtedly reinforce one's opinion.

(c) Measuring compliance (see Chapter 12)

7.4.8. The importance of steady-state concentrations

If plasma drug concentrations are measured before steady state has occurred (i.e. before about four half-times of continual administration) then one may be led into misinterpreting the relationship between dose and steady-state plasma concentration. Remember that if you measure the plasma concentration on a day when steady state has not yet been achieved the plasma concentration you measure will *underestimate* the eventual steady-state concentration. This may happen during the early stages of therapy, or when patient compliance is poor or variable, or when renal function is decreasing and the half-time of the drug consequently lengthening.

7.4.9. Timing of blood sampling in relation to dose

The importance of blood sampling time in relation to dose can be seen in the case of digoxin illustrated in Fig. 7.2. After oral administration the

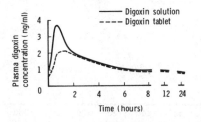

Fig. 7.2. Plasma digoxin concentrations during the 24 h following a single dose during daily maintenance dose therapy. In the 6 h after administration the plasma digoxin concentration is a poor guide to the mean steady-state plasma concentration. [Adapted from Lloyd *et al.* (1978) *Am. J. Cardiol.* **42**, 129–136, with permission.]

plasma concentration changes within quite a wide range before complete tissue distribution has occurred, even at steady state. One may be misled about the true steady-state plasma concentration if the sample is taken before that time. It is generally *simplest* to take the blood sample just before the next dose when one will measure the *minimum* steady-state concentration. In the case of aminoglycoside antibiotics, however (see gentamicin below) one should also measure the 'peak' concentration. Specific guidelines are given below for individual drugs.

7.4.10. Specific drug plasma concentrations in practice (see also Table 7.2)

(a) Phenytoin

The 'therapeutic' range is 40–80 µmol/l. Above 80 µmol/l the incidence of toxicity rises. However, patients with values above the range may not be toxic and patients with values below the range may not be undertreated. Although in the toxic range plasma phenytoin concentrations are quite well related to its *acute* toxic effects (see Fig. 7.3), they are not well related to its long-term adverse effects, such as gingival hyperplasia, hirsutism and acne, and folate and vitamin D deficiencies.

Because of the non-linearity of phenytoin kinetics it is unwise to increase the dose by increments of daily dose of more than 25–50 mg every two weeks or so, when an increase in dose is thought necessary. When the plasma phenytoin concentration is below 60 µmol/l an increase of 50 mg in the daily dose is sufficient; if above 60 µmol/l the increase should be no more than 25 mg.

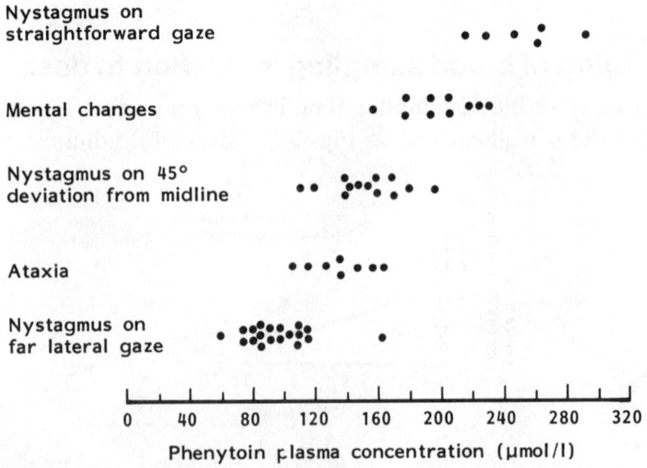

Fig. 7.3. Relationship between plasma concentrations of phenytoin and its acute effects. [Adapted from Kutt *et al.* (1964) *Arch. Neurol.* (*Chicago*) **11**, 642–648, with permission. Copyright 1967, American Medical Association.]

Table 7.2 *Usual therapeutic and toxic plasma concentrations of commonly measured drugs (see text for discussion)*

Drug	Usual therapeutic range	Usual toxic range
Aminoglycosides		
Amikacin	Peak: ≈34 μmol/l (20 μg/ml)	Peak: >55 μmol/l (32 μg/ml) Trough: >17 μmol/l (10 μg/ml)
Gentamicin	Peak: ≈5 μg/ml*	Peak: >12 μg/ml* Trough: >2 μg/ml*
Kanamycin	Peak: ≈50 μmol/l (25 μg/ml)	Peak: >80 μmol/l (40 μg/ml) Trough: >20 μmol/l (10 μg/ml)
Aspirin (salicylate)	Analgesic: 0.15–0.75 mmol/l (20–100 μg/ml) Anti-inflammatory: 1.1–2.2 mmol/l (150–300 μg/ml)	>2.2 mmol/l (300 μg/ml)
Carbamazepine	17–42 μmol/l (4–10 μg/ml)	>42 μmol/l (10 μg/ml)
Cardiac glycosides		
Digitoxin	20–35 nmol/l (15–25 ng/ml)	>39 nmol/l (30 ng/ml)
Digoxin	1.0–2.6 nmol/l (0.8–2.0 ng/ml)	>3.8 nmol/l (3.0 ng/ml)
Lithium	0.4–1.0 mmol/l	>1.0 mmol/l
Paracetamol		>1.0 mmol/l†
Phenytoin	40–80 μmol/l (10–20 μg/ml)	>80 μmol/l (20 μg/ml)
Theophylline	55–110 μmol/l (10–20 μg/ml)	>110 μmol/l (20 μg/ml)

* Gentamicin is given as a mixture of related compounds (see structure on p.632), and cannot therefore be measured in molar units.
† The toxicity of paracetamol relates not only to its plasma concentration, but also to the time after overdose (see discussion on p.576).

Steady state occurs at one to two weeks of maintenance therapy after a change in dose at low doses, and the higher the plasma concentration the longer it takes (up to two to three weeks or even longer in some patients). For this reason one should not make too frequent changes in dose.

The time of sampling is probably of little importance for phenytoin since plasma concentrations fluctuate very little during a dosage interval.

Alterations in phenytoin plasma protein binding (usually about 90 per cent) set in train a sequence of events which can further complicate plasma concentration interpretation (see Chapter 10 and Fig. 10.1):

1. Displacement of phenytoin from plasma protein binding sites results in an increase in free concentration without a change in total concentration. Toxicity may then occur if displacement has occurred rapidly enough.

2. Because phenytoin has a low hepatic extraction ratio its total body clearance is proportional to the *fraction* of unbound drug in the plasma (see Chapter 3). With the increase in unbound fraction, therefore, its total body clearance increases proportionately, and within a few days the *total concentration falls*. Since the unbound *fraction* remains increased, however, the unbound *concentration* returns to what it was before the displacement. Toxicity then resolves.

3. The doctor measures the *total* plasma concentration, thinks it is inadequate, and increases the dose. Toxicity results.

The main circumstances in which decreased phenytoin plasma protein binding may occur are:

renal failure;
severe hypoalbuminaemia (<25 g/l);
the third trimester of pregnancy (probably because of hypo-albuminaemia);
displacement by other drugs (see Chapter 10).

(b) Other anti-epileptic drugs

(i) Carbamazepine

The therapeutic plasma range is 17–42 μmol/l (4–10 μg/ml). Carbamazepine induces its own metabolism and thus its half-time shortens during chronic therapy. Thus after an initial peak of plasma concentrations three or four days after starting therapy, a steady state at a lower concentration is reached a few weeks later. Blood samples should be taken immediately before a dose. Plasma carbamazepine concentrations may be increased by dextropropoxyphene and decreased by phenytoin and barbiturates.

(ii) Others

The value of measuring the plasma concentrations of other anti-epileptic drugs has not been clearly established. Rough guides to the sorts of plasma concentration ranges encountered during therapy are given in the section on treatment of epilepsy (p.504).

(c) Digitalis

The therapeutic range for digoxin is 0.8–2.0 ng/ml (1.0–2.6 nmol/l). Below 0.8 ng/ml there is little associated therapeutic effect and in patients who are clinically well digoxin may be withdrawn, usually without subsequent clinical deterioration. Above 2.0 ng/ml the incidence of toxicity increases, and toxicity is highly likely above 3.0 ng/ml. The corresponding range for digitoxin is 15–25 ng/ml, with toxicity highly likely above 30 ng/ml.

There are several factors which alter the relationship between dose and plasma concentration of digoxin. The most important are:

(i) *Renal impairment*
(ii) *Drug interactions*
Quinidine, amiodarone, verapamil, nifedipine, and spironolactone.

In these cases doses of digoxin need to be reduced. Digitoxin is not affected by these circumstances.

There are also several factors which alter the link between the pharmacokinetic and pharmacodynamic phases of therapy with both digoxin and digitoxin, and in such circumstances the plasma concentration can be difficult to interpret.

(i) Hypokalaemia

A low extracellular potassium concentration increases the affinity of digitalis for Na^+, K^+-ATPase and increases the pharmacodynamic effect of a given concentration of digitalis. For this reason one should never try to interpret the plasma digitalis concentration without also knowing the plasma potassium concentration. In circumstances in which digitalis toxicity is suspected a low plasma potassium concentration (i.e. < 3.5 mmol/l) is sufficient to warrant withdrawal of digitalis on the assumption that toxicity *has* occurred.

(ii) Thyroid disease

Hyperthyroidism causes both a decrease in plasma digitalis concentrations at a given dose, *and* a decrease in responsiveness. Hypothyroidism has the opposite effects. There are no guidelines to the interpretation of plasma digitalis concentrations in these circumstances.

(iii) Age

Children under 6 months of age have lower plasma concentrations at a given dose, *and* are resistant to the effects of digitalis. In the elderly the reverse of these effects occurs.

The time of blood sampling should be at least 6 h after the previous dose, and 12 h is the optimum time in patients taking once-daily treatment (Fig. 7.2). During regular maintenance dosage without a loading dose, steady state will be reached after about 7 days (digoxin, normal renal function), 18 days (digoxin, anephric patients), or 25 days (digitoxin).

(d) Lithium

The therapeutic range is 0.4–1.0 mmol/l. At 1.0–1.5 mmol/l there is an increase in the incidence of both acute toxicity and long-term adverse effects. Concentrations above 1.5 mmol/l should be avoided.

Regular plasma lithium monitoring is necessary for several reasons:

1. Lithium is nephrotoxic and is excreted by the kidneys. Toxicity is thus self-perpetuating since toxicity causes renal damage, further retention of lithium, and further toxicity.

2. Systemic availability varies from individual to individual, is altered by diarrhoea, and varies from formulation to formulation (see Pharmacopoeia).

3. Changes in sodium balance alter the renal excretion of lithium. For example, renal sodium loss induced by diuretics leads to lithium retention.

Blood samples should be taken 12 h after the previous dose.

It takes about 3 days for steady state to be reached during regular maintenance therapy, but there is wide variation and in some patients it may require a week of treatment before steady state is reached.

(e) Aminoglycoside antibiotics

We shall restrict discussion here to gentamicin. Corresponding concentrations for other aminoglycosides are given in Table 7.2 and similar considerations apply.

The relationship between plasma gentamicin concentration and therapeutic efficacy is complicated by the fact that different organisms have different sensitivities to the antibiotic. A peak plasma concentration of 5–9 µg/ml is generally considered to be necessary. However, when gentamicin is used in combination with benzylpenicillin in the treatment of bacterial endocarditis lower plasma gentamicin concentrations may be efficacious.

The relationship between plasma gentamicin concentration and its toxic effects on the ears and kidneys is of great importance. To understand this relationship we must first define 'peak' and 'trough' concentrations. 'Peak' concentration means the concentration measured about 1 h after intramuscular (i.m.) administration or 15 min after the end of a half-hour infusion. 'Trough' concentration means the concentration measured at least three half-times (i.e. about 6 h) after the previous dose; the trough concentration is usually measured just before the next dose.

Ototoxicity is thought to be related to the trough concentration and its relationship to the peak concentration is not clear. The relationship between plasma concentration and nephrotoxicity is not clear and is complicated by the fact that renal damage will itself alter the plasma concentration. It is recommended that peak plasma gentamicin concentrations be *below* 12 µg/ml at peak and *below* 2 µg/ml at trough in order to avoid toxicity. The corresponding values for amikacin and kanamycin are given in Table 7.2.

Since toxicity of these drugs may be related to both peak and trough concentrations it may be necessary to change both *size of dose* and *timing of administration* if target plasma concentrations at both peak and trough are to be achieved. This principle is illustrated for gentamicin in three different cases (see Fig. 7.4).

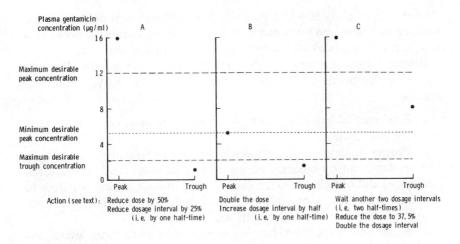

Fig. 7.4. Some theoretical problems in gentamicin therapy in relation to peak and trough plasma gentamicin concentrations (see text).

Case A

In this case the peak is too high (16 μg/ml) but the trough is acceptable (1 μg/ml). The dosage interval is obviously equal to about four half-times (allowing for the extra hour between administration and measurement of the peak). If the dose is halved immediately the peak will be about 8 μg/ml, and only three half-times will be required before the same trough of 1 μg/ml is reached. The dosage interval should therefore be reduced by 75 per cent.

Note that if one halved the dose and halved the dosage interval the peak would be 8 μg/ml and the trough 2 μg/ml. Despite the fact that one would be giving the same total dose over a given period of time, the range of plasma concentrations found during that time would be more acceptable than before, simply because of the alteration in timing (compare Fig. 3.10).

Case B

The peak here is a little low (5 μg/ml) and the dose could be doubled. The dosage interval is equal to about two half-times (trough 1.25 μg/ml) and the dosage interval should therefore be increased by a half (i.e. one half-time).

Case C

In this case the peak concentration is too high (16 μg/ml). The trough is also too high (8 μg/ml). The dosage interval is equivalent to about one half-time. The next dose should be delayed until the plasma concentration has fallen to 2 μg/ml (i.e. another two dosage intervals). At that time $^{2}/_{16}$, i.e. 12.5 per cent of the original body load will be present in the body and one wants to raise it to 50 per cent (i.e. a plasma concentration of 8 μg/ml).

One therefore gives 50−12.5 per cent, i.e. 37.5 per cent of the original maintenance dose and waits two half-times before repeating the dose. This should result in a peak of 8 μg/ml and a trough of 2 μg/ml.

We must stress that these are theoretical examples discussed to illustrate the principles involved. In practice things are not so easy, for several reasons:

1. Estimates of half-time from two concentration measurements only are very inaccurate.

2. Plasma aminoglycoside concentration measurements take at least 24 h to carry out by bioassay (using *in vitro* measurements of bacterial inhibition) and one cannot make decisions about dosage from one dose to the next (usual dosage intervals 8–12 h). Immunoassay of aminoglycosides is considerably faster but the results are less accurate.

3. Renal function may be changing more rapidly than dosage alterations can be calculated.

Despite these problems an understanding of the principles involved will be some help in guiding dosage in these difficult circumstances.

(f) Theophylline

Therapeutic plasma concentrations vary between 10 and 20 μg/ml and the incidence of toxicity increases at over 20 μg/ml. For routine plasma theophylline measurements to be of value in the treatment of acute asthma they must be available very rapidly so that adjustments in dose may be made quickly. In practice this means the use of fast immunoassay techniques and these are available in few centres. For chronic therapy other assays are equally useful.

The time to steady state is usually less than a day but the half-time varies in disease and the time to steady state may be as long as 2–3 days.

Blood samples are best taken just before a dose, and because of diurnal variations in trough concentrations should ideally be taken at the same time of day in an individual.

8 Pharmacogenetics

Pharmacogenetics is the study of the influence of heredity on the pharmacokinetic and pharmacodynamic responses to drugs.

8.1. PHARMACOKINETIC DEFECTS

The extent to which an individual metabolizes a drug is, at least in part, genetically determined. This fact has emerged from studies on monozygotic (i.e. identical) and dizygotic (i.e. non-identical) twins. Monozygotic twins metabolize drugs similarly while dizygotic twins often do not (see Fig. 8.1). For most drugs in population studies the variability in drug

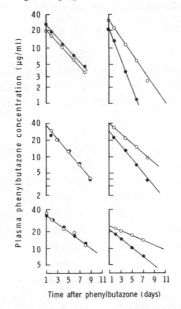

Time after phenylbutazone (days)

Fig. 8.1. Plasma phenylbutazone concentrations following administration to three pairs of monozygotic twins (left hand panels) and three pairs of dizygotic twins (right hand panels). The monozygotic twins show virtually identical kinetics while the dizygotic twins differ. [Adapted from Vesell and Page (1968) *Science* **159**, 1479–1480, with permission. Copyright 1968, The American Association for the Advancement of Science.]

metabolism shows a unimodal, normal distribution. This is illustrated in Fig. 8.2 for sodium salicylate. Sodium salicylate is conjugated in the liver to the glucuronide, the acylphenolic conjugate, and the glycine conjugate. Some is oxidized to gentisic acid. This metabolism accounts for about 90 per cent of its elimination at low doses. After a therapeutic dose of sodium salicylate to a population of subjects the plasma salicylate concentrations show a unimodal normal distribution, suggesting that the rates of metabolism of sodium salicylate within the population have a continuous distribution of variability.

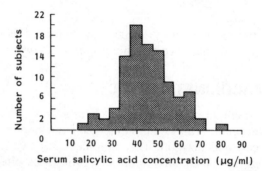

Fig. 8.2. Unimodal drug metabolism. The frequency distribution of serum salicylic acid concentrations (3 h after the same dose of aspirin in 100 individuals) is unimodal. [Adapted from Evans and Clarke (1961) *Br. med. Bull.* **17**, 234–240, with permission.]

However, for some drugs the distribution is bi- or tri-modal indicating the existence of separate populations of subjects capable of metabolizing those drugs at discretely different rates. The important pathways of drug metabolism subject to pharmacokinetic variability are detailed below.

8.1.1. Acetylation

Several drugs are acetylated by the hepatic enzyme *N*-acetyl transferase and the distribution of rates of acetylation in the population is bimodal (Fig. 8.3). The difference between fast and slow acetylation depends upon the *amount* of hepatic *N*-acetyl transferase, rather than a change in its properties. It is known that rapid acetylation is inherited as an autosomal dominant character while slow acetylation is thought to be recessive. The ratio of fast:slow acetylators is 40:60 in Europe, 85:15 in Japan and 100:0 in Eskimos.

Drugs whose acetylation is genetically determined in this way are isoniazid, hydralazine, procainamide, phenelzine, dapsone, and some sulphonamides (e.g. sulphadimidine, sulphamethoxypyridazine). Not all drugs which are acetylated are affected, the exceptions including sulphanilamide, *para*-aminobenzoic acid, and *para*-aminosalicylic acid, which are acetylated by a different enzyme outside the liver.

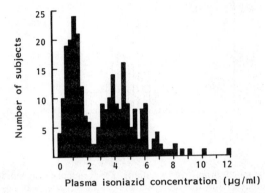

Fig. 8.3. Bimodal metabolism (acetylation). The frequency distribution of plasma isoniazid concentrations (6 h after an oral dose of 9.7 mg/kg in 267 individuals of 53 families) is bimodal. Those with lower plasma isoniazid concentrations are fast acetylators, those with higher plasma isoniazid concentrations are slow acetylators. [Adapted from Evans *et al.* (1960) *Br. med. J.* **ii**, 485–491, with permission.]

The clinical consequences of these differences are increased drug toxicity, usually among slow acetylators, but also sometimes an enhanced response to treatment in those patients. Thus slow acetylators have been reported to require lower doses of isoniazid and hydralazine than fast acetylators in the treatment of tuberculosis and hypertension respectively. On the other hand slow acetylators are more likely to develop the lupus erythematosus-like syndrome caused by isoniazid, hydralazine, and procainamide, and the peripheral neuropathy caused by isoniazid (which can be prevented or treated with pyridoxine). The interaction between isoniazid and phenytoin, resulting in phenytoin toxicity due to inhibition of phenytoin metabolism, occurs more frequently among slow acetylators. When a *metabolite* is toxic, however, fast acetylators are more at risk, and that may be so in the case of the hepatic damage associated with isoniazid.

The acetylator status of a patient may be easily assessed by giving 1 g of sulphadimidine orally and measuring the relative proportions of acetylated and total sulphonamide in a sample of urine passed 5–6 h later.

8.1.2. Hydroxylation

Poor hydroxylation of debrisoquine has been reported in 9 per cent of the population (Fig. 8.4) and has an autosomal dominant inheritance. Other drugs affected include phenytoin and phenformin. Poor hydroxylators are more likely to develop adverse effects than extensive hydroxylators.

8.1.3. Succinylcholine hydrolysis

Succinylcholine is metabolized in the plasma by a pseudocholinesterase. Metabolism is normally fast, the blood is quickly cleared of the drug, and

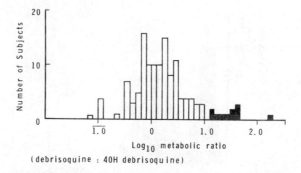

Fig. 8.4. Bimodal metabolism (hydroxylation). The frequency distribution of the ratio of urinary debrisoquine to 4-hydroxydebrisoquine (in the 8 h after a 10 mg oral dose of debrisoquine in 128 individuals) is bimodal. Those with a lower ratio are extensive hydroxylators, those with a higher ratio are poor hydroxylators. [Adapted from Babanunmi *et al.* (1980) *Br. J. clin. Pharmacol.* **9**, 112–113P, with permission.]

therefore neuromuscular blockade lasts only a few minutes. In some individuals, however, the pseudocholinesterase is abnormal and does not metabolize the succinylcholine so rapidly. In these patients the drug persists in the blood and continues to produce neuromuscular blockade for several hours. This results in respiratory paralysis (sometimes called 'scoline apnoea') which requires prolonged ventilation until the succinylcholine is cleared. In this enzyme abnormality the affinity of the enzyme for its substrate, e.g. succinylcholine, is decreased, and the amount of normal enzyme is also reduced.

The abnormalities of pseudocholinesterase are of three main types, each of which is inherited in autosomal recessive fashion.

(a) Dibucaine resistant (see Fig. 8.5)

The normal pseudocholinesterase is about 80 per cent inhibited by the local anaesthetic dibucaine at a concentration of 10^{-5}M. The percentage inhibition of a subject's enzyme by dibucaine is called the 'dibucaine number'. In some people there is a homozygous defect which results in the production of an abnormal enzyme with a reduced affinity for succinylcholine. This variant is resistant to inhibition by dibucaine and these individuals have low dibucaine numbers (about 15) and are at risk of scoline apnoea.

Individuals who are heterozygous for the defect have dibucaine numbers (45–70) intermediate between those of normal individuals and homozygotes. Heterozygotes are not at risk of scoline apnoea.

This is the commonest form of abnormality and occurs in about 1:2500 of the population.

(b) Fluoride resistant

This is a rare variant of pseudocholinesterase abnormality. The enzyme has a variable response to dibucaine but is resistant to inhibition by fluoride. Homozygotes are at risk of scoline apnoea.

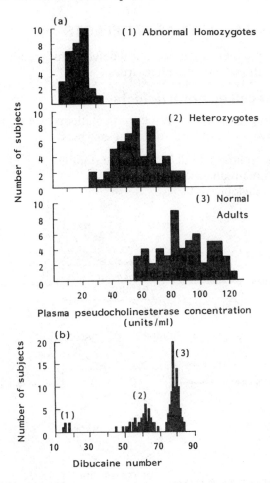

Fig. 8.5. Pseudocholinesterase deficiency.
(a) The frequency distribution of plasma pseudocholinesterase concentrations is trimodal, homozygotes and heterozygotes having lower concentrations than normal individuals.
[Adapted from Lehmann and Silk (1961) *Br. med. Bull.* **17**, 230–233, with permission.]
(b) The frequency distribution of dibucaine numbers (a measure of the affinity of the inhibitor for the enzyme) is trimodal, in similar fashion to the plasma pseudocholinesterase concentration, but the dibucaine number more readily differentiates the groups from each other. [Adapted from Kalow and Staron (1957) *Can. J. Biochem. Physiol.* **35**, 1305–1317, with permission.]

(c) 'Silent' gene

Another rare variant associated with scoline apnoea is the so-called 'silent' gene variety. Homozygotes for this defect have little or no enzyme activity at all and cannot hydrolyse succinylcholine.

8.2. PHARMACODYNAMIC DEFECTS

In some people there are biochemical defects which render them peculiarly sensitive to the effects of certain drugs.

8.2.1. Red cell enzyme defects

Unusual drug reactions may occur in patients whose erythrocytes are deficient in any one of three different enzymes:

(a) glucose 6-phosphate dehydrogenase (G6PD);
(b) glutathione reductase;
(c) methaemoglobin reductase.

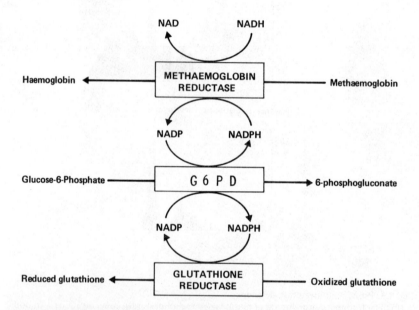

Fig. 8.6. The reactions catalyzed by glucose 6-phosphate dehydrogenase (G6PH), methaemoglobin reductases, and glutathione reductase in red cells, and their metabolic inter-relationships. Deficiency of G6PD or of glutathione reductase may result in haemolysis following exposure to certain drugs (see Table 8.1). Deficiency of methaemoglobin reductase following exposure to those drugs may result in methaemoglobinaemia.

The metabolic inter-relationships of the reactions catalyzed by these enzymes are shown in Fig. 8.6. G6PD catalyzes the oxidation of glucose 6-phosphate to phosphogluconate from which pentose 5-monophosphate is eventually generated. Although this phosphogluconate pathway is relatively unimportant as a route of glycolysis, it *is* important as a source of reduced NADP (i.e. NADPH). NADPH in turn is an important electron donor in the reactions catalysed by glutathione reductase, in which oxidized glutathione is converted to reduced glutathione, which in turn is necessary for the prevention of the oxidation of various cell proteins. Although NADPH also acts as an electron donor for the reduction of methaemoglobin by one of the enzymes in the methaemoglobin reductase complex this is a relatively unimportant pathway for methaemoglobin reduction and the enzyme for which NADH acts as electron donor is more important (see below).

(a) Glucose 6-phosphate dehydrogenase deficiency

Lack of G6PD in erythrocytes results in diminished production of NADPH. Consequently oxidized glutathione (and, to a lesser and insignificant extent, methaemoglobin) accumulates. When the erythrocyte is exposed to oxidizing agents haemolysis occurs, probably because of unopposed oxidation of sulphydryl groups in the cell membrane, which are normally kept in reduced form by the continuous availability of reduced glutathione.

The incidence varies with race. The defect is rare among Caucasians and has its highest incidence (50 per cent or more) among Sephardic Jews of Asiatic origin. The incidence in Negros is between 10 and 20 per cent.

Inheritance of the defect is complex, the enzyme being heterogeneous.

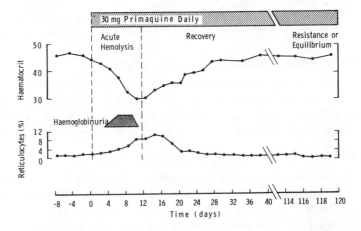

Fig. 8.7. The time-course of haemolysis following exposure to primaquine in a subject with the Negro variety of G6PD deficiency. The abnormality in this variety is accelerated degradation of G6PD. [Adapted from Alving *et al.* (1960) *Bull. Wld. Hlth. Org.* **22**, 621–31, with the permission of the WHO.]

There are broadly speaking two enzyme varieties, the Negro and the Mediterranean. In the Negro variety G6PD production is probably normal but its degradation is accelerated so that only old red cells (those older than about 55 days) are affected. In this form acute haemolysis occurs on first administration of the drug and lasts only for a few days. Thereafter continued administration of the precipitating drug causes chronic mild haemolysis (see Fig. 8.7). In the Mediterranean variety the enzyme is abnormal and both young and old cells are affected. In this form severe haemolysis occurs on first administration and is maintained.

The commonly used drugs which may cause haemolysis in susceptible individuals are listed in Table 8.1. The reaction is sometimes called 'favism' because it may result from eating broad beans (*Vicia faba*) which contain an oxidant alkaloid.

Table 8.1   *Drugs which may precipitate haemolysis in subjects with G6PD deficiency*

(a) *Drugs with the most marked effect*

Nitrofurantoin
Phenacetin
Primaquine
Probenecid
Sulphonamides—sulphafurazole, sulphanilamide, sulphapyridine, sulphasalazine

(b) *Other commonly used drugs*

Analgesics—antipyrine, salicylates
Antimalarials—chloroquine, mepacrine, quinine
Sulphonamides other than those listed in (a) above
Others—chloramphenicol, dapsone and other sulphones, dimercaprol, quinidine, vitamin K

(b) Glutathione reductase deficiency

This enzyme deficiency may result directly in reduced glutathione deficiency (see Fig. 8.6) and haemolysis results from the effects of the oxidizing agents listed in Table 8.1. In addition warfarin and phenylbutazone have been implicated. The defect is of autosomal dominant inheritance.

(c) Methaemoglobin reductase deficiency

Although there are several mechanisms for preventing the accumulation of methaemoglobin in the red cell, the methaemoglobin reductase complex of enzymes, and particularly the enzyme dependent on NADH, are the most important. In normal individuals methaemoglobin is continuously being reduced to haemoglobin and forms only 1 per cent of the total red cell haemoglobin. Following exposure to the oxidant drugs listed in Table 8.1 (and in addition to glyceryl trinitrate and related compounds) more methaemoglobin is formed but can be rapidly reduced. In methaemoglobin reductase deficiency this reduction cannot be carried out so efficiently and methaemoglobin accumulates causing tissue hypoxaemia because methaemoglobin causes impairment of oxygen delivery to the tissues.

Treatment is with the reducing agent methylene blue (1–2 mg/kg body weight).

Inheritance of the defect is autosomal recessive.

8.2.2. Resistance to drug effects

(a) Coumarin resistance

There is a wide range of dosage requirements of coumarin anticoagulants in the general population, partly because of genetic variability in both the metabolism of the drugs and the synthesis of clotting factors. However, there is also a very rare type of resistance to the effects of these drugs in which 20 times the usual dose may be required to produce anticoagulation. In affected subjects the metabolism of drug is normal as is the availability of vitamin K_1 and the mechanism is unknown. The defect has autosomal dominant inheritance and has been described in only a few families.

(b) Vitamin D-resistant rickets

This is a more common form of genetic defect, inherited in sex-linked dominant fashion. The precise cause of the disorder is unknown but it results in rickets which responds only to very large doses (more than 1000 times usual) of vitamin D (see also Table 25.4).

8.2.3. Porphyria

The hepatic porphyrias, acute intermittent porphyria and porphyria cutanea tarda, are characterized by abnormalities in haem biosynthesis. The biochemical pathways involved are shown in Fig. 8.8.

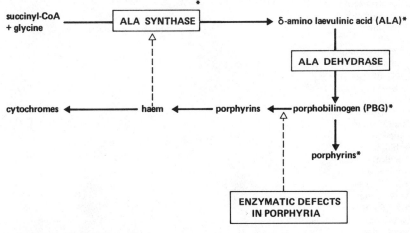

* Increased in hepatic porphyria

Fig. 8.8. Abnormalities in haem biosynthesis in patients with porphyria.

Table 8.2   *Drugs which may precipitate an attack of porphyria*

Alcohol (ethanol)
Antipyrine and related compounds
Barbiturates
Carbamazepine
Chlordiazepoxide†
Chloroquine*
Chlorpropamide*
Dichloralphenazone
Ergot preparations
Eucalyptol
Female sex hormones
Glutethimide†
Griseofulvin†
Hydantoins (e.g. phenytoin)†
Imipramine
Meprobamate†
Methyldopa†
Rifampicin
Succinimides (e.g. ethosuximide)†
Sulphonamides†
Tolbutamide

* Reported to precipitate porphyria cutanea tarda but not acute intermittent porphyria.
† Reported to precipitate acute intermittent porphyria but not porphyria cutanea tarda.

Table 8.3   *Drugs which do not precipitate an attack of porphyria*

Atropine
Choral hydrate
Chlorpromazine
Corticosteroids
Diazepam
Digoxin
Diphenhydramine
Guanethidine
Hyoscine
Meclozine
Methadone
Neostigmine
Opiates
Penicillins
Pethidine
Prochlorperazine
Promazine
Promethazine
Propoxyphene
Prostigmine
Reserpine
Streptomycin
Trifluoperazine
Vitamins B and C

The activity of δ-aminolaevulinic acid (ALA) synthase, the rate-limiting enzyme, is increased in porphyria, resulting in excess production of ALA and porphobilinogen (PBG), and of porphyrias down the pathway alternative to haem biosynthesis. Haem normally acts as a repressor of ALA synthase activity. The mechanisms by which some drugs may precipitate an attack of porphyria are not fully understood but involve an increase in ALA synthase activity. Drugs which are enzyme inducers may act by diverting haem to the synthesis of cytochrome P450 thereby derepressing ALA synthase activity.

The drugs which can precipitate an acute attack of porphyria are listed in Table 8.2 and those which are known *not* to precipitate an attack are listed in Table 8.3. There is little information about the clinical effects of most other drugs. Although the drugs listed in Table 8.2 have all been reported to precipitate acute attacks of porphyria in affected subjects, they do not always do so and drug-induced attacks of porphyria are unpredictable.

8.2.4. Malignant hyperthermia

This is a serious, potentially fatal complication of general anaesthesia with halothane, methoxyflurane, and succinylcholine. It occurs in about 1 in 20 000 anaesthetized patients and is inherited in autosomal dominant fashion. It is characterized by an acute rise in body temperature to 40–41°C, muscle stiffness, tachycardia, sweating, cyanosis, and tachypnoea. The cause is not fully known but there are abnormalities in the response of the muscles of affected individuals to caffeine and halothane *in vitro*, and the defect may involve abnormalities in the compartmentation of sarcoplasmic calcium. Dantrolene, which decreases the amount of calcium released from sarcoplasmic reticulum, should be used in the treatment, and given intravenously in an initial dose of 1 mg/kg repeated as necessary to a total of 10 mg/kg.

9 Adverse reactions to drugs

9.1. HISTORY

From the earliest times pharmaceutical preparations have been recognized as being potentially dangerous. It is a maxim that unless a drug is capable of doing some harm it is unlikely to do much good!

Public and professional concern about these matters first arose in the late nineteenth century. Between 1870 and 1890 committees and commissions were established in order to investigate sudden deaths occurring during chloroform anaesthesia, now known to be due, probably, to the effect of chloroform to sensitize the myocardium to catecholamines, causing an increased risk of cardiac arrhythmias. In 1922 there was an inquiry into jaundice associated with the use of salvarsan, an organic arsenical, in the treatment of syphilis. In the USA in 1937, 107 people died as a result of taking an elixir of sulphanilamide which contained as a solvent diethylene glycol. Although the toxic effects of the solvent were known, they were not known to the manufacturer. This led to the establishment in the USA of the Food and Drug Administration (FDA), which was given the task of enquiring into the safety of new drugs before allowing them to be marketed.

There are many other examples, but the major modern catastrophe which changed professional and public attitudes all over the world toward modern medicines was the thalidomide incident. In 1961, in West Germany, it was reported that there was an outbreak of phocomelia (hypoplastic or aplastic limb deformities) in newborn children. It was shown that thalidomide, a non-barbiturate hypnotic, was to blame. The crucial period of pregnancy during which thalidomide is teratogenic is the first three months. Of course, not all pregnant women who took thalidomide gave birth to deformed babies, but it is estimated that in West Germany about 10 000 children were born deformed, of whom 5000 survived (the high mortality being due to deformities other than phocomelia). In the UK 600 children were born deformed and 400 survived. In the USA the FDA had held up the marketing of the drug because of evidence that the drug caused hypothyroidism and a peripheral neuropathy. Thus only a few cases of phocomelia occurred in the children of women taking part in clinical trials. At that time teratogenicity testing was not undertaken as a routine. It was later confirmed that thalidomide was teratogenic in experimental animals if given early in pregnancy.

This incident led to a public outcry, to the institution all around the world of drug regulatory authorities, to the development of a much more sophisticated approach to preclinical testing and clinical evaluation of drugs before marketing, and to a greatly increased awareness of adverse effects of drugs and methods of detecting them.

9.2. INCIDENCE OF ADVERSE DRUG REACTIONS

All sorts of numbers get quoted about the incidence of adverse reactions to drugs. It is, in fact, very difficult to be certain how commonly adverse reactions occur overall, and what proportion are trivial on the one hand or serious on the other. The following are the sorts of figures generally quoted:

(a) *Hospital in-patients* 10–20 per cent suffer an adverse drug reaction;

(b) *Deaths in hospital in-patients* 0.24–2.9 per cent are due to adverse drug reactions;

(c) *Hospital admissions* 0.3–5.0 per cent of hospital admissions are due to adverse drug reactions.

Thus there is a considerable problem with adverse reactions to drugs, although its precise quantitative nature is unclear.

9.3. CLASSIFICATION OF ADVERSE DRUG REACTIONS

No classification of adverse drug reactions is entirely satisfactory. However, it has been suggested that adverse drug reactions be classified into two types:

(a) dose-related (so-called Type A, or augmented);

(b) non-dose-related (so-called Type B, or bizarre).

Since some adverse reactions do not fit neatly into this classification we shall add two further groups:

(c) long-term effects;

(d) delayed effects.

Even then not all adverse drug reactions can be neatly classified, but that is in the nature of classification.

The various subdivisions of these four categories are shown in Table 9.1 and we shall deal with them in the order shown there. We shall deal mainly with the principles underlying the mechanisms involved, giving appropriate examples. Discussions of drugs which cause damage to particular organs are dealt with in the therapeutics section (e.g. hepatotoxic drugs in the section on the treatment of liver disease, etc.).

Table 9.1 *Classification of adverse drug reactions*

---

1. Dose-related (Type A, or augmented)
  (a) Pharmaceutical variation
  (b) Pharmacokinetic variation
    (i)   Pharmacogenetic variation
    (ii) Hepatic disease
    (iii) Renal disease
    (iv) Cardiac disease
    (v)   Thyroid disease
  (c) Pharmacodynamic variation
    (i) Hepatic disease
    (ii) Altered fluid and electrolyte balance

2. Non-dose-related (Type B or bizarre)
  (a) Immunological reactions
  (b) Pharmacogenetic variation

3. Long-term effects
  (a) Adaptive changes
  (b) Rebound phenomena
  (c) Other long-term effects

4. Delayed effects
  (a) Carcinogenesis
  (b) Effects connected with reproduction
    (i)   Impaired fertility
    (ii) Teratogenesis
    (iii) Drugs in breast milk

9.4. DOSE-RELATED ADVERSE REACTIONS

These are due usually to a pharmacokinetic or pharmacodynamic abnormality producing *an excess of a known pharmacological effect of the drug*, resulting in an adverse effect. The pharmacological effect which proves adverse may be that through which one hopes to achieve the therapeutic effect (e.g. hypoglycaemia due to insulin), or some other effect (e.g. the anticholinergic action of tricyclic antidepressants, producing a dry mouth or urinary retention).

Dose-related adverse reactions have led to the concept of the therapeutic index, or the toxic:therapeutic ratio. This indicates the margin between the therapeutic dose and the toxic dose. The bigger the ratio the better. For example, if a patient is not hypersensitive to penicillins then for that patient penicillin G will have a high therapeutic index or a high toxic:therapeutic ratio, since one can safely use much higher doses than one needs to treat the patient satisfactorily. Some examples of commonly used drugs with a low toxic:therapeutic ratio (i.e. for which a small increase in dose beyond the therapeutic dose may result in toxicity) are:

anticoagulants (e.g. warfarin, heparin);
hypoglycaemic drugs (e.g. insulin, sulphonylureas);
anti-arrhythmic drugs (e.g. lignocaine, disopyramide);
digitalis compounds;
aminoglycoside antibiotics (e.g. gentamicin);
oral contraceptives;
cytotoxic and immunosuppressive drugs (e.g. methotrexate,
   azathioprine);
antihypertensive drugs (e.g. β-adrenoceptor antagonists, hydralazine).

Dose-related adverse reactions may occur because of variations in the pharmaceutical, pharmacokinetic, or pharmacodynamic properties of a drug, often due to some disease or pharmacogenetic characteristic of the patient. The following are examples of such mechanisms.

9.4.1. Pharmaceutical variation

From time to time adverse drug reactions can occur because of alterations in the systemic availability of a preparation. The most dramatic example was the outbreak of phenytoin intoxication amongst epileptic patients in Australia in the late 1960s. This was found to be due to a change in one of the excipients in the phenytoin capsules from calcium sulphate to lactose. This caused an increase in the systemic availability of phenytoin.

Sometimes an adverse reaction can occur because of the presence of a contaminant, e.g. pyrogens or even bacteria in i.v. preparations, if quality control breaks down. If a febrile reaction occurs in a patient receiving an infusion the drip should be taken down and all its components sent for bacteriological investigation. Urgent action in notifying the manufacturer should be taken if ever this sort of contamination is suspected.

Out-of-date formulations may sometimes cause adverse reactions, as in the case of out-dated tetracycline which may cause Fanconi's syndrome because of a degradation product. Avoid using out-of-date formulations.

9.4.2. Pharmacokinetic variation

There is a great deal of variation among normal individuals in the rate of elimination of drugs. This variation is most marked for drugs which are cleared by hepatic metabolism and is determined by several factors which may be genetic, environmental (e.g. diet, smoking, alcohol), or hepatic (blood flow and intrinsic drug metabolizing capability). On top of this normal variation there may occur specific pharmacogenetic or hepatic abnormalities which may be associated with adverse reactions. In addition renal and cardiac disease can cause alterations in drug pharmacokinetics.

(a) Pharmacogenetic variation

Pharmacogenetic abnormalities are discussed in detail in Chapter 8.

Examples of the pharmacokinetic kind associated with adverse reactions include the increased incidence of peripheral neuropathy in slow acetylators treated with isoniazid, and the prolongation of apnoea following succinylcholine administration in patients with pseudocholinesterase deficiency.

(b) Hepatic disease

It might be expected that, considering the central role of hepatic metabolism in the pharmacokinetic behaviour of many drugs, hepatic disease would frequently be associated with impaired drug elimination. However, such is the reserve of the liver parenchyma that in practice adverse reactions due to impaired hepatic metabolism are not all that common. Nevertheless in the presence of severe liver disease care must be taken, particularly with drugs with a low toxic:therapeutic ratio.

Theoretically liver dysfunction can affect drug disposition and elimination in several ways, and the outcome in an individual case may be complex and difficult to predict.

1. Hepatocellular dysfunction, as in severe hepatitis or advanced cirrhosis, may reduce the clearance of drugs for which the capacity of the liver is limited, for example phenytoin, theophylline, and warfarin.

2. Portosystemic shunting in portal hypertension, associated with cirrhosis, reduces the clearance of drugs normally cleared by the liver, for example morphine and other narcotic analgesics, propranolol, labetalol, and chlorpromazine.

3. Reduction in hepatic blood flow, as in heart failure, can reduce the hepatic clearance of drugs which have a high extraction ratio (see Chapter 3). Such drugs include lignocaine, propranolol, morphine, and pethidine.

4. Decreased plasma protein (albumin) production by the liver in cirrhosis may lead to reduced protein binding of drugs. The clinical significance of this effect is discussed in Chapter 10.

5. The effects of drugs. Certain drugs are hepatotoxic and need to be avoided or used with caution in patients with liver disease (see pp.383–6). If they cause impaired liver function in patients with previously normal liver function they may in turn cause decreased clearance of other drugs.

(c) Renal disease

If a drug or active metabolite is excreted either by glomerular filtration or tubular secretion, it will accumulate in renal failure and toxicity will occur. Examples of drugs which may accumulate in renal failure are given in Table 3.5, along with guidance to dosage reduction in those circumstances. Certain pharmacokinetic principles apply in drug dosage in renal failure:

1. The loading dose is not changed, unless the apparent volume of distribution of the drug is also altered by renal failure (as in the case of

digoxin, whose apparent volume of distribution is lowered by about one third).

2. Because less drug is being cleared per unit time from the body, maintenance doses can be made smaller, or their frequency of administration reduced, or both.

3. The time to steady state during repeated dosage will be longer than expected since the half-time will be prolonged.

4. Protein binding of drugs may be lowered in severe renal failure because of physicochemical changes in plasma albumin (see Chapter 10 for a discussion of the clinical relevance of this effect).

There are some drugs which are nephrotoxic and which should be avoided or used with caution in patients with renal disease (see p.416).

(d) Cardiac disease

Cardiac failure, particularly congestive cardiac failure, can alter the pharmacokinetic properties of drugs by several mechanisms:

1. Impaired absorption due to mucosal oedema and a poor splanchnic circulation. This can alter the efficacy of some oral diuretics, such as frusemide.

2. Hepatic congestion and reduced liver blood flow may impair the metabolism of some drugs (e.g. lignocaine).

3. Poor renal perfusion may result in decreased renal elimination of some drugs (e.g. procainamide).

4. Changes in apparent volume of distribution. By mechanisms which are not understood the apparent volumes of distribution of some cardioactive drugs (e.g. procainamide, lignocaine, and quinidine) are reduced in patients with congestive cardiac failure. This will not affect steady-state dosages but will result in reduced loading dose requirements.

(e) Thyroid disease

Hepatic metabolism of some drugs is increased in hyperthyroidism and decreased in hypothyroidism, but it is not possible to make general statements about all drugs which are metabolized. Drugs reportedly affected are methimazole (the active metabolite of carbimazole), propranolol, practolol, tolbutamide, and hydrocortisone.

Plasma digoxin concentrations are increased in hypothyroidism and decreased in hyperthyroidism partly because of changes in the apparent volume of distribution, and partly because of changes in renal clearance. In addition there are changes in the pharmacodynamic effects of cardiac glycosides in thyroid disease (decreased in hyperthyroidism, increased in hypothyroidism), and finding the optimum therapeutic dose while avoiding toxicity can be very difficult.

9.4.3. Pharmacodynamic variation

As with pharmacokinetic variability there is a great deal of pharmacodynamic variability within the general population, and that underlying variability may be compounded by the effects of disease.

(a) Hepatic disease

There are several mechanisms whereby hepatic disease may influence the pharmacodynamic response to certain drugs:

1. Reduced blood clotting. In cirrhosis and acute hepatitis production of clotting factors may be impaired and patients may bleed more readily. There is also a bleeding hazard in patients with oesophageal and gastric varices caused by portal hypertension in cirrhosis. Drugs which themselves impair clotting, which may impair haemostasis, or which may predispose to bleeding by causing gastric ulceration, should be avoided. These include anticoagulants, and non-steroidal anti-inflammatory drugs (e.g. aspirin, phenylbutazone, and indomethacin; paracetamol in usual doses is probably safe).

2. Hepatic encephalopathy. In patients with, or on the borderline of, hepatic encephalopathy (hepatic coma or hepatic pre-coma), the brain appears to be more sensitive to the effects of drugs with a sedative action. If such drugs are used coma may result. It is wise to avoid opiates and other narcotic analgesics, and barbiturates. Doses of chlorpromazine should be reduced. Chlormethiazole or short-acting benzodiazepines may be used cautiously as tranquillizers.

Diuretics used for the treatment of ascites and peripheral oedema may precipitate hepatic encephalopathy, particularly if diuresis occurs too rapidly. This seems to be associated with the production of a hypokalaemic alkalosis which in turn causes increased renal ammonia synthesis, resulting in ammonia retention, one of the factors contributing to hepatic encephalopathy.

3. Sodium and water retention. In hepatic cirrhosis sodium and water may be exacerbated by drugs which cause fluid retention. Drugs which should be avoided or used with caution include carbenoxolone, carbamazepine, phenylbutazone, indomethacin, corticosteroids, and preparations containing large amounts of sodium, e.g. antacid mixtures and sodium salts of penicillins.

All of these problems may, of course, be exacerbated by drug-induced hepatotoxicity (see pp.383–6).

(b) Altered fluid and electrolyte balance

The pharmacodynamic effects of some drugs may be altered by changes in fluid and electrolyte balance. For example the effects of cardiac glycosides are potentiated by hypokalaemia and hypercalcaemia, while the effects of Class I anti-arrhythmic drugs, such as lignocaine, quinidine, procainamide, and disopyramide, are reduced by hypokalaemia. Hypocalcaemia prolongs the action of skeletal muscle relaxants such as tubocurarine and fluid depletion enhances the hypotensive effects of antihypertensive drugs.

9.5. NON-DOSE–RELATED ADVERSE REACTIONS

Under this heading we shall deal with immunological and pharmacogenetic mechanisms of adverse reactions.

9.5.1. Immunological reactions (drug allergy or hypersensitivity reactions)

The following are the features of allergic drug reactions:

there is no relation to the usual pharmacological effects of the drug;
there is often a delay between first exposure to the drug and the occurrence of the subsequent adverse reaction;
there is no formal dose–response curve, and very small doses of the drug may elicit the reaction once allergy is established;
the reaction disappears on discontinuation of the drug;
the illness is often recognizable as an immunological reaction, e.g. rash, serum sickness, anaphylaxis, asthma, urticaria, angio-oedema, etc.

The factors involved in drug allergy concern *the drug*, *the patient*, and *incidental diseases*.

(a) The drug

Macromolecules, such as proteins (e.g. vaccines), polypeptides (e.g. insulin), and dextrans can themselves be immunogenic. Smaller molecules may act as haptens and combine with body proteins to form antigens. Little is known about the exact nature of many of the haptens (drugs or their metabolites) involved in immunological reactions to drugs. One exception is penicillin, for which the major antigenic determinant is the penicilloyl group formed after splitting of the β-lactam ring.

(b) The patient

Some patients are more likely to develop allergic drug reactions than others. These include patients with a history of atopic disease (eczema, asthma, or hay fever), those with hereditary angio-oedema, and those with a history of previous allergic drug reactions.

There is evidence that the syndrome mimicking systemic lupus erythematosus (see below), at least when it occurs in patients taking hydralazine, depends on the presence of the HLA DR4 tissue type. Slow acetylators (see Chapter 8) are also more prone to this reaction.

(c) Incidental diseases

Although there is some controversy as to whether it is an allergic reaction or not, the ampicillin/amoxycillin skin rash, distinct from skin rashes due to penicillin hypersensitivity, is much more common in patients with infectious mononucleosis (glandular fever) and other viral infections, leukaemia, and lymphomas. This rash is also more common, for unknown reasons, in patients also taking allopurinol.

9.5.2. Drug allergy—mechanisms and types

Theoretically drug allergy and its manifestations should correspond to the types of hypersensitivity reactions classified as Types I to IV. In practice it is not so easy to classify allergic drug reactions in this fashion because they present as clinical syndromes. We shall therefore start by giving examples which fit this classification, and continue with examples based on the clinical presentations.

Type I reactions (anaphylaxis; immediate hypersensitivity)

In this type the drug or metabolite interacts with antibody IgE molecules fixed to cells, particularly tissue mast cells and basophil leucocytes. This triggers a process leading to release of pharmacological mediators, which cause the allergic response (histamine, kinins, 5-hydroxytryptamine, and arachidonic acid derivatives).

Clinically Type I reactions manifest as urticaria, rhinitis, bronchial asthma, angio-oedema, and anaphylactic shock.

Drugs likely to cause anaphylactic shock include penicillins, streptomycin, local anaesthetics, and radio-opaque iodide-containing X-ray contrast media.

Type II reactions (cytotoxic reactions)

In Type II reactions a circulating antibody of the IgG, IgM, or IgA class interacts with a hapten (drug) combined with a cell membrane constituent (protein), to form an antigen–antibody complex. Complement is then activated, and cell lysis occurs. Most examples are haematological: thrombocytopenia associated with quinidine or quinine ('gin and tonic purpura'), digitoxin, and occasionally rifampicin; 'immune' neutropenia is difficult to distinguish in incidence from direct toxic effects of drugs on the bone marrow, but phenylbutazone, carbimazole, tolbutamide, anticonvulsants, chlorpropamide, and metronidazole have all been incriminated; haemolytic anaemias can also be produced by this mechanism by penicillins, cephalosporins, rifampicin, quinine, and quinidine.

Type III reactions (immune-complex reactions)

In Type III reactions antibody (IgG) combines with antigen (drug hapten–protein) in the circulation, the complex is deposited in the tissues, complement is activated, and damage to capillary endothelium results.

Serum sickness is the typical drug reaction of this type and is manifested most commonly by fever, arthritis, enlarged lymph nodes, urticaria, and maculo-papular rashes. Penicillins, streptomycin, sulphonamides, and antithyroid drugs may be responsible. This reaction is called 'serum sickness' because it used to occur most commonly as a reaction to injections of foreign serum (e.g. antitetanus serum).

Type IV reactions (cell-mediated, or delayed hypersensitivity reactions)

In Type IV reactions, T lymphocytes are 'sensitized' by a drug hapten–protein antigenic complex. When the lymphocytes come into contact with the antigen an inflammatory response ensues. Type IV reactions are exemplified by contact dermatitis caused by local anaesthetic creams, antihistamine creams, and topical antibiotics and antifungal drugs.

This then is the mechanistic view of allergic drug reactions. In clinical practice, however, one is usually faced with one of a variety of syndromes.

(a) Fever

Drug fever as an isolated phenomenon may occur with penicillins, phenytoin, hydralazine, and quinidine. Such fevers are usually of low grade and the patient is generally not very ill. The fever subsides within a few days of stopping the drug.

(b) Rashes

These are of several types.

(i) Toxic erythema
This is the commonest skin reaction to drugs. The lesions are macular or maculo-papular and can look like those of measles or scarlet fever; sometimes they are more like erythema multiforme; occasionally an urticarial element is present. Antibiotics (e.g. penicillins), sulphonamides, thiazide diuretics, frusemide, sulphonylureas, and phenylbutazone are commonly implicated.

(ii) Urticaria
Urticarial rashes occur sometimes in response to penicillins, aspirin, codeine, dextrans, and X-ray contrast media.

(iii) Erythema multiforme
In this form of rash target-like lesions often occur on the extensor surfaces of the limbs, and vesicles and bullae may form. In severe cases the mucous membranes of the mouth, throat, eye, urethra, and vagina may also be involved (Stevens–Johnson syndrome). Penicillins, sulphonamides, barbiturates, and phenylbutazone may be responsible.

(iv) Erythema nodosum
This may be produced by sulphonamides, and occasionally oral contraceptives.

(v) Cutaneous vasculitis
Here palpable purpura, vesicles and pustules, and necrotic ulcers may occur. Sulphonamides, phenylbutazone, thiazide diuretics, allopurinol, indomethacin, phenytoin, and alclofenac have all been implicated.

(vi) Purpura
Drugs which produce thrombocytopenia may cause purpura (see Type II reactions above). Non-thrombocytopenic purpura may result from capillary damage or fragility caused by drugs such as corticosteroids, thiazide diuretics, and meprobamate.

(vii) Exfoliative dermatitis and erythroderma
Red, scaly, and exfoliative skin lesions, which may on occasions involve extensive areas of skin, may be caused by gold, phenylbutazone, isoniazid, and carbamazepine.

(viii) Photosensitivity
Increased sensitivity to sunlight (u.v. light) may be produced by sulphonamides, thiazide diuretics, sulphonylureas, tetracyclines, phenothiazines, and nalidixic acid. Amiodarone can cause a phototoxic reaction in the skin.

(ix) Fixed eruptions
These are well-demonstrated, round, erythematous plaques occurring repeatedly at the same site, and associated with local pigmentation. They may occur in association with the use of phenolphthalein, barbiturates, sulphonamides, and tetracyclines.

(x) Toxic epidermal necrolysis (Lyell's syndrome)
This severe eruption consists of shearing of sheets of epidermis leaving the appearance of scalded skin. It may occur with the use of phenytoin, sulphonamides, gold salts, tetracyclines, allopurinol, and phenylbutazone.

(c) Connective tissue disease
A syndrome mimicking systemic lupus erythematosus, often with joint involvement, may result from treatment with hydralazine, procainamide, phenytoin, or ethosuximide. It is more common, when occurring with hydralazine or procainamide, in slow acetylators (see Chapter 8). The features which distinguish this syndrome from the idiopathic form of lupus erythematosus are listed in Table 9.2.

It is possible that sulphonamides may on rare occasions cause polyarteritis nodosa.

Table 9.2 *Features distinguishing drug-induced from idiopathic lupus erythematosus (LE)*

Feature	Idiopathic LE	Drug-induced LE
Age and sex	Usually young women	Any (depends on treatment)
Renal involvement	Common	Rare
Serum complement	Often low	Usually normal
DNA antibodies	Usual (double-stranded DNA)	Uncommon

(d) Blood disorders

Thrombocytopenia, neutropenia (or agranulocytosis), haemolytic anaemia, and aplastic anaemia may all occur as adverse drug reactions (see above).

(e) Respiratory disorders

Asthma may occur as part of a Type I reaction, particularly to aspirin (q.v. Pharmacopoeia). Aspirin-sensitive asthmatics are often sensitive to other analgesics or anti-inflammatory drugs, and care should be taken when using such drugs. In addition, a high proportion of aspirin-sensitive asthmatics are also sensitive to tartrazine, a yellow dye used as a colouring agent in some drug formulations and foodstuffs. Other adverse drug reactions in the lung include pneumonitis associated with systemic lupus erythematosus (see above), pulmonary eosinophilia, and fibrosing alveolitis.

9.5.3. Pharmacogenetic variation causing non-dose-related reactions

Pharmacogenetic abnormalities have been discussed in Chapter 8. The pharmacodynamic type of abnormalities are generally non-dose-related and include the precipitation of haemolysis by a variety of drugs (see Table 8.1) in patients with glucose 6-phosphate dehydrogenase (G6PD) deficiency, and of an acute attack of porphyria by a large number of drugs (see Table 8.2) in susceptible individuals.

9.6. LONG-TERM EFFECTS CAUSING ADVERSE REACTIONS

Adverse effects listed under this heading are related to the *duration* of treatment as well as to the *dose*, and may be regarded as being related to some function of the two.

9.6.1. Adaptive changes

Adaptive changes which can occur in response to drug therapy have been discussed in detail in Chapter 4. Sometimes such changes can form the basis of an adverse reaction. Examples include the development of tolerance to and physical dependence on the narcotic analgesics (see p. 77) and the occurrence of tardive dyskinesia in some patients receiving long-term neuroleptic therapy for schizophrenia (see p.79).

9.6.2. Rebound phenomena

When adaptive changes occur during long-term therapy sudden withdrawal of the drug may result in rebound reactions (see also Chapter 4). Examples include the typical syndromes which occur following sudden withdrawal of narcotic analgesics (see p.77) or of alcohol (delirium tremens). Sudden withdrawal of barbiturates may result in restlessness, mental confusion, and convulsions and a similar syndrome in which anxiety features prominently may occur following sudden withdrawal of benzodiazepines. Sleeplessness may also be a feature of sudden withdrawal of these and a variety of other hypnotic drugs. Sudden withdrawal of some antihypertensive drugs may result in rebound hypertension and is particularly common with clonidine, which should always be withdrawn slowly. Sudden withdrawal of β-adrenoceptor antagonists may also cause rebound effects, especially cardiac ischaemia.

In a separate category is the effect of sudden withdrawal of corticosteroids. During long-term treatment with corticosteroids there is interference with the normal feedback system involving the hypothalamus, pituitary gland, and adrenal gland. As a result, the hypothalamus and pituitary become unable to react normally to the stimulus of low circulating concentrations of corticosteroids and the adrenal gland atrophies. Following sudden withdrawal the syndrome of acute adrenal insufficiency occurs. The extent to which this effect occurs depends on both the daily dose and the duration of treatment, and it can to some extent be minimized by giving twice the usual daily dose but only on alternate days. If corticosteroids have to be given every day, in cases where the therapeutic response is poor with alternate day therapy, hypothalamic–pituitary–adrenal axis suppression can be reduced by giving the dose in the morning. Withdrawal of corticosteroids should be very slow after long-term treatment, e.g. for prednisolone reduce the daily dose by only 1 mg at intervals of no less than a month.

In passing it is worth pointing out that withdrawal of oral anticoagulants, such as warfarin, is not accompanied by a rebound hypercoagulability, although, of course, thromboembolism may nonetheless occur subsequently. However, reversal of the effects of heparin with protamine sulphate may be associated with rebound hypercoagulability with an increased risk of thromboembolism. This risk may, however, have to be taken when there is life-threatening bleeding due to heparin overdosage.

9.6.3. Other long-term effects

Chloroquine, which has a particular affinity for melanin, may accumulate in the corneal epithelium, causing a keratopathy, and in the retina, causing a pigmentary retinopathy. The former occurs in about 30–70 per cent of patients after 1–2 months of therapy, but the latter is much less common, although more serious. The risk increases with daily doses over 500 mg and in patients also taking probenecid.

Chronic ingestion of analgesic mixtures, particularly those containing phenacetin, causes papillary and medullary necrosis in the kidney, accompanied by renal tubular atrophy. Later the degenerative and fibrotic changes may extend into the cortex and produce glomerular damage and an overall interstitial nephritis. Clinically these changes can result in renal pain, haematuria, and ureteric obstruction. Eventually chronic renal failure may occur. There is still some confusion about the precise type of analgesic responsible for analgesic nephropathy. Undoubtedly phenacetin has been the main culprit in the past, and for this reason it has been taken off the market in the UK, Sweden, and Denmark, and replaced by its active metabolite, paracetamol. However, some have suggested that the nephropathy associated with phenacetin was due to the *combination* of phenacetin with aspirin, and it is possible that phenacetin metabolites are concentrated in the medullary region of the kidney, and that the normal tissue response there to oxidative damage is impaired by aspirin. This hypothesis is unproven, but what is certain is that the analgesic abuse must be prolonged and heavy for renal damage to occur, e.g. six or more tablets per day of a combined analgesic preparation containing phenacetin for 3 y or more.

It is still not absolutely certain that chronic ingestion of large doses of aspirin cannot by itself cause analgesic nephropathy, but paracetamol seems to be safe.

9.7. DELAYED EFFECTS CAUSING ADVERSE REACTIONS

A simple example of a delayed adverse drug effect is that of hypothyroidism occurring years after the treatment of hyperthyroidism with radioactive iodine, ^{131}I. However, this is a recognized and acceptable risk of this form of treatment, whereas our other examples under this heading are adverse effects which are highly unacceptable.

9.7.1. Carcinogenesis

The subject of the production of tumours in man through the use of drugs is a confused and difficult one. The causes and mechanisms of cancers are, in the majority of cases, still unknown. It is seldom possible, on clinical and pathological grounds, to distinguish, in an individual, a 'naturally occurring' tumour from one produced by an identifiable chemical carcinogen. In man, therefore, one has to rely on statistical associations and these are not easy to observe in a condition whose pathogenesis involves an indefinite period of exposure to a carcinogen (and possibly other chemical substances), and a latent period for development.

Much time, effort, and money is expended in testing drugs for carcinogenic potential and it is likely that the incidence of cancer produced by drugs is low, although precise numerical estimates are hard to come by.

There are three major mechanisms which are currently considered to be potentially important in carcinogenesis.

(a) Hormonal

There is a probable increase in the incidence of uterine endometrial carcinoma in women receiving oestrogen replacement therapy for menopausal symptoms. There is a clear increase in the occurrence of vaginal adenocarcinoma in the daughters of women who have received stilboestrol during pregnancy for the treatment of threatened abortion. Oral contraceptives increase the incidence of benign liver tumours.

(b) 'Gene toxicity'

This term is used to cloak the mystery of what happens when certain molecules bind to nuclear DNA, and produce changes in gene expression, leading to abnormalities of cell growth and the production of tumours. In man it is sometimes difficult to divorce this mechanism from suppression of the immune response (discussed below).

There are some examples which might fall into this class:

(i) the increased risk of bladder cancer in patients taking long-term cyclophosphamide;

(ii) carcinomas of the renal pelvis associated with phenacetin abuse;

(iii) the occurrence of non-lymphocytic leukaemias in patients receiving alkylating agents such as melphalan, cyclophosphamide, and chlorambucil.

(c) Suppression of immune responses

In recent years it has become apparent that patients receiving immunosuppressive drug regimens, such as azathioprine with corticosteroids, have a greatly increased risk of developing lymphomas. This has mainly been noted after renal transplantation, but has been seen in other patients. In immunosuppressed patients there also seems to be an increased risk of cancers of the liver, biliary tree, and bladder, of soft-tissue sarcomas, bronchial adenocarcinoma, squamous carcinoma of the skin, and malignant melanoma.

There is probably an association between the occurrence of lymphoma and the long-term use of phenytoin, although at present this does not influence the prescribing of phenytoin for the treatment of epilepsy.

9.7.2. Adverse effects associated with reproduction

(a) Impaired fertility

While impaired fertility due to drugs in women is usually a desired effect when using oral contraceptives, it may be an unwanted effect of other drugs. For example cytotoxic drugs may cause female infertility through ovarian failure with amenorrhoea.

Impairment of male fertility can be caused by impairment of spermatozoal production or function, and may be either reversible or irreversible:

(i) reversible impairment may be caused by sulphasalazine, nitrofurantoin, monoamine oxidase (MAO) inhibitors, and antimalarials;

(ii) reversible impairment leading to irreversible impairment, due to azoospermia, can be caused by cytotoxic drugs, such as the alkylating agents cyclophosphamide and chlorambucil.

(b) Teratogenesis (see also Chapter 11)

Teratogenesis is the effect of a drug to cause a developmental abnormality in a fetus. For a drug to affect the development of a fetus it must first pass across the placental barrier. The mechanisms whereby drugs pass across the placenta are similar to those by which they cross any lipoid cell membrane, and most drugs pass across by simple diffusion. This diffusion depends in part on molecular size, degree of ionization, and lipid solubility. Thus, drugs of low molecular weight, poorly ionized at physiological pH, and very fat soluble will pass across the placenta readily. However, most drugs in the maternal circulation do reach the fetus in greater or lesser amounts, and since the thalidomide incident great care has been taken about prescribing drugs during pregnancy. Furthermore, during the development of a drug its potential for teratogenesis has to be explored if there is any likelihood of its being promoted for the treatment of women while pregnant.

If a drug is known to be teratogenic then the drug information sheet will say so. If, however, teratogenicity has not been demonstrated in animals, that does not necessarily mean that the drug is not teratogenic in man, and a warning such as the following may be given: 'This drug has not been shown to be teratogenic in animals, and so far there is no evidence that it is teratogenic in man. However, the use of this drug should be avoided in pregnant women if possible.' If one is tempted to prescribe a drug in a pregnant woman especially during the first trimester, it is very important to be aware of the current trend of opinion concerning its safety (see Chapter 18 on sources of information).

The problem often occurs that a woman of child-bearing potential, who does not know that she is pregnant, is given a drug, and then finds out days or weeks later that she *is* pregnant. Cases like this must be dealt with individually when considering terminating the pregnancy, and such a decision will depend on various factors, the most scientifically decisive being the degree of teratogenicity, if known. Thus, even if a woman is not known to be pregnant, but is of child-bearing age, care should be taken in prescribing, and the risks discussed with the patient.

The first trimester of pregnancy, and particularly the period from the second to the eighth weeks of gestation, the period of organogenesis, is the most critical. During this time drugs may cause structural abnormalities. Later in fetal life drugs may affect the subsequent growth, development, and integrity of body structures, particularly the brain. Drugs given immediately before and during labour can cause problems in the neonate.

In Table 9.3 are listed the drugs which should be avoided during early pregnancy because of the listed effects on the fetus, or because of a slightly increased risk of fetal abnormality.

Table 9.3 *Drugs to avoid during early pregnancy*

1. Drugs with a high risk of producing abnormalities (known teratogens)

Androgens	Virilization, and multiple congenital defects
Antineoplastic agents, e.g. methotrexate	Multiple congenital defects
Corticosteroids in high dosage	Cleft palate
Diethylstilboestrol	Vaginal adenosis and adenocarcinoma in daughters
Tetracyclines	Yellow discolouration of teeth, inhibition of bone growth
Warfarin	Multiple congenital defects

2. Drugs under strong suspicion of producing abnormalities (slightly increased risk)

Chloroquine (do not withhold in acute malaria)	Deafness
Lithium	Cardiovascular defects
Phenytoin (do not withhold if necessary for control of epilepsy)	Multiple congenital defects

3. Other drugs to avoid (theoretical risk from animal and other studies)

Co-trimoxazole, rifampicin, sulphonylureas, trimethoprim
There is a possible teratogenic risk from general anaesthesia during early pregnancy

Some drugs should be avoided or used with care during later pregnancy and they are listed in Table 9.4:

1. Aminoglycoside antibiotics should be used during pregnancy only if absolutely essential, because of their effects on the eighth nerve.

2. Antithyroid drugs may be used during pregnancy but at the minimum dosage necessary to control maternal hypothyroidism. Some recommend using half the usual doses of these drugs during pregnancy.

Table 9.4 *Drugs to be avoided or used with care during later pregnancy* (*see text for discussion*)

Drug(s)	Effect on fetus or neonate
Aspirin	Kernicterus, haemorrhage (also maternal haemorrhage)
Aminoglycoside antibiotics	Eighth nerve damage
Antithyroid drugs	Goitre and hypothyroidism
Benzodiazepines	'Floppy infant syndrome'
Chloramphenicol	Peripheral vascular collapse
Oral anticoagulants	Fetal or retroplacental haemorrhage, microcephaly
Oral sulphonylurea hypoglycaemics	Hypoglycaemia
Pethidine	Respiratory depression
Reserpine	Bradycardia, hypothermia, and nasal congestion with respiratory distress
Sulphonamides and novobiocin	Kernicterus
Tetracyclines	See Table 9.3
Thiazide diuretics	Thrombocytopenia

3. Aspirin has been suggested to be teratogenic in early pregnancy but the case has not been proven. However, in high doses in late pregnancy it may displace fetal bilirubin from plasma proteins and thus cause kernicterus (see sulphonamides below), and if taken within about a week before delivery can cause impaired haemostasis in the mother at time of delivery and haemorrhage in the neonate.

4. Benzodiazepines given at around the time of labour may cause the 'floppy infant syndrome' with muscular hypotonia, hypothermia, respiratory difficulties, and difficulty with suckling.

5. Chloramphenicol is poorly metabolized by the immature liver and can cause peripheral vascular collapse if given to neonates in weight-corrected adult doses. It should not, therefore, be used in pregnancy.

6. Oral anticoagulants are not only teratogenic during the first trimester, but if given later in pregnancy may also cause microcephaly, or fetal or retroplacental haemorrhage. They should be avoided altogether during early and late pregnancy. Heparin does not cross the placenta and should be used instead at those times.

7. Oral sulphonylurea hypoglycaemics may cause fetal and neonatal hypoglycaemia, and insulin should be used to control diabetes during pregnancy.

8. The effects of pethidine on the neonate after administration to the mother as a pain-killer during labour do not constitute a contra-indication to its use, but care should be taken not to administer too high a dose. Neonatal respiratory depression can be reversed by naloxone. In this context it should be noted that neonates born to mothers who are addicted to narcotic analgesics may have a withdrawal syndrome.

9. Sulphonamides and novobiocin should be avoided completely during

the third trimester. They displace bilirubin in the fetal circulation from plasma proteins, and the free bilirubin enters the brain and is deposited in the basal ganglia, causing the condition known as kernicterus, in which there may be any of a variety of neurological abnormalities including lethargy, muscular hypotonia, and poor feeding, progressing to spasticity and convulsions, with extrapyramidal movement disorders later on in those who survive.

10. Tetracyclines should not be used because of their effects on growing teeth and bones (see Table 9.5 and Pharmacopoeia).

11. Thiazide diuretics may cause thrombocytopenia in the neonate, probably by a direct toxic effect on the marrow, and should be avoided in late pregnancy.

There are certain drugs which may be prescribed during pregnancy. Iron and folic acid are routinely prescribed to prevent their deficiency. Because of the frequency of nausea and vomiting early in pregnancy it is frequently necessary to prescribe an anti-emetic—meclozine, cyclizine, and dicyclomine, despite recent scares, are almost certainly safe and may be prescribed when necessary. As a mild analgesic paracetamol is recommended —the case against aspirin as a teratogen in early pregnancy has been raised but not proved, but in high doses in late pregnancy it may cause kernicterus by displacing bilirubin from plasma proteins. As antibiotics the penicillins are safe to use. No tranquillizers or hypnotics can be said to be completely safe (see, for example, benzodiazepines above) and all should be avoided. The uses of insulin in the treatment of diabetes, and of heparin as an anticoagulant have been mentioned above. For the treatment of hypertension in pregnancy see pp. 186 and 300.

(c) Adverse reactions to drugs in breast milk

The problem of adverse effects in suckling infants because of the passage of drugs into the breast milk is determined by the following factors:

the passage of the drug from the maternal blood into the milk;
the concentration of drug in the milk;
the volume of milk sucked;
the ability of the infant to eliminate the drug.

Certain drugs are excreted in breast milk to an extent likely to affect the infant, while others are known to be safe. Lists of these drugs are given in Table 9.5.

Included in the list of drugs to be avoided by breast-feeding mothers are antibiotics such as penicillins and streptomycin, which may cause hypersensitivity reactions even in the small quantities excreted in breast milk, and drugs such as nitrofurantoin which are only hazardous in babies with G6PD deficiency (see Chapter 8). Some drugs are hazardous for more than one reason (e.g. sulphonamides, which can cause kernicterus in any baby, and haemolysis in G6PD deficient babies).

Table 9.5 *Drugs in breast-feeding mothers*

(*a*) *Some drugs to be avoided in breast-feeding mothers*

Antineoplastic drugs	Metronidazole
Antithyroid drugs	Nalidixic acid
Benzodiazepines	Nitrofurantoin
Chloral derivatives	Oral contraceptives
Chloramphenicol	Oral hypoglycaemics
Corticosteroids (high dosages)	Penicillins
Ergot alkaloids	Phenytoin
Erythromycin (intravenously)	Radioactive iodine
Immunosuppressive drugs	Streptomycin
Indanedione anticoagulants	Sulphonamides
Isoniazid	Tetracyclines
Lithium	Vitamin D
Methysergide	Xanthines

(*b*) *Some drugs which appear to be safe*

ACTH (corticotrophin)	Hydralazine
Adrenaline	Imipramine
β-adrenoceptor antagonists (but	Insulin
monitor neonate for bradycardia	Methyldopa
and hypoglycaemia)	Neuroleptics in moderate dosage
Amitriptyline	(e.g. chlorpromazine, haloperidol)
Anti-asthmatic drugs (inhalations)	Nortriptyline
Antihistamines (H_1 antagonists)	Thyroxine
Carbamazepine	Valproate
Heparin	Warfarin

Included in the list of drugs known to be safe are drugs which are destroyed in the gut (e.g. insulin, adrenaline) and drugs whose concentrations in milk have been measured and found to be very low (e.g. warfarin).

If there is any doubt about the safety of a drug, it is best either to choose another drug, or, if the drug must be used, to advise the mother not to breast-feed.

9.8. SURVEILLANCE METHODS USED IN DETECTING ADVERSE REACTIONS

During the clinical trial period a drug undergoes before its general release, none but the most frequent of adverse reactions will be picked up, despite meticulous monitoring, because so few patients are studied.

In Table 9.6 are shown the numbers of patients usually studied during the various stages of the development of a drug before it goes on general release. The total is usually less than 2500. In contrast, in Table 9.7 are shown the numbers of patients one would have to study in order to detect only one, two, or three adverse events for a given incidence of adverse reactions in the treated population. On this basis only adverse reactions with a relatively high incidence will be picked up before marketing. Note, however, that the numbers in Table 9.7 refer to an adverse event which has no background incidence as 'a natural or induced disease. But not many adverse drug reactions are like that—they tend to mimic the signs and symptoms of non-drug-induced diseases. In these circumstances it becomes even more difficult to detect an adverse effect of a drug.

Table 9.6   *Numbers of patients usually recruited in pre-marketing studies*

Phase I	Volunteer or very early patient studies	25–50
Phase IIa	Clinical pharmacology in patients	50–100
Phase IIb	Dose-finding studies and early efficacy studies	100–250
Phase III	Extended clinical studies leading to marketing	250–1000 (rarely >2000)
Total		Usually fewer than 2500

Table 9.7   *Numbers of patients required to detect 1, 2, or 3 cases of an adverse reaction*

Expected incidence of adverse reaction	Numbers of patients required to detect one, two, or three events		
	1	2	3
1 in 100	300	480	650
1 in 200	600	960	1300
1 in 1000	3000	4800	6500
1 in 2000	6000	9600	13 000
1 in 10 000	30 000	48 000	65 000

These numbers are based on the following assumptions:
  (a) that there is no background incidence of the adverse effect;
  (b) that the number of adverse events follows a Poisson distribution.

With these considerations in mind adverse reactions can be classified as follows:

1. The drug *commonly* produces an otherwise *rare illness*. An example is thalidomide-induced phocomelia. Such an event is relatively easily detected by clinical observation.

2. The drug *rarely* produces an otherwise *rare illness*. Phenylbutazone-induced aplastic anaemia is an example, again detected by clinical observation, but with more difficulty than 1 above.

3. The drug *commonly* produces an otherwise *common illness*. It has been suggested that tolbutamide may cause an increased incidence of myocardial ischaemic damage in diabetics. There is, in fact, evidence that

that is not the case, but were it so it would only be detected by large formal studies. The controversy which surrounded the first publication of this suggestion underlines the difficulty of proving such associations.

4. The drug *sometimes* induces an illness which itself has a *moderate incidence*. An example of this is the production of endometrial carcinoma by oestrogens. Such an occurrence can only be detected by formal epidemiological studies.

5. The drug *rarely* produces an otherwise *common illness*. This would be extremely difficult to detect by any means.

If only the most common of adverse reactions are going to be detected during the clinical trial stage, then it is important to devise methods for detecting adverse reactions as quickly as possible after marketing, for confirming that the events detected are truly adverse reactions, and for assessing their overall incidence, in order to be able to make some evaluation of the benefit versus risk balance.

9.8.1. Methods of surveillance

(a) Anecdotal reporting

We are still largely dependent upon anecdotal reports from individual doctors that a patient has suffered some peculiar event for the majority of 'first reports' of adverse drug reactions. This anecdotal reporting is only likely to be useful and effective when the adverse reaction is of Type 1 or 2 (Table 9.1). An example of the value of astute observation by individuals was the detection in 1974 of the oculomucocutaneous syndrome (dry eyes, corneal damage, a psoriatic-like skin rash, and sclerosing peritonitis) due to practolol. The propensity of halothane to cause jaundice on repeated administration was first brought to light by anecdotal reports, as was the effect of chloramphenicol in causing agranulocytosis.

Of course, such anecdotal reports need to be verified by further studies which sometimes fail to confirm a problem. Nevertheless, the skill of individual observant clinicians is still a valuable force in the detection of adverse drug reactions.

(b) Voluntary but organized reporting

In Fig. 9.1 is shown the 'yellow card' used in the UK for voluntary reporting of suspected adverse drug reactions to the Committee on Safety of Medicines (CSM). If a doctor observes what he suspects to be an adverse drug reaction he should fill out one of these cards and send it to the CSM. At a later date he may receive a follow-up request for more information.

This system suffers from various problems and artefacts. For example, it is difficult to be ingenious enough to spot an adverse reaction which you do not actually know to exist. Furthermore, there is a natural desire to report adverse drug reactions that one has just heard about, and not to report those everybody already knows about. This introduces an element of bias into the system. Finally because of natural human indolence there is a tendency to under-report.

IN CONFIDENCE – REPORT ON SUSPECTED ADVERSE REACTIONS

1. Please report all suspected reactions to recently introduced drugs (identified by a black triangle in the British National Formulary), vaccines, dental or surgical materials, IUCD's, absorbable sutures, contact lenses and associated fluids, and serious or unusual reactions to all agents.

2. Record all other drugs etc, including self-medication, taken in the previous 3 months. With congenital abnormalities, record all drugs taken during pregnancy, and date of last menstrual period.

3. Do not be deterred from reporting because some details are not known.

4. Please report suspected drug interactions.

NAME OF PATIENT (To allow for linkage with other reports for same patient. Please give record number for hospital patients.)	Family name					SEX	AGE or DATE OF BIRTH	WEIGHT (Kg.)
	Forenames							

DRUGS, VACCINES (Inc. Batch No.), DEVICES, MATERIALS etc. (Please give Brand Name if known)	ROUTE	DAILY DOSE	DATE		INDICATION
			STARTED	ENDED	
Suspected drug, etc.					
Other drugs, etc. (Please state if no other drug given..					

SUSPECTED REACTIONS	STARTED	ENDED	OUTCOME (eg. fatal, recovered)

ADDITIONAL NOTES	REPORTING DOCTOR (Block letters please)
	Name:
	Address:
	Tel. No: / Specialty:
	Signature: / Date:

If you would like information about other reports associated with the suspected drug, please tick box –

AR/20 250M/10/82 51-2835/PRINT PROCESSES LTD

Fig. 9.1. The 'Yellow Card' used to report suspected adverse reactions to the Committee on Safety of Medicines. [Reproduced by permission of the CSM.]

Despite these difficulties the voluntary 'organized' system of reporting in the UK has provided extremely useful information on the occurrence of adverse reactions in the national community. Coupling these occurrence figures with the figures on the numbers of prescriptions issued (information which is available from the Prescription Pricing Authority) the incidence of a given adverse drug reaction can be very roughly calculated. Every so often extracts from the Register of Adverse Reactions kept by the CSM are published, and can be a valuable source of reference.

Every doctor is urged to report a suspected adverse reaction to the CSM on a yellow card. At that stage it does not matter whether the suspected reaction can be fully validated since the system is geared to detecting *patterns* of reporting which may implicate a particular drug from the conjunction of a handful of similar reports. Although the system has not often been responsible for the *initial* detection of an adverse reaction, it has been helpful in monitoring adverse reactions in the national community, in validating adverse reactions, and in assessing in a large population the risk of an adverse reaction relative to the potential benefit of treatment with the resultant formulation of specific prescribing advice or warnings to doctors not to prescribe a drug in particular circumstances. In serious cases a drug may be taken off the market because of this kind of monitoring, as happened with practolol and benoxaprofen. In those cases the risk of adverse reactions was thought to be greater than the potential benefits.

(c) Other systems of post-marketing surveillance

Because of the imperfections of voluntary reporting systems other surveillance systems have been tried or considered. For various reasons none has yet proved completely satisfactory. What one requires is *speed* of detection, an estimate of the *incidence* of the reaction in the population receiving the drug, and clues as to the *factors involved* (e.g. age, sex, concurrent diseases, concurrent drug therapy). From information of this kind one might be able to estimate the benefit:risk ratio and even be able to give prescribing advice to avoid the adverse reaction.

(i) Intensive event recording

The aims of certain hospital-based adverse reaction reporting schemes has been to designate a medical group to screen a defined population specifically to detect adverse reactions and then to relate them to prescribed drugs. Such schemes (e.g. the Boston Collaborative Drug Surveillance Program) have provided interesting statistics on the incidence of adverse reactions in hospitals around the world, but have not generally been effective in reporting anything new. That is partly because the population being studied is relatively small, and, more importantly, each patient is studied for only a short period of time.

(ii) Cohort studies (prospective studies)

In a cohort study patients taking a particular drug are identified and events are then recorded. The weakness of this method is the relatively small number of patients likely to be studied, and the lack of a suitable control group from which to assess the natural incidence of any apparent adverse reactions noted. Such studies are also very expensive and it would be difficult to justify and organize such a study for every new drug coming onto the market.

(iii) Case-control studies (retrospective studies)

In case-control studies patients who present with symptoms or an illness which could be due to an adverse drug reaction are screened to see if they have taken the drug. The prevalence of drug-taking in this group is then compared with the prevalence in a reference population who do not have the symptoms or illness. In a cohort study one starts with a population and looks for an effect, in a case-control study one starts with the effect and looks for the drug. The case-control study is thus suitable for determining whether a drug causes a given adverse effect once some initial indication has been received that it might. It is not, however, a method of detecting new adverse reactions. The relationship between maternal stilboestrol ingestion and vaginal adenocarcinoma in female offspring was confirmed by this method.

(iv) Use of population statistics

Registers of causes of deaths and of congenital malformations are held in the UK by the Office of Population Censuses and Surveys, and other information may be available from other sources (e.g. hospital and other records, see next item). If a change in the pattern of deaths occurred (as happened, for example, among young asthmatics in the early 1960s), it might stimulate an investigation of a possible drug-induced cause. In the case of the young asthmatics it was subsequently shown that the increase in deaths could be attributed to the increased use of bronchodilator aerosols containing non-selective (i.e. β_1 and β_2) adrenoceptor agonists. More recently a similar increase in deaths of young asthmatics in New Zealand has been attributed to some effect of theophylline, although the case has not been confirmed. Following the suggestion that Debendox® (Bendectin®) was teratogenic a study was made of congenital malformation data in Northern Ireland. No association was found and in this case it was possible to provide reassurance of the probable safety of this preparation. It has, nonetheless, been withdrawn from the market.

(v) Record linkage

The idea here is to bring together a variety of patient records:

general practice records of illness events;
general practice records of prescriptions;

hospital records of illness events;
hospital records of prescriptions.

In this way it may be possible to match illness events with drugs prescribed. Particularly interesting are studies in which general practice prescribing is related to hospital admissions and diagnosis. One such analysis suggested a link between antihistamine prescribing and motorcycle accidents. Retrospective linkage of drugs prescribed in general practice with illness events noted confirmed the association between practolol prescribing and eye complaints.

A particular example of the use of record linkage is the so-called Prescription–Event Monitoring scheme, in which all the prescriptions issued by selected practitioners for a particular drug are obtained from the Prescription Pricing Authority. The prescribers are then asked to inform those running the scheme of any events (whether attributable to adverse reactions or not) in the patients taking the drug. This scheme promises to be less expensive and time-consuming than other surveillance methods.

The debate on how best to monitor adverse drug reactions continues. No system, either existing or proposed, is perfect. The various advantages and disadvantages of the different schemes are outlined in Table 9.8.

Table 9.8 *Advantages and disadvantages of various post-marketing surveillance schemes*

Scheme	Advantages	Disadvantages
Anecdotal reports	Simple; cheap	Relies on individual vigilance and astuteness; only detects relatively common effects
Voluntary 'organized' reporting	Simple	Under-reporting; bias by 'bandwagon' effect
Intensive event monitoring	Easily organized	Selected population studied for a short time
Cohort studies	Can be prospective; good at detecting effects	Very large numbers required; very expensive
Case-control studies	Excellent for validation and assessment	Will not detect new effects; expensive
Population statistics	Large numbers	Difficult to co-ordinate; quality of information may be poor; too coarse
Record linkage	Excellent if comprehensive	Time-consuming, expensive; retrospective; relies on accurate records

10 Drug interactions

Most drug interactions are special kinds of adverse drug reactions in which the effects of a drug are altered by the effects of another drug. In a few cases such an interaction may prove beneficial.

Drug interactions involve one drug which precipitates the change in effects of another. For clarity of discussion we shall call the drug which precipitates the interaction the *precipitant* drug and the drug whose action is affected the *object* drug. Occasionally in an interaction the effects of both drugs may be altered, as, for example, in the complex interaction of phenytoin with phenobarbitone. In such cases our nomenclature does not apply.

10.1. INCIDENCE OF DRUG INTERACTIONS

Although hundreds of interactions have been described relatively few are of clinical importance, and we shall deal here only with those. The incidence of such interactions is difficult to gauge. One must, for example, distinguish between the frequency with which two potentially interacting drugs are prescribed together, and the frequency with which clinically important interactions occur in those cases in which two potentially interacting drugs have been prescribed. Unfortunately, there are problems in collecting incidence figures of this kind. For example, it may often be difficult to determine whether an adverse effect of a drug occurs as a result of a drug interaction rather than as a result of, say, misuse of the drug, or of an interaction between the drug and some peculiarity of the patient (e.g. his disease, renal function, or liver function). In regard to the general incidence of drug interactions of clinical importance a further difficulty is created by geographical differences in drug prescribing habits. Therapeutic fashions around the world differ greatly. In the USA, for example, the number of drugs being taken by patients on admission to hospital is nearly twice that in the UK. Furthermore, it is clear that polypharmacy is an important factor—the more drugs a patient is taking the greater the chance of an interaction.

It has been estimated that interactions form about 7 per cent of all adverse drug reactions, and that among the few patients who die from adverse drug reactions (about 4 per cent of all deaths) about a third are due to interactions.

10.2. WHICH DRUGS ARE LIKELY TO BE INVOLVED IN INTERACTIONS?

Although it is not always possible to be sure about the clinical importance of a drug interaction, it *is* possible to predict which types of drugs are *likely* to be involved in important interactions. The following are some examples.

Precipitant drugs

1. Those which are highly protein bound, and therefore likely to displace object drugs from protein binding sites, e.g. aspirin, phenylbutazone, sulphonamides, and trichloracetic acid (a metabolite of chloral hydrate and its congeners).
2. Those which alter (stimulate or inhibit) the metabolism of other drugs. Examples of drugs which may *stimulate* drug metabolism are various anticonvulsants (phenytoin, carbamazepine, and phenobarbitone), rifampicin, and griseofulvin. Examples of drugs which may *inhibit* drug metabolism are metronidazole, cimetidine, chloramphenicol, phenylbutazone and related drugs, monoamine oxidase (MAO) inhibitors, and allopurinol.
3. Those which affect renal function and alter the renal clearance of object drugs, e.g. diuretics, probenecid.

Object drugs

The drugs which are most likely to be the object drugs in interactions are those which have a steep dose–response curve (i.e. drugs for which a small change in dose results in a relatively large change in therapeutic effect, important in interactions causing *decreased efficacy* of the object drug) and drugs which have a low toxic : therapeutic ratio (i.e. drugs for which the dose at which toxic effects start to occur is little more than the therapeutic dose, important in interactions causing *toxic effects* of the object drugs). These criteria are two sides of the same coin and are fulfilled by anticoagulants, anticonvulsants, hypoglycaemic drugs, anti-arrhythmics, cardiac glycosides, antihypertensives, oral contraceptives, aminoglycoside antibiotics, cytotoxic and immunosuppressant drugs, and drugs acting on the central nervous system.

10.3. PHARMACEUTICAL INTERACTIONS

Pharmaceutical interactions are physicochemical interactions either of a drug with an intravenous infusion solution or of two drugs in the same solution. Such interactions result in the loss of activity of the object drug(s). Such interactions can be avoided by adhering to the following principles:

1. Give i.v. drugs by bolus injection if possible or via a burette.
2. Do not add drugs to infusion solutions other than dextrose or saline. Even in those solutions some drugs are unstable, while others are light-sensitive and must be protected from the light to prevent rapid loss of activity. These drugs are listed in Table 10.1.

Table 10.1   *Stability of drugs in saline and dextrose*

I *Unstable—infuse within 2–4 h*
Ampicillin (dextrose only; stable in saline for 12 h)
Erythromycin

II *Stable for 6–8 h*
Benzylpenicillin
Dacarbazine
Diazepam
Frusemide (use only in saline)
Tetracosactrin

III *Stable for 12 h*
Flucloxacillin
Oxytetracycline
Tetracycline

IV *Photosensitive drugs*
Amphotericin
Dacarbazine
Sodium nitroprusside

V *Drugs which must not be infused after 6 h in solution*
Cephaloridine
Colistin

---

3. Avoid mixing drugs in the same infusion solution, unless you know the mixture to be safe (e.g. potassium chloride and insulin).
4. Check the manufacturer's literature for specific warnings and to check that the drug is suitable for i.v. administration (for example, the data sheets for dopamine and dobutamine warn against mixing these drugs with alkaline solutions such as bicarbonate, a procedure which would also be avoided by following principle 2 above).
5. Mix the drug thoroughly in the infusion solution and check soon after, and later during infusion, for visible changes (turbidity, precipitation, or colour change). Absence of such changes, however, does not guarantee the absence of an interaction.
6. Prepare solutions only when needed. The exceptions to this rule are those drugs which are available in pre-packed infusion solutions, e.g. potassium chloride, lignocaine, metronidazole, chlormethiazole.

7. Label all infusion bottles clearly with the name and dose of drug added and the times of starting and ending the infusion.

8. Use two separate infusion sites if you must infuse two drugs simultaneously, unless you know that there is no interaction.

9. Consult your local hospital pharmacist if in doubt.

10.4. PHARMACOKINETIC INTERACTIONS

Such interactions occur when the absorption, distribution, metabolism, or excretion of the object drug is altered by the precipitant drug.

10.4.1. Absorption interactions

Although there are several mechanisms whereby the absorption of a drug may be altered by another drug (for example, the decrease in gastrointestinal motility caused by morphine-like drugs and drugs with anticholinergic effects, such as the tricyclic antidepressants; chelation of calcium, aluminium, magnesium, and iron salts by tetracyclines), such effects are rarely of clinical importance. Among the exceptions are the interactions of cholestyramine with warfarin and digitoxin, whose initial absorption and reabsorption after biliary excretion is reduced, resulting in increased requirements of the object drugs. An example of a beneficial absorption interaction is that between metoclopramide and analgesics in the treatment of an acute attack of migraine (see Chapter 28, p.508).

10.4.2. Protein-binding displacement interactions

If an object drug is highly protein bound (greater than 90 per cent), and has a low apparent volume of distribution (see Chapter 3, p.20) then displacement by a precipitant drug will result in a relatively large increase in the free concentration of object drug in the plasma, and therefore to an increased effect. If the precipitant drug is withdrawn the reverse will occur. The important object drugs which fulfil the criteria of high protein binding and low apparent volume of distribution (V_d) are warfarin (99 per cent protein bound, V_d 9 l), phenytoin (90 per cent bound, V_d 35 l), and tolbutamide (96 per cent bound, V_d 10 l). The commonest precipitant drugs involved in such interactions are the sulphonamides, the salicylates, derivatives of chloral (because of their metabolite trichloroacetic acid), and phenylbutazone and related drugs (oxyphenbutazone, azapropazone). Valproic acid displaces phenytoin.

The importance of protein binding displacement interactions has been exaggerated, however, and such interactions are often of no clinical importance. The reason is that for drugs such as warfarin, phenytoin, and tolbutamide, whose hepatic extraction ratio is low (see Chapter 3, p.53 and Table 3.4), the total clearance rate is proportional to the fraction of drug unbound in the plasma. Following displacement of the object drug its rate of total clearance from the body is increased in proportion to the degree of displacement. Thus at steady state the total concentration of drug in the plasma will have fallen to a new equilibrium value such that the free *concentration* is the same as it was before the precipitant drug was introduced despite an increase in the free *fraction*. In some cases the change in free fraction occurs so slowly that the compensatory increase in clearance reduces the transient increase in free concentration of the object drug to negligible proportions. Provided the patient can 'weather' the increase, if any, in free concentration of the object drug for as long as it takes to reach the new steady state, such an interaction will not be of importance. Furthermore, such interactions can be avoided by slow introduction of the precipitant drug.

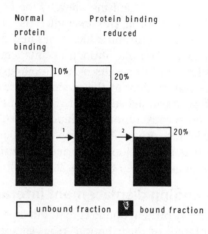

Fig. 10.1. The events following displacement of a drug from its binding sites on plasma proteins.

1. Displacement of drug leads to an increase in unbound fraction from 10 per cent to 20 per cent. This leads to increased effects of the drug.

2. If the drug has a low extraction ratio its total clearance is proportional to the unbound fraction, and clearance increases. Eventually the total concentration is reduced so that, although the unbound *fraction* is still increased, the unbound *concentration* is as it was before displacement occurred.

There is, however, another effect, important for phenytoin, in regard to the 'therapeutic' plasma concentration range. The principle is illustrated in Fig. 10.1. Suppose a patient has a therapeutically effective *total* plasma phenytoin concentration of 60 μmol/l ('therapeutic' range 40–80 μmol/l) of which 10 per cent is free (i.e. free *concentration* 6 μmol/l). If the free fraction is doubled to 20 per cent very rapidly, the free concentration will rise to 12 μmol/l. However, the clearance rate of total phenytoin will then double and at the new equilibrium the total phenytoin concentration will fall to 30 μmol/l, of which 20 per cent is free (i.e. a free concentration of 6 μmol/l). As far as the patient is concerned the new equilibrium is no different from the old but it is clear that his 'therapeutic' plasma concentration range (measured as total drug) is lower than before the interaction.

10.4.3. Cellular distribution interactions

Rifampicin is thought to diminish the effects of warfarin by inhibiting its uptake by hepatocytes. However it also induces warfarin metabolism and diminishes its effects by that mechanism (see below).

The active transport of some antihypertensive drugs (bethanidine, guanethidine, debrisoquine) into sympathetic nerve-endings, where they exert their therapeutic effects, is inhibited by tricyclic antidepressants (and perhaps also by phenothiazines), with resultant loss of blood pressure control. This may also be the basis for the similar interaction of clonidine with the tricyclic antidepressants.

10.4.4. Metabolism interactions

Drug interactions involving metabolism occur when the metabolism of an object drug is either inhibited or decreased by a precipitant drug. Of the different metabolic pathways (see Chapter 3) it is Phase I oxidation which is usually affected. 'Oxidation' is a term which embraces several different metabolic transformations all of which involve oxidation by the so-called 'mixed function' oxidase system. Such transformations include hydroxylation (e.g. phenytoin, debrisoquine), deamination (e.g. amphetamine), dealkylation (e.g. morphine, azathioprine), sulphoxidation (e.g. chlorpromazine, phenylbutazone), desulphuration (e.g. thiopentone), and dehalogenation (e.g. DDT, halogenated anaesthetics). The hallmark of these reactions is their dependence on the presence of both NADPH and a haem-containing protein called cytochrome P450. The biochemical processes involved in these reactions are shown in Fig. 10.2.

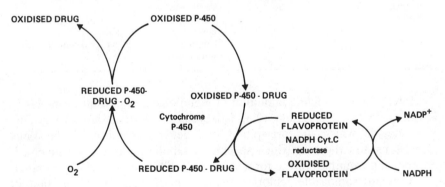

Fig. 10.2. The role of cytochrome P450 in hepatic microsomal drug oxidation.

The combination of drug with oxidized cytochrome P450 is reduced by the oxidation of a flavoprotein, cytochrome c reductase, which is itself returned to the reduced state, NADPH being the electron donor. The reduced P450–drug complex is then oxidized with the resultant formation of oxidized drug and oxidized P450.

This process occurs in hepatic microsomes and drugs which increase ('induce') drug metabolism do so by increasing the amount of endoplasmic reticulum in hepatocytes and by increasing the content of cytochromes P450 and c reductase. The mechanisms whereby these changes occur are not fully understood.

The important interactions of this type are listed in Table 10.2. The result of the induction of metabolism of the object drug by the precipitant drug will be a reduction in the plasma concentration and therefore of the effect of the object drug (e.g. epileptic fits while on phenytoin, pregnancy while on an oral contraceptive). If such failure of treatment results in an increase in dose of the object drug then withdrawal of the precipitant drug may lead to an enhanced effect of the former (e.g. bleeding after barbiturate withdrawal from a patient otherwise well controlled on warfarin).

Table 10.2   *Drug interactions due to induction of drug metabolism*

Precipitant drug(s)	Object drug(s)
Alcohol	Coumarin anticoagulants, phenytoin
Barbiturates	Chlorpromazine, corticosteroids, coumarin anticoagulants, doxycycline, oral contraceptives, phenytoin
Carbamazepine	Phenytoin
Dichloralphenazone	Warfarin
Glutethimide	Coumarin anticoagulants
Griseofulvin	Warfarin
Orphenadrine	Chlorpromazine
Phenylbutazone	Corticosteroids
Phenytoin	Corticosteroids, coumarin anticoagulants, oral contraceptives, tolbutamide
Rifampicin	Coumarin anticoagulants, oral contraceptives, tolbutamide

Interactions involving inhibition of metabolism, important examples of which are listed in Table 10.3, fall broadly speaking into two groups —those in which the precipitant is a general inhibitor of metabolic reactions and those in which specific metabolic pathways are involved. Important examples of the former are the inhibition of warfarin metabolism by metronidazole, chloramphenicol, and phenylbutazone, that of phenytoin metabolism by isoniazid (particularly in slow acetylators, see Chapter 8), and that of tolbutamide metabolism by phenylbutazone.

The metabolism interaction of phenylbutazone with warfarin is complicated. Phenylbutazone inhibits the metabolism of the $S(-)$ stereoisomer but enhances the metabolism of the $R(+)$ stereoisomer. Although there is no overall effect on the clearance of the racemic mixture the clinical result is one of increased anticoagulant effect, since the $S(-)$ stereoisomer is about five times more potent than the $R(+)$ stereoisomer. The interaction with metronidazole is similarly stereospecific.

Table 10.3 *Drug interactions due to inhibition of drug metabolism*

I Non–specific

Precipitant drug(s)	*Object drug(s)*
Chloramphenicol	Phenytoin, tolbutamide, warfarin
Cimetidine	Diazepam, propranolol, warfarin
Disulfiram	Alcohol, phenytoin, $S(-)$ warfarin
Isoniazid (slow acetylators)	Phenytoin
Metronidazole	Alcohol, $S(-)$ warfarin
Phenylbutazone	Chlorpropamide, phenytoin, tolbutamide, $S(-)$ warfarin

II Specific

Precipitant drug(s)	*Object drug(s)*
Allopurinol (xanthine oxidase)	Azathioprine, 6-mercaptopurine
Carbidopa and benserazide (dopa decarboxylase)	L-dopa
MAO inhibitors (e.g. tranylcypromine, iproniazid)	Amine-containing foods (see below) amphetamine

III Amine–containing foods which may interact with MAO inhibitors

Cheese (matured, especially Cheddar. Cream and cottage cheeses are safe)
Meat or yeast extracts
Wines (especially Chianti)
Unfresh protein (especially hung poultry or game). Canned or frozen foods are safe if eaten immediately after opening or thawing.

An inhibitory interaction which has been put to therapeutic use is that of disulfiram with alcohol. Alcohol is metabolized to acetaldehyde which is metabolized in turn to carbon dioxide and water. Disulfiram inhibits the metabolism of acetaldehyde, which accumulates and causes an unpleasant reaction which includes abdominal colic, flushing, dizziness, breathlessness, tachycardia, and vomiting. Disulfiram has therefore been used to try to break the drinking habit in alcoholics.

The interaction of allopurinol with azathioprine and 6-mercaptopurine is an example of the effect of inhibiting a specific metabolic pathway. During allopurinol therapy xanthine oxidase activity is inhibited. 6-mercaptopurine and azathioprine (of which 6-mercaptopurine is a metabolite) are metabolized by xanthine oxidase and their dosage requirements are reduced (see Pharmacopoeia). This is of practical importance in the treatment of leukaemia when allopurinol is given to prevent the hyperuricaemia resulting from increased cell turnover induced by cytotoxic drugs such as 6-mercaptopurine.

An example of a therapeutically beneficial interaction involving inhibition of a specific enzyme is that of L-dopa with the dopa decarboxylase inhibitors, benserazide and carbidopa. L-dopa is decarboxylated to dopamine by dopa decarboxylase. In the brain this leads to a therapeutic increase in dopamine concentrations but peripheral decarboxylase activity diverts much of the administered L-dopa to dopamine, which cannot itself enter the brain. Dopa decarboxylase inhibitors decrease this peripheral metabolism and do not enter the brain where dopamine formation can continue. The therapeutic dose of L-dopa can therefore be reduced and its peripheral adverse effects, such as hypotension, minimized.

The interaction between MAO inhibition and dietary tyramine (see Table 10.3) is caused by inhibition of tyramine metabolism and results in severe hypertension which may be fatal. The sequence of events is complex:

1. Inhibition of MAO results in an increase in the noradrenaline content of sympathetic nerve-endings.

2. When tyramine is ingested and MAO is inhibited then tyramine is not, as is usually the case, metabolized but passes through the gut wall and liver to the systemic circulation.

3. Tyramine releases noradrenaline from its increased stores in nerve-endings and a hypertensive crisis results.

The α-adrenoceptor antagonist, phentolamine, is highly effective in the treatment of the hypertension due to this interaction.

10.4.5. Excretion interactions

Most interactions involving drug excretion occur in the kidneys. The important interactions are listed in Table 10.4.

Table 10.4   *Drug interactions involving altered drug excretion*

Precipitant drug(s)	Object drug(s)	Result
Diuretics	Lithium	Lithium retention
Loop diuretics	Gentamicin	Nephrotoxicity
Phenylbutazone	Acetohexamide, chlorpropamide	Hypoglycaemia
Salicylate (low dose)	{ Sulphinpyrazone Methotrexate	Decreased uricosuric effect Methotrexate retention
Quinidine Verapamil Spironolactone }	Digoxin	Digoxin retention

Competition for renal tubular secretion is an important mechanism. For example, probenecid inhibits the tubular secretion of penicillin so that the blood concentration of penicillin is increased and its therapeutic effects prolonged—a beneficial interaction. Quinidine inhibits the tubular secretion of digoxin and the consequent rise in plasma digoxin concentrations (on average twofold) may be associated with toxicity. However, quinidine also limits the distribution of digoxin and the interaction may also result in a decrease in the positive inotropic effect of digoxin on the heart. Salicylates inhibit the active secretion of methotrexate thereby potentiating its toxic effects.

An interesting example of a pharmacokinetic interaction which results from a pharmacodynamic effect is that of frusemide and thiazide diuretics with lithium. By their effects on renal tubular sodium transport diuretics cause retention of lithium with consequent toxicity. If diuretics and lithium are used concurrently (e.g. because of fluid retention or nephrogenic diabetes insipidus caused by lithium) lithium doses should be reduced using plasma concentration measurements as a guide. Frusemide may alter the excretion of gentamicin and enhance its nephrotoxicity.

10.5. PHARMACODYNAMIC INTERACTIONS

Pharmacodynamic interactions are those in which the precipitant drug alters the effect of the object drug at its site of action. Such interactions may be termed either *direct* or *indirect*. The important examples are listed in Table 10.5.

10.5.1. Direct pharmacodynamic interactions

Direct pharmacodynamic interactions occur when two drugs either act on the same site (antagonism or synergism) or act on two different sites with a similar end result.

(a) Antagonism at the same site

There are numerous examples of such interactions, some of which are therapeutically beneficial, for example the reversal of the effects of opiates with naloxone, and treatment of arrhythmias due to tricyclic antidepressant overdose with physostigmine.

(b) Synergism at the same site

Warfarin is frequently involved in such interactions with drugs such as the tetracyclines, clofibrate, and corticosteroids and oestrogens. Some of these interactions may involve alterations in the synthesis rates of clotting factors (e.g. anabolic steroids, corticosteroids, oestrogens) while others may involve an alteration in the affinity of vitamin K for clotting factor receptors (e.g. D-thyroxine, tetracyclines).

Table 10.5   *Pharmacodynamic drug interactions*

Precipitant drug(s)	Object drug(s)	Result
I *Direct*		
Aminoglycosides, quinidine, quinine	} Depolarizing skeletal muscle relaxants	} Enhanced skeletal muscle relaxation
Centrally-acting drugs	Centrally-acting drugs	Potentiation
β-adrenoceptor antagonists	Verapamil	Arrhythmias, asystole
Physostigmine	Tricyclic antidepressants	Reversal of anticholinergic effects
Naloxone	Opiate analgesics	Reversal of opiate effects
Vitamin K_1	Warfarin	Diminished anticoagulation
Anabolic steroids		
Clofibrate		
Corticosteroids	} Warfarin	Increased anticoagulation
Oestrogens		
Tetracyclines		
II *Indirect*		
Drugs affecting platelet adhesiveness*	Anticoagulants	Impaired haemostasis
Drugs causing gastro-intestinal ulceration*	Anticoagulants	Increased chance of bleeding
Drugs causing potassium loss*	} Cardiac glycosides Anti–arrhythmics*	Increased effects Decreased effects
Drugs causing hypercalcaemia (e.g. calcium salts, vitamin D)	} Cardiac glycosides	Increased effects
Drugs causing fluid retention*	Diuretics	Decreased effects
Diuretics*	Oral hypoglycaemics	Decreased effects
β-adrenoceptor antagonists	Vasodilators	Improved control of hypertension/angina

* See text for examples

   The effects of depolarizing skeletal muscle relaxants are potentiated by some antibiotics (e.g. aminoglycosides, polymixin B, and colistin) and by quinidine and quinine. These interactions are due to the curare-like effects of the precipitant drugs on the motor end-plate of skeletal muscle.

   β-adrenoceptor antagonists and verapamil, when used in combination, cause arrhythmias in a higher incidence than either does alone, presumably because of an interaction in the specialized cardiac conducting tissues.

(c) Summation or synergism of similar effects at different sites

Any drug which has a depressant action on central nervous function may potentiate the effect of another such drug whether or not they have effects on the same receptors. The most common example is that of alcohol with any centrally-acting drug, but any two centrally-acting drugs may participate in such an interaction. The therapeutically beneficial combination of phenytoin with phenobarbitone, used in the treatment of epilepsy where the response to phenytoin alone is poor is an example of this type of interaction but is complicated by the fact that each drug alters the metabolism of the other in an unpredictable way.

Other examples include the numerous combinations of cytotoxic drugs used in the treatment of lymphomas and leukaemias, and the use of combinations of antibiotics in the treatment of infection, even when only one organism is implicated (e.g. gentamicin with penicillin in the treatment of bacterial endocarditis).

10.5.2. Indirect pharmacodynamic interactions

In indirect pharmacodynamic interactions the precipitant drug has an effect which is unrelated to the effects of the object drug. The result of that effect in some way secondarily alters the effects of the object drug.

Warfarin and other anticoagulants may be involved in indirect interactions of this kind in two ways:

1. Some drugs decrease the ability of platelets to aggregate (e.g. salicylates, dipyridamole, sulphinpyrazone, phenylbutazone, mefenamic acid) thus impairing haemostasis if warfarin-induced bleeding occurs. Thrombocytopenia caused by the precipitant drug would have a similar effect.

2. If a drug causes gastro-intestinal ulceration it provides a site for bleeding in patients on anticoagulants (e.g. aspirin, phenylbutazone, indomethacin, and other non-steroidal anti-inflammatory drugs).

Drugs which alter body potassium content may alter the therapeutic effects of cardiac glycosides and some anti-arrhythmics. The effects of cardiac glycosides are enhanced by potassium depletion while the effects of some anti-arrhythmics (e.g. lignocaine, quinidine, procainamide, phenytoin) are decreased. The common precipitant drugs in such interactions are potassium-wasting diuretics, corticosteroids, carbenoxolone, and purgatives.

β-adrenoceptor antagonists potentiate the effects of vasodilators in the treatment of hypertension and angina pectoris both by preventing reflex tachycardia and by their own distinct therapeutic effects.

The effects of diuretics may be attenuated by fluid-retaining drugs (e.g. carbamazepine, phenylbutazone) while diuretics (frusemide, bumetanide, thiazides) may attenuate the effects of oral hypoglycaemic drugs.

10.6. LISTS OF CLINICALLY IMPORTANT INTERACTIONS

In Table 10.6 are listed the important interactions in which the effects of object drug are either potentiated [Table 10.6(a)] or diminished [Table 10.6(b)].

Table 10.6   *Clinically important drug–drug interactions*

In the following two parts of this table the interactions discussed in Chapter 10 and listed in tables 10.2 to 10.5 are iterated and others added. They are not classified, however, according to mechanism but according to the nature of the result of the interaction.

(A) Interactions in which the effects of a drug are potentiated

Object drug(s)	Precipitant drug(s)
Acetohexamide	β-adrenoceptor antagonists, phenylbutazone
Alcohol	Centrally-acting drugs, disulfiram, metronidazole
Amine-containing foods	MAO inhibitors
Amphetamines	Centrally-acting drugs, MAO inhibitors
Azathioprine	Allopurinol
β-adrenoceptor antagonists	Verapamil
Cardiac glycosides	Hypokalaemia (diuretics, purgatives, carbenoxolone, corticosteroids, amphotericin B), hypercalcaemia (vitamin D, calcium), quinidine, spironolactone, verapamil
Cefoxitin	Probenecid
Cephaloridine	Potent diuretics (frusemide, ethacrynic acid)
Chlorpropamide	β-blockers, phenylbutazone
Coumarin anticoagulants	Anabolic steroids, chloral hydrate, chloramphenicol, clofibrate, dipyridamole, disulfiram, D-thyroxine, indomethacin, mefenamic acid, metronidazole, neomycin, oxyphenbutazone, phenylbutazone, salicylates, sulphinpyrazone, tetracyclines
Digitalis—see cardiac glycosides	
Gentamicin	Potent diuretics (ethacrynic acid, frusemide)
Hypoglycaemic agents (see also under individual names)	β-adrenoceptor antagonists
L-dopa	Dopa decarboxylase inhibitors (carbidopa, benserazide)
Lithium	Diuretics
Local anaesthetics	Adrenaline
Mercaptopurine	Allopurinol
Methotrexate	Salicylates
Penicillin	Probenecid
Pethidine	MAO inhibitors
Phenytoin	Azapropazone, chloramphenicol, coumarin anticoagulants, disulfiram, isoniazid, phenylbutazone
Tolbutamide	Chloramphenicol, clofibrate, coumarin anticoagulants, phenylbutazone, salicylates, sulphonamides
Vasodilators	β-adrenoceptor antagonists
Verapamil	β-adrenoceptor antagonists

Table 10.6 (continued)

(B) Interactions in which the effects of a drug are diminished

Object drug(s)	Precipitant drug(s)
Bethanidine	Tricyclic antidepressants
Chlorpromazine	Barbiturates, orphenadrine
Hydrocortisone	Barbiturates, phenylbutazone, phenytoin
Clonidine	Tricyclic antidepressants
Coumarin anticoagulants	Alcohol, barbiturates, cholestyramine, dichloralphenazone, glutethimide, griseofulvin, hydrocortisone, nortriptyline, phenytoin, rifampicin, vitamin K_1
Debrisoquine	Tricyclic antidepressants
Guanethidine	Tricyclic antidepressants
Oral contraceptives	Barbiturates, phenytoin, rifampicin
Phenytoin	Alcohol, barbiturates, carbamazepine
Salicylates	Sulphinpyrazone
Sulphinpyrazone	Salicylates
Tolbutamide	Rifampicin

11   Drug therapy in the young, in the elderly, and in pregnancy

11.1. DRUG THERAPY IN THE YOUNG

Paediatricians tell us that neonates, infants, and children are not just little adults, and this is certainly true for the ways in which they absorb, distribute, metabolize, excrete, and respond to drugs.

Most dosage schedules for children are based upon some formula relating body weight, age, or body surface area of the child to the adult dose. This is better than nothing, but it will become apparent that because of the variability of drug kinetics at various ages, the variability of responses at various ages, and the variability in the properties of individual drugs, there never can be a simple all-embracing formula relating the children's dose to the adult dose. There can be no substitute for carefully executed clinical studies and trials defining what the optimal paediatric dosage should be and the intelligent application of those dosage schedules in the individual case. Yet because of the ethical constraints placed upon such investigations in children it often happens that drugs which might be useful in children arrive on the market without proper information on dosage schedules in children.

We shall discuss here the general principles underlying the problems of drug therapy in children, but first a word of general advice: if you find it necessary to prescribe a drug to a child, and if you are not certain of the paediatric dosage or indeed whether the drug has been used in children, look it up in the *British National Formulary*, *Martindale's Extra Pharmacopoeia*, a paediatric source-book (such as the *Paediatric Vade-mecum*), or the manufacturer's data sheet, and if still in doubt ask an experienced paediatrician. This is particularly important for drugs with a low therapeutic index. In this respect at least children are just like adults! Differences between neonates, infants, toddlers, older children, and adults occur in respect of:

1. *Pharmaceutical factors*   Mode of administration.
2. *Pharmacokinetic factors*   Absorption, distribution, metabolism, and excretion.

3. *Pharmacodynamic factors* Different pharmacological sensitivity to drug effects.

4. *Therapeutic and toxic effects peculiar to children* Differences in the disease process and in its interaction with drugs.

5. *Practical matters* Compliance, dosage schedules, behavioural problems, problems with school.

11.1.1. Pharmaceutical factors

Children do not at all like injections, so oral formulations are preferable. However, vomiting is a common symptom with febrile illnesses in children, and antibiotics may have to be given parenterally. Small children find swallowing tablets and capsules difficult, so liquid medicines are made available. In practice it is less easy to be precise about dosages when using a 5 ml teaspoon, particularly when nasty-tasting medicine is spat out, drooled down the lower lip, and so on. The use of pleasant-tasting medicine incurs the risk of accidental overdose.

All these common-sense factors have to be taken into account when deciding upon the route of administration and the formulation chosen.

11.1.2. Pharmacokinetic factors

(a) Absorption

Although there is reduced gastric acid secretion in the neonate, the practical importance of this in regard to the absorption of drugs and the efficacy of oral therapy has not been well documented.

Oral absorption of drugs in older infants and children is similar to the adult.

Percutaneous absorption is generally enhanced in neonates, infants, and children, particularly if the skin is excoriated or burned. Several cases of toxicity due to excessive percutaneous absorption have been recorded, e.g. corticosteroid excess from ointments and creams; boric acid toxicity (diarrhoea, vomiting, convulsions, and occasionally death in infants) from boric acid lotion and ointment; and deafness from aminoglycoside/polymyxin antibacterial sprays on burns.

(b) Distribution

Premature babies, neonates, infants, and young children differ from adults in the distribution of their body's water and fat, as illustrated in Table 11.1. Since drugs are distributed between water and fat according to their physicochemical characteristics, it would be expected that the distribution between various body compartments would be different in children, particularly the neonate. This difference would be most evident for the water-soluble drugs mainly distributed within the extracellular space, and is documented for sulphonamides, the apparent volume of distribution in the neonate being about twice that in the adult. However, overall the effect of these theoretical changes in the apparent volume of distribution is confounded by concomitant changes in elimination, and well–documented examples of how this theory affects practice are not available.

Table 11.1   *Relative amounts of body water and fat at different ages*

	Total body water (% of wt)	Extracellular fluid (% of wt)	Intracellular fluid (% of wt)	Fat (% of wt)
Premature baby	85	50	35	1
Full-term neonate	70	40	30	15
Infant (6 months)	70	35	35	15
Child	65	25	40	15
Adult	60	15	45	20
Elderly adult	45	10	35	

Plasma protein binding of drugs is diminished in the neonate and reaches adult values by about one year. This is because of lower concentrations of plasma albumin and a lower capacity of that albumin to bind drugs. This is particularly important in the infant with malnutrition and hypoalbumin-aemia. It is thought that lowered plasma protein binding is one factor causing the increased apparent volume of distribution of phenytoin in neonates (1.3 L/kg in neonates compared with 0.6 L/kg in adults).

The interaction of drugs with the plasma protein binding of bilirubin in the neonate is important. Free bilirubin can cross the blood–brain barrier in the neonate and cause kernicterus (see p.149). Sulphonamides, aspirin, novobiocin, diazoxide, and vitamin K analogues can displace bilirubin from plasma albumin binding sites and if hepatic conjugating mechanisms for bilirubin are immature its free concentration in blood may rise and predispose to kernicterus.

The blood–brain barrier is less mature and efficient in neonatal animals and is thought to be so in neonatal humans. This may be one of the reasons why neonates are sensitive to the effects of certain centrally-active drugs, such as morphine, but other factors may be involved, and the exact role of an immature blood–brain barrier in the neonatal response to drugs remains undefined.

(c) Metabolism

In general hepatic *oxidative metabolism* and *glucuronide* conjugation are deficient in the newborn, and the maturation of these drug-metabolizing systems is variable. The following are examples of changing drug metabolism in the young.

(i) Diazepam

The hydroxylation of diazepam is reduced in the newborn: $t_{1/2}$ in premature neonates, 38–120 h; $t_{1/2}$ in full-term neonates, 22–46 h; $t_{1/2}$ in infants of one month, 10–12 h; $t_{1/2}$ in children 1–15 yr, 15–21 h; and $t_{1/2}$ in adults, 24–48 h.

(ii) Phenytoin
Phenytoin is normally hydroxylated and its elimination in the newborn may be impaired: $t_{1/2}$ in neonates, 30–60 h; $t_{1/2}$ in infants of 1 month, 2–7 h (NB shorter than adult); $t_{1/2}$ in children 1–15 yr, 2–20 h; $t_{1/2}$ in adults, 20–30 h. Remember that the apparent half-time of phenytoin is also dose-dependent, being longer at higher doses. Phenytoin, in common with phenobarbitone, theophylline, carbamazepine, ethosuximide, and some sulphonamides, has a shorter $t_{1/2}$ in young children (1–8 y) than in neonates or adults, and children of this age therefore require a relatively higher dosage. This illustrates the dangers of global assumptions about drug dosage in the young.

(iii) Theophylline
Theophylline is an important drug in this context because it is being used increasingly for the treatment of apnoea of the newborn. The $t_{1/2}$ of theophylline for the premature neonate is 14–58 h; $t_{1/2}$ in adults is 3.5–8 h. Compare the advocated aminophylline i.v. infusion dosage protocols for the treatment of adult asthma with those for the treatment of apnoea of preterm neonates:

	Loading dose	Infusion dose
Adult (asthma)	5–6 mg/kg	0.9 mg/kg/h
Preterm neonate (apnoea)	5–6 mg/kg	0.1–0.2 mg/kg/h

Note: in practice the loading dose turns out to be about the same but the infusion dose is several-fold lower because of decreased clearance of the drug in the neonate. In the neonate, monitoring of the plasma concentration is advisable (see Chapter 7).

(iv) Chloramphenicol
Chloramphenicol may be indicated in the treatment of *Haemophilus influenzae* meningitis in the newborn, but great care should be taken because of the occurrence of the 'grey syndrome', which is due to the accumulation and toxicity of chloramphenicol. Chloramphenicol is normally conjugated with glucuronate by glucuronyl transferase in the liver. However, this enzyme activity is inadequate during the first month of life. In addition, the newborn child is unable to excrete adequately unconjugated chloramphenicol in the urine.

The drug may therefore accumulate and cause vomiting, difficulty in feeding, failure to suck, poor and rapid respiration, cyanosis, and loose green stools. The child becomes ashen-grey, flaccid, and hypothermic. Death may ensue.

Because of this toxicity, dosage in infants less than one month should not be greater than 25 mg/kg daily in four divided doses at six–hourly intervals. In older infants and children doses of 50 mg/kg daily in four divided doses may be given.

(d) Renal excretion

In the neonate, both glomerular filtration rate (GFR) and tubular function are immature, and take about 6 months to reach adult levels. For example, GFR in the neonate is (per unit of body surface area) about 30–40 per cent of that of the adult.

Drugs and active metabolites excreted in the urine tend, therefore, to accumulate in the neonate and young infant. Gentamicin and the penicillins are examples, the dosages of which need adjustment particularly in the premature neonate. Because the urinary excretion of gentamicin improves markedly over the first weeks of life a dose which was safe and effective initially can become inadequate as therapy proceeds and plasma concentration monitoring is important (see Chapter 7). Initial gentamicin $t_{1/2}$ in week 1 of life is 5 h, and in weeks 2–3 is 3 h.

The situation in relation to digoxin is very complicated and is discussed below.

11.1.3. Pharmacodynamic factors

Knowledge of true pharmacodynamic sensitivity to drugs in the young is sparse.

There is evidence to suggest that infants are truly less pharmacodynamically sensitive to digoxin, but several things confuse the clinical pharmacology of digoxin in the neonate and infant. GFR is reduced in the neonate, particularly in premature neonates, and digoxin $t_{1/2}$ is prolonged to twice or three times the adult value. Some studies have also shown an increased apparent volume of distribution in the neonate. In the end with digoxin

Table 11.2 *Digoxin dosages at different ages as used in therapy* *

	Loading dose (μg/kg)	Maintenance dose (μg/kg)	Maintenance dose (μg/m^2/day)	Maintenance plasma concentration (ng/ml)
Premature or neonate	20–30	13	200	2.1
Infants 1–12 months	40–60	20	300	2.1
Infants 1–10 yr	30	12	280	1.4
Adults	15	5	200	1.2

* Assuming normal renal function for age.

one relies upon long-established empirical dosage schedules which work out for the neonate, infant, child, and adult as shown in Table 11.2. This illustrates how complex children's dosage can be.

Neonates have increased sensitivity to non–depolarizing neuromuscular blocking agents such as tubocurarine, while neonates and children seem *less* sensitive to depolarizing neuromuscular blocking agents such as succinylcholine.

11.1.4. Therapeutic and toxic effects peculiar to children

Whereas in adults amphetamine increases motor and behavioural activity, in so-called 'hyperkinetic' or 'hyperactive' children it increases attention span and decreases disruptive social behaviour. This may be due to an effect of amphetamine to induce in animals and man stereotyped behaviour, i.e. to reduce the numbers of behavioural responses the animal needs to make at any time. Thus a child who will not pay attention, and who disrupts a school class, may be made to pay attention and concentrate on the task in hand. It is beyond our scope to discuss whether or not such behavioural control is desirable.

Systemic corticosteroid therapy in children is particularly dangerous because it may result in stunted growth. The systemic steroid-sparing effect of disodium cromoglycate and aerosol corticosteroids in the treatment of childhood asthma have been particularly important in avoiding this complication.

11.1.5. Practical matters

There is good advice on prescribing for children in the *British National Formulary* and you should read the relevant section.

We shall mention here some obvious problems:

1. Dosage difficulties with teaspoons and liquids.
2. Children do not like injections and tablets can be difficult to swallow.
3. Children vomit easily.
4. Parents give in to fractious children so that compliance can be bad, and the duration of antibiotic therapy curtailed (the child seems better so the course of therapy is not completed).
5. Young children will try anything and will poison themselves with their own pleasant-tasting medicines or anyone else's drugs. Therefore keep medicines out of their way.
6. Nursing staff responsible for children (and casualty staff may be forgotten in this) need to be reminded from time to time about drug and drug dosage problems in children.

11.1.6. Dosage calculations in children

Ideally drug dosages for children should be individualized, taking into account the age, weight, body surface area, general condition, and so on, as discussed above. Sometimes dosages have already been determined by clinical trial or experience and regimens based on those dosages should be followed. If such information is not available, however, probably the safest way to scale down dosages from adult dosages is the body surface method:

$$\text{Dose} = \frac{\text{adult dose} \times \text{patient's body surface area(m}^2)}{\text{adult body surface area (i.e. } 1.7 \text{ m}^2)}.$$

The infant's body surface area can be calculated from tables or a nomogram if one knows its height (length) and weight (see *Martindale's Extra Pharmacopoeia*, 28th edition). The dose so calculated is only approximate and is not reliable for preterm neonates and infants.

11.2. DRUG THERAPY IN THE ELDERLY

The importance of considering drug therapy in the elderly adult specifically is illustrated by the following facts:

(a) In most developed countries the elderly constitute about 12 per cent of the population but they consume 25–30 per cent of health service expenditure on drugs.

(b) Adverse drug reactions are two to three times more common in the elderly than in young and middle-aged adults.

(c) Polypharmacy in the elderly is common. In one survey 34 per cent of patients over 75 years of age in a general practice were taking three to four different drugs daily. The scope for drug interactions is therefore large.

(d) The error rate in taking drugs is about 60 per cent in patients over 60 years of age and the rate of error increases markedly if more tha.1 three drugs are prescribed. More of these errors are potentially fatal in the elderly than in the young and middle-aged.

The reasons for the high prescribing rate in the elderly, and for the occurrence of polypharmacy are easy to understand. Old people get ill and frequently have multiple diseases and symptoms requiring treatment. The nature of illness in the elderly has to be faced, drugs do have a part in the treatment of that illness, and our task is to learn how to use drugs in the elderly to maximize their efficiency and to minimize their adverse effects.

The term 'elderly' implies a homogeneous group, and the first thing to understand is that this is totally wrong as far as drug therapy is concerned. The elderly do not form a neat package and are very variable in both their handling of and their response to drugs.

There are several factors in the elderly which by common experience signal potential trouble, and the more of these factors which are common to an elderly patient, the more likely it is that one will encounter difficulty with drug therapy. The important factors are: frailty, the degree of illness, inability to look after themselves, poor appetite and nutrition, poor fluid intake, immobility, multiple illnesses, confusion and forgetfulness, and lack of supervision. Some of these factors lead to problems with compliance, confusion over treatment, the use of wrong dosages and wrong drugs (e.g. from hoarded past prescriptions). Other factors impinge upon drug handling and action and it is these factors we shall discuss here.

As in the discussion of drug therapy in children the problem can be considered according to the all-pervading themes of clinical pharmacology:

  (a) pharmaceutical factors;
  (b) pharmacokinetic factors;
  (c) pharmacodynamic factors;
  (d) therapeutic and toxic factors;
  (e) practical matters.

11.2.1. Pharmaceutical factors

Many elderly patients find tablets difficult to swallow and the more frail, the more ill, the more dehydrated, and the more confused they are, the more difficult it becomes. Elixirs help, but you have to be sure they are swallowed. For example, many potassium tablets are quite large and can cause difficulty (particularly as the diuretic they are given with may be causing dehydration). Effervescent potassium tablets have to 'fizz' in water and dissolve and instructions as to their use (and for that matter the use of any medicines) are particularly important for the elderly. Counselling as to the use of medicines is important.

It is known that tablets or capsules may adhere to the oesophageal mucosa and dissolve there. This has been demonstrated, for example, in the case of the 200 mg tablets of emepromium bromide, an anticholinergic drug used for the treatment of incontinence, which can thus cause oesophageal ulceration. Emepromium bromide 100 mg tablets, the form now on the market, is said not to produce this effect but to avoid hold-up in the oesophagus they should be swilled down with at least 60 ml of fluid.

It is quite an education to go round a geriatric ward after a drug round looking in patients mouths to see how much medication is still in the oral cavity slowly dissolving away, even in those patients who are not obviously confused or somnolent.

11.2.2. Pharmacokinetic factors

(a) Absorption

There are no well-documented examples to show that this is important as a factor specifically in the elderly.

(b) Distribution

It is important to make adjustments in dosage for body weight when faced with elderly patients particularly for drugs with a low therapeutic index.

There are reductions in plasma protein binding of some drugs in the elderly (e.g. phenytoin), for which the decrease is accounted for by the decrease in plasma albumin with age.

The distribution of body water and fat is altered in the elderly (see Table 11.1) and because of an increased proportion of fat lipid-soluble drugs tend to accumulate to a greater extent than in younger patients.

Because of different sources of variability it is exceedingly difficult to predict what might happen to the apparent volume of distribution of a drug in the elderly. For instance, the apparent volume of distribution of diazepam is increased in the elderly, but that of nitrazepam is not.

(c) Metabolism

Evaluation of drug metabolism in the elderly and the relation of any changes to clinical practice is very difficult, and there are many pitfalls. The following questions will illustrate the problem.

Do you compare normal elderly people (and if so how old) with normal young people (and if so how young)? Do you compare ill old people with ill young people? Do you compare smokers and non-smokers (smoking may affect drug metabolism)? Do you control comparisons for nutrition (diet may affect drug metabolism)? Do you compare elderly patients on other medications with younger people on or off similar medications (because so many elderly people are on chronic drug therapy anyway, and some drugs cause induction of hepatic drug metabolizing enzymes)?

When one examines the literature on the subject of drug metabolism in the elderly the subject becomes confusing because there are so many variables to take into account. For example, various authorities state that the hepatic clearance of such drugs as propranolol, lignocaine, chlormethiazole, theophylline, phenobarbitone, and paracetamol decrease with age, while clearance of warfarin, indomethacin, phenylbutazone and ethanol is apparently unaffected.

(d) Renal excretion

There is a well-documented decrease in glomerular filtration rate with age such that by the age of 80 the GFR may have fallen to 60–70 ml/min. Tubular function also declines with age.

Drugs and active metabolites which are mainly excreted in the urine may therefore require downward adjustment of dosage, just as they might in renal failure in younger patients (see Chapter 24), e.g. digoxin, gentamicin and other aminoglycosides, lithium, and procainamide (see Table 3.5).

Some drugs are best avoided in the elderly, for example tetracyclines, which because of poor renal function may accumulate, producing nausea and vomiting, which cause dehydration and further deterioration in renal function. In addition, they have an anti-anabolic action which worsens uraemia and promotes muscle wasting. All these adverse effects are particularly hazardous in the elderly.

11.2.3. Pharmacodynamic factors

For various reasons drug sensitivity (independent of pharmacokinetics) may be altered in old age.

There appears to be a diminished sensitivity of β-adrenoceptor function in the elderly, which decreases the pharmacological efficacy of β-adrenoceptor agonists and antagonists.

Elderly patients appear to be more sensitive to the anticoagulant effects of warfarin and generally require smaller dosages to produce adequate anticoagulation.

The elderly brain, particularly where there is hypoxia or fever, seems especially sensitive to centrally-active drugs, e.g. hypnotics, sedatives, tranquillizers, antidepressants, and neuroleptics, such that in confusional states in the elderly the first cause to exclude is a centrally-active drug.

11.2.4. Therapeutic and toxic factors and drug–disease, drug–physiology interactions

There are all sorts of practical problems which arise in the treatment of elderly patients, due to the interaction of drugs with diseases or aged physiology.

The elderly cerebral circulation does not autoregulate efficiently. Elderly patients easily become hypovolaemic with diuretics (or even without, if not eating and drinking normally). Peripheral autonomic responses may be sluggish in response to hypotension. All these factors accumulate to make the treatment of hypertension in the elderly a matter to be cautious about, as it is often very easy to inadvertently produce hypotension, causing syncope, which results in a fall, injury (e.g. fractured femur, subdural haematoma), immobilization, and all the consequent complications, such as hypostatic pneumonia and pulmonary emboli, which can be fatal. Unless one can be reasonably sure of prolonging life or reducing morbidity in the asymptomatic patient over the age of 70, hypotensive therapy should be viewed with caution.

The elderly are particularly prone to diuretic-induced hypokalaemia, which may interact with digoxin to predispose to digoxin toxicity. Some authorities prefer to prescribe thiazides or loop diuretics with a potassium-sparing diuretic in the elderly, to be on the safe side. A brisk diuresis in an elderly man with prostatic hypertrophy can produce acute urinary retention. The elderly who are at an increased risk of gout anyway may have gout more easily precipitated by diuretics. Diuretics may also produce urinary incontinence in women.

Confusion and hyperactivity in an elderly person is often treated with a neuroleptic agent, e.g. chlorpromazine or haloperidol, and this can result in severe Parkinsonism.

Whether or not non-steroidal anti-inflammatory drugs have a decreased clearance in the elderly, and whether or not the elderly stomach is more prone to peptic erosion or ulceration are uncertain, but there have been reports of worrying numbers of cases of upper gastro-intestinal haemorrhage in elderly patients taking such drugs.

Lastly, always guard against the temptation to treat the adverse effect of one drug with another; in this way some of the polypharmacy seen in the elderly can be avoided.

11.2.5. Practical matters

Remember that the elderly may be slow of comprehension, forgetful, and hard of hearing. They may have difficulty in understanding what to you seem simple instructions. It is worth taking the time to write things down so that the patient can consult the written instructions when required. Writing the names of drugs on bottles may not be enough. In some cases it is worth writing 'water tablets' on a bottle of diuretic tablets, or 'heart tablets' on a bottle of digoxin tablets. Remember that the elderly may have poor eyesight and write large!

The elderly may have difficulty in manipulating bottles and tablets. Some modern 'child-proof' medicine containers are also elderly-proof.

In general, when prescribing, try to use as few drugs as possible, start with low doses and increase carefully only if required. Remember to choose easily swallowed formulations and try to keep therapy as simple as possible (e.g. with once-a-day drugs).

11.3. DRUG THERAPY IN PREGNANCY

The potential for doing harm to the fetus by prescribing drugs for the mother during pregnancy is considerable. This fact was brought home by the thalidomide disaster. All involved in drug therapy, patient, doctor, and nurse, should now be aware of the potential dangers of drug therapy in pregnancy. Drugs should only be given to pregnant women if the likely benefit outweighs the risks to the fetus, and in general only those drugs of which there is extensive experience in pregnancy should be prescribed. It is a good rule to avoid new drugs in pregnancy.

The problems associated with drugs in pregnancy are as follows.

11.3.1. The placental transfer of drugs

Most drugs in the maternal circulation pass across the placenta into the fetal circulation to a greater or lesser extent, although there are a few exceptions. For example, heparin does not pass because it is ionized and of high molecular weight; tubocurarine is ionized and relatively lipid insoluble, and does not cross the placenta. The usual principles governing the passage of drugs across cell membranes apply to the passage of drugs across the placenta. Lipophilicity, non-ionization at physiological pH, and low molecular weight (i.e. < 1000 daltons) favour transfer (e.g. thiopentone, anti-thyroid drugs, steroid hormones).

11.3.2. Adverse effects of maternal drugs on fetus and neonate (see Chapter 9)

The adverse effects of maternal drugs on the fetus and neonate, which are discussed in Chapter 9, consist of:

(a) Teratogenesis (Table 9.3);
(b) Fetal toxicity and abnormalities of growth and development (Table 9.4);
(c) Perinatal adverse effects (drugs given to mother before and/or during labour having adverse effects on the fetus and neonate; Table 9.4).

11.3.3. Altered maternal pharmacokinetics

(a) Absorption

The absorption of drugs seems to be generally unaltered during pregnancy.

(b) Distribution

Plasma volume and total body water increase during later pregnancy. The plasma concentrations of drugs with a normally small apparent volume of distribution, and those particularly water soluble may be found to be low when the drugs are given in conventional doses (e.g. ampicillin). Ampicillin dosages need to be increased during pregnancy.

Plasma protein drug binding may alter during pregnancy. Plasma albumin concentrations fall, and consequently the bound fraction of drugs normally highly bound to albumin may also fall. Total phenytoin concentrations in the plasma fall during pregnancy because of decreased albumin binding and increased body water but this does *not* mean that phenytoin dosage should be increased because the concentration of *free* drug may remain unchanged. This principle is discussed in Chapter 10 (p.161). Phenytoin dosages should only be increased in pregnancy if fit frequency increases.

(c) Metabolism

Because of the ethical problems of doing drug studies in pregnant women there is not much information about drug-metabolizing capacity in pregnancy. Indirect evidence such as liver histology, and urinary D-glucaric acid and 6-β-hydroxycortisol excretion suggest that drug-metabolizing activity may be increased in pregnancy, but the importance of this is as yet unknown.

(d) Excretion

In pregnancy the glomerular filtration rate increases by about 70 per cent. Thus, drugs which are mainly eliminated by renal excretion will be cleared more quickly. The dosage requirements of lithium and digoxin may therefore increase during pregnancy. Ampicillin and gentamicin plasma concentrations on conventional dosages have also be found to be low in pregnancy. In all three cases, of course, plasma concentration measurement will help to guide therapy (see Chapter 7).

11.3.4. Common practical problems of drug therapy during pregnancy

(a) Anaemia (see also Chapter 26, p.458 and iron salts in the Pharmacopoeia, p.693).

Iron supplements are now routinely given to pregnant women, and because the needs for folic acid double during pregnancy combined iron and folic acid preparations are usually given as prophylaxis against both iron deficiency anaemia and the megaloblastic anaemia of pregnancy. There are numerous preparations available (see Table 26.2), but the aim should be to provide a minimum daily dose of 30 mg of iron in the form of a ferrous salt, and of between 200 and 500 micrograms of folic acid.

(b) Antibiotic therapy

Antibiotic therapy is commonly indicated for urinary tract infection during pregnancy. However, the antibiotics shown in Table 11.3 should not be given unless absolutely necessary, because of the risks indicated.

Table 11.3 *Antibiotics to be avoided in pregnancy unless absolutely necessary*

Antibiotic	Risk
Chloramphenicol	Infant 'grey syndrome' (circulatory collapse, hypothermia, ashen-grey cyanosis, abdominal distension)
Co-trimoxazole	Neonatal hyperbilirubinaemia (sulphonamide)
	Folate antagonist (?significant)
	Teratogenesis
Streptomycin	Ototoxicity in fetus
Sulphonamides	Neonatal hyperbilirubinaemia leading to kernicterus (see p. 149)
Tetracyclines	Infant teeth discoloration
	Acute hepatic toxicity in mother

Ampicillin, amoxycillin, and cephalosporins appear to be safe to both mother and baby, if penicillin hypersensitivity is not a problem. Genta-micin and amikacin are potentially harmful to the fetal eighth nerve, and the risks of this should be balanced against the benefits of their use in severe infections.

(c) Maternal hyperthyroidism

If it becomes necessary to treat maternal hyperthyroidism with drugs then carbimazole or methimazole, or propylthiouracil are indicated. There is then about a 10 per cent risk of fetal hypothyroidism with goitre, and because of this the lowest dose of antithyroid drug which will control maternal hyperthyroidism is indicated, particularly during late pregnancy.

Antithyroid drugs are secreted in breast milk and will therefore cause hypothyroidism and goitre in the baby. Breast feeding is therefore not recommended for women who are taking antithyroid drugs.

(d) Diabetes mellitus

Because of the potential complications to mother and child of badly controlled diabetes during pregnancy careful management is very important.

(i) Pre-existing insulin-dependent diabetes
Maternal insulin requirements reach their maximum during the third trimester of pregnancy, and patients may require from two-thirds more insulin to three times as much as usual. Ketoacidosis may occur with only mild precipitants, e.g. a mild infection or a short period of food deprivation. Diabetic control should if possible be monitored using blood glucose rather than the less accurate urinary glucose measurements, and pregnant diabetic women should learn how to measure blood glucose themselves. The blood glucose concentration should be kept at or below 7 mmol/l.

Insulin therapy should be changed to a twice-a-day regimen, and such a regimen established before the second half of the pregnancy. Short- and intermediate-acting highly purified porcine insulins are the types usually used.

The complexities of diet and of overall management of diabetes in pregnancy are beyond our scope. Suffice it to say that this is a most important subject requiring the careful attention of physicians and obstetricians, and the organization of careful and skilled antenatal care.

(ii) Gestational diabetes
This is diabetes diagnosed for the first time during pregnancy. It is usually mild (sometimes called chemical diabetes of pregnancy), and management usually consists of diet with or without insulin. In this case once-daily insulin may be sufficient.

Oral hypoglycaemics are not favoured during pregnancy because of the risks of teratogenesis and prolonged neonatal hypoglycaemia.

During labour the continuous i.v. regimen described for use during operations (p.451) can be used to control blood glucose satisfactorily.

After delivery insulin requirements fall rapidly, but dosage regimens can be further complicated by breast-feeding.

(e) Hypertension in pregnancy

(i) Pre-eclamptic hypertension

Drug therapy forms but a small part of the management of pre-eclamptic hypertension, which is hypertension occuring in the third trimester. Delivery produces a rapid and complete cure, but drug therapy can be used to protect the mother from eclamptic complications, although it has not been shown to improve fetal prognosis.

Oral therapy with methyldopa 0.5–1 g t.d.s. is usually effective in lowering the blood pressure, and has not been shown to be harmful to the fetus, or to the infant on follow-up for 4 years. Methyldopa may be given intravenously if it cannot be taken by mouth. If this is not completely effective then oral hydralazine may be added in a dosage of not more than 300 mg daily.

Occasionally it is necessary to lower the blood pressure more rapidly, when hydralazine as an i.v. infusion of 20–40 mg is often effective.

Diuretics are not used because they are not very effective and aggravate the already existing hypovolaemia. β-adrenoceptor antagonists are not generally used because of their potential adverse effects on the fetus (e.g. fetal bradycardia), but they are being evaluated and further information on their benefits and risks will be forthcoming.

It may be necessary to prevent fits from occurring or to treat fits before delivery. In the UK i.v. diazepam or chlormethiazole are used, in the USA parenteral magnesium sulphate.

(ii) Chronic hypertension and pregnancy

Although pre-existing chronic hypertension in pregnancy predisposes to pre-eclampsia with its consequent risks to mother and child, mild to moderate hypertension without the problem of pre-eclampsia does not in itself appear to be a particular hazard to the fetus. Some believe that chronic hypertension with blood pressures of below 170/110 mm Hg may not need treatment during pregnancy since the duration of pregnancy is short, blood pressures may fall during pregnancy, and pre-eclampsia will be dealt with as a separate condition. Others feel that if the pregnant woman is on antihypertensive therapy this should be continued and she should be carefully observed for the occurrence of pre-eclampsia.

Certain points about continuing with antihypertensive drug therapy in pregnancy should be emphasized. Reserpine and captopril are hazardous and should be withdrawn. Diuretics may be continued if essential for blood pressure control, but they should be discontinued if pre-eclampsia supervenes. Occasional cases of neonatal thrombocytopenia have been reported with thiazide diuretics. The β-adrenoceptor antagonists have not yet been fully evaluated in pregnancy but do not appear to be teratogenic. There are, however, potential risks to the fetus, e.g. inadequate responses to hypoxaemia, pre-term labour, and neonatal hypoglycaemia and respiratory depression. However, so far these risks have not been confirmed. Trials of β-adrenoceptor antagonists in the treatment of all forms of hypertension in pregnancy are under way, and guidance as to their efficacy and adverse effects should be available soon.

The effects of other antihypertensive agents in pregnancy (e.g. clonidine, bethanidine, debrisoquine, prazosin) have not been adequately studied, and these drugs should be avoided.

(f) Anticoagulation during pregnancy

Warfarin is associated with major hazards to mother and child:

Maternal haemorrhage;
Fetal haemorrhage (cerebral);
Multiple congenital abnormalities (teratogenesis during first three months of development).

For these reasons it has become common practice to substitute heparin subcutaneously during the first trimester, to use warfarin if necessary from 13–36 weeks, and then again to use heparin subcutaneously well before delivery. There is however no entirely safe or ideal anticoagulant for use during pregnancy, and the above advice is a compromise.

(g) Epilepsy

The treatment of epilepsy during pregnancy poses the problem of the assessment of the teratogenicity of the anticonvulsant drugs against a background of an increased risk of congenital abnormalities in children born of epileptic mothers (which may or may not be drug-related). Most authorities believe that there is a slight risk of teratogenicity from phenytoin. The position with valproate is confusing and the data are insufficient to exonerate it completely. Experience with carbamazepine is insufficient to allow a definitive statement one way or the other. So what does one do? Since epileptic fits are definitely dangerous to both mother and child current advice is that if an epileptic woman on an anticonvulsant, including phenytoin, becomes pregnant, the treatment should be continued with careful plasma concentration monitoring if possible, to avoid toxic plasma concentrations. Remember that because of changes in plasma protein binding, the effective plasma concentration of phenytoin is probably in the lower part of the usual therapeutic range, e.g. about 40–60 μmol/l or lower (10–15 μg/ml; see Chapter 7).

(h) Vomiting (see p.370.)

12   Patient compliance

Patient compliance with drug therapy may be defined as the extent to which the patient follows a prescribed drug regimen.

The extent of non-compliance varies widely depending on numerous different factors and in different studies has been recorded as low as 10 per cent and as high as 92 per cent.

12.1. FACTORS WHICH AFFECT COMPLIANCE

Numerous studies have shown that many different factors may affect compliance. Those factors may be considered under the following headings:

1. The nature of the treatment.
2. Characteristics of the patient.
3. The type of illness.
4. The behaviour of the doctor.

12.1.1. The nature of the treatment

Here two factors are important, the complexity of the regimen, and adverse effects. These are discussed below.

(a) The complexity of the prescribed regimen

This involves the *frequency of administration* (the more often during the day a patient has to take a drug, the less likely he is to take it), and the *number of drugs* prescribed (the more drugs prescribed the less likely is overall compliance).

When several different tablets (or other formulations) have to be taken, at different dosages (i.e. numbers of tablets), and at different times of the day, compliance suffers (see for example the prescription outlined on p.245).

(b) Adverse effects

If patients experience symptoms which they attribute to adverse effects of the medicine then, unless they can be persuaded that the potential benefits of treatment outweigh the disadvantages, they will stop taking the medicine.

12.1.2. Characteristics of the patient

These are nebulous factors mostly involving the shortcomings of human behaviour.

People tend to forget, or can't be bothered; they may feel no need for treatment (e.g. in asymptomatic hypertension); they may be unclear about the prescribing instructions; they may not want to feel dependent or be thought to be dependent on 'pills'.

In addition there may be social or physical problems about their getting to the chemist's shop, difficulties over paying prescription fees, or inconveniences, during every-day use, in carrying and taking the medication.

Some patients, notably children, have problems with certain formulations, e.g. sickly elixirs or large dry bitter tablets.

12.1.3. The type of illness

Compliance is poor in people who are severely mentally disturbed. For example, in the long-term treatment of schizophrenia, medical follow-up and patient compliance are made more predictable by the use of depot neuroleptic therapy and special clinics to provide it.

Physical disability may interfere with compliance despite the patient's desire to comply. It may sound silly, but if the patient with rheumatoid or osteo-arthritis cannot get the top off the childproof container, he will not be able to take the tablets.

Dysphagia may make it difficult for a patient to swallow tablets, particularly if they are large.

Some diseases may promote compliance. Patients with severe, insulin–dependent diabetes may easily become very ill, quite quickly, if they forget their insulin and that is likely to make them comply, although they may not comply precisely with the prescribed instructions. Patients in whom β-blockers have significantly decreased the incidence of anginal attacks will be conditioned to good compliance.

12.1.4. The behaviour of the doctor

The enthusiasm and confidence with which a treatment is prescribed, and the extent to which these attitudes are transmitted to the patient, may influence not only compliance, but response to therapy (the placebo response, see Chapter 13).

There is also good evidence that education of the patient improves compliance. Such education involves discussion of the nature of the disease and its complications, and of the benefits and possible adverse effects of treatment.

12.2. METHODS OF MEASURING COMPLIANCE

Measurement of compliance is of importance both in everyday practice and in research. It is important, for example, to know the extent of a patient's compliance before attributing the failure of a particular therapy to incorrect or inappropriate prescribing, while in clinical trials the need to measure compliance is obvious.

12.2.1. Pharmaceutical methods

The fact that the patient collects his prescription is at least evidence of the first stage of compliance. However, the patient often complies no further, and more useful in assessing the extent of his compliance is the tablet count. This method may be misleading in the case of a patient who throws his tablets away and tablet counts will therefore tend to lead to an overestimate of the extent of compliance. However, the method is better than estimation by the doctor on the basis of his knowledge of the patient's personality, a method which overestimates even more the extent of compliance.

Recently the development of the silicon chip has led to the use of a recording device fitted in the cap of the medication bottle. Such a device allows one to monitor both the frequency and timing of the opening of the bottle and, although it does not allow for the patient who throws his tablets away at regular intervals (an unlikely event), it promises to provide accurate information about compliance.

12.2.2. Pharmacokinetic methods

Measurement of some compounds in the plasma or urine may give a good indication of compliance, but does not allow for the patient who takes his treatment only on the day of the visit to the doctor. The compound measured will usually be the drug itself, but it may be a marker of some sort. Examples of the former are the measurement of digoxin, phenytoin, or lithium in the plasma, or of salicylates or penicillin in the urine. An example of a marker for compliance is the incorporation of riboflavin, easily detected in the urine, into the medication.

12.2.3. Pharmacodynamic methods

If the pharmacological effect of a drug can be measured then that may afford evidence of compliance. Thus measurement of the response of the heart rate to exercise may give information about β-blockers, measurement of prothrombin time may give information about oral anticoagulants, and measurement of the reticulocyte count may give information about haematinics. Non-detection of the pharmacological effect of the drug implies either non-compliance, inadequate dosage, or inappropriate therapy.

12.2.4. Therapeutic methods

If the desired therapeutic effect occurs then in routine practice the question of compliance is unimportant. One should remember, however, that a good therapeutic outcome may occur irrespective of the treatment used. It would then be wrong to attribute the good outcome to the effect of a drug which the patient may not have taken and this principle is important in clinical trials (see Chapter 14).

12.3. METHODS OF IMPROVING COMPLIANCE

Compliance may be improved by:

1. Simplifying the therapeutic regimen.
2. Educating and reminding the patient of the need to take the treatment.

Simplification of the therapeutic regimen consists of reducing the number of drugs a patient has to take, and reducing the frequency of dosage. The first of these objectives may be achieved by trying to avoid the unnecessary use of a drug or by using combinations of drugs in single tablet formulations (although using such formulations carries the difficulty of adjusting drug dosages individually, see Chapter 2, p.14).

Reduction in the frequency of drug administration may be achieved either by using drugs with long durations of action in preference to those with shorter durations (e.g. chlorpropamide vs tolbutamide), or by using a slow-release formulation in preference to a conventional one (e.g. aminophylline). An alternative method is to use depot injections at intervals of a few weeks instead of daily injections or oral medication (e.g. phenothiazine treatment of schizophrenia).

Sometimes compliance may be ensured by giving a single injection of drug at the time of consultation, rather than a short course of tablets (e.g. i.m. antibiotics in the treatment of gonorrhoea, which not only solve the problem of treatment of the individual patient, but in this case prevent the spread of the disease).

Education undoubtedly improves compliance, but is not often applied properly, partly because it is so time-consuming. Nevertheless, the patient with asymptomatic hypertension, or glaucoma, for example, who learns the importance of taking drugs when he is feeling well is more likely to comply than the patient who is simply given a prescription without instructions.

Finally, reminding the patient may help to improve compliance. A simple method consists of the 'calendar pack', commonly used for prescriptions of oral contraceptives (see Fig. P9 in the Pharmacopoeia, p.747).

One imponderable in all this is one's view of who is responsible for the patient's taking the treatment. It is our view that the responsibility of the doctor extends to the proper education of the patient about the therapy, and encouragement to comply, but that the final responsibility lies with the patient. Sometimes, however, problems crop up in which the responsibilities of the doctor are more difficult to define. For example, the treatment of tuberculosis or other infections in large populations with a high rate of infection, when poor compliance may make widespread control difficult; the use of certain immunization procedures (e.g. whooping cough); the use of mass sterilization or contraception programmes in over-populated countries; the addition of fluoride to water supplies. Some of these problems are controversial, all are difficult, and there are no simple answers.

13 Placebos

The translation of the word 'placebo' is 'I shall please'. Originally a placebo was a preparation of a pharmacologically inactive compound 'adopted to please rather than to benefit the patient' (OED), although it could be argued that anything which pleases a patient also benefits him. The term, as now used, goes further than that.

Placebos are of two types, those which contain pharmacologically inactive ingredients, and those which contain some compound with pharmacological activity. Although the former are always used as placebos knowingly by the physician, the latter are given either in the knowledge that their pharmacological action is not appropriate or in the mistaken belief that it *is* appropriate. Some examples are given below.

13.1. USES AND ABUSES OF PLACEBOS

13.1.1. Inert placebos

(a) Clinical trials

The commonest use of the inert placebo is as a dummy for the real treatment in clinical trials, in order to reduce the element of subjective bias (see Chapter 15).

(b) The misuse of the placebo as a 'therapeutic test'

Occasionally inert placebos, rather than drugs known to have pharmacological activity, are given to patients who are incessantly complaining of some symptom, and who are thought to be exaggerating. Pain is the symptom usually involved. If the patient responds to the placebo then it is often assumed that the patient was making an unnecessary fuss. However, it is quite wrong to assume that, because the pain is reported by the patient to have been relieved by an intramuscular injection of saline, the symptom did not exist, or was not severe, or that the patient was exaggerating. A third of all people are placebo reactors, i.e. will report symptomatic relief following the administration of an inert compound. It would therefore not be surprising if on occasion, and despite real pain appropriate to the pathology, relief was obtained from a placebo. A positive response to a placebo does not automatically mean that the patient is either exaggerating or malingering.

13.1.2. 'Active' placebos

(a) To terminate a visit

The issue of a prescription is a common way of ending a patient's visit to the doctor. Not infrequently the doctor will prescribe a compound whose pharmacological action is irrelevant to the case at hand. The practitioner may be aware of this as, for example, in the case of the prescription of a vitamin preparation, the patient being informed of the nature of the prescription and being told that it is a 'tonic'. On the other hand, the practitioner may misunderstand the proven indications for which a drug has been shown to be effective, as for example in the case of the prescription of cimetidine for symptoms of 'dyspepsia' in the absence of proven ulceration or oesophagitis.

(b) To 'treat' the untreatable

Some doctors find it difficult to accept that there is *no* effective treatment for their patient and they feel constrained to try something. There are plenty of examples of pseudotherapy based on apparently good ideas which, when examined scientifically, just do not hold up, for example the use of cerebral vasodilators in the treatment of senile dementia. Some patients cannot believe that there is not a 'pill' to cure their disease, and sometimes no amount of talk will persuade them otherwise. Often, in exasperation, something is prescribed which, however tenuously, could be interpreted as rational, for example the use of diuretics and so-called appetite suppressants in the treatment of obesity, despite lack of evidence of their long-term efficacy.

13.2. ADVERSE EFFECTS OF PLACEBOS

If a doctor uses placebos unthinkingly he may ignore the patient's real problem and that may lead to delayed diagnosis of a treatable condition. Delay in diagnosis and hence in instituting proper treatment will be prolonged if the patient initially responds to the placebo. An example is the use of a benzodiazepine to treat endogenous depression which may present with symptoms of anxiety.

Strangely, placebos may cause direct adverse effects. Whether this occurs as an artefact of the natural incidence of trivial symptoms in normal people, as an adverse consequence of doctor–patient interactions, or through some other mechanism, is not known. For example, in a survey of placebo studies common symptoms were dry mouth (9 per cent), nausea

(10 per cent), fatigue (18 per cent), difficulty in concentrating (15 per cent), and headache (25 per cent). Note that these complaints fall within the common experience of healthy people.

13.3. FACTORS WHICH INFLUENCE THE RESPONSE TO PLACEBOS

Certain factors are thought to increase the likelihood of a response to a placebo.

13.3.1. The doctor's attitude

If a placebo is to be prescribed, then it should be prescribed with enthusiasm and some show of belief in its efficacy.

13.3.2. The doctor–patient relationship

One would suppose that a placebo is more likely to work if there is a respectful rapport between doctor and patient, although there is no proof that that is the case.

13.3.3. The formulation

Several studies have shown that the placebo response may be affected by the presentation or route of administration of the drug. For example, in a study on pain relief, different colours (red, green, blue, and yellow) of placebo were compared for their analgesic efficacy. The order of analgesic potency was red > blue > green > yellow (Figure 13.1).

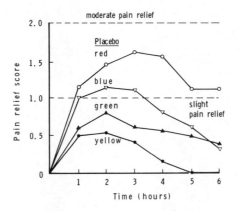

Fig. 13.1. The effect of the colour of a placebo formulation on the analgesic effects of its administration. [Adapted from Huskisson (1974) *Br. med. J.* **iv**, 196–200, with permission.]

13.4. MODE OF ACTION OF PLACEBOS

The way in which placebos produce symptomatic relief is not known.

Recently there has been interest in the role which endorphins and enkephalins might have in the placebo response, but at present the position is quite unclear. It would be interesting, though, if placebos did act, at least in relieving pain, by psychological mechanisms which secondarily caused the release of enkephalins in the areas of the brain mediating pain sensation, thereby producing analgesia.

14 Drug development: the pharmaceutical industry and the regulatory authorities

Almost all the drugs mentioned in this book have been synthesized and developed by the pharmaceutical industry. Broadly speaking those drugs fall into two categories—those which are new and which have been developed through a long period of research and development, and those which are well known, out of patent, and which a pharmaceutical company may decide to formulate and market as a particular preparation. The standards of the pharmaceutical industry in regard to both of these types of preparation are high and regulated by law. Doctors and patients are dependent on high and predictable standards of quality of formulation and proper ethical evaluation of safety and efficacy.

At the time of writing (1983) the total cost of discovering, developing, and marketing a new drug which is pharmacologically and therapeutically innovative is in the region of £30–50 million. Considerable commercial risks are involved. At any point during the development process the drug might come to grief because of problems with safety, lack of efficacy, changes in therapeutic fashion, or a better competitor. The duration of a drug's patent from the time of its registration with the UK Patent Office is 16 years. Seven to nine of those years will be taken up with research and development, so that after marketing there will be 7–9 years left in which the company can recoup its investment and make a profit, some of which will be ploughed back into the research and development of another drug. That is why drugs cost what they do, why pharmaceutical companies are anxious to sell their drugs through various marketing techniques such as advertising and the drug representative, and why, when a drug's patent expires and other formulations are marketed by competitors, the price often drops considerably.

14.1. DRUG DISCOVERY

Drug discovery comes about in several ways.

14.1.1. As a development from herbal or traditional remedies

Examples are the isolation of morphine from the poppy (*Papaver somniferum*) and the subsequent synthesis of related analgesics, the isolation of digitoxin and digoxin from foxgloves, and of atropine from the deadly nightshade (*Atropa belladonna*) and the subsequent development of related anticholinergic drugs.

14.1.2. Serendipity plus hard work and good sense

Alexander Fleming's observation of the effects of *Penicillium* mould on bacterial growth had a touch of serendipity about it, but his conclusions about the observation revealed the mind of a man of an observant and inquiring nature. The development of penicillin into a therapeutic agent 14 years later by Florey, Chain, and Heatley is an excellent example of applied science at its very best.

Another form of serendipity is the discovery of a useful effect as a side effect of the original effect desired. Clonidine was originally tested as a nasal decongestant when it was found to lower blood pressure. The hypoglycaemic effect of sulphonamides in patients being treated for typhoid fever led to the development of the oral sulphonylurea hypoglycaemic drugs.

Sometimes faulty reasoning leads to a lucky discovery. In the early 1940s Svartz in Sweden reasoned that rheumatoid arthritis, which was thought to be an infective disease, would respond to a molecule containing a sulphonamide with a salicylate as an anti-inflammatory agent. She therefore synthesized sulphasalazine (see Pharmacopoeia) but it had no effect in rheumatoid arthritis. However, a rheumatoid type of arthropathy sometimes occurs in patients with ulcerative colitis, and the therapeutic efficacy of sulphasalazine in ulcerative colitis was noted when those patients were given the drug. Further study of sulphasalazine has yielded another drug (see section 14.1.4 below).

14.1.3. Empirical chemistry coupled with good pharmacology

To date this has been the most productive process of discovery. One takes a 'reactive' molecule, chemically alters it on the basis of known structure/activity relationships, on an intuitive hunch, or out of curiosity. One then tests its pharmacological activity in a number of carefully chosen pharmacological screening tests for some sort of pharmacological activity. If some activity is found, refinement of the molecule is carried out and a new drug may result. It is reckoned that several thousands of compounds are synthesized and screened for every one which appears as a new entity worthy of clinical testing.

Usually in this process there is a chemical, biological, or pharmacological starting point. For example, many synthetic penicillins and cephalosporins have been developed in this fashion.

14.1.4. Metabolites of existing drugs

Sometimes active metabolites of drugs (see Chapter 3) are found to have therapeutic advantages over the original parent compound. For example, paracetamol is the main metabolite of phenacetin and is effective as an analgesic but does not cause renal damage; chlordiazepoxide is metabolized to a variety of other active benzodiazepines which have shorter actions than chlordiazepoxide itself—this has led to the introduction of drugs such as oxazepam; the active metabolite of procainamide, N-acetylprocainamide, is an effective anti-arrhythmic drug but does not cause the lupus-like syndrome that can occur with procainamide; the example of sulphasalazine mentioned above is another case, since sulphasalazine is metabolized to 5-aminosalicylic acid and sulphapyridine, the former being the active therapeutic moiety and the latter causing the adverse effects—5-aminosalicylic acid is now being used in the treatment of ulcerative colitis.

14.1.5. Rational molecular design

This is the approach to drug discovery and development of the future. Take the development of L-dopa and peripheral dopa decarboxylase inhibitors. The sequence was as follows:

1. The discovery of dopamine in the brain and the suggestion that it was a neurotransmitter (1957).
2. Pathway of dopamine synthesis already known.
3. Localization of dopamine in the basal ganglia (1958).
4. Reserpine already known to produce Parkinsonian-like symptoms.
5. The discovery that reserpine depletes brain dopamine in animals (1958).
6. The discovery that dopamine was deficient in the brains of patients with Parkinson's disease (1960).
7. The administration of the dopamine precursor, L-dopa, to patients with Parkinsonism, initially in too low a dose (1962) but later in therapeutic doses (1967).
8. The recognition that many of the adverse effects of L-dopa were due to its peripheral decarboxylation to dopamine.
9. The use (1967) of already available peripheral dopa decarboxylase inhibitors which do not enter the brain, thus diminishing the peripheral adverse effects of dopamine, and allowing the use of lower doses with the same effect on the brain as higher doses without the use of the inhibitors.

The discovery of β-adrenoceptor antagonists by modification of the structure of isoprenaline, and of histamine (H_2) receptor antagonists by modification of the structure of histamine, represent other examples of the rational approach to drug development.

14.2. DRUG DEVELOPMENT

Once a new chemical entity has been discovered it has to be put through the developmental process.

14.2.1. Pre-clinical pharmacology and toxicology

The potential drug undergoes extensive pharmacological testing *in vivo* in animals, and on *in vitro* preparations, so that as much as possible may be learnt about those of its properties which will be of importance in its therapeutic application, and about its dose-related adverse effects. At the same time studies of its pharmacokinetic properties are carried out in animals. It undergoes acute and chronic toxicity testing in animals, so that its toxicological properties may be defined in a rough dose–response fashion at various multiples of the proposed human dose. The duration of this toxicological testing is geared to the likely duration of therapeutic use. Similarly the routes of administration used are related to those likely to be used in man.

In addition at this stage special testing, such as mutagenicity and carcinogenicity testing, tests of the effects on fertility and reproduction, and teratogenicity testing may be required.

14.2.2. Clinical testing (volunteer studies)

At some point during the pre-clinical toxicological testing programme a decision will be made that enough is known about the safety of the drug to allow it to be given to healthy volunteers, if that is appropriate (while one would give, for example, a new diuretic, β-adrenoceptor antagonist, or benzodiazepine to healthy volunteers, one would not give a new cytotoxic drug). The drug's pharmacokinetic behaviour is studied following single and multiple doses, and if it has measurable effects in healthy people (e.g. anticholinergic drugs, histamine (H_2) antagonists, β-adrenoceptor antagonists) the human pharmacology can also be monitored. Adverse effects are also recorded, and its general tolerance and clinical, bio-chemical, and haematological toxicity assessed.

14.2.3. Phase I clinical studies in patients

These early studies concentrate upon the clinical pharmacology of the drug, its short-term safety, its promise of efficacy, its pharmacological effects, and its pharmacokinetics in disease. These early studies will also provide information as to the likely effective dose. These studies are searching and scrupulously monitored.

14.2.4. Phase II clinical studies in patients

In these studies one gathers further evidence of safety and efficacy in larger numbers of patients (see Table 9.7) with further attention to dose-ranging and tolerance. Although monitoring for adverse effects and efficacy is still extremely important, the intensity of investigation is a little less at this stage, particularly in so far as invasive investigations are concerned.

14.2.5. Phase III clinical studies in patients

These are full-scale clinical trials (see Chapter 15) which, if successful in demonstrating safety and efficacy, will precede marketing. The numbers of patients studied are usually larger still (Table 9.7), and although careful monitoring is still carried out, the number of investigations is less and their intensity more relaxed than in Phases I and II.

14.2.6. Marketing

If all is well, and the regulatory authority is convinced about quality, safety, and efficacy, the drug will then receive its product licence and be marketed. This is accompanied by advertising to the profession through the mail and the medical press, by visits to doctors and pharmacists by the company's representatives, and by promotional meetings for doctors.

14.3. POST-MARKETING ASSESSMENT

As sales of the drug increase, post-marketing assessment gradually takes place, although there is no formalized routine. Articles start to appear in medical journals on various aspects of the use of the drug, the regulatory authority and other bodies receive notification of adverse effects (see Chapter 9), and the profession gradually makes up its corporate mind about the overall safety and efficacy of the drug. In fact it takes a long time for a drug to find its eventual place in therapeutic practice and, if it is a good drug, for its full potential to be appreciated.

Medical practitioners may be involved in this process of post-marketing surveillance and assessment at all sorts of stages. The pharmaceutical industry employs suitably qualified medical practitioners to help plan and execute clinical studies. Clinical pharmacologists both in industry and in academic departments are commonly involved in Phase I and Phase II studies, and sometimes in Phase III studies. Those practitioners who regularly deal with the patients for whom the drug is relevant, whether in hospital or in general practice, will often be involved in subsequent early clinical investigations. Later on all medical practitioners who may be in a position to prescribe the drug will have a chance to assess the safety and efficacy of the drug for their own particular patients.

14.4. ADVERTISING

The advertising of a drug plays an important part in disseminating information about the drug to medical practitioners. Unfortunately, most of the drug advertisements in the medical press are an insult to the knowledge and scientific sensibility of their readers. It would be better if they contained more medical and scientific information and fewer slogans, although doubtless market research would reveal that it is the slogans which sell the drugs. Read advertisements critically, question drug representatives carefully about their claims, try to assess the claims of clinical trials (see Chapter 15), and whatever you do, do not automatically prescribe the newest drug. Always ask:

Is this drug generally safe?
Will it be safe for this particular patient?
Is it efficacious, and if so is it *more* efficacious than an existing drug about which more is known?
If it is equally efficacious is it safer?

One of the reasons for scientific training in medicine is to allow doctors to make up their own minds critically about the answers to such questions.

14.5. REGULATORY AUTHORITIES

Throughout the world, and particularly in the 'developed' countries, there exist drug regulatory authorities, whose task, to a greater or lesser extent, is to ensure that drugs are of acceptable quality, efficacious, and within given limits safe.

In the United Kingdom the responsibility for ensuring the quality, safety, and efficacy of drugs lies with the Health Ministers responsible for the populations of England, Wales, Scotland, and Northern Ireland. These ministers constitute the Licensing Authority, and it is this Authority which actually issues the various licences and certificates for drugs, and with whom the statutory legal responsibility rests.

The Licensing Authority is served by a civil service department known as the Medicines Division of the Department of Health and Social Security (DHSS). This Division is composed of administrative staff, pharmacists, and doctors, to whom all regulatory matters concerning medicines are referred.

The Medicines Division also serves the Committee on Safety of Medicines (CSM). This Committee is composed of a number of medical experts covering a wide spectrum of medical knowledge, and serving both on the main Committee and on a number of expert subcommittees. The CSM advises the Licensing Authority on all matters referred to it, and in practice it is the CSM to which the medical profession looks for guidance and assurance about the quality, safety, and efficacy of drugs.

The CSM reviews the evidence supplied to it by the pharmaceutical industry and advises the Licensing Authority on the issuing of certificates and licences. For example, it can advise the Authority that a drug may be licensed for clinical trial (i.e. Clinical Trial Certification), although the Authority itself can speed up drug development by issuing Clinical Trials Exemption certificates for new drugs if there appear to be no problems from the results of pre-clinical studies.

More important, however, is the role of the CSM in advising the Licensing Authority whether or not to grant a *Product Licence* for a new drug, based on its assessment of the drug's quality, safety, and efficacy.

The CSM is also responsible for post-marketing surveillance (at present mainly carried out through the Yellow Card reporting system, see p.153), for encouraging doctors to report adverse reactions, and for communicating with doctors about current problems in drug therapy (e.g. through its 'Current Problems' leaflet, which is issued at intervals and sent to all registered practitioners, and occasionally by a special letter about an urgent, serious problem).

Every practitioner is, sooner or later, going to receive such communications and may be in a position to report problems to the CSM through the Yellow Card system, and it is as well to have some idea of the way the system works.

14.4.1. Local drug and therapeutics committees

Practically all District Health Authorities in the UK have a Drug and Therapeutics Committee which advises on local prescribing policy, disseminates information on drug matters, and advises the Health Authority on drug costs and economics. Such committees may also sometimes take responsibility for certain research into matters concerning drugs.

On these committees serve physicians, surgeons, nurses, pharmacists, and administrators, who together help to formulate local policies suited to local needs.

14.4.2. Drug information

Many Regional Health Authorities have set up their own drug information services, staffed by pharmacists. Drug information pharmacists are responsible for collecting, collating, and disseminating information about all aspects of drug use, often in collaboration with an academic department of clinical pharmacology. They may be consulted by any doctor about any drug-related problem.

15 Clinical trials

Medicines should be effective. In other words, they should alleviate a symptom, or ameliorate or cure a disease. In an individual the efficacy (or benefit of treatment) should outweigh the potential hazard (the risk) and the decision to use a drug depends on assessing the benefit:risk ratio.

Experience has shown that clinical impressions of the efficacy of treatments can be misleading, partly because of bias on the part of both doctors and patients in favour of the treatment, and partly because of the placebo response (see Chapter 13). The dangers of having ineffective medicines on the market are that they may be hazardous, that really effective treatment may be denied the patient, and that time and resources may be wasted.

The clinical trial is a means whereby the efficacy of a drug may be tested. It may also give some guidance to the risks involved, but usually this is not the primary consideration.

In general the more predictable and clear-cut the outcome of an illness or disease, and the more efficacious the therapy, the easier it is to demonstrate that efficacy. For example, the effect of benzylpenicillin in the treatment of pneumococcal pneumonia is dramatic and easy to demonstrate. However, dramatic effects of this kind are rare in therapeutics, and most treatments require a formal trial of some sort. This is especially important in the treatment of diseases with an uncertain outcome in the individual (e.g. mild hypertension, myocardial infarction, stroke), and in cases where treatment may improve outcome only slightly (e.g. the use of β-adrenoceptor antagonists to reduce the incidence of sudden death after myocardial infarction, or the use of low-dose subcutaneous heparin to prevent deep venous thrombosis and pulmonary embolism after myocardial infarction). In such cases the doctor can never be sure that his treatment is doing any good in the individual patient—for example, if a patient's blood pressure is lowered there is a *chance* that his outlook will be improved, but one never knows. In such circumstances the rationale for therapeutic action will depend entirely upon the results of carefully designed and carefully executed clinical trials.

It is also important never to assume, simply because a treatment seems logically right, that it is either efficacious or safe. This point is underlined, for example, by the failure of paediatricians to appreciate, until it had been used for some years in premature babies, that 100 per cent oxygen therapy in incubators was associated with the occurrence of retrolental fibroplasia.

15.1. DEFINITION OF A CLINICAL TRIAL

A clinical trial of a drug in a patient has been defined in the UK Medicines Act of 1968 as an investigation or series of investigations which:

(a) consists of the administration of one or more medicinal products by, or under the direction of, a doctor or dentist to patients where
(b) there is evidence that the products have effects which may be beneficial to the patients and
(c) the administration is for the purpose of ascertaining whether, or to what extent, the products have those or any other effects, whether beneficial or harmful (i.e. assessment of efficacy and risks).

This definition is specifically designed to cover trials of drugs in patients. It could be extended to include, for example, therapeutic *procedures* (such as a surgical operation) and volunteer trials in which benefit would not be expected, or indeed required.

15.2. THE CONDUCT OF A CLINICAL TRIAL

We cannot emphasize too strongly that the reliability of the conclusions based upon the results of a clinical trial depend entirely upon the care with which the trial is designed, carried out, and analysed. Many clinical trials are poorly designed, carried out with insufficient attention to detail, and analysed inappropriately. Publication of the results of a clinical trial in a medical journal does not necessarily guarantee their validity.

As experience of clinical trials has increased over the last 50 years or so, certain principles have come to be recognized as being important in regard to the conduct of such trials. These principles are related to:

1. The aims of the trial.
2. Its design.
3. The drugs to be tested.
4. The subjects to be studied.
5. The analysis and interpretation of the results.
6. Ethical considerations.

A checklist of the important facets of each of these considerations is given in Table 15.1, and we shall discuss the conduct of clinical trials under those headings, as if we were designing and conducting a clinical trial.

Table 15.1   *A checklist of factors to be considered when designing and evaluating clinical drug trials*

---

1. *Aims*
Should be few and simple
End-point should be carefully defined
Pilot study

2. *Basic design*
Choice of subjects
Choice of controls
Randomization
Blindness
Placebos
One or more centres
Prospective or not
Methods of assessment
Records

3. *Subjects*
Numbers
Controls
Inclusions and exclusions
Disease characteristics
In-patients or out-patients
Age and sex
Race
Other diseases or drugs

4. *Drugs*
Prescribing characteristics
'Run-in' and 'wash-out' periods
Compliance
Other therapy

5. *Analysis and interpretation*
Appropriate statistical tests
A priori hypotheses
Exclusions from analysis
Intermittent analysis
Statistical versus clinical significance
Extrapolation to other populations

6. *Ethics*
Invasive techniques
Placebos
Informed consent
Children
Correct design
Control of ethical problems

15.2.1. Aims

The aims of the trial should be carefully formulated before embarking on any other aspect. It is generally best to ask one or two specific questions, and to design the trial to answer those questions and those questions only. Usually the main aim is to answer the question 'how effective is this therapy in this condition, compared with another therapy or no therapy at all?' If one tries to answer too many questions in one study then the trial design becomes more and more complex and organization becomes difficult. Even if such a study is well organized there may be difficulty in interpreting the data, as in the Multiple Risk Factor Intervention Trial, a large and complex trial carried out in the USA to assess the benefit of a multifactorial therapeutic strategy called 'stepped care' on the mortality from coronary heart disease. The study involved 12 866 men and was operationally successful, but no difference was found in mortality in the treated group compared with controls. The trial group concluded that the likeliest explanation for the lack of difference was that some of the measures in the programme reduced mortality but that the benefit was annulled by an increased mortality from other factors. A trial of a single therapeutic measure would at least have demonstrated the effect of that one measure.

In addition to assessing the efficacy of a particular treatment a drug trial will also be designed to assess, however inadequately (see Chapter 9), the benefit:risk ratio for the treatment, at least by measuring the incidence of adverse reactions. Sometimes, however, the aim is more circumscribed, such as the determination of the most appropriate dosage regimen—for example, in the treatment of urinary tract infections one might compare a 10-day course of low-dose antibiotic treatment with a 3-day course of high-dose treatment. Whatever the aim of a trial, its formulation will also involve a careful decision about the exact end-point to be measured.

Sometimes it is desirable to evaluate the feasibility of a trial by a *pilot study* before embarking on the full-scale trial. In a pilot study a small number of patients may be studied without recourse to blindness (see below). The main aim of a pilot study is to pinpoint problems with the trial design, and so to help in designing the formal study.

15.2.2. Basic design

(a) Subjects to be studied

See below, section 15.2.3.

(b) Control subjects

See below, section 15.2.3.

(c) Randomization

The purpose of randomization is to eliminate bias, for example to avoid recruiting patients who are different in some respect to one treatment group and not to the other. Randomization should not be carried out until immediately before treatment begins. There may therefore be a delay between the time when the patient is approached and asked to take part and the time of randomization. Sometimes this delay can be useful—it may allow the patient to have second thoughts about participating, or it may allow the investigator to have second thoughts about admitting the patient to the study (e.g. if he feels the patient's compliance will be poor). Once randomization has occurred the investigator is committed to including that patient's data in the final analysis (see below under analysis of results).

Simple methods of randomizing can be designed using, for example, published tables of random numbers, but whatever technique is used certain principles must be observed. Firstly, the order in which the subjects are to be allocated to the different treatment groups when they are recruited should be decided *before* the trial starts. Code lists should be drawn up so that the main investigators may be kept blind to the treatment an individual is receiving, but so that at the same time the treatment an individual is receiving can be readily discovered at any time by breaking the code. Secondly, the code used to identify treatments should be such that if the code has to be broken the knowledge of what treatment a patient was taking does not yield information about the treatments other patients are taking. For example if two separate treatments are coded 'A' and 'B' then as soon as the code for one patient is broken the code for every patient is broken automatically. Thirdly, it is best if the information on which patient is to receive which treatment is left to one person, say the pharmacist holding the tablets or some trial co-ordinator. Then, for example, a telephone call would be made to the co-ordinator and he would issue instructions as to treatment, e.g. 'Give this patient treatment number 34'. Only he knows what treatment 34 is, and his choice is randomly predetermined. All this may seem excessively tedious, but the outcome of a trial may depend on the success with which randomization is carried out and blindness maintained. The use of stratification to try to minimize chance differences between randomly allocated groups is discussed below, section 15.2.3(b).

(d) Blindness

Blindness in a trial means that the individual (investigator or patient) does not know what treatment is being administered. The purpose of blinding the investigator is to eliminate bias. For example, an investigator who knows what treatment the patient is taking may in some way influence a measurement or an outcome by his own actions in a fashion such as to shift the outcome in one way or another. Such bias may occur both consciously and unconsciously. Only if he is blind to the treatment can the investigator have full confidence in his own judgement of a patient's progress. The purpose of blinding the patient is to eliminate the differences in responses that can occur because of differences in the patient's expectation of what a particular treatment, or no treatment, may do. For example, a patient supposedly receiving a pain-killer and expecting relief of pain may report an effect of pain relief in excess of the true effect.

A trial may be *single-blind* (i.e. the patient does not know what treatment he is receiving), or *double-blind* (i.e. neither the patient nor the investigator knows what treatment the patient is receiving) and the latter is generally preferable. In the double-blind trial some investigator other than those directly involved in observing the patient, must hold the treatment code (see 15.2.2.(c), above).

Sometimes it may be difficult to keep the investigator blind. For example, it is impossible for an investigator comparing the effects of a β-adrenoceptor antagonist with those of a placebo to be blind to the obvious clinical effects of the former (e.g. bradycardia). In such cases it may be possible for the results of some of the objective measurements to be assessed by a different investigator who does not see the patient and who *can* therefore be kept blind to the treatment.

By a similar token it may sometimes be difficult to keep the patient blind to the treatment, if it has a distinctive adverse effect (e.g. drowsiness with antihistamines, discolouration of the urine by rifampicin).

(e) Use of placebos

Placebos are used in order to achieve blindness. It is important, therefore, that placebos be made to match the active treatment as closely as possible. This means that the placebo formulation should as far as possible be of the same size, shape, colour, texture, weight, taste, and smell as the active formulation.

If two different doses of an active drug are being compared then the differences in the numbers of tablets must be balanced by placebo tablets. If two different formulations are to be compared then each must be administered at the same time as the placebo form of its counterpart (the so-called 'double dummy' technique).

(f) Number of centres

Ideally a clinical trial should be carried out in one place only, in order to minimize variations in population, and variations in investigators' techniques, and to avoid the problems of communication, collection of data, and follow-up. However, because the need for adequate numbers of patients in a trial overrides everything else except the elimination of bias, it is often necessary to involve more than one centre in order to obtain sufficient numbers of patients. Large numbers, and therefore multicentre trials, may be necessary when studying a rare disease, or when the effect one is looking for is a small one albeit occurring in many patients, or when the number of patients in whom an effect can be expected is small. As an example of the last problem consider the influence of drugs on the rate of pulmonary embolism due to deep venous thrombosis after myocardial infarction. Although the effect of a treatment (e.g. low-dose subcutaneous heparin) may be large (say a 50 per cent reduction in incidence) the actual numbers of patients suffering a pulmonary embolism is very small compared with the number suffering a myocardial infarction. Thus very many patients with myocardial infarction must be studied before enough cases of pulmonary embolism occur for even a large effect to be detectable.

In multicentre trials the desirability of asking only one or two questions and of making those questions simple ones becomes more obvious. For example, in a study of the effects of a β-adrenoceptor antagonist in patients who have had a myocardial infarction one might simply ask the question 'Does treatment with a β-adrenoceptor antagonist for one year after myocardial infarction result in a reduced death rate?' With an easily detectable end-point, and simple, but carefully applied selection criteria, such a study could readily be organized among a large number of centres, and be expected to produce an answer in a relatively short space of time, even though several thousands of patients might have to be recruited.

(g) Prospective design or not?

Clinical trials designed to evaluate the efficacy of *new* drugs are always prospective. In other words, the characteristics of the population to be studied are identified before the study begins, and the results of treatment are observed thereafter. For example, if one randomized all patients with heart failure to treatment with either digoxin or a new positive inotropic drug, and then studied the outcome over the following 6 months, that would be a prospective trial.

It is possible, however, to study aspects of existing treatments by methods other than that of the prospective clinical trial, for example by a case-control study. In such a study the outcome is first identified and then comparisons are made retrospectively between the characteristics of patients who did or did not have that outcome. Such studies have, for example, shown that lignocaine is beneficial in the management of ventricular arrhythmias after myocardial infarction, and that oral anti-coagulants can reduce the incidence of reinfarction in patients who have had a myocardial infarction. Studies of this kind may be carried out some time after the introduction of a drug therapy to get some idea of its place in the overall management of the disease, or to evaluate adverse effects (see Chapter 9, p.156).

Case-control studies are cheap and easy to carry out. However, it is not possible to ensure random allocation to treatment groups, or blindness, and the results may be less reliable than those of a randomized prospective trial. Nevertheless the results of a case-control study may prompt a proper prospective trial in order to confirm the original findings and to extend investigation of the problem.

(h) Methods of assessment

Methods of assessment may be *subjective* or *objective*. Investigators often feel that subjective ('soft') data are of less value than objective ('hard') data. However, subjective assessments may be essential (for example, in studies of anti-depressants), and if analysed appropriately may provide as much useful information as objective measurements. Although the patient's feelings will always be subjective it is sometimes possible to eliminate the investigator's subjective interpretation of the patient's feelings by the use of visual analogue scales, in which the patient might, for example, mark on a line the extent to which he feels happy or sad, tired or energetic (see Fig. 27.2).

Objective assessments, on the other hand, should not necessarily be regarded as incontrovertibly accurate. Assessment criteria should be shown to be reproducible in terms of within-subject, between-observer, day-to-day, diurnal, or other variability.

Of particular importance is the choice of the *scale* of measurement, since that influences the statistical technique to be used in later analysis (see section 15.5.5(a) below). Scales of measurement are of three kinds:

(i) Nominal scales
A nominal scale is one in which different attributes are codified. For example, one might code the time of day at which an event occurred as 1 = morning, 2 = afternoon, 3 = evening, 4 = night (the exact times of each period being defined). It is then convenient to record the data as frequencies.

(ii) Ordinal scales
Here some form of ranking is generally involved. For example, one might rank grades of consciousness from 0 to 4 on the basis of a patient's response to stimuli (see the scheme outlined in the chapter on self-poisoning, pp.566–7).

(iii) Interval scales
Here continuous measurements are possible, e.g. blood urea or plasma drug concentrations, white cell count.

(i) Records

The importance of keeping careful, simple, accurate records during a trial is obvious. Suitable forms for keeping such records should be compiled before the trial begins, and should contain reminders to the investigator of the questions to be asked and the routine to be followed in each case.

15.2.3. Subjects

(a) Numbers

Having enough patients in your study is, after elimination of bias, the most important consideration in a clinical trial. Before discussing how to decide on the number of patients you will need we must first introduce the statistical concept of the *null hypothesis*. Although the aim of a drug trial is generally to find out if there is a difference between different treatments, the statistical approach is to assume that there is *no* difference between the two treatments and then to test the validity of that assumption. The assumption that there is no difference is called the null hypothesis. If the results of the trial lead one to *reject* the null hypothesis it is then accepted that there *is*, or is likely to be, a difference between the treatments. It is important to appreciate this inverted thinking before tackling the question of numbers.

The number of patients necessary for a trial depends on three factors:

1. The expected difference in efficacy between treatments (often designated δ or θ).

2. The level of chance one will accept for the so-called *Type I* (or α) error. This is the error of *rejecting* the null hypothesis *incorrectly*. For example if a trial showed a difference between treatments at a probability value of $\alpha = 0.05$, one would have to accept that there was a 5 per cent ($\frac{1}{20}$) chance that the apparent difference was not a true difference. The value of 0.05 is, by convention only, the value which is usually taken as the upper limit of chance of a Type I error that one is prepared to take when rejecting the null hypothesis. If the value found on comparing results is *less than* 0.05 (e.g. 0.02), the null hypothesis is rejected, and the difference regarded as a true difference.

3. The level of chance one will accept for the so-called *Type II* (or β) error. This is the error of *accepting* the null hypothesis *incorrectly*. For instance, let us suppose that because of incorrect trial design too few patients had been recruited, and that the results of the trial showed no apparent difference between treatments where in fact a difference did exist, the incorrect conclusion that there was no difference would be a Type II error. The numbers studied would have been too small to pick up the real difference between treatments.

The level of probability for the Type II error is often more liberal than that for the Type I error. For example it might be set at 0.8, accepting that there is a 20 per cent ($\frac{1}{5}$) chance that the Type II error has been made. This is sometimes called the 'power' of a trial. As in the case of the Type I error, the choice of level at which the chance of error is accepted is arbitrary. When reporting trials with negative results it is important to report the power of the trial to detect a difference of a given size, and the exact confidence limits of one's measurements, so that a quantitative assessment can be made of the chance that the treatment really does not work, or is not different from the comparison treatment.

The smaller the difference between the results of two treatments, the more patients will need to be studied to have a reasonable chance of detecting that difference at given values of probability of Type I and Type II errors. If one can estimate the likely size of the difference (θ), and set arbitrary values of α and β, then one can calculate the minimum number of subjects required in the study to detect the difference between treatments one expects with the given probabilities of being correct. The exact algebra need not concern us, but we can take a practical example.

If we expect that treatment with an antidepressant will increase the response to treatment from 30 per cent (placebo group) to 50 per cent (active drug), i.e. an increase of 20 per cent ($\theta = 0.2$), and if we set $\alpha = 0.05$ (for a 'one-tailed' test, i.e. expecting a result in a specified direction), how many subjects would we need to study to be reasonably confident that if we detect a difference, then there really is a difference? The answer is that if we study 32 patients in each treatment group, a total of 64 patients, we will have a 95 per cent chance of being correct if the expected difference occurs. If we want to guard against the possibility that we will, by chance, detect no difference in such a study, when in fact there is a difference, and if we set β at 0.9, we will need to increase our numbers of patients to a minimum of 127 in each group.

Now suppose that we have a new antidepressant to test, and that it is considered unethical to withhold existing effective treatment from the 'control' group. We will therefore have to compare our new treatment with our existing treatment. In this case the expected relative benefit will be smaller, say a difference in response from 50 to 60 per cent ($\theta = 0.1$). If we set α at 0.05 and β at 0.9 as before we would have to study a minimum of 533 patients in each group to be reasonably sure that our final conclusion was correct.

Note that when making these calculations we assumed that the new treatment was better than the established treatment and calculated the numbers on the basis of a 'one-tailed' probability for α. In practice it is rarely possible to be sure of the direction of an effect when comparing two treatments and one generally therefore uses 'two-tailed' tests (i.e. making no assumptions about the direction of the effect). In our last example this would increase the number of patients required to 640 in each group.

These figures should emphasize firstly how important it is to plan carefully on the numbers of patients needed to be reasonably sure of getting an answer that is not by chance wrong, and secondly how difficult it can be to carry out a proper controlled trial. The problems of recruiting nearly 1300 patients with depression into a clinical trial would be enormous.

(b) Control subjects

Subjects allocated to a control group may receive no treatment at all, or a placebo. If no treatment is given the trial cannot be blind (see above) and control subjects, therefore, usually receive a placebo. In such cases the trial is called a 'placebo-controlled' trial. For ethical reasons it is sometimes not possible to deny a group of subjects treatment, and in such cases the control group is replaced by a group receiving some standard treatment with which the new treatment will be compared.

Control subjects are used to eliminate the effect of natural variability of the disease, since proper randomization should produce similar variability among control and treated subjects. However even the best randomization procedure cannot *guarantee* that chance differences between the groups will be avoided, although the bigger the groups the less likely there are to be chance differences. If it is considered important to match the groups in respect to particular characteristics (e.g. age, sex), then stratification can be carried out to ensure that like is being compared with like. Stratification can be done either before entry to the trial or, more satisfactorily, retrospectively at the analysis stage. Retrospective stratification involves splitting all the patients in a trial into several strata on the basis of say age and/or sex, and comparing the results for patients allocated to one treatment regimen with those allocated to the other within the same strata.

If the outcome of a trial can be easily measured, and can be expected to occur within a relatively short space of time, then variability can be reduced even further by using a 'cross-over' design. In a cross-over trial the patient takes one treatment during the first half of the study, and the alternative treatment during the second half. Patients are randomized to take one or other treatment first. A wash-out period between treatments may be necessary to avoid overlap effects. If more than two treatments are to be studied then similar cross-over designs may be used. One such design, commonly used, is the 'Latin Square' design. Take for example a study of the effects of three different treatments, A, B, and C. Ideally one would want to study the effects of these treatments given in every conceivable order, i.e. ABC, ACB, BAC, BCA, CAB, and CBA (with or without wash-out periods in between each treatment period). However, studying all possible combinations is cumbersome and requires more patients. If there are more than three treatments being studied the number of possible combinations increases alarmingly. The Latin Square design takes care of that. One writes down the treatments in the form of a square in which each treatment is contained once only in each row and column, for example:

I   A   B   C
II   B   C   A
III   C   A   B

One then allocates patients at random to protocol I, II, or III. The result of this design is that if the effect of say treatment A when studied in group I is consistently greater or smaller than its effect in Group II, even so the difference will not affect the overall mean results. Systematic variation between the groups is thus eliminated.

In cross-over trials the patient acts as his own control and the advantages are that fewer subjects may be needed to demonstrate an effect, since the random variability between subjects is avoided.

Occasionally the natural history of a condition is highly predictable, and the results of a new treatment can be compared with one's knowledge of the natural history. In this case the subjects in the comparison groups are said to be 'historical controls'. Historical controls can be used, for example, when the natural history is known with a fair degree of certainty, for example, when there is a high rate of fatality and the result of treatment is fairly large. The advantage of this kind of study is that all the control information is available before the study starts and all patients can then be given the new treatment. Thus nobody is denied the chance of potential benefit and it takes a shorter length of time to collect the number of treated patients required. However, the method of historical controls has certain disadvantages. Firstly, since all subjects receive the new treatment blindness is not possible. Secondly, incorrect comparisons may be made if the disease varies with time (obvious examples are scarlet fever and influenza), or if changes in other forms of management occur between the gathering of control data and the start of the new treatment (e.g. changes in the treatment of cardiac arrhythmias after myocardial infarction). It should be noted, therefore, that the circumstances in which such studies can be carried out with the confidence of obtaining a clear-cut result are very few, and restricted to treatments such as the use of penicillin in lobar pneumonia. However this approach has occasionally been used, for example because of ethical problems, and proved valuable. Thus the effects of cysteamine and acetylcysteine in limiting the extent of liver damage after paracetamol overdose were first compared with the outcome in patients who had been studied before the use of these treatments. Although these studies cannot be said to have proved beyond doubt the efficacy of these treatments the results are good enough to warrant the recommendation that acetylcysteine be given to selected patients following paracetamol overdose (see Chapter 32, p.576).

(c) Criteria for selection or exclusion

There are several factors influencing the selection of patients for inclusion in a trial or their exclusion from the trial.

Certain groups of individuals are generally excluded from clinical drug trials, unless the trial is designed specifically to study those individuals, for example pregnant women, children, and seriously ill patients. Patients at particular risk of an adverse reaction would also usually be excluded (e.g. asthmatic patients from a trial of a β-adrenoceptor antagonist, patients with peptic ulcer from a trial of a non-steroidal anti-inflammatory drug). This principle also applies to the avoidance of drug interactions.

There are specific problems about studying the elderly. Drug trials are frequently carried out in younger patients because of the difficulties of studying the elderly—they are less mobile, are likely to be on more drugs and to have other diseases both of which may interact with the treatment being tested, they are easily confused and their compliance may be poor. However it is the elderly who most commonly receive drugs, and unforeseen adverse effects may then occur. For example the anti-inflammatory drug benoxaprofen was found to be toxic, especially to the elderly in dosages which were relatively safe in younger patients; it was widely prescribed in the elderly before that was realized, since most of its earlier use was in younger patients. This was particularly important in the considerations leading to its withdrawal. If possible, therefore, one should try not to exclude elderly patients from drug trials and it is often worthwhile studying the data from elderly patients separately to try to pick up adverse effects early on.

Because poor compliance may reduce the power of a trial it is useful to try to identify poor compliers before randomization. This can be done by having a run-in period during which compliance is specifically studied. Poor compliers may then be excluded before randomization. This does not introduce bias. A run-in period can also be useful to allow the patient to decide whether or not he or she wants to be included in the trial, or is capable of meeting the demands of participation.

It is always important to be sure of the diagnosis before admitting a patient to a trial and one would exclude patients who did not fulfil certain pre-determined criteria of diagnosis. For example, one might define criteria for the diagnosis of myocardial infarction in terms of chest pain and ECG and plasma enzyme changes. Patients in whom the preset criteria were not fulfilled would not be admitted to a trial of, say, secondary prevention with aspirin.

(d) Disease characteristics

The choice of subjects for a trial may be determined by the characteristics of their disease.

(i) Severity

The value of treating moderate and severe hypertension has been demonstrated. Recently trials have been designed to test the benefit of treating mild hypertension.

(ii) Duration

It might be best to study an anti-diarrhoeal drug only in patients with diarrhoea of a more than a few days duration to eliminate the problem that the majority of acute diarrhoeal illnesses resolve quickly and spontaneously.

(iii) Failure to respond to other treatment

If the risks of treatment with a drug are likely to be considerable at first, and if one therefore wants to proceed cautiously, one might study only those patients in whom other treatment had failed. Examples include the use of captopril or minoxidil initially in the treatment of severe, refractory hypertension, or of bromocriptine in patients with Parkinsonism whose response to L-dopa had been poor.

(e) In-patients or out-patients

Some diseases can be studied only in in-patients (e.g. the prevention of cerebral arterial vasospasm after subarachnoid haemorrhage), while for others an in-patient study may be impracticable (e.g. oral hypoglycaemic treatment of maturity-onset diabetes). The choice will usually be straightforward.

(f) Age and sex

Differences in drug handling between the sexes and in different age groups (see Chapter 11) must be taken account of. It is best, if possible, first to establish the efficacy of a treatment in adults and then in older children before trying it in the very young. This does not apply, of course, to the treatment of a disease which is limited to the very young (e.g. the respiratory distress syndrome). The ethics of trials in the young are discussed below.

(g) Race

Occasionally a genetic factor may alter the nature of a disease, the nature of its response to treatment, or the chance of an adverse reaction (see, for example, Chapter 8 on pharmacogenetics).

(h) Complicating diseases or drugs

These are usually factors which lead to exclusions of patients from trials, as discussed above.

15.2.4. Drugs used

(a) Dosage regimens

The various features of routine dosage must all be carefully considered–they are formulation, dose, frequency of administration, time of administration, and total duration of treatment (see also Chapter 16 on prescribing). At the time the clinical trial is carried out the drug must be used to obtain the best possible effect, using the knowledge available at that time.

(b) 'Run-in' and 'wash-out' periods

It is sometimes important to wait some time after deciding that a patient is eligible for a trial before actually starting the formal treatment (the 'run-in' period). One may, for example, want to establish a set of pre-trial 'base-line' measurements in an individual, and to demonstrate their reproducibility. A run-in period may also be used in conditions which alter spontaneously with the passage of time while under observation, for example hypertension–it is well known that the blood pressure of a patient who presents with apparent hypertension may settle to within the normal range over a few weeks of simple observation and repeated measurement.

In cross-over designs a 'wash-out' period may be required during the trial to ensure that the effects of one treatment are not carried over into the next treatment period. For example if one were studying a drug with a very long half-time one would have to wait four or five half-times between treatment periods to be sure that there was no carry-over effect due to persistence of the drug in the body.

The use of the run-in period to study compliance, or to allow the patient to have second thoughts is discussed above.

(c) Compliance

The methods used for assessing patient compliance are outlined in Chapter 12. Careful consideration should be given to the best method in individual cases.

(d) Other therapy

The question of avoiding drug interactions has been mentioned above, but one has to consider what other drugs a patient may be allowed to take during a trial, and if possible to control their prescription. If therapy is complex this may be a factor to consider in stratification (for example, separately randomizing all patients taking thiazide diuretics).

15.2.5. Analysis and interpretation

These are complex subjects about which only a few points can be made here.

(a) Choice of statistical tests

All too often data are analysed using the wrong tests, such as parametric tests (e.g. Student's *t*-test) for discontinuous data (e.g. ordinal scores, see section 15.2.2(h) above), or *t*-tests for comparing sets of data with different degrees of variability. There are many different ramifications of statistical analysis, and it is wise, in the early stages of *planning* a trial (not when the trial has already started) to consult a statistician for advice on the design of the trial and its later analysis. When approaching the statistician one should be well prepared. He will want to know what you want to study, what your intended design is, and above all what the numbers are likely to be: how many patients you will be able to recruit and how many you expect to respond to one treatment and how many to the other (i.e. what is the likely size of the effect).

(b) A priori hypotheses

Before starting a trial one must formally state one's hypotheses, and when the trial is complete the data will be tested on the basis of those hypotheses. However, other questions will often arise, not based on properly formulated *a priori* hypotheses. If many such questions arise and are tested then, not surprisingly, from time to time statistically significant differences will crop up. This is because the more statistical tests you perform, the more likely it is that at least one comparison will be found to be statistically significant simply by chance. After all if a hundred comparisons are made at least five will be statistically significant at the 5 per cent level by chance alone! If the hypotheses thus tested were not formulated *a priori* (i.e. *before* the trial started) then it is necessary to be more rigorous about testing them. For example, if one were to analyse a set of data in terms of five different subgroups (e.g. male versus female, over-60s versus under-60s) one would be wise to reduce the acceptable value of α from 0.05 to say 0.01. One would not then be prepared to accept the hypothesis at a lower level of significance than 1 per cent. However, it is also wise in these circumstances to be flexible about one's interpretation of the data since there is always a chance that one might incorrectly reject a correct hypothesis by being too rigorous. One should therefore always be prepared to consider carrying out another trial specifically designed to confirm the new related hypothesis or hypotheses that had been generated by these apparently significant comparisons.

(c) Exclusions from analysis

Once an individual has been randomized to a treatment group in a study then even if he subsequently defaults from the study, for whatever reason, his case should be analysed as if he had continued with the treatment to which he was allocated. This is because one cannot guarantee that the reasons for default will be the same in two different groups, and the analysis of the remaining data may, therefore, be subject to bias. Unfortunately this approach reduces the power of one's study, since one will inevitably have to include in one's analysis of the effects of treatment data from patients who defaulted from treatment. However, that is the price one pays for avoiding bias. In order to minimize default one should at least do one's best to encourage good compliance (see Chapter 12).

Rarely it may be necessary to omit a patient from the analysis if it transpires after random ization that there has been a gross violation of the entry criteria. In such cases careful judgement may be necessary to decide whether the degree of violation of the criteria is sufficient to warrant exclusion from analysis, and if there is any doubt the patient should be included. When the results of a trial are published all such exclusions, with the outcome, should be reported. In Fig. 15.1 is shown a simple method for reporting data from clinical trials, including the outcome in patients who have been withdrawn.

(d) Intermittent analysis

Intermittent analysis of data as they accrue in a clinical trial is often desirable but great care must be taken in the application of such analysis. The chief purpose of intermittent analysis is to detect any beneficial or adverse effects of treatment as soon as possible so that the trial may be stopped if necessary. In this way both the risk of adverse effects and the number of patients from whom a useful treatment has to be withheld (the control group) may be minimized. However it must be remembered that by chance a beneficial effect of a treatment may appear to have occurred at some time during a trial and not be borne out by the final results. For this reason it is important that one's criteria for stopping a trial on the basis of an apparent interim beneficial effect should be more rigorous than one's criteria for accepting that there is a beneficial effect once the trial is complete. On the other hand if a clear *adverse* effect is seen to occur during the trial that might be grounds for stopping the trial. In this respect it is important to analyse the incidence of adverse effects in the elderly as a separate group since the apparent incidence of adverse effects may be diluted by the absence of adverse effects in younger patients.

There is a particular form of intermittent analysis called 'sequential' analysis in which one analyses the results for each patient as the trial progresses. When it becomes clear (and specific tests are available) that there is either a difference or no difference between treatments the trial is stopped. Such a procedure has the advantage that the number of patients to be studied can be kept to a minimum, but there are disadvantages—it is easy to miss small differences with this type of design, and when a difference is detected the size of the difference tends to be over-estimated. Sequential trials should be reserved for specific cases, particularly when one thinks that a large difference may occur in a short space of time.

(e) The difference between statistical significance and clinical significance

In a clinical trial it may be found that although the effect of a drug is *statistically* significantly better than placebo or the comparison treatment, the overall effect is very small. It may be that the *clinical* importance of such an effect is minimal, despite the statistical demonstration of a 'significant' effect. This problem is rare in drug trials but is an important

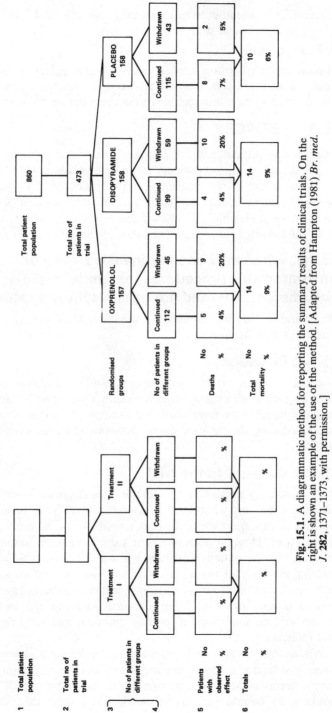

Fig. 15.1. A diagrammatic method for reporting the summary results of clinical trials. On the right is shown an example of the use of the method. [Adapted from Hampton (1981) *Br. med. J.* **282**, 1371–1373, with permission.]

principle to remember when assessing the practical importance of the results of any clinical study.

(f) Extrapolation

Clinical trials are often carried out on highly selected populations. No matter what the result, it would be wrong to assume that the same result would occur were a less highly selected population to be studied.

15.3.   ETHICS

This is a very difficult subject, but everyone who is about to be involved in a clinical trial, or whose patients are to be involved in someone else's trial, should be aware of the problems, and be prepared to make up his or her own mind about how those problems should be tackled or avoided. The Declaration of Helsinki was formulated by the 18th World Medical Assembly in 1964 to offer guidelines. The following are some of the issues involved.

15.3.1. When may one use invasive, risky or uncomfortable procedures that under ordinary circumstances would not be clinically indicated?

For example, the determination of the haemodynamic effects of a drug by cardiac catheterization.

15.3.2. Placebos

The use of a placebo in a randomized, double-blind, controlled trial of a new drug when an existing drug is already thought to be efficacious might be considered to be unethical. For example, in the evaluation of a new antidepressant should one use a placebo when an effective treatment already exists?

15.3.3. Consent to the trial

It is customary nowadays to seek 'informed consent' from any patient entering a trial, but what does 'informed consent' really mean? Can anyone but the most expert properly understand all the nuances surrounding a clinical trial? How far does one go in explaining them to the patient? (Not infrequently the patient's attitude will be 'I'll leave it to you doctor, the hospital wouldn't let you do this if it wasn't all right'). Can one really obtain 'informed consent' from the elderly, demented patient, from patients with mental illness, or from other patients who are not in a position to understand the explanations, such as children, and what rights do parents and relatives have?

Where the patient can be expected to understand at least some of the issues involved it is customary to discuss the trial with him, explaining in simple terms what is involved and what the risks are. If the patient is unlikely to benefit directly from the trial then that should also be explained. The patient should be given a brief written explanation of the trial, couched in simple terms and then given time to think it over. Later on he should have an opportunity to discuss the trial again with the investigator if he wants. It should always be made clear to the patient that there is no compulsion to take part in a trial and that his non-participation in the trial will not alter the quality of medical care he expects to receive. It should also be made clear that he may withdraw from the trial at any time if he so chooses. One should not try to convince a patient that he should take part in a trial.

Sometimes the timing of requesting consent may be important. One should try to avoid moments when the patient may be under pressure, for example when the patient is about to have an operation, or when a woman is in labour.

The legality and ethics of trials in children (anyone under the age of 18 years) are very difficult. However, ethical guidelines have been formulated by the 1978 Working Party on Ethics of Research in Children and have been accepted by the British Paediatric Association. The guidelines depend on four premises:

(i) That research in children is important for their benefit;

(ii) That research in children should not be carried out if the same investigation could be carried out in adults;

(iii) That research which involves a child and which is not beneficial to that child is not necessarily unethical or illegal;

(iv) That the benefit:risk ratio should be estimated.

In the context of the last premise risk is defined as 'negligible' (less than that run in everyday life), 'minimal' (risk questionably greater than negligible risk), and 'more than minimal'. Benefit is defined on the basis of 'therapeutic' research (of potential benefit to the subject) and 'non therapeutic' research (which may either potentially benefit others, or add to basic biological knowledge).

The guidelines are discussed in detail in the issue of the *British Medical Journal* for January 26, 1980 (pp.229–231).

(d) Study design

It is unethical to carry out an improperly designed trial. In effect, it is unethical to subject patients or volunteers to the various hazards and discomforts of a clinical trial if the trial is too badly designed to yield an answer to one's original question.

(e) The control of ethical problems

Various bodies may exert control of one kind or another on the ethics of a clinical trial:

(i) The Committee on Safety of Medicines

No drug should undergo a clinical trial in patients unless it has a Clinical Trials Certificate (CTC), or an exemption certificate (CTX), issued in the UK by the Licensing Authority (see p.202).

(ii) Ethics committees

All major centres of clinical research, and some pharmaceutical companies, have independent committees whose job it is to scrutinize clinical research proposals and advise as to whether or not they consider them to be ethical. Serving on such committees are lay members of the public as well as doctors, nurses, and administrators. While the approval of an ethics committee is not essential, and does not carry legal authority, one would be ill-advised to embark on a clinical trial without such approval. Guidelines for such committees are published in a variety of journal articles and books, e.g. the British Medical Association's *Handbook of Medical Ethics* (see the bibliography in Chapter 18).

(iii) Insurers

If a pharmaceutical company commissions a piece of research on one of its products, then it is important that it provides indemnification in case adverse effects occur during the trial (i.e. the company must be prepared to accept responsibility, short of negligence on the part of the investigator).

(iv) The law

Very little is clear about the influence of British law on clinical trials, since there have been very few cases tested in the courts. However there are two basic principles involved—those of consent and negligence. Of these, negligence has been the more widely tested, albeit in circumstances other than clinical trials, and the principle that a doctor is expected to exercise 'reasonable care' is well understood.

SECTION II

Practical prescribing

SECTION II

Surgical prescriptions

16 Principles of prescribing

Before writing a prescription there are several questions one should ask.

16.1. IS DRUG THERAPY INDICATED?

This question really has two parts:

(a) Is the intended treatment necessary?
(b) Is the potential benefit likely to be greater than the attendant risk?

Unnecessary prescribing is not uncommon, and the following are examples:

1. The prescription of broad-spectrum antibiotics (e.g. neomycin) for bacillary dysentery. It has been shown that such treatment confers no benefit, and may even prolong diarrhoea.

2. The prescription of cerebral vasodilators for patients with senile dementia. There is very little evidence that this type of drug confers any benefit at all, and there is evidence that they may do harm by diverting blood flow from compromised areas of the brain to areas already quite well perfused.

3. The prescription of vitamin and mineral (e.g. iron) preparations as 'tonics' in the absence of any evidence of vitamin or mineral deficiency. These preparations act only as placebos in such circumstances, and should be recognized as such by the prescriber.

The reasons for unnecessary prescribing are numerous, and include imprecision of diagnosis, the lack of time and resources to deal adequately with the sadnesses and anxieties of life (relevant to the wide prescribing of psychotropic drugs), and the need of patients for comfort and action. The question of placebos is dealt with in Chapter 13.

The question of relative benefit and risk arises once it has been decided that treatment is necessary and stems from the particular treatment contemplated in the particular patient. Because this question arises at every stage of decision-making in drug therapy we shall leave discussion of it to the end of this chapter.

16.2. WHICH DRUG?

If one has decided that drug therapy is indicated then one has to go through the process of deciding which particular drug to use. This involves further detailed questions:

16.2.1. Which therapeutic class of drug?

This is sometimes straightforward—for example, one would prescribe an antibiotic for an infection, an antidepressant for depression, and a bronchodilator for an acute attack of asthma. At other times, however, the decision can be more complicated—for example, in the treatment of congestive heart failure the choice lies among diuretics, positive inotropic drugs, and vasodilators, and in the treatment of hypertension among diuretics, β-adrenoceptor antagonists, and vasodilators.

16.2.2. Which group of drugs within the therapeutic class?

Take, for example, the treatment of an infection. The therapeutic class of drugs is the antibiotics, but within that class there will be a choice among several different groups, e.g. penicillins, cephalosporins, tetracyclines, aminoglycosides, macrolides, and many more.

16.2.3. Which particular drug in the group?

Finally when prescribing, the name of an individual drug has to be written on the prescription and a final choice must be made. With antibiotics, if one has chosen to use a tetracycline, for example, one will have the choice of tetracycline, oxytetracycline, minocycline, doxycycline, and others.

Is there a rational way of arriving at a best choice of drug? To some extent there may be. In some cases it may be a choice among equals. For example, there is little to choose among the large variety of thiazide diuretics available (e.g. bendrofluazide, cyclopenthiazide, chlorothiazide, hydrochlorothiazide, polythiazide, and several others). In such cases the prescriber is well advised to use the drug with which he is most familiar. In other cases, however, it may be possible to choose one drug in favour of another. The factors dictating one's decision are numerous and the following are examples.

(a) Pharmacokinetic considerations

1. *Absorption* For example, one might choose bumetanide rather than frusemide for a patient with congestive heart failure because frusemide may be erratically absorbed in congestive heart failure and bumetanide better absorbed. Of course, as an alternative, one could give frusemide intravenously, thereby circumventing the problem of absorption.

2. *Distribution* If an antibiotic is well distributed to a particular site where there is an infection then that antibiotic may be the antibiotic to use. For example, tetracyclines are concentrated in the bile, and lincomycin and clindamycin in bones.

3. *Metabolism* Drugs which are extensively metabolized may be less useful in patients with severe liver disease. For example, one might avoid using opiate analgesics in patients with hepatic cirrhosis.

4. *Excretion* Similar considerations apply in renal failure. One would usually avoid using chlorpropamide in patients with renal failure and choose instead, say, glibenclamide, a sulphonylurea which is mostly metabolized. If a tetracycline is to be used in a patient with renal impairment then doxycycline would be the drug of choice since it does not accumulate in renal failure.

(b) Pharmacodynamic considerations

Sometimes the pharmacological effect of a drug or group of drugs is appreciably greater than that of another. For example, the sulphonylurea drugs as a whole are more potent hypoglycaemic agents than the biguanides and are generally used as first-line treatment. If the resultant effect is not sufficient then a biguanide may be added but the additional effect will be small. In patients with myocardial infarction the positive inotropic effects of adrenoceptor agonists, such as dopamine or dobutamine, may be greater than those of cardiac glycosides, such as digoxin.

(c) Therapeutic considerations

(i) Features of the disease

If one knows, or has good reason to suspect, the identity of an infective organism then one would choose one's antibiotic appropriately. For example one might choose a penicillin, a tetracycline, or co-trimoxazole for a patient with bronchopneumonia since the likeliest organisms involved will be the pneumococcus or *Haemophilus influenzae*. Sputum culture with identification of the organism and of its sensitivity to different antibiotics will help in making the choice. Other factors may also help—one would avoid most tetracyclines in patients with renal impairment, penicillins in patients with penicillin hypersensitivity, and co-trimoxazole in patients with sulphonamide hypersensitivity.

The severity of the disease may influence one's choice of drug. For example mild pain will generally respond to aspirin or paracetamol, while more severe pain may require more potent analgesics such as codeine phosphate, or even morphine. Moderate hypertension often responds to either a diuretic or a β-adrenoceptor antagonist while more severe hypertension may require treatment with a combination of a β-adrenoceptor antagonist and hydralazine.

(ii) Co-existing diseases

For example, in the treatment of moderate hypertension one's choice lies between a thiazide diuretic such as bendrofluazide, and a β-adrenoceptor antagonist, such as atenolol. In a patient with left ventricular failure a diuretic is the logical choice, while one would choose a β-adrenoceptor antagonist in a patient with co-existing angina pectoris. In a patient with asthma one would generally avoid β-adrenoceptor antagonists, but if a patient with mild, intermittent asthma were likely to benefit greatly from such treatment then a cardioselective agent would be preferred. Selective β-adrenoceptor antagonists are probably also preferable in patients with diabetes mellitus.

(iii) Avoidance of adverse effects

A short-acting benzodiazepine, such as temazepam, may be preferred as a sedative to a longer-acting compound, such as nitrazepam, in the hope of avoiding excessive sedation during the day. In patients with drug hypersensitivity an alternative drug may be necessary. For example, one would use chloramphenicol to treat meningococcal meningitis in a patient with penicillin hypersensitivity, or trimethoprim to treat a urinary tract infection in a patient with sulphonamide hypersensitivity.

(iv) Avoidance of adverse drug interactions

In patients on warfarin one often needs to be careful in one's choice of other drugs. For example, aspirin and other non-steroidal anti-inflammatory drugs are to be avoided and drugs such as benorylate and diflunisal may be safer in treating arthritis, and paracetamol and opiate analgesics in treating pain; barbiturates and chloral derivatives are to be avoided as sedatives, and benzodiazepines and chlormethiazole to be preferred; tetracyclines, sulphonamides, and chloramphenicol are to be avoided in the treatment of infections and penicillins, cephalosporins and aminoglycosides, among others, to be preferred.

(d) Patient compliance

Sometimes a drug may be chosen simply because it can be taken once a day, in the hope that by minimizing the frequency of drug administration one may improve patient compliance (see Chapter 12). Thus one might choose once daily atenolol in preference to twice daily propranolol, once daily chlorpropamide in preference to twice daily glibenclamide or thrice daily tolbutamide.

16.3. WHAT ROUTE OF ADMINISTRATION SHOULD ONE USE?

Routes of administration of drugs are dealt with in Chapter 2. The route of administration may depend on the drug chosen in which case this question answers itself. However, sometimes the prescriber may choose a particular route of administration because it confers some particular therapeutic benefit.

For example, glyceryl trinitrate is most commonly given sublingually, since it is rapidly absorbed through the oral mucosa straight into the systemic circulation avoiding first-pass metabolism in the liver. It thus acts rapidly in relieving angina pectoris during an acute attack. However, it can also be applied as an ointment to the skin (usually the anterior chest), through which it is slowly absorbed over a prolonged period of time. In this way it can be used to *prevent* attacks of angina pectoris.

Indomethacin is usually given by mouth, but if there is gastric ulceration it may be given by suppository instead, in the hope of avoiding its direct adverse effects on the stomach.

The intramuscular route may sometimes be chosen to ensure compliance; for example, in the single dose treatment of gonorrhoea with intramuscular penicillin supplemented by oral probenecid, or in the regular treatment (once every 2–4 weeks) of schizophrenia with depot injections of phenothiazines such as fluphenazine.

The subcutaneous route may be chosen because it allows administration by the patient or nurse (e.g. heparin, insulin). In these cases the subcutaneous route also provides a more prolonged effect.

The intravenous route may be chosen in order to circumvent problems of systemic availability (e.g. i.v. frusemide in a patient in whom poor absorption results in a lack of diuresis in congestive heart failure).

16.4. WHICH FORMULATION?

There is a large number of different drug formulations for different circumstances. For example, oral formulations include tablets, capsules, granules, elixirs, and suspensions. Drugs for injection may come as lyophilized powders for reconstitution before injection, or as solutions ready for injection; solutions may come in single dose ampoules, single or multiple dose vials, and in half litre or 1 litre bottles for infusion.

Usually the drug is available in one form only and no choice is necessary. There are some exceptions, however, and we give a few examples here.

Aspirin is available in several different tablet formulations including soluble, buffered, and enteric-coated. In each case the aim of the formulation is to avoid the direct gastric irritation caused by using an ordinary formulation. However, for the treatment of acute pain the rapidly acting formulations (i.e. soluble and buffered aspirin) will be preferred, whereas for the treatment of the symptoms of chronic rheumatoid arthritis one might prefer to use an enteric-coated form.

Potassium salts are available in either slow-release formulations or as effervescent tablets which dissolve in water and are drunk. One's choice here usually depends on patient preference, but one might choose an effervescent formulation in a patient with gastro-intestinal hurry in whom the slow-release formulation might pass through the gut unabsorbed.

Iron salts are available as ordinary tablets for twice daily administration or as slow-release formulations for once daily administration. One would often choose the latter in the hope of improving patient compliance and diminishing adverse gastro-intestinal effects. However the iron in slow-release formulations is more erratically absorbed and one might choose the ordinary tablets in a patient whose iron deficiency was not being corrected by a slow-release formulation.

The acceptability of some preparations may influence their use. For example a child may prefer a pleasant-tasting suspension of paracetamol to a less pleasant elixir, while the elderly may prefer a tasteless solution of benorylate to tablets which they may find hard to swallow.

16.5. WHAT DOSAGE REGIMEN?

This question covers two aspects of treatment:

(a) What should the dosage be?
(b) How frequently, and when during the day, should the dose be given?

There are certain principles governing dosage regimens of drugs, and they depend on the pharmacokinetic and pharmacodynamic properties of the drug, certain characteristics of the patient, and the characteristics of the symptoms or disease being treated. Because each patient and each illness varies, dosage regimens also vary within limits to suit the individual case.

It is often forgotten that one of the fundamental tenets of pharmacology, the dose–response curve, demonstrates how effect varies with dose. For example it is the dose–response curve which determines the dose of frusemide in oedematous states, of hydralazine in hypertension, of diamorphine in the treatment of severe pain, of insulin in the treatment of diabetes mellitus. Because the nature of the dose–response curve varies from patient to patient, for reasons we may not understand, flexibility in dosage prescribing is essential.

Besides this essentially pharmacodynamic variability there is of course pharmacokinetic variability, i.e. differences in absorption, distribution, and elimination, often leading to wide differences in the plasma concentrations resulting from the same dose in different patients.

One must admit that precision in dosage is, in practical clinical circumstances, often a bit vague! How then does one go about tailoring a dosage regimen for an individual patient?

(a) Look up the dosage regimens recommended in a reliable source of information (see Chapter 18). These have been constructed through careful study and clinical experience.

(b) Consider the dose-related toxicity of the drug, i.e. does it have a low therapeutic ratio, the toxic dose being little more than the therapeutic dose (e.g. digoxin, phenytoin, lithium, gentamicin, warfarin)? If so, it will be necessary to take particular care not to overdose.

(c) Consider the dose–response curve for the patient, and where on the curve you are aiming for, and the possible variation of the dose–response curve with the illness, e.g. insulin requirements are lower in non-ketotic patients than in ketotic patients, neuroleptic requirements in previously untreated patients are lower than in patients on chronic treatment.

(d) Consider the characteristics of the patient, e.g. age, weight, and renal and hepatic function. Does any of these factors indicate a dose towards the extremes of the usual dosage range? If so, there are usually guidelines in the reference sources to help decide.

(e) Consider potential drug interactions. For example the dose of gentamicin in patients also receiving benzyl penicillin for infective endocarditis need not be as large as in patients with Gram-negative septicaemia because of synergy between the two antibiotics.

(f) Consider whether a loading dose is required. This is discussed in detail in Chapter 3. Conversely, consider whether one needs to start with a low dose and gradually increase to achieve a desired effect. Take for instance L-dopa combined with a peripheral dopa decarboxylase inhibitor (see p.696). Toxicity may occur readily if one starts with high doses and because the effective dosage range is so wide it is best to start at the lower end and slowly increase the dosage until the desired effect is achieved. The same applies to several other drugs, e.g. antihypertensives, oral hypoglycaemics, diuretics. In general, if in doubt, it is better to start at the lower end of the recommended dosage range.

When one has decided on and instituted one's dosage regimen there may still be room for improvement and the patient's progress should be monitored carefully for evidence that the treatment regimen is satisfactory. The different methods whereby the effects of drug therapy may be monitored are detailed in Chapter 7.

Frequency of dosage is usually fixed for a given drug and there is no need to make a decision. However, there may sometimes be circumstances which lead one to alter the frequency of administration. For example, although spironolactone may be given once daily, some patients complain of gastro-intestinal symptoms and benefit from splitting the dose into two parts, one to be taken in the morning and one in the evening. Occasionally the half-time of the drug in the individual may be crucial, as in the case of gentamicin when doses may have to be given eight-hourly or as infrequently as once every 24 or 36 h; in this case plasma concentration measurement guides one's therapy. In cases where symptomatic treatment is being given the frequency of symptoms may regulate frequency of dosage, as in the case of the use of glyceryl trinitrate in the relief of acute attacks of angina pectoris; some patients may need to take 10 or 20 tablets at different times during the day because of the frequency of attacks. The use of prednisolone in some diseases provides a special case in which the adverse effects of corticosteroids may be diminished by giving twice the usual daily dose but only on every alternate day.

Because it is thought that patient compliance with dosage regimens is improved by giving the drug only once a day one frequently tries to simplify dosage regimens in this way. Because of this some pharmaceutical companies have manufactured slow-release formulations which allow minimal frequency of administration. An example of one such preparation is that of slow-release aminophylline which provides theophylline plasma concentrations in the therapeutic range for several hours at a time and is particularly useful, for example, in preventing bronchospasm overnight.

Timing of dosage depends on several factors. Once-daily treatment is often most simply taken first thing in the morning, but for some drugs adverse effects may be minimized by administration last thing at night, as for example in the case of tricyclic antidepressants which, early on in treatment, may cause drowsiness and a dry mouth shortly after the dose, and cytotoxic drugs which may cause nausea and vomiting soon after administration. On the other hand potent diuretics, such as frusemide and bumetanide, are best given first thing in the morning to avoid the inconvenience of diuresis later in the day. Prednisolone is also best taken first thing in the morning in order to minimize its inhibitory effects on ACTH secretion by the pituitary and glucocorticoid secretion by the adrenal glands. The occurrence of symptoms often dictates the timing of dosage, as for example in the treatment of angina pectoris, or the use of antacids. Some drugs are best taken before food (e.g. most penicillins, whose absorption is impaired by food, and tetracyclines whose absorption may be impaired by calcium and other salts), while others may be better taken *with* food (e.g. aspirin, in order to reduce gastro-intestinal adverse effects, and griseofulvin whose absorption is improved).

16.5.1. Nomograms as guidelines to dosage regimens

A nomogram is a diagram in which the relationship among three or more variables is represented in the form of a number of straight or curved scales. These scales are so arranged that the value of one variable corresponding to given values of the others can be read off its scale by drawing straight lines intersecting the other scales at the appropriate given values.

Nomograms have been devised to help decide on dosage regimens of various drugs (notably digoxin, gentamicin, kanamycin, phenytoin, and theophylline). They have been devised from pharmacokinetic equations using variables whose values are the mean values estimated from population studies.

We cannot stress too heavily that while such aids may be useful as guides to the range of doses most likely to be therapeutically effective in an individual patient they should not be depended upon to give accurate predictions. If they are used they should be backed up by appropriate plasma concentration measurements (see Chapter 7).

16.6. WHAT SHOULD BE THE DURATION OF TREATMENT?

The duration of treatment depends on the nature of the disease or symptoms and to a great extent on collective experience.

At one end of the scale a single dose of aspirin may be sufficient to treat a headache, or a single dose of diamorphine sufficient to treat the pain of myocardial infarction. In the latter case further doses may be necessary but it is not likely that treatment will need to be continued for more than a day.

At the other end of the scale chronic therapy for the individual's lifetime is usually required for the treatment of diabetes mellitus, essential hypertension, hypothyroidism, pernicious anaemia, and several other diseases.

Difficulties and controversy often arise in relation to treatments of intermediate duration. For example in the use of cimetidine in the treatment of peptic ulceration, symptoms generally resolve in about a week and healing occurs within about 6 weeks; however, if treatment is then withheld there is an appreciable incidence of recurrence and it is not clear for how long one should continue treatment thereafter. This is particularly a problem in view of the current worries about the long-term toxicity of histamine (H_2) antagonists.

The duration of treatment of infections with antibiotics varies from infection to infection, and depends on the infective organism, the site of infection, and the response to treatment. For example, streptococcal tonsillitis and pneumococcal pneumonia might require treatment with penicillin for 7–10 days, non-gonococcal urethritis tetracycline for 10–21 days, and infective endocarditis due to *Streptococcus viridans* intravenous penicillin for up to 6 weeks. In the last case it is not clear what the minimum duration of treatment should be and it may be that treatment for 6 weeks is unnecessarily long. Gentamicin, given in conjunction with penicillin, is generally continued in this infection only for the first 10–14 days. Therapy of tuberculosis is very complex. Triple drug therapy, e.g rifampicin, isoniazid, and ethambutol, is usually given in the initial phase for 8 weeks, or until the organism's sensitivities are known. This regimen is used because it takes several weeks to culture the Mycobacterium and the risk of resistance to therapy is reduced by using several different drugs. Treatment is then continued with two drugs (e.g. rifampicin and isoniazid) for 9 months in pulmonary infections or 12 months in extrapulmonary infections. However, there are many different antituberculous regimens in use around the world, taking into account drug costs, patient compliance and the problems of delivery of medical care to the population, and resistance of the Mycobacterium to antituberculous therapy.

16.7. THE BENEFIT:RISK RATIO IN PRESCRIBING

It should have become clear from the above account that good prescribing is not an easy discipline to master. It requires detailed knowledge of the pathophysiology of disease, and of the clinical pharmacology of the drugs one intends to use.

Most difficult of all is the weighing up of the benefit:risk ratio in an individual. Every time one prescribes a drug which is potentially the least bit toxic one should try to balance the likely benefit against the risk. Some of the statistical aspects of adverse drug reactions are discussed in Chapter 9, and in the end it is those statistics which govern our evaluation of the risk. Sometimes such risks cannot be stated, but sometimes they can. For example, the incidence of marrow aplasia in patients taking phenylbutazone is from 1 in 30 000 to 1 in 100 000 and is at the higher end of the scale in the elderly and during prolonged therapy. So although phenylbutazone is a very effective non-steroidal anti-inflammatory drug it is not now recommended even for short periods of time, e.g. in the treatment of gout. The assessment of the potential benefit of a drug of this kind can be very complex. In the case of painful osteoarthritis other, less toxic, compounds are available for treatment, and the extent of symptomatic relief varies widely from patient to patient. Often one's appreciation of the potential benefit only comes *after* one has tried the treatment and assessed its effects.

To illustrate the difficulties which can arise in assessing the benefit:risk ratio take the following examples:

(a) In a patient with moderate left ventricular failure is the benefit which is likely to accrue from adding digoxin to the diuretic and other anti-hypertensive therapy likely to outweigh the risk of digoxin toxicity engendered by the renal impairment secondary to hypertensive renal disease?

(b) Is the benefit likely to be gained from a course of co-trimoxazole in treating a urinary tract infection in a woman who is two months pregnant likely to be outweighed by the unknown risk of teratogenesis in the fetus?

(c) Is the benefit to be gained from treating an old lady with giant cell arteritis with prednisolone likely to be greater than the risks of making her osteoporosis worse, of increasing the difficulty of treating her diabetes mellitus, and of exacerbating her hypertensive heart failure because of sodium and water retention?

Questions such as these can be extremely difficult to answer because until appropriate studies on benefit and risk are carried out we have no data to go on and one has to try to decide each case on its own merits.

However, by thoughtful prescribing one may be able to lessen the risks, and by following through the sequence we have outlined in this chapter one may be able to achieve one's aim of optimal therapy with minimal toxicity or adverse effects.

17 How to write a prescription

17.1. PRACTICAL PRESCRIPTION-WRITING

The common types of prescription are four in number:

1. Hospital prescriptions for in-patients.
2. Hospital prescriptions for an 'external' pharmacy.
3. Prescriptions in general practice.
4. Private prescriptions.

In all cases there are certain principles to be followed. A prescription should be a precise, accurate, clear, and readable set of instructions. The instructions should be sufficient for a nurse to administer a drug accurately in hospital, or for a pharmacist to provide a patient with both the correct drug and the instructions on how to take it.

The following information must be given:

17.1.1. The date

17.1.2. Identification of the Patient

(a) In hospital

Name, initials, and number. If there are two patients of the same name in the ward this should be clearly stated.

(b) For non-hospital pharmacies

Name, initials, and address. In all cases the *age* must be given for a child under the age of 12. Giving the age of an adult may sometimes be useful (e.g. for the elderly), but it is not essential.

17.1.3. The name of the drug

Preferably in capitals.

17.1.4. The dose of the drug

The following important points should be noted:
    (i) Quantities of 1 g or more should be written in grams, e.g. 2 g.

(ii) Quantities less than 1 g but more than 1 mg should be written in milligrams, e.g. 100 mg, *not* 0.1 g.

(iii) Quantities less than 1 mg should be written in micrograms, or nanograms as appropriate, e.g. 100 micrograms.

(iv) Do *not* abbreviate micrograms or nanograms (e.g. to μg or ng) since this may lead to prescribing errors.

(v) If a decimal point cannot be avoided for values less than one, write a zero before it, e.g. 0.5 ml, *not* .5 ml.

(vi) Use ml for millilitres.

(vii) For liquid oral medicines the dose should be stated as the number of mg in either 5 ml or 10 ml, since these are readily measured amounts, and special spoons are given to patients for measurement. If, for children, the dose of a drug is contained in less than 5 ml the pharmacist will dilute the preparation so that the volume to be given will be 5 ml.

(viii) For some drugs a maximum dose may need to be stated (e.g. ergotamine in migraine or colchicine in gout). For example, 'Ergotamine 1 mg at onset of attack and repeat every 30 minutes if necessary. Do not take more than 6 mg in one day or more than 12 mg in one week.'

17.1.5. Frequency of administration

This should be clearly indicated. Accepted abbreviations may be used (see below). For example:

Atenolol 100 mg once daily.
Amoxycillin 250 mg t.d.s.

Generally speaking the simpler the instruction the better. Patients outside of hospital are often unable to follow a rigid six-hourly or eight-hourly regimen and compromises have to be made. Sometimes it is worth telling patients what you mean by 'three times a day'. To most people 'three times a day' would mean 'with or after breakfast, lunch, and dinner'. Obviously whether or not that is optimal depends on the timing of the meals, and the pharmacokinetics of the drug. If it is important that dosage intervals be as near to 6 or 8 h as possible, that should be made clear to the patient.

In hospital the frequency of administration is determined by two factors:

(a) The demands of the treatment.

If, for example, you want to give gentamicin eight-hourly, then it must be given eight-hourly, and not as a haphazard three-times-a-day regimen. The times of administration must be clearly stated on the prescription chart, *but* the times should be chosen for maximum convenience to both patient and nursing staff. If intramuscular (i.m.) gentamicin is to be given it may be kinder to the patient to give the night time dose by i.v. infusion over half an hour instead.

Prescriptions for drugs to be given as required ('p.r.n.') should have exact instructions as to the maximum frequency, e.g. paracetamol tabs 2 p.r.n., not more than four-hourly.

(b) The nursing drug round

Drug rounds are held in some form, on most acute medical and surgical wards four-hourly or six-hourly and treatment should, if possible, be organized to fit in with those times. Remember that a drug round takes time (as much as 1–2 h in many cases) and the *actual* time at which a patient receives a drug may be different from the *notional* time of the round.

Every clinical student should take the opportunity of accompanying the nurses on a drug round. To see at first-hand the use of the prescription, the process of drug administration, the patient's response, and the nurse's problems is very revealing.

17.1.6. Route and method of administration

The route of administration should be clearly indicated, e.g. oral, sublingual, i.v., i.m., s.c. (subcutaneous), unless the route is obvious (.e.g. 'beclomethasone inhaler, 2 puffs four-hourly'). In hospital the method of giving a drug intravenously may need to be indicated separately. For example one may want to give the contents of a one-dose ampoule as a single undiluted injection, as an infusion in a small volume of saline (e.g. in an infusion burette) over a few minutes, or in a larger volume over a longer period of time. In some cases it may be necessary to indicate the precise rate of flow of a precisely specified solution of drug (e.g. dopamine, see Pharmacopoeia).

17.1.7. Amount to be supplied

In hospital the pharmacist will organize this. Many hospitals have a policy to supply drugs sufficient for a predetermined period on discharge, and a prescription written for drugs for the patient to take home after a stay in hospital will generally have to take account of that.

In general practice one should indicate the quantities of drugs you want dispensed. This may be done by indicating, for example, the precise number of tablets required, but it is often simpler to indicate the period of treatment. There is a space on the prescription form (see Fig. 17.1) for indicating the duration of treatment.

17.1.8. Instructions for labelling

In the NHS a drug container will be labelled with whatever drug name the practitioner uses on the prescription, whether it be an approved or a proprietary name (see below). The standard prescription sheet used in general practice (the FP10, see Fig. 17.1) contains the instruction 'NP' (*nomen proprium* or 'proper name'). If the prescriber does not want the

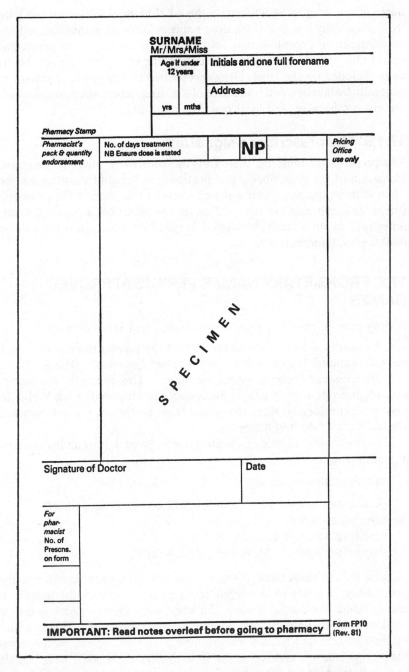

Fig. 17.1. The FP10—the prescription form used in the UK by general practitioners. [Reproduced with the permission of the Controller of Her Majesty's Stationery Office. Crown copyright.]

name of the drug to be written on the label he must strike out the letters 'NP'. Generally it is best if the drug name is included in the label although occasionally an exception may arise. Drugs given by private prescription need to be labelled 'NP' by the prescriber if he wants the name of the drug to be included on the label. Drugs prescribed by a hospital pharmacy will generally be labelled with the name of the drug, unless specific instructions are given otherwise, but local practices may vary.

17.1.9. The prescriber's signature

The prescription must be signed by the prescriber, must contain some indication of the prescriber's qualifications, and should show his address. Then if there are any queries the pharmacist can contact the prescriber. Private prescriptions are best written on the prescriber's personal headed notepaper or on a specially printed prescription form, in order to avoid doubts about authenticity.

17.2. PROPRIETARY NAMES VERSUS APPROVED NAMES

A drug may be called by one of several different kinds of name:

1. Its *chemical* name, whose form generally follows the rules issued by the International Union of Pure and Applied Chemistry. (IUPAC).

2. Its *approved* (official, or generic) name. This is usually the International Nonproprietary Name, recommended or proposed by the WHO, but may be some locally approved name (e.g. British Approved Name, or United States Adopted Name).

3. Its *proprietary* (brand-, or trade-) name, given to it by a pharmaceutical manufacturer.

Take the following example:

chemical name—4-amino-5-chloro-*N*-(2-diethylamino)ethyl-2-methoxybenzamide;
approved name—metoclopramide;
proprietary names—Maxolon®, Primperan®.

Since the chemical name is often, as in this case, unsuitable for routine prescribing, one has to use either the approved name or the proprietary name. Which should one choose? For some drugs the question is somewhat academic, since only one proprietary formulation exists. When a pharmaceutical firm produces a unique new drug their brand, which carries their proprietary registered name (trademark), is the only one available (e.g. cimetidine is available only as Tagamet®). Sometimes, on the basis of a commercial agreement, a new drug might be marketed by two different firms with two different proprietary names e.g. Bactrim® and Septrin®

(both co-trimoxazole) or Norpace® and Rythmodan® (both disopyr-amide).

Several proprietary formulations of the same chemical entity with one approved name may become available when the patent expires on a drug with a previously unique proprietary name. For instance, diazepam (approved name) was first marketed as Valium® (proprietary name). When the patent on Valium® expired the number of proprietary brands of diazepam multiplied. Tablet forms now available include Alupram®, Atensine®, Evacalm®, Solis®, and Valium®. When this happens prescribing and dispensing problems may arise. For example, if the prescriber writes 'cimetidine BP' or 'Tagamet', the patient will receive Tagamet®. However, if the prescriber writes 'metoclopramide BP' the pharmacist may dispense any formulation of metoclopramide he chooses, provided the formulation conforms to the description laid out in the BP (British Pharmacopoeia, see Chapter 18). Thus he might dispense Maxolon®, or Primperan®, or some other acceptable product, and would generally choose the cheapest variety available.

By writing the proprietary name the prescriber can ensure that a particular *formulation* of a drug is prescribed. However, in hospitals in the UK it is frequently the case that the hospital pharmacy stocks only one formulation, and even if the hospital doctor writes 'Primperan' on an in-patient prescription the pharmacist may dispense Maxolon®, or some other approved preparation of metoclopramide. For this reason it is generally best in hospital to prescribe drugs by their generic names.

There are certain advantages and disadvantages to the prescribing of drugs by their generic names as opposed to their proprietary names.

17.2.1. Advantages of prescribing by proprietary name

(a) Remembering names

Proprietary names are chosen by pharmaceutical companies because they are easy to remember, and catchy. They are often easier to remember than the corresponding generic name and may be shorter and easier to spell (compare, for example, 'Librium®' with 'chlordiazepoxide'). Furthermore, a single proprietary name will do when the formulation may in fact contain two or more drugs (compare, for example, 'Distalgesic®' with 'paracetamol and dextropropoxyphene'). This makes for ease of prescription and helps in communication with patients, who may have difficulty in remembering more complicated approved names.

(b) Quality of product

For some drugs a change in tablet excipients may have important effects on the absorption of the drug from the formulation. This has been demonstrated for drugs such as digoxin and phenytoin, and is an argument for prescribing such drugs by the same proprietary name every time for the same patient, so that variations in formulation do not lead to variations in systemically available dose. See also the discussion of formulations of lithium (pp.96 and 702).

(c) Continuity of treatment

Patients not infrequently become confused if the drug they are being given changes its form with every prescription. Continuity can be achieved by prescribing the same proprietary name every time.

17.2.2. Disadvantages of prescribing by proprietary name

(a) Awareness of one's prescription

Consider the list of proprietary names in the left hand column of Table 17.1. This list of proprietary names was actually typed on the formal referral letter that a patient brought into hospital (reproduced in Fig. 17.2). It is hard to imagine that the practitioner who prepared that referral letter really knew what the drugs were that the prescribed formulations contained. If he had, he would not have prescribed two formulations containing trimethoprim, two containing paracetamol, two containing different benzodiazepines, and three containing different phenothiazines! There is a danger that in prescribing by proprietary name the nature of the drugs being prescribed will be forgotten.

Table 17.1 *Proprietary and approved names of the drugs listed on one patient's referral letter (see also Fig. 17.2)*

Proprietary name	Approved name(s)
Maxolon®	Metoclopramide monohydrochloride
Largactil®	Chlorpromazine hydrochloride
Stemetil®	Prochlorperazine maleate
Triptafen Minor®	Perphenazine + amitriptyline hydrochloride
Merital®	Nomifensine hydrogen maleate
Valium®	Diazepam
Halcion®	Triazolam
Tegretol®	Carbamazepine
Epilim®	Sodium valproate
Stugeron®	Cinnarizine
Norgesic®	Orphenadrine citrate + paracetamol
Solpadeine®	Paracetamol + codeine phosphate + caffeine
Dolobid®	Diflunisal
Zomax®	Zomepirac
Ipral®	Trimethoprim
Co-Fram®	Trimethoprim + sulphamoxole

<u>INDICATION OF DRUG TREATMENT FROM GENERAL PRACTITIONERS</u>

Please take this form to your General Practitioner *before* coming into hospital so that he may fill in the relevant details below.

PLEASE BRING TO HOSPITAL WITH YOU

Doctor,

        Could you please list the drugs etc., if any, that this patient is taking:

Zomax, Valium, Stemetil, Merital 50mg, Norgesic,
....

Solpadeine, Maxolon, Ipral, Dolobid, Triptafen Minor,

PLEASE PRINT   ....

Epilim, Halcion, Tegretol, Stugeron, Co Fram, Largactil
....

Has patient been on *STEROIDS* during the past 2 years?

      Yes   ....

      No   NO..

Has this patient any known *ALLERGIES* (Drug or otherwise)?

                NO
....

If patient is taking one of the tranquillisers containing a *MONO-AMINE OXIDASE INHIBITOR* then he/she should be off these drugs for two weeks prior to surgery. If necessary, could you please notify the Waiting List Clerk so that the patient's admission may be delayed.

Fig. 17.2. Part of the referral letter brought by a patient on admission to hospital. The list of drugs involved is given in Table 17.1 in both brand-name and generic-name forms.

(b) Drug stocks

If one prescribes, say, 'Ceporex®' rather than 'cephalexin', and the pharmacist who is to dispense the prescription stocks only Keflex®, he cannot legally dispense the prescription without first consulting the doctor. Clearly this can cause inconvenience to all concerned.

(c) Expense

It will generally be cheaper to prescribe by the approved name, since the pharmacist will dispense the cheapest variant he holds in stock. The actual cash saving will vary widely from drug to drug. That is because firstly many drugs are still available only in one manufacturer's formulation (e.g. cimetidine, as mentioned above), and no saving will be made by prescribing by approved name; and secondly, because competition between manufacturers often means that the difference between the cheapest and dearest brands may not be large.

However it has been estimated, at 1980 prices, that the difference between the costs of dispensing the most expensive and the cheapest formulations could be as much as £50 million in the UK, out of a total expenditure on medicines of around £1000 million.

It is clear that there is no simple answer to the question: Should I prescribe by proprietary name or approved name? In hospital it is usually better to prescribe by approved name since the pharmacy will dispense whatever formulation is held in stock. However, the proprietary name may be used when combination products are prescribed, e.g. 'Burinex-K®'. In general practice if proprietary names are used the prescriber must know precisely what drug or drugs he is prescribing, but in general prescribing by approved name is to be preferred.

17.3. PRESCRIBING CONTROLLED DRUGS

Because of the problems of drug addiction and misuse of drugs, drugs likely to be abused are the subject, in the UK, of the Misuse of Drugs Act (1971), and the Misuse of Drugs Regulations (1973).

Drugs are divided into three classes.

Class A includes: cocaine, diamorphine, morphine, pethidine, and LSD.

Class B includes: oral amphetamines, cannabis, codeine, and methylphenidate.

Class C includes: certain drugs related to the amphetamines, such as benzphetamine, chlorphentermine, and pipradrol.

Practitioners in the UK have an obligation to notify drug addicts to the Home Office. Only medical practitioners who hold a special licence may prescribe diamorphine or cocaine *for addicts*. Other practitioners must refer addicts to a treatment centre. All general practitioners may prescribe diamorphine and cocaine for the treatment of pain and organic disease (see below).

All practitioners have a responsibility to try to curb drug dependence by careful and thoughtful prescribing, and by avoiding being duped by addicts skilled in wheedling drugs out of doctors.

Prescriptions for controlled drugs must:

(a) be signed and dated;
(b) carry the prescriber's address;
(c) be completely written in the prescriber's handwriting in ink;
(d) carry the name and address of the patient;
(e) state the total quantity of the drug or number of dose units in both *words* and *figures*;
(f) state the exact dose in both *words* and *figures*.

If these rules are not followed the pharmacist will not dispense the prescription.

17.4. ABBREVIATIONS

Some abbreviations are used in prescribing and one should be familiar with them. The following (Table 17.2) are commonly used and are acceptable. Others, more obscure, should be avoided and instructions written in plain English.

Table 17.2 *Common abbreviations in prescribing*

Abbreviation	Latin meaning	English translation
b.d. or b.i.d.	*bis in die*	twice a day
gutt.	*guttae*	drops
i.m.	—	intramuscular(ly)
i.v.	—	intravenous(ly)
NP	*nomen proprium*	proper name
o.d.	*omni die*	(once) every day
o.m.	*omni mane**	(once) every morning
o.n.	*omni nocte**	(once) every night
p.o.	*per os*	by mouth
P.R.	*per rectum*	by the anal route
p.r.n.	*pro re nata*	whenever required
PV	*per vaginam*	by the vaginal route
q.d.s.	*quater die sumendum†*	four times a day
s.c.	—	subcutaneous(ly)
stat.	*statim*	immediately
t.d.s.	*ter die sumendum†*	three times a day

* Sometimes written simply as *mane* or *nocte*.
† The abbreviations t.i.d. or q.i.d. (*ter* or *quater in die*) are sometimes used instead.

18 Sources of information on drugs

There are several different forms of sources of information on the different aspects of clinical pharmacology and therapeutics:

 (i) textbooks;
 (ii) monographs;
 (iii) review articles in journals;
 (iv) manufacturers' literature (see Chapter 14);
 (v) original scientific papers.

It is as well to become familiar with a handful of reference texts in which you will be able to find information for most problems (see the bibliography below), going only to the more detailed texts when studying a particular topic in greater depth. In addition you may be able to find out information about drugs from your local pharmacy (particularly if it has a drug information pharmacist) or department of clinical pharmacology. Pharmaceutical manufacturers may also sometimes be useful sources of information, but some pieces of information are confidential and you will not always be able to find out about, say, details of tablet excipients or other pharmaceutical matters.

18.1. PHARMACEUTICAL INFORMATION

For general information relevant to clinical practice, *The Pharmaceutical Handbook* (edited by R.G. Todd) is useful, and itself contains an extensive list of other sources of information.

The British Pharmacopoeia and *The Pharmaceutical Codex* contain information about the pharmaceutical requirements for formulations in Great Britain, and there are comparable publications in other countries (e.g. the *US Pharmacopoeia and National Formulary*).

The British National Formulary (Joint Formulary Committee) contains comprehensive lists of the different drug formulations available, as does *Martindale's Extra Pharmacopoeia*, edited by Reynolds.

18.2. PHARMACOKINETICS

18.2.1. General

There are several texts of varying degrees of inscrutability in which the principles of pharmacokinetics are outlined. The shortest introduction to the subject is *An Introduction to Pharmacokinetics* by Clark and Smith, but for those who want a more comprehensive introductory text *Clinical Pharmacokinetics* by Rowland and Tozer may be preferred. *Fundamentals of Clinical Pharmacokinetics* by J.G. Wagner is useful for those who are conversant with the basic principles and want to explore further. It also contains a large range of references.

Drug disposition and metabolism are discussed in detail in *Fundamentals of Drug Metabolism and Disposition*, edited by La Du, Mandel, and Way. *Variability in Human Drug Response* by Smith and Rawlins contains highly readable introductory accounts of the various aspects of clinical pharmacokinetics.

18.2.2. Specific

We have given only a limited amount of pharmacokinetic information on specific drugs in the Pharmacopoeia and in the tables in Chapter 3. More detailed information on individual drugs is to be found in the *Handbook of Clinical Pharmacology* by Bochner, Carruthers, Kampmann, and Steiner, and in the lists published in *Drug Treatment*, edited by G.S. Avery and in *The Pharmacological Basis of Therapeutics*, edited by Gilman, Goodman, and Gilman.

The monthly journals *Clinical Pharmacokinetics* and *Drugs* publish long review articles about specific drugs. They contain much useful and readily accessible information, and extensive lists of references.

18.3. PHARMACOLOGICAL EFFECTS OF DRUGS

The standard texts on basic pharmacology are *The Pharmacological Basis of Therapeutics*, edited by Gilman, Goodman and, Gilman, and the *Textbook of Pharmacology* by Bowman and Rand. These texts also contain a large selection of primary and secondary source references. The review journal *Drugs* is also informative. A general discussion of relevant pharmacological principles is contained in *Principles of Drug Action*, by Goldstein, Aronow, and Kalman.

18.4. THERAPEUTICS

There are few texts devoted solely to therapeutics, and unfortunately large textbooks of medicine and medical monographs tend to concentrate more on other aspects of disease. The following are devoted mainly to therapeutics: *Current Treatment*, edited by H.F. Conn; *Drug Treatment*, edited by G.S. Avery; *Emergencies in Medical Practice*, edited by C.A. Birch.

Self-poisoning is dealt with as a separate subject in several monographs, of which the following may be found useful: *Treatment of Common Acute Poisoning* by Matthew and Lawson, and *Diagnosis and Management of Acute Poisoning*, by A.T. Proudfoot.

18.5. PHARMACOGENETICS

There are few monographs on pharmacogenetics and they are not widely available. The chapter in *Principles of Drug Action* by Goldstein, Aronow, and Kalman is useful as are *Pharmacogenetics* by I. Szorady, and *Pharmacogenetics* by W. Kalow.

18.6. ADVERSE EFFECTS OF DRUGS

The most useful sources of information about adverse effects of specific drugs are *Meyler's Side Effects of Drugs*, both in its various editions (edited by Meyler and Herxheimer, and by Dukes) and in its companion annual update volumes (edited by Dukes), and *Martindale's Extra Pharmacopoeia*, edited by Reynolds.

Adverse drug effects are also discussed in terms of the ways in which organ systems may be affected in the *Textbook of Adverse Drug Reactions*, edited by D.M. Davies, and *Iatrogenic Diseases*, by D'Arcy and Griffin (with companion update volumes).

Mechanisms of adverse effects of drugs are discussed in *The Pharmacological Basis of Therapeutics*, edited by Gilman, Goodman, and Gilman.

18.7 DRUG INTERACTIONS

Comprehensive listings of drug interactions are to be found in *Drug Interactions*, by P.D. Hansten, and *Drug Interactions*, by I. Stockley.

18.8. CLINICAL TRIALS

Clinical Trials, edited by Johnson and Johnson, and *The Principles and Practice of Clinical Trials*, edited by C.S. Good, deal with the subject in different ways. For statistical discussions see the texts by Bradford Hill and by Armitage.

18.9. PATIENT COMPLIANCE

The monograph edited by Sackett and Haynes is very informative. Other information must largely be gleaned from primary sources.

18.10. PRESCRIBING INFORMATION

Notes on writing prescriptions are to be found in *The Pharmaceutical Handbook*, (edited by R.G. Todd), *The British National Formulary* (Joint Formulary Committee), and in the *Medicines and Poisons Guide* by Hay and Pearce.

Information about the different available preparations of drugs, proprietary or otherwise, is to be found in the *British National Formulary* (Joint Formulary Committee), *MIMS* (the *Monthly Index of Medical Specialties*), and the *Data Sheet Compendium*, complied by the Association of British Pharmaceutical Industries.

All of these texts are described in the bibliography which follows, along with some additional texts to which we have not alluded.

18.11. BIBLIOGRAPHY

In this bibliography we have listed some textual sources of information which may be useful either for reference or for general reading.

Adverse Drug Reaction Bulletin. Adverse Drug Reaction Research Unit, Co. Durham. Published bimonthly.
  Distributed free to final year medical students and recently qualified doctors. Contains review articles on various different aspects of adverse drug reactions. Clear and concise, well referenced.
Armitage, P. (1971). *Statistical methods in medical research*. Blackwell Scientific, Oxford.
  Good introductory textbook, but does not deal specifically with clinical trials. Easy to read, but has a lot of mathematics (cf. Bradford Hill).
*Association of British Pharmaceutical Industries. *Data sheet compendium*. Datapharm Publications, London*. Published annually.
  Voluntary compilation of most data sheets, as issued by individual pharmaceutical companies in compliance with legal requirements for drug marketing. Listed in groups of preparations under the name of each manufacturer. Each describes the formulations available, the drug's licensed indications for use, notes on dosages and administration, adverse effects, precautions and contra-indications, treatment of overdosage, and interactions, and adds a little pharmaceutical information (e.g. special storage instructions). Two indexes, one of proprietary names, the other of approved names with corresponding proprietary names.
Avery, G.S., ed. (1980). *Drug treatment* (2nd edn.). Adis Press, Sydney; Churchill Livingstone, Edinburgh and London.
  Introductory chapters on basic clinical pharmacology followed by chapters on therapeutics of disease discussed by system. Appendices contain numerous tables listing physicochemical and pharmacokinetic properties of drugs, adverse reactions, interactions, and details of antibacterial drugs.
Birch, C.A., ed. (1976). *Emergencies in medical practice* (10th edn). Churchill Livingstone, Edinburgh.
  Comprehensive reviews of medical emergencies and their treatment. Many useful appendices containing addresses of specialist centres in the UK.

*Sources most likely to be found useful as initial references.

*Bochner, F., Carruthers, G., Kampmann, J. and Steiner J. (1983). *Handbook of clinical pharmacology* (2nd edn.). Little, Brown, Boston.

Monographs on individual drugs or groups of closely related drugs (e.g. penicillins) containing notes on mode of action, pharmacokinetic properties, dosages, therapeutic concentrations, adverse reactions, and interactions. Well referenced. Abbreviated introductory chapters on some aspects of basic clinical pharmacology.

*Bowman, W.C., and Rand, M.J. (1980) *Textbook of pharmacology* (2nd edn.). Blackwell Scientific, Oxford.

Excellent reference text covering the basic pharmacology of drugs mostly by organ systems (e.g. the blood, the heart) but in some cases by indication (e.g. pain, anaesthesia, hypnotics and sedatives). Introductory six chapters deal with some relevant matters of anatomy, physiology, and biochemistry. Last five chapters deal with principles of drug action, pharmacokinetics, relevant statistics, 'social' pharmacology, and diet.

*Bradford Hill, A. (1971). *Principles of medical statistics* (9th edn.). The Lancet, London.

Good introductory text, well oriented towards specific problems (e.g. chapters on clinical trials, problems of sampling, collection of statistics). Very little maths.

British Medical Association (1980). *The handbook of medical ethics*. British Medical Association, London.

A general guide to ethics in medical practice. Includes sections or notes on clinical trials, compensation for drug damage, prescribing, pharmacists, oral contraception, treatment in children, placebos, and ethics committees.

British Pharmacopoeia (1980; 2 vols) and *Addenda* (1981, 1982). HMSO, London.

Monographs on individual therapeutic agents giving (Vol.1) structural formulae, chemical properties, preparations, notes on storage, assay techniques, and (Vol.2) descriptions of individual formulations describing identification, strengths available, and details of requirements for dissolution rates and uniformity of content where necessary.

British Pharmacopoeia Commission (1981). *British approved names* 1981. HMSO, London.

Lists approved names alphabetically, giving corresponding chemical names, proprietary names, and a note on the actions and uses.

Clark, B., and Smith, D.A. (1982). *An introduction to pharmacokinetics*. Blackwell Scientific, Oxford.

A simple introduction to pharmacokinetics without excessive emphasis on maths—but you would still have to follow the maths to understand it thoroughly. Contains practical examples.

Clinical Pharmacokinetics. ADIS Press, Australia. Published bimonthly.

Journal containing detailed review articles on all aspects of the pharmacokinetics of drugs relevant to clinical practice. Well referenced.

*Committee on Safety of Medicines (1977). *Extracts from the register of adverse reactions* (2 sets of 7 vols) CSM, London.

A summary of the numbers of reports of specific adverse reactions received by the CSM. In the first seven volumes the *reactions* are listed under the names of specific drugs; in the second seven the drugs are listed under the types of reactions they have been reported to have been associated with. Also contains the numbers of prescriptions issued for individual drugs in specified years.

Conn, H.F., ed. *Current therapy*. W.B. Saunders, Philadelphia. Published annually.

*Sources most likely to be found useful as initial references.

Individualistic accounts of the management of specific diseases arranged in monographs under systematic headings.

Dale, J.R., and Appelbe, G.E. (1976). *Pharmacy, law and ethics*. The Pharmaceutical Press, London.

Deals with most legal aspects of drugs. Mainly intended for pharmacists but has much information of interest to doctors.

D'Arcy, P.F., and Griffin, J.P. (1979; 1st update 1981). *Iatrogenic diseases* (2nd edn). Oxford University Press, Oxford.

Three introductory chapters on interactions, and monitoring and epidemiology of adverse reactions, followed by chapters in which adverse reactions in body systems (e.g. blood dyscrasias) are discussed in relation to the drugs which may cause them. Well referenced. Two appendices contain lists of interactions and matching of approved with proprietary names.

Davies, D.M., ed. (1977). *Textbook of adverse drug reactions*. Oxford University Press, Oxford.

Adverse drug reactions classified by organ systems. Four introductory chapters deal with history, epidemiology, pathogenesis, detection, and investigation. The final chapter covers medico-legal aspects, and there are four useful appendices (e.g. 'Effect of drugs on laboratory tests').

*Diem, K. and Lentner, C., eds. (1970). *Documenta Geigy—scientific tables* (7th edn.). J.R. Geigy, Basle.

Invaluable set of tables for most branches of medical science. Includes mathematical and statistical tables and tables of chemical and biochemical data. Also has a large section on descriptive statistics useful for reference.

Drug and Therapeutics Bulletin. Consumers' Association, London. Published fortnightly.

Distributed free to final year medical students and recently qualified doctors. Contains reviews of new drugs or treatment procedures, providing advice on the relative value of such therapies, generally in comparison with other available therapies. Clear and concise, with primary references.

Drugs. Adis Press, Australia. Published monthly.

Journal containing detailed review articles on the pharmacology and clinical pharmacology of drugs. Includes information on basic pharmacology, pharmacokinetics, therapeutic trials, adverse effects, interactions, dosage and administration, and assessments of the value of the drugs in clinical practice. Also contains other, more specific, reviews.

*Dukes, M.N.G., ed. (1975, 1980, 1983). *Meyler's side effects of drugs* (Vols 8, 9, 10). Excerpta Medica, Amsterdam. See also Meyler.

Adverse reactions to drugs discussed under the headings of the individual drugs or groups of drugs, arranged in chapters according to class of drug. The earlier volumes sometimes contain information not included in later volumes, whose format is slightly different. Good indexes with separate listings for drugs and diseases.

Dukes, M.N.G., ed. *Side effects of drugs annuals*. Excerpta Medica, Amsterdam. Published annually since 1977.

Companion volumes to *Meyler's side effects of drugs* (ed. Dukes), using the same format, but mostly covering only reports published during the relevant year. A special feature is the 'reviews' in which specific topics are reviewed carefully and distinguished from the rest of the text typographically.

*Gilman, A.G., Goodman, L.S., Gilman, A. (1980). *The pharmacological basis of therapeutics* (6th edn.). MacMillan, New York.

*Sources most likely to be found useful as initial references.

Thorough, comprehensive account of basic pharmacology as relevant to therapeutics, arranged by groups of drugs. Useful appendices on prescribing, pharmacokinetic data of individual drugs, and interactions. Very well referenced with both primary and secondary sources.

*Goldstein, A., Aronow, L., and Kalman, S.M. (1974). *Principles of drug action : the basis of pharmacology*, (2nd edn). John Wiley, New York.

Broad-ranging text on numerous aspects of both basic and clinical pharmacology, including molecular aspects of drug action (mostly about drug–receptor interactions), descriptive pharmacokinetics, drug toxicity in its various aspects, pharmacogenetics, and drug development and evaluation.

Good, C.S., ed. (1976). *The principles and practice of clinical trials*. Churchill Livingstone, Edinburgh.

Proceedings of a symposium covering the setting up, running, and evaluation of clinical trials. Well illustrated with examples throughout, with references.

Gross, F.H., and Inman, W.H.W., eds. (1977). *Drug monitoring*. Academic Press, London.

Proceedings of a symposium on methods of monitoring for adverse drug reactions. Covers virtually every aspect, with references to primary sources.

Hansten, P.D. (1971). *Drug interactions* (2nd edn.). Lea and Febiger, Philadelphia.

Drug interactions listed by class of drug (e.g. anti-arrhythmics, oral anticoagulants), and within classes subdivided according to whether the effect of the object drug is increased or decreased. Clinical significance of the interactions is both shown typographically and discussed. Management is also mentioned. Also contains detailed lists of drug effects on laboratory tests.

Hay, C.E., and Pearce, M.E. (1980). *Medicines and poisons guide* (2nd edn.). The Pharmaceutical Press, London.

Legal classification of medicinal products and non-medicinal poisons. Includes sections on prescriptions, dispensing, and labelling. Comprehensive lists of medicines for human and veterinary use and of non-medicinal poisons for retail use or supply.

Johnson, F.N. and Johnson, S. eds. (1977). *Clinical trials*. Blackwell Scientific, Oxford.

Clear, comprehensive descriptions of most aspects of clinical trials, including Phase I and Phase II trials during drug development, organization of trials, statistical analysis, interpretation, and ethics.

*Joint Formulary Committee. *British National Formulary*. British Medical Association and The Pharmaceutical Society of Great Britain, London. Published every 6 months since 1981.

Excellent guide to currently available formulations, with notes on doses, uses, adverse effects, and interactions. Appendices include lists of interactions and intravenous additives. Introductory chapters on prescribing, especially in renal failure, in liver disease, in pregnancy, and during breast-feeding

Kalow, W. (1962). *Pharmacogenetics, heredity and the response to drugs*. W.B. Saunders, Philadelphia.

Thorough, well-referenced review covers pharmacokinetic and pharmacodynamic types of genetic variability, and the effect of race, in addition to drug resistance in bacteria and insects.

La Du, B.N., Mandel, H.G., and Way, E.L., eds. (1971). *Fundamentals of drug metabolism and drug disposition*. Williams and Wilkins, Baltimore.

---

*Sources most likely to be found useful as initial references.

Thorough review of all aspects of drug disposition and metabolism including sections on absorption, protein binding, tissue distribution, placental transfer, renal and non-renal excretion, pathways of biotransformation, various chapters on mechanisms of drug metabolism and on techniques for studying biotransformation.

*Matthew, H., and Lawson, A.A.H. (1979). *Treatment of common acute poisoning* (4th edn.). Churchill Livingstone, Edinburgh.

Introductory chapters on epidemiology, diagnosis, principles of management and psychiatric treatment, and special methods for removing drug from the body. Subsequent chapters deal with the treatment of poisoning by specific drugs, including drug addiction. Final chapter on prevention. Very well referenced throughout. Sensible and clear.

*Meyler, L. and Herxheimer, A. (1972). *Side effects of drugs* (Vol. 7). Excerpta Medica, Amsterdam. See Dukes, ed.

MIMS (*Monthly index of medical specialities*). Medical Publications, London. Published monthly.

Lists proprietary formulations by the proprietary names arranged alphabetically within class headings. Gives names of manufacturers, approved name(s) of the drug(s) contained in the formulations, types of formulation available, costs, doses, indications, contra-indications, and special precautions. Each month's issue contains a list of newly issued formulations with a little extra pharmacological information. MIMS is sent free to all GPs and to a few other selected doctors.

Notari, R.E. (1975). *Biopharmaceutics and pharmacokinetics. An introduction* (2nd edn.). Marcel Dekker, New York.

Step-by-step account of pharmacokinetics. A lot of algebra and good sample problems. Mainly aimed at pharmacists.

The Pharmaceutical Codex (1979) (11th edn.). The Pharmaceutical Press, London.

Monographs on specific therapeutic agents and diseases, arranged alphabetically. The drug monographs include the following information to a greater or lesser extent: chemical characteristics, means of identification, available formulations, pharmacokinetic characteristics, adverse effects, contra-indications and precautions, interactions, and uses. Has references for further reading.

Proudfoot, A.T. (1982). *Diagnosis and management of acute poisoning*. Blackwell Scientific, Oxford.

Clearly written text with introductory chapters on classification, diagnosis, and general plan for management of acute poisoning, followed by monographs on individual drugs.

*Reynolds, J.E.F., ed. (1982). *Martindale: the extra pharmacopoeia* (28th edn.). Pharmaceutical Press, London.

Lists virtually every therapeutic agent, with notes on dosages, relevant chemical and pharmaceutical properties, adverse effects, precautions, absorption and fate, uses, and preparations (both proprietary and non-proprietary). Extensively illustrated by quotations from published reports, with references.

Riggs, D.S. (1963). *The mathematical approach to physiological problems. A critical primer*. The MIT Press, Cambridge, Mass.

Essential reading for anyone who intends making any kind of scientific calculations.

Rowland, M. and Tozer, T.N. (1980). *Clinical pharmacokinetics. Concepts and applications*. Lea and Febiger, Philadelphia.

An excellent introductory text which needs to be worked through systematically.

*Sources most likely to be found useful as initial references.

Covers basic concepts, principles of kinetics as applied to drugs, therapeutic
regimens, and individualization of therapy. Well illustrated with practical
problems throughout. Light on maths, but appendices deal with some of the
practicalities of mathematical treatment of kinetic data.

Sackett, D.L. and Haynes, R.B. eds. (1976). *Compliance with therapeutic
regimens*. Johns Hopkins University Press, Baltimore.

A lively collection of papers on a variety of aspects of patient compliance.

Smith, S.E., and Rawlins, M.D. (1973). *Variability in human drug response*.
Butterworth, London.

Excellent, easy-to-read introduction to basic clinical pharmacology including
descriptive and mathematical pharmacokinetics, pharmacogenetics, tissue sensitivity, and monitoring drug therapy.

*Stockley, I. (1981). *Drug interactions*. Blackwell Scientific, Oxford.

Monographs on individual drug interactions arranged in chapters by object drug.
Each well-referenced monograph contains a description of the interaction and its
mechanism, and an assessment of its importance, with guidance on management.
The introductory chapter contains an abbreviated account of basic mechanisms.

Szorady, I. (1973). *Pharmacogenetics. Principles and paediatric aspects*. Akademiai
Kiado, Budapest.

Comprehensive, well-referenced text, but difficult to read.

Today's treatment (4 vols. to date). British Medical Association, London. Published periodically.

Collections of review articles, originally published in the *British Medical Journal*,
dealing with a variety of different aspects of clinical pharmacology and therapeutics. Concise and clear.

Todd, R.G., ed. (1980). *Pharmaceutical handbook* (19th edn.). The Pharmaceutical Press, London.

Contains a wide variety of information on numerous pharmaceutical matters,
including the preparation of medicines, posology, microbiology, immunology,
nomenclature, mensuration. Contains several comprehensive glossaries (e.g.
'Terms used in pharmacology', 'Approved names and their synonyms').

Wagner, J.G. *Biopharmaceutics and relevant pharmacokinetics* (1st edn.). *Drug
Intelligence Publications*, Hamilton, Ill.

Technical account mostly of pharmaceutical matters, e.g. disintegration and
dissolution of dosage forms, special formulations (sustained-release, enteric-
coated), bioavailability, and quality control. Useful chapters on mechanisms of
drug transport in the body.

Wagner, J.G. *Fundamentals of clinical pharmacokinetics*. *Drug Intelligence Publications*, Hamilton, Ill.

Eclectic text on various aspects of pharmacokinetics. Contains many useful
equations, but is difficult to use without a good basic understanding of the
subject. Deals extensively with compartmental models (linear and non-linear),
dosage regimen calculations, the effects of disease on pharmacokinetics, and
concentration–response relationships.

Windholz, M., Budavari, S., Stroumtsos, L.Y., and Fertig, M.N., eds. (1976) *The
Merck index* (9th edn.). Merck, Rahway, N.J.

Comprehensive list of chemical substances. Includes structures, chemical information, a few references (usually on synthesis but sometimes on uses etc), and
occasionally other information (e.g. LD_{50}, pharmaceutical incompatibilities).
Useful appendices, containing miscellaneous tables and other information.

*Sources most likely to be found useful as initial references.

SECTION III

The drug therapy of disease

19 Introduction to drug therapy

In section I we discussed the basic principles of clinical pharmacology, breaking down the therapeutic process into its component phases (pharmaceutical, pharmacokinetic, pharmacodynamic and therapeutic). In Section IV (the Pharmacopoeia) the properties of individual drugs are discussed.

In this section it is our aim to marry the properties of the drugs with the basic principles, and with the pathology and abnormal physiology of disease and its manifestations, to illustrate the way drugs are used in the treatment of disease.

	Pathophysiology	Symptoms	Therapeutic points
Cause:	Coronary atheroma and obstruction (thrombosis) factors		
	- diet		? reduce cholesterol intake
	- smoking		stop smoking
	- hypertension		treat hypertension early
	- genetic		treat hyperlipidaemia
	- thrombotic potential		? aspirin ? sulphinpyrazone ? warfarin
Primary pathology:	myocardial ischaemia (± previous episodes of myocardial infarction)	angina, acute chest pain	nitrates, nifedipine, β-adrenoceptor antagonists
	ventricular dysfunction (poor pump)		rest, positive inotropic drugs (digoxin, β-adrenoceptor agonists, aminophylline, vasodilators)
	altered haemodynamics reduced cardiac output increased left ventricular end-diastolic pressure pulmonary oedema ⟶ hypoxia increased venous pressure ⟶ hepatomegaly	breathlessness ⎱ liver pain ⎰	acutely diamorphine/morphine, vasodilators; diuretics, vasodilators, oxygen
Secondary pathology:	poor renal perfusion (+ congestion) ⟶ oedema poor tissue perfusion (including brain)	legs swell exhaustion	diuretics

Fig. 19.1. Pathophysiological changes in acute myocardial infarction with corresponding therapeutic points.

It is not always easy to state precisely the molecular mechanisms responsible for causing disease (e.g. hypertension, depression, cancer), nor in fact the precise mechanisms through which drugs exert their therapeutic effects (e.g. β-adrenoceptor antagonists in hypertension, ergotamine in migraine, carbenoxolone in gastric ulcer), and in such cases attempts at a purely rational approach to drug therapy are thwarted. Nevertheless, an interpretation at some level of understanding (see Chapter 4) is usually possible. For example, although we do not understand precisely how corticosteroids act at the molecular level, many of their actions at the cellular and organ levels are known and can be related to their observed therapeutic effects.

Take the treatment of cardiac failure as an example. In Fig. 19.1 are shown the underlying pathophysiological changes and the drugs or other manoeuvres one would use in treatment. Of course there are various different possible presentations of cardiac failure, each demanding some fine tuning of drug therapy and other approaches, but the broad essentials are shown in the figure. Compare the treatment of acute left ventricular failure associated with a myocardial infarct with the treatment of chronic congestive cardiac failure associated with chronic, severe myocardial ischaemia.

Acute left ventricular failure will require:
oxygen;
diamorphine or morphine i.v.;
frusemide i.v.;
then perhaps aminophylline i.v.;
then perhaps a vasodilator i.v. (e.g. sodium nitroprusside).

Chronic congestive cardiac failure will require:

oral diuretics—e.g. thiazides, frusemide or bumetanide, potassium-sparing diuretics;
digitalis, e.g. digoxin orally;
then perhaps an oral vasodilator, e.g. hydralazine or captopril.

In each case our knowledge of the pathophysiology of the disease and of the properties of the drugs especially in relation to the patient, and our cumulative, corporate experience of the results of using those drugs in these circumstances guide our hand.

Where appropriate, in the chapters which follow in this section, we shall describe drug therapy starting with the relevant pathophysiology, stating the nature of the problem, and continuing with the details of specific drug usage, referring to the Pharmacopoeia (Section IV) as necessary.

20 The drug therapy of infectious diseases

For practical reasons, our aim in this chapter is to deal with the general principles governing the use of the drugs used in the treatment of diseases caused by infective agents. These can be classified according to the type of infective agent the drug is directed against:

1. Antibacterial drugs.
2. Antiviral drugs.
3. Antiprotozoal drugs.
4. Anthelminthics.
5. Antifungal drugs.

We shall deal with each class separately. Many specific infections are dealt with in other relevant chapters (e.g. infective endocarditis in Chapter 21, pneumonias in Chapter 22, and so on).

20.1. ANTIBACTERIAL DRUGS—THE TREATMENT OF BACTERIAL INFECTIONS

Table 20.1 *List of antibiotics (those drugs underlined are first-choice antibiotics)*

Penicillins (p.723)
  Penicillinase-sensitive penicillins
    Benzylpenicillin (Penicillin G)
    Procaine penicillin (a benzylpenicillin salt)
    Benethamine penicillin (a benzylpenicillin salt)
    Phenoxymethylpenicillin (Penicillin V)
  Penicillinase-resistant penicillins
    Flucloxacillin
    Methicillin
  Broad-spectrum penicillins
    Ampicillin
    Amoxycillin (+ clavulanic acid: Augmentin®)
    Mezlocillin
    Piperacillin

Table 20.1   *Continued*

Antipseudomonal penicillins
   <u>Azlocillin</u>
   Ticarcillin
   Carbenicillin
   Carfecillin
Other penicillins
   Mecillinam (parenteral)
   Pivmecillinam (oral)

Cephalosporins (p.653)
   Orally-active cephalosporins
      Cephradine
      <u>Cephalexine</u> ⎫
      <u>Cefaclor</u>   ⎬ either
   Injectable cephalosporins
      <u>Cefuroxime</u> (cephamandole alternative)
      Cefotaxime
      Latamoxef
      Cefoxitin .

Tetracyclines (p.758)
   <u>Tetracycline</u>
   Doxycycline
   Minocycline

Aminoglycosides (p.632)
   <u>Gentamicin</u>
   Kanamycin
   Amikacin
   Tobramycin
   Netilmicin
   (Neomycin—topical and oral only)

Macrolides
   <u>Erythromycin</u> (p.678)
   Oleandomycin
   Troleandomycin

Lincomycin and clindamycin (p.701)

Sulphonamides (p.755)
   Sulphamethizole

Trimethoprim (p.669)

Co-trimoxazole (trimethoprim + sulphamethoxazole) (p.669)

Chloramphenicol (p.658)

Metronidazole (p.707)

Sodium fusidate (p.682)

Spectinomycin

Vancomycin (p.765)

Table 20.1 *Continued*

Antituberculous drugs
   Rifampicin (p.740)
   Ethambutol (p.679)
   Isoniazid (p.695)
   Streptomycin (p.632)

Antileprotic drugs
   Dapsone (p.673)
   Rifampicin
   Clofazimine

Urinary antimicrobials
   Nitrofurantoin (p.720)
   Nalidixic acid

The list of antibacterial drugs which one has at one's disposal is a formidable one, and is given in Table 20.1. It is possible, however, to pare back this list to a much shorter list of drugs, covering about 85 per cent of all the antibiotics prescribed in hospitals in the UK. The list is as follows:

benzylpenicillin ⎫
amoxycillin   ⎬ penicillins
flucloxacillin ⎪
azlocillin   ⎭
erythromycin
co-trimoxazole/trimethoprim
tetracycline
gentamicin
metronidazole
cefuroxime
rifampicin ⎫
ethambutol ⎬ anti-tuberculous drugs
isoniazid   ⎪
streptomycin ⎭

20.1.1. Mechanisms of action of antibiotics relative to their clinical use

The whole basis of antibacterial therapy depends upon the action of a drug either to kill or to prevent the growth of bacteria without harming the host. Antibacterial drugs do this by two main mechanisms:

(a) Impairment of cell (bacterial) wall synthesis

Penicillins, cephalosporins, vancomycin.

(b) Impairment of bacterial nucleic acid and protein synthesis

Several antibiotics do this, but by different mechanisms (see Pharmacopoeia). They include sulphonamides, trimethoprim, tetracyclines, aminoglycosides, erythromycin, rifampicin, chloramphenicol, lincomycin, and clindamycin.

Antibacterial agents, when tested on bacterial cultures *in vitro*, can be shown to be either bacteriocidal (they actually kill bacteria) or bacteriostatic (they arrest the growth of bacteria; see Table 20.2). To some extent bacteriostatic agents rely upon the host's immune and cellular defence mechanisms to clear the bacteria, and this is a factor to consider in patients whose cellular defence mechanisms or immune responses are compromised. In such patients a *bacteriocidal* drug might be preferable. Outside of this important consideration, however, the distinction between bacteriocidal and bacteriostatic drugs is not of great clinical importance.

Table 20.2   *Some bacteriocidal and bacteriostatic antibiotics*

Bacteriocidal	*Bacteriostatic*
Penicillins	Sulphonamides
Cephalosporins	Tetracyclines
Aminoglycosides	Chloramphenicol
	Erythromycin
	Trimethoprim

A crucial factor in antibacterial chemotherapy is the minimal inhibitory concentration (MIC) of the drug against a specified bacterium. The MIC for a given culture system is that concentration of agent below which bacterial growth is not prevented. Plainly the lower this concentration, the more potent the antibiotic. The clinical value of the drug then depends upon the relationship between the MIC and the plasma concentrations at which adverse effects occur. For instance, the MIC for benzylpenicillin against the pneumococcus is generally greatly below the plasma concentrations of penicillin associated with adverse effects (excluding penicillin hypersensitivity), whereas the MIC of gentamicin for *Escherichia coli* is generally closer to the plasma concentrations of gentamicin associated with renal toxicity and ototoxicity. The MIC is the factor which determines the denominator in the therapeutic index (see p.134) for an antibiotic.

The MIC, however, is determined in a homogeneous culture system *in vitro*. *In vivo* the drug must pass from the plasma into the infected tissue to destroy bacteria, and if the concentration within that tissue is lower than that in the plasma, treatment failure may occur. For instance, the penetration of antibiotics into abscess cavities may be poor, and surgical drainage is often necessary. Antibiotics may enter cells poorly and intracellular pathogens may therefore be quite difficult to eradicate, e.g. *Salmonella, Brucella, Toxoplasma, Mycobacteria*.

20.1.2. Bacterial resistance to antibiotics

True resistance of bacteria to antibacterial agents is a factor affecting the whole approach to the chemotherapy of infectious disease. Profligate prescription of antibiotics without consideration of their indications leads to the emergence of resistant strains. The sensible use of antibiotics guards against this.

The known mechanisms of bacterial resistance to antibiotics are detailed below.

(a) Selection (chromosome-mediated)

If within a bacterial population there exist bacteria with a natural resistance to an antibiotic, then the antibiotic will eliminate the sensitive organisms and the resistant forms will proliferate. This factor operates particularly in hospitals.

(b) Mutation (chromosome-mediated)

Within a population of bacteria mutants which are resistant to an antibiotic may arise spontaneously. These bacteria are then 'selected' for proliferation as described above.

(c) Transferred resistance

Resistance may be transferred from one organism to another by the exchange of genes conferring antibiotic resistance. Such genes may either be contained within bacteriophages (viruses which infect bacteria) or within plasmids (the so-called R factor : R for 'resistance'). Plasmids conferring resistance are transferred into other bacteria by conjugation and the actual passage of the DNA material from one bacterial cell to another. Either way, new DNA enters the bacterium and therein codes for a mechanism which confers resistance. Such mechanisms involve:

(i) Enzymatic inactivation of the antibiotic
For example, β-lactamases conferring resistance to some penicillins and cephalosporins.

(ii) Substitution of a metabolic pathway resistant to the antibacterial agent
For example, in the case of sulphonamides and trimethoprim.

(iii) Altered permeability of the bacterium to the drug
For example, tetracycline.

Emergence of bacterial resistance can be minimized by prescribing antibiotics only when really necessary, by ensuring adequate dosage, by reserving certain drugs carefully for certain infections (to preserve their efficacy), and by using drug combinations when appropriate (e.g. in tuberculosis).

20.1.3. Principles of antibacterial chemotherapy

There is a great deal of unnecessary prescribing of antibiotics. The hazards of this are several.

(a) Resistant organisms may arise

This is a particular hazard in the hospital environment and can lead to disastrous wound infections on surgical wards, and cross-infections in intensive care units.

(b) Superinfection

The patient being treated is always at risk of a superinfection with a resistant bacterium (e.g. *Clostridium difficile*, causing pseudomembranous colitis) or, very frequently, with *Candida albicans*.

(c) Adverse effects

Unnecessary antibiotic prescribing produces unnecessary adverse effects, e.g. hypersensitivity, and drug toxicity.

(d) Difficulty in diagnosis

If antibiotics are prescribed in a bacterial infection before a diagnosis is made, then if the treatment does not eradicate the infection subsequent diagnosis can be very difficult because of confusion caused by alteration of clinical signs, alteration in bacterial flora, and the problems of culturing bacteria and determining their sensitivities.

The following principles will, if followed, avoid many of these problems:

(1) Make a diagnosis

It would be perfect if before starting antibiotic therapy a precise bacteriological diagnosis were available in every case. However, this perfection of antibiotic prescribing is not always possible. For instance, in life-threatening infections 'best guess' antibiotic therapy must be started quickly on the basis of the clinical features of the illness, although in all such cases specimens (blood, urine, sputum, etc.) must be taken *before treatment*, so that rational antibiotic therapy can be applied later if an organism is identified.

Sheer numbers of patients and economic realities in various parts of the world pose the problem of whether the precise laboratory bacteriological diagnosis of some common infections with a reasonably predictable bacterial cause is necessary. Examples of such infections would be uncomplicated urinary tract infection in women (mostly due to *E. coli*), acute follicular tonsillitis (*Streptococcus pyogenes*), acute bronchitis complicating chronic bronchitis (*Haemophilus influenzae* and pneumococcus). If circumstances permit, then one should certainly take a specimen of urine for bacteriological examination in a woman with an uncomplicated urinary tract infection before the administration of amoxycillin (with or without clavulanic acid) or trimethoprim, so that the appropriateness of antibiotic therapy and any further action can be assessed later. Likewise, treatment of acute follicular tonsillitis with phenoxymethylpenicillin in a child ideally should be preceded by a throat swab for bacterial culture. A case can also be made out for taking a specimen of sputum for bacteriological examination from a patient with chronic bronchitis who is having recurrent attacks of acute bronchitis before giving amoxycillin in an acute attack.

Whether or not such bacteriological procedures are undertaken in such conditions depends upon the prevailing clinical practice in the particular socio-economic climate. The conditions just described do have a reasonable chance of being due to particular bacteria, and a fair guess can be made in a given local environment as to their likely sensitivities to antibiotics. However, there are many conditions in which the likelihood that a clinical guess about the responsible bacterium and/or its antibiotic sensitivities will be correct is statistically much poorer, and indeed where the correct answer is essential for the successful outcome of therapy. Meningitis is a case in point. A Gram stain of the cerebrospinal fluid (CSF) may show numerous polymorphs and Gram-negative kidney-shaped diplococci. Bacteriological culture may later reveal *N. meningitidis* (meningococcus) in blood or CSF, but treatment with benzylpenicillin can be started on the results of the Gram stain of the CSF alone. Gram-positive diplococci in the CSF are likely to be pneumococci, which likewise should be responsive to benzylpenicillin. Small Gram-negative bacilli in the CSF are likely to be *H. influenzae* for which chloramphenicol ± ampicillin is the treatment of choice. The Gram stain of the CSF can thus be very useful in indicating the likely bacteriological diagnosis and initial antibiotic therapy which can be undertaken swiftly in a life-threatening condition.

In summary, therefore, the counsel of perfection is to make a bacteriological diagnosis before treatment. If, because of practical circumstances or the urgency of the problem, this is not possible, one should take appropriate specimens for bacteriological examination, make a clinical and presumptive guess at the responsible organism and then begin a 'best guess' antibiotic. If there are problems about the bacterial diagnosis then consult the bacteriologist at the earliest opportunity.

(2) Decide whether antibiotic therapy is really necessary

Not all boils need antibiotic therapy, although this needs careful clinical judgment as to the likelihood of complications and spread, and the necessity for surgical drainage. Generally speaking bacillary dysentery and food poisoning due to *Salmonella* spp. do not require antibiotic therapy.

(3) Choose the correct antibiotic

Several different factors influence one's choice of antibiotic:

(i) spectrum of antibacterial activity;

(ii) bacterial resistance;

(iii) pharmacokinetics (e.g. distribution to specific tissues);

(iv) adverse effects and drug interactions;

(v) empirical (clinical trials) evidence for efficacy in the clinical problem;

(vi) synergy of other antibiotics (combination therapy).

(i) Spectrum of antibacterial activity

Ideally this should be tested *in vitro* by determining the ability of an antibiotic to inhibit the growth of the causative organism. However, in cases in which the organism has not, or not yet, been isolated it has to be assumed that the organism presumed to be causing the infection is sensitive to a particular antibiotic because of the known characteristics of such organisms in general. In Table 20.3 are listed the infections for which particular antibiotics are generally the first choice, and in Table 20.4 are shown the usual sensitivities of organisms to the commonly used antibiotics.

Table 20.3 *Infections for which the given antibiotics are usually of first choice*

Benzylpenicillin	
Streptococcus pyogenes	Acute follicular tonsillitis (acute otitis media over 5 years—see also amoxycillin)
Streptococcus viridans	Endocarditis (+ gentamicin)
Streptococcus faecalis	Endocarditis (+ gentamicin)
Streptococcus pneumoniae	Pneumococcal pneumonia
Neisseria gonorrhoeae	Gonorrhoea
Neisseria meningitidis	Meningococcal meningitis
Treponema pallidum	Syphilis
Amoxycillin	
Haemophilus influenzae and *Streptococcus pneumoniae* }	Exacerbations of chronic bronchitis, acute bronchitis/pneumonia
Streptococcus pyogenes or *H. influenzae*	Acute otitis media (under 5 years)
Streptococcus pneumoniae *Streptococcus pyogenes* *H. influenzae* }	Sinusitis
E. coli	Pyelonephritis Urinary tract infection (+ clavulanic acid if resistant)
Flucloxacillin	
Staphylococcus aureus (penicillin-resistant)	Wounds, boils (if necessary), and abscesses Septic arthritis Osteomyelitis Pneumonia Endocarditis Impetigo

Table 20.3 *Continued*

Erythromycin
  Mycoplasma pneumoniae   Pneumonia
  Legionella pneumophila   Legionnaires' pneumonia

Co-trimoxazole (trimethoprim alone may be just as effective)
  E. coli   Pyelonephritis
         Urinary tract infection

  H. influenzae and   ⎫
  Streptococcus pneumoniae ⎬   Exacerbations of chronic bronchitis
        ⎭

Tetracyclines
  Rickettsiae   Typhus, Q fever
  Chlamydiae   Trachoma
         Psittacosis
         Lymphogranuloma venereum
         Non-specific urethritis

Gentamicin
  Streptococcus viridans ⎫
  Streptococcus faecalis ⎬ Endocarditis (+ penicillin G)
  E. coli
  Klebsiella   ⎫ In *severe* infections, e.g. septicaemia, acute
  Enterobacter   ⎬ pyelonephritis, pneumonia, biliary tract infection
  Proteus   ⎭
  Pseudomonas aeruginosa   (+ azlocillin) urinary tract infection, pneumonia

Azlocillin
        ⎫ Septicaemia (+ gentamicin)
  P. aeruginosa ⎬ Urinary tract infection
        ⎭ Pneumonia (+ gentamicin)

Metronidazole
  Bacteroides spp.   Intra-abdominal infections
         e.g. liver abscess
             pelvic inflammatory disease
             cholangitis
             peritonitis
             female genital tract infections
         Lung infections—abscess
         Endocarditis

Chloramphenicol
  Salmonella typhi   Typhoid fever
  H. influenzae   Meningitis

(ii) Bacterial resistance

This is also ideally tested by examination of the causative organism, but may have to be assumed. For example, the staphylococci found in hospitals are generally resistant to certain penicillins because they produce penicillinase. In such circumstances one would choose a penicillinase-resistant penicillin such as flucloxacillin, or add clavulanic acid, a penicillinase inhibitor, to the penicillin regimen.

Table 20.4   *The sensitivities of some organisms to commonly used antibiotics*

	Staphylococcus aureus (penicillin-sensitive)	Staphylococcus aureus (penicillin-resistant)	Streptococcus pyogenes	Streptococcus pneumoniae	Streptococcus faecalis	Streptococcus viridans	N. meningitidis	N. gonorrhoeae	H. influenzae	E. coli	Klebsiella	Proteus mirabilis	Pseudomonas aeruginosa	Brucella	Legionella pneumophila	Salmonella typhi	Bacteroides	spp. and other anaerobes	Mycoplasma pneumoniae	Chlamydiae	Rickettsiae
Benzylpenicillin	+		+	+			+	+													
Amoxycillin				+[2]					+[1]	+[1]											
Flucloxacillin		+																			
Erythromycin															+				+		
Co-trimoxazole				+[3]					+[3]	+[4]											
Tetracycline																				+	+
Gentamicin					+[5]					+[6]	+	+	+								
Azlocillin													+[7]								
Metronidazole																		+			
Chloramphenicol																+					

[1] Resistant strains + clavulanic acid.
[2] Acute otitis media in young children.
[3] Exacerbation of chronic bronchitis.
[4] Trimethoprim alone probably just as effective.
[5] Endocarditis (+ benzylpenicillin).
[6] Severe *E.coli* infections.
[7] Combined with gentamicin.

(iii) Pharmacokinetics

Various different aspects of the pharmacokinetics of an antibiotic may govern its use in different circumstances, but particularly important is distribution to specific tissues for the treatment of infections in those tissues.

For example, in meningitis one must be assured that the antibiotic will enter the CSF in a concentration sufficient to kill the organism. Some antibiotics penetrate the CSF well across normal meninges, while others penetrate well only when the meninges are inflamed (see Table 20.5). It is always a little worrying to consider how much inflammation is necessary to influence penetration by what degree, but the information in Table 20.5 has good validation from studies of clinical efficacy.

Table 20.5 *Penetration of antibiotics into CSF*

Meninges normal—good penetration	*Meninges inflamed—good penetration*	*Meninges inflamed—poor penetration*
Sulphonamides	Benzylpenicillin	Streptomycin
Trimethoprim	Ampicillin	Gentamicin (used though)
Metronidazole	Tetracycline	Most cephalosporins
Rifampicin		Macrolides
Ethambutol		
Isoniazid		
Chloramphenicol		

The ability of lincomycin, clindamycin, fusidic acid and penicillinase-resistant penicillins to penetrate bone is of importance in the treatment of staphylococcal osteomyelitis.

Ampicillin, amoxycillin, and tetracyclines are concentrated in the functioning gall-bladder and may therefore be useful in the treatment of biliary tract infections.

Abscesses should be drained whenever possible as they are poorly penetrated by antibiotics.

In infective endocarditis relatively high doses of antibiotics, particularly penicillins, are usually advised for two reasons: penetration of vegetations and valve tissue (which is relatively avascular) may be poor, and tissue defence mechanisms in the area are often inadequate.

In the treatment of urinary tract infection, where there is tissue inflammation, with many pus cells and bacteria in the urine, it would seem logical to employ antibiotics which not only reach the bacteria in the tissues of the urinary tract but also reach sufficiently high concentrations in the urine to act on the bacteria there. Amoxycillin, sulphonamides, trimethoprim, gentamicin, tetracycline, nitrofurantoin, and nalidixic acid do that.

(iv) Adverse effects and drug interactions
These are discussed in section (5) below.

(v) Empirical evidence of efficacy
The use of chloramphenicol in the treatment of typhoid fever rests on the clinical observations that it works and that other antibiotics (e.g. co-trimoxazole) may not be as effective. Sometimes it is clinical experience of this kind which alone determines the choice of antibiotic.

(vi) Synergy
In the treatment of bacterial endocarditis penicillin and gentamicin are used because they have been demonstrated to be synergistic in killing

bacteria *in vitro*. The synergy of trimethoprim with sulphamethoxazole (co-trimoxazole) is discussed in the Pharmacopoeia (p.669).

(4) Consider patient (host) factors

(i) Severity of infection
If the infection is very severe then the general condition of the patient may be poor, and oral absorption unpredictable (e.g. because of nausea, vomiting, gastric stasis). It is wiser in such cases to give antibiotics i.m. or i.v., and the i.v. route would be preferred in hospital.

After the infection is brought under control, and the patient's general condition has improved, it may be possible to achieve appropriate antibiotic concentrations by the oral route. An exception to this would be infective endocarditis (see p.336).

(ii) Host defence mechanisms
The patient's ability to mount a complete defence response against a bacterial infection is of great importance in determining the overall outcome of treatment. If there is depression of defence mechanisms (e.g. in old age, malignant disease, treatment with immunosuppressive drugs, malnutrition), then bacteriocidal drugs are preferred to bacteriostatic drugs.

(iii) Individual pharmacokinetic factors
Age—the newborn (poor renal and hepatic function) and the elderly (mainly poor renal function) may have altered rates of elimination of antibiotics, and dosage adjustments have to be made accordingly (see Chapter 11).

Renal failure—severe infections may be associated with impairment of renal function, particularly in the elderly. Infections of the urinary tract, both acute and chronic, particularly when associated with urinary obstruction can produce renal failure. In addition some antibiotics are themselves nephrotoxic (see Table 24.6). For example, gentamicin (particularly when used with frusemide) can produce tubular damage; the penicillins may produce acute interstitial nephritis.

In all grades of renal failure the dosage of cephalosporins and of ethambutol should be reduced: the plasma concentrations of gentamicin must be monitored if ototoxicity and renal damage are to be avoided and efficacy maintained (see Chapter 7). In more severe grades of renal failure the dosages of metronidazole, co-trimoxazole, and the penicillins need modification. Tetracyclines, nitrofurantoin, vancomycin, and nalidixic acid should be avoided in renal failure.

Hepatic disease—The dosages of antibiotics which are excreted by the liver may have to be reduced in liver disease, e.g. erythromycin, clindamycin, lincomycin, and chloramphenicol.

In cirrhosis of the liver the half-times of rifampicin and isoniazid are prolonged and this poses problems in the treatment of tuberculosis in patients with alcoholic cirrhosis, a not uncommon problem. Dosages of these drugs may need to be reduced, particularly as both rifampicin and isoniazid may themselves produce hepatic damage.

It is now believed that erythromycin in the estolate, stearate, and ethyl succinate forms are all equally liable to produce hepatic impairment and jaundice.

(iv) Pharmacogenetic factors
Sulphonamides, nitrofurantoin, and chloramphenicol can produce acute haemolysis in patients with glucose 6-phosphate dehydrogenase (G6PD) deficiency (see Chapter 8). Sulphonamides (and griseofulvin) should be avoided in patients with porphyria.

(5) What is the likelihood of adverse reactions?

(i) Allergic responses
Never administer an antibiotic to a patient without having taken, as best you can, a history of allergic responses to antibiotics. This applies particularly to the penicillins, with which anaphylactic shock occurs not uncommonly—particularly with i.m. or i.v. benzylpenicillin. It is estimated that 1 in 2000 patients treated with a penicillin will have a Type I hypersensitivity reaction. Although this seems a small frequency, very large numbers of patients are treated with penicillins, and thus the actual number of patients affected may be quite large. Some patients allergic to penicillin will also be allergic to cephalosporins (see p.654), and unfortunately it is not possible to tell whether a particular patient is allergic to both.

Ampicillin and amoxycillin produce a measles-like rash in almost all patients with infectious mononucleosis, and in some with cytomegalovirus infections and chronic lymphatic leukaemia, but this reaction is not a Type I hypersensitivity (nor apparently any sort of hypersensitivity reaction).

(ii) General comments
If patients are not allergic to the penicillins they are fairly safe drugs with a high toxic/therapeutic ratio (high therapeutic index).

Sulphonamides quite frequently produce hypersensitivity reactions and co-trimoxazole contains sulphamethoxazole.

Trimethoprim does not seem to produce hypersensitivity reactions frequently, but it can produce marrow depression with agranulocytosis and thrombocytopenia.

Erythromycin can produce hepatic damage, but rarely. Otherwise it is a safe antibiotic.

Tetracyclines may worsen renal failure and should not be used in patients with renal impairment (doxycycline is an exception). They stain teeth in children up to 7 years of age. They can produce pseudo-membranous colitis and antibiotic-associated diarrhoea (in up to 50 per cent of patients). Overgrowth of *Candida albicans* is common. Skin rashes often occur. So tetracyclines are moderately toxic but serious adverse reactions with them are uncommon.

The aminoglycosides are ototoxic and nephrotoxic, and dosages need careful control.

The adverse effects of the cephalosporins, if one excludes allergy, are not frequent. Occasionally neutropenia and thrombocytopenia occur. Nephrotoxicity was a problem with cephaloridine and cephalothin, but these have been superseded by safer cephalosporins and their use is not advised.

Clindamycin and lincomycin may produce pseudomembranous colitis, a serious and potentially fatal adverse reaction (see pp.701–2). Their use should be reserved for the treatment of severe anaerobic infections, and for bone and joint infections.

Chloramphenicol may produce aplastic anaemia and is reserved for the treatment of typhoid fever and of meningitis due to *H. influenzae*.

Adverse effects with metronidazole are uncommon. Peripheral neuropathy can occur with prolonged use.

(iii) Drug interactions

Drug interactions may produce toxicity or inefficacy. Some more common interactions with antibiotics are shown in Table 20.6.

Table 20.6 *Antibiotics/drug interactions* (see also individual antibiotics in Pharmacopoeia)

Antibiotic	Interacting drug	Mechanism	Effect
Gentamicin	{ Frusemide Ethacrynic acid	Additive	Ototoxicity
Chloramphenicol } Metronidazole }	Warfarin	Inhibition of metabolism	Potentiation of anti-coagulation
Metronidazole	Alcohol	Inhibition of aldehyde dehydrogenase	'Disulfiram reaction'
Rifampicin	Warfarin	Induction of metabolism	Diminished warfarin effect
Rifampicin	Oral contraceptive	Induction of metabolism	Decreased contraceptive effect
Tetracycline	Antacids	Decreased absorption	Tetracycline ineffective
Isoniazid	Phenytoin	Inhibition of metabolism (slow acetylators)	Phenytoin toxicity
Tetracycline	Warfarin	Altered clotting factor activity	Potentiation of anti-coagulation

(6) Consider the chance of superinfection

There is always a risk of superinfection. This is particularly so in the frail and immunosuppressed. Careful oral and general hygeine, and attention to nutritional factors, particularly in the elderly, are essential in any severe infection during treatment with antibiotics. The commonest superinfection is oral candidiasis which can be treated effectively with nystatin suspension.

(7) Decide route of administration, dose, and frequency and duration of therapy

The dose must be designed to produce adequate bacteriocidal or bacteriostatic concentrations at the site of the infection. The frequency of dosage must be sufficient to maintain appropriate concentrations for an appropriate period. The duration of treatment should be sufficient to eradicate the infection.

Each of these factors needs careful consideration in each individual patient. The guidelines on dosage in the Pharmacopoeia indicate the usual dosage ranges, but adjustments must be made according to age, weight, renal, and hepatic function, and the severity of the infection. In severe infections in hospital dosage schedules may be determined by the MIC of the antibiotic against the offending organism.

Take, for example, the use of amoxycillin in different circumstances. An uncomplicated *E. coli* urinary tract infection in a young woman may be treated effectively with two 3g doses of amoxycillin spaced 10–12 h apart. On the other hand, an episode of acute bronchitis associated with *H. influenzae* or pneumococcal infection may require amoxycillin 250 mg q.d.s. for a week or more.

Or take the treatment of infective endocarditis caused by *Streptococcus viridans*. Assuming the streptococcus is sensitive to benzylpenicillin 0.2 µg/ml, a usual initial regimen would be benzylpenicillin 12 million i.u. (international units) daily i.v. (in four divided doses), together with gentamicin 5 mg/kg body weight daily divided into three doses at eight-hourly intervals i.v. if renal function is normal. However, there are various opinions as to how this treatment should be continued thereafter. If the streptococcus is very sensitive to penicillin, and the patient is not very ill, then some physicians would discontinue the gentamicin after a week, and continue the benzylpenicillin for 4 weeks. Others would discontinue the gentamicin after a week, and change from i.v. benzylpenicillin to oral amoxycillin plus probenecid. Others more conservative would continue both benzylpenicillin and gentamicin for a full 4 weeks. In the USA streptomycin is preferred to gentamicin. Whichever regimen is adopted the treatment should be based upon the MICs of the organism, adequate plasma concentrations of the antibiotics, avoidance of gentamicin toxicity (see Pharmacopoeia), and the patient's clinical condition.

Finally, take the example of pulmonary tuberculosis. Around the world there are various regimens for the treatment of active pulmonary tuberculosis depending upon local socio-economic conditions. In the UK treatment is divided into two phases, an initial phase using three drugs, and a continuation phase using two drugs:

Initial phase (8 weeks)

Rifampicin 450–600 mg, once daily.
Isoniazid 200–300 mg, once daily.
Ethambutol 15 mg/kg body weight, once daily.

Continuation phase (assuming organism sensitive)

Isoniazid 200–300 mg, once daily.
Rifampicin 450–600 mg, once daily.
All these are adult doses.

Currently it is recommended that the continuation phase should last 7 months (a total of 9 months). In extrapulmonary tuberculosis the total duration of treatment should be 12 months.

Where socio-economic conditions do not allow the above regimen, various combinations of *para*-aminosalicylic acid (PAS), isoniazid, and streptomycin are used, tailoring the therapeutic regimen to produce the best balance between cost, patient acceptability and compliance, efficacy, and the prevention of resistance to antituberculous drugs.

20.2. ANTIVIRAL CHEMOTHERAPY

Until recently the only therapeutic approach to viral illnesses was to attempt to prevent them. Immunization has been very effective for smallpox, measles, rubella (German measles), poliomyelitis, and yellow fever. Although immunization against influenza viruses is effective, the influenza virus changes its antigenic properties so frequently and unpredictably that it is difficult to provide effective vaccines to order.

During the past few years important chemotherapeutic agents have been produced which, although of limited use, are effective and which pave the way for further advances. These drugs are listed in Table 20.7.

Table 20.7 *Antiviral drugs*

Idoxuridine (p.687)
Vidarabine
Acyclovir
Amantadine

20.2.1. Mechanisms of action and uses of antiviral drugs

(a) Idoxuridine

Idoxuridine is similar in structure to thymidine. It inhibits an enzyme involved in DNA synthesis and is incorporated into DNA. It thereby inhibits DNA synthesis. Because it is not specific for the synthesis of viral DNA, when used systemically it causes bone marrow depression with leucopenia. It is therefore used *locally* for *Herpes simplex* infections of the eye, skin, and external genitalia and also for the skin lesions of *Herpes zoster*.

(b) Vidarabine (adenosine arabinoside)

Inside the host cells adenosine arabinoside is converted to a triphosphate derivative which inhibits DNA polymerase and therefore DNA synthesis. It will inhibit DNA synthesis in all cells, producing bone marrow suppression, but it seems to have greater potency on DNA synthesis in DNA viruses than on host cell DNA synthesis.

It is used systemically for the treatment of chickenpox and *H. zoster* infections in immunosuppressed patients where such infections are life-threatening, and as topical therapy in the treatment of *Herpes simplex* infections of the eye.

(c) Acyclovir

Acyclovir enters all cells, but is only phosphorylated by a virus-specific enzyme, thymidine kinase, to produce the active triphosphate derivative, which then inhibits DNA polymerase, thus blocking viral replication. Because of the selectivity of its activation it has a high therapeutic index compared with idoxuridine and vidarabine.

Acyclovir is active topically and is used as an ointment in the treatment of *H. simplex* eye infections. Topically it is also effective in herpetic labial and genital lesions if started early. It is also available for i.v. administration in the treatment of systemic infections caused by the DNA viruses *H. simplex* and *Varicella zoster*. Acyclovir represents a considerable advance in viral chemotherapy.

(d) Amantadine

Amantadine is active against RNA viruses of which influenza A virus is most important. It is thought that amantadine inhibits either viral penetration into the cell, or viral uncoating within the cell.

Amantadine has to be taken prophylactically against influenza A infection and thus must be administered during the whole course of an epidemic, for perhaps 8 weeks or so. Adverse effects such as confusion, depression, insomnia, and agitation are not uncommon, and although usually mild, they can be a nuisance in the elderly. Because of the need for prophylactic therapy for weeks and the occurrence of adverse effects amantadine has never become popular. It accumulates in renal failure when doses should be reduced.

It was during trials for its prophylactic effect against influenza A in the elderly that its anti-Parkinsonian effect was discovered.

The mode of administration and current uses of the antiviral agents are shown in Table 20.8.

Table 20.8   *Uses and routes of administration of antiviral drugs*

Drug	Route of administration	Disease
Idoxuridine	1% eye drops	*Herpes simplex* keratitis
	0.1% paint	Oral herpes
	5% in dimethyl sulphoxide	*H. simplex* and *Herpes zoster* of skin (must be started early)
Vidarabine	3% eye ointment	*H. simplex* keratitis
	i.v.	Chickenpox and zoster infections in immuno-suppressed patients
Acyclovir	3% eye ointment	*H. simplex* keratitis
	i.v.	Systemic *H. simplex* and *Varicella zoster* infections
Amantadine	Oral	Prophylaxis of influenza

20.3. ANTIPROTOZOAL CHEMOTHERAPY

The chemotherapy of protozoal disease is a complex subject. The full clinical pharmacology of many of the drugs has not been well worked out, largely because facilities for doing so are not easily available in the parts of the world where many of these illnesses are prevalent.

In the development of drugs for diseases which afflict the impoverished parts of the world there is a harsh economic fact which has to be faced. Drug development is very costly, and the price of drugs reflects this. Even if, with a great deal of investment, new drugs for the treatment of diseases peculiar to the impoverished parts of the world are developed, those countries afflicted will be unable to afford either the drugs or the medical system required to apply them to the therapy of disease.

Because of increased international travel it is not uncommon in the UK to encounter patients with malaria, amoebiasis, and giardiasis, and an acquaintance with the therapy of these diseases is important, although facility in its application requires experience. For this reason when an imported protozoal illness which is uncommon in local medical practice occurs, expert advice should be sought.

The drugs used in the treatment of protozoal infections are listed in Table 20.9.

20.3.1. Drug therapy of malaria

(a) Mechanisms of drug action

In Fig. 20.1 is shown the life-cycle of the malaria parasite and the sites of action of the various antimalarial drugs. The molecular mechanisms of the actions of the antimalarials are still somewhat obscure. Their selective toxicity probably depends either upon their concentration by the parasite, or on their binding to high-affinity binding sites in the parasites. Chloroquine, primaquine, and quinine are thought to interfere with the replication of parasite DNA. Proguanil, pyrimethamine, and the sulphones interfere with folinic acid production and therefore inhibit parasitic nucleic acid synthesis.

(b) Aims of therapy

The aims of therapy are:

(i) *acute attack*—elimination of parasitaemia;
(ii) *prevention*—chemoprophylaxis.

The problems are as follows:

(i) Resistance of parasites to antimalarials
This requires tailoring the treatment to the known sensitivities in particular geographical areas.

(ii) Prevention of relapse due to persistent hepatic schizonts (Plasmodium vivax and Plasmodium ovale)
The principle here is to follow a course of 'acute antimalarials' by a course of primaquine.

(iii) Prevention of recrudescence of falciparum malaria (asymptomatic persistence of erythrocyte forms)
Because the combination of pyrimethamine + sulphadoxine (Fansidar®) usually clears the red cells of the parasite it may be given after acute therapy.

(iv) Treatment of complications in falciparum malaria
The principal complications in falciparum malaria are:

cerebral malaria;
acute haemolysis ⎫
acute renal failure ⎬ blackwater fever;
acute pulmonary oedema. ⎭

The complications of falciparum malaria require prompt chemotherapy and full supportive treatment (maintenance of fluid and electrolyte balance, renal dialysis, blood transfusion). Dexamethasone is not effective in the treatment of the cerebral oedema associated with cerebral malaria, and may in fact be deleterious.

Table 20.9   *Drugs used in treatment of protozoal infections*

1. *Drug therapy of malaria*

Treatment	Prophylaxis
Chloroquine (p.660)	Chloroquine
Quinine (p.737)	Proguanil
Primaquine	Pyrimethamine + sulfadoxine (Fansidar®)
	Pyrimethamine + dapsone (Maloprim®)
	(p.673)

2. *Drug therapy of amoebiasis*
   Metronidazole (p.707)
   Diloxanide furoate
   Chloroquine

3. *Drug therapy of giardiasis*
   Metronidazole

4. *Drug therapy of trichomonal infections*
   Metronidazole

5. *Drug therapy of leishmaniasis* (not dealt with further)
   Sodium stibogluconate

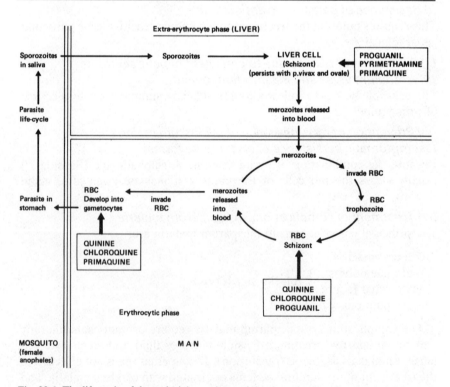

Fig. 20.1. The life-cycle of the malarial parasite, and the sites of action of antimalarial drugs.

(c) Treatment

(i) Malarial attacks in adults with P. vivax, P. ovale, and P. malariae infections

Treatment with chloroquine and oral therapy is usually sufficient, unless the patient cannot take it.

First day: chloroquine 600 mg base followed in 8 h by chloroquine 300 mg base.

Second day: chloroquine 300 mg base.

Third day: Chloroquine 300 mg base.

Days 4–18: Primaquine 7.5 mg b.d.

(ii) Uncomplicated falciparum malaria

Chloroquine-sensitive areas (chloroquine)—usually oral therapy.

First day: chloroquine 600 mg base; 8 h later further dose of chloroquine 600 mg base.

Second day: chloroquine 300 mg base.

Third day: chloroquine 300 mg base.

Fourth day: chloroquine 300 mg base.

This regimen should clear P. *falciparum* infection.

Chloroquine-resistant areas (quinine)—usually oral therapy.

Quinine 600 mg base is given every 12 h for a total of six doses. This is followed by pyrimethamine 75 mg plus sulphadoxine 1500 mg (three tablets of Fansidar®).

(iii) Complicated attacks of falciparum malaria

Chloroquine-sensitive areas—i.v. quinine or chloroquine followed by oral chloroquine.

Chloroquine-resistant areas—i.v. quinine followed by oral quinine plus a final dose of Fansidar®.

(d) Prophylaxis

Because drug resistance varies with the geographical area, advice should be sought from the appropriate advisory body on which drug to use for which area. Treatment should be started with the drug *before* entering the area, and should be continued for *4 weeks after leaving it*.

Chloroquine-resistant falciparum malaria—Fansidar® or Maloprim® one tablet weekly. Add chloroquine (300 mg chloroquine base weekly) if *P. vivax* is also endemic.

Chloroquine-sensitive areas—chloroquine 300 mg base weekly or proguanil 100–200 mg daily.

NB *G6PD deficiency*—Acute haemolysis may occur with chloroquine (not commonly), primaquine, and quinine (see Chapter 8).

20.3.2. Drug therapy of amoebiasis

(a) Mechanisms of action of amoebicides

Entamoeba histolytica exists in two forms:

(i) *trophozoites*—these are found in the stools of patients with active and acute amoebic dysentery;

(ii) *cysts*—these are characteristically found in the stools of patients with chronic intestinal amoebiasis whether or not they have symptoms.

Metronidazole is most active against trophozoites. Diloxanide furoate is active against cysts.

Metronidazole is thought to act via a reduced derivative which interferes with protozoal DNA function. The mechanism of action of diloxanide is unknown.

(b) Treatment of amoebiasis

(i) Acute amoebic dysentery

Metronidazole 800 mg t.d.s. for 5 days followed by diloxanide furoate 500 mg t.d.s for 10 days (to eradicate cysts).

In severe cases emetine hydrochloride i.m. may be necessary.

(ii) Cysts in stools with minimal or no symptoms

Diloxanide furoate 500 mg t.d.s for 10 days.

(iii) Hepatic amoebiasis

Metronidazole 400 mg t.d.s. for 5 days followed by diloxanide furoate 500 mg t.d.s. for 10 days (to eradicate cysts in the intestine).

Hepatic abscesses may require aspiration.

20.3.3. Drug therapy of giardiasis

Giardiasis is an infection of the duodenum and jejunum with the protozoon *Giardia lamblia*.

The protozoon exists in two forms:

(a) The *trophozoite* which attaches itself to the small intestinal mucosa, and somehow causes diarrhoea;

(b) the *cyst* form which is spread in the faeces and transmits the infection.

Chronic giardial infestation may cause chronic diarrhoea, and chronic intestinal malabsorption may also result, although the association is still not fully understood.

Treatment is with metronidazole, 2 g daily, orally for 3 days.

Patients should be warned that they may experience a metallic taste, nausea, vomiting, headache, and discoloured urine. They may also feel dizzy and should not drive or be involved with complex and dangerous machinery.

20.3.4. Drug therapy of trichomonal infections

Trichomonas vaginalis most commonly causes vaginitis, and sometimes urethritis.

Treatment is with metronidazole. Various dosage regimens are recommended:

(a) Metronidazole in a single dose of 2 g. (Sexual partners should be treated also).

(b) Metronidazole 800 mg in the morning and 1.2 g at night for 2 days.

(c) Metronidazole 200 mg t.d.s. for 7 days.

Compliance is likely to be best with the regimen (a).

20.4 ANTHELMINTHICS

The drugs used in the treatment of helminthic infections are listed in Table 20.10. These drugs are not discussed in the Pharmacopoeia. For information consult the *British National Formulary* or manufacturers' literature. Other therapies are available, but currently the drugs listed are usually first choice in the UK for the indications shown.

Table 20.10   *Drug therapy of infestations*

Worm	*Drug*	*Comments*
Ascariasis (roundworm)	Piperazine	Mild nausea and vomiting
Trichuriasis (whipworm)	Mebendazole	Teratogenic in animals—avoid in pregnancy
Ankylostomiasis (hookworm)	Bephenium	Mild nausea and vomiting
Strongyloidiasis	Thiabendazole	Nausea, dizziness, and sedation
Enterobiasis (threadworm or pinworm)	Piperazine	As above
Taenia saginata (tapeworm)	Niclosamide	Occasional nausea and abdominal pain
Taenia solium	Niclosamide	Risk of cysticercosis

20.5. ANTIFUNGAL CHEMOTHERAPY

The drugs used in the treatment of fungal infections are listed in Table 20.11 and their pharmacological properties in the Pharmacopoeia.

In Tables 20.12 and 20.13 are shown the indications and routes of administration. Adverse effects and dosages are listed in the Pharmacopoeia.

Table 20.11   *Drugs used in the treatment of fungal infections*

Nystatin (p.720)
Amphotericin (p.635)
Flucytosine
Imidazoles (p.636)
   Clotrimazole
   Econazole
   Ketoconazole
   Miconazole
Griseofulvin (p.684)

Table 20.12   *Preferred antifungal therapy for superficial mycoses*

	Topical amphotericin	Topical clotrimazole	Topical miconazole	Topical econazole	Topical nystatin	Oral griseofulvin	Oral ketoconazole	
Candidiasis								
Skin	++	++	++	++	++	–	+[1]	[1] Chronic muco-cutaneous candidias
Mouth	++	–	+	–	+	–	+[2]	[2] Not responding to local therapy or chronic and recurrent
Vagina	+	++	++	++	++	–	+[2]	
Dermatophytes								
Tinea cruris, Tinea pedis, Tinea corporis[3]	–	++	++	++	–	–	–	[3] Don't forget Whitfield's ointment
Tinea capitis, Tinea corporis, Tinea unguium	–	++	++	++	–	+++[4]	++	[4] If at all severe use griseofulvin. Ketoconazole is also active
Tinea versicolor[5] (pityriasis)	–	–	–	–	–	–	++	[5] 1% selenium sulphide is also used

NB   See amphotericin, griseofulvin, and antifungal imidazoles in Pharmacopoeia.

The following points should be particularly noted in using these drugs:

1. Drug interactions may occur with griseofulvin (see p.684).

2. Amphotericin has a low toxic:therapeutic ratio and can be very toxic when used systemically (see p.635). It penetrates the CSF poorly.

3. The most important adverse effect of flucytosine is bone marrow suppression, which is dose-related.

4. Imidazoles can cause hepatic dysfunction and jaundice.

Table 20.13   *Drug therapy of some systemic mycoses*

	Amphotericin B, i.v.	Flucytosine, oral or i.v.	Miconazole, i.v. or oral	Ketoconazole, oral[‡]
Systemic candidiasis	+[†]	+	+	+
Histoplasmosis	+[†]			?
Coccidioidomycosis	+[†]		+	?
Blastomycosis	+[†]			?
Cryptococcosis (meningitis)	+[†]	+[†]		
Systemic aspergillosis	+			

NB   See amphotericin and antifungal imidazoles in Pharmacopoeia.
[*] Not aspergilloma or allergic bronchopulmonary aspergillosis.
[†] First choice. Cryptococcal meningitis—combine amphotericin with flucytosine.
[‡] Ketoconazole being evaluated.

20.6 PREVENTION OF INFECTIONS USING VACCINES AND IMMUNOGLOBULINS

20.6.1. Vaccines

The term 'vaccine' was originally used to describe the extract of cowpox (Latin vacca = cow) used to inoculate against smallpox in the 18th century. However, it is now used to describe any preparation used for active immunization against any infectious disease.

Vaccines are available for immunization against both bacterial and viral infections, and are of three types:

1. Live organisms, in attenuated form.
2. Inactivated organisms.
3. Extracts of organisms or exotoxins produced by organisms (toxoids).

Live organisms usually require to be administered in only a single dose and produce immunity lasting almost as long as that of a natural infection. This group includes vaccines against tuberculosis (BCG), influenza, measles, poliomyelitis (oral formulation), rubella, smallpox, and yellow fever.

Inactivated organisms usually require a series of doses intially to stimulate antibody production, and booster doses may be required at later times. This group includes cholera, pertussis, hepatitis B, poliomyelitis (s.c. and i.m. formulations), rabies, and typhoid.

Toxoids require schedules similar to those for inactivated organisms. This group includes diphtheria and tetanus.

Table 20.14   *Immunization schedules*

Vaccine	Source	Usual times of administration
BCG	Live, attenuated bovine *M. tuberculosis*	Age 10–13 years (if tuberculin-negative)
Cholera	Killed *Vibrio cholerae*	Before entering an endemic zone; six-monthly in endemic zones.
Diphtheria	Toxoid, prepared from toxin of *C. diphtheriae*	First dose at 3 months, second dose 6–8 weeks later, third dose 4–6 months later
Tetanus	Toxoid, prepared from toxin of *C. tetani*	
Pertussis	Killed *Bordetella pertussis*	
Hepatitis B	Inactivated hepatitis B virus surface antigen	When risk of infection is high
Influenza	Live, attenuated influenza viruses (grown in chick embryos)	In high-risk patients when infection is anticipated
Measles	Live, attenuated measles virus (grown in chick embryos)	Age 2 years
Poliomyelitis	(a) Live, attenuated poliomyelitis virus (oral)	As for diphtheria. tetanus, and pertussis
	(b) Inactivated poliomyelitis virus	If live vaccine contra-indicated (e.g. pregnancy and immune suppression)
Rabies	Inactivated rabies virus	Following infection (combined with antirabies immunoglobulin) and when risk of infection is high
Rubella	Live, attenuated rubella virus	Girls aged 10–13 years and women of child-bearing age (if seronegative for rubella)
Smallpox	Live, attenuated smallpox virus	Research workers studying pox viruses
Typhoid	Killed *Salmonella typhi*	Before entering an endemic zone; every 2–3 years in endemic zones
Yellow fever	Live, attenuated yellow fever virus	Before entering an endemic zone

Schedules of immunization

A list of commonly used vaccines is given in Table 20.14, showing their sources and usual times of initial administration. In the UK the DHSS has laid down a recommended schedule of administration for many of these vaccines, and an outline is given in Table 20.15.

Table 20.15 *Recommended immunization schedules in the UK*

Time	Vaccine(s)	Comments
First year	{ Diphtheria/tetanus/pertussis Poliomyelitis	Pertussis may be omitted if contra-indicated or refused
2 years	Measles	
On first going to school	{ Diphtheria/tetanus Poliomyelitis	At least 3 years after initial course
10–12 years	{ BCG Rubella	Girls only (rubella)
On leaving school	{ Poliomyelitis Tetanus	
Adults	Poliomyelitis	If previously unvaccinated and travelling to endemic area, or if own child being vaccinated
	Rubella	Women, if sero-negative; exclude pregnancy first and avoid pregnancy for 3 months
	Tetanus	If unvaccinated for 5 years

Table 20.16 *Recommended immunization for travellers*

Region[1]	Immunization[4]
S. Europe	Poliomyelitis
Central and S. America	Yellow fever, typhoid, polio, rabies[3], hepatitis[2]
Middle East and N. Africa	Typhoid, polio, cholera, rabies, hepatitis
Central, E., and W. Africa	Yellow fever, typhoid, polio, rabies[3], hepatitis[2]
S. Africa	Typhoid, polio, hepatitis[2]
Indian subcontinent, China, and S.E. Asia	Typhoid, polio, rabies, hepatitis[2]

[1] Precautions are not necessary for travel in N. Europe, N. America, Japan, Australia and N. Zealand.

[2] Immunization against hepatitis is with normal human immunoglobulin.

[3] Anti-rabies immunization is not always necessary, but should be offered to travellers to primitive areas or if medical facilities will not be available.

[4] Malaria prophylaxis should also be used for all the areas listed in the table except for S. Europe and S. Africa to the south of Johannesburg.

Recommendations on vaccination before travelling abroad are issued by government agencies. A set of recommendations is summarized in Table 20.16, but requirements change from time to time and it is always best to obtain up-to-date information locally (for the UK see the *British National Formulary*).

Adverse effects of vaccines

Reactions at the site of injection of a vaccine are very common, and in many cases provide evidence of a good antibody response. In most cases when this occurs there will be some local swelling and inflammation. In some cases there may also be local lymph node enlargement, and occasionally this may be accompanied by fever, headache, and general malaise, lasting up to a few days.

Hypersensitivity reactions may occur with vaccines made from viruses grown in chick or duck embryos (e.g. influenza and measles vaccine), and it is important to ask about hypersensitivity to eggs before giving these vaccines. Hypersensitivity reactions may also be caused by antibiotics or animal serum present in the vaccine (e.g. neomycin in rubella and poliomyelitis vaccines). Care should be taken when vaccinating patients who have allergic disorders, such as eczema or asthma. Smallpox vaccine should never be given to patients with eczema because of the danger of vaccinatum gangrenosum.

Vaccines containing live organisms may cause severe local reactions, or even systemic infection in patients with infections and other acute febrile illnesses, and in patients whose immune responsiveness is impaired for any reason (e.g. due to disease, radiotherapy, or drugs—see below). Live vaccines should, therefore, not be used in such patients.

Pertussis vaccine has been reported to have caused on rare occasions neurological complications resulting in convulsions and permanent brain damage. The issue of whether children should be immunized against whooping cough has therefore become controversial recently, but it is generally felt that the benefit of immunization outweighs the risk of complications. However, if a child has had a severe local or general reaction on one occasion then pertussis vaccine should not be given again. The vaccine should not be given at all to a child with a history of disorders of the central nervous system, or who has any acute infection at the time.

Live vaccines should not be used in pregnancy, because of the risk of congenital malformations. This is especially important for rubella virus, which is well-documented as a cause of congenital malformations, and pregnancy should be avoided for 3 months after rubella immunization.

Interactions with vaccines

Vaccines prepared from live organisms should not be given to patients taking cytotoxic chemotherapy, because of the risks of severe local reactions, and even overwhelming systemic infection. Patients on long-term corticosteroid therapy may be similarly at risk.

20.6.2. Immunoglobulins

Immunoglobulins are used to provide immediate protection against infection, and their effects last for 1–6 months.

(a) Normal immunoglobulin

Normal immunoglobulin is gamma globulin prepared from normal human plasma. It is used as short-term prophylaxis against and in the modification of infective hepatitis (A and B) and measles, and in the prevention of rubella in women exposed to infection. It is also used in the treatment of hypogammaglobulinaemia. Its effect lasts for 4–6 months.

The recommended dosages of the 16 per cent solution are as follows:

Infective hepatitis: 0.02–0.04 ml/kg i.m. as routine prophylaxis, and 0.06–0.12 ml/kg i.m. in circumstances where the risk of infection is high.

Measles: 0.2 ml/kg i.m. within 5 days of exposure.

Rubella: in pregnant women 20 ml i.m. as soon as possible after exposure.

(b) Specific immunoglobulins

Immunoglobulins for specific disorders are prepared from the plasmas of patients who have had the disorders. They include immunoglobulins for the prevention of rhesus incompatibility, and as short-term prophylaxis against and in the modification of hepatitis B, measles, pertussis, rabies, tetanus, and vaccinia infections.

Important adverse effects of immunoglobulins

Hypersensitivity reactions may occur and occasionally result in anaphylaxis. Pain and tenderness at the site of intramuscular injection are common.

Anti-D (rhesus negative) immunoglobulin should not be given to rhesus-positive or rhesus-immunized patients, since it may cause haemolysis.

Gamma globulin should not be given at the same time as measles, mumps, oral polio, and rubella vaccines.

21 The drug therapy of cardiovascular disorders

21.1. HYPERTENSION

Hypertension may either be of unknown cause ('essential'), or secondary to some definite abnormality, e.g. renal parenchymal disease, renovascular disease, a variety of endocrine disorders, coarctation of the aorta, and drugs. Where the primary abnormality can be reversed (e.g. renal artery stenosis, phaeochromocytoma) there may be no need to treat the hypertension chronically with antihypertensive drugs. However, in many cases treatment of the underlying cause is not possible and generally treatment of secondary hypertension follows the same principles as treatment of essential hypertension. In the following discussion we shall deal principally with essential hypertension and note some special points about secondary forms of hypertension. A list of drugs which may commonly cause or exacerbate hypertension, or which may oppose the effects of antihypertensive drugs is given in Table 21.1.

Table 21.1 *Drugs which may commonly cause or exacerbate hypertension, or oppose the effects of antihypertensives*

---

1. *By sodium and water retention*
Sodium salts of drugs (e.g. sodium penicillin, sodium-containing antacids)
Steroids—glucocorticosteroids
   mineralocorticosteroids
   androgens and anabolic steroids
   oestrogens and progestogens (e.g. oral contraceptives)
Carbenoxolone
Non-steroidal anti-inflammatory drugs (e.g. indomethacin, phenylbutazone)

2. *By vasoconstriction*
Sympathomimetics (e.g. adrenaline, noradrenaline)
Monoamine oxidase (MAO) inhibitors (in interaction with vasoactive amines such as dietary tyramine—the 'cheese reaction')

3. *Following withdrawal of antihypertensive drugs (rebound hypertension)*
Clonidine (potentially dangerous)
α-methyldopa
β-adrenoceptor antagonists

When the blood pressure is increased there is an increased risk of the complications of hypertension (myocardial ischaemia, cardiac failure, renal failure, and stroke). In addition severe hypertension may be associated with necrotizing vascular changes, so-called 'malignant' or 'accelerated' hypertension. The extent of the increase in risks is now known. For example, there is a 50 per cent increase in mortality from ischaemic heart disease among middle-aged men with blood pressures of 140/95 mmHg. Furthermore the risks of complications increase with increasing blood pressure (b.p.).

Although it is difficult to define precisely degrees of severity of hypertension, a rough working guide is as follows:

mild hypertension, b.p. 130/90–140/100 mmHg;
moderate hypertension, b.p. 140/100–160/120 mmHg;
severe hypertension, b.p. > 160/120 mmHg;
hypertensive emergency, diastolic b.p. > 130 mmHg.

These values apply to adults in the age range 20–65 (roughly). In young children increases in blood pressure to 160/110 mmHg can result in malignant or accelerated hypertension (e.g. in acute glomerulonephritis). Conversely people in their 70s may have no arteriolar change and be asymptomatic with a blood pressure of 220/120. Hard and fast rules are therefore difficult to apply. Nonetheless the individual doctor has to make up his mind when to treat, and some guidance is necessary.

The therapeutic hope is that by lowering a raised blood pressure the complications of hypertension may be avoided, or the risks at least reduced, and indeed that seems to be the case under certain circumstances. There is no doubt that effective treatment of accelerated or malignant hypertension is life-saving. The natural history of malignant hypertension is that 90 per cent of untreated patients will die within a year. On the other hand treated patients have a similar prognosis to patients with chronic hypertension.

Lowering the blood pressure in patients with moderate or severe chronic hypertension considerably reduces the risk of stroke, renal failure, and cardiac failure, and may also reduce the risk of myocardial ischaemia. In all of these cases the beneficial effects of therapy undoubtedly outweigh the risk of adverse drug effects.

However in mild hypertension, i.e. b.p. in the region 130/90–140/100 mmHg, the case for antihypertensive drug therapy is still not absolutely proven and large-scale studies are under way to clarify the problem. The difficulty stems from the fact that because the morbidity and mortality among patients with mild hypertension without tissue damage is only slightly greater than those in the non-hypertensive population studies of the effects of drug therapy require very large numbers of patients, treated over prolonged periods of time, to determine whether or not drug therapy has a beneficial effect (see Chapter 15 on numbers in clinical trials). Such trials are consequently difficult to carry out. One might also expect differences in efficacy of treatment according to whether or not arterial damage had already occurred, i.e. the treatment would be too late to prevent it. To date the results of such trials have been difficult to interpret, and in addition there is insufficient information on the risks of adverse effects in relation to the small benefit which might accrue from treatment.

Table 21.2   *Drugs used in the treatment of hypertension*

1. *Diuretics*
Thiazides (p.761)
Other thiazide-like diuretics—chlorthalidone, clopamine, clorexolone, mefruside, metolazone, quinethazone, xipamide

2. *β-adrenoceptor antagonists* (p.622)
e.g. propranolol, atenolol, oxprenolol, metoprolol

3. *α-adrenoceptor antagonists*
Selective (α_1):
    Prazosin (p.734)
    Indoramin (p.688)
Non-selective (generally used only in phaeochromocytoma):
    Phentolamine and phenoxybenzamine (p.621)

4. *Mixed α- and β-adrenoceptor antagonist*
Labetalol (p.695)

5. *Peripheral vasodilators*
Hydralazine (p.686)
Minoxidil (p.709)
Diazoxide
Sodium nitroprusside (p.751)

6. *Drugs affecting nervous control of blood pressure*
(a) Centrally acting
    α-methyldopa (p.705)
    Clonidine (p.663)
    Reserpine
(b) Peripherally acting
    Adrenergic neurone blocking drugs (p.619)—bethanidine, debrisoquine, guanethidine

7. *Angiotension converting enzyme inhibitors*
Captopril (p.649)

8. *Calcium 'antagonists'*
Nifedipine (p.719)

There appear to be two schools of thought. There are those who offer antihypertensive drug therapy to all patients with a diastolic blood pressure of greater than 90 mmHg measured resting on at least three occasions. Others generally withhold treatment until a sustained diastolic blood pressure of 100 mmHg or greater is observed, except for those patients with high risk factors, e.g. left ventricular hypertrophy, a history of angina, left ventricular failure, cerebral ischaemia, evidence of hyperlipidaemia, a strong family history of vascular disease, or evidence of renal damage or retinopathy.

If it is decided to treat them, the aim of treatment in young and middle-aged patients should be to reduce blood pressure to about 130/90 if possible.

21.1.1. Mechanisms of action of drugs used in hypertension

In Fig. 21.1 are shown the mechanisms involved in the actions of antihypertensive drugs, and in Table 21.2 are listed the various drugs used according to their modes of action.

(a) Diuretics

The mode of action of the thiazide diuretics in hypertension is not yet understood and cannot be solely related to their effects on salt and water balance. More potent diuretics such as frusemide are not more potent antihypertensive drugs, and diazoxide, a chemically related compound causing sodium retention, is a powerful antihypertensive acting by peripheral vasodilatation. Although intravascular fluid volume and total body sodium fall during the first few weeks of diuretic therapy there follows an increase in circulating renin and within a few weeks the intravascular volume and sodium content return to normal but the antihypertensive effect persists. Diuretics may be acting by a direct effect on vascular smooth muscle causing vasodilatation, and that effect may be mediated through a decrease in vessel wall sodium content.

(b) β-adrenoceptor antagonists

The mechanism of action of the β-adrenoceptor antagonists is not fully understood. Currently favoured is the idea that they produce a fall in cardiac output, that baroreflex mechanisms do not fully compensate for this, that the baroreflex receptors are reset, and so peripheral resistance decreases. All the details of this suggested mode of action have not been worked out. Other hypotheses are that the β-adrenoceptor antagonists have a central effect altering sympathetic tone (unlikely since β-adrenoceptor antagonists which enter the brain poorly, such as atenolol, are equally good antihypertensives) or that they inhibit renin release from the kidney (possible, but currently not favoured).

(c) Vasodilators

Several drugs act as direct vasodilators of arterioles. These include hydralazine and minoxidil, used in the treatment of chronic hypertension, and diazoxide and sodium nitroprusside, used for rapid lowering of blood

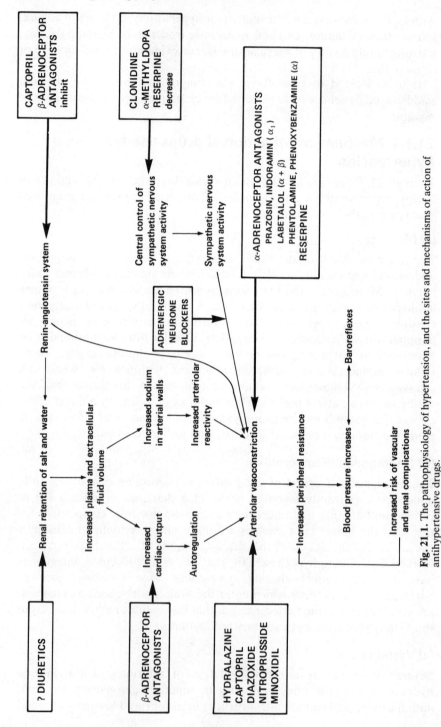

Fig. 21.1. The pathophysiology of hypertension, and the sites and mechanisms of action of antihypertensive drugs.

pressure in hypertensive crises. The mechanisms of the vasodilatation caused by these drugs are unknown. Since most of these vasodilators cause salt and water retention they are generally used in combination with a diuretic. Furthermore, since hydralazine causes a reflex tachycardia its effects are enhanced by concurrent administration of a β-adrenoceptor antagonist.

(d) α-adrenoceptor antagonists

Prazosin and indoramin are also peripheral dilators through their actions as post-synaptic α-adrenoceptor antagonists. Labetalol combines non-specific α- and non-specific β-adrenoceptor antagonist properties.

(e) Angiotensin converting enzyme inhibitors

Captopril acts by inhibiting the angiotensin converting enzyme, thus causing decreased production of angiotensin II. This results in vasodilatation (and thus decreased peripheral resistance) and decreased aldosterone production (and thus decreased sodium retention), all of which favour a decrease in blood pressure. Captopril also decreases the inactivation of the vasodilator peptide bradykinin, but the exact role of this action is unclear.

(f) Drugs affecting nervous control of blood pressure

These drugs act in diverse ways. It is thought that α-methyldopa acts centrally in those parts of the brain controlling sympathetic nervous system function. It is converted in noradrenergic neurones to α-methylnoradrenaline, a potent α-adrenoceptor agonist. Clonidine is a direct α-adrenoceptor agonist. In both cases the stimulation of α-adrenoceptors in the brain stem results in a decrease in peripheral sympathetic nervous system function.

Reserpine acts by causing depletion of neuronal stores of catecholamines both centrally and peripherally.

The adrenergic neurone blocking drugs, bethanidine, debrisoquine, and guanethidine inhibit the release of noradrenaline from peripheral sympathetic nerve endings.

21.1.2. Practical use of antihypertensive drugs

The different choices of drug regimens in essential hypertension are summarized in Table 21.3 in the order in which they would be used.

(a) Moderate hypertension

In the initial treatment of moderate hypertension the choice of drug lies between a diuretic and a β-adrenoceptor antagonist. The decision which to use may sometimes be purely arbitrary, or may depend on the doctor's personal preference and habits of medical practice. However, in a hypertensive patient with cardiac failure a diuretic would be the logical choice while a β-adrenoceptor antagonist would be preferred in a hypertensive patient who also had angina pectoris. Sometimes the choice may depend on likely patient preference or on adverse effects, either experienced or anticipated. For example, one would prefer to avoid a β-adrenoceptor antagonist in most patients with symptomatic bronchial asthma (even a $β_1$-selective antagonist), or with peripheral vascular disease. Diuretics, on the other hand, might worsen pre-existing diabetes in a patient with hypertension.

Table 21.3 *Summary of the drug therapy of essential hypertension*

---

1. Moderate hypertension

(a) *β-adrenoceptor antagonist not contra-indicated*

   (i)   Diuretic or β-antagonist (e.g. bendrofluazide or atenolol)
  (ii) Diuretic + β-antagonist
 (iii) Diuretic + β-antagonist + hydralazine
       or Diuretic + labetalol

(b) *β-adrenoceptor antagonist contra-indicated*

   (i)   Diuretic
  (ii) Diuretic + prazosin *or* α-methyldopa

2. Severe hypertension

(a) *β-adrenoceptor antagonist not contra-indicated*

   (i)   β-antagonist and/or diuretic
  (ii) β-antagonist + diuretic + hydralazine *or* prazosin
 (iii) β-antagonist + diuretic + hydralazine or prazosin + captopril

(b) *β-adrenoceptor antagonist contra-indicated*

   (i)   Diuretic + prazosin or α-methyldopa

(c) *Patients not responding to these regimens*

   Add α-methyldopa *or* captopril *or* minoxidil *or* an adrenergic neurone blocking drug (e.g. bethanidine)

(i) Diuretics

The choice of a diuretic is restricted to a thiazide or thiazide-like diuretic (see Table 21.2), other diuretics conferring no advantage. The loop diuretics in particular (e.g. frusemide, bumetanide) are more potent in causing adverse effects, and no more effective in lowering the blood pressure when used alone. Commonly one would use a thiazide such as bendrofluazide 5–10 mg o.d. orally, or cyclopenthiazide 0.5–1 mg o.d. orally. The use of potassium supplements and potassium-sparing diuretics to conserve potassium in patients taking diuretics is discussed in detail in

Chapter 24. In hypertension the potassium-losing effect of thiazide diuretics is less than in patients being treated for cardiac failure and potassium-conserving measures are usually not necessary.

Besides hypokalaemia the major adverse effects of the thiazides are excessive salt and water loss, hyperuricaemia, and impairment of glucose tolerance. There is also an increased incidence of erectile impotence in patients with hypertension taking thiazide diuretics. Patients do not often complain about this symptom since they generally do not link it with the drug and in any case do not like to talk about it.

(ii) β-adrenoceptor antagonists and alternatives

Of the wide variety of β-adrenoceptor antagonists atenolol is the drug of choice—it penetrates the brain poorly and consequently has fewer central adverse effects, it can be given once daily in the hope of improving compliance (see below), and it is relatively β_1-cardioselective. The usual dosage is 50–200 mg o.d. orally. Metoprolol is similar but needs to be given twice daily, and is slightly less cardioselective than atenolol. The usual dosage is 50–200 mg b.d. orally. Despite their relative cardioselectivity these drugs may nonetheless cause bronchoconstriction in some patients with asthma or chronic bronchitis in whom great care must be taken. The other adverse affects include bradycardia and impairment of cardiac output which may result in heart failure, an increased susceptibility of the hands and feet to the cold especially in patients with peripheral vascular disease, producing Raynaud's phenomenon, and a general feeling of fatigue, particular muscular weakness and fatigue on severe muscular effort.

The use of either a diuretic or a β-adrenoceptor antagonist will lower the blood pressure satisfactorily in 50–80 per cent of patients with moderate hypertension and this figure can be increased to about 90 per cent by combining the two types of treatment.

As an alternative to combining a β-adrenoceptor antagonist with a diuretic it may instead be combined with a vasodilator such as hydralazine or prazosin. Hydralazine alone is an effective vasodilator but its blood pressure lowering effect is counteracted by reflex tachycardia. Unacceptably high doses of hydralazine producing a high incidence of systemic lupus erythematosus are therefore required if it is to be an effective antihypertensive when used alone, but in combination with a β-adrenoceptor antagonist which blocks the reflex tachycardia it is effective in lower doses (less than 200 mg daily in all). The usual dose is 25–50 mg t.d.s. or q.d.s. Its important adverse effects are postural hypotension, nausea, vomiting, and diarrhoea.

Prazosin is an alternative to hydralazine, and is useful in the treatment of patients on a diuretic and in whom a β-adrenoceptor antagonist is contra-indicated, and also in the treatment of hypertension in patients with heart failure, for which its vasodilator properties are also helpful. It is important that the very first dose (0.5 mg) be given when the patient is lying down in order to avoid postural hypotension. This is not often a problem with subsequent doses. The usual dosage is 0.5 mg t.d.s. initially increasing gradually to a maximum of 5 mg q.d.s.

Labetalol is an alternative to the combination of a peripheral vasodilator and a β-adrenoceptor antagonist, since it combines α- and β-adrenoceptor antagonist properties. Its effects are however non-selective. It is given in a dosage of 100–800 mg t.d.s. orally. It is often combined with a thiazide diuretic.

Indoramin is another α-adrenoceptor antagonist, and its effects are enhanced by combination with a diuretic or a β-adrenoceptor antagonist.

(b) Severe hypertension

In severe hypertension one would generally start with a β-adrenoceptor antagonist, such as atenolol 100 mg o.d., increasing to 200 mg if the desired response was not achieved within a few days, and then adding hydralazine or prazosin. Prazosin with a diuretic could be used instead in those patients in whom a β-adrenoceptor antagonist was contra-indicated. In patients not fully responding to atenolol with hydralazine, prazosin should be added.

(c) Alternative drugs

Well over 90 per cent of patients will respond to treatment with one of the above four types of drugs (diuretics, β-adrenoceptor antagonists, hydralazine, and prazosin), either alone or in combination. In those few patients who do not respond satisfactorily, or who cannot tolerate these drugs, other drugs must be added. The main alternatives are α-methyldopa, captopril, the adrenergic neurone blocking drugs, and minoxidil.

(i) α-methyldopa

α-methyldopa is an effective antihypertensive drug which, with diuretics, was first-line treatment for moderate and severe hypertension before the advent of β-adrenoceptor antagonists. However, it frequently makes patients feel depressed and generally lacking in physical and mental energy, and is now a reserve drug for that reason. It is still useful, however, in pregnancy (see below). It is given in an initial dosage of 250 mg t.d.s. orally and may be increased to a maximum of 3 g daily. Dosages should be reduced in renal failure (Table 3.5).

(ii) Captopril

Captopril has been introduced cautiously into the treatment of hypertension. Currently it is indicated for the treatment of severe hypertension refractory to other forms of treatment. The dosages recommended are up to 150 mg t.d.s. and at high dosages proteinuria and neutropenia may occur. However it is possible that such adverse effects are less likely at lower dosages (e.g. 25 mg t.d.s.). The hypotensive effects of captopril are greatly enhanced by diuretics.

(iii) Adrenergic neurone blocking drugs
These drugs (bethanidine, debrisoquine, and guanethidine) are now little used because of their adverse effects, which include severe postural hypotension, diarrhoea, and erectile impotence.

(vi) Minoxidil
Minoxidil is a potent vasodilator which causes marked fluid retention, hirsutism, and reflex tachycardia. It is therefore reserved for the treatment of hypertension which has failed to respond to the above measures, and must be used in combination with both a diuretic and a β-adrenoceptor antagonist. Fluid retention may be severe enough to require the use of a loop diuretic (as for captopril).

21.1.3. Some aspects of the treatment of secondary hypertension

(a) Renal disease
The treatment of hypertension secondary to renal disease is similar to that of essential hypertension. However, fluid retention can be a particular problem when vasodilators are used and a loop diuretic may then be necessary in preference to a thiazide diuretic. Some antihypertensive drugs are excreted unchanged by the kidneys and have to be used in lower dosages in renal impairment. The important examples are the β-adrenoceptor antagonists sotalol and nadolol, and α-methyldopa. Captopril may prove to be particularly effective in patients with renal hypertension and impairment of renal function.

(b) Specific uses of α-adrenoceptor antagonists
There are some circumstances in which the non-selective α-adrenoceptor antagonists phenoxybenzamine and phentolamine should be used in treating hypertension. They are as follows:

(i) Phaeochromocytoma (see also p.431)
For chronic treatment of hypertension due to phaeochromocytoma before surgery or when surgery is not possible, oral phenoxybenzamine should be used (10 mg o.d. to start with, increasing to a maximum of 60 mg t.d.s. if required). At operation an i.v. infusion of phentolamine should be used to prevent sudden severe hypertension due to release of noradrenaline during handling of the tumour. The mixed α- and β-adrenoceptor antagonist labetalol is an alternative to α-antagonists both before and during surgery.

(ii) Certain causes of acute hypertensive crisis
There are several circumstances in which an acute hypertensive crisis

should be treated with i.v. phentolamine (5–15 mg). They are:

acute hypertension following abrupt clonidine withdrawal;

hypertensive crisis in patients on MAO inhibitors (e.g. 'cheese reaction', see p.166);

in overdose with α-adrenoceptor agonists.

(c) Endocrine disorders

In hypertension due to Conn's syndrome (primary hyperaldosteronism) if surgical treatment is not possible, the aldosterone antagonist spirono-lactone may be used. In Cushing's syndrome β-adrenoceptor antagonists may provide non-specific hypotensive effects, although more specific medical or surgical therapy may be indicated. In both these conditions hypokalaemia is a particular risk and care must be taken with thiazides and loop diuretics because of potassium loss.

(d) Hypertension in pregnancy (see also Chapter 11)

Hypertension in pregnancy may be due either to pre-existing chronic hypertension (e.g. essential or renovascular hypertension) or to the specific entity known as pre-eclampsia, or toxaemia of pregnancy, which occurs in the third trimester, and in which there is hypertension with persistent proteinuria and peripheral oedema. The risks of pre-eclampsia are of slowed intra-uterine fetal growth, of an increased incidence of stillbirth and of the occurrence of eclampsia (fits) with danger to the life of mother and fetus. Other complications include disseminated intravascular coagulation, renal failure, acute left ventricular failure, and stroke.

Since the blood pressure normally falls during pregnancy the criteria for diagnosis of hypertension are difficult and usually one would define pre-eclampsia hypertension as a persistent blood pressure of at least 30/15 mmHg higher than the pressure when first recorded at before 20 weeks of gestation. In some women with chronic hypertension it is possible to withhold treatment during pregnancy, but if drug therapy is necessary, either for chronic hypertension or pre-eclampsia, then the drug of choice is α-methyldopa. β-adrenoceptor antagonists have also been used, but pro-pranolol has been reported to cause fetal and neonatal bradycardia and respiratory depression. Diuretics should be avoided because intravascular fluid volume is reduced. The aim should be to reduce diastolic pressure to 90–95 mmHg.

If pre-eclampsia occurs rapidly late in pregnancy the best treatment is rapid termination (i.e. delivery of the child), but if the blood pressure needs to be lowered rapidly hydralazine or diazoxide should be given parenterally. If fits occur they should be treated with chlormethiazole.

21.1.4. Hypertensive crises

There are some circumstances in which the blood pressure needs to be lowered relatively quickly. These include:

accelerated or malignant hypertension, with or without hypertensive encephalopathy;
acute dissecting aneurysm of the aorta;
hypertensive left ventricular failure;
pre-eclampsia (see above).

The definition of a hypertensive emergency used here is a diastolic blood pressure greater than 130 mmHg.

Although it is desirable to reduce the diastolic blood pressure below 120 mmHg within 24 h in accelerated or malignant hypertension it is usually unnecessary to reduce it more rapidly, and indeed it may be dangerous to do so. That is because the mechanisms which maintain cerebral blood flow at a constant level independent of peripheral blood pressure are impaired in hypertension. If the blood pressure is lowered too rapidly in such cases cerebral blood flow may fall and brain damage and death can occur from cerebral anoxia, cerebral oedema, and even frank infarction. Only occasionally does the need to lower the blood pressure rapidly outweigh the risk of reducing cerebral blood flow—as in patients with an acute dissection of an aortic aneurysm, with acute left ventricular failure secondary to hypertension, with severe pre-eclampsia, and with hypertensive encephalopathy, i.e. conditions very acutely threatening to life.

If the blood pressure has to be lowered very rapidly the choice of drugs includes sodium nitroprusside, labetalol, and diazoxide. Sodium nitroprusside has a rapid 'on–off' effect. Its half-time is very short and its effects come on and wear off in a few minutes. It is thus possible to control the blood pressure by varying the infusion rate (usual dosage 0.5–1.5 micrograms/kg/min increasing if necessary to 8 micrograms/kg/min). It is therefore the ideal drug for control of the blood pressure, but because of the rapidity of its effects its use requires constant medical supervision with frequently repeated, or preferably continuous, blood pressure measurement. It should not be given to patients with renal failure because of the danger of cyanide poisoning, nor in pregnancy.

The alternative is labetalol, given either as a continuous i.v. infusion at a rate of 1–4 mg/min or as 50 mg i.v. bolus doses repeated at 5–15 min intervals up to a maximum total of 200 mg. Patients should always be supine because of the risk of severe postural hypotension. Its effects after bolus injection occur within a few minutes and last for up to 6 h, and in some cases as long as 24 h.

Diazoxide is given as a rapid i.v. bolus of 150 or 300 mg, but should be used with great care since the blood pressure may fall markedly within a few minutes of administration. It has a very long half-time (25 h) and is excreted mostly unchanged in the urine. Dosages should not therefore be repeated too frequently in renal failure. It is not now used in the long-term treatment of hypertension because of its adverse effects, including impairment of glucose tolerance, salt and water retention, hyperuricaemia, hirsutism, and hypersensitivity reactions (skin rashes, thrombocytopenia, and leucopenia). Its adverse effects after acute administration include tachycardia and cardiac pain. Occasionally on bolus i.v. administration it can cause acute pancreatitis with severe epigastric pain. It is sometimes preferred for rapid lowering of blood pressure in pre-eclampsia but hydralazine is safer, albeit slower.

When lowering of the blood pressure is not so urgent the treatment of choice is parenteral hydralazine (e.g. 10 mg i.m. not more frequently than four-hourly, as long as the diastolic pressure is greater than 120 mmHg). Treatment should be started at the same time with an oral β-adrenoceptor antagonist such as propranolol 80 mg b.d., so that the reflex tachycardia is blocked and also to ensure that when the blood pressure has fallen parenteral hydralazine can be withdrawn and blood pressure control can be maintained.

21.1.5. Contra-indications to treatment of hypertension

There are two circumstances in which treatment of hypertension must be carried out cautiously—in patients with stroke or with acute myocardial infarction. Only if there is severe hypertension (diastolic blood pressure greater than 120 mmHg) should antihypertensive drugs be used acutely to treat hypertension. In stroke thiazide diuretics and/or β-adrenoceptor antagonists are safe, and in acute myocardial infarction treatment of pain with opiates and of sodium and fluid retention with diuretics may result in lowering of the blood pressure satisfactorily without the need for other specific measures.

Treatment of hypertension in the elderly is still controversial. The controversy concerns the value of the blood pressure at which treatment is indicated. Many would give treatment when the diastolic blood pressure is over 110 mmHg. Others would treat at lower values and some at higher. Diuretics and β-adrenoceptor antagonists are then the drugs of choice.

21.1.6. Monitoring therapy in hypertension

It is always wise to measure blood pressures when the patient is supine and when standing in order to detect postural falls in blood pressure. In addition it may be valuable to measure the blood pressure after a small amount of exercise (e.g. stepping up and down on a step half-a-dozen times). This is particularly useful for patients on β-adrenoceptor antagonists in whom the blood pressure may fall on exercise. It is relatively simple for patients to measure their own blood pressures at home and self-monitoring in this way yields useful information on the variability of the blood pressure and its response to treatment.

21.1.7. Compliance in hypertension

There is a special case for discussing compliance in the treatment of mild to moderate asymptomatic hypertension. Patients with hypertension usually feel well and often do not understand the need to take drugs which may make them feel unwell. It is very important to take the time to explain carefully to every hypertensive patient the need to take antihypertensive treatment, and careful education has been shown to improve compliance. Once-daily therapy may also help but is not always possible.

One can usually tell whether the patient is complying with β-adrenoceptor antagonist therapy by taking the pulse rate at rest and on exercise.

21.2. ANGINA PECTORIS

The syndrome of angina pectoris occurs when there is an acute imbalance between the oxygen requirements of the myocardium and the oxygen available to it. This occurs either when there is sudden spasm of a coronary artery (so-called 'variant' or 'Prinzmetal' angina), or a sudden increase in demand for oxygen in a chronically ischaemic heart. An increase in oxygen demand may result from any stimulus which causes an increase in systolic ventricular pressure or size, an increase in heart rate, or an increase in the rate or force of contractility of the myocardium. The commonest precipitating factor of an acute attack of angina is exercise but angina pectoris can also occur in response to other forms of stress such as emotion, cold, or a heavy meal. Other factors which may be associated with attacks of angina pectoris in patients with chronic myocardial ischaemia include anaemia (poor oxygen-carrying capacity of the blood), aortic stenosis (inadequate supply of blood to the coronary arteries during diastole), paroxysmal arrhythmias (impaired blood supply), and thyrotoxicosis (increased metabolic requirements).

Table 21.4 *Drugs used in angina pectoris*

---

1. *Treatment of an acute attack in chronic stable angina*
Glyceryl trinitrate (p.682)
Isosorbide dinitrate (p.682)

2. *Prevention of acute attacks and treatment of unstable angina*
Glyceryl trinitrate (topical application)
Isosorbide dinitrate
β-adrenoceptor antagonists (p.622)
Nifedipine (p.719)

21.2.1. Mechanisms of action of drugs used to relieve or prevent angina pectoris

The drugs used in the treatment of an acute attack of angina pectoris, or in the prevention of attacks are listed in Table 21.4, and their modes of action are illustrated in Fig. 21.2.

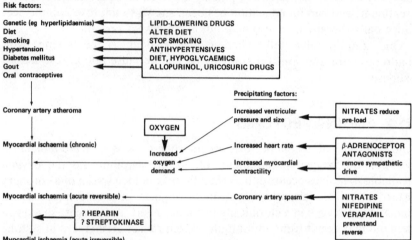

Fig. 21.2. The pathophysiology of ischaemic heart disease, and the sites and mechanisms of action of drugs used in its treatment.

Nitrates relieve angina pectoris by several mechanisms:

1. By causing arteriolar vasodilatation, lowering peripheral resistance, and reducing myocardial work and oxygen demand.

2. By causing peripheral venous dilatation, decreasing venous return, and thereby reducing left ventricular end-diastolic pressure and volume, and again reducing myocardial work and oxygen demand.

3. By relieving coronary arterial spasm in variant angina, and any spasm occurring as part of common angina.

4. By redistribution of myocardial blood flow to improve the perfusion of ischaemic areas.

β-adrenoceptor antagonists act by blocking the action of noradrenaline released from sympathetic nerve-endings, thereby decreasing the effects of the nervous system on the heart. This has two effects—firstly, the increase in heart rate in response to physical or emotional stress is reduced, and secondly, the contractility of the myocardium is reduced. Both of these effects result in prevention of increased oxygen requirements at times of stress.

Nifedipine is an antagonist of calcium ion flux and causes peripheral arterial and venous vasodilatation. In this respect it acts like the nitrates (see above). It also dilates normal coronary arteries.

21.2.2. Use of anti-anginal drugs

(a) Treatment of acute attacks of angina pectoris in chronic stable angina

If a patient has acute attacks of angina pectoris, whether on a background of chronic ischaemic myocardial disease or because of coronary artery spasm, the treatment of choice for the *acute* attack is a nitrate, and glyceryl trinitrate is the nitrate usually chosen. It is taken as a tablet which is allowed to dissolve under the tongue, because the rapid absorption of glyceryl trinitrate through the oral mucosa provides rapid relief of anginal pain, and because this route of administration also avoids the extensive first-pass metabolism of glyceryl trinitrate in the liver following oral administration (i.e. the sublingual route improves the rate and extent of systemic availability). The anti-anginal action of glyceryl trinitrate begins within a minute or two and lasts for up to half an hour. The chief adverse effects when it is taken in this way are secondary to vasodilatation and include palpitation, headache, flushing, dizziness, and postural hypotension.

Usually one tablet (0.5 mg) is sufficient to relieve the pain of an attack, but two tablets may sometimes be necessary. The patient should be told that if pain relief does not occur within a few minutes, however, he should not continue to use glyceryl trinitrate tablets but should consult a doctor. He should also be advised of the use of a glyceryl trinitrate tablet taken sublingually in order to *prevent* an acute attack of angina pectoris which may be anticipated (e.g. just before unusual exertion, in anticipation of an emotional stress, or before going out on a cold morning). There is no limit on the number of tablets a patient may use for the treatment of repeated attacks.

Glyceryl trinitrate is unstable, tablets have a relatively short shelf-life, and deterioration can lead to lack of efficacy. Patients should be told to keep their tablets in a dark container, only taking out enough tablets for a day's supply at a time if it is their habit to carry tablets loose. The bottle in which tablets are stored should have an aluminium-foil lined top. Neither cotton wool nor other drugs should be kept in the same bottle.

(b) Prevention of acute attacks in chronic stable angina

The choices of therapy in the prevention of acute anginal attacks in chronic stable angina are shown in Table 21.4.

Glyceryl trinitrate and isosorbide dinitrate may both be used. Glyceryl trinitrate is now available for chronic use as an ointment which is rubbed into the skin (usually of the anterior chest) and which is slowly absorbed, maintaining therapeutic plasma concentrations for up to 8 h. It is also available in adhesive pads which are applied to the skin and from which slow release occurs into the blood via the skin. These methods are expensive and a bit inconvenient, and have not become routinely established in the prevention of attacks of angina pectoris.

Most commonly used is orally administered isosorbide dinitrate in a usual dosage of 10 mg t.d.s. (but ranging from 5 mg b.d. to 20 mg q.d.s.). The adverse effects are the same as those of glyceryl trinitrate sublingually.

If attacks of angina are very frequent, if many tablets of glyceryl trinitrate have to be taken, or if isosorbide dinitrate is not wholly effective, then it would be usual next to prescribe a β-adrenoceptor antagonist. This provides a background of β-blockade and decreased myocardial oxygen demand at times of stress upon which, if still necessary, the patient can take glyceryl trinitrate as indicated.

It is likely that all β-adrenoceptor antagonists are equally effective in preventing acute anginal attacks. Atenolol is a good choice, for the reasons outlined under the treatment of hypertension. It is given in a dose of 50–200 mg o.d. orally. Alternatives include propranolol, metoprolol, and oxprenolol (see Pharmacopoeia, p.622). Cardiac failure is usually a contra-indication to the use of β-adrenoceptor antagonists. If there is concern about left ventricular function in a patient with angina on β-adrenoceptor antagonists, then it is wise to prescribe a diuretic and consider further the possible treatment of cardiac failure (see p.328).

Contra-indications to the β-adrenoceptor antagonists are the same as for their use in hypertension.

If angina continues on a background of β-blockade with isosorbide, then treatment with nifedipine would be considered. It is given in a dosage of 10–20 mg t.d.s. Important adverse effects are tachycardia and hypotension and rarely it can worsen angina.

Verapamil (40–80 mg t.d.s.) is an alternative to nifedipine, but it has a negative inotropic effect on the heart which may result in heart failure, and it is therefore of less value than nifedipine.

When the nitrates, nifedipine, or verapamil are used in patients with chronic myocardial ischaemia or in patients with variant angina, the reflex tachycardia which opposes their beneficial effects on myocardial oxygen requirements is inhibited by the administration of the β-adrenoceptor antagonist. One should be aware however that occasionally β-adrenoceptor antagonists may exacerbate variant angina.

Treatment with a vasodilator or a β-adrenoceptor antagonist or both will either prevent or markedly reduce the frequency of attacks of angina pectoris in over 90 per cent of patients, but it is not known whether effective treatment leads to a reduction in mortality from coronary artery disease. However there is some evidence that long-term therapy with β-adrenoceptor antagonists may result in a decreased incidence of subsequent myocardial infarction.

Patients who do not respond satisfactorily to drugs should be referred to a cardiologist with a view to considering coronary angiography followed by coronary artery by-pass graft surgery. This technique is now also being used increasingly as a first-line treatment for certain selected patients with angina pectoris.

(c) Unstable angina

Unstable angina (also known as crescendo angina, pre-infarction angina, acute coronary insufficiency, and intermediate coronary syndrome) is a state in which there is acute continuous cardiac pain, unresponsive to sublingual glyceryl trinitrate, which may lead on to frank myocardial infarction (i.e. irreversible ischaemic damage). Attacks may last for up to 45 min at a time and are generally unassociated with obvious precipitating factors, such as exercise or emotional stress.

The patient should be put to bed, preferably in hospital, and given oxygen by facial mask in a high concentration. Chest pain should be immediately relieved using an opiate (see treatment of myocardial infarction), and nitrates and β-adrenoceptor antagonists should be given in increasing dosages until the pain is prevented. If this does not happen within 24 h nifedipine should be added. If that is not effective coronary angiography should be considered with a view to coronary artery by-pass graft surgery or coronary angioplasty.

Isosorbide dinitrate orally is the nitrate of choice in these circumstances, starting in a dose of 10 mg t.d.s. and increasing if required to 20 mg t.d.s. Glyceryl trinitrate ointment is an alternative (1–2 inches rubbed into the skin every 4 h). A β-adrenoceptor antagonist should also be given, e.g. metoprolol 50 mg b.d. initially, increasing if required to 100 mg q.d.s. Metoprolol has the advantages here that it is a cardioselective β-adrenoceptor antagonist and has a relatively shallow dose–response curve, so that one can carefully titrate the response of the patient to increasing doses over a short period of time and determine to what extent the drug has been effective. If the combination of isosorbide and a β-adrenoceptor antagonist proves ineffective nifedipine should be added (10 mg t.d.s. orally increasing to 20 mg t.d.s. if required).

Careful review of the patient should be undertaken twice a day and dosages of drugs increased if the pain is not under control.

There have been some experiments with heparin given i.v. and streptokinase infused directly into the coronary arteries, but there is no conclusive proof that either of these manoeuvres prevents the development of irreversible myocardial ischaemic damage (i.e. infarction).

21.3. ACUTE MYOCARDIAL INFARCTION

Acute myocardial infarction occurs when there is occlusion of a coronary artery, because of thrombosis, spasm, or rarely embolism, with subsequent irreversible tissue damage. Treatment can be considered in terms of prevention and treatment of the acute attack.

21.3.1. Prevention of myocardial infarction

The risk factors for coronary atheroma are illustrated in Fig. 21.2. Drugs may be indicated for treatment of hyperlipidaemias, diabetes, and hypertension. So far there have been no studies showing overall benefit from any drug therapy in the primary prevention of myocardial infarction—outside of the treatment of risk factors. The *secondary* prevention of myocardial infarction is discussed below.

21.3.2. Mechanisms of action of drugs used in the treatment of acute myocardial infarction

The drugs used in the treatment of acute myocardial infarction and its complications are listed in Table 21.5.

Table 21.5   *Drugs used in the treatment of acute myocardial infarction and its major complications*

---

1. Oxygen

2. Relief of pain and distress—opiate analgesics (p.713)

3. Nausea and vomiting—anti-emetics (e.g. phenothiazines, p.727)

4. Cardiac failure:
     oxygen
     loop diuretics (pp.646 and 681)
     opiates
     vasodilators (Table 21.9)
     dopamine (p.675)
     β-adrenoceptor agonists (p.620)

5. Arrhythmias—anti-arrhythmics (Table 21.6)

6. Prevention of secondary venous thrombosis—heparin (p.685)

7. Limiting infarct size—β-adrenoceptor antagonists (p.622)

8. Pericarditis and Dressler's syndrome:
     aspirin (p.740)
     corticosteroids (p.664)

(a) Oxygen

The rationale for the use of oxygen in acute myocardial infarction is that the partial pressure of oxygen in the arterial blood (P_AO_2) is often decreased and an increase in inhaled oxygen will correct that, thereby increasing tissue oxygenation. Oxygen should therefore be used if there is evidence of arterial hypoxia, e.g. in patients with acute left ventricular failure or cardiogenic shock. Oxygen must be used with caution in patients with chronic obstructive airways disease (see p.348).

(b) Opiate analgesics

Opiate analgesics have several different valuable properties for use in myocardial infarction. They relieve pain and mental distress, and presumably reduce sympathetic nervous system activity. They are dilators of peripheral blood vessels, both arterioles and venules, thereby reducing the cardiac preload and afterload, and relieving cardiac failure. They may, however, cause hypotension, and nausea and vomiting. They should be used with caution in patients with chronic lung disease because they depress the respiratory centre.

(c) Anti-emetics

Patients with acute myocardial infarction frequently feel sick and vomit. Opiate analgesics make this worse and anti-emetics are therefore given. There is no clear guidance to the correct choice of anti-emetic and a phenothiazine, such as prochlorperazine, is often used. Great care must be taken, however, with such drugs since they too can cause hypotension, because of α-adrenoceptor blockade, particularly in patients with hypovolaemia.

(d) Diuretics

Many patients have some degree of left ventricular failure following an acute myocardial infarction. Intravenous frusemide is used and causes both peripheral venous vasodilatation reducing cardiac pre-load, and of course a diuretic effect, both of which may be beneficial.

(e) Anti-arrhythmics

See section 21.4 on the treatment of arrhythmias (p.316).

(f) Heparin

Patients who have had an acute myocardial infarction have an increased risk of deep venous thrombosis and therefore of pulmonary embolism. Normally low-dose heparin subcutaneously is given to prevent this (see pp.311 and 341).

(g) Drugs used to limit infarct size

Acute coronary occlusion produces an area of irreversibly damaged (i.e. dead) myocardium surrounded by normal myocardium. Between these two regions there is an intermediate zone of tissue which is ischaemic but which theoretically might recover, and if so useful myocardium could be saved from permanent damage. In recent years, therefore, efforts have been made to prevent irreversible damage in this intermediate ischaemic zone. Since prognosis appears to be related to infarct size this approach might be of considerable importance.

Chief among the treatments studied has been the use of β-adrenoceptor antagonists. The rationale is that decreased myocardial contractility and heart rate results in decreased myocardial oxygen requirements and thus the compromized tissue is more likely to survive the ischaemic insult. Several studies suggest that the early use of β-adrenoceptor antagonists may limit the size of a myocardial infarction and also relieve pain. However the overall benefit versus risk of the administration of β-adrenoceptor antagonists in the acute phase of myocardial infarction has been insufficiently assessed for firm recommendations to be made.

Other approaches which have been tried but which have not been fully validated include nitrates (to reduce myocardial oxygen requirements), hyaluronidase, corticosteroids, and the combination of glucose, potassium, and insulin.

21.3.3. Drug therapy in acute myocardial infarction

About 50 per cent of those who die following an acute myocardial infarction die immediately or within the first few hours, mostly because of arrhythmias, such as ventricular fibrillation. This observation has led to the introduction in some centres of schemes to improve the availability of facilities for cardiopulmonary resuscitation. Such schemes include the provision of rapidly mobilized coronary-care ambulances whose staff are specifically trained in the necessary techniques, and the education in some areas of members of the general population in those techniques.

(a) General measures

(i) Oxygen

Oxygen should be administered if there is suspicion of hypoxia, for instance in patients with cardiac failure or cardiogenic shock. It should be given via either a face-mask capable of delivered high concentrations in the inspired air (it is rarely possible to get a higher oxygen content than 60 per cent) or via nasal tubing (2–4 l/min). If the patient has chronic obstructive airways disease only 24 or 28 per cent oxygen should be used because of the danger of CO_2 narcosis with higher concentrations (see p.348).

(ii) Pain relief

The treatment of choice for pain relief is either morphine or diamorphine. Diamorphine is slightly to be preferred because it enters the brain more rapidly than morphine and may therefore act a little more quickly than morphine after parenteral administration. However, diamorphine is rapidly metabolized to morphine ($t_{1/2}$ 10 min) and there are therefore no other important differences between the two besides dosage—morphine 10–20 mg i.m. or i.v.; diamorphine 5–10 mg i.m. or i.v. A single dose is usually enough to relieve the pain of myocardial infarction but the dose may be repeated if it has not taken effect within 15 min of an i.v. injection or within 30 min of an i.m. injection. The opiate analgesics cause peripheral venous and arteriolar vasodilatation, and while this may be beneficial in patients with left ventricular failure, too much opiate may cause severe hypotension and excessive doses must be avoided. Because they depress the respiratory centre opiates should be used with caution in patients with chronic lung disease.

Because the opiate analgesics commonly cause nausea and vomiting or exacerbate that associated with acute myocardial infarction, anti-emetics are often given as well. There is no clear-cut guidance as to the best choice of anti-emetic in such circumstances, but phenothiazines or related antihistamines are commonly used (e.g. prochlorperazine 12.5 mg i.m., or cyclizine 50 mg i.m.). These drugs are liable to cause hypotension, via α-adrenoceptor blockade, which may add to the effects of the opiates.

The opiates and phenothiazines have the added benefits of causing sedation and this is generally a welcome effect. If it is felt necessary, however, to continue to relieve mental distress after the initial acute stage, when opiates are no longer required, then a benzodiazepine, such as diazepam 5–10 mg t.d.s., may be helpful and may also help the patient to sleep, especially if he is being treated in the unfamiliar, and perhaps worrying environment of the coronary care unit. The use of a benzodiazepine in such circumstances should only be regarded as a temporary measure.

(iii) Anticoagulation
As noted above there is an increased risk of deep venous thrombosis after acute myocardial infarction, and consequently of pulmonary embolism. The risk can be reduced by the use of heparin given subcutaneously in the low dose of 5000 i.u. b.d. or t.d.s. Patients should also be encouraged to move their leg muscles in order to reduce the risk of venous thrombosis in the deep veins of the calves. If deep venous thrombosis occurs, or if the patient develops a left ventricular aneurysm which is associated with ventricular clot and systemic emboli, full anticoagulation may be indicated firstly with heparin i.v. followed by warfarin (see treatment of thromboembolism p.342). Patients with pericarditis should not be given full anticoagulant therapy because of a real risk of pericardial haemorrhage and tamponade.

There is some evidence that streptokinase given i.v. or infused through a cardiac catheter directly into a coronary artery may hasten lysis of a coronary thrombosis and thereby reduce mortality after a myocardial infarction. However it is too soon to make any definitive statement about the benefit : risk ratio for streptokinase or to recommend its use.

(iv) Limiting infarct size

If β-adrenoceptor antagonists are used in an attempt to limit infarct size they should be given soon after the onset of pain, and only in those patients who are suitable for such treatment. This excludes patients with asthma or chronic bronchitis with bronchoconstriction, with moderate or severe left ventricular failure, with heart block of any degree, with bradycardia, or with a systolic pressure below 100 mmHg. Treatment, if used, should start with i.v. administration (e.g. propranolol 2 mg i.v. over 1 min repeated at 5 min intervals to a total dose of 6 mg) and continue with usual oral dosages. Generally such treatment should only be undertaken in coronary-care units, with continuous ECG monitoring and facilities for resuscitation. If excessive bradycardia or hypotension occurs treatment should be withheld immediately. The use of a β-adrenoceptor antagonist may have the additional advantage of relieving ischaemic pain. Note that this use of β-adrenoceptor antagonists to limit infarct size is quite different from their use in the secondary prevention of myocardial infarction.

(b) Treatment of immediate complications

(i) Acute left ventricular failure with pulmonary oedema

This is diagnosed on the basis of the signs and symptoms of pulmonary oedema where present (orthopnoea, crackles at the lung bases), evidence of pulmonary congestion on the chest X-ray, and haemodynamic measurements (if available) showing raised pulmonary capillary wedge pressure.

In myocardial infarction left ventricular failure may be transient, and often responds to oxygen and the opiate given to relieve pain. However, not infrequently it is also necessary to give a diuretic, such as frusemide (either 40–80 mg orally or if more severe 20–40 mg i.v.) or bumetanide (1–2 mg orally or i.v.). The dosage and frequency of administration of diuretics may have to be increased in more severe cases, for instance to doses of 160 mg i.v. of frusemide or 5 mg i.v. of bumetanide. However, great care should be taken not to over-use diuretics since that may cause a reduction in cardiac output due to a decreased intravascular volume.

Severe left ventricular failure may be fatal, and requires vigorous treatment. If large doses of diuretics, e.g. frusemide 250–500 mg i.v., are ineffective then one should quickly start treatment with vasodilators to reduce afterload. This should preferably be carried out in a coronary care unit under haemodynamic control with measurement of right atrial (i.e. central venous) pressure, and pulmonary capillary wedge pressure (left ventricular filling pressure). The choice of vasodilator is from glyceryl trinitrate i.v., isosorbide dinitrate i.v., or sodium nitroprusside i.v. The administration of these drugs requires meticulous attention to cardiac haemodynamic state. For the use of vasodilators see below under cardiogenic shock.

(ii) Cardiogenic shock

In cardiogenic shock the patient is hypotensive (systolic pressure < 90 mmHg), cold, clammy, cyanosed, hyperventilating, and oliguric. The peripheral veins are constricted and the pulse rapid and thready. The prognosis is very poor with a 90 per cent mortality, even with modern methods of management. Ideally all drug therapy in cardiogenic shock should be accompanied by haemodynamic monitoring of central venous pressure and pulmonary capillary wedge pressure, but of course that may not be possible. The first aim should be to reduce afterload with a vasodilator and thereby to improve the circulation so that in turn the left ventricular filling pressure (preload) falls.

The vasodilator of choice is sodium nitroprusside given initially in a dosage of 0.5–1.5 micrograms/kg/min, increasing if required to 8 micrograms/kg/min, with careful continuous monitoring. Nitroprusside should be combined with a low dose of dopamine (5 micrograms /kg/min) in order to cause renal vasodilatation and thus maintain renal blood flow. Dopamine also causes mesenteric and coronary arterial dilatation. Alternative vasodilators are glyceryl trinitrate which is given by i.v. infusion (100–200 micrograms/min), and isosorbide dinitrate (2–7 mg/h).

If vasodilator therapy fails to result in improvement in cardiac output then one should try a β-adrenoceptor agonist such as dopamine or dobutamine. For this purpose dopamine is used at higher dosages than are used for renal vasodilatation and can be given at rates of up to 20 micrograms/kg/min. However, its use carries the risk of cardiac arrhythmias and peripheral vasoconstriction, since at high doses it has α-adrenoceptor agonist properties. Dobutamine on the other hand does not have the dopaminergic effect necessary to dilate renal arteries but is equally arrhythmogenic and may cause peripheral vasoconstriction.

In general cardiac glycosides should be avoided as positive inotropic drugs in myocardial infarction. For the patient in mild heart failure they tend to increase myocardial oxygen consumption and enhance the risk of arrhythmias. Their inotropic effect is in any case relatively small and in severe heart failure dobutamine at least is a more potent inotropic drug. However i.v. ouabain or oral digoxin should be used in patients with fast atrial fibrillation (for treatment of arrhythmias see p.316).

(ii) Arrhythmias

The common arrhythmias in acute myocardial infarction are: ventricular extrasystoles, which may lead to ventricular tachycardias and cardiac arrest due to ventricular fibrillation; sinus tachycardia; atrial fibrillation and flutter; supraventricular tachycardia; and heart block (which we include for convenience under this heading). Their treatment is dealt with in the section on arrhythmias.

(iii) Pericarditis

Acute pericarditis occurs in about 10 per cent of patients with an acute myocardial infarction, and causes severe, sharp, stabbing chest pain, made worse by coughing and inspiration, and by sitting back. It may be associated with breathlessness. Treatment of choice for mild or moderate pain due to acute pericarditis is aspirin, 600 mg q.d.s. if required. Other non-steroidal anti-inflammatory drugs may be used, such as indomethacin 50 mg t.d.s., but some of these drugs may cause fluid retention and are better avoided.

(c) Treatment of late complications

(i) Dressler's syndrome

This consists of fever, with pericarditis and sometimes pleurisy, and occurs in about 4 per cent of patients. In some cases aspirin or other non-steroidal anti-inflammatory drugs may be sufficient. In patients not responding to aspirin, or if there is severe pain, a short course of corticosteroids should be given (e.g. prednisolone 60 mg o.d. reducing the dose to complete withdrawal in 4–6 days, or hydrocortisone 100 mg i.v. six-hourly). Occasionally attacks may be recurrent, requiring repeated courses of corticosteroid therapy.

(ii) Ventricular aneurysm

Surgical removal is the definitive treatment for ventricular aneurysm. Full dosages of oral anticoagulants should be used to minimize the risk of mural thrombus and consequent cerebral embolism. These patients may also require treatment for recurrent ventricular tachycardia (see treatment of arrhythmias, p.316).

(iii) Recurrent ischaemic pain

If ischaemic chest pain recurs without evidence of re-infarction or extension of infarction it should be treated in the same way as unstable angina [see section 21.2.2(c)].

21.3.4. Treatment in the post-infarction period

Rehabilitation after myocardial infarction includes attention to physical and psychological well-being. Patients should be told to stop smoking. They should be instructed on how much exercise to take, on how to modify their diet, on when to return to work, when to drive again, and when and how sexual activity can be resumed. We shall not discuss these matters in detail.

Drug therapy after myocardial infarction generally consists of treatment for heart failure and arrhythmias (which are dealt with elsewhere, see pp.328 and 316). There is also the question of secondary prevention of myocardial infarction which we shall consider here.

21.3.5. Secondary prevention of myocardial infarction

Various types of therapy have been investigated in the hope that it may be possible to prevent a recurrence of myocardial infarction after a first episode.

(a) Drugs which reduce platelet aggregation

Drugs such as aspirin, sulphinpyrazone, and dipyridamole have been used for this purpose. The evidence that dipyridamole and sulphinpyrazone are effective in secondary prevention is limited. There is considerable evidence that aspirin may reduce re-infarction rate by about 10 per cent but it does not affect mortality. However doubts about the correct dosage of aspirin, worries about the risk of acute gastro-intestinal bleeding, and the difficulties in ensuring compliance with a life-long treatment have so far resulted in little application of aspirin treatment in secondary prevention. The results of studies of its effects in preventing myocardial infarction in patients who have not previously had a myocardial infarction ('primary prevention') are still awaited.

(b) β-adrenoceptor antagonists

There is now convincing evidence that β-adrenoceptor antagonists given after myocardial infarction reduce the subsequent incidence of both myocardial infarction and sudden death. The precise mechanism of this effect is unknown and could involve prevention of arrhythmias, reduction of myocardial oxygen requirements, and prevention of increased blood pressure.

Propranolol, sotalol, timolol, and metoprolol have individually been shown to be effective in the secondary prevention of myocardial infarction. However the exact place of such therapy remains to be worked out—it is not clear, for example which patients are most likely to benefit from this therapy, which (if any) of the numerous β-adrenoceptor antagonists is the drug of choice, what the optimum dose should be, and for how long therapy should be continued.

(c) Anticoagulants

There was a vogue some years ago for the use of long-term anticoagulant therapy with coumarin anticoagulants after myocardial infarction. The early studies which were purported to show efficacy in the secondary prevention of myocardial infarction were later heavily criticized, and the practice was dropped. Recently there has been a revival of interest in this mode of treatment, and some believe in its efficacy. However, the current clinical consensus is that if anticoagulants such as warfarin are effective in the secondary prevention of myocardial infarction, even so the benefits of using them do not outweigh the risks.

21.4. CARDIAC ARRHYTHMIAS

Cardiac arrhythmias are most commonly associated with ischaemic heart disease, but may also be due to congential abnormalities of conduction pathways, to arrhythmogenic drugs such as cardiac glycosides, and to metabolic disturbances, such as hypokalaemia. The drugs used in treating arrhythmias are listed in Table 21.6.

Table 21.6   *Drugs used in treating arrhythmias*

Sinus node arrhythmias	
Sinus tachycardia	Treat cause
Sinus bradycardia	Atropine (p.616)
Supraventricular arrhythmias	
Atrial fibrillation	(d.c. cardioversion)
	Cardiac glycosides (p.652)
	Amiodarone (p.634)
	β-adrenoceptor antagonists (p.622)
	Disopyramide (p.674)
Atrial flutter	(d.c. cardioversion)
	(Atrial pacing)
	Amiodarone
	Cardiac glycosides
	Quinidine (p.737)
Supraventricular tachycardia	(Carotid sinus massage, etc.)
	(d.c. cardioversion)
	β-adrenoceptor antagonists
	Verapamil
	Amiodarone
	Cardiac glycosides
	Disopyramide
Ventricular tachyarrhythmias	(d.c. cardioversion)
	Lignocaine (p.697)
	Quinidine
	Procainamide (p.735)
	Disopyramide
	Mexiletine
	Tocainide
	N-acetylprocainamide
	Amiodarone
Digitalis-induced arrhythmias	(Withdraw digitalis)
	Potassium chloride (p.732)
	Phenytoin (p.730)
	Lignocaine
	β-adrenoceptor antagonists
	Cholestyramine (p.661)
	Atropine

The various actions of the different anti-arrhythmic drugs on the action potentials of cardiac fibres are discussed in detail in the Pharmacopoeia under the relevant drug headings, particularly under lignocaine (lidocaine). However it is not clear how those actions relate to the therapeutic effects of anti-arrhythmic drugs. In practice therefore the uses of these drugs are determined by empirical observations in studies of their efficacy, rather than on any strictly rational application of pharmacological understanding.

21.4.1. Principles underlying anti-arrhythmic drug therapy

There are certain practical principles at the root of anti-arrhythmic drug therapy which must be considered in each case before prescribing an anti-arrhythmic drug.

(a) Does the arrhythmia require treatment?

This question must be considered carefully with respect to two different aspects:

(i) Are there any treatable precipitating factors?

Not infrequently it may be possible to treat an arrhythmia by treating an underlying precipitating abnormality. Important precipitating factors in the ischaemic heart yielding to this approach are:

    hypokalaemia;
    acidosis and hypoxia;
    drugs, especially cardiac glycosides;
    heart failure;
    pulmonary embolism;
    pericarditis and myocarditis.

It is particularly important to identify and treat hypokalaemia, not only because treatment may cause resolution of an arrhythmia, but because hypokalaemia decreases the therapeutic effect on the Class I anti-arrhythmics such as lignocaine, quinidine, procainamide, disopyramide, and phenytoin.

(ii) Does the benefit of treatment outweigh the risk?

Compare, for example, recurrent ventricular tachycardia, which carries a high risk of ventricular fibrillation and must be treated, with, at the other end of the spectrum, multiple supraventricular extrasystoles which are harmless and generally need no treatment. Atrial fibrillation with a fast ventricular response rate will eventually impair myocardial contractility and the ventricular rate should be slowed. However atrial fibrillation with a normal ventricular rate does not need specific treatment, though in some cases anticoagulation will be necessary because of the risk of systemic emboli.

(b) Is there a non-drug treatment?

In some circumstances drug therapy can be avoided by the use of some other procedure. Examples include:

> carotid sinus massage in acute supraventricular tachycardia;
> d.c. cardioversion in acute supraventricular tachycardia, atrial fibrillation, ventricular tachycardia and ventricular fibrillation;
> surgical treatment in Wolff–Parkinson–White syndrome;
> a permanent pacemaker in complete heart block;
> programmed electrical stimulators for certain paroxysmal arrhythmias.

(c) Choice of drug

Consideration should be given to the following:

(i) Class of drug

The anti-arrhythmic drugs are classified into at least four classes depending on their electrophysiological effects on the action potential (see lignocaine in the Pharmacopoeia, p.697). Generally, treatment with Class I drugs should be limited to the use of a single drug, because the effects of two Class I drugs on the heart will be additive. It may also be dangerous to use amiodarone in combination with those Class I anti-arrhythmics which prolong the QT interval of the electrocardiogram (quinidine, procainamide, and disopyramide).

Non-cardiac adverse effects of anti-arrhythmic drugs may constitute contra-indications to their use and are listed in Table 21.7. For example, atropine, quinidine, and disopyramide have anticholinergic effects and would be contra-indicated in patients with glaucoma or prostatic enlargement.

Table 21.7 *Important non-cardiac adverse effects of some anti-arrhythmic drugs*

Drug	Class	Important non-cardiac adverse effects
Atropine	—	Anticholinergic effects
Lignocaine	I	Central nervous toxicity
Quinidine	I	Cinchonism
		Anticholinergic effects
		Hypersensitivity reactions
Procainamide	I	Lupus-like syndrome
		Hypersensitivity reactions
Disopyramide	I	Anticholinergic effects
Phenytoin	I	CNS toxicity
		Long-term effects (see Pharmacopoeia)
Tocainide	I	CNS toxicity
β-adrenoceptor antagonists	II	Bronchoconstriction
		Peripheral vasoconstriction
Amiodarone	III	Corneal opacities
		Skin pigmentation and photosensitivity
		Thyroid dysfunction
		Fibrosing alveolitis

Table 21.8 *Drug interactions with anti-arrhythmic drugs*

Object drug	Precipitant drug	Result of interaction
Class I drugs	Class I drugs	Potentiation
Quinidine, procainamide, disopyramide, amiodarone	The same drugs	Prolongation of the QT interval
Class I drugs	Drugs causing hypokalaemia	Decreased anti-arrhythmic effects
Digoxin	Quinidine, amiodarone, verapamil	Digoxin toxicity
Warfarin	Amiodarone	Warfarin toxicity
Anticholinergic drugs	Quinidine, disopyramide	Potentiation
Class I drugs	β-adrenoceptor antagonists	Negative inotropy
Verapamil	β-adrenoceptor antagonists	Negative inotropy/ arrhythmias/asystole
Antihypertensive drugs	Bretylium	Severe hypotension

Various drug interactions with phenytoin are discussed in the Pharmacopoeia (p.730)

(ii) Drug interactions
Drug interactions involving anti-arrhythmic drugs are listed in Table 21.8 and it is necessary either to avoid such interactions altogether (e.g. verapamil and β-adrenoceptor antagonists) or at least to reduce the dose of object drug when its effects are increased (e.g. the dose of digoxin should be reduced in patients given amiodarone).

(iii) The type of arrhythmia or underlying cardiac disease
Tachycardias arise from one of two separate mechanisms. They may be due to abnormal pacemaker activity (either normal or ectopic) or to a 're-entry' mechanism. Increased ectopic pacemaker activity occurs when the automaticity of excitable cardiac tissue initiates impulses at a rate greater than that of the normal pacemaker, the sinus node. In re-entry tachycardias, once the arrhythmia is initiated it perpetuates itself by recirculation of impulses to the site of initiation of the abnormal impulse. Re-entrant arrhythmias are commonly associated with abnormal conduction pathways (e.g. the Wolff–Parkinson–White syndrome) and in such cases verapamil, quinidine, and amiodarone are particularly effective.

(iv) The presence of heart failure or heart block
Those anti-arrhythmic drugs which have pronounced negative inotropic effects and those which delay conduction through the AV node should be avoided or used with care in patients in heart failure or with heart block. Anti-arrhythmic drugs particularly likely to exacerbate heart failure are quinidine, procainamide, disopyramide, β-adrenoceptor antagonists, and verapamil. Drugs likely to delay conduction through the AV node include quinidine, procainamide, disopyramide, β-adrenoceptor antagonists, and cardiac glycosides. Lignocaine does not decrease conduction velocity in

normal conducting tissue but does if the tissue is ischaemic. Phenytoin tends to increase conduction velocity and is therefore the drug of choice for the treatment of ventricular arrhythmias due to cardiac glycosides. Nonetheless care should still be taken in patients with second or third degree heart block.

(d) Dose of drug

The pharmacokinetics of certain anti-arrhythmic drugs are altered by cardiac failure and dosages may need to be altered (see Chapter 9, p.137 and Pharmacopoeia). For example, the apparent volumes of distribution of lignocaine, quinidine, and procainamide are reduced in heart failure and loading doses should be reduced. In hepatic congestion the hepatic metabolism of these drugs will be affected and maintenance dosages will also have to be reduced.

21.4.2. Practical treatment of cardiac arrhythmias

(a) Sinus node arrhythmias

(i) Sinus tachycardia

There is no specific treatment for sinus tachycardia and attention should be paid to the underlying cause. In hyperthyroidism the administration of a β-adrenoceptor antagonist will, among other things, slow a sinus tachycardia (see Chapter 25, p.433).

(ii) Sinus bradycardia

Chronic sinus bradycardia (ventricular rate < 60/min) may be due to a number of different causes including hypothyroidism, and drugs such as β-adrenoceptor antagonists, the phenothiazines, cardiac glycosides, and acetylcholinesterase inhibitors. In these conditions treatment of the underlying cause is all that is required and in many instances when drugs are at fault no treatment at all is required provided cardiac function otherwise remains normal. Sinus bradycardia is a normal feature in highly trained athletes and requires no treatment.

Sinus bradycardia is very common following an acute myocardial infarction and need be treated only if clinically obvious lowering of cardiac output results. In that case atropine 0.5 mg i.v. should be given every 5 min until the heart rate rises above 60/min to a maximum total dose of 2 mg.

(b) Supraventricular arrhythmias

(i) Atrial fibrillation

The most common causes of atrial fibrillation are acute or chronic myocardial ischaemia, mitral stenosis, and hyperthyroidism. Less commonly it may be due to pericarditis, myocarditis, other acute infections, cardiomyopathies, sick sinus syndrome, Wolff–Parkinson–White syndrome, or an unknown cause (so-called 'lone' fibrillation).

In atrial fibrillation of recent origin (e.g. following an acute myocardial infarction) the aim would be to convert the rhythm to sinus rhythm using d.c. shock. In some circumstances, however, there is a high chance of recurrence after d.c. shock (e.g. in mitral stenosis, severe left ventricular failure, sick sinus syndrome, and untreated hyperthyroidism) and drug therapy will be indicated. If atrial fibrillation persists in hyperthyroidism despite restoration of normal thyroid function then d.c. cardioversion would be indicated.

Drug therapy is also indicated if atrial fibrillation is of prolonged duration, since reversion to sinus rhythm is unlikely. The aim of treatment will be to slow the ventricular rate to within normal limits (60–90 beats/min at rest).

Patients who are to receive attempted cardioversion are at risk of embolism from atrial thrombus when the atria start to contract normally. It is customary therefore, unless contra-indicated, to anticoagulate patients with warfarin before elective cardioversion, although it has not been satisfactorily proven that this prevents embolism. Full anticoagulation should be achieved for at least two weeks before and after cardioversion.

When the aim is to control the ventricular rate in atrial fibrillation a cardiac glycoside (digitalis) is almost always the treatment of choice. In patients with hyperthyroidism one would start with a β-adrenoceptor antagonist, such as propranolol, and add digitalis if there was a poor response or in the presence of heart failure. If a β-adrenoceptor antagonist were contra-indicated one would use digitalis alone (see treatment of hyperthyroidism, p.433). Digitalis should also be used to maintain sinus rhythm when d.c. cardioversion has been successful. In this case long-term treatment is not necessary and after successful cardioversion digitalis need be continued only for a few weeks. Digitalis should not be used in sick sinus syndrome or Wolff–Parkinson–White syndrome (see below).

There is no hard and fast rule about the choice of cardiac glycoside, and it is best to become thoroughly acquainted with the use of one and to stick to it. We prefer digoxin, and a suitable dosage regimen is outlined in the Pharmacopoeia.

If digoxin is ineffective then the alternatives are to add a β-adrenoceptor antagonist or to use amiodarone.

In sick sinus syndrome digitalis is not helpful and may worsen arrhythmias. Amiodarone or disopyramide should be used instead (see Pharmacopoeia for dosages). In some cases it may be necessary to cut the bundle of His and insert a pacemaker.

Atrial fibrillation in Wolff–Parkinson–White syndrome is particularly difficult to treat. Digitalis should not be used. A single episode may be treated with d.c. cardioversion but if drug therapy is required to prevent recurrent atrial fibrillation oral disopyramide or amiodarone may be used. If these are unsuccessful then surgery is indicated.

In patients with chronic atrial fibrillation secondary to mitral stenosis there is an increased risk of embolism from atrial mural thrombus, and lifelong anticoagulation with warfarin is required. Anticoagulants should also be used in patients in whom elective cardioversion is contemplated.

(ii) Atrial flutter with a fast ventricular rate

The causes of atrial flutter with a fast ventricular rate (e.g. > 150/min) are the same as those of atrial fibrillation. Digoxin should be tried first, but it is less likely to be effective than in atrial fibrillation, and if it is ineffective then d.c. cardioversion should be used. Because of the increased risk of digitalis-induced arrhythmias following d.c. shock it is important to start with very low energies (10 J) in patients who have had digoxin within the previous 2 or 3 days, increasing the energy gradually until cardioversion occurs.

The main alternative to digoxin or cardioversion is to use quinidine, 200 mg orally four-hourly to a total of 1.2 g in an attempt to convert the rhythm to atrial fibrillation, followed by digoxin. The dose of digoxin should be reduced by about half in patients on quinidine because of their interaction (see Table 21.8 and pp.653 and 738). Recently i.v. amiodarone has emerged as another alternative.

(iii) Supraventricular tachycardia

Acute supraventricular tachycardia can occur in acute myocardial infarction, in digitalis intoxication, and in myocarditis and following cardiac surgery. Paroxysmal supraventricular (or 'atrial') tachycardia may be due to chronic ischaemia, the pre-excitation syndromes (e.g. Wolff–Parkinson–White syndrome), other congenital conduction defects, and digitalis toxicity. Digitalis toxicity should be strongly suspected if there is paroxysmal supraventricular tachycardia with block ('PAT with block').

Acute supraventricular tachycardia may not need treatment if the patient is otherwise well with a good cardiac output and in such cases may revert spontaneously to sinus rhythm. However, if it persists or if cardiac function is being impaired treatment is indicated, and the first recourse is to try manoeuvres aimed at stimulating the vagal innervation of the heart. Carotid sinus massage is the most commonly used of these manoeuvres but should not be carried out if there is evidence of carotid artery disease (e.g. a carotid bruit or a history of transient cerebral ischaemic attacks) and should always be performed with continuous electrocardiographic monitoring since some individuals have a sensitive carotid sinus and may go into asystole following even light pressure on the carotid sinus. Firm pressure with circular massage using the thumb over the right carotid artery for 10–20 seconds is recommended.

If carotid sinus massage has no effect and there is severe embarassment of cardiac function then d.c. cardioversion is the treatment of choice and will successfully restore sinus rhythm in over 90 per cent of patients.

If there is no urgency or if d.c. cardioversion fails then drugs should be used. The main choices are verapamil or a β-adrenoceptor antagonist. If there is evidence (e.g. from a history of a pre-excitation syndrome) that the arrhythmia may be a re-entry arrhythmia then verapamil is the drug of choice. It is given as a slow i.v. injection of 10 mg at a rate of 1 mg/min, stopping if the ventricular rate goes below 100/min. Verapamil should not be used in digitalis toxicity or sick sinus syndrome and is best avoided if there is severe cardiac failure because of its negative inotropic effect. It should not be used within 24 h of having given a β-adrenoceptor antagonist (see p.768).

If there is no indication whether or not the arrhythmia is of the re-entrant variety then a β-adrenoceptor antagonist is the drug of choice, especially in myocardial infarction. Practolol should be used i.v. in an initial test dose of 1 mg, followed 5 min later by up to 20 mg at a rate of 1 mg/min. During its infusion the blood pressure must be continually monitored and it should not be used in severe heart failure.

For those in whom both of these drugs are contra-indicated, i.v. amiodarone is a suitable alternative, but it should not be used in digitalis intoxication. Some prefer to use a cardiac glycoside in patients not previously treated with digitalis.

Phenytoin is the treatment of choice for digitalis-induced supraventricular tachycardia (see section below on treatment of digitalis toxicity).

Attacks of paroxysmal supraventricular tachycardia may be prevented by treatment with either a β-adrenoceptor antagonist (e.g. propranolol), or a cardiac glycoside, or a combination of the two.

(c) Ventricular arrhythmias

The most common ventricular arrhythmias are ventricular extrasystoles (premature beats), ventricular tachycardia, and ventricular fibrillation. They most commonly occur after acute myocardial infarction, but can also occur in otherwise healthy individuals, or because of chronic ischaemia, digitalis toxicity, and the effects of other anti-arrhythmic drugs (e.g. quinidine, disopyramide) and of tricyclic antidepressants.

(i) Treatment of ventricular arrhythmias after acute myocardial infarction

The treatment of ventricular extrasystoles in acute myocardial infarction is highly controversial. The difficulty is that there is a high risk of the fatal or potentially fatal arrhythmias, ventricular tachycardia, and ventricular fibrillation in myocardial infarction and it has been presumed that these arrhythmias can be prevented by suppressing the ventricular extrasystoles, any one of which might initiate tachycardia or fibrillation. However, there is still no clear guidance as to when to use anti-arrhythmic drugs in these circumstances and little understanding of the exact benefit:risk ratios. The difficulty is enhanced by the fact that the drugs used in the suppression of ventricular extrasystoles are all cardiotoxic and liable to cause cardiac failure or arrhythmias, especially in patients with myocardial infarction.

The most commonly quoted guidelines for the use of anti-arrhythmic drugs are as follows:

more than five ventricular extrasystoles per minute; or
multifocal extrasystoles; or
salvos of extrasystoles (i.e. runs of more than two extrasystoles at a time); or
recurrent bouts of ventricular tachycardia; or
premature extrasystoles (so-called 'R on T' phenomenon).

In recent years, however, these guidelines have been challenged. For example, the premise for treatment of extrasystoles which fall very shortly after the T wave of the preceding sinus beat is based on the experimental observation that introducing an extrasystole during ventricular repolarization (i.e. at the same time as the T wave) virtually always results in a fatal ventricular arrhythmia. However, there is no clear evidence that the nearer an extrasystole is to the preceding T wave the more likely is the next extrasystole to occur during ventricular repolarization. Furthermore not all patients who develop ventricular tachyarrhythmias have 'warning' extrasystoles, nor do all those with extrasystoles go on to develop serious tachyarrhythmias.

Different authorities adopt different attitudes, therefore, to the use of anti-arrhythmic drugs after myocardial infarction. Some recommend using drugs in all patients on the assumption that the incidence of ventricular arrhythmias will thereby be decreased. At the opposite extreme others prefer merely to observe patients with ventricular extrasystoles, using drugs only if ventricular tachycardia or fibrillation occur. If the latter policy is adopted then it should be adopted only in circumstances where facilities for resuscitation are immediately available (see cardiac arrest below).

We feel that the following set of guidelines is a reasonable one:

1. Since there is no evidence that the use of anti-arrhythmic drugs prevents serious arrhythmias in patients without arrhythmias to start with, the risk of such treatment with, for example, lignocaine outweighs the benefit and should be avoided.

2. Ventricular extrasystoles should be treated (especially if facilities for resuscitation are not readily available) if they are occurring more frequently than 10/min, if they are multifocal, or if they occur repeatedly in salvos.

3. If suppression of ventricular extrasystoles does not occur with a single or at most two drugs then it is best to observe since the use of more anti-arrhythmic drugs increases the risk of adverse effects.

Not only is there no general agreement as to when to treat ventricular extrasystoles, but there is also no general agreement as to the best drug to use when treatment is indicated! However, i.v. lignocaine is still widely regarded as the drug of choice. The usual loading dose is 100 mg, followed by a maintenance infusion at decreasing rates (see the recommended regimen in the Pharmacopoeia, p.700). In this way therapeutic concentrations may be rapidly achieved and then maintained. Because it has active and potentially toxic metabolites which may accumulate, lignocaine cannot be used for longer than 24–48 h, but in most cases suppression of ventricular extrasystoles after myocardial infarction does not need to be continued for longer than 48 h.

If lignocaine does not depress ventricular extrasystoles then other possibilities are amiodarone or a Class I anti-arrhythmic other than lignocaine. Amiodarone is given in a dose of 5 mg/kg i.v. over 1 min. For patients who have already had lignocaine it carries the advantage over the Class I anti-arrhythmics that it has different effects on the action potential.

The choice for i.v. therapy from the Class I anti-arrhythmics lies among procainamide, quinidine, mexiletine, and disopyramide, of which the first is preferred. Disopyramide cannot be given rapidly i.v. since it is likely to cause hypotension due to a negative inotropic effect on the heart. Mexiletine has a high rate of dose-related adverse effects, particularly on the CNS, and since its adverse effects are closely similar to those of lignocaine it is better avoided after lignocaine has already been used. Quinidine is not available as an i.v. preparation in some countries and is pharmaceutically quite difficult to prepare. Procainamide is given at a rate of 25 mg/min until either the extrasystoles are abolished or 1000 mg have been given. An i.v. infusion can then be continued at a rate of 0.25–2 mg/min.

There are some newer Class I anti-arrhythmic drugs which may be alternatives to the better established drugs. They include tocainide, encainide, lorcainide, flecainide, and *N*-acetylprocainamide (the active metabolite of procainamide). Of these tocainide, flecainide, and *N*-acetylprocainamide have been best studied, but it is not yet clear whether or not they are preferable to the better-known drugs.

If persistent ventricular tachycardia occurs it should be treated with d.c. cardioversion and drug therapy started or continued as discussed above. However, care should be taken with drug therapy in patients with the form of ventricular tachycardia known as '*torsade de pointes*' since that may be caused by anti-arrhythmic drugs.

Ventricular fibrillation requires immediate cardioversion and other measures discussed below under cardiac arrest.

(ii) Treatment and prevention of ventricular arrhythmias in the post-infarction period
After a ventricular arrhythmia requiring treatment continued prophylactic

drug therapy is usually given for about six weeks, but if ventricular extrasystoles persist then the duration of treatment might be increased to 3–6 months, because of the increased risk of sudden death during that time attributable to ventricular arrhythmias. The treatment is as for chronic ventricular arrhythmias.

(iii) Chronic ventricular arrhythmias

If ventricular extrasystoles are symptomatic they should be treated. Treatment is also indicated to prevent recurrent ventricular tachycardia.

Choice of treatment is from among the Class I anti-arrhythmic drugs and amiodarone, and currently the main choice is between amiodarone and quinidine. Amiodarone is given in an initial oral dosage of 200 mg t.d.s. for 1–4 weeks depending on response, thereafter reducing gradually to a suitable maintenance dosage, often 200 mg o.d. Quinidine has a short half-time, and is usually given as slow-release formulations of quinidine bisulphate. The usual oral dosage is two to five 250 mg tablets b.d. A test dose of 250 mg should always be given first in case of hypersensitivity.

(d) Digitalis-induced arrhythmias

Digitalis toxicity commonly causes ectopic ventricular and supraventricular arrhythmias, or heart block, or a combination of the two. It is rarely necessary to do more than three things in treatment:

withhold digitalis;

measure the plasma potassium concentration and if it is low give oral or i.v. potassium (e.g. 16 mmol potassium chloride orally q.d.s.);

if digitoxin is to blame give a steroid-binding resin such as cholestyramine 12–24 g daily in divided doses.

If an arrhythmia is life-threatening then specific treatment should be given. The following are the choices.

(i) Ventricular tachyarrhythmias

Phenytoin is the treatment of choice. Of all the Class I anti-arrhythmics it is the only one to increase conduction velocity in the AV node. Very careful electrocardiographic monitoring is necessary, however, since serious arrhythmias may occur during its use. It should not be used if there is second or third degree heart block, since it decreases ventricular automaticity. The dose is 4 mg/kg given i.v. at a rate not exceeding 50 mg/min. This does may be repeated after 10 min if necessary, and oral therapy can then be given in dosage similar to those used in epilepsy. If phenytoin is ineffective then the alternatives are i.v. lignocaine or an i.v. β-adrenoceptor antagonist. If there is concurrent heart block then these drugs should be used only if there is a transvenous pacemaker in position. Direct current cardioversion is not contra-indicated in the face of a life-threatening arrhythmia.

(ii) Paroxysmal atrial tachycardia with block

Phenytoin, lignocaine, or an i.v. β-adrenoceptor antagonist should be used with a transvenous pacemaker in position in case of worsening block.

(iii) Sinus bradycardia

This should be treated only if it is causing hypotension. It will often respond to atropine (see above), but sometimes a pacemaker may be necessary.

The treatment of digitalis overdose is discussed in Chapter 32 (p.581). Recently F_{ab} fragments of anti-digoxin antibody have been successfully used to treat digitalis overdose and may in time become the definitive treatment for life-threatening digitalis toxicity.

(e) Cardiac arrest after myocardial infarction

Cardiac arrest is usually due to acute ventricular tachycardia or fibrillation, or to cardiac asystole, the latter having a worse prognosis. Cardiac arrest is an acute medical emergency since cerebral hypoxia lasting more than 2–4 min results in irreversible brain damage. The aims of treatment are therefore to provide oxygen to the tissues and to restore normal cardiac rhythm.

First-aid measures are as follows:

1. Give a sharp blow over the sternum with the clenched fist. This wastes little time and occasionally restores normal rhythm.

2. Make sure the patient is on a hard surface (e.g. in a bed with a hard base or on the floor). If he is not effective cardiac massage will be difficult.

3. Make sure the airways are patent. If possible insert an endotracheal tube and give oxygen. Otherwise give respiration by the mouth-to-mouth method or with an Ambu bag.

4. Start cardiac massage.

5. Correct acidosis by giving sodium bicarbonate 50 mmol i.v. (50 ml of an 8.4 per cent solution). All patients should be given sodium bicarbonate in this way. The bicarbonate, and all other drugs, should be given via a cannula inserted into a jugular or subclavian vein rather than via a more peripheral vein.

6. Direct current cardioversion. This should be carried out as soon as possible. Ideally one should first identify the cardiac rhythm since d.c. cardioversion is of no use in asystole, but if an electrocardiogram cannot be obtained then blind cardioversion should be carried out at a high energy (200–400 J). If ventricular fibrillation or ventricular tachycardia are not terminated then cardioversion should not be tried again for another 2 min or so and in the meantime cardiac massage and oxygenation should be continued and further treatment of acidosis with another 25 mmol of sodium bicarbonate given. If a second cardioversion fails then i.v. bretylium should be given (5 mg/kg) followed by a third cardioversion. This

regimen may be repeated once if unsuccessful. If the ventricular fibrillation is of a fine pattern then adrenaline may be used to convert it to a more coarse pattern, and it may then respond more readily to cardioversion. The dose of adrenaline is 0.5 ml of a 1:1000 solution (i.e. 0.5 mg). Do not mix adrenaline with sodium bicarbonate.

7. If there is cardiac asystole give calcium gluconate i.v. (10 ml of a 10 per cent solution). Calcium acts by enhancing ventricular automaticity and increasing myocardial contractility. It is important not to infuse calcium salts at the same time as sodium bicarbonate since this will result in the precipitation of the insoluble salt calcium carbonate.

8. There are three main indications for the use of other drugs. Firstly to treat arrhythmias, secondly to treat asystole if calcium is not effective, and thirdly to treat cardiac failure.

Not infrequently the result of cardioversion of a ventricular tachy-arrhythmia is not sinus rhythm but some other rhythm, such as sinus or nodal bradycardia, or idioventricular rhythm. If cardioversion results in some supraventricular rhythm, whether sinus or not, lignocaine therapy should be given to try to prevent recurrence of the ventricular arrhythmia. If there is a bradycardia, atropine 0.5 mg i.v. should be used and heart block should be treated by transvenous pacing. Idioventricular rhythm may also respond to atropine, which increases the rate of sinus depolarization, or to overdrive pacing (i.e. pacing the right atrium at a faster rate then the ventricular rate). It is important at this stage to continue assessing cardiac output by feeling the volume of the carotid pulse and to continue cardiac massage until the heart rate increases.

Cardiac asystole is very difficult to treat. If it does not respond to cardiac massage and calcium then adrenaline should be given in doses of 0.5 mg (0.5 ml of a 1:1000 solution) i.v. at 5 min intervals. It may be necessary to use a pacemaker in these cases.

Cardiac failure should be treated as discussed above in the section on myocardial infarction.

21.5. CARDIAC FAILURE

21.5.1. Mechanisms of action of drugs used to treat cardiac failure

The way in which drugs affect the major pathophysiological abnormalities of cardiac failure are shown in Fig. 21.3 and a list of the drugs used is given in Table 21.9.

The principles of the treatment of cardiac failure are three in number.

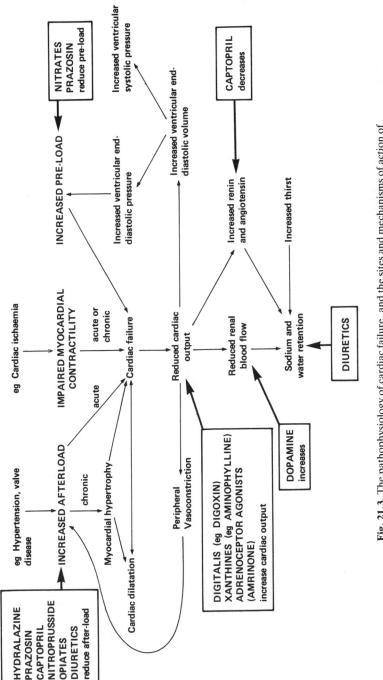

Fig. 21.3. The pathophysiology of cardiac failure, and the sites and mechanisms of action of drugs used in its treatment.

Table 21.9   *Drugs used in the treatment of cardiac failure*

1. *Diuretics*
Thiazide diuretics (p.761)
Thiazide-like diuretics (see Table 21.2)
Loop diuretics
    Frusemide (p.681)
    Bumetanide (p.646)
Potassium-sparing diuretics
    Spironolactone (p.751)
    Amiloride (p.629)
    Triamterene

2. *Positive inotropic drugs*
Cardiac glycosides (p.652)
Xanthine derivatives (e.g. aminophylline; p.779)
Adrenoceptor agonists (p.620)
(Amrinone)

3. *Vasodilators*
Morphine (p.713)
Nitrates (p.682)
Sodium nitroprusside (p.751)
Hydralazine (p.686)
Prazosin (p.734)

4. *Angiotension converting enzyme inhibitors*
Captopril (p.649)

Table 21.10   *Causes of cardiac failure*

1. *Decreased contractility*
Chronic ischaemia
Acute infarction
Cardiomyopathies
Drugs
    Negative inotropic drugs (β-adrenoceptor antagonists, Class I anti-arrhythmics, verapamil)
    Drug-induced cardiomyopathy (doxorubicin)

2. *Increased afterload*
Hypertension
Aortic valve disease
Hypertrophic obstructive cardiomyopathy

3. *Increased output*
Mitral incompetence
Arrhythmias
Anaemia
Hyperthyroidism
Peripheral shunts (e.g. arteriovenous shunts, Paget's disease)

4. *Pulmonary heart disease* (cor pulmonale)
Chronic airways obstruction
Recurrent pulmonary embolism

(a) Removal of the underlying cause

Cardiac failure due to valvular disease, hypertension, anaemia, and hyperthyroidism is amenable to this approach. In Table 21.10 are listed the major causes of cardiac failure.

(b) Control of the signs and symptoms of cardiac failure

This can be done using three types of drug:

    (a) diuretics—to remove excess sodium and water;
    (b) positive inotropic drugs—to increase cardiac contractility;
    (c) vasodilators—to reduce the workload of the heart.

Before discussing these facets of the drug therapy of cardiac failure we must first consider the relationship between cardiac output and ventricular end-diastolic pressure. This relationship is called the Frank–Starling curve since it derives from the observations originally made by those physiologists relating cardiac output to venous pressure in the isolated heart–lung preparation. The relationship is illustrated in Fig. 21.4A. The normal curve shows that cardiac output increases with an increase in ventricular end-diastolic pressure but only up to a certain point, past which cardiac output starts to decrease. In established cardiac failure the curve is set lower down, that is at any given value of ventricular end-diastolic pressure cardiac output is lower than normal. If cardiac output can be increased (e.g. by increased sympathetic drive) that can only happen at the expense of an increased ventricular end-diastolic pressure and eventually congestive signs and symptoms occur. If cardiac output cannot be increased then the signs are of low output (e.g. in cardiogenic shock).

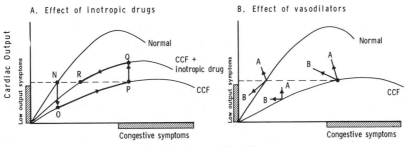

Fig. 21.4. The Frank–Starling curve illustrated here for the relationship between ventricular end-diastolic pressure and cardiac output.
    A. *The effect of positive inotropic drugs*—inotropic drugs increase the cardiac output for any given value of end-diastolic pressure.
    B. *The effects of vasodilators*—the effects of vasodilators depend on whether they are predominantly arterial vasodilators (A—e.g. hydralazine) or mixed vasodilators (B—e.g. prazosin). [(A) Adapted from Mason (1973) *Am. J. Cardiol.* **32**, 437–448 and (B) from Braunwald (1980) *Heart Disease*, p.548, W. B. Saunders, Philadelphia, with permission.]

(i) Diuretics

The mechanisms whereby sodium and water retention occur in cardiac failure involve a combination of a variety of different mechanisms, including reduced renal blood flow, increased ADH secretion, and increased renin secretion leading to increased angiotensin and aldosterone secretion. Diuretics act to reduce the body sodium and water content. Spironolactone is an aldosterone antagonist counteracting the hyperaldosteronism which can result from cardiac failure itself and as a secondary response to the natriuresis produced by other diuretics. In the treatment of acute left ventricular failure the effects of frusemide and bumetanide occur more quickly than would be expected from the rate of onset of their diuretic actions and vasodilator effects may be involved in their acute actions in left ventricular failure. The effect of diuretics on the Frank–Starling curve is to lower the ventricular end-diastolic pressure (e.g. from P towards O in Fig. 21.4A).

(ii) Positive inotropic drugs

The end effect of positive inotropic drugs is to increase the cardiac output at any given value of ventricular end-diastolic pressure. Thus the Frank–Starling curve is shifted upwards (see Fig. 21.4A). Consider, for example, a patient whose normal state is at point N in Fig. 21.4A. In heart failure with the same ventricular end-diastolic pressure his cardiac output would fall to point O, and if he were able to increase his cardiac output by increasing sympathetic drive he would do so at the expense of an increased ventricular end-diastolic pressure (point P) and would develop signs and symptoms of congestion. A positive inotropic drug would increase the cardiac output (point Q) and that would allow the ventricular end-diastolic pressure to fall without cardiac output falling below normal (point R). Thus a normal cardiac output can be maintained, albeit with an increased ventricular end-diastolic pressure and signs and symptoms will be relieved if the end-diastolic pressure is low enough.

The most commonly used inotropic drugs are the cardiac glycosides. They probably act by inhibition of sodium transport out of cells through inhibition of the enzyme Na^+, K^+-ATPase. The resultant increase in intracellular sodium leads to a decreased efflux of calcium via the Na^+/Ca^{++} exchange mechanism, and thus to an increase in intracellular calcium, necessary for the translation of electrical stimulation into contraction ('excitation–contraction coupling'). This leads to increased contractility.

β-adrenoceptor agonists cause an increase in myocardial cellular cyclic AMP concentration, and this increases the rate of availability of calcium to contractile sites.

Xanthines, such as aminophylline, are inhibitors of phosphodiesterase and also therefore cause an increase in tissue cyclic AMP. Xanthines also have a slight vasodilatory effect.

Amrinone is a new inotropic drug with some vasodilating effects. Its mode of action is unknown. It is too soon to discuss its place in the treatment of heart failure.

(iii) Vasodilators

Vasodilators reduce the work-load of the heart by dilating either arterioles or venules or both. Dilatation of arterioles results in a reduction in cardiac after-load and dilatation of venules results in a reduction in cardiac pre-load. A pure reduction in after-load will increase the cardiac output at a given ventricular end-diastolic pressure, while a pure reduction in pre-load will reduce the ventricular end-diastolic pressure and hence the cardiac output along the Frank–Starling curve. In practice vasodilators cause both of these effects. That is because a reduction in arterial resistance increases ventricular emptying which reduces pre-load, and venous dilatation decreases ventricular volume which reduces afterload, with the result that in both cases cardiac output increases and ventricular end-diastolic pressure falls. However, the *extent* to which these two effects occur does depend on whether the vasodilator acts predominantly on arterioles or venules. For example, in a patient with congestive cardiac failure hydralazine, which is a pure arterial dilator, has a larger effect on cardiac output than on ventricular end-diastolic pressure, while prazosin, which is both an arterial and a venous vasodilator, alters both cardiac output and end-diastolic pressure equally (see Fig. 21.4B). However, the extent and direction of the effects of these vasodilators also depend on the severity of disease as shown in Fig. 21.4B—compare the effects in normal individuals with those in patients with cardiac failure with normal end-diastolic pressure and those in patients with congestive cardiac failure.

Note that the blood pressure generally does not fall much when arterial vasodilators are used in cardiac failure because cardiac output rises. However, the blood pressure may fall if excessive dosages are used, or if a pure venous vasodilator is used in patients with low output failure (see Fig. 21.4B). The hypotensive effects of vasodilators may also be increased in patients with a reduced intravascular volume due to diuretics.

21.5.2. Practical treatment of cardiac failure

(a) Left ventricular failure

Acute left ventricular failure producing pulmonary oedema is a medical emergency requiring treatment with oxygen, morphine, a loop diuretic, aminophylline, and vasodilators if required, as described above under the treatment of acute left ventricular failure in myocardial infarction. Oxygen should be given in a high concentration by facial mask. Frusemide is given i.v. in a dose of 40 mg; bumetanide can be given instead (1 mg i.v.). This is followed by i.v. morphine, 10 mg, via the same needle. Aminophylline (6 mg/kg i.v. over 10 min) may then be given. However, some now prefer to proceed to vasodilators, if necessary, because of the arrhythmogenic actions of aminophylline.

If there is a poor response to this regimen then the dose of morphine may be repeated and higher doses of diuretic given. However, in severe left ventricular failure i.v. vasodilators should be used as described under the treatment of left ventricular failure and cardiogenic shock in the section on myocardial infarction.

Cardiac glycosides may also be used in acute left ventricular failure, particularly when it is associated with fast atrial fibrillation. The use of oral digoxin is described in the Pharmacopoeia (p.652).

In acute left ventricular failure due to acute severe hypertension the blood pressure should also be lowered using nitroprusside or diazoxide (see under hypertension).

Acute left ventricular failure due to iatrogenic fluid overload can be prevented by the use of a loop diuretic. For example, during blood transfusion in a patient with chronic anaemia, and therefore a normal intravascular fluid volume, frusemide 20 mg i.v. should be given immediately before each unit of blood.

(b) Congestive cardiac failure

Initial treatment of cardiac failure is generally with diuretics, adding a cardiac glycoside later if the response is felt to be inadequate. However, some would use a combination of a diuretic with a cardiac glycoside from the start, especially in severe cardiac failure.

(i) Diuretics
The choice of diuretic depends on the severity of cardiac failure. In mild cardiac failure a thiazide or thiazide-like diuretic is indicated. The most commonly used of these diuretics in the UK are bendrofluazide (5–10 mg o.d. orally) and cyclopenthiazide (0.5–1 mg o.d. orally) but there is no particular advantage of using any one of these diuretics rather than another.

In more severe cardiac failure oral loop diuretics are used, e.g. frusemide 40–160 mg o.d. or bumetanide 1–5 mg o.d.

Care must be taken to avoid hypokalaemia when prescribing diuretics in the elderly, and in patients on cardiac glycosides. Generally potassium chloride supplements or a potassium-sparing diuretic will be required. Thus it is common to prescribe a thiazide diuretic or a loop diuretic in combination with a potassium-sparing diuretic (spironolactone, triam-terene, or amiloride). The use of potassium chloride supplements and of potassium-sparing diuretics is discussed in Chapter 34. In some cases it may be necessary to use a combination of all three types of diuretic.

(ii) Cardiac glycosides
A cardiac glycoside should be added to diuretic therapy if diuretics have

not been completely effective. Alternatively, a cardiac glycoside together with diuretics may be used as first-line treatment.

Cardiac glycosides should not be used, or are ineffective in the following conditions:

left ventricular outflow obstruction (e.g. aortic stenosis, hypertrophic obstructive cardiomyopathy), since they increase the force of contraction against a fixed obstruction;

constrictive pericarditis, for a similar reason;

chronic cor pulmonale, because of their decreased efficacy and increased risk of toxicity, perhaps secondary to acidosis and hypoxia;

hyperthyroidism, because of their decreased efficacy and increased risk of toxicity, although they may be useful in addition to a β-adrenoceptor antagonist in patients with atrial fibrillation.

The question of the long-term efficacy of cardiac glycosides in cardiac failure in sinus rhythm is currently controversial. The following are practical guidelines:

1. If the patient is in a stable condition and there has been some identifiable precipitant of cardiac failure which has since been treated (e.g. anaemia, hyperthyroidism) then it is justified to withdraw the glycoside.

2. If the patient's condition is stable and the plasma glycoside concentration is below the lower end of the accepted therapeutic range (e.g. < 0.8 ng/ml for digoxin, see Chapter 7), then it is justified to withdraw the glycoside.

3. If digitalis is withheld from other patients whose condition is stable then in about a third of cases there will be subsequent clinical deterioration. In general it is simpler to continue treatment in all these patients rather than embark upon a trial of withdrawal involving careful observation of the patient over a period of a few weeks.

(iii) Vasodilators

Although it is customary at present to reserve the use of vasodilators for those patients whose cardiac failure has not responded fully to diuretics plus a cardiac glycoside, their use as first-line treatment for mild or moderate heart failure is being assessed.

The choice of vasodilator is from among those with predominantly arterial effects and those with arterial and venous effects (see Table 21.11). An arterial vasodilator such as hydralazine will be preferred in patients whose problem is principally in systole, i.e. those who have signs and symptoms principally of low output. Venous vasodilators will be preferred in patients whose problem is principally in diastole, i.e. those with congestive signs and symptoms (see Fig. 21.4B).

Table 21.11 *Effects of different vasodilators on arterioles and venules*

Drug	Arterial dilatation	Venous dilatation
Hydralazine	+ +	−
Prazosin	+ +	+ +
Nitrates	+	+ +
Nifedipine	+ +	+
Nitroprusside	+ +	+ +
Salbutamol	+ +	+ +
Opiates	+	+ +

The angiotensin converting enzyme inhibitor captopril acts both as an arterial and venous vasodilator, but also reduces circulating aldosterone thus reducing renal sodium reabsorption. It thus has a dual action.

Hydralazine is usually the choice when an arterial vasodilator is preferred, but it may cause a lupus-like syndrome in dosages over 200 mg/day, and nifedipine is being evaluated as an alternative. One of the nitrates, such as isosorbide dinitrate (10 mg t.d.s. orally) is the preferred choice if a venodilator is preferred. Frequently the best choice is a drug which has balanced vasodilatory properties, such as prazosin (up to 20 mg/day orally). Captopril is an alternative to prazosin but at present its use is restricted to the treatment of severe cardiac failure refractory to other treatment because it can cause neutropenia and renal toxicity at high dosages (see Pharmacopoeia, p.649). It has theoretical advantages over other vasodilators since it also reduces circulating aldosterone concentrations by reducing angiotensin II.

(iv) Anticoagulants
In patients with severe cardiac failure, with swollen legs due to oedema, and who are immobile, there is an increased risk of venous thrombosis. Prophylactic anticoagulation is therefore advisable in such patients, using either an oral anticoagulant (e.g. warfarin) or low-dose subcutaneous heparin.

21.6. INFECTIVE ENDOCARDITIS

The principles of the treatment of infection are outlined in Chapter 20. In infective endocarditis the aims are:

1. To prevent the infection from occurring.
2. To identify the infective organism when infection occurs.
3. To eradicate the organism by using the appropriate antibiotics in sufficient dosages for a sufficient period of time.
4. To make continual careful observations of the patient's condition and to consider the indications for surgical intervention.

21.6.1. Prevention of infective endocarditis

There are two factors which combine to cause infective endocarditis. They are as follows:

(a) The presence of a cardiac abnormality

For example a valvular or septal defect, or an artificial valve, which provides a site for infection. Some abnormalities are associated with a high risk of endocarditis and some with a lower risk (see Table 21.12).

Table 21.12 *Cardiac abnormalities associated with a risk of infective endocarditis*

---

1. *High risk*
Aortic valve disease (acquired or congenital)
Aortic coarctation
Mitral regurgitation
Prosthetic valves
Ventricular septal defect
Atrial septal defect (ostium primum)
Tetralogy of Fallot
Transposition of the great vessels
A previous episode of infective endocarditis

2. *Intermediate risk*
Mitral valve prolapse
Hypertrophic obstructive cardiomyopathy
Pulmonary stenosis
Marfan's syndrome

3. *Low risk*
Mitral stenosis
Tricuspid valve disease (but high risk in drug addicts)
Atrial septal defect (other than ostium primum)

(b) The occurrence of bacteraemia

Infective endocarditis occurs when an abnormal heart is infected by bacteria released into the circulation from an infected site, e.g. bad teeth or a skin abscess, or after some surgical procedure. The most commonly incriminated procedure is dental surgery, but other procedures carry a risk, including gastro-intestinal, biliary, and genito-urinary surgery, upper respiratory surgery, and cardiac surgery with extra-corporeal circulation. Drug addicts (main-liners) have an increased risk of endocarditis, particularly right-sided.

For each of these types of procedure different prophylactic regimens are recommended since the organisms likely to cause infection vary. In Table 21.13 are listed the various therapeutic regimens appropriate to the different surgical procedures. A few points about these regimens should be stressed:

Table 21.13 *Surgical procedures associated with a risk of infective endocarditis and the prophylactic regimens appropriate to each*

Procedure	Likely organisms	Prophylactic regimen (30–60 min beforehand)*	Alternative in penicillin hypersensitivity
1. Dental surgery: (a) Artificial valves (b) General anaesthetic (c) Other procedures (excluding fillings)	Streptococci, enterococci, staphylococci	Penicillin G + gentamicin i.v. Penicillin G + gentamicin i.m. Amoxycillin p.o.	Vancomycin i.v. Vancomycin i.v. + gentamicin i.m. Erythromycin p.o.
2. Tonsillectomy, adenoidectomy, and other ENT surgery	Streptococci, enterococci, staphylococci	Penicillin G + gentamicin i.m.	Vancomycin i.v. + gentamicin i.m.
3. Gastro-intestinal, biliary, and genito-urinary surgery	Streptococci, Gram-negative bacteria, bacteroides	Gentamicin i.v. + ampicillin i.v.	Gentamicin i.v. + erythromycin i.v.
4. Cardiac surgery	Staphylococcus aureus	Gentamicin i.v. + cloxacillin i.v.	Gentamicin i.v. + vancomycin i.v.

*Intramuscular and i.v. drugs 30 min before procedure; oral drugs 60 min before procedure.

Dosages: penicillin G (i.m. and i.v.): 2 megaunits (1.2 g);
gentamicin (i.v.): 1.5 mg/kg up to a maximum of 80 mg;
vancomycin (i.v.): 1 g (see text and Pharmacopoeia for administration and contraindications);

    ampicillin (i.v.): 1 g;
    cloxacillin (i.v.): 2 g;
    erythromycin (i.v.—lactobionate): 500 mg;
    erythromycin (oral): 2 g;
    amoxycillin (oral): 3 g.

1. All involve a penicillin. If the patient gives a history of penicillin hypersensitivity then an alternative should be used, either vancomycin or erythromycin, as shown in Table 21.13.

2. Vancomycin is ototoxic and nephrotoxic and should not be used in patients with pre-existing hearing impairment or renal damage. In a patient who is hypersensitive to penicillin and in whom vancomycin is contraindicated a cephalosporin should be used, such as cephotaxime 1 g, i.v. or i.m.

3. Intramuscular or i.v. antibiotics should be given only 30 min before and oral antibiotics only 60 min before any procedure. If pre-operative treatment is more prolonged there is a risk that resistant organisms will emerge and cause an infection which will be difficult to treat. The main aim of prophylaxis is to cover the transient bacteraemia during surgical procedures.

4. Although only one dose of antibiotics is required *before* the procedure there should also be follow-up treatment for up to 2 days *after* treatment. The following follow-up regimens are suggested:

after dental procedures give oral penicillin V 500 mg six-hourly for eight doses (alternative erythromycin 500 mg six-hourly for eight doses);

after gastro-intestinal and other surgery (Table 21.13) repeat doses of gentamicin and ampicillin (or erythromycin) i.v. eight-hourly for two doses;

after cardiac surgery give cloxacillin 1 g i.v. plus gentamicin i.v. according to renal function four-hourly for twelve doses (alternative gentamicin i.v. + vancomycin 1 g i.v. twelve-hourly for four doses).

5. There is no universally agreed set of prophylactic regimens in this controversial area. The regimens suggested here merely represent one view.

21.6.2. Identification of the organism

If you suspect infective endocarditis do not give antibiotics before taking blood samples. In a clear-cut case of infective endocarditis it is best to proceed with treatment as soon as blood specimens have been taken for culture and serological examination (for *Chlamydia* and *Coxiella*). Because streptococcal infections are commonest treatment should initially be with benzylpenicillin and gentamicin and when the organism has been identified therapy may be changed if required. Culture- and serology-negative endocarditis should be treated as for enterococcal endocarditis with ampicillin and gentamicin.

21.6.3. Antibiotics

(a) Choice of antibiotic

The choice of antibiotic depends as always on the type and sensitivities of the infecting organism. The usual treatments for a variety of different organisms in infective endocarditis are listed in Table 21.14.

Table 21.14   *Choice of antibiotic in infective endocarditis*

Organism	First choice	Alternatives
Streptococcus viridans	Penicillin G + gentamicin	Vancomycin
Enterococci (e.g.		
Streptococcus faecalis)	Ampicillin + gentamicin	Vancomycin
Streptococcus bovis	Penicillin G	Cephalosporin/vancomycin
Streptococcus pneumoniae	Penicillin G	Cephalosporin/vancomycin
Staphylococcus aureus		
Penicillin-sensitive	Penicillin G	Cephalosporin/vancomycin
Penicillin-resistant	Flucloxacillin	Vancomycin
Staphylococcus epidermidis	Gentamicin + flucloxacillin	Vancomycin
Haemophilus	Ampicillin	Cephalosporin/vancomycin
E. coli	Cephalosporin	Ampicillin
Proteus	Ampicillin	Cephalosporin/vancomycin
Klebsiella	Cephalosporin	Gentamicin
Pseudomonas	Tobramycin + anti–pseudomonal penicillin (e.g. azlocillin or ticarcillin)	Gentamicin or amikacin + cephalosporin
Yeasts and fungi	Amphotericin B + flucytosine	—
Chlamydia and *Coxiella*	Tetracycline + clindamycin	Chloramphenicol
Culture and serology negative	As for enterococci	

(b) Route of administration and dosage of antibiotics

For most of the antibiotics used in infective endocarditis the dosages are as given in the Pharmacopoeia. However the following points should be noted:

1. The route of administration should be i.v., and bolus doses are said to be more effective than continuous infusion. After the first two or three weeks oral antibiotics may be substituted.

2. Recommended penicillin dosages vary widely. The dosage in an individual should be tailored to the sensitivity of the organism, and as a rule the antibiotic should be present in the plasma in a peak plasma concentration which is in at least eight-fold excess of the minimum inhibitory concentration (MIC) for the organism (see Chapter 20, p.264). This is so that enough penicillin can get into the cardiac vegetations and valves to kill the organism. A typical dose of benzylpenicillin (penicillin G) would be 4 megaunits (2.4 g) four-hourly.

3. When oral penicillin is substituted for i.v. penicillin it may be given in combination with probenecid to decrease the tubular secretion of penicillin and thus to maintain plasma concentrations for a longer period of time (see Pharmacopoeia p.735).

21.6.4. Duration of treatment

In most cases treatment should be continued for 4 weeks, but infections with *Streptococcus faecalis* and *Staphylococcus* spp. need 6–8 weeks of treatment.

21.7. VENOUS THROMBOEMBOLIC DISEASE

There are three aspects to the treatment of venous thromboembolic disease:

1. Prevention.
2. Treatment of established venous thrombosis.
3. Treatment of pulmonary embolism.

21.7.1. Prevention of venous thrombosis

The circumstances in which there is an increased risk of venous thrombosis are listed in Table 21.15. In some cases short-term prophylaxis may be indicated and occasionally long-term prophylaxis may also be appropriate.

Table 21.15 *Circumstances in which there is an increased risk of venous thrombosis*

1. *Conditions associated with an increased risk*
*Myocardial infarction
†*Severe congestive cardiac failure
*Surgical operations:
  General surgery
  Fractured hip
  Elective hip surgery   }   higher risk than general surgery
  Pelvic operations
*Trauma
Malignant disease
Pregnancy
Severe varicose veins
Polycythaemia
Oral contraceptive therapy

2. *Factors increasing the risk*
A previous episode of venous thrombosis
Advanced age
Immobility

*Short-term prevention may be appropriate.
†Long-term prevention may be appropriate.

For short-term prophylaxis heparin is the usual choice. It decreases the incidence of venous thrombosis when given to patients with acute myocardial infarction and to patients undergoing general surgical operations. It is given in a dose of 5000 i.u. b.d. or t.d.s. subcutaneously into the abdominal wall, varying the site of injection each time. For patients undergoing general surgery an extra dose should be given 2 h before the operation. Treatment should be continued for as long as the patient is immobile. The major worry concerning its use after surgery is that of bleeding and some surgeons are not keen on taking this risk as a routine.

The effect of heparin in patients undergoing orthopaedic surgery on the leg (e.g. hip replacement) or pelvic surgery (e.g. prostatectomy or gynaecological operations) is not so marked as in other forms of surgery and the alternative is dextran. Dextran has been shown to reduce the incidence of post-operative thrombosis in hip surgery, but is no more effective than heparin in urological and gynaecological surgery. It acts by decreasing blood viscosity, decreasing platelet aggregation, and promoting fibrinolysis. Dextran 40 or dextran 70 (molecular weights 40 000 and 70 000 daltons respectively) are used. They are given as an initial 500 ml infusion over 30 mins, followed by 1000–2000 ml/day for 2 days and 500–1000 ml/day for 3 days by continuous i.v. infusion. The main adverse effects are allergic reactions which are rare and occur less commonly with dextran 40, and bleeding which is usually not excessive. Fluid overload can occur if care is not taken.

Because of the high risk of venous thrombosis in patients undergoing hip surgery, and the relative ineffectiveness of heparin and dextran some recommend full oral anticoagulation with warfarin in selected patients (for dosages see below and in the Pharmacopoeia, p.775). Warfarin is effective in patients with fractured hips but in elective hip surgery is not recommended because of the increased risk of bleeding.

Because of the adverse effects of heparin and dextran many surgeons prefer to use mechanical methods for preventing venous thrombosis. These methods include electrical calf muscle stimulation during the operation and intermittent calf compression during the operation and for one or more days after. Intermittent compression using an inflatable pulsatile stocking or other methods reduces the incidence of venous thrombosis after most forms of surgery and is free of adverse effects. It is of no value in hip surgery for fractures.

Long-term prophylaxis can be carried out using either subcutaneous heparin (5000 i.u. b.d. or t.d.s.) or oral anticoagulants (e.g. warfarin). This may be required in high-risk patients who are rendered immobile for long periods of time (e.g. patients with severe congestive cardiac failure).

21.7.2. Treatment of venous thrombosis

(a) Deep vein thrombosis in the calf

Definite thrombosis in the calf should be treated with full anticoagulation in the absence of contra-indications (see Table 21.16). However, some would treat thrombosis in the soleal veins with an elastic stocking only, provided the patient is mobile. The aims of treatment are to prevent extension of the existing clot, to prevent contralateral thrombosis, and to prevent pulmonary embolism.

Table 21.16 *Contra-indications to the use of anticoagulants and thrombolytic drugs*

1. *Contra-indications to the use of heparin and warfarin*
(a) Absolute
   Current gastro-intestinal bleeding
   Recent intracranial or intra-ocular bleeding
   Pericarditis
   (Pregnancy—warfarin contra-indicated in early and late pregnancy. Heparin is safe—see sections on the use of drugs in pregnancy, Chapters 9 and 11)
(b) Relative
   Haemostatic disorders (congenital or acquired, e.g.liver disease)
   Past history of gastro-intestinal bleeding
   Thrombocytopenia
   Drug interactions (see Pharmacopoeia)

2. *Contra-indications to the use of thrombolytic drugs (streptokinase and urokinase)*
(a) Absolute
   Active bleeding (including menstruation)
   Recent intracranial or intra-ocular bleeding
   Children (urokinase)
(b) Relative
   Recent surgery (< 10 days)
   Recent obstetric delivery
   Recent puncture of a non-compressible blood vessel
   Recent gastro-intestinal bleeding
   Recent trauma
   Severe hypertension (systolic pressure > 200 mmHg or diastolic pressure > 110 mmHg)
   Haemostatic disorders (congenital or acquired, e.g. liver disease)
   Pregnancy
   Infective endocarditis
   Age > 75 yr
   Diabetic haemorrhagic retinopathy
   Streptococcal infection
   Recent cavitating pulmonary tuberculosis

Treatment should begin with heparin given by continuous i.v. infusion. It is usual to give a loading dose of 5000 i.u. i.v. followed by an infusion of 1000–1500 i.u./h. It is important to control the rate of infusion carefully and to this end it is best to use an infusion pump, if available, rather than the usual, less easily controlled i.v. infusion methods.

Therapy may be monitored by measuring the partial thromboplastin time and adjustments in dose made as required to prolong the time about two-fold.

Bleeding is the only important short-term adverse effect of heparin. If minor bleeding occurs stop the infusion and measure the partial thrombo-plastin time. Generally no specific treatment will be needed since heparin has a rapid half-time at these dosages (about 1 h). If there is major bleeding, however, protamine sulphate should be given to reverse the effects of heparin. The dose of protamine can be calculated on the basis of the calculated amount of heparin in the body, since 1 mg of protamine neutralizes 100 i.u. of heparin. If bleeding occurs within 15 min of a single dose the dose can be calculated directly on this basis, if later it can be calculated on the basis of the predicted amount left given that the half-time is 1 h (e.g. 50 per cent left after 1 h, 25 per cent after 2 h, etc.; see Table 3.3). During steady-state administration the amount of heparin in the body can be calculated from the following relationship [see eqn (3.35), p.56]:

$$\text{rate of infusion} = (\text{amount in body} \times 0.7)/t_{1/2}$$

Thus if the rate of infusion is 1500 i.u./h and $t_{1/2}$ is 1 h the amount in the body at steady state is $(1500 \times 1)/0.7$, i.e. about 2100 i.u.

Protamine is given by slow i.v. injection of no more than 50 mg (see heparin in Pharmacopoeia). Rebound hypercoagulability can occur after reversal of heparin.

Once heparin therapy has been started there is no rush to start oral anticoagulation, and warfarin can be started the following day after the prothrombin time has been measured in order to be sure that it is not already reduced because of parenchymal liver disease or hepatic conges-tion secondary to cardiac failure. When the prothrombin time result is known warfarin can be given using the sort of regimen described in detail in the Pharmacopoeia, i.e. daily loading doses of 10 mg until the prothrom-bin time is between 20 and 30 per cent or 1½–2 times normal (depending on the test used), followed by a maintenance dose depending on the loading dose. Remember that lower dosages than normal will be required in patients:

   (i) with liver disease;
   (ii) with congestive cardiac failure;
   (iii) with hypothyroidism;
   (iv) on a variety of different drugs, the most important of which are phenylbutazone, metronidazole, chloramphenicol, cimetidine, and iso-niazid (all inhibit warfarin metabolism), clofibrate, tetracyclines, and anabolic steroids (all increase the effect of warfarin on clotting factor synthesis). Avoid phenylbutazone and tetracycline altogether.

Higher dosages of warfarin may be required in patients on enzyme-inducing drugs such as phenytoin, primidone, phenobarbitone, rifampicin, carbamazepine, and griseofulvin.

Care should be taken in patients on aspirin, dipyridamole and sulphin-pyrazone, not because warfarin dosage requirements are altered in regard to the prothrombin time, but because if bleeding occurs haemostasis may be impaired.

As with heparin the most important adverse effect of warfarin is bleeding. In most cases withdrawal of warfarin is all that will be required but if bleeding is serious then give fresh frozen plasma as a source of clotting factors. If plasma is not available give vitamin K_1 10 mg i.v. (not i.m. because of the risk of haematoma).

Heparin treatment should be continued until the prothrombin time has been stable for at least 3 days on a regular maintenance dose of warfarin. Warfarin should then be continued for at least 3 months before it is withdrawn.

It should be noted that there is no guarantee that by prolonging the clotting time as long as it can be prolonged without bleeding, you will necessarily prevent pulmonary embolism from an existing clot. That is because neither heparin nor warfarin is thrombolytic in action. Their use is aimed at preventing extension of the existing clot, and preventing clot forming elsewhere (e.g. in the other leg), thereby allowing the body a chance to disperse the existing clot by natural thrombolysis, and to recanalize the affected vessel.

21.7.3. Iliofemoral and other large vein thrombosis

Thrombosis in large veins is a more serious condition than thrombosis in veins of the calf, carrying a high risk of pulmonary embolism. The risk of pulmonary embolism is higher in thigh and pelvic vein thrombosis than in the axillary vein in the arm.

Here there is a choice of treatment between heparin plus warfarin on the one hand and the thrombolytic agents streptokinase or urokinase on the other.

The advantages of the thrombolytic agents are as follows:

1. They cause lysis of the clot resulting in a reduced risk of embolism and relief of local signs and symptoms.

2. They reduce the risk of damage to the venous valves and therefore of subsequent symptoms due to venous stasis.

The combination of heparin and warfarin does neither of these things.

The main disadvantage of the thrombolytic agents is that the risk of bleeding is higher than with heparin/warfarin. However, if patients are chosen carefully according to the contra-indications listed in Table 21.16 the risk of bleeding is outweighed by the therapeutic benefit. In addition thrombolytic agents should not be used unless the diagnosis has been established by venography or some other detection technique (e.g. [125]I fibrinogen uptake) and should not be used unless the thrombosis is of recent origin (< 7 days).

Before treatment starts the thrombin time, activated partial thromboplastin time, prothrombin time, platelet count, and packed cell volume should be measured, to check that there are no important coagulation abnormalities and to provide a baseline for monitoring therapy. Treatment should be given as described in the Pharmacopoeia (see p.753) with monitoring by thrombin time or thromboplastin time measurement. Heparin and warfarin should be discontinued before thrombolytic drugs are started, and the thrombin time and prothrombin time should not be prolonged more than twofold.

Bleeding from puncture sites is almost inevitable and does not usually necessitate withdrawal. The number of such sites should be kept to a minimum (e.g. one venous line, and if blood gas measurements are required one arterial line). If major bleeding occurs stop therapy and give whole fresh blood, packed cells, or fresh frozen plasma. It may also be necessary to give tranexamic acid (see p.630).

Streptokinase is the thrombolytic drug of choice and urokinase should be used only in patients with a history of streptokinase hypersensitivity. Streptokinase is given for 7 days following which heparin and warfarin should be started, the heparin being continued until the prothrombin time is stable for at least 3 days during the same dose of warfarin. Warfarin should then be continued for at least 6 months.

If a thrombolytic drug is contra-indicated then heparin and warfarin should be used, in the absence of contra-indications (Table 21.16).

21.7.4. Treatment of pulmonary embolism

Here the choice of drug treatment lies between heparin plus warfarin on the one hand and thrombolytic drugs on the other.

Heparin and warfarin are used in patients with a small pulmonary embolism in whom there is little or no haemodynamic disturbance, and in patients in whom thrombolytic drugs are contra-indicated (Table 21.16).

In large pulmonary embolism when there is haemodynamic disturbance heparin should be used in the first instance, but if there is no haemodynamic improvement after 24 h or if there is deterioration thrombolytic agents should be used, provided that:

(i) there are no contra-indications;
(ii) the diagnosis has been definitely established, preferably by angiography;
(iii) the event is of recent origin (< 7 days).

The advantages of the thrombolytic drugs over heparin/warfarin are that they cause lysis of clots and hence more rapid relief of haemodynamic and pulmonary disturbance, and that they minimize damage to the pulmonary vascular bed. There is probably no difference in mortality, however, with the two types of treatment.

The dosages of drugs in pulmonary embolism are the same as in venous thrombosis. The warfarin therapy given after heparin or streptokinase treatment should be continued for at least 6 months.

22 The drug therapy of respiratory disorders

22.1. THE USE OF OXYGEN IN RESPIRATORY DISEASE

When there is hypoxia (as in the conditions listed in Table 22.1) it is therapeutically useful to increase the percentage of oxygen in the inspired air, whose oxygen content is about 20 per cent.

Table 22.1 *Common conditions in which oxygen therapy may be useful*

Chronic bronchitis and emphysema (acute exacerbations)
Asthma
Pneumonia
Pulmonary oedema of any cause
Pulmonary embolism
Pneumothorax
Fibrosing alveolitis

Oxygen may be added to the inspired air to produce percentages ranging from 24 to 60 per cent, and the dose one chooses depends not on the degree of hypoxia but on the presence or absence of *hypercapnia*. If the partial pressure of carbon dioxide in arterial blood (P_ACO_2) is normal (5.3 kPa or 40 mmHg) then high concentrations of oxygen may usually be given safely. However, if there is hypercapnia ($P_ACO_2 > 6.6$ kPa or 50 mmHg) then high concentrations of oxygen may be dangerous for the reasons discussed below.

Generally, therefore, the concentration of oxygen administered should be altered according to monitoring of the blood gases. This is especially important in finding the optimal concentration of oxygen in patients with hypercapnia.

Concentrations of oxygen in the inspired air of up to 60 per cent can be given via either nasal catheters or facial mask. Nasal catheters may be more comfortable for some patients but tend to produce uncomfortable drying of the nasal mucosa and ideally oxygen so given should be first humidified.

Lower concentrations of oxygen (24–35 per cent) can be given using masks which are designed to deliver different concentrations of oxygen in the inspired air, depending on the design of the mask and on the flow rate of oxygen. Examples are the Edinburgh mask and 'Venturi' masks. The Edinburgh mask can be tuned to give any desired concentration depending on the oxygen flow rate. 'Venturi' masks on the other hand come in different varieties giving different concentrations of inspired oxygen depending on the size of the holes admitting air to the mixture—three types are available giving 24, 28, or 35 per cent oxygen at oxygen flow rates of 4 to 8 l/min.

When low concentrations of oxygen are required it is best to start with 24 per cent and increase the concentration only if the blood gases show continuing hypoxia ($P_AO_2 < 8$ kPa) without worsening hypercapnia compared with pre-treatment values. The problem of avoiding hypercapnia most commonly occurs in patients with chronic obstructive airways disease.

Oxygen is not without potential adverse effects. The most important is worsening hypercapnia in patients with chronic obstructive airways disease. The respiratory centre responds mainly to the P_ACO_2 and arterial pH, and to a lesser extent to the P_AO_2. When there is hypercapnia the respiratory centre responds poorly to carbon dioxide and relies on hypoxia as a stimulus. If arterial hypoxia is removed by giving a high concentration of inspired oxygen then the hypoxic drive to respiration is lost and hypercapnia worsens.

Prolonged inhalation of high concentrations of inspired oxygen may have adverse effects in both neonates and adults. In neonates it can result in the serious adverse effect of retrolental fibroplasia. In adults it may cause irritation of the respiratory tract with coughing, sore throat, tracheobronchitis, pulmonary oedema, and atelectasis.

22.2. COUGH

If a cough is irritating and unproductive of sputum it may be suppressed. If it is associated with production of sputum, but difficulty in expectoration, then some would use expectorant drugs. These measures are used only for the *symptomatic* treatment of cough, and where possible the underlying condition should be treated.

22.2.1. Cough suppressants

Opiates are used as cough suppressants and act directly on the medullary mechanisms subserving cough. Codeine phosphate and pholcodine are indicated when a dry cough is disturbing the sleep, but rarely otherwise. They may cause sputum retention and should therefore be used with caution in chronic bronchitis or bronchiectasis. The potent opiates, such as morphine and diamorphine, may sometimes be useful in the treatment of intractable dry cough in patients with terminal illness, particularly bronchial carcinoma.

In addition to drugs which suppress cough directly, symptomatic relief may be obtained from sedation with an antihistamine, such as diphenhydramine.

22.2.2. Expectorants

Various compounds have been purported to act as expectorants, but there is little evidence that any of them is of any practical value. The inhalation of steam, with or without a volatile inhalant, such as menthol or benzoin, is soothing in bronchitis and bronchiectasis, and is harmless. It may be used as an adjunct to physiotherapy to aid expectoration of viscid sputum.

Mucolytic expectorants act by decreasing sputum viscosity. Although they can be shown to have that effect *in vitro* their clinical efficacy is unproven, and they may be no better than inhalations of steam or menthol. There is a wide variety of other expectorants available, containing drugs which increase watery bronchial secretions, but which probably act as expectorants only if they cause vomiting (e.g. squill, ipecacuanha, ammonium chloride). There is no evidence that such preparations are of any value.

22.3. PNEUMONIAS

A list of infective causes of pneumonias is given in Table 22.2 along with the first-line and alternative antibiotics indicated in such case.

Table 22.2   *Common causes of pneumonia and their treatment*

Organism	Antibiotic(s) of choice	Alternative(s)
1. *Bacterial*		
Strep. pneumoniae	Benzylpenicillin or amoxycillin	Erythromycin
Staph. aureus (penicillin-sensitive)	Benzylpenicillin	Erythromycin
Staph. aureus (penicillinase-producing)	Flucloxacillin	According to local sensitivities
Kl. pneumoniae	Gentamicin + cephalosporin	Chloramphenicol/ co-trimoxazole
H. influenzae	Amoxycillin or ampicillin	Cephalosporin/ chloramphenicol
Legionella pneumophila	Erythromycin	Tetracyclines/rifampicin
Mycobacterium tuberculosis	See text	
2. *Viral*	Treat secondary bacterial infection	
3. *Others*		
Coxiella burneti	Tetracyclines	Erythromycin
Mycoplasma pneumoniae	Tetracyclines	Erythromycin
Chlamydia spp.	Tetracyclines	Erythromycin

The principles of treatment of infections are outlined in Chapter 20, but the following points are emphasized in regard to pneumonia.

22.3.1. Route of administration of antibiotics

In severe cases (e.g. if the patient is ill enough to be admitted to hospital) parenteral antibiotics should generally be used. A change to oral treatment should be possible when clinical improvement occurs. In mild or moderate cases the oral route will usually be sufficient.

22.3.2. Duration of treatment

Treatment for 7–10 days is usually sufficient but should be continued for at least 3 days after the temperature has returned to normal. However infections with *Staph. aureus* and *Kl. pneumoniae* can be very difficult to eradicate and relapse readily. Parenteral treatment should be continued until the temperature is consistently normal and the sputum has cleared. Thereafter oral therapy should be continued for at least 2 weeks.

Because of the tendency to relapse of mycoplasmal infections treatment should be continued for 2–3 weeks.

22.3.3. Alternatives to first-line antibiotics

The alternative antibiotics to those of first choice are listed in Table 22.2. They should be used if the first choice is contra-indicated (e.g. penicillin in a patient with penicillin hypersensitivity, or tetracycline in a young child or a patient with renal failure), or if the organism proves to be resistant to the first choice (e.g. penicillinase-producing *Staph. aureus*).

22.3.4. Drug therapy besides antibiotics

Oxygen should be given for hypoxia. Pleuritic pain can often be helped by mild analgesics, such as aspirin. More severe pain may be treated with more potent analgesics, such as buprenorphine, morphine, or pethidine, but care must be taken in patients with hypercapnia, since the opiates can cause respiratory depression.

22.4. CHRONIC AIRWAYS OBSTRUCTION

In chronic airways obstruction the main aims of treatment are to prevent infections, to relieve reversible airways obstruction (due to bronchospasm and secretions), and to treat acute exacerbations and heart failure. In addition patients should be advised to stop smoking.

22.4.1. Infection

Antibiotics are not used prophylactically as continuous therapy, since their use in this way leads to the emergence of resistant organisms. Instead patients may be given a supply of an antibiotic (amoxycillin, co-trimoxazole, or tetracycline) to take when they get an upper respiratory tract infection (e.g. a winter cold) or at the first signs of acute infective bronchitis, so that the risks of infection can be reduced. Influenza vaccine should be given in the winter, since serious bacterial infection often occurs in these patients secondary to viral infections.

22.4.2. Bronchospasm

Chronic airways obstruction may be both reversible and irreversible. Reversible obstruction is due to mucus secretion and bronchospasm, and the latter can be treated in the same way as in chronic asthma, with aerosol inhalation of bronchodilators and corticosteroids (see below). There is little evidence that drugs used as expectorants are of value in relieving obstruction due to viscid mucus, but steam inhalations soothe and may be used in combination with physiotherapy.

22.4.3. Acute exacerbations

Acute exacerbations are generally caused by infections and prompt treatment of infection is important.

In an acute exacerbation hypoxia should be treated with oxygen, starting with low concentrations (e.g. 24 per cent) and increasing slowly according to response (see above under oxygen).

Infection is usually due to *H. influenzae* or *Strep. pneumoniae* and treatment with amoxycillin, co-trimoxazole, or a tetracycline is indicated. Bronchospasm should be treated as in acute asthma with inhaled and i.v. bronchodilators, such as aminophylline and salbutamol.

22.4.4. Cardiac failure

Congestive cardiac failure should be treated with diuretics as described in Chapter 21 (p.328). In the acute stage loop diuretics should be used and later it may be possible to switch to a thiazide diuretic. In some cases, however, long-term treatment with a loop diuretic or with a combination of diuretics, including potassium-sparing diuretics, may be necessary. Potassium chloride supplements or a potassium-sparing diuretic are usually necessary in these patients (see Chapter 24, p.401).

Cardiac glycosides should not be used in chronic cor pulmonale since they are poorly effective, and the risk of digitalis toxicity with cardiac arrhythmias is high.

22.5. BRONCHIAL ASTHMA

22.5.1. Pharmacological factors in the production of asthma and the mechanisms of action of drugs used in its treatment

Impairment of air-flow in asthma is caused by three bronchial abnormalities:

1. Constriction of bronchial smooth muscle (bronchoconstriction). The extent to which bronchoconstriction occurs in response to a stimulus at any time varies with bronchial 'reactivity'.

2. Swelling of bronchial mucosa (bronchial oedema).

3. Excessive bronchial mucus secretion.

These abnormalities are caused by the release of chemical inflammatory mediators within the bronchial wall, mainly from mast cells. The mediators involved include histamine, peptides (kinins), and arachidonic acid derivatives (prostaglandins and leukotrienes). The release of these substances from cells, and their actions on bronchial tissues involves intracellular mediators such as cyclic AMP and cyclic GMP (so-called 'second messengers').

Occasionally asthma may be precipitated by hypersensitivity to aspirin. In such patients there is generally a history of nasal polyps and some patients have attacks of urticaria. About half of these patients are also allergic to tartrazine, a yellow dyestuff found in many foods and in some drugs. The mechanism whereby aspirin induces asthma is not known, but may be related to inhibition of prostaglandin synthesis.

Asthma may also be precipitated by a β-adrenoceptor antagonist, particularly non-cardioselective antagonists such as propranolol and oxprenolol.

The pathogenetic mechanisms in asthma are summarized in Fig. 22.1 in which are also shown the effects of drugs used to treat asthma. The drugs are listed in Table 22.3.

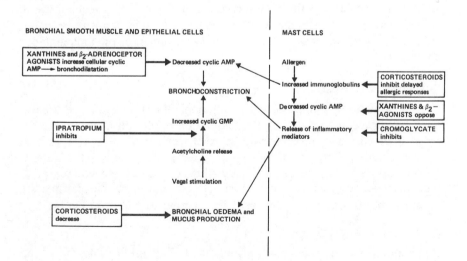

Fig. 22.1. The pathophysiology of bronchial asthma and the sites and mechanisms of action of drugs used in its treatment.

Table 22.3   *Drugs used in the treatment of bronchial asthma*

β₂-adrenoceptor agonists (p.620)
Salbutamol (albuterol)
Terbutaline
Rimiterol
Fenoterol
Reproterol

Anticholinergic drugs (p.616)
Ipratropium

Xanthine derivatives (p.779)
Aminophylline

Mast cell stabilizers
Cromoglycate (p.670)
Ketotifen

Corticosteroids (p.664)
Beclomethasone
Betamethasone

(a) β_2-adrenoceptor agonists

These drugs (salbutamol, terbutaline, rimiterol, fenoterol, and reproterol) are direct β-adrenoceptor agonists with some selectivity for β_2-adrenoceptors. They therefore act mainly on adrenoceptors in bronchial tissue, and when used in the recommended dosages have much less effect on cardiac (β_1) adrenoceptors. Their action on mast cells and bronchial smooth muscle cells results in an increase in adenylate cyclase activity and an increase in cellular cyclic AMP concentrations. This leads to bronchodilatation, and in mast cells to decreased release of inflammatory mediators.

(b) Xanthine derivatives

Theophylline and its congeners (e.g. aminophylline) decrease the breakdown of intracellular cyclic AMP by inhibition of phosphodiesterase. The result is an increase in cellular cyclic AMP concentrations, with similar effects to those of the β_2-adrenoceptor agonists. Since the two different types of drug produce the same effect by different routes one would expect their therapeutic effects to be at least additive and there is experimental evidence that this might be the case (see Chapter 4, p.67, and Fig. 4.5).

(c) Anticholinergic drugs

Ipratropium, an atropine analogue, inhibits the action of acetylcholine at tissue cholinoceptors, and thereby inhibits the bronchoconstrictive effects of vagus nerve activity. It also decreases bronchial mucus secretion.

(d) Mast-cell stabilizers

Cromoglycate and ketotifen inhibit the release of mediators from sensitized mast cells. They do not, however, reverse the effects of the mediators and do not therefore cause bronchodilatation, relieve bronchial oedema, or decrease mucus production. They are therefore used in the *prevention* of acute attacks, not in their treatment.

(e) Corticosteroids

The mechanisms of action of corticosteroids in asthma are not fully understood, but they probably act in several different ways:

1. They have anti-inflammatory effects, thereby decreasing bronchial oedema and bronchial mucus production;

2. They enhance the actions of β-adrenoceptor agonists, both endogenous (adrenaline and noradrenaline) and exogenous (e.g. salbutamol), and increase their bronchodilating properties.

3. They inhibit the IgE- and IgG-mediated, delayed (Type III) allergic responses to extrinsic allergens, but not the immediate (Type I) IgE-mediated response.

Table 22.4 *Some types of inhalational formulations used in the treatment of bronchial asthma*

Formulation	Drug	Dose (mg) in one puff	Dose (mg) in one tablet (oral use)
Aerosol	β_2-adrenoceptor agonists		
	Fenoterol	0.2	—
	Reproterol	0.5	20
	Salbutamol	0.1	2–4
	Terbutaline	0.25	5
	Corticosteroids		
	Beclomethasone	0.05	—
	Betamethasone	0.1	0.5
	Anticholinergic drugs		
	Ipratropium	0.018	—
	Mast-cell stabilizers		
	Cromoglycate	1.0	100
Aerosol (breath-activated)	β_2-adrenoceptor agonists		
	Rimiterol	0.2	—
Micro-fine powder (breath-activated)	Salbutamol	0.2–0.4	2–4
	Beclomethasone	0.1	—
	Cromoglycate	20.0	100
Solution for nebulizing	Cromoglycate		
Respirator solution	Salbutamol Terbutaline		

22.5.2. Routes of administration of drugs in asthma

(a) Inhalation

The administration of some anti-asthmatic drugs by inhalation confers two advantages—firstly it allows rapid relief of bronchospasm with β_2-adrenoceptor agonists, and secondly it allows the use of smaller dosages of drugs with the result that there are fewer systemic adverse effects. In Table 22.4 are listed some of the different kinds of inhalational formulations available.

It is important when prescribing these formulations to ensure that the patient understands how to use them properly. There are two important points to be made—the first is in regard to the *mechanics* of using inhalational formulations, the second to the *regularity* of their use.

(i) Mechanics of inhalation

Incorrect technique in using inhalational formulations is a common cause of failure to respond to treatment. The patient must be taught the correct method of inhalation by demonstration, and the doctor should confirm that the patient can use the inhaler correctly. The correct method is as follows: breathe out fully with the inhaler in the mouth; depress the cannister and at the same time breathe in slowly and as deeply as possible; hold the breath for a few (up to 10) seconds and then breathe out slowly.

Some patients have difficulty in timing this procedure and for them alternative types of inhaler are available. These include inhalers which merely require the patient to breathe in without separately activating a drug-release mechanism (e.g. Ventolin Rotacaps®), and inhalers which have a 'spacer' fitted to the mouthpiece, which allow a little extra time after depression of the canister before inhalation is required (e.g. Bricanyl Spacer Inhaler®).

(ii) Frequency of administration

The β_2-adrenoceptor agonists act very rapidly in relieving bronchospasm and are therefore often used to treat acute attacks (although patients with chronic asthma may derive benefit from regular, three or four times daily, administration). Because of this intermittent use of β_2-adrenoceptor agonists patients often believe that other drugs can be taken intermittently. That is not the case—corticosteroids, cromoglycate, and ipratropium should be taken at regular intervals during the day, usually four times.

22.5.3. Practical treatment of bronchial asthma

The practical treatment of bronchial asthma has several aspects:

    (a) The avoidance of precipitating factors.
    (b) Treatment of reversible airways obstruction:
        (i) acute, severe (status asthmaticus);

(ii) acute, mild to moderate;
(iii) chronic.
3. Prevention of attacks.

(a) Avoidance of precipitating factors

If precipitating factors can be identified then attacks may be avoidable by avoidance of the allergen. The role of desensitization is controversial, and there is little evidence to support its use.

Drugs which can cause asthma should be avoided. Non-selective (i.e. β_1 and β_2) adrenoceptor antagonists should never be used in a patient with asthma, and the relatively selective β_1-adrenoceptor antagonists (atenolol, metoprolol, and practolol) should be used with great caution.

Aspirin and other salicylates should not be used in patients with known aspirin hypersensitivity (see p.742), and such patients should be warned of the vast number of over-the-counter medicines which contain aspirin. These patients may also be sensitive to other non-steroidal anti-inflammatory drugs and to tartrazine, a yellow dye used in some foods and drugs.

Infection is an important complication to avoid, and patients whose asthma is clearly associated with chest infections should be given a supply of an antibiotic, such as amoxycillin, to take at the first sign of an upper or lower respiratory tract infection. In all asthmatics lower respiratory tract infections should be treated vigorously, and in patients with influenza prophylactic antibiotics should be given to prevent secondary bacterial infection. Influenza vaccine should be given in the winter.

(b) Treatment of reversible airways obstruction

(i) Acute severe asthma (status asthmaticus)

Acute severe asthma is an acute medical emergency characterized by severe wheeze, incapacitating breathlessness, to the extent that the patient can hardly speak, tachycardia, central cyanosis, and sometimes pulsus paradoxus.

An acute severe attack of asthma should be treated with oxygen, i.v. bronchodilators, i.v. fluids, i.v. corticosteroids, antibiotics, and artificial ventilation if required. Although these patients are excessively anxious it is important not to sedate them unless artificial ventilation is intended.

Oxygen—oxygen should be given in a high concentration (up to 60 per cent), only if there is hypoxia and a *low* P_ACO_2. A *normal* or *raised* P_ACO_2 is a sign of very severe asthma, and the initial concentration of oxygen in the inspired air should be 24 per cent, increasing if necessary according to the blood gases (see above under oxygen).

Bronchodilators—a β_2-adrenoceptor agonist and a xanthine may be given intravenously (e.g. salbutamol and aminophylline). Initially salbutamol is given as a continuous i.v. infusion starting at a rate of

5 micrograms/min and adjusting the rate according to the clinical response up to 20 micrograms/min. Aminophylline is given as an i.v. loading dose of 6 mg/kg over 10 min followed by a continuous i.v. infusion at a rate of 0.9 mg/kg/min. Lower maintenance dosages should be used if there is concurrent emphysema, congestive cardiac failure, or impaired liver function, and in patients over 50 years of age (for dosages see Table P.10, p.780). The loading dose should be omitted in a patient who has previously been taking long-term oral treatment with a theophylline derivative.

A β_2-adrenoceptor agonist given by inhalation via a nebulizer is an alternative to the i.v. route, but is likely to be ineffective if there is very severe bronchoconstriction. Nebulizer treatment can replace i.v. treatment as bronchoconstriction becomes less severe during treatment.

Corticosteroids—corticosteroids should be given i.v., e.g. hydrocortisone 200 mg six-hourly, until oral prednisolone can be given, starting in a dosage of 20 mg q.d.s.

Antibiotics—chest infections should be treated with appropriate antibiotics. Ampicillin i.v. should be used, with a cephalosporin as an alternative in patients with penicillin hypersensitivity. If oral therapy is possible co-trimoxazole and tetracyclines are alternatives.

Intermittent positive pressure ventilation (IPPV)—in patients who do not respond to the above treatment IPPV is necessary. IPPV should be started if the $P_A O_2$ remains low (< 6.6 kPa, 50 mmHg), if the $P_A CO_2$ rises above 6.6 kPa, if acidosis persists (pH < 7.3), or if there is severe drowsiness, confusion, or exhaustion leading to worsening hypoxia.

If the patient improves in response to these measures then oral and inhaled therapy should be continued using oxygen and nebulized salbutamol or terbutaline, oral corticosteroids gradually reducing in dosage to eventual withdrawal, and an oral antibiotic. Physiotherapy should be started. Later bronchodilators by nebulizer may be replaced by regular aerosols with or without oral bronchodilators as required (see below).

(ii) Acute mild or moderate attacks of asthma

Acute intermittent asthmatic attacks are best treated with a β_2-adrenoceptor agonist by inhalation (see Table 22.4). These drugs relieve bronchospasm within a few minutes, reach a peak at 15–30 min and last for 3–4 h. Ipratropium by inhaler is an alternative, but its effects take longer to come on and it is probably better reserved for the regular treatment of chronic asthma.

An inhalation of a β_2-adrenoceptor agonist before exposure to a known precipitant (e.g. in patients with cold-induced or exercise-induced asthma) may help to prevent the anticipated acute attack.

(iii) Chronic asthma

In maintenance therapy of chronic asthma a β_2-adrenoceptor agonist (e.g. salbutamol) by aerosol is the treatment of choice, and should be given up to four times daily. Ipratropium is an alternative and patients who do not respond to one or the other should be given both.

If the response to this combined treatment is not complete then an oral theophylline derivative should be added. Because the toxic:therapeutic ratio of theophylline is low initial dosages should be low, and ideally therapy should be monitored by plasma theophylline concentration measurements (see Chapter 7). Slow-release aminophylline is particularly useful for patients who have nocturnal or early-morning symptoms.

(c) Prevention of attacks

Prevention of asthmatic attacks may be achieved by regular maintenance therapy with inhaled corticosteroids or sodium cromoglycate.

Inhaled steroids and cromoglycate are given up to four times a day even if the patient is not chronically wheezy. Cromoglycate may also be a useful alternative to a β_2-adrenoceptor agonist in preventing exercise-induced asthma.

The oral analogue of cromoglycate, ketotifen, is an alternative, but is no better than cromoglycate and may cause drowsiness.

In patients with severe asthma, in whom other drug therapy has been ineffective, *oral* corticosteroids may be required. They may also be used in short courses in the case of a severe attack when the patient's usual treatment becomes ineffective in controlling symptoms.

22.5.4. Adverse effects of drugs in asthma

Adverse effects are very uncommon with the use of inhaled drugs, because the dosages used are much lower than the equivalent oral dosages (see Table 22.4). Occasionally with high dosages of β_2-adrenoceptor agonists sinus tachycardia and arrhythmias may occur; this is particularly important in patients being treated with β_2-agonists by inhalation via a nebulizer. Inhalation of corticosteroids may occasionally cause oropharyngeal infection with *Candida albicans*. Some suppression of the hypothalamic-pituitary axis may rarely occur with high dosages (> 20 puffs per day).

Orally or i.v. administered β_2-adrenoceptor agonists can cause tachycardia and cardiac arrhythmias. They may worsen glucose tolerance in diabetics particularly when given i.v. with hydrocortisone in acute severe asthma, and increased insulin dosages may be required.

Xanthines can cause cardiac arrhythmias and ideally cardiographic monitoring should be available when xanthines and β_2-agonists are given together i.v. in acute severe attacks. During chronic therapy adverse effects of theophylline derivatives can be minimized by monitoring plasma concentrations.

The numerous adverse effects of oral corticosteroids are detailed in the Pharmacopoeia (p.666).

22.5.5. Monitoring therapy in asthma

It is important to measure either the forced expiratory volume in one second (FEV_1) or more simply the peak expiratory flow rate (PEFR) during treatment of asthma. This has been discussed in Chapter 7, but it is worth stressing that these measurements can vary widely within a patient depending on the time of day. There is often a dip early in the morning, and apparently normal lung function later in the day may be misleading in regard to the severity of disease. Patients should be encouraged to measure their own PEFR at home, thus enabling them to monitor their own progress.

Monitoring of plasma theophylline concentrations is discussed in Chapter 7.

22.6. PULMONARY TUBERCULOSIS

The principles of treating infections (see Chapter 20) apply to the treatment of pulmonary tuberculosis. However, at least two drugs are used concurrently because the causative organisms are often resistant to one or more antituberculous drug, and resistance develops readily if only one drug is used.

Drug regimens vary throughout the world, depending on socio-economic conditions. The drugs used are listed in Table 22.5 with details of adult dosages, important adverse effects, drug interactions, comments about monitoring various aspects of therapy, and comments about circumstances in which the drugs should be avoided.

22.6.1. Developed countries

The most usual regimen used in initial therapy in developed countries is the combination of rifampicin, isoniazid (with pyridoxine), and ethambutol.

In the *initial phase* these drugs are each given once daily as a single oral dose (see Table 22.5), 30–60 min before food. Initial treatment should be continued for at least 2 months. When the results of drug sensitivity are known, treatment in the *continuation phase* can be with two drugs only, one of which should be isoniazid. The usual combination is isoniazid with rifampicin, and treatment should be continued for a further 7 months (i.e. 9 months in all).

Sometimes alternative drugs may be used for the following reasons.

(a) Resistant organisms

If a patient is failing to improve on the standard regimen of isoniazid, rifampicin, and ethambutol, and if sensitivity testing suggests that bacterial resistance is the cause then alternative drugs may be used as indicated by sensitivity tests (see Table 22.5).

Table 22.5   *Drugs used in the treatment of tuberculosis*

Drug	Adult dosage	Important adverse effects/interactions	Comments
(a) Routine therapy (developed countries)			
1. Isoniazid (p.695)	5 mg/kg o.d. (maximum 300 mg)	Peripheral neuropathy (must be given with pyridoxine); hepatitis	Monitor liver function tests; pharmacogenetic variability in metabolism (see Chapter 8)
2. Rifampicin (p.740)	8–12 mg/kg o.d.	Hepatotoxicity; induces metabolism of warfarin and oral contraceptive	Monitor liver function tests; avoid in pregnancy
3. Ethambutol (p.679)	15 mg/kg o.d.	Optic neuritis	Monitor visual fields/colour vision; reduce dosage in renal failure
(b) Second-line drugs (developing countries, and for resistant organisms)			
Streptomycin (p.632)	7.5–15 mg/kg o.d. i.m.	Hypersensitivity; nephrotoxicity (enhanced by frusemide and ethacrynic acid); ototoxicity; enhances effects of neuromuscular blocking agents	Wear gloves when administering; avoid in pregnancy; (monitor plasma concentrations if possible)
para-aminosalicylic acid (PAS)	150 mg/kg/day in divided doses	Anorexia, nausea, vomiting; liver damage; hypersensitivity	Avoid in renal failure
Pyrazinamide (TB meningitis in particular)	30 mg/kg/day in three or four doses (maximum 3 g)	Liver damage; hyperuricaemia	Monitor liver function tests
(c) Other drugs for resistant organisms			
Thiacetazone	2 mg/kg o.d.	Anorexia, nausea, vomiting; jaundice; vestibular toxicity	Initial dose 0.5 mg/kg
Ethionamide	0.75–1.0 g/day in three doses	Anorexia, nausea, vomiting; mental disturbances; peripheral neuropathy	Avoid in liver disease and in pregnancy
Capreomycin	1 g o.d. i.m. (maximum 20 mg/kg/day)	Ototoxicity; hypokalaemia; nephrotoxicity; hepatotoxicity	Avoid in pregnancy; monitor auditory, renal, and hepatic function
Cycloserine	250 mg b.d. or t.d.s.	CNS toxicity; psychosis; convulsions	Reduce dosages in renal failure; avoid in epilepsy or psychosis

(b) Poor compliance

If oral therapy fails because of poor compliance, supervised therapy with twice weekly streptomycin (1 g i.m.) plus isoniazid (14 mg/kg orally with pyridoxine 10 mg orally) can be given. Treatment in such cases should be continued for 18 months.

(c) Contra-indications

The main contra-indications to antituberculous drugs are shown in Table 22.5. For example, in pregnancy rifampicin, streptomycin, ethionamide, and capreomycin should not be used. Isoniazid and ethambutol would be the drugs of choice.

(d) Adverse reactions

If a serious adverse reaction occurs and can be attributed to a single drug (e.g. visual disturbance due to ethambutol) then that drug should be withdrawn and therapy continued with the other two drugs. Alternative drugs can be added later if there is a poor response.

Infrequently serious blood dyscrasias or hypersensitivity reactions occur, and in such cases all antituberculous therapy should be withdrawn for at least two weeks. Alternative drugs should then be used.

22.6.2. Developing countries

In countries in which the cost of expensive drugs, such as rifampicin, cannot be met, regimens of cheaper drugs are used. A typical regimen employs streptomycin, *para*-aminosalicylic acid (PAS), and isoniazid (with pyridoxine). Thiacetazone is an alternative to PAS. Streptomycin is continued in these regimens for 1–2 months, and thereafter therapy is continued with two drugs only. Ideally treatment should be continued for a total of 18 months, following which relapse is uncommon.

22.6.3. Relapse

If a first-line regimen (e.g. rifampicin + isoniazid + ethambutol) is complied with strictly there should be eradication of the tubercle bacillus in 100 per cent of cases. In patients treated with a twice-weekly regimen because of poor compliance 5–10 per cent will need to be re-treated at a later time. Relapse rates are higher following the cheaper regimens (e.g. streptomycin + PAS + isoniazid) and increase with shorter courses of therapy. For example, the relapse rate following 18 months of therapy with streptomycin, isoniazid, and PAS is about 3 per cent, but is up to 15 per cent following a 12-month course.

Initial treatment in relapse should be with isoniazid plus two drugs which the patient has not previously been given. Subsequently changes may be made in the light of *in vitro* sensitivities.

22.6.4. Monitoring therapy

It is usually unnecessary to monitor therapy when treating tuberculosis. In patients in whom poor compliance is suspected, it is possible to detect antituberculous drugs, such as isoniazid, PAS, and ethambutol in the urine. Rifampicin colours the urine reddish-brown and is readily detected by eye.

If streptomycin is used then ideally plasma concentrations should be monitored, so that dosages can be altered to minimize the risk of eighth nerve damage. Unfortunately in developing countries, in which streptomycin is most commonly used, monitoring is too expensive. The steady-state plasma concentration, measured 24 h after a daily dose, should be no higher than 20 μg/ml.

22.7. DRUG-INDUCED RESPIRATORY DISORDERS

A variety of drugs can cause respiratory disorders. Some important examples are given in Table 22.6.

Table 22.6 *Drug-induced respiratory disorders*

Type of disorder	Drugs commonly involved
Acute infiltration and eosinophilia	Nitrofurantoin
Interstitial pneumonia and fibrosis	Amiodarone
	Bleomycin
	Busulphan
	Cyclophosphamide
	Methotrexate
	Nitrofurantoin
Lupus-like syndrome	Hydralazine
	Phenytoin
	Procainamide
Asthma	Aspirin
	β-adrenoceptor antagonists
	Tartrazine
	Anaphylaxis due to any drug
Pulmonary embolism	Oral contraceptives
Respiratory depression	Alcohol
	Antidepressants
	Antihistamines
	Benzodiazepines
	Chloral derivatives
	Opiate analgesics

23 The drug therapy of gastro-intestinal, hepatic, and biliary disorders

23.1. ANTACIDS

Antacids are used for the symptomatic relief of dyspepsia, whether it be 'functional' or associated with identifiable pathology, e.g. heartburn due to oesophageal reflux, pain and discomfort associated with peptic ulceration, or gastritis.

23.1.1. Mechanisms of action of antacids

Antacids are bases which raise the pH of the gastric contents. Examples of commonly used antacids are listed in Table 23.1 along with additives which are often incorporated in proprietary preparations.

Table 23.1 *Examples of commonly used antacids and antacid preparations*

1. *Antacids*
(a) Aluminium salts, e.g. aluminium hydroxide
(b) Magnesium salts, e.g. magnesium trisilicate
(c) Sodium salts, e.g. sodium bicarbonate

2. *Common additives*
(a) Foaming agents, e.g. alginates
(b) Anti-foaming agents, e.g. dimethicone (simethicone)
(c) Surface (local) anaesthetics, e.g. oxethazaine

3. *Examples of common combinations*
Aluminium + magnesium salts
Aluminium + magnesium salts + dimethicone
Sodium bicarbonate + alginic acid
Sodium + aluminium + magnesium salts + alginic acid

The normal pH of gastric contents is 1–2, although this may increase with food to as much as pH 5. The administration of 5–10 ml of a liquid antacid formulation may raise the pH to 3–4 on average, but the alkalinizing effect of proprietary formulations of antacids varies widely. The relative neutralizing capacities of some antacid preparations are listed in Table 23.2.

Table 23.2 *Relative neutralizing capacities and sodium content of some antacid preparations*

Antacid preparation	Relative neutralizing capacity (aluminium hydroxide = 1)	Sodium content
Aluminium hydroxide gel BPC	1.00	
Magnesium hydroxide BP	1.00	
Magnesium trisilicate BPC	0.62	High
Magnesium carbonate BPC	0.57	High
Magnesium trisilicate BPC (tablets)	0.25	

Other effects of antacids include the inhibition of acid and gastric secretion, decreased pepsin activity secondary to the increase in gastric pH, and increased oesophageal sphincter pressure. Some antacids also adsorb bile acids.

The duration of action of antacids depends on the rate of gastric emptying. If taken on an empty stomach the buffering effect lasts for about 30 min, if after a meal up to 2 h or more.

Calcium-containing antacids may cause rebound hyperacidity and are better avoided.

Alginates are often added to antacid formulations as foaming agents. They act by forming a layer of foam on top of gastric contents and are thereby supposed to reduce oesophageal reflex. In contrast the anti-foaming agent dimethicone decreases the surface tension of gastric fluid thereby reducing bubble formation—it too is supposed to reduce oesophageal reflux.

Oxethazaine is sometimes also added, particularly for the treatment of symptoms associated with oesophageal reflux, and is supposed to act as a surface anaesthetic.

23.1.2. Uses of antacids

Antacids are widely used in the population for the following purposes:

(a) Symptomatic relief of dyspeptic symptoms

Antacids are commonly used for symptomatic relief of dyspeptic symptoms, whether or not a cause, such as oesophageal reflux, has been found. Usual dosages are 5–10 ml of a liquid formulation or one to two tablets whenever required, but higher dosages can be used if necessary to relieve symptoms.

(b) Peptic ulceration

In small doses antacids relieve pain but do not heal the ulcer. *Large* doses of antacids, on the other hand, (e.g. 30 ml seven times a day) have been shown to be effective in *healing* duodenal ulcers. However, the large volumes of antacids required for such therapy, the need for obsessive compliance, and the high incidence of adverse effects make this approach to the treatment of duodenal ulcer unacceptable as compared with the use of the histamine (H_2) antagonists.

(c) During labour

Antacids are given regularly to women in labour, who may have to have an emergency operation. The rationale is that if buffered gastric acid is inhaled during the operation it is less likely to damage the lungs than unbuffered acid. The use of the histamine (H_2) antagonists is an alternative to antacids in these circumstances.

23.1.3. Choice of antacid

The following considerations may influence the choice of an antacid:

1. Liquid antacids act faster than tablets, but have a shorter duration of action.

2. Aluminium salts may cause constipation and magnesium salts diarrhoea. The choice may therefore be dictated by the patient's bowel habit.

3. In patients with congestive cardiac failure or hypertension in whom a high sodium intake is undesirable, one would choose an antacid with a low sodium content. Some examples of antacids of high sodium content are given in Table 23.2.

23.1.4. Adverse effects of antacids

Antacids are generally safe, but certain adverse effects peculiar to individual antacids should be noted.

(a) Sodium bicarbonate

Sodium bicarbonate is water soluble and is readily absorbed from the gastro-intestinal tract. It therefore acts as a *systemic* alkali as well as having a local effect in the stomach. In patients who take large volumes of sodium bicarbonate systemic alkalosis may occur and result in hypercalcaemia with nephrocalcinosis and renal failure. This has been termed the 'milk–alkali' syndrome.

(b) Magnesium and aluminium salts

These antacids are water-insoluble and are less well absorbed than sodium bicarbonate. Their most common adverse effects are therefore on the bowel. Aluminium salts tend to cause constipation, while magnesium salts are laxative. Magnesium and aluminium salts are therefore often combined in antacid preparations.

These salts (particularly aluminium hydroxide) also decrease phosphate absorption. Normally little aluminium is absorbed and it is in any case cleared rapidly by the kidneys. However, in patients with renal failure, being treated with high doses of aluminium hydroxide for hyperphosphat-aemia, and being subjected to aluminium in dialysis fluids, accumulation of aluminium may lead to aluminium toxicity, and cause the encephalopathy known as 'dialysis dementia'.

23.1.5. Interactions with antacids

Antacids may bind other drugs and prevent their absorption. Drugs which may be affected include tetracyclines (but not doxycycline), digoxin, iron, and prednisone.

L-dopa absorption has been shown to be increased by antacids, with enhancement of its effects in Parkinsonism.

If urinary pH is increased by large dosages of sodium bicarbonate the passive reabsorption of some drugs may be altered. This may lead to an increased excretion of salicylates and a decreased excretion of quinidine and quinine.

It is not clear how important the interactions involving altered absorption of other drugs may be, but it is wise to advise patients to take drugs at a different time of day from antacids (at least 30 min apart).

23.2. ANTI-EMETICS

The primary aim in the treatment of vomiting is to remove the underlying cause, but anti-emetics may be given for symptomatic relief.

23.2.1. Mechanisms of action of drugs used to treat vomiting

The drugs used in the treatment of vomiting are listed in Table 23.3, and some current views on their mechanisms of action are illustrated in Fig. 23.1. Stimuli from peripheral tissues, such as the stomach and lungs, pass via afferent nerves to the group of nuclei known collectively as the vomiting centre in the medulla oblongata in the brain stem. The vomiting centre also receives impulses from the labyrinth via the vestibular nucleus and reticular formation, from higher centres following stimuli such as sight and emotion, and from the chemoreceptor trigger zone in the area postrema in the floor of the fourth ventricle, which itself receives input from various stimuli, such as drugs with emetic effects. It is known that nerve impulses in these areas are subserved by different neurotransmitters: acetylcholine (muscarinic) and histamine (H_1) in the vestibular system and vomiting centre; dopamine (D_2) in the chemoreceptor trigger zone. It may be that anti-emetic drugs which act at these sites do so by their effects on neurotransmission there, but the mechanisms whereby these drugs act as anti-emetics are not fully understood.

Table 23.3   *Drugs of choice in the treatment of nausea and vomiting*

Antihistamines (p.637)
Hyoscine hydrobromide (p.616)
Metoclopramide (p.705)
Phenothiazines (p.727)

Disorder	Drugs
Motion sickness	Hyoscine hydrobromide
	Antihistamines (e.g. promethazine)
Opiate-induced	Phenothiazines (e.g. prochlorperazine)
Post-operative	Metoclopramide or phenothiazines
Migraine	Metoclopramide
Pregnancy (if necessary)	Antihistamines (e.g. promethazine)
Vertigo	Antihistamines (see Chapter 28)
Cytotoxic drug therapy and	Phenothiazines + antihistamines
radiotherapy (treatment of cancer)	(e.g. prochlorperazine + diphenhydramine)
	Nabilone (a synthetic cannabinoid)

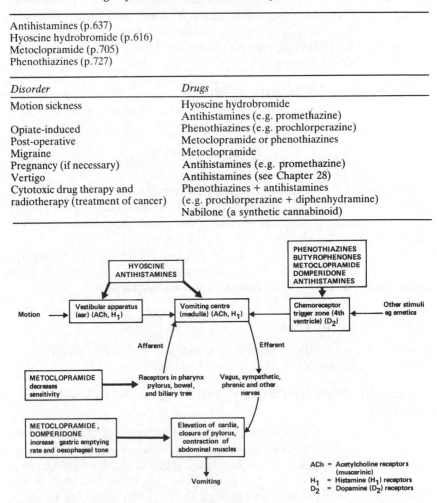

Fig. 23.1. The pathophysiology of vomiting and the sites and mechanisms of action of anti-emetic drugs.

Hyoscine seems to act principally on the vomiting centre in the medulla, where it has an anticholinergic (antimuscarinic) action. It also has an effect on the vestibular apparatus, which would explain its efficacy in motion sickness.

The phenothiazines, butyrophenones, domperidone, and metoclopramide are all dopamine antagonists acting on the chemoreceptor trigger zone.

Antihistamines act on the vestibular apparatus, vomiting centre, and chemoreceptor trigger zone. Their effects in these areas vary, however, since the potency of these drugs as anticholinergic, antihistaminic, and antidopaminergic agents varies.

Some anti-emetics also have peripheral effects. For example, hyoscine decreases gastro-intestinal motility and metoclopramide decreases the sensitivity of the afferent impulses to the brain, and alters gastric function by increasing oesophageal tone, stimulating pyloric contraction, and increasing the rate of gastric emptying, effects which it shares with domperidone.

23.2.2. Uses of anti-emetics in different circumstances

The drugs of choice in the treatment of vomiting due to different disorders are summarized in Table 23.3. For dosages, adverse effects, and interactions of these drugs see the Pharmacopoeia.

(a) Motion sickness

Hyoscine is the most effective drug available. It is usually given orally, but recently a transdermal formulation has become available—a patch impregnated with the drug is stuck on to the skin, and there is slow continuous absorption into the bloodstream providing a prolonged effect. It should not be used in patients with glaucoma or prostatic enlargement. The alternatives are the antihistamines, but they may cause more drowsiness than hyoscine. Travellers should be cautious about driving when taking hyoscine or an antihistamine for travel sickness.

(b) Drug-induced nausea and vomiting

Withdrawal of the drug is best but if it has to be continued then treatment depends on the mechanism of the drug-induced emesis. Local gastric irritation may be minimized by spreading the doses out during the day (e.g. L-dopa, spironolactone) and by taking the drug with food. Central effects, such as opiate-induced vomiting after myocardial infarction, may be treated with a phenothiazine such as prochlorperazine.

(c) Post-operative vomiting

Post-operative vomiting may be due to several causes including surgically remediable abnormalities (e.g. intestinal obstruction), intestinal stasis (e.g. gastric stasis, ileus), and drugs (e.g. opiate analgesics).

Metoclopramide or a phenothiazine are the treatments of choice. Metoclopramide should not be used, however, after intestinal surgery or if there is intestinal obstruction. If there is intestinal stasis gastric suction may be required.

(d) Migraine

The nausea and vomiting of migraine is accompanied by gastric stasis, and there may therefore be delayed absorption of analgesics such as paracetamol. To speed gastric emptying and increase the rate of analgesic absorption metoclopramide is given orally.

(e) Pregnancy

Because of the fear of teratogenicity, drug therapy of vomiting in pregnancy should be undertaken only when it is very troublesome. Then the general opinion is that promethazine or thiethylperazine are not harmful to the fetus, and can be effective.

(f) Vomiting during cytotoxic drug therapy and radiotherapy

Frequently nausea and vomiting occur during treatment of cancer with cytotoxic drugs or irradiation (see Chapter 33). No treatment is entirely satisfactory, but phenothiazines and butyrophenones are used regularly with some effect. Some use combinations of drugs with different pharmacological effects (e.g. prochlorperazine plus diphenhydramine). Cannabinoids have recently been shown to have some efficacy, and a synthetic cannabinoid, nabilone, has been introduced for this indication.

(g) Symptomatic relief

If the underlying cause is either self-limiting or cannot be removed in circumstances other than those discussed above, then metoclopramide is usually the drug of choice, in the absence of gastro-intestinal obstruction. If, however, a sedative effect is also required then a phenothiazine or an antihistamine might be preferred.

23.3. PEPTIC ULCERATION

23.3.1. Mechanisms of action of drugs used in treating peptic ulceration

The two main identifiable factors involved in the pathogenesis of peptic (gastric and duodenal) ulceration are:

(i) acid and pepsin secretion;
(ii) mucosal resistance to acid and pepsin.

However, the precise pathophysiological mechanisms are not yet known. Certain drugs which cause peptic ulceration (e.g. aspirin, other non-steroidal anti-inflammatory drugs, and corticosteroids) are thought to do so by impairing mucosal resistance.

The drugs commonly used in treating peptic ulceration are listed in Table 23.4.

Table 23.4 *Drugs used in the treatment of peptic ulceration*

Antacids (p.364)
Histamine (H$_2$) antagonists (p.685)
   Cimetidine
   Ranitidine
Carbenoxolone (p.651)
Tripotassium dicitratobismuthate

(a) Antacids

Antacids give symptomatic relief as described in the section on antacids above.

(b) Histamine (H$_2$) antagonists

The H$_2$ antagonists cimetidine and ranitidine decrease gastric acid secretion occurring in response to histamine, gastrin, and food.

(c) Carbenoxolone

The mechanism whereby carbenoxolone acts is not fully understood, but it enhances mucus secretion, prolongs the life of gastric mucosal cells, and increases mucosal defences to acid and pepsin.

(d) Colloidal bismuth

Colloidal bismuth (tripotassium dicitratobismuthate) must also have a local action, since it is not absorbed and is effective after oral administration, but its mode of action is not known.

23.3.2. Treatment of peptic ulceration

(a) Antacids

The use of antacids in providing symptomatic relief is discussed above under antacids.

(b) Histamine (H$_2$) antagonists

The H$_2$ antagonists cimetidine and ranitidine are effective in increasing the rate of healing of gastric and duodenal ulcers, of stomal ulcers, of ulceration due to oesophageal reflux, and of the multiple ulcers due to the hypergastrinaemia of the Zollinger–Ellison syndrome. They are the initial treatment of choice in all these conditions. Cimetidine and ranitidine appear to be equally effective, and while experience is greater at present with cimetidine it is possible that ranitidine may have fewer adverse effects. The effects of the two are contrasted in Table 23.5. Either of these drugs may be given for 4–8 weeks in initial therapy. Antacids should be continued until symptoms are relieved, which may take a week or more. Healing takes at least 4 weeks. Thereafter maintenance therapy should be given for 6–12 months.

Table 23.5 *Contrast between cimetidine and ranitidine*

	Cimetidine	Ranitidine
Initial dosage	400 mg b.d. or 200 mg t.d.s. + 400 mg o.n. (maximum 400 mg q.d.s.)	150 mg b.d. (maximum 300 mg t.d.s.)
Maintenance dosage	400 mg at night	150 mg at night
Healing rate in duodenal ulcer	45–84% (4 weeks) 92–95% (8 weeks)	63–78% (4 weeks) 85–92% (8 weeks)
Hyperprolactinaemia	+	–
Antiandrogenic effect	+	–
Inhibition of hepatic drug metabolism	+	–
Increased systemic availability of high extraction ratio drugs (Table 3.6)	+	–

There have been fears about the possible carcinogenicity of the H_2 antagonists since they decrease gastric acidity and may therefore increase the risk of formation of carcinogenic nitrosamines from dietary nitrites. In addition the drugs are themselves nitrosylated. Although the possibility that these drugs may cause gastric cancer remains an unproven hypothesis, most doctors prefer to restrict maintenance therapy to a total of 6–12 months, and to treat exacerbations when they occur. However, in the Zollinger–Ellison syndrome long-term treatment is necessary and justifiable.

The usual dosages of H_2 antagonists are shown in Table 23.5. If there is a poor response to initial dosages then the dosage can be increased. Ulcer-causing drugs may obviate the therapeutic effects of the H_2 antagonists and should be withdrawn.

(c) Carbenoxolone

Carbenoxolone should be used if peptic ulcer fails to respond to H_2 antagonists, or if there are unacceptable adverse effects. It is given in a dosage of 100 mg t.d.s. orally for 2 weeks, followed by 50 mg q.d.s. for 2 months. It is of proven value in gastric ulcer, but is of less use in duodenal ulcer and oesophageal reflux, perhaps because it acts locally. There are, however, special preparations of carbenoxolone which are formulated so as to release the drug near or at the oesophagus (Pyrogastrone®) or duodenum (Duogastrone®) and these may also be effective. However, because of its adverse effects carbenoxolone remains a second-line drug —it causes sodium and water retention and hypokalaemia, which need to be treated with a diuretic (thiazide or loop) plus potassium chloride (see Chapter 24). The potassium-sparing diuretic spironolactone should be avoided since it may inhibit the therapeutic effect of carbenoxolone on the stomach.

(d) Tripotassium dicitratobismuthate (De-Nol®)

There is evidence that this is effective in the treatment of gastric and duodenal ulcer, but it is not widely used.

23.3.3. Bleeding from peptic ulcer

Chronic bleeding from a peptic ulcer may result in iron-deficiency anaemia requiring iron replacement therapy (see Chapter 26).

Acute and obvious bleeding, e.g. haematemesis or melaena, is a medical emergency requiring blood transfusion to replace losses. There is so far no evidence that H_2 antagonists are of any value in arresting acute bleeding from gastric or duodenal ulcer.

23.4. LAXATIVES

Table 23.6 *Commonly used laxatives*

---

1. *Bulk-forming agents*
Bran
Ispaghula husk
Methylcellulose
Psyllium preparations
Sterculia

2. *Faecal softeners and lubricants*
Arachis oil
Dioctyl sodium sulphosuccinate
Glycerol

3. *Gastro-intestinal stimulants*
Frangula ⎫
Senna   ⎬ Anthraquinones
Danthron ⎭
Bisacodyl
Castor oil

4. *Osmotic laxatives*
Lactulose
Magnesium salts ⎫
Sodium salts   ⎬ 'Saline purgatives'

The commonly used laxatives are listed in Table 23.6, in which they have been subdivided into broad categories according to their mechanisms of action. There are numerous formulations of laxatives available and dosages are to be found in standard references such as the *British National Formulary*. The important principle in using laxatives is to vary the dosage until, by trial and error, the most suitable dosage for the patient is found, i.e. the dosage which regularly produces a comfortable formed stool.

Furthermore, in all patients with simple constipation it is important to give advice about diet and regularity of bowel habit, so that eventually a regular pattern can be established without the use of purgatives. Patients should be encouraged to take foods with a high content of 'fibre', e.g. fruit and vegetables, whole wheat and bran cereals, and wholemeal bread.

23.4.1. Bulk-forming agents

These are hydrophilic compounds which act by absorbing water, swelling, and increasing stool bulk. The increased bulk stimulates rectal reflexes and promotes defaecation.

The bulk laxatives are given orally and take a few days to have their full effect. They are used to establish a normal bowel habit in patients with chronic constipation, and are particularly useful in patients with simple constipation (i.e. constipation without associated colonic pathology) and with constipation associated with diverticular disease, irritable bowel syndrome, and pregnancy.

The bulk laxatives can cause intestinal obstruction in patients with intestinal diseases (e.g. intestinal adhesions, stenosis, or ulceration, scleroderma, or autonomic neuropathy), and they should be avoided in those circumstances.

Flatulence is a common adverse effect. Occasionally sterculia can cause hypersensitivity reactions, including skin rashes, asthma, and rhinitis.

23.4.2. Faecal softeners and lubricants

Vegetable and mineral oils act by lubricating and softening the stool. Arachis (peanut) oil is usually given as an enema. Glycerol lubricates the stool and is given by suppository. It is free of adverse effects, but is not always effective.

Dioctyl sodium sulphosuccinate is an anionic surface-active detergent which increases the volume of the stool by unknown mechanisms. Because it inhibits secretion of bile and may damage gastric mucosa it is better reserved for rectal use only.

The faecal softeners and lubricants are used in cases in which bulk laxatives would be indicated but cannot be used because of intestinal pathology (see above). They are also indicated in patients with anal fissure or haemorrhoids, in whom constipation may be caused by fear of pain during defaecation. They are also of value when a rapid purgative effect is required.

Paraffin oil ('liquid paraffin'), widely used in the past, is no longer recommended because of a wide range of adverse effects. It can cause malabsorption of fat-soluble vitamins (A, D, and K), foreign body reactions in the small bowel ('paraffinomas'), and faecal leakage at the anus, causing pruritus ani.

23.4.3. Gastro-intestinal stimulants

These drugs act on the bowel, stimulating peristalsis and reducing net reabsorption of water and electrolytes by unknown mechanisms. Frangula, senna, and danthron (the anthraquinones), and bisacodyl (a phenyl-methane) act on the colon, and take about 6–8 h to act after oral administration. Bisacodyl can also be given rectally for a faster action. Castor oil has its effects on the small bowel, and acts within 1–3 h.

The gastro-intestinal stimulants are used when rapid evacuation of the bowel is required, e.g. in preparation for radiological examination of the bowel or colonic surgery. They are also used in the initial phases after the treatment of faecal impaction following severe chronic constipation.

The main adverse effects of these drugs occur with repeated abuse, leading to fluid and electrolyte, particularly potassium, loss, and colonic atony leading to constipation and further abuse. In such cases fluid and potassium losses should be replaced and a saline purgative, such as magnesium sulphate, given instead. Later on gradual withdrawal of the saline purgative should be attempted, and it is important to educate the patient in the dangers of continued purgation and in the need for regular bowel habits.

Certain phenylmethane derivatives, used in the past, are no longer recommended because of adverse effects. They include oxyphenisatin, which is hepatotoxic, and phenolphthalein, which frequently causes hypersensitivity reactions.

23.4.4. Osmotic laxatives

Osmotic laxatives act by decreasing water reabsorption in the bowel. The magnesium and sodium salts used as purgatives (e.g. magnesium sulphate or hydroxide) cause large amounts of water to be retained in both small and large bowel and thus cause increased peristalsis throughout the bowel. Because of their severe and rapid effects they are usually reserved for rectal use only.

Lactulose is a disaccharide of galactose and fructose. It is hydrolysed by colonic bacteria to its component sugars which are then fermented to acetic and lactic acids, which act as osmotic laxatives. In contrast to the saline purgatives it takes several days to act and is given orally. It is used in the treatment of hepatic encephalopathy and is not frequently used purely for its laxative properties. It may cause abdominal discomfort and flatulence.

23.4.5. Treatment of faecal impaction

In cases of faecal impaction a suppository of glycerol or bisacodyl should be tried first. If there is no response a colonic stimulant should be tried but if that is ineffective then rectal washout will be necessary. Start with a retention enema of arachis oil or another vegetable oil (100–150 ml) or of dioctyl sodium sulphosuccinate (40 ml plus 80 ml warm water). Run the enema into the rectum with the patient supine and the foot of the bed raised. The enema should be retained for 15–30 min to allow time for it to soften the stool. This should be done twice daily for one to two days, followed by rectal wash-outs with warm saline (500 ml). If treatment is urgent then digital evacuation of the rectum may be required—use a well-lubricated glove and sedate the patient well, e.g. with pethidine 50–100 mg i.m. or diazepam 5–10 mg i.m. Following disimpaction start treatment with a colonic stimulant and re-education of the patient.

23.5. ANTIDIARRHOEAL DRUGS

The commonly used antidiarrhoeal drugs are listed in Table 23.7 and dosages are to be found in standard references, such as the *British National Formulary*.

Table 23.7   *Drugs used in the symptomatic treatment of diarrhoea*

---

1. *Drugs altering gastro-intestinal motility*
Codeine (p.713)
Diphenoxylate (combined with atropine in Lomotil®) (p.713)
Loperamide (p.703)
Morphine (p.713)

2. *Fluid adsorbents*
Kaolin

3. *Fluid absorbents*
Bulk-forming agents (see Table 23.6)

4. *Drugs used in specific circumstances*
Indomethacin (post-irradiation diarrhoea)
Cholestyramine (diarrhoea due to excess bile acids)
Pancreatic enzymes (pancreatic malabsorption)

When treating diarrhoea the underlying cause should be treated if possible, and fluid and electrolyte losses replaced if necessary. The anti-diarrhoeal drugs are used for symptomatic relief and do not constitute specific therapy.

23.5.1. Drugs altering gastro-intestinal motility

This group of drugs includes opiate analgesics, such as codeine phosphate and morphine, and opiate analogues, such as loperamide and diphenoxylate. They decrease bowel motility giving more time for fluid reabsorption to occur. They also cause an increase in the tone of the anal sphincter and a decrease in the central awareness of the sensory reflex arc for defaecation. These effects are caused by stimulation of opioid receptors in the bowel and these drugs are most useful in cases of chronic diarrhoea where there is increased motility of the small or large bowel.

Dosage requirements vary widely from patient to patient. Initial dosages should be at the lower end of the dosage range, increasing gradually until the diarrhoea is controlled. Note, however, that there are maximum dosages for these drugs—codeine phosphate 120 mg/day, loperamide 16 mg/day, and diphenoxylate (in combination with atropine as Lomotil®) 20 mg/day. In addition dosages must be carefully titrated so as to avoid constipation.

The opiates should not be used in patients with acute inflammatory disease of the large bowel (e.g. ulcerative colitis, Crohn's disease, or pseudomembranous colitis) since they may precipitate the serious condition of acute 'toxic' dilatation of the colon.

Morphine and codeine should not be used in patients with chronic liver disease (see p.387). In chronic diarrhoea codeine is to be preferred to morphine since it is less likely to cause dependence. Morphine is used in short-term symptomatic treatment, usually in combination with kaolin.

23.5.2. Fluid adsorbents

About 1–1.5 l of water enter the colon every day, of which most is reabsorbed, about 100–200 ml being excreted in the faeces. Relatively small changes in faecal fluid volume (10–20 ml) can make the difference between a hard stool and a soft stool, or between a soft stool and a watery stool. This accounts for the efficacy of fluid adsorbents, such as kaolin, in treating diarrhoea. Kaolin is used principally in the short-term symptomatic treatment of diarrhoea and is often combined with a small dose of morphine. Its main adverse effect is constipation.

23.5.3. Fluid absorbents

The bulk-forming agents have been discussed above under laxatives. They act in diarrhoea by absorbing water and are therefore of value in the irritable bowel syndrome, in which intermittent diarrhoea may co-exist with constipation, and in which they are often combined with drugs having an antispasmodic effect on the large bowel (e.g. mebeverine and dicyclomine). They are also used to control the consistency of the stool in patients with ileostomy. Their adverse effects and contra-indications have been discussed above.

23.5.4. Drugs used in specific circumstances

In some form of diarrhoea specific agents may be indicated. For example, anti-inflammatory drugs, such as indomethacin, may be of value in post-irradiation enteritis. Cholestyramine binds bile acids in the gut and is therefore useful in treating diarrhoea due to bile acids (e.g. in Crohn's disease and post-vagotomy diarrhoea). Pancreatic enzymes may help in controlling diarrhoea due to pancreatic malabsorption.

23.6. GASTRO-INTESTINAL INFECTIONS

The principles of diagnosing and treating infections in general are discussed in Chapter 20. The treatment of helminthic infestations, amoebiasis, and giardiasis are also dealt with in Chapter 20 and we shall deal here with other infections.

In all cases of infective diarrhoea, especially during the acute phase, it is important to avoid dehydration. This may be achieved simply by increasing oral fluid intake, but in severe cases i.v. fluids may be required.

Rehydration in severe infective diarrhoea (e.g. cholera) is best achieved using the oral rehydration solution recommended by the WHO. It can be made up by adding to 1 l of water the following constituents: sodium chloride (3.5 g), sodium bicarbonate (2.5 g), potassium chloride (1.5 g), and glucose (20 g) or sucrose (40 g). Absorption of the fluid and electrolytes in this solution is enhanced by the glucose, even in severe diarrhoea. If the solution cannot be taken orally it should be given by nasogastric tube. If dehydration is severe it can be given both orally and by i.v. infusion. Whether the oral or i.v. route is chosen care must always be taken not to cause fluid overload.

Oral salt and sugar solutions in water (salt, 1 level teaspoon per litre, and sugar, 8 level teaspoons per litre), plus some source of potassium (e.g. orange juice) can be used as alternatives in an emergency.

23.6.1. Specific infections

(a) Travellers' diarrhoea

There is no specific therapy for travellers' diarrhoea, and symptomatic relief of diarrhoea is all that is required.

(b) Shigellosis

Acute *Shigella* infections are usually self-limiting and require no therapy besides oral fluids. Antibiotics should not be used because of the danger of producing resistant organisms. However, in severe cases or in cases which are prolonged antibiotics may be necessary, and the choice depends on local sensitivities. If the organism is sensitive to sulphonamides then a sulphonamide such as sulphadiazine or co-trimoxazole may be used; if not the best choice is ampicillin. Five days' treatment is usually sufficient.

(c) *Salmonella* infections

(i) Typhoid fever

In typhoid antibiotic therapy is indicated, the first choice being chloramphenicol. It is given in a dosage of 50 mg/kg/day in divided doses for 2 weeks. Children need larger dosages than adults (100 mg/kg/day), but these high dosages should not be used in neonates (see pp.658–9). The oral route is usually adequate, but i.v. therapy can be given to patients who cannot take oral therapy. Do not give chloramphenicol i.m. unless both oral and i.v. routes are unsuitable—absorption does occur after i.m. injection but it is variable and erratic.

When the organism is resistant to chloramphenicol, amoxycillin (1 g six-hourly orally) or co-trimoxazole (two tablets twelve-hourly orally) may be given instead, each for 2 weeks.

If there are complications, such as meningitis, osteomyelitis, or abscesses, treatment may have to be continued for longer than 2 weeks in high dosages.

A small percentage of patients will relapse about 2 weeks after adequate antibiotic therapy and will require another course of antibiotics. The choice is the same as before but the decision will depend on the sensitivity of the organism, which may have altered.

A small percentage of patients who recover go on to become chronic carriers, continuing to excrete the organism in the stool or urine, and often harbouring a growth in the gallbladder. Chronic carriers are asymptomatic but spread the infection. Eradication of organisms can be very difficult but may sometimes be achieved by a course of amoxycillin (1 g q.d.s. for 3 months with probenecid). If there is also chronic biliary disease cholecystectomy may be required, followed by oral amoxycillin for a month. Chloramphenicol is of no value in these cases since it does not penetrate the gallbladder.

(ii) Salmonella gastroenteritis

Treatment is by maintenance of fluid balance, and symptomatic relief of vomiting and diarrhoea (e.g. with a phenothiazine and an opiate respectively). Antibiotics should not be used except if there is a bacteraemia or in patients with immune suppression. In such cases intravenous chloramphenicol should be used as for typhoid. The alternative is i.v. ampicillin. If the organism is resistant to both ampicillin and chloramphenicol then oral co-trimoxazole may be used instead.

(d) Cholera

There is no specific antibiotic therapy for cholera, since it is due to an exotoxin produced by the *Vibrio*, and the most important aspect of therapy is to maintain fluid balance by replacing orally or intravenously the large volumes of fluid lost via the bowel. However, there is some evidence that antibiotics may shorten the duration of the disease, and all patients should be given tetracycline (500 mg q.d.s. orally) or co-trimoxazole (two tablets b.d. orally). Cholera vaccine should be used during an epidemic to try to contain the spread of the disease, although the results are relatively poor.

(e) *Clostridium difficile*

The syndrome known as antibiotic-induced pseudomembranous colitis is now known to be due to superinfection of the large bowel by *Clostridium difficile* in patients who have received broad-spectrum antibiotics. It occurs most commonly in patients who have taken clindamycin or lincomycin, but has also been reported following ampicillin, amoxycillin, tetracycline, co-trimoxazole, some cephalosporins, and metronidazole in combination with aminoglycoside antibiotics.

In mild cases withdrawal of the antibiotic and fluid replacement may be sufficient, but in more severe cases vancomycin should be given (500 mg six-hourly orally for 1–2 weeks). Antidiarrhoeal opiates should not be used because of the risk of acute colonic dilatation.

(f) *Campylobacter* enteritis

This is probably the most common cause of infective diarrhoea in the UK, accounting for 10–15 per cent of cases. It is usually self-limiting, lasting only a few days, but severe cases may need treatment with erythromycin or a tetracycline.

(g) *Yersinia* enteritis

This is usually self-limiting and needs no treatment. In severe cases a tetracycline should be used.

(h) Tuberculosis

Treatment of gastro-intestinal tuberculosis is carried out on the same principles as for pulmonary tuberculosis (see Chapter 22). Treatment should be given for a year. If there is obstruction or fistula formation surgery will be necessary.

(i) Viral infections

No specific therapy is indicated. Supportive therapy with fluid replacement and symptomatic relief of diarrhoea if prolonged are sufficient.

23.7. ULCERATIVE COLITIS

The drugs used in the treatment of ulcerative colitis are listed in Table 23.8.

Table 23.8   *Drugs used in the treatment of ulcerative colitis*

1. *Acute attack*
Corticosteroids (e.g. prednisolone, p.664)
Antibiotics (e.g. metronidazole, p.707)

2. *Prevention of recurrence*
Sulphasalazine (p.754)

3. *Chronic active ulcerative colitis*
Sulphasalazine
Corticosteroids

23.7.1. Acute severe ulcerative colitis

This is characterized by severe diarrhoea, blood in the stool, fever, tachycardia, anaemia, and a raised erythrocyte sedimentation rate (e.s.r.).

Patients with acute severe ulcerative colitis should be treated in hospital. The following are the important points of management.

(a) Fluid and electrolytes

At first no food or oral fluids should be given. Intravenous infusion of fluid and electrolytes (e.g. potassium) should be used to replace losses. Plasma or albumin infusions may be required to treat hypoalbuminaemia, and blood transfusion to treat anaemia.

(b) Corticosteroids

Corticosteroids have been found empirically to be of value in the treatment of an acute attack of ulcerative colitis and may act by suppressing the inflammatory and immunological responses which occur in ulcerative colitis (see Chapter 34). They should be given both i.v. and rectally —prednisolone phosphate 60–80 mg/day i.v. and hydrocortisone enemas (100 ml) 100 mg b.d.

(c) Diarrhoea

Bed rest plus the regimen of i.v. fluids and i.v. and rectal corticosteroids will reduce the frequency of attacks of diarrhoea. A small dose of an anticholinergic drug, such as propantheline 15 mg, may help severe diarrhoea, but should be used with great care in case of precipitating acute colonic dilatation. Opiates should not be used for the same reason.

(d) Antibiotics

Antibiotics are used empirically in the treatment of acute severe ulcerative colitis on the supposition that the normal bowel flora may be more pathogenic when the bowel is inflamed. Sometimes secondary systemic infection may occur with anaerobic bacteria and require specific treatment. Currently metronidazole (500 mg i.v. eight-hourly) is preferred to other antibiotics.

The above treatment will lead to improvement in about 75 per cent of patients. In those who get worse or who do not improve within 5 days, colectomy will be necessary. In those who respond oral fluids and a light diet can be introduced after 5 days and oral steroids (prednisolone 40 mg daily) can be given instead of i.v. steroids. Steroid enemas (prednisolone 20 mg in 100 ml) should be continued and sulphasalazine should be started (0.5 g q.d.s. orally). The dosage of prednisolone should be tailed off and withdrawn within a few weeks. If full remission occurs then it will also be possible to withhold the steroid enemas. Sulphasalazine should be continued indefinitely, however, since it decreases the risk of relapse. In a few patients, however, steroid enemas or even oral steroids may need to be continued (see chronic ulcerative colitis below).

23.7.2. Mild to moderate acute attacks of ulcerative colitis

For the mild or moderate attack steroid enemas (e.g. prednisolone 20 mg in 100 ml) should be given at night and sulphasalazine started (0.5 g q.d.s. orally, increasing if necessary to 1 g q.d.s.). A short course of oral prednisolone should be used starting with 40 mg daily and tailing off over the next few weeks.

23.7.3. Chronic ulcerative colitis

Chronic ulcerative colitis in remission usually requires only treatment with regular oral sulphasalazine (0.5–1 g q.d.s.). A few patients however, have chronic active ulcerative colitis and require continued treatment with daily prednisolone enemas and in some cases oral prednisolone.

23.8. CROHN'S DISEASE

Unlike ulcerative colitis the drug therapy of Crohn's disease is very unsatisfactory. Corticosteroids may be useful in an acute attack but do not prevent relapse. Sulphasalazine is used by some to treat active colonic disease, but its efficacy is not proven. Azathioprine is generally reserved for those who have a poor response to steroids or in whom steroids have caused serious adverse effects. In a dose of 2.5 mg/kg/day it may reduce steroid requirements.

Specific deficiencies due to malabsorption should be treated as indicated (e.g. with folic acid, iron, vitamin B_{12}, and vitamin D). Diarrhoea may respond to cholestyramine.

23.9. DRUGS AND THE LIVER

23.9.1. Effects of drugs on bilirubin metabolism and liver function

Drugs can alter bilirubin metabolism leading to hyperbilirubinaemia. They can also cause liver damage by direct hepatotoxicity or by biliary obstruction (cholestasis).

(a) Drugs which alter bilirubin metabolism

(i) Haemolysis

Drugs can cause hyperbilirubinaemia through haemolysis (see Chapter 26). Because bilirubin conjugation is saturable this leads to an increase in circulating unconjugated bilirubin. There is thus jaundice without impairment of liver function. Drugs which cause haemolysis are listed in Table 26.9.

(ii) Displacement of bilirubin from plasma albumin

Drugs such as salicylates and sulphonamides can displace bilirubin from plasma albumin, causing an increase in circulating unbound bilirubin. This is of importance in the fetus and neonate, since the unbound bilirubin enters the brain and can cause kernicterus (see Chapter 9, p.150).

(b) Drugs causing hepatocellular damage

A variety of different drugs can cause hepatocellular damage resulting in different clinical syndromes. These syndromes include acute hepatocellular damage (acute hepatitis), chronic active hepatitis, hepatic cirrhosis, and hepatic tumours, and the commonly implicated drugs are listed in Table 23.9.

The following examples illustrate some specific drug-related hepatic problems.

(i) Paracetamol

The liver damage associated with paracetamol overdose is due to the formation of a hepatotoxic metabolite. Therapeutic doses of paracetamol are metabolized mostly (95 per cent) to sulphate and glucuronide conjugates. The rest is metabolized to a reactive intermediate which is detoxified by conjugation with glutathione. In overdose the sulphate and glucuronide conjugation pathways are saturated and more drug is converted to the reactive metabolite. The glutathione available for its detoxification is rapidly depleted, and the metabolite accumulates and binds covalently to liver cell proteins, causing irreversible damage. Liver damage can be prevented by providing glutathione-like substances, such as acetylcysteine, so that the reactive metabolite can be removed by conjugation, and the liver cell protected (see Chapter 32).

Table 23.9   *Drugs causing liver damage*

---

1. *Acute hepatocellular damage*

Dose-related
Alcohol
Azathioprine
Chlorambucil
Hydrocarbons (e.g. glue sniffing)
Iron salts (overdose)
Mercaptopurine
Methotrexate
Paracetamol (overdose)
Salicylates
Tetracycline (large i.v. doses)

Non-dose-related
Antituberculous drugs
  Ethionamide
  Isoniazid
  PAS
  Pyrazinamide
  Rifampicin
Halothane
Methoxyflurane
Methyldopa
Monoamine oxidase inhibitors
Phenylbutazone
Quinidine
Tricyclic antidepressants
  Amitriptyline
  Imipramine
  Iprindole
Valproate

2. *Chronic active hepatitis (non-dose-related)*
Dantrolene
Isoniazid
Methyldopa
Nitrofurantoin
Oxyphenisatin

3. *Cirrhosis*
Alcohol
Methotrexate

4. *Hepatic tumours (benign and malignant)*
Anabolic steroids
Oestrogens (combined oral contraceptives)

5. *Intrahepatic cholestasis*
Dose-related
Anabolic steroids
  Methyltestosterone
  Norethandrolone
Azathioprine
Mercaptopurine
Oestrogens

Non-dose-related
Antithyroid drugs
  Carbimazole
  Methimazole
  Methylthiouracil
Erythromycin salts
Gold salts
Phenothiazines (e.g. chlorpromazine)
Sulphonylureas
  Chlorpropamide
  Tolbutamide

6. *Gallstones*
Clofibrate
Oestrogens

(ii) Halothane

Halothane-induced liver damage can follow a single exposure, but is very rare, occurring in about 1 in 30 000 patients. However, a repeated exposure within about 3 months of the first causes acute liver damage in about 20 per cent of patients. The liver damage is rarely fatal and full recovery usually occurs without residual impairment of hepatic function. The first sign is fever, followed a week or two later by jaundice and biochemical evidence of hepatocellular damage. There may be other evidence of hypersensitivity (e.g. eosinophilia, rash, arthralgia, myalgia).

Halothane is metabolized mostly to a non-toxic metabolite, trifluoro-acetic acid, by oxidation. However, it is also reduced to other metabolites, and it has been proposed that an intermediate metabolite can bind covalently to liver tissue leading to damage. In patients with severe reactions there may be an additional immunological mechanism involving the production of antibodies to hepatocytes and increased hepatocyto-toxicity of circulating lymphocytes.

(iii) Isoniazid

Long-term treatment with isoniazid causes liver damage in about 15 per cent of patients, and in about 0.5 per cent liver damage is severe. Liver damage is caused by a metabolite. Isoniazid is predominantly acetylated to acetylisoniazid, which is in turn converted to acetylhydrazine. Acetyl-hydrazine is thought to be converted to a reactive metabolite which binds covalently to liver cell proteins, causing damage. Although it was originally thought that fast acetylators (see Chapter 8) were more likely to develop liver damage due to isoniazid this finding has not been confirmed. Since acetylhydrazine is itself detoxified by the same *N*-acetyltransferase, acety-lator status may not play a part in the pathogenesis of isoniazid hepato-toxicity.

(c) Drugs causing intrahepatic cholestasis

The drugs which can cause intrahepatic cholestasis are listed in Table 23.9. The drug most commonly associated with intrahepatic cholestasis is chlorpromazine. Chlorpromazine-induced cholestasis is part of a hypersen-sitivity reaction occurring in about 0.5 per cent of patients. It starts within 1–4 weeks of beginning treatment and is accompanied by fever, chills, nausea and vomiting, and itching. There may be eosinophilia. It is usually reversible on withdrawal but full recovery may take several weeks or months to occur. In common with other hypersensitivity reactions involv-ing the liver it has been suggested that it is due to conjugation of the drug or a metabolite with liver cell proteins, and that the hapten–protein complex is antigenic, provoking attack by lymphocytes and the production of antibody.

(d) Drugs associated with an increased risk of gallstones

The incidence of gallstones is increased in patients taking combined oral contraceptives or clofibrate; this may lead to obstructive jaundice.

23.9.2. The effects of impairment of liver function on drug elimination and action

In Table 23.10 is given a list of drugs which should be avoided or used with care in patients with liver disease. Drug use may be affected in such patients for several different reasons.

(a) Pharmacokinetics altered

(i) Hepatic clearance reduced
If a drug is metabolized in the liver then liver failure may result in decreased metabolism and accumulation with toxicity. The functional capacity of the liver is large, and generally chronic impairment of hepato-cellular function has to be considerable before important changes in hepatic drug clearance occur. However, hepatic drug clearance may be reduced in acute hepatitis, in hepatic congestion due to cardiac failure, and if there is intrahepatic arteriovenous shunting.

In contrast to renal failure (see Chapters 3 and 24) there is no easy way of calculating changes in dosages required in patients with hepatic failure, partly because there is no single clear-cut test of hepatic metabolizing capacity, even by a single metabolic route, comparable to the creatinine clearance in renal failure, and partly because the rate of *metabolism* of a drug by the liver is only one index of hepatic *clearance*, which also involves transport into the bile and excretion of bile.

Dosages of drugs which are metabolized by the liver therefore have to be altered, where possible, according to the patient's therapeutic response, and with careful clinical monitoring for signs of toxicity, particularly if the clinical response is hard to measure.

For drugs which have a high hepatic extraction ratio and a large first-pass metabolism by the liver (see Chapter 3 and Table 3.6), hepatic impairment may increase the systemic availability thus reducing oral dosage requirements. In such cases i.v. dosage requirements may be unaltered. For example, oral dosages of chlormethiazole may need to be reduced in liver disease because of increased systemic availability, but i.v. dosages are not altered.

(ii) Biliary clearance reduced
Biliary excretion is quantitatively important for very few drugs, notably fusidic acid and rifampicin. Biliary obstruction, therefore, reduces dosage requirements of these drugs.

Table 23.10 *Drugs to be avoided or used with care in patients with liver disease*

(a) Pharmacokinetics altered

1. *Hepatic clearance reduced*
   Chloramphenicol
   Clindamycin
   Isoniazid
   Drugs with a high hepatic extraction ratio (see Table 3.6)

2. *Biliary clearance reduced*
   Fusidic acid
   Rifampicin

3. *Decreased binding to plasma albumin*
   Phenytoin

(b) Pharmacodynamics altered

4. *Drugs which inhibit clotting factor synthesis*
   Oral anticoagulants

5. *Drugs whose adverse effects are enhanced*
   Biguanides (lactic acidosis)
   Chloramphenicol (bone marrow suppression)
   Cimetidine (confusional states)
   Methyldopa (idiosyncratic reactions)
   Niridazole (CNS toxicity)
   Non-steroidal anti-inflammatory drugs (gastro-intestinal bleeding)
   Sulphonylureas (hypoglycaemia)

(c) Drugs contributing to the pathophysiology of liver disease

6. *Hepatotoxic drugs*
   See Table 23.9

7. *Drugs containing a lot of sodium*
   Some antacids (see Table 23.2)
   Sodium salts of penicillins

8. *Drugs causing sodium and water retention*
   Carbenoxolone
   Corticosteroids
   Phenylbutazone

9. *Drugs causing potassium loss*
   Carbenoxolone
   Corticosteroids
   Thiazide and loop diuretics (may also precipitate encephalopathy)

10. *Drugs which may precipitate hepatic encephalopathy*
    Opiate analgesics
    Sedatives and hypnotics
    Potassium-wasting diuretics

(iii) Decreased binding to plasma albumin

If there is hypoalbuminaemia below 25 g/l binding of drugs to plasma albumin will be reduced. The most important example of a drug which may be affected by chronic changes in plasma protein binding is phenytoin. For a discussion of the relevance of this effect see Chapter 10.

(b) Pharmacodynamics altered

The effects of the oral anticoagulants are increased in liver disease because of impaired clotting factor synthesis.

In addition there is a miscellaneous list of drugs which have adverse effects which are increased in liver disease (see Table 23.10).

(c) Drugs contributing to the pathophysiology of liver disease

(i) Fluid and electrolyte balance

In patients with portal hypertension, oedema, and ascites, drugs which contain sodium or which cause sodium and water retention (see Table 23.10) may worsen the condition. If there is secondary hyperaldosteronism drugs causing potassium loss are more likely to cause hypokalaemia and that may in turn lead to hepatic encephalopathy.

(ii) Drugs which may precipitate hepatic encephalopathy

Many drugs with central nervous depressant actions may precipitate hepatic encephalopathy (Table 23.10). Chlormethiazole (in reduced oral dosages), or a benzodiazepine which is not metabolized and which has a relatively short half-time (see Table 29.3) are relatively safe if a hypnotic is required.

An excessively brisk diuresis may precipitate hepatic encephalopathy, so care must be taken when prescribing diuretics, particularly the potent loop diuretics, such as frusemide or bumetanide.

23.10. DRUG THERAPY IN THE TREATMENT OF CHRONIC LIVER DISEASE

23.10.1. Oedema and ascites

Sodium and water retention occurs in chronic liver disease for a variety of reasons: hypoalbuminaemia reduces the colloid oncotic pressure of the plasma leading to transudation of fluid; portal hypertension also causes transudation of fluid, because of increased hydrostatic pressure in the splanchnic veins; reduced renal blood flow due to the decreased intravascular volume leads to increased renal sodium retention and this is partly mediated by increased aldosterone production.

Management of hepatic oedema and ascites is with a low-salt diet and diuretics. Usually moderate salt restriction (to 80 mmol/day) is all that can be achieved, by advising the patient not to add salt to his food. Spironolactone alone should be used at first since it is an aldosterone antagonist. It may be combined with a loop diuretic such as frusemide, but care must be taken not to produce too brisk a diuresis because of the risk of precipitating acute electrolyte disturbances and hepatic encephalopathy. Therapy should be carefully monitored by daily weighing and weight loss should be no greater than 0.5 kg/day in ascites alone, or 1 kg/day if there is peripheral oedema as well as ascites.

If hypokalaemia does not respond to spironolactone additional potassium supplements may be required (see Chapter 24).

23.10.2. Hepatic encephalopathy

The pathogenesis of hepatic encephalopathy in chronic liver failure is not fully understood. It is known that there is retention of nitrogenous toxins such as ammonia, and an imbalance of amino acids with an increase in circulating concentrations of aromatic amino acids and a decrease in branched-chain amino acids. How these changes might cause hepatic encephalopathy is not known, but there is evidence that central neurotransmitter function may be altered, with a decrease in brain noradrenaline and dopamine and an increase in brain 5-hydroxytryptamine. These changes might occur secondary to alterations in the transport of amino acids into the brain.

Treatment of acute hepatic encephalopathy is aimed at reducing the absorption of the nitrogenous breakdown products of dietary protein, which are the source of most of the nitrogen-containing toxins in hepatic encephalopathy, and at reducing or eliminating any precipitating factors, e.g. by withholding diuretics, by treating infections, or by treating gastro-intestinal bleeding and consequent hypovolaemia.

Protein intake should be reduced to 20 g per day or less, and calories provided in the form of carbohydrate. The lower bowel should be evacuated using enemas and saline purgatives (e.g. magnesium sulphate). Finally oral neomycin should also be used in acute hepatic encephalopathy in a dosage of 1–2 g orally q.d.s. It acts by eliminating the gastro-intestinal urease-producing bacteria responsible for metabolizing urea to ammonia, and perhaps also by causing malabsorption of dietary protein.

In chronic hepatic encephalopathy the protein intake may be increased to the maximum tolerated (usually about 50 g/day) and instead of neomycin lactulose should be used (see laxatives above). It may act by altering bacterial metabolism in the colon with decreased production of ammonia, or by reducing colonic transit time. It is given in a dosage of 30 ml t.d.s.

orally, increasing if required to a maximum total of 200 ml daily. The dosage should be titrated according to the stools, which should be soft and two or three in number per day.

23.10.3. Acute bleeding from gastro-oesophageal varices

Acute variceal bleeding is a medical emergency.

Blood transfusion should be given using fresh whole blood or packed red cells. Fresh frozen plasma may also be required if there is defective clotting.

Vitamin K 10 mg i.v. should be given to reverse clotting defects.

Oesophageal tamponade should be carried out using a Sengstaken tube.

If the bleeding does not stop after these measures vasopressin should be given. It acts by peripheral arterial vasoconstriction, which causes reduced venous pooling in the splanchnic veins with a consequent reduction in portal venous pressure. It is given i.v. in a dose of 20 i.u. in 100 ml of 5 per cent dextrose infused over 20 min. It causes facial pallor, intestinal colic, and defaecation, and these are signs that it is having a pharmacological effect. It should not be given to patients with a history of myocardial ischaemia since it can cause coronary artery spasm. Treatment with vasopressin can be repeated four-hourly, but its effectiveness diminishes with repeated administration.

Treatment for hepatic encephalopathy (see above) should be started immediately.

Surgical measures to control bleeding include transhepatic sclerosis and oesophageal transaction, but surgery during acute bleeding carries a high mortality and should be avoided if possible.

Long-term management of oesophageal varices involves sclerotherapy, the veins being injected with a sclerosant under direct vision every few months, and the oral administration of a histamine (H_2) antagonist in the hope of preventing acute bleeding, although it has not been demonstrated that this is effective.

23.10.4. Chronic active hepatitis

Corticosteroids are of value in treating this form of chronic hepatitis and may act by immunosuppression (see Chapter 34). They may prevent the progression to cirrhosis in patients with severe disease. Treatment should be limited to patients in whom the disease is progressive or severe. A typical regimen would be prednisolone 40 mg daily orally reducing over a period of a few weeks to a maintenance dose of 10–15 mg daily. In those who need higher dosages, or in whom severe adverse effects occur, the dosage of prednisolone may be reduced by adding azathioprine. The hazards of using corticosteroids and azathioprine in patients with liver disease must be weighed against the potential benefits, and great care must be taken to avoid adverse effects by careful monitoring.

23.10.5. Pruritus

Jaundice due to chronic liver disease is often accompanied by pruritus. Cholestyramine (4–8 mg daily orally) may give symptomatic relief and acts by binding bile acids in the gut and preventing their reabsorption via the ileum. It is of no value, however, if there is *complete* biliary obstruction, since in that case there will be no biliary excretion of bile acids.

23.11. DRUG TREATMENT OF GALLSTONES

About 80 per cent of all gallstones are pure cholesterol stones or stones containing mostly cholesterol. The rest are bile stones or mixed stones containing calcium. Only cholesterol stones are susceptible to drug therapy.

The pathogenesis of cholesterol stones is incompletely understood. It is partly due to supersaturation of cholesterol in the bile with cholesterol precipitation but other factors must operate since gallstones do not always occur in people whose bile is supersaturated with cholesterol. There are several factors which lead to increased cholesterol content in bile, e.g. obesity, during pregnancy, and in patients taking clofibrate or oestrogens. Decreased bile salt absorption in ileal disease (e.g. Crohn's disease) also causes an increase in biliary cholesterol both proportionately and absolutely, since bile salts normally inhibit cholesterol synthesis.

Cholesterol stones may be treated with bile acids. They inhibit cholesterol production and increase the proportion of bile salts in the bile, thereby decreasing the proportion of cholesterol. Stone formation is halted and with long-term treatment dissolution occurs.

Chenodeoxycholic acid (10–15 mg/kg/day) and its epimer ursodeoxycholic acid (8–10 mg/kg/day) are used, and need to be given for at least 3 months to allow even the smallest stones to dissolve. The larger the stone the longer dissolution takes and treatment may have to be continued for up to 2 years. Because the rate of dissolution is proportional to the ratio of surface area : volume of stone, very large stones (> 20 mm diameter) are not treated in this way. For stones less than 10 mm in diameter 6 months of treatment will usually be sufficient.

The recurrence rate after dissolution is high (70 per cent in 5 years) and repeated treatment may be needed. For this and other reasons medical treatment of gallstones is restricted to certain patients:

1. Patients with translucent stones.
2. Those with few or no symptoms. Symptomatic patients are best treated surgically.
3. Those in whom surgery is contra-indicated for any reason.
4. Those who do not have a contra-indication to bile acid treatment.

This excludes from treatment patients with biliary obstruction, a nonfunctioning gall-bladder, ileal disease with poor absorption of bile acids, patients with peptic ulceration, and pregnant women.

The major adverse effect of the cholic acids is diarrhoea, less so with ursodeoxycholic acid than chenodeoxycholic acid. It occurs in about a third of patients and there is some tolerance with long-term treatment. Lipid-lowering drugs (see Chapter 25) and drugs which increase the biliary excretion of cholesterol (e.g. oestrogens) oppose the therapeutic effects of the cholic acids.

24 The drug therapy of renal, urinary tract and sexually transmitted disorders

24.1. DIURETIC THERAPY

24.1.1. Mechanisms of action of diuretics in relation to disease

The main uses of diuretics are in the treatment of oedema due to cardiac failure, renal disease (nephrotic syndrome), and cirrhosis of the liver, and in the treatment of hypertension (particularly the thiazides). The place of the diuretics in the practical management of those conditions is discussed under those disease headings. Here we shall present a broad view of diuretic action and therapy. Details about important members of each class of diuretics can be found in the Pharmacopoeia.

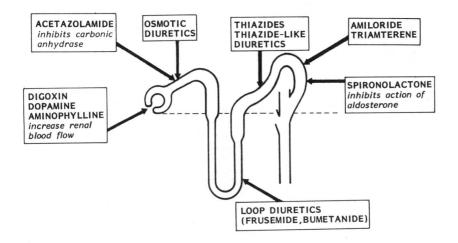

Fig. 24.1. The sites of action of diuretics on the nephron.

There are important differences between the actions of diuretics which can be usefully exploited in their therapeutic use. The various diuretics used are listed in Table 24.1 and in Table 24.2 are shown the main points of action of the various classes of diuretics, and some qualitative differences between their effects. In Fig. 24.1 are shown their sites of action in the nephron.

Table 24.1   *Diuretics*

1. *Thiazides* (Benzothiadiazines; p.761)
Bendrofluazide
Hydrochlorothiazide
Cyclopenthiazide

   Other thiazides available are benzthiazide, chlorothiazide, hydroflumethiazide, methylclothiazide, and polythiazide.
   Other sulphonamide diuretics with similar actions and adverse effects to the thiazides include chlorthalidone, clopamide, clorexolone, metolazone, quinethazone, and xipamide. Mefruside is related to frusemide but in action more closely resembles the thiazides.

2. *Loop diuretics*
Frusemide (p.681)
Bumetanide (p.646)
Ethacrynic acid

3. *Potassium-sparing diuretics*
Amiloride (p.629)
Triamterene
Aldosterone antagonists
   Spironolactone (p.751)
   Potassium canrenoate

4. *Osmotic diuretics*
Mannitol

5. *Carbonic anhydrase inhibitors*
Acetazolamide

6. *Combined diuretics*
(a) Combinations with potassium
Many preparations are available (see *British National Formulary*). Examples are:
   Cyclopenthiazide 250 μg + potassium 8 mmol (Navidrex-K®)
   Frusemide 20 mg + potassium 10 mmol (Lasikal®)
   Frusemide 40 mg + potassium 8 mmol (Diumide-K®)
   Bumetanide 500 μg + potassium 7.7 mmol (Burinex-K®)

(b) Combinations of thiazide or loop diuretics with potassium-sparing diuretics include:
   Hydrochlorothiazide 50 mg + amiloride 5 mg (Moduretic®)
   Hydrochlorothiazide 25 mg + triamterene 50 mg (Dyazide®)
   Benzthiazide 25 mg + triamterene 50 mg (Dytide®)
   Hydroflumethiazide 50 mg + spironolactone 50 mg (Aldactide 50®)
   Frusemide 20 mg + spironolactone 50 mg (Lasilactone®)

Table 24.2 *Pharmacological comparison of diuretics*

Diuretic	Site of action	Urinary excretion				Potency on Na$^+$ excretion	Potency as diuretic
		Na$^+$	K$^+$	Cl$^-$	HCO$_3^-$		
Thiazides	Cortical segment—early part of distal tubule	↑	↑	↑	↓	++	++
Loop diuretics	Medullary segment—ascending limb of the loop of Henle	↑	↑	↑	↓ or ↔	+++	+++
Potassium-sparing diuretics	Distal tubule	↑	↓	↕	←	+	+
Aldosterone antagonists	Distal tubule	↑	↓	↕	←	+*	++*
Mannitol	Throughout tubule (depends on osmotic load)	↑	↕	↓	←	+	+++
Carbonic anhydrase inhibitors	Proximal tubule	↑	↑	↕	↑	+	+

*Na$^+$ excretion and diuresis are more marked when there is significant secondary hyperaldosteronism (e.g. oedema due to cirrhosis of the liver).
Symbols used in text: ↑ =increased; ↓ = reduced; ↔ = unchanged.

24.1.2. Clinical importance of the differences in action between the diuretics

(a) Efficacy and maximal diuretic effect

If a brisk, large diuresis is required (e.g. in acute left ventricular failure) then frusemide or bumetanide (the loop or 'high-ceiling' diuretics) are indicated. They are capable of achieving at least a 2½ times greater increase in sodium excretion than the thiazides and act much more rapidly. Thiazides produce a smaller diuresis and usually it is spread out over a longer period of time. In patients with mild cardiac failure the lesser diuretic effect of the thiazides may be more acceptable to the patient. A fierce diuresis with frequent passage of large volumes of urine can be quite uncomfortable particularly for the elderly. In addition in elderly women there is the problem of incontinence, which is made much worse by diuretics (particularly the loop diuretics), and in elderly men with benign hypertrophy of the prostate acute large volume diuresis may produce acute retention of urine.

(b) Antihypertensive effect

There is no doubt that the thiazide diuretics are just as effective if not more effective than the loop diuretics as antihypertensive drugs. The mode of action of the thiazide diuretics in hypertension is still undecided but one or more of three mechanisms might be involved:

1. Sodium diuresis producing lower intracellular sodium concentrations within vascular smooth muscle cells and decreased reactivity of vascular smooth muscle to noradrenaline released from sympathetic nerve-endings.
2. Haemodynamic changes consequent upon an initial hypovolaemia produced by diuresis.
3. A direct vasodilating action on arterioles. Diazoxide, which is a thiazide, is a vasodilator, decreases peripheral resistance, and lowers the blood pressure despite the fact that it produces sodium retention.

In the treatment of hypertension thiazide diuretics are preferred as hypotensive agents to loop diuretics or any of the other classes of diuretics.

(c) Effects on potassium balance (see also next section on hyper- and hypokalaemia)

From the information given in Table 24.2 it will be seen that the thiazide diuretics and the loop diuretics produce potassium loss. There are certain circumstances where this loss may be excessive, in which case it may be dangerous and replacement therapy becomes advisable. Action to replace potassium or to prevent its excretion must be taken if the plasma potassium concentration is below 3.5 mmol/l or if it is below 4.0 mmol/l with evidence of total body potassium depletion (e.g. alkalosis, ECG changes). If using potassium supplements potassium *chloride* should be used (see p.732).

The following are guidelines to potassium replacement during diuretic therapy.

(i) Digoxin therapy
Potassium replacements should be given to patients in cardiac failure who are being treated with both diuretics and digoxin, since the effects of digoxin are potentiated by hypokalaemia. Plasma potassium concentrations should be monitored.

(ii) Secondary hyperaldosteronism
For example in cirrhosis of the liver with oedema and ascites, thiazide or loop diuretics may produce significant hypokalaemia. Potassium replacements, or potassium-sparing diuretics, especially aldosterone antagonists, may be necessary. Plasma potassium concentrations should be monitored.

(iii) The elderly
The elderly appear to be particularly prone to develop hypokalaemia with thiazides, frusemide, and bumetanide. Malnutrition increases the risk. Many geriatricians routinely use a thiazide or loop diuretic with a potassium-sparing diuretic to avoid this complication.

(iv) Intercurrent illness
Intercurrent illness during diuretic therapy is not unusual and may produce severe hypokalaemia. Vomiting and diarrhoea are common causes.

(v) Drugs
Laxatives (which may be taken without the doctor's knowledge) increase potassium loss from the bowel. Carbenoxolone, used for the treatment of benign gastric ulcer, produces greatly increased urinary potassium loss and very serious hypokalaemia can be produced, particularly if at the same time the patient is taking diuretics. Corticosteroids may cause sodium and water retention, particularly in the elderly, and diuretics may be required. However, they also produce potassium loss and potassium supplements or potassium-sparing diuretics may be required.

Conversely potassium supplements must sometimes be avoided because of an increased risk of *hyper*kalaemia. This is most important in patients with renal impairment, and monitoring of plasma potassium is necessary when treating such patients with diuretics. It can be very difficult to predict exactly what effects diuretics will have on the plasma potassium in patients with renal impairment.

In most circumstances, other than those outlined above, routine potassium supplements, or potassium-sparing diuretics are not required, for example in uncomplicated essential hypertension being treated with thiazides, or mild cardiac failure being treated with thiazides alone.

24.1.3. Choice of agent as prophylaxis against hypokalaemia during diuretic therapy

The choice lies among:

1. Potassium supplements as separate formulations (see potassium chloride in the Pharmacopoeia).
2. Combination tablets of a diuretic with potassium.
3. Combination of a thiazide or loop diuretic with a potassium-sparing diuretic as separate formulations.
4. Combination tablets of a thiazide or loop diuretic plus a potassium-sparing diuretic.

Examples of combination tablets available are given in Table 24.2 and in the Pharmacopoeia (see also the *British National Formulary*).

It is sometimes said that the combination tablets of diuretic with potassium contain too little potassium. The normal dietary intake of potassium is about 50 mmol/day, which is balanced by urinary excretion of 50 mmol/day. The usual daily dose of a thiazide, or frusemide when given acutely causes an extra urinary potassium loss of about 20 mmol/day. More potassium than this will be lost in the treatment of severe oedema, and supplements of 48 mmol KCl/day (e.g. two tablets of Slow-K® t.d.s.) may be needed. Since most combinations of diuretic with potassium contain 8 mmol of K^+ per tablet and half the usual dose of diuretic, a whole dose of diuretic will provide 16 mmol of K^+ which may well be insufficient. In the treatment of oedema therefore, and in heart failure, combinations of diuretic with potassium are too inflexible for a correct diuretic/K^+ balance to be achieved and probably do provide too little potassium.

In uncomplicated hypertension potassium supplements to thiazide treatment are usually unnecessary, and the combination diuretic/potassium tablets are an unnecessary expense. There is little place therefore for the use of diuretic/potassium combination tablets.

For these reasons, or when a further diuretic effect is required, a potassium-sparing diuretic may be prescribed. These can be given separately which allows for flexibility of dosage, or in combination with a thiazide (spironolactone, amiloride, and triamterene) or frusemide (spironolactone). Such combinations should be used only when the patient's diuretic therapy is stabilized and a potassium-sparing effect is required. Care should be taken not to produce *hyper*kalaemia with potassium-sparing diuretics. Amiloride and triamterene should not be used in patients with renal failure (serum creatinine > 150 μmol/l) and never with potassium supplements unless during active and careful controlled replenishment of dangerous potassium depletion.

24.1.4. Resistance to diuretics

Various factors in oedematous states may make adequate diuresis difficult to achieve.

(a) Secondary hyperaldosteronism

This becomes a significant factor fairly late in cardiac failure, is of more significance in the nephrotic syndrome, and is particularly important in cirrhosis of the liver.

Spironolactone may therefore be helpful in controlling oedema in late-stage cardiac failure (usually in combination with loop diuretics). Spironolactone is frequently given together with frusemide or bumetanide in the nephrotic syndrome.

In cirrhosis with oedema and/or ascites, diuretics have to be used with care because of the dangers of hypokalaemia, hepatic encephalopathy, hyponatraemia, and alkalosis. The treatment should be monitored with frequent plasma electrolyte determinations. Diuresis and loss of weight should not be too rapid.

Initially in the cirrhotic patient with ascites and oedema, dietary sodium restriction is undertaken. Usually both frusemide 40 mg daily and spirono-lactone 100 mg daily are given together initially. The patient should be weighed daily checking the rate of diuresis, and plasma electrolytes and urea should be measured twice weekly. When a satisfactory response has been achieved, maintenance diuretic therapy may often be continued with spironolactone alone.

(b) Lowered renal blood flow and glomerular filtration

Generally when renal blood flow decreases, increased proximal tubular reabsorption of sodium occurs. In severe cardiac failure this is probably the most common mechanism through which oedema becomes resistant to diuretic therapy, although the precise intrarenal mechanisms by which it occurs are still not fully worked out. Certainly improvement in cardiac output (with positive inotropic agents) and renal arteriolar vasodilatation (with dopamine) can on occasions overcome this resistance and allow diuretics to act.

(c) Renal failure

One of the complications to avoid in renal failure is sodium and water overload. It can be very difficult to get rid of sodium and water by diuresis in patients with renal failure and a low glomerular filtration rate. It has recently been suggested that one reason for this is that in the uraemic state organic acids accumulate and that these block the transport of thiazides, frusemide, bumetanide, and ethacrynic acid into their site of action in the tubular lumen. Large doses of frusemide can overcome this inhibition of transport but care must be taken because of the increased risk of ototoxicity with high doses of frusemide.

(d) Decreased absorption due to oedematous bowel wall

On occasions it appears that in severe congestive cardiac failure there may be failure of absorption of thiazides or loop diuretics with consequent poor response. It is always worthwhile giving 20–40 mg frusemide by i.v. injection in such patients to see if this route of administration will overcome apparent resistance. If it does and the heart failure improves oral therapy may later become effective.

24.1.5. Adverse effects of diuretics

Although they are dealt with under the individual drug entries in the Pharmacopoeia, certain of the common adverse effects of diuretics are worth emphasizing and are listed in Table 24.3.

Table 24.3   *Adverse effects of diuretics*

Thiazides and loop diuretics
Hyponatraemia
Hypovolaemia (dehydration)
Raised blood urea
Hypokalaemia and alkalosis
Hypomagnesaemia
Hyperuricaemia and gout
Carbohydrate intolerance

Frusemide and ethacrynic acid (high dose)
Ototoxicity

Bumetanide
Myalgia

Potassium-sparing diuretics
Risk of hyperkalaemia

Spironolactone
Dyspepsia, peptic ulceration
Gynaecomastia (particularly in cirrhosis)

24.1.6. Drug interactions with diuretics

(a) Indomethacin, possibly because of actions on renal prostaglandin synthesis, inhibits the diuretic effect of frusemide.

(b) Drugs which promote sodium reabsorption antagonize the effects of diuretics, e.g. corticosteroids, carbenoxolone, oestrogens.

(c) Drugs which promote potassium excretion may act additively with the thiazides and loop diuretics to produce serious hypokalaemia, e.g. carbenoxolone, corticosteroids.

(d) Potassium-sparing diuretics and potassium supplements may produce serious hyperkalaemia in patients taking captopril particularly if there
is a degree of renal failure.

(e) The hypokalaemia produced by thiazides and loop diuretics may
significantly enhance the actions of digoxin and produce digitalis toxicity.

(f) The combination of gentamicin and frusemide is nephrotoxic.

24.2. HYPOKALAEMIA

The causes of hypokalaemia are listed in Table 24.4.

Table 24.4   *Causes of hypokalaemia*

---

1. *Iatrogenic (drug-induced)*
Laxatives (chronic)
Diuretics
Corticosteroids
Carbenoxolone
Insulin in diabetic ketoacidosis

2. *Gastro-intestinal loss*
Vomiting
Diarrhoea
Malabsorption (e.g. coeliac disease)

3. *Renal loss*
Primary and secondary hyperaldosteronism
Tubular damage (e.g. during diuretic phase of acute tubular necrosis)

4. *Old age*
Usually a number of factors are operative in the elderly presenting with hypokalaemia:
malnutrition, poor potassium intake, vomiting, diarrhoea, and drugs are common causes

---

The treatment of diuretic-induced hypokalaemia with potassium supplements or potassium-sparing diuretics has been discussed above under
diuretics. In other circumstances potassium should be given as potassium
chloride, either orally (as elixir, effervescent tablets or sustained-release
tablets, according to patient preference), or in some circumstances by i.v.
infusion.

Oral replacement of potassium loss has the obvious hazard of going too
far and producing hyperkalaemia. Anorexia, nausea, and vomiting are not
uncommon. The slow-release potassium preparations now available uncommonly cause serious adverse effects. Small intestinal ulcers (which
were commoner with enteric-coated potassium chloride tablets) occur
rarely. Oesophageal ulceration has been described as resulting from
sustained-release potassium chloride tablets and patients should be advised
to wash down their tablets with a glassful of water.

When hypokalaemia is severe and/or the patient is unable to take oral
formulations then i.v. administration is necessary.

Take great care in the i.v. administration of potassium salts because hyperkalaemia may cause a fatal cardiac arrhythmia. Potassium should never be injected as a bolus, but should be given by infusion at a rate of 10 mmol/h unless depletion is very severe when a rate of up to 20 mmol/h, with careful monitoring of plasma potassium concentrations and the ECG (T wave peaking with hyperkalaemia) is necessary.

Usually not more than 120 mmol of potassium should be given per day.

Potassium chloride should *never* be added to blood, blood products, mannitol, or solutions of lipids or amino acids.

Very great care must be taken when giving potassium to patients with renal impairment.

24.3. HYPERKALAEMIA

The causes of hyperkalaemia are listed in Table 24.5. When plasma potassium concentrations reach 6.5 mmol/l peaked T waves on the ECG usually become apparent. As the concentration rises to 7–8 mmol/l, the PR interval becomes prolonged and the QRS complex widens. The ECG signs are a good guide to serious hyperkalaemia.

Table 24.5   *Causes of hyperkalaemia*

---

1. *Iatrogenic (drug-induced)*
Potassium supplements and potassium-sparing diuretics

2. *Decreased renal loss*
Acute and chronic renal failure
Hypoaldosteronism—Addison's disease

3. *Shifts across cell membranes from inside to outside*
Acidosis
Cell destruction (e.g. haemolysis, tumour lysis, burns)
Diabetic ketoacidosis
Hyperkalaemic periodic paralysis

24.3.1. Treatment of hyperkalaemia

(a) When hyperkalaemia is severe, and ECG signs present then calcium gluconate should be given at a rate of 10–30 ml of a 10 per cent solution i.v. over 5 min, preferably with ECG monitoring. This treatment should be used with great caution in patients taking cardiac glycosides, since calcium salts given intravenously may precipitate glycoside toxicity. Calcium gluconate is the immediate treatment in life-threatening hyperkalaemia, but its effects are only temporary since calcium acts by decreasing cardiac membrane excitability and thus prevents potassium-induced arrythmias. It does not, however, affect the hyperkalaemia itself.

(b) Insulin is given to shift potassium into cells and thus lower plasma potassium. Glucose is also given to prevent hypoglycaemia. Rule out Addison's disease before using this form of treatment, since patients with adrenocortical failure are very sensitive to the effects of insulin.

Give 50 g of glucose (e.g. as 100 ml of 50 per cent dextrose) with 20 i.u. (international units) of soluble insulin i.v. over 15–30 min. Beware of hypoglycaemia.

In diabetic ketoacidosis hyperkalaemia, if present, is reversed by insulin alone and in fact extra potassium is often given to avoid resultant *hypo*kalaemia as potassium passes into cells and the acidosis is corrected (see treatment of diabetes, Chapter 25).

(c) Sodium bicarbonate 50–100 ml of an 8.4 per cent solution (50–100 mmol) is given i.v. over 15–30 min. This will correct acidosis if present and help shift potassium into cells. Care should be taken in renal failure not to overload with sodium and increase extracellular fluid volume.

The hypokalaemic effect of sodium bicarbonate occurs within an hour and lasts several hours.

(d) If the serum potassium is between 5.5 and 6.5 mmol/l administration of sodium polystyrene–sulphonate resin (Resonium A®) should be started. It can be given orally 15 g 3–4 times daily or rectally as a retention enema, 30 g. The sodium on the ion-exchange resin exchanges for potassium and potassium is removed from the body as the resin passes through (oral) and is expelled rectally. This exchange of ions, however, may produce sodium overload, and if this is a danger in patients with heart failure then *calcium* polystyrene–sulphonate (Calcium Resonium®) can be used.

Obviously further treatment will be determined by the cause.

24.4. THE PLACE OF DRUGS IN THE MANAGEMENT OF ACUTE RENAL FAILURE

Drugs have only a small part to play in the management of acute renal failure.

24.4.1. Diuretics and dopamine in acute tubular necrosis

The use of diuretic therapy in acute tubular necrosis is complex and controversial.

(a) There is some evidence that frusemide and/or mannitol might prevent or lessen the degree of acute tubular necrosis if they are administered before or very soon after a potentially causative event, e.g. an episode of significant renal hypoperfusion.

(b) Once acute tubular necrosis is established frusemide may, in some patients, produce a flow of urine without altering blood urea or creatinine. However the establishment of urine flow can help the management of plasma potassium concentrations and intravascular volume problems.

(c) In some circumstances, if there is uncertainty about the actual level of central venous pressure, (Is the patient hypovolaemic or not? Is the oliguria due simply to renal hypoperfusion?) then mannitol i.v. may produce an increase in urine volume over the subsequent hour or two in the hypovolaemic patient in whom acute renal failure is not established.

(d) In hypovolaemic states, and sometimes despite adequate volume replacement, oliguria persists even though the syndrome of acute tubular necrosis is not established. In some patients a low-dose i.v. infusion of dopamine can produce renal arteriolar vasodilatation and increase urine flow. The addition of frusemide i.v. can increase this urine flow even more.

However, great care needs to be taken in using diuretics in this situation, and specialist advice should be sought. The dangers are as follows:

(a) Mannitol i.v.

There is a risk of osmotic overload, an increase in intravascular volume, and consequent pulmonary oedema due to left ventricular failure. In the oliguric patient phlebotomy or dialysis will be the only methods of decreasing intravascular volume.

(b) High-dose i.v. frusemide

High-dose i.v. frusemide may be ototoxic and the combination of frusemide and gentamicin is particularly so.

(c) Dopamine i.v. infusion

Too high dosage can produce renal vasoconstriction and worsen acute tubular necrosis.

The rules therefore are:

(i) Monitor *central venous pressure* if the intention is to use diuretic therapy in any patient with suspected, incipient, or established acute renal failure due to acute tubular necrosis.

(ii) Do not give mannitol i.v. to patients with myocardial disease.

(iii) Do not overdose with dopamine (see below).

(iv) Do not rely on diuretic therapy to prevent or reverse oliguria and do not delay dialysis if it is otherwise indicated. In other words diuretic therapy is not reliable in acute tubular necrosis.

The dosage regimens of mannitol, frusemide and dopamine used in acute renal failure are as follows:

(i) Mannitol

An i.v. infusion 12.5–25 g (as 50–100 ml of a 25 per cent solution given over 5–10 min) as a first dose. A favourable response is indicated by an increase in urine flow to > 50 ml per hour. Some combine mannitol with a conventional i.v. dose of frusemide, e.g. 40–80 mg. These dosages can be repeated in say 1 h (remember to check central venous pressure and keep the patient normovolaemic). Generally not more than two of these doses of mannitol should be given.

(ii) Frusemide (high-dose)

Some combine high-dose frusemide with mannitol, others use frusemide alone, which is probably safer and does not carry such a hazard of fluid overload in the event that urine flow does not increase. As an example, high-dose frusemide 250 mg/25 ml is diluted in 225 ml of sodium chloride injection BP which is given over 1 h (a rate of about 4 mg/min). If urine volume does not increase to 40–50 ml per hour with this first infusion, double the amount (i.e. 500 mg) should be given at a rate of 4 mg/min. If again there is no response a third infusion of 1000 mg over 4 h can be given. If there is still no response then dialysis will be required.

If with this regimen of high-dose frusemide infusion fluid overload is likely the frusemide may be given in a more concentrated form by infusion pump at a rate not exceeding 4 mg/min.

(iii) Dopamine

Dopamine can be particularly useful in the incipient stage of acute renal failure when a renal vasodilating dose of 1–5 microgram/kg/min together with diuretics may reverse oliguria.

24.4.2. Drug-induced iatrogenic disease in renal failure

In patients who are seriously ill with acute (or chronic) renal failure there is a temptation to use drugs to treat various symptoms and complications. Always consider drug usage very carefully because many drugs are cleared by the kidney and the risks of dose-related adverse effects is considerable.

Problems with drugs in renal failure are dealt with in section 24.11 below, but because of the special place of antibiotics in acute renal failure we shall deal with them in the next paragraph.

24.4.3. Antibiotics in acute renal failure

Special attention must be paid to antibiotics in acute renal failure for four reasons:

1. Acute septicaemia may cause acute renal failure.
2. Patients with acute renal failure are particularly prone to secondary infection.
3. Some antibiotics may cause acute renal failure or if improperly used may worsen it.
4. The handling of several antibiotics is considerably changed by renal failure thus predisposing to adverse reactions.

The antibiotics to which particular attention must be paid are listed in Table 24.6.

Table 24.6　*Antibiotics which can cause renal damage and/or which accumulate in renal failure*

Drug	Type of renal damage (if nephrotoxic)	Hazards of excess accumulation	Comments
Aminoglycosides (e.g. gentamicin)	Renal tubular necrosis	Ototoxicity; further renal damage	Reduce dosages; monitor plasma concentrations
Amphotericin B	Renal tubular necrosis		Common; dose related
Cephaloridine	Renal tubular necrosis		More modern cephalosporins safe
Nitrofurantoin		Peripheral neuropathy	Avoid
Penicillins (e.g. benzylpenicillin, methicillin)	Acute interstitial nephritis	Convulsions, haemolytic anaemia	Reduce large dosages (normal dosages not affected)
Sulphonamides (e.g. co-trimoxazole)	Renal tubular obstruction Acute interstitial nephritis		Due to crystalluria. ?Due to hyper-sensitivity. Reduce dosages (or avoid if possible)
Tetracyclines	Accumulate in renal failure causing nausea, vomiting, and dehydration	Renal damage Increased uraemia due to antianabolic effect	Avoid. Doxycycline is probably safe
Vancomycin (i.v.)	Interstitial nephritis	Ototoxicity	Avoid

24.4.4. Drug treatment of hyperkalaemia in acute renal failure

See drug therapy of hyperkalaemia above.

24.5. THE PLACE OF DRUGS IN THE MANAGEMENT OF CHRONIC RENAL FAILURE

There is a restricted place for drugs in the management of patients with chronic renal failure. While chronic dialysis or renal transplantation solve many of the metabolic problems of renal failure, hypertension and renal bone disease (with hyperparathyroidism) may still pose management problems.

24.5.1. Drug treatment of hyperkalaemia (see p.402)

24.5.2. Drug treatment of hypertension (see p.290)

Captopril and minoxidil may be particularly useful in the treatment of hypertension in the patient with chronic renal failure. Otherwise the treatment of hypertension is as outlined in Chapter 21.

Thiazides are ineffective when glomerular filtration rate falls below

20 ml/min. The effects of prazosin will be influenced by intravascular blood volume and care should be taken in patients who may be water- or salt-depleted.

24.5.3. Management of calcium, phosphate, and vitamin D problems, and renal bone disease

This is a complex subject, and the correct management of some of these problems is still being worked out.

To set the background for a rational approach to treatment a simple understanding of the effects of chronic renal failure on calcium and phosphate metabolism is helpful (see Fig. 24.2).

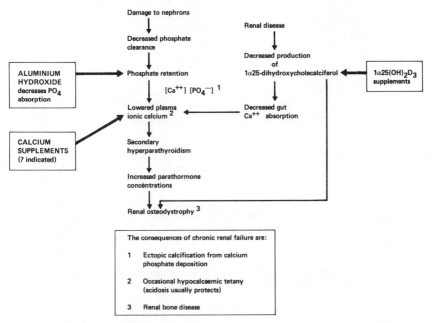

Fig. 24.2. Effects of chronic renal failure on calcium and phosphate metabolism, and the sites and mechanisms of action of drugs used to treat those effects.

(a) Phosphate retention

To reduce the hyperphosphataemia of chronic renal failure and the consequent renal and extrarenal calcification, agents which bind phosphate in the gut lumen and prevent its absorption are given, for example aluminum hydroxide 30 ml immediately after meals. Lowering plasma phosphate increases plasma calcium.

(b) Calcium supplementation

The dangers of calcium supplements to correct hypocalcaemia in chronic renal failure are ectopic calcification, the production of pseudogout, and the inadvertant swing into hypercalcaemia. If there is moderate to severe hyperphosphataemia calcium supplements should probably be avoided.

Calcium supplements are certainly necessary at least temporarily in those patients who develop hypocalcaemic tetany.

(c) Vitamin D derivatives

It is unusual for renal osteodystrophy to cause a great deal of trouble unless life is prolonged by dialysis. Nevertheless treatment of renal osteodystrophy in the patient with chronic renal failure has recently been undertaken with 1 α-hydroxycholecalciferol (alfacalcidol) or 1 α,25-dihydroxycholecalciferol (calcitriol). A glance at Fig. 24.3 will remind the reader of the vitamin D metabolic activation pathway.

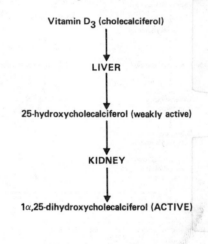

Vitamin D$_3$ (cholecalciferol)

↓

LIVER

↓

25-hydroxycholecalciferol (weakly active)

↓

KIDNEY

↓

1α,25-dihydroxycholecalciferol (ACTIVE)

Orally administered 1α-hydroxycholecalciferol undergoes rapid conversion to 1α,25-dihydroxycholecalciferol in the liver.

Fig. 24.3. The metabolic activation of vitamin D (see also Fig. P11, p.770).

The dose of alfacalcidol is initially 1 microgram orally daily, and most patients respond to 1–3 micrograms daily. The dose of calcitriol initially is 1 microgram daily, increasing to 2–3 micrograms daily according to the response. With either of these vitamin D derivatives serum calcium should be monitored at least weekly during the early stages of treatment to avoid hypercalcaemia, and monitoring should be carried out monthly thereafter.

24.6. DRUG TREATMENT OF GLOMERULONEPHRITIS

The drug treatment of glomerulonephritis, apart from the use of diuretics, and corticosteroids with or without cyclophosphamide treatment in minimal-change disease, is generally disappointing, and rather confused. Too few controlled clinical trials have been done in most cases to show definite efficacy. What follows is a brief summary of current attitudes.

24.6.1. Acute post-streptococcal glomerulonephritis (a form of acute proliferative glomerulonephritis)

Oral phenoxymethylpenicillin treatment is indicated, to eradicate Group A haemolytic streptococci.

Other drug treatment seems not to influence the course of the renal pathology.

24.6.2. Rapidly progressive glomerulonephritis (crescentic)

Drug therapy is confused, with advocates of various different drug regimens, e.g.—

    (a) high dose corticosteroid (prednisolone) therapy;
    (b) heparin + dipyridamole + cyclophosphamide.

Definitive clinical trials have not yet been done. Plasmapheresis may have a role to play in treatment.

24.6.3. Diffuse mesangiocapillary (membranoproliferative) glomerulonephritis

Corticosteroids and immunosuppressive therapy are used but are of unproven efficacy.

24.6.4. Acute glomerular basement-membrane disease

The renal pathology of this is part of Goodpasture's syndrome. Corticosteroids and immunosuppressive therapy are used but are of unproven efficacy. Plasmapheresis, at least in Goodpasture's syndrome, may have a place in therapy, in combination with cyclophosphamide and prednisolone.

24.6.5. Minimal-change glomerulonephritis (lipoid nephrosis)

This is commonly associated with the nephrotic syndrome.

(a) Diuretic therapy

Frusemide or bumetanide orally, with or without spironolactone, are usually given; see diuretic therapy, p.393.

(b) Immunosuppression (see Chapter 34)

Prednisolone, 1 mg/kg body weight daily for children, or in adults a usual dosage of 60 mg daily, are given for 3 weeks. Diuresis usually occurs at about the 10th day of treatment. After 3 weeks the dose is usually reduced to 0.3 mg/kg body weight daily and continued for 3–6 months. There are various sorts of corticosteroid regimen advocated and local specialist advice is needed. About 95 per cent of children respond and 45 per cent become free of proteinuria. About 70 per cent of adults respond but 55 per cent relapse. If relapses cannot be controlled with prednisolone or if steroid toxicity is a great problem then cyclophosphamide 1.5–2.5 mg/kg body weight daily for 6–12 weeks is usually tried.

24.6.6. Membranous glomerulonephritis

The nephrotic syndrome should be treated with diuretics. The results of immunosuppressive therapy with corticosteroids or cyclophosphamide (which has also been combined with heparin and dipyridamole) are not entirely conclusive.

24.6.7. Glomerulonephritis associated with systemic disease

(a) Systemic lupus erythematosus

Prednisolone therapy is usually advocated, and in appropriate cases may be combined with azathioprine or cyclophosphamide.

(b) Polyarteritis nodosa

Again prednisolone is advocated, and in uncontrolled trials cyclophosphamide or azathioprine seem to have added benefit.

(c) Wegener's granulomatosis

Cyclophosphamide is the treatment of choice, as it seems to be in several of the necrotizing vasculitic syndromes, presumably acting as an immunosuppressant. Prednisolone therapy may be additionally beneficial in some cases.

24.7. DRUGS IN THE TREATMENT OF URINARY TRACT INFECTION

For the general principles of antibiotic therapy, which apply to the treatment of urinary tract infection, see Chapter 20.

The clinical problems of urinary tract infection include the following:

urethritis
cystitis
acute and chronic pyelonephritis
prostatitis
asymptomatic bacteriuria
recurrent urinary tract infection.

The commonest infecting organism in uncomplicated cases of urinary tract infection is *E. coli* (about 80 per cent of cases). When recurrent infection exists or when there are other complicating factors, such as surgical instrumentation or catheterization, then other organisms such as *Proteus* (very common), *Klebsiella, Enterobacter, Pseudomonas aeruginosa,* enterococci, and *Staphylococcus aureus* occur.

The following practical points should be noted:

1. Establish the diagnosis of urinary tract infection by urinary microscopic examination and by sending a urine specimen for culture and sensitivity testing.

2. After treatment is complete check for cure by a repeat examination and culture of the urine.

3. One attack of lower urinary tract infection in a male and more than two attacks in a female are signals to investigate the urinary tract for underlying pathology in urethra, bladder, ureters, kidneys, or prostate.

24.7.1 Uncomplicated infections of the lower urinary tract

If the infection at first sight appears to be uncomplicated by other abnormalities of bladder, ureters, or kidneys assume that the infection is due to *E.coli.*

For cystitis the choices are generally:

co-trimoxazole or trimethoprim
amoxycillin ($\pm$ clavulanic acid)
sulphamethizole.

The duration of therapy is usually about a week, but one single dose of amoxycillin 3 g may cure uncomplicated lower urinary tract infections.

24.7.2. Acute pyelonephritis

(a) In hospital

The choices are generally:

first—gentamicin;
second—co-trimoxazole;
third—ampicillin or amoxycillin;
fourth—cephalosporins (cefotaxime, latamoxef): relapse is common.

Parenteral antibiotic therapy is often necessary because of nausea and vomiting.

(b) In domiciliary practice

Co-trimoxazole or amoxycillin ($\pm$ clavulanic acid) are the usual choices.

If severe, gentamicin i.m. can be used, but if the infection is that severe, depending on circumstances, it is generally better treated in hospital. Duration of therapy is 1–2 weeks. The choice of antibiotic for the total course of therapy will depend crucially on the results of the pretreatment culture.

24.7.3. Chronic pyelonephritis

Antibiotic therapy of exacerbations of pyelonephritis will depend upon the infecting organism and the factors rendering the urinary tract prone to infection (e.g. anatomical abnormalities, bladder dysfunction, stones). Suppressive or prophylactic therapy is dealt with below.

24.7.4. Prostatitis

The penetration into the prostate of antibiotics active against Gram-negative organisms is generally poor. Therapy is usually begun with co-trimoxazole until the results of prostatic secretion culture and sensitivity are known. Treatment should be continued (usually with co-trimoxazole) for 4 weeks. Suppressive treatment is sometimes necessary with co-trimoxazole one tablet each night or nitrofurantoin 100 mg each night.

24.7.5. Recurrent urinary tract infections

In women with normal urinary tracts who suffer recurrent urinary tract infections (often associated with sexual intercourse) in whom simple measures—such as pre- and post-coital micturition and the application of an antiseptic cream to the periurethral area—do not prevent attacks, co-trimoxazole, one tablet each night, or nitrofurantoin, 50 mg each night, or nalidixic acid 0.5 g every night for 6 months followed by reassessment is often used as prophylaxis.

If there are irremediable abnormalities of the urinary tract associated with recurrent symptomatic urinary tract infections, similar therapy may be indicated in the long term, with periodic reassessments. Resistance of infecting organisms often occurs and therapy may need to be adjusted appropriately.

24.7.6. Asymptomatic bacteriuria

If there is no structural or functional neurological abnormality of the urinary tract in a young woman then probably treatment is not indicated.

Asymptomatic bacteriuria should probably be treated with the appropriate antibiotic in the following circumstances:

(a) Pregnancy (symptomatic urinary tract infections frequently follow on).

(b) Other patients with a high risk of developing symptomatic infection (e.g. those with abnormalities of the urinary tract).

The management of asymptomatic bacteriuria in the elderly is difficult. If it is truly asymptomatic, if the patient is fit, well, and mobile, and if there are not associated urinary tract abnormalities treatment is probably unnecessary. However, if there is incontinence or increased frequency of micturition, or if the patient is ill and has to be in bed or resting for long periods of time during which florid infection may occur, then probably the appropriate antibiotics should be administered.

24.7.7. Urinary tract infection in pregnancy

The problem of treating urinary tract infections in pregnancy is common. What drugs are safe?

One should avoid co-trimoxazole, because of the risk of teratogenicity and kernicterus if used in late pregnancy, gentamicin because of the slight potential for ototoxicity, and tetracyclines because of discolouration of teeth and interference with bone growth in the fetus.

Ampicillin, amoxycillin, and other penicillins are apparently safe. The safety of clavulanic acid has not been established in pregnancy. So far there are no suggestions that cephalosporins are unsafe in pregnancy.

24.7.8. Urinary infections and catheterization

Generally prophylactic antibiotics in catheterized patients, particularly those with long-term catheters, do little to prevent urinary tract infections and lead to problems with resistant organisms. Antibiotic therapy should be limited to the treatment of acute infections.

24.7.9. Genito-urinary tuberculosis

The drug treatment of genito-urinary tuberculosis is undertaken on similar principles to that of pulmonary tuberculosis (Chapter 22). The following regimen has been found to be effective in the vast majority of cases:

rifampicin 600 mg o.d. orally;
isoniazid 300 mg o.d. orally;
pyridoxine 100 mg o.d. orally;
ethambutol 25 mg/kg o.d. orally for 2 months followed by 15 mg/kg o.d. orally.

This therapy should be continued for at least 2 years (i.e. longer than in pulmonary tuberculosis).

Corticosteroids (e.g. prednisolone 20 mg o.d.) may be of value in relieving ureteric strictures, but surgical intervention may be necessary, as it may be in other aspects of genito-urinary tuberculosis.

24.8. DRUG TREATMENT OF URINARY CALCULI

24.8.1. Acute—treatment of renal colic

For pain give:

> pethidine 100 mg i.m.; or
> morphine 10 mg or diamorphine 5 mg s.c. plus atropine 0.3–0.6 mg s.c.
> (as an antispasmodic).

> Avoid pethidine in renal failure.

24.8.2. Chronic—prevention of stone formation

(a) Calcium oxalate and apatite stones with hypercalciuria

A high fluid intake is essential (2–3 l/day). Calcium in the diet should be restricted as should oxalate, if appropriate. A thiazide diuretic such as bendrofluazide 5–10 mg daily, reduces renal tubular calcium reabsorption. Sodium cellulose phosphate, 12–15 g daily, reduces dietary calcium absorption from the gut. If calcium stone-formers have high uric acid excretion allopurinol may also be helpful.

(b) Uric acid stones (see also the treatment of gout, Chapter 27)

Avoid excess purines in the diet and ensure a high fluid intake. Maintain an alkaline urine—keep urinary pH at around 7.5, for example by giving potassium citrate mixture 10 ml t.d.s. Unfortunately excess alkalinization may result in calcium stone formation so care must be taken and in many patients a high fluid intake and allopurinol will suffice.

(c) Cystinuria

High fluid intake. Alkalinization of the urine—potassium citrate mixture as above or sodium bicarbonate 12 g daily to keep the urine at pH $\geq$ 7.5.

If high fluid intake and alkalinization of the urine are ineffective then give penicillamine 250 mg t.d.s. to a maximum of 500 mg q.d.s.

24.9. DRUGS AND THE URINARY BLADDER

As the bladder fills, stretching of its wall initiates afferent nerve impulses which pass to the cerebral cortex and result in the sensation of wanting to pass urine. At the act of micturition parasympathetic activity results in contraction of the detrusor muscle and co-ordinated urethral sphincter relaxation, and urine is passed.

In the elderly particularly, increased frequency of micturition, urgency of micturition, vesical suprapubic pain, and urethral pain can occur commonly. These symptoms are almost certainly associated with bladder pathology, usually inflammatory due to infection.

The bladder symptoms can be very disturbing to the patient and difficult to control. Attempts have therefore been made to control bladder irritability medically by inhibiting parasympathetic drive to the bladder with antimuscarinic drugs.

This has not been altogether successful because of the generalized atropinic effects of these drugs. Nevertheless in some elderly patients suffering from distressing increase of frequency of micturition and incontinence, particularly at night, in whom urinary infection and other urinary tract abnormalities have been investigated and treated, anticholinergic drugs can bring some relief. Excessive dosages should not be given, adverse effects should be carefully monitored, and if within a day or two symptoms are not relieved treatment should be stopped. The efficacy of these drugs is limited and they are frequently prescribed unnecessarily.

Emepronium is given orally in doses of not more than 200 mg t.d.s. or for nocturnal problems 200–400 mg at night. Tablets of emepronium contain 100 mg. Previously there were 200 mg tablets but these appeared to stick in the oesophagus and caused serious oesophageal ulceration. The 100 mg tablets do not appear to do this but the drug should not be given to patients suspected of having any oesophageal pathology, and the tablets should always be washed down with at least 60 ml of fluid and the patient should be instructed to remain upright for 15 min following ingestion.

Flavoxate (dose 200 mg t.d.s.) is an alternative to emepronium. It has a direct effect on bladder muscle causing relaxation. Adverse effects include nausea and diarrhoea, and blurred vision.

These drugs should never be used in patients with urinary outflow tract obstruction or glaucoma.

24.10. DRUG THERAPY OF TUMOURS OF THE KIDNEY AND PROSTATE

The two important malignancies to consider here are nephroblastoma and carcinoma of the prostate.

24.10.1. Nephroblastoma (Wilms's tumour)

This is the second most common abdominal malignant tumour in infants and children (neuroblastoma being the most common). The peak incidence is at 3–4 years. Five to ten per cent are bilateral. About 38 per cent have pulmonary metastases by the time of diagnosis, and some of those will have liver secondaries as well.

The overall treatment is complex but three approaches are used:

(a) *Surgical removal* of the primary tumour.

(b) *Post-operative radiation* may or may not be indicated depending upon local spread of the tumour.

(c) *Adjuvant chemotherapy* has been extremely successful in this condition, and at 2 years 80 per cent of cases are free of disease.

Combination chemotherapy is usually given using actinomycin D and vincristine (see cancer chemotherapy, Chapter 33).

24.10.2. Carcinoma of the prostate

Controversy surrounds the choice of surgical and/or medical treatment appropriate for the various stages of prostatic carcinoma. However, hormonal therapy or cytotoxic drug therapy are only indicated in metastatic disease. It has been shown that stilboestrol treatment of non-metastatic, non-symptomatic prostatic carcinoma results in no prolongation of lifespan, and in fact may shorten life through increased likelihood of death due to cardiovascular disease.

There is apparently nothing to be gained from stilboestrol therapy before symptoms occur (e.g. bone pain from metastases). The usual recommended dose of stilboestrol for symptoms from metastatic carcinoma of the prostate is 1–3 mg daily. The adverse effects are gynaecomastia, loss of libido, sodium and water retention with oedema and cardiac failure, and nausea and vomiting.

Various cytotoxic drug regimens have been tried in metastatic carcinoma of the prostate and these have used, singly or in various combinations, including doxorubicin, cyclophosphamide, cisplatin, and mustines.

24.11. THE EFFECTS OF IMPAIRMENT OF RENAL FUNCTION ON DRUG DISPOSITION, ELIMINATION, AND ACTION

Various aspects of this subject are discussed throughout the book—in the chapter on pharmacokinetics (Chapter 3), in each drug section in the

Table 24.7   *Drugs to be avoided in patients with renal failure*

Drug	Reason
p-aminosalicylic acid (PAS)	Potentiates acidosis, increased risk of gastro-intestinal bleeding
Cephaloridine	Nephrotoxic
Chlorpropamide	Hypoglycaemic effect cumulative and prolonged
Nitrofurantoin	Peripheral neuropathy due to accumulation
Phenformin	Increased risk of acidosis, ketosis, and hyperuricaemia
Potassium and potassium-sparing diuretics	Risk of hyperkalaemia
Probenecid and sulphinpyrazone	Ineffective
Tetracyclines	See Table 24.6
Vancomycin (i.v.)	Ototoxicity due to accumulation

Pharmacopoeia, and earlier in this chapter when discussing antibiotic therapy in renal failure.

It is a very important subject because renal impairment is common, sometimes unsuspected, and drug toxicity in renal impairment frequently occurs and is usually avoidable. Drugs which should be avoided in renal impairment are listed in Table 24.7.

For drugs which are used in renal impairment there are three main problems.

24.11.1. Retention of drugs and/or metabolites normally wholly or in large part eliminated by the kidney

If less drug is being excreted, more will accumulate, and once a toxic concentration is reached dose-dependent adverse effects will occur.

In practice the information one needs to tailor dose according to the degree of renal impairment is:

1. The fraction of drug and/or active metabolite normally excreted by the kidney. The smaller that fraction the less influence will renal failure have on overall drug clearance from the body.

2. The degree of renal failure. This is best assessed in ordinary clinical practice by the fall in creatinine clearance as an index of glomerular filtration rate. The greater the fall in creatinine clearance the more will drugs with high rates of renal clearance be retained.

3. Knowledge of the appropriate dosage for the particular patient if renal function were normal (to which adjustments are going to have to be made).

4. Knowledge of the likelihood that raised plasma concentrations will lead to dose-related adverse effects, i.e. knowledge of the toxic:therapeutic ratio—the therapeutic index. For instance, drugs like digoxin and gentamicin which have a low therapeutic index, and which accumulate in renal failure are very likely to cause adverse effects, while penicillin G which is largely eliminated in the urine has such a high therapeutic index that in spite of renal failure adverse reactions are still uncommon (which is not to say that one should not consider appropriate dose reduction when using high doses of penicillins).

A useful *dose adjustment formula* which can be used in practice has been discussed in Chapter 3, and is shown below.

Let *P* be the percentage of drug which is cleared from the body in a given time (say 1 h). Let *NR* be the non-renal contribution to that clearance (say per cent/h) and let *R* be the renal contribution corrected for creatinine clearance.

Then the following relationship is obtained:

$P = NR + (R \times \text{Creatinine clearance})$.

Values for *NR* and *R* for a variety of different drugs are given in Table 3.5.

The example of digoxin was discussed in Chapter 3 (p.47). Let us here consider the example of gentamicin in a patient whose usual requirements would be 80 mg every 8 h.

For gentamicin $NR = 2$
$$R = 0.3.$$
Let normal creatinine clearance ($CL_{Cr.N}$) be 100 ml/min.
Let the patient's creatinine clearance ($CL_{Cr.RF}$) be 20 ml/min.
Then $P_N = 2 + (0.3 \times 100) = 32$
and $P_{RF} = 2 + (0.3 \times 20) = 8$.
Thus the ratio $P_{RF}/P_N = 0.25$.
In this patient one would therefore do one of three things:

(a) reduce the maintenance dose by one quarter, i.e. 20 mg every 8 h;
(b) increase the dosage interval fourfold;
(c) both reduce the dose and increase the dosage interval, e.g. 40 mg every 16 h.

With gentamicin the precise way in which one changes the dose will depend on the peak and trough plasma concentrations found during treatment—the problems are discussed in detail in Chapter 7 (p.118).

Using these principles we can create Table 24.8 for gentamicin, comparable with that for digoxin (p.47).

Table 24.8 *Ratio of renal failure dose: usual dose of gentamicin for different values of creatinine clearance*

Creatinine clearance (ml/min)	Hourly elimination rate (%)	Ratio $\dfrac{Renal\ failure\ dose}{Usual\ dose}$
100	32	32/32 = 1
50	17	17/32 ≈ ½
30	11	11/32 ≈ ⅓
20	8	8/32 = ¼
15	6.5	6.5/32 ≈ ⅕
10	5	5/32 ≈ ⅙

These calculations provide a guide to the dosage regimens one would first use in patients with given levels of renal impairment. However, one would subsequently adjust the doses of drug, or the frequency of administration, or both, depending on measurement of plasma gentamicin concentrations (see Chapter 7).

These calculations in practice assume:

1. That drug elimination follows first-order kinetics (see p.29).

2. That the drug's metabolites are inactive.

3. That absorption, distribution, or metabolism are unchanged in patients with renal failure. Remember, however, that changes in the apparent volume of distribution do not affect calculations of steady-state maintenance dosages.

4. That there is a linear relationship between the renal clearance of the drug and the creatinine clearance.

5. That renal function does not change during dosing.

6. That there is no change in the response sensitivity to the drug in renal impairment.

Commonly used drugs which are mainly cleared by the kidney and for which dosage alterations may have to be made in renal failure are listed in Table 3.5 (p.48). In any patient with renal failure particulars about any drug you are going to prescribe should be checked unless you already have knowledge of that drug's behaviour in renal failure.

There are two further points. One is obvious: monitor plasma concentrations when possible in renal failure (digoxin, lithium, gentamicin). The other is the matter of the loading dose. If it is known that the apparent volume of distribution is unchanged in renal failure then the usual loading dose may be given to achieve adequate therapeutic concentrations. This may be important for drugs with long half-times because if the $t_{1/2}$ is prolonged in renal failure (and since four half-times of regular maintenance therapy are required before steady state is reached) it can take much longer than usual to achieve steady state. It so happens that for digoxin the apparent volume of distribution is decreased by about 50 per cent in severe renal failure so that the loading dose also needs reduction.

24.11.2. Plasma protein binding of drugs in renal failure

Acidic drugs such as phenytoin and warfarin are increasingly less bound to plasma proteins as the degree of renal failure increases and the uraemic state worsens. This decreased binding is due both to changes in the structure and binding properties of plasma albumin and the competitive role of organic acids.

The importance of this in relation to the interpretation of plasma phenytoin concentrations is discussed in Chapter 7 (p.115).

The binding of basic drugs is little affected in renal failure.

24.11.3. Changes in drug action in renal failure

It seems to be a general rule that a brain which is clouded by disease will be more sensitive than usual to the CNS depressant effects of tranquillizers, sedatives, and opiate analgesics. Renal failure has to be quite advanced, however for this to occur.

In renal failure control of body fluid volumes may be disturbed, and if for any reason patients are hypovolaemic they become very sensitive to hypotensive agents, particularly α-adrenoceptor antagonists such as prazosin.

Patients with uraemia have an increased bleeding tendency. The effects of anticoagulants may therefore be enhanced and aspirin and other non-steroidal anti-inflammatory agents are more liable to produce significant gastro-intestinal bleeding.

Drugs which cause sodium retention (e.g. carbenoxolone, phenylbutazone, indomethacin) may produce fluid overload, oedema, and heart failure.

Hyperkalaemia is often a consequence of renal failure so that potassium supplements, triamterene, amiloride, and spironolactone should usually be avoided in patients with renal failure.

Finally patients in renal failure may be more sensitive to the effects of acetylcholinesterase inhibitors, such as neostigmine, because of reduced esterase activity.

24.12. DRUGS AND DIALYSIS

The factors which determine the extent to which a drug is removed from the body relate to characteristics of the drug and (for haemodialysis) of the equipment.

The important characteristics of the drug are as follows.

24.12.1. Molecular weight

The larger the drug molecule the lower the rate of clearance by dialysis. The dialysis of drugs with a molecular weight less than 500 daltons depends in turn on the effective membrane surface area, and the rate of flow of blood and dialysate. For drugs with molecular weights above 500 daltons only membrane area is of importance.

24.12.2. Water solubility

Poorly water-soluble drugs are poorly dialysed since dialysis fluids are aqueous. For example, glutethimide which has a low molecular weight is nonetheless not well dialysed, being poorly water-soluble.

24.12.3. Protein binding

Drugs which are highly protein bound are poorly cleared by dialysis since the rate of transfer across the dialysis membrane is proportional to the concentration gradient between unbound drug in the plasma and drug in the dialysis fluid. For example, propranolol is highly protein bound and is poorly removed by dialysis even though its molecular weight is low.

24.12.4. Apparent volume of distribution

If a drug is extensively bound to body tissues then even if it passes readily across dialysis membranes there may be little removal of the total drug from the body. For example, digoxin is poorly removed by dialysis because it is so widely distributed to body tissues.

24.12.5. Usual route of drug clearance

If a drug is mostly eliminated by hepatic metabolism at a rate of clearance appreciably greater than the rate of dialysis clearance then dialysis will affect total clearance to only a small extent.

24.12.6. Body weight

Since total body clearance of a drug is roughly proportional to body weight but dialysis clearance is constant for a given piece of equipment, it follows that the smaller the patient the greater will be the contribution to total body clearance of clearance by dialysis.

The important characteristics of the haemodialyser are as follows:

24.12.7. The membrane

As surface area and porosity increase so does the rate of drug clearance. Partly because the peritoneal membrane has different characteristics to haemodialysis membranes some drugs are removed by peritoneal dialysis but not by haemodialysis and vice versa (see Table 24.9).

Table 24.9 *Drugs for which dialysis may be expected to remove significant quantities from the body*

Aminoglycoside antibiotics (HP)	Meprobamate (HP)
Amoxycillin (H)	Methaqualone (HP)
Ampicillin (H)	Methotrexate (H)
Azathioprine (H)	Methyldopa (HP)
Carbenicillin (H)	Metronidazole (H)
Cephalosporins (most) (HP)	Nitrofurantoin (H)
*Chloral hydrate derivatives (HP)	Nitroprusside (HP)
Colistimethate (P)	Nortriptyline (P)
Co-trimoxazole (H)	Paracetamol (H)
Cyclophosphamide (H)	Pentazocine (H)
Diazoxide (HP)	*Phenobarbitone (HP)
Diphenhydramine (H)	*Phenytoin (H)
Ethambutol (HP)	Primidone (H)
5-Fluorocytosine (HP)	Procainamide (H)
5-Fluorouracil (H)	Quinidine (H)
Gallamine (HP)	Quinine (H)
Isoniazid(HP)	*Salicylates (HP)
*Lithium (HP)	*Sulphonamides (HP)

H = haemodialysis, P = peritoneal dialysis.
* Dialysis may be useful in self-poisoning. In addition to these drugs dialysis may be of value in treating severe cases of self-poisoning with ethanol, methanol, bromides and fluorides, and mushrooms.

24.12.8. Rate of flow of dialysis fluid

This is important for drugs with low molecular weights (see above).

The relationship between drugs and dialysis has four aspects:

(a) Routine dialysis may cause loss of drugs from the body with subsequent loss of therapeutic effects.

(b) Routine dialysis may cause alterations in the body, for example changes in electrolyte balance, which may affect the response to the drug.

(c) Drugs may alter the kinetics of dialysis.

(d) Dialysis may be useful in hastening the elimination of drugs from the body after self-poisoning.

(a) Loss of therapeutic effect

A list of drugs which are significantly affected by dialysis is given in Table 24.9. However it is not always possible to predict the *extent* to which removal will occur nor the *rate* at which it will occur, because of differences in haemodialysis equipment and because there is relatively little information from formal studies of individual drugs.

However, if one knows that a drug is likely to be lost from the body during dialysis one should monitor treatment closely to try to determine how to adjust dosages (see Chapter 7). For example, one would measure plasma gentamicin concentrations to determine how much extra gentamicin to give during or after dialysis.

(b) Changes in fluid and electrolyte balance

It is important to avoid hypokalaemia in patients taking cardiac glycosides or anti-arrhythmic drugs (see Pharmacopoeia and Chapter 10).

(c) Alteration of dialysis kinetics

Drugs which alter peripheral blood flow, for example vasodilators such as hydralazine or vasoconstrictors such as adrenoceptor agonists, may alter the rate of clearance of drugs by dialysis (see above).

(d) Treatment of self-poisoning

See Chapter 32.

24.13. DRUG TREATMENT OF SEXUALLY TRANSMITTED DISEASES

The drugs used are listed in Table 24.10.

Table 24.10 *Drugs used in the treatment of sexually transmitted diseases*

Disease	Antibiotic	Alternative
Syphilis	Procaine penicillin or benzylpenicillin	Erythromycin or tetracycline
Gonorrhoea	Procaine penicillin or ampicillin + probenecid	Co-trimoxazole, spectinomycin, cefuroxime
Non-gonococcal urethritis	Tetracycline	Erythromycin

24.13.1. Syphilis

The drug of choice in all forms of syphilis is penicillin. In patients who are allergic to penicillin erythromycin or tetracycline should be used.

In primary and secondary syphilis procaine penicillin is given in a dosage of 600 mg i.m. daily for 8 days. The alternatives are erythromycin (1 g orally b.d. for 2 weeks) or tetracycline (500 g orally q.d.s. for 2 weeks). Similar dosages are used in other forms of syphilis but for differing (usually longer) periods of time, the exact duration of treatment depending on the form of the disease. In some cases benzylpenicillin is used rather than procaine penicillin (e.g. in congenital syphilis).

In addition to the usual risk of penicillin hypersensitivity (see Pharmacopoeia, p.725) there is an additional risk in early syphilis of the Jarisch–Herxheimer reaction. This is a systemic reaction which is thought to be due to the release of endotoxin from killed spirochaetes. It comes on within a few hours of the first injection of penicillin, and lasts up to a day. It consists of fever, flushing, tachycardia, myalgia, and hypotension. It is rare in late syphilis, but when it occurs it can cause progression of neurosyphilis or exacerbation of the local effects of gummata. Pre-treatment with prednisolone, 40 mg, on the day before treatment and in subsequently decreasing doses can mitigate the effects, and aspirin may give symptomatic relief.

Asymptomatic sexual contacts of syphilitic patients should be traced and treated, and patients should be warned to avoid intercourse for 2 weeks.

24.13.2. Gonococcal infections

(a) Gonorrhoea

A single dose of penicillin is the treatment of choice in most cases of uncomplicated gonorrhoea (e.g. procaine penicillin 2.4 g for men, 4.8 g for women) in combination with oral probenecid, 1 g. Ampicillin, 2 g orally once for men, repeated for women, can be used as an alternative to procaine penicillin. Alternatives to penicillins (e.g. in penicillin hyper-sensitivity or when the organism is not sensitive) are:

co-trimoxazole, four tablets b.d. for 2 days or five tablets repeated after 8 h;
spectinomycin, 2 g i.m. in men, 4 g i.m. in women;
cefuroxime, 1.5 g i.m.

When gonorrhoea is complicated by pelvic inflammation or is affecting other organs, eight-day courses of penicillin or one of its alternatives are required.

(b) Gonococcal conjunctivitis

Gonococcal conjunctivitis may be prevented in the newborn child of an infected mother by the use of silver nitrate eye drops (1 per cent) immediately after delivery. However, this treatment may cause a chemical conjunctivitis, and many doctors prefer to treat only those in whom infection has occurred.

In an established infection penicillin eye drops 10 000 i.u./ml should be given four-hourly plus procaine penicillin 300 000 i.u./day i.m. for 5 days. Chloramphenicol ointment, 1 per cent applied four-hourly is an alternative to penicillin eye drops.

24.13.3. Non-gonococcal urethritis

Non-gonococcal (or 'non-specific') urethritis is most commonly caused by *Chlamydia trachomatis* or *Ureaplasma urealyticum* organisms. Both are sensitive to tetracyclines, which should be used (e.g. tetracycline 250 mg orally q.d.s. for 1 week). Erythromycin is the alternative (500 mg orally b.d. for 1 week), for example in pregnancy.

25 The drug therapy of endocrine and metabolic disorders

25.1. DISORDERS OF THE PITUITARY GLAND

25.1.1. Hypopituitarism

Reduced function of the anterior pituitary results in underactivity of the organs which are normally stimulated by the pituitary trophic hormones, of which the most important are ACTH (adrenocorticotrophic hormone) and TSH (thyroid stimulating hormone). In children growth hormone deficiency is also important. Gonadal deficiency may also require treatment.

(a) ACTH deficiency

For adrenal insufficiency secondary to hypopituitarism it is usual to use a glucocorticosteroid which also has some mineralocorticoid effect, such as cortisone 12.5–37.5 mg orally o.d. Occasionally, however, it may also be necessary to use a mineralocorticoid, in which case one would use 9-α-fluoro-hydrocortisone (fludrocortisone) 50–200 micrograms orally o.d.

If there is severe, acute hypopituitarism (so-called pituitary 'apoplexy') then i.v. hydrocortisone should be used in the same dosages as described below under acute adrenocortical insufficiency.

(b) TSH deficiency

Hypothyroidism secondary to hypopituitarism is treated in exactly the same way as primary hypothyroidism (p.432). It is important to note, however, that when hypothyroidism is due to hypopituitarism corticosteroid replacement must be undertaken before thyroid replacement, or at least concurrently, since thyroid replacement alone may precipitate acute adrenocortical insufficiency in these patients.

(c) Gonadotrophin deficiency

In hypopituitarism if it is necessary to achieve or maintain sexual maturity then steroid sex hormones are used. If infertility is the problem then one uses gonadotrophins.

Gonadal steroids are discussed in detail in the Pharmacopoeia (p.744). In men testosterone is used and in women a combination of an oestrogen and a progestogen (e.g. ethinyloestradiol plus norethisterone acetate as in one of the conventional oral contraceptive preparations). In children the use of gonadal steroids should be delayed until full skeletal growth has occurred, since the gonadal steroids cause epiphyseal fusion and stunting of growth.

The uses and dosages of gonadotrophins are discussed in the Pharmacopoeia.

(d) Growth hormone deficiency

In children with hypopituitarism whose epiphyses have not fused human growth hormone is used. It is given i.m. in dosages of at least 0.6 i.u./kg/week in two or three divided doses, and individual requirements vary greatly.

25.1.2. Pituitary overactivity

(a) ACTH

Increased pituitary ACTH production is dealt with under adrenocortical hyperactivity (p.429).

(b) Gigantism and acromegaly

These conditions arise from increased growth hormone production, usually due to a pituitary adenoma. Surgical removal of the tumour is the definitive treatment, but if surgery is not possible, or if growth hormone hypersecretion persists after surgery, then bromocriptine may be used to reduce growth hormone secretion (see Pharmacopoeia, p.645).

(c) Hyperprolactinaemia

Hyperprolactinaemia may be due to a variety of causes, including drugs (see Table 25.1), some of which are treatable. Drug-induced hyperprolactinaemia, for example, resolves on withdrawing the drug, but if that is not possible or desirable then bromocriptine can be used. Other circumstances in which bromocriptine is of value include other causes for which treatment of the primary abnormality is not possible, or when hyperprolactinaemia is due to an adenoma which has not extended outside of the sella turcica. For larger prolactin-secreting tumours surgical removal is indicated, but bromocriptine is used post-operatively to reduce circulating prolactin concentrations, which often remain high. In patients with large prolactinomas in whom surgery is not possible bromocriptine can be used to reduce the size of the tumour and to counteract hyperprolactinaemia. Some also use bromocriptine routinely before surgical removal of a prolactinoma in order to shrink its size and make surgical removal of large tumours easier.

Table 25.1 *Causes of hyperprolactinaemia*

Prolactin-secreting pituitary adenoma
Other endocrine abnormalities
    Destructive lesions of the hypothalamus and pituitary stalk
    Primary hypothyroidism
Drugs
    Benzodiazepines
    Cimetidine
    Methyldopa
    Metoclopramide
    Oestrogens
    Phenothiazines
    Reserpine
Chest wall lesions
    Chronic breast stimulation
    Herpes zoster
    Trauma and surgery
Ectopic prolactin production

25.1.3. Diabetes insipidus

Diabetes insipidus occurs either when there is failure of secretion of antidiuretic hormone (ADH or vasopressin) from the neurohypophysis (cranial diabetes insipidus) or when neurohypophyseal ADH production is adequate but the kidney fails to respond (nephrogenic diabetes insipidus).

(a) Mechanisms of action of drugs used to treat diabetes insipidus

The various vasopressins all act by increasing the permeability of the distal parts of the renal tubule to water, thus enhancing water reabsorption.

The thiazide diuretics have a paradoxical effect in *reducing* urine flow rate in diabetes insipidus. They probably act by causing sodium depletion, which leads to increased water reabsorption in the proximal tubule. Increased dietary sodium intake prevents the therapeutic effects of diuretics and patients should be instructed to limit their salt intake when using diuretics for diabetes insipidus. The main use of the thiazide diuretics is in the nephrogenic form of diabetes insipidus, but they can also be used in the cranial form if there is only partial deficiency of vasopressin.

Chlorpropamide, clofibrate, and carbamazepine act by increasing ADH release from the pituitary. They are ineffective in nephrogenic diabetes insipidus and, because of their adverse effects they are generally not used in the treatment of cranial diabetes insipidus.

(b) Practical aspects of the treatment of cranial and nephrogenic diabetes insipidus

(i) Cranial diabetes insipidus
Cranial diabetes insipidus may be due to one of a number of different types

of pituitary or hypothalamic lesion, but whatever the cause the treatment is the same.

Mild cranial diabetes insipidus (urine output < 4 l/day) may not need treatment, although a thiazide diuretic (e.g. hydrochlorothiazide 50–100 mg o.d. or chlorothiazide 0.5–1.0 g o.d.) may be useful to reduce urine output if required.

For more severe diabetes insipidus desmopressin is the treatment of choice since it has a longer duration of action than other vasopressins and has much less of a constricting effect on vascular and other smooth muscle. It is usually given by nasal insufflation of a solution containing 100 micrograms/ml. The dosage of desmopressin must be tailored to each individual's requirements according to the clinical response. Start with a single dose of 10 micrograms intranasally in the evening. The antidiuretic effect should come on within an hour and last at least 8 h. If the antidiuretic effect is not maintained the following day an extra dose will be required in the morning. The dosage should then be titrated according to response, aiming to use the smallest total daily dose which results in a urine output of 2 l per day. Usual maintenance dosages are 10–20 micrograms b.d. If a patient cannot take desmopressin nasally (e.g. at times of operations) it can be given i.m. It has a longer duration of action by this route and can usually be given once daily (1–2 micrograms).

In cases where cranial diabetes insipidus may be expected to be transient (e.g. in association with acute head injury) i.m. vasopressin or desmopressin, or intra-nasal lypressin or desmopressin may be used temporarily (for dosages see the Pharmacopoeia, p.766).

(ii) Nephrogenic diabetes insipidus

Nephrogenic diabetes insipidus is usually either congenital or drug-induced, lithium and demethylchlortetracycline being the most important drug causes. Because pituitary function is normal there is hypersecretion of endogenous vasopressin and exogenously administered vasopressin is ineffective. Treatment is with a thiazide diuretic (e.g. hydrochlorothiazide 50–100 mg orally o.d.). In patients with lithium-induced nephrogenic diabetes insipidus treatment with a thiazide diuretic causes lithium retention and lithium dosages should be reduced.

25.2. DISORDERS OF THE ADRENAL GLAND

25.2.1. Primary adrenocortical insufficiency

Chronic adrenocortical insufficiency

Chronic adrenocortical insufficiency due to primary disease of the adrenal cortex (Addison's disease) requires treatment with cortisone (12.5–37.5 mg orally o.d.). Most patients also require fludrocortisone

(100–200 micrograms orally o.d.). In contrast, patients with adrenocortical insufficiency secondary to pituitary ACTH deficiency often do not require fludrocortisone.

At times of stress (e.g. during acute infections or at times of operation) corticosteroid requirements are increased and replacement dosages of corticosteroids should therefore be doubled temporarily in order to avoid acute adrenocortical insufficiency. If oral therapy cannot be taken then i.m. cortisone or i.m. or i.v. hydrocortisone should be used instead.

Patients with chronic adrenocortical insufficiency should carry a steroid card (see Fig. 34.2), or preferably should wear some form of identification (e.g. a bracelet or a locket) containing information about their condition. They should also be warned that in the event of an acute stress (e.g. acute infection, a major dental procedure) they should immediately both double the dose of corticosteroid and seek medical advice.

Acute adrenocortical insufficiency

Addisonian crisis is a medical emergency requiring immediate treatment. Salt, water, and glucose replacement should be undertaken using i.v. dextrose (5 per cent) plus isotonic saline. The usual fluid requirement is about 4 l in the first 24 h, 2 l being given during the first 4 h. Subsequently fluid requirements are less and can be judged according to the previous day's urinary output, adding 500 ml for 'insensible' losses (e.g. in sweat, perspiration, and faeces). As soon as possible after diagnosis hydrocortisone should be given i.v. in a dose of 100 mg and this may be repeated six-hourly. At the same time cortisone acetate should be given orally (or i.m. if the oral route is not possible, e.g. due to vomiting), starting with a high dose (e.g. 100 mg) and reducing over the next few days to a maintenance dosage according to requirements.

25.2.2. Adrenocortical hyperactivity

Adrenocortical hyperactivity is known as Cushing's disease when it is due to hypersecretion of ACTH by a pituitary adenoma, and Cushing's syndrome when due to any other cause. The different causes are listed in Table 25.2. The sites of action of drugs affecting steroid synthesis are shown in Fig. 25.1.

Table 25.2 *Causes of adrenocortical hyperactivity*

---

1. *Primary*
Adrenocortical adenoma
Adrenocortical carcinoma

2. *Secondary*
Pituitary adenoma (Cushing's disease)
Drug-induced (ACTH or corticosteroids)
Ectopic ACTH secretion

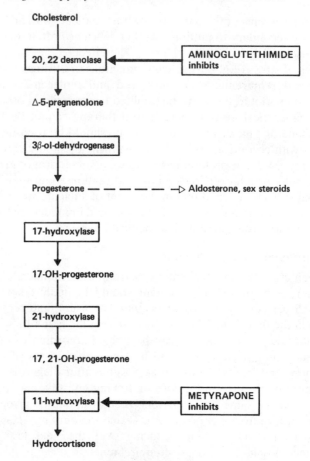

Cholesterol

20, 22 desmolase ◄———— AMINOGLUTETHIMIDE inhibits

Δ-5-pregnenolone

3β-ol-dehydrogenase

Progesterone — — — — — —▷ Aldosterone, sex steroids

17-hydroxylase

17-OH-progesterone

21-hydroxylase

17, 21-OH-progesterone

11-hydroxylase ◄———— METYRAPONE inhibits

Hydrocortisone

Fig. 25.1. The effects of aminoglutethimide and metyrapone on steroid hormone biosynthesis.

Where possible the lesion causing adrenocortical hyperactivity should be removed surgically—this applies to primary adrenal tumours, pituitary tumours, and primary tumours producing ectopic ACTH. The following specific drug treatments are also appropriate.

(a) Adrenal adenoma

Metyrapone is given for a few weeks or months before surgical removal of an adenoma in order to inhibit corticosteroid synthesis and thus decrease the risks of surgery by correcting the metabolic abnormalities associated with Cushing's syndrome. After surgical removal replacement corticosteroid therapy will be required for up to 2 years.

(b) Adrenal carcinoma

If surgical removal is not possible or is incomplete the cytotoxic drug mitotane (*o,p*-DDD), which is relatively selective for cells of the adrenal cortex, may be used. It very commonly causes nausea and vomiting, and also commonly causes somnolence, lethargy, and skin rashes. However, these dose-related effects can be reduced by using low dosages and by supplementing treatment with either metyrapone or aminoglutethimide, both of which reduce adrenal steroid production.

(c) Pituitary adenomas

If surgical removal of a pituitary ACTH-secreting adenoma is not possible then bilateral adrenalectomy plus pituitary irradiation are indicated. 'Chemical adrenalectomy' with aminoglutethimide is an alternative to surgical adrenalectomy. Replacement corticosteroid therapy is necessary in both cases, and thyroid replacement may also be necessary.

(d) Ectopic ACTH production

Removal of the ACTH-producing tumour is curative if complete. Otherwise treatment with metyrapone or aminoglutethimide will help reduce corticosteroid production.

25.2.3. Primary hyperaldosteronism

Primary hyperaldosteronism (Conn's syndrome) may be due either to an adrenal adenoma secreting aldosterone, or rarely to bilateral adrenal hyperplasia. If surgical removal of an adenoma is not possible, or in bilateral adrenal hyperplasia producing hyperaldosteronism, spironolactone is used. Antihypertensive drugs may also be required.

25.2.4. Phaeochromocytoma

Surgical removal is the treatment of choice for phaeochromocytoma. Drugs are used either in relation to surgery, or to control the blood pressure in patients in whom surgery is not possible or has not proved successful, or in disseminated malignant phaeochromocytoma.

Before surgery patients should be treated with a combination of α- and β-adrenoceptor antagonists (e.g. phenoxybenzamine 10 mg orally b.d. plus propranolol 40 mg orally b.d.) whether or not they are hypertensive. Treatment with the β-adrenoceptor antagonist should be started only after full α-blockade has been achieved, otherwise severe hypertension may occur because of inhibition of skeletal muscle vascular dilatation.

For anaesthesia methoxyflurane and enflurane are the inhalational anaesthetics of choice, and during surgery phentolamine and noradrenaline should be immediately available for blood pressure control. Severe hypertension can be treated with i.v. phentolamine 1–5 mg as required. Tachycardias and ventricular ectopic arrhythmias can be treated with i.v. propranolol 0.5–1 mg as required. If the blood pressure falls after removal of the tumour it should be maintained using i.v. noradrenaline. If hypertension persists post-operatively it may be treated with a β-adreno-ceptor antagonist.

For patients in whom it has not proved possible to effect a surgical cure long-term medical management is indicated with a combination of α- and β-adrenoceptor antagonists as described above for pre-operative management. In cases which are resistant to this approach an alternative is α-methyl-*para*-tyrosine which inhibits catecholamine biosynthesis in the tumour.

25.3. DISORDERS OF THE THYROID GLAND

25.3.1. Hypothyroidism

The treatment of hypothyroidism is the same no matter what the cause.

In the absence of evidence of heart disease it is usual to start treatment with a low dose of thyroxine, 50 micrograms orally o.d. The dosage can then be increased at 6-week intervals by 50 microgram increments until the serum T_4 (and the TSH in primary hypothyroidism) are normal. The usual maintenance dosage of thyroxine is 100–200 micrograms orally o.d.

In patients with a history of heart disease it is best to start with a lower dose of thyroxine, say 25 micrograms, or in severe cases 10 micrograms. This is because treating hypothyroidism too quickly in such cases may lead to severe angina or myocardial infarction, heart failure, or cardiac arrhythmias. In a few cases it may prove impossible to restore thyroid function completely to normal without incurring severe anginal symptoms.

Rarely hypothyroidism may present as myxoedema coma, which is a medical emergency. There is no universally agreed method of treating myxoedema coma. However the principles are:

(a) the administration of thyroid hormone;

(b) the administration of hydrocortisone; and

(c) adjunctive therapy of dehydration, hyponatraemia, hypercapnia, and infection.

A suggested dosage of thyroid hormone is liothyronine 25 micrograms six-hourly until improvement is seen. Most physicians also give hydrocortisone i.v. in doses of 100–300 mg/day although its efficacy is unproven. The rationale for its use is that the 'hypothyroid' adrenal cortex cannot supply the amount of steroid necessary for the increase in metabolism produced by replacement thyroid hormone.

25.3.2. Hyperthyroidism

(a) Mechanisms of action of drugs which affect thyroid function

The mechanisms of action of drugs which affect thyroid function are illustrated in Fig. 25.2. The thionamides (carbimazole, its active metabolite methimazole, and propylthiouracil) act by inhibition of iodide oxidation, of iodination of tyrosine, and of coupling of the iodotyrosines to form the thyronines, T_3 and T_4. Propylthiouracil also inhibits the conversion of T_4 to T_3 in the plasma. These drugs are used in the long-term treatment of hyperthyroidism and to reduce thyroid function before surgery.

Iodine acts by inhibition of release of T_3 and T_4 by the thyroid into the plasma. It very rapidly reduces thyroid function in this way and is used to treat thyrotoxic crisis (thyroid storm).

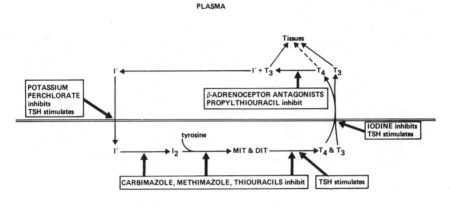

Fig. 25.2. The effects of drugs on thyroid hormone metabolism.

Radioactive iodine (^{131}I) acts by destroying functioning thyroid cells.

The β-adrenoceptor antagonists act rapidly to relieve the acute symptoms of hyperthyroidism. They do so principally by blocking the β-adrenergic effects of the sympathetic nervous system. They also inhibit the peripheral conversion of T_4 to T_3 (Fig. 25.2).

(b) Practical treatment of hyperthyroidism

The *acute symptoms* of hyperthyroidism (tachycardia, tremor, anxiety, and restlessness) can be rapidly controlled using a non-selective β-adrenoceptor antagonist, such as propranolol. Initial dosages should be relatively high (say 80 mg orally t.d.s.) since the metabolism of propranolol is accelerated in hyperthyroidism. If the acute symptoms are not relieved within 24–48 h the dosage of propranolol should be increased. Exophthalmos is unaffected by β-adrenoceptor antagonists. Propranolol is also of value in treating atrial fibrillation in hyperthyroidism, and is often used in combination with digitalis (see treatment of atrial fibrillation, p.320). In patients with heart failure a β-adrenoceptor antagonist may be used cautiously, but should be combined with digitalis and, if necessary, diuretics. For the contra-indications to β-adrenoceptor antagonists see the Pharmacopoeia (p.623).

Treatment with propranolol should be continued until thyroid function has been made normal with an antithyroid drug, and then withdrawn.

Long-term treatment of hyperthyroidism involves three options— antithyroid drugs, radioactive iodine (^{131}I), and surgery.

It is usual in most patients to start with antithyroid drugs, but if there is a large goitre or evidence of local compression then surgery would be preferred. Radio-iodine would be used in such a case if surgery were contra-indicated.

(i) Drug therapy

The full effects of drug therapy take several weeks to occur. Carbimazole (in the UK) or methimazole (in the USA) are the drugs of choice. The initial dosages of these drugs are 10–20 mg orally t.d.s., continuing until the patient is euthyroid (usually after 4–8 weeks). The dose is then reduced gradually to a daily oral maintenance dose, usually of 5–15 mg o.d. If adverse effects occur, such as skin rashes or agranulocytosis, then propyl-thiouracil may be substituted in a dosage of 300–450 mg orally o.d. Although propylthiouracil can also cause skin rashes and agranulocytosis, as well as other blood dyscrasias, cross-reactivity with carbimazole or methimazole is uncommon.

Drug therapy if effective should be continued for at least 12–18 months and then withdrawn. After withdrawal the rate of relapse is very high, being about 50 per cent in the first 2 years, with a small continuing rate of relapse thereafter. For this reason all patients should be seen regularly even after treatment has been withdrawn. If relapses occur repeated courses of drug therapy may be given, but in such cases, or in patients in whom serious adverse effects have occurred, surgery or radio-iodine treatment may be preferred.

The important adverse effect shared by all the antithyroid drugs is agranulocytosis. It is uncommon and reversible, but dangerous, and patients should be warned to stop the drug immediately if they develop a sore throat and to consult a doctor for a full blood count. Routine blood counts are not helpful since agranulocytosis occurs rapidly and without warning with these drugs. The treatment of agranulocytosis is outlined in Chapter 26.

(ii) Radioactive iodine (^{131}I)

Treatment with radioactive iodine is virtually always curative if a large enough dose is used. However, there are several disadvantages to its use. Firstly, it is better reserved for men over 40 and post-menopausal women. This is mainly because of the risk of gonadal irradiation, there being little evidence that therapeutic ^{131}I administration is associated with an increased risk of leukaemia or other malignancies later in life. Radio-iodine should not be used in pregnancy nor in breast-feeding women. Secondly, there is a high incidence of hypothyroidism after ^{131}I treatment—about 15 per cent of patients are hypothyroid within 2 years and about 60 per cent within 20 years.

There is no simple way to calculate the optimum dose of ^{131}I for an individual, so that one starts with a therapeutic dose which carries a minimal chance of causing hypothyroidism. Calculations based on thyroid size and on tests of ^{131}I uptake by the thyroid are imprecise, but give some guidance to the first dose that may be tried. The usual dose is 80 micro-curies/g of thyroid (the normal thyroid weighs 20 g), and this can be corrected upwards if the 24 h ^{131}I uptake is also known (e.g. doubled if the uptake is only 50 per cent). Some patients will require a second dose to effect a cure, and a few will require more than two doses. However, the full effects of a single dose of ^{131}I take 6 months to occur and repeat dosage should not be considered for that period of time.

Because of the continuing risk of hypothyroidism follow-up should be indefinite after [131]I. Some therefore prefer to give a large dose of [131]I (e.g. 15 mCi) and start replacement treatment immediately with thyroxine.

(iii) Surgery

Where there is a single toxic adenoma surgical removal is the treatment of choice. Otherwise surgery should be considered in those in whom repeated drug treatment has failed and radio-iodine treatment is undesirable (i.e. pre-menopausal women and men under 40 years of age). It is often proposed when the goitre is very large.

Subtotal thyroidectomy is curative in the majority of cases, but there is a small relapse rate of about 10 per cent overall. Hypothyroidism after operation is quite common, being about 30 per cent in 10 years.

It is important to make the patient free of symptoms and signs of hyperthyroidism before surgery. This can be done by giving carbimazole 30–60 mg orally per day for 8 weeks followed by iodine for 2 weeks (Lugol's aqueous iodine solution containing iodine 5 per cent and potassium iodide 10 per cent, total iodine 130 mg/ml, 0.1–0.3 ml orally t.d.s.). In patients in whom antithyroid drugs have caused serious adverse effects propranolol can be used instead, but it must be remembered that propranolol does not cause remission, but merely controls some of the effects of hyperthyroidism.

(c) Special problems in hyperthyroidism

(i) Pregnancy

Radio-iodine should not be used in pregnancy nor during breast feeding. Pregnancy should be avoided for at least 3 months after a dose of radio-iodine. An antithyroid drug should be used in these circumstances, but since all cross the placenta and can cause fetal goitre or hypothyroidism, very low dosages should be used (< 30 mg/day of carbimazole or methimazole, or 300 mg/day of propylthiouracil), in order to control symptoms without necessarily producing normal thyroid function.

(ii) Thyrotoxic eye disease

Ophthalmopathy may improve with treatment of hyperthyroidism. In severe exophthalmos there may be difficulty in closing the eyes, with consequent drying and corneal ulceration. 'Artificial tears' can help in these cases—1 per cent methylcellulose drops. Guanethidine eye drops, 5 per cent, applied 1–2 times daily may help to reduce periorbital and eyelid oedema.

In very severe cases a short course of high dosage steroid therapy (e.g. prednisolone 60 mg per day, tapering off after a few days) may be successful. Otherwise surgical treatment may be necessary.

(iii) Thyrotoxic crisis ('thyroid storm')

Thyrotoxic crisis is a medical emergency requiring immediate treatment. It may occur after partial thyroidectomy if the patient has not been properly prepared by preoperative treatment of the thyrotoxicosis (see above) or if hyperthyroidism was not recognized in a patient undergoing any form of surgery; it may also be precipitated by infection, myocardial infarction, thrombo-embolic disease, or other severe stresses of illness. A β-adrenoceptor antagonist should be given parenterally at first, e.g. propranolol 0.5–2.0 mg i.v. six-hourly, followed by oral therapy when signs and symptoms have subsided. Antithyroid drugs should be given in high dosages orally, or by naso-gastric tube if required, e.g. carbimazole 60–120 mg or propylthiouracil 600–1200 mg per day, in combination with Lugol's aqueous iodine solution 0.3 ml t.d.s. Corticosteroids are given to inhibit the peripheral conversion of T_4 to T_3, hydrocortisone 100 mg i.v. q.d.s. or dexamethasone orally or i.v. 2 mg q.d.s. Complications should be treated as required, e.g. dehydration with i.v. fluids, and hyperpyrexia by direct cooling and with chlorpromazine if there is also need for sedation.

25.3.3. Drugs and thyroid disease

Drugs can interact with thyroid disease in one of four ways.

(a) Thyroid function tests

Some drugs can alter thyroid function tests in the absence of thyroid disease (see Table 25.3).

(b) Thyroid disease

Some drugs can cause hypothyroidism or hyperthyroidism. Drugs causing hypothyroidism also frequently produce a goitre because TSH secretion by the pituitary increases in response to the decrease in thyroid hormone secretion. Some important examples of drugs which cause thyroid disease are given in Table 25.3.

Table 25.3 *The effects of drugs on thyroid function tests and on thyroid function*

---

1. *Drugs which interfere with thyroid function tests*
(a) Increased thyroid binding globulin (increased PBI and T_4)—oestrogens and oral contraceptives
(b) Decreased thyroid binding globulin (decreased PBI and T_4)—androgens, salicylates, phenylbutazone, phenytoin
(c) Decreased serum T_3—phenytoin, phenobarbitone, carbamazepine, amiodarone
(d) Increased serum T_4—orphenadrine, amiodarone

2. *Drugs which can cause hypothyroidism*
Aminoglutethimide
Amiodarone
Antithyroid drugs
Lithium
Phenylbutazone
Sulphonamides
Sulphonylureas (chlorpropamide, tolbutamide)

3. *Drugs which can cause hyperthyroidism*
Amiodarone
Iodides

(c) Altered pharmacokinetics

Thyroid disease can alter the disposition and elimination of drugs.

(i) Distribution

The apparent volume of distribution of digoxin is altered in thyroid disease, being increased in hyperthyroidism and decreased in hypothyroidism. The resultant changes in plasma digoxin concentrations after loading doses may partly explain the apparent resistance to digoxin in hyperthyroidism and increased sensitivity in hypothyroidism.

(ii) Metabolism

Important examples of increased drug metabolism in hyperthyroidism are methimazole (and hence carbimazole), propranolol and practolol, and hydrocortisone. The metabolism of propranolol is reduced in hypothyroidism.

(iii) Renal elimination

Glomerular filtration rate is increased in hyperthyroidism and reduced in hypothyroidism. One would therefore expect changes in the clearance of drugs which are mostly excreted by the kidneys (see Chapter 3). Such an effect has been suggested, for example, for digoxin.

(d) Altered pharmacodynamics

There is evidence that the pharmacological effects of cardiac glycosides are increased in hypothyroidism and decreased in hyperthyroidism, independently of pharmacokinetic changes.

The prothrombin time is prolonged in hyperthyroidism and shortened in hypothyroidism, perhaps because of altered catabolism of clotting factors. This leads to reduced requirements of warfarin in hyperthyroidism and increased requirements in hypothyroidism—always be guided by the prothrombin time.

25.4. DISORDERS OF CALCIUM METABOLISM

25.4.1. Hypocalcaemia

The main causes of hypocalcaemia are listed in Table 25.4. The dosages of vitamin D analogues and of calcium salts which are used in the treatment of these conditions are listed in the Pharmacopoeia (pp.770 and 649).

Table 25.4   *Causes of disorders of calcium metabolism*

1. *Hypocalcaemia*	
Hypoparathyroidism	
Vitamin D deficiency	
Renal osteodystrophy	
(see Chapter 24)	
Congenital rickets	X-linked dominant (vitamin D-resistant)
	Autosomal recessive
	(1,25-dihydroxycholecalciferol responsive)
	Autosomal recessive
	(1,25-dihydroxycholecalciferol resistant)
Acute pancreatitis	
2. *Hypercalcaemia*	
Endocrine	Hyperparathyroidism
	Hyperthyroidism
	Adrenocortical insufficiency
Drugs	Vitamin D
	Calcium
	Thiazide diuretics
	Vitamin A
Malignancy	Multiple myeloma
	Metastatic bone disease
	Non-metastatic (hormone-secreting tumours)
Sarcoidosis	

The aims of treatment are to maintain the plasma calcium concentration within the normal range (2.25–2.75 mmol/l, 9–11 mg/dl) and to avoid hypercalcaemia. Thus, measurements of the plasma calcium concentration should be made as often as is necessary.

(a) Hypoparathyroidism

Hypoparathyroidism responds readily to 1α-hydroxycholecalciferol (alfacalcidol) which is converted to the active 1,25-dihydroxycholecalciferol (calcitriol) in the liver. Alternatively one can use calcitriol itself, or dihydrotachysterol. Vitamin D (e.g. calciferol) can also be used but very high dosages are required and the onset of action is very slow.

Calcium supplements are usually also given, since lack of parathyroid hormone decreases calcium absorption and increases urinary calcium loss.

(b) Malabsorption

Alfacalcidol is usually indicated since very high dosages of vitamin D are required and dosage requirements vary enormously. Oral calcium supplements are also given.

(c) Nutritional

Nutritional rickets and osteomalacia, and osteomalacia of pregnancy respond to ordinary dosages of vitamin D.

(d) Anticonvulsant-induced osteomalacia

Since anticonvulsant-induced osteomalacia is probably due to diversion of the relatively inactive precursors of 1,25-dihydroxycholecalciferol it can be treated using alfacalcidol.

(e) Hypocalcaemic tetany

Hypocalcaemic tetany should be treated with i.v. calcium gluconate, 10–20 ml of a 10 per cent solution.

25.4.2. Hypercalcaemia

The causes of hypercalcaemia are listed in Table 25.4.

(a) Emergency treatment of severe hypercalcaemia

Emergency treatment of hypercalcaemia consists firstly of i.v. fluid replacement with saline, and several litres may be required to make good the deficit.

If fluid replacement alone is insufficient then mithramycin should be used. Mithramycin is a cytotoxic drug which in low dosages has a specific effect on osteoclasts and blocks calcium resorption. In a dose of 15 micrograms/kg it can reduce plasma calcium concentrations to normal within 1–2 days.

Mithramycin is locally irritant and causes inflammation if it leaks outside a vein; it should be infused in 1 l of 5 per cent dextrose over 6 h. Nausea and vomiting are common, and it can also cause bleeding, liver damage, and renal damage. The dose of 15 micrograms/kg can be repeated two or three times on consecutive days.

Calcitonin is an alternative which may be given i.v. and has a rapid but short-lasting effect in hypercalcaemia. It is particularly effective in cases where there is an increased turnover of bony calcium, e.g. Paget's disease and hyperthyroidism. It may also be of value in hypercalcaemia due to malignancy, vitamin D intoxication, and hyperparathyroidism. For dosages and adverse effects see the Pharmacopoeia (p.648).

(b) Drug therapy of chronic hypercalcaemia

Where possible the underlying cause should be treated (e.g. parathyroidectomy for parathyroid adenoma). If that is not possible then drugs can be used to produce symptomatic relief, i.e. to lower plasma calcium concentrations without altering the underlying cause.

Oral corticosteroids are effective in reducing the plasma calcium concentration in patients with sarcoidosis, multiple myeloma, metastatic bone involvement, and vitamin D intoxication. Prednisolone may be used in the usual doses (see Chapter 34), starting with 30–60 mg orally per day. Response to corticosteroids is slow, taking about 2 weeks.

If corticosteroids are contra-indicated, or ineffective (i.e. in those conditions not mentioned above) then dietary calcium restriction should be tried and sodium cellulose phosphate can be given in an oral dosage of 5 g t.d.s. with meals. It may cause diarrhoea, and is contra-indicated in patients with renal failure and cardiac failure.

25.5. DIABETES MELLITUS

25.5.1. Mechanisms of action of drugs used in the treatment of diabetes mellitus

The drugs used in the treatment of diabetes mellitus are listed in Table 25.5.

(a) Insulin

Insulin has several different effects on carbohydrate, fat, and protein metabolism through its action on specific cell membrane receptors. It promotes glucose uptake and utilization in fat and muscle, increases hepatic glycogen formation and inhibits gluconeogenesis. It also inhibits lipolysis and increases protein synthesis.

(b) Sulphonylureas

The sulphonylureas act principally by stimulating insulin release from the pancreas, although they may also have some long-term effects by increasing the numbers of cell membrane insulin receptors. They are of no value therefore in treating patients who are severely insulin deficient.

(c) Biguanides

The biguanides have several actions including inhibition of intestinal glucose absorption, inhibition of gluconeogenesis, and an increase in peripheral glucose utilization.

Table 25.5. *Drugs used in the treatment of diabetes mellitus*

1. *Insulin* (p.689)
(a) Short-acting
   Soluble insulin
   Neutral insulin
(b) Intermediate-acting
   Semilente
   Isophane
   Globin zinc
   Biphasic (mixtures)
(c) Long-acting
   Ultralente
   Lente
   Protamine zinc insulin

2. *Sulphonylureas* (p.756)
(a) Most commonly used
   Chlorpropamide
   Glibenclamide
   Tolbutamide
(b) Others
   Acetohexamide
   Glibornuride
   Gliclazide
   Glipizide
   Gliquidone
   Glymidine
   Tolazamide

3. *Biguanides* (p.643)
   Metformin

25.5.2. Practical treatment of the different acute clinical presentations of diabetes mellitus

(a) Acute ketoacidotic hyperglycaemia

This is a medical emergency, requiring immediate treatment. The aims are as follows:

(a) to correct dehydration with *fluid*;
(b) to lower the blood glucose concentration to normal with *insulin*;
(c) to correct acidosis if severe with *bicarbonate*;
(d) to maintain *potassium* balance; and
(e) to treat underlying associated factors (e.g. infections).

Treatment is summarized in Table 25.6.

(i) Intravenous fluids and electrolytes

Patients with diabetic ketoacidosis have the following average deficits: fluid, 5 l; sodium, 500 mmol; potassium 300–1000 mmol; chloride, 350 mmol. These deficits should be corrected as follows:

Table 25.6   *A summary of the treatment of acute ketoacidotic hypergly-caemia*

---

1. *Fluid*
Isotonic saline—1 *litre* in the first 30 min
   1 *litre* in the next hour
   1 *litre* in the next hour
   1 *litre* in the next 2 hours
   1 *litre* in the next 2 hours
   500 ml four-hourly thereafter
Change to 10 per cent dextrose when blood glucose 10–16 mmol/l

2. *Potassium*
20 mmol/h by continuous i.v. infusion in the saline
Reduce to 13 mmol/h if plasma K^+ > 5.0 mmol/l
Withdraw if plasma K^+ > 6.0 mmol/l
Reduce to 13 mmol/h when blood glucose 10–16 mmol/l

3. *Insulin*
(a) 6 i.u./h by continuous i.v. infusion
Reduce to 2 i.u./h when blood glucose 10–16 mmol/l
or
(b) 6 i.u. hourly by i.m. injection after initial dose of 20 i.u.
Reduce to 12 i.u. four-hourly s.c. when blood glucose 10–16 mmol/l

4. *Bicarbonate*
50–150 ml of an 8.4 per cent solution if arterial pH < 7.0

5. *Other measures*
Nasogastric tube
Bladder catheterization
Antibiotics

6. *Monitoring*
Blood glucose—initially, at 2 h after start of treatment, and four-hourly treatment
Plasma potassium—initially and four-hourly thereafter
Arterial pH—initially and again after bicarbonate
ECG—continuously if possible during potassium infusion
General clinical state (pulse, blood pressure, respiration, consciousness)—regularly

---

Isotonic saline should be given by continuous i.v. infusion of 5 l over 6½ h (see Table 25.6), switching to 10 per cent dextrose when the blood glucose falls to 10–16 mmol/l.

Potassium should be given by i.v. infusion at a rate of 20 mmol/h as soon as insulin treatment is begun, even if the plasma potassium is normal, since insulin drives potassium into cells and can rapidly cause hypokalaemia. Check the plasma potassium concentration every 4 h and adjust the rate of potassium infusion accordingly, reducing for example to 13 mmol/h if the plasma potassium rises above 5 mmol/l and withdrawing potassium if it rises above 6 mmol/l. Monitoring the ECG for changes in the T wave is a good way of detecting hyperkalaemia quickly. Reduce to 13 mmol/h when the blood glucose falls to 10–16 mmol/l.

(ii) Insulin

Give soluble or neutral insulin either by continuous i.v. infusion or in repeated doses i.m. By i.v. infusion the rate is 6 i.u./h, reducing to 2 i.u./h when the blood glucose falls to 10–16 mmol/l. By repeated i.m. injection the dose should be 20 i.u. initially followed by 6 i.u. every hour, reducing to 12 i.u. s.c. four-hourly when the blood glucose falls to 10–16 mmol/l.

If the blood sugar does not begin to fall within 2 h of initial insulin administration the insulin dosage by i.v. infusion should be doubled. In the case of the i.m. regimen intermittent i.v. therapy can be tried instead.

(iii) Acidosis

Sodium bicarbonate should be given to correct acidosis only if the blood pH is below 7.0. Usually it is sufficient to give 50–100 mmol (e.g. 50–100 ml of an 8.4 per cent solution) over half an hour, but in severe cases 150 mmol may be required.

(iv) Other measures

Nasogastric tube—because diabetic ketoacidosis causes gastric dilatation a nasogastric tube should be passed if there is impairment of consciousness, to reduce the risk of vomiting and aspiration.

Bladder catheterization—this should be done after 4 h if the patient has not passed urine.

Antibiotics—antibiotics should be used appropriately (see Chapter 20) for proven or suspected infection.

(v) Treatment after the acute phase

Eventual treatment depends on whether the patient's diabetes is insulin-dependent or not, but in the first few days after acute ketoacidosis it is customary to continue treatment using soluble or neutral insulin (e.g. Actrapid®) s.c. q.d.s. Because insulin requirements vary so much from patient to patient this is generally done according to a 'sliding scale' in which the amount of insulin is altered according to the blood or urine glucose at the time. An example of the sort of regimen that might be used at first is shown in Table 25.7.

The technique is as follows: measure urinary or preferably capillary blood glucose (e.g. Clinitest® tablets for urine and BM Stix® or Dextrostix® for blood) four times a day (usually just before meals) and give the dose of insulin appropriate to the concentration. On the following day increase all the doses (except the lowest) by 4 i.u. if the mean blood glucose during the previous day was greater than 10–13.3 mmol/l (180–240 mg/dl) or if there was consistently 0.5 per cent or more of glucose in the urine. It is possible to keep on increasing insulin doses in this way day by day until control is achieved, but with experience it is possible to gauge likely daily requirements within a couple of days.

Table 25.7   *An example of a sliding scale of insulin doses for treatment of diabetes mellitus where dosage requirements are not known*

Urine glucose	Blood glucose mmol/l (mg/dl)	Dose of soluble or neutral insulin (i.u.)
2%	22.2(400)	20
1%	13.3(240)	16
0.5%	10.0(180)	12
0.25%	6.7(120)	8
0	<6.7(<120)	4

The sliding scale can be used either in conjunction with urinary glucose measurements or with capillary blood glucose measurements using impregnated sticks (e.g. BM Stix®), the latter being preferred for accuracy.

Using such a scale soluble or neutral insulin is given subcutaneously four times daily. The scale should be revised daily according to the previous day's responses.

The daily insulin requirement (e.g. the total amount of insulin required to maintain the blood glucose at or below 10 mmol/l) should then be given in one or two daily doses as discussed below under chronic treatment of diabetes mellitus. It is usual to start with doses in the ratio of 1:2, short-acting:intermediate- or long-acting, as a first approximation.

If the patient is known to be non-insulin-dependent or may be expected to be (e.g. an elderly diabetic with no previous history) then it should be possible to withdraw insulin over a few days after once or twice daily therapy has been established, having first instituted treatment with an oral hypoglycaemic drug.

For example, one might start with a small dose of glibenclamide (2.5 mg orally b.d.). One would then reduce each insulin dose by 4 i.u. every day until the blood sugar started to increase above 10 mmol/l. If necessary one would then increase the dose of glibenclamide and continue reducing the doses of insulin. Eventually one should be able to withdraw insulin entirely and continue on the oral hypoglycaemic drug alone.

For details of the chronic overall* treatment of diabetes mellitus see below.

(b) Non-ketotic acute hyperglycaemia

This condition is sometimes called 'hyperosmolar' coma but the term is a little misleading since the plasma osmolarity is also increased in ketoacidosis. The important feature here is the relative absence of ketones, and often there is hypernatraemia (plasma sodium > 150 mmol/l).

Treatment is along the same lines as for ketoacidosis but with some important differences.

(i) Fluid replacement

There is some controversy as to the correct strength of saline to use if there is hypernatraemia. There is a danger of causing cerebral oedema if half-isotonic saline is given rapidly at first because of excessive intravascular sodium dilution, but it is nonetheless clearly desirable to reduce the plasma sodium concentration. A rational approach to this problem is to first replenish the intravascular volume with 1–1.5 l of isotonic saline over about 1 h and then, if there is hypernatraemia, to continue with half-isotonic saline until the plasma sodium falls below 150 mmol/l.

(ii) Insulin dosages
Non-ketotic patients require less insulin than ketotic patients, but the regimens described above involve low dose infusion or repeated low doses intramuscularly, and if regular blood glucose measurements are made the dose can be reduced at the appropriate time (i.e. when the blood glucose falls to 10–16 mmol/l).

(iii) Arterial thrombosis
Non-ketotic patients run a high risk of arterial thrombosis and should be fully heparinized (see Chapter 21, p.343).

Most of these patients will not require insulin after treatment of the acute phase and can be switched to oral hypoglycaemics or even diet alone (see below).

Any drugs which may have precipitated non-ketotic hyperglycaemia (e.g. diuretics, phenytoin) should be reviewed and withdrawn if possible.

(c) Hypoglycaemia
Treatment in the unconscious hypoglycaemic patient is with i.v. dextrose, 50 ml of a 50 per cent solution, repeated if necessary. In severe cases (e.g. hypoglycaemia due to sulphonylurea overdose) it may be necessary to use a continuous i.v. infusion of 10 per cent dextrose to maintain the blood glucose within normal limits. Glucagon may also be used in such cases (1 mg i.v., i.m., or s.c.) but takes several minutes to act and should not be given until dextrose treatment has been started.

In the conscious patient with symptoms of hypoglycaemia (dizziness, sweating, palpitation, a feeling of hunger, tingling round the mouth) dextrose should be given orally (e.g. as a sugary drink, or as a soluble dextrose tablet or sugary sweet). All diabetics and their immediate family should be taught to recognize the signs and symptoms of hypoglycaemia so that immediate treatment can be instituted when necessary.

It is important to note that a single bout of hypoglycaemia may be followed for 24–36 h by poor diabetic control with high blood glucose concentrations. It is important not to increase insulin doses during that time and indeed it is often necessary to *reduce* doses in order to avoid recurrence.

25.5.3. Chronic treatment of diabetes mellitus

Treatment of diabetes mellitus may take one of three forms: diet alone, diet plus oral hypoglycaemic drugs, or diet plus insulin.

The aim of treatment is to control blood glucose concentrations within reasonable limits, avoiding both hyperglycaemia and hypoglycaemia. It is generally accepted at present that it is desirable to maintain mean blood glucose concentrations at below 10 mmol/l (180 mg/dl) and preferably at around 7 mmol/l (125 mg/dl). Although it has not been completely proven, it is generally assumed, and there is experimental evidence to support the assumption, that good control of the blood glucose concentration will result in a reduced incidence of the long-term complications of diabetes mellitus. For this reason, patients should monitor their own therapy, at least by measuring urinary glucose concentrations, or better still by measuring capillary blood glucose concentrations at home. Monitoring of blood glucose in diabetes is discussed in Chapter 7.

(a) Diet

All patients with diabetes mellitus should be given advice about diet. If the patient is overweight then calories should be restricted so that weight may be lost, but even in a patient whose weight is ideal it is desirable to alter the balance of the types of food he or she takes.

Dietary management in diabetes is complicated, but certain simple principles apply:

1. Advice should be tailored to the individual's own habits and abilities. This is important in the elderly in whom it may be totally impractical to alter the dietary habits of a lifetime, and who may not be able to afford to do so.

2. It is not simply the *quantity* of carbohydrate to which the diabetic is exposed but the *rapidity with which it is absorbed* which is important. Rapidly absorbed carbohydrate will lead to high peak plasma glucose concentrations which may cause increased glycosylation of tissue proteins and hence tissue damage. Slowly absorbed carbohydrate will lead to a smoother pattern of lower blood glucose concentrations, despite the same carbohydrate intake. This principle is discussed in Chapter 3 and illustrated in Fig. 3.1. Thus rapidly absorbed carbohydrates (e.g. sugary drinks) should be reserved for hypoglycaemic emergencies. Foods containing slowly absorbed carbohydrates include bread, potatoes, rice, cereals, and pasta.

3. It is generally agreed that dietary fat intake should be reduced, particularly animal fat intake, in favour of carbohydrate. Foods with a high fibre ('roughage') content, such as pulses, raw vegetables, wholemeal bread, and bran as cereals or bran supplements, are also recommended.

(b) Oral hypoglycaemic drugs

For most elderly diabetics ('mature onset' diabetics) oral hypoglycaemic drugs are usually sufficient. It is common at present to start with a sulphonylurea in general, and many use glibenclamide in particular. That is because it has a relatively wide dosage range (2.5–20 mg daily), is metabolized and therefore can be safely given to patients with renal impairment (in contrast to chlorpropamide) and can be given once, or at most twice a day (in contrast to tolbutamide). None of the other numerous sulphonylureas (see Table 25.5) has any established advantage over glibenclamide. Always start at the lower end of the range (i.e. 2.5 mg orally o.d.) and increase the dose at intervals of one or two weeks until control is achieved.

If good control is not achieved with maximum dosage of a sulphonylurea (e.g. glibenclamide 10 mg b.d., chlorpropamide 500 mg o.d.) then it is usual to add a biguanide such as metformin (500 mg orally t.d.s.). However, this addition is unlikely to lower the average blood glucose concentration by more than 1 or 2 mmol/l and many patients who require a biguanide have to go on sooner or later to insulin therapy instead.

Table 25.8 *Important drug interactions with sulphonylurea hypoglycaemic drugs*

Object drug(s)	Precipitant drug(s)	Effect of the interaction
Tolbutamide, chlorpropamide, glibenclamide	Phenylbutazone	Inhibition of metabolism or of renal excretion, i.e. increased hypoglycaemic effect
Tolbutamide (? other sulphonylureas)	Rifampicin	Enhancement of metabolism, i.e. reduced hypoglycaemic effect
Tolbutamide	Salicylates, chloral derivatives, sulphinpyrazone, sulphonamides	Protein-binding displacement, i.e. temporarily increased hypoglycaemic effect (see Chapter 10)
All sulphonylureas (and insulin)	Diabetogenic drugs (corticosteroids, diazoxide, frusemide, thiazide diuretics, thyroid hormones)	Reduced hypoglycaemic effects
All sulphonylureas (and insulin)	β-adrenoceptor antagonists (selective drugs may be safer)	(a) Increased hypoglycaemic effects (b) Inhibition of signs and symptoms of hypoglycaemia (except sweating)
Alcohol	Chlorpropamide	Flushing (see also alcohol in Pharmacopoeia)
All sulphonylureas (and insulin)	Monoamine oxidase inhibitors	Increased hypoglycaemic effects

The major adverse effect of the oral hypoglycaemic drugs is hypo-glycaemia, about which patients should be carefully warned. They should be advised to carry with them at all times a source of rapidly absorbable glucose to take in case of hypoglycaemic symptoms. They should also be told that when in doubt it is safer to take glucose than not.

Other adverse effects occur most commonly with chlorpropamide and include the unusual reaction to alcohol of facial and bodily flushing in about a third of patients. This effect has only rarely been described with other sulphonylureas. Chlorpropamide may also occasionally cause cholestatic jaundice.

Drug interactions with oral hypoglycaemics are important. They are summarized in Table 25.8. Insulin may also interact with some drugs as is also indicated in the table.

(c) Insulin

Insulin therapy is required for young ('juvenile-onset' or Type I) diabetics, and in older diabetics in whom oral therapy has become inadequate. It may also be required in some forms of secondary diabetes.

There are three basic types of insulin regimen.

(i) An intermediate-acting insulin plus a short-acting insulin, given together in the morning and the evening

With this type of regimen the day can be regarded as being split into four sections. The periods after injection (i.e. morning and evening) are controlled by the short-acting insulin, and the other periods (i.e. afternoon and overnight) are controlled by the intermediate-acting insulin. An example of such a regimen would be soluble + isophane insulins morning and evening. In some patients one or even two of the four components of this type of regimen may be unnecessary.

(ii) A long-acting insulin in the morning plus a short-acting insulin morning and evening

The rationale underlying this type of regimen is that the long-acting insulin will provide a continuous background of insulin in the circulation on the top of which short-acting insulins given in the morning and evening provide control of the fluctuations in blood glucose concentrations due to meals. Example of this type of regimen would be lente or ultralente in the morning plus soluble insulin morning and evening.

(iii) A long-acting insulin with or without a short-acting insulin in the morning only

This regimen is essentially the same as (*ii*) above, but omits the evening insulin. It is used for patients in whom the evening rise in blood glucose is not large enough to require an extra dose of short-acting insulin. It is also useful for patients who prefer to use only a single injection a day and is particularly useful, therefore, for the elderly. An example would be lente or ultralente + soluble in the morning. In some patients the short-acting insulin may be unnecessary.

In Table 25.9 are shown the ways in which the dosages of the insulins used in these regimens can be changed in patients who are able to monitor their blood or urine glucose concentrations at the appropriate times. It is usual when altering insulin dosages to make alterations of no more than 4 i.u. at a time.

Table 25.9 *Guidelines for altering insulin dosages according to blood and urine glucose concentrations*

Example (a): a.m.—isophane + soluble 　　　　　　 p.m.—isophane + soluble	
If control poor (e.g. blood glucose > 10 mmol/l) at: 　pre-breakfast* 　pre-lunch 　pre-evening meal 　late evening	Alter dose of: p.m. isophane a.m. soluble a.m. isophane p.m. soluble
Example (b): a.m.—ultralente + soluble 　　　　　　 p.m.—soluble	
If control poor (e.g. blood glucose > 10 mmol/l) at: 　pre-breakfast* 　pre-lunch 　late evening	Alter dose of: ultralente a.m. soluble p.m. soluble

* Remember that hyperglycaemia or excess of glycosuria before breakfast may be a rebound response to nocturnal *hypo*glycaemia in which case the relevant insulin dose should not be increased! A careful history may elucidate symptoms of nocturnal hypoglycaemia (e.g. a drenching overnight sweat or disturbed dreams).

25.5.4. Some practical aspects of insulin therapy

(a) Dosages

Individual insulin dosage requirements vary enormously, but the majority of patients are controlled with total daily doses of between 20 and 60 i.u. When starting treatment with insulin combinations it is usual to apportion a third of the total dose to the short-acting insulin and two-thirds to the intermediate or long-acting insulin. In addition for the regimens involving twice daily intermediate-acting plus short-acting insulins it is usual to start off by giving a third of the total dose in the evening. For example in a patient requiring a total of 60 i.u. of insulin one might give 40 i.u. in the morning and 20 i.u. units in the evening as follows:

　　a.m.—isophane 24 i.u. + soluble 16 i.u.;
　　p.m.—isophane 12 i.u. + soluble 8 i.u.

Fine adjustments to these doses would then be made along the lines described in Table 25.9.

(b) Strength of formulation

As discussed in the Pharmacopoeia (p.689) there has been in many parts of the world a change to insulin of strength 100 i.u./ml, and there are special syringes available (0.5 and 1 ml) graduated in units of insulin. This is now the preferred strength, therefore, since it avoids some of the confusion which arose with weaker preparations (see Pharmacopoeia), and since it reduces the total volume of insulin to be injected.

(c) Formulation

Where the economic climate allows all new diabetics should be treated with highly purified ('mono-component' or 'pro-insulin-free') insulins. Patients who are on older insulins need not be changed to newer insulins unless there is a specific indication (e.g. insulin resistance or subcutaneous lipodystrophy).

(d) Use of the syringe

Patients should be carefully instructed in how to fill the syringe accurately and how to give a subcutaneous injection properly. It is important to avoid intracutaneous injection since that will result in poor diabetic control and local tissue damage at the sites of injection. Disposable syringes may be re-used for up to at least a week without running any risk of infection. Some patients may prefer to change the needle more often if it becomes too blunt. Plastic syringes should be kept in the refrigerator in their original wrapping. Any two different types of insulin may be freely mixed in the same syringe.

(e) Sites of injection

The usual sites of self-injection are the skin over the thighs and abdomen, but the arms may also be used, particularly if a nurse or relative is giving the injection. Whatever the site it is important to alternate the sites of injection (e.g. first left thigh, then right thigh, then lower left quadrant of abdomen, etc.), and to use a different area of each site each time.

(f) Recognition of hypoglycaemia

Most patients will, sooner or later, experience an attack of hypoglycaemia, and it is important that they (and their relatives) learn to recognize the signs and symptoms so that prompt treatment may be instituted when necessary. For this reason it is a common practice for a patient to be deliberately rendered hypoglycaemic in hospital as a demonstration.

(g) Avoidance of complications

As explained above, it is thought that careful control of the blood glucose may result in a reduction in the extent of eventual tissue damage due to diabetes. It is important that this principle be carefully explained to patients to help them understand the importance of careful, regular monitoring.

In addition they should be warned about the dangers of injury to the feet, which can result in ischaemic damage, and in severe cases may lead to the need for amputation. Elderly patients and those with peripheral neuropathy should especially be recommended to attend a chiropodist regularly.

On the physician's part regular checks of the blood pressure and optic fundi are important for the early detection of treatable complications.

25.5.5. Special circumstances in the treatment of diabetes mellitus

(a) Intercurrent infections

During infection insulin dosage requirements increase. Patients should be educated in two important aspects of their treatment at such times (e.g. during a bout of 'flu):

(a) They should increase their dosages as indicated by blood and urine tests during infections (e.g. using the method outlined in Table 25.9).

(b) If they are vomiting or not eating they will still need some insulin to maintain normal metabolism, although total insulin dosages may be reduced. For example a patient taking ultralente in the morning with once or twice daily soluble would continue to take the ultralente but omit the soluble.

(b) Operations

(i) Elective surgery
Diabetics having planned surgical operations requiring general anaesthesia should ideally be first on the operating list in the morning.

For all diabetics treatment should be omitted on the day of the operation and post-operative hyperglycaemia can be controlled using a sliding-scale of the type shown in Table 25.7 until the patient is once more eating and can be given his or her usual dose of oral hypoglycaemic drug or insulin. During long operations a continuous i.v. infusion of insulin and potassium should be given as 3 i.u. soluble insulin/h with 2 mmol potassium/h in 10 per cent dextrose, 100 ml/h. Patients on long-acting insulins should ideally be changed to short- and intermediate-acting insulins before operation. Patients who had a dose of long-acting insulin on the day before the operation may need an extra 10–20 g of dextrose i.v. before the operation.

Patients with poor diabetic control should be admitted early for proper control with short- and intermediate-acting insulins before operation.

(ii) Emergency operation

When diabetic control is required during an emergency operation careful repeated measurements of blood glucose should be made. Good control can usually be attained by giving a low-dose continuous infusion of soluble insulin and potassium in 10 per cent dextrose, 100 ml/h, as described above, provided care is taken to check the blood glucose frequently.

(c) Pregnancy

It is generally agreed that good control of diabetes mellitus during pregnancy improves the outcome for the fetus. Careful control of the blood concentration at or below 7 mmol/l is the aim and this should be achieved with a twice-daily regimen of short- and intermediate-acting insulins. Monitoring should be by blood glucose rather than urine glucose measurements. For details see Chapter 11 (p.185).

25.6. DISORDERS OF LIPID METABOLISM

25.6.1. Mechanisms of action of drugs which lower plasma lipid concentrations

Plasma lipids comprise a group of compounds including cholesterol (esterified and non-esterified), triglycerides, phospholipids, and free fatty acids. Because these compounds are relatively insoluble in water they are found in the plasma either as lipoproteins, or (in the case of free fatty acids) bound to albumin.

Table 25.10 *The lipid and protein content (per cent) of various lipoproteins*

	Content (%)			
	HDL	*LDL*	*VLDL*	*Chylomicrons*
Triglycerides	5	8	50	85
Cholesterol				
Esterified	15	40	15	3
Non-esterified	3	10	7	3
Phospholipid	27	22	18	7
Protein	50	20	10	2

Plasma lipoproteins may be classified in different ways, but the usual method relates to their densities: HDL, LDL, and VLDL (high, low, and very low density lipoproteins respectively), and chylomicrons (of a density similar to VLDL). The lipid and protein content of these lipoproteins is shown in Table 25.10. The main functions of the lipoproteins are as follows:

chylomicrons—transport of exogenous (i.e. dietary) triglycerides;
VLDL—transport of endogenous triglycerides;
LDL—transport of cholesterol to the tissues;
HDL—transport of cholesterol out of the tissues.

The drugs used to lower plasma lipid concentrations are listed in Table 25.11 along with the effects they have on circulating lipids and lipoproteins.

Table 25.11 *Drugs used to lower plasma lipid concentrations and their effects on circulating lipids and lipoproteins*

	Effect of drug on lipid category				
Drug	*Cholesterol*	*Triglycerides*	*VLDL*	*LDL*	*HDL*
Clofibrate (p.662)	↓ or ↔	↓	↓	↓ or ↑	↔
Bezafibrate	↓	↓	↓	↓	↑
Cholestyramine (p.661) and colestipol	↓	↔	↔	↓	↔
Nicotinic acid and nicofuranose	↓	↓	↓	↓	↓
Probucol	↓	↔	↔	↓	↔

Symbols in table: ↑ = increased; ↓ = reduced; ↔ = unchanged.

Clofibrate

Clofibrate and its analogue bezafibrate reduce hepatic cholesterol synthesis and increase the rate of removal of VLDL from the blood. As a result the concentrations of both cholesterol and VLDL fall. Triglyceride concentrations also fall, as may LDL. Clofibrate increases biliary cholesterol excretion, and thus predisposes to cholesterol gallstones.

Cholestyramine

Cholestyramine and colestipol are exchange resins whose main action is in sequestering bile acids in the gut, thus reducing their reabsorption after biliary excretion. In doing so they reduce the inhibitory effect of bile acids on cholesterol metabolism to bile acids. Their effect, therefore, is to reduce plasma cholesterol and LDL concentrations. In some cases a compensatory increase in cholesterol synthesis may obviate the therapeutic effect and this in turn may be prevented by adding nicotinic acid.

Nicotinic acid

Nicotinic acid and nicofuranose have a variety of actions, including inhibition of hepatic lipid and lipoprotein synthesis, and of lipolysis in fat.

They reduce the plasma concentrations of cholesterol, triglycerides, VLDL, LDL, and HDL.

Probucol

Probucol lowers plasma cholesterol and LDL by increasing bile acid excretion (compare cholestyramine).

There are no drugs currently available for lowering chylomicron concentrations.

25.6.2. Practical treatment of disorders of lipid metabolism

Plasma lipid concentrations require consideration in three circumstances:

(a) coronary heart disease in the absence of definitive lipoprotein abnormalities;

(b) secondary hyperlipoproteinaemias;

(c) primary hyperlipoproteinaemias.

(a) Coronary heart disease

Because of the evidence that accumulation of lipids in vascular tissue is an important early step in the development of arterial atheroma, and because of the epidemiological evidence relating increased plasma lipid concentrations to an increased risk of coronary heart disease, it has been thought that the use of lipid-lowering manoeuvres might be of value in either the primary or the secondary prevention of coronary artery disease (see also Chapter 21). To this end two approaches have been used—diet and drugs.

(i) Diet

Plasma cholesterol concentrations can be lowered by reducing dietary intake of cholesterol and saturated fats, and by increasing intake of polyunsaturated fats. Although the results of dietary measures in trials of primary prevention of myocardial infarction have not been conclusive there is a suggestion that cardiovascular mortality in younger age groups may be reduced. However, there is little evidence that dietary intervention is of value in preventing recurrence of myocardial infarction after a first infarct (i.e. secondary prevention).

(ii) Drugs

There is evidence that clofibrate may be effective in the primary prevention of non-fatal myocardial infarction. However, total mortality is not affected and there may be an increased incidence of cholelithiasis and cholecystitis, and an increased death rate from diseases of gallbladder, liver, and intestine. It is currently felt that the risks of treatment with clofibrate outweigh the potential benefits in the individual, and the results of other drug trials are awaited.

The effects of lipid-lowering drugs in secondary prevention have been inconsistent, although clofibrate and nicotinic acid may reduce the incidence of non-fatal infarcts.

At present, therefore, there is no justification for the use of lipid-lowering drugs in either the primary or secondary prevention of coronary heart disease in patients without hyperlipidaemia. Dietary measures can be recommended for primary prevention in young subjects, but it should be noted that the therapeutic efficacy of dietary intervention has not been proven, and its risks are not known.

(b) Secondary hyperlipoproteinaemias

Hyperlipoproteinaemias, particularly hypertriglyceridaemia, may occur secondary to a variety of conditions, including diabetes mellitus, obesity, alcoholism, chronic renal failure, liver disease, and oestrogen therapy. Hypothyroidism, nephrotic syndrome, and renal transplantation may be associated with hypercholesterolaemia in combination with hypertriglyceridaemia.

Treatment in these cases should be by treatment of the primary condition. Lipid-lowering drugs should not be used.

(c) Primary hyperlipoproteinaemias

The primary, genetically determined, hyperlipoproteinaemias are most commonly classified by the Frederickson system as Types I to V. The characteristics of these disorders are shown in Table 25.12 along with the drugs commonly used in their treatment.

The decision on whether or not to treat a patient with primary hyperlipoproteinaemia can be difficult, but the aims of treatment when given, are to decrease the risk of atheroma (Types II, III, IV), and to decrease the risk of acute pancreatitis (Types I, IV, V). In addition treatment may lead to regression of xanthomatous eruptions in the skin and deposits in tendons.

Treatment consists of diet and drugs.

(i) Diet

Obesity should be tackled by reducing caloric intake, and if there is hypercholesterolaemia a cholesterol-lowering diet should be recommended, i.e. one low in cholesterol-containing food and saturated fats, and high in polyunsaturated fats. A low fat diet without cholesterol restriction may benefit Type I hyperlipoproteinaemia. If the cholesterol is not within normal limits after 6 weeks of diet, or if there is hypertriglyceridaemia, lipid-lowering drugs should be used.

(ii) Drugs

Hypercholesterolaemia resistant to diet may be treated with cholestyr-

Table 25.12   *The Frederickson classification of the primary hyperlipoproteinaemias and the drugs used in their treatment*

Type	Cholesterol	Triglycerides	HDL	LDL	VLDL	Chylomicrons	Drugs
I(rare)‡		↑ ↑				↑	(Low fat diet)
IIa†	↑			↑			Cholestyramine Nicotinic acid
IIb†	↑	↑		↑	↑		Cholestyramine Clofibrate Nicotinic acid
III*	↑	↑			Abnormal		Cholestyramine Clofibrate Nicotinic acid
IV*‡		↑			↑		Clofibrate Nicotinic acid
V‡	↑	↑			↑	↑	Clofibrate Nicotinic acid

* Increased risk of coronary heart disease.
† Greatly increased risk of coronary heart disease.
‡ Increased risk of pancreatitis.
Symbol used in table: ↑ = increased.

amine, 12–24 g o.d. or in divided doses, or colestipol, 15–30 g daily in two to four divided doses. If these are ineffective, nicotinic acid or the related compound nicofuranose should be tried. These latter compounds may be particularly useful in those cases of Type IIa, in which plasma triglyceride concentrations rise after cholestyramine, or in cases of Type IIb, in which triglycerides are raised in addition to cholesterol. Dosages are: nicotinic acid, 250 mg o.d. initially, increasing to 1–2 g t.d.s.; nicofuranose, 0.5–1 g t.d.s. These drugs commonly cause flushing in the initial stages of treatment, but tolerance usually develops within a few days. Other common effects include nausea and vomiting, dizziness, hypotension, impaired glucose tolerance, hyperuricaemia, and impaired liver function. In Type IIb clofibrate is an alternative to nicotinic acid to lower triglyceride concentrations if cholesterol concentrations fall in response to cholestyramine or colestipol.

Hypertriglyceridaemia without hypercholesterolaemia may be treated either with clofibrate, 30 mg/kg daily p.o. in two divided doses, or with nicotinic acid or nicofuranose.

Bezafibrate, a clofibrate analogue, and probucol are newer drugs which should at present be reserved for resistant cases or where adverse effects limit the use of the better-established drugs.

26 The drug therapy of blood disorders

26.1. ANAEMIAS

26.1.1. Iron deficiency anaemia

The aims in treating iron deficiency are to remove the cause and to increase red cell mass by giving iron. The main causes of iron deficiency anaemia are listed in Table 26.1.

Table 26.1 *Causes of iron deficiency anaemia*

---

1. *Chronic blood loss*
Gastro-intestinal
  Disease of the gastro-intestinal tract (e.g. hiatus hernia, peptic ulcer, carcinoma of the large bowel, intestinal parasites)
  Drug-induced (e.g. aspirin and other non-steroidal anti-inflammatory drugs; see Table 27.1)
Menstrual (> 80 ml/cycle = 46 mg iron)
Recurrent haemoptysis (e.g. vascular abnormalities, pulmonary haemosiderosis)

2. *Increased requirements*
Pregnancy
Treatment of megaloblastic anaemia

3. *Malabsorption*
Malabsorption syndromes
Post-gastrectomy

4. *Dietary deficiency*

Iron may be given orally or parenterally and in almost all patients the oral route is satisfactory. Iron in oral preparations is in the ferrous form since that is the form in which it is absorbed. Most of the iron so given is absorbed from the upper jejunum. Normal dietary iron absorption is 1–2 mg from a dietary intake of 10–20 mg. This absorption balances the daily loss which is mainly due to sloughing of cells from the gastro-intestinal tract and skin, and to urinary loss. In iron deficiency gastro-intestinal iron absorption increases but is not sufficient to replace losses due to, say, bleeding from a hiatus hernia.

The total body iron deficit may be roughly calculated from the following equation:

iron deficit = Hb deficit × body weight × 0.65 × 3.4
  (mg)   (g/dl)   (kg)   (dl/kg)   (mg/g)

This equation derives from the fact that the normal blood volume is 65 ml/kg (i.e. 0.65 dl/kg) and the amount of iron in 1 g of haemoglobin is 3.4 mg. Thus in a 70 kg man with a haemoglobin of 8 g/dl (normal 15.5 g/dl) the deficit would be:

(15.5–8) × 70 × 0.65 × 3.4 = 1160 mg.

The normal total body iron content is 3–5 g so that such a deficit is a major one.

(a) Choice of oral iron preparation

The seventh edition of the *British National Formulary* lists 73 different oral iron preparations containing ferrous salts. The following categories are available:

ferrous salt preparations in fluid formulations, ordinary tablets and capsules, and slow-release tablets and capsules;
formulations containing both a ferrous salt and folic acid (for use in pregnancy);
formulations containing both a ferrous salt and a wide variety of different vitamins and minerals.

The ranges of amounts of iron available in unit dosage form of these different formulations are given in Table 26.2.

The total daily dose of elemental iron should usually be 150–300 mg. Dose for dose there is no difference among the different available salts, so that one's choice of preparation is dictated by three things—patient acceptability, efficacy, and cost.

(i) Patient acceptability

Two main factors influence patient acceptability of ferrous formulations. The major factor is adverse effects, particularly gastro-intestinal disturbances (e.g. nausea, abdominal discomfort, diarrhoea, or constipation). The other factor is compliance—once-a-day therapy is more likely to be acceptable than thrice-a-day therapy. These factors may lead patients to prefer slow-release formulations, but these have disadvantages as discussed below.

Table 26.2   *A summary of the elemental iron content of a wide variety of iron formulations*

Type of formulation	Ferrous salts available	Range of elemental iron content (mg/dose*)	Comments
1. *Iron alone*			
(a) Elixirs and mixtures	Sulphate, fumarate, succinate, and glycine sulphate	12–45	
(b) Tablets and capsules	Sulphate, fumarate, gluconate, succinate, and glycine sulphate	35–100	
(c) Slow-release formulations	Sulphate and glycine sulphate	45–105	
2. *Iron + folic acid*			
(a) Tablets and capsules	Sulphate, fumarate, gluconate, and glycine sulphate	35–100	Folic acid 150–1700 µg
(b) Slow-release formulations	Sulphate, fumarate, and glycine sulphate	45–110	Folic acid 350–500 µg
3. *Iron + minerals/vitamins*			
(a) Elixirs	Sulphate, gluconate, and glycine sulphate	35–60	
(b) Tablets and capsules	Sulphate, fumarate, gluconate, succinate, and glycine sulphate	25–100	Most contain vitamin C and members of the vitamin B complex. A few contain folic acid.
(c) Slow-release formulations	Sulphate and fumarate	45–100	

* One tablet, one capsule, or 5 ml of fluid.

(ii) Efficacy

The efficacy of an iron preparation depends on how much of its iron content is released in the upper part of the small intestine whence it is mostly absorbed. In this respect fluids and ordinary tablets or capsules are preferable, since slow-release formulations release iron into the gut slowly and iron absorption from such preparations may be variable (e.g. in patients with gastro-intestinal hurry).

(iii) Cost

Here the ordinary tablets and capsules are to be preferred, slow-release and fluid formulations being generally more expensive.

Initially therefore start treatment with an ordinary formulation, such as ferrous sulphate tablets 200 mg (= 60 mg elemental iron) t.d.s. If the patient complains of gastro-intestinal disturbances reduce the dosage to 200 mg b.d. Alternatively a change to ferrous gluconate or ferrous fumarate may help. If the symptoms persist one may be forced to switch to a slow-release formulation. The problem of failure to respond to treatment is dealt with below.

In the prevention of iron deficiency in pregnancy it is customary to give a formulation containing both a ferrous salt and folic acid which acts as a prophylactic against megaloblastic anaemia of pregnancy. The choice of preparation here can be made almost entirely on grounds of cost, since in this case the ordinary tablets or capsules can be used once a day and are generally free of adverse effects. Total iron requirements during pregnancy amount to about 900 mg (i.e. about 3–4 mg/day). This requires a minimum daily intake of 30 mg elemental iron, and this is provided by all the available iron/folic acid formulations (Table 26.2). Folate requirements in pregnancy are increased by four to ten times but normal requirements are so low (about 50 micrograms per day) that only a small daily dose is required. Most iron/folic acid preparations, therefore, contain folic acid in excess of requirements (Table 26.2).

In a patient with established iron deficiency adequate replacement should result, after a delay of a few days, in an increase in haemoglobin of 0.1–0.2 g/dl per day (i.e. about 1 g/dl per week). Treatment should be stopped when the haemoglobin is normal but should be continued if the underlying cause cannot be remedied.

(b) Failure to respond to oral iron

If a patient's anaemia fails to respond to oral iron several possibilities must be considered.

(i) Pharmaceutical
If the patient is taking a slow-release formulation absorption may not be adequate. A switch to an ordinary formulation or to an elixir may help. If poor compliance is suspected then a switch from an ordinary formulation to a once-a-day slow release formulation may help.

(ii) Pharmacokinetic
Absorption of iron may be reduced in malabsorptive states and this may affect medicinal iron as well as dietary iron. Malabsorption of *dietary* iron due to achlorhydria does not affect *medicinal* iron.

(iii) Excessive loss
Continued heavy blood loss may outstrip the rate at which medicinal iron is replacing loss. An increase in dosage, if tolerated, may help (not neglecting the need to treat the underlying cause). In such cases, however, blood transfusion may be required.

(iv) The diagnosis may be wrong
Hypochromic anaemia may be due to causes other than iron deficiency.

If the diagnosis is not in doubt and manipulation of the oral regimen fails to produce a response then parenteral iron therapy should be considered.

(c) Parenteral iron therapy

Parenteral iron should be used only if there is failure to respond to oral therapy in the following circumstances:

excessive adverse effects from oral iron or poor compliance;
malabsorption of oral iron;
continued excessive loss when the underlying cause cannot be remedied, and even then intermittent blood transfusion may be sufficient.

Two parenteral iron preparations are available—iron dextran and iron sorbitol. Iron dextran may be given i.v. and i.m. However, the occasional occurrence of severe allergic reactions after i.v. infusion dictates that the i.v. route be used rarely and with caution. Iron sorbitol may only be given i.m.

The administration of parenteral iron is discussed in the Pharmacopoeia (p.693).

26.1.2. Vitamin B$_{12}$ and folate deficiency anaemia

The main causes of megaloblastic anaemias are given in Table 26.3. If eradication of the underlying cause is not possible then long-term treatment with vitamin B$_{12}$ and/or folic acid will be necessary.

(a) Pernicious anaemia

Daily requirements of vitamin B$_{12}$ are 2–5 micrograms and total body stores are 2000–5000 micrograms. Treatment therefore consists of giving large doses of vitamin B$_{12}$ initially to replenish body stores and thereafter to give large doses intermittently at long intervals. Vitamin B$_{12}$ is the term used for a variety of different cobalamins. Hydroxocobalamin is now the preparation of choice in the treatment of vitamin B$_{12}$ deficiency and it is converted in the body to adenosylcobalamin. It is given in a dosage of 1000 micrograms i.m. every 2–3 days to a total of six doses, followed by a single injection of 1000 micrograms every 3 months for life.

The response to initial therapy with hydroxocobalamin is very rapid, and reticulocyte counts start to rise within 3 or 4 days, reaching a maximum in 6–8 days, and gradually returning to normal in 2–3 weeks. The height of the reticulocyte response depends on the severity of the anaemia and in severe cases may reach 40–50 per cent. Haemoglobin then returns to normal within 5–6 weeks, as do platelet and white cell counts.

If red cell production is very fast iron stores may be depleted, due to excessive demands. If iron deficiency results during treatment of pernicious anaemia, or if you suspect that body iron stores may already be depleted (e.g. in a woman with heavy menstrual periods) then treatment with oral iron should be given (e.g. ferrous sulphate 200 mg b.d.).

Table 26.3 *Causes of megaloblastic anaemia*

1. *Vitamin B$_{12}$ deficiency*

(a) Malabsorption
  Gastric causes
    Pernicious anaemia
    Gastrectomy
  Intestinal causes
    Stagnation (e.g. jejunal diverticula, blind loops, ileo-colic fistula)
    Tropical sprue
    Ileal resection and Crohn's disease
    Fish tapeworm (*Diphyllobothrium latum*)
(b) Inadequate intake
  Strict vegetarianism

2. *Folate deficiency*

(a) Inadequate intake
  Dietary deficiency—predisposing factors include old age, alcoholism, and scurvy
(b) Malabsorption
  Coeliac disease
  Dermatitis herpetiformis with malabsorption
  Tropical sprue
(c) Increased demands
  Pregnancy and lactation
  Haemolytic anaemias
  Malignancy and chronic inflammatory diseases
(d) Drugs
  Anticonvulsants (e.g. phenytoin, barbiturates)
  Dihydrofolate reductase inhibitors (e.g. pyrimethamine, trimethoprim, traimterene, methotrexate)

In pernicious anaemia therapy with folic acid is not necessary. Indeed, if folic acid alone is inadvertently given to a patient with pernicious anaemia the neurological effects of B$_{12}$ deficiency may be exacerbated or even precipitated. This underlines the need to make an accurate diagnosis in a case of megaloblastic anaemia.

Blood transfusion in pernicious anaemia should be reserved for those with a haemoglobin below 4 g/dl and evidence of tissue hypoxia, when even the rapid response to hydroxocobalamin would not be fast enough, e.g. in patients with severe congestive cardiac failure, angina pectoris, or evidence of cerebral hypoxia.

(b) Other causes of vitamin B$_{12}$ deficiency

The treatment of vitamin B$_{12}$ deficiency due to causes other than pernicious anaemia is in most cases the same as for pernicious anaemia, but if the cause can be found and remedied (e.g. antibiotic therapy and surgery to remedy bacterial overgrowth in gastro-intestinal blind loops) then hydroxocobalamin therapy need be continued for only so long as is required to return the haemoglobin to normal.

(c) Folate deficiency

Total body folate stores are about 5 mg and daily requirements of folic acid are less than 0.5 mg, a value which is not greatly exceeded by dietary intake. In pregnancy folic acid requirements may increase up to tenfold, and folic acid supplements should be given to avoid anaemia (see iron deficiency above).

In other conditions associated with folic acid deficiency the usual dosage of folic acid is 10–20 mg o.d. orally for a week or two, followed by a maintenance dosage of 5 mg o.d. orally. These dosages will be suitable in all cases of megaloblastic anaemia due to folate deficiency (Table 26.3) except those due to dihydrofolate reductase inhibitors, since they inhibit the conversion of folic acid to its active metabolites. In such cases folinic acid may be used instead, 15 mg orally o.d.

26.2. MYELOPROLIFERATIVE DISORDERS

The myeloproliferative disorders include polycythaemia rubra vera, myelofibrosis, chronic myeloid leukaemia, and acute myeloblastic leukaemia. They are grouped together because of common relationships amongst them. For example, patients with polycythaemia or myelofibrosis may go on to develop chronic myeloid or acute myeloblastic leukaemia.

26.2.1. Polycythaemia rubra vera

In polycythaemia rubra vera there is an increase in circulating red cell mass with an increase in the numbers of circulating white cells and platelets. It must be distinguished from the other causes of polycythaemia, such as those secondary to chronic hypoxia, or to abnormal erythropoietin production by a tumour or renal abnormality.

Treatment of polycythaemia rubra vera is directed at reducing the numbers of circulating red cells and platelets. Three forms of treatment are available—venesection, radioactive phosphorus (^{32}P), and alkylating agents (e.g. busulphan).

Venesection is effective in reducing red cell mass and in some cases may be all the treatment that is required. However, venesection does not reduce the numbers of circulating platelets and does not alter the risk of thromboembolism. The use of ^{32}P and busulphan decreases the numbers of circulating red cells and platelets thus reducing the mortality from thromboembolism, but there is an increased mortality from other causes, particularly haemorrhage (perhaps due to abnormal platelet function). Busulphan should therefore be reserved for short courses of treatment in patients with very high platelet counts (above 800×10^9/l), ^{32}P may be used if short-term treatment is insufficient.

The aim of venesection should be to reduce the haematocrit to between 45 and 50 per cent. Iron deficiency will eventually occur, since 200 mg of iron are removed with every 500 ml of whole blood, but iron treatment should be given only if symptoms of iron deficiency occur.

Busulphan is given in an initial dosage of 4–6 mg orally o.d., reducing to 2 mg o.d. when the platelet count is reduced by 50 per cent. Treatment can be withdrawn when the platelet count falls below 250×10^9/l. The adverse effects of busulphan are listed in the Pharmacopoeia (p.646).

^{32}P is given in a single dose of 3–5 mCi i.v. One dose will be effective in well over half of all patients, but some may need a second dose at 8–12 weeks (2–3 mCi). The main adverse effect of ^{32}P is an increased risk of leukaemia.

Most patients have hyperuricaemia which will require treatment (e.g. with allopurinol 300 mg daily).

26.2.2. Myelofibrosis

Myelofibrosis results in anaemia, splenomegaly, and hepatomegaly. Bleeding may occur because of thrombocytopenia, and gout because of hyperuricaemia.

Treatment is usually symptomatic and may be limited to blood transfusion to keep the haemoglobin at or above 9 g/dl. Busulphan may also be used, especially if there is symptomatic splenomegaly (pain, abdominal swelling, and discomfort). It is given in a dosage of 2–4 mg orally o.d. for 3–4 weeks, followed by 2 mg two to three times a week. The blood count should be monitored regularly.

Allopurinol may be used to treat hyperuricaemia.

26.2.3. Chronic myeloid and acute myelogenous leukaemias (see also Chapter 33)

It is beyond our scope to discuss the treatment of leukaemias in detail. The principles of cancer chemotherapy are outlined in Chapter 33 and we shall limit ourselves here to a few observations on the drugs used in chronic myeloid and acute myelogenous leukaemias.

In *chronic myeloid (or granulocytic) leukaemia* the aim of drug therapy is to treat symptoms, since current drug therapy does not prolong survival. Reduction of the circulating load of neoplastic cells and of spleen size produces symptomatic relief and this can be achieved with busulphan. One recommended regimen is to give 4–6 mg orally o.d. until the white cell count is 10×10^9/l; then withhold treatment until the count is 25×10^9/l and repeat. The alternative to busulphan is hydroxyurea (0.5–2 g orally o.d.). It may be of value in those who develop pulmonary fibrosis or thrombocytopenia on busulphan. Since it is cleared unchanged via the urine dosages should be reduced in renal failure. Its major adverse effects are those of all other cytotoxic drugs (see p.595). Drug treatment is preferable to splenic irradiation. Hyperuricaemia should be treated with allopurinol.

The term *acute myelogenous leukaemias* encompasses several different varieties of leukaemias, including monocytic, myelomonocytic, and different forms of promyelocytic leukaemias. They are also called 'non-lymphoblastic' leukaemias.

The ideal aims of treatment in each case are to produce a *complete* haematological remission and then to treat relapses. Cytarabine is the most useful drug used to induce a remission, and it is generally combined with daunorubicin in which case remission can be achieved in 60 per cent of cases. A typical dosage regimen would be as follows: daunorubicin 45 mg/m^2 i.v. for 3 days plus cytarabine 100 mg/m^2 by i.v. infusion o.d. for 7 days; repeat every 4 weeks until remission is obtained.

Regimens of this sort improve survival from a few months to a few years. The use of drugs to try to maintain remissions once induced has not been successful in prolonging survival time.

Supportive therapy is often necessary in these patients to treat anaemia, bleeding due to thrombocytopenia, and infections (see below).

Allopurinol should be used to treat or prevent hyperuricaemia.

26.3. LYMPHOPROLIFERATIVE DISORDERS

The term lymphoproliferative disorders is used to describe the group of malignancies arising from lymphatic tissue. These disorders include acute lymphoblastic leukaemia, chronic lymphocytic leukaemia, and the lymphomas (Hodgkin's and non-Hodgkin's lymphomas).

26.3.1. Acute lymphoblastic leukaemia (see also Chapter 33)

The aims of treatment of acute lymphoblastic leukaemia, which most commonly affects children and young adolescents, are to induce a haematological remission, to maintain that remission, and to eradicate leukaemic cells from the CNS or to prevent their invasion there. Examples of typical regimens used are given in Chapter 33 (p.597).

(a) Induction

Induction is commonly carried out using vincristine and prednisolone. The addition of daunorubicin or L-asparaginase may improve the remission rate.

(b) Maintenance

Maintenance therapy is usually carried out using a combination of methotrexate and 6-mercaptopurine. If allopurinol is being used to treat hyperuricaemia the dosage of mercaptopurine should be reduced from, say, 50 mg/m^2 o.d. to 15 mg/m^2 o.d. Treatment should be adjusted to keep the peripheral white cell count at around $3 \times 10^9/l$. Maintenance therapy is continued for 3 years.

(c) Treatment of the CNS

Two methods are used, often in combination—radiotherapy and intra-thecal methotrexate. This is necessary because systemically administered drugs do not eradicate leukaemia cells from the brain. In some centres methotrexate alone is used because of the long-term adverse effects thought to be due to cranial irradiation.

26.3.2. Chronic lymphocytic leukaemia (see also Chapter 33)

In contrast to acute lymphoblastic leukaemia, chronic lymphocytic leukaemia almost always affects the middle-aged and elderly, and fre-quently needs no drug treatment. The aim of treatment is to reduce the total body load of lymphocytes, but only in patients who have evidence of a marked increase of lymphocytes in the bone marrow *and* who develop anaemia, thrombocytopenia, and neutropenia. Other indications for treat-ment are severe lymph node or splenic enlargement.

Chlorambucil is the drug treatment of choice, in a usual dosage of 0.1–0.2 mg/kg orally o.d. initially, reducing to a maintenance dosage after 3–6 weeks depending on the response. The usual maintenance dosage is 2 mg o.d. Improvement will occur in over 50 per cent of cases.

In patients with auto-immune thrombocytopenia or haemolytic anaemia a short course of prednisolone may be used (60 mg daily initially tailing off to a maintenance dosage as improvement occurs). Prednisolone should also be used before starting chlorambucil in patients who present with features of bone-marrow suppression. Large masses of lymph nodes may require treatment with radiotherapy, and splenomegaly may require splenectomy.

The overall prognosis is not improved by drug therapy, but symptomatic relief can improve the quality of survival, if judiciously used.

26.3.3. Hodgkin's lymphoma

The approach to the patient with a Hodgkin's lymphoma depends on the stage of the disease, as outlined in Table 26.4. The reason for staging is that the prognosis in stages I and II is very good with the use of irradiation only, while in stages IIIB and IV the prognosis is not as good, and chemotherapy is required.

There are several different suitable regimens used in the treatment of Hodgkin's lymphoma, and that currently considered to be the best (the 'MOPP' regimen) is outlined in Chapter 33 (p.598). Remission occurs in over 70 per cent of cases with such regimens, usually by the third to sixth course and there is little evidence that maintenance treatment thereafter improves survival. The 5 year survival is about 75 per cent.

Table 26.4   *Therapeutic approaches to Hodgkin's lymphoma based on staging (Ann Arbor modification of the Rye system)*

Stage	Definition	Therapy
I	Disease limited to one group of lymph nodes or to a single non-lymphatic site	Irradiation of affected sites
II	Disease limited to more than one group of nodes, with or without localized non-lymphatic involvement, all on one side of the diaphragm only	Irradiation of affected sites
III	Involvement of nodes and/or spleen on both sides of the diaphragm, with or without localized non-lymphatic involvement	IIIA Irradiation IIIB Chemotherapy
IV	Disseminated disease	Chemotherapy

These stages are subdivided into Types A (asymptomatic) and B (symptomatic, i.e. weight loss, fever, night sweats).

26.3.4. Non-Hodgkin's lymphomas

In contrast to Hodgkin's lymphoma the non-Hodgkin's lymphomas have a poor prognosis. They may be classified clinically in a similar fashion to Hodgkin's lymphoma, but there is no clear-cut allied therapeutic strategy, mainly because most patients have stage III or IV disease at time of presentation. Histologic classification is therefore used as a guide to treatment. The non-Hodgkin's lymphomas may be classified histologically according to whether they are nodular or diffuse, lymphocytic or histiocytic, and if lymphocytic well differentiated or poorly differentiated.

For the histological types associated with a relatively good prognosis (median survival > 5 yr) no treatment is usually necessary. These include all the nodular lymphocytic types and the diffuse lymphocytic well-differentiated type. However, if the disease is progressive and symptomatic, treatment with a single agent such as chlorambucil may be of value, and is associated with remission rates of over 60 per cent.

For the histological types associated with a poor prognosis (median survival < 3 yr) combination chemotherapy is indicated. A typical example of one such regimen is the 'CHOP' combination:

C = cyclophosphamide 750 mg/m^2 i.v. on day 1;
H = doxorubicin (hydroxyldaunomycin) 50 mg/m^2 i.v. on day 1;
O = vincristine (Oncovin®) 1.4 mg/m^2 i.v. on days 1 and 5;
P = prednisolone 25 mg q.d.s. orally on days 1–5.

This cycle is repeated every 3 weeks to a total of six courses.

In the non-Hodgkin's lymphomas with a favourable prognosis drug therapy does not improve survival but may help symptoms. In the lymphomas with an unfavourable prognosis combined chemotherapy plus irradiation in certain cases may prolong survival. For example, the diffuse histiocytic lymphoma has a median survival time untreated of about a year with a 5–20 per cent 5-year survival. Treatment results in long-term remission in 20–40 per cent of patients.

26.4. MULTIPLE MYELOMA

Multiple myeloma belongs to the group of conditions known as the monoclonal gammopathies, which also includes localized plasmacytomas, Waldenström's macroglobulinaemia, heavy chain diseases, and primary amyloidosis.

In multiple myeloma there is neoplastic proliferation of plasma cells with anaemia, lytic bone lesions, hypercalcaemia and renal failure, and an increased susceptibility to infection. Patients can be classified into those with small, intermediate, or large tumour cell mass, on the basis of haematological, biochemical, and X-radiological findings (Table 26.5). This classification allows one to assess the prognosis before treatment, and to assess the response to chemotherapy. The aims of treatment are to induce a remission, to maintain that remission, and to treat complications of the disease.

Table 26.5 *Prediction of tumour mass in multiple myeloma*

	Small tumour mass	*Large tumour mass*
Haemoglobin	> 10 g/dl	< 8.5 g/dl
Serum calcium*	< 3 mmol/l	> 3 mmol/l
Immunoglobulins	IgG < 50 g/l	IgG > 70 g/l
	or	or
	IgA < 30 g/l	IgA > 50 g/l
Bone X-ray	Normal or one lesion	Many lesions
	(*All* of the above = low tumour mass†)	(*Any* of the above = high tumour mass†)

* Corrected for serum albumin [corrected calcium, mmol/l = measured calcium + 0.025 × (40 minus albumin in g/l)].
† Patients who do not fulfil either of these criteria are classified as having an intermediate tumour mass.

(a) Induction

The best results currently come from treatment regimens involving melphalan.

The following is a typical regimen:

> melphalan, 10 mg/m² orally o.d.;
> prednisolone, 40 mg orally o.d.
> Give for four days and repeat at 4-week intervals.

The dosage of melphalan can be altered depending on the response or the occurrence of toxicity. The dosage should be reduced if there is a fall in the cell count to below 4.5×10^9/l or in the platelet count to below 100×10^9/l. Treatment should be withdrawn if the counts falls below 3×10^9/l (white cells) or 75×10^9/l (platelets). Therapy should also be monitored by regular measurement of haemoglobin, serum calcium (if increased), serum IgG and IgA, and urinary light chain excretion.

Remission rates are about 50 per cent, irrespective of the tumour cell mass before treatment.

(b) Maintenance

If an improvement occurs with induction therapy (a fall to below 50 per cent in the concentration of serum myeloma protein from the pre-treatment value) maintenance therapy should be continued using melphalan and prednisolone in intermittent courses as before. For those with a small tumour cell mass, treatment should be given for 1 year, but patients with a large tumour cell mass may require treatment for longer.

Dosages of melphalan should be reduced in patients with renal failure proportionately with the creatinine clearance.

Survival time in multiple myeloma is dependent on the time spent in remission. Patients with a small tumour mass who respond to therapy have a median survival time of 40–46 months, while those with a large tumour mass and who are unresponsive have a median survival time of 9–14 months.

(c) Treatment of complications

(i) Hypercalcaemia

Hypercalcaemia usually responds to melphalan/prednisolone therapy, but it should also be treated by other methods since it is associated with a high risk of renal damage. A high fluid intake should be encouraged and some recommend the use of frusemide, which increases urinary calcium excretion. However, great care must be taken since dehydration can precipitate renal failure in these patients. In some patients mithramycin may be of value in lowering serum calcium when other methods fail. It is given in a dose of 25 micrograms/kg in 1 l of 0.9 per cent saline by i.v. infusion over 4–6 h. It probably lowers serum calcium by a direct effect on bone and when used in a single dose is less toxic than when used in repeated doses as a cytotoxic agent, e.g. in testicular carcinoma. Local extravasation can cause local irritation and cellulitis. It should not be used in patients with thrombocytopenia since it may impair clotting factor synthesis, thus increasing the likelihood of bleeding. If mithramycin is ineffective calcitonin may be of value.

(ii) Bone pain
Symptomatic relief of bone pain may be achieved with local radiotherapy. If there is bony involvement without hypercalcaemia then bone formation may be encouraged by the use of sodium fluoride (50 mg orally b.d.) with calcium carbonate (1 g orally q.d.s.).

(iii) Hyperuricaemia
Hyperuricaemia should be treated with allopurinol. Allopurinol should also be given for 2 days before starting chemotherapy in order to prevent hyperuricaemia.

(iv) Hyperviscosity
Increased plasma viscosity may cause visual defects, changes in mental state, neurological deficits, or haemorrhage, and should be treated by encouraging a high fluid intake and, if severe, with plasmapheresis.

(v) Renal impairment
Dehydration must be avoided. If renal failure occurs dialysis may be considered.

(vi) Infections
Patients with multiple myeloma are more susceptible to infections because of impaired white cell function and decreased amounts of normal immunoglobulins. If there is any evidence of infection specimens should be obtained for culture and aggressive antibacterial therapy should be started immediately (see below).

26.5. DRUG-INDUCED BLOOD DYSCRASIAS

In this section we shall deal with the prevention and management of drug-induced pancytopenia, thrombocytopenia, and leucopenia.

Drugs can cause selective thrombocytopenia, selective leucopenia (usually neutropenia, or so-called agranulocytosis), or pancytopenia, in which all the formed elements of the blood are affected. They can also cause haemolytic anaemia. Virtually any drug can cause any of these adverse effects, but some do it more commonly than others, and they are listed in Tables 26.6–26.9.

(a) Prevention
Before using a drug which carries a relatively high risk of causing a blood dyscrasia the relative benefit:risk ratio must be assessed. For example, in

the treatment of some infections (e.g. *Haemophilus influenzae* meningitis, typhoid fever) chloramphenicol remains the drug of first choice because it is considerably more effective than other drugs. However, for other infections alternative antibiotics may be equally good or better and the risk of neutropenia from chloramphenicol too great.

In the treatment of malignancies the risk of pancytopenia has to be set against the potential benefit. Assessment of the benefit:risk ratio for various cytotoxic drug combination schedules may sometimes be difficult, and eventually has to be determined by clinical trial.

Table 26.6.   *Drugs which can cause pancytopenia**

Cytotoxic and immunosuppressive drugs (see Table 33.2)
Antibiotics
   Chloramphenicol
   Sulphonamides
   Streptomycin
   Isoniazid
Anticonvulsants
   Hydantoins (e.g. phenytoin)
   Succinimides (e.g. ethosuximide)
   Primidone
   Troxidone
Antimalarial drugs
   Pyrimethamine
Antirheumatic drugs
   Phenylbutazone and oxyphenbutazone
   Gold salts
   Penicillamine
   Colchicine
   Indomethacin
Antithyroid drugs
   Potassium perchlorate
   Thiouracils
   Carbimazole
Psychotropic drugs
   Meprobamate
   Phenothiazines (e.g. chlorpromazine)
   Tricyclic antidepressants (e.g. amitriptyline)
Oral hypoglycaemic drugs
   Tolbutamide
   Chlorpropamide
Others
   Acetazolamide

---

* These drugs can also cause selective neutropenia or thrombocytopenia.

Table 26.7 *Drugs which can cause selective neutropenia*

Drugs which can also cause pancytopenia
Amodiaquine
Antihistamines
Captopril
Metronidazole
para-amino salicylic acid
Phenindione
Sulphasalazine
Thiacetazone

Table 26.8 *Drugs which can cause selective thrombocytopenia*

Drugs which can also cause pancytopenia
Carbamazepine
Chloroquine
*Digitoxin
Mepacrine
Meprobamate
*Methyldopa
*Quinidine
*Quinine
*Rifampicin
*Salicylates
Tetracyclines
Thiazide diuretics

* These drugs may cause thrombocytopenia by a direct effect on circulating platelets, similar to that caused by apronal (Sedormid®), rather than by an effect on the bone marrow (see Chapter 9, p.140).

Table 26.9 *Drugs which can cause haemolytic anaemia*

1. *Immune (i.e. due to the combination of drug hapten with antibody)*
Penicillins and cephalosporins
Quinidine
Quinine
Stibophen
Sulphonamides

2. *Autoimmune (i.e. due to an antibody directed against the red cell membrane)*
L-dopa
Mefenamic acid
Methyldopa
Phenacetin

3. *In association with glucose 6-phosphate dehydrogenase (G6PD) deficiency (see Table 8.1)*

4. *Through altered red cell metabolism (effects enhanced by G6PD deficiency)*
Dapsone
Phenacetin

(b) Identification of patients at risk

This is generally not possible, but patients with a history of drug allergy or of a previous blood dyscrasia should be monitored closely. Any drug known to have caused a blood dyscrasia in a patient should not be used again.

(c) Monitoring

Patients should be warned of the possibility of a blood dyscrasia when the risk is relatively high and should be educated as to the warning signs: general malaise, fever, sore mouth or throat, signs of bruising, haemorrhage (e.g. nose-bleeds), skin rashes.

Regular monitoring of blood counts is necessary for drugs which cause dose-dependent inhibition of marrow function, e.g. cytotoxic drugs. It is of less value for other drugs, since the blood dyscrasia may occur suddenly. A pre-dose full blood count should be done before starting treatment with a high risk drug (e.g. phenylbutazone, chloramphenicol) and at regular intervals during therapy.

(d) Treatment

With cytotoxic drugs careful monitoring of the full blood count will allow anticipation of blood dyscrasias with appropriate adjustment of dosage. However, if inadvertently overtreatment occurs, or if a blood dyscrasia occurs unexpectedly with another drug, the drug should be withdrawn immediately. Unfortunately there are no tests which will identify the causative drug in an unexpected case, and all drugs must be suspected.

(i) Anaemia
Treat anaemia by transfusion to bring the haemoglobin to above 12 g/dl. Transfusion should be repeated if the haemoglobin falls to 9 g/dl.

(ii) Thrombocytopenia
If thrombocytopenia results in haemorrhage, blood losses should be replaced by transfusion. Platelet transfusion may sometimes be necessary to help the patient over an acute haemorrhagic crisis.

(iii) Neutropenia
It is very important to prevent infection in patients with neutropenia and to treat infections vigorously when they occur. Infection in these patients is usually due to the organisms which they themselves carry. The risk of infection with those organisms can be reduced by maintaining scrupulous hygiene. A typical regimen involves daily washing or bathing and regular shampooing with a disinfectant such as chlorhexidine, daily hydrogen peroxide and nystatin mouthwashes, the application of nystatin cream to armpits and groins, and the use of an antibiotic spray (e.g. framycetin) to eradicate nasal *Staphylococcus aureus*.

The use of sophisticated techniques for 'reverse barrier nursing' has not been shown to be of value in preventing infection, but it is common to nurse the patient in a single room and to have as few people as possible concerned with his or her regular care as possible, to reduce the chance of the transfer of organisms.

Prophylactic antibiotics should *not* be used since they may lead to the emergence of resistant organisms.

When infection occurs it should be identified immediately by culture of blood, urine, sputum, and of any obviously infected lesions. Treatment should be begun immediately with bactericidal drugs, without waiting for the results of culture. The antibiotics chosen should, in combination, be effective in treating both Gram positive and Gram negative organisms, particularly *Staph. aureus*, *Pseudomonas spp.*, *E. Coli*, and *Proteus spp.* One recommended combination is gentamicin (80 mg i.m. or i.v. six-hourly, adjusting the dose according to renal function if impaired) plus a penicillin with antipseudomonal activity, such as ticarcillin or azlocillin (e.g. azlocillin 5 g eight-hourly i.v.). When the results of culture and organism sensitivities are known the antibiotics may be changed or supplemented if necessary. Fungal and yeast infections should be treated with oral nystatin, nystatin cream or pessaries, or, if systemic, with amphotericin B. In patients whose infection does not respond to anti-microbial therapy, and whose white cell count is below $5 \times 10^9/l$, granulocyte transfusions may be necessary.

Various drugs have been used to try to accelerate recovery of marrow function but none has proven efficacy. Those which have been used are androgens (e.g. oxymetholone), corticosteroids, and lithium carbonate.

26.6. COMPLICATIONS OF BLOOD TRANSFUSION

We shall not deal in detail with blood transfusion, but a few points are worth making in relation to the prevention and treatment of its complications (listed in Table 26.10).

26.6.1. Immune reactions

Immune reactions to blood products are not uncommon despite careful cross-matching. The most serious, however, is when incompatible blood is transfused. When any transfusion reaction occurs, immediately stop the transfusion and replace the i.v. giving set, but continue infusing with saline to maintain access to the circulation. Check that the correctly labelled blood was being given for that patient and send the packet of blood to the laboratory for repeat cross-matching. If the wrong blood has been given make sure that another patient is not also at risk because of a mix-up. Send blood and urine samples to the laboratory for diagnosis of haemolysis. If haemolysis has occurred then specialist management of shock, renal failure, and disseminated intravascular coagulation may be required. It is most important to maintain renal blood flow in such cases by giving i.v. frusemide 40–80 mg initially, making sure at the same time that the patient remains well hydrated.

Table 26.10   *Complications of blood transfusion*

1. *Immediate*
Acute allergic reactions
   Haemolysis
   Fever
   Anaphylaxis
Air embolism
Circulatory overload
Infections causing acute septicaemia
Hyperkalaemia
Hypocalcaemia (due to excess citrate) ⎫ complications of massive transfusion
Hypothermia   ⎬
Coagulation defects due to dilution of clotting factors ⎭

2. *Delayed*
Infections, particularly hepatitis
Iron overload (transfusion siderosis)
Delayed hypersensitivity
Delayed haemolytic reactions

In the case of febrile or allergic reactions where the correct blood was given and in which haemolysis has not occurred (the commonest form of transfusion reaction) it is usually sufficient to treat by removing the blood and giving an antihistamine (see p.637). In cases of severe allergic reactions hydrocortisone 100 mg i.v. may be required and bronchospasm may have to be treated (see treatment of asthma, p.357). Anaphylactic shock should be treated as outlined on p.606.

26.6.2. Circulatory overload

Circulatory overload causing cardiac failure in patients with a normal intravascular volume is an avoidable complication. Such patients should be given frusemide 20 mg i.v. just before each unit of blood or packed cells. If cardiac failure occurs the transfusion should be stopped and frusemide given i.v.

26.6.3. Complications of massive transfusion

In patients who require large volumes of blood, hyperkalaemia, hypocalcaemia, hypothermia, and bleeding may occur.

Hyperkalaemia may occur because the potassium in the red cells of citrated blood used in transfusion leaks into the plasma. Careful monitoring of children and patients with renal failure must be undertaken to avoid this complication.

Hypocalcaemia may occur because of sequestration of calcium by citrate. Calcium gluconate should be given (10 ml of a 10 per cent solution).

Hypothermia may occur because of the transfusion of a large amount of blood which has been stored at 4°C. It can be avoided by warming the blood before transfusion, but care must be taken during warming not to cause haemolysis by overheating.

If bleeding occurs, because of dilution of clotting factors, an infusion of fresh frozen plasma to replace them should be given.

26.6.4. Transfusion siderosis.

In patients receiving treatment with large amounts of blood repeatedly (e.g. in thalassaemia) iron overload may occur. When the total body load of iron is greater than 0.7 g/kg it causes damage to the tissues in which it is deposited, analogous to the tissue damage found in haemochromatosis, resulting in failure of growth in children, hepatic and cardiac failure, and sometimes endocrine disorders (e.g. diabetes mellitus, hypoparathyroidism).

Treatment is with desferrioxamine as outlined in the Pharmacopoeia (p.673). Vitamin C in an oral dose of 100–200 mg o.d. is given to enhance the therapeutic efficacy of desferrioxamine.

27 The drug therapy of disorders of bones and joints

27.1. ARTHRITIS

Under the heading of 'arthritis' we shall consider the therapy of rheumatoid arthritis (and all its variants, including its involvement in other system connective tissue diseases such as systemic lupus erythematosus), of osteoarthritis, of ankylosing spondylitis, and of soft tissue rheumatism.

Drug treatment in these conditions can be considered in two parts:

1. Control of symptoms by analgesics and non-steroidal anti-inflammatory drugs.

2. Specific measures in rheumatoid arthritis, aimed at controlling the disease process using gold, penicillamine, chloroquine, or azathioprine. (Systemic corticosteroids are now used only infrequently in rheumatoid arthritis.)

27.1.1. Mechanisms of action of non-steroidal anti-inflammatory drugs in relation to arthritis

This is a difficult field of drug therapy. So many non-steroidal anti-inflammatory drugs are on the market that the choice is bewildering. In the list given in Table 27.1 most of the non-steroidal anti-inflammatory drugs available are listed; those asterisked are in the Pharmacopoeia. The student should be acquainted with those drugs marked with a dagger.

There are two aspects of the actions of the non-steroidal anti-inflammatory drugs to consider—their analgesic effect and their anti-inflammatory effect. The analgesic effect of these drugs comes on quickly and goes away within a few hours. In contrast, the anti-inflammatory effect comes on over a few days and requires regular and repeated dosage.

It seems extremely likely that non-steroidal anti-inflammatory drugs produce their anti-inflammatory effects by inhibition of prostaglandin synthesis. Prostaglandins are normally released in inflammatory responses and are involved in the production of hyperalgesia, erythema, and exudation, and are synergistic with the effects of other inflammatory mediators. Non-steroidal anti-inflammatory drugs block the conversion of arachidonic acid to cyclic endoperoxides by an inhibitory effect on the enzyme cyclo-oxygenase, and this results in a decreased production of the prostaglandins, such as PGE_2 and prostacyclin, which mediate inflammatory responses (see Fig.27.1).

Table 27.1 *Non-steroidal anti-inflammatory drugs*

1. *Salicylates* (p.740)
   Aspirin*†
   Benorylate*
   Diflunisal*
   Aloxiprin
   Salsalate
   Trilisate

2. *Arylalkanoic acids* (p.639)
   (a) Phenylpropionic acid derivatives
   Ibuprofen*†
   Ketoprofen*
   Flurbiprofen*
   Fenoprofen*
   Fenbufen
   (b) Naphthylpropionic acid derivates
   Naproxen
   (c) Phenylacetic acid derivatives
   Fenclofenac*
   Diclofenac*
   Alclofenac

3. *Anthranilic acids* (p.635)
   Mefenamic acid*†
   Flufenamic acid*

4. *Pyrazolones*
   Phenylbutazone* (p.729)
   Oxyphenbutazone* (p.729)
   Azapropazone
   Feprazone

5. *Cyclic acetic acids*
   Indomethacin*† (p.687)
   Sulindac
   Tolmetin

6. *Oxicams*
   Piroxicam

*† See text, p.478

It is probably the inhibition of prostaglandin synthesis which is responsible for the gastro-intestinal mucosal damage, peptic erosions and ulcers, and gastro-intestinal bleeding associated with the non-steroidal anti-inflammatory drugs. It is thought that prostaglandins, particularly prosta-cyclin, are involved in the maintenance of the gastric mucosal micro-circulation, and that when their production is inhibited areas of gastric mucosa may become ischaemic and more susceptible to attack by acidic peptic juices, and erosions are thereby formed.

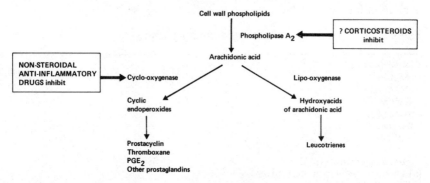

Fig. 27.1. Biosynthetic pathways of leukotrienes and prostaglandins, and the mechanisms of actions of drugs which inhibit their production.

The bleeding tendency produced by non-steroidal anti-inflammatory drugs is caused by inhibition of platelet cyclo-oxygenase. Decreased production of thromboxane interferes with platelet aggregation and there is an increased bleeding tendency, which adds to the dangers of gastric and duodenal erosions.

Inhibition of prostaglandin synthesis in patients taking non-steroidal anti-inflammatory drugs has been demonstrated by showing decreased excretion of prostaglandin metabolites in the urine.

The pharmacological action of the non-steroidal anti-inflammatory drugs is translated into a therapeutic effect by a reduction in pain, tenderness, swelling, and temperature in the affected joints, by decreased stiffness and increased joint movement, and by improved function and strength of movement, as the inflammatory reaction is controlled.

Such clinical improvement can be measured on scales of pain intensity. For instance, one can use visual analogue scales in which a line 10 cm (say) in length is marked at one end 'Pain unbearable' or 'As bad as it has ever been', and at the other 'No pain'. The patient marks the point on the line corresponding to the intensity of the pain at that moment. An example of a visual analogue scale is shown in Fig. 27.2. Such measurements can be quite reliable. Joint size can be measured, for example using rings round the proximal interphalangeal joints. The strength of grip can also be quantitatively assessed. The duration of morning stiffness can be recorded. Walking and general mobility are important. There are indices for assessing the degree of joint inflammation.

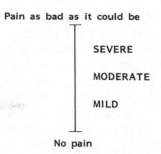

Pain as bad as it could be

SEVERE

MODERATE

MILD

No pain

Fig. 27.2. A visual analogue scale used in rating severity of pain. When the descriptive terms 'severe', 'moderate', and 'mild' are included it is called a graphic rating scale. [Adapted from Huskisson (1974) *Lancet* **ii**, 1127–1131, with permission.]

Last but not least the patient's overall assessment of the effect of the drug (i.e. benefit versus adverse effects) is important. In the end whether or not the patient feels better is the real test of therapy.

27.1.2. Clinical usage of non-steroidal anti-inflammatory drugs

Early on, and with mild rheumatoid arthritis or osteoarthritis, all that may be needed to control symptoms is intermittent analgesia with mild analgesics.

When symptoms become more severe and are not controlled by simple analgesics then non-steroidal anti-inflammatory drugs are prescribed.

There are different therapeutic fashions in various parts of the world as regards first and subsequent choices of these drugs in the treatment of arthritis. While in the USA there are many proponents of aspirin, 600–900 mg six times daily, as first choice, in the UK many rheumatologists feel that these doses of aspirin have an unacceptably high incidence of adverse reactions, and they prefer to start with an arylalkanoic acid derivative such as naproxen, which has a lower incidence of adverse effects and can be given twice daily (e.g. 500 mg b.d.). Alternative first choices might be diflunisal, fenoprofen, flurbiprofen or sulindac. Those who start with an arylalkanoic acid derivative, or for that matter with any non-salicylate anti-inflammatory drug, recognise that if, in adequate dosage, the first choice does not appear to be working well within 2–3 weeks then a switch to another drug is indicated, even a drug of the same class, for example from naproxen to flurbiprofen. Many rheumatologists will then back up the first choice if necessary with indomethacin 100 mg at night (sustained-release tablets and suppositories are available if adverse effects prove a nuisance). This improves morning stiffness and relieves pain at night which can be very distressing. Many patients with rheumatoid arthritis or osteoarthritis may also need, in addition to their non-steroidal anti-inflammatory drug therapy, a further supply of a drug to be used specifically as an analgesic, for example paracetamol ± codeine or dextropropoxyphene. Some patients find that a small dose of aspirin, in addition to their other non-steroidal anti-inflammatory drug therapy, is effective as an acute analgesic while others 'top up' with an extra dose of their non-steroidal anti-inflammatory drug, which can produce extra analgesia for a time.

It may be necessary to try a range of non-steroidal anti-inflammatory drugs. There is great patient variability in response, and it is impossible to predict which drug will be the most effective in an individual. Whatever drug is chosen, however, it is very important to use an adequate dosage. Care should be taken in the elderly who seem to be particularly liable to the adverse effects of these drugs, particularly gastro-intestinal bleeding.

The duration of treatment depends upon the disease. In osteoarthritis there may be short-term symptoms from one or two joints, in which case the treatment can be tailed off. On the other hand the affected joints may cause chronic pain, stiffness, and functional disability, in which case prolonged treatment may be necessary. Physical treatments and surgery may be required in such cases.

In rheumatoid arthritis an acute flare-up may require only short-term non-steroidal anti-inflammatory drug treatment, or the disease may be chronically active, in which case therapy is continued in the long term. If the disease is active and causing serious symptoms and disability after 6 months of what is thought to be optimal therapy then 'disease-modifying' drugs may be necessary (see below).

This then constitutes the approach to non-steroidal anti-inflammatory drug therapy for rheumatoid arthritis and its variants, osteoarthritis, ankylosing spondylitis, and soft tissue rheumatism. In rheumatoid arthritis before considering 'disease-modifying' drugs, problem joints may need special attention, e.g. with intra-articular steroids or orthopaedic procedures.

27.1.3. Mechanisms of action of disease-modifying drugs in rheumatoid arthritis

Certain drugs seem able not simply to relieve the symptoms of rheumatoid arthritis, but actually to alter the course of the disease. These drugs are listed in Table 27.2.

Table 27.2 *Drugs which may modify the disease process in rheumatoid arthritis*

Penicillamine (p.721)
Gold salts: sodium aurothiomalate (p.683)
Chloroquine (p.660)
Corticosteroids (p.664)
Immunosuppressive drugs: azathioprine (p.640)

(a) Penicillamine

It is possible to catalogue some of the actions of penicillamine which might be relevant to its therapeutic effect in rheumatoid arthritis. For example, penicillamine chelates metals, affects cross-linking of collagen, affects the production of some immunoglobulins, decreases the concentrations of some circulating complexes, suppresses lymphocyte stimulation by some agents, and improves neutrophil chemotaxis. None of these, however, convincingly explains its therapeutic effect.

(b) Gold salts

Gold salts are taken up by macrophages. They inhibit phagocytosis and lysosomal enzyme activity. Cell-mediated immune reactions are suppressed. In rheumatoid arthritis they reduce the circulating concentrations of rheumatoid factor and immunoglobulins. Again none of these effects explains fully their therapeutic effect. The mechanisms by which gold produces its adverse effects are not clear either.

(c) Chloroquine

For the pharmacological actions of chloroquine relevant to its therapeutic effect in rheumatoid arthritis and systemic and discoid lupus erythematosus see the Pharmacopoeia. Again the basis of its action is very poorly understood.

(d) Corticosteroids and immunosuppressive drugs (azathioprine)

See the chapter on immunosuppression (Chapter 34).

27.1.4. Clinical usage of disease-modifying drugs in rheumatoid arthritis

What are the indications for disease-modifying drugs? The general indications are:

(a) non-steroidal anti-inflammatory drug therapy for 6 months with continuing active disease or sooner if the disease is very severe; or

(b) progressive disease with deformities, erosions, and worsening disabilities.

Extra-articular manifestations, such as nodules, neuropathy, skin ulcers, and purpuric rashes, may also be indications.

The disease-modifying drugs are toxic and one must therefore have good reasons for using them. Generally specialist advice on this should be sought.

The first choice usually lies between penicillamine and gold.

(a) Penicillamine

The clinical effects of penicillamine are only seen after several weeks of therapy, and over a period of months 75 per cent of patients will be improved. Joint swelling is reduced and nodules disappear. The e.s.r. and rheumatoid factor fall. If after 6 months there has been no response, there is unlikely to be one. In adults 250 mg daily orally is the initial dose of penicillamine, and after 4–6 weeks the dose is increased to 500 mg daily. Some patients may require 750 mg or 1 g daily.

Certain aspects of toxicity are dose-related. The rather high incidence and serious nature of the adverse effects of penicillamine are the main problems. The adverse effects are listed in Table 27.3. Because of these adverse effects clinical supervision of the patients taking penicillamine is very important. This should include monthly examination of the urine, blood count (including platelets), and renal function (blood urea and creatinine).

Table 27.3 *Adverse effects of penicillamine*

Adverse effect	Comment
Anorexia and nausea	Often resolves; do not decrease dosage
Loss of taste	Transient; resolves on continuation
Rash	Stop therapy; lower the dosage; may not recur
Mouth ulcers	Stop drug
Thrombocytopenia	Stop drug if platelet count $< 50 \times 10^9/l$
Pancytopenia	Stop drug
Proteinuria	Observe carefully; monitor 24 h urinary protein and check renal function. Not always necessary to stop therapy
Nephrotic syndrome (proteinuria + oedema)	Stop drug

If the patient tolerates penicillamine then it should be continued for as long as that patient's rheumatoid arthritis remains active, at the lowest effective dose.

(b) Gold salts

Like penicillamine the therapeutic effects of gold salts develop slowly, reaching a maximum after about 4–6 months of treatment.

Gold is given i.m. as sodium aurothiomalate. Initially a 10 mg test dose is given to exlude hypersensitivity. Then sodium aurothiomalate i.m. 50 mg is given weekly until the patient responds, so that if this takes 10 weeks the total dose will be 500 mg. If the disease is controlled the interval between doses can be lengthened to 2 weeks and longer, a change in dosage interval being undertaken only every 6 months because of the time it takes for the effects of increases and decreases in dosage to be reflected in the clinical state.

Again adverse effects are a problem. Rashes occur in about 30 per cent of patients and can lead to exfoliative dermatitis, so that when a rash occurs treatment is usually stopped. As with penicillamine, thrombo-cytopenia, neutropenia, and pancytopenia can occur, and, since they are potentially fatal, treatment must be stopped. Proteinuria and the nephrotic syndrome also occur, and treatment must be stopped.

Like penicillamine therefore gold therapy is fairly toxic and careful supervision in the same way is necessary.

If gold is effective and non-toxic in a patient then maintenance therapy at the lowest effective dose is usually given.

Chloroquine

Chloroquine has the same sort of clinical effects as gold and penicillamine, and is an alternative to them for patients with less severe rheumatoid arthritis in whom the response to non-steroidal anti-inflammatory drugs is suboptimal. It is also used in systemic and discoid lupus erythematosus. It does not prevent progression of bony erosions.

Its main drawback is its *ocular toxicity*. It causes retinopathy, the incidence of which increases as dosage exceeds 250 mg daily for longer than one year. Any patient taking chloroquine should have a full ophthal-mological examination every 3 months. The recommended dosage is chloroquine phosphate 250 mg daily for 10 months of the year.

(e) Corticosteroids

The general anti-inflammatory and immunosuppressive actions of cortico-steroids are dealt with in Chapter 34.

In relation to rheumatoid arthritis it is important to note that:

(a) They may suppress inflammation but do not alter the course of the disease.

(b) They have no effect on the extra-articular manifestations of the disease.

(c) The dosages required to suppress inflammation usually produce Cushing's syndrome with all its serious implications.

(d) Experience shows that initial doses have to be increased to suppress symptoms with consequent increased likelihood of Cushingoid adverse effects.

(e) Once having started patients on corticosteroids it is very difficult to withdraw them.

(f) The adverse effects of excessive corticosteroid therapy can cause as much suffering as the disease.

The general rule therefore is to *avoid* the use of corticosteroids in the treatment of rheumatoid arthritis. With extreme care and keeping in mind all the points made above there may occasionally be a case for their use, as for example when non-steroidal anti-inflammatory drugs have been unsuc-cessful in the elderly. Then small doses of prednisolone (not more than

5–7.5 mg daily), gradually reducing to complete withdrawal over a subsequent period of a few months, can control an acute attack of rheumatoid arthritis. We would advise that such treatment only be instituted by a specialist rheumatologist.

Intra-articular steroids have a special place in active rheumatoid arthritis, being used to relieve symptoms confined to one or two joints. Joint damage may occur with repeated injections.

(f) Immunosuppressive drugs (see Chapter 34)

The action of immunosuppressive drugs like azathioprine is slow in onset like penicillamine and gold. Generally azathioprine or other immunosuppressive drugs are not used until both penicillamine and gold have been tried, and only when the disease process is severe.

Azathioprine is the drug usually chosen in the UK, and it is given in a dosage of 2.5 mg/kg/day. Marrow suppression, infection, nausea, vomiting, and diarrhoea are adverse effects. Full blood counts every month are necessary.

27.2. GOUT AND HYPERURICAEMIA

27.2.1. Mechanisms of action of drugs used in the treatment of gout and hyperuricaemia

The drugs used in the treatment of gout and hyperuricaemia are listed in Table 27.4 and their mechanisms of action are shown in Fig. 27.3. We shall deal here with the mechanisms in relation to the clinical problems.

Table 27.4   *Drugs used in the treatment of gout and hyperuricaemia*

Acute attacks of gout
Non-steroidal anti-inflammatory drugs, e.g. indomethacin (see Table 27.1)
Colchicine (p.664)

Long term control of gout or hyperuricaemia
Allopurinol (p.628)
Probenecid (p.735)
Sulphinpyrazone (p.755)

(a) Acute attacks of gout

(i) Non-steroidal anti-inflammatory drugs
The drugs in this group which are used in the treatment of acute attacks of gout include indomethacin, naproxen, and diclofenac. They have effects similar to their effects in rheumatoid arthritis.

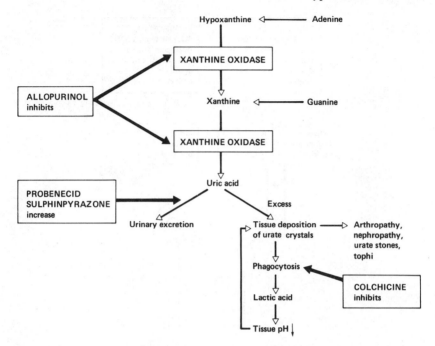

Fig. 27.3. Pathophysiology of gout, and the sites and mechanisms of action of drugs used in its treatment.

(ii) Colchicine

Colchicine is concentrated by leucocytes within which it binds to micro-tubular protein. This is thought to cause inhibition of the migration of leucocytes into the area where sodium mono-urate crystals are deposited in the acute gouty attack, thereby reducing the inflammatory response.

(b) Long-term control of gout and hyperuricaemia

(i) Allopurinol

Allopurinol inhibits the breakdown of xanthines to uric acid. It is not effective in the treatment of an acute attack of gout. It is given to prevent attacks of gout and to prevent deposition of urate crystals in the kidney, thus preventing gouty nephropathy. It also prevents the deposition of urate crystals in other soft tissues and thereby prevents the formation of gouty tophi, and can cause their disappearance.

(ii) Probenecid and sulphinpyrazone

These drugs inhibit the active reabsorption of uric acid in the proximal tubule, and thus increase its urinary excretion (see Fig. 27.4).

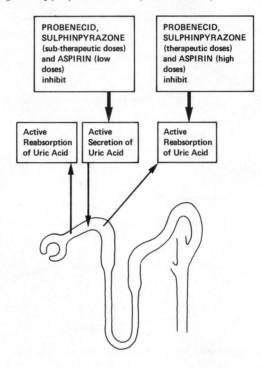

Fig. 27.4. Mechanisms of action of uricosuric drugs on uric acid secretion and reabsorption in the nephron.

27.2.2. Clinical treatment of acute gout

First-choice treatment for a patient with acute gout is now a non-steroidal anti-inflammatory drug, and most would use indomethacin (50–100 mg orally initially, then 50 mg repeated every 4–6 h until the acute symptoms subside). Treatment is then continued with lower doses at longer intervals for about a week (e.g. 25 mg t.d.s.). Headache, nausea, and vomiting are adverse effects.

An alternative anti-inflammatory drug is naproxen, 750 mg initially then 250 mg eight-hourly until the attack subsides.

Colchicine is effective and specific in acute gout, but it causes gastro-intestinal toxicity and in routine therapy of proven gout is now not first choice. It is not easy to use optimally. It should be started as early as possible in an attack since it becomes less effective the longer the attack has proceeded. The initial dose is 1 mg followed by 0.5 mg every 2 h until the pain is relieved, or vomiting or diarrhoea occurs. No more than a total of 10 mg should be given in a single course. Single courses should not be repeated within 3 days.

Systemic corticosteroids have no place in the treatment of acute gout, but in certain circumstances, for example in post-operative gout, or when the above therapy is ineffective ACTH (corticotrophin) is effective (80 i.u. i.m. repeated the next day or after 2 days as necessary). Rebound gout may occur on stopping treatment and colchicine should be given to prevent this (0.5 mg t.d.s. for one week).

27.2.3. Treatment of threatened attacks

Patients who suffer from gout may, despite the preventive treatment described below, still have attacks, and these patients can abort such attacks by the early and judicious use of indomethacin, 25 or 50 mg six-hourly for a few doses when they get the symptoms they recognise as prodromal to an attack.

27.2.4. Long-term management of gout

In a patient with hyperuricaemia (serum or plasma uric acid concentrations >0.42 mmol/l or 7 mg/dl in adult men, or >0.36 mmol/l or 6 mg/dl in adult women) therapy to lower the uric acid concentration should be considered:

(a) if there have been acute attacks of gout;
(b) if there are tophi;
(c) if there is evidence of renal failure.

The choice of drug lies between allopurinol, which blocks the production of uric acid, and one of the uricosuric drugs (probenecid or sulphin-pyrazone), which promote the excretion of uric acid. In both cases the aim is to lower plasma concentrations of uric acid.

Ideally not only should serum uric acid concentrations be measured, but so should the *urinary* uric acid and excretion rate. Then rationally a choice can be made as follows:

(a) If the serum uric acid is high, and the 24 h urinary excretion of uric acid is consistently elevated (on a restricted purine diet) to >3.6 mmol (600 mg) per day then that patient is an overproducer of uric acid and allopurinol is the first choice.

(b) If the serum uric acid is high but the 24 h urinary excretion of uric acid is consistently lower than 2.4 mmol (400 mg) per day then diminished renal excretion of uric acid is present and uricosuric agents may be preferred. Note, however, that uricosuric agents are contra-indicated in nephrolithiasis.

In practice, however, allopurinol is now probably the drug of first choice in all cases. It should not be started within 3 weeks of an attack of acute gout as it may precipitate another attack. The initial dose is 300 mg daily. After 3 months' treatment the serum uric acid concentration should be checked and the dose may have to be adjusted. The usual maintenance dosages are from 200 to 600 mg daily. It is likely that treatment will be life-long. Note that during the initiation of therapy with allopurinol acute attacks of gout may occur and for this reason colchicine 0.5 mg twice daily *or* indometha-cin 25 to 50 mg twice daily should be given for the first 1 or 2 months of allopurinol therapy.

Rashes constitute the most common adverse effect and may necessitate a switch to uricosuric drugs.

Asymptomatic hyperuricaemia is not currently treated unless the serum uric acid concentration is markedly elevated, or if there is a family history of tophaceous gout, or renal or heart disease. Then allopurinol is the treatment of choice.

(a) Uricosuric drugs

If patients are intolerant of allopurinol, probenecid or sulphinpyrazone may be used. They are, however, relatively ineffective in patients with poor renal function.

Probenecid should be started in low dosage and gradually increased, e.g. probenecid 250 mg b.d. increasing to 500 mg b.d. after a week, and then to 2 g daily in divided doses over the next few weeks, depending upon the effect on the serum uric acid concentration, with subsequent reduction in dose if possible to keep the serum uric acid in the normal range.

An alternative to probenecid is sulphinpyrazone, initially 100–200 mg daily in divided doses, increasing to 600 mg daily in divided doses, and then decreasing to a maintenance dose according to serum uric acid concentrations.

Uricosuric drugs should not be given within 3 weeks of an acute attack. Their initial use should be accompanied by prophylactic therapy against an acute attack, using colchicine or indomethacin, as for allopurinol (see above).

During the first few weeks of therapy with uricosuric drugs it is necessary to ensure adequate clearance of the extra urinary load of uric acid, and to avoid uric acid gravel. The fluid intake should therefore be at least 2 l per day, and it may be necessary to alkalinize the urine using potassium citrate or sodium bicarbonate mixtures (see *British National Formulary*), or by giving acetazolamide 250 mg daily at night.

Salicylates must be avoided in patients taking uricosuric drugs since salicylates block their uricosuric action.

Uricosuric drug therapy is contra-indicated in patients with renal failure or uric acid stones and in patients with a history of uric acid stone. It should also be avoided in those patients with high uric acid excretion in the untreated state (urinary uric acid per 24 h >3.6 mmol (600 mg) on a restricted purine diet).

Both probenecid and sulphinpyrazone may cause rashes, and nausea and vomiting. Rarely probenecid may cause a nephrotic syndrome.

(c) Uric acid stones

See Chapter 24 (p.414).

27.2.5. Drugs causing hyperuricaemia and gout

Certain drugs can cause hyperuricaemia and precipitate gout.

(a) Diuretics

The following diuretics inhibit tubular secretion of uric acid:

thiazide diuretics
frusemide
bumetanide
ethacrynic acid.

(b) Aspirin

Aspirin in low doses inhibits tubular secretion of uric acid.

(c) Cytotoxic drugs

During cytotoxic drug therapy of leukaemias and lymphomas, a high rate of cell kill may increase purine production with a consequent increase in the production of uric acid which may result in an acute attack of gout. Allopurinol is often given to prevent this but note that allopurinol inhibits the metabolism, decreases the clearance and therefore potentially enhances the toxicity of 6-mercaptopurine and azathioprine. The dosages of these drugs therefore must be reduced when allopurinol is given.

Table 27.5 *Musculo-skeletal disorders induced by drugs*

Disorder	Drugs associated
Muscle pain, cramps	Diuretics (reduced Na^+ and K^+)
	Clofibrate
	Corticosteroid withdrawal
	Carbenoxolone (reduced K^+)
	Succinylcholine
Arthralgia and arthritis	Drug hypersensitivity, e.g. sulphonamides
Haemarthrosis (can masquerade as acute arthritis or gout)	Anticoagulants
Osteoporosis	Corticosteroids
	Long-term heparin
Osteomalacia	Long-term phenytoin
	Diphosphonates (see Paget's disease)
Aseptic necrosis	Corticosteroids
Gout	Diuretics
	Cytotoxic drugs (see text)
Systemic lupus erythematosus-like syndrome (with joint manifestations; see Chapter 9)	Hydralazine
	Procainamide
	Phenytoin
	Ethosuximide

27.3. MUSCULO-SKELETAL DISORDERS INDUCED BY DRUGS

Muscle pain, joint pain, bone pain, and associated syndromes may be caused by drugs. Some of the more important associations are shown in Table 27.5.

27.4. PAGET'S DISEASE OF BONE

This is undoubtedly the field of the specialist, but it is worth remembering that every patient being seen regularly by a specialist is also under continuing care by the general practitioner who may have to evaluate problems and difficulties ensuing from specialist treatment, and indeed may have to monitor the effects of that treatment.

27.4.1. Mechanisms of action of drugs used in the treatment of Paget's disease

In Paget's disease of bone there is excessive osteoclastic activity leading to resorption of bone. There is also, probably as a secondary response, an increase in bone formation by increased osteoblast activity. So bone destruction is followed by bone formation, and this occurs in an abnormal mosaic pattern of lamellar bone (woven bone). During the end stage of the disease osteoclastic activity declines, sclerosis predominates, and the disease becomes quiescent.

While the disease is active and bone destruction and formation are increased the marrow becomes fibrotic and the whole bone is very vascular. The increased vascularity of bones in Paget's disease may effectively produce functional arterio-venous fistulae with a high cardiac output which rarely may lead to cardiac failure.

This bone pathology leads to:

(i) pain;
(ii) deformity and enlargement of bones;
(iii) fractures;
(iv) neurological problems in the eighth nerve, or nerve roots or spinal cord;
(v) osteosarcoma in affected bone.

Biochemically the increased bone turnover leads to:

(i) raised serum alkaline phosphatase;
(ii) increased urinary hydroxyproline excretion.

Serum calcium usually remains normal but can rise if there is prolonged bed-rest.

The drugs used in the treatment of Paget's disease are listed in Table 27.6.

Table 27.6 *Drugs used in the treatment of Paget's disease*

Non-narcotic analgesics (see drug therapy of pain, Chapter 30)
Calcitonin
Diphosphonates: disodium etidronate

Calcitonin

Calcitonin reduces osteoclastic activity and inhibits bone resorption. This relieves pain. It rarely seems to alter eighth nerve symptoms but can improve nerve root or spinal cord compression. It reduces the vascularity of bone. During calcitonin therapy the serum alkaline phosphatase and urinary hydroxyproline excretion are reduced.

Diphosphonates

Diphosphonates are pyrophosphate analogues, resistant to chemical and enzymatic degradation. They inhibit the growth and dissolution of hydroxyapatite crystals, and retard bone resorption and formation, generally reducing bone turnover.

27.4.2. Treatment of Paget's disease

Indications for specific drug treatment (as opposed to analgesics only) in Paget's disease of bone are:

(a) severe bone pain;
(b) neurological complications;
(c) serious osteolytic lesions in weight-bearing bones;
(d) hypercalcaemia due to immobilization and rapid bone resorption.

Evaluation of drug therapy is based upon the clinical response, standardized radiological measurement techniques, and the serum alkaline phosphatase, urinary hydroxyproline, and serum calcium and phosphate if appropriate.

Calcitonin is probably preferred to disodium etidronate at present, because

(a) we have more experience with it;
(b) etidronate does not regularly heal osteolytic lesions;
(c) if the dose of etidronate is too high it may cause an increase in demineralization of bone and lead to osteomalacia.

Other diphosphonates are being developed and seem less likely to produce demineralization (e.g. dichloromethylene diphosphonate).

Calcitonin (porcine) is given in a dosage of 160 i.u. daily s.c., reducing after 2–3 months to 80 i.u. three times a week. If there is no improvement in pain after 6–8 weeks then stop the calcitonin. If there is improvement continue for a year, stop therapy, and if symptoms recur restart. There are no hard and fast rules and each patient must be treated individually. Antibodies to porcine calcitonin may form, in which case a switch to salmon calcitonin may be indicated. The adverse effects of calcitonin which may occur are nausea, vomiting, diarrhoea, flushing, paraesthesiae, and an unpleasant taste in the mouth. The occurrence of these adverse effects is variable and there does not seem to be other serious toxicity. Points against calcitonin are its expense and the need for injection.

Disodium etidronate is given in a single daily oral dose of 5 mg/kg for up to 6 months and then withdrawn. Food should be avoided for 2 h before and after a dose to improve its absorption. Some advocate the higher dose of 10 mg/kg daily for 3 months, although demineralization of bone is more likely at this dose.

Adverse effects are nausea and diarrhoea. In about 5 per cent of patients there may be an increase in bone pain during the first month or so of treatment. Because of demineralization, an increased incidence of spontaneous fractures may occur at higher dosages.

28 The drug therapy of neurological disorders

28.1. MENINGITIS

The main causes of meningitis are shown in Table 28.1, along with the drugs used in their treatment. The principles of treating infections are outlined in Chapter 20, but there are some additional points worth emphasizing in regard to meningitis.

Table 28.1 *Treatment of bacterial and fungal meningitis*

Organism	Treatment of choice	Alternative
Meningococcus (*N. meningitidis*)	Benzylpenicillin	Chloramphenicol
Pneumococcus (*Strep. pneumoniae*)	Benzylpenicillin	Chloramphenicol
H. influenzae	Ampicillin + chloramphenicol	Chloramphenicol alone
E. coli	Ampicillin	Co-trimoxazole
Staph. aureus	Benzylpenicillin + cloxacillin	Vancomycin
Salmonella spp.	Ampicillin	Chloramphenicol
M. tuberculosis	Rifampicin+ isoniazid + ethambutol	As for pulmonary tuberculosis (see Table 22.5)
Listeria monocytogenes	Ampicillin	Chloramphenicol
Cryptococcus neoformans	Amphotericin B + flucytosine	

28.1.1. Initial treatment

Start treatment as soon as blood and CSF specimens have been obtained. It is important to try to identify the infecting organism immediately by the microscopic examination of a Gram-stained sample of centrifuged CSF, so that appropriate therapy can be given. If, however, the organism cannot be identified start with benzylpenicillin (penicillin G) i.v. and wait for the results of bacteriological culture for further guidance. If the patient is allergic to penicillin start with chloramphenicol i.v.

In children under 6 years of age, in whom meningitis is more likely to be due to *H. influenza* or, in neonates, *E. coli*, start instead with ampicillin and chloramphenicol. Remember to use dosages of chloramphenicol appropriate for children (see pp. 175–6).

28.1.2. Route of administration

All antibiotics used in the treatment of acute meningitis, with the exceptions of co-trimoxazole and those used in the treatment of tuberculous meningitis, should be given intravenously. Use of the intrathecal route is unnecessary, since the drugs commonly used either penetrate well into the CSF normally or do so when the meninges are inflamed (see Table 20.5).

28.1.3. Duration of treatment

Treatment should be continued for 5–7 days after the patient has become afebrile, and the repeat examination of the CSF should show only a few cells ($<50/mm^3$). In pneumococcal meningitis continue to 14 days after the fever has remitted, and for at least 3 weeks in infections with Gram-negative organisms, since the rate of relapse is high in such cases.

28.1.4. Complications of meningitis

In addition to the usual general care of a severely ill patient (e.g. maintenance of fluid and electrolyte balance, maintenance of a clear airway, and prevention of aspiration in the comatose patient) particular complications may need specific treatment. Convulsions should be treated with i.v. diazepam or chlormethiazole. Cerebral oedema may respond to i.v. mannitol (500 ml of a 25 per cent solution, given over 30–60 min); corticosteroids have not been shown to be of value in treating cerebral oedema in patients with meningitis. Headache should be treated with simple analgesics.

28.1.5. Prevention

Patients with CSF rhinorrhoea or otorrhoea are at risk of meningitis, and should be treated prophylactically with penicillin V, 500 mg orally q.d.s. until the leak stops.

Close contacts of a case of meningococcal meningitis (i.e. close family and friends, schoolmates) should be given prophylactic antibiotics. The choice lies between rifampicin (600 mg orally b.d. for 2 days) and minocycline (100 mg orally b.d. for 5 days). Sulphadiazine (1 g orally b.d. for 2 days) is an alternative, particularly in developing countries because it is less expensive, but unfortunately many strains of meningococcus are nowadays resistant to sulphonamides. Immunization with meningococcal vaccines is sometimes an alternative in widespread epidemics.

28.1.6. Tuberculous meningitis

The principles in treating tuberculous meningitis are the same as those for pulmonary tuberculosis (see Chapter 22). Fortunately most antituberculous drugs penetrate the CSF well, the one exception being streptomycin. Treatment can start with rifampicin, isoniazid, and ethambutol for 2 months, continuing with rifampicin and isoniazid for up to a total of 2 years. Because pyrazinamide penetrates the CSF so well some authorities prefer to add it during the first two months. Despite the relatively poor penetration of streptomycin into the CSF some use it i.m. in the initial phase of treatment instead of ethambutol. Intrathecal streptomycin is not required.

All patients with neurological signs should be given corticosteroids during the first few days of treatment (e.g. prednisolone 20–40 mg orally per day), and many would use corticosteroids in all patients, in the hope of minimizing exudation and consequent adhesions in the subarachnoid space.

28.2. PARKINSON'S DISEASE AND PARKINSONISM

Parkinson's disease is so called because it was first described by Sir James Parkinson (1755–1824) in his classic text *Essay on Shaking Palsy* (1817).

Parkinson's disease is characterized by hypokinesia, rigidity, and tremor, and this symptom complex is due to decreased dopamine function in the corpus striatum. When the complex occurs secondary to some identifiable cause it is called Parkinsonism.

28.2.1. Mechanisms of actions of anti-Parkinsonian drugs

The following clinical classification relates to the pathophysiology of Parkinson's disease and Parkinsonism.

(a) Idiopathic Parkinson's Disease

For reasons unknown there is degeneration of the neurones with melanin-containing cell bodies in the substantia nigra. This leads to degeneration of the nigrostriatal neuronal tract for which dopamine is the neurotransmitter at nerve endings in the corpus striatum (caudate nucleus and putamen). There is thus deficient dopamine function.

(b) Secondary Parkinsonism

(i) After encephalitis lethargica
(Post-encephalitic) Parkinsonism may occur, and this too is due to degeneration of nigrostriatal dopaminergic fibres.

(ii) Toxins
Manganese and carbon monoxide poisoning may cause degeneration of the nigrostriatal pathway and striatal dopamine deficiency.

(iii) Drugs
Neuroleptic drugs (e.g. phenothiazines, butyrophenones) are dopamine

antagonists in the corpus striatum and therefore decrease the functional activity of dopamine.

(iv) Cerebrovascular and CNS degenerative diseases

Occasionally secondary Parkinsonism may be associated with cerebro-vascular disease and a range of other CNS degenerative diseases and abnormalities (e.g. Wilson's disease or hepatolenticular degeneration).

All the causes of Parkinsonism result in a decrease in functional activity of striatal dopamine. The corpus striatum is involved in modulating voluntary movements by an effect upon the function of the pyramidal tract motor system (the exact connections are still unclear). This function of the striatum is inhibited by nigrostriatal neurones releasing dopamine in the striatum and stimulated by the release of acetylcholine (onto muscarinic receptors) from excitatory cholinergic neurones within the striatum. There is therefore a functional balance between striatal dopaminergic neuronal activity and cholinergic neuronal activity such that anything decreasing dopamine activity, leaving a relative excess of cholinergic activity, will result in Parkinsonism. Drug treatment is therefore aimed at increasing dopaminergic activity and/or decreasing cholinergic activity. The various drugs used in Parkinson's disease are listed in Table 28.2, and their effects on striatal dopaminergic cholinergic function are shown in Table 28.3.

Table 28.2 *Drugs used in the treatment of Parkinsonism*

---

1. *Acting through dopaminergic mechanisms*
Levodopa (L-dopa) plus a peripheral decarboxylase inhibitor, such as carbidopa (Sinemet®) or benserazide (Madopar®) (p.696)
Bromocriptine (p.645)
Amantadine
Selegiline (p.709)

2. *Acetylcholinergic antagonists (anticholinergics)* (p.616)
Benzhexol
Benztropine
Orphenadrine

Table 28.3 *The effects of drugs used in Parkinson's disease on striatal dopaminergic and cholinergic functions*

	Striatal dopaminergic function	Striatal cholinergic function
Parkinson's disease	↓	Relatively ↑
L-dopa		
Bromocriptine	↑	No effect
Amantadine		
Selegiline		
Acetylcholine antagonists	No effect	↓

Symbols used in table: ↑ = increased; ↓ = reduced

28.2.2. Practical aspects of treatment

When the illness is mild and not at all disabling drugs are not necessary.

(a) Anticholinergic drugs

As symptoms progress, but before they are severe, anticholinergic drugs should be tried, starting with a small dose and increasing gradually. Anticholinergic drugs are the drugs of choice in post-encephalitic and drug-induced Parkinsonism (since in the latter the effects of L-dopa are blocked). In acute Parkinsonian crisis benzhexol or benztropine would be given i.v. (each in a dose of 2 mg).

(b) Amantadine

In mild Parkinsonian illness amantadine (which is thought to cause dopamine release and to inhibit its uptake) may also be effective. Amantadine 100 mg b.d. is given and an effect is usually seen in 3 days. If the disease remains mild its efficacy may continue; as the disease progresses its efficacy tends to wear off. The adverse effects of amantadine include livedo reticularis (a bluish mottling of the skin of the extremities, dose-related), erythema and oedema of the ankles, insomnia, and hallucinations.

(c) L-dopa + a peripheral decarboxylase inhibitor

As the illness progresses, or the above treatment becomes ineffective, therapy with Sinemet® or Madopar® becomes necessary. Again the principle is to start with a low dose, gradually increasing the dose every 2–3 days (see Pharmacopoeia for dosages, adverse effects, and interactions). Remember that the point of the peripheral decarboxylase inhibitor is to decrease the peripheral adverse effects of L-dopa, e.g. hypotension, arrhythmias, and nausea, and to maximise the central anti-Parkinsonian effects (which might also result in central adverse effects such as dystonic movements and psychiatric disturbances). For each individual patient it is a matter of finely tuning the disability and the adverse effects with the drug preparation.

Several problems occur with long-term L-dopa therapy:

(i) Gradual ineffectiveness

Unfortunately L-dopa does not influence the progression and final outcome of Parkinson's disease. It does however prolong survival, improve functional ability very markedly, and greatly enhance the quality of life. Over a period of years in many cases L-dopa therapy becomes less effective and with increasing dosage, adverse effects increase.

(ii) 'Wearing-off' phenomenon

This phenomenon has a pharmacokinetic explanation in that towards the end of a dosage period the patient notes the wearing off of the therapeutic effect as hypokinesia returns. Some patients then benefit from shorter dosage intervals, although usually at the risk of increased dyskinetic reactions.

(iii) 'On-off' phenomenon

This is not related to the pharmacokinetics of L-dopa and consists of a sudden loss of the anti-Parkinsonian effects with consequent rigidity and hypokinesia. The loss of effect occurs irregularly and may last for some hours. The switch 'on' is rapid and unrelated to the dose of L-dopa. The episodes may occur several times a day and be very disabling. Occasionally the 'on-off' phenomenon responds to increased L-dopa dosage or to bromocriptine, but generally is very difficult to treat.

(d) Bromocriptine

Some patients cannot tolerate L-dopa preparations because of adverse effects, and in them bromocriptine may be beneficial. It may also have some use in those patients suffering fluctuations of their clinical illness while on L-dopa. In the uncomplicated case it has no advantages over L-dopa. When combined with L-dopa it tends to produce dyskinetic reactions and confusion.

It should be started at a dose of 1.25 mg at night, and gradually increased to between 40 and 100 mg per day, in divided doses taken with food.

Bromocriptine is a dopamine agonist. It has a wide spectrum of adverse effects in high dosage (see Pharmacopoeia), particularly when combined with L-dopa, and is only moderately effective in the treatment of Parkinson's disease. The reason it is the treatment of choice in the suppression of lactation is that the effective dosage is low, i.e. 5 mg daily for suppression of lactation as compared with up to 100 mg daily for Parkinson's disease.

(e) Selegiline (deprenyl)

There are two main isoenzyme subtypes of the enzyme monoamine oxidase (MAO), Types A and B. MAO is in part responsible for the metabolism of the monoamines 5-hydroxytryptamine, noradrenaline, and dopamine. Type A MAO preferentially metabolizes 5-hydroxytryptamine and noradrenaline. Tyramine and dopamine are metabolized by both Type A and Type B. However, human brain, particularly the striatum, contains a preponderance of Type B.

Selegiline (deprenyl) is a selective Type B MAO inhibitor, and it therefore inhibits the metabolism of dopamine in the striatum. It does not however produce the 'cheese and wine' hypertensive reaction associated with the non-selective MAO inhibitors (see Chapter 10) for the following reasons:

1. Because Type A MAO is still active when selegiline is being given, noradrenaline is still metabolized in the periphery so that sympathetic nerve-ending stores of noradrenaline do not increase.

2. Tyramine, which is the trigger of the hypertensive cheese reaction, is a substrate for MAO types A and B so it is metabolized as it passes through the gut and liver.

Therefore with only inhibition of Type B MAO, tyramine does not circulate after cheese, wine and other foods and there is in any case no excess of noradrenaline to be released from sympathetic nerve endings. There appears, therefore, to be no risk of a hypertensive reaction from this drug.

It has only recently been introduced but it appears to be effective in the following circumstances:

(a) In potentiating and prolonging the anti-Parkinsonian effects of L-dopa, allowing reduction in L-dopa dosage and reduction in peripheral adverse effects.

(b) It may be helpful as adjunctive therapy with L-dopa to prevent the fluctuations of 'wearing-off' and 'on-off', though this has not yet been fully evaluated.

28.3. EPILEPSY

28.3.1. Mechanisms of action of anticonvulsant drugs

An epileptic fit is caused by a paroxysmal disturbance of brain function, consequent upon a brief, unphysiological synchronous discharge of neurones. It is still unclear whether all generalized seizures result from a paroxysmal discharge of a focus of neurones (as occurs in 'focal' epilepsy) with a rapid generalized spread of depolarization, or whether in generalized epilepsy (idiopathic grand mal, petit mal) the discharge can be synchronously generalized.

Anticonvulsants act to prevent the spread of the neuronal excitation by mechanisms that are not fully understood, but which can be roughly divided into those which involve a stabilizing effect on excitable cell membranes, and those which involve an enhanced functional activity of neurotransmitters, such as γ-aminobutyric acid (GABA), which then act to inhibit spread of seizure activity by blocking synaptic transmission at some point.

One or other of these mechanisms has been proposed for all the anticonvulsants.

In Table 28.4 are listed the drugs used in the treatment of epilepsy with a summary of the currently favoured ideas regarding their mechanisms of action.

Table 28.4   *Drugs used in the treatment of epilepsy*

Drug	Membrane effects	Neurotransmitter effects
Phenytoin (p.730)	+	± (5HT)
Phenobarbitone ⎫ (p.726) Primidone ⎭	−	+ (GABA)
Valproate (p.764)	−	+ (?GABA)
Carbamazepine (p.650)	?	?
Benzodiazepines (p.642) ⎫ (diazepam, clonazepam) ⎭	−	+ (GABA)
Ethosuximide	?	−
Paraldehyde	+	−?

All these drugs raise seizure threshold to either electroconvulsive shock or to the convulsant drug pentylenetetrazol (leptazol)

28.3.2. Practical use of anticonvulsants

(a) Which drug for which epilepsy?

The epilepsies have been classified according to whether they are (a) generalized (e.g. grand mal, petit mal, myoclonic seizures) or (b) partial (focal epilepsy). Partial seizures are further subclassified according to whether there are psychomotor symptoms (complex partial seizures, such as in temporal lobe epilepsy) or not (simple partial seizures, such as Jacksonian epilepsy). Although this classification is useful for the specialist who needs to identify patients by specific syndromes, it bears no more than a purely empirical relationship to the effectiveness of anticonvulsant drugs, which is not surprising considering their actions are largely unknown. Here we shall therefore consider the more common types of epilepsy in relation to their treatment. Complicated forms of epilepsy become the treatment province of the specialist.

Some anticonvulsants have been shown to be effective in particular forms of epilepsy and these are listed in the usual order of their choice in each case in Table 28.5.

(b) How should the drugs be used?

The aim of treatment is to suppress fits without impairing mental or motor function, and in children particularly without producing behavioural disorders which may result in difficulties at school.

All the anticonvulsants have a fairly low therapeutic index and it is therefore of paramount importance to tailor dosages carefully in the individual, to try to maximise efficacy while minimizing adverse effects.

For improved compliance once-a-day dosage would be preferable but this may not be possible because of concentration-related adverse effects associated with the peak plasma concentrations occuring after a large single dose. Most antiepileptic drugs can be given twice daily at the most.

Table 28.5 *Drugs of choice in the treatment of particular types of epilepsy*

Type of epilepsy	Drugs of choice
Grand mal	Phenytoin
(generalized tonic–clonic seizures)	Carbamazepine
	Valproate
	Primidone
	Phenobarbitone
Petit mal	Valproate
(generalized absence seizures)	Ethosuximide
Focal epilepsies	Carbamazepine
(temporal lobe and Jacksonian	Phenytoin
epilepsy)	Primidone
	Phenobarbitone
Myoclonic seizures	Clonazepam
	Valproate
Grand mal + petit mal	Valproate
	Phenytoin + ethosuximide

The aim should be to use only one drug, and usually this is possible with careful attention to dosage. A second drug should only be added if the fits are still not controlled (a) in the presence of 'adequate' plasma anticonvulsant concentrations (see Chapter 7) or (b) if there are adverse effects of the first drug of choice. Combined therapy may also be necessary in patients with complex epilepsy, e.g. grand mal together with petit mal.

In order to individualize drug therapy more carefully, plasma or serum drug concentrations should be monitored if relevant and possible. The details of drug dosages and pharmacokinetics can be found in the Pharmacopoeia under each drug heading. In Table 28.6 are shown the usual adult dosages and therapeutic ranges for plasma concentrations of anticonvulsant drugs, and some indication as the usefulness of measuring these concentrations in the practical management of patients (see also Chapter 7).

The dose-related adverse effects of the anticonvulsants are generally sedation, nystagmus, ataxia, and psychological changes, such as confusion, memory loss, and depression. Anticonvulsants can in the individual cause mild mood change and behavioural symptoms.

As an example, consider the details of starting treatment with phenytoin in an adult:

(a) Start phenytoin 300 mg daily (in one dose at night or in two divided doses).

After about 2 weeks, steady-state plasma concentrations should have been reached and the plasma concentration should be measured.

Table 28.6 *Dosages and therapeutic plasma concentration ranges of different anticonvulsants*

Drug	Usual adult dosage range at steady state after gradual introduction	Reported 'therapeutic' plasma concentration range	Usefulness of measuring plasma concentrations
Phenytoin	300–400 mg daily	40–80 μmol/l (10–20 μg/ml)	Must be measured to help individualization of dosage
Phenobarbitone	90–180 mg daily	43–172 μmol/l (10–40 μg/ml)	Only moderately useful
Primidone	500–1000 mg daily	Monitored by measuring phenobarbitone	Not very useful
Carbamazepine	600–1200 mg daily	17–42 μmol/l (4–10 μg/ml)	Useful
Valproate	1000–1600 mg daily	350–700 μmol/l (50–100 μg/ml)	Not very useful
Ethosuximide	1000–2000 mg daily	284–710 μmol/l (40–100 μg/ml)	May be helpful, but base dosage more on clinical response
Clonazepam	4–8 mg daily (in 3–4 divided doses per day)	41–285 nmol/l (13–90 μg/ml)	Usefulness unknown

(c) According to the plasma concentration and the clinical response adjust the dose by 50 mg/day at a time, and not more frequently than every 4 weeks. At each stage repeat the plasma concentration measurement. If plasma concentrations get toward 60 or 70 μmol/l reduce the size of increments in dose to 25 mg/day over 4-week periods because of saturation kinetics (see p.47).

(d) If the patient becomes fit-free there is no need to increase the dose of phenytoin further, but keep a careful watch for signs of toxicity since accumulation of phenytoin can sometimes occur over periods of more than 2–4 weeks.

(e) Use the plasma concentration as a guide to help you to control therapy, but do not alter the dose simply to obtain a particular plasma concentration—treat the patient and the fits. The following examples illustrate this principle:

1. If plasma concentrations on the initial dose of 300 mg/day are in or even below the therapeutic range and the patient is free of fits and of adverse effects do not adjust the dose.

2. If plasma concentrations are about 80 μmol/l and the patient is free of toxicity but still having fits, then cautiously increase the dose, since in some cases freedom from fits may be associated in some patients only when

plasma phenytoin concentrations are greater than 80 μmol/l. In such cases, however, watch carefully for signs of toxicity.

Remember that in patients with reduced plasma protein binding of phenytoin (e.g. in renal failure or pregnancy) the free phenytoin concentration is greater than one would expect from the total phenytoin concentration measurement, and consequently the 'therapeutic' range of plasma concentrations is reduced (see Chapter 10 for a full discussion).

The principles of treating epilepsy with other drugs are similar to those for phenytoin, although without the problems of saturable metabolism. Remember, however, that carbamazepine induces its own metabolism, and after a week or two of treatment plasma concentrations may fall without change in daily dosage.

(c) Continuation of anticonvulsant drug therapy

Some experts advise a cautious and slow withdrawal of anticonvulsants after a fit-free period of 2 years. Others believe that relatively few patients can continue without medication, and that continued anti-convulsant drug therapy is frequently the rule for patients with established grand mal and temporal lobe epilepsy.

In considering whether or not to withdraw anticonvulsant therapy one important point to remember is that, if the patient has a fit while awake he or she will not be allowed, in the UK, to drive a car for a further 2 years. Before withdrawing therapy the implications must be discussed with the patient. The patient should be advised not to drive for about 6–12 months during and after withdrawal.

28.3.3. Status epilepticus

Status epilepticus is potentially fatal and is a medical emergency requiring swift and effective treatment to minimize the risk of brain damage.

There are almost as many methods of treating status epilepticus as there are authorities who write about it and there are preferred methods in individual medical centres. We suggest the following approach:

1. It is essential to establish an airway and to have the patient in a physical environment where he cannot hurt himself.

2. Administer diazepam i.v., if possible as an emulsion (Diazemuls®), 10–20 mg slowly i.v., over 3–6 min. Slow i.v. injections can be difficult in patients having a fit, as can the insertion of i.v. lines, so one copes as best one can.

3. The initial dose is repeated in 30 min if necessary and can be followed by a continuous i.v. infusion of 100 micrograms/kg/h to a maximum of 30 mg/kg body weight over 24 h.

Most status is terminated by i.v. diazepam. Clonazepam i.v. may be more effective than diazepam in the emergency treatment of status but is more likely to produce hypotension and apnoea.

4. If the fits have not stopped various choices are available.

(a) Chlormethiazole

Chlormethiazole is given by i.v. infusion of a 0.8 per cent solution (8 mg/ml), 40–100 ml (320–800 mg) initially over a period of 5–10 min to stop the convulsions, monitoring respiration carefully, particularly if following on diazepam. This is followed usually by 1–3 ml/min (8–24 mg/min) for 24 h, assuming respiratory circulatory functions are well maintained, to ensure that the epileptic state has settled down.

(b) Phenytoin

Slow intravenous injection of 13–15 mg/kg at a rate of no more than 100 mg/min. Ideally the i.v. injection of phenytoin should be carried out with cardiographic monitoring in case of cardiac arrhythmias.

(c) Paraldehyde

Paraldehyde may be given i.v., but should be used only by those with experience. It can be very effective in terminating very *resistant* status epilepticus.

Paraldehyde for injection is *freshly* diluted with sodium chloride 0.9 per cent to produce a 10 per cent (v/v) solution of paraldehyde. The total dose depends upon the patient's response, but to start with it is infused at a rate of 1 ml/min for 10 min. This dose is repeated with each fit, to a total dose of not more than 100 ml in an hour. When seizures have stopped for 2 h a slow i.v. infusion of 5 ml of 10 per cent solution is given.

Some still treat status epilepticus with paraldehyde i.m. giving 5 ml by deep i.m. injection into each buttock, but this is unreliable in its effects.

(d) Barbiturates

In the USA i.v. barbiturates are frequently used. Phenobarbitone is injected at a rate of 50 mg/min i.v., to a total dose of 7 mg per kg body weight (e.g. 500 mg infused over 10 min). If seizures continue after 30 min then another 3 mg/kg may be given slowly i.v. Sodium amylobarbitone, 50 mg/min i.v., can also be used.

Barbiturates may cause respiratory depression and severe hypotension, and facilities for full resuscitation must be available.

(e) Complete paralysis

In severe cases in which there is little or no response to the above measures it is necessary to terminate status epilepticus by giving i.v. thiopentone, with or without curare or related drugs. This requires the assistance of an anaesthetist.

28.4. MIGRAINE

28.4.1. Mechanisms of action of drugs to treat migraine

Migraine is a difficult subject from almost every point of view. Although classical migraine is fairly easy to describe, there are all sorts of paroxysmal headaches, without obvious neurological cause, which can cause diagnostic problems. Not only is diagnosis difficult but the aetiology is unknown. There is most likely a paroxysmal disturbance of arterial calibre in the cerebral vessels, consisting of an initial vasoconstriction of intracranial vessels, causing cortical or brain-stem ischaemia (giving prodromal symptoms), followed by vasodilatation of particularly the extracranial arteries, causing pain (i.e. headache) apparently through stimulation of pain-mediating sensory nerve-endings in the arterial wall. Exactly how these changes might be brought about is still a mystery, but hypotheses abound. For example, dietary substances (e.g. alcohol and tyramine in chocolate and cheese) might release vasoactive substances (e.g. catecholamines, 5-hydroxytryptamine, kinins) from stores in platelets or nerve-endings or other tissues, thus triggering an attack. These mechanisms or vessel reactivity may be subject to the influence of genetic inheritance, sex hormonal state in women (e.g. premenstrual migraine and oral-contraceptive-induced migraine occur), and psychosomatic factors. Certainly most theories implicate the release of vasoactive substances, altered arterial reactivity in and around the head, and neurogenic factors.

In classical migraine there is a phase in which patients may know that an attack is going to occur in the near future; they may feel particularly well, mood may alter, or they may feel listless or drowsy. Then the acute prodromal phase occurs with neurological features, often visual, such as scintillating lights and visual scotomas, and less frequently hemiplegic and rarely hemisensory features. Then after 20–30 min or so the headache comes on. It usually begins in one spot behind an eye, or in the temporal region, and classically spreads unilaterally (the hemicrania which gives the disease its name), but the side can vary and it can become bilateral. The pain is often severe and throbbing. The patient feels awful and there is often photophobia, nausea, and vomiting. The episode usually lasts a few hours, but it can go on for a day or two. The further away from this classical description the symptoms become the more difficult it is to diagnose migraine, but paroxysmal headaches without prodromata are often called 'common migraine' or 'migrainous headaches'. It is always important to consider intracranial causes of such symptoms, e.g. tumours and vascular abnormalities such as aneurysms.

The drugs used in the treatment of migraine are listed in Table 28.7. It is difficult to propound the rationale of the drug therapy of migraine because of the lack of understanding of the cause of the illness and the mechanisms of action of some of the drugs.

Table 28.7   *Drugs used in the treatment of migraine*

---

1. *Treatment of an acute attack*
Analgesics
   Aspirin (p.740)
   Paracetamol (p.721)
   Codeine (p.713)
Anti-emetics
   Buclizine }
   Cyclizine } both antihistamines (H_1 receptor antagonists) (see p.637)
   Metoclopramide (p.705)
   There are several effective combinations of analgesics and anti-emetics (see *British National Formulary*)
Ergotamine (p.678)

2. *Prophylaxis*
Serotonin (5-hydroxytryptamine) antagonists
   Pizotifen (p.732)
   Methysergide
Other agents
   Propranolol (p.622)
   Clonidine (p.663)

The use of analgesics and anti-emetics is obviously as symptomatic therapy.

Ergotamine could act through one of several mechanisms. It is an α-adrenoceptor antagonist, a weak serotonin (5-hydroxytryptamine) antagonist, and itself a direct vasoconstrictor. Any of these actions might modify the abnormal arterial vasoconstriction and vasodilatation thought to be operating in migraine.

In prophylaxis the serotonin antagonists pizotifen and methysergide are thought to block the actions of serotonin after its release from platelets and other sites.

Exactly how propranolol works is unknown, but apart from its β-adrenoceptor blocking actions which could interfere with a 'stress' response, it is also a serotonin antagonist.

Clonidine, in the low doses used, reduces arterial reactivity, but the mechanism involved is obscure.

28.4.2. Use of drugs in migraine

(a) Treatment of an acute attack

(i) Analgesics and anti-emetics

Patients often find that during an acute attack of migraine they need to lie down in a quiet, darkened room. The initial drug treatment of an acute attack should be based upon the use of analgesics with or without anti-emetics. Because nausea and vomiting may occur in acute attacks and may be associated with gastric stasis due to inhibition of gastric motility, metoclopramide not only relieves the nausea and vomiting but by increasing the speed of gastric emptying it improves the absorption of oral drugs mainly absorbed from the small intestine (e.g. analgesics).

Aspirin 600 mg every 4–6 h as necessary, or paracetamol 1 g every 4–6 h as necessary may be sufficient, combined with rest, to see the patient through an attack. Metoclopramide 5–10 mg orally t.d.s., the first dose given very early in the attack, relieves the nausea. Metoclopramide 10 mg i.m. may be necessary in a severe attack.

Various proprietary preparations with mixtures of analgesics and antiemetics are available (see *British National Formulary*), and some patients find these suitable.

(ii)Ergotamine

Ergotamine is most effective when given early in an attack preferably during the prodromal phase. Unreliability of absorption because of gastric stasis, vomiting, and the emetic action of ergotamine itself may prove difficult. It can be given sublingually or orally (see Pharmacopoeia for dosages), but to overcome the problems of absorption an aerosol inhalation is available.

If ergotamine is effective, then in a competent patient a self-administered subcutaneous or intramuscular injection may be preferred.

Ergotamine may produce nausea. Overdosage itself will produce headaches. Take great care not to overdose patients or to allow them to overdose themselves; vasoconstriction and peripheral limb gangrene can occur. Do not give ergotamine to pregnant or breast-feeding women, and avoid its use in patients with ischaemic heart disease and peripheral vascular disease.

Ergotamine should not be used prophylactically.

(b) Prophylaxis

(i) Pizotifen

In patients with frequent, disabling attacks pizotifen can be effective. It may produce some drowsiness and interacts with alcohol.

(ii) Clonidine

Clonidine is used in doses much smaller than those used in the treatment of hypertension (see Pharmacopoeia), and it can abolish or reduce the frequency of attacks.

(iii) Propranolol

Propranolol is used in a dosage of 80–160 mg daily in divided doses.

(iv) Methysergide

In patients who actually have migraine and do not respond to the above prophylactic drugs methysergide can be tried in a dosage of 1 mg once at night initially, increasing to 1–2 mg b.d. or t.d.s.

The long-term use of methysergide may be associated with retroperitoneal fibrosis and occasionally fibrotic cardiac valvular disease. If effective it should be given in the minimum effective dose for 6 months at a time, with withdrawal for a month's 'drug holiday' before reinstitution of therapy. Patients should be asked to report any urinary symptoms or loin pain suggestive of retroperitoneal fibrosis. Methysergide may also produce peripheral limb ischaemia like ergotamine, hypotension, and oedema. It is not a drug to be used lightly because of these serious adverse effects.

(c) General management

The physician must try to understand the factors which may be involved in the patient's migraine; the psychological factors and the stresses, the possibility of dietary factors, the association with the menstrual cycle, the oral contraceptive, and alcohol. All these are important to explore, and it may be that the frequency of attacks can be diminished by quite simple measures. The nature of migraine should be explained. If treatment is not very effective, and in some cases it may not be so, the patient must be reassured that the illness is not dangerous and that ways of coping with the condition have to be found, even although this may involve no more than symptomatic treatment as outlined above.

28.5. MYASTHENIA GRAVIS

28.5.1. Mechanisms of action of drugs used in the treatment of myasthenia gravis

In Fig 28.1 is shown the hierarchy of events involved in both the causation of myasthenia gravis and its treatment (see also Chapter 4).

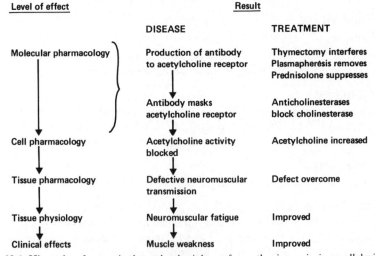

Fig. 28.1. Hierarchy of events in the pathophysiology of myasthenia gravis, in parallel with the mechanisms of action and effects of drugs used in its treatment.

Essentially the disease results, for reasons unknown, from the production of antibodies to nicotinic acetylcholine (ACh) receptors in skeletal muscle. This results in acetylcholine blockade with symptoms and signs resembling intoxication with curare, i.e. a competitive neuromuscular block. The clinical manifestations include: weakness of the eye muscles resulting in ptosis or diplopia; difficulties in chewing, swallowing, and speaking. Proximal limb weakness is common and there may be distal limb weakness with weak hands; rarely respiratory muscle weakness occurs requiring artificial ventilation. Characteristically the weakness worsens as muscles fatigue.

The particular pattern of weaknesses and its fluctuating character from day to day or hour to hour are characteristic for the individual patient.

The drugs used in treating myasthenia gravis are listed in Table 28.8. Anticholinesterases inhibit cholinesterase which metabolises acetylcholine, and the concentration of acetylcholine at the neuromuscular junction increases, overcoming the effect of the antibody.

Table 28.8   *Drugs used in the treatment of myasthenia gravis*

Acetylcholinesterase inhibitors (p.617)
Neostigmine
Physostigmine
Edrophonium (in diagnosis)

Immunosuppressive therapy
Corticosteroids (p.664)

Prednisolone presumably acts by suppressing lymphocyte production of ACh receptor antibody.

Plasmapheresis is sometimes used in myasthenic crisis to reduce antibody concentrations, and therefore the degree of block.

28.5.2. The use of drugs in myasthenia gravis

(a) In diagnosis

(i) Edrophonium
Edrophonium has a very short action, and can be used in making the initial diagnosis, and in different ... of *myasthenic* crisis (due to severe disease or to too little cholinesterase inhibition) from *cholinergic* crisis (too much cholinesterase inhibition and excess acetylcholine at the neuromuscular junction). Edrophonium will make a cholinergic crisis very transiently worse but will greatly improve a myasthenic crisis. In these circumstances it as well to have facilities for artificial ventilation available.

Edrophonium is usually given i.v. in an initial dose of 2 mg. If no response or untoward effect occurs in 30 seconds, give a further 3 mg, and if there is still no response give a further 5 mg.

In diagnosis this drug is particularly useful when the facial muscles are weak and being evaluated.

In the differentiation of a myasthenic crisis from a cholinergic crisis it is crucial to observe the effect on the respiratory muscles.

(b) Treatment

(i) Neostigmine and pyridostigmine

The dosages of these drugs vary from patient to patient and must be tailored to the individual. They are similar in their efficacy but features distinguishing them are:

1. The action of neostigmine (orally) lasts 30–45 min, which is shorter than the duration of action of pyridostigmine.
2. Muscarinic adverse effects, particularly abdominal cramps, nausea, and diarrhoea may be worse with neostigmine.
3. Some patients find that neostigmine gives a quicker and slightly greater improvement in muscle strength.
4. Pyridostigmine is sometimes more effective in bulbar muscle weakness.

Initially neostigmine should be given in doses of 7.5–15 mg orally q.d.s. Dosage may be increased by decreasing the interval between doses, for example to three-hourly during the day, and by increasing each individual dose. A total daily dose of over 300 mg daily is rarely tolerated and the usual dosage is 120–180 mg daily, taken in equally divided doses at four-hourly intervals during the day.

The effects of pyridostigmine last slightly longer than those of neostigmine. Pyridostigmine 60 mg is equivalent to neostigmine 15 mg. Pyridostigmine should be started at a dosage of 30–60 mg six to eight-hourly, adjusting the dosage as necessary to a total dosage of 0.3–1.2 g daily in appropriate divided doses.

Anticholinesterase drugs restore strength to about 80 per cent of normal, and there is no point in pushing the dosage to try and achieve absolute normality as this will result in unacceptable muscarinic adverse effects.

Parenteral preparations are available, but the dosage is much smaller parenterally than orally, e.g. neostigmine 15 mg orally equals 1.5 mg neostigmine i.m.; pyridostigmine 60 mg orally equals 2 mg pyridostigmine i.m.

The edrophonium test can be used to test the adequacy of anticholinesterase therapy. About 1 h after a dose of the oral anticholinesterase, when its action should be at its peak, edrophonium is given (2 mg i.v.) and the patient's strength is tested before and after. If strength improves significantly the dose of the oral anticholinesterase may be increased.

(c) Treatment of crisis

(i) Myasthenic crisis

The myasthenic patient's oropharyngeal, laryngeal, and respiratory muscles may become so weak that it becomes impossible to maintain an adequate airway or respiratory movement.

Infections, non-compliance with medication, and vigorous physical activity may produce a crisis.

Any of the following may interact with the disease to produce a crisis:

aminoglycosides (e.g. gentamicin, streptomycin)
quinine and quinidine
sedatives and hypnotics (e.g. barbiturates)
anti-arrhythmics (lignocaine, procainamide, propranolol)
phenytoin
phenothiazines.

Myasthenic patients are exquisitely sensitive to curare and other competitive neuromuscular blocking agents, but less sensitive to succinylcholine.

Diagnosis of myasthenic crisis involves using the edrophonium test as an aid (see above). Treatment is by artificial ventilation (endotracheal intubation with a cuffed tube, aspiration, positive pressure ventilation), and one may have to proceed to tracheostomy with ventilation. These cases should be cared for in intensive therapy units by anaesthetists. Patients in a true myasthenic crisis may be resistant to anticholinesterases, and often these are withdrawn while ventilation and intensive care are given. They may be reinstituted with effect later when the crisis has passed (e.g. by resolution or removal of the precipitating cause, see above). Plasmapheresis with removal of ACh receptor antibody from the circulation may restore responsiveness to anticholinesterases.

(ii) Cholinergic crisis

Muscle fasciculation, pallor, sweating, small pupils, and excessive salivation are signs of both excessive nicotinic and muscarinic cholinergic activity induced by anticholinesterase overdose. Again the edrophonium test can be helpful in diagnosis. Drug withdrawal is necessary and atropine may be used as an antidote for excessive muscarinic activity.

(d) Other measures

(i) Thymectomy

This operation should be performed if a thymoma is demonstrated, if there is severe progressive myasthenia, and particularly if bulbar muscles are involved.

(ii) Immunosuppression

Views on treatment with prednisolone vary. Some delay prednisolone therapy until after thymectomy has been performed and found not to be very successful in severe disease. Others will prescribe prednisolone to those with incapacitating disease. Dosage is usually about 50 mg prednisolone daily. Short courses can be helpful during transient bouts of deterioration. Initially steroid therapy may worsen the condition, and the patient should be closely supervised.

(iii)Plasmapheresis

Although the place of plasmapheresis in the routine treatment of myasthenia gravis has not been established, it can be helpful in severe cases resistant to other treatments, and before thymectomy.

28.6. MUSCLE SPASTICITY

28.6.1. Mechanisms of action of drugs used in the treatment of muscle spasticity

Muscle spasticity occurs as a result of upper motor neurone lesions, and most commonly requires treatment in those patients with spinal cord injuries and tumours, degenerative disease of the spinal cord, and multiple sclerosis. Spasticity can interfere markedly with remaining voluntary movement, and flexor spasms can be very painful.

The problem is that of the adverse effects of the drugs, limiting their usefulness. The drugs used in the treatment of muscle spasticity are listed in Table 28.9. Diazepam acts at the supraspinal and spinal cord levels by suppressing neuronal transmission in polysynaptic more than monosynaptic reflex pathways. Whether this occurs through its effect to enhance GABA function is unknown.

Table 28.9   *Drugs used in the treatment of muscle spasticity*

Diazepam (p.642)
Baclofen (p.641)
Dantrolene (p.672)

Baclofen is an analogue of GABA which penetrates the CNS poorly. Its precise mode of action is unknown, but it is known to inhibit monosynaptic and polysynaptic neurotransmission at the spinal cord level.

Dantrolene is thought to act at the skeletal muscle cell level to inhibit excitation–contraction coupling by decreasing the amount of calcium released from the sarcoplasmic reticulum.

28.6.2. Use of drugs in the treatment of muscle spasticity

Treatment with drugs is generally only moderately effective.

(a) Diazepam

This is usually tried first, the dosage being limited by sedation and muscular hypotonia. The starting dosage of diazepam is usually 2–5 mg t.d.s. The dosage can be increased by 5 mg daily, and some patients can tolerate 30–40 mg daily.

(b) Baclofen

Dosages are begun at 5 mg t.d.s. and increased to a maximum of 100 mg daily. Adverse effects, including hypotonia, can be limiting.

(c) Dantrolene

This is quite a toxic drug, and spasticity should be bad and complaints realistically open to improvement before this drug is used. Initial dosages are 12.5–25 mg daily increased gradually at weekly intervals over a 4–7 week period to a maximum of 400 mg daily. If there is no worthwhile benefit after 6–7 weeks discontinue treatment. Common adverse effects are drowsiness (and patients should take great care with machinery and when driving), muscle weakness, nausea and vomiting. Liver function should be tested before dantrolene is given and 6 weeks after starting. Hepatic toxicity can be serious, and women over 30 years of age taking 300 mg or more daily seem most susceptible.

28.7. VERTIGO

28.7.1. Mechanisms of action of drugs used in the treatment of vertigo

The drugs used in the treatment of vertigo are listed in Table 28.10. None of these drugs acts on any of the *causes* of vertigo. They all interfere in one way or another with the labyrinthine or neuronal mechanisms by which the *sensation* is mediated or appreciated, and therefore provide symptomatic relief only.

The diagnosis of vertigo is not easy, and before being tempted to treat vague dizziness with these drugs it is essential to take a most careful history to ensure that the dizziness of which the patient complains is of a vertiginous type, and that all has been done to exclude a serious cause.

There are many causes of vertigo, some of which are listed in Table 28.11. Sorting these out can be a formidable task.

It would be folly to suppose that we understand how antivertiginous drugs act. The following hypotheses, none of which is watertight, have been proposed.

Antihistamines have been thought to act via their muscarinic blocking activity but recent studies have revealed histamine (H_1) receptors in the

Table 28.10   *Drugs used in the treatment of vertigo*

1. *Antihistamines (H₁ antagonists; p.637)*
See list in Pharmacopoeia, but the following antihistamines are favoured:
Dimenhydrinate
Cyclizine
Cinnarizine
Buclizine
Betahistine

2. *Phenothiazines (p.727)*
Prochlorperazine
Thiethylperazine
Chlorpromazine

3. *Anticholinergics (p.616)*
Scopolamine (hyoscine)—motion sickness

4. *Tranquillizers*
Diazepam (p.642)

Table 28.11   *Causes of vertigo*

1. *Vestibular disorders*
Labyrinthine disease (inflammation, post-traumatic)
Vestibular nerve or nucleus disease (neuronitis, tumours, drug toxicity)
Menière's disease
Benign positional vertigo
(Drug induced vestibular disease may result from toxicity of aminoglycoside antibiotics, frusemide, or ethacrynic acid)

2. *Central neurological disorders*
Brain-stem ischaemia
Demyelinating disease (multiple sclerosis)
Cerebellopontine angle tumours

3. *Systemic disease*
Hypotension (cardiac causes, e.g. arrhythmias, postural)
Vasculitis (brain stem)

4. *Miscellaneous associations*
Polycythaemia
Diabetes mellitus
Anaemia
Dysproteinaemias

CNS, and it is possible that they are blocking the central actions of histamine. It has been suggested that they interfere with the function of the vestibular nucleus and the reticular formation.

Phenothiazines have anti-dopaminergic activity and anticholinergic activity, and may act at several different points in the pathways leading to vertigo. It is worth noting that antihistamines and phenothiazines are also effective in the treatment of nausea, with or without vertigo.

Anticholinergics, of which the use of hyoscine in motion sickness is the best example, presumably act by blocking muscarinic neurotransmission at various 'central' points.

There are all sorts of other hypotheses about how some antihistamines might work, for example by vasodilatation and improvement of blood flow in the labyrinth or brain stem or by an antagonistic effect on calcium transport, but none of them has been proven.

28.6.2. Use of drugs in the treatment of vertigo

(a) Symptomatic therapy of acute severe vertigo associated with nausea and vomiting

Parenteral treatment is necessary because of vomiting. Prochlorperazine by deep intramuscular injection, 12.5 mg, may relieve the vertigo, nausea, and vomiting, relieve the anxiety and distress, and sedate the patient. This may be followed by oral therapy. Note that the elderly are prone to extrapyramidal reactions with prochlorperazine.

(b) Moderate vertigo not associated with vomiting

Oral therapy with conventional doses of one of the antihistamines or phenothiazines is usually undertaken.

In Menière's disease drug therapy is complex. Because of the suggested excessive endolymph production in the labyrinth, diuretic therapy is usually given. Antihistamines and anticholinergics are also employed.

Apart from the use of parenteral phenothiazines in the symptomatic treatment of vertigo, drug therapy of vertigo is generally disappointing.

(c) Motion sickness

Various medications can be tried for susceptible individuals.

(a) Scopolamine (hyoscine hydrobromide) 300–600 micrograms as necessary, q.d.s. Recently it has become possible to give scopolamine transdermally by means of a drug-impregnated pad which when applied to the skin (e.g. behind the ear) leads to the continuous absorption of drug at a slow rate, providing prolonged action.

(b) One of the listed antihistamines such as cinnarizine or promethazine in conventional dosage. Remember the interaction of antihistamines with alcohol and the consequent increase in drowsiness and interference with psychomotor performance (particularly with driving).

The neuroleptic phenothiazines and metoclopramide are not very effective against motion sickness. If prophylactic treatment is required drugs should be taken 1–2 h before the journey is begun.

29 The drug therapy of psychiatric disorders

In Table 29.1 are listed the drugs used in the treatment of psychiatric disorders. It looks a formidable list, but the student should not be put off by it. Try to remember something about the following drugs as members of each class; they may not be the ideal for every patient but they act as an introduction to each therapeutic class upon which further experience can be built:

    Hypnotics—benzodiazepines : DIAZEPAM
    Anxiolytics—benzodiazepines : DIAZEPAM
    Antidepressants—tricyclics : AMITRIPTYLINE
    Antipsychotic drugs—phenothiazines : CHLORPROMAZINE
             —butyrophenones : HALOPERIDOL
             —lithium salts   : LITHIUM CARBONATE OR CITRATE

Table 29.1 *Drugs used in the treatment of psychiatric disorders*

1. *Hypnotics*
Benzodiazepines (p.642)
Chlormethiazole (p.659)
Antihistamines (promethazine—in children—p.637)
Chloral derivatives (p.657)

2. *Anxiolytics*
Benzodiazepines
β-adrenoceptor antagonists (propranolol; p.622)

3. *Antidepressant drugs*
Tricyclic and related antidepressants (pp.763 and 708)
Monoamine oxidase inhibitors (p.709)

4. *Antipsychotic drugs*
Phenothiazines (p.727)
Thioxanthenes (p.727)
Butyrophenones (p.647)

5. *Lithium* (p. 702)

29.1. MECHANISMS OF ACTION OF DRUGS USED IN PSYCHIATRIC DISORDERS

Although it would be silly to pretend that the mechanisms by which any of the drugs in this section act to benefit any of the disorders mentioned are fully understood, it would be equally unnecessarily nihilistic to deny that nothing is known. In recent years advances in neuropharmacology have revealed much about the pharmacological actions of psychotropic drugs, but the problems come when one tries to relate the known actions to the therapeutic action.

29.1.1. Antipsychotic drugs

Take, for example, the antipsychotic drugs, such as chlorpromazine and haloperidol. There is no doubt that these drugs inhibit the action of the neurotransmitter dopamine on a certain class of post-synaptic dopamine (D_2) receptors. This is the cause of their Parkinsonian adverse effects. Is this the mechanism of action by which their therapeutic action is exerted in schizophrenia? There are other leads to suggest that dopamine 'overactivity' might play a part in schizophrenia. For example, amphetamine abuse can lead to a paranoid psychotic state, on occasions indistinguishable from schizophrenia. So far, however, no certain endogenous changes in the post-mortem schizophrenic brain not previously exposed to neuroleptics, or in the CSF of patients with schizophrenia have been found which incontrovertibly show an abnormality in dopamine synthesis, turnover, or function. If antipsychotics are acting as dopamine antagonists (and it is most likely they are) they are probably acting at some secondary level.

As a parallel consider the actions of diuretics in heart failure. Diuretics act on the kidney to cause a sodium diuresis, and prevent sodium retention brought about by poor renal perfusion and secondary hyperaldosteronism. They reduce blood volume, venous and pulmonary congestion, cardiac preload, and to some extent afterload, and the clinical state of heart failure improves without any direct action of the drug on the primary site of disorder of the heart.

It might well be that the abnormal brain function responsible for schizophrenia is 'channelled' through dopamine pathways in the brain, and that the antipsychotics block this 'channel'.

Another point of interest about the dopamine-blocking antipsychotics is that during long-term treatment they tend to produce abnormal movements, so called tardive dyskinesia, characterized by oro-facial grimacing and sometimes bizarre athetoid movements of the head, neck, and upper limbs. Experiments in animals have shown that chronic administration of antipsychotics leads to increased numbers of dopamine receptors in certain brain areas, producing dopamine supersensitivity in the extrapyramidal system, and resulting in dyskinesias. It is impossible to say whether increased dopamine sensitivity plays any part in the chronic therapeutic effects of antipsychotics.

Although the various antipsychotics have a differing pharmacological spectrum of activity, e.g. α-adrenoceptor antagonism, histamine antagonism, anticholinergic effects, and direct membrane actions, the one feature they share is that of dopamine-blocking activity.

29.1.2. Hypnotics and anxiolytics

Benzodiazepines act at post-synaptic sites sensitive to the actions of GABA to enhance GABA function and thus causing increased inhibitory neurotransmission, which leads to sedation and decreased anxiety. The exact molecular interactions underlying this process are unknown, but it is a mechanism of great importance. Because there are specific binding sites for benzodiazepines in the brain, it has been proposed that there is an endogenous substance binding to them normally and modulating GABA function, and that interference with this process might underlie anxiety. Chemicals have been identified, β-carbolines, which interact with specific benzodiazepine binding sites in animal brain. There are also different types of benzodiazepine binding sites in brain with different chemical specificites. These differences open up the possibilities of differentiating pharmacologically between say anticonvulsant, anxiolytic, and hypnotic benzodiazepines. To be able to modulate different behavioural and physiological functions of GABA in the brain by such means could lead to the production of more specific drugs for the treatment of insomnia, anxiety, and epilepsy.

29.1.3. Antidepressants

Most, but not all, of the tricyclic and tetracyclic antidepressants inhibit the high affinity pump which takes up either noradrenaline or 5-hydroxytryptamine from the synaptic cleft after their release, thereby terminating their action. Some of the antidepressants inhibit noradrenaline uptake more than 5-hydroxytryptamine uptake, some the reverse, while others are non-selective for the two monoamines (see Table 29.2).

Mianserin does not inhibit monoamine uptake at all. Thus although there are good reasons for supposing that blockade of noradrenaline and/or 5-hydroxytryptamine uptake can somehow result in antidepressant activity there may be other pharmacological routes to achieving the same effect.

It is generally agreed that the antidepressants take 1–2 weeks to act and this has brought to the fore the possibility that adaptive pharmacological responses to the initial blockade of monoamine reuptake are responsible for the therapeutic effect of antidepressants. In experimental animals the chronic administration of tricyclic antidepressants leads to decreased numbers of α_2-adrenoceptors, decreased cortical β-adrenoceptors, and decreased activity of cortical noradrenaline-sensitive adenylate cyclase. A whole array of adaptive responses occurs, and currently attention is focusing on these types of changes as an explanation for antidepressant activity. In this context it is interesting to note that mianserin is an α_2-adrenoceptor and a 5-hydroxytryptamine receptor blocking agent which brings its effects at least within the monoamine 'orbit', particularly if the adaptive responses to its acute effects were to prove similar to those of the tricyclics.

Table 29.2   *Effects of antidepressants on monoamine reuptake*

Drug	Inhibition of uptake	
	Noradrenaline	*5–hydroxytryptamine*
Amitriptyline (metabolite nortriptyline)	+ +	+ +
Nortriptyline	+	+
Imipramine	+ + (through metabolite desipramine)	+ +
Desipramine	+ +	−
Mianserin	−	−
Maprotiline	+	−
Nomifensine	+ +	−

Many cyclic antidepressants have anticholinergic and antihistaminic effects, but these are not thought to be linked to their antidepressant activity.

It is of interest to note that in experimental animals electroconvulsive shock given in a manner similar to that in which electroconvulsive therapy is given to depressed patients produces, with a latent period, several of the effects of antidepressant drugs discussed above, with the addition of enhancement of dopamine function, which generally is not produced by antidepressants.

However, none of this actually explains how antidepressants relieve depression! Nevertheless, there is a large body of work suggesting that abnormalities of brain noradrenaline or 5-hydroxytryptamine function occur in patients with depression, and these include studies on post-mortem brains of suicide patients, and measurements of monoamine metabolites in the CSF and of neuroendocrine responses to monoamine agonists (e.g. decreased growth hormone responses to the α_2-adrenoceptor agonist clonidine in endogenous depression).

Monoamine oxidase (MAO) inhibitors inhibit the metabolism of noradrenaline, 5-hydroxytryptamine, and dopamine. There is little doubt that in adequate clinical dosage they do this, and it is likely that the concentrations of brain monoamines rise as a result. Again adaptive responses occur, not dissimilar to those found with the cyclic antidepressants, e.g. decreased β-adrenoceptor sensitivity in the cortex of experimental animals. Presumably MAO inhibitors by their effect on monoamine metabolism, and cyclic antidepressants by their effects on monoamine reuptake, both cause an increase in monoamine concentrations in the synaptic cleft, leading to common effects.

29.1.4. Lithium

There are several hypotheses concerning the mode of action of lithium in benefiting patients with acute mania (which is an interesting but not particularly useful property because the neuroleptics act more quickly), and in preventing attacks of mania and depression in patients with manic–depressive disease.

The hypotheses involve effects:

to 'stabilize' neurotransmitter receptors against stimuli causing up- and down-regulation;

to alter responses to receptor stimulation;

to increase the synthesis, turnover, and functional activity of brain 5-hydroxytryptamine;

to alter certain aspects of the neuronal membrane function by effects on sodium and potassium fluxes.

Which of these, if any, is responsible for the therapeutic effect of lithium is unknown, but each hypothesis is backed by good experimental evidence which shows that lithium has quite marked effects on brain function.

29.2. THE USE OF DRUGS IN THE TREATMENT OF PSYCHIATRIC DISORDERS

It would not be appropriate here to enter into discussions of the diagnostic problems in psychiatry, of the pros and cons of drug therapy versus psychotherapy in particular illnesses, or the general role of psychotherapy and psychosocial manipulation in the treatment of mental illness. Here diagnostic categories will be assumed as appropriate, drug therapies known to be effective in those categories will be described, and important points made about their methods of use and adverse effects.

29.2.1. Insomnia

No drug available at present induces normal sleep. All have drawbacks such as dependency, withdrawal reactions, and hangover effects. Thus there is nothing which cures insomnia, i.e. which allows normal sleep without hangover, puts the sleep cycle right, and leaves it right when the drug is stopped.

Our understanding of sleep disorders is improving. We know, for instance, that somehow or other sleep fits in with circadian rhythms dependent upon the function of biological clocks within the nuclei of the hypothalamus. The sleep EEG cycle has been described with its alternating phases of slow-wave or non-rapid-eye-movement (NREM) sleep and fast-wave or rapid-eye-movement (REM) sleep. These phases are thought to be dependent upon the reciprocal functioning of aminergic inhibitory and cholinergic excitatory sets of neurones situated in the pontine brain stem. This neuronal control of the sleep cycle ties up with alterations in sleep produced by respiratory abnormalities, such as sleep apnoea, either central or obstructive. It superficially explains why psychiatric disturbances such as anxiety, mania, and endogenous depression may, through aminergic mechanisms, alter sleep patterns.

However, when it comes to the drug treatment of insomnia we still use rather blunderbuss therapy and we are gradually realising that it is probably not all that effective or desirable.

Before prescribing hypnotic therapy the physician must satisfy himself about the following points:

(a) Is there an important decrease in the time and quality of sleep in this patient? Is the patient's assessment of his sleep pattern accurate? Elderly people naturally sleep shorter hours than the young. Lying awake in the dark when the rest of the world is asleep is unpleasant and time passes very slowly, causing errors in assessment. Whether or not one wakes from sleep feeling refreshed depends upon many factors in one's life, mood, and personality other than the quality of a night's sleep.

(b) Is there a medical reason for poor sleep? Pain, endogenous depression, alcoholism, caffeine-induced anxiety, stress, increased frequency of micturition, itching, cough, and breathlessness all interrupt sleep.

In practical terms one is left with a large group of patients who do feel that their sleep is inadequate. However, treatment with hypnotic drugs should be reserved for those with significant distress caused by what is likely to be temporary insomnia.

It is said that tolerance to the effects of hypnotic agents occurs over a 2-week period. Most authorities now recommend that hypnotic therapy should not be continued for longer than a week or two because of the occurrence of dependence and the problem of withdrawal (see Chapter 31). This causes rebound insomnia for which the patient again consults the doctor who might be tempted to re-prescribe a hypnotic, thus establishing a vicious circle. If patients have developed a dependent state, then explanation about the withdrawal phase must be given, and hypnotics should not be prescribed for it.

The elderly are particularly sensitive to hypnotic drugs. They may become confused. They wake in the night, need to micturate, get up, are ataxic, and fall and injure themselves. Do not indiscriminately prescribe hypnotics to the elderly.

Much has been made of the relevance of the pharmacokinetics of the benzodiazepines to their hypnotic actions. Studies have been done to show that those with a short half-time and few or no active metabolites, such as temazepam or triazolam have less hangover effect and are less cumulative than, say, nitrazepam or diazepam, both of which have long half-times and are metabolized to active metabolites with long half-times, but which nonetheless are commonly used as hypnotics. The half-times of the benzodiazepines commonly used in the treatment of insomnia are shown in Table 29.3.

Table 29.3   *Mean half-times of benzodiazepines commonly used in the treatment of insomnia*

Drug	Half-time (h)
Diazepam*	72
Chlordiazepoxide*	24
Nitrazepam	24
Clobazam*	20
Temazepam	15
Oxazepam	12
Lorazepam	12
Triazolam	5

* All benzodiazepines so marked are partly metabolized to active compounds with long half-times (e.g. desmethyldiazepam).

  Some other benzodiazepines (clorazepate, prazepam, and flurazepam) are completely metabolized to active metabolites with long half-times.

If *early waking* is a problem then a longer-acting benzodiazepine, such as diazepam 2–10 mg, or nitrazepam 5–10 mg, might be beneficial. If *getting to sleep* is a problem then temazepam 10–30 mg or lorazepam 1–4 mg would be preferred. Hypnotic benzodiazepines should be taken 30 min before going to bed. Dosages should be reduced in the elderly to the minimum necessary.

  Chloral hydrate and dichloralphenazone are still used as hypnotics, especially in the elderly (see Pharmacopoeia).

  Barbiturates are no longer normally used as hypnotics in the UK because of problems with tolerance and withdrawal symptoms.

  In depressed patients with early waking a sedative antidepressant given at night may be sufficient, e.g. amitriptyline.

29.2.2. Anxiety

Do not prescribe benzodiazepines for every patient who complains of mild anxiety reactions to various social or family stresses. Reserve drug treatment for those who are really likely to benefit from it. Simple understanding, psychotherapy, the passage of time, and adaptation of the patient to his or her circumstances solve many problems. Those who do not recover by these simple measures may need anxiolytics.

  Benzodiazepines are the safest and most efficacious drugs available for the treatment of anxiety. Several are available, but there is little evidence that one is more effective than another. The treatment of anxiety with benzodiazepines should be limited to about 6 weeks, because of tolerance to their effects and the occurrence of dependence, which on withdrawal leads to recrudesence of anxiety with dysphoria, tremor, sleeplessness, and occasionally psychotic reactions and convulsions, a syndrome not unlike that of delirium tremens. Diazepam is a commonly prescribed anxiolytic in doses of 2 mg t.d.s. in mild anxiety to 10 mg t.d.s. in more severe anxiety states. It may be given i.v. in doses of 10 mg for the treatment of acute panic attacks.

Patients with troublesome somatic symptoms in anxiety, e.g. palpitation, sweating, or tremor, may benefit from a β-adrenoceptor antagonist, such as propranolol 20–40 mg t.d.s.

29.2.3. Depression

In the treatment of neurotic depression, drug therapy, apart from the symptomatic therapy of associated anxiety with say diazepam, has a minor role to play. In more severe depression, particularly when associated with bodily disturbances such as loss of appetite, constipation, early wakening, and psychomotor retardation, antidepressant drug therapy tends to be more effective. In all studies on antidepressant drug therapy there has been a large placebo response (about 30 per cent), partly because in many cases the depressive episode is self-limiting. The problem is that among similar patients, with appropriate criteria for treatment, there is no way of telling who will respond. Given those appropriate criteria treatment is commenced.

(a) Tricyclic and tetracyclic antidepressants

The choice amongst cyclic antidepressant drugs is wide, and the points to bear in mind are these:

(a) Is there a need for sedation and is insomnia a problem? If so amitriptyline may be prescribed, i.e. in agitated patients.

(b) Is lethargy a particular problem? If so imipramine is less sedating. Protriptyline may be mildly stimulant.

(c) Is there likely to be a problem with cardiotoxicity, e.g. in the elderly or patients with ischaemic heart disease? If so consider mianserin.

(d) Is there likely to be a problem with anticholinergic activity, e.g. in glaucoma or prostatism? If so mianserin might be preferable to tricyclics, such as amitriptyline or imipramine.

Suicide is an ever-present risk in patients with depression. Whenever such a risk is apparent restrict the amounts of benzodiazepines or antidepressants prescribed. Antidepressant drug overdose can be particularly dangerous (see p.578). In any case, patients who are sufficiently depressed to require antidepressant medication should be seen frequently to assess their response to treatment, and to ensure that their depression is not worsening during the latent period before the drug begins to bring benefit.

In the specialist literature much has been made of the use of plasma drug concentration measurements in monitoring and optimizing antidepressant drug therapy. In carefully controlled studies of nortriptyline, low plasma drug concentrations were associated with lack of response, intermediate concentrations with response, but high concentrations with a diminution of therapeutic effect—the so-called inverted U curve (see Fig. 7.1).

Such studies as have been done with amitriptyline show either the inverted U curve or a linear relationship between response and dose. With imipramine the relationship has been found to be linear. Such studies have shown that for a given dose different patients will have remarkably different plasma concentrations, due to polymorphism of hepatic metabolism and variability in other pharmacokinetic characteristics of the drugs. This is a situation where plasma concentration measurements might in fact be useful, but the rather poor correlation between plasma concentration and response, the variability of the illness itself, and the expense of having the measurements done have militated against general acceptance of routine antidepressant plasma concentration measurements. There has been no study comparing the outcome of antidepressant drug therapy with and without access to drug plasma concentration measurement. Until that is done we shall not know whether it is really helpful or not.

The pharmacokinetics, adverse effects, drug interactions, and dosages of tricyclic antidepressants are dealt with in the Pharmacopoeia. There are no hard and fast rules about dosage. It is most important to recognize that the effective dosage in an individual is very variable, and that unfortunately there is a latent period of 2 weeks or so before the therapeutic effects of a given dosage regimen are seen. Adverse effects, particularly the anticholinergic effects, are seen before that and to some extent indicate the patient's tolerance to a given dose.

Take amitriptyline as an example of an antidepressant being used to treat an otherwise healthy 55 year-old woman with endogenous depression as an out-patient (out-patient dosage regimens tend to be less aggressive than in-patient dosage regimens).

Start with low dosages and build up gradually. In this way the patient comes to tolerate adverse effects and excessive dosage is avoided. Begin with 50 mg amitriptyline at night before bedtime. Increase the dose by 25 mg at night every 3 days, if the dose is tolerated, to a maximum of 150 mg daily in an out-patient. Many patients will have anticholinergic effects at this dosage. If the adverse effects are intolerable, lower the daily dosage by 25 mg. Whatever the maximum tolerated dosage is, some therapeutic effect should be seen within 3 weeks. Some patients might find it preferable to spread the dosage out over the day but most find night-time dosage preferable since it aids sleep and the peak anticholinergic effects occur during sleep. There are two reasons why daily dosage is just as effective as divided dosage. Firstly, the half-time of these drugs is generally 12 h or more. Secondly, the pharmacological action through which the therapeutic effect is mediated is probably not related to the moment-to-moment plasma drug concentration but more related to adaptive responses which will have their own long half-time.

In the elderly dosage should be more cautious. For instance, with amitriptyline begin with 25 mg at night and increase as necessary every 2–3 days by increments of 10 mg. In this way one will pick up troublesome adverse effects earlier. Many elderly patients will not tolerate more than 75 mg a day, because of decreased clearance and increased pharmacodynamic sensitivity, particularly in relation to cardiotoxicity and hypotension. It is for this reason that mianserin is often preferred in the elderly, beginning with doses of 30 mg at night and increasing to 60 mg if necessary.

In all patients treatment should be continued at the dosage finally chosen for about 3 months, assuming that some recovery has occurred. In first episodes of depression the dosage may then be gradually reduced over a few weeks and tapered off. One is here relying on one's assessment that natural remission of the depression has occurred against the background of drug therapy. If there is a history of previous attacks of depression it might be preferable to continue dosage after 3–4 months at about half the previous dosage to try to prevent relapse for some months.

(b) Monoamine oxidase (MAO) inhibitors

Although effective antidepressants these drugs are not nowadays very popular because of their potential to produce the hypertensive 'cheese reaction' and because of the risk of drug interactions. They tend, therefore, to be reserved for patients who have not responded to other antidepressant drugs, and for those who have phobic, hypochondriacal, or hysterical symptoms. As for the other antidepressants there is a latent period of about 2–3 weeks between starting treatment and the onset of the therapeutic benefit.

The dosages, adverse effects, and interactions of MAO inhibitors are dealt with in the Pharmacopoeia but the following important points should be remembered:

(a) A hypertensive crisis may occur if a patient on an MAO inhibitor takes certain amine-containing foods, such as cheese, meat or yeast extracts, unfresh poultry or game, and wines (especially Chianti). All patients receiving MAO inhibitors must be informed and educated about the risks of eating or drinking such foods.

(b) Certain proprietary medicines, some of which may be bought at the chemist's contain sympathomimetic amines (e.g. decongestants in tablets and capsules or in nose drops or sprays, for the relief of the symptoms of the common cold). Such amines interact with MAO inhibitors in the same way as the amine-containing foods described above and patients should be warned about them.

(c) All patients taking an MAO inhibitor should be given a card (of the kind issued in the UK by the DHSS) warning them of these dangers (see Fig. P7, p.711).

29.2.4. Mania

The principles of treating mania lie in the use of antipsychotic (neuroleptic) drugs with the 'take-over' effect of lithium in the acute phase, followed by maintenance lithium therapy as prophylaxis against recurrences of either manic or depressive episodes.

(a) Acute phase of mania

If the patient is very hyperactive, a parenteral dose of chlorpromazine or haloperidol i.m. may be needed. Once the patient is less active and more amenable, oral therapy with chlorpromazine, thioridazine, or haloperidol can be instituted. Dosages can be found in the Pharmacopoeia but must be tailored to each patient. These drugs at the dosages required may produce Parkinsonism, and as the manic phase comes under control the extra-pyramidal signs require treatment with one of the anticholinergic anti-Parkinsonian agents, such as benzhexol or benztropine (see p.499). It is a fascinating pharmacological phenomenon that the acutely psychotic patient (whether manic or schizophrenic) may require very large doses of neuroleptic drugs which essentially are competitive dopamine antagonists. This is telling us something about the functional activity of dopamine in the acutely psychotic brain, but we do not know what! As the acute phase wears off or comes under control the maintenance dose can often be much lower.

The initiation of lithium therapy should generally be a specialist deci-sion, but it is effective and can take over from antipsychotic drug therapy in the acute phase. Lithium (probably because of the time taken to reach effective, steady-state brain concentrations) takes a few days to exert its anti-manic effect, and so antipsychotic (neuroleptic) drug cover must be continued. If the patient is given lithium, then when the acute manic phase is under control, it may be possible to taper off the neuroleptic drug therapy gradually.

Important aspects of lithium dosage, with preparations to use, and the monitoring of plasma concentrations because of the low toxic:therapeutic ratio, are discussed in the Pharmacopoeia and in Chapter 7.

(b) Prophylaxis of manic–depressive disease

Manic–depressive disease is characterized by recurrent episodes of mania or depression, between which the patient may be fairly well. The nature of the episodes is variable, although recurrent depressive episodes seem to be most common, but alternate manic and depressive episodes can occur, as occasionally can repetitive manic episodes.

Whether or not lithium prophylaxis is indicated depends upon the frequency of episodes of affective illness and their severity. Treatment may need to be continued indefinitely.

In an illness in which manic episodes occur lithium is the preferred prophylactic agent. There is evidence that lithium is effective in the prevention of recurrent depressive episodes (unipolar depression), although the choice here is between lithium and long-term tricyclic antidepressant drug therapy. The evidence for the efficacy of lithium in the control of manic–depressive illness in which episodes of mania occur is better than that for unipolar depression. Whether or not in recurrent unipolar depression one uses lithium or a tricyclic antidepressant depends upon the patient's ability to tolerate the adverse effects of each drug, and the psychiatrist's judgement of their importance for that patient.

The dosages of lithium salts for prophylaxis, their adverse effects, and the importance of monitoring plasma concentrations are all discussed in the Pharmacopoeia and in Chapter 7.

29.2.5. Schizophrenia

A brief (albeit inadequate) description of schizophrenia is necessary for an understanding of the aim of drug therapy in the illness, and a realistic attitude of what is likely to be achieved by it.

The illness commonly occurs during adolescence or young adult life. Its onset may be insidious or acute. An acute attack may remit completely or may be followed by further attacks after each of which there remain defects in personality and mental state which increase in severity.

Many patients who develop schizophrenia have normal premorbid personalities, while others have had more withdrawn, quiet, unsociable personalities.

Certain manifestations of the schizophrenic illness are characteristic. Auditory hallucinations and delusions, often paranoid, are most important. Thought disorders occur—patients may feel that their thoughts are being influenced or disrupted from without, or that thoughts are being inserted, withdrawn, or jumbled. A patient may also feel his or her thoughts are being broadcast. Communication can be difficult. Thinking is vague and unfocused on the point at hand. Replies to questions do not constitute answers and ramble on into irrelevancies. It often takes some time for the physician to realize that it is the patient's thinking that is at fault rather than the doctor's ability to ask questions clearly and to conduct the interview coherently. There is disturbance of affect—the schizophrenic is characteristically cold and distant, and lacking in sympathy. Emotional attitudes may be incongruous, for example the patient may suddenly laugh inappropriately at something serious or unfunny.

Psychomotor abnormalities may occur with abnormalities of posture and movement, of which catatonia is the most striking and classically described.

During the 'active' phase of the illness hallucinations, delusions and florid symptoms tend to occur. In the 'chronic' phase thought disturbances, emotional passivity, and social difficulties occur and vary in severity.

In the treatment of this incredibly variable and complex psychiatric state drug treatment, although very important, is but a small part of the total therapeutic approach. We can, however, only deal with the drug therapy here.

What effect do the antipsychotic drugs have on the manifestations of schizophrenia, and what does one expect to happen to a patient treated with them?

Initially there is a rapid change in the patient over the first few weeks, a slower improvement for up to 3 months, and a very small change thereafter. Generally the florid symptoms respond well, i.e. hallucinations, delusions, and gross thought disorder. Withdrawn states, apathy, and emotional passivity are less responsive. The acute phases of schizophrenia are more responsive than the chronic state. Long-term antipsychotic drug therapy may be necessary to prevent relapse and perhaps to prevent the establishment of serious chronic illness in some patients.

Great care should be taken during withdrawal of antipsychotic drug therapy since relapse may occur, particularly in the event of psychosocial stresses, against the effects of which the antipsychotic drugs seem to have a protective effect.

Outcome from the presenting illness (i.e. what is likely to happen eventually) is variable. Good prognostic features include high intelligence, normal premorbid personality, the occurrence of an acute illness and catatonic features during the acute phase. Bad prognostic features are low intelligence, abnormal premorbid personality, an insidious onset of the illness and a preponderance of the less flamboyant features of the syndrome, such as thought disorder and emotional passivity.

(a) Choice of drug in schizophrenia

There are differences in the overall spectrum of effects (both therapeutic and adverse) of the antipsychotic drugs but their essential 'antischizophrenic' action is similar. Differences lie in the degree of sedation produced (good for the agitated patient), the degree of quietening in the hyperactive state (good for the patient in the florid acute schizophrenic state) and in the degree of production of extrapyramidal symptoms. For instance, chlorpromazine is quite sedative and is useful for violent, difficult patients who may quieten down without becoming stuporose. Haloperidol is generally accepted as being particularly useful in patients with marked hyperactivity. Fluphenazine and trifluoperazine have rather marked extrapyramidal effects, while thioridazine has fewer.

Here we shall restrict our discussion to chlorpromazine and fluphenazine with which many of the aspects of treatment can be illustrated.

In the acute phase the patient may be so disturbed that parenteral therapy is indicated, and this could be given as chlorpromazine i.m. injection, 25–50 mg every 6–8 h. However, larger doses may be needed initially, and dosages should be tailored to the patient's needs. Chlorpromazine (probably because of its α-adrenoceptor blocking action) can produce profound hypotension when given parenterally and patients should, if possible, remain supine for 30–60 min after injection. Some authorities now prefer to use haloperidol 2–10 mg i.m. six-hourly. If and when the patient can take oral therapy doses of chlorpromazine are given which vary enormously, from a small dosage of 25 mg t.d.s. to a moderate dosage of 100 mg t.d.s. to huge dosages, in some very disturbed in-patients, of 400 mg t.d.s. or more. Apart from great variability in the clearance rate of chlorpromazine and its metabolites from patient to patient there are plainly differences in the 'sensitivity' of the schizophrenic state to the drug. Flexibility in dosage to meet the patient's needs is essential.

After the acute phase of the illness has come under control and stabilized it may be decided after some weeks or months to switch to maintenance therapy. If oral therapy with chlorpromazine is continued the dose might be cut down gradually to, for example, 75 mg at night, from an acute phase dosage of 400 mg daily. Sudden large downward changes in dosage are inadvisable because of unpredictability of response.

Chronic oral therapy can be unreliable because of poor compliance, and from time to time uncertain bioavailability. For this reason intramuscular preparations have been developed which slowly release their drug from an intramuscular depot site over 1–3 weeks. Such a preparation is fluphenazine decanoate in oil (Modecate®). This is given by deep intramuscular injection initially in a test dose of 12.5 mg and then, after an interval of 4–7 days, 25 mg is given and then repeated at intervals usually of 2–4 weeks, the dose and interval being determined by response.

The ritual of the depot injection clinic has helped to regularize the treatment of a class of patient notoriously unpredictable in taking medication, and in addition has regularized their psychiatric supervision.

(b) Adverse effects of antipsychotic drugs

The adverse effects of antipsychotic drugs are catalogued in the relevant sections of the Pharmacopoeia. They can be problematic in the treatment of schizophrenia, and further discussion is warranted here. The types of problem are listed in Table 29.4.

Table 29.4   *Adverse effects of antipsychotic drugs*

Psychiatric	Sedation
	Depression
Extrapyramidal and motor	Parkinsonism
	Tardive dyskinesia
	Restlessness (akathisia)
Autonomic	Hypotension
	Acute cholinergic effects
	Cardiac arrhythmias
Skin	Photosensitivity
Endocrine and metabolic	Gain in weight
	Hyperprolactinaemia
	Galactorrhoea, gynaecomastia
	Loss of libido in men
Other	Hepatitis
	Blood dyscrasias
	Corneal and lens opacities (chlorpromazine)

The main problems are the treatment of Parkinsonism and tardive dyskinesias.

(i) Parkinsonism
In most patients improvement can be obtained with one of the anti-Parkinsonian anticholinergics such as benzhexol or benztropine. Most authorities do not recommend the use of these drugs routinely but prefer to wait until the individual patient shows signs of needing them.

(ii) Tardive dyskinesia
This condition is exceedingly difficult to treat effectively. Anticholinergic drugs may worsen it so these should be withdrawn. Very gradual reduction of the dosage of antipsychotic medication may be attempted, trying to strike a balance between keeping the psychosis under control and minimizing the tardive dyskinesia. Although tardive dyskinesia may be irreversible, sometimes if antipsychotic therapy can be withdrawn without relapse or worsening of the psychotic state then after a time (weeks or months) improvement may occur and it may be possible to reinstitute drug therapy at a lower dosage. Conversely, removal of the antipsychotic medication, even gradually, may *worsen* the tardive dyskinesia, and the former dosage must be resumed.

Medications which have been tried include reserpine and tetrabenazine (which deplete dopamine), lithium which may 'desensitize' dopamine receptors, and various means of increasing acetylcholine activity by providing more choline, for example as lecithin. Unfortunately none of these has proved very effective.

30 The relief of pain, and anaesthesia

In this chapter we shall consider the *symptomatic* treatment of pain, remembering that the treatment of pain should always also take account of the *cause* of the pain (see below).

Pain is a subjective symptom which is difficult to measure. It is affected by a variety of psychological factors, some patients complaining of pain when seemingly negligibly painful stimuli are present ('low pain threshold'), others being uncomplaining in the face of severely painful stimuli ('high pain threshold'). Even in the individual, pain intensity is subject to variation according to the presence or absence of various factors, including anxiety, depression, boredom, or distraction. Pain can be reduced in intensity by simple reassurance, by hypnosis, by trance-like meditative states, and by acupuncture. It can also be alleviated by the administration of inactive material—the placebo response, which occurs in about one-third of patients with pain (see Chapter 13). It is fashionable to ascribe these strange phenomena to functions of the endogenous opioid peptides, the endorphins and enkephalins, in the brain and spinal cord, but the role of these substances in the physiological control of the nervous system mechanisms processing pain sensation has yet to be fully defined.

In practical terms, however, these observations emphasize that management of the *whole* patient, rather than the uncritical prescription of analgesics alone, is of great importance in the treatment of pain.

30.1. ANATOMICAL AND NEUROPHARMACOLOGICAL MECHANISMS UNDERLYING PAIN SENSATION

The chain of nervous system mechanisms underlying pain sensation is illustrated in Fig. 30.1. The sequence is as follows:

1. Noxious stimuli are detected by pain receptors ('nociceptive' nerve-endings) in pain-sensitive tissues.
2. The signal generated by these receptors is transferred by sensory

nerves, through the dorsal root ganglia, to the dorsal horn of the spinal cord.

3. The signal received through the peripheral sensory mechanisms is processed by the spinal cord segment, and transferred via various ascending spinal cord pathways to various parts of the brain.

4. The signals received in the thalamic nuclei, periventricular grey matter, and brain-stem reticular formation are processed and passed on to the sensory cortex, giving the patient the sensation of pain.

5. Signals received in several sites, but particularly in the reticular formation and medulla, descend, through polysynaptic pathways to the dorsal horn of the spinal cord, where they may either facilitate or inhibit activity.

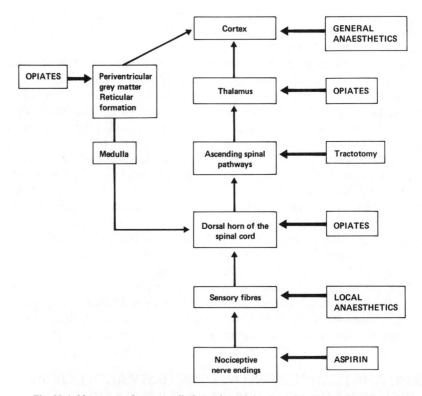

Fig. 30.1. Nervous pathways mediating pain and the sites of action of analgesics.

Although the precise functions of some of the central nervous system relays are not understood, the relevant neuropharmacology is becoming clearer. Opiate receptors and opioid peptides, particularly the enkephalins, are found in the dorsal horn of the spinal cord, in the periventricular grey matter, and in the thalamus. The opioid peptides probably function as neurotransmitters in these areas. Substance P is highly concentrated in the dorsal horn of the spinal cord, where it might function as a neurotransmitter for the relay of nervous impulses. 5-hydroxytryptamine is the neurotransmitter of the system originating in the medulla and descending to the dorsal horn, where it probably modulates sensory inputs from the periphery.

30.2. MECHANISMS OF ACTION OF ANALGESICS

Against this background the actions of analgesic drugs can be partly understood. Their sites of action are illustrated in Fig. 30.1.

Non-narcotic analgesics almost certainly act peripherally. Aspirin is a potent inhibitor of prostaglandin synthetase (cyclo-oxygenase), and thus inhibits the formation of the prostaglandins. Through this mechanism it produces at least its anti-inflammatory activity, and even if inflammation is not primarily involved in the syndrome of pain, the inhibition of prostaglandin synthesis is thought to remove the effect of prostaglandins in lowering the threshold at which the pain nerve-endings fire—i.e. it makes them less sensitive to painful stimuli.

The analgesic action of paracetamol is not easy to explain. It is a poor inhibitor of peripheral prostaglandin synthesis, but it has been suggested that it may inhibit brain prostaglandin synthetase activity, and somehow produce an analgesic effect centrally. However, the matter is not settled.

The narcotic analgesics all act as complete or partial agonists at opiate receptors, of which several types are now known to exist, in the brain and spinal cord, and in the periphery (e.g. in the gut). Presumably they mimic the actions of the endogenous opioid peptides, albeit in great excess, and thereby inhibit both the spinal and central processing of pain sensation.

Local anaesthetics block sensory nerve conduction, and general anaesthesia renders the brain incapable of perceiving pain.

30.3. PRINCIPLES UNDERLYING THE USE OF ANALGESICS IN THE TREATMENT OF PAIN

There are certain principles to be observed in the treatment of pain.

30.3.1. Identification of the cause

If the cause of the pain can be identified then it may be possible to treat the pain by specific measures aimed at treating the cause. For example, one would not treat angina pectoris with an analgesic, since glyceryl trinitrate, by decreasing myocardial oxygen requirements, relieves the pain directly. Often, however, even when the cause of the pain is known and treatable, interim symptomatic relief with analgesics may be required. For example, although the treatment of acute peritonitis involves surgery and antibiotic therapy, narcotic analgesics are also used to relieve the pain. In the discussion that follows we shall deal only with the symptomatic relief of pain.

30.3.2. The need for adequate dosage

When treating pain it is important to give effective doses of analgesics and to give treatment sufficiently frequently to provide continuous control. This means that one does *not* control continuing severe pain on the basis of doses 'when required', thus allowing the pain to recur before giving further treatment. Instead doses of analgesics in such cases should be given *in anticipation of pain*, based on careful observation of the pattern of symptoms in the individual patient. In severe continuous pain, continuous control of the pain allows the use of lower doses of narcotic analgesics, avoids to some extent analgesic tolerance, and is generally more therapeutically effective.

30.3.3. The use of adjunctive therapy

There are several circumstances in which drugs other than analgesics may be needed as adjunctive therapy.

(a) Anti-emetics

Morphine and diamorphine both cause nausea and vomiting, and their use in short-term treatment is often accompanied (e.g. in coronary care units) by the administration of anti-emetics, such as cyclizine or prochlorperazine. During chronic therapy, when narcotic analgesics are given orally, they are often given in elixirs containing anti-emetics, such as chlorpromazine (see Pharmacopoeia, p.714). In such cases cocaine is also often added, to act as a mental stimulant and mild euphoriant, although its therapeutic value in the relief of pain has not been proven.

(b) Psychotropic drugs

Whether tricyclic antidepressants have some effect on pain perception is not known, but the effectiveness of analgesic therapy in the treatment of chronic pain can sometimes be improved by tricyclic antidepressants, particularly if there are depressive symptoms. Tricyclic antidepressants have also been found of value in the treatment of post-herpetic neuralgia when used in combination with carbamazepine or sodium valproate.

If anxiety is an important component of pain a benzodiazepine may be of value, and benzodiazepines or chloral hydrate derivatives may also be useful in treating insomnia associated with pain.

(c) Laxatives

These may be necessary to relieve the constipation which may result during the long-term use of narcotic analgesics.

30.3.4. Differences in analgesic and anti-inflammatory properties of analgesic drugs

It is important to note that drugs used as analgesics and non-steroidal anti-inflammatory drugs vary in their analgesic and anti-inflammatory activities as shown in Table 30.1. Drugs which have both analgesic and anti-inflammatory properties are specifically useful in the treatment of rheumatic and other arthropathies (see Chapter 27) and in the treatment of painful bony metastases.

Table 30.1 *Analgesic and anti-inflammatory properties of some commonly used analgesics and non-steroidal anti-inflammatory drugs*

Drug	Analgesic activity	Anti-inflammatory activity
Aspirin	+	+
Paracetamol	+	−
Indomethacin	±	+
Phenylbutazone	±	+
Mefenamic acid	+	+
Flufenamic acid	−	+

Table 30.2 *Drugs used in the symptomatic treatment of pain*

Non-narcotic analgesics (*mild to moderate pain*)
Aspirin (p.740)
Paracetamol (p.721)
Some non-steroidal anti-inflammatory drugs (see Table 30.1)

Combinations of non-narcotic and weak narcotic analgesics (*mild to moderate pain*)
Aspirin or paracetamol plus codeine
Aspirin or paracetamol plus dextropropoxyphene

Narcotic analgesics (p.713)
Mild to moderate pain
   (Codeine)
   (Dextropropoxyphene)
   Dihydrocodeine
   Buprenorphine
   Pentazocine
Severe pain
   Morphine
   Diamorphine
   Buprenorphine
   Pethidine
   Dextromoramide
   Dipipanone
   Methadone

30.4. PRACTICAL USE OF ANALGESICS

The various analgesics we shall discuss are listed in Table 30.2, and some examples of the conditions in which they are used are given in Table 30.3. In addition some pain syndromes which have specific forms of treatment are listed in Table 30.4.

Table 30.3 *Examples of appropriate analgesics for some clinical problems*

Condition	Analgesic
Sprained ankle	Aspirin
Simple headache	Aspirin or paracetamol
Pain following dental extraction	Aspirin + codeine or
Mild sciatic pain	Paracetamol + dextropropoxyphene
Severe sciatic pain	Dihydrocodeine or buprenorphine
Moderately severe post-operative pain (e.g. orthopaedic)	Dihydrocodeine or buprenorphine
Severe post-operative or traumatic pain	Morphine, diamorphine, or buprenorphine
Severe intractable pain of malignant disease	Morphine, diamorphine, dipipanone, dextromoramide etc. (see text)
Acute myocardial infarction	Morphine or diamorphine
Acute abdominal pain	Pethidine
Pain of labour	Pethidine

Table 30.4 *Some pain syndromes with specific analgesic treatments*

Condition	Treatment
Dysmenorrhoea	Mefenamic acid
Bone pain from metastatic malignant disease	Narcotic analgesics + indomethacin
Bone pain from metastatic prostatic carcinoma	Stilboestrol
Trigeminal neuralgia	
Diabetic neuropathy	Carbamazepine
Lightning pains of tabes dorsalis	
Migraine	Acute—ergotamine, paracetamol + metoclopramide
	Prophylaxis—pizotifen (see p.509)
Pains associated with giant cell arteritis and polymyalgia rheumatica	Corticosteroids
Post-herpetic neuralgia	Carbamazepine or valproate + a tricyclic antidepressant

30.4.1. Non-narcotic analgesics for mild to moderate pain

The chief indications for non-narcotic analgesics are:

somatic pain in the musculoskeletal tissues;
simple headaches;
other mild to moderate non-visceral pain in general.

Aspirin is the analgesic of choice for musculoskeletal pain and simple headache. It is particularly effective if there is an inflammatory element. The main problem with aspirin is gastric irritation, which at its mildest may result in dyspepsia, and at its most severe may cause peptic ulceration and symptomatic gastro-intestinal bleeding (see p.741). Symptomatic dyspepsia due to aspirin may be lessened by taking the drug with food, and by using soluble or buffered preparations. These preparations are particularly useful for the treatment of acute pain since they are relatively quickly absorbed. For chronic pain one may use preparations such as micro-encapsulated or enteric-coated aspirin, or other types of salicylate which cause less gastro-intestinal irritation (e.g. benorylate or diflunisal, see p.740).

Paracetamol is an alternative to aspirin, and should be used in patients with an increased tendency to gastric irritation, because it does not cause gastro-intestinal bleeding or ulceration, in patients who are sensitive to aspirin, and in patients taking warfarin (see p.777).

30.4.2. Weak narcotic analgesics for mild to moderate pain

The indications for drugs such as dextropropoxyphene and codeine are similar to those for the non-narcotic analgesics, with which they are often used in combination. Although they add little in the way of analgesic effect, they may have a slight euphoriant effect which potentiates the overall analgesic effect. These narcotic analgesics should not be prescribed for long periods for trivial reasons, since they carry a slight potential for abuse. In addition codeine can cause severe constipation.

30.4.3. Moderately potent analgesics for the treatment of moderate pain

Dihydrocodeine is more potent than codeine or dextropropoxyphene, and can be useful in patients with moderate to severe visceral pain. However, like codeine it causes constipation, and can also be quite sedative. It also causes dizziness and, especially in the elderly, confusion.

Pentazocine is more potent still. It is a narcotic analgesic with agonist/antagonist properties and is roughly half as potent as morphine. It does not generally produce much sedation or respiratory depression, but neither is it very effective in relieving anxiety or in producing euphoria. In fact it may cause dysphoria and hallucinations. Because it causes a rise in systemic and pulmonary arterial pressures it should not be used for the treatment of the pain of acute myocardial infarction. It has potential for abuse but less than that of morphine. If used in patients with narcotic addiction it causes withdrawal reactions because of its antagonist properties.

Buprenorphine (p.541) is now to be preferred to pentazocine.

30.4.4. Narcotic analgesics for the treatment of severe pain

Potent narcotic analgesics are particularly indicated for the relief of visceral pain, post-operative pain, severe pain in trauma, and the pain of advanced malignant disease. Morphine and diamorphine have the additional very useful actions of relieving anxiety, producing drowsiness, and allowing sleep. Because they also cause peripheral vasodilatation they are the narcotics of choice in the treatment of the pain of acute myocardial infarction. For the relief of pain in labour pethidine is generally chosen if only short-term relief is required (epidural anaesthesia being preferred for longer-term relief). That is because it causes less respiratory depression in the newborn than other potent narcotic analgesics. It is also sometimes preferred to morphine in the treatment of biliary and ureteric colic, since it causes less smooth muscle contraction. In such cases the alternative is to use morphine in conjunction with atropine.

Although there are quantitative differences between the narcotic analgesics they all share the potential to produce similar adverse effects, such as respiratory depression, suppression of cough reflex, nausea and vomiting, constipation, tolerance, and dependence.

Beware of prescribing narcotic analgesics for any of the following:

patients with impaired liver function (see p.387);

patients with increased intracranial pressure, since the level of consciousness and the diameter and reactivity of the pupils in such cases are important guides to the aetiology and prognosis;

patients with decreased respiratory function;

patients with hypotension;

patients with impaired renal function (this is important only for pethidine, whose metabolite norpethidine is pharmacologically active, and is excreted in the urine).

Details of formulations available, dosages, routes of administration, and so on, are given in the Pharmacopoeia (see p.713) but some of the points are worth expanding.

For short-term treatment of pain morphine and diamorphine are given parenterally. The choices of parenteral route are:

subcutaneous (not a favoured route because of variability of absorption);

intramuscular (usually the preferred route);

intravenous (usually reserved for very severe, acute pain or in acute left ventricular failure with pulmonary oedema).

More recently opiates such as morphine have been given into the spine, intrathecally or extradurally, for the treatment of post-operative pain (e.g. after urological procedures), but these routes are still mainly experimental.

For more chronic pain oral preparations are available, e.g. as elixirs, particularly in combinations with anti-emetics such as chlorpromazine (see Pharmacopoeia).

The usual dose of morphine i.m. is 10 mg. It has effects in 15–30 min, reaching a maximum in 1–1½ h, and lasting 3–6 h. The effective dose when given orally, whether by elixir or as controlled-release tablets is unpredictable and usually a larger dose is needed than by the parenteral routes because of first-pass metabolism. If one uses the controlled-release preparation one should first determine the dose the individual patient requires using elixir and then substitute the controlled-release tablets. This is because the time to steady state (see p.34) will depend on the rate-limiting half-time, which in this case is prolonged, being the half-time of release of morphine from the controlled-release tablet.

Dosages of diamorphine by any route are about half those of morphine.

Pethidine is generally given i.m. since its systemic availability after oral administration is unpredictable, mostly because of extensive first-pass metabolism.

Dextromoramide, dipipanone, and methadone are generally used in the long-term treatment of intractable pain, as alternatives to morphine or diamorphine (e.g. in the pain associated with malignant disease). They are all liable to produce tolerance and dependence.

Buprenorphine is a relatively new narcotic analgesic with low potential for dependence, because of its agonist/antagonist profile. It has a duration of action of 6–8 h and can be given not only parenterally (i.m. or i.v.) but also sublingually, for both acute and chronic pain. The sublingual route obviates the first-pass metabolism by the liver and is especially useful in treating transient, moderate to severe visceral pain. Buprenorphine can cause respiratory depression, and naloxone (see p.713) is not very effective as an antagonist—in such cases artificial ventilation and respiratory stimulants, such as doxapram, may be required.

30.5. THE TREATMENT OF INTRACTABLE PAIN IN TERMINAL MALIGNANT DISEASE

Analgesia is only one factor in the treatment of the pain and distress of advanced, metastatic, and terminal malignant disease, the management of which has become a specialty of its own in recent years.

In the treatment of pain in these patients there are certain important principles to be observed, similar to the general principles outlined above.

1. Analgesic drug therapy must be carefully tailored to suit the needs of the individual.

2. Pain should be relieved quickly and effectively by the administration of adequate doses, sufficiently frequently. The aim should be to remove pain altogether and to prevent its recurrence.

3. Although tolerance to narcotic analgesics may occur, the principle of giving the appropriate dose sufficiently often will minimize the develop-

ment of tolerance. One should not withhold analgesics in these circumstances simply because of a concern that dependence may occur.

Treatment can begin with simple non-narcotic analgesics and these may be effective when combined with other general management. If and when the pain becomes worse an oral narcotic agent will be indicated—some use the synthetic narcotics such as oral dipipanone, dextromoramide, or methadone, while others prefer morphine or diamorphine elixirs. Whichever preparation is used the starting dose should be at the lower end of the dosage range (e.g. 10 mg morphine four-hourly) increasing the dose every 24 h until the pain is controlled. If the pain is very severe dosages may be increased more frequently. For morphine the steps in dosage should be 10, 20, 30, 45, 60, 90, 120, and 150 mg. As soon as the pain is controlled the effective dose should be repeated at the usual dosage interval (e.g. four-hourly for morphine), or more frequently if the patient's pain is recurring before the next dose is due.

Parenteral analgesics should be necessary only for the patient who cannot swallow or who is vomiting.

Phenothiazines should be used to prevent nausea and vomiting due to opiate analgesics (see Pharmacopoeia for lists of some available elixir preparations of narcotic analgesics with chlorpromazine).

30.6. GENERAL ANAESTHESIA

Anaesthetists are amongst the best practical clinical pharmacologists. Through the skilled use of drugs the patient is tranquillized and prepared for operation, quickly and pleasantly rendered unconscious and unfeeling, and kept so at a finely-tuned level throughout the operation. During this time muscle relaxants are administered to facilitate surgery, the patient's airways are carefully kept patent, and meticulous attention is paid to oxygenation and the preservation of normal blood gases and respiratory acid–base balance. Cardiovascular function and blood pressure are monitored and kept within well-defined 'normal' limits. All of this requires careful handling of the drugs used in anaesthetic practice. Any untoward physiological disturbance during the operation has to be handled, often with drugs. After the operation the sooner the patient's normal functions are restored the better. He should be independently breathing normally and fully (i.e. reversed respiratory depression and neuromuscular block), with stable circulation and normal consciousness, but without post-operative pain (requiring the judicious use of post-operative analgesic drugs).

It is a tribute to anaesthetic skill in the use of drugs and the maintenance of physiological functions that serious adverse events are so infrequent during anaesthesia.

Our purpose here is to examine briefly the clinical pharmacology of the main agents used in anaesthetic practice, and some principles of their use. Precise details of anaesthetic practice will not be dealt with, nor, except when it is productive (e.g. muscle relaxants), will we pay much attention to basic mechanisms of action. (The actions of opiates, benzodiazepines, anticholinergic drugs, and analgesics are discussed elsewhere, and the mechanism of action of the volatile anaesthetics is still obscure.)

The usual requirements during general anaesthesia are:

narcosis (unconsciousness);
analgesia (reflex suppression);
muscle relaxation;
control of physiological stability and suppression of visceral reflexes.

A brief reflection will reveal that no one agent is likely to achieve all of these effects in the correct proportions, so various agents are used in combination to produce balanced anaesthesia.

Procedurally, drug use can be considered for the various parts of the general anaesthetic process:

1. Premedication.
2. Induction of anaesthesia.
3. Muscle relaxation.
4. Maintenance of narcosis.
5. Reflex suppression (analgesia).
6. Post-operative medication:
    (a) reversal of neuromuscular block;
    (b) analgesia.

The list of drugs used is given in Table 30.5.

Let us examine briefly the way that some of the drugs listed are used in anaesthetic practice.

30.6.1. Premedication

The aims of premedication are:

(a) reduction of anxiety;
(b) reduction of salivary secretions;
(c) suppression of autonomic reflexes (e.g. cardiac arrhythmias);
(d) amnesia;
(e) to aid in various aspects of the anaesthetic technique and process.

The most commonly used premedication is an opiate together with an antimuscarinic agent. The opiate is usually morphine or papaveretum (omnopon), which in addition to relieving anxiety provide some intra-operative analgesia. Atropine or hyoscine are used to dry up secretions and to suppress the parasympathetic overactivity induced by suxamethonium and operative procedures.

Table 30.5   *Drugs used in anaesthesia*

A. *Premedication*
1. Sedatives and analgesics
   Narcotic analgesics, e.g. morphine, pethidine, papaveretum (p.713)
   Benzodiazepines, e.g. diazepam (p.642)
2. Anticholinergic drugs (p.616)
   Atropine
   Hyoscine

B. *Induction: intravenous anaesthetics (induction and maintenance)*
   Thiopentone
   Diazepam
   Methohexitone
   Alphaxalone/alphadolone
   Etomidate
   Propanidid
   Ketamine

C. *Maintenance of narcosis: inhalational anaesthetics*
   Nitrous oxide
   Halothane
   Enflurane
   Cyclopropane
   Ether
   Methoxyflurane
   Trichloroethylene

D. *Muscle relaxation*
1. Non-depolarizing muscle relaxants (p.717)
   Tubocurarine
   Pancuronium
   Gallamine
   Alcuronium
   Fazadinium
2. Depolarizing muscle relaxants (p.718)
   Suxamethonium

E. *Neuroleptic and narcotic analgesic drugs (specially used during anaesthesia)*
   Droperidol (p.647)
   Fentanyl
   Phenoperidine
   Morphine (p.713)

Depending upon the operative procedure being undertaken alternative premedication procedures may employ:

(a) Benzodiazepines (which provide no analgesia).

(b) Droperidol (a neuroleptic drug) with fentanyl (a narcotic analgesic), both given i.v. providing swift sedation with analgesia.

(c) Phenothiazines—trimeprazine is sometimes used as a premedication in children.

30.6.2 Induction of anaesthesia

Thiopentone i.v. is the most commonly used inducing agent for major surgery. Narcosis occurs within 10–30 s. Other options are mentioned in the list of drugs. Suxamethonium i.v. is usually used immediately following thiopentone prior to tracheal intubation if that is to be performed, to provide muscle relaxation of short duration.

30.6.3.Maintenance of anaesthesia

The above induction may then be followed by maintenance anaesthesia appropriate to the type of surgical operation being undertaken. This might involve the administration of a nitrous oxide/oxygen mixture, with or without halothane, supplemented when necessary by the i.v. administration of a narcotic analgesic such as fentanyl, or occasionally by additional doses of an i.v anaesthetic drug. Muscle relaxation during maintenance anaesthesia of appreciable duration can be provided by the use of non-depolarizing muscle relaxants.

It is important to note that halothane is a potent inhalational anaesthetic but a rather poor analgesic whereas nitrous oxide is a potent analgesic but a weak anaesthetic, the two together providing controlled and balanced anaesthesia and analgesia.

The anaesthesia and analgesia produced by inhalational anaesthetics quickly reverse as the anaesthetic agent is cleared from the brain. Analgesia and respiratory depression from narcotic analgesics given during anaesthesia may persist into the post-operative phase. Post-operative analgesia may be desirable but respiratory depression is not. Naloxone (an opiate antagonist) is used to reverse narcotic-induced respiratory depression, but careful dosage is needed to avoid reversal of analgesia.

Non-depolarizing neuromuscular block persisting after the operation is reversed by the administration of neostigmine i.v., which may need to be repeated. The muscarinic effects of neostigmine are prevented by the concurrent administration of i.v. atropine.

Post-operative analgesia is usually provided by the administration of narcotic analgesics.

The above general type of routine is subject to great variation depending upon the age and medical condition of the patient, the type of operation and surgical technique, the wishes and experience of the anaesthetist, and the peri-operative anaesthetic technology available.

There are also points of general principle about some of the agents used in anaesthetic practice which require some explanation.

30.6.4. Intravenous anaesthetic agents
(a) Thiopentone

This barbiturate is the most commonly used i.v. anaesthetic, and is often used as the sole anaesthetic agent for short and minor operations, and for electroconvulsive therapy. The solution for injection is alkaline and can produce tissue necrosis if injected extravascularly, and arterial spasm if injected into an artery.

The onset and duration of action of thiopentone illustrate some interesting clinical pharmacology. An effective anaesthetic dose (up to 4 mg/kg) produces loss of consciousness within the time of circulation of the total blood volume (i.e. 1 min). This is because the drug is highly lipid soluble and enters the brain very readily. This fast induction of anaesthesia occurs while plasma concentrations are at a peak after injection. Then the drug starts to distribute to other body tissues and the plasma concentrations start to fall as the drug is distributed first into muscle and later into fat. It is mainly the fall in plasma concentrations produced by the distribution phase ($t_{1/2}$ 2.5 min) which is responsible for the short duration of anaesthesia after an initial injection.

However, if large or repeated doses of thiopentone are given the drug enters fat depots, and because hepatic metabolism is slow ($t_{1/2}$ 6 h), a distribution equilibrium is set up between blood, fat (and other tissues), and brain, and this can lead to prolonged anaesthesia and unconsciousness, which post-operatively is a serious hazard. This cumulative effect must be allowed for when calculating dosages for administration by intermittent injection or infusion. This is one reason why maintenance anaesthesia with an inhalational anaesthetic is generally preferred.

In states of circulatory shock, with peripheral circulatory failure and hypovolaemia, the speed and effectiveness of the distribution phase may be reduced, and prolonged high blood concentrations may cause prolonged and deep anaesthesia, unexpectedly severe depression of all cerebral functions, and depression of cardiac function (hypotension and a fall in cardiac output).

Adverse effects of thiopentone include: respiratory depression, hypotension due to vasodilatation and depressed myocardial function, and laryngeal spasm.

Thiopentone is best avoided in patients with renal failure, marked congestive cardiac failure, acute intestinal obstruction, and in gravely ill patients with anaemia, debilitation, or circulatory shock.

Contra-indications to the use of thiopentone include a history of thiopentone sensitivity and, because it is a barbiturate, porphyria (see Chapter 8).

(b) Methohexitone

Methohexitone is a barbiturate, more potent than thiopentone, and producing a shorter duration of anaesthesia. Recovery from its anaesthetic effects depends upon the redistribution of drug from brain to tissues as with thiopentone. Hepatic metabolism is faster than with thiopentone ($t_{1/2}$ 100 min).

Methohexitone is used for out-patient and dental procedures because of its short duration. Its disadvantages are that it may cause tremor, involuntary movements, hiccups, and coughing, it is not anticonvulsant, and it can cause Type I hypersensitivity reactions.

(c) Alphaxalone/alphadolone combination (Althesin®)

Althesin® is a mixture of two steroids. Alphadolone is about half as potent as alphaxalone as an anaesthetic agent, but has an effect in the mixture to increase the solubility of aphaxalone about threefold. Even so the mixture has to be made up in polyoxyethylated castor oil (Cremophor EL®) which can cause adverse effects of an anaphylactoid type, e.g. bronchospasm, hypotension, flushing. Care should be taken in individuals with an allergic history. It has a tendency to cause thrombophlebitis. These reactions have limited its use.

Following i.v. administration it rapidly produces general anaesthesia which lasts about 8–12 min. It is not a potent analgesic. Elimination occurs through rapid hepatic metabolism.

(d) Etomidate

Etomidate is an imidazole with a short duration of action, probably due to rapid hepatic metabolism. Repeated doses are not cumulative. Its drawbacks are pain at the site of injection and muscle movements. The latter usually require that premedication with a narcotic analgesic such as fentanyl be given.

(e) Propanidid

Propanidid is an i.v. anaesthetic agent, a phenoxyacetic amine, which is also prepared in polyoxyethylated castor oil (Cremophor EL®) with its attendant problems as outlined for Althesin®. It has a very short duration of action because it is hydrolysed by serum and tissue (liver) cholinesterases ($t_{1/2}$ 5 min). Its duration of action is therefore prolonged in patients with pseudocholinesterase deficiency. It may prolong the action of suxamethonium. Its important potential adverse effects are cardiovascular depression with hypotension, hyperpnoea followed by apnoea, and the anaphylactoid-like reactions due to the castor oil vehicle.

30.6.5. Inhalational anaesthetic agents

The depth of anaesthesia produced by these agents is determined by their partial pressure in cerebral arterial blood (which determines their diffusion into, and partial pressure within, brain tissue).

The partial pressure of the anaesthetic agent in arterial blood is determined by the following factors:

(a) The partial pressure of the agent in alveolar gas.

This depends on several factors.

(i) The concentration of the anaesthetic agent in the inspired gas
This is controlled by the anaesthetist.

(ii) The alveolar ventilation
This can be controlled by the anaesthetist.

(iii) The removal (rate of diffusion) of the agent from alveolus to blood
This depends upon the partial pressure gradient of the agent between alveolus and mixed venous blood (which changes as the duration of administration proceeds), pulmonary blood flow, carrying the agent in the blood away from the diffusion point, and the solubility of the anaesthetic agent in the blood (see below). The alveolar membrane itself provides no appreciable barrier to diffusion.

(b) The solubility of the anaesthetic agent in the blood

The solubility of an anaesthetic agent in the blood is expressed as the blood/gas partition coefficient. This is the ratio of the concentration in the blood to the concentration in a gas phase across a diffusing membrane when the partial pressures in both phases are equal, i.e. at equilibrium. The more soluble the agent in the blood the higher the partition coefficient. Some blood/gas coefficients are shown below.

Cyclopropane	0.46
Nitrous oxide	0.47
Halothane	3.6
Diethyl ether	12.1 (very soluble)

When blood solubility is high, more of the anaesthetic must be dissolved in the blood to raise its partial pressure there to levels which will produce anaesthesia, and in addition more agent is removed from the alveolar gas phase thus reducing the diffusion gradient. When blood solubility is low the partial pressure in the blood increases more quickly and anaesthesia is more rapid.

One measure often used to express the potency of anaesthetic gases is the Minimum Alveolar Concentration (MAC) which will produce a state of anaesthesia in 50 per cent of patients. Some values for MAC are given below.

Halothane	0.77
Diethyl ether	1.92
Cyclopropane	9.2
Nitrous oxide	101

Recovery from anaesthesia involves a reversal of the effects described for its production. When ventilation with gas free of anaesthetic is given, the partial pressure of the agent in arterial blood quickly falls, partial pressures in the brain quickly follow, and consciousness returns. The anaesthetic agent persists for longer in muscles and fat because of lower blood supply.

Of the inhalational anaesthetics in the list of drugs in Table 30.5 only nitrous oxide and halothane will be discussed briefly here.

(a) Nitrous oxide

Nitrous oxide is quite a potent analgesic but a relatively weak anaesthetic (MAC=101).

It is frequently used with narcotic analgesic premedication and i.v. thiopentone for *induction* of anaesthesia (nitrous oxide 70 per cent with 30 per cent oxygen), and then as a background anaesthetic together with a volatile anaesthetic, e.g. halothane, and oxygen 30–35 per cent in *maintenance* anaesthesia.

Nitrous oxide–oxygen mixture (50 per cent N_2O : 50 per cent O_2—Entonox®) is useful as a rapid analgesic agent in subanaesthetic doses, and is used for this purpose in obstetric analgesia, and for procedures requiring short periods of analgesia, e.g. burns dressings, orthopaedic manipulations.

It is generally non-toxic, but hypoxia must be avoided. It may potentiate respiratory depression due to narcotic analgesics.

Bone marrow depression has occurred with prolonged administration of nitrous oxide (e.g. in the treatment of tetanus). It quickly diffuses into air-containing spaces, and pressure may build up in the paranasal sinuses, and the middle ear. Pneumothorax may also result.

(b) Halothane

Halothane is a colourless, non-inflammable, volatile liquid anaesthetic, the vapour of which is pleasant to inhale, and non-irritating, and with which there is a low incidence of post-operative vomiting. It is a powerful anaesthetic (MAC=0.75) and rapid in its action, but in low concentrations is a rather poor analgesic. Recovery from its anaesthetic effects is rapid. It is used in the maintenance of anaesthesia. Although most of it is eliminated by expiration, some is metabolized in the liver, and the metabolites are cleared slowly.

Halothane itself produces some degree of muscle relaxation, although insufficient for major abdominal surgery when muscle relaxants should be used. The actions of d-tubocurarine on the motor end-plate and at autonomic ganglia are potentiated, and the latter may result in hypotension. Gallamine and pancuronium have no ganglionic blocking effects and so when used with halothane do not produce hypotension.

The effects on the cardiovascular system are important. Halothane normally slows the heart rate by reducing cardiac sympathetic activity. However, it also predisposes to ventricular arrhythmias: ventricular extrasystoles, ventricular tachycardia, and occasionally ventricular fibrillation. Carbon dioxide retention worsens this tendency. Halothane also renders the heart more sensitive to the arrhythmogenic effects of injected adrenaline.

Halothane causes a dose-dependent fall in blood pressure which is thought to be due to a combination of peripheral vasodilatation, depressed myocardial contractility producing a fall in cardiac output, and disordered baroreceptor function.

Halothane is a respiratory depressant, and the tendency to hypoventilation must be corrected by assisted ventilation. Bronchodilatation, lack of stimulation of secretions and its lack of irritation to bronchi, pharynx, and larynx make it a suitable agent for patients with asthma, chronic bronchitis, and emphysema.

The main problem outside the actual procedure of anaesthesia has been the effect of halothane on the liver. There is a very small risk of hepatitis occurring after halothane, the severity of which can range from acute massive necrosis of the liver, which is very rare indeed, to disturbances of liver function with or without jaundice. The risk of liver damage is increased by repeated exposure (particularly when the last exposure was within 6 weeks), in the middle-aged, and in the obese. The hepatitis may be a hypersensitivity reaction perhaps due to metabolite (hapten)–protein interaction, or possibly due to direct toxicity of halothane metabolites.

The precise incidence and cause of hepatitis following halothane anaesthesia are still somewhat unclear, but most authorities now accept that there is a small risk and if possible avoid repeated exposure at short intervals.

30.6.6. Muscle relaxants—neuromuscular blocking drugs

The detailed clinical pharmacology of the muscle relaxants is dealt with in the Pharmacopoeia. They are of two types:

(a) Non-depolarizing or competitive blocking agents—tubocurarine, pancuronium, gallamine, alcuronium, and fazadinium.
(b) Depolarizing agents—suxamethonium.

Non-depolarizing competitive blocking agents compete with and antagonize the actions of acetylcholine at the muscle motor end-plate. These drugs can be antagonized by acetylcholinesterase inhibitors (e.g. neostigmine) which prevent the metabolism of acetylcholine and cause its build-up at the motor end-plate, thereby overcoming the competitive block.

The depolarizing agent suxamethonium, which is similar in structure to acetylcholine, causes a prolonged depolarization of the motor end-plate and prevents the response to acetylcholine. Its effects are not reversed by neostigmine.

Suxamethonium is used for short periods of muscle relaxation during tracheal intubation or electroconvulsive therapy.

If longer periods of muscle relaxation are required, e.g. during abdominal surgery, non-depolarizing drugs such as pancuronium or tubo-curarine are used.

All these drugs are administered i.v., they are highly charged, and do not pass across cell membranes. Muscle blood flow therefore determines the speed of onset of neuromuscular blockade.

Ventilation is, of course, essential when the patient is paralysed with neuromuscular blocking agents, and one of the main problems with these drugs is prolonged apnoea requiring maintenance of assisted ventilation. Prolonged apnoea after non-depolarizing relaxants may be caused by metabolic acidosis, myasthenia gravis, potassium depletion, hypo-natraemia, drugs, and decreased elimination (e.g. renal failure). Prolonged apnoea after depolarizing agents may be due to congenital pseudo-cholinesterase deficiency (Chapter 8), dehydration and electrolyte imbalance resulting in 'dual block' (which is the development of a non-depolarizing block following the primary depolarizing block, usually due to repeated doses of suxamethonium), overdose, and relatively low serum cholinesterase, e.g. in liver disease, malnutrition, or because of drugs.

30.7. LOCAL ANAESTHETICS

Local anaesthetics (see list in Table 30.6) block nerve conduction by reducing membrane permeability to sodium ions.

Table 30.6 *Commonly used local anaesthetics*

Lignocaine (p.697)
Mepivacaine
Bupivacaine
Prilocaine
Amethocaine

Small unmyelinated fibres are blocked first, and large myelinated fibres last. Loss of nerve function proceeds through pain, temperature, touch, proprioception, and finally skeletal muscle power.

The procedures undertaken to apply local anaesthetics to nervous tissues in appropriate concentrations without producing systemic toxicity are the province of surgical and anaesthetic texts.

Local anaesthetics are used in the following ways to produce local anaesthesia:

30.7.1. Local and regional anaesthesia

(a) Topical—lignocaine, amethocaine.
(b) Infiltration—lignocaine, mepivacaine, prilocaine.
(c) Field block—lignocaine, mepivacaine, prilocaine.

(d) Nerve block—bupivacaine, lignocaine, mepivacaine, prilocaine.
(e) Intravenous local anesthesia—lignocaine, prilocaine.
(f) Epidural—bupivacaine, lignocaine, mepivacaine, prilocaine.
(g) Caudal—bupivacaine, lignocaine, mepivacaine, prilocaine.
(h) Spinal (intradural)—prilocaine, mepivacaine.

Taking the potency of lignocaine, mepivacaine, and prilocaine as one, the potencies of bupivacaine and amethocaine are 0.25.

Consider in further detail the use of lignocaine as a local anaesthetic. Lignocaine is a weak base with a pK_a of 7.86. It is prepared in aqueous solution as the soluble hydrochloride salt. At the physiological pH of the tissues (which is less than 7.86) most of the drug will be in the ionized form, but some will be in the non-ionized form. The non-ionized form is important because it is in this form that the drug most easily penetrates the lipid barriers around and within nerve tissues, and thus gets to the site of action, but it seems likely that it is the ionized form which combines with the excitable membrane to inhibit sodium permeability.

The onset of the action of lignocaine is rapid. Alone in a 1 per cent solution its duration of action is about 1 h, but when adrenaline is present in the solution this may be prolonged to 1½–2h.

When used as a local anaesthetic the duration of effect of lignocaine is governed by its diffusion from the site of injection, the drug eventually being cleared from the body by hepatic microsomal amidases. Plainly systemic toxicity (see lignocaine in the Pharmacopoeia) can occur if the amounts injected for local anaesthesia are large. In adults it is suggested that 200 mg lignocaine (i.e. 20 ml of a 1 per cent solution) is the maximum when no adrenaline is in the solution and 500 mg (i.e. 50 ml of a 1 per cent solution) with solutions which contain adrenaline.

The systemic toxicity of all the local anaesthetics is similar. These are discussed in detail for lignocaine in the Pharmacopoeia. The main effects are on the CNS and cardiovascular system.

Allergic reactions occasionally occur with bronchospasm, urticaria, and angio-oedema. Such reactions occur more commonly with amethocaine, cocaine, and procaine. The local application of amethocaine and benzocaine may cause a local allergic reaction on skin or mucous membranes.

Some special points need to be made to avoid adverse reactions in the use of local anaesthetics.

1. Take care not to overdose because of the risks (particularly in the frail elderly) of systemic toxicity.
2. Beware of overdosing with local anaesthetic solutions containing adrenaline or felypressin (a vasoconstrictor vasopressin analogue).

These vasoconstrictors are added to diminish local blood flow and therefore to prolong anaesthesia. Their dangers are:

(a) The production of local ischaemia.

(b) Adrenaline may produce systemic toxicity in the susceptible patient and overdose must be avoided. The total dose of adrenaline should not exceed 500 micrograms, and if more than 50 ml of a solution is to be injected the adrenaline concentration should not be more than 1:200 000.

(c) Adrenaline in local anaesthetics can be potentiated by tricyclic antidepressants. This is potentially a very important drug interaction in dental anaesthetic practice. Solutions containing felypressin should be safer in such patients.

The preparations of lignocaine which are available are worth examining so that one is aware of the availability of a particular preparation for a particular use, and so that haphazard use of the inappropriate preparation is avoided.

30.7.2. Local anaesthetic preparations of lignocaine

(a) Lignocaine hydrochloride injection

Solutions of 0.5, 1, 1.5, and 2 per cent lignocaine are available (1 per cent solutions are usually adequate for local anaesthesia).

(b) Lignocaine and adrenaline injections

Lignocaine	–	*Adrenaline*
0.5 per cent (5 mg/ml)	–	1:200 000 (5 micrograms/ml)
1 per cent (10 mg/ml)	–	1:100 000 (10 micrograms/ml)
1 per cent (10 mg/ml)	–	1:200 000 (5 micrograms/ml)

(c) Lignocaine preparations for surface anaesthesia

Most of these preparations contain lignocaine in concentrations of 2–4 per cent.

(d) Spinal anaesthesia

In spinal (intradural) anaesthesia local anaesthetic preparations are sometimes used (e.g. mepivacaine) which contain glucose and are of high specific gravity. By positioning of the patient the local anaesthetic effect can be limited to a desired level of the cord. This requires a great deal of skill.

31 Drug dependence and abuse

The important classes of chemical agents most commonly subject to abuse are listed below:

   (i) opiates (and related narcotic analgesics);
   (ii) CNS stimulants—amphetamine and related drugs, and cocaine;
  (iii) cannabis;
  (iv) lysergic acid diethylamide (LSD) and other psychedelic agents;
   (v) alcohol;
  (vi) hypnotics and tranquillizers;
 (vii) nicotine (tobacco).

Some authorities tend to be pedantic about the use of terms in this subject, and we shall therefore define the commonly used terms.

Psychological dependence indicates a state in which an individual has become dependent on taking the drug to achieve a level of everyday function which he perceives as being satisfactory. In this state the patient has got 'into the habit' of taking the drug and is therefore *habituated*. If the individual requires continued administration of the drug to prevent the occurrence of physical withdrawal symptoms then *physical dependence* exists. If the individual spends a good deal of the time in drug-seeking and drug-taking behaviour then this indicates *compulsive drug abuse*. The term *drug addiction* indicates compulsive drug abuse plus psychological and physical dependence.

31.1. FACTORS PREDISPOSING TO DRUG DEPENDENCE

31.1.1. The nature of the individual

(a) Psychological factors.

Although the psychological factors predisposing to drug dependence are beyond the scope of this text they form one aspect of a number of different factors which predispose to or perpetuate drug dependence in an individual. There are no sure predictive tests to indicate who may or may not seek to abuse drugs.

(b) Neurochemical and neuropharmacological factors

These may well operate in the initiation of drug abuse, and certainly operate in addiction. Presumably there is some pattern of neuronal function, either at the level of the integration of neuronal systems, or at a biochemical/pharmacological level, rendering an individual more or less likely to react to a drug in such a way as to lead that individual to want to repeat the experience. This biological substrate will then be one of the factors which might continue to predispose the individual to further repetitions of the experience. Repeated exposure then leads to the occurrence of pharmacological adaptive changes in the CNS causing the addictive state. When this state is reached the adaptive changes which occur are such that in the absence of the drug, neuronal patterns of activity are unveiled or activated, and cause the withdrawal syndrome.

There are various pharmacological hypotheses about the basis of opiate addiction, and alcohol and benzodiazepine dependence. Although they are unproven these hypotheses show the way science is approaching the problem.

In opiate addiction it is proposed that the exogenous opiate (addictive drug) acts on the endogenous opiate receptor (enkephalin receptor). This agonist action may either turn off endogenous enkephalin synthesis by negative feedback or function in some way such that when the exogenous opiate is withdrawn endogenous enkephalin function is inadequate. Through a series of events, which probably involve the activation of central noradrenergic systems, the withdrawal syndrome is activated. It is of note that clonidine, an α_2-adrenoceptor agonist, which can inhibit the activity of certain central noradrenergic systems, can, in some addicts, suppress the withdrawal syndrome.

In alcohol, barbiturate, and benzodiazepine dependence attention is being focused currently on GABA (γ-aminobutyric acid) function. It is proposed that in their different ways alcohol, barbiturates, and benzodiazepines all lead to an increase in the functional activity of GABA in certain brain areas. If this is continued then there might be an adaptive response whereby endogenous GABA function is decreased, whether this be at the level of the whole neurone, or at a biochemical or pharmacological level. If endogenous GABA function is deficient, and the exogenous GABA 'prop' is withdrawn then GABA-mediated inhibitory influences in the brain are removed and the alcohol, barbiturate, and benzodiazepine withdrawal syndromes result. All of these syndromes have some gross features in common, including anxiety, insomnia, fits, and tremor, although the severity and quality differ in each.

Amphetamine addiction may well be dependent upon adaptive changes in dopamine or noradrenaline function, occurring as a result of the release by amphetamine of these neurotransmitters. Cocaine dependence may result from changes brought about by inhibition of noradrenaline reuptake.

LSD dependence relates to 5-hydroxytryptamine function. The pharmaco-logical mechanisms by which cannabis and nicotine bring about depend-ence are still very much a mystery.

31.1.2. Environmental factors

These comprise factors which operate outside the patient, and which lead to the initial drug-taking and its perpetuation.

Social environment, participation in drug sub-culture, and access to the drug are important psychosocial factors. As with most mental illness, in which abnormalities of cognitive function, affect, and behaviour are products of both brain function and environmental influence, so drug dependence is a result of the factors allowing or promoting access to the drug and its use, and the receptivity of the brain to its effects.

31.2. OPIATES

Opiate dependence is a potential public health menace around the world with a great deal of criminal activity surrounding it. Heroin is the most frequently socially abused opiate. First experiences may occur through sniffing ('snorting'), with graduation to subcutaneous ('joy-popping'), and then intravenous ('mainlining') administration. On first usage nausea, vomiting, and anxiety often ensue, but these symptoms disappear with subsequent use, and euphoria becomes predominant. As tolerance develops the addict uses the i.v. route with increasing dosage to try to produce the euphoria and the 'kick' which results from high plasma drug concentrations producing pleasurable bodily sensations. Tolerance to constipation and pupillary constriction does not occur to any great extent. Eventually the addict becomes most concerned with combating withdrawal symptoms and must have the drug to avoid these.

Withdrawal symptoms begin about 8 h after the last dose, and mount to a peak at about 36–72 h. Symptoms occur in the following order:

1. First psychological symptoms—anxiety, depression, restlessness, irritability, drug craving.

2. At 8–15 hours, lacrimation, rhinorrhoea, yawning, and sweating.

3. Restless sleep after which the above symptoms are accompanied by sneezing, anorexia, nausea, vomiting, abdominal cramps, diarrhoea, bone and muscle pain, tremor, weakness, chills and goose-flesh ('cold turkey'), and insomnia. Hypertension, cardiovascular collapse, and convulsions occur rarely.

4. Symptoms gradually fade over about 5–10 days, during which time general malaise and abdominal cramps persist.

The medical complications of narcotic addiction are due to the drugs, infected materials injected, and adulterants.

(a) Acute heroin reactions

Some acute reactions are due to overdose. Some may be due to adulterants, such as quinine, or to allergic reactions. These reactions tend to present as hypoxia with cyanosis, pulmonary oedema, respiratory depression, and decreased levels of consciousness progressing to coma. Fever and leucocytosis may occur. Treatment consists of establishing a good airway, maintaining adequate oxygenation, through an endotracheal tube if necessary, giving i.v. glucose and thiamine, and the cautious administration of naloxone i.v. in amounts necessary (initially 0.4 mg) to lighten consciousness if a real overdose is responsible. Naloxone may need to be repeated (see p.580). Take care not to produce an acute withdrawal reaction in an addict.

Depending upon the nature of the acute reaction, tracheal and bronchial suction, treatment of acute allergic reactions (with corticosteroids and antihistamines), and antibiotic therapy of infection may also be necessary.

(b) Infections due to repeated septic injections

Skin—abscesses, cellulitis, thrombophlebitis
Septicaemia
Endocarditis, which may be right-sided (*Staph. aureus* common)
Osteomyelitis
Viral hepatitis
Pneumonia, lung abscess

(c) Neurological complications

Transverse myelitis
Peripheral neuropathy
Meningitis
Brain abscess
Myopathy

(d) Cardiovascular/pulmonary complications

Cardiac arrhythmias
Emboli
Pulmonary aspiration
Pulmonary collapse
Coma/hypoxia

(e) Venereal disease

There is a high rate of venereal disease in female addicts because of prostitution.

(f) Pregnancy

Addicted mothers may give birth to addicted babies who may suffer withdrawal syndromes at birth.

31.2.1. Treatment of opiate dependence (see also Pharmacopoeia, p.715)

This is extremely difficult, and overall not very successful. In the UK addiction clinics have been established to try to contain the great (mainly heroin) addiction problem. At these clinics addicts can receive controlled amounts of drugs, and psychiatric and social help. Dosage reduction, with or without methadone maintenance therapy, may be possible.

Methadone maintenance aims at substituting a dose of methadone which will prevent withdrawal symptoms. Methadone is begun and heroin is gradually withdrawn. Methadone is given orally, has a prolonged action, and in appropriate doses can remove the craving for opiates. In some addicts it does become possible after a time to withdraw the methadone gradually.

Every prescriber has a duty not to foster dependency, and must avoid unwise prescribing in the individual or prescribing in such a way that controlled drugs become available in a community. One should always be on the lookout for the addict who is trying to use the unwitting doctor as a source of supply. Forging prescriptions is not uncommon.

The requirements of the Misuse of Drugs Act 1971 are summarized in the *British National Formulary*, as are the procedures for finding out about addicts from the Home Office and for notifying their occurrence. In the UK addicts may only be given diamorphine or cocaine for the purpose of addiction needs by practitioners holding a special licence, and addicts must be referred to Drug Addiction Treatment centres for such prescriptions.

The aim of all these restrictions is to prevent the spread of narcotic addiction which is a serious threat to the well-being of society let alone responsible for countless tragedies in the lives of young people.

31.3. COCAINE AND AMPHETAMINE

The clinical effects of cocaine (also known as 'coke' or 'snow') and amphetamine (also known as 'speed') are not dissimilar, although distinguishable by those with experience. The effects include euphoria, increased drive, increased confidence, increased sociability, loquacity, and increased physical and mental capacity. Decreased need for food, rest, and sleep also occur.

Amphetamine abuse usually occurs by oral administration, and i.v. use is uncommon. Cocaine is sniffed and also taken i.v.

Tolerance occurs to the peripheral and central effects of amphetamines.

Tolerance to the psychoactive effects of cocaine does not occur. There is no cross-tolerance between cocaine and amphetamines. Prolonged and high dosages may lead to amphetamine- or cocaine-induced psychosis, not dissimilar from acute paranoid schizophrenia. There are no major physiological withdrawal phenomena from amphetamines or cocaine.

31.4. CANNABIS

Cannabis sativa, the hemp plant, gives rise to marijuana and hashish. The active chemicals in the plant are δ-9-tetrahydrocannabinol (δ-9-THC), δ-8-THC, and numerous other cannabinols.

Marijuana is the dried mixture of crushed leaves and stalks of the plant. The flowering tops of the plant secrete the resin which when compressed forms hashish (or 'hash') which is more potent than marijuana. These preparations are also known under a variety of other names including 'ganja', 'bhang', 'grass', 'pot', and 'kef'. Marijuana is smoked in home-made cigarettes, hashish in small pipes.

There is widespread controversy as to whether cannabis should be legalized, like alcohol and tobacco. On balance the current opinion is that the adverse effects, psychological and physical, are likely to outweigh the benefits to society. This is bound to remain a value judgement since it is unlikely that there will ever be a clinical trial of sufficient size to find out whether the current opinion is correct or not.

When smoked, effects begin within minutes, and consist of physiological and mental effects. The physiological effects include an increase in heart rate, conjunctival suffusion, bronchodilatation, peripheral vasodilatation, dryness of the mouth, and in large doses tremor, ataxia, nystagmus, nausea, and vomiting. The mental effects vary from person to person, depending on such variables as personality, mood, surroundings, expectations, and previous cannabis experience. Generally there is a feeling of enhanced sensory perception in many sensory modalities, and a feeling of well-being. Drowsiness or hyperactivity may occur. Ideas flow rapidly and may be disconnected. Time passes slowly. Motor performance may be altered, as it may by any sedative drug, and this may impair the individual's driving skills.

Mild tolerance can occur and a mild withdrawal syndrome, a little like a mild benzodiazepine withdrawal syndrome, can occur. Physical dependence is not a big problem.

Heavy use of marijuana is associated with social apathy. Adverse psychological effects include occasional cases of depression, anxiety, acute panic reactions, and paranoid ideas. Single large doses may cause an acute toxic psychosis with confusion and hallucinations. There is controversy as to whether marijuana can produce a prolonged psychosis.

31.5. LSD AND OTHER PSYCHEDELIC DRUGS

The psychedelic drugs include lysergic acid diethylamide (LSD, also called 'acid'), psilocybin, psilocin, dimethyltryptamine, diethyltryptamine, mescaline, and some molecular analogues of the amphetamines.

LSD is the group example. Effects usually occur at doses of 200 μg, but may be seen at lower doses down to 20 μg. Within 20 min autonomic effects are apparent, including mydriasis, hyperthermia, tachycardia, increased blood pressure, piloerection, and sometimes nausea.

Mental effects are present within 1–2 h and their nature and intensity depend upon the environment and state of mind of the individual.

The mental changes noted include heightened perception, after-images fusing with true images, wave-like images, melting visual impressions, an increased sense of clarity, increased awareness, the impression that one's thoughts are of great importance (although they are generally exceptionally mundane or even trivial), a sensation of a slowing of time, and impressions of distorted body images. Mood varies, there can be euphoria or dysphoria, calmness or anxiety, elation or depression, sociability or paranoia.

Tolerance to LSD develops quickly. Physical dependence does not occur.

'Bad trips' with acute panic reactions occur sometimes and many lead to suicide.

'Flashback' is a most curious phenomenon, and is the recurrence of some aspect of the drug experience at a time when the patient is drug-free.

Acute intoxication with LSD and the flashback phenomenon can be treated with chlorpromazine.

31.6. ALCOHOL

The morbidity and mortality associated with alcohol abuse are considerable public health problems. There are three main medical and psychiatric problems:

(a) Acute alcoholic intoxication (see Pharmacopoeia, p.624).

(b) Chronic alcoholism (with its attendant physical effects, e.g. cirrhosis).

(c) Alcohol withdrawal reactions (delirium tremens).

Drug therapy plays little part in (a) and (b), except for aversion therapy with disulfiram, but does have a place in the management of delirium tremens, which in itself is an interesting drug withdrawal reaction.

Delirium tremens

This is important to recognize because it has a high rate of mortality. It can occur in a chronic alcoholic who simply cannot get a drink, but in general medical practice it more frequently occurs in a chronic alcoholic admitted to hospital with an intercurrent illness, such as trauma, pneumonia, stroke, or coronary thrombosis. It also occurs in patients with alcoholic cirrhosis admitted to hospital with gastro-intestinal bleeding. Symptoms tend to come on within a few hours after the last drink and mount over the next 2–3 days. At first there is anxiety, agitation, tremulousness, and tachycardia. These are accompanied later by confusion, severe agitation, and frank hallucinations (often visual). The patient is tremulous, sweating, and tachypnoeic. He has a tachycardia, and may be pyrexial. The blood pressure may be high, low, or normal. Nausea and vomiting are common. Seizures may occur and are serious.

The management of delirium tremens, in terms of drugs given, varies around the world. Important measures are:

1. The maintenance of fluid and electrolyte balance.
2. The administration of vitamins, particularly thiamine to guard against Wernicke's encephalopathy.
3. High carbohydrate, high calorie diet.
4. Drug treatment.

Choices for treatment of the delirium are from among benzodiazepines, barbiturates, and chlormethiazole. Besides the delirium another important consideration is the prevention of seizures, and in those with a previous history of convulsions during withdrawal phenytoin may be indicated.

Most physicians treating alcohol withdrawal states now use chlordiazepoxide, diazepam, or chlormethiazole.

Chlordiazepoxide is given in doses of 50–100 mg by deep intramuscular injection for the treatment of delirium tremens when the patient is very agitated or confused. This is followed by 50–100 mg orally six-hourly. Dosages should be tailored to the individual patient, and once the patient is stabilized gradual withdrawal can be commenced and carried out over a 2–3 week period.

Diazepam can be given in doses of 10 mg i.v. four-hourly as necessary. Oral diazepam can be substituted as the critical stage passes.

Chlormethiazole can be given as an i.v. infusion of a 0.8 per cent solution, 40–100 ml (320–800 mg) over 5–10 min to produce drowsiness and to remove restlessness and agitation. The subsequent infusion rate is adjusted according to the response.

Oral chlormethiazole therapy can be substituted for the infusion at doses of three capsules six-hourly for 2 days, two capsules six-hourly for 3 days and then one capsule six-hourly for 4 days (one capsule = 192 mg chlormethiazole). Chlormethiazole has a tendency to produce its own dependency in alcoholic patients, so there is this hazard in its use. It should not be given for longer than is necessary.

31.7. HYPNOTICS AND TRANQUILLIZERS

31.7.1. Benzodiazepine dependence

Recently it has become apparent that patients may become tolerant to and dependent upon benzodiazepine tranquillizers when these are given in therapeutic doses for period of longer than about 6 weeks. The withdrawal symptoms are anxiety, agitation, restlessness, irritability, insomnia, and sometimes convulsions.

31.7.2. Barbiturate dependence

In the UK this is now generally due to illicit drug abuse with marked tolerance occurring. It is often associated with i.v. usage. Withdrawal symptoms can be severe and are very similar to delirium tremens.

31.8. TOBACCO (NICOTINE)

The adverse effects of smoking, and particularly of smoking cigarettes, pervade a great deal of medical practice. Acute and chronic bronchitis, emphysema, carcinoma of the bronchus, and some other carcinomas, peripheral arterial disease, coronary artery disease, and peptic ulceration, are all associated. It is reckoned that one-third to a half of all smokers die of a smoking related disease.

It is difficult to pin down just what pleasure smoking brings. It is a habit which generally needs working at to establish its pleasure, but once it is established then perhaps it can engender both relaxation of mind and increased drive at different times and in different circumstances.

Withdrawal symptoms include craving for tobacco, increased appetite, and irritability.

Smoking increases the metabolism of caffeine, theophylline, and imipramine by induction of liver drug-metabolizing enzymes. A history of smoking should always be considered as a factor in variable drug response.

Recently chewing-gum containing nicotine has been claimed to be helpful to those attempting to give up smoking, However, the main factor in successfully breaking the tobacco habit is the will of the individual. Anti-smoking clinics function to help people give up smoking and they provide encouragement and reassurance.

31.9. PERSONAL ACCOUNTS

Several well-known writers have described their own experiences with drugs of abuse. The following works may be of interest:

Confessions of an English opium-eater, Thomas de Quincey (1822).
Opium. The diary of a cure, Jean Cocteau (1930).

Junkie, William Burroughs (1953; heroin).

The doors of perception, Aldous Huxley (1954; mescalin).

Return trip to nirvana, Arthur Koestler (1961). Reprinted in *Drinkers of infinity* (Hutchinson, 1968; psilocybin).

32 The management of self-poisoning

The vigour with which one treats a case of self-poisoning varies from doing little or nothing to large-scale intensive action to maintain vital body functions. Almost all poisoned patients will survive with intensive supportive treatment if necessary, and only a few patients will need antidotes or special treatment to hasten elimination of the poison from the body.

32.1. IMMEDIATE MANAGEMENT OF THE ACUTELY ILL PATIENT

In Table 32.1 are summarized the various components of the immediate management of the acutely ill patient.

Table 32.1 *Management of acute self-poisoning*

(a) Respiratory function	Check cough reflex Clear out oropharyngeal obstructions/debris/secretions Lay on left side with head down Insert oral airway or endotracheal tube Give oxygen Assist respiration

(b) Circulatory function	Check heart rate and blood pressure
	 If blood pressure < 90 mmHg systolic:
	    Raise end of trolley/bed
	    Give volume expanders
	 If fluid overload and oliguria give dopamine or dobutamine
	 Monitor urine output

(c) Consciousness	Assess conscious level in response to standard stimuli (see text)
(d) Temperature	Take temperature rectally If <36°C reheat slowly ('space blanket') If < 30°C reheat more rapidly (arm in water at 40°C if elderly, whole body if young) Warm all inspired air and i.v. fluids

Table 32.1 *Continued*

(e) Convulsions	Treat with diazepam, chlormethiazole, or anaesthesia with muscle paralysis and assisted ventilation
(f) Cardiac arrhythmias	Treat as required (see Chapter 21)
(g) Gastric lavage and ipecac-induced emesis	Within 4 h of all drugs (but see below) Within 8 h of anticholinergic drugs (e.g. tricyclic antidepressants) At any time for salicylates Ipecac-induced emesis for choice in children (cough reflex must be intact) Gastric lavage for choice in adults (except digitalis, when emesis) Add non-specific or specific antidotes to lavage fluid or leave in stomach after lavage Contra-indicated after corrosive acids or alkalis, or volatile substances (e.g. paraffin)
(h) Fluid and electrolyte balance	Oral fluids usually enough in dehydration If patient unconscious use dextrose/saline and insert a CVP line Treat hypokalaemia (see p.401)
(i) Specific emergency measures	Cyanide—dicobalt edetate Paraquat—fuller's earth Paracetamol—acetylcysteine Carbon monoxide—oxygen Opiates—naloxone
(j) Chest X-ray	In drowsy or comatose patients who have vomited After endotracheal intubation
(k) Collection of specimens	Gastric aspirate (drugs) Urine (drugs) Blood (drugs, arterial gases, electrolytes)

32.1.1. Respiratory function

It is important to maintain a clear airway at all times. In most cases it is sufficient to ensure an open airway, in a drowsy or unconscious patient, by keeping the patient semi-prone with the neck extended, by inserting an oral airway, and by regularly sucking out secretions. If unconscious, the patient should be turned onto the left side. Remove all obstructions from the patient's mouth (including dentures), and suck out any secretions or debris. If there is no cough reflex, an endotracheal tube should be inserted, and in all such cases blood gases should be measured. If there is hypoxia, oxygen should be given in amounts depending on the blood gases according to the following guidelines:

P_AO_2 between 8 and 11 kPa (62 and 85 mmHg), and P_ACO_2 between 5 and 7 kPa (38 and 54 mmHg)—give 24 per cent O_2 increasing to 28 per cent after 30 min if the P_ACO_2 has not risen.

P_AO_2 below 8 kPa or P_ACO_2 above 7 kPa—assisted ventilation will be required. For oxygen therapy in carbon monoxide poisoning see under carbon monoxide (p.580). If the patient is not breathing spontaneously, insert a cuffed endotracheal tube and begin assisted respiration with an Ambu bag or at least by mouth-to-mouth breathing. Move the patient as soon as possible to facilities for mechanically assisted ventilation. Respiratory function may be assessed formally by measuring tidal volume and arterial blood gases.

32.1.2. Cardiovascular function

Measure the heart rate and blood pressure. The minimum acceptable systolic blood pressure is 80 mmHg if the patient is aged less than 50 y, or 90 mmHg if aged more than 50 y. If the patient is hypotensive, raise the foot of the trolley or bed about 8 in. If the blood pressure remains low, set up an intravenous infusion and give plasma volume expanders such as fresh frozen plasma or colloid solutions. However, patients are often already in positive fluid balance, or at least not fluid-depleted, and great care must be taken not to cause fluid overload. For this reason a central venous pressure line should be inserted so that fluid requirements can be assessed precisely. If plasma volume expanders do not cause an increase in blood pressure, or if fluid overload occurs, then cautious drug therapy is indicated. Some would recommend the use of a β-adrenoceptor agonist such as dobutamine (2.5–10 micrograms/kg/min by continuous i.v. infusion) but if one's chief concern is renal blood flow then low doses of dopamine (e.g. 5–10 micrograms/kg/min) may be sufficient, or may be combined with dobutamine. Higher doses of dopamine (10–20 micrograms/kg/min) also have a β-adrenoceptor agonist effect, but at higher doses both drugs have α-adrenoceptor agonist effects, resulting in peripheral and renal vasoconstriction. Whatever agent is used it is wise not to raise the systolic blood pressure above 100 mmHg. The urine output should also be carefully monitored, if necessary by catheterization.

32.1.3. Level of consciousness

This will already have been roughly assessed while assessing respiratory and cardiovascular functions, but now is the time to assess it more rigorously according to the following scheme, so that progress can be monitored:

Grade 0. Patient fully conscious.
Grade 1. Patient drowsy but responds to commands, or asleep but easily roused.

Grade 2. Patient unconscious, but responds to standard minimally painful stimuli.

Grade 3. Patient unconscious, but responds to standard maximally painful stimuli.

Grade 4. Patient does not respond to any stimuli.

Useful 'standard' stimuli are rubbing the sternum vigorously with the knuckles or pinching the Achilles' tendon. Pressure over the supra-orbital fissure should not be used because of the risk of damage to the eye if the hand slips.

The main virtue of this system is that it may be used to provide objective evidence of a change in conscious state over a period of time. In addition any patient who is in grade 2 or worse should not have gastric lavage carried out without being intubated with an endotracheal tube first. Impairment of consciousness to any level in patients who have taken salicylates is an important sign and suggests serious poisoning.

32.1.4. Temperature

In the unconscious patient measure the temperature rectally with a low-reading clinical thermometer or thermocouple. Hypothermia (rectal temperature below 36°C) should be treated slowly by keeping the patient in a warm environment and by the use of a foil blanket ('space blanket'). In severe cases (rectal temperature below 30°C) more rapid warming is necessary. In the middle-aged or elderly put one arm into water at 40°C. In the young immersion of the whole body in water at 40°C is safe. All inspired air and infusion solutions should be warmed before administration.

Hyperthermia should be treated by fanning and tepid sponging. In severe cases give chlorpromazine 100 mg i.m.

32.1.5. Convulsions

Convulsions may be treated with either diazepam (10 mg i.v., repeated at 30 min intervals to a total of 30 mg, and followed if required by a continuous infusion at a rate of 100 micrograms/kg/h in saline) or chlormethiazole (40–100 ml of an 0.8 per cent solution given by i.v infusion over 5–10 min, followed if necessary by a continuous i.v. infusion at a rate depending on the patient's response). If this fails, the patient should be anaesthetized and treated with neuromuscular blocking drugs and assisted ventilation.

32.1.6. Cardiac arrhythmias

Record a full ECG and monitor the cardiac rhythm in patients who are deeply unconscious or hypothermic, or who have taken digoxin, anti-arrhythmic drugs, β-adrenoceptor antagonists, anticholinergic drugs (e.g.

tricyclic antidepressants), potassium, or sympathomimetic drugs. If arrhythmias occur check for and correct electrolyte abnormalities (especially hypokalaemia), hypoxia, and acidosis.

In general it is better to avoid treating arrhythmias if the blood pressure is satisfactory, but continuous ventricular tachycardia and ventricular fibrillation should be treated by direct current shock. If other ventricular arrhythmias need to be treated then conventional drug treatment should be used (see Chapter 21). For digitalis-induced arrhythmias, however, phenytoin is the treatment of choice. Supraventricular arrhythmias generally do not need treatment. If sinus bradycardia needs to be treated atropine may be used, but a transvenous pacemaker may be required.

32.1.7. Removal of poison from the gut and prevention of further absorption

If the patient is seen within 4 h of self-poisoning then it is worthwhile attempting to remove tablets or capsules from the stomach by induced emesis or gastric lavage. Such procedures may also be of value up to 24 h or even longer after self-poisoning with iron salts or aspirin, which can cause pylorospasm, and up to 8 h after drugs with anticholinergic effects, which decrease gastro-intestinal motility (e.g. tricyclic antidepressants). The procedures are as follows:

(a) Induced emesis

This should only be carried out in a patient with a normal cough reflex. In an emergency, vomiting may be induced by pharyngeal stimulation with a finger or the back of a spoon. In hospital, syrup of ipecacuanha, or paediatric ipecacuanha emetic draught is used in a dose of 15 ml (10 ml in a child under 18 months) with 200 ml of water or fruit juice. It should have an effect within 15–30 min but if not the dose should be repeated. This regimen is effective in almost all cases. If vomiting does not occur within 30–60 min, however, one should proceed with gastric lavage.

(b) Gastric lavage

Before carrying out gastric lavage check that the cough reflex is intact. If it is not, a cuffed endotracheal tube must be inserted before gastric lavage is carried out in order to avoid aspiration, and suction apparatus should be available. The patient should be laid upon the left side, the head below the level of the rest of the body, and a wide-bore tube should be passed via the mouth into the stomach. We use a 150 cm tube with a 7 mm internal diameter and extra perforations in the final 10 cm or so. The usual lavage fluid is warm water, but in young children saline should be used. In some cases special antidotes may be added to the lavage fluid (see Table 32.2). The lavage fluid in volumes of 300 ml is passed, via a large funnel held above the patient, down the tube into the stomach. The funnel is then lowered beneath the level of the patient and the gastric contents allowed to drain into a bucket or aspirated with a large syringe. This procedure is repeated until the fluid returning from the stomach is clear. Some of the initial return should be kept for chemical analysis if later required.

Table 32.2 *Agents used in decreasing the absorption of poisons*

Poison	Additions to lavage fluid* (warm water or saline)	Agent(s) to be left in stomach after lavage or to be given orally
Cyanide	Sodium thiosulphate 5%	Sodium thiosulphate 25%, 300 ml
Digitoxin		Colestipol or cholestyramine; activated charcoal
Hydrofluoric acid		Calcium gluconate 10%, 300 ml
Iron	Desferrioxamine (see text)	Desferrioxamine (see text)
Opiates	Potassium permanganate (one tablet, BPC, in 3.5 l)	Wash all permanganate out of stomach
Oxalic acid (e.g. in bleach)	Calcium gluconate 1%	Calcium gluconate 1%, 300 ml
Paraquat	Fuller's earth, 150 g/l	Fuller's earth, 150 g/l (see text)
Phenol, cresol, lysol	Castor oil in water, 1:2	Castor oil, 50 ml (or other vegetable oil, such as arachis oil or olive oil)
Phosphorus	Copper sulphate 0.1%	Copper sulphate 0.1%, 50 ml
Sodium hypochlorite (e.g. in bleach)	Sodium thiosulphate 5%, or milk, or milk of magnesia (magnesium hydroxide 8.5%)	Copper sulphate 0.1%, 100 ml
Various (see text under 'gastric lavage')		Activated charcoal (see text)

*Never delay gastric lavage simply because the appropriate lavage fluid is not available.

Neither induced emesis nor gastric lavage should be carried out in patients who have taken corrosive acids (give antacids), or alkalis (give dilute acetic or citric acid), or any volatile substances (e.g. petroleum products, such as paraffin).

In children, ipecacuanha-induced emesis is the procedure of choice. In adults, however, gastric lavage is still to be preferred. While ipecacuanha-induced emesis is easier to carry out it carries the risk of emetine toxicity, albeit in a minority of patients, and even when successful it does not cause complete emptying of the stomach. Aspiration is a risk if the patient becomes drowsy after having taken ipecacuanha. An added advantage of gastric lavage is that antidotes may be instilled directly into the stomach (see Table 32.2). Activated charcoal instilled into the stomach (5–10 g in 100 ml of water) may adsorb various drugs thereby reducing their absorption (e.g. salicylates, barbiturates, tricyclic antidepressants, dextropropoxyphene, digitalis, and paraffin). Activated charcoal may also be given orally (to a maximum of 50 g) but should not be given with ipecacuanha which it renders ineffective by adsorption.

There are some other more specific agents which may be given orally or instilled into the stomach after lavage to decrease further absorption of poison. These are listed in Table 32.2.

32.1.8. Fluid and electrolyte balance

Most patients have either normal fluid and electrolyte balance or slight fluid overload. For those who are fluid depleted (e.g. because of vomiting), but conscious, oral fluids are usually sufficient. In most unconscious patients simple replacement with two 500 ml units of 5 per cent dextrose for every 500 ml unit of physiological saline is usually sufficient. Central venous pressure monitoring may be required in severely ill patients. Hypokalaemia may be treated with either oral or i.v. potassium chloride (see p.401).

32.1.9. Specific measures

Some drugs require immediate specific treatment. The most important are cyanide and paraquat, discussed below. The treatment of paracetamol poisoning should be instituted as soon as possible, without waiting for the plasma concentration result, in patients seen within 10–12 h of ingestion. Opiate poisoning should be treated as soon as possible with naloxone, and carbon monoxide poisoning with oxygen.

Other specific measures which are not so urgent are dealt with under the specific drug headings listed below.

32.1.10. Chest X-ray

A chest X-ray should be taken in any drowsy or comatose patient who has vomited, to rule out aspiration pneumonia. A chest X-ray is not usually necessary in a fully conscious patient even after induced emesis or gastric lavage. Chest X-ray should also be carried out in any patient who requires endotracheal intubation, to check the position of the endotracheal tube.

32.1.11. Collection of specimens

Gastric aspirate, admission urine sample, and admission blood sample (20 ml in two lithium–heparin tubes) should be kept in case later analysis is required in:

suspected criminal poisoning;
unconscious or severely poisoned patients;
any unusual poison (especially new drugs).

Label containers carefully with full name, date and *time*.

Emergency analysis of drugs in blood is indicated only if the result will affect the patient's management, and is usually restricted to aspirin and paracetamol. These are discussed under their separate headings. Measurement of barbiturate concentrations serves principally in making the diagnosis in cases of coma of unknown cause and in identifying the type of barbiturate involved (i.e. long-, intermediate-, or short-acting). It does not reflect prognosis, however, because of wide interindividual variability, and should not be used as a guide to treatment.

Paraquat may be identified in gastric aspirate and urine by a simple colorimetric test. This test is useful in *excluding* the diagnosis and in monitoring progress.

In the majority of cases routine plasma urea and electrolyte measurements are not necessary, but they should be performed in all ill patients to assess renal function, hepatic function, and state of hydration. In some cases tests should be carried out specific to the effects of the drug (e.g. blood glucose, arterial blood gases, and prothrombin time for aspirin, liver function tests for paracetamol).

The indications for the various blood tests are summarized in Table 32.3.

Table 32.3 *Indications for laboratory tests in self-poisoning*

Test	Indication
Plasma drug concentration	Aspirin, paracetamol (barbiturates, iron, lithium)
Urine drug concentration	Paraquat
Arterial blood gases	Coma
	Aspirin
	Unexplained hyperventilation
	Hypoxia (e.g. due to carbon monoxide)
Plasma electrolytes (especially potassium)	Severe aspirin poisoning
	Digoxin
	Potassium
	Insulin
	Sulphonylureas
	Sympathomimetics
Blood glucose	Unexplained coma
	Alcohol
	Hypoglycaemic drugs
	Aspirin
Prothrombin time	Aspirin
	Paracetamol (not urgent)
Liver function tests	Paracetamol (not urgent)

32.2. DETAILED MANAGEMENT OF SELF-POISONING

There are seven components to management:

1. Diagnosis.
2. Clinical assessment.
3. Removal of the poison from the gut.
4. General supportive and non-specific therapeutic measures.

5. Hastening of drug elimination.
6. Measures specific to the drug.
7. Psychiatric assessment (not discussed here).

32.2.1. Diagnosis

The diagnosis may be straightforward, and patients may give the history themselves or be accompanied by a friend or relative who will do so. The drugs used may be produced. However, not infrequently the history is not straightforward, and self-poisoning should always be a differential diagnosis in the assessment of an unconscious patient, particularly in young adults in cases where there are decreased or absent tendon reflexes, or hypothermia without an obvious cause. Even in cases where a history has been given, one should keep in mind the possibility that the incriminated drug may not have been the drug involved, and that other drugs may have been taken instead, or in addition.

History-taking should not stop at the identification of the drug. Other useful pieces of information to be elicited are as follows:

(a) The number of tablets, capsules, etc. taken

This is in order to try to assess the probable severity of the problem. In addition it may be helpful to know if alcohol was also taken, and if so how much, in order to assess to what extent impairment of consciousness is due to alcohol, rather than to the drug. However, assessment of the extent and severity of self-poisoning from the history is frequently unreliable.

(b) The time of overdose

This serves two purposes: firstly, to help decide whether induced emesis or gastric lavage are necessary, and secondly, to help in the interpretation of plasma drug concentration measurements, especially paracetamol (see below).

(c) If the patient has vomited and if haematemesis has occurred

If vomiting has occurred in a drowsy or unconscious patient, the possibility of aspiration must be considered.

(d) Past history

This may give a clue to drugs which might have been readily available to the patient. In patients who have been taking drugs which induce liver enzymes (e.g. phenobarbitone, phenytoin) the effects of paracetamol on the liver may be increased. A past history of renal or hepatic disease may influence management. For example, forced diuresis is contra-indicated in a patient with renal failure and the effects of certain drugs (e.g. the opiates) may be expected to be more prolonged or severe in a patient with liver disease.

(e) Assessment of the seriousness of the attempt

Although strictly speaking this is not part of the acute management of self-poisoning, it is important to do it early on in order that medical and nursing staff be made aware of the seriousness of a particular case, and in order that psychiatric help be sought at a relatively early stage. Nowadays, there is a growing trend to discharge patients on the same day as their presentation to the hospital, sometimes without even admitting them to the ward and it is important that a patient who has made a serious attempt on his or her life should not be allowed to leave without having had the opportunity of being properly assessed by a trained psychiatrist. The signs of a serious attempt are:

Self-poisoning in a middle-aged or elderly patient.
An admission that suicide was truly contemplated.
A history of depression.
A suicide note.
An attempt not to be discovered.

32.2.2. Clinical assessment

(a) Level of consciousness

It is useful to grade loss of consciousness using a standard grading system (see section 32.1.3 above).

(b) Respiratory function

In the comatose patient this can be assessed by direct observation, by measuring the tidal volume or minute volume if appropriate equipment is available, and by measuring the blood gases.

(c) Cardiovascular and renal function

In comatose patients it is important to assess peripheral circulatory and renal function by measuring heart rate, blood pressure, and urine output. If necessary the patient should be catheterized. Continuous ECG monitoring is necessary if the patient has taken a drug which may cause arrhythmias.

(d) Rectal temperature

Hypothermia (rectal temperature below 36°C) occurs not uncommonly in patients who are unconscious through self-poisoning. However, poisoning with salicylates and monoamine oxidase (MAO) inhibitors can cause hyperthermia. It is important when taking the temperature to use a low-reading thermometer, so that hypothermia is not missed.

(e) Other signs

Certain drugs may produce signs which may be of value. For example, pupillary constriction due to narcotic analgesics, the syndrome of tinnitus, hyperpyrexia, hyperventilation, and sweating due to salicylates, and skin blisters due to barbiturates (although this is not a specific sign and can occur in poisoning with other drugs, such as tricyclic antidepressants, and carbon monoxide). Puncture marks and perivenous ulcers in the skin of the arms should be looked for to identify the drug addict.

(f) Chest X-ray

See section 32.1.10 above.

(g) Blood and urine tests

See section 32.1.11 above and Table 32.3.

32.2.3. Removal of the poison from the gut

Induced emesis and gastric lavage are discussed above in section 32.1.7. Drugs which should be used to decrease absorption of the poison are listed in Table 32.2.

32.2.4. General supportive and non-specific therapeutic measures

These have been discussed in section 32.1 above under the following headings:

Respiratory function
Cardiovascular function
Temperature
Convulsions
Cardiac arrhythmias
Fluid and electrolyte balance.

32.2.5. Hastening of drug elimination

(a) Diuresis in alkaline or acidic urine

For drugs which are subject to extensive passive reabsorption by the renal tubules, and whose rate of renal clearance is proportional to the rate of urine flow, forced diuresis at an altered urine pH will hasten elimination of the drug. Thus the rates of salicylate and lithium renal clearance are increased by alkaline diuresis and those of amphetamine, quinine, quinidine, and tranylcypromine by acid diuresis. A useful regimen for salicylates is discussed below.

(b) Dialysis

Removal of drug by dialysis (either haemodialysis or peritoneal dialysis) is reserved for severe cases of poisoning. It is useful only for drugs which are not widely distributed to body tissues and which are not highly bound by plasma proteins. It may be of value in serious poisoning with salicylates, barbiturates, chloral hydrate and its derivatives, iron, and lithium, among others. For a list of drugs which are removed from the body to haemodialysis or peritoneal dialysis see Table 24.9, p.421.

(c) Charcoal haemoperfusion

Because charcoal adsorbs many drugs it can be used to remove drug from the circulation. It is of value even when there is high plasma protein binding; but wide distribution of drug to the tissues limits its usefulness. The problems of thrombocytopenia, leucopenia, febrile reactions and charcoal emboli encountered with earlier forms of charcoal columns have been diminished by more modern preparations, but the pharmacokinetics of column clearance of drugs from the body have not yet been completely worked out. If available, charcoal haemoperfusion may be of value in serious poisoning with salicylates, barbiturates, glutethimide, meprobamate, methaqualone, theophylline, and derivatives of chloral hydrate.

32.2.6. Measures to be taken in specific cases of self-poisoning

In Table 32.4 (see the end of this chapter) are listed the drugs used in the specific treatment of cases of self-poisoning. Some of the aspects of their uses are also summarized. The following merit extra discussion:

(a) Salicylates

The clinical features of salicylate poisoning are tinnitus, deafness, hyperventilation, hyperpyrexia with sweating and dehydration, and epigastric pain and vomiting. Patients are generally fully conscious, and *any impairment of consciousness is a sign of serious poisoning*. There may be hypoglycaemia. Bleeding may occur because of a reduction in the prothrombin time.

Salicylates directly stimulate the respiratory centre, causing a respiratory alkalosis due to hyperventilation. A metabolic acidosis occurs due to the presence of salicylic acid which uncouples oxidative phosphorylation. In adults the respiratory alkalosis usually predominates, but in children the metabolic acidosis tends to predominate and poisoning in children is more serious at any given plasma salicylate concentration than it is in adults.

The plasma salicylate concentration may be measured as a guide to therapy, but because salicylate is highly protein-bound, the total (protein-bound and unbound) plasma concentration is not a good guide to the severity of poisoning, and should always be considered in conjunction with the patient's clinical state. The arterial blood gases often give a better indication of the severity of poisoning.

Gastric lavage should always be carried out no matter how long after ingestion. If the plasma salicylate concentration is above 3.0 mmol/l (1.8 mmol/l in children) and the patient has obvious signs and symptoms of toxicity, then forced alkaline diuresis should be commenced. The following i.v. regimen is considered safe:

A mixture of physiological saline (500 ml), 5 per cent dextrose, (1 l), and 1.26 per cent sodium bicarbonate (500 ml) is infused as a 2 l mixture over 3 h and thereafter at 1 l/h until clinical improvement occurs. Potassium chloride should be added at a rate of 20 mmol/h. In children the infusion rate of this solution should be 30 ml/kg/h. Plasma electrolyte measurements should be made every 2–4 h. Great care must be taken to avoid fluid overload. Urinary output should be monitored carefully and if necessary a central venous pressure line should be inserted.

Forced alkaline diuresis should *not* be carried out in patients with circulatory failure, renal failure, or fluid overload. In such cases sodium bicarbonate alone should be infused (1500 ml of a 1.26 per cent solution over 4 h). Peritoneal dialysis or haemodialysis are alternatives.

Hypoglycaemia is usually reversed by the dextrose in the mixed infusion. If the prothrombin time is prolonged, vitamin K_1 should be given (10 mg i.v.).

In drowsy or unconscious patients acidosis should be corrected with i.v. sodium bicarbonate before starting other treatment. Haemodialysis or peritoneal dialysis are to be preferred to forced alkaline diuresis in these patients.

(b) Paracetamol

In paracetamol poisoning there is usually little in the way of acute symptoms apart from nausea and vomiting. However, in severe poisoning (more than 15 g) there are several delayed effects, the most important of which is the toxic effect on the liver. Paracetamol, in the usual analgesic doses, is metabolized about 85 per cent by conjugation with glucuronide and sulphate and about 10 per cent by conjugation with glutathione. However, in overdose glucuronide pathways are saturated, and the excess of paracetamol is metabolized via the glutathione pathway. Hepatic glutathione in turn is rapidly depleted, and an intermediate hydroxylamine metabolite accumulates and binds to liver cell proteins causing irreversible damage. Compounds which provide sulphydryl (SH) groups for the conjugation of the toxic hydroxylamine metabolite can prevent liver damage. The most useful of these is *N*-acetylcysteine.

The signs of serious paracetamol toxicity occur late, but careful observations in poisoned patients have led to the development of guidelines to treatment, based on the value of the plasma paracetamol concentration and the time since ingestion. These guidelines allow one to decide whether or not to institute treatment soon after ingestion. A simple method of applying the guidelines is illustrated in Fig.32.1 which consists of a graph which can be (and in this case was) constructed on plain paper as follows:

(i) draw vertical and horizontal axes;

(ii) mark on the vertical axis values of 0.3, 0.6 and 1.2 mmol/l (plasma paracetamol concentrations) at equal intervals;

(iii) mark on the horizontal axis values of 4, 8 and 12 h (time after ingestion) at equal intervals;

(iv) draw a dot at the point marking 4 h and 1.2 mmol/l and a second dot at the point marking 12 h and 0.3 mmol/l;

(v) join the two dots with a straight line—plot the value of the patient's plasma concentration against the time after ingestion;

(vi) if the point falls above the line treatment is indicated;

(vii) in patients in whom ingestion occurred less than 4 h before sampling, the plasma concentration is unreliable because absorption is still continuing.

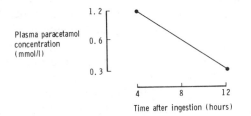

Fig. 32.1. Criteria for treatment with acetylcysteine following self-poisoning with paracetamol to prevent liver damage. Plot the value of the paracetamol concentration in the patient's plasma against the time of sampling. If the plotted point is above the line treatment is indicated.

If more than 10 g has been taken treatment should be started before the plasma paracetamol concentration result becomes available. This is particularly important for patients who present at 8 h or more after ingestion since after about 10–12 h treatment is probably of no value and may even be harmful, if reports that liver damage is worse following treatment after 10–15 h are correct.

·In patients who have been taking drugs which induce hepatic drug-metabolizing enzymes (e.g. phenobarbitone, phenytoin, rifampicin, griseofulvin) the toxic effects of paracetamol may be enhanced. There is no good guidance, however, as to when treatment should be given in such cases and it is probably wise at present to treat all such patients.

Treatment should be with intravenous acetylcysteine as follows:

(i) 150 mg/kg i.v. over 15 min;

(ii) 50 mg/kg i.v. in 500 ml of 5 per cent dextrose over 4 h;

(iii) 100 mg/kg i.v. in 1 l of 5 per cent dextrose over 16 h.

Methionine is sometimes used as an alternative to i.v. acetylcysteine but it is less reliable because it is given orally, and its usefulness may be limited by vomiting.

Liver function tests (including the prothrombin time) should be measured on admission in all patients who require treatment. Such patients should be kept in hospital for 48 h for observation and reassessment of liver function. Abnormal liver function tests at 48 h presage severe liver damage.

In patients who take paracetamol as Distalgesic® or Cosalgesic® remember also to treat dextropropoxyphene poisoning with naloxone (see below).

(c) Tricyclic antidepressants

The features of poisoning with these drugs are due to peripheral and central anticholinergic effects and to the potentiation of sympathetic nervous activity. The clinical results are dry mouth, dilated pupils and blurred vision, urinary retention, tachyarrhythmias and heart block, hypotension, impairment of consciousness, impairment of respiration, hallucinations, and convulsions.

The majority (over 80 per cent) of patients require only supportive measures, but if there are life-threatening tachyarrhythmias, hypotension, or serious cerebral effects (e.g. respiratory depression, convulsions), physostigmine should be used. It acts by inhibiting acetylcholinesterase, thereby antagonizing the anticholinergic effects of tricyclic antidepressants, and, unlike other cholinesterase inhibitors, such as neostigmine, it enters the brain. It is given up to a total of 2 mg by i.v. injection at a rate of 0.2 mg/min and the full dose need not be given if a therapeutic response occurs rapidly. The effects of physostigmine are very variable. When it is efficacious its effects are dramatic and occur within a few minutes. The patient wakes up, and tachyarrhythmias are abolished. However, quite often it has no effect at all. Furthermore, its effect is short-lived and doses need to be repeated at intervals of about half an hour. Even if a first dose has worked, subsequent doses may sometimes have little or no effect. Physostigmine should only be used to treat life-threatening tachyarrhythmias, respiratory depression, or serious cerebral effects, because it has its own adverse effects, including bronchospasm, hypersalivation and an increase in bronchial secretions, vomiting, diarrhoea, gastro-intestinal spasm, and convulsions.

If physostigmine is not effective, tachyarrhythmias may be treated with a β-adrenoceptor antagonist, such as practolol, and convulsions with diazepam or chlormethiazole. Acidosis should be corrected with sodium bicarbonate. Bradycardia and heart block should be treated by artificial transvenous pacing.

In passing, it may be noted that physostigmine has been reported to be of value in treating poisoning with phenothiazines, such as chlorprom-azine, and some antihistamines. Its use in these circumstances, however, has not been properly evaluated. It is, of course, also of value in reversing the anticholinergic effects of atropine and other anticholinergic drugs.

(d) Barbiturates

Barbiturate poisoning presents with the signs and symptoms of CNS depression, including any degree of impairment of consciousness from drowsiness to coma, restlessness, delirium, hallucinations, convulsions, and respiratory depression. Other effects include hypotension and shock, sometimes causing renal failure, hypothermia, and the characteristic but non-specific skin blisters, which may also be seen in poisoning with, for example, tricyclic antidepressants, and carbon monoxide. The effects of poisoning may persist for several days with the long-acting barbiturates, such as phenobarbitone and pentobarbitone.

Gastric lavage and supportive measures are indicated. In seriously ill patients haemodialysis or charcoal haemoperfusion may be required if deterioration occurs despite intensive support.

(e) Paraquat

This is a serious and often fatal poisoning with a herbicide used in various proprietary weed killers (e.g. Weedol®, Gramoxone®, Pathclear®). Fatalities are much less common after ingestion of granular (domestic) forms of paraquat than after liquid (commercial) forms, which can be fatal in ingested volumes of 10 ml. Paraquat irritates skin and mucous membranes, producing burning sensations in the mouth and abdomen, followed by local ulceration, and nausea and vomiting. The major effect takes some days to develop, however, and consists of pulmonary oedema secondary to alveolitis and bronchiolitis due to the effects of a toxic superoxide. It usually results in fatal respiratory failure. Treatment should be started immediately, therefore, and may be withdrawn if urine testing fails to reveal the presence of paraquat. The poison should be vigorously washed away from the skin and eyes and antibiotic drops applied to the eyes if affected. In an emergency, vomiting should be induced by pharyngeal irritation. Gastric lavage must be carried out as soon as possible, preferably with a 15 per cent solution of fuller's earth (i.e. 150 g/l). After lavage, 1 l of a suspension of 150 g fuller's earth as an adsorbent, with 200 ml of 20 per cent mannitol as a purgative, should be left in the stomach. Bentonite 7 g may be used instead of fuller's earth but is less effective. Fuller's earth 100 g will irreversibly bind 5 g of paraquat. Thereafter this treatment should be repeated as often as the patient can tolerate it (say half-hourly) until fuller's earth appears in the stools. During this time a nasogastric tube should be kept in position and the treatment given through the tube directly into the stomach. In addition forced diuresis as for salicylate poisoning should be carried out, as should charcoal haemoperfusion if available. Fluid losses by purgation should be replaced intravenously.

(f) Cyanide

Cyanide poisoning is a medical emergency, requiring rapid treatment. Following gastric lavage with 5 per cent sodium thiosulphate if available, 300 ml of 25 per cent sodium thiosulphate should be left in the stomach. The traditional method of treating cyanide poisoning (see below) has been replaced by the use of dicobalt edetate (dicobalt EDTA). It is given i.v., in a dose of 600 mg in 40 ml over 1 min, and followed by 50 ml of 5 per cent dextrose. If recovery does not occur within a minute or two, another 300 mg of dicobalt edetate should be given. In patients who have not taken cyanide, dicobalt edetate may cause vomiting, hypotension, and tachycardia, and these may require treatment. The traditional alternative to dicobalt edetate is the administration of 10 ml of 3 per cent sodium nitrite, given i.v. over 3 min, and followed by 25 ml of 50 per cent sodium thiosulphate, given by slow i.v. injection. This regimen may be repeated if necessary, using half the doses. Oxygen (100 per cent) should be given. Acidosis should be corrected with sodium bicarbonate.

(g) Carbon monoxide

Carbon monoxide poisoning can still occur, despite the replacement of coal gas by North Sea gas in the home, because of incomplete combustion with the formation of carbon monoxide, and of course in patients who poison themselves with car exhaust gases. Treatment is by removal from the source of gas, and by administration of 100 per cent oxygen with assisted ventilation in patients not breathing spontaneously. Hyperbaric oxygen should be used if available. Treat cerebral oedema with mannitol (500 ml of a 20 per cent solution), and cardiac arrhythmias as required.

(h) Narcotic analgesics

Naloxone rapidly reverses the effects of opiate analgesics and other narcotic analgesics (e.g. pethidine, pentazocine, dextropropoxyphene). It is given in a dose of 0.4 mg i.v. initially, repeated every 2–3 min if required. A total dose of 1.2 mg is usually sufficient. In buprenorphine poisoning only partial reversal occurs and in severe cases a respiratory stimulant, such as doxapram, may be required. Naloxone is eliminated from the body with a half-time of about 1 h, i.e. faster than the narcotic analgesics. Its effects may therefore wear off.

(i) Organophosphorus insecticides

These are very toxic and are absorbed through the skin. Rubber gloves should therefore be worn when in contact with the patient or the patient's clothes. Intensive respiratory support is required and when cyanosis has been reversed atropine should be given, 2 mg i.v. every 10 min until the skin is dry and there is a sinus tachycardia, or other evidence of full atropinization. Since these compounds inhibit acetylcholinesterase irreversibly, a cholinesterase reactivator should be given, such as pralidoxime 30 mg/kg i.v., at a rate of no more than 500 mg/min, and repeated after 30 min. Convulsions should be treated with diazepam or chlormethiazole.

(j) Digitalis

In this instance, for removal of the drug from the stomach ipecacuanha-induced emesis is preferable to gastric lavage, since there is a risk of cardiac asystole during lavage. Activated charcoal may help reduce the absorption of digitalis, particularly digitoxin, and an anion exchange resin, such as cholestyramine or colestipol, is also effective in reducing digitoxin absorption. A temporary pacemaker should be inserted as soon as possible, even in the absence at the time of arrhythmias or heart block. Hypokalaemia should be treated with potassium chloride i.v., at a rate of no more than 20 mmol/h, but *hyper*kalaemia may occur and is a poor prognostic sign. It should be treated with insulin, 20 i.u. i.v., and 50 ml of 50 per cent dextrose. In severe cases dialysis may be required to treat hyperkalaemia, but dialysis does not remove digitalis from the body. Tachyarrhythmias should be treated with phenytoin, lignocaine, or propranolol, and bradycardia and heart block by transvenous pacing or with atropine if a pacemaker is not available.

Charcoal haemoperfusion has been advocated for digitalis poisoning but its usefulness has not been established. It may be of value for digitoxin poisoning, particularly if started very soon after ingestion.

(k) Notes on some other important poisonings (see also Table 32.4)

1. Benzodiazepines. Only supportive measures are required.
2. Major tranquillizers (phenothiazines, such as chlorpromazine, butyrophenones, such as haloperidol). Intensive supportive measures may be required. Dyskinesias should be treated with benztropine, 2 mg i.v., and convulsions with diazepam or chlormethiazole.
3. MAO inhibitors. Dopamine or dobutamine should *not* be used for treating shock since their metabolism is inhibited by MAO inhibitors. Use instead hydrocortisone, 100 mg i.v. six-hourly. For hyperthermia use a fan and tepid sponging or chlorpromazine, 100 mg i.m. Chlorpromazine is also useful for treating the cerebral stimulatory effects of MAO inhibitors.
4. Lithium. Lithium excretion is hastened by forced alkaline diuresis,

but very careful plasma electrolyte monitoring must be carried out. Dialysis or charcoal haemoperfusion may be required.

5. Iron. Gastric lavage should be carried out with a solution of desferrioxamine, in a concentration of 2 g/l, and 10 g of desferrioxamine in 50 ml water should be left in the stomach at the end. Desferrioxamine should also be given as soon as possible both i.m. and i.v. The doses are: i.m. 2 g (1 g in a child) repeated after 12 h; i.v. 15 mg/kg/h to a maximum of 80 mg/kg/day. If there is oliguria dialysis should be started immediately.

6. Methanol. Give ethyl alcohol 1 ml/kg of a 50 per cent solution orally immediately, followed by an i.v. infusion of 5 per cent ethyl alcohol in 5 per cent dextrose at a rate of 5–10 ml/h, aiming for a minimum blood ethanol concentration of 100 mg/dl (22 mmol/l). Increase the dose by 8 ml/h during dialysis. Treat acidosis with sodium bicarbonate. In severe cases haemodialysis or peritoneal dialysis is necessary, e.g. if the blood methanol concentration is over 500 mg/l (16 mmol/l), or if there are neurological or ophthalmic complications, or severe acidosis.

32.3. SOURCES OF INFORMATION

For the names of some textbooks describing the presentation and management of acute poisonings see the bibliography (Chapter 18). For information on individual drugs one of the following poisons centres should be contacted:

> Belfast: 0232–240503, ext.2140
> Cardiff: 0222–33101 (8 am–5 pm)
>   0222–35159 (5 pm–8 am)
> Edinburgh: 031–229–2477, ext.2233
> London: 01–407–7600, ext.4001.

For specific advice on paraquat poisoning one of the many paraquat treatment centres should be contacted (see *Brit.med.J.* (1979) **ii**, 619).

32.4. AGENTS USED IN THE TREATMENT OF SELF-POISONING

In Table 32.4 are shown the various therapeutic agents which may be used in the treatment of self-poisoning, arranged alphabetically in order of agent. There is also a cross-index to the table, arranged alphabetically in order of the poisons to be treated.

Table 32.4 *Agents used in the treatment of self-poisoning*

Agent	Used in poisoning by	Mode of action	Dosage	Comments
N-acetylcysteine	Paracetamol	Sulphydryl compound: prevents hepatic necrosis by assisting conjugation of toxic hydroxylamine metabolites of paracetamol	See text (p.576)	Ineffective if given more than 10–15 h after overdose.
Acids, dilute acetic acid 1% w/v, lemon juice, vinegar, 1 in 4 dilution	Caustic alkalis (e.g. ammonia, potassium or sodium hydroxide)	Neutralizing effect	*Oral:* 100–200 ml or as much as can be tolerated	
Alcohol (ethanol, ethyl alcohol) (p.624)	Methyl alcohol, ethylene glycol (and other glycols)	Competes with methyl alcohol for metabolism by hepatic enzyme alcohol dehydrogenase preventing formation of toxic formic acid and formates; prevents breakdown of glycols into toxic oxalic acid and oxalates	See text	
Ascorbic acid	As an alternative to methylene blue (but less effective)	See methylene blue	*i.v.:* 1 g slowly *Oral:* 200 mg, three times daily	
Atropine sulphate (p.616)	1. Organophosphorus insecticides, e.g. malathion, parathion, and other acetylcholinesterase inhibitors, including carbamates	Competes with acetycholine at parasympathetic nerve endings; no effect at neuromuscular sites	1. *im., s.c.:* initially 0.6–1.2 mg (*i.v.* for severe cases). *Mild cases:* this dose will relieve symptoms. *Severe cases:* 0.25–2 mg repeated at 15–30 min intervals to maintain atropinization	Not to be used in cyanosed patients (acetylcholinesterase reactivator)
	2. Neostigmine and other parasympathomimetics		2. *i.m., s.c.:* 0.6–1.2 mg to control muscarinic effects (may be given i.v. for severe cases)	

Table 32.4   *Continued*

Agent	Used in poisoning by	Mode of action	Dosage	Comments
Benztropine (p.616)	Butyrophenones Phenothiazines Reserpine	Acetylcholinergic antagonist for control of the extra-pyramidal effects of these drugs	*i.v.*: 2 mg will provide rapid relief of symptoms; dose may be repeated	
Calcium gluconate	1. Hydrofluoric acid	Binds fluoride ion in less soluble complex	*Oral*: after ingestion, 30 g well diluted. *Eye-drops*: 10% sterile solution, instil a few drops *Topical*: applied to affected skin repeatedly for 15 min after pain subsides. May be used as a dressing. *i.v.*: for convulsions 10 ml, 10% solution repeated as necessary	Administer by slow *i.v.* injection; high blood concentrations of calcium ions may depress cardiac function. Solution irritant, take care to avoid extravasation during *i.v.* injection
	2. Lead	Relieves pain of colic after acute poisoning	*i.v.*: 10–20 ml. 10% solution	
	3. Oxalic acid	Prevents tetany	*Oral*: after ingestion, 100 ml of a 1% solution *i.v.*: 10–20 ml, 10% solution	
Chlormethiazole (p.659)	Agents causing convulsions	Anticonvulsant	See text	
Chlorpromazine hydrochloride (p.727)	LSD, amphetamines, MAO inhibitors	Tranquillizer. Reduces hyperpyrexia	*i.m.*: 100–200 mg	Contra-indicated in comatose patients
Desferrioxamine mesylate	Iron	Iron chelating agent: renders non-toxic any iron remaining in the alimentary tract; administered parenterally, increases the urinary excretion of iron. 100 mg desferrioxamine chelates approximately 8.5 mg iron	See text	Rapid *i.v.* injection may cause allergic reaction. Local pain may occur with *i.m.* injection.

Table 32.4 *Continued*

Agent	Used in poisoning by	Mode of action	Dosage	Comments
Dextrose	1. Hypoglycaemic agents 2. Cyanide (see cobalt edetate)	To maintain blood glucose	1. *Oral, i.v.*: as required 2. *i.v.*: following dicobalt edetate therapy, through same needle, 50 ml 50% dextrose	
Diazepam (p.642)	Agents causing convulsions	Anticonvulsant	See text	
Dicobalt edetate	Cyanide	Forms stable complex with cyanides	*i.v.*: 300 mg (20 ml) over 1 min, followed immediately by 50 ml dextrose injected through the same needle. If the response is inadequate, a further dose of 300 mg may be given, followed by 50 ml 50% dextrose.	*Note:* if there is no improvement with dicobalt edetate start nitrite/thiosulphate therapy (see text).
Dimercaprol (synonym BAL)	Arsenic, mercury, antimony, bismuth, gold, thallium, lead (combined with sodium calcium edetate for encephalitis), nickel	Chelating agent: combines in the body with heavy metals which inhibit the pyruvate oxidase system by competing with sulphydryl groups in proteins: dimercaprol has a greater affinity for these metals than the proteins, and the resultant chelates are stable and rapidly excreted by the kidneys	4 mg/kg *i.m.* every 4 h for 2 days followed by 3 mg/kg b.d. for up to 8 days if required	High doses produce adverse effects in 50% of patients (nausea, vomiting, headache, burning sensation of lips, mouth, throat and eyes, salivation, lachrymation, hypertension, tachycardia, muscle spasm); these are at a maximum 20 min after injection, and subside in 2 h. There may be pain at site of injection. Do not use in patients with impaired hepatic function. Contra-indicated for cadmium and iron poisoning
Fuller's earth suspension (150 g/l)	Paraquat, diquat, and other bipyridylium compounds	Adsorption of poison in the gastro-intestinal tract, preventing absorption	See text	

Table 32.4   *Continued*

Agent	Used in poisoning by	Mode of action	Dosage	Comments
Glucagon	1. Hypoglycaemic agents	1. Increases hepatic glycogen mobilisation to increase plasma glucose	1. *i.m.*, *s.c.*, or *i.v.*: 0.5–2 mg may be repeated to one or two additional doses if no response	1. Response takes 5–20 min so i.v. dextrose is the treatment of choice (to prevent cerebral effects of prolonged hypoglycaemia)
	2. *β*-adrenoceptor antagonists	2. Stimulates adenyl cyclase activity	2. *i.v.*: 2 mg repeated according to response, (*i.v.* to 40 mg over 12 h has been used)	2. Diluent of glucagon may contain phenol 0.2% which may cause toxic effects if repeated doses necessary
Methylene blue (Ascorbic acid is an alternative but less effective)	Chlorates, phenacetin, glyceryl trinitrate, phenazone, nitrobenzene, toluidine, nitric acid, nitrites, dinitrophenol, aniline derivatives	For methaemoglobinaemia: hastens the conversion of methaemoglobin to haemoglobin	*i.v.*: 10 ml 1% solution repeated as required (1–4 mg/kg body weight)	Take care to avoid extravasation
Naloxone hydrochloride	Narcotic analgesics	Narcotic antagonist, counteracts respiratory depression	*i.v.*: initially 0.4–1.2 mg repeated once or twice at 2–3 min intervals	Pure antagonist—does not induce respiratory depression
D-*penicillamine* (p. 721)	1. Lead—chronic poisoning or in control of plumbism following acute overdose. (NOT tetra-ethyl lead poisoning) 2. Gold—if adverse reaction to dimercaprol occurs	Chelating agent, aids elimination of metallic ion	*Oral*: 1–4 mg daily in divided doses. Children: 5 y 150 mg twice daily; 6–12 y 300 mg twice daily	Allergic reactions: patients sensitive to penicillin may react to penicillamine
Phentolamine mesylate (p.621)	Sympathomimetic agents such as ephedrine, and amphetamines. Clonidine. Hypertensive crisis in patients receiving MAO inhibitors	*α*-adrenoceptor antagonist	*i.v.*: 5–10 mg repeated as necessary	

Table 32.4 *Continued*

Agent	Used in poisoning by	Mode of action	Dosage	Comments
Physostigmine (p.617)	1. Anticholinergic drugs, such as atropine, hyoscine, propantheline	Acetylcholinesterase inhibitor. Reverses both peripheral and central effects	1. *i.v., i.m., s.c.*: 1–2 mg every 1–2 h or as required	
	2. Cardiac arrhythmias in poisoning with tricyclic antidepressants (but see text)		2. See text	2. See text
Salbutamol (p.620)	β-adrenoceptor antagonists	Selective β₂-agonist: relieves β-blocker-induced bronchoconstriction	*Inhalation*: 1–2 mg/h via nebulizer of a suitable intermittent positive pressure ventilator	
Sodium calcium edetate	Lead (acute and chronic) More effective if used in combination with dimercaprol	Exchanges calcium ions for lead ions in the blood and forms a stable, non-ionizable, water-soluble lead compound which is readily excreted unchanged in the urine	*i.v.*: 40 mg/kg/day in two divided doses for 3–5 days; combined with dimercaprol *Note*: if there is encephalopathy and increased intracranial pressure, the dose may be given *i.m.* to avoid giving excess fluid	Nausea, diarrhoea, and abdominal pains often occur during *i.v.* injection as can a burning sensation at the injection site. Thrombophlebitis can occur if the concentrated solution is injected quickly. Nephrotoxicity can cause albuminuria, casts and cells in urine, oliguria, and renal failure
Sodium nitrite	Cyanide	Converts haemoglobin to methaemoglobin which competes with cytochrome oxidase for cyanide forming cyanmethaemoglobin	See text	Used with sodium thiosulphate. Cobalt edetate is the usual first-line therapy for cyanide poisoning
Sodium thiosulphate	Cyanide	Hastens conversion of cyanmethaemoglobin to thiocynate by the action of tissue rhodanase	See text	Used with sodium nitrite

Cross-index for Table 32.4

Poisoning by	Agent(s) used (Table 32.4)	Poisoning by	Agent(s) used (Table 32.4)
Acetylcholinesterase inhibitors	Atropine	Lead	Calcium gluconate, dimercaprol, penicillamine, sodium calcium edetate
β-adrenoceptor antagonists	Glucagon, salbutamol	LSD	Chlorpromazine
Alkalis, caustic	Acids	Malathion	Atropine
Ammonia	Acids	MAO inhibitors	Chlorpromazine
Amphetamines	Chlorpromazine, phentolamine	MAO inhibitors (hypertension after withdrawal)	Phentolamine
Analgesics, narcotic	Naloxone	Mercury	Dimercaprol
Aniline derivatives	Ascorbic acid, methylene blue	Methyl alcohol (methanol)	Alcohol (ethanol)
Anticholinergic drugs	Physostigmine	Narcotic analgesics	Naloxone
Antidepressants, tricyclic	Physostigmine	Neostigmine	Atropine
Arsenic	Dimercaprol	Nickel	Dimercaprol
Atropine	Physostigmine	Nitric acid	Ascorbic acid, methylene blue
Bipyridylium compounds	Fuller's earth	Nitrites	Ascorbic acid, methylene blue
Bismuth	Dimercaprol	Nitrobenzene	Ascorbic acid, methylene blue
Butyrophenones	Benztropine	Organophosphorus insecticides	Atropine
Carbamates	Atropine	Oxalic acid	Calcium gluconate
Caustic alkalis	Acids	Paracetamol	*Acetylcysteine
Chlorates	Ascorbic acid, methylene blue	Paraquat	Fuller's earth
Clonidine	Phentolamine	Parasympathomimetic agents	Atropine
Convulsive agents	Chlormethiazole, diazepam	Parathion	Atropine
Cyanide	Dicobalt edetate+dextrose; sodium nitrite+sodium thiosulphate	Phenacetin	Ascorbic acid, methylene blue
Dinitrophenol	Ascorbic acid, methylene blue	Phenazone	Ascorbic acid, methylene blue
Diquat	Fuller's earth	Phenothiazines	Benztropine
Ephedrine	Phentolamine	Potassium hydroxide	Acids
Ethylene glycol	Alcohol (ethanol)	Propantheline	Physostigmine
Glyceryl trinitrate	Ascorbic acid, methylene blue	Reserpine	Benztropine
Glycols	Alcohol (ethanol)	Sodium hydroxide	Acids
Gold	Dimercaprol, penicillamine	Sympathomimetic agents	Phentolamine
Hydrofluoric acid	Calcium gluconate	Thallium	Dimercaprol
Hyoscine	Physostigmine	Toluidine	Ascorbic acid, methylene blue
Hypoglycaemic agents	Dextrose, glucagon	Tricyclic antidepressants	Physostigmine
Insecticides, organophosphorus	Atropine		
Iron	Desferrioxamine		

33 The principles of cancer chemotherapy

The use of drugs in the treatment of malignant neoplastic disease is, in its detail, a very complicated matter requiring much experience and skill. However, as cancer chemotherapy routines become more effective they will be given to more patients, and although such treatment will be carried out in specialist units, the general continuing care of these patients will become part of the responsibility of every surgeon, physician, and general practitioner. A knowledge of the principles of cancer chemotherapy is therefore of increasing importance.

The first point to note is that cancer chemotherapy never stands alone in the treatment of the patient with malignant neoplastic disease. The general management of the patient and family, the control of symptoms such as pain, the treatment of complications such as urinary flow obstruction in carcinoma of the prostate, and the place of surgery and radiotherapy in overall management are of vital importance. Because the toxic:therapeutic ratio for all cytotoxic drugs is low, and because the results of toxicity are symptomatically very distressing and can be fatal, the judgement as to when such treatment should be used is based on assessments of its known efficacy in similar cases, and of the mental, physical, and social condition of the individual patient. Very many factors must be taken into consideration in each case. The mixture of skills required, and the integration and organization of surgical, radiotherapeutic, and chemotherapeutic programmes have in recent years produced the specialties of medical and surgical oncology.

Although the 5-year survival rates for the major solid neoplasms (e.g. colon, rectum, lung, breast, uterus) have not increased dramatically since the 1940s, there have been startling successes in some neoplastic conditions, and some of these are listed in Table 33.1.

In other neoplastic conditions chemotherapy, with or without surgery or radiotherapy, is less effective, but in appropriate cases may produce worthwhile remissions and may prolong life. In other malignancies, all solid tumours, there is no response and current chemotherapy is not indicated (see Table 33.1).

Table 33.1   *Examples of tumour responsiveness to cancer chemotherapy*

1. *Highly responsive (treatment may be curative—normal life expectancy common)*

Hodgkin's lymphoma	Combination chemotherapy (pp.467,598)
Choriocarcinoma	Methotrexate, actinomycin D
Wilms's tumour (children)	Surgery, radiotherapy, chemotherapy
Burkitt's lymphoma	Cyclophosphamide
Rhabdomyosarcoma	Surgery, radiotherapy, chemotherapy

2. *Responsive (responders have prolonged life and some are cured)*

Acute lymphoblastic leukaemia (children)	Combination chemotherapy (pp.466, 598)
Non-Hodgkin's lymphoma	Combination chemotherapy (p.468)
Retinoblastoma	Radiotherapy, cyclophosphamide
Testicular carcinoma	Surgery, radiotherapy, chemotherapy (p.598)

3. *Moderately responsive (clinical remissions frequent, may be increased survival)*

Breast carcinoma	Surgery, radiotherapy, chemotherapy
Multiple myeloma	Combination chemotherapy (p.469)
Adult acute leukaemias	Combination chemotherapy (p.466)
Ovarian carcinoma	Combination chemotherapy
Small cell, undifferentiated lung carcinoma	Combination chemotherapy
Endometrial carcinoma	Hormonal and cytotoxic chemotherapy ± surgery/radiotherapy
Carcinoma prostate	Stilboestrol

4. *Partly responsive (occasional worthwhile regression, remission rare, little prolongation of survival)*

Pancreatic islet cell carcinoma	Combination chemotherapy
Head and neck cancer	Chemotherapy ± surgery, radiotherapy
Adrenocortical carcinoma	Combination chemotherapy

5. *Minimally responsive to current chemotherapy*
Non-small cell bronchial carcinoma
Bladder carcinoma
Colorectal carcinoma (surgery can be effective)
Malignant melanoma
Pancreatic adenocarcinoma
Glioblastoma

33.1. ACTIONS OF DRUGS RELEVANT TO THEIR CLINICAL USE

Some of the drugs used in cancer chemotherapy are listed in Table 33.2 and their modes of action are summarized in the Pharmacopoeia. However, there are certain points to emphasise in relation to their use in cancer chemotherapy.

33.1.1. Sites of action

There are several different sites at which cytotoxic drugs act in interfering with cell growth and division. The different sites of action in regard to the

Table 33.2   *Some drugs used in cancer chemotherapy*

Alkylating agents
Busulphan (p.646)
Chlorambucil (p.658)
Cyclophosphamide (p.670)
Melphalan (p.703)
Mustine (p.712)

Antimetabolites
Cytarabine (p.671)
Fluorouracil (p.680)
Methotrexate (p.704)
Mercaptopurine (p.640)

Cytotoxic antibiotics
Actinomycin D (p.618)
Bleomycin (p.644)
Doxorubicin (p.677)

Hormones and hormone antagonists
Anti-oestrogen—tamoxifen (p.757)
Glucocorticoids (p.664)
Oestrogens, e.g. stilboestrol (p.752)
Progestogens, e.g. medroxyprogesterone (p.744)

Vinca alkaloids (p.769)
Vinblastine
Vincristine

Others
Cisplatin (p.662)

---

molecular biochemistry of the cell are illustrated in Fig. 33.1. The fact that cytotoxic drugs differ in their effects in these ways gives the opportunity for producing cumulative biochemical lesions in the cell during therapy. This is the basis for the development of combination drug therapy.

33.1.2. Effects of cytotoxic drugs on different phases of the cell cycle

All cells which are synthesizing DNA go through a regular cycle which has several different phases (illustrated in Fig. 33.2).

G_1 *phase*—this is a resting phase which occurs after cell division (mitosis) is complete. During this phase there is no DNA synthesis, but RNA and protein synthesis occur normally. After mitosis cells may go into a different kind of resting phase, G_0, in which they are out of the cycle but are capable of proliferating. During G_0 cells are very resistant to the effects of cytotoxic drugs.

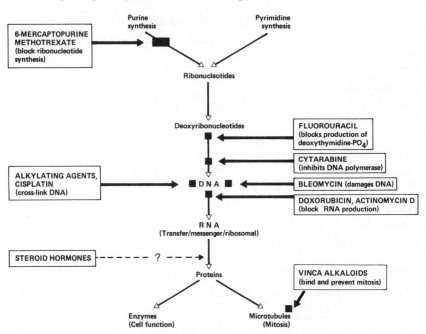

Fig. 33.1. Cellular molecular biochemistry and the sites and mechanisms of action of cytotoxic drugs.

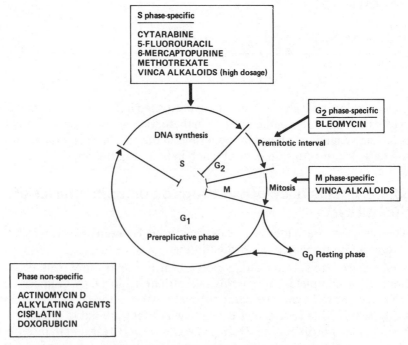

Fig. 33.2. The cell cycle and the timing of the actions of cytotoxic drugs.

S phase—this is a phase of DNA synthesis which is preceded at the end of G_1 by an increase in the rate of RNA synthesis.

G_2 *phase*—in this phase DNA synthesis once more stops while RNA and protein synthesis continue.

M phase (*mitosis*)—during mitosis there is a decrease in the rate of RNA and protein synthesis and after mitosis the resting phase occurs again.

Different cytotoxic drugs may act at different phases of the cell cycle, as illustrated in Fig. 33.2. Certain principles follow from these observations:

(a) The faster the cell cycles are turning over the more likely are treatments with cytotoxic drugs to 'catch' cells in a sensitive phase. Unfortunately, the faster the cell cycles the more malignant the condition. As a corollary of this, *normal* tissues with fast cell cycles, e.g. bone marrow, gastro-intestinal mucosa, lymphoid tissue, and skin, suffer most from cytotoxic drug therapy.

(b) Theoretically the more cells there are in the tumour in synchrony of cycle, the more cells will be likely to be 'caught' by a pulse of cytotoxic drug therapy. The fewer cells there are in synchrony the more necessary is prolonged therapy, with a consequent increase in toxicity.

Sometimes an attempt may be made to recruit cells into synchrony. For example, it is thought that surgical removal of large tumour masses will sometimes provoke the remaining cells to proliferate, at which point they can be 'caught' by cytotoxic drug therapy (adjuvant chemotherapy to surgery).

(c) Theoretically treatment with a mitotic spindle poison, such as a vinca alkaloid, might arrest cells in their cycle, after which they could be treated with an inhibitor of DNA synthesis, say cytarabine, just when they are in S phase. Whether in practice such a combination works this way in man is difficult to prove, but it does work with experimental mouse leukaemias.

(d) The effects of tumour size on treatment—Large tumours are relatively unresponsive to cytotoxic drugs for two reasons. Firstly, many cells tend to be in G_0, the resting phase, when cells are unresponsive to drugs, and secondly, penetration of the drug through a rather poor vasculature is insufficient to achieve cytotoxic concentrations for long enough without also producing severe systemic toxicity. Better, if possible, to remove large tumour bulk and to treat remaining small tumour masses (adjuvant chemotherapy).

Generally speaking both on the basis of cell-growth kinetics and vascularity, small tumours tend to be more sensitive to chemotherapy. It follows theoretically that the sooner treatment is instituted the better.

(e) Kinetics of cell kill—Because cytotoxic drugs affect only those cells in a particular phase they kill a *proportion* of all cells of a type, rather than a fixed number of cells. Since many human tumours are heterogeneous in their cell populations there may be great variability in the responses of individual cell types. It is difficult therefore to kill off every tumour cell, although if cure is the aim this is essential. Because of this proportionality of cell kill, chemotherapy can reduce tumour mass sufficiently to result in clinical remission, often quite easily, but without eradicating the tumour. Remember that the faster the cells divide, the more easily they are killed by the cytotoxic drugs, and the faster the onset of clinical remission. Unfortunately, if the tumour cells are not completely cleared, quickly-dividing cells also produce clinical relapse quickly, e.g. acute myeloid leukaemia.

33.2. PRE-TREATMENT EVALUATION

Because of the serious toxicity of cancer chemotherapy it is vital that patients be properly assessed to evaluate their likely response and progress. Careful histopathology and clinical staging (by radiological techniques such as CAT (computed axial tomographic) scanning, lymphangiography, and surgical exploration, (as in Hodgkin's lymphoma) are essential. These procedures enable some prediction of response. During therapy such evaluation may have to be repeated to give guidance as to the advisability of further chemotherapeutic courses.

In some cases tumour markers may be measurable: for example, gonadotrophic hormones in choriocarcinoma, myeloma proteins, α-fetoprotein in hepatocellular carcinoma, ectopic hormones in oat cell carcinoma of bronchus, acid phosphatase in prostatic carcinoma.

33.3. COMBINATION CHEMOTHERAPY

Combinations of chemotherapeutic agents are used because:

1. Human malignancies tend to be resistant to one agent; this may or may not be due to cell heterogeneity.

2. Cell resistance is often acquired with treatment with a single agent, probably because of the proliferation of mutant cells with biochemical properties conferring resistance to particular agents.

3. Multiple sites of attack on tumour cells are possible with drugs which have different toxic effects on normal cells. Thus greater overall efficacy of treatment can be achieved without unacceptable toxicity. For instance, vincristine and prednisolone do not have great marrow toxicity, and can be combined successfully with doxorubicin in the treatment of acute lymphoblastic leukaemia.

33.4. REGIMENS OF CANCER CHEMOTHERAPY

The main aim of any regimen used in the treatment of cancer is to try and get enough drug to the tumour cells for long enough to achieve a reasonable kill, while at the same time avoiding unacceptable toxicity.

Most regimens are based upon an intermittent administration of drugs, with intervals of a few weeks between courses. This allows time for recovery of normal bone marrow and immune functions in between courses. There are, however, exceptions: for example, in the maintenance treatment of chronic lymphocytic leukaemia with chlorambucil, in stilboestrol therapy of carcinoma of the prostate, and in the maintenance treatment of chronic myeloid leukaemia with busulphan.

Sometimes special action must be taken to get at cells in sites not easily accessible to drugs administered systemically, for example pleural or peritoneal malignant effusions, and CNS spread. The instillation of cytotoxic drugs such as thiotepa into malignant effusions can be palliative, reducing the size of the effusion.

The CNS 'sanctuary' for malignant cells has proved a particular problem in the treatment of leukaemia. For instance, intrathecal methotrexate and radiotherapy to the cranium are now routinely used with great success in preventing CNS involvement in acute lymphoblastic leukaemia in children.

33.5. ADVERSE EFFECTS OF DRUGS USED IN CANCER CHEMOTHERAPY

The main problem limiting the use of cytotoxic drugs is the occurrence of adverse effects. Although these are listed under the individual agents in the Pharmacopoeia, some generalizations are important. The adverse effects common to many cytotoxic drugs are as follows:

33.5.1. Nausea and vomiting

These are most common during high-dose pulse therapy. The worst offenders are the mustines, cisplatin, and doxorubicin, but nausea and vomiting can be caused by many cytotoxic drugs, and can be a major factor in some patients' tolerance of cancer chemotherapy. Treatment and prevention of nausea and vomiting are not yet satisfactory. Various anti-emetics, such as prochlorperazine and domperidone are given routinely, and cytotoxic drugs are often given at night so that sedation and sleep can add to the anti-emetic effect. Recently cannabinoid (marijuana) derivatives have also been introduced for this purpose.

33.5.2. Bone marrow toxicity

Bone marrow suppression can result in decreased production of any or all of the formed elements of the blood with resulting anaemia, leucopenia, and thrombocytopenia.

Neutropenia (granulocytopenia or agranulocytosis) and lymphocytopenia are associated with an increased risk of infections such as candidiasis, and unusual nosocomial (hospital-derived) infections may occur, including infection with *Pneumocystis carinii* and cytomegalovirus.

Thrombocytopenia leads to haemorrhagic complications, and anaemia, common as part of the disease, is worsened by bone marrow toxicity.

The adverse effects of high doses of methotrexate on the bone marrow can be reversed by 'folinic acid rescue', although the precise place of this procedure in practical chemotherapy has yet to be defined. Since the action of methotrexate is to block the synthesis of folinic acid its action can be bypassed by giving folinic acid. Of course the cytotoxic action of methotrexate would be nullified by this so the procedure is to give a high dose of methotrexate over a short period, wait for a few hours for the methotrexate to 'catch' a reasonable number of cells going through S phase, then give folinic acid, thus protecting the bone marrow. A regimen of this kind is described in the Pharmacopoeia (p.704).

33.5.3. Gastro-intestinal toxicity

Stomatitis and oral ulceration are common. Superinfection with *Candida albicans* may occur, causing oral moniliasis (thrush). Intestinal ulceration and mucosal shedding may be associated with diarrhoea and again nosocomial (hospital-associated) infections can supervene.

33.5.4. Alopecia

Hair falls out because of effects on the hair follicle, but it does regrow.

33.5.5. Gonadal effects

In women menstrual irregularities and amenorrhoea are common, and occasionally sterility may result. In men impaired spermatogenesis is common, and infertility may result.

33.5.6. Hyperuricaemia

Because of cell breakdown during cytotoxic drug therapy there may be large amounts of purines released. The purines are metabolised to uric acid and thus can lead to gout and renal damage. Allopurinol may be given to prevent the conversion of hypoxanthine and xanthine to insoluble uric acid. If possible allopurinol therapy should be started a day or two in advance of cytotoxics in order to allow allopurinol to reach its full effect. Beware, however, of interactions with allopurinol. Allopurinol inhibits the metabolism of 6-mercaptopurine, and thus enhances its toxicity; it may also enhance the bone-marrow toxicity of cyclophosphamide (see Pharmacopoeia, p.629).

33.5.7. Carcinogenesis and mutagenesis

Because of the mutagenic potential of cytotoxic therapy it is suggested that 6 months should elapse after treatment of either partner before attempts at conception are made.

Cytotoxic drug therapy is associated with an increased risk of other malignant tumours. Whether this is because of the induction of mutations or because of immunosuppression is unknown. This risk must be weighed against the efficacy of the treatment.

Besides these adverse effects, common to a greater or lesser extent to most cytotoxic drugs, there are some special adverse effects to individual drugs shown in Table 33.3.

Table 33.3 *Special adverse effects of individual drugs (see also Pharmacopoeia)*

Drug	Adverse effect
Bleomycin	Pulmonary fibrosis
Busulphan	Pulmonary fibrosis
Cisplatin	Renal toxicity
	Ototoxicity
	Peripheral neuropathy
Cyclophosphamide	Haemorrhagic cystitis
Doxorubicin	Cardiac arrhythmias
	Cardiomyopathy
5–fluorouracil	Skin pigmentation
Methotrexate	Hepatic damage (chronic treatment)
Vincristine	Peripheral neuropathy
	Autonomic neuropathy

33.5.8. Drug interactions

Specific interactions of cytotoxic drugs with other drugs are described in the Pharmacopoeia. However, it should also be noted that there is a theoretical risk of using live vaccines (see p.288) in patients on cytotoxic drug therapy, since their immune responses may be diminished. This may result in an exaggerated local reaction to the vaccine or even severe systemic infection. Such an effect has been reported, for example, after smallpox vaccination in patients taking methotrexate.

33.6. THE PRACTICAL USE OF CYTOTOXIC DRUGS

The following three examples of chemotherapeutic regimens will give an idea of the practicalities involved. Note that many of the dosages are expressed as a number of mg/m^2. This is because animal experiments have shown a closer relationship between dose and effect when dose is corrected for body surface area rather than weight. As a rough guide the surface area of a 70 kg man is generally taken to be about $1.7 \ m^2$.

33.6.1. Acute lymphoblastic leukaemia in children

(a) Induction therapy (to induce remission)

Vincristine 1.5 mg/m^2 i.v. weekly for 4–6 weeks.
Prednisolone 40 mg/m^2 orally daily for 4–6 weeks.

Response is monitored by peripheral blood count and bone marrow aspiration.

(b) CNS prophylaxis

Cranial irradiation and/or intrathecal methotrexate are used. There is some concern about the toxicity to the brain of combined cranial irradiation and intrathecal methotrexate, and in some centres intrathecal methotrexate alone is used.

(c) Maintenance therapy (to maintain remission)

6-mercaptopurine 50 mg/m^2 orally, once daily.
Methotrexate 20 mg/m^2 orally, once weekly.

Depending on the severity of the leukaemia this may be backed up by a single dose of vincristine i.v once a month and prednisolone orally for 5 days a month. Other cytotoxic drugs may be added to maintenance therapy if required, but on a monthly basis. Maintenance therapy should be continued for 2–3 years. Children remaining in remission for 4 years after completing 2–3 years of treatment have a very good chance of cure.

33.6.2. Testicular carcinoma

The testis is removed and the disease staged according to the extent of spread. Radiotherapy is given according to the extent of spread.

If there is any evidence of spread chemotherapy is also commenced:

Cisplatin—20 mg/m^2 i.v daily for 5 days every 3 weeks for three courses.

Vinblastine—0.15 mg/kg i.v daily for 2 days every 3 weeks (give 6 h before bleomycin). After five such treatments switch to 0.3 mg/kg i.v. every 4 weeks for 2 years.

Bleomycin 30 mg i.v. on days 2, 9, and 16 of each course of cisplatin, then weekly for a total of 13 weeks. Stop at 360 mg.

33.6.3. Hodgkin's lymphoma

In the literature on cancer chemotherapy one is frequently confronted with acronyms for combination cytotoxic drug therapy, each letter standing for either the approved or proprietary name for the drug.

One such example is the 'MOPP' regimen for Hodgkin's lymphoma:

M = mustine—6 mg/m^2 IV on days 1 and 8;
O = vincristine (Oncovin®)—1.5 mg/m^2 IV on days 1 and 8;
P = procarbazine—100 mg/m^2 orally daily on days 1–14;
P = prednisolone—40 mg orally daily on days 1–14.

This treatment is repeated every 4 weeks for a minimum of six treatments. Combination therapy in Hodgkin's lymphoma is currently recommended for the more severe forms (some classes of stage III and all stage IV).

It will be seen from the demands of these regimens on the patients, the occurrence of adverse effects, the monitoring of haematological and biochemical functions required, and the medical care necessary to cope with infection, that cancer chemotherapy must be carried out by teams experienced in it and equipped to do it properly.

34 Immunosuppression and the drug therapy of allergies and connective tissue diseases

34.1. IMMUNE DISEASE: PATHOGENESIS AND MECHANISMS OF ACTION OF DRUGS

Although the precise details of the actions of drugs used in the treatment of allergic and immune diseases have not been fully worked out, sufficient is known to fit the actions of the drugs into a scheme dependent upon an understanding of the four different types of immune reaction. The drugs used are listed in Table 34.1.

Table 34.1 *Drugs used in the treatment of allergic disorders and in immune suppression*

A. *Allergic disorders*
1. Antihistamines (p.637)
    Chorpheniramine
    Mebhydrolin
    Promethazine
    Trimeprazine
2. Adrenaline (p.620)
3. Glucocorticoids (p.664)
4. Mediator-release inhibitors
    Sodium cromoglycate (p.670)

B. *Immune suppression*
1. Glucocorticoids
2. Cytotoxic drugs
    Azathioprine (p.640)
    Methotrexate (p.704)
    Cyclophosphamide (p.670)
    Cyclosporin A.

The actions and uses of gold and penicillamine are dealt with in the Pharmacopoeia and in Chapter 27.

34.1.1. Type I: Immediate hypersensitivity (anaphylactic reaction)

Previous contact with the offending antigen in a predisposed individual leads to the production of IgE antibodies which bind to cell surfaces, particularly those of mast cells. Subsequent exposure of the individual to the antigen leads to an antigen–antibody reaction at the mast cell surface, and activation of a system which leads to the release of inflammatory mediators from the mast cell. These mediators include histamine, leukotrienes (previously slow reacting substance of anaphylaxis; SRSA), 5-hydroxytryptamine, and kinins. These substances together cause vasodilatation, increased capillary permeability, and tissue oedema. Histamine release in the skin causes itching.

Clinically acute allergic rhinitis (hay fever) results when the antigen reaches sensitized mast cells in the nasal mucosa. Extrinsic allergic asthma occurs when the antigen reaches sensitized bronchial mast cells. Urticaria occurs when skin mast cells are affected. Systemic anaphylaxis (anaphylactic shock) occurs when there is massive mediator release from mast cells in many tissues. In angio-oedema release of inflammatory mediators from mast cells in skin and the mucous membranes of the respiratory tract lead to the typical facial oedematous swelling, with urticaria and erythema of the face and neck, laryngeal oedema which threatens the airway, and sometimes bronchoconstriction.

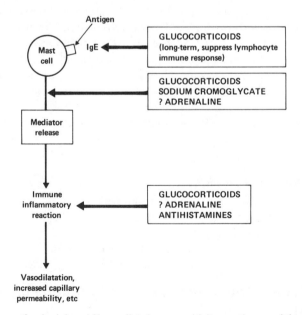

Fig. 34.1. The pathophysiology of immediate hypersensitivity reactions, and the sites of action of drugs used in their treatment.

Hereditary angio-oedema is complement-mediated. There is decreased production or function of the inhibitor of the esterase of the first complement protein, C_1, of the complement activation, and release of inflammatory mediators from mast cells.

The actions of the drugs used to treat acute immediate hypersensitivity reactions are illustrated in Fig. 34.1.

(a) Histamine (H_1)-receptor antagonists (e.g. chlorpheniramine)

These drugs block the H_1-receptor-mediated actions of histamine.

(b) Adrenaline

This is used as immediate treatment in life-threatening acute angio-oedema and anaphylactic shock. Exactly how it works is not known, but the suggestions are that it inhibits the mechanisms of release of inflammatory mediators, decreases capillary permeability, and if there is broncho-constriction relaxes bronchial smooth muscle.

(c) Glucocorticosteroids

Glucocorticoids (e.g. hydrocortisone or prednisolone) have multiple pharmacological effects which interfere with immune reactions. They inhibit the release of inflammatory mediators and suppress the components of the inflammatory reaction, including vasodilatation, increased capillary permeability and tissue oedema. It has been shown that corticosteroids inhibit the release of arachidonic acid from cell membrane phospholipid, and thereby interfere with prostaglandin and leukotriene synthesis.

These effects on mediator release and the inflammatory reaction take some time to come on, and although glucocorticoids should be given as soon as possible in a severe allergic crisis (e.g. angio-oedema with laryngeal oedema, anaphylactic shock), adrenaline and antihistamines have immediate effects and should be used first.

In the longer term corticosteroids suppress the immune function of lymphocytes and interfere with both humoral- and cell-mediated immune reactions.

(d) Mediator-release inhibitors

Sodium cromoglycate, by a mechanism which is not fully understood, prevents the antigen-induced increased permeability of the mast cell membrane to calcium, a process which is an essential precursor of the release of inflammatory mediators. It must therefore be given before antigen challenge, and for this reason is used prophylactically.

34.1.2. Type II: Membrane reactive immunity (cytotoxic reaction)

In this type of reaction an antigen on the surface of a cell combines with antibody, the antigen–antibody complex fixes complement, and damage to the cell membrane results in cell lysis.

Examples of Type II reactions are autoimmune haemolytic anaemia and haemolytic anaemia of the newborn (Rhesus incompatibility). This immune mechanism is also involved in the autoimmune haemolytic anaemia occasionally produced by α-methyldopa. The antibodies in this case are in fact directed against components of the Rhesus complex. Although positive direct Coombs's antibody tests occur in as many as 5–10 per cent of patients taking α-methyldopa for longer than a few months, the occurrence of frank haemolysis is rare. The antibody disappears on stopping the drug.

Glucocorticoids are used to suppress lymphocyte function and immunoglobulin production in autoimmune haemolytic anaemia.

34.1.3. Type III: Immune complex disease

Immune complex disease is caused by the deposition of antigen–antibody complexes in the capillary beds of tissues with local inflammatory injury. Immune complex damage can produce at least part of the pathological picture of serum sickness, glomerulonephritis, rheumatoid arthritis, and infective endocarditis. Serum sickness may occur as an immune response to penicillin, streptomycin, and sulphonamides.

Glucocorticoids suppress the inflammatory response, and reduce lymphocyte function and immunoglobulin production.

34.1.4. Type IV: Cell-mediated immune reactions

In this type of reaction the antigen stimulates T lymphocytes to produce lymphokines. Antibody is not involved. Lymphokines cause the tissue changes associated with cell-mediated hypersensitivity in various ways. There are lymphokines affecting macrophage function which cause macrophages to accumulate at the site of the reaction. Some lymphokines have chemotactic properties for polymorphonuclear leukocytes, while others promote or suppress lymphocyte antibody production. Interferon is a lymphokine produced by T cells in response to viral infections, and it inhibits viral multiplication.

Type IV reactions are most commonly produced by viral and bacterial agents having a predominantly intracellular site of action, e.g. tuberculosis, brucellosis, pertussis, syphilis, and viral infections.

Organ transplant rejection, and contact dermatitis occur mainly through type IV reactions. Cell-mediated hypersensitivity is also of importance in autoimmune diseases.

Cell-mediated hypersensitivity reactions can be suppressed with glucocorticoids or with cytotoxic drugs used as immunosuppressive agents.

Glucocorticoids act to suppress the inflammatory reaction (and when applied to an area of contact dermatitis do so locally). They also suppress lymphocyte function.

The cytotoxic immunosuppressive drugs act by inhibiting the proliferation of lymphocytes produced by antigen.

34.2. DRUG THERAPY OF ALLERGIC DISORDERS

34.2.1. Allergic rhinitis (hay fever)

Avoidance of the allergen and the induction of desensitization with specific allergens are alternatives to drug therapy.

(a) Antihistamines

Symptomatic therapy usually begins with the antihistamines (H_1 antagonists). They are usually only partially effective. The main adverse effect is drowsiness, and this can be dangerous when driving or operating machinery. Individual variability in effectiveness and severity of drowsiness is unpredictable and it is worthwhile finding the best drug for the individual, being prepared to change from one to another if a satisfactory response is not obtained. An example of prescribing for hay fever could be chlorpheniramine, 4 mg 3–4 times daily. Some newer antihistamines, e.g. terfenadine and astemizole, are said to cause less sedation.

(b) Sodium cromoglycate

This is used as prophylactic therapy. It can be given as a nasal spray, drops, or insufflation. These preparations must be applied up the nose 4–6 times daily. Cromoglycate can also be applied in drops to the eyes if they are also affected as happens not uncommonly in this condition.

(c) Glucocorticoids

Nasal applications of beclomethasone (spray), betamethasone (drops), or flunisolide (spray) are available. They are applied 2–3 times daily. In the prescribed dosage there is very little danger of significant systemic absorption, and adverse effects in the nose are few.

Oral and i.m. preparations of glucocorticoids are very effective in the treatment of acute allergic rhinitis but generally should NOT be used because of the serious risk of adverse effects. In *very* severe cases of seasonal allergic rhinitis when sleep is disturbed and the patient's critical duties are being interfered with, a short course of prednisolone may be given (e.g. 30 mg daily reducing by 5 mg a day, every other day). One should check carefully for contra-indications beforehand (see p.608).

(d) Decongestants

Unfortunately all the sympathomimetics, such as ephedrine (an indirect sympathomimetic causing release of noradrenaline) or xylometazoline (a direct α-agonist), are subject to tolerance and rebound vasodilatation, and cause damage to the nasal mucosa and cilia.

They are not generally effective for more than a few days and therefore have limited usefulness. They all act as vasoconstrictors and reduce congestion and oedema of the nasal mucosa.

Systemic nasal decongestants, of which 19 brands are listed in the *British National Formulary*, contain mixtures of paracetamol, antihistamines, and nasal decongestants. Many are available 'over the counter' and generally they are not very effective. So many are available because people use them when they have a cold or nasal congestion. They are not without risk. The antihistamine causes drowsiness and the sympathomimetic may cause tachycardia and a rise in blood pressure. They should not be used by patients with ischaemic heart disease, hypertension, or thyrotoxicosis, and they are potentially fatal for patients taking monoamine oxidase (MAO) inhibitors.

34.2. Urticaria and angio-oedema

For acute attacks of mild to moderate urticaria due to exposure to an allergen an antihistamine, such as chlorpheniramine 4 mg q.d.s., may be sufficient until the reaction has run its course.

If the urticaria is extremely severe then a short course of corticosteroids may be indicated (see below).

Calamine lotion is a suitable cooling local application. If there is associated angio-oedema, particularly if laryngeal oedema develops or if there is bronchoconstriction, then this should be treated as a serious medical emergency.

Adrenaline 0.5 to 1 ml of a 1:1000 solution should be given i.m. This can be life-saving if laryngeal obstruction is present. Also give as soon as possible an antihistamine i.m., e.g. chlorpheniramine 10–20 mg (some authorities recommend this dose by slow i.v. injection). Follow this up with chlorpheniramine 4–8 mg four-hourly until all signs have gone.

In addition administer hydrocortisone 200 mg i.v., and follow this up with prednisolone 30 mg orally, gradually tailing this off over the following week.

34.2.3. Hereditary angio-oedema

In acute attacks the above treatment should be given. If the attack is very severe give fresh frozen plasma which will supply temporarily at least the C_1 esterase inhibitor which is lacking.

Anabolic steroids have been used to prevent attacks. The may increase C_1 esterase inhibitor concentrations but even if they do not they may suppress attacks. Danazol 100–400 mg daily can be used. Increased weight, and in women some androgenic changes will occur, and the benefits must be weighed against these adverse effects.

Antifibrinolytic drugs such as ε-aminocaproic acid and tranexamic acid have also been used to try to suppress attacks on the basis that their action to inhibit proteolysis might spare the C_1 esterase inhibitor. They are not first choice because of adverse effects, such as vascular thrombosis.

34.2.4. Anaphylactic shock

When anaphylactic shock occurs it does so with such swiftness and ferocity that controlled clinical studies of treatment have never been possible (nor would be ethical). What follow are the usual treatment procedures applied.

Prevention is, of course, most essential. A history of previous drug, vaccine, serum, or blood transfusion allergies must be sought from everyone undergoing any treatment with the slightest hazard of this kind. Patients predisposed to allergic reactions should wear an alerting bracelet or necklace (e.g. Medic-Alert®).

If an injection is given which causes an anaphylactic reaction a tourniquet should be placed proximal to the site of injection to minimize further absorption. In another limb adrenaline (0.5–1 ml of a 1:1000 solution) should be given i.m. (withdraw the plunger of the syringe to ensure that the needle is not in a vein). If laryngeal and/or epiglottic oedema is present intubation or emergency tracheostomy may be necessary to establish an airway. If bronchospasm is present inhaled or i.v. salbutamol and/or i.v. aminophylline will be necessary (see asthma, Chapter 22). The administration of adrenaline should also greatly alleviate bronchospasm. Oxygen may also be necessary.

The hypotension of anaphylactic shock is presumably due to vasodilatation and increased capillary permeability. Adrenaline will help, but rapidly infused i.v. fluids (e.g. sodium chloride 0.9 per cent) should be given to correct relative hypovolaemia. If hypotension continues despite adrenaline, i.v. fluids, corticosteroids, and antihistamines (see below) should be given. This is one condition in which α-adrenoceptor agonists *might* be of help (e.g. metaraminol 2–10 mg i.m. or noradrenaline by i.v. infusion 8–12 micrograms/min). Monitor for arrhythmias and treat appropriately.

Hydrocortisone 200 mg i.v. followed by 100 mg i.v four-hourly over the emergency period should be given. This can be followed by oral prednisolone. Chlorpheniramine 10–20 mg i.m. or slowly i.v. should also be given.

34.3. THE USE OF GLUCOCORTICOIDS AS ANTI-INFLAMMATORY, ANTI-ALLERGIC, AND IMMUNOSUPPRESSIVE AGENTS

Glucocorticoids are used for their pharmacological actions on the processes of inflammation and the immune response (lymphocyte function) in diverse situations, some examples of which are shown in Table 34.2.

Table 34.2 *Examples of the use of glucocorticoids as anti-inflammatory or immunosuppressive agents*

	Anti-inflammatory action	*Immunosuppressive action*
Pneumonitis following aspiration of vomit	+++	–
Systemic lupus erythematosus	++(joints)	++
Status asthmaticus	++(allergic response)	–(?)
Autoimmune haemolytic anaemia	–	++
Prevention of transplant rejection	+(in rejection episode)	++

Despite the potential hazard of their adverse effects, which should never be underestimated, and in spite of the circumspect use of glucocorticoids generally in medicine, the justified indications for their systemic use, particularly in hospital practice are numerous and include the following (see also Pharmacopoeia):

severe allergic reactions;
acute severe asthma (status asthmaticus);
complicated sarcoidosis;
connective tissue disorders (e.g. systemic lupus erythematosus, a very few patients with rheumatoid arthritis, polyarteritis nodosa, giant cell arteritis);
minimal-change glomerulonephritis associated with the nephrotic syndrome;
ulcerative colitis;
cerebral oedema;
pemphigus;
acute leukaemias and lymphomas (in combination therapy);
autoimmune haemolytic anaemia;
idiopathic thrombocytopenic purpura;
organ transplantation.

It is as well therefore to have some general guidelines for their use.

1. Make sure of the 'state of the art' for steroid therapy in the disease you wish to treat, because new assessment of benefit versus risk with steroids and refinement of their usage occurs frequently.

2. Although adequate dosage must be used initially, once the disorder seems under control cut back the dose to the smallest effective dose necessary, and if the particular condition allows, e.g. status asthmaticus, acute rheumatoid flare-up, temporal (giant-cell) arteritis, tail off the treatment gradually. In some acute allergic conditions only a few days' therapy may be necessary. If you do decide to treat with steroids treat with adequate dosage, and if no response occurs withdraw gradually. Nothing is

worse than to treat a potentially steroid-responsive condition with an inadequate dosage, since the adverse effects may then occur without the therapeutic benefits.

3. General dosages and adverse effects are given in the Pharmacopoeia, but certain conditions may be aggravated by glucocorticoids and may constitute contra-indications to therapy which should be borne in mind when contemplating treatment with glucocorticoids:

(a) A history of *peptic ulcer*.

(b) *Diabetes mellitus*.

(c) *Sodium retention* (heart failure, oedema; there is here the additional risk of hypokalaemia, particularly in patients taking diuretics).

(d) *Osteoporosis*.

(e) *Depressive disease*.

(f) *Tuberculosis*.

(g) *Children* (growth suppression).

4. Get used to certain preparations. For example hydrocortisone hemi-succinate suffices for most i.v. uses (except when huge doses are given as in the treatment of states of shock, when methylprednisolone is usually used). Prednisolone is generally preferred for oral therapy. Dexamethasone is traditionally used for the treatment of cerebral oedema.

5. To get some perspective on dosages of prednisolone commonly used consider the following facts:

(a) the usual replacement dose of hydrocortisone for patients with bilateral adrenalectomy is 20–30 mg daily;

(b) hydrocortisone 20 mg is equivalent to prednisolone 5 mg in gluco-corticoid potency.

Therefore a dose of prednisolone of 40 mg daily is about eight times the normal glucocorticoid output of the adrenal cortex, which will completely suppress ACTH secretion and cause adrenocortical atrophy. At a dosage of prednisolone of 5 mg daily, ACTH secretion might not be completely suppressed. At prednisolone dosages of 10 mg daily or more Cushingoid adverse effects are frequent.

6. Alternate-day glucocorticoid therapy has become popular for patients on high dosages. It is believed that the anti-inflammatory and immuno-suppressive effects continue over 48 h, that the undesirable catabolic actions are minimized and that the degree of suppression of hypo-thalamic–pituitary–adrenal function is lessened. With this kind of regimen it might, for example, be possible to reduce a daily dosage of prednisolone 60 mg to prednisolone 80 mg every other day, an equivalent decrease in total dosage of 20 mg daily.

7. Patients must be informed of the dangers of sudden withdrawal of therapy, of the hazards of intercurrent infection, of the necessity of careful medical care, and of the need to inform all doctors, nurses, and dentists

attending them that they are taking steroids. Warning cards are available and should be carried by the patient (see Fig. 34.2).

INSTRUCTIONS

1 DO NOT STOP taking the steroid drug except on medical advice. Always have a supply in reserve.

2 In case of feverish illness, accident, operation (emergency or otherwise), diarrhoea or vomiting the steroid treatment MUST be continued. Your doctor may wish you to have a LARGER DOSE or an INJECTION at such times.

3 If the tablets cause indigestion consult your doctor AT ONCE.

4 Always carry this card while receiving steroid treatment and show it to any doctor, dentist, nurse or midwife whom you may consult.

5 After your treatment has finished you must still tell any new doctor, dentist, nurse or midwife that you have had steroid treatment.

Dd8311496 165m 2/82 J.I.H. Ltd.,

I am a patient on—

STEROID TREATMENT

which must not be stopped abruptly

and in the case of intercurrent illness may have to be increased

full details are available from the hospital or general—▶ practitioners shown overleaf

STC1

Fig. 34.2. An example of the kind of warning card which should be carried by patients taking corticosteroid therapy. [Issued by the Department of Health and Social Security, UK, and reproduced with the permission of the Controller of Her Majesty's Stationery Office.]

8. Withdrawal or termination of glucocorticoid therapy is a hazardous, difficult, and variable business. Any patient who is on glucocorticoid therapy and who cannot take oral steroids (for example, during a surgical operation, or when vomiting) must be covered with an adequate dose of intramuscular or intravenous hydrocortisone or methylprednisolone.

Therapeutic withdrawal of glucocorticoid therapy after long-term administration should be undertaken very slowly because of suppression of ACTH secretion and consequent adrenocortical atrophy. With dosages of prednisolone of 20–30 mg daily for a few months, it can take many months for the pituitary–adrenal axis to regain its normal responsiveness (see Fig.4.8).

When glucocorticoid therapy is discontinued the dosage should be decreased gradually over a period of weeks or months at a rate which depends on the dosage and previous duration of therapy. If in doubt do not reduce the daily dosage by more than 1 mg every month.

During and after withdrawal it is necessary to be on the lookout for signs of flare-up of the disease process and for the occurrence of major stress such as infection, trauma, or surgery, which will need extra steroid cover because of the relative unresponsiveness of pituitary–adrenal function.

It is possible during withdrawal to monitor pituitary (ACTH) and adrenal (cortisol) function and responsiveness if this is deemed necessary.

Polymyalgia rheumatica and temporal arteritis are examples of connective tissue diseases where glucocorticoid therapy is the treatment of choice.

(a) Polymyalgia rheumatica

Prednisolone 10–15 mg daily for 1–3 months is usually enough to induce a remission, after which dosage is very gradually reduced over the next 2 years as described above, and then stopped.

(b) Temporal (giant cell) arteritis

Prednisolone 40–60 mg daily is usually effective, the higher dose being necessary in those patients in whom retinal arteritis threatens. Once a remission is induced the dosage can be gradually tailed off over a period of 2–3 years as described above.

Flare-ups of both these conditions are common on reduction of dosage and it is then necessary to return to a higher dosage and to begin dosage reduction again.

34.4. IMMUNOSUPPRESSIVE DRUG THERAPY

In contrast to drug therapy which aims to block some component of the inflammatory response, immunosuppressive drug therapy aims to suppress the immune response by interfering with lymphocyte function.

Glucocorticoids produce a lymphopenia, particularly of T lymphocytes, by a redistribution into lymphoid tissue. They interfere with lymphocyte proliferation, activation, and differentiation, and with many aspects of lymphocyte function involved in the immune response. They are not very effective in indirectly suppressing B cell antibody production, and the beneficial effects of corticosteroids in antibody and immune-complex-mediated diseases is more likely to be due to their anti-inflammatory effects.

The cytotoxic drugs azathioprine, methotrexate, and cyclophosphamide are aimed mainly at preventing lymphocyte proliferation and function. The actions of these drugs on the cell growth cycle are dealt with under cancer chemotherapy (Chapter 33).

34.4.1. Azathioprine

Azathioprine is most active on dividing cells acting through its metabolite 6-mercaptopurine. It inhibits Type IV immune reactions (cell-mediated) and does not interfere so much with normal humoral antibody production, presumably because it is more active on T cells than on B cells. Although marrow suppression is always a risk, an effect of azathioprine on lymphocyte proliferation and function can be attained with doses lower than those which usually produce marrow suppression and lower than those used (equivalent to 6-mercaptopurine) in cancer chemotherapy.

Azathioprine, in combination with corticosteroids, was (until the advent of cyclosporin) the mainstay of immunosuppression therapy in renal and other organ transplantation. Azathioprine has also been used when corticosteroids have been relatively ineffective, in the treatment of some autoimmune diseases which can be life-threatening, such as systemic lupus erythematosus, particularly with nephritis, and chronic active hepatitis.

Cyclophosphamide has effects on both T and B cell function, it reduces antibody production, depresses cell-mediated immunity, and suppresses the inflammatory reaction. It is used in minimal-change glomerulonephritis when the disease cannot be adequately controlled with steroids, and has recently been found to be beneficial in a number of diseases characterized by necrotizing vasculitis, e.g. Wegener's granulomatosis, and polyarteritis nodosa.

The action of methotrexate in severe psoriasis is undoubted. Whether it acts by inhibiting proliferation of epidermal cells or as an immunosuppressive agent, since it also benefits the arthritis in psoriatic arthritis, is difficult to know.

Immunosuppressive therapy using combinations of glucocorticoids with one or other of azathioprine, cyclophosphamide, or occasionally chlorambucil has been tried in systemic lupus erythematosus, necrotizing vasculitis, scleroderma, polymyositis, rheumatoid arthritis, Wegener's granulomatosis, regional enteritis (Crohn's disease), ulcerative colitis, chronic active hepatitis, glomerulonephritis, auto-immune haemolytic anaemia, idiopathic thrombocytopenic purpura, and several other conditions. These are disorders for which specialist care is essential since these drugs are very dangerous:

(a) There is the problem of marrow toxicity.

(b) There is the problem of immunosuppression with increased risk of viral, fungal and bacterial infections.

(c) There are direct toxic effects such as hair loss and infertility in men with cyclophosphamide.

(d) There is an increased risk of neoplasia, usually of lymphoid origin, after long-term immunosuppressive therapy.

34.4.2. Cyclosporin A

Cyclosporin A is a cyclical polypeptide, derived from soil fungi, which has been introduced for the prevention of organ graft rejection. It probably acts mainly by inhibition of T lymphocyte proliferation and it therefore inhibits cell-mediated immunity. Success has been achieved with its use in kidney, bone marrow, liver, pancreas, and heart transplants. There is little experience so far in autoimmune disease. Nephrotoxicity, abnormalities in liver function, transient hirsutism, gum hypertrophy, and lymphomas (particularly with high dosages) are adverse effects. Again one should note the occurrence of neoplasia, particularly lymphomas in immunosuppressed patients.

Cyclosporin A is an important advance because it has little effect in the dosages used on the myeloid system of the bone marrow. Nor does it have the wide cytotoxic actions of azathioprine or cyclophosphamide.

SECTION IV

Pharmacopoeia

INTRODUCTION

In this Pharmacopoeia we have listed those drugs most commonly used in clinical practice (a total of about 300 compounds). Each drug is dealt with either on its own (e.g. allopurinol) or in conjunction with other drugs with which it forms a distinct group (e.g. the aminoglycoside antibiotics). Each section contains the following information.

1. Structure

This is given in full in the case of a single drug. In the case of a group the general structure is given and individual differences listed below or indicated.

2. Mode of action

By this we mean the mechanisms of the effects a drug produces at a relevant level of discrimination, e.g. physiological, cellular, or molecular (see Chapter 4).

3. Uses

In the case of a group of drugs comprising several different compounds, having a number of different indications, those drugs which are usually prescribed for a particular indication are specifically indicated as such, e.g. see acetylcholinesterase inhibitors.

4. Dosages

The dosages given are those most commonly used. One should remember, however, that it may be necessary to go outside the usual range on occasion (see p.232. For some drugs with complicated dosage regimens larger texts should be consulted. We have generally not taken account of the differences in dosages occasioned by special formulations (e.g. enteric-coated or slow-release tablets) and manufacturers' literature (i.e. Data Sheets or package inserts) should be consulted. All dosages relate to adults unless specifically stated. Information on paediatric dosages should be sought elsewhere.

5. Kinetic data

Absorption after oral administration has been designated as 'well absorbed' (usually > 70%) or 'poorly absorbed' (usually < 50%). In some cases we have given percentage values. Values of $t_{1/2}$ quoted are means culled from published literature and there may be wide individual variations from these means. Extent of metabolism or urinary excretion has generally been approximately graded using terms such as 'mostly metabolized' or 'mainly excreted unchanged'. We have indicated the major route of elimination of pharmacologically active compounds and in some cases given more specific information. Information on the apparent V_d and protein binding of some important drugs is given in Tables 3.2 and 3.3.

6. Important adverse effects

Where we have not given percentage incidence figures we have used terms such as the following: 'common' (usually > 5 per cent); 'occasional' (1–5 per cent); 'unusual' or 'rare' (< 1 per cent).

In sections 6 and 7 we have also, where relevant, discussed the interactions of drugs with diseases, since such interactions may lead the prescriber to use caution in particular circumstances when using the drug. Occasionally such considerations will dictate a contra-indication.

7. Interactions

Of the numerous reported drug interactions (see Chapter 10) we have tried to list only those of clinical relevance.

Abbreviations:

i.v.—intravenously;
i.m.—intramuscularly;
s.c.—subcutaneously;
o.d.—once daily;
b.d.—twice daily;
t.d.s.—three times daily;
q.d.s.—four times daily.

ACETYLCHOLINERGIC AGONISTS
(CHOLINOCEPTOR AGONISTS)

Structures

Bethanecol and carbachol are related to acetylcholine:

$$R-CH-CH_2N^+(CH_3)_3$$
$$O-CO-NH_2$$

Pilocarpine has a more complicated structure, and is not related to acetylcholine.

Mode of action

Direct agonist effect on acetylcholinergic receptors leading to:

(a) stimulation of the smooth muscle of bowel and bladder and relaxation of their sphincters;

(b) pupillary constriction.

The effects of pilocarpine and bethanecol are chiefly muscarinic. Carbachol has some nicotinic activity in addition.

Uses

Relief of post-operative urinary retention of bowel distension (bethanecol and carbachol).

Glaucoma (pilocarpine).

Reversal of pupillary dilatation (pilocarpine).

Dosages

Bethanecol: 5 mg s.c.
Carbachol: 250–500 micrograms s.c.
Pilocarpine: glaucoma, two drops of an 0.5–4 per cent solution t.d.s., to the eyes.

Kinetic data

Neither compound is metabolized by cholinesterases.

Important adverse effects

Commonly abdominal colic, urinary urgency or bladder pain, pupillary constriction, bradycardia, bronchial constriction, flushing, and sweating. These effects are readily reversed by atropine. Do not give these drugs to patients with asthma (bronchoconstriction), hyperthyroidism (may precipitate atrial fibrillation), ischaemic heart disease (may precipitate angina/infarction), or peptic ulcer (increased gastric acid secretion). Do not use i.v. or i.m. route. Remember that urinary retention in old men is usually due to prostatic obstruction which will not be relieved by stimulating the bladder.

ACETYLCHOLINERGIC ANTAGONISTS
(CHOLINOCEPTOR ANTAGONISTS)

Structures

Atropine and hyoscine (scopolamine) are stereoisomers. Atropine is shown here:

The other drugs discussed here have widely different structures. We give benzhexol hydrochloride as an example:

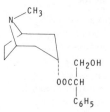

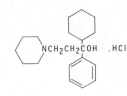

Mode of action

Direct antagonist effect on muscarinic cholinergic receptors leading to:

(a) relaxation of the smooth muscle of bowel and bladder and stimulation of their sphincters;
(b) pupillary dilatation;
(c) decrease in secretions from sweat, bronchial, and other glands;
(d) increased heart rate;
(e) bronchiolar dilatation.

Uses

To decrease glandular secretions preoperatively (atropine, hyoscine).

To dilate pupils (cyclopentolate, tropicamide).

To speed the heart rate in sinus bradycardia (atropine).

To relieve bronchoconstriction in asthma (ipratropium).

To prevent bowel spasm during radiological procedures (hyoscine butyl bromide).

To treat Parkinson's disease.

To reverse drug-induced Parkinsonism and dystonias (e.g. benzhexol, benztropine, orphenadrine).

To prevent travel sickness (hyoscine hydrobromide).

Dosages

Atropine: sinus bradycardia, 500 micrograms, i.v.; pre-operatively, 600 micrograms, i.m.

Hyoscine hydrobromide: travel sickness, 600 micrograms, orally, six-hourly for up to 48 h; pre-operatively, 600 micrograms, s.c.

Hyoscine butyl bromide: prevention of bowel spasm, 20 mg, i.v. or i.m.

Cyclopentolate: to the eyes, two drops of a 0.5 per cent solution.

Tropicamide: to the eyes, two drops of an 0.1 per cent solution.

Ipratropium: inhalation, one or two puffs (each 20 micrograms) t.d.s.

Benzhexol: orally, 1 mg o.d. initially, increasing in 2 mg increments every 3–5 days as required up to 15 mg daily; i.v., 2 mg.

Benztropine: orally, 0.5 mg o.d. initially, increasing in 0.5 mg increments every 5–6 days as required to 6 mg daily; i.v., 2 mg.

Orphenadrine: orally, 50 mg b.d. initially, increasing as required to 300–400 mg daily.

Kinetic data

Atropine is well absorbed but metabolized during its first passage through the liver. Only about 50 per cent appears unchanged in the urine and parenteral routes are therefore more reliable. $t_{1/2} = 24$ h.

Hyoscine hydrobromide is well absorbed and almost completely metabolized. Its effects last about 2 h.

In the eye the effects of cyclopentolate last up to 24 h, of tropicamide up to 8 h.

Important adverse effects

Unwanted effects are almost unavoidable, especially drying of the mouth, blurred vision, and constipation. In patients with prostatic hypertrophy, acute urinary retention may occur. Glaucoma may be precipitated in susceptible individuals. Common central nervous effects include confusion, restlessness, and hallucinations, but hyoscine hydrobromide causes sedation. Tachycardia occurs with all but hyoscine, which may cause bradycardia.

These adverse effects may be reversed with an acetylcholinesterase inhibitor such as physostigmine.

Interactions

The anticholinergic effects of other drugs (e.g. tricyclics, disopyramide) may be potentiated.

ACETYLCHOLINESTERASE INHIBITORS

Structures

These drugs are quaternary ammonium compounds. Neostigmine is given as an example:

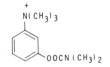

Mode of action

Inhibition of acetylcholinesterase, leading to accumulation of endogenous acetylcholine in cholinergic synapses. This results in:

(a) stimulation of the smooth muscle of bowel and bladder and relaxation of their sphincters;

(b) pupillary constriction;

(c) increased secretion from sweat, salivary, bronchial and other glands;

(d) depolarization of the motor end-plates of skeletal muscle.

Uses

Myasthenia gravis—diagnosis (edrophonium) and treatment (neostigmine, pyridostigmine).

Reversal of curariform effects (neostigmine).

Tricyclic antidepressant overdose (physostigmine).

Dosages

Neostigmine: myasthenia gravis, 75–300 mg daily, orally, in divided doses, taken when most needed; reversal of curariform effects of skeletal muscle relaxants 1–2.5 mg, i.v.

Pyridostigmine: myasthenia gravis, 0.3–1.2 g daily, orally, in divided doses when most needed; i.v., 2–5 mg.

Physostigmine: tricyclic overdose, up to 2 mg, i.v., over 5 min repeated as required at intervals of 30–60 min if a therapeutic effect is obtained.

Edrophonium: myasthenia gravis diagnosis, 2 mg, i.v., initially followed by 8 mg if no adverse reaction occurs.

Kinetic data

Absorption after oral administration generally poor. Values of $t_{1/2}$ and of duration of action are mostly short. The very short duration of action of edrophonium makes it a useful drug for the diagnosis of myasthenia gravis and the differential diagnosis of myasthenic crisis from overdose of other cholinesterase inhibitors. Physostigmine crosses the blood–brain barrier, a property which is useful in treating tricyclic antidepressant overdose.

Important adverse effects

Common are symptoms of excessive cholinergic effects, e.g. abdominal cramps, hypersalivation, sweating, bradycardia (all muscarinic effects) and muscle cramps (nicotinic). The muscarinic effects are reversible by atropine.

Acetylcholinesterase inhibitors should be given cautiously to patients with cardiac disease, e.g. bradycardia, hypotension, myocardial ischaemia.

ACTINOMYCIN D

Structure

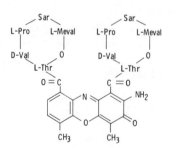

Mode of action

Actinomycin D (or dactinomycin) is a cytotoxic antibiotic. It inhibits DNA-dependent RNA synthesis, especially ribosomal RNA, by intercalating between DNA base pairs. It is not specific for any phase of the cell cycle.

Uses

Wilms's tumour of kidney.

Choriocarcinoma.

A variety of sarcomas.

Dosage

Actinomycin D is given i.v. and usually in combination with other cytotoxic drugs. Dosages vary widely, but a typical dosage regimen (for example in choriocarcinoma) would be 15 micrograms/kg i.v., daily for 5 days every 2–3 weeks.

Kinetic data

Poorly absorbed and therefore given i.v. Excreted mostly in bile as unchanged drug and doses should therefore be reduced in liver disease. $T_{1/2} = 36$ h.

Important adverse effects

Anorexia, nausea, vomiting, diarrhoea, and stomatitis are common. Bone-marrow suppression is dose-related (see cancer chemotherapy, Chapter 33). Alopecia and skin rashes may occur.

Interaction

For the possible interaction with live vaccines see p.288.

ADRENERGIC NEURONE BLOCKING DRUGS

Structures

Bethanidine:

Debrisoquine:

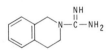

Guanethidine:

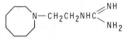

Mode of action

Inhibition of sympathetic nerve impulse release of noradrenaline by mechanisms not yet understood.

Use

Hypertension. With the advent of β-adrenoceptor antagonists these drugs now have limited usefulness.

Dosages

Bethanidine: 10 mg t.d.s., orally, initially, increasing in increments of 5 mg t.d.s. every few days, if required, to a maximum of 65 mg t.d.s.

Debrisoquine: 10 mg b.d., orally, initially, increasing in increments of 10–20 mg daily every few days, if required, to a maximum of 100 mg t.d.s.

Guanethidine: 20 mg o.d., orally, initially, increasing in increments of 10 mg daily at weekly intervals to a maximum of 300 mg o.d.

Only in the most severe cases of hypertension will the highest doses in these ranges be required.

Kinetic data

Bethanidine and debrisoquine are well absorbed but guanethidine is metabolized by the liver and has low systemic availability. The $t_{1/2}$ may not be related to the duration of action.

Debrisoquine hydroxylation in the liver has a bimodal population distribution—about 9 per cent are poor hydroxylators, the rest extensive (see Chapter 8). There is evidence that this polymorphism is shared by other hydroxylated drugs (e.g. phenytoin, phenformin).

Important adverse effects

Postural and exercise hypotension, failure of ejaculation, dry mouth, and diarrhoea are common.

Interactions

Effects are antagonized by tricyclic antidepressants and perhaps by phenothiazines.

**ADRENOCEPTOR AGONISTS
(EXCEPT DOPAMINE)**

Structures

General:

Examples: see below

Mode of action

Direct agonist effects on α- and β-adrenoceptors with the following relative specificities:

	α	β_1	β_2
Adrenaline	++	++	++
Noradrenaline	++	+	+
Isoprenaline	+	++	++
Salbutamol	0	±	++
Dobutamine	0	++	±

α-receptor stimulation leads to arteriolar vasoconstriction and pupillary constriction.

β-receptor stimulation leads to arteriolar vasodilatation (mainly in muscle—β_2), bronchodilatation (β_2), uterine relaxation (β_2), and cardiac effects (increase in heart rate and contractility—β_1).

The mode of action in glaucoma is not understood.

Uses

To relieve bronchoconstriction in asthma (salbutamol).

To treat allergic reactions, especially anaphylactic shock (adrenaline).

To produce local vasoconstriction and enhance the effects of local anaesthetics (adrenaline).

To prevent and treat premature labour (salbutamol).

To treat open angle glaucoma (adrenaline).

To treat myocardial pump failure, e.g. cardiogenic shock, after cardiopulmonary bypass (dobutamine).

Dosages

Adrenaline: acute allergic reactions, 0.5 ml of a 1:1000 solution, i.m.; glaucoma, one drop of a 1 per cent solution o.d. or b.d.

Salbutamol: asthma, orally, 2–4 mg t.d.s.; i.v., 5 micrograms/min, increasing as required up to 20 micrograms/min; inhalation, one puff (100 micrograms) once or twice daily as required, up to q.d.s.; premature labour, 10 micrograms/min i.v., increasing as required up to 45 micrograms/min.

Dobutamine: 2.5–10 micrograms/kg/min by continuous i.v. infusion depending on response. Doses should be reduced gradually on withdrawal.

Important adverse effects

Adverse effects are dose-related. They commonly include anxiety, restlessness, tremor, tachycardia, nausea, hypertension, cardiac arrhythmias, and angina.

Examples:

	R_1	R_2
Adrenaline (epinephrine)	OH	$C(OH)HCH_2NHCH_3$
Noradrenaline (norepinephrine)	OH	$C(OH)HCH_2NH_2$
Isoprenaline (isoproterenol)	OH	$C(OH)HCH_2NHCH(CH_3)_2$
Salbutamol (albuterol)	CH_2OH	$C(OH)HCH_2NHC(CH_3)_3$
Dobutamine	OH	$(CH_2)_2NHC(CH_3)H(CH_2)_2C_6H_4OH$

Kinetic data

	Absorption	Elimination	$T\frac{1}{2}$
Adrenaline	Nil	Metabolized	Minutes
Salbutamol	Good	40% metabolized	4 h
Dobutamine	Nil	Metabolized	Minutes

α-ADRENOCEPTOR ANTAGONISTS
(α-BLOCKERS)

Structures

Phentolamine:

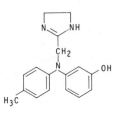

Phenoxybenzamine:

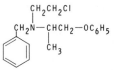

Prazosin and indoramin, which have α-blocking activity, are dealt with in full separately.

Mode of action

Direct effect on adrenoceptors, preventing the pharmacological action of released noradrenaline on α_1 (post-synaptic) and/or α_2 (mostly pre-synaptic) receptors. The drugs dealt with in this section are not selective for α_1 and α_2 receptors (cf. prazosin and indoramin).

Uses

Treatment of hypertension due to:
  phaeochromocytoma;
  overdose of α-adrenoceptor agonists;
  clonidine withdrawal;
  tyramine–MAO inhibitor interaction;
  vasospastic states (e.g. ergotism).

For these conditions i.v. phentolamine would normally be used. In chronic treatment of phaeochromocytoma oral phenoxybenzamine is used. The value of these drugs in peripheral vascular disease is minimal.

Dosages

Phenoxybenzamine: orally, 10 mg o.d., increasing as required in 10 mg increments at 4 day intervals to a maximum of 60 mg t.d.s.
Phentolamine: i.v., 5–15 mg.

Kinetic data

Little is known about the eliminatory pathways of these drugs but they are probably metabolized in the liver.

Important adverse effects

Common are vasodilatation leading to sinus tachycardia, other arrhythmias, angina pectoris, and orthostatic hypotension. Nasal congestion and failure to ejaculate are common during long-term treatment.

β-ADRENOCEPTOR ANTAGONISTS
(β-BLOCKERS)

Structures

Propranolol:

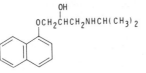

Others—general:

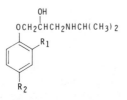

Examples:

	R₁	R₂
Oxprenolol	$OCH_2CH=CH_2$	H
Atenolol	H	CH_2OCNH_2
Metoprolol	H	$CH_2CH_2OCH_3$
Practolol	H	$NHOCCH_3$

Uses

In certain aspects of ischaemic heart disease:

(a) angina pectoris;
(b) in acute myocardial infarction to limit extension of the infarct;
(c) following myocardial infarction to prevent recurrence ('secondary prevention').

These last two uses are not yet applied widespread in routine fashion.

Hypertension.
Treatment and prevention of supraventricular tachyarrhythmias.
Symptomatic relief in thyrotoxicosis.

Dosages

Oral:

Propranolol, 20–160 mg b.d.
Oxprenolol, 120–480 mg daily in two or three divided doses.

Atenolol, 100–200 mg o.d.
Metoprolol, 100–400 mg daily in two or three divided doses.

Intravenous:

Practolol, 5–20 mg.

Mode of action

These drugs are competitive antagonists of adrenaline and noradrenaline at β-adrenoceptors, which are of two types. Blockade of cardiac $β_1$ receptors slows the heart rate and decreases myocardial contractility (negative inotropic effect). In general clinical practice the degree of β-blockade can be assessed by the decreased response of the heart rate to exercise.

In angina pectoris these effects result in decreased cardiac work and decreased oxygen requirements with less likelihood of the metabolic consequences of ischaemia. During exercise the prevention of tachycardia contributes to these effects.

In hypertension the mechanism of the hypotensive effects of β-blockers is difficult to explain. Most would agree that an effect of β-blockade on the heart is the first in a chain of events, that this leads to a variety of adaptive responses, e.g. changes in sensitivity of baroreflex mechanisms, both central and peripheral, and perhaps to long-term changes in cardiac function, all of which compound to lower the blood pressure continuously. A decrease in renal renin secretion has also been invoked as playing a role.

The mechanism of the effect in supraventricular tachyarrhythmias is by a direct effect on the heart.

In thyrotoxicosis, while β-blockade does result in a clinically obvious decrease in sympathomimetic symptoms, it is not clear that the effect is by antagonism of sympathetic nervous activity since true increases in such activity in thyrotoxicosis have been difficult to demonstrate.

Blockade of $β_2$ receptors is mainly of importance in relation to adverse effects (see below). The different β-blockers have different effects on β_1 and β_2 receptors, some being relatively selective for β_1 receptors, others being non-selective. In addition some have partial agonist activity and penetration into the brain is variable. The differences are shown on the next page.

Kinetic data

Most β-blockers are well absorbed (atenolol is an exception at about 50 per cent). Propranolol and metoprolol are extensively metabolized during their first passage through the liver to active (hydroxylated) compounds which are excreted in the urine. The other drugs are eliminated unchanged.

In angina pectoris, and probably in supraventricular tachyarrhythmias, it is likely that the degree of β-blockade is directly related to therapeutic efficacy, and that the $t_{1/2}$ of a β-blocker roughly correlates with its duration of action. Therefore propranolol is given b.d. or t.d.s. for angina, atenolol once daily. In hypertension, because of the complex mode of action (see above) the $t_{1/2}$ of a β-blocker is not related to its duration of action, which is generally 12 h and often greater than 24 h. In practice, however, this has not resulted in dosage regimens different from those used in angina pectoris or arrhythmias.

Important adverse effects

Blockade of β_2 receptors in the lungs may cause bronchoconstriction in susceptible subjects and may lead to life-threatening status asthmaticus. Non-selective β-blockers should therefore not be given to asthmatics. Even relatively selective β-blockers should be used with caution, since none is completely devoid of some β_2 receptor antagonism.

Because of their negative inotropic effects β-blockers may cause or worsen heart failure. It is important, therefore, to look out for symptoms and signs of heart failure when using β-blockers in patients with cardiac disease.

Central nervous effects (depression, hallucinations, sleep disturbances) can be avoided by using a β-blocker which penetrates the brain poorly (see next page).

Peripheral vasoconstriction, which results in Raynaud's phenomenon, and is particularly troublesome in the cold weather, is a common complaint, the precise mechanism of which is still not understood.

Practolol, in long-term oral use, causes a syndrome consisting of dry eyes (progressing to corneal ulceration and perforation), a skin rash, and peritoneal fibrosis. For this reason its use is restricted to intravenous short-term therapy of arrhythmias. There are reports of dry eyes in patients taking other β-blockers but this complaint does not presage the occurrence of the practolol syndrome. It may, however, be sufficiently unpleasant to warrant withdrawal of therapy. There have also been reports of peritoneal fibrosis in patients on β-blockers but so far it has not been proven that this occurs with greater frequency than in the untreated population.

The normal sympathetic response to hypoglycaemia is blocked by β-blockers. Sweating still occurs, however, since it is a sympathetic nervous function not served by adrenaline or noradrenaline.

If β-blocker therapy is to be withdrawn it should be withdrawn slowly since abrupt withdrawal may result in a rebound increase in anginal symptoms or frank myocardial infarction, possibly related to adaptive β-receptor supersensitivity in response to chronic blockade.

Interactions

Cimetidine inhibits the first-pass metabolism of propranolol. When β-blockers and verapamil are used concurrently there is an increased incidence of arrhythmias. There have also been reports of asystole attributed to the use of the combination (see also p.768).

The effects of insulin and oral hypoglycaemic drugs may be potentiated by β-blockers with resulting hypoglycaemia. There is some evidence that this effect is more pronounced with non-cardioselective β-blockers. This interaction is distinct from the effects of β-blockers on the clinical *response* to hypoglycaemia (see above). β-blockers interact beneficially with some other drugs used in the treatment of cardiovascular disease.

Thus, for example, the negative inotropic effects of β-blockers can be diminished by cardiac glycosides; the combination of α- and β-adrenoceptor antagonists is useful in the treatment of hypertension (see labetalol) as is the combination of β-blockers and the peripheral vasodilator hydralazine, since the former prevent the reflex tachycardia caused by the latter, allowing lower doses of hydralazine to be therapeutically effective and avoiding the toxic effects of higher doses.

Drug	Receptor specificity	Partial agonist	Brain penetration
Propranolol	$\beta_1 \beta_2$	−	+
Oxprenolol	$\beta_1 \beta_2$	+	+
Atenolol	β_1	−	−
Metoprolol	β_1	−	+
Practolol	β_1	+	−

ALCOHOL

Alcohol is the name commonly given to ethyl alcohol, or ethanol, C_2H_5OH. It is present in a wide range of drinks in a wide range of concentrations, e.g. in beers (2.5–11 per cent v/v), cider (3.5–5.0 per cent), table wines (9.5–15.5 per cent), fortified wines (16–23 per cent), liqueurs (25–55 per cent), and spirits (35–55 per cent).

In addition to alcohol, alcoholic drinks may contain other constituents called congeners, the commonest of which is fusel oil. Congeners may be present in quantities up to 0.3 per cent of the volume of alcohol, and they contribute to the taste of the drink.

Effects of alcohol

Alcohol has a wide range of effects on different tissues.

(a) Central nervous system

In the brain alcohol acts as a dose-dependent depressant, producing the well-known features of intoxication. At plasma concentrations of around 40 mg/dl (400 μg/ml or 8.7 mmol/l) learned skills are impaired, including the ability to maintain self-restraint. Other early effects include loss of attentiveness, loss of concentration, and impaired memory, and there may be lethargy.

At progressively higher concentrations there are further changes in mood, behaviour, and a variety of sensory and motor functions.

Mood

The effects of alcohol on mood depend on the individual's personality, mental state, and social environment. Commonly there is euphoria, but any kind of mood change can occur. Libido is often enhanced, but sexual performance impaired.

Behaviour

Alcohol generally increases confidence, often resulting in aggressive or silly behaviour; loss of self-restraint leads to increased loquacity with immoderate speech content, such as swearing or the use of lewd language.

Motor functions

Unsteadiness of gait, slurred speech, and difficulty in carrying out even simple tasks become obvious at plasma concentrations of about 80 mg/dl (the concentration above which motor-driving is illegal in the UK and many other countries). Driving skills are therefore impaired, and are affected even at concentrations below 80 mg/dl. Impaired coordination leads to excessive movement of the steering wheel and inaccurate cornering; overconfidence leads to attempts at dangerous manoeuvres which, combined with impaired judgement and prolonged reaction time, may lead to accidents (see Fig. P1); sensory changes may also contribute to impaired driving skills (see next section).

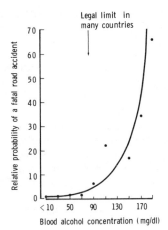

Fig. P1. The relative probability among drivers of a fatal road accident in relation to the blood alcohol concentration. [Adapted from Perrine *et al.* (1971). Alcohol and highway safety: behavioural and medical aspects. NHTSA Report, DOS HS–800–599, with the permission of the US Department of Transport.]

Sensory functions

Recovery from dazzle is delayed and this may impair night-time driving. Visual acuity and peripheral vision are reduced, and colour vision and visual tracking are impaired. Hearing and taste may also be impaired, and the pain threshold is increased. At high concentrations there may be vertigo and nystagmus.

Consciousness

Alcohol causes acute drowsiness, deep sleep, and in high concentrations may cause coma and respiratory depression. In some individuals sleep may later be impaired. On waking there is the characteristic 'hangover', which usually consists of irritability, headache, thirst, abdominal cramps, and bowel disturbance. The cause of hangover is not known.

Chronic effects

Alcohol may cause a variety of neurological abnormalities including Wernicke's encephalopathy (due to thiamine deficiency), retrobulbar neuropathy (so-called alcohol amblyopia), cerebral atrophy, and polyneuropathy. Encephalopathy may occur as a result of chronic hepatic cirrhosis.

Dependence occurs during chronic ingestion, and withdrawal results in a typical syndrome, including delirium tremens (see Chapter 31).

(b) Cardiovascular system

In moderate amounts alcohol causes peripheral vasodilatation, resulting in skin flushing. At higher doses there may be hypotension.

Chronic ingestion may cause a cardiomyopathy.

(c) Skeletal muscle

Chronic ingestion can result in a skeletal myopathy.

(d) Gastro-intestinal tract

In moderate doses alcohol stimulates gastric acid production and enhances back-diffusion of hydrogen ions. At higher doses gastric acid output decreases, gastric mucus production increases, and the gastric mucosa becomes congested and hyperaemic. There may be vomiting, and in severe cases acute gastritis. These effects are lessened by food.

Chronic ingestion may result in chronic atrophic gastritis, with hypochlorhydria.

(e) Metabolism and nutrition

Alcohol is oxidized in the liver at the expense of other compounds such as those in the tricarboxylic acid (citric acid) cycle, which is thus inhibited. Blood glucose usually rises during acute alcohol ingestion, because of increased sympathetic nervous system activity. However, if glycogen stores are depleted because of malnutrition (e.g. in chronic alcoholics) hypoglycaemia may occur, because of impaired gluconeogenesis, via the effects on the tricarboxylic acid cycle.

Alcohol impairs fatty acid utilization and induces hepatic microsomal enzymes, causing increased lipoprotein synthesis. There may, therefore, be hyperlipoproteinaemia.

Because it induces hepatic enzymes alcohol may precipitate an acute attack of porphyria (see Chapter 8).

Chronic alcoholics tend to eat less than normal, partly because they prefer to spend their money on drink, and partly because chronic alcohol ingestion impairs the appetite. They do not lose weight, because alcohol provides all the energy they need, but may develop nutritional deficiencies. These include the following:

Wernicke's encephalopathy (or Wernicke–Korsakoff syndrome)

This is due to thiamine deficiency and the features include ocular disturbances (weakness of the lateral rectus muscles, nystagmus, and paralysis of conjugate gaze), ataxia, and impaired mental function, including Korsakoff's psychosis (a disorder of memory and other cognitive functions). There may also be delirium tremens.

Neuropathy

This is also due to thiamine deficiency, but may also be due in part to a direct effect of alcohol on peripheral nerves.

Anaemia

Alcoholics become anaemic through iron, folate, or even vitamin B_{12} deficiency. However, the most common change in the blood is a macrocytosis, without megaloblastosis and without anaemia. Its cause is unknown.

(f) Renal function

Alcohol acts as a diuretic by decreasing water reabsorption in the renal tubules, perhaps by inhibiting ADH secretion in the pituitary.

Alcohol inhibits uric acid excretion and may cause hyperuricaemia or acute gout.

(g) Hepatic function

Acutely alcohol inhibits hepatic enzymes, but chronically causes enzyme induction. However, if liver function is impaired because of chronic cirrhosis enzyme activity will become impaired.

Acutely alcohol causes fat deposition in the liver and this may be associated with an acute alcoholic hepatitis. Chronically it may cause cirrhosis, the pathogenesis of which is not fully understood.

(h) The fetus

Alcohol inhibits fetal growth, and may cause the 'fetal-alcohol' syndrome if taken in large amounts during pregnancy. Babies born to mothers with severe chronic alcoholism may have craniofacial, limb, and cleft deformities, and cardiovascular and brain defects.

Medical uses

Alcohol has a few medical uses:

(a) Local uses

Alcohol kills bacteria, and is therefore used to swab the skin before venepuncture or other surgical procedures.

It is rubefacient (i.e. it makes the skin red) and is therefore used as a counter-irritant in some liniments. It is also used to harden the skin to prevent bedsores, and to harden the nipples before breast-feeding.

It decreases sweating, and is therefore incorporated into some antihidrotic solutions.

(b) Pain relief

Alcohol may be injected directly into nerve ganglia or around nerve trunks to destroy them and relieve severe or chronic pain (e.g. trigeminal neuralgia), but the results are generally short-lasting only.

(c) Treatment of acute methanol poisoning

Ethyl alcohol competes with methyl alcohol

(methanol) for hepatic metabolism and is therefore used in the treatment of acute methanol poisoning (for dosage see Chapter 32, p.582).

(d) Pharmaceutical uses

Alcohol is widely used as a solvent in pharmaceutical preparations.

Kinetic data

(a) Absorption

Alcohol is rapidly absorbed from all parts of the gut. The rate of absorption is concentration-dependent, e.g. in the stomach it is maximal at a concentration of about 30 per cent (v/v).

(b) Distribution

Alcohol is distributed throughout body tissues in an apparent volume of distribution roughly equal to that of total body water (i.e. 0.6 l/kg). Thus about 32 g of alcohol (about 2–3 pints of beer or two double measures of spirits) will produce a blood alcohol concentration of 80 mg/dl in a 70 kg individual. This figure, however, is calculated from mean data. It will vary greatly from individual to individual and may depend on the type of drink and whether or not food is taken with it.

(c) Metabolism

Alcohol is metabolized 98 per cent by the route shown in Fig. P2. It is first oxidized to acetaldehyde by alcohol dehydrogenase, and this step is rate-limiting and has a K_m of about 10 mg/dl. Thus since blood alcohol concentrations are usually above 10 mg/dl the kinetics of alcohol metabolism are predominantly zero-order at most concentrations (see Chapter 3, p.28 and Fig. 3.3.). At whole blood concentrations over 10 mg/dl the clearance rate of alcohol is constant at about 6 g/h. For some drinks the clearance rate may be slower since some congeners may compete with alcohol for metabolic sites.

The second step in alcohol metabolism is to acetate under the influence of aldehyde dehydrogenase. This step is rapid and blood aldehyde concentrations are usually low (< 2 mg/dl).

Alcohol does not induce the activity of its own metabolizing enzymes.

(d) Excretion

Most of the small amount of alcohol which is not metabolized is excreted unchanged in the urine and breath. The concentration in the expired air is about 0.05 per cent of that in the blood, i.e. 0.04 mg/dl at a blood concentration of 80 mg/dl—sufficient for detection by a 'breathalyser'.

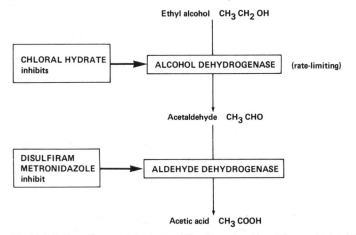

Fig. P2. Metabolic pathway of alcohol and the sites of action of drugs which inhibit its metabolism.

Interactions

(a) Pharmacodynamic

(i) Centrally-acting drugs
The most important interactions of drugs with alcohol are those with other centrally-acting drugs, such as the phenothiazines, butyrophenones, barbiturates, benzodiazepines, tricyclic antidepressants, antihistamines, and lithium. In all cases the effects of alcohol and the drug may be mutually enhanced, and patients taking centrally-acting drugs should be advised not to take any alcohol at all if they are going to drive or operate machinery.

(ii) Hypoglycaemic drugs
In about a third of patients taking chlorpropamide, alcohol causes facial flushing. The precise mechanism of this interaction is not known. It happens only rarely with other sulphonylureas.

Patients taking insulin should be advised not to drink, or to drink only small amounts of particular beverages (e.g. 'diabetic' lager, dry wine, or dry cider). This is because:

alcohol impairs gluconeogenesis which is the main source of blood glucose when glycogen stores are depleted;

alcohol provides extra carbohydrate;

if drunk the diabetic may become careless about his general care and treatment.

(iii) Intravenous feeding
Alcohol and fructose should not be used together as energy sources in i.v. feeding since alcohol encourages the formation of lactic acid by its effects on glucose metabolism and fructose is metabolized to lactic acid. There is thus an increased risk of lactic acidosis.

(b) Pharmacokinetic

(i) Inhibition of alcohol dehydrogenase
Chloral hydrate inhibits alcohol dehydrogenation and thus potentiates its effects. It also has a potentiating pharmacodynamic effect as a sedative. The combination of alcohol and chloral hydrate or other sedatives has been called a 'Mickey Finn'.

(ii) Inhibition of aldehyde dehydrogenase
Disulfiram and metronidazole are aldehyde dehydrogenase inhibitors and cause accumulation of acetaldehyde. This causes an unpleasant set of symptoms, including colic, flushing, dizziness, breathlessness, tachycardia, and vomiting. Disulfiram (Antabuse®) has therefore been used as aversion therapy in chronic alcoholism.

(iii) Hepatic microsomal enzyme induction
Chronic alcohol injection causes an increase in the activity of the mixed-function oxidative enzymes in the liver. This leads to an increased rate of metabolism of drugs such as phenytoin and warfarin. However, chronic liver damage due to alcohol may result in decreased drug metabolism and the changes in kinetics of these drugs in chronic alcoholics may therefore be unpredictable.

ALLOPURINOL

Structure

(Note the similarity to hypoxanthine.)

Mode of action
Inhibition of xanthine oxidase by both allopurinol and its metabolite, alloxanthine (oxypurinol). As shown below this enzyme is involved in the production of uric acid from xanthines, as well as in the metabolism of allopurinol itself:

There is therefore decreased production of uric acid and the purine load needing elimination is spread out amongst hypoxanthine, xanthine, and uric acid, the individual solubilities of which are not exceeded.

Uses

Treatment of chronic hyperuricaemia (both primary and secondary), and prevention of its complications (tophi, uric acid nephropathy, and acute attacks of gout).

Dosages

300–600 mg o.d., orally.

Kinetic data

Well absorbed. $T_{1/2}$ of allopurinol is 2 h, of alloxanthine 24 h. Thus alloxanthine accumulates to a greater extent than allopurinol but, since it inhibits its own formation, the extent of its accumulation is dose-dependent. Both compounds are excreted in the urine.

Important adverse effects

During the first few days of treatment there is an increased risk of acute gout. This may be prevented by the concurrent use of colchicine (q.v.). Allergic reactions are common but generalized hypersensitivity reactions are rare. Skin rashes occur with an incidence of 2 per cent when allopurinol alone is given. However, when allopurinol is combined with ampicillin the incidence of skin rashes rises to 22 per cent (ampicillin alone 8 per cent). Renal failure, hepatitis, and eosinophilia have been occasionally reported.

Interactions

When 6-mercaptopurine is used in the treatment of leukaemia, the cell death which occurs results in the production of large amounts of purines, which are metabolized to uric acid with consequent hyperuricaemia and its attendant complications. Allopurinol is often used to guard against these but allopurinol inhibits the metabolism of 6-mercaptopurine to 6-thiouric acid (by xanthine oxidase) and leads to accumulation of 6-mercaptopurine. For this reason the dosage requirements of 6-mercaptopurine are *reduced by 75 per cent* when allopurinol is also given. Because azathioprine is metabolized to 6-mercaptopurine it is also subject to this interaction.

The toxic effect of cyclophosphamide on the bone marrow is potentiated by allopurinol.

The interaction between allopurinol and ampicillin is mentioned above under 'adverse effects'.

AMILORIDE

Structure

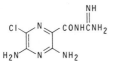

Mode of action

Amiloride causes increased sodium and chloride excretion in the distal convoluted tubule of the nephron causing an increase in water excretion. In contrast to other diuretics (such as thiazides and loop diuretics), and in common with spironolactone and triamterene, it inhibits potassium secretion in the distal convoluted tubule. Its use is therefore associated with potassium retention. The mechanism of these effects is unknown but is independent of the action of aldosterone (contrast spironolactone).

Uses

In combination with potassium-depleting diuretics (e.g. Moduretic®, a combination of hydrochlorothiazide and amiloride) in the treatment of oedema due to cardiac failure, liver disease, nephrotic syndrome.

Dosages

10–20 mg o.d., orally.

Kinetic data

Very poorly absorbed. Almost completely excreted unchanged in the urine. $T_{1/2} = 6$ h.

Important adverse effects

Hyperkalaemia, dehydration and hyponatraemia are common. The incidence of hyperkalaemia (about 5 per cent) is unaffected by concurrent administration of potassium-depleting diuretics. Nausea and vomiting occur occasionally.

ε-AMINOCAPROIC ACID AND TRANEXAMIC ACID

Structures

ε-aminocaproic acid:

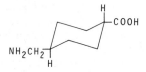

$$NH_2CH_2(CH_2)_4COOH$$

Tranexamic acid:

Mode of action

ε-aminocaproic acid and tranexamic acid are antifibrinolytic agents which competitively inhibit the activation of plasminogen to plasmin (see Fig. P3, and compare with streptokinase and urokinase which have opposite actions).

Uses

These drugs are used in circumstances in which excessive bleeding cannot be controlled. They are best reserved for short-term use only, and conditions in which they have been found valuable include post-operative haemorrhage, particularly after prostatectomy and bladder surgery, menorrhagia associated with an intra-uterine contraceptive device, epistaxis, and dental extraction in haemophiliacs. Their usefulness in preventing re-bleeding after subarachnoid haemorrhage is controversial and has not been proven satisfactorily.

Tranexamic acid is also used to reverse the effects of streptokinase or urokinase if excessive (see p.753), and in the treatment of hereditary angio-oedema as second choice after an anabolic steroid such as danazol.

Dosages

Intravenous: Tranexamic acid, 1–2 g t.d.s. by infusion over at least 5 min.

Oral: Tranexamic acid, 1–1.5 g, two to four times daily; ε-aminocaproic acid, 3 g four to six times daily.

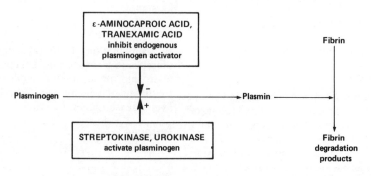

Fig. P3. The activation of plasminogen and the effects of drugs which activate it or inhibit its activation.

Kinetic data

These drugs are well absorbed. They are mostly excreted unchanged by the kidneys, and dosages should be reduced in renal failure. $T_{1/2}$ of aminocaproic acid is 2 h, and of tranexamic acid 14 h.

Important adverse effects

The incidence of adverse reactions to tranexamic acid is lower than for ε-aminocaproic acid, but the contra-indications are the same and are as follows:

1. Massive haematuria from the upper urinary tract, since these drugs promote clotting which may cause ureteric obstruction.
2. A recent history of thrombo-embolism, and in cases where there is an increased risk of thrombosis even in the presence of bleeding (e.g. disseminated intravascular coagulation).

3. Pregnancy.

Adverse reactions to tranexamic acid are uncommon and consist mostly of nausea, vomiting, and diarrhoea, which are dose-related. Rarely giddiness may occur during over-rapid infusion.

ε-aminocaproic acid may cause nausea, vomiting, diarrhoea, nasal congestion, conjunctival suffusion, dizziness, hypotension, and skin rashes. Rarely an acute myopathy may occur during long-term therapy (> 4 weeks) and cause muscle weakness and tenderness, and myoglobinuria which may cause renal failure.

Interactions

The risk of thrombosis due to these drugs is increased by concomitant therapy with oral contraceptives.

AMINOGLUTETHIMIDE

Structure

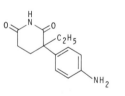

Mode of action

Aminoglutethimide inhibits the first step in steroid synthesis, the conversion of cholesterol to pregnenolone. It thus reduces the production of all endogenous steroids, including cortisone, aldosterone, and the sex steroids (see Fig. 25.1).

Uses

1. To cause 'medical adrenalectomy' in women with metastatic breast cancer, after the menopause or after oophorectomy.
2. To reduce adrenal steroid production in Cushing's syndrome due to adrenal tumours, ectopic ACTH production, or (in combination with metyrapone) excess pituitary ACTH production.

Dosages

250 mg b.d. orally for 2 weeks, increasing to 250 mg q.d.s. in the absence of severe adverse effects.

Supplementary therapy is discussed below.

Important adverse effects

Because aminoglutethimide inhibits steroid synthesis in general, supplementary steroid therapy is necessary, using oral cortisone (12.5–37.5 mg orally o.d.) and fludrocortisone (50–200 micrograms orally o.d.), to prevent Addison's disease.

Central nervous system effects are common and include dizziness, lethargy, and somnolence. Nausea, vomiting, and diarrhoea occur less often. All these effects are dose-related

Drug rash with fever may occur after 1–2 weeks' treatment but is self-limiting and usually resolves within a further 1–2 weeks without withdrawal of treatment.

Occasionally aminoglutethimide may cause hypothyroidism.

Interactions

Aminoglutethimide increases the rate of metabolism, and therefore the dosage requirements, of warfarin, oral hypoglycaemics, and dexamethasone.

AMINOGLYCOSIDE ANTIBIOTICS

Structures

These drugs contain different amino sugars in glycosidic linkage. Gentamicin is shown as an example:

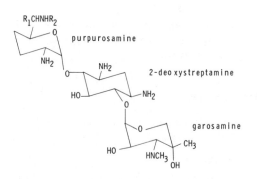

gentamicin C_1 : R_1 = R_2 = CH_3

C_2 : R_1 = CH_3 ; R_2 = H

C_{1a} : R_1 = R_2 = H

Other aminoglycosides in common clinical use are streptomycin, neomycin, kanamycin, tobramycin, and amikacin.

Mode of action

Inhibition of protein synthesis in bacterial ribosomes and disruption of the translation process from RNA to DNA. This leads to a bacteriostatic effect but the aminoglycosides are also bacteriocidal through a mechanism not yet fully understood. Neomycin acts, in hepatic encephalopathy, perhaps by reducing the gut flora which possess urease activity, thus reducing ammonia production in the gut, but perhaps also by inhibition of protein absorption.

Uses

Below are listed some of the common examples of bacteria sensitive to the aminoglycosides, and the associated diseases for which they are particularly used. Neomycin is also used in the treatment of hepatic encephalopathy.

Bacteria	Disease	Aminoglycoside
Gram +ve cocci	Streptococcal endocarditis	Gentamicin (in combination with penicillin G)
Gram −ve bacilli	Infections with *E. coli, Proteus, Pseudomonas,* and *Klebsiella pneumoniae*	Gentamicin Tobramycin Amikacin
Mycobacteria	Tuberculosis	Streptomycin
Various	Skin, ear, and eye infections	Neomycin

Dosages

Intramuscular or intravenous (assuming normal renal function):

Gentamicin, 2–2.5 mg/kg initially then 1–2 mg/kg eight-hourly; adjust doses according to plasma concentrations (see below). Doses may need to be reduced after about a week of continuous therapy because of slow accumulation.

Streptomycin (i.m. only), 7.5–15 mg/kg o.d.

Kanamycin, 10 mg/kg initially then 5–10 mg/kg b.d.; adjust doses according to plasma concentrations.

Intravenous doses of these drugs should be given by infusion over half-an-hour.

Oral:

Neomycin, 0.5–1 g four to six times daily.

Kinetic data

All are poorly absorbed and are therefore given parenterally (neomycin is given orally for its effect on the gastro-intestinal tract) or topically.

Gentamicin, kanamycin, and streptomycin each have an apparently short half-time of about 2 h but long-term studies have shown that gentamicin has a terminal half-time of about 5 days, the plasma concentrations usually found during therapy being too low to detect this very long phase. Because of this long $t_{1/2}$ accumulation of gentamicin may become a problem after about 1–2 weeks of continuous treatment and dosage reductions should be anticipated.

Therapeutic plasma concentrations should be:

Gentamicin: less than 2 μg/ml just before a dose ('trough' concentration) at steady state, and near, but less than, 12 μg/ml about 1 h after an i.m. dose, or 15 min after an i.v. dose ('peak' concentration).

Kanamycin: the corresponding values are 10 μg/ml and 40 μg/ml.

Streptomycin: 15–20 μg/ml at steady state. See also Chapter 7.

The aminoglycosides are almost completely eliminated via the kidneys. For this reason doses should be reduced in renal failure, using creatinine clearance as a guide. Doses should be reduced in direct proportion to creatinine clearance (normal 80–120 ml/min); thus creatinine clearance = 50 ml/min, dose = 50 per cent of usual dose.

Important adverse effects

Hypersensitivity reactions are common, especially skin rashes (about 5 per cent). Streptomycin may cause dermatitis by a direct effect on the skin and it should be handled with gloves.

Auditory and vestibular dysfunction may occur as toxic effects. Gentamicin and streptomycin tend to affect vestibular function more commonly, resulting in nausea, vomiting, difficulty in standing, vertigo, and nystagmus. Kanamycin and amikacin, on the other hand, tend to affect auditory function more, resulting in tinnitus, reduction in high-tone perception, and deafness. The aminoglycosides have sometimes been used deliberately to produce these affects in patients with disabling Menière's disease.

Acute renal impairment due to tubular damage may occur as a toxic effect of aminoglycosides. This is more likely to occur in patients who already have renal disease and in patients who are being treated with frusemide and ethacrynic acid.

The aminoglycosides have neuromuscular blocking effects and may exacerbate symptoms in patients with myasthenia gravis.

Neomycin may cause malabsorption, and superinfection of the oropharynx with yeasts and fungi.

Interactions

Frusemide and ethacrynic acid may potentiate the ototoxic and nephrotoxic effects of the aminoglycosides.

The aminoglycosides potentiate the effects of neuromuscular blocking agents.

Neomycin inhibits the absorption of dietary vitamin K and destroys vitamin K-producing bacteria in the gut—it may, therefore potentiate the effects of oral anticoagulants.

AMIODARONE

Structure

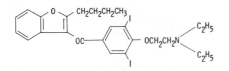

Mode of action

Amiodarone has been categorized as a Class III anti-arrhythmic drug. Its effects on the action potential (see lignocaine) resemble those of hypothyroidism. It prolongs the duration of the action potential by slowing repolarization (phase 3). It does not prolong phase 4 depolarization, does not alter the threshold potential, and does not alter the rate of depolarization during phase 0 (cf. Class I anti-arrhythmics—see lignocaine).

Because it prolongs the action potential the refractory periods are also prolonged. These effects occur in the atria, ventricles, AV node, SA node, and conducting system. The QT interval is prolonged by amiodarone.

Uses

Supraventricular and ventricular arrhythmias:

(a) Paroxysmal atrial fibrillation and flutter.
(b) Recurrent supraventricular tachycardias associated with the Wolff–Parkinson–White syndrome.
(c) Recurrent ventricular tachyarrythmias.

Dosages

Intravenous: 5 mg/kg by infusion over 20–120 min in 250 ml of 5 per cent dextrose. Maximum dose 15 mg/kg (over 24 h).

Oral:
Initial dose, 200 mg t.d.s. for 1 week, followed by 200 mg b.d. for 1 week, then reducing to a maintenance dose.
Average maintenance dose, 100–200 mg/ day.

Kinetic data

The pharmacokinetic properties of amiodarone have not yet been fully described. It appears to have a very long $t_{1/2}$ (of the order of a month or more), and its effects have been observed to last for weeks after its discontinuation.

Important adverse effects

In virtually all patients on long-term therapy amiodarone causes corneal microdeposits of lipofucsin, which can be seen with a slit lamp. They do not usually affect vision, but if central may cause visual haloes. They are not considered serious or requiring withdrawal of therapy, but some authorities still recommend regular ophthalmic examination. These microdeposits are reversible and disappear on withdrawal of amiodarone.

Photosensitization is very common and may cause reactions varying in intensity from an increased propensity to suntan to severe erythematous reactions requiring withdrawal. A slate-grey, cosmetically undesirable pigmentation of the skin may also occur.

Amiodarone affects the thyroid in two ways. Firstly it decreases the peripheral conversion of T_4 to T_3 (see Fig. 25.2) causing an increase in serum T_4 and a decrease in serum T_3. Thyroid-binding globulin is unaffected and the secretion of TSH in response to TRH is usually, but not always, normal. These changes occur in the absence of functional thyroid disease, but amiodarone can also cause both hypothyroidism and hyperthyroidism in about 4 per cent of cases. Routine monitoring of thyroid function is not recommended, however, and in patients in whom abnormal thyroid function is suspected clinically it may be difficult to interpret the results of thyroid function tests.

A reversible peripheral neuropathy has been described and attributed to demyelination.

Recently a few cases of interstitial pneumonitis have been reported, some of which have been fatal.

Miscellaneous effects include constipation, headache, nausea, vomiting, fatigue, tremor, and nightmares.

Interactions

Amiodarone potentiates the effects of warfarin by an unknown mechanism.

Plasma concentrations of digoxin are increased by amiodarone and the mechanism is not yet known. Digitalis toxicity may thus occur.

Amiodarone should not be used with other drugs which prolong the QT interval (e.g. quinidine, disopyramide, and procainamide).

AMPHOTERICIN B

Structure

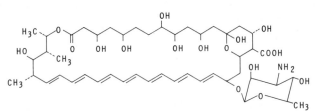

(Compare nystatin)

Mode of action

As for nystatin.

Uses

Local and systemic yeast and fungal infections (*Candida spp., Coccidioides, Histoplasma, Blastomyces, Mucor, Cryptococcus, Aspergillus*).

Dosages

Oropharyngeal infections: 10 mg lozenges q.d.s.

Intravenous therapy: 0.25–1.0 mg/kg daily by continuous infusion.

Kinetic data

Unabsorbed after oral administration. $T_{1/2} = 1$ day. Almost completely metabolized.

Important adverse effects

Renal impairment is almost unavoidable due to renal vasoconstriction and a direct effect on the tubules, resulting in diminished glomerular filtration rate and renal plasma flow, with consequent tubular acidosis and hypokalaemia. These effects can be reduced by concomitant mannitol infusion, are generally reversible, but may become irreversible at total doses of over 5 g.

Fever is common (50 per cent) and may be reduced by hydrocortisone.

A normochromic, normocytic anaemia occurs in most patients because of bone marrow depression.

The incidence of adverse effects may be reduced by alternate day therapy of twice the dose.

ANTHRANILIC ACIDS (MEFENAMIC AND FLUFENAMIC ACIDS)

Structures

General:

	R_1	R_2
Mefenamic acid	CH_3	CH_3
Flufenamic acid	H	CF_3

Mode of action

These drugs are derivatives of phenylanthranilic acid. They have analgesic, antipyretic, and anti-inflammatory properties, and these actions may be related to their inhibitory effects on prostaglandin synthesis.

Uses

For the relief of mild to moderate pain, particularly in musculoskeletal conditions, such as rheumatoid arthritis, osteoarthritis, and ankylosing spondylitis.

Relief of menorrhagia due to dysfunctional causes and the presence of an intra-uterine contraceptive device (mefenamic acid).

Dosages

Mefenamic acid: 500 mg t.d.s., orally.
Flufenamic acid: 200 mg t.d.s., orally.

Kinetic data

Slowly absorbed (peak concentrations occurring at 2–3 h). Extensively metabolized; $t_{1/2} =$ 4 h. Highly bound to plasma proteins.

Important adverse effects

Gastro-intestinal adverse effects are common and include nausea, vomiting, symptoms of 'dyspepsia', and diarrhoea. Peptic ulceration and haematemesis are serious and fairly common complications.

Skin rashes may occur, and if so treatment should be stopped.

It is often recommended that treatment with these drugs should be limited to seven days. If longer term administration is required blood tests should be carried out because of the risk of leucopenia, thrombocytopenia, and an autoimmune haemolytic anaemia.

ANTIFUNGAL IMIDAZOLES

Structures

In common with metronidazole (q.v., p.707) the antifungal imidazoles consist of an imidazole ring with different substituents attached. We give here miconazole as an example.

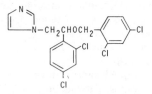

Other members of the group are clotrimazole, econazole, and ketoconazole.

Mode of action

The mode of action of the antifungal imidazoles has not been fully established, but several of their effects on fungal metabolism are known. For example, they increase membrane permeability by several mechanisms, including inhibition of membrane ATPase, inhibition of ergosterol synthesis, and an interaction with cell membrane phospholipids. They also inhibit cellular oxidative and peroxidative enzymes, leading to accumulation within the cell of toxic peroxides.

The effects of the antifungal imidazoles on fungal cells include leakage of essential cell constituents, swelling of the cells, and abnormalities of cell division.

Uses.

The antifungal imidazoles are active against a wide variety of fungi, including mould fungi and yeast fungi. They are used in the treatment of the following infections:

1. Dermatophyte infections due to *Trichophyton*, *Microsporum*, and *Epidermophyton spp.*, e.g. *Tinea pedis*, *Tinea capitis*, *Tinea cruris*.

2. *Candida* infections, e.g. acute oral and vaginal candidiasis, intertrigo, paronychia, and chronic mucocutaneous candidiasis.

3. Vaginal trichomoniasis.

4. Certain systemic mycoses, including histoplasmosis, coccidioidomycosis, paracoccidioidomycosis, and systemic candidiasis.

Dosages

Intravenous: Miconazole, initially 600 mg eight-hourly by i.v. infusion in 200–500 ml of 5 per cent dextrose or isotonic saline, over at least 30 min.

Oral: Ketoconazole, 200 mg orally o.d., until at least one week after symptoms have cleared and cultures have become negative.

Miconazole, 250 mg orally q.d.s., until at least two days after symptoms have cleared and cultures have become negative.

Other routes: There is a wide variety of formulations of clotrimazole, econazole, and miconazole available for local application to skin and vagina, e.g. creams, lotions, powders, vaginal creams, and pessaries. Miconazole may also be given intrathecally in fungal meningitis.

Kinetic data

Only small amounts of these drugs are absorbed after local application to the skin or vagina.

Ketoconazole and miconazole are poorly absorbed after oral administration, ketoconazole better than miconazole. They are widely distributed to body tissues, particularly joints, skin, and the eyes, but do not penetrate the CSF well. They are highly bound to plasma proteins and are mostly metabolized in the liver to inactive metabolites. $T_{1/2}$ for miconazole is 24 h, and for ketoconazole 8 h.

Important adverse effects

There may be local irritation following local application of these drugs.

After intravenous infusion miconazole very commonly causes thrombophlebitis. Other common effects after i.v. infusion include pruritus, nausea and vomiting, fever, rashes, drowsiness, and hyponatraemia. Diarrhoea occurs occasionally and may also occur after oral administration. Rapid infusion may cause cardiac arrhythmias and should be avoided.

In addition there may be adverse reactions to the vehicle, a polyethoxylated castor oil called Cremophor EL® (see p.547). These include hyperlipidaemia, blood abnormalities (e.g. erythrocyte clumping, thrombocytosis), and hypersensitivity reactions.

After oral administration of miconazole and ketoconazole there are few adverse effects, nausea, vomiting, diarrhoea, and pruritus occurring occasionally. Ketoconazole may cause changes in liver function tests and may rarely cause hepatitis. Ketoconazole should be withdrawn if jaundice occurs.

Interactions

Miconazole has been reported to enhance the effects of oral anticoagulants and phenytoin by inhibition of metabolism.

The absorption of ketoconazole is in part dependent on its dissolution in an acid medium. Co-administration of antacids or histamine (H_2) antagonists such as cimetidine reduces its absorption.

ANTIHISTAMINES (H_1 ANTAGONISTS)

Structures

The antihistamines form a heterogeneous group of compounds. Some, such as promethazine and trimeprazine, are related to the phenothiazines; others, such as buclizine, cinnarizine, and cyclizine, are related to piperazine; yet other antihistamines are related to other compounds (e.g. mepyramine is an ethylenediamine). As examples we give here cinnarizine and promethazine.

Cinnarizine:

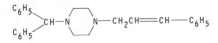

Promethazine (cf. phenothiazines):

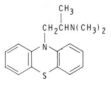

Mode of action

Inhibition of the effects of histamine on H_1 receptors, particularly the effects of increased capillary permeability, vasodilatation, and itching. Antihistamines inhibit these effects but do not reverse them, once established. The H_1 antagonists do not block the effects of histamine on gastric acid secretion (see H_2 antagonists, p.685). The adverse effects of the H_1 antagonists are related mainly to their direct effects on the brain, causing sedation, and on muscarinic cholinergic receptors. Cinnarizine blocks transmembrane calcium ion transport in a manner similar to verapamil and nifedipine. It consequently has vasodilator properties, but is not anti-arrhythmic.

Uses

Treatment of allergic reactions, e.g. hay fever, urticaria and angio-oedema, insect bites and stings, drug reactions, and transfusion reactions.

Prevention of motion sickness.

Symptomatic treatment of Menière's disease and vertigo.

Symptomatic treatment of pruritus.

Treatment of peripheral vascular disease (cinnarizine).

Dosages

The commonly used adult dosages are given in Table P1. If antihistamines are given by i.v. injection they should be given slowly and in dilute solution.

Table P1 *Usual adult dosages and relative sedative and anticholinergic potencies of some antihistamines*

Drug	Dosages		Relative effects	
	Oral	*i.m. or i.v.*	*Sedative*	*Anticholinergic*
Astemizole	10 mg o.d.		±	−
Betahistine	8–16 mg t.d.s.		+	++
Buclizine	25 mg t.d.s.		+	++
Chlorpheniramine	4 mg t.d.s.	10–20 mg	++	
Cinnarizine	15–30 mg t.d.s. (75 mg t.d.s.†)		+	+
Cyclizine	50 mg t.d.s.	50 mg	++	++
Cyproheptadine	4–20 mg/day*		++	
Dimenhydrinate	50–100 mg 4 hrly (max. 300 mg/day)	50 mg	+++	
Diphenhydramine	50–200 mg/day*		+++	++
Mebhydrolin	50–100 mg t.d.s.		+	
Mepyramine	100 mg t.d.s.		++	+
Oxatomide	30–60 mg b.d.		+	−
Promethazine	10–25 mg b.d. or t.d.s.	25–50 mg	++++	+++
Terfenadine	60 mg b.d.		±	
Trimeprazine	10–40 mg/day*		++++	+++
Triprolidine	2.5–5 mg t.d.s.		++	

* in divided doses.
† in peripheral vascular disease.

Kinetic data

All are well absorbed. Most are extensively metabolized with a $t_{1/2}$ of a few hours. Most enter the brain, but terfenadine less so than the rest.

Important adverse effects

Adverse effects occur in up to 50 per cent of cases. Sedation is common but varies in severity from compound to compound (see Table P1) and from individual to individual. Patients should be warned of the hazards of driving or operating machinery while taking antihistamines. Rarely central nervous stimulation may occur, resulting in nervousness, tremor, insomnia, and convulsions.

Anticholinergic effects are common, including dry mouth, blurred vision, constipation, and urinary retention. Caution should be taken in patients with glaucoma or prostatic obstruction.

Direct application to the skin should be avoided, because of a high risk of sensitization.

Interactions

Antihistamines potentiate the effects of other drugs with central nervous depressant effects (e.g. alcohol, benzodiazepines, phenothiazines).

ARYLALKANOIC ACIDS (IBUPROFEN ETC.)

Structures

(a) Phenylpropionic acid derivatives

General:

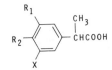

Examples: see below

(b) Naphthylpropionic acid derivatives

Naproxen:

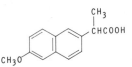

(c) Phenylacetic acid derivatives

Example:
Diclofenac:

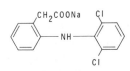

(Others include alclofenac and fenclofenac.)

Mode of action

These drugs are all non-steroidal anti-inflammatory agents, whose total mode of action is unknown. Inhibition of prostaglandin synthesis may play an important part.

Uses

All may be used as analgesic and anti-inflammatory agents in the treatment of rheumatoid arthritis, osteoarthritis, and ankylosing spondylitis. Ibuprofen may be used in Still's disease (juvenile rheumatoid arthritis) and in sero-negative (non-rheumatoid) arthropathies. Naproxen and diclofenac may be used in the symptomatic treatment of acute gout.

Dosages

(Oral)
Fenoprofen, 300–600 mg q.d.s.
Flurbiprofen, 50–100 mg t.d.s.
Ibuprofen, 200–400 mg t.d.s. or q.d.s.
Ketoprofen, 50 mg b.d. to q.d.s.
Naproxen, 250–500 mg b.d. (acute gout —750 mg initially and 250 mg eight-hourly until relief is obtained).
Diclofenac, 25–50 mg b.d. or t.d.s. (75 mg o.d. or b.d. i.m.).
Fenclofenac, 300–600 mg b.d.

Examples:

	R_1	R_2	X
Fenoprofen	C_6H_5O	H	H
Flurbiprofen	H	C_6H_5	F
Ibuprofen	H	$(CH_3)_2CHCH_2$	H
Ketoprofen	H	C_6H_5CO	H

Kinetic data

All are extensively metabolized to inactive compounds and have half-times of 2–6 h (naproxen and fenclofenac 14 h). Excretion is via the urine and bile (the latter up to 50 per cent).

Important adverse effects

Gastro-intestinal adverse effects occur in up to 30 per cent of patients, and include nausea, vomiting, symptoms of 'dyspepsia', and diarrhoea. Some of these symptoms can be reduced by taking the tablets with or just after food. Gastro-intestinal bleeding occurs with a frequency and severity varying from compound to compound. Naproxen, for example, causes gastro-intestinal bleeding less frequently than some of the other drugs of its type but when bleeding occurs it may be very severe; this is a particular problem in the elderly. In general, however, daily occult blood loss is less than with aspirin.

Skin rashes occasionally occur, particularly with fenclofenac, and some patients with hypersensitivity to aspirin may have cross-sensitivity to an arylalkanoic acid.

AZATHIOPRINE AND 6-MERCAPTOPURINE

Structures

Azathioprine:

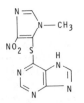

6-mercaptopurine, which is a metabolite of azathioprine, has SH instead of *S*-methylnitro-imidazolyl.

Mode of action

Azathioprine has some therapeutic activity of its own but is almost completely metabolized to 6-mercaptopurine. 6-mercaptopurine is converted within cells to its 5-phosphate ribonucleotide, thio-inosinate, which inhibits the synthesis of DNA from its purine precursors during S phase. The precise link between this effect and the cytotoxic and immunosuppressant effects of these drugs has not been fully worked out.

Uses

Azathioprine: immunosuppressant effects used in inhibiting rejection of transplanted organs (e.g. kidney) and in treating various autoimmune disorders including systemic lupus erythematosus, dermatomyositis, polyarteritis nodosa, and rheumatoid arthritis.

6-mercaptopurine is used in the treatment of acute leukaemias.

Dosages

Azathioprine: average daily oral dose is 2–5 mg/kg.

6-mercaptopurine: initially 2.5 mg/kg o.d., orally, increasing to 5 mg/kg if required.

In both cases dosages should be altered depending on both the clinical responses and adverse effects.

Kinetic data

Both are well absorbed, azathioprine somewhat better than 6-mercaptopurine. Azathioprine is converted to 6-mercaptopurine which is further metabolized ($t_{1/2} = 1$ h) to inactive compounds.

Important adverse effects

Azathioprine: bone marrow depression is dose-related. Infections are common and may arise because of leucopenia and general immunosuppression. Long-term therapy with azathioprine, and indeed perhaps any effective immunosuppressant, is associated with an increased incidence of malignant tumours, particularly lymphoma. The effects of azathioprine on the fetus have not been firmly established but its use should be avoided in pregnancy, if possible.

6-mercaptopurine: nausea, vomiting, and diarrhoea are common with high dose therapy. Other adverse effects are similar to those of azathioprine.

Interactions

The metabolism of 6-mercaptopurine is inhibited by allopurinol (for a full discussion see under allopurinol). Doses of azathioprine and 6-mercaptopurine should be *reduced by 75 per cent* during treatment with allopurinol.

BACLOFEN

Structure

$$H_2NCH_2-CH-CH_2-COOH$$

Cl

Mode of action

Baclofen is the 4-chlorophenyl derivative of γ-aminobutyric acid (GABA). GABA is an inhibitory neurotransmitter whose action in the spinal cord would be expected to lead to muscle relaxation, and it was originally thought that baclofen's action in relieving muscle spasm was as a post-synaptic GABA receptor agonist in the spinal cord. However, it has since been suggested that it may act as a GABA agonist, but at *pre*-synaptic sites, where it has the effect of decreasing the release of excitatory neurotransmitters.

Uses

To alleviate muscle spasm in conditions of the spinal cord associated with spasticity, e.g. multiple sclerosis, spinal cord tumours, and transverse myelitis.

Dosages

Start with low dosages to reduce the incidence of adverse effects and increase slowly according to response. Initial oral dosage should be 5 mg t.d.s., increasing every three days by a total of 5 mg t.d.s. to 20 mg t.d.s. Occasionally higher dosages may be used but the maximum total daily dose should be 100 mg.

Kinetic data

Baclofen is well absorbed. It is mostly excreted unchanged by the kidney, $t_{1/2} = 4$ h. Reduce dosages in renal failure.

Important adverse effects

Adverse effects of baclofen are dose-related. Nausea, vomiting, drowsiness, vertigo, confusion, and fatigue are all common. Nausea can be reduced by taking baclofen with food. As with other drugs used for muscle spasticity baclofen can cause muscular hypotonia especially at high dosages (60 mg per day or more).

Sudden withdrawal of baclofen should be avoided since it can result in hallucinations.

Baclofen can cause convulsions, and should be used with caution in patients with epilepsy or cerebrovascular disease.

Unpredictable psychiatric changes may occur particularly in patients with psychiatric disease, in whom it should be used with caution.

Interactions

Baclofen can cause hypotension and may therefore potentiate the effects of antihypertensive drugs.

BENZODIAZEPINES

Structures

General:

Examples: see next page

Mode of action

Benzodiazepines appear to act on specific receptors in the brain to facilitate GABA inhibitory neurotransmission, which is assumed to result in the anxiolytic, sedative, and anti-epileptic effects.

Uses

Relief of anxiety (particularly chlordiazepoxide, diazepam, oxazepam).

Night-time sedation (particularly nitrazepam, temazepam, lorazepam).

Epilepsy—status epilepticus (diazepam), and myoclonic seizures (clonazepam).

Sedation for operative procedures (e.g. bone-marrow trephine, endoscopy).

Dosages

Anxiety:

Chlordiazepoxide, 10 mg t.d.s., orally.
Diazepam, 2–5 mg t.d.s., orally.
Oxazepam, 10–20 mg t.d.s., orally.

Night-time sedation:

Nitrazepam, 2.5–5 mg orally.
Temazepam, 10–20 mg orally.
Lorazepam, 1–4 m.g. orally.

Status epilepticus:

Diazepam: 10–20 mg i.v. initially and repeated if necessary after 30 min. If effective this may be followed by a continuous i.v. infusion.

Myoclonic seizures:

Clonazepam, 2 mg t.d.s., orally.

Sedation for operative procedures:
Diazepam, 10–20 mg i.v.

Kinetic data

For half-times see Table 29.3, p.524.

Clonazepam and nitrazepam are metabolized to inactive compounds. The following diagram illustrates the metabolic interrelationships of some other compounds:

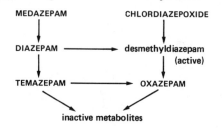

Important adverse effects

Drowsiness and ataxia are common adverse effects with day-time therapy and patients should take care when operating dangerous machinery (e.g. when driving). Because of the cumulative effects of the long-acting benzodiazepines, adverse psychomotor effects may become progressively marked after a week or two of continuous treatment. Disinhibitory effects may occur, causing behavioural abnormalities such as aggression. Psychological dependence is common, but physical dependence also occurs and withdrawal may result in anxiety, agitation, tremulousness, and seizures. Rebound sleeplessness may occur, with EEG abnormalities. Intravenous administration of diazepam sometimes causes thrombophlebitis (3.5 per cent of injections, but less commonly with emulsions). Rarely it may cause transient hypotension and apnoea.

Interactions

Benzodiazepines potentiate the central nervous depressant effects of other drugs (e.g. alcohol, barbiturates). Cimetidine inhibits benzodiazepine metabolism.

Examples:

	R$_1$	R$_2$	X$_1$	X$_2$
Chlordiazepoxide	H	H	NHCH$_3$	Cl
Clonazepam*	H	H	O	NO$_2$
Diazepam	CH$_3$	H	O	Cl
Lorazepam*	H	H(OH)	O	Cl
Nitrazepam	H	H	O	NO$_2$
Oxazepam	H	H(OH)	O	Cl
Temazepam	CH$_3$	H(OH)	O	Cl

* These compounds have 5-*o*-chlorophenyl instead of 5-phenyl

BIGUANIDES

Structures

General:

Examples:

	R$_1$	R$_2$
Metformin	CH$_3$	CH$_3$
Phenformin	H	CH$_2$CH$_2$

Mode of action

Inhibition of intestinal absorption of glucose; increase in peripheral glucose utilization; decrease in gluconeogenesis. Biguanides do not have an effect on insulin release (compare sulphonylureas).

Use

Diabetes mellitus of mature onset type. Phenformin is no longer used in the UK and some other countries because of the risk of lactic acidosis (see below).

Dosage

Metformin: 500 mg t.d.s., orally.

Kinetic data

Both metformin and phenformin are about 60 per cent absorbed. $T_{1/2}$: metformin = 3 h; phenformin = 13 h. Metformin is excreted mostly unchanged in the urine, while phenformin is 50 per cent metabolized (bimodal hydroxylation, see debrisoquine under adrenergic neurone blockers), the rest being excreted unchanged in the urine.

Important adverse effects

Nausea, vomiting, and diarrhoea are common. Lactic acidosis is a serious adverse effect of phenformin and may occasionally also occur with metformin. It is thought to be due to inhibition of electron transport and tissue oxidation at the levels of succinic dehydrogenase and cytochrome oxidase. The presentation consists of nausea, vomiting, abdominal pain, hyperventilation or dyspnoea, drowsiness, and, in severe cases, coma. It occurs more frequently in patients taking phenformin when renal or hepatic function is impaired. There is evidence that poor hydroxylators of phenformin may be more prone to developing lactic acidosis.

BLEOMYCIN

Structure

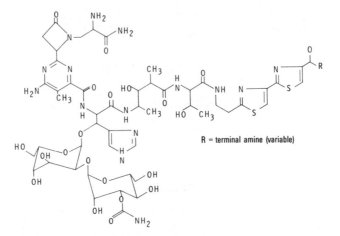

R = terminal amine (variable)

Mode of action

Bleomycin acts on DNA in several different ways. It inhibits DNA synthesis by inhibiting DNA polymerase; it causes breakage of single-stranded DNA; and it prevents DNA repair by inhibiting DNA ligase. It is specific to the G_2 phase of cell division, but is also active during other phases.

Uses

In the cytotoxic chemotherapy of:

1. Testicular carcinoma.
2. Hodgkin's disease.
3. Non-Hodgkin's lymphoma.
4. Various squamous cell carcinomas.

Dosages

Dosages of bleomycin vary with the therapeutic regimen, and it is usually used in combination chemotherapy (see p.594). For example in testicular carcinoma it may be used, in combination with cisplatin and vinblastine, in a dosage of 30 mg i.v. weekly, stopping at a total dose of 360 mg.

Kinetic data

Not effective after oral administration. Bleomycin is widely distributed in the body but does not readily penetrate the brain. It is rapidly inactivated enzymatically in most tissues, especially lung and skin: $t_{1/2} = 4$ h.

Important adverse effects

Anorexia, nausea, and vomiting are relatively common but mild with bleomycin. Stomatitis can occur.

Allergic reactions are frequent in patients with lymphoma, and include fever and chills following injection, and hypotension and cardiovascular collapse.

Effects on the skin are common and include hyperpigmentation, alopecia, and desquamation of the hands and feet, and over areas subject to pressure. The most serious adverse effect is pulmonary fibrosis, and lung function should be monitored during therapy. If impairment of lung function occurs, or if changes are seen in the chest X-ray, treatment should be withheld immediately.

Interaction

For the possible interaction with live vaccines see p.288.

BROMOCRIPTINE

Structure

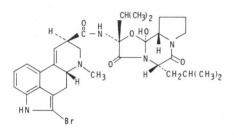

Mode of action

Bromocriptine is an agonist at dopamine receptors.

In Parkinson's disease it directly stimulates nigrostriatal dopamine receptors, thus replacing the effects of the deficient dopamine, although it is not very potent in this respect.

In hyperprolactinaemia it inhibits the release of prolactin from the pituitary. It also inhibits lactation by this mechanism in normal women.

Its action in acromegaly is paradoxical—in normal individuals dopamine causes an increase in growth hormone release from the pituitary, as does bromocriptine. However, in acromegaly bromocriptine *inhibits* the release of growth hormone.

Uses

Parkinson's disease (idiopathic Parkinsonism).

Prevention and suppression of lactation after pregnancy.

Hyperprolactinaemia.

Acromegaly.

Cyclical breast disease and cyclical menstrual disorders.

Dosages

Note the wide differences in dosages in different conditions.

1. Prevention of lactation

2.5 mg orally on the day of delivery, then 2.5 mg b.d. for 14 days.

2. Suppression of lactation

2.5 mg orally on the first day, increasing after 2–3 days to 2.5 mg b.d. for 14 days.

3. Parkinson's disease

1.25 mg orally at night with food initially; increase as required by 2.5 mg every 2–3 days to a total of 40–100 mg per day in divided doses with food.

4. Hypogonadism with galactorrhoea (hyperprolactinaemia)

As for Parkinson's disease initially. Usual daily maintenance dose is 7.5 mg but up to 30 mg may be required.

5. Acromegaly

As for Parkinson's disease initially. Usual daily maintenance dose is 20–60 mg.

6. Cyclical breast and menstrual disorders

As for Parkinson's disease initially increasing to a maintenance dosage of 2.5 mg b.d.

Kinetic data

Bromocriptine is variably absorbed. It is mostly metabolized in the liver ($t_{1/2} = 66$ h), and excreted in the bile.

Important adverse effects

Adverse effects with bromocriptine are numerous, frequent, and dose-related. They can be minimized by slow introduction of dosage (see regimens above), and by taking the daily dosage in divided doses and with food.

At total daily dosages below 20 mg adverse effects are uncommon, the most troublesome being nausea, vomiting, and constipation. Hypotensive reactions can occur during the first few days of treatment, but tolerance occurs.

It is wise to avoid bromocriptine in pregnancy, although there is currently no evidence that it is teratogenic. Treatment of hyperprolactinaemia may make a woman fertile and contraceptive precautions should be taken. Oestrogens should not be used, however, since they may stimulate prolactin secretion.

In acromegaly there is an increased risk of peptic ulceration, particularly in patients taking bromocriptine.

With the high dosages used in acromegaly and Parkinson's disease adverse effects are common and include drowsiness, confusion, dyskinetic reactions (particularly in patients also taking L-dopa), dry mouth, leg cramps, hallucinations, spasm of digital arteries, and cardiac arrhythmias. Care should be taken in patients with a history of psychosis or cardiovascular disease.

BUMETANIDE

Structure

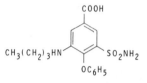

(Compare frusemide.)

Mode of action

Bumetanide inhibits sodium and chloride reabsorption in the ascending limb of the loop of Henle and perhaps also in the proximal convoluted tubule, but how it does this is unknown. It also increases potassium secretion in the distal convoluted tubule but to a lesser extent than frusemide (q.v.).

Uses

Oedema due to cardiac failure, liver disease, nephrotic syndrome, and drugs.

Dosages

1–5 mg o.d., orally or i.v.

Kinetic data

Well absorbed. $T_{1/2} = 1\frac{1}{2}$ h. Excreted 60 per cent unchanged in the urine; the rest is metabolized and excreted in urine and bile.

Important adverse effects

Muscle pain and cramps are common. The other adverse effects of bumetanide are similar to those of frusemide (q.v.). However, it is said to have slightly less potassium-depleting and uric acid-retaining properties and is not magnesium-depleting. It is much less ototoxic than frusemide in high doses.

Interactions

Hypokalaemia potentiates the effects of cardiac glycosides and diminishes the effects of anti-arrhythmic drugs such as quinidine and procainamide.

BUSULPHAN

Structure

$$CH_3SO_2O(CH_2)_4OSO_2CH_3$$

Mode of action

Busulphan is an alkylating agent with specific effects on the myeloid series of cells. Alkylating agents react with guanine moieties in DNA, resulting in a variety of effects which cause mismatching of base pairs during replication, direct damage to the DNA molecule, or cross-linking of nucleic acid chains.

Uses

Myeloproliferative disorders, especially chronic myeloid leukaemia.

Dosages

A general formula for the treatment of chronic myeloid leukaemia might be as follows:

Induction of a remission: 60 micrograms/kg o.d., orally, until the white cell count falls to between 20 and 25 × 10^9/l.

Maintenance of remission: 0.5–2.0 mg o.d., orally.

However, each case needs careful individualization of dosage according to response.

Kinetic data

Well absorbed. About 30 per cent appears in the urine in 24 h as metabolites, principally methane sulphonic acid.

Important adverse effects

Bone-marrow suppression is dose-related, the main effect being on the myeloid cells and platelets. Care should be taken if the platelet count falls below $100 \times 10^9/l$ during treatment. Hyperuricaemia is common and may be prevented by allopurinol (q.v.). Increased skin pigmentation occurs in up to 10 per cent of cases and may occasionally accompany a syndrome similar to that of hypoadrenalism. Other, rare adverse effects include pulmonary fibrosis, cataract, and pulmonary infection with *Pneumocystis carinii* and cytomegalovirus. Busulphan should not be used during pregnancy.

Interaction

For the possible interaction with live vaccines see p.288.

BUTYROPHENONES

Structures

Haloperidol is illustrated here. Other butyrophenones share the 4-fluorobutyrophenone structure but have different substituents at the fourth carbon of the butyrate moiety.

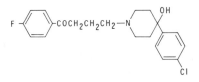

Mode of action

The butyrophenones are classified as neuroleptics or major tranquillizers. They inhibit the action of dopamine and block dopamine receptors reversibly. It is probable that this effect in the brain is the basis of their mode of action in the treatment of acute psychoses (mania and schizophrenia), and of acute confusional and psychotic states. Their actions in the chronic treatment of psychosis are perhaps not quite so straightforward, however, and may depend on the development of adaptive pharmacological responses to the acute dopamine inhibitory effects.

Uses

In the treatment of acute psychotic and confusional states, and in the treatment of mania and schizophrenia.

Droperidol is also used as an anti-emetic and in pre-medication before general anaesthesia.

Dosages

Haloperidol: oral therapy may be given in single or divided doses. Initially 10 mg is given daily, increasing as required to 200 mg. Some patients may respond to less than 10 mg daily. Whenever a therapeutic effect is achieved the dose should be reduced gradually to the minimum effective dose.

Intramuscular: 10–30 mg as a single dose, repeated six-hourly if required.

Droperidol:

i.v., 5–15 mg;
i.m., 5–10 mg
orally, 5–20 mg

as a single dose, repeated six-hourly if required.

Kinetic data

The butyrophenones are mostly metabolized in the liver to inactive compounds. $T_{1/2}$ for haloperidol = 20 h; $t_{1/2}$ for droperidol = 3 h, but its effects last much longer (up to 48 h).

Important adverse effects

The commonest adverse effects are extrapyramidal disorders, including Parkinsonism, dyskinesias, and akathisias. These effects are dose-dependent, occurring most often at daily doses of haloperidol of over 30 mg, and may be treated with anticholinergic drugs (e.g. benztropine). Occasionally cardiovascular effects may occur (e.g. tachycardia, hypotension, and ventricular extrasystoles).

During long-term therapy tardive dyskinesias may occur.

Interactions

The butyrophenones potentiate the effect of alcohol and other drugs acting on the brain.

CALCITONINS

Structure

Calcitonin is a naturally occurring single-chain polypeptide containing 32 amino acids (molecular weight 3600 daltons), which circulates in the plasma both as the monomer and in polymeric forms up to a molecular weight of about 60 000. Porcine calcitonin is used therapeutically and synthetic human calcitonin is now also available.

Salcatonin is synthetic calcitonin with the structure of salmon calcitonin.

Mode of action

Calcitonin is secreted in the parathyroids and in the parafollicular cells of the thyroid. It lowers plasma calcium and phosphate concentrations principally by a direct effect on bone, decreasing osteoclastic and osteocytic activity, thus decreasing bone resorption. This effect is most marked when bone turnover rate is high (e.g. in Paget's disease). It also increases urinary calcium and phosphate excretion and decreases calcium absorption from the gut, but these are minor effects.

Uses

Paget's disease with bone pain or hypercalcaemia.

To lower the plasma calcium concentration acutely in hypercalcaemia (calcitonin is not very effective and should be used in combination with other methods of treatment, see p.439).

Dosages

Dosage units

100 i.u. (international units) of porcine calcitonin = 1 mg.

100 i.u. of salcatonin = 0.025 mg.

Paget's disease

Porcine calcitonin, 0.5–2 i.u./kg daily s.c. or i.m.

Salcatonin, 50 i.u. three times weekly to 100 i.u. per day, s.c. or i.m.

Hypercalcaemia

Porcine calcitonin, 4–8 i.u./kg daily s.c. or i.m..

Salcatonin, 400 i.u. every 6–9 h, s.c. or i.m.

Kinetic data

Human calcitonin has a half-time of about 5 h, and since its metabolism is mostly in the kidney the $t_{1/2}$ is prolonged in renal failure. Salcatonin has a longer duration of action than human and porcine calcitonins.

Important adverse effects

Calcitonins may cause nausea, vomiting, and flushing, effects which diminish with continued treatment. Unpleasant taste sensations, tingling of the hands, and pain at the site of injection may also occur.

Porcine calcitonin and salcatonin are immunogenic and antibodies may be formed. During long-term therapy, therefore, there may be resistance to the pharmacological effects of these calcitonins.

Allergic reactions may also occur, and in patients with a history of allergy a skin test should first be carried out using a 1:100 dilution. Salcatonin is less immunogenic than porcine calcitonin and is to be preferred in these patients, but a preliminary skin test is still necessary.

Calcitonins may impair glucose tolerance and lead to increased hypoglycaemic drug requirements in diabetes mellitus.

CALCIUM SALTS

Uses

Chronic hypocalcaemia due to hypoparathyroidism or malabsorption (with vitamin D).

Acute hypocalcaemic tetany.

To stimulate myocardial contractility in cardiac arrest.

Kinetic data

Total body calcium in adults is about 500 mmol/kg (20 g/kg), of which nearly all is in the bony skeleton, about 25 mmol in all forming an exchangeable pool.

The normal plasma calcium concentration is between 2.25 and 2.5 mmol/l, about 40 per cent of which is protein bound, 10 per cent in the form of diffusible salts (e.g. phosphate), and 50 per cent ionized. It is the ionized fraction which determines the amount of pharmacologically active calcium in the plasma.

Daily requirements of calcium are about 10–15 mmol (400–600 mg) increasing to 30 mmol (1200 mg) in pregnancy. The main sources of calcium in the normal diet are dairy products (milk, butter, cheese). Absorption of calcium is about 40 per cent but is very variable. Absorption is increased by parathyroid hormone and vitamin D, and decreased by fatty acids and oxalates.

About 3 mmol (120 mg) of calcium are lost every day via the gastro-intestinal tract and about 4 mmol (160 mg) via the urine. Renal tubular reabsorption is enhanced by parathyroid hormone in the distal renal tubules, and by vitamin D in the proximal tubules.

Dosages

In the treatment of chronic hypocalcaemia dosages of calcium salts should be adjusted according to the response of the plasma calcium concentration. The maximum recommended dosage is 20 mmol/day. This can be given in the form of a number of salts (e.g. calcium gluconate, 8.9 g; calcium lactate, 6 g).

In the treatment of acute hypocalcaemic tetany, i.v. calcium gluconate is used, 10–20 ml of a 10 per cent solution (i.e. 1–2 g of calcium gluconate, or 2.25–4.5 mmol of calcium).

In cardiac arrest with asystole, i.v. calcium gluconate may be given, 10 ml of a 10 per cent solution.

Important adverse effects

Excessive dosages may cause hypercalcaemia resulting in general malaise, headache, anorexia, nausea and vomiting, constipation and abdominal pain, muscle weakness, thirst, polyuria and nocturia, and drowsiness and confusion. In severe cases there may be psychosis and cardiac arrhythmias. Prolonged hypercalcaemia may cause tissue damage with renal stone formation, nephrocalcinosis, and deposition of calcium in other tissues, such as skin, blood vessels, and eyes. In children hypercalcaemia may retard growth.

If calcium is given rapidly i.v. it can cause peripheral vasodilatation with consequent hypotension. Cardiac arrhythmias, nausea and vomiting, hot flushes, and sweating may also occur.

Interactions

Calcium salts should not be given i.v. in patients taking cardiac glycosides because of an increased risk of cardiac arrhythmias. They should not be given through the same i.v. line as bicarbonate salts (e.g. in cardiac arrest) because of precipitation of the insoluble salt calcium carbonate.

CAPTOPRIL

Structure

Mode of action

Captopril is a competitive inhibitor of the angiotensin converting enzyme dipeptidyl carboxypeptidase, or kininase II. Inhibition of this enzyme results in a decrease in the conversion of angiotensin I to the vasoactive peptide angiotensin II, and also in an accumulation of bradykinin, a vasodilator which is normally inactivated by kininase II.

The therapeutic effects of captopril in both hypertension and cardiac failure result from direct peripheral vasodilatation, due mainly to a decrease in the amount of circulating angiotensin II. Circulating aldosterone is also reduced because of reduced angiotensin II formation.

Uses

Severe hypertension, resistant to other antihypertensive therapy.

Severe congestive cardiac failure.

Dosages

Treatment should be started with low oral doses, and the dosage increased at 2 week intervals according to the patient's response. The initial oral dosage is 25 mg t.d.s., up to a maximum of 150 mg t.d.s.

Kinetic data

Well absorbed, but absorption is reduced to 50 per cent by food. Captopril is 50 per cent excreted unchanged and 50 per cent metabolized to inactive compounds. $T_{1/2} = 2$ h.

Important adverse effects

Because of its adverse effects captopril should be reserved for the treatment of patients in whom other treatment has been unsuccessful, or has caused unacceptable adverse effects.

Rashes are common (about 10 per cent) and may be accompanied by fever and eosinophilia. Rarely angio-oedema may occur.

Taste disturbance, which is usually transient, occurs in about 5 per cent of patients.

Proteinuria occurs in about 1 per cent of patients and the nephrotic syndrome in about 0.3 per cent. The latter is due to a membranous glomerulonephritis.

Neutropenia occurs in about 0.3 per cent of patients and may progress to agranulocytosis.

Interactions

Hypotension is common among patients treated with other antihypertensive drugs and particularly in patients who are volume-depleted by diuretics. This is especially a problem during the first few hours of administration of captopril.

Captopril causes an increase in the plasma potassium concentration and the effects of other drugs with a similar effect may be potentiated (e.g. potassium-sparing diuretics or potassium chloride supplements).

Cyclo-oxygenase inhibitors, such as indomethacin, may reduce the hypotensive effects of captopril.

CARBAMAZEPINE

Structure

(Compare tricyclic antidepressants.)

Mode of action

Unknown.

Uses

As an anticonvulsant (especially in the generalized seizures of grand mal and the focal seizures of temporal lobe epilepsy).

Trigeminal neuralgia.

Relief of post-herpetic neuralgia (in combination with a tricyclic antidepressant).

Dosages

100 mg o.d., orally, increasing at intervals of a few days up to 1600 mg, if required.

Kinetic data

Extensively metabolized $T_{1/2} = 36$ h during chronic dosage. One metabolite may be active. Therapeutic plasma concentrations are in the range 17–42 μmol/l.

Important adverse effects

Visual symptoms are common at high doses (diplopia and blurred vision occurring at daily doses above 1200 mg). At all doses leucopenia may occur after a few months' treatment (6 per cent of all cases) but resolves after withdrawal. Central nervous effects, including drowsiness, loss of balance, and paraesthesiae, occur in up to 50 per cent of cases depending on dose. Water retention may occur (inappropriate ADH syndrome).

CARBENOXOLONE

Structure

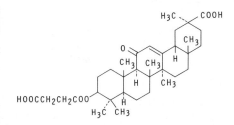

(Note the similarity to spironolactone—see below under 'adverse effects'.)

Mode of action

Carbenoxolone enhances gastric mucus secretion, prolongs the life of gastric mucosal cells, and inhibits pepsin activity. How it does all that is not known.

Use

Treatment of gastric ulceration.

Dosages

100 mg t.d.s., orally, for 6 weeks.

Kinetic data

Well absorbed in the stomach at an acid pH. Absorption is thus impaired by the presence of food but this does not affect steady-state plasma concentrations. Carbenoxolone is mostly excreted unchanged in the bile and there is some enterohepatic recirculation. $T_{1/2}$ = 15 h.

Important adverse effects

Fluid retention and hypokalaemia are common. Fluid retention may be treated with a diuretic but great care must be taken not to worsen hypokalaemia. For this reason full doses of potassium supplements should be given if carbenoxolone is continued. Spironolactone should not be used since it may diminish the ulcer-healing effects of carbenoxolone.

Interactions

Spironolactone (see above).

The effects of cardiac glycosides are enhanced, and the effects of anti-arrhythmic drugs, such as quinidine and procainamide, are diminished by hypokalaemia.

CARBIMAZOLE

Structure

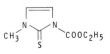

Mode of action

Inhibition of the iodination of tyrosine and perhaps inhibition of the coupling of iodotyrosines by inhibition of thyroid peroxidase. The end result is the inhibition of the synthesis of triiodothyronine and thyroxine.

Use

To treat hyperthyroidism.

Dosages

Initially 30–60 mg daily, orally, in divided doses, reducing the daily dose by 10–20 mg every 3–6 weeks to a daily maintenance dose of 5–20 mg o.d. Continue treatment for 1–2 years (see therapy of hyperthyroidism, p.432).

Kinetic data

Carbimazole is rapidly metabolized to the active derivative methimazole, which has a $t_{1/2}$ of 6 h. Methimazole is mostly metabolized. Its duration of effect is longer than would be expected from its $t_{1/2}$.

Important adverse effects

Adverse effects occur in up to 7 per cent of cases, usually in the first 2 months of treatment. They are usually limited to gastrointestinal disturbances, headache, and skin rashes. In about 1 in 800 cases agranulocytosis occurs. When it occurs it usually comes on rapidly and patients should be warned to stop treatment and see their doctor if they develop a fever or sore throat. Over-treatment may result in hypothyroidism. Mothers should not breast-feed during treatment to avoid neonatal goitre.

CARDIAC GLYCOSIDES (DIGITALIS)

Structures

General:

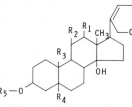

Examples: see below:

Mode of action

Cardiac glycosides inhibit the ATPase responsible for the sodium pump. Their electrophysiological effects are thought to be due to the changes in transmembrane potential brought about directly by that inhibition. Their effects on cardiac muscle are thought to be due to changes in intracellular free calcium concentration or disposition secondary to the changes in intracellular sodium concentrations brought about by that inhibition. The electrophysiological effects include slowing of the heart rate (*negative chronotropic effect*) due to decreased conduction velocity and prolongation of the effective refractory period in the AV node, in addition to effects on the other specialized conduction tissues and on various reflex arcs. The effect on cardiac muscle is that of increasing the rate of myocardial contractility (*positive inotropic effect*).

Uses

Treatment of atrial fibrillation (to slow the ventricular rate, although sometimes reversion to sinus rhythm occurs) and other supraventricular tachyarrhythmias (to slow the heart rate and to restore sinus rhythm). Treatment of cardiac failure especially when due to ischaemic, valvular, and hypertensive heart disease. It should not be used in the treatment of hypertrophic obstructive cardiomyopathy. Its value in other cardiomyopathies and constrictive pericarditis is unclear. It is of little value in the treatment of heart failure due to chronic cor pulmonale.

Dosages

Oral:

Digoxin: loading dose 15 micrograms/kg in three divided doses over 12 h reducing the dose if evidence of toxicity occurs before the full dose has been given. Maintenance dose depends on renal function varying between 5 micrograms/kg o.d. with normal renal function and 2 micrograms/kg o.d. in the anephric state.

Examples:

	R_1	R_2	R_3	R_4	R_5
Digoxin	OH	H	CH_3	H	(Digitoxose)$_3$
Digitoxin	H	H	CH_3	H .	(Digitoxose)$_3$
Ouabain	H	OH	CH_2OH	OH	Rhamnose

Digitoxin: loading dose 20 micrograms/kg given as described for digoxin. Maintenance dose 1–2 micrograms/kg o.d.

Intravenous:

Digoxin: two-thirds of oral doses.
Digitoxin: same as oral doses.
Ouabain: 0.25–0.5 mg as initial dose and continue with digoxin. When given i.v. digoxin and digitoxin should be infused over 0.5–1 h. Ouabain may be given over 5–10 min.

Important adverse effects

Adverse effects are dose-related. Common non-cardiac effects include anorexia, nausea, vomiting, and diarrhoea; confusion and acute psychiatric disturbances; visual disturbances (photophobia, blurring of vision, colour visual disturbances). Virtually any cardiac arrhythmia may occur, the commonest being those related to ventricular and supraventricular ectopic beats, and AV nodal conduction impairment leading to heart block. The combination of ectopic arrhythmias and heart block is particularly suggestive of glycoside toxicity. Bradycardia occurs occasionally.

Kinetic data

The adverse effects of cardiac glycosides are enhanced by the following factors:

(a) electrolyte disturbances, especially *hypokalaemia*, hypercalcaemia, hypomagnesaemia;
(b) hypoxia and acidosis;
(c) hypothyroidism;
(d) old age.

Patients with hyperthyroidism are relatively resistant to the therapeutic effects of cardiac glycosides.

Interactions

Hypokalaemia due to other drugs (e.g. diuretics) enhances the effects of cardiac glycosides.

Quinidine administration results in an increased incidence of adverse effects in patients on digoxin due to diminished renal clearance and altered tissue distribution of digoxin.

Other drugs may cause an increase in plasma digoxin concentrations and increase the risk of toxicity. These include amiodarone, verapamil, and nifedipine.

	Absorption	Elimination	$T\frac{1}{2}$
Digoxin	67% (tablets) 80% (elixir)	Renal	40 h
Digitoxin	100%	Metabolic	5 days
Ouabain	Virtually 0%	Renal	20 h

Plasma concentrations should be below 3 ng/ mg (digoxin) or 30 ng/ml (digitoxin) but toxic-ity may occur even below these concentrations (see above and Chapter 7).

CEPHALOSPORINS AND RELATED COMPOUNDS

Structures

The penicillins and cephalosporins share a common structure, the β-lactam ring, as seen in the following general structures:

Penicillins:

Cephalosporins:

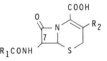

R, R_1, and R_2 indicate a variety of different substituents. Cephamycins are related to the cephalosporins, having a methoxy group in the 7-position. Latamoxef is also related but has oxygen instead of sulphur in the general structure.

We shall refer here to the cephalosporins and related compounds collectively as 'cephalosporins'. The following are some of those available:

Orally active—cephradine, cephalexin, cefaclor.

Injectable—cefuroxime (alternative cephamandole), cefotaxime, cefoxitin (a cephamycin), latamoxef (see 'structure' above).

The earlier cephalosporins, cephaloridine and cephalothin, have been supplanted by less toxic and more efficacious successors.

Mode of action

As for penicillin—inhibition of bacterial cell wall synthesis.

Bacterial resistance results mainly from bacterial production of β-lactamases (cephalosporinases), which open the β-lactam ring, destroying the activity. Usually, however the β-lactam ring of the cephalosporins tends to be somewhat more stable than that of many penicillins toward the common β-lactamases. Nevertheless with increasing use resistance to cephalosporins is emerging, and some bacteria now produce specific cephalosporinases.

Uses

In the treatment of infections caused by sensitive bacteria. The main bacterial sensitivities to cephalosporins and the usual indications for their use are shown in the Tables (P2 and P3).

Because new cephalosporins and related antibiotics with varying antibacterial spectra are continually being produced, there are changing opinions about the place of cephalosporins in the chemotherapy of infections. At the moment most authorities agree that the cephalosporins are usually second-choice antibiotics. They are seldom preferred to other first-line antibiotics on bacteriological grounds alone. With the extended spectrum of some of the newer cephalosporins, however, this opinion may change, particularly with regard to some Gram-negative bacterial infections.

About 10 per cent of patients who give a history of an allergic reaction to penicillin will also be allergic to cephalosporins, so one cannot prescribe cephalosporins to penicillin-sensitive patients with absolute confidence, although they are in practice often used as alternatives to penicillin in penicillin-sensitive patients when the potential benefits outweigh the risks.

Dosages

Cephradine: 250–500 mg, six-hourly, orally or 0.5–1 g six-hourly i.m. or i.v.

Cephalexin: 250–500 mg, six-hourly, orally.

Cefaclor: 250 mg eight-hourly, orally.

Cefuroxime: 750 mg eight-hourly, i.m. Up to 1.5 g, six-hourly, i.v.

Cefotaxime: 1 g six-hourly, i.m. or i.v.

Latamoxef: 1 g eight-hourly, i.m. or i.v.

Cefoxitin: 1–2 g every 6–8 h, i.m. or i.v.

Kinetic data

Elimination of the cephalosporins usually occurs by renal excretion. Cefotaxime is 40 per cent metabolized.

Because of preponderant renal excretion dosages should be reduced in renal failure. See Table P2 for values of $t_{1/2}$.

Important adverse effects

Allergic reactions occur in about 5 per cent of patients and are similar to those produced by the penicillins. Some patients allergic to penicillins may also be allergic to cephalosporins (see above). Thrombophlebitis at the site of an i.v. infusion can be a problem. Infrequently the cephalosporins produce a positive Coombs's test, but haemolytic anaemia is very rare.

The older cephalosporins, e.g. cephaloridine, were undoubtedly nephrotoxic, but this does not seem to be a problem with the cephalosporins listed here.

Interactions

The nephrotoxicity of the older cephalosporins was enhanced by frusemide, ethacrynic acid, and aminoglycosides. It is doubtful that this is likely to be a problem with the cephalosporins discussed here, but it is still probably wise to be cautious about the use of large doses of cephalosporins in very ill patients receiving gentamicin, frusemide, or ethacrynic acid.

Table P2 Sensitivities of various bacteria to some cephalosporins

	Staphylococcus aureus	Streptococcus pyogenes	Streptococcus pneumoniae	Streptococcus faecalis	N. meningitidis	N. gonorrhoeae	Haemophilus influenzae	Escherichia coli	Klebsiella spp.	Proteus spp.	Pseudomonas aeruginosa	Bacteroides fragilis	Route	T½ (h)
Cephradine	++	++	++	0	0	0	0	++	++	++	0	0	Oral, i.m., i.v.	0.9
Cephalexin	++	++	++	0	+	+	0	++	++	+	0	0	Oral	0.9
Cefaclor	++	++	++	0	0	0	++	++	++	++	0	0	Oral	0.6
Cefuroxime	+++	+++	+++	0	+++	+++	+++	+++	+++	+++	±	++	i.m., i.v.	1.5
Cefotaxime	++	++	++	±	++	++	+++	+++	+++	+++	++	+	i.m., i.v.	1.0
Latamoxef	++	+++	±	0			+++	+++	+++	+++	+++	++	i.m., i.v.	2.5
Cefoxitin	++	++	++	0	++	++	++	+++	+++	+++	0	++	i.m., i.v.	0.7

+++ Usually very sensitive.
++ Quite sensitive.
+ Sensitive.
± Some activity but not useful.
0 Usually resistant.

Table P3   *Some infections in which cephalosporins would be commonly used as second-line agents*

Infection	First-line antibiotic	Cephalosporin
Acute otitis media (*Strep. pyogenes, H. influenzae*)	Amoxycillin	Cefaclor
Pneumonia (*H. influenzae and Strep. pneumoniae*)	Amoxycillin	Cefuroxime
Hospital-acquired urinary infections (resistant enterobacteria)	Gentamicin	Cefotaxime Latamoxef
Intra-abdominal infection (anaerobic bacteria: *Bacteroides fragilis*)	Metronidazole	Cefoxitin
Skin and soft tissue infections:		
Strep. pyogenes	Benzylpenicillin	Cephalexin or
Staph. aureus	Flucloxacillin	Cephradine
Gram-negative septicaemia:		
E. coli ⎫ Klebsiella spp. ⎭	⎰ Azlocillin ⎱ Gentamicin	Cefotaxime or Latamoxef

CHENODEOXYCHOLIC AND URSODEOXYCHOLIC ACIDS

Structure

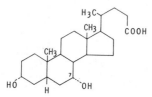

Mode of action

Chenodeoxycholic acid (illustrated) is a naturally occurring bile acid. Ursodeoxycholic acid is its 7β-epimer. They are used to dissolve gallstones and act by at least two mechanisms:

1. By increasing the proportion of bile salts in the bile. This reduces the proportion of cholesterol in the bile below the value at which cholesterol precipitation occurs. Cholesterol reabsorption from formed cholesterol stones then results in dissolution of the stones.

2. By reducing cholesterol synthesis. The cholic acids inhibit microsomal 3-hydroxy-3-methylglutaryl coenzyme A (HMG-CoA) reductase which converts HMG-CoA to mevalonate, which is in turn metabolized to cholesterol. This is probably the main mode of action.

Use

In the treatment of radiotranslucent cholesterol-containing gallstones. Other types of stones are not affected.

Dosages

Chenodeoxycholic acid : 10–15 mg/kg daily as a single night-time dose or in two divided doses if more than 500 mg. Continue treatment for up to 2 years, depending on the size of the stone.

Ursodeoxycholic acid: 8–10 mg/kg daily in two doses for up to 2 years, depending on the size of the stone.

In both cases treatment should be continued for 3 months after the stones have dissolved.

Kinetic data

In common with other bile salts these drugs are 95 per cent absorbed via the terminal ileum. Absorption is saturable and reduced at single doses of more than 500 mg. They are conjugated with taurine and glycine in the liver and are excreted into the bile. The conjugates are reabsorbed in the terminal ileum, but about 5 per cent is deconjugated by intestinal bacteria and converted to lithocholic acid which is excreted in the faeces. The normal daily endogenous production of bile salts (the sodium salts of the bile acids) is about 10 mg/kg.

Important adverse effects

The major adverse effect is diarrhoea due to impaired intestinal water and electrolyte reabsorption. Tolerance to this effect occurs with prolonged treatment. Ursodeoxycholic acid causes less diarrhoea than chenodeoxycholic acid. Chenodeoxycholic acid may impair liver function.

The cholic acids should not be used in patients who have alimentary disorders which interfere with bile salt disposition (e.g. regional ileitis, cholestasis, a non-functioning gall-bladder, and severe chronic liver disease).

These drugs may exacerbate peptic ulceration, and should not therefore be used in patients with peptic ulcers.

Interactions

Drugs which lower blood cholesterol (e.g. clofibrate) and drugs which increase cholesterol elimination in the bile (e.g. oestrogen) oppose the effects of the cholic acids.

CHLORAL DERIVATIVES

Structures

General:

$$Cl_3C - \underset{\underset{R_2}{|}}{C}H - R_1$$

Examples:

	R_1	R_2
Chloral hydrate	OH	OH
Dichloralphenazone*	OH	OH
(Trichloroethanol	H	OH)

*Two molecules of chloral hydrate combined with one of antipyrine.

Mode of action

Cerebral depressant action of unknown mechanism.

Use

Hypnotic.

Dosages

Chloral hydrate: 500–1000 mg, orally.
Dichloralphenazone: 650–1300 mg, orally.

Kinetic data

Well absorbed. Completely hydrolyzed to the active compound trichloroethanol which is in turn partly metabolized to the therapeutically inactive compound trichloracetic acid, which does, however, participate in some drug interactions (see below). $T_{1/2}$ of trichloroethanol = 6 h.

Important adverse effects

The commonest adverse effect is the sensation of an unpleasant taste. This may be trivial but may sometimes be severe enough to require withdrawal of therapy. Gastric irritation with nausea and vomiting are also common.

Interactions

Stimulation of drug metabolism may result in diminished effects of oral anticoagulants.

Trichloracetic acid displaces other drugs from protein binding sites and this particularly effects phenytoin, warfarin, and tolbutamide. For a discussion of the clinical relevance of this effect see Chapter 10.

Alcohol potentiates the effects of chloral derivatives (e.g. 'Mickey Finn').

CHLORAMBUCIL

Structure

(ClCH₂CH₂)₂N—⟨benzene ring⟩—CH₂CH₂CH₂COOH

(Compare cyclophosphamide, melphalan.)

Mode of action

Alkylating agent (see busulphan).

Uses

Chronic lymphatic leukaemia.
Primary (Waldenström's) macroglobulin-aemia.

Dosages

A general formula for the treatment of chronic lymphatic leukaemia might be as follows: Induction of a remission: 0.1–0.2 mg/kg o.d., orally, for 3–6 weeks, monitoring the peripheral white cell count as a guide. Maintenance of remission: 2 mg o.d., orally, How-ever, each case needs careful individualization of dosage according to response.

Kinetic data

Well absorbed. $T_{1/2}$ = 1.5 h. Mostly metabolized to phenylacetic acid mustard.

Important adverse effects

The most important adverse effects of chlorambucil are on the bone-marrow and on spermatogenesis. Bone-marrow suppression is dose-related and is potentiated by concurrent radiotherapy or other cytotoxic chemotherapy. All alkylating agents may inhibit spermatogenesis resulting in oligospermia which may be reversible but which may progress to irreversible azoospermia with sterility. Chlorambucil should not be used during pregnancy because it is potentially teratogenic.

Interaction

For the possible interaction with live vaccines see p.288.

CHLORAMPHENICOL

Structure

NO₂

HOCH
|
HCNHCOCHCl₂
|
CH₂OH

Mode of action

Inhibition of bacterial protein synthesis by an effect on the 50S ribosomal subunit.

Uses

Infections due to:
Gram +ve cocci (anaerobic streptococci, *Strep. pneumoniae*).
Gram −ve cocci (*N. meningitidis*).
Gram −ve bacilli (*E. coli*; *Kl. pneumoniae*, *S. typhi*, *Serratia*, *H. influenzae*, *Brucella abortus*).
Rickettsiae.
Chlamydiae.

The use of chloramphenicol should be severely restricted in therapeutic practice because of its adverse effects. However, it is still drug of first choice in meningitis due to *H. influenzae* and in acute typhoid fever. It is also first alternative in penicillin-sensitive patients who have meningococcal or pneumococcal meningitis, and in Rickettsial infections in patients in whom tetracyclines are contra-indicated (e.g. pregnant women). In bacterial infections of the eye it is very commonly used.

Dosages

25–50 mg/kg/day in four divided doses, orally or i.v. Dosages should be adjusted if salts such as the palmitate are used, to allow for different molecular weights (e.g. 1.7 g palmitate = 1 g base).

Kinetic data

Well absorbed. Extensively metabolized by the liver. $T_{1/2} = 2$ h.

Important adverse effects

Neonates, who are unable to metabolize chloramphenicol as well as adults, may develop the 'grey syndrome' if ordinary doses are used. The syndrome consists of peripheral circulatory collapse with cyanosis, vomiting, irregular respiration, abdominal distension, and diarrhoea. Neonates should either not be given chloramphenicol or given it only in low doses (less than 25 mg/kg/day).

Chloramphenicol has two effects on the bone marrow:

(a) A dose-related inhibition of erythropoeisis and other marrow functions. This effect usually occurs at high dosages (over 50 mg/kg/day) or after prolonged therapy (> 2 weeks), and is probably due to the same mechanism involved in the effect of chloramphenicol on bacterial protein synthesis. There is also inhibition of incorporation of iron into haem.

(b) A hypersensitivity reaction resulting in granulocytopenia, agranulocytosis, aplastic or hypoplastic anaemia, or thrombocytopenia. This adverse effect is uncommon (occurring in between 1 in 20 000 and 1 in 400 000 patients) but carries a high mortality, particularly if the clinical onset of the reaction is more than 2 months after the course of treatment.

Because of these effects blood tests should be carried out regularly in patients taking chloramphenicol, and treatment courses should not be prolonged beyond 1 or 2 weeks if possible.

Interactions

Chloramphenicol inhibits hepatic microsomal drug-metabolizing enzymes. It thereby increases the effects of oral anticoagulants.

CHLORMETHIAZOLE

Structure

Mode of action

Although chlormethiazole is structurally related to vitamin B_1 (aneurine or thiamine) there is no evidence that its mode of action is exerted through an effect involving that vitamin. Its mode of action is not yet understood.

Uses

As a hypnotic and anxiolytic, especially in the elderly.

To treat the symptoms of acute alcohol withdrawal.

As an anti-epileptic in status epilepticus (i.v. use).

Dosages

Chlormethiazole edisylate 250 mg = chlormethiazole (base) 192 mg. The dosages that follow are for the edisylate.

Oral:

Sedation—250–500 mg at night.
Anxiety—250 mg t.d.s.
Acute alcohol withdrawal—1 g initially followed by 750 mg six-hourly for 2 days, 500 mg six-hourly for 3 days, and 250 mg six-hourly for 4 days. Do not continue for more than 9 days in all.

Intravenous: Chlormethiazole edisylate solution contains 8 mg/ml (i.e. 0.8 per cent).

Status epilepticus and acute alcohol withdrawal—40–100 ml (i.e. 320–800 mg) at a rate of 4 ml/min initially, followed by continuous infusion at a rate of 1 ml/min, adjusting the rate subsequently to a rate sufficient to stop convulsions.

Kinetic data

Chlormethiazole is well absorbed, but subject to extensive first-pass metabolism by the liver. Its systemic availability is therefore reduced in chronic liver disease and oral (but not i.v.) dosages should be reduced. $T_{1/2} = 4$ h.

Important adverse effects

The most common adverse effect is nasal irritation, causing sneezing soon after administration. Conjunctival irritation, headache, and nausea and vomiting may also occur.

Sedation is common with regular daytime dosages and patients should be warned to take care when driving or operating machinery.

There is a risk of dependence of the barbiturate–alcohol type (see Chapter 31), especially in patients being treated for alcohol withdrawal symptoms, and in those patients treatment should be restricted to 9 days as detailed above.

When given i.v. chlormethiazole may cause superficial phlebitis. Other adverse effects during i.v. administration occur with high dosages, and constant observation of the patient is necessary during continuous i.v. infusion. These effects include sedation and respiratory depression.

Interactions

The effects of chlormethiazole are potentiated by other drugs acting on the central nervous system (e.g. alcohol, benzodiazepines).

Cimetidine inhibits the metabolism of chlormethiazole, reducing dosage requirements.

CHLOROQUINE

Structure

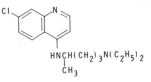

$$HN\underset{\underset{CH_3}{|}}{C}H(CH_2)_3N(C_2H_5)_2$$

Mode of action

Chloroquine has many actions, listed below.

1. As an antimalarial

(a) Interference with plasmodial DNA replication.

(b) Possibly metabolic effects upon plasmodia (chloroquine is concentrated in infected erythrocytes).

2. As an anti-inflammatory agent

The mechanism by which chloroquine exerts its effect in rheumatoid arthritis is uncertain. While chloroquine probably has a direct anti-inflammatory effect by stabilizing lysosomes, thereby inhibiting the release of lysosomal enzymes and preventing their inflammatory actions, the drug seems to have a more profound effect upon the disease process, more like penicillamine or gold (q.q.v.).

Uses

1. Treatment of malaria due to chloro-

quine-sensitive *Plasmodium vivax*, *P. ovale*, *P. falciparum*, or *P. malariae*.

2. Rheumatoid arthritis and lupus erythematosus (especially of the discoid variety).

Dosages

Dosages here are expressed in terms of chloroquine base (150 mg chloroquine base = 200 mg chloroquine sulphate = 250 mg chloroquine phosphate).

1. Malaria

See therapy of malaria, p.278, for details:

(a) Acute attack: 300–600 mg daily.

(b) Prophylactic dose: 300 mg weekly.

2. Rheumatoid arthritis and lupus erythematosus

150–300 mg orally daily (see 'adverse effects').

Kinetic data

Rapidly and completely absorbed. Chloroquine is concentrated in erythrocytes, liver, spleen, kidney, heart, and lung. It binds to melanin, and may be deposited in the cornea, forming characteristic opacities, and in the retina, causing retinal damage (see below and p.145). It is mainly (75 per cent) metabolized in the liver, the rest being excreted unchanged in the urine. $T_{1/2}$ = 5 days. The long $t_{1/2}$ is mainly due to extensive tissue binding.

Important adverse effects

In the doses used in the treatment of malaria serious adverse effects are rare. Mild headaches, nausea and vomiting, pru..itus, and skin rashes occur occasionally.

The larger doses used in rheumatoid arthritis and lupus erythematosus may cause corneal opacities and, more seriously, a retinopathy associated with visual loss (see p.145). All patients receiving long-term chloroquine treatment should be carefully monitored for ophthalmic changes.

Other effects of prolonged treatment include bleaching of the hair, bluish pigmentation of the skin and mucous membranes, lichenoid skin lesions, and ototoxicity. Occasionally thrombocytopenia occurs.

Chloroquine may cause haemolysis in subjects with G6PD (glucose 6-phosphate dehydrogenase) deficiency (see Chapter 8).

Chloroquine is best avoided during pregnancy because of the danger of ototoxicity in the fetus, a hazard which is probably dose-related. It may, however, be used in acute malaria, when the benefit outweighs the risk.

Some patients are hypersensitive to chloroquine and they should not be given the drug. Chloroquine may precipitate psoriasis in susceptible patients, and is best avoided in patients with psoriasis.

Because it is cleared by both liver and kidneys dosages should be reduced in patients with hepatic or renal disease.

Interactions

There is an increased risk of exfoliative dermatitis when chloroquine is used together with gold or phenylbutazone, and these combinations should not be used.

CHOLESTYRAMINE

Structure

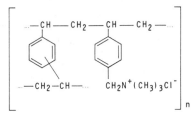

Typified structure of main polymeric groups.

Mode of action

Cholestyramine is an exchange resin. It sequesters bile acids in the gut leading to a reduction in the amount of bile acid subject to enterohepatic recirculation. Because bile acids inhibit the breakdown of cholesterol to bile acids, their reduction results in increased breakdown of cholesterol and consequent lowering of plasma cholesterol concentrations. Furthermore removal of bile acids from the gut may reduce cholesterol absorption.

These effects may, however, be offset by an increase in cholesterol synthesis.

Uses

Familial hypercholesterolaemia (Type IIa).
Pruritus of obstructive jaundice (due to accumulation in the skin of bile acids).
Diarrhoea due to ileal disease or resection (due to excess bile acids).
Digitoxin toxicity.

Dosages

Cholesterol reduction and diarrhoea: 12–24 g o.d. or in divided doses, orally.

Pruritus: 4–8 g o.d., orally.

Kinetic data

Cholestyramine is not absorbed and is excreted unchanged in the faeces.

Important adverse effects

Constipation occurs in up to 50 per cent of

cases and patients may complain of other gastro-intestinal symptoms such as nausea and heartburn. The absorption of vitamins A and K may be impaired.

Interactions

Cholestyramine inhibits the absorption of warfarin, thyroxine, and digitoxin.

CISPLATIN

Structure

Cisplatin is a platinum complex, *cis*-diamminedichloroplatinum:

$$(NH_3)_2 PtCl_2$$

Mode of action

Cisplatin inhibits DNA synthesis by cross-linking complementary strands of DNA, particularly at guanine residues. It is not specific for any particular phase of the cell cycle.

Uses

In the combination therapy of various malignancies, such as testicular carcinoma, ovarian carcinoma, and carcinomas of head and neck.

Dosages

Dosage regimens vary with indication. For example, in testicular carcinoma cisplatin may be used, in combination with vinblastine and bleomycin, in a dose of 20 mg/m^2 of body surface area, given i.v. for 5 days every 3 weeks and for three courses.

Because it is nephrotoxic cisplatin must be given only after hydration of the patient with 1–2 l of i.v. fluid 8–12 h beforehand. Hydration must be also maintained for 24 h thereafter since vomiting is common.

Kinetic data

Not absorbed after oral administration. It is rapidly cleared from the plasma but the metabolites are extensively bound to tissues and consequently the overall $t_{1/2}$ of platinum in the body is long (about 3 days). Platinum may be detected in tissues 4 months or more after a dose. Platinum is excreted in urine, and doses of cisplatin should be reduced in renal failure.

Important adverse effects

Severe nausea and vomiting often occur after treatment, starting within a few hours, and usually lasting for a day, but sometimes up to a week. Bone marrow toxicity is dose-related (see Chapter 33, p.595).

Nephrotoxicity is important and results in reduced creatinine clearance and necrotic changes in the kidney. Patients with renal failure are more at risk because of accumulation, and the toxicity is therefore self-perpetuating.

Ototoxicity is common and results in tinnitus and deafness. Formal audiometry should be carried out before each dose. When high dosages are used a peripheral neuropathy can occur.

Interactions

Gentamicin may potentiate the nephrotoxic effects of cisplatin. For the possible interaction with live vaccines see p.288.

CLOFIBRATE

Structure

Cl—⟨benzene ring⟩—OCCOOC$_2$H$_5$ with CH$_3$ groups above and below

Mode of action

Clofibrate inhibits cholesterol synthesis in the liver and increases the rate of removal of VLDL from the blood. As a result, plasma triglyceride and (to a lesser extent) cholesterol concentrations fall.

Uses

Hyperlipoproteinaemias, particularly of Types IIb, III, and IV, or in the presence of xanthomata.

Dosage

30 mg/kg daily, orally, in two divided doses.

Kinetic data

Well absorbed. The protein binding of clofibrate is saturable leading to non-linear kinetics at high doses or in the presence of hypoalbuminaemia (see below). It therefore has a very variable 'half-time' (about 10 h at low doses). It is about 60 per cent metabolized by glucuronidation but otherwise excreted unchanged in the urine.

Important adverse effects

The incidence of gallstones is increased two- to three-fold in patients taking clofibrate because of altered bile composition. In patients with hypoalbuminaemia, e.g. in the nephrotic syndrome, a syndrome consisting of muscle pain, stiffness and weakness may occur. Daily doses should not exceed 500 mg in patients with renal impairment.

Interactions

Clofibrate potentiates the anticoagulant effects of warfarin by increasing the turnover rate of factors II and X, and by displacing warfarin from its plasma protein binding sites. It also decreases the adhesiveness of platelets and this may contribute to impaired haemostasis if bleeding occurs.

CLONIDINE

Structure

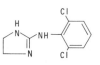

Mode of action

The actions of clonidine in hypertension are very complex. It does seem, however, that its primary action is exerted in the brain with secondary peripheral effects. It is believed that clonidine acts as a central α_2-adrenoceptor agonist, and that stimulation of α-adrenoceptors centrally decreases sympathetic nervous system activity peripherally, resulting in decreased noradrenaline release from peripheral sympathetic nerve endings. There is consequently decreased vascular tone, decreased peripheral vascular resistance, and a lowering of blood pressure.

In migraine its mechanism of action is unknown.

Uses

Hypertension ⎫
Migraine ⎬ Note differences in dosages.

Dosages

Hypertension: 50–100 micrograms t.d.s., orally, initially, increasing as required in increments of 100–200 micrograms to a maximum daily dose of 1.8 mg.

Migraine: 50–75 micrograms t.d.s., orally.

Kinetic data

Well absorbed. Excreted at least 50 per cent unchanged in the urine with a variable $t_{1/2}$ (mean about 12 h).

Important adverse effects

Drowsiness and a dry mouth are very common with doses used for treating hypertension. When withholding treatment dosage should be tailed off gradually, since sudden withdrawal results in severe hypertension which may be treated with an α-adrenoceptor antagonist (e.g. phentolamine i.v.).

Interactions

The effects of clonidine are blocked by α-adrenoceptor antagonists, and by desipramine and perhaps other tricyclic antidepressants.

COLCHICINE

Structure

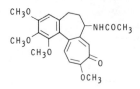

Mode of action

A plausible explanation of the action of colchicine in gout is that it inhibits the migration of phagocytes to gouty tissue, and thereby prevents both the phagocytosis of urate crystals and the subsequent increase in local lactate release following phagocytosis, which is responsible for further urate deposition.

Uses

Acute gout.

Prevention of acute gout during the early phases of treatment of hyperuricaemia (e.g. with allopurinol, q.v.)

Dosages

Acute gout: 1 mg orally initially, then 0.5 mg every 2–3 h until the pain subsides, *or* vomiting or diarrhoea occur, *or* until a total dose of 10 mg has been given. Colchicine should then not be given for a further 3 days.

Prophylaxis of acute gout: 0.5 mg b.d., orally.

Dosages should be decreased in hepatic failure and severe renal failure.

Kinetic data

Although colchicine is said to have a short $t_{1/2}$ (about 1 h), its presence in leucocytes may be detectable for several *days* after a single dose, and clearly accumulation occurs. It is mostly metabolized (80 per cent) in the liver and its metabolites are excreted in the bile.

Important adverse effects

Gastro-intestinal symptoms are dose-related and include abdominal pain, diarrhoea, nausea, and vomiting, and in severe poisoning an enteritis resembling cholera.

Rarely bone marrow suppression, resulting in leucopenia and thrombocytopenia, may occur during chronic administration, as may steatorrhoea, and peripheral neuropathy or myopathy.

CORTICOSTEROIDS

1. Glucocorticoids

Structures

The general structure of the glucocorticoids is illustrated here by the case of hydrocortisone.

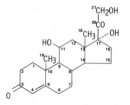

Various groups in this general structure can be substituted to form compounds with greater or lesser glucocorticoid or mineralocorticoid activity. For example, hydroxylation or methylation at the C19 position decreases mineralocorticoid activity, while α-fluoro-substitution at the C9 position increases mineralocorticoid activity. Thus betamethasone and dexamethasone are potent glucocorticoids with little mineralocorticoid activity, whereas 9-α-fluorohydrocortisone (fludrocortisone) is a potent mineralocorticoid (see p.667) with little glucocorticoid activity.

Mode of action

Glucocorticoids have the following effects:

1. *Effects on protein and carbohydrate metabolism.* Glucocorticoids induce the mobilization of proteins and amino acids from skeletal muscle, skin, and bone. Enzymes involved in gluconeogenesis are induced by glucocorticoids, the mobilized amino acids are converted in the liver to glucose, and glycogen stores are built up. There is therefore a negative nitrogen balance. Large doses of glucocorticoids cause high blood glucose concentrations and diabetes mellitus may occur.

2. *Effects on fat metabolism.* Body fat is redistributed leading to truncal obesity, and the so-called 'buffalo hump' and 'moon face'. Glucocorticoids also facilitate the actions of lipolytic agents such as adrenaline, glucagon, ACTH, and TSH.

3. *Mineralocorticoid effects (see below).* The extent of mineralocorticoid effects varies from glucocorticoid to glucocorticoid.

4. *Anti-inflammatory and immunosuppressive actions.* Glucocorticoids are widely used for these effects. They prevent the vascular response (i.e. capillary dilatation) and increased vascular permeability which normally lead to tissue oedema and swelling. They have inhibitory effects on the cellular components of the acute inflammatory response, inhibiting the migration of leucocytes and phagocytic activity. They also inhibit certain aspects of chronic inflammation, e.g. capillary and fibroblast profileration and the deposition of collagen. The precise mechanisms by which these effects are produced are unknown.

Glucocorticoids have immunosuppressive effects. They inhibit lymphocyte functions; the responses of both B-cells and T-cells to antigens are suppressed and this results in impairment of humoral and cellular immunity. Again the precise mechanisms underlying these effects are unknown.

Although from the above discussion it would appear that nothing is known about the mechanisms by which glucocorticoids exert their effects, that is not quite true. It *is* known that corticosteroids combine with cytosolic receptor proteins, and that this complex then binds to chromatin in the cell nucleus. RNA polymerases are activated and the transcription of specific mRNAs occurs. This results in the synthesis of protein in the ribosomes. Thus, many of the actions of glucocorticoids depend on protein synthesis and one must presume that such proteins, either as enzymes or as regulatory factors, control the appropriate cell functions which result in the pharmacological effects described above.

Uses

1. Replacement therapy
(hypopituitarism, hypoadrenalism).

2. Anti-inflammatory and immunosuppressive therapy:

(a) Diseases characterized by vasculitis (e.g. lupus erythematosus, polyarteritis nodosa, dermatomyositis, polymyalgia rheumatica, giant cell arteritis, Wegener's granulomatosis).

(b) Sarcoidosis.

(c) Rheumatoid arthritis.

(d) Bronchial asthma.

(e) Skin diseases of various kinds (especially eczema and psoriasis — local treatment; pemphigus — systemic treatment).

(f) Eye diseases of inflammatory origin (but not *Herpes simplex*).

(g) Some gastro-intestinal disorders (ulcerative colitis, Crohn's disease).

(h) Liver diseases, especially chronic active hepatitis.

(i) Renal diseases, especially minimal change glomerulonephritis.

(j) Prevention of transplant rejection.

(k) Blood disorders, especially some haemolytic anaemias, idiopathic thrombocytopenia, and some haematological malignancies (acute leukaemias and lymphomas).

(l) Septicaemic shock.

(m) Cerebral oedema.

3. Malignancy.
In patients with terminal illness prednisolone may for a short time induce a general sense of well-being.

Dosages

The relative potencies of available glucocorticoids are as follows, with hydrocortisone as reference:

Cortisone	0.8
Hydrocortisone	1
Prednisolone	4
Methylprednisolone	5
Triamcinolone	5
Betamethasone	25
Dexamethasone	25
Beclomethasone	50

The following are examples of commonly used dosages for the relevant conditions. There is a wide dosage variation for many of the conditions.

Oral therapy

Replacement—cortisone, 12.5–37.5 mg daily.

Anti-inflammatory and immunosuppressive dosage—prednisolone, initially 40–60 mg daily in three divided doses for a few days, then reducing gradually over a week or two to a maintenance dosage (usually 5–15 mg once daily). In some conditions (e.g. status asthmaticus) it may be possible to treat the acute condition without continuing with a maintenance dose simply by tailing off the dose completely. In some conditions, requiring a regular maintenance dose, it may be possible to achieve a therapeutic effect with minimal adverse effects by giving twice the usual daily dose every other day (i.e. the same total dose).

Parenteral therapy:

An Addisonian crisis may be precipitated, in susceptible patients, by stress such as infection, trauma, or a gastro-intestinal disturbance. In such circumstances replacement therapy should be given in high doses, e.g. hydrocortisone 100 mg, eight-hourly.

Substitution for oral therapy—there will be occasions (e.g. during surgical procedures) when patients taking oral corticosteroids need to have treatment continued i.v. One would then use hydrocortisone in a dose equipotent with the therapy being replaced (see examples of relative potencies above). Often, however, higher doses may be required because of the clinical circumstances (e.g. increased stress during surgical procedures).

Septicaemic shock—the use of corticosteroids in septicaemic shock is controversial, but if they are to be used the dose should be high, e.g. hydrocortisone i.v. in doses up to 500 mg repeated at four-hourly intervals for a short period. During short-term therapy the risk of serious adverse effects, even with such high doses, is minimal.

Cerebral oedema—dexamethasone, 10 mg i.m., then 4 mg six-hourly until a clinical response occurs. Dosage should then be gradually reduced over the following week and oral therapy may be used where possible.

Rectal therapy: Ulcerative colitis—prednisolone, 20 mg enema, once nightly until a clinical response occurs.

Inhalation therapy: Asthma—betamethasone, one puff (100 micrograms) or beclomethasone, two puffs (100 micrograms) by aerosol q.d.s.

Kinetic data

All are well absorbed. Cortisone and hydrocortisone are extensively metabolized ($t_{1/2}$ 30 min and 1½ h respectively). The others are also metabolized, but at a slower rate, e.g. prednisolone $t_{1/2}$ 3 h, dexamethasone $t_{1/2}$ 4 h.

Important adverse effects

Oral therapy

The appearance of adverse effects is related to the duration of treatment and the dosage used. The following effects are common:

Suppression of the pituitary–adrenal axis occurs inevitably to a greater or lesser extent, depending on the duration of treatment. Steroid withdrawal will then result in hypoadrenalism, which may cause an Addisonian crisis. Withdrawal of steroids after long-term treatment should be very slow to allow recovery of normal adrenocortical function. Sometimes total withdrawal is not possible.

All the features of Cushing's syndrome, i.e. moon-face, bruising, hirsutism, impaired glucose tolerance, hypertension, acne, weight gain, osteoporosis with an increased risk of spontaneous fractures, and an increased susceptibility to infections.

Gastro-intestinal disturbances are common, and at daily doses of prednisolone of 15 mg and over there is an increased incidence of peptic ulceration.

Corticosteroids may interfere with the normal inflammatory responses. This may result in the suppression of the clinical signs and symptoms of perforation of a peptic ulcer, or of any abdominal viscus ('silent abdomen'). The signs or symptoms of septicaemia or tuberculosis may be suppressed, and fever may be absent in conditions where it would ordinarily provide useful information.

Salt and water retention may result in peripheral oedema which, in combination with hypertension, may cause heart failure. Mental disturbances can occur, including any kind of mood change. Ischaemic necrosis of the femoral head occurs commonly and is often bilateral.

Hypokalaemia may require potassium supplementation. Muscle weakness is common and may be accompanied by a myopathy. Glaucoma may be precipitated occasionally during systemic therapy. Cataracts are common and usually posterior in position.

In children retardation of growth occurs and epiphyseal closure may be delayed. Corticosteroid administration during pregnancy may suppress fetal adrenal function and cause cleft palate.

Inhalation therapy
Local irritation of the oropharynx, and fungal infections of the upper respiratory tract occur.

Local application to skin
This may cause atrophy with scarring and telangiectasia. Systemic effects from local treatment are uncommon, but may occur if large areas are treated under occlusive dressings.

Local application to the eyes
Infections may be exacerbated with resultant corneal damage. This is particularly important in herpetic infections. Glaucoma may occur and is unpredictable; it is usually reversible. Cataracts occur occasionally.

Interactions
Enzyme-inducing drugs may enhance the rate of metabolism of corticosteroids.

Hypokalaemia due to corticosteroids potentiates the effects of cardiac glycosides and decreases the effects of Class I anti-arrhythmics (see lignocaine). Other drugs causing potassium depletion may potentiate the hypokalaemic effects of corticosteroids.

The effects of antihypertensive and hypoglycaemic drugs may be attenuated by corticosteroids.

Corticosteroids may potentiate the effects of warfarin.

2. Mineralocorticoids

Structures
For fludrocortisone see under glucocorticoids.

Mode of action
Mineralocorticoids act on the distal convoluted tubule of the kidney, enhancing sodium reabsorption and potassium and hydrogen ion excretion. Water is retained along with the sodium. Aldosterone is the most potent naturally occurring mineralocorticoid (500 times more potent than hydrocortisone), but the semi-synthetic compound $9\text{-}\alpha\text{-fluoro}$-hydrocortisone (fludrocortisone), which is less potent, is used in therapy.

Uses
Replacement therapy in adrenocortical or pituitary insufficiency.

Postural hypotension—temporary benefit, probably due to an increase in intravascular volume, may be gained in the treatment of postural hypotension. However, the danger of fluid overload in these circumstances is considerable.

Dosages
Fludrocortisone:

Replacement therapy: 100–200 micrograms orally od.

Postural hypotension: 500 micrograms orally od.

Kinetic data

Well absorbed. Extensively metabolized; $t_{1/2}$ = 30 min.

Important adverse effects

Sodium and water retention result in oedema and cardiac failure in susceptible individuals.

CORTICOTROPHINS
(ACTH AND TETRACOSACTRIN)

```
  1     2     3     4     5     6     7     8     9    10    11    12    13    14    15
Ser - Tyr - Ser - Met - Glu - His - Phe - Arg - Trp - Gly - Lys - Pro - Val - Gly -Lys
                                                                                    |
                                                                                   16
                                                                                   Lys
                                                                                    |
                                                                                   17
                                                                                   Arg
                                                                                    |
 32    31    30    29    28    27    26    25    24    23    22    21    20    19    18
Ala - Ser- Glu- Asp- Glu- Ala - Gly - Asn- Pro - Tyr- Val - Lys- Val - Pro- Arg
  |
 33
Glu
  |
 34    35    36    37    38    39
Ala - Phe- Pro- Leu - Glu - Phe        Human ACTH
```

Structure

ACTH is a single-chain polypeptide containing 39 amino acids, of which the first 24 are identical in all species. Tetracosactrin (Synacthen®) is a synthetic, single-chain polypeptide containing those 24 amino acids. It has the same pharmacological effects as ACTH, but a shorter duration of action.

Mode of action

ACTH is the endogenous adrenocortical-stimulating hormone synthesized in cells of the anterior pituitary. Its release is stimulated by the action of the corticotrophin-releasing factor, CRF, synthesized in the hypothalamus.

ACTH acts on the adrenal gland, stimulating the production of glucocorticoids, having little effect on the production of aldosterone. Increases in circulating corticosteroid concentrations decrease ACTH secretion (negative feedback).

Uses

1. In the diagnosis of adrenocortical insufficiency.
2. As a short-term alternative to corticosteroids.

Dosages

Note: 1 mg of tetracosactrin i.v. is equivalent to 100 international units (i.u.) of ACTH.

(a) ACTH test of adrenal gland responsiveness to ACTH

(i) Tetracosactrin (Synacthen®)
0.25 mg i.m., with blood samples immediately before and 30 min after for measurement of plasma cortisol concentrations.

(ii) ACTH
40 i.u. i.m., with blood samples immediately before and 4 h after for measurement of plasma cortisol concentrations.

(b) As a short-term alternative to corticosteroids

(i) Tetracosactrin
As Synacthen Depot®, a slow-release formulation of tetracosactrin with a zinc phosphate complex, 0.5–1 mg i.m. twice a week.

(ii) ACTH
Initial dose 40 i.u. i.m. o.d. After a few days the dose and dosage interval should be altered according to the individual patient's response, in order to achieve a therapeutic effect with as low a dosage as possible.

Important adverse effects
The corticotrophins are polypeptides and may, therefore, cause allergic reactions, including (rarely) fatal anaphylactic reactions. Even a mild allergic reaction should be a sign to withhold treatment.

Overtreatment can result in Cushing's syndrome, hyperglycaemia, and hypokalaemia.

The contra-indications to the use of corticotrophins are the same as those for the glucocorticosteroids (p.666).

Interactions
As for glucocorticosteroids (p.667).

CO-TRIMOXAZOLE
(TRIMETHOPRIM + SULPHAMETHOXAZOLE)

Structures
Sulphamethoxazole — see sulphonamides.
Trimethoprim:

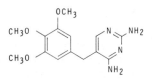

Mode of action
The original aim of this combination (and, subsequently, of others like it) was to interfere with two different metabolic steps in folic acid metabolism, essential for bacterial integrity. The sequence is as follows:

2-amino-4-hydroxy-6-
hydroxymethyldihydropteridine +
para-aminobenzoic acid

$$\downarrow 1$$

dihydropteroic acid

$$\downarrow$$

dihydrofolic acid

$$2 \downarrow \text{ dihydrofolate reductase}$$

tetrahydrofolic acid

Sulphonamides inhibit the production of dihydropteroic acid at step 1, and trimethoprim is a dihydrofolate reductase inhibitor, decreasing the production of tetrahydrofolate at step 2.

Uses
These two compounds are used in the combination known as co-trimoxazole in infections due to bacteria sensitive to these agents (see sulphonamides). The combination is used most frequently in Gram-negative infections of the urinary tract (e.g. *E. coli*, *Proteus*) and chest (e.g. *H. influenzae*). It may also be of value in the treatment of typhoid fever and brucellosis.

In recent years it has been realized that trimethoprim alone is as clinically efficacious as co-trimoxazole for most indications, especially in infections of the urinary tract and chest.

Dosages
Co-trimoxazole: One tablet b.d., orally (each tablet containing 800 mg sulphamethoxazole and 160 mg trimethoprim).
Trimethoprim: 200 mg b.d., orally.

Kinetic data

Trimethoprim is rapidly absorbed, but both are well absorbed. $T_{1/2} = 16$ h (trimethoprim) and 10 h (sulphamethoxazole). The resulting steady-state concentrations during repeated dosage are in the ratio 20:1 (trimethoprim:sulphamethoxazole), which is said to be the optimum ratio. Both are excreted mainly in the urine, and dosages should be reduced in renal failure.

Important adverse effects

Those attributable to sulphonamides (qq.v.) but crystalluria does not occur. Folate deficiency may occur in those who are already relatively folate depleted.

CROMOGLYCATE (DISODIUM SALT) (CROMOLYN)

Structure

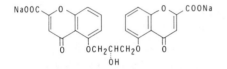

Mode of action

Cromoglycate acts by inhibiting the release of histamine and the slow-reacting substance of anaphylaxis from mast cells in the mucosae of the bronchial tree, nose, and eye.

Uses

Prophylaxis of asthma, allergic rhinitis, and allergic conjunctivitis.

Dosages

Asthma: 20 mg powder q.d.s., by inhalation, via a 'spinhaler'; 2 mg q.d.s. by aerosol; or 20 mg q.d.s. via a nebulizer.

Allergic rhinitis: Two drops of a 2 per cent solution q.d.s., intranasally.

Allergic conjunctivitis: One or two drops of a 2 per cent solution q.d.s., to the eyes.

Important adverse effects

The common adverse effects are trivial but occasionally bronchiolar irritation, causing bronchoconstriction, may follow inhalation. This may be overcome by the use of 0.2 mg isoprenaline incorporated into the powder formulation.

CYCLOPHOSPHAMIDE

Structure

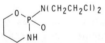

(Compare melphalan, chlorambucil.)

Mode of action

Cyclophosphamide is an alkylating agent (see busulphan).

Uses

A wide variety of malignant diseases, including Hodgkin's and non-Hodgkin's lymphomas, and multiple myeloma. It is also used in the treatment of various forms of necrotizing vasculitis, e.g. Wegener's granulomatosis, in which conditions it may act as an immunosuppressant.

Dosages

Dosages vary widely and, as with all cytotoxic agents, specialist advice on dosage regimens should be sought.

Kinetic data

Cyclophosphamide itself is relatively inactive. In the liver it is metabolized to aldophosphamide, which circulates to other tissues where it is converted to cytotoxic alkylating derivatives, t_{12} 7 h. Cyclophosphamide and its metabolites are filtered by the renal glomerulus, but undergo extensive passive tubular reabsorption; thus only about 10 per cent of the administered dose is excreted unchanged in the urine. The polar metabolites are probably the cause of the chemical cystitis (see below).

Important adverse effects

Bone marrow suppression is dose-related. Hair loss is common. Anorexia, nausea, and vomiting occur at higher dosages.

A haemorrhagic cystitis occurs in about 10 per cent of cases, and bladder fibrosis may occur. This effect is thought to be due to toxic polar metabolites of cyclophosphamide, particularly acrolein. Measures taken to try to reduce its incidence include increasing fluid intake, alkalinizing the urine, and bladder irrigation. However, recently the administration of mesna (sodium-2-mercapto-ethane sulphonate), which forms a non-toxic compound with acrolein, has been shown to decrease the incidence of haemorrhagic cystitis. Because mesna has a shorter half-time than cyclophosphamide (1.5 h) it has to be given several times after each dose. Its use does not prevent the other adverse effects of cyclophosphamide.

Water retention and hyponatraemia may occur at high dosage, probably due to an effect on the distal renal tubule.

Cyclophosphamide should not be used during pregnancy. The dose may have to be reduced in patients with severe liver disease.

Infertility, caused by a testicular effect, resulting in diminished numbers of normal sperm, may occur during long-term therapy.

Interactions

Cyclophosphamide inhibits pseudocholinesterase and prolongs the neuromuscular blocking effect of suxamethonium. An alternative muscle relaxant should be used in patients taking cyclophosphamide, and perhaps other alkylating agents (see p.591).

Allopurinol potentiates the toxic effect of cyclophosphamide on the bone marrow.

For the possible interaction of cytotoxic drugs with live vaccines see p.288.

CYTARABINE

Structure

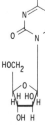

Mode of action

Cytarabine (cytosine arabinoside, or Ara-C) is converted within the cell to phosphorylated derivatives which competitively inhibit DNA polymerase, thus inhibiting the synthesis of DNA. This effect is specific to the S phase of cell division.

Uses

Acute leukaemias.

Dosages

Cytarabine is given i.v., usually in combination therapy (see Chapter 33, p.594). Recommended dosages vary, but an example would be 2 mg/kg by rapid i.v. injection daily until a response or toxicity occurs. Cytarabine may also be given by i.v. infusion, the total dose being infused over 24 h.

Kinetic data

Cytarabine is rapidly metabolized in the liver and many other cells, $t_{1/2} = 3$ h. It is mostly (90 per cent) excreted in the urine as the inactive metabolite, uracil arabinoside (Ara-U).

Important adverse effects

Anorexia, nausea, and vomiting are common, especially after rapid i.v. injection.

Stomatitis is uncommon.

Bone marrow suppression is dose-related (see Chapter 33, p.595).

Interaction

For the possible interaction with live vaccines see p.288.

DANTROLENE

Structure

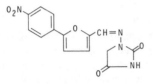

Mode of action

Dantrolene relieves muscle spasticity by a direct effect on skeletal muscle. This effect may be related to a decrease in the amount of calcium released from the sarcoplasmic reticulum, leading to a dissociation of excitation–contraction coupling.

Uses

To alleviate muscle spasm in spasticity e.g. in multiple sclerosis, spinal cord injury, and cerebral palsy.

In the treatment of malignant hyperpyrexia (see Chapter 8).

Dosages

Oral: In order to minimize adverse effects start treatment with a low dosage, increasing according to response. Initial oral dosage should be 25 mg o.d., increasing at weekly intervals to 25 mg b.d., 50 mg b.d., 50 mg t.d.s., and 75 mg t.d.s. In a few cases up to 100 mg q.d.s. may be required.

Intravenous: In malignant hyperpyrexia, after discontinuing anaesthetic drugs, give 1 mg/kg dantrolene, and repeat as required up to a maximum of 10 mg/kg.

Kinetic data

Dantrolene is slowly and incompletely absorbed. It is mostly metabolized in the liver and excreted in the bile (50 per cent) and urine (25 per cent); $t_{1/2} = 9$ h.

Important adverse effects

Adverse effects are most common during prolonged oral treatment, and rarely occur after i.v. administration. The main effects are on the muscles and nervous system. Dantrolene causes muscle weakness and hypotonia, and that tends to reduce its efficacy as a treatment for spasticity. Common central nervous system effects include drowsiness, dizziness, vertigo, and nervousness. Patients should be warned to take care when driving or operating machinery.

Dantrolene may rarely cause liver damage, usually after prolonged treatment with high dosages. Furthermore, because it is mostly metabolized by the liver caution must be taken in patients with liver disease. Liver function should be monitored before and during therapy. Dantrolene should not be used in patients with *active* liver disease.

Dantrolene should be used with caution in patients with cardiac or pulmonary disease.

Interactions

Other drugs acting on the central nervous system (e.g. alcohol, tranquillizers) potentiate the central effects of dantrolene.

The risk of liver damage may be increased in patients taking oestrogens.

DAPSONE

Structure

$$H_2N-\!\!\langle\rangle\!\!-SO_2-\!\!\langle\rangle\!\!-NH_2$$

(Compare sulphonamides.)

Mode of action

Antibacterial—see sulphonamides.
Its mode of action in dermatitis herpetiformis is unknown.

Uses

Malaria prophylaxis (with pyrimethamine).
Leprosy.
Dermatitis herpetiformis.

Dosages

Malaria prophylaxis: given as Maloprim® tablets, one tablet each week (one tablet contains 100 mg dapsone and 12.5 mg pyrimethamine).

Kinetic data

Slowly, but well absorbed. Metabolism—see sulphonamides. $T_{1/2} = 24$ h.

Important adverse effects

Allergic reactions are common, particularly skin reactions, but fever and hepatitis may also occur.

A dose-related, reversible, haemolytic anaemia may occur, due to a metabolite, and is more pronounced in patients with G6PD deficiency (see Chapter 8).

DESFERRIOXAMINE (DEFEROXAMINE)

Structure

$$NH_2(CH_2)_5\overset{|}{\underset{HO}{N}}-\overset{\parallel}{\underset{O}{C}}(CH_2)_2\overset{\parallel}{\underset{O}{C}}NH(CH_2)_5\overset{|}{\underset{HO}{N}}-\overset{\parallel}{\underset{O}{C}}(CH_2)_2\overset{\parallel}{\underset{O}{C}}NH(CH_2)_5\overset{|}{\underset{HO}{N}}-\overset{\parallel}{\underset{O}{C}}CH_3$$

Mode of action

Desferrioxamine is an iron-chelating drug which chelates iron mole for mole (i.e. 1 g of desferrioxamine chelates a maximum of 85 mg of iron). It removes all the iron bound to ferritin and haemosiderin but much less from transferrin and none from haemoglobin, myoglobin, and iron-containing enzymes such as the cytochromes.

Uses

Acute iron poisoning.
Chronic iron overload secondary to repeated blood transfusion (e.g. in thalassaemia).

Dosages

Acute iron poisoning

Gastric lavage with desferrioxamine 2 g/l. Leave 10 g in 50 ml water in the stomach. Give 2 g i.m. and repeat after 12 h (1 g in a child). Give 15 mg/kg/h by continuous i.v. infusion to a maximum of 80 mg/kg/day.

Chronic iron overload

Intramuscular: 25 mg/kg/day.

Subcutaneous: Initially 2 g daily by continuous s.c. infusion over 6–12 h. In most patients this will produce a maximum effect on urinary iron excretion which should be checked. In all patients however higher dosages should be tried since in a few greater effects may be obtained from daily dosages of up to 16 g.

Kinetic data

Desferrioxamine is poorly absorbed and must be given parenterally. It is metabolized by enzymes in the plasma and also excreted unchanged in the urine.

Important adverse effects

The most important adverse effect during i.v.

infusion is hypotension, perhaps because of histamine release. It should not be injected rapidly i.v. Other adverse effects are rare and include skin rashes, dizziness and convulsions, pain after i.m. injections, and gastro-intestinal irritation after oral administration. It is not yet known if there are serious adverse effects associated with the long-term subcutaneous administration of high dosages in chronic iron overload.

Interactions

Vitamin C (100–200 mg orally o.d.) improves the therapeutic effect of desferrioxamine in chronic iron overload.

DIPYRIDAMOLE

Structure

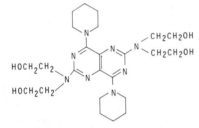

Mode of action

Dipyridamole inhibits ADP-induced platelet aggregation *in vitro*, and is thought to have a similar effect *in vivo*, thus inhibiting intra-vascular clot formation.

Uses

Prevention of emboli from prosthetic heart valves (in combination with aspirin, q.v. under salicylates).

Dosages

100–200 mg t.d.s. or q.d.s., orally.

Kinetic data

Well absorbed.

Important adverse effects

The most common effects are headache, and diarrhoea. Peripheral vasodilatation may result in facial flushing.

Interactions

Because of its effects on platelets, dipyridamole may impair haemostasis in patients who bleed while taking anticoagulants.

DISOPYRAMIDE

Structure

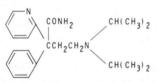

Mode of action

Disopyramide is a Class I anti-arrhythmic drug whose direct actions on the cardiac conducting tissues are virtually identical to those of quinidine and procainamide. These effects are discussed under lignocaine.

In addition, and in common with quinidine, disopyramide has potent anticholinergic effects. It also has a negative inotropic action.

Uses

Although it has been shown that disopyramide can be of use in the treatment of both supraventricular and ventricular arrhythmias, it is more useful in the latter.

Dosages

Intravenous: Loading dose 2 mg/kg over 30 min followed by an i.v. infusion of 400 micrograms/kg/h to a total of 800 mg daily.
Oral: 100–200 mg six hourly.

Kinetic data

Disopyramide is moderately well absorbed. About 50 per cent of a dose is eliminated unchanged by renal excretion, and 20 per cent as the mono-*N*-dealkylated metabolite. $T_{1/2} =$ 6 h. The clearance is reduced in renal failure and dosages should be reduced.

At therapeutic plasma concentrations the percentage of disopyramide bound to plasma proteins varies between 30 and 80 per cent, because its binding to plasma proteins is saturable. Thus the unbound fraction of drug in the plasma is increased at higher concentrations and this results in a higher renal and metabolic clearance. The exact clinical significance of this has not yet been worked out.

Important adverse effects

(a) Cardiac

The negative inotropic effect of disopyramide may cause hypotension and aggravate cardiac failure. This is particularly important during i.v. treatment, and it is important to avoid too rapid infusion during the loading phase. Disopyramide prolongs the QT interval but less so than quinidine, and ventricular arrhythmias as a result are also less common.

(b) Anticholinergic

Dry mouth, blurred vision, and constipation are common. Disopyramide may exacerbate glaucoma.

(c) Other

Nausea, vomiting, and diarrhoea sometimes occur. Hypoglycaemia has been reported.

Interactions

Disopyramide should not be used with other drugs which prolong the QT interval (e.g. quinidine, procainamide, and amiodarone).

The anticholinergic effects of other drugs (e.g. tricyclic antidepressants, anti-Parkinsonian anticholinergics) will add to the anticholinergic effects of disopyramide.

The negative inotropic effects of other drugs, e.g. β-adrenoceptor antagonists, will be potentiated.

Hypokalaemia, e.g. due to diuretics, decreases the effects of Class I anti-arrhythmic drugs on the cardiac action potential, and the hypokalaemia should be corrected when using disopyramide.

DOPAMINE

Structure

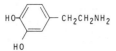

Mode of action

In low doses (1–5 micrograms/kg/min) dopamine is active on dopamine receptors in renal arterioles and causes renal vasodilatation, which results in increased renal flow and diuresis. This action is useful in circumstances in which poor renal perfusion has led to the vicious circle of oliguria and worsening renal function.

In higher does (5–20 micrograms/kg/min) dopamine may also act on cardiac β_1-adrenoceptors and produce a positive inotropic effect.

Large doses of dopamine (above 20 micro-grams/kg/min) may result in an effect on α-adrenoceptors causing tachycardia, cardiac arrhythmias, and vasoconstriction, with deleterious effects such as hypertension, angina, and even renal vasoconstriction.

Uses

Dopamine is used in the treatment of shock accompanied by poor perfusion, low cardiac output, and impending renal failure associated with such conditions as myocardial infarction (cardiogenic shock), severe trauma, septicaemia, and after cardiac surgery. It has also been used in the treatment of severe heart failure.

Because of its tendency to decrease peripheral resistance in low to medium doses, and also to reduce intravascular volume, the blood volume should be restored with plasma expanders when necessary before dopamine is used.

Dosages

The mode of administration of dopamine is important. It is infused i.v. generally in a final concentration of 1600 micrograms/ml (i.e. 800 mg dopamine in 500 ml of physiological saline or 5 per cent dextrose). Infusion is usually started at 2 micrograms/kg/min and the dose should be increased in increments of 5 micrograms/kg/min according to the patient's response, monitored by measuring urine output, blood pressure, vascular perfusion, heart rate, and, if available, central venous pressure. The maximum dose should usually be 20 micrograms/kg/min. Higher doses have been used but careful monitoring for adverse effects is necessary.

Kinetic data

Dopamine is eliminated mainly by metabolism (oxidative deamination, conjugation, and other routes). The $t_{1/2}$ is short (2 min) and it is therefore given by continuous i.v. infusion.

Important adverse effects

In high dosage (see 'mode of action' above) sinus tachycardia, ectopic beats and other arrhythmias, and vasoconstriction, with a risk of angina, hypertension and renal impairment, are almost inevitable. Other common adverse effects include nausea, vomiting, and dyspnoea. If accidental overdosage occurs the α-adrenergic effects, such as hypertension, can be quickly controlled by discontinuing the infusion and administering the α-adrenoceptor antagonist phentolamine.

Interactions

Dopamine should not be used in patients taking MAO inhibitors, since they inhibit its metabolism.

DOXAPRAM

Structure

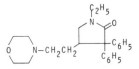

Mode of action

Doxapram is an analeptic drug, i.e. it is a non-specific stimulant of the central nervous system. However, in low doses it is relatively specific in stimulating respiration principally by stimulating carotid chemoreceptors, but also by stimulating the respiratory centre in the medulla oblongata (cf. nikethamide).

Uses

Respiratory stimulants have a limited role in the short-term management of ventilatory failure in patients with chronic obstructive airways disease. A doxapram infusion may be of use to stimulate respiration in those patients with hypoxia and hypercapnia who cannot tolerate even as low a concentration of inspired oxygen as 24 per cent without worsening of CO_2 narcosis, and in whom artificial ventilation is contra-indicated. A single i.v. dose of a respiratory stimulant (e.g. nikethamide) may also be useful in rousing a patient for long enough to help cough up bronchial secretions.

They should not be used if there is no retention of carbon dioxide, or in patients with respiratory failure secondary to neurological or muscle disease, or in overdose. They are of no value in the long-term treatment of chronic respiratory failure.

Dosages

0.5–4 mg/min by continuous i.v. infusion depending on response. Monitor progress frequently with arterial blood gas and pH measurements.

Kinetic data

Doxapram has a half-time after i.v. injection of about 3 h.

Important adverse effects

Adverse effects are common and dose-related. They include tachycardia and cardiac arrhythmias, nausea and vomiting, dizziness, restlessness, tremor, and convulsions.

Doxapram should not be given to patients with respiratory failure in association with neurological disease (including cerebral oedema), or to patients with status asthmaticus, coronary artery disease, hyperthyroidism, or severe hypertension. It should be administered only with great care to patients with a history of epilepsy.

It is not helpful, and may be dangerous, in patients with respiratory depression due to overdose with hypnotics or sedatives. However, it may be used to treat respiratory depression due to buprenorphine if naloxone has not proved successful.

Interaction

The effects of doxapram are potentiated by MAO inhibitors and the combination should be avoided.

DOXORUBICIN

Structure

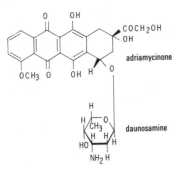

adriamycinone

daunosamine

Mode of action

Doxorubicin (former generic name adriamycin) is a cytotoxic antibiotic. It inhibits DNA-dependent RNA and DNA synthesis, by intercalating between DNA base pairs. It is not specific for any phase of the cell cycle.

Uses

Acute leukaemias.

Many different malignant tumours, including a variety of carcinomas, sarcomas, and lymphomas.

Dosages

Doxorubicin is frequently used in combination therapy (see Chapter 33, p.594). A typical i.v. dose is 60 mg/m^2 body surface area given once every 3 weeks. It should be administered through a fast-running infusion line to avoid thrombophlebitis and local extravasation. The total dose should not normally exceed 600 mg/m^2 because of the adverse effects on the heart.

Kinetic data

Poorly absorbed and therefore not used orally. Highly bound to tissues resulting in a long $t_{1/2}$ (17 h). Metabolized by the liver with 75 per cent excretion in bile as drug and active metabolite (adriamycinol). Dosages should be reduced if liver function is poor. Urine excretion accounts for about 10 per cent.

Important adverse effects

Nausea and vomiting are common and usually moderate in severity. Diarrhoea and stomatitis may also occur. Bone marrow suppression is dose-related (see Chapter 33). Doxorubicin is cardiotoxic and can cause a cardiomyopathy. This effect is dose-related (see dosages above). Treatment should be withheld if there is evidence of a cardiomyopathy or of ECG changes (e.g. sinus tachycardia or other arrhythmias, T wave flattening or inversion, ST segment depression). Doxorubicin should not be used in patients with pre-existing heart disease.

Interactions

For the possible interaction with live vaccines see p.288. Doxorubicin may enhance the hepatotoxicity of 6-mercaptopurine and azathioprine.

ERGOTAMINE

Structure

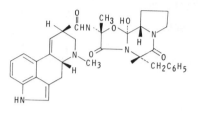

Mode of action

Ergot compounds cause vascular constriction, and contraction of uterine muscle. The mode of action in migraine is unknown.

Uses

Migraine.

Dosages

2 mg orally or sublingually at the onset of an attack, and repeated in 30–60 min if required. Not more than 6 mg in one day or 16 mg in one week.

In severe attacks parenteral ergotamine may be used—125–500 micrograms, i.m. or s.c.

Kinetic data

Poorly absorbed, especially during an attack of migraine. Mostly metabolized; $t_{1/2} = 3$ h.

Important adverse effects

Peripheral vasoconstriction is common and ergotamine is contra-indicated in patients with established arterial disease. Overdosage is extremely dangerous, and proper instructions as to the correct dosage must be given to patients. Even in those without vascular disease overdosage may lead to severe peripheral vasoconstriction and gangrene of toes and feet. Vasoconstriction may be relieved by the use of an α-adrenoceptor antagonist (e.g. phenoxybenzamine) or by a directly acting vasodilator such as sodium nitroprusside.

Its use is contra-indicated in pregnancy because of the direct effect on the uterus, and during breast-feeding because of its passage into the milk.

Nausea and vomiting are common during prolonged use and withdrawal may result in headache.

ERYTHROMYCIN

Structure

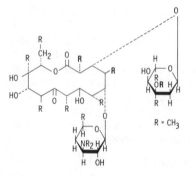

Mode of action

Inhibition of bacterial protein synthesis by binding to 50S ribosomal subunits.

Uses

Erythromycin is active against Gram-positive cocci, Gram-negative cocci, *Haemophilus influenzae, Mycoplasma pneumoniae, Legionella pneumophila*, and Gram-positive rods such as *Clostridium perfringens* and *C. diphtheriae*.

It is used in many infections with the above organisms in which penicillin would be the treatment of choice but where the patient is penicillin-sensitive. The most important exception is meningococcal meningitis in which chloramphenicol is the best alternative to penicillin. Erythromycin is the treatment of choice in Legionnaires' disease.

Dosage

250–1000 mg q.d.s., orally or i.v.

Kinetic data

Absorption is variable and dependent on the salt form used—the estolate is best absorbed (the stearate and ethylsuccinate being the two other available salts). Erythromycin is 50 per cent metabolized and most of the remainder is excreted unchanged in the bile. $T_{1/2} = 2$ h.

Important adverse effects

Until quite recently it was thought that intrahepatic cholestasis due to erythromycin was generally due to the estolate. Recent studies, however, suggest that jaundice may occur equally frequently with all the salts of erythromycin, and that the estolate may be preferable for some patients and for children, who may find that other salts cause nausea, vomiting, or anorexia.

Intravenous administration often results in thrombophlebitis, particularly if high doses are used. Otherwise the most frequent adverse effects are gastro-intestinal, and include nausea, vomiting, epigastric pain, and diarrhoea. Allergic reactions, particularly skin rashes, occur rarely.

ETHAMBUTOL

Structure

$$CH_3CH_2\overset{\overset{\displaystyle CH_2OH}{|}}{C}HNHCH_2CH_2NH\overset{\overset{\displaystyle CH_2OH}{|}}{C}HCH_2CH_3$$

(Note the similarity to EDTA.)

Mode of action

Bacteriostatic to mycobacteria by an unknown mechanism.

Uses

Tuberculosis.

Dosages

Initially 25 mg/kg/day given as a single oral dose. After a few weeks the dose is usually reduced to 15 mg/kg/day.

Kinetic data

Well absorbed. $T_{1/2} = 4$ h. Mostly excreted unchanged by the kidney.

Important adverse effects

Optic neuritis frequently occurs at dosages of over 25 mg/kg/day. It may result in loss of visual acuity, ocular scotomata, or colour vision defects.

ETHOSUXIMIDE

Structure

Mode of action

Although the precise mode of action is not understood, in animals ethosuximide raises seizure thresholds to various convulsant stimuli.

Uses

Generalized absence seizures (petit mal).

Dosages

Adults and children over 6 years: 500 mg orally o.d. initially, increasing no more frequently than weekly to the minimal effective dose (usually no more than 1.5–2.0 g).

Kinetic data

Well absorbed. Mostly metabolized. $T_{1/2}$ 60 h. Optimal control of absence seizures is attained at serum concentrations of 280–700μmol/l (40–100μg/ml).

Important adverse effects

Adverse effects are few and usually limited to gastro-intestinal disturbances and CNS effects such as drowsiness, mood change, and dizziness.

5-FLUOROURACIL

Structure

Mode of action

5-fluorouracil inhibits thymidylate synthetase, and hence decreases the production of thymidylic acid, the deoxyribonucleotide of thymine (5-methyluracil), a DNA pyrimidine base. Thus DNA synthesis is blocked. It is specific to the S phase of the cell cycle.

Uses

Carcinomas of breast, ovary, and skin.
Adenocarcinomas of the gastro-intestinal tract.

Dosages

5-fluorouracil may be given i.v. or topically. There is a variety of different regimens but an example would be the palliative treatment of colorectal carcinoma in which 5-fluorouracil may be given in a dose of 12 mg/kg i.v. daily for 5 days every 4 weeks.

Kinetic data

Poorly absorbed. After i.v. administration the apparent $t_{1/2}$ is about 20 min, but intracellular concentrations persist for much longer. 5-fluorouracil is converted inside the cell to its deoxynucleotide, 5-fluorodeoxyuridylate, which is pharmacologically active. Further metabolism occurs in the liver, and the inactive products are excreted in the urine (10–15 per cent) and as CO_2 in the breath (60–90 per cent).

Important adverse effects

Anorexia, nausea and vomiting are common. Stomatitis and diarrhoea are less so, but are indications for withholding treatment. Bone marrow suppression is dose-related (see Chapter 33, p.595).
Alopecia and dermatitis can occur.
Cerebellar ataxia occurs rarely.

Interaction

For the possible interaction with live vaccines see p.288.

FOLIC ACID (PTEROYLGLUTAMIC ACID)

Structure

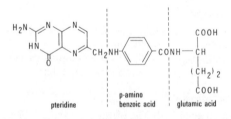

Mode of action

Folic acid is converted to several congeners of tetrahydrofolic acid, each of which plays an essential role in intracellular metabolism. The metabolic processes involved are as follows: synthesis of purines and thymidylate; conversion of serine to glycine and of homocysteine to methionine; metabolism of histidine; and the utilization and generation of formate.

Uses

Folate deficiency (prevention and treatment).

Dosages

Prevention of folate deficiency: the daily requirement of folate is 50 micrograms but in pregnancy this increases to 200 micrograms or more. Because dietary folate intake may not be sufficient folate is administered in a usual daily oral dose of 200–500 micrograms during pregnancy, in combination with an iron salt.
Treatment of folate deficiency: 10–20 mg o.d., orally for a week or two followed by a maintenance dose of 5 mg o.d.

Kinetic data

Folic acid is mostly absorbed in the upper jejunum. Its metabolism to active compounds (e.g. tetrahydrofolate) is dose-dependent, being almost complete at low doses (100 micrograms), but only 10–50 per cent at higher doses (5–15 mg). If folate does not enter the body the total stores are depleted within 4 months (contrast vitamin B_{12}).

Important adverse effects

Folic acid is well tolerated even in high doses and adverse effects are exceedingly rare, and limited to hypersensitivity reactions.

It should never be administered to patients with pernicious anaemia without concurrent administration of vitamin B_{12} since it does not prevent, and may precipitate, the onset of subacute combined degeneration of the spinal cord.

FRUSEMIDE (FUROSEMIDE)

Structure

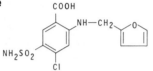

Mode of action

Frusemide is a loop diuretic, capable of producing a greater diuresis than thiazides, triamterene, or amiloride. Its efficacy is similar to that of bumetanide (q.v.) It is called a loop diuretic because it inhibits sodium and chloride reabsorption in the ascending limb of the loop of Henle, with a resulting increase in sodium excretion with a decrease in free water clearance. Potassium secretion in the distal convoluted tubule is increased because of exchange of potassium for sodium, under the influence of both aldosterone and the increased intraluminal sodium concentration. This leads to increased potassium excretion.

The action of frusemide in the treatment of acute pulmonary oedema is complex. Intravenously administered frusemide will reduce pulmonary vascular congestion and pulmonary venous pressure within a few minutes, well before it has an appreciable diuretic effect. This action is thought to be due to systemic venous dilatation (i.e. a reduction in cardiac pre-load).

Uses

Oedema due to cardiac failure, hepatic disease, nephrotic syndrome, and drugs (e.g. carbenoxolone).

Acute pulmonary oedema.

Acute and chronic renal failure (note dose).

Dosages

As a diuretic:
orally: 40–160 mg o.d.
i.v.: 20–160 mg (also acute pulmonary oedema).
In renal failure:
i.v. infusion 250–2000 mg at a rate not exceeding 4 mg/min.
orally: 250–2000 mg/day.

Kinetic data

Poorly absorbed (about 50 per cent). Absorption may be impaired in severe cardiac failure. $T_{1/2} = 1$ h. Mainly excreted unchanged in the urine.

Important adverse effects

Hypokalaemia, hyponatraemia, and dehydration are the most important. Hypokalaemia may be prevented or treated with potassium supplements (q.v.) or potassium-sparing diuretics (e.g. spironolactone, amiloride, or triamterene). Hypomagnesaemia may also occur.

Hyperglycaemia is usually not of clinical importance, although in diabetics increased doses of oral hypoglycaemics may be needed.

Hyperuricaemia occurs but rarely causes frank gout.

In patients with prostatic hypertrophy acute urinary retention may be precipitated.

In hepatic insufficiency encephalopathy may be precipitated, particularly if hypokalaemia occurs.

Rapid intravenous injection of high doses may result in cochlear damage (usually reversible).

Interactions

Frusemide diminishes the excretion of lithium. The dose of lithium should be halved.

Hypokalaemia potentiates the effects of cardiac glycosides and diminishes the effects of anti-arrhythmic drugs such as procainamide and quinidine.

The nephrotoxic effects of cephaloridine and the nephrotoxic and ototoxic effects of the aminoglycoside antibiotics are potentiated.

FUSIDIC ACID (SODIUM FUSIDATE)

Structure

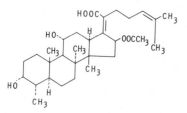

Mode of action

Fusidic acid is bactericidal to staphylococci, and acts by inhibition of bacterial protein synthesis.

Uses

Infections due to penicillin-resistant staphylococci, particularly osteomyelitis.

Dosages

Fusidic acid 250 mg = sodium fusidate 175 mg. The dosages given here are for sodium fusidate.

Oral: 500 mg eight-hourly.

Intravenous: 500 mg by infusion over 6 h, t.d.s.

Local applications: Formulations contain 2 per cent fusidic acid or sodium fusidate, and are applied up to four times daily.

Kinetic data

Fusidic acid is well absorbed. It is widely distributed to body tissues, including bone, but does not normally penetrate into the CSF. It is mostly metabolized in the liver and excreted in the bile; $t_{1/2} = 5$ h.

Important adverse effects

After oral therapy adverse effects are usually limited to nausea, vomiting, and skin rashes. Rarely reversible liver damage may occur.

After i.v. infusion thrombophlebitis can occur and infusion ideally should be via a large cannula in a large vein, and at a slow rate (see dosages above). Liver damage is more likely after high dosages of i.v fusidic acid than after oral therapy.

GLYCERYL TRINITRATE AND ISOSORBIDE DINITRATE

Structures
Glyceryl trinitrate:

$$
\begin{array}{l}
CH_2 \!-\! ONO_2 \\
| \\
CH \!-\! ONO_2 \\
| \\
CH_2 \!-\! ONO_2
\end{array}
$$

Isosorbide dinitrate (sorbide nitrate):

Mode of action

The action of the nitrates in relieving angina pectoris is complex. Three main mechanisms are involved:

1. Peripheral arteriolar vasodilatation with reduction in peripheral resistance and lowering of blood pressure. This leads to a decrease in cardiac work, and a reduction in myocardial oxygen requirements.

2. Peripheral venous vasodilatation results in peripheral venous pooling, a reduction in left ventricular end-diastolic pressure, and a reduction in resistance to coronary blood flow during diastole.

3. The vasodilatory effects of the nitrates may also affect certain areas of the coronary arteriolar bed, redistributing blood flow to areas of myocardial ischaemia. This may be of particular importance in angina due to coronary arterial spasm.

The action of nitrates in heart failure depends on venous and arterial vasodilatation, with consequent reduction in preload and afterload.

Uses

Angina pectoris.
Cardiac failure.

Dosages

Glyceryl trinitrate:
Angina, one to two 0.5 mg tablets sublingually on occurrence of pain or in immediate anticipation of the pain (e.g. before exercise or an expected emotional stress); ointment, 1–2 in (2.5–5 cm) of a 2 per cent ointment rubbed into the skin, usually of the anterior chest.
Isosorbide dinitrate:
Angina, 5–20 mg b.d., t.d.s., or q.d.s., orally;
Heart failure, 10–30 mg q.d.s., orally.

Kinetic data

Because glyceryl trinitrate undergoes extensive first-pass metabolism in the liver it is administered sublingually and is well and rapidly absorbed through the oral mucosa whence it enters the systemic circulation.

Isosorbide is absorbed from the gut and is extensively metabolized to active metabolites. It is therefore active by oral administration.

The $t_{1/2}$ of glyceryl trinitrate and isosorbide is 30 min.

Important adverse effects

Vasodilatation may result in throbbing headache, sinus tachycardia, and hypotension. Tolerance to headache may develop with prolonged use. Patients should be advised to swallow any remnants of a sublingual tablet of glyceryl trinitrate once relief of anginal pain has occurred, to try to minimize these acute effects.

GOLD SALTS (SODIUM AUROTHIOMALATE)

Structure

```
        CH₂COONa
        |
AuSCHCOONa
```

Mode of action

Although the detailed pharmacological actions of gold in rheumatoid and related arthritides are unknown, broadly speaking it suppresses inflammatory and immune responses. It is taken up by macrophages and inhibits phagocytosis and lysosomal enzyme activity; it reduces the concentrations of rheumatoid factor, and immunoglobulins; and it suppresses cell-mediated immune reactions.

Uses

Severe, active rheumatoid arthritis. Gold is toxic and its use should be restricted to cases particularly likely to benefit from its use — this usually needs specialist opinion.

Dosages

The patient's tolerance should first be tested by i.m. doses of 1, 5, and 10 mg at weekly intervals. Then, if no adverse effects occur, 50 mg is given i.m. once weekly until a therapeutic response occurs, following which the frequency of dosing may be reduced according to the clinical response. Many patients can be managed on 50 mg i.m. every 4–6 weeks.

If the patient relapses the dose should be

increased to 50 mg i.m. weekly then read-justed as above. Treatment should be continued indefinitely.

Kinetic data

Erratically absorbed after i.m. injection (time to peak plasma concentrations = 4–6 h). Eliminated unchanged in the urine. $T_{1/2}$ 6 days.

Important adverse effects

Adverse effects are common, occurring in up to 40 per cent of cases. They may be serious in about 10 per cent.

Skin rashes occur in about 25 per cent of cases.

Blood disorders occur occasionally, and may be severe and fatal. They consist of thrombocytopenia, agranulocytosis, and aplastic anaemia.

Traces of proteinuria are common and unimportant, but heavy proteinuria indicates more serious renal damage, and may be associated with the nephrotic syndrome due to a membranous glomerulonephritis.

Stomatitis with oral ulceration occurs in about 8 per cent of cases, and other gastro-intestinal symptoms, such as nausea, vomiting, and abdominal discomfort, are common.

Severe reactions to gold therapy may be controlled by the use of corticosteroids, with or without the addition of dimercaprol or penicillamine to hasten elimination.

Interaction

When gold salts are used in combination with chloroquine there is an increased risk of exfoliative dermatitis, and this combination should not be used.

GRISEOFULVIN

Structure

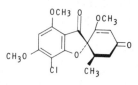

Mode of action

Griseofulvin binds to keratin and renders it resistant to fungal infection. New growths of skin, hair, and nails are the first to become free of infection and then as the fungus-infected tissues are shed they are replaced by uninfected tissues. It follows, therefore, that treatment should be continued until the diseased tissue has been shed (see below under 'Dosages').

Uses

Griseofulvin is used in the treatment of ring-worm (*Tinea*) infections of skin, hair, and

nails, particularly when these are widespread and intractable.

Dosages

0.5–1 g o.d., orally for at least 4 weeks (hair and skin infections), 6 months (fingernails), or 12 months (toenails). It should be taken after meals, when its absorption is improved.

Kinetic data

Almost completely metabolized by the liver. $T_{1/2}$ = 15 h.

Important adverse effects

Headaches are the most common adverse effect and may be severe. Griseofulvin may precipitate an attack of acute intermittent porphyria (see Chapter 8).

Interactions

Griseofulvin induces the metabolism of warfarin by the liver and may reduce its effects.

HEPARIN

Structure

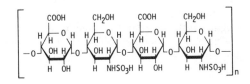

The value of *n* is variable, yielding molecular weights in the range 6000–20 000

Mode of action

Heparin is a mucopolysaccharide which is acidic and carries a negative charge at a physiological pH. It enhances the interaction between antithrombin III and both thrombin and those factors involved in the intrinsic clotting cascade. It also inhibits fibrin-induced platelet aggregation.

Uses

As an anticoagulant in the treatment of deep venous thrombosis and pulmonary embolism, or in the prevention of deep venous thrombosis.

Dosages

Prophylaxis: 5000 i.u. every 8–12 h, s.c.

Treatment: loading dose, 5000 i.u., i.v.; maintenance dose, 1000–1500 i.u./ h, by i.v. infusion.

These are usual doses, and adjustments may be made on the basis of the partial thromboplastin time.

Kinetic data

Mostly metabolized in the liver. $T_{1/2}$ is dose-dependent — at low doses (<5000 i.u. i.v.) it is about 1 h, increasing to 2–6 h at higher doses.

Important adverse effects

Haemorrhage is a common complication. The effects of heparin may be reversed by an injection of protamine sulphate: 1 mg of protamine neutralizes 100 i.u. of heparin and the dose of protamine can be calculated on this basis within 15 min of a single dose of heparin. Obviously the longer the time after a single dose of heparin, the less heparin there will be in the blood, and the less protamine will be necessary to neutralize its effects. Protamine sulphate should not be given in doses greater than 50 mg and it should be given slowly i.v. (over 10 min) to avoid hypotension, bradycardia and flushing, and nausea and vomiting. Occasionally allergic reactions occur.

HISTAMINE (H₂) ANTAGONISTS

Structures

Cimetidine:

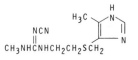

Ranitidine:

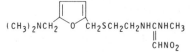

Mode of action

These drugs are specific antagonists of histamine (H₂) receptors in the stomach and thereby reduce gastric acid secretion.

Uses

Gastric ulceration.
Duodenal ulceration.
Reflux oesophagitis.

Dosages

Cimetidine:
Gastric and duodenal ulceration—200 mg t.d.s. and 400 mg at night, orally for 4–6 weeks;

maintenance therapy—400 mg nightly for 6 months;

Reflux oesophagitis—400 mg q.d.s., orally for 6 weeks.

Ranitidine:

150 mg b.d., orally for 4–6 weeks; maintenance therapy—150 mg at night.

Kinetic data

	Cimetidine	Ranitidine
Absorption	Well absorbed	50 per cent
$T_{1/2}$	2 h	2 h
Elimination	Both are mostly excreted unchanged in the urine	

Important adverse effects

These drugs have few adverse effects during short-term treatment. Cimetidine causes an increase in plasma prolactin concentrations and may sometimes cause gynaecomastia; ranitidine does not cause a rise in prolactin.

Although the question has been raised of the potential of these drugs to cause gastric carcinoma, overall there is no evidence that this happens. The suggestion that nitrosamine formation in the stomach, either from the drugs themselves, or from dietary nitrates because of the raised pH of gastric juice, might result in gastric carcinoma is purely speculative. Nonetheless, it is prudent to limit the use of the drug to short-term therapy.

Interactions

There are two mechanisms whereby cimetidine interacts with other drugs:

1. Inhibition of hepatic drug-metabolizing enzymes. Interactions of this type with cimetidine have been described for warfarin, benzodiazepines, and phenytoin.

2. Decrease in liver blood flow, diminishing clearance of drugs with a high extraction ratio (see Chapter 3). Interactions of this type have been described for propranolol and labetalol, whose systemic availability is increased.

Ranitidine has been reported not to interact in either of these ways with other drugs.

HYDRALAZINE

Structure

Mode of action

Peripheral arteriolar dilatation by a direct relaxing effect on vascular smooth muscle. This peripheral dilatation causes a fall in blood pressure with a resultant reflex tachycardia, which can nullify the fall in blood pressure. The reflex tachycardia is prevented by β-adrenoceptor antagonists which therefore potentiate the effect of hydralazine. For this reason hydralazine is now usually used in combination with a β-adrenoceptor antagonist in the treatment of hypertension. In the treatment of heart failure, on the other hand, peripheral vasodilatation lessens cardiac afterload with a resultant increase in cardiac output and little change in blood pressure—no appreciable reflex tachycardia occurs and the heart rate may slow because of improvement in cardiac function.

Uses

Hypertension.
Cardiac failure.

Dosages

Oral: 25–50 mg t.d.s. or q.d.s.
Intravenous or i.m.: 10–20 mg.

Kinetic data

Well absorbed. Extensively metabolized, principally by acetylation, with a bimodal distribution in the general population (see Chapter 8). The $t_{1/2}$ is about 4 h and because the acetylation of hydralazine occurs mainly during the first passage through the liver, the subsequent rate of clearance is not appreciably related to the rate of acetylation, and is therefore unaffected by the patient's acetylator status. Thus the $t_{1/2}$ does not much differ between slow and fast acetylators. The hydralazine which is not acetylated is hydroxylated.

Important adverse effects

Palpitation and tachycardia, nausea, vomiting and diarrhoea, and postural hypotension are all common.

In dosages over 200 mg daily an arthropathy resembling rheumatoid arthritis or a syndrome similar to that of systemic lupus erythematosus (so-called LE or lupus-like syndrome) may occur, especially in slow acetylators. Recently it has been shown that hydralazine-induced lupus is more common in patients with the HLA phenotype DR4.

IDOXURIDINE

Structure

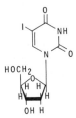

Mode of action

Incorporation into viral DNA of idoxuridine results in faulty transcription leading to failure of viral replication.

Uses

Infections with DNA viruses particularly of the herpes group, e.g. superficial *Herpes simplex* keratitis (dendritic keratitis), and *Herpes zoster* infections (shingles).

Dosages

Skin: application of a 5 per cent solution in dimethylsulphoxide q.d.s.

Eyes: application of a 0.5 per cent ointment five times daily.

Important adverse effects

When applied locally idoxuridine has few adverse effects. Pain or stinging at the site of application occurs transiently, and inflammatory reactions may occur in the eye.

INDOMETHACIN

Structure

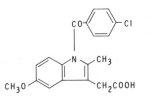

Mode of action

Indomethacin has analgesic, antipyretic, and anti-inflammatory actions. The mechanism of these effects is not fully understood but is probably related to inhibition of prostaglandin synthesis.

Uses

For the relief of the painful symptoms of osteoarthritis, ankylosing spondylitis, rheumatoid arthritis, gout, and acute musculoskeletal disorders.

Dosages

Indomethacin, when used orally, should always be taken with food to minimize gastrointestinal disturbances.

Oral therapy: 25 mg b.d. initially increasing gradually according to clinical response. The usual range of daily dosage is 50–200 mg in divided doses (b.d. or t.d.s.).

Rectal therapy: 75 mg b.d.

Kinetic data

Well absorbed after both oral and rectal administration. Metabolized 80 per cent by various routes to inactive compounds which are excreted in the urine and bile with enterohepatic recycling (50 per cent). $T_{1/2} = 9$ h.

Important adverse effects

Symptomatic adverse effects are very common (35–50 per cent). Gastro-intestinal adverse effects are very common and consist of nausea, vomiting, symptoms of 'dyspepsia', and peptic ulceration, sometimes with haemorrhage. Headache is very common and may be associated with other central nervous system effects such as vertigo, sleep disturbance, and psychiatric problems. Allergic reactions (rashes, angioneurotic oedema, and bronchospasm) occur occasionally, as do blood disorders (e.g. thrombocytopenia). Fluid retention occurs and may occasionally cause peripheral oedema. Hypertension has been reported.

Interactions

Indomethacin may counteract the effects of diuretics because it causes fluid retention.

It antagonizes the hypotensive effect of propranolol, possibly by inhibition of prostaglandin synthetase (cyclo-oxygenase) activity in the kidney.

Since it inhibits platelet aggregation and may cause peptic ulceration, indomethacin should be used with care in patients also taking anticoagulants.

INDORAMIN

Structure

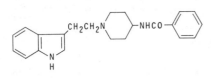

Mode of action

Indoramin is a selective α_1 (post-synaptic)-adrenoceptor antagonist (cf. prazosin), which acts as a peripheral vasodilator and causes little or no reflex tachycardia.

Use

Hypertension

Dosages

25 mg orally b.d. initially, increasing at two-weekly intervals by daily dosages of 25–50 mg to a maximum of 100 mg b.d.

Kinetic data

Indoramin is well absorbed, but almost completely metabolized on its first passage through the liver. The $t_{1/2}$ of indoramin is 5 h. It is not clear how active the metabolites are by comparison with indoramin itself.

Important adverse effects

The most common adverse effect of indoramin is sedation, which is dose-related. Postural hypotension occurs occasionally, particularly at high dosages. Other occasional adverse effects include failure of ejaculation, depression, dizziness, dry mouth, and nasal congestion.

Interactions

The therapeutic effects of indoramin are enhanced by other antihypertensive drugs such as diuretics and β-adrenoceptor antagonists.

Indoramin should not be used in combination with MAO inhibitors.

INSULIN

Structure

Human insulin:

```
Gly
 |
Ile
 |
Val
 |
Glu                              CHAIN A
 |
Gln— Cys— Cys-Thr—Ser —Ile—Cys—Ser—Leu—Tyr—Gln—Leu—Glu—Asn—Tyr—Cys-Asn
                                                                    |
      His— Leu— Cys— Gly—Ser—His—Leu—Val—Glu—Ala—Leu—Tyr—Leu—Val — Cys
             |                                                       |
            Gln              CHAIN B                                Gly
             |                                                       |
            Asn                                                     Glu
             |                                                       |
            Val                                                     Arg
             |                                                       |
            Phe              Thr—Lys—Pro—Thr—Tyr—Phe—Phe—Gly
```

Mode of action

Insulin has multiple effects on the metabolism of carbohydrates, fat, and protein, and acts on specific receptors on cell membranes to regulate various processes as follows:

1. It promotes the transport of glucose into cells and its utilization therein.
2. It increases hepatic glycogen formation and inhibits gluconeogenesis.
3. It inhibits lipolysis.
4. It increases protein synthesis and decreases protein breakdown.

When insulin promotes glucose uptake by cells, potassium influx is also enhanced. This is important because during treatment of diabetic ketoacidosis with insulin the plasma potassium concentration may fall to dangerously low values unless intravenous potassium is given (see p.441). This principle is also applied in the treatment of hyperkalaemia with insulin and glucose.

Uses

Diabetes mellitus.

Dosages and formulations

The dosage of insulin varies widely from individual to individual (see the treatment of diabetes mellitus, Chapter 25).

Until recently insulin formulations were available in three different strengths—20 i.u./ml, 40 i.u./ml, and 80 i.u./ml (U20, U40, and U80). The 1 ml insulin syringes used for the administration of these strengths of insulin are graduated in 20 'marks' and thus one mark on the syringe does not necessarily correspond to one international unit of insulin. For example one mark of U80 insulin equals 4 i.u. of insulin. In an attempt to standardize insulin administration in the UK and elsewhere, a change-over to U100 preparations (i.e. 100 i.u./ml) and to new syringes has recently been implemented.

New 0.5 ml insulin syringes are graduated in international units to a maximum of 50 i.u. and new 1.0 ml syringes are graduated in international units to a maximum of 100 i.u. The marks on these syringes can be ignored for descriptive purposes and dosages can always be expressed in international units. This will avoid the confusion that not infrequently occurs when, for example, the patient talks in marks while the doctor talks in units. Even so, it is important that especial care be taken that there is precise communication between patient and doctor as to the exact dose of insulin the patient is taking, in case this type of confusion arises. The brand names of available insulins are listed in Table P4. They are all available in U100 strengths.

Table P4 *Brand names of preparations of purified insulins available in the UK in U100 (100 i.u./ml) strength (all are highly purified)*

Type of insulin	Boots	Nordisk	Novo	Weddel	Wellcome	Evans	Lilly
Soluble insulin (acid)	—	—	—	—	No brand name	—	—
Soluble insulin (neutral)	Quicksol	Velosulin & Human Velosulin	Actrapid & Human Actrapid	Hypurin Neutral	Neusulin	No brand name	Humulin S
Protamine zinc insulin	—	—	—	Hypurin Protamine Zinc	—	—	—
Isophane insulin	Monophane	Insulatard & Human Insulatard	—	Hypurin Isophane	Neuphane	No brand name	Humulin I
Insulin zinc suspension (semilente)	—	—	Semitard	—	—	—	—
Insulin zinc suspension (lente)	Tempulin	—	Lentard, Monotard, & Human Monotard	Hypurin Lente	Neulente	No brand name	—
Insulin zinc suspension (ultralente)	—	—	Ultratard	—	—	—	—
Biphasic							
Crystalline 75%, neutral 25%	—	—	Rapitard	—	—	—	—
Isophane 70%, neutral 30%	—	Mixtard & Human Mixtard	—	—	—	—	—
Isophane 50%, neutral 50%	—	Initard & Human Initard	—	—	—	—	—

Kinetic data

Insulin is not absorbed from the gut because it is metabolized by the proteolytic enzymes in gut and liver. It is therefore administered parenterally, usually subcutaneously, but in emergencies intravenously.

One must distinguish between insulin itself (or so-called 'soluble' insulin) and the various preparations of insulin designed to alter the absorption characteristics of insulin after parenteral administration. After intravenous injection soluble insulin is rapidly metabolized by the liver and kidney with a $t_{1/2}$ of about 6 min. However, numerous different preparations of insulin are available which release insulin at different rates from the site of injection, and it is the $t_{1/2}$ of *release* of insulin from those preparations (differing from preparation to preparation) which is the prime determinant of the duration of action of the preparation.

The rate of release of insulin from subcutaneous preparations is also influenced, for any one preparation, by the site of injection and by exercise. In general absorption is slightly faster from legs and arms than from the abdomen, and the rate of absorption is increased by exercise.

It should be remembered that if injections are given at intervals of less than about four half-times of release of a preparation (e.g. daily for ultralente, or twice daily for soluble insulin), then a steady state will not occur until four or five half-times of release have elapsed. For example, in the case of ultralente a steady state will not be reached for about 5–7 days. Thus the effect of insulin treatment will be cumulative over that period of time.

Table P5 *Characteristics of commonly used insulin preparations*

---

1. Short-acting insulins
Subcutaneous kinetics
   Time to peak action 2–4 h
   Duration of action 6–12 h
Preparations
   Insulin injection (*soluble* insulin)
   Neutral insulin injection
   Neutral insulin is also a component of some of the preparations listed under 'intermediate-acting insulins'. In those combinations the neutral insulin confers a rapid onset of action.

2. Intermediate-acting insulins
Subcutaneous kinetics
   Time to peak action 3–8 h (but earlier with preparations also containing neutral insulin)
   Duration of action 12–20 h
Preparations
   Insulin zinc suspension (amorphous), *semilente*
   Isophane insulin injection
   Globin zinc insulin injection
   Biphasic insulin injection:
      (a) crystalline insulin 75%, neutral insulin 25%
      (b) isophane insulin 70%, neutral insulin 30%
      (c) isophane insulin 50%, neutral insulin 50%

3. Long-acting insulins
Subcutaneous kinetics
   Time to peak action 6–12 h
   Duration of action 16–30 h
Preparations
   Insulin zinc suspension (crystalline), *ultralente*
   Insulin zinc suspension (mixed), *lente*
   Protamine zinc insulin

Name of Patient..

Address..

....

Tel. No..

Tel. No. of next of kin..

OWN DOCTOR/HOSPITAL CLINIC

Name..

Address..

....

Telephone..

Always carry this Card with you

Issued by The British Diabetic Association
10 Queen Anne Street London W1M 0BD

LB 20580

DAILY INSULIN DOSAGE
MORNING

TYPE OF INSULIN	DOSE In Units	STRENGTH Units per ml. (c.c.)	MARKS on SYRINGE

EVENING

Date of diagnosis ....19.......　Daily carbohydrate intake

Date of issue of card.............................. 19......　.. Grams

Fig. P4. An example of the kind of warning card which should be carried by patients taking insulin therapy. A similar card is available for patients taking oral hypoglycaemic drugs. [Reproduced with the permission of the British Diabetic Association.]

The subcutaneous absorption kinetics of the commonly used insulin preparations are given in Table P5. Most of these formulations are prepared from either beef or porcine pancreas, but there are now also some formulations of human insulin which are prepared either semi-synthetically (by altering a single amino-acid in the structure of porcine insulin) or biosynthetically (by introducing genetic material coding for the production of insulin into *E. coli*).

Important adverse effects

Acute hypoglycaemic reactions are common and result from either insulin overdose or mismanagement of diet. Chronic hypoglycaemia may result in neurological or psychiatric disturbances.

Allergy occurs occasionally, resulting in local skin reactions at the site of injection, or less commonly, generalized reactions.

Lipodystrophy (either atrophy or hypertrophy) may occur at the site of injection. It may be avoided by the use of the modern purified preparations. Lipodystrophy may be reversed by changing from an old-fashioned insulin formulation to a purified variety.

Insulin resistance may occur, necessitating increased doses. This happens to a lesser extent with the use of purified preparations.

Interactions

Numerous hormones and drugs antagonize the effects of insulin, including β-adrenoceptor agonists, corticosteroids, growth hormone, thyroxine, glucagon, diazoxide, and thiazide diuretics.

Non-selective β-adrenoceptor antagonists (e.g. propranolol) may worsen hypoglycaemia, because they block the glycogenolytic effects of adrenaline. They may also block some of the clinical manifestations of an attack of hypoglycaemia.

IRON SALTS

Uses

Iron deficiency anaemia (treatment and prevention).

Dosages

Normal daily iron requirements are 1–2 mg, average daily dietary intake in the UK being 10–20 mg.

Oral iron

In pregnancy daily requirements increase to 3–4 mg and dietary intake should be increased to 30–40 mg daily. This can be achieved using one tablet or capsule of any formulation available in the UK containing a mixture of a ferrous salt and folic acid (see Table 26.2).

Oral treatment of iron deficiency anaemia usually requires between 120 and 180 mg of elemental iron daily. Examples of commonly used dosages are:

Ferrous sulphate, 200 mg t.d.s. (= 60 mg iron t.d.s.).

Ferrous fumarate, 200 mg t.d.s. (= 65 mg iron t.d.s.).

Ferrous succinate, 200 mg b.d. (= 70 mg iron b.d.).

Ferrous gluconate, 600 mg b.d. (= 70 mg iron b.d.).

Numerous slow-release formulations are available for those who cannot tolerate ordinary formulations.

Parenteral iron

Calculate the total body deficit of iron from the following equation (see p.459 for a discussion of its derivation).

iron deficit (mg) =
Hb deficit (g/dl) $\times$ body weight (kg) $\times$ 2.21

Thus a 50 kg woman with a haemoglobin of 8 g/dl (normal 14) will require $(14-8) \times 50 \times 2.21 = 663$ mg of iron.

Intravenous therapy

Note that the intravenous route is hazardous because of the risk of allergic reactions. It is therefore reserved for special cases (e.g.

women with severe anaemia in the third trimester of pregnancy). Intravenous iron is given as iron dextran (50 mg/ml, the total doses required being made up in 500–1000 ml of saline and infused over 6–8 h. It is important to give first a test dose of 50 mg over 10 min and wait a further 10 min for signs of allergy before continuing with the infusion. Careful observation is necessary throughout the infusion and for an hour after. Be prepared to stop the infusion and to treat allergic reactions (see p.604).

Intramuscular therapy

Iron dextran (50 mg iron/ml), 1 ml on the first day, 2 ml on subsequent days.

Iron sorbitol (50 mg iron/ml), 1.5 ml/kg up to a maximum of 100 mg daily or on alternate days.

The number of injections likely to be required can be calculated from the calculated deficit (see above).

Because staining at the i.m. injection site can occur due to leakage of iron along the needle track, a special injection technique is required: draw back the skin over the intended injection site in the buttock as far as it will go; inject deeply into the muscle using a long (5 cm) long-bevelled needle; after injection and removal of the needle the tissues which have been drawn back over the injection point will fall back and create a zigzag needle track. In this way staining can be reduced, although not completely eliminated.

Kinetic data

Medicinal iron behaves in the same way as dietary iron. Normally about 10 per cent of oral intake is absorbed, but absorption increases in iron deficiency and decreases in iron overload. In haemochromatosis iron absorption is abnormally increased. Absorption from slow-release formulations is less reliable than from ordinary formulations.

Of the daily losses of 1–2 mg from a total load of 3–5 g most is lost via epithelial sloughing of the gastro-intestinal tract, and via the urine and skin but in small amounts.

After i.m. injection iron dextran is very slowly absorbed (about 50 per cent in 3 days), and 20 per cent may remain after 1 month. Iron sorbitol on the other hand is rapidly absorbed (about 80 per cent within 12 h).

Important adverse effects

The commonest adverse effects with oral iron are gastro-intestinal symptoms — nausea, abdominal discomfort, vomiting, and constipation or diarrhoea. These effects are dose-related and are reduced by using slow-release preparations.

Iron salts make the faeces black and this may cause alarm because it may be mistaken for melaena. However, stools which are black because of iron are negative for occult blood and look and smell differently from melaena.

After parenteral injection allergic reactions can occur. They are rare but may be severe, and great care must be taken, especially in patients with a history of allergy of any sort (see dosage recommendations above). Do not give i.v. iron to patients with a history of asthma. Allergic reactions are more likely after i.v. injection but can also occur after i.m. injection, especially with the rapidly absorbed form, iron sorbitol.

Staining of the skin after i.m. injection has been mentioned above.

Other adverse effects after parenteral injection include thrombophlebitis after i.v. infusion, a metallic taste in the mouth, hypotension and bradycardia, abdominal pain, lymph node enlargement, arthralgia, and myalgia.

Parenteral iron should not be given to patients with severe hepatic or renal disease or to patients with active renal infections.

Interactions

Iron absorption is enhanced by vitamin C, but the addition of vitamin C to oral iron preparations does not influence the therapy of iron deficiency.

A chelating interaction of iron with tetracycline results in the formation of an insoluble precipitate and the absorption of both compounds is impaired.

ISONIAZID

Structure

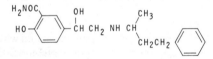

Mode of action

Isoniazid is an antituberculous drug, but the precise mechanism by which it produces its bacteriostatic and bacteriocidal effects on mycobacteria is unknown.

Uses

All forms of tuberculosis, in combination with other antituberculous drugs.

Dosages

5 mg/kg/day, usually up to 300 mg/day, commonly given as a single daily dose. Extensive caseous disease, tuberculous meningitis, and isoniazid-resistant infections may require higher dosages, when pyridoxine (10–20 mg o.d.) will also be needed (see below).

Kinetic data

Well absorbed. Metabolized principally by acetylation with a bimodal distribution in the general population (see Chapter 8). $T_{1/2} = 1$ h in fast acetylators, 3 h in slow acetylators.

Important adverse effects

Peripheral neuropathy is common with high doses, is more frequent among slow acetylators, and may be prevented or treated by administration of pyridoxine. Other neurological effects include optic neuritis or atrophy, various mental disturbances, dizziness, paraesthesiae, ataxia, and convulsions, all of which may be prevented or reduced by pyridoxine. Hepatic damage occurs occasionally and may be more common among fast acetylators.

LABETALOL

Structure

H₂NOC, OH, CH₃ ... HO— ...CH CH₂ NH CH... CH₂CH₂

Mode of action

Labetalol combines the actions of non-selective β (i.e. β_1 and β_2)-adrenoceptor antagonists and α-adrenoceptor antagonists. It is about three times more potent as a β-antagonist than as an α-antagonist and causes peripheral arteriolar vasodilatation without reflex tachycardia. It has no sympathetic agonist effects.

Use

Hypertension.

Dosages

Oral: 100–800 mg t.d.s. Start with a low dose and increase the dosage gradually in order to minimize adverse effects. Increases in dosage may be made every 1–2 weeks if required.

Intravenous: 1–4 mg/min by continuous infusion to a maximum of 200 mg. Alternatively give 50 mg i.v. over 1 min and repeat if necessary at 15 min intervals to a maximum total of 200 mg.

Kinetic data

Well absorbed but subject to extensive first-pass metabolism in the liver (hence the large difference between oral and i.v. dosages). Almost completely metabolized, $t_{1/2}$ 4 h. Dosages should be reduced in liver disease.

Important adverse effects

Labetalol commonly causes postural hypotension, probably because of its α-antagonist effect.

Other adverse effects are uncommon, but include a lichenoid skin rash, tingling of the scalp, and difficulty in ejaculation and micturition.

Care should be taken in patients with heart block, heart failure, and asthma.

Interactions

The effects of labetalol are enhanced by other antihypertensive drugs, such as diuretics, and labetalol is best used in combination therapy.

Cimetidine increases the systemic availability of labetalol after oral administration from about 40 per cent to about 80 per cent.

L-DOPA AND DECARBOXYLASE INHIBITORS

Structures

General:

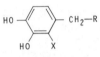

L-dopa (Levodopa) and the clinically used decarboxylase inhibitors share similar structures. Examples are:

	R	X
L-dopa	–CHCOOH | NH$_2$	H
Carbidopa	–CH$_3$ | –CCOOH | NHNH$_2$	H
Benserazide	–NHNHCOCHCH$_2$OH | NH$_2$	OH

Mode of action

Exogenously administered L-dopa crosses the blood–brain barrier and is assumed to enter dopaminergic nerve-endings in the basal ganglia. There it is converted to dopamine which is released by nerve impulse. This can only occur in viable dopaminergic neurones, but it is presumed that this sequence corrects the dysfunction brought about by the dopamine deficiency accompanying the loss of normally functioning dopaminergic neurones in Parkinsonism.

Dopa decarboxylase inhibitors inhibit the metabolism of L-dopa outside the brain, thus allowing more L-dopa to enter the brain. They do not themselves enter the brain and thus do not inhibit the production of dopamine there. This allows the use of lower doses of L-dopa with fewer peripheral adverse effects.

Uses

Parkinsonism, but not that associated with the use of neuroleptic drugs (e.g. phenothiazines, thioxanthenes, and butyrophenones).

Dosages

The following preparations, of L-dopa plus a decarboxylase inhibitor, are available:

	L-dopa	Decarboxylase inhibitor
Sinemet 110 (L-dopa + carbidopa)	100 mg	10 mg
Sinemet 'Plus'	100 mg	25 mg
Sinemet 275	250 mg	25 mg
Madopar 62.5 (L-dopa + benserazide)	50 mg	12.5 mg
Madopar 125	100 mg	25 mg
Madopar 250	200 mg	50 mg

Several preparations containing L-dopa alone are also available.

Generally, dosage is begun with one of the above preparations, containing 50 or 100 mg of L-dopa, given t.d.s. or q.d.s. Dosage is then increased every few days by using the same combination in increments of 100 mg of L-dopa until a satisfactory therapeutic response is achieved. Most patients achieve a therapeutic response and can be maintained on an L-dopa dosage for Sinemet® of 750–1500 mg daily and for Madopar® of 400–800 mg daily. The large range of dosage forms available give flexibility in producing the best response.

Kinetic data

L-dopa is poorly absorbed. It is completely metabolized with a $t_{1/2}$ of 3 h, but when given with a decarboxylase inhibitor its metabolism is 80 per cent decreased ($t_{1/2} = 15$ h).

Important adverse effects

Common general adverse effects include:

changes in bowel habit;
epigastric and abdominal pain;
anorexia, nausea, and vomiting;
cardiac arrhythmias;
orthostatic hypotension;
dizziness;
polyuria, difficulty with micturition, incontinence, discolouration of urine and other body fluids (e.g. sweat);

unpleasant body odour.

These adverse effects are reduced by using a decarboxylase inhibitor.

Common mental symptoms include euphoria, excitement, confusion, hallucinations and delusions, agitation, and anxiety.

Abnormal movements may limit dosage. The 'on–off' effect, characterized by fluctuations in the ability to perform voluntary movements, may be troublesome. It usually occurs suddenly and may be so frequent as to be as disabling as the original illness.

L-dopa is contra-indicated in patients with closed angle glaucoma, and caution should be taken in patients with a history of psychiatric illness or dementia, and in patients with a history of myocardial ischaemia or cardiac arrhythmias.

Interactions

The effects of L-dopa are potentiated by MAO inhibitors, which should be withdrawn at least 2 weeks before L-dopa is started.

Neuroleptic drugs decrease the effects of L-dopa by blocking its effects on dopamine receptors.

Pyridoxine is a co-factor for dopa decarboxylase and enhances its activity. It may therefore increase the dosage requirements of L-dopa if a decarboxylase inhibitor is not used.

LIGNOCAINE (LIDOCAINE)

Structure

Mode of action

Lignocaine is a Class I anti-arrhythmic drug which is grouped together with a number of

other anti-arrhythmic drugs because they have similar effects on the action potential of cardiac conducting tissues. Other drugs in Class I are quinidine, procainamide, disopyramide, and phenytoin. Other classes of action are discussed under amiodarone and verapamil.

To understand the actions of these drugs it is necessary first to examine the cardiac action potential itself. In Figs. P5 and P6 is shown an example of a fast action potential recorded in a Purkinje fibre. The action potential is divided into five phases:

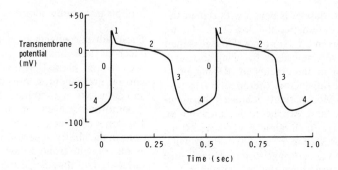

Fig. P5. An example of two consecutive action potentials recorded from a single cardiac Purkinje fibre. The phases of the action potential are numbered 0–4 (see text).

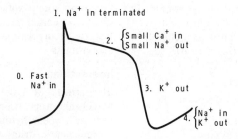

Fig. P6. The cationic changes which take place during the period of an action potential in a Purkinje fibre. The numbers 0–4 correspond to the defined phases of the action potential (see Fig. P5).

Phase 4

In cells normally capable of spontaneous depolarization, e.g. cells in the sino-atrial (SA) node, atrioventricular (AV) node and His–Purkinje system, during the resting phase (phase 4) there is a slow drift from the maximum negative potential (around -90 mV in Purkinje fibres, although in the SA node the potential is never less than -60 mV), to a more positive potential (around -70 mV in Purkinje fibres). This slow drift of potential during phase 4 is due to a small influx of sodium ions and efflux of potassium ions. This spontaneous depolarization to the threshold at which the action potential is initiated confers automaticity on these tissues. In contrast atrial and ventricular myocardial cells do not normally exhibit spontaneous depolarization and are therefore at rest until stimulated by a propagatory impulse.

Phase 0

When the threshold potential is reached there is then a fast inward flux of sodium ions, causing a rapid rise in transmembrane potential to positive values (i.e. depolarization).

Phase 1

When the transmembrane potential reaches a given positive value (e.g. about $+20$ mV in Purkinje fibres) the fast inward sodium flux is rapidly terminated. The potential then starts to fall towards zero.

Phase 2

During this phase, often called the plateau phase of the action potential, the transmembrane potential remains relatively stable due to low conductance of ions. There is a small inward current of calcium ions which is balanced by a small outward current of potassium ions. Eventually the small inward calcium current is slowly terminated. The time taken before the slow inward calcium current is terminated may be a factor determining the duration of Phase 2, and therefore the time of onset of repolarization (Phase 3).

Phase 3

The major portion of repolarization to the maximum negative potential occurs during this phase and is primarily due to outward flux of potassium. As the transmembrane potential falls to its maximum negative value this outward flux is terminated and phase 4 begins again with a small influx of sodium ions and efflux of potassium ions.

Refractory periods

During the phases of *re*polarization (phases 1–3) the fibres are refractory to further *de*polarization, although when about 50 per cent of repolarization has occurred a larger than normal stimulus *can* cause depolarization. The period during which depolarization cannot normally occur is called the *effective* refractory period, and the period during which depolarization cannot occur, no matter how large a stimulus occurs, is called the *absolute* refractory period.

The effects of the Class I anti-arrhythmic drugs on the action potential are of two types, which can be compared by considering the effects of lignocaine and quinidine separately.

(a) Lignocaine

(i) Automaticity
Lignocaine slows the rate of depolarization during phase 4, but without a change in the threshold at which phase 0 depolarization occurs. Automaticity is thus suppressed.

(ii) Rate of depolarization and conduction velocity
There is a decrease in the rate of the fast inward sodium current during phase 0, and thus a slowing of the rate of depolarization. This effect does not result in a change in conduction velocity in normal conducting tissues; however, in ischaemic conduction tissues conduction velocity is reduced.

(iii) Effective refractory period and total action potential duration
There is enhancement of the outward potassium flux during phase 3, with increase in the rate of repolarization and shortening of the total action potential duration (APD). The effective refractory period (ERP) is also shortened, but to a lesser extent. Thus the *proportion* of the total duration of the action potential during which the fibres are effectively refractory (i.e. the ratio ERP/APD) is *increased*. This means that during the period of the action potential the conduction tissue is refractory to new depolarizing stimuli for a relatively longer period of time.

These effects of lignocaine are exerted principally on normal Purkinje fibres, ventricular muscle fibres, and ventricular ectopic foci. The SA node, AV node, atrial muscle fibres, and atrial ectopic foci are generally unaffected. The ECG is usually unaffected by lignocaine.

Phenytoin and tocainide have effects similar to those of lignocaine, but phenytoin tends to *increase* conduction velocity in ischaemic tissue.

(b) Quinidine

(i) Automaticity
Quinidine slows the rate of depolarization during phase 4, but in contrast to lignocaine also increases the threshold at which phase 0 depolarization occurs. Automaticity is thus suppressed to a greater extent.

(ii) Rate of depolarization and conduction velocity
There is a decrease in the rate of the fast inward sodium current during phase 0, and thus a slowing of the rate of depolarization (as for lignocaine). However, this results in a reduction in conduction velocity in both normal and ischaemic tissues (in contrast to lignocaine).

(iii) Effective refractory period and total action potential duration
In contrast to lignocaine, quinidine increases slightly the duration of the action potential. It also increases the effective refractory period,

but to a greater extent. Thus, as for lignocaine, the proportion of the total action potential duration during which the fibres are effectively refractory (i.e. the ratio ERP/APD) is *increased*.

These effects of quinidine occur in normal Purkinje fibres, ventricular muscle fibres, and ventricular ectopic foci, but in contrast to lignocaine also occur in the fibres of the AV node, atrial muscle fibres, and atrial ectopic foci. Quinidine prolongs the QRS complex and QT interval of the ECG.

Procainamide and disopyramide have effects similar to those of quinidine, but disopyramide has greater effects on atrial and ventricular muscle fibres and lesser effects on Purkinje fibres. These compounds also differ in the potency of their anticholinergic effects —lignocaine, phenytoin, and procainamide have no anticholinergic properties in contrast to quinidine and disopyramide.

Despite the detailed knowledge about the actions of these drugs on cardiac electrophysiological events, it is still difficult to relate these actions in any precise way to their therapeutic effects on various arrhythmias. Likewise there is still much to be learned about the precise molecular events by which these drugs produce their electrophysiological effects.

Local anaesthetic action of lignocaine

In common with other local anaesthetics, such as procaine, amethocaine, cocaine, bupivacaine, mepivacaine, and prilocaine, lignocaine acts by decreasing the large transient increase of sodium permeability resulting from slight depolarization of the membrane and thereafter by increasing the threshold for electrical excitability. This results in blockade of the nervous impulse.

Uses

Lignocaine is used in the treatment and prevention of acute ventricular arrhythmias (ventricular extrasystoles, ventricular tachycardia, and ventricular fibrillation), e.g. after myocardial infarction and cardiac surgery. It is also used as a local anaesthetic.

Dosages

(a) Anti-arrhythmic dosages

Lignocaine is given by i.v. injection in an initial dose of 100 mg given as 10 ml of a 1 per cent solution over 2 min. In order to maintain therapeutic plasma concentrations thereafter, it is usual to continue treatment with an i.v. infusion, starting at a high rate and gradually decreasing to a maintenance rate. This is because lignocaine has a short half-time and the initial bolus dose will be subject to elimination which is too rapid for a low fixed rate maintenance infusion to replace. A suggested regimen after the initial bolus is:

4 mg/kg/h for 1 h;
3 mg/kg/h for 1 h;
2 mg/kg/h thereafter for 24 h.

Lignocaine has also been used by the i.m. route (50–100 mg) as a prophylactic against cardiac arrhythmias outside hospital practice before admission of the patient to hospital. The therapeutic value of this approach is uncertain.

(b) Local anaesthetic dosages

There are two important matters here. The first is to appreciate the general toxicity of lignocaine and related local anaesthetics, and therefore to limit the total dosage given in a single injection or infiltration. Under these circumstances the total dose of lignocaine should not exceed 200 mg, or 500 mg when given with adrenaline.

The second is to appreciate that some preparations of lignocaine, and other local anaesthetics, contain adrenaline. For instance lignocaine is available in solutions of 0.5 per cent, 1 per cent, and 2 per cent both alone and in combination with adrenaline 1 in 200 000 (i.e. 500 micrograms/100 ml). The maximum dose of adrenaline at any one time is 500 micrograms.

Kinetic data

After oral administration lignocaine is almost completely metabolized on its first passage through the liver. For this reason it has to be given i.v. Metabolism ($t_{1/2}$, 1.5 h) is to two active metabolites, monoethylglycinexylidide (MEGX) and glycinexylidide (GX), both of which have less anti-arrhythmic activity than lignocaine but which are more toxic, and are probably responsible for CNS toxicity. Since the half-times of these metabolites are longer than that of lignocaine, continuous i.v. infusion of lignocaine should be limited to 24–48 h to limit the extent of their accumulation.

In liver disease the metabolism of lignocaine may be decreased, and dosages must be reduced. In patients with heart failure there may be reduced clearance because of hepatic congestion and the apparent volume of distribution may also be reduced; these changes result in lower dosage requirements.

Plasma concentration measurements

The therapeutic range of plasma lignocaine concentrations is 1–5 μg/ml, although in some patients concentrations of up to 9 μg/ml may be required. The routine application of plasma lignocaine measurement has not yet been proved useful.

Important adverse effects

Adverse effects of lignocaine are dose-related, and occur in about 6 per cent of patients treated by i.v. infusion. The common effects are central nervous system toxicity, including nausea, vomiting, drowsiness, convulsions and coma, and cardiac effects, including sinus bradycardia, tachyarrhythmias, asystole, and hypotension. Lignocaine should be used with caution in patients with pre-existing impairment of conduction in the AV node and bundle of His, and in patients with the sick sinus syndrome, in whom it may further impair sinus nodal function.

Interactions

Since lignocaine has a high hepatic extraction ratio (see Chapter 3) its clearance by the liver is reduced by drugs which reduce liver blood flow, e.g. β-adrenoceptor antagonists such as propranolol, and histamine (H_2) antagonists such as cimetidine and ranitidine.

Hypokalaemia, e.g. due to diuretics, decreases the effects of Class I anti-arrhythmic drugs on the action potential. Hypokalaemia should be corrected when using lignocaine.

LINCOMYCIN AND CLINDAMYCIN

Structures

General:

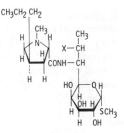

Lincomycin: X = OH
Clindamycin: X = Cl

Mode of action

Inhibition of bacterial protein synthesis by an effect on ribosomal RNA.

Uses

The following organisms are generally sensitive to these antibiotics:

Gram-positive cocci (Streptococci, penicillin-resistant Staphylococci).
Gram-negative bacilli (*Bacteroides*).
Gram-positive bacilli (*C. diphtheriae, Clostridium spp.*).

Because of their adverse effects these antibiotics are generally reserved for infections in bones and joints, for severe intra-abdominal sepsis, and for severe infections of the skin.

Dosages

Oral therapy:
lincomycin 500 mg every 6 to 8 h;
clindamycin 150–300 mg every 6 h.
Parenteral therapy:
lincomycin i.m. 600 mg every 12 or 24 h;
i.v.* 600 mg every 8 or 12 h.

clindamycin i.m. or i.v.* 0.6–2.4 g daily, in 2–4 divided doses.

*Intravenous infusion of these drugs should be carried out over 1 h in 250 ml of a solution of 5 per cent dextrose or physiological saline. Rapid infusion carries a risk of cardiopulmonary arrest.

Kinetic data

	Lincomycin	Clindamycin
Absorption	20–40%	90–100%
$T_{1/2}$	5 hours	2 hours
Metabolism	80%	90%
Excretion	20% unchanged in urine	10% unchanged in urine

Important adverse effects

Diarrhoea is common (up to 50 per cent) and may occasionally be due to pseudomembra-

nous colitis, which is a serious complication and which, untreated, has a high mortality. Pseudomembranous colitis may present as mild diarrhoea, or as an acute fulminant colitis with profuse bloody diarrhoea. Sigmoidoscopy shows raised white plaques on the colonic mucosa. It is caused by overgrowth in the colon of *Clostridium difficile*, which produces a necrotizing toxin. Treatment is with oral vancomycin (500 mg six-hourly).

Pseudomembranous colitis may occur with other antibiotics including ampicillin, the cephalosporins, chloramphenicol, co-trimoxazole, gentamicin, kanamycin, metronidazole, and tetracycline. The incidence is lower with these antibiotics than with lincomycin and clindamycin.

Interactions

Lincomycin and clindamycin may potentiate the effects of neuromuscular blockers.

LITHIUM

Mode of action

Lithium has several pharmacological effects on the function of brain monoamines, possibly through its effect on transmembrane sodium flux, but the relationship of these effects to its therapeutic action is unknown.

Uses

1. Manic depression—prevention of mood swings.
2. Unipolar depression—prevention of recurrent depressive episodes.
3. Mania—lithium is effective in the treatment of acute mania, but its slow onset of action is a disadvantage, and for this reason acute manic episodes are usually treated with a neuroleptic drug.

Dosages

Lithium salts are available in both conventional formulations and in sustained-release formulations. The latter have been devised in order to reduce the frequency of dosage. The following preparations are available:

Lithium carbonate (300 mg = 8 mmol Li⁺):
      Camcolit® 250 (250 mg)
      Camcolit® 400 (400 mg)
      Liskonum® (450 mg, sustained-release)
      Phasal® (300 mg, sustained-release)
      Priadel® (400 mg, sustained-release);
Lithium citrate (564 mg = 6 mmol Li⁺):
      Litarex® (564 mg).

The initial dose of lithium is 6 mmol orally daily (i.e. lithium carbonate 250 mg, lithium citrate 564 mg). The dose is then gradually increased, depending on the plasma concentration, to a final maintenance dose of up to about 50 mmol daily (i.e. lithium carbonate 2g, lithium citrate 4.5g).

Kinetic data

Well absorbed. Lithium is eliminated unchanged in the urine and its $t_{1/2}$ therefore varies with age, being about 20 h in young adults, and up to 36 h in the elderly. Therapeutic plasma concentrations vary between 0.4 and 1.0 mmol/l. At concentrations above 1.5 mmol/l adverse effects become common (see Chapter 7).

Important adverse effects

The effects of lithium intoxication are gastro-intestinal disturbances (anorexia, nausea, vomiting, and diarrhoea), and CNS disturbances (drowsiness, lethargy, giddiness, ataxia, tremor, lack of co-ordination, and dysarthria). Severe overdose (plasma concentrations above 3 mmol/l) may cause coma, fits, toxic psychoses, oliguria, circulatory failure, and occasionally death.

Less serious adverse effects commonly experienced are mild gastro-intestinal disturbances, tremor, and either fluid retention with weight gain and oedema, or polyuria and polydipsia.

In the long term nephrogenic diabetes insipidus may occur, and hypothyroidism is not uncommon.

Interactions

Diuretics, such as thiazides and frusemide, cause lithium retention, and care should be taken to avoid lithium intoxication in patients taking this combination. Lithium dosage should be halved if diuretic therapy is prescribed and the dosage of lithium then adjusted according to its plasma concentration.

LOPERAMIDE

Structure

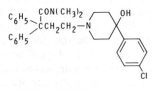

(Compare haloperidol.)

Mode of action

Loperamide binds to opiate receptors in the gastro-intestinal tract where it has morphine-like effects. It also has anticholinergic effects on the bowel. It does not penetrate the brain well and is therefore relatively free of central opiate effects.

Use

Symptomatic relief of diarrhoea.

Dosages

4 mg initially followed by 2 mg after each loose stool. During long-term treatment the total dose, titrated against the effect on bowel movement, may be given in two divided doses. Maximum daily dose is 16 mg.

Kinetic data

Loperamide is poorly absorbed, partly because it decreases gastro-intestinal motility, and it is therefore mostly excreted unchanged in the faeces.

Important adverse effects

Constipation will occur with over-treatment. Tolerance does not develop to the constipating effect during long-term therapy. Loperamide occasionally causes abdominal pain, dry mouth, dizziness, headache, and rashes.

MELPHALAN

Structure

$$HOOCCHCH_2-\text{（aryl）}-N(CH_2CH_2Cl)_2$$
$$\overset{|}{NH_2}$$

(Compare chlorambucil, cyclophosphamide.)

Mode of action

Alkylating agent (see busulphan).

Uses

Multiple myeloma.

Some solid tumours, e.g. malignant melanoma, and advanced carcinoma of the breast.

Dosages

0.15 mg/kg o.d., orally for 7 days repeated at six-weekly intervals, according to the response.

Kinetic data

Variably absorbed. Mostly metabolized.

Important adverse effects

Bone marrow suppression is dose-related. Prolonged therapy results in an increased incidence of leukaemia.

Melphalan should not be used during pregnancy.

Interaction

For the possible interaction with live vaccines see p.288.

METHOTREXATE

Structure

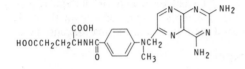

Mode of action

Methotrexate inhibits the activity of dihydrofolate reductase (see co-trimoxazole). This leads to decreased production of tetrahydrofolic acid which is required for the synthesis of thymidylic acid and purine nucleotides. This effect prevents the synthesis of nuclear material in the S phase, and causes cell death.

Uses

Acute lymphoblastic leukaemia—to maintain remission and to prevent or treat CNS infiltration.

Choriocarcinoma.

Other solid tumours, such as those of head, neck, breast, and lung.

Severe psoriasis not responding to other treatment.

Dosages

Dosage regimens vary with the indication:

1. Maintenance therapy during remission in acute leukaemia is carried out with low dosages, e.g. 15 mg/m^2 once weekly.
2. Intrathecal methotrexate is given in doses up to 15 mg at weekly intervals for the prevention and treatment of CNS infiltration in lymphoblastic leukaemia.
3. High dose regimens—it is possible to give methotrexate in higher doses for the treatment of certain solid tumours, and to avoid bone marrow suppression by giving folinic acid (so-called 'rescue').

For example, in the treatment of choriocarcinoma, methotrexate is given in a dose of up to 60 mg i.m. every 48 h for four doses. This is followed by an intravenous infusion of folinic acid in a dose of up to 120 mg, followed by 12–15 mg i.m. every 6 h for eight doses.

The idea behind this regimen is that because the cells of the tumour are turning over very rapidly the methotrexate affects them before it affects the cells of the bone marrow. The effect on the tumour occurs early, and then the actions of methotrexate are reversed by the folinic acid before the full effect occurs on the bone marrow.

4. Psoriasis—10–25 mg orally once weekly.

Kinetic data

Absorption is saturable. Methotrexate is mostly excreted unchanged in the urine and is subject to active tubular secretion. $T_{1/2} = 4$ h.

Important adverse effects

Bone marrow suppression is dose-related, and may be prevented by the use of folinic acid (see above).

Oral ulceration, stomatitis, pharyngitis, glossitis, and gingivitis are common (up to 30 per cent of cases), as are gastro-intestinal disturbances including anorexia, nausea, vomiting, and diarrhoea.

During prolonged treatment (e.g. in psoriasis), hepatotoxicity is common. In about 20 per cent of cases it may result in hepatic fibrosis.

The use of intrathecal methotrexate is often

accompanied by headache and vomiting, and occasionally neurological disturbances may occur.

Methotrexate should not be used in pregnancy because of its teratogenic effects. Contraceptive precautions should be taken during and for 3 months after its use because of its effects on spermatogenesis and oogenesis.

Dosages should be reduced by half in patients with renal failure, and methotrexate should not be used in patients with liver damage.

Interactions

Methotrexate potentiates the effects of other dihydrofolate reductase inhibitors.

Aspirin and probenecid inhibit the tubular secretion of methotrexate and thus enhance its effects.

α-METHYLDOPA

Structure

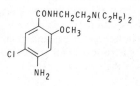

(Compare adrenoceptor agonists, L-dopa, dopamine.)

Mode of action

α-methyldopa enters the brain and neurones. In noradrenergic neurones it is decarboxylated to α-methyldopamine which is then β-hydroxylated to α-methylnoradrenaline. It is thought that this potent $α_2$-adrenoceptor agonist is then released by inhibitory noradrenergic neurones in vasomotor centres controlling sympathetic outflow. The net result is central inhibition of peripheral sympathetic nervous system function.

Use

Hypertension.

Dosages

Initially 250 mg b.d., orally, increasing as required in increments of 250 mg to a maximum of 3 g daily.

Kinetic data

The bioavailability of α-methyldopa is variable because it is metabolized in the gut wall. It is extensively metabolized and the metabolites are excreted in the urine. Very little of the drug actually enters the brain to produce a pharmacological effect; $t_{1/2} = 2$ h.

Important adverse effects

The commonest adverse effects are on the central nervous system—depression, drowsiness, sleep disturbances, and dizziness. Other important effects are postural hypotension and erectile impotence.

Although a positive Coombs's test occurs in about 20 per cent of patients, autoimmune haemolytic anaemia occurs in only 0.02 per cent.

α-methyldopa should be used with caution in patients with active liver disease since it can cause liver damage. In patients with severe renal impairment dosages should be reduced.

If treatment is being stopped α-methyldopa dosage should be tailed off gradually since sudden withdrawal may result in severe rebound hypertension.

METOCLOPRAMIDE

Structure

CONHCH$_2$CH$_2$N(C$_2$H$_5$)$_2$
OCH$_3$
Cl
NH$_2$

Mode of action

Metoclopramide has several different effects at different sites, all of which contribute to its anti-emetic action:

(a) Its most important effects are directly

on the gastro-intestinal tract. It increases oesophageal tone, increases pyloric contraction, and enhances the rate of gastric and duodenal emptying. These effects may be mediated by both cholinergic and antidopaminergic effects.

(b) It is a central dopamine antagonist, and may block the action of dopamine released within the chemoreceptor trigger zone in the floor of the fourth ventricle, which is thought to be one of the neurotransmitter functions involved in the process of emesis.

(c) It may also decrease afferent impulses to the brain from emetic foci, e.g. gastric mucosa.

Its major adverse effects are caused by its antidopaminergic effects in the brain.

Uses

As an anti-emetic in the following conditions:

gastro-duodenal disorders;
drug-induced nausea and vomiting (but not with cytotoxic drugs);
post-operatively.

To increase gastro-duodenal transit time during radiological procedures.

As an anti-emetic and to increase the rate of absorption of analgesics in migraine.

Dosage

Anti-emetic: 10 mg orally, i.m. or i.v. May be given t.d.s. if required.

In radiology: 10 mg i.m. or i.v.

Migraine: 10 mg orally at the onset of the attack repeated twice at most if required (i.e. a total of 30 mg). Metoclopramide is available in proprietary formulations suitable for use in migraine:

Migravess® : metoclopramide 5 mg, aspirin 325 mg, sodium bicarbonate 1180 mg, citric acid 850 mg.

Paramax® : metoclopramide 5 mg, paracetamol 500 mg.

Note that all these dosages refer to adults over 20 years of age. The dosages in other age groups corresponding to an adult dosage of 10 mg t.d.s. are:

children under 1 year, 1 mg b.d.;
children 1–3 years, 1 mg b.d. or t.d.s.;
children 4–5 years, 2 mg b.d. or t.d.s.;
children 6–14 years, 2.5–5 mg t.d.s.;
young adults 15–20 years, 5–10 mg t.d.s.

Always start at the lower end of the dosage range increasing only if required.

Kinetic data

Metoclopramide is well absorbed. It is extensively metabolized in the liver to inactive metabolites, $t_{1/2}$ 4 h.

Important adverse effects

The most important adverse effects of metoclopramide are extrapyramidal reactions caused by its antidopaminergic action in the nigrostriatal tracts. These reactions occur in about 1 per cent of patients and are usually dystonic in nature, including facial muscle spasm, trismus, titubation, extra-ocular muscle spasm and oculogyric crisis, torticollis, and opisthotonos. Parkinsonian features occur during chronic therapy and metoclopramide should be avoided in patients with Parkinsonism. These dystonic reactions are dose-dependent, and dosages should be reduced in children and young adults (see above). In the elderly start with doses of 5 mg, increasing to 10 mg only if necessary. Dystonic reactions should be treated with benztropine 2 mg i.v. or diazepam 10 mg i.v.

Metoclopramide may also occasionally cause central nervous symptoms, such as dizziness and drowsiness.

In common with other dopamine receptor antagonists it stimulates the release of prolactin from the pituitary and may cause galactorrhoea.

Interactions

Metoclopramide potentiates the antidopaminergic actions of other dopamine receptor antagonists (phenothiazines, thioxanthenes, and butyrophenones) with an increased risk of dystonic reactions.

Anticholinergic drugs antagonize its effects on the gastro-intestinal tract and L-dopa its effects on the oesophagus.

Because it increases gastric emptying rate metoclopramide may increase the *rate* of absorption of some drugs. This is important in the treatment of migraine where a rapid analgesic effect is required but gastric stasis prevents the absorption of analgesic drugs (see dosages above). It is probably of little importance in other circumstances, since the *extent* of absorption of drugs is usually not affected.

METRONIDAZOLE

Structure

Mode of action

Metronidazole kills bacteria and protozoa whose metabolism is anaerobic or micro-aerophilic. In such organisms it is reduced to active metabolites which interfere with nucleic acid function.

Uses

Infections due to:

Trichomonas (genital);
Anaerobic bacteria (e.g. *Bacteroides*);
Amoeba enterohepatica (amoebiasis);
Giardia lamblia (giardiasis);
Vincent's organisms (acute ulcerative gingivitis).

Dosages

Trichomoniasis: 200 mg t.d.s., orally to each sexual partner for 7 days.

Anaerobic infections: 400 mg t.d.s., orally for 7 days, or 1 g t.d.s. by suppository for 3 days, followed by oral therapy.

Amoebiasis: 400–800 mg t.d.s., orally for 5–10 days depending on the form of the infection.

Giardiasis: 2 g o.d., orally for 3 days.

Acute ulcerative gingivitis (Vincent's angina): 200 mg t.d.s., orally for 3 days.

In severe sepsis due to sensitive organisms i.v. administration may be necessary.

Kinetic data

Well absorbed after oral and rectal administration. Mostly metabolized. $T_{1/2}$ 6 h.

Important adverse effects

Adverse effects are infrequent. During long-term therapy a peripheral neuropathy may occur.

Interactions

Metronidazole inhibits hepatic microsomal drug-metabolizing enzymes. It thus enhances the effects of warfarin (see Chapter 10) and may cause a disulfiram-like reaction to alcohol.

METYRAPONE

Structure

Mode of action

Metyrapone inhibits the 11-hydroxylation of 17, 21-hydroxyprogesterone to cortisol (hydrocortisone). It is thus more selective in its inhibition of steroid biosynthesis than aminoglutethimide which inhibits synthesis at an early stage and thus inhibits the synthesis of other steroids (see Fig. 25.1). Although metyrapone does also inhibit the synthesis of aldosterone, that is a relatively small effect.

Inhibition of cortisol synthesis should normally cause the release of ACTH from the pituitary resulting in increased formation of the 11-desoxycorticosteroids (17-hydroxy-corticoids), precursors of cortisol. The change in concentrations of those steroids in the urine after metyrapone forms the basis of the use of metyrapone to test hypothalamic–pituitary function. For example, in Cushing's syndrome due to pituitary overactivity there is an exaggerated response to metyrapone, while in ectopic ACTH production there is no response.

Uses

Assessment of anterior pituitary function.
Suppression of adrenal corticosteroid production in Cushing's syndrome and in metastatic breast carcinoma ('medical adrenalectomy').

Dosages

Diagnostic: 750 mg orally four-hourly for six doses.

Measure urinary 17-oxogenic steroids before, during, and after metyrapone.

Therapeutic (e.g. Cushing's syndrome): 250 mg t.d.s. to 1 g q.d.s. depending on the response of plasma cortisol concentrations.

Important adverse effects

Because metyrapone can precipitate acute adrenocortical insufficiency it should be used with great care in patients suspected of having hypopituitarism.

Metyrapone can cause nausea and vomiting. These can be lessened by taking it with food.

MIANSERIN

Structure

(Compare tricyclic antidepressants.)

Mode of action

Mianserin is a tetracyclic antidepressant drug whose mode of action is not clearly understood, although thought to be mediated via effects on brain monoamine neurotransmitter function.

The sedative effects of mianserin may be related to its antihistaminic properties. In contrast to the tricyclic antidepressants mianserin has weak peripheral anticholinergic action.

Use

Endogenous depression.

Dosages

30 mg orally at night initially, increasing if required to a maximum of 200 mg a day in divided doses.

Kinetic data

Mianserin is well absorbed. It is mostly metabolized in the liver, $t_{1/2}$ 10 h. In the elderly its clearance is decreased and the $t_{1/2}$ prolonged to 30 h. Dosages should therefore be reduced in the elderly. Its main metabolites, desmethyl- and 8-hydroxy-mianserin have some pharmacological activity.

Important adverse effects

Mianserin is less likely than the tricyclic antidepressants to cause anticholinergic adverse effects, but nonetheless should be used with caution in patients with glaucoma and prostatic enlargement. It is also less likely to cause cardiac arrhythmias. Its most common adverse effect is of sedation which may be sufficiently pronounced to necessitate withdrawal. Mianserin may rarely cause neutropenia.

Interactions

Unlike the tricyclic antidepressants mianserin does not seem to interact with centrally-acting antihypertensive drugs such as clonidine.

The sedative effects of mianserin may be enhanced by other centrally-acting drugs.

MINOXIDIL

Structure

Mode of action

Minoxidil has a direct effect on arteriolar smooth muscle causing vasodilatation. It does not affect venules. Most of its adverse effects are due to vasodilatation but it causes fluid retention both by reducing renal blood flow and by inhibition of sodium reabsorption in the proximal tubule.

Use

Hypertension.

Dosages

Initially 5 mg o.d. orally, increasing to 10 mg and then in increments of 10 mg every three days as required to a maximum of 50 mg daily.

Kinetic data

Minoxidil is well absorbed. It is mostly meta-

bolized in the liver to relatively inactive compounds; $t_{1/2}$ of minoxidil is 4 h but its therapeutic effects last for at least 16 h, perhaps because it remains bound to arteriolar smooth muscle.

Important adverse effects

Adverse effects are common and mostly attributable to vasodilatation. Reflex tachycardia and fluid retention necessitate the use of minoxidil only in combination with other antihypertensive drugs, namely a β-adrenoceptor antagonist and a diuretic. Although a thiazide diuretic may suffice, fluid retention may be severe enough to warrant the use of frusemide or bumetanide. Reflex tachycardia due to minoxidil may sometimes precipitate an acute attack of angina.

Increased hair growth (hypertrichosis) is common, occurring after about 3 weeks' treatment. It is reversible on withdrawing therapy, but may be cosmetically unacceptable, particularly in dark-haired women.

Flattening or inversion of the T wave in the ECG occurs in most patients within a few days of starting minoxidil, but usually resolves within a few weeks. This may make interpretation of the ECG difficult. Cardiac ischaemic pain irrespective of ECG changes should be a sign to withhold the drug. Rarely minoxidil may cause pericardial effusion.

MONOAMINE OXIDASE (MAO) INHIBITORS

Structures

The MAO inhibitors form a group of compounds of differing structures, some of which are hydrazines (e.g. phenelzine, isocarboxazid, and iproniazid), and others which are not (e.g. tranylcypromine, which is a derivative of amphetamine). We give here phenelzine as an example:

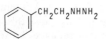

Mode of action

MAO has a variety of isoenzymes which have been classified as Type A (present in gut and liver) and Type B (present in the brain). The commonly used MAO inhibitors, phenelzine, isocarboxazid, tranylcypromine, and iproniazid are non-selective inhibitors of MAO Types A and B. Pargyline is a selective inhibitor of MAO Type A at low doses but is non-selective in clinically effective doses. Selegiline (deprenyl) is a relatively selective inhibitor of MAO Type B.

These different types of isoenzyme have

different selectivities for amine substrates, but the physiological importance of this is not clear.

Since MAO is one of the two main enzymes involved in the metabolism of 5-hydroxytryptamine (5-HT) and catecholamines (e.g. adrenaline, noradrenaline, and dopamine), the MAO inhibitors cause an increase in 5-HT and catecholamine concentrations in the brain and other nervous tissues. It is this effect that is thought to be the primary action leading to the therapeutic effect of the MAO inhibitors in relieving endogenous depression, although how this is achieved is as yet unknown.

Uses

Endogenous depression.

Phobic anxiety states with depression.

Because of drug and food interactions with MAO inhibitors (see below) they are less popular currently in the treatment of endogenous depression than the tricyclic and other antidepressants. They are usually reserved for patients who have failed to respond to other forms of drug therapy. Selegiline is used in the treatment of Parkinson's disease, to reduce the adverse effects of L-dopa.

Dosages

Depression

Phenelzine, 15 mg orally t.d.s. initially, increasing to q.d.s. after 2 weeks if necessary, then reducing gradually to the lowest effective maintenance dosage.

Isocarboxazid, 10–20 mg orally o.d.

Tranylcypromine, 10 mg orally b.d. initially, increasing if required to t.d.s. after 1 week, then reducing to a maintenance dosage (usually 10 mg o.d.).

Iproniazid, 100–150 mg orally o.d., initially, reducing gradually to a maintenance dosage of 25–50 mg o.d.

As an adjunct to L-dopa in Parkinson's disease

Selegiline, 5–10 mg orally o.d.

Kinetic data

The MAO inhibitors are all well absorbed. The hydrazine derivatives are metabolized by acetylation which is genetically polymorphic (see Chapter 8). The duration of action of the hydrazine derivatives does not depend on their half-times since they cause irreversible inhibition of MAO. After withdrawal therefore their effects last for as long as it takes for MAO stores to be repleted by fresh synthesis (i.e. about 2 weeks).

Tranylcypromine is also extensively metabolized. Its inhibitory effect on MAO is reversible and its duration of action after withdrawal is about 4 days.

Important adverse effects

The most important adverse effect of the MAO inhibitors is an acute hypertensive crisis due to the interaction of MAO inhibitors with amines, particularly that with tyramine in foods. The important interactions of MAO inhibitors can be classified as follows:

(a) Monoamines

(i) Tyramine

MAO inhibitors interact with tyramine in foods and the interaction can result in a serious, potentially fatal, reaction consisting of severe hypertension associated with severe headache, sweating, flushing, nausea, vomiting, and palpitation. The mechanism of this interaction (the so-called 'cheese interaction') has been discussed in Chapter 10, and a list of foods particularly to be avoided is given in Table 10.3. Patients should be warned about such interactions and be given a warning card of the type illustrated in Fig. P7. Treatment of the hypertension in these cases is with i.v. phentolamine (see pp.299 and 621).

Because the first step in this interaction involves inhibition of MAO in the gut, and since gut MAO is of Type A, it would be expected that a Type B MAO inhibitor, such as selegiline, would not cause this interaction, and in practice that seems to be so.

TREATMENT CARD

Carry this card with you at all times. Show it to any doctor who may treat you other than the doctor who prescribed this medicine, and to your dentist if you require dental treatment.

INSTRUCTIONS TO PATIENTS

Please read carefully

While taking this medicine and for 10 days after your treatment finishes you must observe the following simple instructions:-

1 Do not eat CHEESE, PICKLED HERRING OR BROAD BEAN PODS.

2 Do not eat or drink BOVRIL, OXO, MARMITE or ANY SIMILAR MEAT OR YEAST EXTRACT.

3 Do not take any other MEDICINES (including tablets, capsules, nose drops, inhalations or suppositories) whether purchased by you or previously prescribed by your doctor, without first consulting him.

   NB *Cough and cold cures, pain relievers and tonics are medicines.*

4 Drink ALCOHOL only in moderation and avoid CHIANTI WINE completely.

Report any severe symptoms to your doctor and follow any other advice given by him.

Prepared by The Pharmaceutical Society and the British Medical Association on behalf of the Health Departments of the United Kingdom.

11530/1963 R16S 558906 250m 11/77 AG 3640/4

Fig. P7. An example of the kind of warning card which should be given to a patient taking MAO inhibitors. [Reproduced with the permission of The Pharmaceutical Society of Great Britain and the British Medical Association.]

(ii) Other indirectly acting amines

The effects of other amines, such as ephedrine, pseudoephedrine, phenylpropanolamine, and amphetamines, which release noradrenaline from nerve-endings, may be potentiated by MAO inhibitors, since the amount of noradrenaline in nerve-endings is increased by MAO inhibitors, and the increased amount of noradrenaline so released is less well metabolized. A severe hypertensive reaction may result. Since indirectly-acting amines are found in proprietary cold and cough 'cures' which can be bought at pharmacists' shops over the counter, patients should be warned not to use such medicines (see Fig. P7).

(iii) Dopamine receptor agonists

L-dopa and dopamine may cause similar hypertensive reactions in patients taking non-selective MAO inhibitors, and generally should be avoided.

(iv) Directly-acting adrenoceptor agonists

For the same reasons, exogenously administered catecholamines, such as adrenaline, noradrenaline, and isoprenaline should not be administered to patients taking MAO inhibitors. This is particularly important when using local anaesthetics, such as lignocaine, which may also contain adrenaline (see p.700).

(b) Tricyclic antidepressants

Since tricyclic antidepressants inhibit monoamine reuptake by nerve endings the combination of tricyclic antidepressants with MAO inhibitors is theoretically hazardous and sometimes is so in practice. Adverse effects of this interaction include flushing, sweating, hyperpyrexia, restlessness, excitement, tremor, muscle twitching, muscle rigidity, convulsions, and coma.

However, there are also reports of the successful and safe use of this combination by some psychiatrists. Nevertheless, such treatment requires experience and care, and should be used only by those expert in the treatment of psychiatric disorders.

(c) Pethidine

The combination of pethidine with MAO inhibitors is a serious and potentially fatal one, and should be avoided. The mechanism of the interaction is not known, but it can result in flushing, sweating, hyperpyrexia, restlessness, increased muscle tone, muscle rigidity, respiratory depression, severe hypotension, and coma. Other narcotic analgesics do not seem to be involved in this type of interaction.

(d) Oral hypoglycaemic drugs

For unknown reasons MAO inhibitors may potentiate the effects of oral hypoglycaemic drugs.

(e) Others

It is generally unwise to combine MAO inhibitors with other drugs which in some way affect monoamine function, e.g. α-methyldopa, L-dopa, reserpine. Selegiline may be combined with L-dopa (see uses above).

Apart from the adverse effects attributable to these interactions MAO inhibitors have mild adverse effects which usually consist of central nervous system and autonomic effects, including dizziness, drowsiness, weakness, dry mouth, blurred vision, and postural hypotension. Overstimulation can occur, particularly with tranylcypromine, and can lead to insomnia, acute anxiety, and agitation. Patients with cerebrovascular disease are more susceptible to these effects and should not be given MAO inhibitors.

The MAO inhibitors are contra-indicated in patients with liver disease, mainly because they are metabolized in the liver. The hydrazine derivatives have been reported to cause liver damage rarely, but with a high mortality rate (20 per cent).

Oedema, and gastro-intestinal effects (nausea, vomiting, and constipation) may occur.

Interactions

See above under 'adverse effects'.

MUSTINE

Structure

$CH_3N(CH_2CH_2Cl)_2$ (Compare melphalan.)

Mode of action

Mustine (other names nitrogen mustard, methchloroethamine, chlorethazine) is an alkylating agent (see busulphan).

Uses

Bronchogenic carcinoma.
Non-Hodgkin's lymphoma.

Dosages

The usual dose is 0.4 mg/kg i.v. as a single dose. Because it is a powerful tissue irritant mustine should be given into the tubing of a fast running i.v. infusion to avoid thrombophlebitis at the site of injection.

Kinetic data

After i.v. injection mustine disappears from the blood within 10 minutes and is metabolized to the reactive ethyleneimmonium ion.

Important adverse effects

Anorexia, nausea, and vomiting are common. Bone marrow suppression is dose-related. Local irritation occurs at the site of injection if there is extravasation or if a fast-running infusion technique is not used (see above). If extravasation occurs infiltrate the area with 3 per cent sodium thiosulphate and apply ice-packs intermittently for 6–12 h thereafter; lignocaine may also be infused locally to relieve pain.

Interaction

For the possible interaction with live vaccines see p.288.

NARCOTIC ANALGESICS

Narcotic analgesics may be classified as follows:

1. *Opiate analgesics*—(a) derived from opium alkaloids (morphine, codeine);
(b) semi-synthetic congeners of morphine (diamorphine, dihydrocodeine, pholcodine).
2. *Non-opiate morphine-like analgesics*—
pethidine (meperidine);
methadone;
dipipanone;
dextromoramide;
dextropropoxyphene;
pentazocine;
diphenoxylate.

1. Opiate analgesics and opiate antagonists

Structures

General:

Examples: see below

Mode of action

In the central nervous system opiate analgesics bind to specific opioid receptors and act as partial and complete agonists, mimicking the effects of the endogenous enkephalins which normally bind to those receptors. This results in a variety of different effects, each of which

depends on the area of the brain affected and the physiological function of that area. For example, the analgesic effects are thought to be mediated by the binding of opiate analgesics to those areas involved in the perception of pain in the spinal cord, spinal trigeminal nucleus, periaqueductal and periventricular grey matter, and medullary raphe nuclei.

There is a multiplicity of CNS effects resulting from the actions of opiates on various areas of the brain and spinal cord:

(i) analgesia;
(ii) drowsiness and sleep;
(iii) mood change—usually euphoria, occasionally dysphoria;
(iv) respiratory depression and suppression of the cough reflex;
(v) nausea and vomiting;
(vi) decreased sympathetic outflow;
(vii) lowering of temperature;
(viii) pupillary constriction.

The peripheral effects of the opiate analgesics are also mediated by their effects on enkephalin receptors. These include a decrease in gastro-intestinal motility with constipation, spasm of the sphincter of Oddi, and increased pressure in the biliary tract which may result in biliary colic.

Morphine and diamorphine are vasodilators, an action which may be due to their effects in releasing histamine, and in suppressing central sympathetic outflow.

The mechanisms by which tolerance and addiction to opiates occur are still unclear, despite the discovery of enkephalins and endorphins.

Examples:

Agonists	X_1	X_2	R
Morphine	OH	OH	CH_3
Diamorphine (heroin)	$COOCH_3$	$COOCH_3$	CH_3
Codeine	OCH_3	OH	CH_3
Dihydrocodeine*	OCH_3	OH	CH_3
(other related agonists include buprenorphine and pholcodine.)			

Antagonists			
Naloxone*	OH	=O	$CH_2CH=CH_2$

* Single bond at C7–8.

Opiate antagonists are competitive antagonists at opioid receptors and reverse the pharmacological effects of the opiate agonists.

Uses

Analgesia:

(a) severe pain—particularly effective in visceral pain (morphine, diamorphine, and buprenorphine);
(b) moderate pain (codeine, dihydrocodeine, buprenorphine).

Acute pulmonary oedema due to left ventricular failure (morphine, diamorphine).
Symptomatic relief of diarrhoea (codeine).
Suppression of cough (morphine, codeine, pholcodine).
Pre-operative medication (morphine).
Naloxone is used to reverse the adverse effects of the opiate analgesics, but is only partially effective in relieving the adverse effects of buprenorphine. Naloxone also reverses the effects of other narcotic analgesics, such as pethidine, dextropropoxyphene, methadone, and pentazocine.

Dosage

There are many different dosage formulations of the opiate analgesics, and individual patients' needs will dictate the use of one or another. A selection of commonly used dosages and formulations is given below. Other formulations are listed in more comprehensive formularies.

Parenteral

Relief of pain (see also p.537), treatment of pulmonary oedema, pre-operative medication (morphine):

Morphine 10–20 mg, i.v., i.m., or s.c.
Diamorphine 5–10 mg, i.v., i.m., or s.c.
Dihydrocodeine 25–50 mg, i.m. or by deep s.c. injection.
Buprenorphine 300–600 micrograms, i.m. or by slow i.v. injection.
Nepenthe (anhydrous morphine, 8.4 mg/ml), 1–2 ml, i.v., i.m., or s.c.

Oral—analgesic elixirs in the treatment of severe pain

Diamorphine and cocaine elixir—each 5 ml contains 5 mg diamorphine and 5 mg cocaine. Initial dose 5–10 ml.

Diamorphine, cocaine, and chlorpromazine elixir—each 5 ml contains 5 mg diamorphine, 5 mg cocaine, and 6.25 mg chlorpromazine. Initial dose 5–10 ml.

Morphine and cocaine elixir—each 5 ml contains 5 mg morphine and 5 mg cocaine. Initial dose 5–10 ml.

Morphine, cocaine, and chlorpromazine elixir—each 5 ml contains 5 mg morphine, 5 mg cocaine, and 6.25 mg chlorpromazine. Initial dose 5–10 ml.

Nepenthe elixir—each 1 ml contains brown anhydrous morphine 8.4 mg. Dose—adults, 1–2 ml; children 1–5 y, 0.25–0.5 ml; 6–12 y, 0.5–1.0 ml.

Other oral or rectal formulations for severe pain

Sustained release tablets—MST-1 Continus® tablets. These each contain morphine 10 mg or 30 mg. Initial dose 10–20 mg b.d.

Sublingual tablets—buprenorphine 0.4 mg (two tablets) every 6–8 h as required.

Suppositories—morphine 15 mg, one to two suppositories.

Oral formulations for the treatment of moderate pain

Codeine phosphate, 10–60 mg, four-hourly when required, to a maximum of 200 mg daily.
Dihydrocodeine, 30–60 mg, every 4–6 h as required.
Buprenorphine, as for severe pain.

Oral formulations for other indications

Diarrhoea—Opium tincture (morphine 10 mg/ml), 1–2 ml; Codeine phosphate, 45–120 mg daily in 3–6 divided doses.
Cough suppression—Linctus codeine, 15 mg/5 ml. Adults 5–20 ml.
Linctus pholcodine, 5 mg/ml, up to 10 ml four-hourly.

Opiate antagonists

Naloxone i.v.—0.4 mg, repeated once or twice at 2–3 min intervals if respiratory function does not improve after a single dose.

Kinetic data

Morphine and diamorphine are extensively metabolized by the liver and after oral administration their systemic availability is about 25 per cent because of the marked first-pass metabolism. Diamorphine is said to enter the brain more readily than morphine, and its earlier effects after parenteral injection may be due to this, but it is rapidly metabolized to morphine ($t_{1/2}$ 2 min) and any early advantage is soon lost. Morphine $t_{1/2}$ = 3 h. Morphine is further extensively metabolized and its metabolites are excreted in the urine.

The systemic availability of codeine is probably more than that of morphine and diamorphine, and it is metabolized by the liver, 10 per cent being demethylated to morphine, $t_{1/2}$ = 3 h.

Naloxone has a $t_{1/2}$ of 1 h. Note that this is shorter than that of morphine.

Important adverse effects

Nausea and vomiting are dose-related and the incidence of these symptoms increases particularly when doses of morphine greater than 10 mg are given (adults). However in clinical practice with judicious dosing it is very often possible to achieve good analgesic effects with minimal emetic effects. Because in many acute clinical situations routine dosage regimens have to be applied, e.g. acute myocardial infarction and post-operative pain, antiemetics are often given routinely with opiates (e.g. cyclizine in Cyclimorph®, chlorpromazine in elixir, and prochlorperazine).

Hypotension is not infrequent due to vasodilatation and may cause concern after myocardial infarction. Confusion, dizziness, and mental clouding often occur, particularly in the elderly. Micturition may be difficult because of effects on the bladder. Dry mouth and constipation are common.

Occasionally instead of euphoria and sedation, dysphoria, restlessness, and even psychiatric mental excitement occur.

Urticaria, pruritus, and itching of the nose may occur because of the histamine-releasing effects.

Physical drug dependence can occur quite quickly, but under usual clinical circumstances, when narcotic analgesics are being given for the relief of pain, addiction is not generally a problem. However, *tolerance*, which is pharmacologically related to dependence, does occur and may result in the need for higher doses. Tolerance to and physical dependence on opiate analgesics occurs at different rates for the different opiates, but typically begins to occur after about 2 weeks of continuous treatment with morphine or diamorphine. Abrupt withdrawal of the opiate, or administration of an opiate antagonist such as naloxone then results in a typical withdrawal syndrome. The first signs of withdrawal are yawning, sweating, lachrymation, and rhinorrhea, occurring at about 12 h after withdrawal. These are followed by restlessness, insomnia, irritability, tremor, anorexia, dilated pupils, and gooseflesh (so called 'cold turkey'). All these symptoms become progressively worse and the syndrome reaches its peak of intensity at about 2–3 days after withdrawal. At that time other symptoms occur, including nausea and vomiting, abdominal cramps, diarrhoea, muscle spasms, sexual orgasm, and an increase in heart rate and blood pressure. Treatment is by giving the patient his usual dose of opiate, but some have found that clonidine is effective in treating the syndrome. Untreated the syndrome disappears in about a week but during that time may be complicated by dehydration with all its consequences.

The syndrome which follows the withdrawal of methadone is less severe than that following withdrawal of morphine or diamorphine and takes longer to occur. For this reason it is possible to treat physical dependence on morphine or diamorphine by substituting methadone in a suitable dose and then slowly withdrawing the methadone. A dose of methadone of 1 mg for every 4 mg of morphine or 2 mg of diamorphine is usually adequate, and withdrawal of methadone can be carried out by small daily reductions in dose over a period of about 2–3 weeks. It is important that this procedure be carried out in hospital so that one may observe any acute withdrawal symptoms which require treatment. During methadone withdrawal minor withdrawal symptoms may be treated symptomatically. Alternatively, withdrawal of methadone may be carried out on an out-patient basis very gradually over several months.

Special problems may arise with the use of opiate analgesics in patients with respiratory or hepatic disease.

(i) Respiratory disease
In acute asthma and chronic obstructive airways disease opiate analgesics are dangerous because they reduce respiratory drive, diminish ventilation, and exacerbate hypoxia and hypercapnia. Catastrophic impairment of respiratory function may then result.

(ii) Hepatic disease
Opiate analgesics are dangerous in moderate or severe hepatic disease for two reasons. Firstly, their metabolism by the liver may be decreased and $t_{1/2}$ prolonged. Secondly, in hepatic failure incipient hepatic encephalopathy may render the brain more sensitive to the effects of opiates, and coma and respiratory depression result.

Naloxone has virtually no adverse effects apart from producing an acute withdrawal syndrome in subjects with physical dependence on opiates.

Interactions

Opiate analgesics and other centrally depressant drugs have additive effects. This is important for the co-administration of, for example, phenothiazines.

2. Non-opiate narcotic analgesics

Structures

Methadone, dextropropoxyphene, dipipanone, and dextromoramide have related structures. Dextropropoxyphene is shown here as an example:

$$(CH_3)_2NCH_2CH{-}\overset{\overset{\displaystyle CH_3}{|}}{\underset{\underset{\displaystyle C_6H_5}{|}}{C}}{-}CH_2C_6H_5$$
(with OOCCH₂CH₃ on the central carbon)

Pethidine and diphenoxylate are related. Pethidine (meperidine) is shown here:

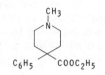

Mode of action
See opiate analgesics.

Uses
Analgesia:

(a) severe pain—particularly effective in visceral pain (pethidine, methadone, dipipanone, and dextromoramide);

(b) mild to moderate pain (dextropropoxyphene, often combined with paracetamol or aspirin).

Diarrhoea (diphenoxylate, combined with atropine sulphate).

Pre-operative medication (pethidine).

Treatment of opiate addiction (methadone).

Dosages

Parenteral
Pethidine, 25–100 mg i.m. or s.c., four-hourly as required.

Methadone, 5–10 mg i.m. or s.c., four-hourly as required.

Oral
Pethidine, 50–100 mg, four-hourly as required.

Methadone, 5–10 mg, four-hourly as required.

Dipipanone, 10 mg initially increasing to 30 mg every 4 h as required.

Dextromoramide, 5 mg initially increasing to 20 mg six-hourly as required.

Dextropropoxyphene. This is commonly used in combination with paracetamol, e.g. as Distalgesic®, Dextrogesic®, or Cosalgesic®, which each contain dextropropoxyphene 32.5 mg with paracetamol 325 mg in each tablet. Dose 1–2 tablets every 6–8 h. Formulations containing aspirin are also available.

Diphenoxylate. This is commonly used in

combination with atropine sulphate, e.g. as Lomotil® or Reasec®, which contain diphenoxylate 2.5 mg and atropine sulphate 25 micrograms in each tablet. Dose, four tablets initially, followed by two tablets six-hourly.

Important adverse effects

The adverse effects of the non-opiate narcotic analgesics are similar to those of the opiate

Kinetic data

	Absorption	Metabolism	$T_{1/2}$
Pethidine	55%	Liver +++	3 h
Methadone	Well absorbed	Extensive first pass	1–2 days
Dipipanone		Liver +++	
Dextromoramide			
Dextropropoxyphene	Well absorbed	Liver +++	12 h

analgesics. However, dextropropoxyphene and diphenoxylate do not commonly cause adverse effects in short courses of therapeutic doses. However, chronic usage can lead to dependence and overdosage has the same effects as morphine.

Interactions

As for opiate analgesics.

NEUROMUSCULAR BLOCKING AGENTS (MUSCLE RELAXANTS)

1. Non-depolarizing muscle relaxants

Structures
Tubocurarine:

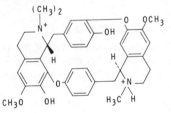

Pancuronium:

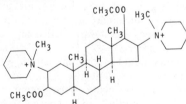

Other non-depolarizing agents include gallamine, alcuronium, and fazadinium.

Mode of action

The non-depolarizing neuromuscular blocking agents act by competitive inhibition of the

action of acetylcholine at the motor end-plate. They thus cause paralysis of voluntary muscle without first causing depolarization (cf. depolarizing agents below).

Their actions are reversible by acetylcholinesterase inhibitors such as neostigmine.

Uses

For the production of muscle relaxation during surgical anaesthesia.

Dosages

Tubocurarine : 10–15 mg i.v. initially, followed by additional doses of 5 mg i.v. to a maximum of 40 mg.

Pancuronium : 60–100 micrograms/kg initially, followed by supplementary doses of 10–40 micrograms/kg according to response.

Kinetic data

The rate of onset, time to peak, and total duration of effect of these drugs are dose-dependent. The following data pertain to usual dosages.

Tubocurarine : Onset of paralysis is rapid, with a peak at 3–5 min and a duration of 20–30 min. Tubocurarine does not cross the blood–brain barrier. Placental transfer is poor and so there is little effect on the fetus. Renal excretion accounts for 30 per cent of the total elimination of the drug. $T_{1/2}$ = 100 min.

Pancuronium : Onset of paralysis is rapid, with a peak at 3 min and a duration of action of 20–30 min. Pancuronium does not cross the blood–brain barrier. Placental transfer is poor and so there is little effect on the fetus. Pancuronium is metabolized by the liver and excreted by the kidney and in the bile. $T_{1/2}$ = 100 min.

Important adverse effects during anaesthesia

Tubocurarine causes some degree of autonomic ganglion blockade and histamine release. It may therefore cause slight hypotension, occasional bradycardia, and a transient erythematous rash. Bronchospasm occurs, but rarely. Pancuronium does not cause autonomic ganglion blockade and causes little histamine release. Thus hypotension is less of a problem than with tubocurarine.

Interactions

The effects of the non-depolarizing muscle relaxants are reversed by acetylcholinesterase inhibitors (q.v.).

Some drugs with direct neuromuscular blocking effects may potentiate the effects of the non-depolarizing muscle relaxants. They include the aminoglycosides, clindamycin and lincomycin, colistin, and quinine and quinidine. Magnesium salts also potentiate the effects of these muscle relaxants.

2. Depolarizing muscle relaxants

Structures

Suxamethonium (succinylcholine) is the most commonly used drug of this type:

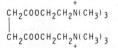

Mode of action

Suxamethonium produces a prolonged depolarization of the motor end-plate and thus prevents any response to acetylcholine. This action is NOT reversible by acetylcholinesterase inhibitors (cf. non-depolarizing muscle relaxants).

Uses

For the production of muscle relaxation during anaesthesia, particularly when only short-term effects are required.

Dosages

20–100 mg i.v. according to the patient's needs and response.

Kinetic data

The onset of action of suxamethonium occurs within 30 s, and its duration of action is 3–5 min in normal individuals. It is rapidly hydrolysed by pseudocholinesterase in the plasma and tissues. $T_{1/2}$ = 2–4 min. However, in patients with pseudocholinesterase deficiency the metabolism is slowed and the $t_{1/2}$ and duration of effect are prolonged (see Chapter 8).

Important adverse effects

Muscle fasciculation occurs during the onset of muscle relaxation because of depolarization, and muscle pains are common after the procedure.

Prolonged apnoea occurs when pseudocholinesterase deficiency is present, either acquired (e.g. due to liver disease, malnutrition, or severe anaemia) or congenital (hereditary pseudocholinesterase deficiency, discussed in Chapter 8).

Suxamethonium has some muscarinic activity, causing a transient rise in intraocular pressure, salivary gland enlargement, increased bowel motility, and increased gastric and salivary secretions. For these reasons premedication with atropine is desirable before suxamethonium is used. It should not be used in patients with glaucoma and during ophthalmic operations.

Dual block may occur with non-depolarizing block (see Chapter 30).

Repeated doses may produce cardiac slowing.

A small rise in plasma potassium (about 0.2–0.4 mmol/l) may occur due to potassium release from muscle.

Interactions

Potentiation of suxamethonium may occur with drugs which have direct neuromuscular blocking effects, including aminoglycosides, clindamycin and lincomycin, colistin, and quinine and quinidine. Magnesium salts also potentiate the muscle relaxant effects of suxamethonium. Drugs which inhibit the activity of pseudocholinesterase decrease suxamethonium metabolism and thus enhance its effects —these include cyclophosphamide, mustine, thiotepa, MAO inhibitors, and inhibitors of acetylcholinesterase. Included in the last group are long-acting acetylcholinesterase inhibitors such as ecothiopate, which is used in eye drops in the treatment of glaucoma, and organo-phosphorus insecticides.

Suxamethonium may potentiate the effects of cardiac glycosides, by an unknown mechanism.

NIFEDIPINE

Structure

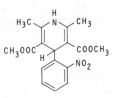

Mode of action

Nifedipine inhibits the transport of calcium across cell membranes and falls into that class of substances called 'calcium antagonists'. Nifedipine affects principally vascular smooth muscle, particularly in peripheral arterioles causing a decrease in peripheral vascular resistance. It also affects normal coronary arteries causing dilatation and preventing spasm.

Uses

Angina pectoris.
Hypertension.

Kinetic data

Nifedipine is well absorbed after oral administration and more quickly after sublingual administration. It is extensively metabolized to inactive metabolites, $t_{1/2} = 5$ h.

Dosages

10–20 mg t.d.s. orally.

Important adverse effects

The commonest adverse effects are related to vasodilatation, and include headache and flushing. In high doses nifedipine may rarely exacerbate acute attacks of angina pectoris.

Interactions

Nifedipine may increase plasma digoxin concentrations by an unknown mechanism. Digoxin dosage should be reduced if required, as assessed by plasma digoxin concentration measurements (see Chapter 7).

NIKETHAMIDE

Structure

Mode of action

Nikethamide is an analeptic, i.e. it is a stimulant of various central nervous system functions. It stimulates respiration by a direct effect on the respiratory centre in the medulla oblongata and does not stimulate carotid chemoreceptors (cf. doxapram).

Uses

For a discussion of the uses of respiratory

stimulants see under doxapram.

Dosages

0.5–2 g i.v. repeated as necessary every 15–30 min. Frequent monitoring of arterial blood gases and pH are required to allow regulation of the dosage.

Important adverse effects

Adverse effects are common and are dose-related. They include nausea and vomiting, tachycardia and cardiac arrhythmias, dizzi-ness, restlessness, tremor, and convulsions.

Nikethamide should not be given to patients with respiratory depression in association with neurological disease (including cerebral oedema), or to patients with status asthmaticus, coronary artery disease, hyperthyroidism, or severe hypertension. It should be administered only with great care to patients with a history of epilepsy.

It is not helpful, and may be dangerous, in patients with respiratory depression due to overdose with hypnotics or sedatives.

NITROFURANTOIN

Structure

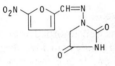

Mode of action

Nitrofurantoin is bacteriostatic by virtue of inhibition of a number of bacterial enzymes, including that responsible for acetyl CoA synthesis, essential for bacterial function.

Uses

Urinary infections due to Gram-negative organisms, particularly *E. coli.*

Dosage

100 mg q.d.s., orally.

Kinetic data

Well absorbed. $T_{1/2}$ 30 min. About 40 per cent of the dose of nitrofurantoin appears unchanged in the urine in concentrations two to four times the usual minimal inhibitory concentration for sensitive bacteria. Blood concentrations are much lower but are increased in renal failure.

Important adverse effects

Nausea and vomiting are common. Mild allergic reactions occur in about 4 per cent of patients. They are usually unimportant in themselves, but their occurrence is a warning to stop treatment since they may herald more serious forms of allergy resulting in lung or liver damage.

Long-term therapy occasionally results in a peripheral neuropathy which is dose-related.

Nitrofurantoin may cause haemolysis in patients with G6PD deficiency (see Chapter 8).

Nitrofurantoin should not be used in patients with renal failure.

NYSTATIN

Structure

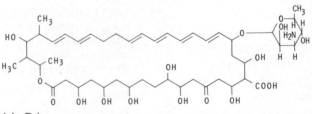

(Compare amphotericin B.)

Mode of action

Alteration of permeability of cell membranes leading to loss of essential cell constituents.

Uses

Infections with *Candida albicans* (moniliasis, candidiasis, thrush) of the gastro-intestinal tract, the vagina, the respiratory tract, and the skin.

Dosages

Depend on formulation and route of administration, e.g.:

oral thrush: nystatin suspension 100 000 i.u. t.d.s.;

vaginal thrush: nystatin pessaries 100 000–200 000 i.u. o.d.

Kinetic data

Not absorbed after oral or topical administration.

Important adverse effects

Adverse effects are rare and generally unimportant.

PARACETAMOL (ACETAMINOPHEN)

Structure

$$CH_3CONH\text{---}\langle\ \rangle\text{---}OH$$

Mode of action

Paracetamol has analgesic and antipyretic properties but little anti-inflammatory activity. The mechanism of these effects is unknown.

Uses

For the treatment of mild pain, particularly in musculoskeletal conditions, headache, and dysmenorrhoea.

Dosages

0.5–1 g every 4–6 h as required, orally. Maximum 4 g daily.

Kinetic data

Well absorbed. Almost completely converted ($t_{1/2}$ 4 h) to metabolites which are excreted in the urine. The route of metabolism is important in understanding the reason for the occurrence of hepatic damage in overdose, and providing the rationale for its prevention.

About 80 per cent of an administered dose of paracetamol is normally conjugated as glucuronide and sulphate, but these pathways are easily saturated; of the remainder about 15 per cent is metabolized to a hydroxylamine derivative which is non-toxic at concentrations resulting from conventional doses, since it reacts with hepatic glutathione intracellularly and is detoxified. When the concentration rises, however, the hepatic stores of glutathione are exhausted and the hydroxylamine combines with cell structures causing cellular damage which results in hepatic necrosis.

Prevention of hepatic necrosis in paracetamol overdose can be achieved by providing sulphydryl groups which react with and detoxify the hydroxylamine. *N*-acetylcysteine and methionine are examples of compounds which are used for this purpose (see p.576).

Important adverse effects

Adverse effects are rare with therapeutic doses. In overdose hepatic necrosis is the most important effect, and when it occurs hepatic enzymes are usually raised by 48 h after overdose. Rarely acute tubular necrosis also occurs, sometimes in the absence of hepatic damage.

PENICILLAMINE

Structure

$$(CH_3)_2C\overset{\overset{\displaystyle SH}{|}}{\text{---}}\overset{\overset{\displaystyle NH_2}{|}}{C}HCOOH$$

(Prepared by the hydrolytic degradation of penicillin, q.v.).

Mode of action

Penicillamine is a chelating agent, and that forms the basis of its mode of action in the treatment of heavy metal poisoning (e.g. lead), and of Wilson's disease, in which there is accumulation of copper. In cystinuria it probably acts by forming a soluble disulphide complex with cystine. The complexes with heavy metals and with cystine are excreted in the urine. The mode of action in the treatment of rheumatoid arthritis and its variants is unknown.

Uses

Wilson's disease (hepatolenticular degeneration).

Chronic lead poisoning.

Active rheumatoid arthritis.

Cystinuria.

Dosages

Wilson's disease: 250 mg b.d., orally initially, increasing to a total of 2 g daily as required, depending on urinary copper excretion.

Lead poisoning: Up to 1 g daily orally, the dose being adjusted according to urinary lead excretion.

Rheumatoid arthritis: 125–250 mg o.d., orally initially, increasing every 4–8 weeks by 125–250 mg. Some patients need as little as 250 mg daily, while others need as much as 1 g daily. It takes up to 12 weeks to see improvement, and if improvement occurs therapy should be continued for 6 months, after which the dose should be gradually reduced.

Cystinuria: 500 mg at night, orally initially, increasing in increments of 250 mg to 2 g daily (range 1–4 g), depending on urinary cystine excretion. An adequate fluid intake should be ensured.

Kinetic data

Penicillamine is well absorbed and is metabolized about 50 per cent in the liver. It is excreted in the urine both as free penicillamine and as disulphide derivatives. Following oral and i.v. administration it disappears from the plasma with a $t_{1/2}$ of a few hours, but continues to be excreted for several days after. Dosages should be reduced in renal failure.

Important adverse effects

Adverse effects are common and on average 30 per cent of patients suffer serious adverse effects.

Allergic reactions include fever (usually transient); syndromes mimicking pemphigus, myositis, systemic lupus erythematosus, and the muscle weakness of myasthenia gravis; nephritis (see below); and skin rashes. Early rashes may necessitate decreased dosage, and late rashes may necessitate the withdrawal of treatment altogether.

Proteinuria occurs in up to 15 per cent of cases, and may herald an immune-complex nephritis which may proceed to the nephrotic syndrome. Treatment may be continued in the presence of proteinuria as long as daily proteinuria is no greater than 2 g, oedema is absent, and other indices of renal function remain normal.

Haematological complications may occur. Thrombocytopenia has been seen in up to 4 per cent of cases, and leucopenia in up to 2 per cent. More rarely, aplastic anaemia and agranulocytosis occur.

In high doses, penicillamine impairs collagen synthesis, and may cause thinning of the skin. Haemorrhage into the skin may then occur.

Anorexia, nausea, and vomiting are common during the early stages of treatment but may be reduced by taking the drug with food, and by very gradual introduction of dosage. Impaired taste occurs during the first few weeks of treatment, but subsequently recovers. Occasionally mouth ulcers may occur.

Because of these adverse effects, blood and urine testing must be carried out at at least monthly intervals, and patients should be carefully observed.

PENICILLINS

Structures

General:

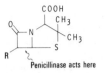

(Compare cephalosporins.)

Various side chains at R alter resistance to gastric acid, resistance to penicillinase, and antibacterial spectrum.

Mode of action

Penicillins are bacteriocidal and act by inhibition of bacterial cell wall synthesis through inhibition of a membrane-bound transpeptidase. Weakening of the cell wall and consequent lysis and cell death result.

Bacterial resistance to penicillin occurs among organisms which produce an enzyme, penicillinase (β-lactamase), which splits the β-lactam ring of the penicillin nucleus (see general structure). The chief organisms which produce penicillinase include *Staph. aureus* (especially those found in hospitals), and some *E. coli, Proteus mirabilis,* and *Pseudomonas aeruginosa.* Some penicillins are resistant to the effects of penicillinase, and they are indicated in the classification below.

Classification

The penicillins may be empirically classified, principally according to certain bacteriological criteria, as follows:

Group I: Penicillinase-sensitive penicillins

(a) Benzylpenicillin (penicillin G), i.v. and i.m. Benzylpenicillin is also formulated as salts to provide slow release from IM injection sites, and therefore longer duration of action. These salts include:

(i) procaine penicillin, i.m., 1–2 times daily;

(ii) benethamine penicillin, i.m., once every 2–3 days;

(iii) benzathine penicillin, i.m., once every 2–3 days.

(b) Phenoxymethylpenicillin (penicillin V), oral.

Group 2: Penicillinase-resistant penicillins

Cloxacillin, i.m. and i.v.
Flucloxacillin, oral, i.m., and i.v.
(Antipseudomonal penicillins–see below.)

Group 3: Broad-spectrum penicillins

Amoxycillin, oral, i.m., and i.v.
Ampicillin, oral, i.m., and i.v. Ampicillin is also formulated as esters (pro-drugs, see Chapter 2), which have better absorption after oral administration and which are then completely converted to ampicillin. These esters include talampicillin and pivampicillin (both for oral use only).

Group 4: Antipseudomonal penicillins

Carbenicillin, i.m. and i.v.
Carfecillin, oral (a pro-drug ester of carbenicillin).
Ticarcillin, i.m. and i.v.
Azlocillin, i.v.

Group 5: Amidinopenicillins

Mecillinam, i.m. and i.v.
Pivmecillinam, oral (a pro-drug ester of mecillinam).

Uses

In Table P6 are listed some of the common examples of bacteria sensitive to the penicillins, and the associated diseases for which they are particularly used.

Kinetic data

Many of the orally administered penicillins are poorly absorbed. The exceptions are the various pro-drug esters which have been specifically designed to improve absorption (see classification above), and amoxycillin. The penicillins are mostly excreted unchanged via the urine but phenoxymethylpenicillin, cloxacillin, and flucloxacillin are about 60 per cent metabolized. Half-times vary between 30 and 60 min but are generally prolonged in renal failure, when dosages should be reduced.

Table P6   *The main indications for the use of penicillins*

Bacteria	Disease	Penicillin
Gram +ve cocci		
Streptococcus pyogenes	Tonsillitis Pharyngitis Otitis media Prophylaxis of rheumatic fever Puerperal sepsis	Penicillinase-sensitive penicillins (group 1), e.g. penicillin V
Streptococcus viridans *Streptococcus faecalis* *Streptococcus bovis* Anaerobic streptococci	Bacterial endocarditis	Penicillin G + gentamicin
Staphylococcus aureus (presume penicillinase-producing)	Boils Pneumonia Endocarditis Osteomyelitis	Penicillinase-resistant penicillins (group 2), e.g. flucloxacillin
Streptococcus pneumoniae	Pneumococcal lobar pneumonia Pneumococcal meningitis	Penicillin G
Gram −ve cocci		
N. meningitidis	Meningococcal meningitis	Penicillin G
N. gonorrhoeae	Gonorrhoea	Penicillinase-sensitive penicillins (group 1), e.g. procaine penicillin + probenecid (q.v.)
Gram −ve bacilli		
Ps. aeruginosa	Urinary tract infection	Antipseudomonal penicillins (group 4) (may be combined with an aminoglycoside)
H. influenzae	Acute or chronic bronchitis Bronchopneumonia Otitis media Sinusitis	Broad-spectrum penicillins (group 3), e.g. amoxycillin
Salmonella spp.	Invasive salmonellosis (typhoid, paratyphoid)	Broad-spectrum penicillins (group 3; probably not first choice)
Vincent's organisms	Acute ulcerative oropharyngitis	Penicillinase-sensitive penicillins (group 1), e.g. penicillin G
Gram +ve bacilli		
Bacillus anthracis	Anthrax	Penicillin G
C. diphtheriae	Diphtheria	Penicillin G
Clostridium perfringens	Gas gangrene	Penicillin G
Clostridium tetani	Tetanus	Penicillin G
Others		
Treponema pallidum	Syphilis	Penicillin G
Actimomyces israelii	Actimomycosis	Penicillin G
Leptospira spp.	Leptospirosis	Penicillin G
Treponema pertenue	Yaws	Penicillin G

Dosages

Dosages vary widely, depending on the clinical indication. Some common dosages are given below.

Group 1: Penicillinase-sensitive penicillins

Benzylpenicillin (penicillin G): 0.3–6.0 g daily, i.m.; up to 24 g by i.v. infusion. For example, pneumococcal pneumonia, 1.2 g six-hourly, i.m. (Note: 600 mg = 1 million i.u. = 1 mega-unit.

Procaine penicillin: 300 mg 1–2 times daily, i.m.

Phenoxymethylpenicillin (penicillin V): 250 mg q.d.s., orally.

Group 2: Penicillinase-resistant penicillins

Flucloxacillin: 250 mg six-hourly, orally i.m. or i.v.

Group 3: Broad-spectrum penicillins

Amoxycillin: 250 mg t.d.s., orally.

Group 4: Antipseudomonal penicillins

Carbenicillin: 5 g every 4–6 h, by i.v. infusion.

Carfecillin: 500–1000 mg t.d.s., orally.

Ticarcillin: 15–20 g daily in divided doses, i.m. or i.v.

Azlocillin: 2–5 g eight-hourly, i.v.

In severe infections dosages may be adjusted by measuring the bacterial inhibitory activity of penicillin in the blood against the infecting organism *in vitro*.

Important adverse effects

Although the penicillins are very safe antibiotics they have important adverse effects.

(a) Hypersensitivity reactions

Anaphylactic shock is a very serious adverse effect which may be fatal, and it is vital to find out if a patient is known to be allergic to penicillin before administering or prescribing any preparation of penicillin. The incidence is between 1 in 2500 and 1 in 10 000, with a fatality rate in those affected of about 10 per cent.

Serum sickness and Stevens–Johnson syndrome occur in up to 5 per cent of patients and usually present 1–3 weeks after starting treatment.

Skin rashes are common (about 10 per cent) and range in severity from mild maculo-papular or urticarial eruptions to the Stevens–Johnson syndrome. The usual onset of these rashes is at between 3 and 10 days. With ampicillin and amoxycillin a specific maculo-papular rash, usually of later onset, and apparently not related to true penicillin hypersensitivity, occurs in up to 18 per cent of patients, but in about 90 per cent of those with infectious mononucleosis. It is also common among patients with infections with some other viruses, such as cytomegalovirus, and in patients with lymphoid malignancies. The ampicillin/amoxycillin rash is not a contra-indication to treatment with penicillins at a later date.

If a patient says that he or she is sensitive or allergic to penicillin (and that information should always be sought), a complete history of the allergy should be taken to confirm that it is so. It may be possible to thus distinguish the late-onset ampicillin/amoxycillin rash from that due to true penicillin hypersensitivity, but if there is any doubt it is usually best to assume that hypersensitivity exists. In such cases an alternative antibiotic should be used. Skin testing for penicillin hypersensitivity is unreliable and sometimes dangerous, and has not found a place in clinical practice.

The problem of whether or not to give a patient with known penicillin hypersensitivity a cephalosporin is a difficult one. About 10 per cent of all patients with penicillin hypersensitivity will develop skin rashes with cephalosporins, and sometimes this risk has to be taken. There is some evidence, however, that the likelihood of a hypersensitivity reaction to cephalosporins is greater in patients with a history of a severe penicillin hypersensitivity reaction (e.g. anaphylaxis), and the cephalosporins should be avoided in such patients.

(b) Other adverse effects

Diarrhoea occurs commonly with oral penicillin formulations but is less frequent with those which are well absorbed (e.g. amoxycillin).

Rarely ampicillin and other penicillins may cause a pseudomembranous colitis (see lincomycin and clindamycin).

Superinfection of the oropharynx with, for example, *Candida albicans*, may occur particularly in the elderly and debilitated.

Hyperkalaemia, and hypernatraemia with fluid retention may occur as a consequence of high intravenous dosages of certain penicillins because of the salt form, e.g. potassium and sodium benzylpenicillin, and disodium carbenicillin.

Penicillin is a neurotoxic in high doses and may cause myoclonic jerks, generalized seizures, or coma. This is a particular hazard with intrathecal therapy.

Acute interstitial nephritis and blood dyscrasias, such as haemolytic anaemia (Coombs's positive), thrombocytopenia, and leucopenia, are all rare complications.

Interactions

Drugs which inhibit renal tubular secretion of the penicillins diminish their excretion and may thus cause accumulation with increased plasma concentrations. Commonly used drugs which have this effect are probenecid, sulphinpyrazone, phenylbutazone, and indomethacin. Advantage is taken of this interaction in the concurrent use of probenecid with penicillin to enhance the therapeutic efficacy of the antibiotic in the treatment of gonorrhoea and of bacterial endocarditis. The dosage of probenecid (q.v.) is 500 mg q.d.s., orally.

Clavulanic acid

Clavulanic acid is used in combination with amoxycillin in the preparation called Augmentin®, which may be used for the treatment of infections with bacteria usually sensitive to amoxycillin, but producing penicillinase, and particularly in infections of the urinary and respiratory tracts. Clavulanic acid is an inhibitor of penicillinase. It will not therefore be of value in treating infections by organisms whose resistance to penicillin is not mediated by penicillinase, such as penicillin-resistant pneumococci or gonococci, or cloxacillin-resistant staphylococci.

PHENOBARBITONE AND PRIMIDONE

Structures

Phenobarbitone: Primidone:

Mode of action

The exact mode of action of these drugs at the molecular level is unknown, although interesting relationships among barbiturate actions, benzodiazepine and GABA receptors, and inhibitory neurotransmitter function are beginning to emerge. At the neurophysiological level they limit the spread of seizure activity, and increase seizure threshold.

Uses

Anticonvulsants in generalized tonic–clonic seizures (grand mal epilepsy). By general agreement phenobarbitone is now restricted to this indication in the U.K.

Dosages

Phenobarbitone: 90–360 mg o.d., orally at night is the usual dosage range but higher doses, to a maximum of 600 mg daily may occasionally be required.

Primidone: 125 mg o.d., orally at night initially, increasing the dose as required at 3-day intervals by 125 mg daily to a dose of 500 mg daily. Then, if necessary, the daily dose should be increased by 250 mg at 3-day intervals until a therapeutic effect is achieved, or a maximum daily dose of 1.5 g is reached. The higher dosages should be divided into two or three equal doses.

Kinetic data

Both are well absorbed, phenobarbitone more slowly than primidone (time to peak concentrations 6–18 h and 2–4 h respectively).

Primidone is slowly metabolized ($t_{1/2}$ = 8 h) to phenobarbitone (about 20 per cent) and phenylethylmalonic acid. The extent of its metabolism, however, is very variable and this results in the large variability in dose. Increases in dose should not be made more frequently than every three days.

Phenobarbitone is mostly metabolized (80 per cent) by parahydroxylation and conjugation ($t_{1/2}$ = 3 days). Its metabolism is saturable in overdose.

Important adverse effects

Effects on the brain are common and include drowsiness, dizziness, headache, and ataxia. The elderly are particularly susceptible. Occasionally allergic skin reactions occur. Barbiturates may precipitate an attack of acute intermittent porphyria (see Chapter 8).

Barbiturate overdose is dealt with on p.579.

Interactions

Phenobarbitone and primidone both induce the hepatic microsomal enzymes involved in drug metabolism. Phenobarbitone therefore induces the metabolism (i.e. increases the rate of clearance) of several drugs, including warfarin, prednisone, digitoxin, and phenytoin. The interaction with phenytoin is complicated by the fact that phenytoin is also an inducer of hepatic microsomal drug-metabolizing enzymes. The resultant effect on the clearance of each drug in the individual patient is completely unpredictable.

Chloramphenicol inhibits phenobarbitone metabolism, resulting in increased plasma phenobarbitone concentrations. Conversely phenobarbitone induces chloramphenicol metabolism.

There are pharmacodynamic interactions with other CNS depressant drugs. For example, the effects of alcohol, hypnotics, tranquillizers, and antihistamines are all potentiated. In addition the CNS adverse effects of phenytoin may be enhanced, increasing the complexity of this interaction.

PHENOTHIAZINES AND THIOXANTHENES

Structures

Phenothiazines, general:

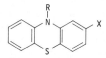

Thioxanthenes, general:

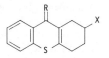

(Compare tricyclic antidepressants.)

The substitution of chemical groups at position R determine the pharmacological actions of these drugs and at position X their potency.

Phenothiazines in common use are chlorpromazine, fluphenazine, perphenazine, prochlorperazine, thioridazine, and trifluoperazine.

Thioxanthenes in common use are flupenthixol and clopenthixol.

Mode of action

Phenothiazines and thioxanthenes inhibit dopamine receptors in the brain. It is thought that this action contributes greatly to their antipsychotic and tranquillizing effects. However, they also have anticholinergic and antihistaminic effects, and block the actions of 5-hydroxytryptamine and the α-adrenergic actions of noradrenaline; the contribution of these effects to their therapeutic efficacy is at present unclear. Their effect in inhibiting dopamine receptors is responsible for their extrapyramidal adverse effects.

These classes of compounds, in common with the butyrophenones, (e.g. haloperidol), are often called 'neuroleptics' (Greek, νευρον =a string or cord, and by extension, a nerve; ληψομαι, from λαμβανειν=to seize). This is a term which has been coined to describe their effects of tranquillizing and causing psycho-motor slowing.

Uses

As sedatives and tranquillizers.

In the treatment of acute and chronic psych-oses, e.g. mania, schizophrenia.

In acute organic confusional states.

As an adjunct to narcotic analgesia in the pain of terminal illness.

In the treatment and prevention of nausea and vomiting, particularly during radiother-apy, and cancer chemotherapy.

Dosages

Dosages vary according to the indication, severity of illness, and the individual. The following dosage recommendations are only a rough guide.

(a) Anti-emetic

Chlorpromazine: a single i.m. dose of 25–50 mg; orally 25 mg t.d.s.

Prochlorperazine: a single i.m. dose of 12.5–25 mg, or 5–25 mg t.d.s., orally.

Trifluoperazine: 1–3 mg daily in divided doses, i.m., or 2–4 mg daily in divided doses, orally.

(b) Ranges of dosages for acute psychoses

Chlorpromazine: 25–50 mg eight-hourly, i.m.

Perphenazine: 5–10 mg i.m. initially, fol-lowed by 5 mg six-hourly, to a maximum of 15 mg daily.

Prochlorperazine: 12.5–25 mg two to three times daily, orally.

Thioridazine: 200 mg orally, followed by up to 800 mg daily.

Trifluoperazine: 1–3 mg daily in divided doses, i.m.

(c) Ranges of dosages and treatment regimens for chronic psychoses

Chlorpromazine: 25 mg t.d.s., orally, ad-justed according to response to 1 g daily or more.

Fluphenazine HCl: 2.5–10 mg o.d., orally, adjusted according to response to a maximum of 20 mg daily.

Fluphenazine decanoate and enanthate (i.m. depot injections): test dose 12.5 mg. Maintenance dosage 25–50 mg every 2–6 weeks (decanoate) or 10–28 days (enanthate).

Perphenazine: 4 mg t.d.s., orally, adjusted according to response to a maximum of 24 mg daily.

Thioridazine: Up to 800 mg daily, orally.

Trifluoperazine: 5 mg b.d., orally, adjusted according to response by 5 mg daily every 3 days.

Flupenthixol decanoate (i.m. depot injec-tion): test dose 20 mg. Maintenance dosage 20–40 mg every 2–4 weeks.

Clopenthixol decanoate (i.m. depot injec-tion): test dose 100 mg. Maintenance dosage 200–400 mg every 2–4 weeks.

Kinetic data

The phenothiazines have variable bioavaila-bility because of extensive metabolism during their first passage through the gut wall and liver. Numerous metabolites of varying de-grees of therapeutic activity and toxicity are formed, and persist in the body for weeks or even months.

Depot preparations

The chronic drug therapy of schizophrenia is dogged by patient non-compliance, and pre-parations have been developed which provide a low, but adequate plasma concentration for several weeks after injection (see dosage regi-mens above). These preparations are formu-lated as esters of the parent drug in vegetable oil, from which the drug is slowly absorbed after intramuscular injection. Because of the prolonged effect of these preparations a test dose should be given initially and regular therapy started a few days later if the patient is free from serious adverse effects. A practi-cal point of management is that the patient is seen every 2–6 weeks or so for the injection and progress can be assessed at the same time.

Important adverse effects

Sedation is common early on but tolerance develops rapidly.

Extrapyramidal signs and symptoms occur

commonly, trifluoperazine and perphenazine being more potent in this respect than chlorpromazine or thioridazine. These may result in Parkinsonism, akathisia, and various acute dystonic reactions. Anticholinergic drugs, such as benzhexol and orciprenaline, are of value in controlling these problems. Tardive dyskinesia may be a serious problem during prolonged therapy. It consists of involuntary dyskinetic movements, most often involving the jaws, lips, and tongue, but the face, limbs, and trunk may also be affected. Such movement disorders may persist despite withdrawal of therapy.

Anticholinergic effects occur at high dosages and include dry mouth, blurred vision, urinary retention, and constipation.

Hypotension may occur, particularly with chlorpromazine, in the critically ill patient with organic confusion who is also hypovolaemic, and care should be taken in these circumstances.

Hypersensitivity reactions occur occasionally. Skin rashes are common and photosensitivity is a particular problem. Cholestatic jaundice is caused by chlorpromazine and has been reported in up to 2 per cent of cases.

In the elderly hypothermia may be a problem.

Endocrine disturbances may be associated with increased prolactin secretion because of dopamine receptor inhibition. These include gynaecomastia, galactorrhoea, and menstrual disturbances.

Prolonged high dosages may cause corneal and lens opacities and pigmentation of the cornea, conjunctiva, and retina.

Blood dyscrasias are rare. Leucopenia and agranulocytosis have been reported.

Interactions

The sedative effects of these drugs are potentiated by alcohol and other sedative drugs.

The effects of hypotensive agents are potentiated.

PHENYLBUTAZONE AND OXYPHENBUTAZONE

Structures

General:

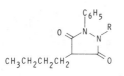

Phenylbutazone: $R = C_6H_5$.
Oxyphenbutazone: $R = C_6H_4OH$.

Mode of action

These drugs belong to the pyrazolone class. They have analgesic, antipyretic, and anti-inflammatory properties and these actions may be related to their inhibitory effects on prostaglandin synthesis. Their uricosuric effect is due to inhibition of tubular reabsorption of uric acid.

Uses

Because of the high incidence of adverse effects during prolonged dosage, the use of these drugs is not now recommended. They have been used in treating acute inflammatory conditions (e.g. thrombophlebitis, acute gout) and acute exacerbations of chronic arthritic conditions, such as rheumatoid arthritis, osteoarthritis, ankylosing spondylitis, and other sero-negative arthropathies, but other safer agents are now preferred.

Dosages

Phenylbutazone: 200 mg t.d.s., orally for 2 days, then 100 mg t.d.s. Rectal route, 250 mg bd.

Oxyphenbutazone: as for phenylbutazone.

These drugs should be taken with food if possible to minimize gastro-intestinal adverse effects.

Kinetic data

Both are well absorbed. Phenylbutazone is metabolized to its active metabolite, oxyphenbutazone and both compounds are excreted in the urine. $T_{1/2} = 3$ days. A second metabolite, γ-hydroxyphenylbutazone has uricosuric effects only and a shorter $t_{1/2}$ (12 h). Both are highly bound to plasma proteins.

Important adverse effects

Both compounds can cause bone marrow suppression resulting in aplastic anaemia, agranulocytosis, or thrombocytopenia. The incidence of aplastic anaemia is about 1:50 000. Anaemia may result from blood loss secondary to thrombocytopenia or gastro-intestinal ulceration.

Gastro-intestinal effects are common, and include nausea, vomiting, and symptoms of 'dyspepsia'. Peptic ulcers occur quite commonly and haematemesis is a serious complication.

Fluid retention may occur, causing peripheral oedema, which may be relieved by diuretics. In severe cases cardiac failure may occur.

Interactions

These drugs should not be used in conjunction with warfarin because of direct and indirect interactions by the following mechanisms:

(a) inhibition of the metabolism of S-warfarin;
(b) peptic ulceration;
(c) inhibition of platelet aggregation;
(d) thrombocytopenia;
(e) displacement of warfarin from protein binding sites.

The effects of sulphonylureas are increased because of inhibition of metabolism and inhibition of renal excretion.

Phenylbutazone increases the risk of methotrexate toxicity by an unknown mechanism.

When phenylbutazone is used in combination with chloroquine there is an increased risk of exfoliative dermatitis, and this combination should not be used.

PHENYTOIN (DIPHENYLHYDANTOIN)

Structure

Mode of action

At the neurophysiological level phenytoin prevents the spread of the epileptic discharge rather than suppressing the activity of the primary focus or altering the seizure threshold. The molecular events which result in these effects are still obscure. Phenytoin inhibits sodium and potassium transmembrane fluxes but the relationship of this action to its anticonvulsant effect is unknown. It also has various effects on the functions of some neurotransmitters (e.g. GABA and 5-hydroxytryptamine), but equally the link between these effects and its anticonvulsant effect is unclear. Phenytoin also possesses a membrane stabilizing effect not unlike that of lignocaine (q.v.), and this may at least account for its actions in the treatment of

cardiac arrhythmias, although its role in the anticonvulsant effect is not clear. However, unlike lignocaine and other Class I anti-arrhythmic drugs, it does not decrease the rate of conduction through the AV node, and this makes it of particular value in the treatment of arrhythmias due to digitalis intoxication.

Uses

Epilepsy: generalized tonic–clonic seizures (grand mal epilepsy); partial seizures (e.g. psychomotor and temporal lobe epilepsy).

Ventricular arrhythmias: particularly those induced by digitalis.

Dosages

Epilepsy: dosages vary widely from individual to individual because of the variability of phenytoin's pharmacokinetics (see below). A typical sort of dosage would be 300 mg o.d., orally.

Cardiac arrhythmias: 4 mg/kg given by slow i.v. infusion with ECG monitoring. If chronic oral treatment is required, anticonvulsant dosages should be used.

Kinetic data

Phenytoin is well, but slowly absorbed (time to peak plasma concentration, 3–10 h). The intramuscular route should be avoided if possible, because of crystallization at the site of injection, and consequent unpredictable bioavailability.

Phenytoin is almost completely metabolized by the liver, and its major metabolite is *para*-hydroxyphenytoin. This oxidative metabolism is saturable within the range of therapeutic doses, and because the point of saturability varies from individual to individual, it is necessary to adjust the dosage in each case according to the plasma concentration and the clinical response (see Chapter 7). The metabolism of phenytoin is also bimodally distributed in the population, about 9 per cent of subjects being poor hydroxylators (see Chapter 8).

Because of its saturable metabolism the $t_{1/2}$ of phenytoin varies with dose, being longer at high doses (up to about 40 h).

Plasma phenytoin concentrations should generally be within the range 40–80 μmol/l (see Chapter 7, p.114). The plasma concentration should be measured at steady state, i.e. after at least one week of continuous treatment. If it is found necessary to increase the dose this should be done in increments of no more than 50 mg before further measurements are made.

In renal failure the therapeutic plasma concentration falls, because of reduced protein binding of the drug. This also happens during the last trimester of pregnancy and in other states producing hypoalbuminaemia, and if there is displacement of phenytoin from its plasma protein binding sites by another drug (see Chapter 10).

Important adverse effects

At plasma concentrations above the therapeutic range toxic effects increase in incidence and are mostly due to effects on the brain. They consist of nystagmus, ataxia, tremor, lethargy, dysarthria, psychological disturbances, seizures, and ultimately coma. Increasing plasma concentrations have been related in rising sequence to nystagmus (80–120 μmol/l), ataxia (120–160 μmol/l), and mental changes (>160 μmol/l).

There are other adverse effects which are not clearly related to dose, and which occur during long-term therapy. These include:

gum hypertrophy and changes in facial features owing to increased collagen thickness;
hirsutism and acne;
megaloblastic anaemia (due to folate deficiency, the reason for which is still not clear);
osteomalacia (due to increased vitamin D metabolism);
lupus erythematosus, erythema multiforme, and other skin rashes;
lymphadenopathy; after prolonged administration there appears to be an increased incidence of lymphoma;

There are certain risks associated with the use of phenytoin in pregnancy. There may be an increased risk of cleft lip and palate and of digital hypoplasia in the fetus, and the neonate may suffer vitamin K deficiency with haemorrhagic consequences. The mother should be treated with vitamin K during the last month of pregnancy.

Interactions

Drugs which induce or inhibit the activity of the hepatic mixed function oxidases will alter the metabolism of phenytoin (see Chapter 10). Phenytoin itself induces the activity of those oxidases and this effect results in increased metabolism of some drugs. The metabolism of warfarin is increased, leading to ineffective anticoagulant control. The oestrogen in the combined oral contraceptive is metabolized more rapidly and the contraceptive may therefore become ineffective. This is usually signalled by mid-cycle spotting, and if that occurs the dose of oral contraceptive should be doubled.

Folic acid, in the doses administered during pregnancy, increases phenytoin clearance by an unknown mechanism, and thus lowers plasma phenytoin concentrations.

PIZOTIFEN

Structure

Mode of action

Pizotifen is a 5-hydroxytryptamine (5-HT) antagonist. The role of 5-HT in migraine is not fully understood, but there is evidence that during the early part of an attack of migraine there is release of 5-HT from platelets, with precipitation of vasoconstriction in the cerebral blood vessels. The aim of pizotifen is to prevent this sequence.

Use

Migraine prophylaxis.

Dosages

0.5 mg o.d., orally initially, increasing to 0.5 mg t.d.s. in 0.5 mg increments every few days. In severe cases up to 2 mg t.d.s. may be required.

Kinetic data

Well absorbed. $T_{1/2} = 26$ h.

Important adverse effects

Mild drowsiness occurs in up to 60 per cent of cases, but tolerance develops within a few weeks. Increased appetite and weight gain are common. Dizziness, nausea, and vomiting may occur.

Interactions

The effects of drugs acting on the brain (e.g. alcohol) may be potentiated.

POTASSIUM CHLORIDE

Uses

Treatment or prevention of potassium depletion from any cause, e.g. in patients taking diuretics, corticosteroids, or carbenoxolone. This is of especial importance in patients taking digitalis preparations, in patients receiving insulin therapy for diabetic ketoacidosis, and in the elderly who are particularly prone to potassium depletion. Potassium chloride is the salt of choice in treating or preventing potassium depletion since retention of potassium will not occur unless the concomitant chloride depletion is also corrected.

Preparations

There are numerous preparations of potassium chloride available for oral and i.v. use and several diuretic preparations containing potassium chloride and a diuretic.

(a) Oral preparations

1. Sustained-release formulations: K-Contin® (tablets), Leo K® (tablets), Nu-K® (capsules), Slow-K® (tablets). Each tablet or capsule contains 8 mmol of potassium as the chloride salt.

2. Effervescent preparations: Potassium tablets, effervescent (6.5 mmol of potassium as the chloride salt in each tablet);

Kloref® (6.7 mmol of potassium as the chloride salt in each tablet);

Sando K® (8 mmol of potassium as the chloride salt in each tablet);

Kloref-S® (20 mmol of potassium as the chloride salt in each sachet of granules).

3. Liquid preparations: Kay-Cee-L® (1 mmol of potassium as the chloride salt in each 1 ml).

4. Combinations of potassium chloride with diuretics: There is a large number of such preparations which contain 6.7–10 mmol of potassium as the chloride salt per tablet.

However, it should be noted that in many of these preparations the dose of diuretic is half the usual dose found in the corresponding preparation without potassium. For example Brinaldix® (clopamide) alone is presented as a 20 mg tablet and Brinaldix-K® also contains 20 mg of clopamide with 8 mmol of potassium chloride. However, Navidrex® (cyclopenthiazide) is presented as a 500 microgram tablet while Navidrex-K® tablets contain 250 micrograms of cyclopenthiazide with 8 mmol of potassium chloride. This is obviously important when considering the required dose of diuretic.

(b) Intravenous preparations

There are two varieties of preparations of potassium chloride for i.v. use—those which can be added to i.v. infusion solutions and those which are already made up for direct infusion.

Because of the hazard of cardiac arrhythmias due to too rapid infusion, solutions containing more than 40 mmol of potassium per litre should not be used. When potassium solutions are infused the rate generally should be about 10 mmol/h and should not exceed 20 mmol/h.

(i) 'Undiluted' solutions

There are several preparations of various strengths, but a commonly used preparation contains 20 mmol of potassium as the chloride salt in 10 ml. This solution must be diluted to a volume of at least 500 ml before administration.

NB Because of the hazards of infusing too large a dose of potassium, which may be fatal, great care must be taken in making up and mixing potassium solutions for infusion. For preference potassium solutions should be used which have already been prepared pharmaceutically.

(ii) Ready prepared solutions

Potassium chloride in sodium chloride solution for i.v. infusion—this solution contains K^+ 40 mmol, Na^+ 150 mmol, and Cl^- 190 mmol in 1 l.

Potassium chloride in dextrose solution for i.v. infusion—this solution contains K^+ 40 mmol and Cl^- 40 mmol in 1 l of 5 per cent dextrose.

Dosages

The total body potassium is about 3500 mmol, of which 90 per cent is intracellular. Daily intake is 60–80 mmol, most of which is eliminated in the urine. A single dose of frusemide or a thiazide diuretic causes the loss of about 16 mmol during the resultant sodium diuresis in a patient who has not previously received a diuretic. However, during repeated administration of these diuretics, at least in patients with hypertension, there is some evidence that total body potassium stores are not depleted by the usual antihypertensive diuretic dosages. In these patients potassium supplements are often not necessary, but occasional plasma potassium estimations are advised.

In patients with oedema due to heart failure, hepatic cirrhosis, and the nephrotic syndrome the administration of diuretics often leads to potassium depletion, and it is wise to use potassium chloride in a dose of 16–48 mmol per day in divided doses to prevent this. In such circumstances a potassium-sparing diuretic may be a useful alternative to potassium chloride.

Intravenous potassium therapy may be indicated to prevent potassium depletion when patients are unable to take oral potassium and this requires about 80 mmol/day.

In the treatment of severe hypokalaemia, and in the prevention of hypokalaemia during insulin therapy of diabetic ketoacidosis, intravenous potassium chloride administration is indicated and should be monitored by frequent plasma potassium concentration measurements.

Important adverse effects

These occur in about 12 per cent of patients taking potassium supplements, and include *hyper*kalaemia, particularly in the elderly, nausea, vomiting, diarrhoea, and abdominal cramps.

Intestinal ulceration is a hazard of using enteric-coated potassium preparations, and such preparations should no longer be used.

Oesophageal ulceration has been reported with the slow-release oral preparations listed above in patients with oesophageal obstruction (e.g. due to left atrial enlargement in mitral stenosis).

Interactions

The risk of hyperkalaemia is greatly increased if potassium supplements are combined with a potassium-sparing diuretic and in general this combination should not be used.

Care should be taken not to make the careless mistake of unwittingly prescribing potassium for a patient being treated with a combination preparation of a thiazide diuretic and a potassium-sparing diuretic, e.g. Aldactide® (containing spironolactone), Dyazide® (containing triamterene), or Moduretic® (containing amiloride).

PRAZOSIN

Structure

Mode of action

Prazosin is an antagonist at α_1 (post-synaptic) adrenoceptors and causes peripheral arteriolar vasodilatation which leads to a fall in blood pressure in hypertension and a decrease in after-load in cardiac failure. In cardiac failure the blood pressure tends not to fall because of a concomitant rise in cardiac output; nevertheless, when prazosin is used in cardiac failure care should be taken to avoid hypotension. The hypotension produced by prazosin is not accompanied by a significant tachycardia because α_2 (presynaptic) adrenoceptors are not affected by prazosin, and noradrenaline in the synapse acts upon these receptors to inhibit further noradrenaline release. This contrasts with phenoxybenzamine and phentolamine which act at both α_1 and α_2 adrenoceptors (see under α-adrenoceptor antagonists).

Phosphodiesterase and dopamine-β-hydroxylase inhibition occur with prazosin, but only at concentrations much higher than are found during therapy, and probably do not contribute to its clinical effects.

Uses

Hypertension.
Cardiac failure.

Dosages

Since profound hypotension often occurs following the first dose of prazosin, in both hypertension and cardiac failure, the first dose should be small (0.5 mg orally) and should be taken with an evening meal or in bed. Thereafter the initial dosage should be 0.5 mg t.d.s. orally, increasing at intervals of a few days if required to a maximum of 5 mg q.d.s.

Kinetic data

Prazosin is well absorbed and is mostly metabolized in the liver. It has a $t_{1/2}$ of 4 h, but its therapeutic effects last for up to about 12 h. The dose of prazosin should be reduced in renal failure, not because there is accumulation, but because of increased sensitivity.

Important adverse effects

Dizziness and loss of consciousness may occur following the first dose of prazosin because of profound hypotension (see above). This effect is especially marked in patients taking diuretics or α-adrenoceptor antagonists. Other common effects include dry mouth, headache, postural dizziness, and tachycardia.

PROBENECID

Structure

$$(CH_3CH_2CH_2)_2NSO_2 - \langle\!\!\!\!\bigcirc\!\!\!\!\rangle - COOH$$

Mode of action

Probenecid inhibits the renal tubular transport of organic acids such as uric acid and penicillin. Since the renal excretion of penicillin is mainly by tubular secretion its elimination is blocked by probenecid. However, uric acid is excreted both by tubular active secretion and by active reabsorption; probenecid in low dosages blocks the active secretion and causes *retention* of uric acid; in higher dosages it also blocks the active reabsorption and the net effect is an *increase in elimination* of uric acid (see Fig. 27.4). This dual dose-dependent effect on uric acid excretion is shared by aspirin and sulphinpyrazone.

Uses

Gout and hyperuricaemia.

To increase the blood concentrations of penicillins and cephalosporins.

Dosages

Gout and hyperuricaemia: 250–500 mg b.d., orally.

As an adjunct to penicillin therapy: 500 mg q.d.s., orally.

Kinetic data

Probenecid is well absorbed. Its $t_{1/2}$ is dose-dependent (usually 6–12 h). It is metabolized 95 per cent to active and inactive compounds, which are excreted in the urine.

Important adverse effects

Adverse effects are uncommon and generally mild. Gastro-intestinal disturbances (about 2 per cent) and skin rashes (about 3 per cent) are the most frequent.

Probenecid may precipitate haemolytic anaemia in patients with G6PD deficiency (see Chapter 8).

Interactions

Probenecid inhibits the tubular secretion of penicillin and has therefore been used as an adjunct to penicillin therapy to cause retention of penicillin.

By a similar mechanism it causes retention of methotrexate and thereby enhances its toxicity.

The risk of chloroquine-induced eye damage is increased in patients taking probenecid.

For the interaction of probenecid with aspirin see under sulphinpyrazone.

PROCAINAMIDE

Structure

$$H_2N - \langle\!\!\!\!\bigcirc\!\!\!\!\rangle - CONHCH_2CH_2N(CH_2CH_3)_2 \cdot HCl$$

Mode of action

Procainamide is a Class I anti-arrhythmic drug with direct actions on cardiac conducting tissues similar to those of quinidine. These effects are discussed under lignocaine. In contrast to quinidine, however, procainamide has no anticholinergic or α-adrenoceptor antagonist properties.

Uses

Acute and chronic ventricular arrhythmias.

Dosages

Intravenous: 100 mg every 5 min with ECG and blood pressure monitoring until the arrhythmia is controlled, or a maximum dose of 1 g is reached. If it is considered necessary to continue with oral or i.v. therapy this would be considered the loading dose. Maintenance i.v. infusion. 0·25–2 mg/min.

Oral: Procainamide is available as ordinary or sustained-release formulations:

ordinary formulation—loading dose 1 g, followed by 250–500 mg four-hourly;

sustained-release—loading dose 2 g, followed by 1·5 g eight-hourly.

Kinetic data

Well absorbed orally. Procainamide is metabolized about 50 per cent to active and inactive metabolites, the remaining 50 per cent being excreted by the kidneys. The active metabolite is an acetylated derivative, *N*-acetylprocainamide (NAPA), and the amount of NAPA produced depends on whether the patient is a slow or fast acetylator (see Chapter 8). Procainamide $t_{1/2} = 3$ h, NAPA $t_{1/2} = 1$ h. NAPA is excreted unchanged in the urine.

In renal failure excretion of both procainamide and NAPA is impaired and dosages should be reduced.

In hepatic disease the metabolism of procainamide is decreased and dosages should be reduced. In congestive cardiac failure metabolism may be reduced because of hepatic congestion, but the apparent volume of distribution is also reduced and both loading and maintenance dosages should be reduced.

The therapeutic range of plasma concentrations of procainamide is 4–10 μg/ml, but this does not take into account the fact that NAPA also has therapeutic activity. Since the production of NAPA varies from individual to individual the interpretation of plasma procainamide concentrations alone is difficult. Perhaps combined measurement of both procainamide and NAPA would improve the usefulness of plasma concentration monitoring in procainamide therapy, but it is more likely that therapy with NAPA itself will replace therapy by procainamide, thus avoiding the problem (see also below under adverse effects).

Important adverse effects

(a) Cardiac effects

These are common and include hypotension (particularly common with i.v. administration), heart block, and ventricular arrhyth-

mias. These effects are commonly dose-related.

(b) Non-cardiac effects

(i) 'Lupus-like syndrome' (see also Chapter 9)

In common with some other drugs (e.g. hydralazine) procainamide may produce a syndrome like systemic lupus erythematosus (SLE), characterized by arthralgia, arthritis, fever, pleurisy, pulmonary involvement, pericarditis, and rashes. Renal involvement is uncommon. Tests for anti-nuclear factor (ANF) are usually positive in patients with the syndrome. However, procainamide therapy is associated with a positive ANF in 60–70 per cent of patients, of whom only 20–30 per cent develop the clinical syndrome if therapy is continued. In patients who are slow acetylators the rate of development of a positive ANF is faster. Usually the syndrome resolves when the drug is stopped, but it may take months and occasionally years to do so.

It is thought that the syndrome is due to procainamide itself or to some non-acetylated metabolite since it resolves on substituting NAPA and since it does not occur with NAPA itself. For this reason in particular NAPA has recently been developed for use as an anti-arrhythmic drug.

(ii) Other non-cardiac effects

Anorexia, nausea, and vomiting may occur. Rarely procainamide may cause giddiness and mental symptoms.

Hypersensitivity reactions may result in fever and blood disorders, including agranulocytosis and leucopenia.

Interactions

Procainamide should not be given together with other drugs which prolong the QT interval (e.g. quinidine, amiodarone, and disopyramide).

Hypokalaemia, e.g. due to diuretics, decreases the effects of Class I anti-arrhythmic drugs on the cardiac action potential, and the hypokalaemia should be corrected when using procainamide.

PROPYLTHIOURACIL

Structure

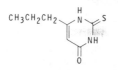

Mode of action

Inhibition of the synthesis of thyroid hormones by interfering with the incorporation of iodine into tyrosyl residues, and possibly with the coupling of those residues into iodothyronines.

Use

Hyperthyroidism.

Dosages

Initially 100–200 mg eight-hourly, orally. As a response is obtained reduce the dose gradually to a maintenance dosage of 50–150 mg daily in one or two divided doses. Treatment is usually continued for 1 or 2 years.

Kinetic data

Propylthiouracil is well absorbed. It is partly metabolized ($t_{1/2}$ = 2 h).

Important adverse effects

Adverse reactions occur in up to 3 per cent of cases and resemble those of carbimazole (q.v.). However, the incidence of agranulocytosis is higher (up to 1:250). Overtreatment, with development of hypothyroidism, is an obvious danger.

QUINIDINE

Structure

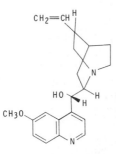

(Quinidine is the dextrorotatory form of quinine.)

Mode of action

Quinidine is a Class I anti-arrhythmic drug, and has direct actions on cardiac conducting tissues. Those effects are discussed in detail under lignocaine.

Quinidine differs from lignocaine in some respects of its actions on the cardiac action potential, and in that it has a more pronounced negative inotropic effect on the heart, and a greater propensity to produce heart block and cardiac arrhythmias.

In addition to its Class I anti-arrhythmic actions it has anticholinergic and α-adrenoceptor antagonist properties.

Uses

Acute and chronic supraventricular and ventricular arrhythmias. Although quinidine is effective in the treatment of supraventricular arrhythmias, such as paroxysmal SVT, and atrial flutter, its use in these conditions has largely been superseded by other drugs (see treatment of arrhythmias, p.316) and by cardioversion, partly because of the toxicity of quinidine. It is still sometimes of value in the treatment of recurrent atrial flutter, when it is generally combined with digitalis (but see interactions below). It also has a place in the treatment of acute and chronic ventricular tachyarrhythmias.

Dosages

Quinidine is available either as quinidine sulphate in ordinary formulation tablets, or as quinidine bisulphate in sustained-release formulations. The latter are to be used for preference because of the reduced frequency of administration and reduced fluctuations of plasma concentrations. Quinidine sulphate 200 mg is equivalent to quinidine bisulphate 250 mg.

Before embarking upon chronic quinidine therapy a single *test* dose of quinidine sulphate 200 mg should be given.

Chronic oral dosages: quinidine sulphate, 200–400 mg, 3–4 times daily; quinidine bisulphate, 500 mg every 12 h, increasing as required to 1·25 g every 12 h.

Kinetic data

Quinidine is well absorbed. It is mostly metabolized but about 20 per cent is excreted unchanged in the urine and its rate of renal elimination is increased by acidification of the urine. $T_{1/2} = 6$ h. Clearance of quinidine is reduced in liver disease. In congestive heart failure not only is clearance reduced because of hepatic congestion, but the apparent volume of distribution is also reduced. Dosages should therefore be reduced by about 25 per cent in patients with hepatic disease or congestive heart failure. The therapeutic range of plasma quinidine concentrations is 3–6 μg/ml. The routine application of plasma quinidine measurement has not yet been proved useful.

Important adverse effects

Adverse effects with quinidine are very common indeed and have limited its usefulness.

(a) Dose-related effects

(i) Cardiac

Quinidine may cause ventricular arrhythmias, particularly ventricular tachycardia which may produce syncope. Patients with a prolonged QT interval are particularly susceptible to ventricular arrhythmias and in such patients quinidine should be avoided. Quinidine may also impair sinus nodal function producing sinus bradycardia and predisposing to supraventricular tachyarrhythmias. This occurs particularly in patients with the sick sinus syndrome. It can also cause atrioventricular

block and worsen pre-existing conduction defects. It should not, therefore, be used in patients with pre-existing AV block. Quinidine may cause postural hypotension by an α-adrenoceptor blocking action.

(ii) Non-cardiac

Overdose with quinidine has long been known to produce a syndrome called *cinchonism*. The manifestations of this syndrome are tinnitus, deafness, blurring of vision, vomiting, diarrhoea, and abdominal pain. In severe toxicity there may also occur headache, diplopia, photophobia, altered colour vision, flushing, confusion, delirium, and psychosis.

(b) Hypersensitivity reactions

Thrombocytopenia is an uncommon but serious effect. Rarely haemolytic anaemia may occur. In addition to these effects nausea, diarrhoea, and vomiting are very common with quinidine in therapeutic doses.

Interactions

Quinidine inhibits the renal tubular secretion of digoxin and doubles steady-state plasma digoxin concentrations. It may also reduce the positive inotropic effects of digoxin and the combination is better avoided in heart failure. If the combination of digoxin and quinidine is used in the treatment of atrial tachyarrhythmias, the dose of digoxin should be halved.

Phenobarbitone, phenytoin, and rifampicin increase dosage requirements of quinidine by increasing its metabolism.

Quinidine should not be used in combination with other drugs which prolong the QT interval (e.g. procainamide, amiodarone, and disopyramide).

Hypokalaemia, e.g. due to diuretics, decreases the effects of Class I anti-arrhythmic drugs on the cardiac action potential, and the hypokalaemia should be corrected when using quinidine.

Quinidine potentiates the anticoagulant effect of warfarin in some patients, by an unknown mechanism.

QUININE

Structure

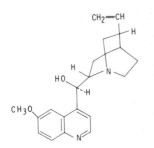

(Quinine is the laevorotatory stereoisomer of quinidine, q.v.).

Mode of action

(a) As an antimalarial

Quinine probably binds to plasmodial DNA and prevents its replication.

(b) In nocturnal leg cramps

Quinine decreases the excitability of motor end-plate and reduces its response to acetylcholine and tetanic stimulation.

Uses

1. In the treatment of chloroquine-resistant falciparum malaria infections.
2. Nocturnal leg cramps.

Dosages

(a) Falciparum malaria (see therapy of malaria, p.280).

Oral: 600 mg every 12 h for a total of six doses.
Intravenous (complicated *P. falciparum* infections): 5–10 mg/kg of base infused over 4 h, and repeated every 12–24 h to a total of four doses, or until oral therapy is possible. The longer dosage interval should be used in patients with liver damage.

(b) Nocturnal leg cramps

Quinine bisulphate, 200–300 mg at bedtime for 2 weeks. In some cases cramps do not recur after a single course, but long-term treatment may be necessary.

Kinetic data

Quinine is almost completely absorbed. It is metabolized 95 per cent in the liver, $t_{1/2} = 10$ h.

Important adverse effects

Toxic effects include tinnitus, deafness, headaches, nausea, and visual disturbances. This cluster of symptoms has been called 'cinchonism' (see also quinidine, p.737).

Hypersensitivity reactions, such as angiooedema, and acute idiosyncratic reactions, such as flushing, dyspnoea, and feeling 'peculiar', also occur.

Intravenous infusions can be associated with CNS toxicity, such as tremor, delirium, fits, and coma.

Haemolytic anaemia may occur, especially in patients with G6PD deficiency (see Chapter 8). Thrombocytopenia occurs occasionally, usually as a Type II allergic reaction (see p.140).

The effects of quinine on the heart are similar to those of quinidine, and care should be taken in patients with cardiac arrhythmias and heart block.

Interaction

In anti-malarial doses quinine may inhibit digoxin renal elimination in a fashion similar to the effect of quinidine.

RIFAMPICIN (RIFAMPIN)

Structure

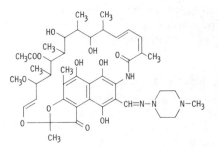

Mode of action

Rifampicin acts by inhibiting the DNA-dependent RNA polymerase in bacteria, but not in mammalian cells.

Uses

Despite its wide and effective antibacterial spectrum, use of rifampicin is largely restricted to the treatment of tuberculosis in combination with other antituberculous drugs.

Other uses include the prevention of meningococcal infection in contacts of a proven case of meningococcal meningitis, and as an adjunct in the treatment of leprosy.

Dosage

450–600 mg o.d., orally.

Kinetic data

Rifampicin is well absorbed. It is partly metabolized to inactive metabolites (35 per cent), and partly excreted into the bile unchanged, with consequent recirculation (35 per cent). The rest is eliminated unchanged in the urine. $T_{1/2} = 3$ h. Biliary excretion increases progressively during the first 2 weeks of treatment and the $t_{1/2}$ shortens. Rifampicin is also excreted in tears and sweat and these, as well as the urine, may turn red as a result.

Important adverse effects

Liver damage can occur and, although it is not common, liver function tests should be monitored regularly, especially in patients with pre-existing liver disease, which is associated with an increased risk of adverse liver reactions. This is partly important because of the association of alcoholic cirrhosis with tuberculosis.

A flu-like illness may occur initially if high doses are used. Thrombocytopenia, a mild leucopenia, and skin rashes are rare.

Interactions

Rifampicin induces hepatic drug-metabolizing enzymes. This is especially important with regard to warfarin and the oral contraceptive, whose effects may be diminished. For advice on the dosage of oral contraceptive see under phenytoin.

SALICYLATES

Structures

Aspirin (acetylsalicylic acid):

Other salicylates include benorylate which is a compound in which aspirin is linked with paracetamol, and diflunisal which is a difluorophenyl derivative.

Mode of action

Salicylates have analgesic, antipyretic, and anti-inflammatory actions. At the molecular level the main known action of salicylates is inhibition of the enzyme cyclo-oxygenase with resultant decrease in prostaglandin synthesis. This action may account for some of the therapeutic and adverse effects of the salicylates, but the total spectrum of their pharmacological actions is difficult to explain on this basis alone. The action in inhibiting platelet aggregation is mediated by inhibition of prostaglandin synthesis.

Recently it has been shown that the effects of aspirin in inhibiting prostaglandin synthesis differ for different prostaglandins. Thus while low doses of aspirin inhibit only the production of thromboxane in platelets, higher doses inhibit the production of both thromboxane in platelets and prostacyclin in vessel walls. This observation suggests that low dose aspirin might be of value in the prevention of such events as myocardial infarction and embolic strokes or transient ischaemic attacks (see below).

Uses

Anti-inflammatory—in rheumatoid arthritis and oesteoarthritis; in acute rheumatic fever; in Dressler's syndrome. It is particularly effective in these last two.

Analgesic—as a mild analgesic, for instance in musculoskeletal pain, simple headache, and dysmenorrhoea.

Antipyretic—for symptomatic relief of fever in viral infections such as influenza and infectious mononucleosis, and sometimes in bacterial infections.

Because of its effects on thromboxane synthesis by platelets low doses of aspirin may be of value in the treatment of transient ischaemic episodes and the prevention of stroke due to cerebral emboli, and in the primary or secondary prevention of myocardial infarction. However, the usefulness of aspirin in these circumstances has not yet been properly proven.

Dosages

(a) Acute rheumatic fever

Aspirin, 0·9–1·2 g every 4 h to a maximum of 8 g daily. In this condition plasma salicylate concentrations of about 1 mmol/l are effectively anti-inflammatory.

(b) Chronic rheumatoid and osteoarthritis

Aspirin, 900 mg orally every 4–6 h.

Benorylate, 1·5 g t.d.s. orally (tablets) or 4 g b.d. orally (elixir).

Diflunisal, 250–500 mg b.d. orally.

(c) Analgesia

Aspirin, 300–900 mg every 4–6 h, orally, to a maximum of 4 g daily.

Diflunisal, 250–500 mg b.d., orally (limit to 750 mg daily during chronic therapy).

The optimal dose of aspirin for the prevention of transient ischaemic attacks or myocardial infarction has not been established. It may be below 300 mg once daily orally.

Kinetic data

All these salicylates are well absorbed.

Aspirin has a short $t_{1/2}$ (about 15 min) in the plasma, but is metabolized to the active metabolite, salicylic acid, whose elimination is saturable. The apparent $t_{1/2}$ of salicylic acid is 3–6 h at low therapeutic doses, but at higher doses the apparent $t_{1/2}$ lengthens and in overdose may be as great as 20 h. This underlines the need to monitor plasma salicylate concentrations during treatment with high doses because of the variability of metabolism from patient to patient. The optimum range of plasma salicylate concentrations for anti-inflammatory effects is 0·7–2·2 mmol/l (100–300 μg/ml). Salicylic acid itself is further metabolized by the liver and also excreted in the urine.

Benorylate is metabolized, after absorption, to salicylic acid and paracetamol.

Diflunisal is excreted as glucuronide by the kidney with a $t_{1/2}$ of 8 h.

Important adverse effects

The commonest adverse effects of the salicylates are gastro-intestinal. Occult blood loss of the order of a few ml per day occurs during aspirin therapy in the majority of patients but is less during treatment with both benorylate and diflunisal. Aspirin may also cause acute gastro-intestinal blood loss, the frequency of severe bleeding being about 15:100 000 per year. In patients with a predisposition to gastro-intestinal haemorrhage (e.g. patients with oesophagitis, gastritis, peptic ulceration) the risk of bleeding is increased. When it occurs bleeding is generally from small gastric erosions, but occasionally larger ulcers may occur. The risk of bleeding may be reduced by using soluble, buffered, or enteric-coated forms of aspirin.

In patients who tend to bleed for other reasons (e.g. patients with haemophilia or von Willebrand's disease, or those taking anticoagulants), this tendency is enhanced by salicylates.

Aspirin hypersensitivity is not common. However, in patients with a history of asthma or hypersensitivity reactions to other drugs, the incidence of hypersensitivity to aspirin is increased. Wheezing and urticaria may result, and such patients often also have nasal polyps. A history of ingestion of proprietary medicines (of which there is a large number) which, unknown to the patient, contain aspirin, should be sought in all patients with gastrointestinal bleeding or unexplained allergic reactions.

Uric acid renal tubular secretion is lowered by low doses of salicylate and gout may occur. Higher doses decrease active reabsorption or uric acid and the net result is increased uric acid excretion (see Fig. 27.4).

Tinnitus is a common toxic effect of salicylates and is usually the first sign that the dose is too high.

For a discussion of salicylate overdose see p.575.

Interactions

The risk of bleeding in patients taking anticoagulants is increased by aspirin for two reasons: firstly, because of the increased risk of gastro-intestinal bleeding and secondly, because of the inhibition of platelet aggregation which leads to measurable impairment in haemostasis. In addition salicylate displaces warfarin from protein binding sites in the plasma leading to a transient increase in warfarin effect (see Chapter 10 for discussion).

Aspirin inhibits the tubular secretion of methotrexate and methotrexate dosage requirements are reduced by about a third. However, this is a potentially fatal interaction and is best avoided altogether.

For the interaction of aspirin with sulphinpyrazone and probenecid see under sulphinpyrazone.

SEX HORMONES (POLYPEPTIDE AND STEROID)

1. Gonadotrophins

Structures

The gonadotrophins are glycoproteins of large molecular weight. FSH (follicle stimulating hormone) and LH (luteinizing hormone) are of pituitary origin, while HCG (human chorionic gonadotrophin) and CFSH (chorionic follicle stimulating hormone) are of placental origin. ICSH (interstitial cell stimulating hormone) was the term used to describe the gonadotrophin in men now recognized to be identical with LH.

Mode of action

Endogenous FSH and LH are produced in the same cell type in the pituitary in response to the effects of the hypothalamic gonadotrophin-releasing hormone (gonadorelin, or GnRH, formerly called LHRH). It is thought that it is the steroid composition of the circulating plasma which determines whether it is FSH or LH which is released in response to gonadorelin.

Following i.v. gonadorelin there is a large rise in serum LH within two minutes, and a smaller and more delayed rise in serum FSH. The changes in serum concentrations of FSH and LH in relation to the normal menstrual cycle are shown in Fig. P8.

During the first 14 days of the cycle (the menstrual and follicular phases) there is an increase in serum FSH concentration which in turn promotes ovarian follicular maturation and stimulates oestradiol secretion. Oestradiol inhibits FSH secretion, but stimulates LH secretion through release of gonadorelin, and this in turn induces ovulation. The follicle differentiates into the corpus luteum which secretes oestradiol and progesterone during the latter half of the cycle (the luteal phase).

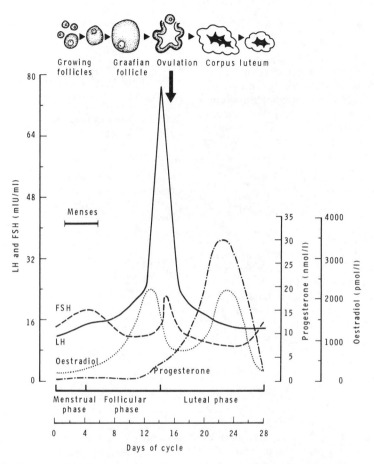

Fig. P8. Changes in circulating concentrations of steroid sex hormones and gonadotrophins during the normal menstrual cycle. [Adapted from Marshall (1981) Amenorrhoea. *Med. Int.* **1**, 291, with permission.]

As the corpus luteum degenerates oestradiol and progesterone concentrations fall and the cycle starts again.

In men serum FSH and LH concentrations do not fluctuate. FSH stimulates the growth of the testicular seminiferous tubules, leading to an increase in testicular weight during maturation. It also stimulates spermatogenesis. LH stimulates androgen production by the interstitial cells of the testis.

HCG is secreted by the placenta and has LH-like actions. During pregnancy it stimulates the corpus luteum which then continues to secrete oestradiol and progesterone until the third month of pregnancy when placental oestrogen and progesterone secretion takes over.

The role of CFSH is not known.

Uses

Infertility secondary to hypopituitarism (FSH and LH).

Cryptorchidism (LH).

Diagnostic tests of hypothalamic–pituitary–gonadal function (GnRH).

Formulations

Pituitary FSH and LH formulations are now available but are very expensive. Alternatives are HCG, with its LH-like properties, prepared from pregnant women's urine, and HMG (human menopausal gonadotrophin or menotrophin) prepared from the urine of post-menopausal women, which contains approximately equal amounts of FSH and LH, but is used principally for its FSH content.

Dosages

The use of these drugs should be limited to specialists.

Gonadorelin: 100 micrograms.

FSH and LH in infertility: various regimens are described of which the following is one —one i.m. dose of HMG (75 i.u. of FSH + 75 i.u. of LH) on alternate days for three doses, followed by a single dose of HCG (5000 i.u. i.m.) 2 days later.

Cryptorchidism: HCG 500–4000 i.u. i.m. three times a week.

Kinetic data

The gonadotrophins must be given parenterally and are generally given i.m. when used therapeutically. Gonadorelin is given i.v. for diagnostic purposes. After i.v. injection FSH, LH, and HCG disappear from the serum with half-times of 20 min, 4 h, and 11 h respectively. However, their eventual half-times are longer (4, 70, and 23 h respectively). HCG is partly excreted unchanged in the urine but little FSH or LH is so excreted.

Important adverse effects

Gonadorelin may cause nausea, abdominal pain, headache, and menorrhagia.

HCG can cause precocious puberty when used in cryptorchidism. It can also cause gynaecomastia, ovarian hyperstimulation (causing abdominal discomfort due to mild ovarian enlargement, or even ovarian rupture and haemoperitoneum), fluid retention, changes in mood, headache, and tiredness. Occasionally allergic reactions may occur.

HMG can cause ovarian hyperstimulation

(see HCG above), fluid retention, arterial thrombo-embolic disease, hypotension, and oliguria. Occasionally it may cause allergic reactions. Pituitary tumours may increase in size. There is an increased risk of multiple births, which are common.

2. Female sex hormones—oestrogens and progestogens

Structures

Naturally occurring oestrogens (oestradiol, oestrone, and oestriol) are synthesized mostly in the ovary under the control of FSH. However, the oestrogens commonly used therapeutically are semi-synthetic and include ethinyloestradiol, mestranol, and diethylstilboestrol (dealt with separately, p.752). Ethinyloestradiol is the most commonly used:

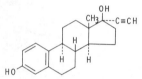

The naturally-occurring progestogen, progesterone, is synthesized mostly in the ovary under the control of LH. There are several semi-synthetic progestogens in use, including norethisterone, levonorgestrel, ethynodiol, lynoestrenol, and desogestrel. Norethisterone is the most commonly used:

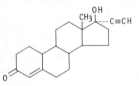

Modes of action

(a) Oestrogens

(i) *Feminizing effects*—oestrogens cause the changes which occur at puberty: growth and development of the vagina, uterus, and Fallopian tubes; breast formation; the pubertal growth spurt and eventual fusion of the bony epiphyses; and other secondary sexual characteristics such as growth of axillary and pubic hair, and pigmentation of the nipples, areolae, and external genitalia.

(ii) *Cyclical ovulation*—oestrogens cause the release of LH at the end of the follicular phase of the menstrual cycle (see Fig. P8) and that in turn leads to ovulation. An increase in circulating oestrogen concentrations in the blood inhibits the release of FSH from the pituitary and this mechanism acts as a negative feedback for the control of oestrogen release (see also gonadotrophins above).

(iii) *Pregnancy*—during pregnancy oestrogens, the major source of which is the placenta, have a variety of effects. They promote uterine growth by increasing the size and number of myometrial cells; they inhibit LH and FSH production thus preventing ovarian follicle development and ovulation; they cause changes in the uterine cervix which allow dilatation at time of labour; and they stimulate breast development in preparation for lactation. They may also be responsible for the increased skin pigmentation in pregnancy and cause changes in haemostatic mechanisms which may help limit blood loss at time of delivery (increased synthesis of clotting factors, increased platelet aggregability, and decreased fibrinolytic activity).

(iv) *Metabolic effects*—oestrogens have effects on metabolism, including sodium and water retention, and an anabolic effect on tissue proteins similar to that of the androgens (see below). They may also impair glucose tolerance in patients with or without a predisposition to diabetes mellitus.

(v) *Contraceptive actions*—see below under progestogens.

(b) Progestogens

(i) *Endometrial effects*—progesterone has direct effects on the endometrium, causing it to become secretory during the luteal phase of the menstrual cycle (see Fig. P8). The sharp fall in circulating progesterone at the end of the cycle is principally responsible for the onset of menstruation. In contrast to the oestrogens, progesterone has no feedback effects on FSH or LH.

(ii) *Effects during pregnancy*—during pregnancy progesterone prevents uterine contrac-

tion and may have effects in preventing the immunological rejection of the fetus. Together with oestrogens it causes breast enlargement in preparation for lactation after delivery.

(iii) *Contraceptive actions*—the mode of action of progestogens alone and of an oestrogen with a progestogen in preventing conception is not fully understood. The oestrogens suppress ovulation by inhibiting gonadotrophin release. Some progestogens, such as norethisterone and norgestrel, are partly metabolized to oestrogen-related compounds which may have some anti-ovulatory effects. However, the main actions of the progestogens are in causing both endometrial changes similar to those found during pregnancy; thus discouraging implantation, and changes in cervical mucus, decreasing its penetrability by spermatozoa.

Oestrogen/progestogen combinations are very effective contraceptives with a failure rate of around 5 per 1000 woman years of therapy. The oral progestogen-only contraceptives have a failure rate of around 25 per 1000 woman years of therapy, as do intramuscular depot progestogen preparations.

Uses

Oestrogens alone

Short-term treatment of menopausal symptoms.

Primary amenorrhoea.

Breast carcinoma in post-menopausal women.

Prostatic carcinoma (see diethylstilboestrol, p.752).

Senile vaginitis and vulvitis (topical preparations).

Progestogens alone

Oral contraception.

Dysfunctional uterine bleeding.

Endometriosis.

Menstrual disturbances (e.g. premenstrual syndrome, dysmenorrhoea).

Oestrogen + progestogen

Oral contraception.

Replacement therapy in ovarian insufficiency.

Menstrual disturbances (e.g. menorrhagia, metropathia haemorrhagica, dysmenorrhoea).

Formulations and dosages

(i) Oestrogens alone

There are several proprietary formulations for oral use containing oestrogens only. Ethinyloestradiol is the oestrogen of choice.

Menopausal symptoms—10–50 micrograms orally t.d.s. reducing to 10–20 micrograms o.d. or b.d. according to symptoms.

Primary amenorrhoea—150 micrograms orally o.d.

Breast carcinoma—1–3 mg orally o.d.

(ii) Progestogens alone

There are several proprietary formulations for oral use containing progestogens only. We give here the recommended dosages for norethisterone.

Oral contraception (progestogen alone)—350 micrograms (one tablet) orally o.d. at the same time of day each day (preferably in the evening), starting on the first day of the cycle.

Dysfunctional uterine bleeding—to stop bleeding 5 mg orally t.d.s. for 10 days; to prevent bleeding 5 mg orally b.d. from days 19 to 26 of the cycle.

Endometriosis—10 mg orally o.d., starting on day 5 of the cycle, increasing if required to 25 mg daily in divided doses to prevent breakthrough bleeding. Continue for at least 6 months.

Pre-menstrual syndrome—10–15 mg orally o.d. from days 19 to 26 of the cycle.

Dysmenorrhoea—5 mg orally t.d.s. from days 5 to 25 for 3–4 cycles.

(iii) Combined oestrogen/progestogen formulations

Many different combination preparations are available, mostly intended for use as oral contraceptives. These preparations can be

Table P7   *Oestrogen/progestogen combination formulations marketed in the UK for oral contraception*

Oestrogen	Progestogen	Brand name(s)
Ethinyloestradiol 20 µg	Norethisterone 1mg	Loestrin-20
Ethinyloestradiol 30 µg	Levonorgestrel 150 µg	Ovranette, Microgynon–30
	Levonorgestrel 250 µg	Ovran–30, Eugynon–30
	Ethynodiol 2 mg	Conova–30.
	Desogestrel 150 µg	Marvelon
Ethinyloestradiol 35 µg	Norethisterone 0.5 mg	Brevinor, Ovysmen
	Norethisterone 0.5/1 mg	Binovum*
	Norethisterone 1 mg	Norimin
Ethinyloestradiol 50 µg	Norethisterone 1 mg	Minovlar, Orlest–21
	Norethisterone 2.5 mg	Norlestrin
	Norethisterone 3 mg	Gynovlar–21
	Norethisterone 4 mg	Anovlar–21
	Levonorgestrel 250 µg	Eugynon–50, Ovran
	Lynoestrenol 2.5 mg	Minilyn
	Ethynodiol 1 mg	Ovulen–50
Mestranol 50 µg	Norethisterone 1 mg	Norinyl, Ortho-novin
Ethinyloestradiol 30/40/30 µg	Levonorgestrel 50/75/125 µg	Logynon*, Trinordiol*

* Phased formulations (see text).

Fig. P9. An example of a 'blister pack' for an oral contraceptive. [Reproduced by permission of the manufacturers, Syntex Pharmaceuticals Ltd. Copyright 1983.]

classified according to their oestrogen content, since the most important adverse effects are caused by the oestrogen and are dose-related. The preparations available for use as oral contraceptives in the UK at the time of writing are shown in Table P7. Note that there is a number of other preparations containing a combination of oestrogen and progestogen which are not licensed for use as oral contraceptives. Before prescribing a combination as a contraceptive check the Data Sheet or manufacturer's literature carefully.

The dosage in most cases is one tablet orally daily, starting on the first or fifth day of the cycle, continuing for 21 days, followed by a 7-day interval of no treatment. In order to aid compliance and to make administration easier, manufacturers pack 21 tablets into a blister pack (see Fig. P9) and some include seven dummy tablets to make up the four-week treatment course.

Some formulations are so-called 'phased' (see Table P7). In these cases the dose of oestrogen and/or progestogen is varied through the cycle. For example, in one such regimen (Logynon® and Trinordiol®) ethinyloestradiol and levonorgestrel are taken in respective doses of 30 and 50 micrograms (6 days), followed by 40 and 75 micrograms (5 days), and finally by 30 and 125 micrograms (10 days). After 7 days treatment-free the cycle is repeated.

Combination products used for purposes *other* than oral contraception may have similar regimens to the non-phased contraceptive formulations, but many have more complicated regimens and the manufacturer's literature should be consulted.

In replacement therapy for ovarian insufficiency sequential therapy is given, starting with an oestrogen (e.g. ethinyloestradiol 10 micrograms orally o.d.) for 21 days, giving a progestogen (e.g. norethisterone 5 mg orally o.d.) on days 17 to 21.

Other formulations

Oestrogens are available for parenteral and topical administration.

Parenteral oestrogen preparations
These are indicated for use in women requiring prolonged oestrogen treatment (e.g. in primary amenorrhoea or breast carcinoma), or in men with prostatic carcinoma, and are available as oily injections (given i.m. every 1–14 days) or as implants (given once every several weeks, the exact time interval depending on the dose—for example a 25 mg implant of oestradiol has a duration of effect of 36 weeks).

Topical oestrogen preparations
These are used for treating senile vaginitis and vulvitis, e.g. dienoestrol cream 0·01–0·025 per cent applied by special applicator o.d.

Parenteral progestogen preparations
Some progestogens are also available as depot injections and have been used both for long-term contraception (medroxyprogesterone— a controversial use of depot progestogens), and to try to prevent abortion in pregnant women with a history of habitual abortion (hydroxyprogesterone—efficacy not proven).

Kinetic data

The commonly used oestrogens and progestogens are well absorbed after oral administration. However, ethinyloestradiol is subject to extensive first-pass metabolism, mostly in the gut wall, and has a systemic availability of about 40 per cent.

The interactions of oestrogens and progestogens with their binding proteins are very complex and their clinical significance is not fully understood. They are highly protein-bound (> 90 per cent). Progestogens are bound both to a sex-hormone-binding globulin and to plasma albumin. The capacity of the globulin is low, but is increased by ethinyloestradiol (> 50 μg/day) and by drugs which induce hepatic microsomal drug-metabolizing enzymes (e.g. phenytoin, phenobarbitone). Ethinyloestradiol is mostly bound to plasma albumin, but not to globulin.

Ethinyloestradiol is extensively metabolized, $t_{1/2}$ = 12 h, and there is enterohepatic recirculation following deconjugation of conjugated ethinyloestradiol in the gut. There is a great deal of variation in the extent of metabolism from individual to individual and for some women the lower doses of ethinyloestradiol (20 or 30 micrograms) may be just sufficient for therapeutic efficacy—this is especially important in regard to the interaction with enzyme-inducing drugs (see interactions below).

Mestranol is predominantly metabolized to ethinyloestradiol by demethylation.

Norethisterone and levonorgestrel are extensively metabolized. $T_{1/2}$ for norethisterone is 8 h, for levonorgestrel 20 h.

Ethynodiol and lynoestrenol are partly converted to norethisterone.

Important adverse effects

Adverse effects due to oestrogens and progestogens are common and dose-related.

(i) Oestrogens
Oestrogens, when given alone, commonly cause fluid retention and hypertension. They cause painful breasts and endometrial bleeding in women, and gynaecomastia in men. There may be impairment of glucose tolerance in diabetics. Oestrogens may precipitate an acute attack of porphyria in susceptible patients (see Chapter 8). Oestrogens can also cause thrombo-embolic disease, and are associated with an increased risk of benign liver tumours and endometrial carcinoma. These are discussed below under oral contraceptives.

(ii) Progestogens
Progestogens, when given alone as contraceptives, commonly cause headache, nausea and vomiting, and abdominal or low back pain. They may occasionally cause breast tenderness. When given for breast cancer they may cause amenorrhoea and hypercalcaemia. If used during early pregnancy they may cause virilization of a female fetus. Long-term (2 y) treatment with depot formulations of progesterone results in a high incidence of amenorrhoea.

(iii) Combined oestrogens and progestogens
Combined oral contraceptives, in addition to the effects described above due to their separate components, commonly cause headache, vaginal discharge, mental depression and loss of libido, and urinary tract infections. Migraine may be precipitated or made worse, although occasionally it may improve.

Hypertension—a small increase in blood pressure is not uncommon, but in about 4 per cent a moderate or severe increase may occur. This hypertension is reversible on withdrawal.

Thrombo-embolism—there is an increased risk of thrombo-embolic disease in women taking combined oral contraceptives. These women are more likely to develop deep venous thrombosis, pulmonary embolism, myocardial infarction, and cerebral infarction. This effect is thought to be related to the oestrogen content. The risk increases with age and is on average about sixfold compared with women not using oral contraceptives. The risk is lower in women taking a 30 microgram oestrogen preparation. Smoking increases the risk of myocardial infarction.

Tumours—there is an increased risk of benign liver tumours in women taking combined oral contraceptives or oestrogens alone. The risk of hepatocellular adenoma increases with age, dose, and duration of use. The risk is low in women taking a 30 microgram oestrogen preparation. If an adverse effect on the liver occurs (e.g. jaundice or acute hepatitis) an alternative form of contraception should be advised.

Oestrogen use during pregnancy is associated with an increased risk of the occurrence in their teens of vaginal adenosis and vaginal adenocarcinoma in the female offspring. There is also an increased risk of fetal malformations.

Oestrogen use during and after the menopause is associated with an increased risk of endometrial carcinoma. The increase is about sixfold and increases with dose and duration of use. It is not clear, however, what the risks are in women taking low-dose (i.e. 30 micrograms oestrogen) oral contraceptives.

There is a *decreased* risk of benign breast tumours in women taking combined oral contraceptives. The effect is related to duration of use. There is some evidence of an increased risk of breast cancer, but this has not been proven. The risk of ovarian carcinoma may be decreased and the risk of carcinoma of the uterine cervix increased.

Gallstones—there is an increased risk of gallstones.

Amenorrhoea—amenorrhoea occurs in about 5 per cent of women after withdrawal of oral contraceptives but usually lasts no longer than a few months. Prolonged amenorrhoea and permanent sterility are rare.

Contra-indications—oral contraceptives are contra-indicated in women with oestrogen-dependent tumours (such as breast cancer), pregnancy, a past history of thromboembolic disease, liver disease, or porphyria. Relative contra-indications include hypertension, diabetes mellitus, age over 35 y, heavy smoking habit, recent menarche, migraine, recurrent urinary tract infections, gallstones, mental depression, and epilepsy.

Interactions

Drugs which induce the activity of hepatic microsomal drug-metabolizing enzymes (e.g. rifampicin, phenytoin, phenobarbitone—see Chapter 10) enhance the metabolism of oestrogens and/or progestogens and can cause failure of therapy in those women in whom the lower doses of oestrogen are only just

sufficient, say to maintain contraception.

Rifampicin

Rifampicin enhances oestrogen and progestogen metabolism and while a course of rifampicin is being given alternative forms of contraception should be used.

Phenytoin and phenobarbitone

Phenytoin and phenobarbitone can cause contraceptive failure, perhaps due to enzyme induction, but perhaps also partly due to an increase in protein binding of progestogen (see kinetic data above). The first sign of contraceptive failure will generally be mid-cycle spotting, and in such cases the daily dose of ethinyloestradiol should be increased to 50, 80, or even 100 μg if necessary.

Because of their adverse effects oestrogens may decrease the therapeutic effects of other drugs, such as warfarin, antihypertensive drugs, oral hypoglycaemic drugs, and antidepressants.

3. Male sex hormones

Structures

The principal male sex hormone is testosterone which is mainly secreted by the interstitial cells of the testis under the influence of LH (ICSH). It is also secreted by the adrenals.

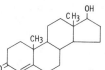

There are several semi-synthetic androgens with different spectra of effects, some (such as methyltestosterone and mesterolone) having both androgenic and anabolic effects, others (such as nandrolone and danazol) having principally anabolic effects, with less androgenic effect than testosterone. Nandrolone is shown here as an example:

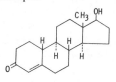

Mode of action

Testosterone has both androgenic and anabolic properties.

The androgenic properties are responsible
for producing male attributes. They cause the
changes which occur at puberty: growth of the
penis, scrotum, and testicles; frequent penile
erections; the pubertal growth spurt and eventual fusion of the bony epiphyses; increased
thickness and oiliness of the skin with acne;
and other secondary sexual characteristics,
such as growth of axillary, pubic, and facial
hair, and deepening of the voice.

The anabolic effects result in increased
muscle mass.

Uses

Replacement therapy in testicular or pituitary insufficiency (testosterone, mesterolone).

Aplastic anaemia (oxymetholone and stanozolol).

To increase muscle bulk (e.g. after debili-
tating disease; ethyloestrenol, nandrolone,
oxymetholone, stanozolol).

Breast carcinoma with metastases (drostanolone, nandrolone).

Dosages

Replacement therapy
Testosterone i.m. is the treatment of choice.
Numerous different formulations of different
salts are available (e.g. testosterone propionate, testosterone enanthate, testosterone decanoate); either alone or in combination, and
the following are examples of suitable regimens:

Testosterone salts (propionate 20 mg/ml +
phenylpropionate 40 mg/ml + isohexanoate
40 mg/ml; Sustanon 100®), 1 ml i.m. every 2
weeks.

Testosterone salts (propionate 30 mg/ml +
phenylpropionate 60 mg/ml + isohexanoate
60 mg/ml + decanoate 100 mg/ml; Sustanon
250®), 1 ml i.m. every 3 weeks.

Testosterone enanthate 250 mg/ml (Pri-
moteston Depot®), 1 ml i.m. every 3 weeks.

In patients who are unsuitable for i.m.
therapy oral treatment may be used as in the
following examples:

Testosterone undecanoate 40–120 mg daily
p.o.

Mesterolone 25 mg t.d.s. p.p.

Aplastic anaemia
Oxymetholone 100–350 mg orally daily in
divided doses.

Stanozolol 50 mg i.m. every 2–3 weeks.

To increase muscle bulk
Ethyloestrenol 2–4 mg orally daily.

Nandrolone 25–50 mg i.m. every 3 weeks.

Oxymetholone 5–10 mg daily for 4–6
weeks, repeated after 10–15 days.

Stanozolol 5 mg orally daily, or 50 mg i.m.
every 2–3 weeks.

Breast carcinoma with metastases
Drostanolone 300 mg i.m. weekly.

Nandrolone decanoate 25–50 mg i.m. every
3 weeks.

Nandrolone phenylpropionate 25–50 mg
i.m. weekly.

Kinetic data

Testosterone is extensively metabolized in the
liver after oral administration and is therefore
usually given i.m. The oily solution of testosterone undecanoate is absorbed via the intestinal lymphatics, avoiding first-pass metabolism. Testosterone is extensively bound in the
plasma to the sex-hormone-binding globulin.

Important adverse effects

The main adverse effects of the male sex
hormones are inherent in their actions as
virilizing hormones. The virilizing effects are,
however, less marked with the specifically
anabolic hormones (such as nandrolone) than
with testosterone itself.

In children growth may be inhibited by
early closure of the bony epiphyses.

In women the virilizing effects cause hirsutism, breast atrophy, acne, clitoral hypertrophy, increased libido, and deepening of the
voice.

In men there is increase of libido, aggressive behaviour, frequent erections, and occasionally priapism.

Other common effects include sodium and
water retention, increased muscle mass (ana-

bolic effect), and hypercalcaemia (in women being treated for metastatic breast cancer).

Ethyloestrenol, oxymetholone, and stanozolol can cause liver damage, and should be used with care in patients with pre-existing liver disease. Methyltestosterone commonly causes cholestatic jaundice and should no longer be used.

In high dosages ethyloestrenol has progestogen-like effects and may cause nausea, vomiting, and amenorrhoea. It has very little androgenic activity.

Androgens should not be used in men with prostatic or breast carcinoma. They should not be used either in pregnancy, since they may cause virilization of a female fetus, or in breast-feeding mothers.

Interactions

Anabolic steroids may increase the effects of warfarin, perhaps by increasing the affinity of warfarin for its receptor site.

SODIUM NITROPRUSSIDE

Structure

$$Na_2Fe(CN)_5NO$$

Mode of action

Sodium nitroprusside has a direct relaxant effect on the smooth muscle of veins and arteries. Peripheral arteriolar dilatation produces the hypotensive effect. It also reduces ergot-induced arterial vasoconstriction. The haemodynamic effects in acute left ventricular failure are due to the combination of both pre- and afterload reduction.

Uses

Accelerated hypertension.

Acute left ventricular failure.

The elective induction of hypotension during surgery.

Ergot-induced arterial vasoconstriction and gangrene.

Dosages

0·5–1·5 micrograms/kg/min by continuous i.v. infusion increasing as required to 8 micro-

grams/kg/min. Meticulous and frequent monitoring of blood pressure is required and treatment should therefore be undertaken only in hospital. Sodium nitroprusside must be protected from light during infusion.

Kinetic data

The $t_{1/2}$ of sodium nitroprusside is only a few minutes, and its effects may therefore be rapidly switched on and off by adjustments in the infusion rate. It is metabolized to thiocyanate, which is eliminated in the urine. Thiocyanate toxicity begins at plasma concentrations over 50 μg/ml.

Important adverse effects

Nausea, vomiting, restlessness, headache, palpitation, sweating, retrosternal discomfort, and abdominal pain all occur with over-rapid infusion, as obviously also does hypotension. In patients with renal impairment thiocyanate toxicity may occur. Sodium nitroprusside should not be used in patients with liver disease, aortic coarctation, or arteriovenous shunts.

SPIRONOLACTONE

Structure

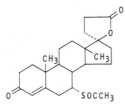

(Compare aldosterone, carbenoxolone, and cardiac glycosides.)

Mode of action

Canrenone, the active metabolite of spironolactone, is an antagonist of the action of aldosterone on the distal convoluted tubule of the nephron. This causes increased sodium and water excretion and potassium retention.

Uses

Fluid retention due to cardiac failure, the nephrotic syndrome, and hepatic disease. In heart failure and the nephrotic syndrome it is usually used in combination with a thiazide or loop diuretic or both.

Dosage

100–200 mg o.d., orally.

Kinetic data

Spironolactone is well absorbed. It has a short $t_{1/2}$ (about 10 min), but is metabolized to the active compound canrenone ($t_{1/2}$ = 16 h) which itself is excreted by the kidney. Partly because of the long $t_{1/2}$ of its metabolite spironolactone has a long duration of action and its maximum effects take several days to occur.

Canrenone is now available for i.v. use as an alternative to spironolactone.

Important adverse effects

Nausea and vomiting are common especially with high doses. If this proves troublesome it may help to give the total daily dose in two divided doses.

Hyperkalaemia occurs in about 8 per cent of patients, even when a potassium-depleting diuretic is also used.

Gynaecomastia is common and often painful. Other less frequent effects include menstrual disturbances, impotence, testicular atrophy, and peptic ulceration.

Interaction

The therapeutic effect of carbenoxolone on peptic ulcer is reversed by spironolactone, and another diuretic should be chosen, therefore, to treat fluid retention due to carbenoxolone.

STILBOESTROL (DIETHYLSTILBOESTROL)

Structure

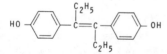

(Compare tamoxifen.)

Mode of action

Stilboestrol is a synthetic oestrogen which is twice as potent as oestradiol.

Uses

In the management of:
  (a) Post-menopausal, oestrogen-sensitive breast carcinoma;
  (b) Metastatic prostatic carcinoma:
    (i) relief of pain from bony metastases;
    (ii) relief of urinary obstruction.

Dosages

Breast carcinoma: 10–20 mg o.d. orally.

Prostatic carcinoma: 1–3 mg o.d. orally.

Kinetic data

Well absorbed. Slowly metabolized in the liver.

Important adverse effects

Nausea and vomiting occur in about 50 per cent of cases. In women tenderness and engorgement of the breasts may occur, and in men gynaecomastia and decreased libido.

There is an increased incidence of cardiovascular deaths in patients on long-term stilboestrol therapy for the treatment of prostatic carcinoma.

Diethylstilboestrol should not be used in pregnancy because of the association with vaginal adenocarcinoma in the female offspring.

Diethylstilboestrol may precipitate an acute attack of hepatic porphyria in susceptible patients.

STREPTOKINASE AND UROKINASE

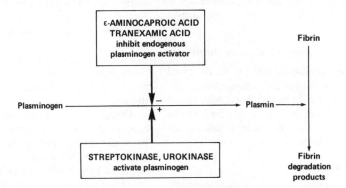

Fig. P10. The activation of plasminogen and the effects of drugs which activate it or inhibit its activation.

Mode of action

Streptokinase is an enzyme made by haemolytic streptococci. Urokinase is an enzyme found in mammalian blood and urine and isolated from human urine. Both are activators of plasminogen by an interaction with its endogenous pro-activator, and this action results in fibrinolysis (see Fig. P10). In this respect they have an opposite action to that of ε-aminocaproic acid and tranexamic acid which inhibit endogenous plasminogen activator and thus discourage fibrinolysis.

Uses

Thrombo-embolic disease of major vessels (e.g. iliofemoral vein thrombosis).

Major pulmonary embolism.

Thrombosis of large arteries.

Thrombosis of arterio-venous shunts (dialysis patients).

The use of thrombolytic drugs given either intravenously or directly into the coronary artery in patients with established acute myocardial infarction is still under investigation.

Dosages

(a) Intravenous dosages

Before starting treatment check the thrombin time, activated partial thromboplastin time, prothrombin time, platelet count, and packed cell volume, to rule out coagulation disorders and to provide a baseline for subsequent monitoring.

Streptokinase

Loading dose: Most patients have antibodies to streptokinase and a large loading dose is required to neutralize them. Generally the loading dose is 250 000 i.u. but may be higher in patients with a history of repeated streptococcal infections or who have previously received streptokinase. The dose is given by i.v. infusion in 0·9 per cent saline over 30 min. Maintenance dosage: 100 000 i.u./h by continuous i.v. infusion initially, then subsequently adjusting the dose according to the thrombin time, which should be prolonged by 2–4 times compared with normal. If prolongation is not sufficient after 8 h of therapy increase the infusion rate to 200 000 i.u./h, if too great reduce to 50 000 i.u./h. Check the thrombin time eight-hourly and alter the infusion rate as required.

Urokinase

Loading dose: 4400 i.u./kg in 15 ml of 0·9 per cent saline by i.v. injection over 10 min. Maintenance dosage: 4400 i.u./kg/h in 180 ml of 0·9 per cent saline by continuous i.v. infusion for 12 h (i.e. 15 ml/h).

Note that while Abbokinase® is formulated in international units, Urokinase Leo® is formulated in Ploug units. 1 Ploug unit = 1·49 i.u. In the USA activity is expressed in CTA units. 1 CTA unit = 0·7 Ploug units = 1·04 i.u.

(b) Thrombosed arterio-venous shunt

Streptokinase 10 000–25 000 i.u. in 10–25 ml of 0·9 per cent saline are injected into the clotted part of the shunt and the venous side is clamped. A sterile syringe is attached on the arterial side so that the artery has an air cushion on which to pulsate.

Important adverse effects

Bleeding is common with thrombolytic drugs, and oozing at puncture sites is to be expected. These drugs should not be used, therefore, in patients with an increased risk of bleeding (for a complete list of contra-indications see Table 21.16). Before giving thrombolytic drugs heparin and warfarin should be withdrawn and the thrombin time and prothrombin time should not be prolonged more than twofold. If severe haemorrhage occurs withdraw therapy and give fresh whole blood, packed red cells, fresh frozen plasma, or cryoprecipitate.

Sometimes it may be necessary to give tranexamic acid (10 mg/kg by i.v. injection over 5 min), or in pregnancy aprotinin (500 000 i.u./h by continuous infusion until bleeding stops).

Mild fever is very common with the use of these drugs and can be minimized by giving hydrocortisone 100 mg i.v. before starting therapy.

Allergic reactions are rare but can be serious (e.g. anaphylaxis) and should be treated by withdrawing therapy and giving corticosteroids, antihistamines, and adrenaline as required (see p.606). Urokinase, in contrast to streptokinase, is not allergenic, and it should be used in patients with a history of streptokinase allergy.

Interactions

Treatment in patients on heparin and warfarin is referred to above.

Drugs which alter platelet function (aspirin, dipyridamole, sulphinpyrazone, phenylbutazone) should be withdrawn for at least 3 days before giving fibrinolytic drugs because of the increased risk of bleeding.

SULPHASALAZINE

Structure

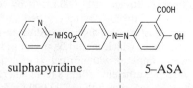

sulphapyridine   5–ASA

Mode of action

Sulphasalazine probably acts, through its metabolite 5-aminosalicylic acid, to suppress the inflammatory reaction in colonic mucosa, perhaps by inhibition of prostaglandin synthesis (see salicylates).

Uses

Ulcerative colitis, both in the treatment of an acute exacerbation, and in the maintenance of remission.

It has also been used in Crohn's disease.

Dosage

500–1000 mg q.d.s., orally.

Kinetic data

Sulphasalazine is hardly at all absorbed. When it reaches the large bowel it is hydrolysed by colonic bacteria to 5-aminosalicylic acid and sulphapyridine. 5-aminosalicylic acid is absorbed only about 25 per cent and is mainly excreted in the faeces. Sulphapyridine, on the other hand is well absorbed from the colon and then metabolized as are other sulphonamides (qq.v.).

Important adverse effects

These are attributable for the most part to sulphapyridine and commonly include nausea, vomiting, and abdominal discomfort. For other adverse effects see under sulphonamides.

SULPHINPYRAZONE

Structure

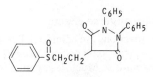

(Compare phenylbutazone.)

Mode of action

Uricosuric effect—by inhibition of the renal tubular reabsorption of uric acid (Fig. 27.4; see also probenecid and salicylates). Inhibition of platelet aggregation in response to various agents—this might be the basis of its suggested effect in reducing the incidence of reinfarction after myocardial infarct.

Uses

Gout and hyperuricaemia.

Efficacy in the secondary prevention of myocardial infarction has been claimed but not proven.

Dosage

100–400 mg b.d., orally.

Kinetic data

Sulphinpyrazone is well absorbed. Its $t_{1/2}$ is about 4 h, but its uricosuric effects persist for up to 10 h during maintenance therapy. It is metabolized 50 per cent to a *para*-hydroxyphenyl derivative, which is also uricosuric but has a short $t_{1/2}$ (1 h). Sulphinpyrazone is also excreted unchanged in the urine.

Important adverse effects

Gastro-intestinal symptoms occur in up to 15 per cent of patients, but are rarely severe. Other adverse effects are rare.

Interactions

The uricosuric effects of sulphinpyrazone and probenecid are antagonized by aspirin at all doses of aspirin. High doses of aspirin are uricosuric and this effect is antagonized by sulphinpyrazone and probenecid.

SULPHONAMIDES

Structures

The general structure of the antibacterial sulphonamides is shown here:

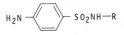

Substitution at R leads to changes in antibacterial activity. The main sulphonamides in use are:

sulphacetamide (for ophthalmic use);
sulphadiazine (in co-trimazine);
sulphadimidine (urinary tract infections);
sulphamethizole (urinary tract infections);
sulphamethoxazole (see co-trimoxazole).

Sulphonamides which are used for non-infective indications include sulphasalazine (in ulcerative colitis—see separate entry), and sulphapyridine (in dermatitis herpetiformis).

Mode of action

Sulphonamides are bacteriostatic, and act by competitive inhibition of the incorporation of *para*-aminobenzoic acid into pteroylglutamic acid (folic acid), which is necessary for bacterial replication. For the effects of a combination of a sulphonamide with trimethoprim see under co-trimoxazole (trimethoprim + sulphamethoxazole). Other similar combinations include co-trifamole (trimethoprim and sulphamoxole), and co-trimazine (trimethoprim and sulphadiazine).

Uses

The organisms against which the sulphonamides may be active include:

Gram-positive cocci (streptococci, pneumococci, staphylococci);

Gram-negative cocci (meningococci, gonococci);

Gram-negative bacilli (*E. coli*, *P. mirabilis*, *H. influenzae*);

Gram-positive bacilli (*B. anthracis*, *C. diphtheriae*).

Other possibly sensitive organisms are *Nocardia*, *Actinomyces*, *Chlamydia*, and *Toxoplasma*.

However, sulphonamides are not so frequently used as previously because of their adverse effects, the emergence of resistant organisms, their limited antibacterial spectrum, and the introduction of more potent and effective antibiotics. The indications for those sulphonamides still in use are very restricted, for example:

Sulphacetamide (used mainly for the topical treatment of infective conjunctivitis);

Sulphamethizole and sulphadimidine (urinary tract infection with Gram-negative organisms);

Sulphadiazine (nocardiasis and, in combination with pyrimethamine, toxoplasmosis).

Dosages

Examples of oral regimens:

Sulphadiazine, 2–4 g initially, then 0·5–1 g q.d.s.

Sulphadimidine, as for sulphadiazine.

Local application: Sulphacetamide, 2–4 drops of a 10 per cent solution four to eight times daily, or an application of a 10 per cent ointment two to four times daily.

Kinetic data

The oral sulphonamides mentioned here are generally well absorbed. Metabolism is very variable, the major route of metabolism being acetylation, the rate of which is bimodally distributed in the population (see Chapter 8). Sulphadimidine is often used as a reference compound for assessing acetylator status, by measuring the proportion of acetylated metabolite present in an aliquot of urine taken 6 h after an oral dose of 1 g.

Important adverse effects

Allergic reactions are common. These include maculopapular skin rashes, drug fever, and photodermatitis. Much less commonly more severe reactions, such as the Stevens–Johnson syndrome and toxic epidermolysis (Lyell's syndrome), are seen.

Sulphonamide crystalluria, the crystallization of the less soluble sulphonamides in the urine may result in renal damage but may be prevented by making the urine alkaline with sodium bicarbonate and by maintaining a high urine flow rate. It is not a complication of the more modern, more soluble sulphonamides such as sulphamethoxazole. It is not wise to use sulphonamides at all in patients with renal failure.

Sulphonamides displace bilirubin from plasma proteins and the increase in unbound bilirubin in the circulation may lead to deposition of bilirubin in the brains of neonates (kernicterus). For this reason sulphonamides should not be given to neonates or to pregnant women in the third trimester.

Occasionally blood dyscrasias may occur, including agranulocytosis, thrombocytopenia, and aplastic anaemia. Sulphonamides may cause haemolysis in patients with G6PD deficiency (see Chapter 8).

Interactions

Sulphonamides bind to plasma albumin and may displace other drugs such as warfarin, phenytoin, and tolbutamide. The clinical relevance of drug interactions of this kind is discussed in Chapter 10.

SULPHONYLUREAS

Structures

General:

$$X-\langle\bigcirc\rangle-SO_2NHCONHR$$

(Compare sulphonamides, thiazide diuretics, diazoxide.)

Substitutions at R and X produce compounds with differing pharmacological activities.

Mode of action

Sulphonylureas enhance the release of insulin from pancreatic islet beta cells and this action accounts for their short-term and long-term effects. Some of their long-term effects may also be mediated by an increase in the numbers of peripheral insulin receptors.

Use

Diabetes mellitus of mature onset.

Dosages

Chlorpropamide, 100–500 mg o.d., orally.

Glibenclamide, 2·5–20 mg daily, orally, in one or two divided doses.

Tolbutamide, 500 mg b.d. or t.d.s., orally.

Kinetic data

See table below.

It is a curious phenomenon that although chlorpropamide is more than 50 per cent metabolized its $t_{1/2}$ is prolonged in renal failure and its effects increased. It is probably better avoided in patients with renal impairment and in the elderly.

Important adverse effects

Hypoglycaemia is common, particularly with glibenclamide, and with chlorpropamide if renal function is impaired.

About a third of patients who take alcohol with chlorpropamide may have a reaction consisting of flushing, vomiting, hypotension, and palpitation. The reaction has also been reported rarely with tolbutamide. The exact mechanism is unknown but it has been reported to be blocked by naloxone.

Nausea, vomiting, and a metallic taste in the mouth occur in about 2 per cent of cases, but tend to resolve after a time.

Interactions

β-adrenoceptor antagonists may enhance the hypoglycaemic effects of sulphonylureas, and also block most of the symptoms of hypoglycaemia (sweating is an exception).

The hypoglycaemic effect of sulphonylureas is reduced by corticosteroids, thiazide diuretics, and diazoxide.

The chlorpropamide–alcohol interaction has been noted above.

	Chlorpropamide	Glibenclamide	Tolbutamide
Absorption	100%	100%	85–100%
Half-time	36 h	6 h	6 h
Elimination	Partly metabolized; metabolites excreted in urine	Almost completely metabolized	Completely metabolized

TAMOXIFEN

Structure

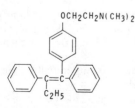

$OCH_2CH_2N(CH_3)_2$

C_2H_5

(Compare stilboestrol.)

Mode of action

Tamoxifen is an antagonist of the effects of oestrogens at tissue receptors. It inhibits the growth of oestrogen-dependent breast cancer cells. In normal pre-menopausal women it decreases plasma prolactin concentrations, perhaps by inhibiting oestradiol-induced prolactin release from the pituitary. In anovulatory women it also increases plasma LH concentrations.

Uses

Breast carcinoma in post-menopausal women.

Stimulation of ovulation in infertility.

Dosages

Breast carcinoma (not to be used in women with functioning ovaries): 10 mg orally b.d. Increase to 20 mg b.d. after 1 month if there is no response.

Treatment of infertility: First exclude pregnancy. If there is regular menstruation give 10 mg b.d. on days 2, 3, 4, and 5 of the cycle increasing during subsequent cycles to 40 mg b.d. if required. Start treatment at any time if menstruation is not occurring.

Kinetic data

Little is known about the pharmacokinetics of

tamoxifen. It seems to be extensively metabolized, but the metabolites are excreted into the gut via the bile and are then hydrolysed to tamoxifen which is reabsorbed. It consequently has a long half-time during chronic therapy (average 7 days) and it may take weeks or even months to reach steady state during maintenance dose therapy.

Important adverse effects

The major and most common (10–20 per cent) adverse effects of tamoxifen are related to its anti-oestrogen actions, namely hot flushes, pruritus vulvae, and occasionally vaginal bleeding. Nausea and vomiting are also very common (10 per cent). It may occasionally cause fluid retention and increase in tumour pain. In women with bony metastases it may occasionally cause hypercalcaemia.

TETRACYCLINES

Structures

Tetracycline:

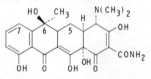

The other commonly used tetracyclines are:
  oxytetracycline;
  doxycycline;
  minocycline;
  chlortetracycline;
  demeclocycline (demethylchlortetracycline).
  These various compounds are formed by making various substitutions at positions 5, 6, and 7 in the structure shown above (e.g. oxytetracycline has a hydroxyl group at position 5).

Mode of action

By inhibition of protein synthesis in bacterial ribosomes, and disruption of the translation process from RNA to DNA. Overall, tetracyclines are bacteriostatic.

Uses

In Table P8 are listed some of the infectious

diseases for which the tetracyclines may be indicated, and the organisms with which those diseases are associated.

Tetracyclines are also used in the prevention of meningococcal infection in the contacts of those with meningoccal meningitis, as an alternative to rifampicin.

Other uses include the treatment of acne vulgaris, and the use of demeclocycline in the syndrome of inappropriate ADH secretion, because of its ability to render the renal tubules relatively insensitive to the effects of ADH.

Dosages

The following are examples of common dosage regimens:

Oral

Tetracycline, 250–500 mg six-hourly.
Oxytetracycline, 250–500 mg six-hourly.
Doxycycline, 200 mg initially then 100 mg once daily.
Minocycline, 200 mg initially, then 100 mg twelve-hourly.
Chlortetracycline, 250–500 mg six-hourly.
Demeclocycline, 150 mg six-hourly or 300 mg twelve-hourly.

Intramuscular and intravenous

	i.m.	i.v.
Tetracycline	100–200 mg 6–8 h	500 mg 12 h (infusion)
Oxytetracycline	100 mg 8–12 h	250–500 mg 12 h (slow infusion)

Local application

Tetracyclines are available for local application in creams and ointments, usually containing the antibiotic in a strength of 3 per cent.

Kinetic data

The tetracyclines are moderately well absorbed (about 70 per cent) except for minocycline and doxycycline, which are well absorbed (90 per cent). The absorption of tetracyclines is reduced by calcium, aluminium, magnesium, and iron, with which they form insoluble chelates (see interactions).

The values of $t_{1/2}$ differ from tetracycline to tetracycline, partly accounting for the differences in dosage frequency: tetracycline, chlortetracycline, and oxytetracycline, $t_{1/2} = 8$ h; demeclocyline, $t_{1/2} = 14$ h; minocycline and doxycycline, $t_{1/2} = 18$ hours.

The tetracyclines are widely distributed to body tissues, but of particular importance is their distribution to growing bones and teeth where they may cause both decoloration and enamel hypoplasia, and decreased growth of long bones (see adverse effects).

Most of the tetracyclines are excreted in the urine 40–60 per cent unchanged, and renal failure causes decreased clearance and accumulation. Minocycline and doxycycline are excreted in the urine to a much lesser extent

Table P8 *The main indications for the use of tetracyclines*

Disease	Organism
1. *Tetracyclines treatment of choice*	
Acute exacerbation of chronic bronchitis	Pneumococcus and *H. influenzae*
'Atypical' pneumonia	
Mycoplasma pneumonia	*Mycoplasma pneumoniae*
Q fever	*Coxiella burnetti*
Psittacosis	*Chlamydia psittaci*
Brucellosis (with streptomycin)	*Brucella abortus*
Leptospirosis (alternative penicillin G)	*Leptospira icterohaemorrhagiae*
Typhus diseases	*Rickettsia spp.*
Lymphogranuloma venereum (LGV)	LGV *Chlamydiae*
Trachoma and inclusion conjunctivitis	*Chlamydia trachomatis*
Non-specific urethritis	*Chlamydia* and *Ureaplasma spp.*
Other rickettsioses (trench fever, rickettsial pox, tick-borne rickettsioses)	
Infections of the skin (local treatment)	
2. *Tetracyclines second-line treatment*	
Syphilis and yaws	*Treponema pallidum* and *T. pertenue*
Actinomycosis	*Actinomyces israelii*
Anthrax	*Bacillus anthracis*
Eye infections (local treatment)	

and are mostly metabolized in the liver. It is generally agreed that if a tetracycline has to be used in a patient with compromised renal function doxycycline is the tetracycline of choice.

All the tetracyclines are to some extent excreted in the bile and undergo enterohepatic recirculation.

Important adverse effects

(a) Renal

In patients with compromised renal function, e.g. patients with renal failure or the elderly, there may be accumulation of tetracyclines to concentrations in the blood which result in toxic effects, such as anorexia, nausea, vomiting, and diarrhoea. These effects lead to dehydration which further compromises renal function and leads to the clinical syndrome of frank acute renal failure.

In addition to this, the *apparent* biochemical degree of renal failure, as judged by the blood urea, may be increased by the anti-anabolic effects of tetracyclines, resulting in a rise in blood urea without a concomitant rise in serum creatinine.

The indirect adverse effects of tetracyclines on renal function should not be confused with the very special effect of direct renal toxicity caused by tetracycline products formed during excessively long storage with chemical breakdown of the drug. This toxicity results in tubular damage with effects similar to those of the Fanconi syndrome. It is important, therefore, that out-of-date tetracyclines should not be used.

The effect of demeclocycline in producing nephrogenic diabetes insipidus, and its consequent value in treating inappropriate ADH secretion has been noted above.

(b) Gastro-intestinal

Tetracyclines commonly produce gastro-intestinal adverse effects, e.g. nausea, vomiting, epigastric discomfort and diarrhoea. Rarely diarrhoea may be caused by superinfection with *Clostridium difficile* resulting in pseudomembranous colitis (see lincomycin). Oral superinfection with *Candida albicans* may result in thrush (moniliasis), especially in the elderly or debilitated.

(c) Bones and teeth

Because of the formation of a tetracycline-calcium or thiophosphate complex, tetracyclines are deposited in growing bones and teeth. In the teeth this causes brown discolouration and hypoplasia of the enamel. The deposit in bone may affect bone growth, but this is reversible.

For these reasons tetracyclines should not be given, unless absolutely necessary, to pregnant women (because of effects on the fetus) or to children up to the age of 12 years.

(d) Other adverse effects

Tetracyclines, particularly demeclocycline, may cause the skin to become very sensitive to light in the u.v. range. This effect does not occur with local application of tetracyclines.

Intravenous administration may be complicated by thrombophlebitis and large doses i.v. may be hepatotoxic.

Rarely thrombocytopenia, haemolytic anaemia, and eosinophilia may occur.

In infants tetracyclines may cause increased intracranial pressure (pseudotumor cerebri) with bulging of the fontanelles. This condition resolves on discontinuation of the drug.

Minocycline may cause vestibular toxicity.

Interactions

Tetracycline absorption is reduction by calcium, aluminium, magnesium, and iron because of the formation of insoluble chelates. The absorption of the ions is thus also decreased.

Tetracyclines increase the effects of warfarin, probably by an effect on clotting factor activity. In patients deficient in *dietary* vitamin K the removal of *bacterial* vitamin K produced in the gut may be an additional factor.

THIAZIDE DIURETICS
(BENZOTHIADIAZINES)

Structures

General:

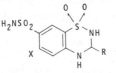

(Compare diazoxide, sulphonamides, sulphonylureas.)

Examples:

	R	X
Hydrochlorothiazide	H	Cl
Bendrofluazide	$CH_2C_6H_5$	CF_3
Cyclopenthiazide	$CH_2C_5H_9$	Cl

Mode of action

Diuretic effect: inhibition of sodium and chloride reabsorption in the distal convoluted tubule of the nephron, resulting in increased sodium and free water clearance. The molecular mechanism of this effect is still unclear. A secondary effect is the loss of potassium by increased secretion in the distal tubule in response to the increased intraluminal sodium concentration.

Antihypertensive effect: the precise details are not known, but a number of factors appear to be involved. There is initially sodium and water loss, leading to relative hypovolaemia, which may result in lowered cardiac output. The hypovolaemia, however, is corrected homoeostatically within a few weeks, while the antihypertensive effect continues. One hypothesis maintains that a lowered sodium concentration in vascular smooth muscle cells leads to a decreased free intracellular calcium concentration, which decreases the reactivity of the vascular smooth muscle to noradrenaline released from sympathetic nerve endings. Overall, therefore, there is a decrease in peripheral resistance and a fall in blood pressure.

Uses

Oedema due to cardiac failure, liver disease, nephrotic syndrome, and drugs.
Hypertension.
Nephrogenic diabetes insipidus.

Dosages

Hydrochlorothiazide: 50–100 mg o.d., orally.
Bendrofluazide: 5–10 mg o.d., orally.
Cyclopenthiazide: 0·5–1 mg o.d., orally.

The thiazide diuretics are also available in combination formulations with potassium-sparing diuretics (spironolactone, triamterene, and amiloride), with potassium chloride (q.v.), or with β-adrenoceptor antagonists. In such cases the dose is usually the same as that which would be given if the thiazide were being used alone.

Kinetic data

All are well absorbed, and are excreted unchanged by the kidney. Although the $t_{1/2}$ is usually short (usually less than 4 h), the duration of action is longer (about 12 h). Thus these drugs should be given in the morning to avoid nocturia.

Important adverse effects

Hypokalaemia, hyponatraemia, and dehydration are the most important. Hypokalaemia may be avoided by using potassium supplements or potassium-sparing diuretics (see under 'potassium chloride' for a discussion of the need for potassium supplements in patients taking potassium-wasting diuretics). Hypomagnesaemia may also occur.

Hyperglycaemia occurs but is usually not of clinical importance, although occasionally diabetes mellitus may be precipitated in a susceptible patient. In diabetics increased doses of oral hypoglycaemics may be required. Hyperuricaemia occurs and occasionally results in acute gout. Hypercalcaemia may occur in susceptible patients, due to decreased urinary calcium excretion.

Rarely bone-marrow suppression may occur, usually resulting in thrombocytopenia. Pancreatitis has also been reported.

In hepatic insufficiency encephalopathy may be precipitated.

Interactions

Thiazide diuretics decrease the clearance of lithium by the kidney, and lithium dosages should be halved initially, and adjusted with careful plasma concentration monitoring (see Chapter 7).

Hypokalaemia potentiates the effects of cardiac glycosides, and diminishes the effects of Class I anti-arrhythmics, such as lignocaine, procainamide, and quinidine.

THYROID HORMONES

Structures

General:

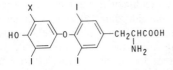

L-thyroxine (T$_4$): X = I.
L-triiodothyronine (T$_3$): X = H.

20 micrograms T$_3$ is equivalent to 100 micrograms T$_4$.

Mode of action and uses

Thyroxine and triiodothyronine are the naturally occurring thyroid hormones, and are therefore used as replacement therapy in hypothyroidism of any cause and in hypothyroid coma. Because an increase in circulating thyroid hormone causes feedback inhibition of TSH output from the normal pituitary they are also used in the treatment of diffuse non-toxic goitre, subacute thyroiditis, Hashimoto's thyroiditis, and thyroid carcinoma.

Dosages

Intravenous: Use triiodothyronine in severe hypothyroidism. There is controversy about the correct dosage of triiodothyronine in this condition. Whatever the dose a glucocorticoid should also be given (e.g. hydrocortisone 100 mg i.v. once daily). Then a dose of triiodothyronine of 25 micrograms every 6–12 h is recommended. This regimen steers a middle course between those who advocate smaller doses (e.g. 10 micrograms six-hourly) and those recommending larger doses (e.g. 100 micrograms immediately and 25 micrograms six-hourly thereafter). (See treatment of thyroid disease p.432).

Oral: Triiodothyronine is used when first treating severe hypothyroidism. After initial treatment one would generally switch to thyroxine. Triiodothyronine: 5 micrograms once daily initially increasing at weekly intervals; when a dose of 60 micrograms is reached change to thyroxine. Thyroxine: 25–50 micrograms once daily initially, increasing as required in 50 microgram increments every four weeks up to 300 micrograms daily.

Kinetic data

Both are well absorbed and very highly bound to plasma proteins (> 99 per cent). Triiodothyronine $t_{1/2} = 36$ h; thyroxine $t_{1/2} = 7$ days. The $t_{1/2}$ of thyroxine is shortened in hyperthyroidism and prolonged in hypothyroidism.

Important adverse effects

In the early stages of treatment of hypothyroidism, patients may suffer angina pectoris, myocardial infarction, or cardiac arrhythmias, especially if they have pre-existing cardiac disease. Later on the signs and symptoms of hyperthyroidism occur if the dose is excessive. Treatment of hypothyroidism with thyroid hormones can be monitored by measuring serum concentrations of triiodothyronine (normal range 1·5–3·0 nmol/l) and TSH (normal range 0–6 mu/l).

TRICYCLIC ANTIDEPRESSANTS

Structures

Examples:

	X_1-R	X_2*
Amitriptyline	$C=CHCH_2CH_2N(CH_3)_2$	C
Imipramine	$N-CH_2CH_2CH_2N(CH_3)_2$	C
Nortriptyline	$C=CHCH_2CH_2NHCH_3$	C

* In other compounds X_2 may be O (e.g. doxepin) or S (e.g. dothiepin).

General:

Mode of action

Tricyclic antidepressants inhibit the reuptake of noradrenaline and 5-hydroxytryptamine (5-HT) at central monoaminergic synapses. The relative potency of inhibition of noradrenaline and 5-HT reuptake varies from drug to drug. Exactly how this action is then translated into an antidepressant effect is not clearly understood. However, it is generally agreed that tricyclic antidepressants take a week or more to show their antidepressant effects, and so attention has recently been directed towards those pharmacological changes in the brain which might occur subsequent to the rises in concentrations of monoamines in the synaptic cleft, i.e. adaptive responses. In experimental animals many such adaptive changes have been found and include down-regulation (i.e. reduction in numbers) of cortical β-adrenoceptors, α-adrenoceptors, and 5-HT receptors. What these changes mean in functional terms is still unknown, but it is now apparent that several adaptive responses occur in the brain as a result of the effects of tricyclic antidepressants, and that perhaps their therapeutic activity is dependent upon this spectrum of adaptive respnses.

Although not perhaps relevant to their antidepressant effects, these drugs also have central and peripheral anticholinergic effects of importance in overdose (e.g. causing cardiac arrhythmias), and in causing some of the common adverse effects (dry mouth, urinary retention). They also have antihistamine (H_1) actions which may be responsible for their effects in causing drowsiness during the early stages of therapy.

Uses

Depression (most active in the endogenous type).

Nocturnal enuresis (mechanism of action unknown).

Post-herpetic neuralgia (in combination with an anticonvulsant such as carbamazepine or valproate).

Dosages

These drugs are probably best given in one daily oral dose at night. Their effects last sufficiently long to allow once-a-day dosage and the anticholinergic and antihistaminic effects may be minimized by taking the tablets last thing at night. Treatment is usually started at a low dosage and increased gradually as required to a maximum. Individual dosages are:

Daily dosage	Amitriptyline	Imipramine	Nortriptyline
Initially	25–75 mg	75 mg	30 mg
Maximum	225 mg	225 mg	100 mg
Usual maintenance	50–100 mg	75–100 mg	30–75 mg

Dosages should not be increased at more than two-weekly intervals because of the long time taken to achieve a therapeutic effect.

Kinetic data

Tricyclic antidepressants are well absorbed but have variable first-pass metabolism. Amitriptyline and imipramine are metabolized in the liver by demethylation to nortriptyline and desipramine respectively, both metabolites being pharmacologically active. Further metabolism by the liver to inactive compounds follows. Metabolism of these compounds is undoubtedly their most important route of elimination and rates of clearance vary widely from individual to individual, possibly for pharmacogenetic reasons. In addition, their apparent volumes of distribution are very high (e.g. 15 l/kg for imipramine) because of extensive tissue distribution, and this is also very variable. This wide variability in both clearance and apparent volume of distribution results in very wide variation in $t_{1/2}$. For amitriptyline a very wide range of values of $t_{1/2}$ has been reported (between 5 and 161 h), and the average is about 40 h. Values for the other drugs are: nortriptyline, 15–95 h; imipramine, 6–20 h; desipramine, 8–28 h.

All this variability leads to a wide variation in the optimum therapeutic dose in an individual (see above).

Important adverse effects

Anticholinergic effects are very common and include dry mouth, blurred vision, constipation, and difficulty with micturition. However, tolerance may develop and patients should be encouraged to persist with treatment. Taking the dose last thing at night may help to minimize these effects. Care should be taken in patients with prostatic enlargement or closed-angle glaucoma.

Cardiovascular effects include tachycardia, ventricular arrhythmias, heart block, and hypotension. Some cases of sudden death in patients on tricyclic antidepressants have been attributed to cardiac arrhythmias. Care should therefore be taken when considering prescribing antidepressants for patients who have had myocardial infarcts. It may then be advisable to prescribe an antidepressant drug with fewer effects on the heart, e.g. mianserin.

Care should also be taken in prescribing tricyclic antidepressants for patients with epilepsy, since they lower seizure threshold.

Confusional states may result from tricyclic therapy, especially in the elderly.

There is some evidence that high doses of nortriptyline may result in a worsening of depression (see Chapter 7).

Interactions

The following are the effects of tricyclic antidepressants on other drugs:

1. They diminish the antihypertensive effects of clonidine and the adrenergic neurone blocking drugs, debrisoquine, bethanidine, and guanethidine.

2. They potentiate the central depressant effects of alcohol.

3. They potentiate the effects of other anticholinergic drugs.

4. They potentiate the effects of adrenaline and noradrenaline (to be noted particularly when administering lignocaine local anaesthetic preparations containing adrenaline—this interaction can be fatal). Occasionally a similar interaction can occur with phenylpropanolamine in 'cold cures', and with amphetamine.

The dose of replacement thyroid therapy may need to be reduced.

VALPROATE SODIUM

Structure

$$(CH_3CH_2CH_2)_2CHCOONa$$

Mode of action

Valproate sodium inhibits γ-aminobutyric acid (GABA) transaminase, and prevents GABA reuptake. This results, at least in animals, in an increase in brain GABA concentrations. It is not clear, however, that its mode of action is related to this effect, because the concentrations of valproate achieved in the human brain are likely to be too low for this effect to occur.

Uses

As an anticonvulsant in:

(a) Generalized seizures

Absences (petit mal).
Tonic–clonic seizures (grand mal).
Myoclonic seizures.

(b) Partial seizures

Psychomotor epilepsy (temporal lobe epilepsy).

(c) Post-herpetic neuralgia

In combination with a tricyclic antidepressant.

Dosages

Initially 200 mg t.d.s. orally, increasing by 200 mg a day at 3-day intervals to a maximum of 2600 mg/day according to the response. Usual maintenance dose, 1000–1600 mg/day.

Kinetic data

Valproate is well absorbed. It is very highly protein bound in the plasma and is mostly metabolized in the liver, $t_{1/2} = 10$ h. Plasma concentrations should be up to 700 μmol/l (100 μg/ml), but there is not a very good relationship between plasma concentrations of valproate and its therapeutic effect.

Important adverse effects

Early on gastro-intestinal symptoms, such as nausea and vomiting, are common, but they resolve on lowering the dose and may be lessened by the use of enteric-coated formulations and by taking the tablets with food. Later on tolerance develops and the dose may be increased without adverse effect.

Ataxia, incoordination, tremor, and drowsiness may occur as toxic effects.

Transient hair loss, oedema, and thrombocytopenia occur infrequently.

Valproate has been reported to impair liver function and in a few patients has led to fatal hepatic failure. It should therefore be used with caution in patients with pre-existing liver disease, and liver function tests should be carried out before treatment is started, and every 2 months thereafter for up to 6 months. If abnormalities in liver function occur the drug should be withdrawn.

Interactions

Valproate displaces phenytoin from plasma protein binding sites. The consequences of this type of interaction are discussed in Chapter 10.

Valproate increases plasma concentrations of phenobarbitone and primidone, perhaps by inhibiting their metabolism.

VANCOMYCIN

Structure

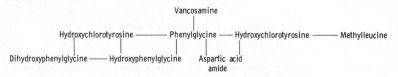

Vancomycin is a complex glycopeptide containing an aminodisaccharide (vancosamine) and several amino acid moieties. Its structure is summarized above.

Mode of action

Vancomycin is bacteriocidal and acts by in-hibiting bacterial cell wall synthesis.

Uses

Pseudomembranous colitis (infection with *Clostridium difficile*—see lincomycin, p.702).
Severe staphylococcal infections.

As an alternative to penicillins in the prophylaxis of infective endocarditis, before dental procedures and cardiac surgery.

As an alternative to penicillins in the treatment of infective endocarditis due to streptococci, enterococci, staphylococci, *Haemophilus spp.*, and *Proteus spp.*

Dosages

Oral (pseudomembranous colitis): 500 mg six-hourly.

Intravenous (infective endocarditis prophylaxis): 1 g 30 min before surgical procedures (see Table 21.13), and after cardiac surgery 1 g i.v. twelve-hourly for four doses.

Intravenous (infective endocarditis treatment): 500 mg i.v. six-hourly.

Vancomycin is very irritant to veins and should be diluted in 200 ml of 5 per cent dextrose or 0·9 per cent saline before i.v. administration. Infusion should be carried out over 20–30 min.

Kinetic data

Vancomycin is very poorly absorbed from the gastro-intestinal tract. It is almost completely eliminated unchanged in the urine, $t_{1/2} = 6$ h, and because of its toxicity it should not be used i.v. in patients with renal impairment (creatinine clearance < 50 ml/min). Renal failure is not a contra-indication to oral use.

Important adverse effects

Vancomycin is both ototoxic and nephrotoxic. Both of these effects are dose-related and i.v. vancomycin should not be used in patients with renal impairment (see above) or in patients with pre-existing hearing impairment. If tinnitus occurs the drug should be withdrawn. If the facilities are available plasma concentration measurement should be used to monitor therapy. Plasma concentrations should be below 30 μg/ml.

Extravasation with i.v. infusion causes tissue necrosis and care should be taken to infuse vancomycin into large veins.

Its effects on the fetus are unknown, and it should not be used i.v. in pregnancy.

Other common adverse effects are hypersensitivity reactions (fever, rash, eosinophilia, anaphylaxis), and nausea.

Interactions

Care should be taken when administering vanomycin i.v. with other nephrotoxic antibiotics (e.g. aminoglycosides, polymixin B, colistin).

VASOPRESSIN AND ITS ANALOGUES

Structures

Vasopressin is a nonapeptide whose alternative name is antidiuretic hormone (ADH). The naturally-occurring human vasopressin is arginine vasopressin:

```
 1    2    3    4    5    6    7    8    9
Cys - Tyr - Phe - Gln - Asn - Cys - Pro - Arg - GlyNH₂
```

There are also semi-synthetic vasopressins including desmopressin (DDAVP or 1-deamino-8-D-arginine vasopressin), and felypressin (2-phenylalanine-8-lysine vasopressin). Lypressin (8-lysine vasopressin) is the naturally occurring porcine vasopressin.

Mode of action

Vasopressin is synthesized in the hypothalamus and transported to the posterior pituitary. It is then released in response to increases in plasma osmolality and decreases in extracellular fluid volume. It acts on the cortical and medullary segments of the distal part of the nephron in the kidney where it increases permeability to water, and thus enhances water reabsorption without altering solute transport.

Vasopressin also has effects on the cardiovascular system but at considerably higher concentrations than are required to inhibit diuresis. It causes vasoconstriction of arteries and arterioles, including the coronary, pulmonary, and splanchnic arteries. The relative potencies of vasopressin and its analogues as antidiuretic agents and as vasoconstrictors are shown in Table P9.

Table P9 *Relative potencies of vasopressin and its analogues as antidiuretic agents and as vasopressors*

Drugs	Relative activity (arginine vasopressin=1)	
	Antidiuretic	Vasopressor
Arginine vasopressin	1	1
Lypressin	0.8	0.6
Desmopressin	12	0.004

Vasopressins which have vasopressor actions also cause smooth muscle contraction elsewhere, notably in the gastro-intestinal tract and uterus, and those effects form the basis of some of the adverse effects of high-dose vasopressin.

Uses

Cranial diabetes insipidus (long-term—desmopressin; short-term—vasopressin, desmopressin, lypressin).

To arrest bleeding from oesophageal varices (vasopressin).

With local anaesthetics, to delay their absorption and thus potentiate their effects (felypressin).

Dosages

(a) Cranial diabetes insipidus

(i) Lypressin: 5–20 i.u., three to seven times a day, intranasally.

(ii) Desmopressin: 10–20 micrograms b.d. intranasally (100 microgram/ml solution). In short-term treatment desmopressin can be given i.m. (1–2 micrograms o.d.).

(iii) Vasopressin 5–20 i.u. s.c. or i.m. at least twice daily.

(b) Oesophageal varices

Vasopressin is given either in single doses (20 i.u. in 100 ml of 5 per cent dextrose infused over 20 min) or by continuous i.v. infusion (0·4 i.u./min for 24 h).

(c) Local anaesthesia

Prilocaine 3 per cent is formulated with felypressin 0·03 i.u./ml. The maximum dose is 20 ml.

Kinetic data

Vasopressin and lypressin are rapidly cleared from the body after i.v. administration ($t_{1/2}$ 10 min), but desmopressin has a much longer half-time (75 min) and can be given less frequently than the other vasopressins.

Elimination of vasopressin is by metabolism by tissue peptidases (e.g. in liver and kidney).

Important adverse effects

Adverse effects are few in low dosages and limited to nausea and occasionally abdominal cramps. The nasal preparations may cause nasal congestion and ulceration.

In the i.v. doses of vasopressin used to stop bleeding from oesophageal varices adverse effects are common and consist of abdominal and uterine cramps and the urgent need to defaecate. Because it can cause coronary artery spasm vasopressin should not be used in patients with a history of coronary artery disease. Care should be taken in patients with a history of hypertension.

Hypersensitivity reactions can occur occasionally.

Interactions

Various drugs can stimulate secretion of vasopressin by the pituitary and cause the syndrome of 'inappropriate ADH secretion'. These drugs include chlorpropamide, clofibrate, cyclophosphamide, tricyclic antidepressants, and vincristine. Ethanol and phenytoin are inhibitors of vasopressin secretion.

Some drugs are antagonists of the effects of vasopressin on the renal tubule, notably lithium and demethylchlortetracycline. These drugs can therefore cause nephrogenic diabetes insipidus. Demethylchlortetracycline has been used to treat the syndrome resulting from increased secretion of ADH.

Chlorpropamide and carbamazepine increase the effects of vasopressin on the renal tubule and may therefore be used in mild cases of nephrogenic diabetes insipidus. (The mechanism whereby thiazide diuretics relieve the polyuria of nephrogenic diabetes insipidus is discussed in Chapter 25).

VERAPAMIL

Structure

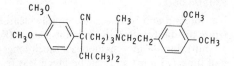

Mode of action

Verapamil has been categorized as a Class IV anti-arrhythmic drug. It impedes the transport of calcium across the myocardial and vascular smooth muscle cell membrane. It therefore prolongs the slow component of the action potential (phase 2, see lignocaine) and prolongs the effective refractory period. This effect occurs particularly in the SA and AV nodes and thus impairs conduction. It also results in a negative inotropic effect.

The effect on vascular smooth muscle results in peripheral vasodilatation, and a reduction in cardiac preload. This, coupled with the reduction in myocardial contractility reduces myocardial oxygen requirements.

Uses

Supraventricular tachycardias, such as paroxysmal supraventricular tachycardia, and the reciprocating tachycardia of the Wolff–Parkinson–White syndrome.

Angina pectoris.

Dosages

Intravenous injection: 5–10 mg at a rate of 1 mg/min.

Intravenous infusion: 5–10 mg/h to a maximum of 100 mg/day.

Oral: 40–120 mg t.d.s.

Kinetic data

Verapamil is well absorbed orally, but subject to 85 per cent first-pass metabolism in the liver. It is not known whether the metabolites have therapeutic activity. The $t_{1/2}$ of verapamil is 5 h and it is prolonged in liver disease.

Important adverse effects

The negative inotropic effect of verapamil may worsen cardiac failure. Hypotension may result from both vasodilatation and the negative inotropic effect.

The effects on the SA and AV nodes may result in sinus bradycardia and impaired AV conduction. Verapamil should therefore be avoided in patients with the sick sinus syndrome, sinus bradycadia, and AV block.

Interactions

β-adrenoceptor antagonists may interact with verapamil—firstly, both are negatively inotropic and cardiac failure and hypotension may result from their combined use; secondly, there have been reports of asystole and an increased incidence of cardiac arrhythmias attributed to their concomitant use. Verapamil should not be used i.v. for at least 8 h after a β-adrenoceptor antagonist but a β-adrenoceptor antagonist may be given within 30–60 min of a verapamil injection.

Verapamil increases steady-state plasma digoxin concentrations by decreasing the renal clearance of digoxin.

VINCA ALKALOIDS

Structures

General:

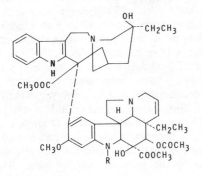

Examples:
Vinblastine: R = CH₃.
Vincristine: R = CHO.

Mode of action

The effects of these drugs may be related to their ability to bind specifically to tubulin, the protein found in cellular microtubules. This results in inhibition of cell division in the metaphase of the mitotic phase, for which they are specific.

Uses

Acute leukaemias (vincristine).

Malignant lymphomas, especially Hodgkin's disease (vincristine and vinblastine).

Dosages

Extreme care must be taken in calculating and administering doses of vincristine and vinblastine. Dosage regimens vary according to age, the disease being treated, and other concurrent therapy. Administration is by the i.v. route, and single doses are usually given once weekly for a set number of times.

It is essential that specialist advice be sought on precise dosage regimens because incorrect dosage can result in serious toxic effects.

Kinetic data

Both are poorly absorbed and are therefore given i.v. They are cleared rapidly from the blood, metabolized in the liver, and excreted in the bile. $T_{1/2} = 3$ h.

Important adverse effects

The most frequent adverse effect is superficial thrombophlebitis at the site of intravenous injection or a local cellulitis if the drug leaks outside of the vein. To avoid this the drug should, if possible, be injected via the tubing of a fast-running i.v. infusion of saline, after reconstitution of the powdered drug in the diluting solution provided by the manufacturers.

Bone marrow suppression is dose-related. It is more frequent with vinblastine than with vincristine in the doses commonly used, and generally affects the neutrophils.

Alopecia is very common.

Peripheral neuropathy is common, more so with vincristine, and generally involves peripheral sensory and motor fibres. Occasionally autonomic innervation of the bowel may be affected leading to constipation and intestinal obstruction. A routine prophylactic laxative regimen is indicated and abdominal pain should be carefully investigated in such patients.

Rarely inappropriate ADH secretion occurs.

Interaction

For the possible interaction with live vaccines see p.288.

VITAMIN D ANALOGUES

Structures

The group of D vitamins includes the following compounds:

 ergocalciferol (calciferol or vitamin D_2);
 cholecalciferol (vitamin D_3);
 dihydrotachysterol;
 25-hydroxycholecalciferol (calcifediol);
 1α-hydroxycholecalciferol (alfacalcidol);
 1,25-dihydroxycholecalciferol (calcitriol);
 24,25-dihydroxycholecalciferol.

We give here the active form of vitamin D, 1,25-dihydroxycholecalciferol (calcitriol):

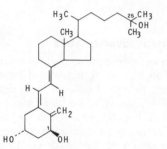

Mode of action

Vitamin D plays a central role in regulating calcium homoeostasis. It is found in the diet and is also synthesized by the skin under the influence of ultraviolet light. Vitamin D_2 (ergocalciferol, found in plants) and D_3 (cholecalciferol, found in animal tissues) are pharmacologically inactive and have to be converted to active compounds (Fig. P11).

Cholecalciferol (vitamin D_3) is hydroxylated in the liver to 25-hydroxycholecalciferol, which is weakly active. This is then further hydroxylated in the kidney either to 24,25-dihydroxycholecalciferol, which is also weakly active, or to 1,25-dihydroxycholecalciferol, the most active form of vitamin D. Under the influence of parathyroid hormone, and in vitamin D or calcium deficiency, the formation of 1,25-dihydroxycholecalciferol is preferred. Orally administered 1α-hydroxycholecalciferol is rapidly converted in the liver to 1,25-dihydroxycholecalciferol.

The main effects of vitamin D are to promote the absorption of calcium and phosphate from the gut and to enhance their reabsorption by the proximal renal tubules. These effects increase plasma concentrations of calcium and phosphate and make them available for mineralization of bone.

Uses

Vitamin D deficiency secondary to inadequate diet, malabsorption, and repeated pregnancy.

Hypoparathyroidism (alfacalcidol).

Renal osteodystrophy (alfacalcidol and calcitriol).

Anticonvulsant-induced osteomalacia.

Congenital rickets.

Dosages

Daily dietary vitamin D requirements are satisfied by 400 i.u. (= 10 micrograms).

In adults over 30 years of age 200 i.u./day are sufficient.

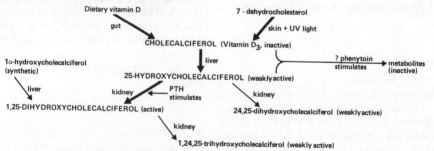

Fig. P11. The metabolic pathways of vitamin D.

(a) Prevention of rickets in children and of osteomalacia in adults

Cholecalciferol or ergocalciferol, 400 i.u./day; dihydrotachysterol, 0·5 mg orally daily.

(b) Dietary deficiency with rickets or osteomalacia

Cholecalciferol or ergocalciferol 3000–5000 i.u. orally o.d. until healing has occurred, then tapering to daily requirements.

Dihydrotachysterol, 1–3 mg daily for 3 days, reducing to a maintenance dosage of 0·25–2 mg daily.

(c) Malabsorption

Dosage requirements vary enormously and may be as high as 500 000 i.u. of vitamin D_3 per day. Alternatively, alfacalcidol may be used in ordinary dosages (see below). Oral calcium salts are also usually given in malabsorption, but care must be taken to avoid hypercalcaemia.

(d) Hypoparathyroidism

Alfacalcidol, 1 microgram orally daily initially. The dosage may be increased to 2 or 3 micrograms daily, and when the full clinical effect has occurred a maintenance dosage of 0·5–1 microgram daily should be sufficient.

(e) Renal osteodystrophy

Alfacalcidol, as above.

Calcitriol, 1–2 micrograms orally daily initially, increasing in increments of 0·25–0·5 micrograms at weekly intervals to a total of 2–3 micrograms daily depending on response.

Kinetic data

Absorption from the gastro-intestinal tract is good. However, vitamin D is fat-soluble and its absorption is reduced in steatorrhoea. Bile is also necessary for its absorption which is therefore reduced in obstructive jaundice.

The metabolic pathway whereby vitamin D_3 is activated to 1,25-dihydroxycholecalciferol is discussed above.

The main route of excretion of vitamin D is via the bile with enterohepatic recirculation, and vitamin D is stored in the body for about 6 months. In malabsorption this enterohepatic recirculation is reduced. The half-time of alfacalcidol in the body is 14 days and of calcifediol 19 days.

Important adverse effects

The most important adverse effect of the vitamin D analogues is hypercalcaemia, which is dose-related. Careful monitoring of the plasma calcium concentration is necessary at least once a week during initial therapy and regularly during maintenance therapy.

Because alfacalcidol has a shorter half-time in the body hypercalcaemia is corrected more quickly after withdrawing it than with other vitamin D analogues. When the calcium returns to normal treatment should be started again, if required, at half the previous dosage.

Interactions

Phenytoin and phenobarbitone can cause osteomalacia, perhaps because of enhanced metabolism of cholecalciferol and calcifediol (see Fig. P11). The metabolism of alfacalcidol is also enhanced by these drugs and increased dosages (up to 5 micrograms daily) may be required.

VITAMIN K

Structure

Vitamin K_1 (phytomenadione, cf. warfarin):

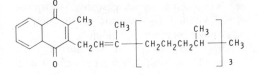

Mode of action

Vitamin K is a cofactor in the synthesis of clotting factors II, VII, IX, and X. It reverses the effects of the coumarin anticoagulants (see warfarin) by acting as a competitive inhibitor of their effects.

Uses

Impaired clotting factor synthesis because of hepatocellular disease, biliary obstruction, or coumarin anticoagulant toxicity.

Vitamin K deficiency from any cause.

Dosages

Vitamin K is available as phytomenadione (vitamin K_1; tablets and injection for i.m. and i.v. administration), and as the synthetic analogue menadiol sodium diphosphate which is water soluble (tablets and injection for i.m. and i.v. administration).

1. Biliary obstruction (e.g. before gall bladder surgery), hepatocellular disease (e.g. before liver biopsy), and coumarin anticoagulant overdose: 10 mg of phytomenadione i.v. slowly.
2. Vitamin K deficiency with malabsorption syndromes and hepatic cirrhosis: 10 mg of the water-soluble menadiol once daily.

3. Vitamin K deficiency in neonates: 1 mg of phytomenadione i.v. (NB synthetic analogues such as menadiol should not be used in the neonate because they may cause haemolysis resulting in hyperbilirubinaemia and kernicterus).

Kinetic data

An assay for vitamin K has only recently been developed.

Important adverse effects

If vitamin K is given by fast i.v. injection flushing, bronchospasm, tachycardia, and peripheral vascular collapse may result. Intravenous administration should therefore be slow. Use of the i.m. route may lead to haematoma formation at the injection site.

Interactions

Vitamin K reverses the effects of the coumarin anticoagulants (e.g. warfarin).

VITAMINS B_{12}

Structures

Several different forms of vitamin B_{12} exist, but their structures are too complex to illustrate here.

Hydroxocobalamin (vitamin B_{12a}) is the most commonly used form in therapy.

Cyanocobalamin is not now recommended for general use in the treatment of pernicious anaemia for two reasons—firstly, because of the remote risk of worsening tobacco amblyopia and Leber's optic atrophy, and secondly, because hydroxocobalamin has a slower rate of clearance.

Mode of action

Vitamin B_{12} is required during the synthesis of purine and pyrimidine bases and their incorporation into DNA. In vitamin B_{12} deficiency maturation of the erythroid series in the marrow is slowed and a megaloblastic, macrocytic anaemia results.

Uses

Vitamin B_{12} deficiency from any cause.

Dosages

Pernicious anaemia: 1 mg initially i.m., repeated every 2–3 days to a total of 6 mg. Maintenance dose, 1 mg i.m. at three-monthly intervals.

Treatment of other causes of vitamin B_{12} deficiency is generally the same as for pernicious anaemia, but other therapy may be required (e.g. folic acid, iron, and treatment of the underlying cause).

Kinetic data

Vitamin B_{12} is not absorbed from the gastrointestinal tract unless it is bound to a cobalamin-binding glycoprotein called intrinsic factor, which is secreted by the gastric parietal cells. Intrinsic factor is absent in pernicious anaemia and after total gastrectomy; its secretion is reduced in chronic gastritis. Absorption of the vitamin B_{12}–intrinsic factor complex takes place mainly in the ileum.

Total body stores of vitamin B_{12} are 3–5 mg. Daily losses are 0·1 per cent of total body stores (i.e. $t_{1/2} = 2$ years), and thus, when total body stores are normal, daily requirements are 3–5 micrograms. There is an enterohepatic recirculation of 0·5–9 micrograms a day the reabsorption of which depends on intrinsic factor, so that daily losses may be slightly greater in pernicious anaemia when total body stores have been repleted.

About 1 microgram of the body's vitamin B_{12} is in the plasma, mostly bound to the binding proteins transcobalamins. Tissue binding and protein binding become saturated when i.m. doses of over 100 micrograms are given and then unbound hydroxocobalamin and cyanocobalamin are excreted unchanged in the urine. Since hydroxocobalamin is bound more tightly by the binding proteins than cyanocobalamin its renal clearance is less rapid and it accumulates to a greater extent.

Important adverse effects

Cobalamins are very safe. Exceptionally rarely an allergic reaction may occur.

WARFARIN

Structure

(Compare vitamin K_1.)

Mode of action

The precise mechanisms by which warfarin acts are not yet completely understood, but some of its actions are, and these can be related to its pharmacological effects.

Consider first the synthesis of the clotting factors II (prothrombin), VII, IX, and X. These are synthesized in the liver and their synthesis requires vitamin K. Although the precise role of vitamin K in the synthesis of these clotting factors is not known, it is clear that its action is required in the conversion of clotting factor precursors into 'complete' clotting factors before their release from the liver into the circulation, and their eventual activation via the clotting cascade.

During the conversion of clotting factor precursors to the 'complete' factor the reduced form of vitamin K is required. It donates protons and is itself converted to the vitamin K epoxide. It is thought that the oral anticoagulants, of which the coumarin warfarin is now the most commonly used, act by preventing the resynthesis of the reduced form of vitamin K from the vitamin K epoxide, by acting as inhibitors of the vitamin K epoxide reductase (see Fig. P12).

There are two aspects of the effect of warfarin on the prothrombin time during therapy.

(a) The direct effect of warfarin

(i) The actual degree of inhibition of the vitamin K epoxide reductase depends on the concentration of warfarin in the liver, which itself depends on the dose and the pharmacokinetic characteristics of the drug in the individual.

(ii) The rate at which warfarin produces this degree of inhibition depends on the rate of accumulation of the drug and that depends on its $t_{1/2}$ (see below).

(b) Clotting factor clearance

Obviously once warfarin has stopped clotting factor synthesis the rate at which an anticoagulant effect appears (as judged by the prothrombin time which is used to assay the various clotting factors) will depend upon the rate at which the amount of each of the clotting factors already present in the body declines. The $t_{1/2}$ of the clotting factors in the blood are: factor VII, 6 h; factor IX, 24 h; factor X, 40 h; Factor II, 60 h. Because of these differences and the long half-times of some of the factors there is a delay before the full effect of a given dose of warfarin on the prothrombin time is seen.

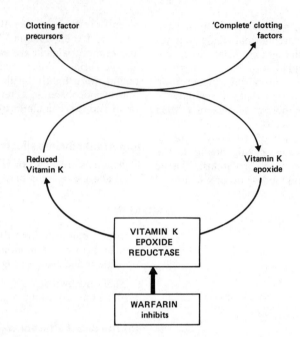

Fig. P12. The effect of vitamin K on clotting factor synthesis and the mechanism of action of warfarin in inhibiting the synthesis of factors II, VII, IX, and X.

Uses

1. Deep venous thrombosis and pulmonary embolism, prophylaxis and treatment.
2. Prevention of emboli in

(a) patients with atrial fibrillation particularly when accompanied by mitral stenosis;
(b) patients with prosthetic heart valves;
(c) patients undergoing elective cardioversion for atrial fibrillation;
(d) patients undergoing hip surgery.

The use of anticoagulants in the secondary prevention of myocardial infarction is controversial.

Monitoring therapy

Therapy with warfarin is monitored by measuring the prothrombin time as a measure of the effect of warfarin on clotting. There are various different ways of measuring the prothrombin time and of expressing the results.

(a) Thrombotest with II, VII, and X reagents

This test measures the extrinsic thromboplastin clotting system and depends on the measurement of the time to clotting of a blood sample related to the activity of factors II, VII, and X after the addition of thromboplastin. The result is expressed as a percentage, being the dilution of control blood which yields the same clotting time as the patient's blood. For example, if the prothrombin time is reported as '20 per cent' that means that the time to clotting is the same as would occur with a 20 per cent solution (i.e. 1 in 5 dilution) of control blood. The optimum range during therapy is 10–20 per cent.

(b) Prothrombin and proconvertin time (Owren)

This test is similar to the thrombotest with II, VII, and X reagents, but before carrying out the clotting time measurement the blood samples are diluted. This has the effect of diluting out the effect of any heparin in the sample but does not alter one's ability to detect the clotting factors. In fact the sensitivity for some of the factors is *increased*. This test is therefore used in patients taking both heparin and oral anticoagulants. The haematologist carrying out the test must be told if the patient is taking heparin, since a falsely low result will be obtained if this dilution is not carried out. The result of the Owren test is expressed in the same way as for the II, VII, X test and the optimum range during therapy is 10–20 per cent.

(c) One-stage prothrombin time (Quick's)

In this test factor V and fibrinogen are detected besides factors II, VII, and X, and this test is usually reserved for patients with other causes of clotting factor defects besides oral anticoagulants. The test has the additional disadvantages that it has to be performed within an hour or two of taking the blood sample and is sensitive to heparin. It is reported as the ratio of the clotting time of the patient's sample to that of the control. The optimum range during therapy is 2–3 times control.

(d) BCR (British Comparative Ratio)

Because the thromboplastin used in the prothrombin tests varies from lab to lab, an attempt has been made to standardize prothrombin time measurement throughout the country by the issue of a standard thromboplastin (the BCT) to all labs. Each lab then calibrates its own thromboplastin against the BCT and translates a test result found with its own thromboplastin (e.g. in the II, VII, X test) into the equivalent BCR value using the calibration curve. The result is expressed as the ratio of the clotting time of the patient's blood to the clotting time of the control sample, and the optimum range during therapy is 2–3 times normal.

Dosages

The following is a suggested regimen of treatment with warfarin:

1. Measure the prothrombin time to check its pre-treatment value. Primary liver disease and congestive cardiac failure with hepatic congestion can alter the prothrombin time and reduce warfarin requirements (see below under adverse effects).

2. Initial dose. 10 mg once daily orally with daily measurements of the prothrombin time. Change to a maintenance dose when the prothrombin time has changed to the following values:

prothrombin time (II, VII, X), 20–30 per cent;

prothrombin time (Owren), 20–30 per cent;

prothrombin time (Quick's), 1½–2 times control value;

BCR, 1½–2 times control value.

(These different measurements are discussed above under 'monitoring therapy'.)

The total initial dose required to produce these changes is usually 20–30 mg, but some patients may require more.

3. Maintenance dose. This is usually one quarter to one fifth of the total initial dose. For example, if after 3 days' treatment with warfarin 10 mg daily (i.e. a total initial dose of 30 mg) the prothrombin time (II, VII, X) has fallen to 30 per cent a daily maintenance dose of 7 mg would be used. One would expect the prothrombin time to fall to between 10 and 20 per cent within the next 2–3 days without further change in dosage. Further small dosage adjustments may, however, be necessary because of interpatient variability. Maintenance doses usually vary between 3 and 8 mg daily.

All this sounds complicated and dangerous, but in practice it turns out to be reasonably efficacious and safe if these guidelines are followed.

If after initial stabilization a change in dosage is made then it takes about 5 days for the prothrombin time to stabilize again, and dosages should generally not be altered again during that time.

Drug interactions and the effect of various diseases may alter warfarin dosage requirements (see below).

Kinetic data

Warfarin is administered as a racemic mixture of its two enantiomorphs, the $R(+)$ and $S(-)$ warfarins. Both are well absorbed but differ in other respects:

(a) Both are extensively metabolized, but at different rates. The $S(-)$ form is metabolized to 7-hydroxywarfarin and has a shorter $t_{1/2}$ (32 h) than the $R(+)$ form (54 h). The $R(+)$ form is metabolized to warfarin alcohols, which may have some anticoagulant effects.

(b) The $S(-)$ form is about four times more potent as an anticoagulant than the $R(+)$ form.

These diffences are important in some drug interactions with warfarin.

Important adverse effects

The commonest adverse effect is bleeding from any organ of the body. This effect is dose-related and usually resolves following withdrawal of the drug. In severe cases, however, vitamin K_1 (10 mg i.v.), or better fresh frozen plasma, which provides clotting factors II, VII, IX, and X, may be given.

Various fetal abnormalities occur in association with the use of warfarin in pregnancy. Its use during the first trimester is associated with a small risk of the syndrome known as chondrodysplasia punctata, in which the formation of cartilage and bone is abnormal, resulting in epiphyseal stippling and nasal hypoplasia. Its use during the third trimester, particularly after 36 weeks of gestation, is associated with retroplacental bleeding and fetal intracerebral bleeding, since fetal concentrations of clotting factors are low in comparison with maternal concentrations. It is therefore recommended that warfarin be used only during the 13th to 36th weeks of pregnancy, and that heparin, which does not cross the placenta, be used instead during the first trimester and after 36 weeks.

Influence of disease on warfarin requirements

Some diseases cause decreased warfarin requirements, and measurement of the prothrombin time before starting treatment is important.

(a) Liver function

Impairment of hepatocellular function both acutely (e.g. viral hepatitis) and chronically (e.g. cirrhosis) decreases warfarin requirements, because of interference with clotting factor synthesis.

In obstructive jaundice there is also decreased vitamin K absorption because of a lack of bile salts, necessary for vitamin K absorption, in the intestinal lumen.

(b) Congestive cardiac failure

Hepatic congestion associated with heart failure results in reduced warfarin requirements and choosing the correct dosage may be very difficult if the heart failure is successfully treated at the same time as anticoagulation is being carried out.

(c) Thyroid function

In hyperthyroidism warfarin requirements are decreased and in hypothyroidism they are increased. The mechanism is not clear but may involve alterations in the rates of clearance of clotting factors from the blood. Treatment of the thyroid disease results in a return to normal of dosage requirements.

Interactions

Drug interactions occur commonly with warfarin and can be classified by mechanism (see also Chapter 10).

(a) Absorption

Warfarin absorption, and reabsorption after biliary excretion, may be decreased by cholestyramine.

(b) Protein-binding displacement

Warfarin is very highly protein bound ($\simeq 99$ per cent), and is displaced from its protein binding sites by salicylates, chloral hydrate derivatives, sulphonamides, and phenylbutazone. The clinical relevance of such interactions is discussed in Chapter 10.

(c) Inhibition of metabolism

Phenylbutazone inhibits the metabolism of S(−) warfarin but induces the metabolism of R(+) warfarin. The overall clearance of the racemic mixture is therefore unaffected. However, because S(−) warfarin is more potent than R(+) warfarin there is potentiation of the pharmacological effect of warfarin, and serious bleeding may occur. (Phenylbutazone interacts with warfarin in other ways—it inhibits platelet aggregation, increases the likelihood of peptic ulceration, and may cause thrombocytopenia).

Other drugs which inhibit warfarin metabolism, and therefore increase its effects, include metronidazole (inhibition of S(−) warfarin metabolism only), and other drugs which are non-selective in their inhibition, including chloramphenicol, cimetidine, disulfiram, isoniazid, and alcohol (acutely).

(d) Induction of metabolism

The metabolism of warfarin is increased, and its effects reduced, by drugs which induce hepatic microsomal drug-metabolizing enzymes. These include phenytoin, phenobarbitone and primidone, carbamazepine, rifampicin, griseofulvin, and alcohol (chronically). If a patient is taking warfarin, and an enzyme-inducing drug is introduced then warfarin requirements will increase over the following few weeks. On stopping the inducing drug bleeding may occur if the dose of warfarin is not again reduced.

(e) Potentiation of the pharmacological effect

Several drugs may increase the pharmacological effect of warfarin by effects at the site of action in the liver. Such drugs include clofibrate, tetracyclines, anabolic steroids, and D-thyroxine. The mechanisms whereby these drugs potentiate the effects of warfarin are not at all clear, but the following hypotheses have been suggested:

(i) Increased affinity of warfarin for its receptor site (clofibrate, D-thyroxine, anabolic steroids).

(ii) Decreased synthesis or increased catabolism of clotting factors (anabolic steroids);

(iii) Modification of the activity of clotting factors (tetracyclines);

(iv) Decreased availability of vitamin K secondary to decreased plasma lipids (D-thyroxine, anabolic steroids).

It has also been suggested that antibiotics may decrease the availability of vitamin K by inhibiting its production by bacteria in the gut. This is unlikely to occur for two reasons: firstly, bacterial vitamin K production occurs principally in the large bowel so that only poorly absorbed antibiotics would be likely to have this effect, and secondly, bacterial vitamin K accounts for only about one third of total intake, the rest coming from food. There have been reports, however, of potentiation of warfarin by antibiotics in patients in whom there was some other reason for vitamin K deficiency (e.g. poor diet). Nonetheless if an antibiotic does not potentiate the effect of warfarin by some other mechanism (e.g. chloramphenicol, tetracyclines, sulphonamides, see above) it is unlikely to participate in an adverse interaction. Thus, antibiotics of the aminoglycoside, penicillin, and cephalosporin groups should generally be safe to use.

(f) Indirect interactions

(i) In patients on warfarin the tendency to bleed may be enhanced and haemostasis reduced by drugs which impair platelet aggregation (e.g. dipyridamole, sulphinpyrazone, and most non-steroidal anti-inflammatory drugs, such as aspirin).

(ii) Drugs which cause peptic ulceration provide a site for potential bleeding in patients on warfarin. These include most non-steroidal anti-inflammatory drugs.

Safe drugs

So numerous are drug interactions with warfarin that it is worth mentioning some drugs which appear to be safe to use in patients taking warfarin.

(a) Analgesics

For mild or moderate pain use paracetamol.

For more severe pain opiate analgesics such as morphine, diamorphine, and buprenorphine are safe.

(b) Anti-inflammatory drugs

All are hazardous because they may cause gastro-intestinal ulceration, and some inhibit platelet aggregation or displace warfarin from protein binding sites. Naproxen, ibuprofen, and indomethacin seem to be relatively safe, but whatever anti-inflammatory drug is prescribed the prothrombin time should be monitored carefully for the first few days, and careful watch kept for signs of gastro-intestinal ulceration or bleeding.

(c) Psychoactive drugs

Benzodiazepines are probably safe. The effects of tricyclic antidepressants are small and do not constitute a contra-indication to the use of warfarin; warfarin dosage requirements may be slightly reduced, however, and prothrombin time monitoring during the first week or two will allow adjustment of dose. There is little information about other antidepressants, but maprotiline seems to be safe.

FOOD AND ALCOHOL

Keep to your normal diet and do not make big changes. You may drink moderate amounts of alcohol; do not make big changes in your food and alcohol consumption.

TREATMENT

The success of your treatment depends on your taking the correct dose of anticoagulant, which varies from person to person. The dose is decided by the clinic doctor after testing your blood.

PREGNANCY

If you are pregnant, or think you may be, you should see your doctor as soon as possible.

Published by The Pharmaceutical Society of Great Britain, 1 Lambeth High Street, London SE1 7JN.

The Society acknowledges the co-operation and sponsorship of certain pharmaceutical companies which include Geigy Pharmaceuticals and WB Pharmaceuticals Limited.

ADVICE FOR PATIENTS ON ANTICOAGULANT TREATMENT

Always carry this card with you and show it to your doctor or dentist when obtaining treatment. Also show it to your pharmacist when you are having a prescription dispensed and when purchasing medicines. As the pharmacist can advise you, it is in your own interest that you purchase all medicines from a pharmacy.

BLOOD

Blood does not usually clot (coagulate) within the blood vessels. When this happens (and it may do so following illness or operation), anticoagulants are used to treat or prevent the condition by reducing the clotting power of the blood to safe levels.

KEEP YOUR TABLETS IN A SAFE PLACE WELL OUT OF THE REACH OF CHILDREN

NAME OF YOUR ANTICOAGULANT

TAKING YOUR TABLETS

Remember the name and strength of the anticoagulant you are taking and always take the correct dose. Take your tablet(s) at the same time(s) each day. If necessary, use a calendar and mark off each dose by a line through the date. In this way you will be unlikely to miss a dose.

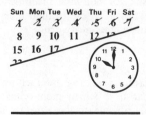

Always make sure that you have at least a week's supply of tablets in hand so that you will not run short.

NEVER miss a dose; if you do, don't take a double dose to make up for it, but tell the clinic doctor when you next go for a blood test. If more than one dose is missed, contact your general practitioner as soon as you can for advice.

ILLNESS OR BLEEDING

In the event of illness, bleeding or apparent severe bruising, consult your general practitioner immediately. If you consult another doctor who might not know that you are having anticoagulant treatment, you must tell him, especially if an operation is necessary. Always tell your dentist.

OTHER MEDICINES

Never take aspirin. Aspirin is most often included in pain relieving remedies but it may be an ingredient of other medicines. When purchasing medicines always advise the pharmacist that you are taking anticoagulants. Some other medicines may also interfere with the action of your anticoagulant, so when you see the doctor who adjusts your anticoagulant dose, always tell him about any new treatments or medicines and mention any changes, even a change of dose. Remember, oral contraceptives and laxatives are medicines. If you have any doubts about your medicines ask the pharmacist or doctor.

Fig. P13. An example of the kind of warning card which should be issued to and carried by a patient taking anticoagulants. [Reproduced with the permission of The Pharmaceutical Society of Great Britain.]

(d) Antibiotics

These are discussed above. Penicillins, cephalosporins, aminoglycosides, nitrofurantoin, nalidixic acid, and lincomycin and clindamycin are all safe. However, lincomycin and clindamycin may cause pseudomembranous colitis with consequent bleeding and care should be taken.

(e) Antihypertensives

Most drugs in this category are safe, including most diuretics, β-adrenoceptor antagonists, α-methyldopa, and vasodilators (e.g. hydralazine, prazosin).

(f) Anti-arrhythmics

Most drugs in this group are safe, the important exceptions being quinidine and amiodarone.

(g) Digitalis

The commonly used cardiac glycosides are safe.

(h) Bronchodilators

Drugs of this type are safe, but proprietary combinations containing a barbiturate should be avoided.

(i) Hypoglycaemics

Insulin is safe. Most sulphonylureas are safe but careful monitoring of prothrombin time and blood glucose is necessary especially early on. Biguanides are fibrinolytic and may indirectly enhance the effects of warfarin without a change in prothrombin time. They are probably best avoided.

XANTHINE DERIVATIVES
(THEOPHYLLINE AND RELATED DRUGS)

Structure

Theophylline:

Mode of action

Xanthine derivatives are inhibitors of the enzyme phosphodiesterase and thus inhibit the metabolism of cyclic AMP. It is not certain, however, that this effect totally underlies the mechanism of action. Attention has recently been paid to the inhibitory effects of theophylline on the actions of purinergic agonists such as adenosine, but the link between this action and the therapeutic effect of xanthines is not clear.

Uses

Reversible airways obstruction (e.g. in bronchial asthma).

Left ventricular failure:

(a) acute left ventricular failure accompanied by pulmonary oedema;

(b) in preventing attacks of acute left ventricular failure.

Dosages

Because theophylline itself is poorly soluble, it is often linked to one of a wide variety of compounds which enhance its solubility. The following compounds are in clinical use, in addition to theophylline itself, and they illustrate this principle:

aminophylline (theophylline ethylenediamine);

choline theophyllinate (choline salt);

diprophylline (dihydroxypropyl derivative);

proxyphylline (hydroxypropyl derivative).

The amounts of theophylline equivalents present in these preparations vary, and this accounts in part for differences in dosage.

The main advantages of these preparations for oral use are improved absorption, and fewer gastro-intestinal adverse effects. The latter can also be reduced by using slow-release formulations and these formulations have also been shown to produce a plasma concentration/time profile with adequate therapeutic concentrations for up to 12 h after a dose, despite the short $t_{1/2}$ of theophylline.

Aminophylline and diprophylline are also formulated for i.v. administration.

Dosages

Oral

Aminophylline, 100–300 mg repeated as necessary.

Slow-release aminophylline (Phyllocontin Continus®), 225 mg tablets, one or two tablets b.d.

Diprophylline, 200–400 mg, 3–4 times daily.

Choline theophyllinate, 200 mg, 2–3 times daily.

Proxyphylline, 300 mg t.d.s. and 600 mg at night.

Theophylline slow-release: Nuelin SA®, 175–500 mg b.d.; Theograd®, 350 mg b.d.

Suppositories

Aminophylline, 360 mg once or twice daily.

Intravenous

Aminophylline—as immediate injection given over 10 min, 250–500 mg (i.e. 5–6 mg/kg); usual maintenance dose 0·9 mg/kg/h by continuous infusion, but dosages vary in disease (see Table P10).

Table P10   *Factors affecting the clearance rate and dosages of theophylline*

1. *Factors increasing the clearance rate of theophylline*
Age: 1–16 years
Diet: Low carbohydrate, high protein intake
      Charcoal broiled meats
Cigarette smoking

2. *Factors decreasing the clearance rate of theophylline*
Age: <1 year
Diet: High carbohydrate intake
      High methylxanthine intake (e.g. coffee and tea)
Obesity (base dosages on estimated lean body weight)
Diseases: Hepatic cirrhosis
      Congestive cardiac failure
      Chronic obstructive airways disease
      Acute pulmonary oedema
      Pneumonia
      Acute febrile illnesses
Drugs: Cimetidine
      Oral contraceptives
      Erythromycin
      Troleandomycin

3. *Maintenance dosages of i.v. aminophylline (e.g. in asthma) as modified by different circumstances*

Modifying Circumstance	Rate of infusion (mg/kg lean body wt/h)
Age <50 years	0.9
Age >50 years	0.7
Co-existing chronic obstructive airways disease	0.6
Co-existing congestive cardiac failure	0.5
Liver function impaired	0.1–0.5 (depends on severity)

Kinetic data

All the derivatives mentioned above are first converted to theophylline, which is itself metabolized to inactive xanthine derivatives. Its average $t_{1/2}$ is 6 h but is very variable and is affected by many factors including diet, smoking, coffee- and tea-drinking, and liver disease (see Table P10).

Plasma concentrations of theophylline most likely to be associated with a therapeutic effect in the acute treatment of bronchial asthma are 55–110 μmol/l (10–20 μg/ml).

Important adverse effects

Adverse effects are dose-related. Nausea, vomiting, fine tremor, anxiety, and nervousness may be the first symptoms, and at higher doses tachycardia and other cardiac arrhythmias, convulsions, and coma may occur.

Interactions

Theophylline potentiates the effects of β-adrenoceptor agonists in the heart and it is thought that cardiac arrhythmias are more likely when this combination is used.

INDEX TO DRUGS LISTED IN THE PHARMACOPOEIA

GENERAL INDEX

albuterol, *see* salbutamol
alclofenac 142, 479 (table), 639
alcohol 624–8
　abuse/dependence 555, 560–1
　apparent vólume of distribution
　　40 (table)
　drugs inhibiting metabolism of 627
　effects 634–6
　glycol poisoning 583 (table)
　interactions 164 (table), 165 (table), 170
　　(table), 171 (table), 274 (table), 628
　　with centrally-acting drugs 168, 170
　　　(table)
　　with chlorpropamide 447 (table)
　　with disulfiram 165, 170 (table)
　kinetic data 627
　liver damage 384 (table)
　medical uses 626–7
　metabolic pathway 627 (fig.)
　metabolic tolerance 75
　methanol poisoning 582, 583 (table)
　in migraine 507, 510
　porphyria precipitated by 130 (table)
　protein binding 21 (table)
　respiratory depression induced by
　　363 (table)
　road accidents,blood concentrations
　　and 625 (fig.)
　self-poisoning, dialysis 421 (table, n.)
　whole blood concentrations 28 (fig.)
　withdrawal syndrome 77, 144, 555, 560–1
　zero-order metabolism 28
alcuronium, *see* neuromuscular blocking
　　agents
aldosterone, *see* mineralocorticoids
aldosterone antagonists 394 (table),
　　395 (table); *see also* canrenone;
　　spironolactone
alfacalcidol
　　(1α-hydroxycholecalciferol) 408,
　　438, 770, 771
　calcium malabsorption 439
　osteomalacia, anticonvulsant-induced 439
alginates 364 (table), 365
alkalis, poisoning by 588 (table)
alkylating agents 591 (table); *see also*
　　individual names
　mechanism of action 592 (figs.)
allergens, cause of extrinsic asthma 86, 88
allergic reactions to antibiotics 273–4
allergic rhinitis, acute (hay fever) 601,
　　604–5
allergies 600–4
　drugs, *see* drug allergy
　drug therapy 604–6
　type I: immediate hypersensitivity
　　(anaphylactic reaction) 601
　type II: membrane reactive immunity
　　(cytotoxic reaction) 602–3

type III: immune complex disease 603
type IV: cell-mediated immune
　　reactions 603–4
allopurinol 71, 628–9
　adverse effects 142, 629
　ampicillin/amoxycillin rash 140
　asymptomatic hyperuricaemia 490
　gout 487, 489–90
　half-time 33 (table)
　hyperuricaemia in cancer
　　chemotherapy 596
　interactions 159, 165 (table), 165–6,
　　170 (table), 466, 491, 629
　lymphoblastic leukaemia, acute 466
　6-mercaptopurine metabolism inhibited
　　by 596, 629
　monitoring therapy with 107
　multiple myeloma 471
　myelofibrosis 465
　myelogenous leukaemia, acute 466
　myeloid leukaemia, chronic 465
　polycythaemia rubra vera 465
　in renal failure 48 (table, n.)
　uric acid stones 414
aloxiprin 479 (table)
alpha blockers, *see* α-adrenoceptor
　　antagonists
alphaxalone/alphadolone combination
　　544 (table), 547
Althesin® 547
aluminium hydroxide 407
aluminium salts 364 (table), 365 (table),
　　366–7
amantadine 277–8, 278 (table)
　Parkinson's disease 498 (tables), 499
amethocaine 551
amikacin 632–3
　adverse effects 64, 633
　infective endocarditis 340 (table)
　interactions 633
　misreading of mRNA code 74
　in pregnancy 185
　therapeutic/toxic plasma
　　concentrations 115 (table)
amiloride 394 (table), 629–30; *see also*
　　diuretics, potassium-sparing
　in renal failure 398, 420
γ-aminobutyric acid, *see* GABA
ε-aminocaproic acid 606, 630–1
aminoglutethimide 631–2
　adverse effects 631
　　hypothyroidism 437 (table)
　　myasthenic crisis 513
　'chemical adrenalectomy' 431
　ectopic ACTH production 431
　effect on steroid biosynthesis 430 (fig.)
aminoglycoside antibiotics 262 (table),
　　632–3; *see also* individual names
　adverse effects 633

Clinical pharmacology 2–256; Drug therapy 258–612; Pharmacopoeia 614–781

azlocillin 475, 723, 725
  as first choice antibiotic 269 (table)
  infective endocarditis 340 (table)
  sensitivity of organisms 270 (table)

bacillary dysentery, antibiotics for 227, 267
baclofen 514, 515, 641
bacterial endocarditis, *see* infective
  endocarditis
bacterial infections 261–76; *see also*
  antibiotics
bacterial resistance to antibiotics 97, 265
bacteriophages 265
bacteriuria, asymptomatic 412–13
Bacteroides spp. 269 (table), 270 (table)
Bactrim® 242
BAL (British Anti-Lewisite), *see*
  dimercaprol
barbiturates
  adverse effects 141, 142
    folate deficiency 463 (table)
    myasthenic crisis 513
    porphyria 130 (table)
    Stevens–Johnson syndrome 141
  charcoal haemoperfusion 575
  dependence 555, 562
  dialysis, effect of 421 (table), 575
  as hypnotics 524
  interactions 164 (table), 170 (table),
    171 (table)
  metabolic tolerance 75
  poisoning 575, 579
  status epilepticus 506
  withdrawal syndrome 78–9, 144, 555
BCG immunization 286
beclomethasone 666
  aerosol 14, 89
  allergic rhinitis (hay fever) 604
Bendectin® 156
bendrofluazide 296, 394 (table), 761
  renal calculi 414
benefit:risk ratio 227, 236–7, 471–2
benethamine penicillin 723
benorylate 479 (table), 740, 741
  gastrointestinal bleeding induced by 24
benoxaprofen, withdrawal from
    market 216
benserazide 696–7
  interactions 165 (table), 170 (table)
  combined with levodopa 14, 498 (table)
Benylin with Codeine® 350
benzathine penicillin 723
benzhexol 616–17
  Parkinsonism 499, 528
  Parkinson's disease 498 (table), 499
benzodiazepines 642–3; *see also* individual
    names
  adverse effects 642
    hyperprolactinaemia 427 (table)

anxiety 520, 524–5
  in breast milk 151 (table)
  dependence 555, 562
  epilepsy 502 (table)
  GABA, effects on 520
  half-times 524 (table)
  hepatic encephalopathy induced by 138,
    388
  as hypnotics 520, 523–4
  interactions 642
  poisoning 581
  pre-anaesthetic medication 544
  in pregnancy 149 (table), 149
  rebound phenomena 77, 144
  withdrawal syndrome 555
benzothiadiazines, *see* thiazide diuretics
benzphetamine 246
benztropine 617
  adverse effects 617
  butyrophenone poisoning 581,
    584 (table)
  chlorpromazine poisoning 581,
    584 (table)
  haloperidol poisoning 581
  interactions 617
  Parkinsonism 499, 528
  Parkinson's disease 498, 499
  phenothiazine poisoning 581, 584 (table)
  reserpine poisoning 584 (table)
benzylpenicillin (penicillin G) 723, 725
  apparent volume of distribution
    40 (table)
  congenital syphilis 423
  CSF penetration 271 (table)
  as first choice antibiotic 268 (table)
  inactivated by gastric acid and proteolytic
    enzymes 19
  infective endocarditis 275, 340 (table), 340
    pre-surgery 338 (table), 339
  meningitis 495 (table), 495
  pneumonia 350 (table)
  renal damage caused by 406 (table)
  in renal failure 406 (table)
  sensitivities of organisms 270 (table)
  stability in saline/dextrose 160 (table)
  syphilis 423
bephenium 283 (table)
beta blockers, *see* β-adrenoceptor
    antagonists
betahistine 516 (table), 638
betamethasone
  aerosol 14
  allergic rhinitis (hay fever) 604
bethanechol 616
bethanidine 619
  adverse effects 619
  hypertension 92, 292 (table), 295, 299
  interactions 163, 170 (table), 619
  in pregnancy 187

Clinical pharmacology 2–256; Drug therapy 258–612; Pharmacopoeia 614–781

carbidopa 696–7
  interactions 165 (table), 170 (table)
  combined with levodopa 14, 498 (table)
carbimazole 433, 434, 651–2
  adverse effects 652
    intrahepatic cholestasis 384 (table)
    neutropenia 140
    pancytopenia 472 (table)
  conversion to methimazole 24
  in hyperthyroidism 437
  mechanism of action 433
  monitoring therapy with 107
  in pregnancy 435–6
  thyrotoxic crisis 436
carbon dioxide
  carbon monoxide poisoning 580
  and oxygen 348–9
carbonic anhydrase inhibitors 394 (table), 395 (table)
carbon monoxide
  Parkinsonism induced by 497
  poisoning 580
carcinogenesis by drugs 145–6
  'gene toxicity' 146
  hormonal 146
  immunosuppression 146
cardiac arrest 327–8
cardiac arrhythmias 316 (table), 316–28
  DC cardioversion 321, 322, 326, 327–8
  digitalis-induced 323, 326–7
  drug therapy 316 (table), 316–20
    adverse effects 318
    choice of drug 318–20
    dose of drug 320
    drug interactions 319 (table), 319
    indicated/not indicated 317–18, 323–4
  principles underlying therapy 317–20
cardiac asystole 328
cardiac failure 328–36
  causes 330 (table)
  congestive 334–6
    adverse drug reactions 137
    choice of treatment 228, 260
    control of signs and symptoms 331–3
    drug distribution effect 23
    drug therapy 328–36
      frusemide 62 (fig.), 63, 99
    left ventricular 260, 312, 333–4
    pathophysiology 329 (fig.)
  in sinus rhythm, digoxin therapy 65–6
cardiac glycosides 652–3; *see also* individual names
  adverse effects 653
  atrial fibrillation 36 (table), 321
  cardiac failure 332
    congestive 334–5
  in heart block 319
  in hyperthyroidism 437
  in hypothyroidism 437

interactions 168 (table), 170 (table), 653
  left ventricular failure 334
  potentiation
    by hypercalcaemia 138–9
    by hypokalaemia 139
    by hypothyroidism 437
    in renal failure 47, 136–7
  sinus bradycardia 320
  specific receptor sites 22
  supraventricular tachycardia 316 (table)
  in thyroid disease 23, 137, 437
  tolerance 77
cardiogenic shock 313
cardioversion, *see* DC cardioversion
carfecillin 23, 723, 725
carotid sinus massage 322
castor oil 373 (table), 375, 569 (table)
caustic alkalis, *see* alkalis
cefaclor 653–6
cefotaxime 653–6
  acute pyelonephritis 411
cefoxitin 653–6
  adverse effects 654
  interactions 170, 654
cefuroxime 424, 653–6
cell cycle, effects of cytotoxic drugs 591–4
cell-mediated immune reactions 141–3, 603–4
cellular biochemistry, effects of cytotoxic drugs 592 (fig.)
cephalexin 653–6
  in coeliac disease 19
  renal/non-renal clearance 48 (table)
cephaloridine 654
  interactions 170 (table)
  renal damage induced by 406 (table)
  in renal failure 416 (table)
  stability in saline/dextrose 160 (table)
cephalosporins 262 (table), 653–6; *see also* individual names
  acute pyelonephritis 411
  adverse effects 654
    haemolytic anaemia 140, 473 (table)
    pseudomembranous colitis 380
  allergic responses 273
  bacterial cell wall, effect on 74
  bacterial sensitivities 655 (table)
  CSF penetration 271 (table)
  dialysis, effect of 421 (table)
  half-time 33 (table)
  infective endocarditis 340 (table)
  interactions 654
  in pregnancy 184–5
  in renal failure 48 (table, n.), 272
  as second-line agents 656
  status asthmaticus 358
  urinary tract infections, in pregnancy 413
cephalothin 654
cephamycins 653–6

Clinical pharmacology 2–256; Drug therapy 258–612; Pharmacopoeia 614–781

cephradine 653–6
cerebral oedema 496, 607
cerebral vasodilators 227
cerebrospinal fluid
    antibiotic penetration into 270–1
    microbiological examination of 267
CFSH, *see* gonadotrophins
charcoal
    activated 569–70
        digitalis poisoning 569 (table), 581
    haemoperfusion 575
        barbiturate poisoning 579
        digitalis poisoning 581
        lithium poisoning 582
        paraquat poisoning 580
chelating drugs 72–3
'chemical adrenalectomy' 431
chemical diabetes of pregnancy 185–6
chemotherapeutic agents, infective
        diseases 73–4, 261–89
chenodeoxycholic acid 391–2, 656–7
chicken pox 271, 278 (table)
children, drug therapy in 172–8
    corticosteroids, systemic 177
    dosage calculations 177–8
    growth stunting 177
    hyperkinetic children 177
    pharmaceutical factors 173
    pharmacodynamic factors 176–7
    pharmacokinetic factors 173–6
    practical matters 177
Chlamydiae 269 (table), 270 (table), 424
chloral hydrate 657
    adverse effects 657
    charcoal haemoperfusion 575
    dialysis, effects of 421 (table), 575
    insomnia 524
    interactions 170 (table), 657
    porphyria not precipitated by
        130 (table)
chloral hydrate derivatives 657; *see also*
        individual names
    adverse effects 657
    in breast milk 151 (table)
    dialysis, effect of 421 (table)
    interactions 161, 447 (table), 657
chlorambucil 591 (table), 658
    adverse effects 658
        liver damage 384 (table)
        male fertility impaired 147
        non-lymphocytic leukaemia 146
    lymphocytic leukaemia, chronic 467, 595
chloramphenicol 658–9, 668
    adverse effects 153, 659
        'grey syndrome' 25
        pancytopenia 472 (table)
    benefit:risk ratio 471–2
    in breast milk 151 (table)
    CSF penetration 271 (table)

enterohepatic recirculation 25
    as first choice antibiotic 269 (table)
    gonococcal conjunctivitis 424
    haemolysis induced by
        in G6PD deficiency 128 (table), 273
        in glutathione reductase deficiency 128
    half-time 33 (table)
    in hepatic disease 273, 387 (table)
    hepatic extraction ratio 55 (table)
    infective endocarditis 340 (table)
    interactions 159, 165 (table), 170 (table),
        274 (table), 659
    meningitis 495, 496
    methaemoglobin
        formation/reduction 128
    in newborn 175–6
    ointment 424
    pneumonia 350 (table)
    in pregnancy 149 (table), 149, 184 (table)
    protein binding 21 (table)
    ribosomal function inhibition 74
    Salmonella gastroenteritis 379
    sensitivities of organisms 270 (table)
    typhoid fever 379
chlorates, poisoning by 588 (table)
chlordiazepoxide 642–3
    adverse effects 642
        porphyria precipitation 130 (table)
    alcohol withdrawal 561
    combined with amitriptyline 15
    half-time 524 (table)
    interactions 624
    metabolism 24, 199
chlorethazine, *see* mustine
chlorhexidine 474
chlormethiazole 659–60
    adverse effects 660
    alcohol withdrawal 561
    chlorpromazine poisoning 581
    convulsions
        in meningitis 496
        in self-poisoning 567, 581, 584 (table)
    eclampsia 186, 300
    haloperidol poisoning 581
    in hepatic disease 386
    hepatic encephalopathy 138, 388
    hepatic extraction ratio 55 (table)
    interactions 660
    status epilepticus 506
    tricyclic antidepressant poisoning 578
chloroquine 280–1, 660–1
    adverse effects 145, 661
        binding to retinal melanin 23, 145
        porphyria precipitation 130 (table)
        thrombocytopenia 473 (table)
    haemolysis induced by
        in G6PD deficiency 128 (table)
        in glutathione reductase deficiency 128
    half-time 33 (table)

connective tissue diseases 142, 607, 610
Conn's syndrome (primary
　　hyperaldosteronism) 300, 431
Conova-30Ⓡ 746 (table)
constipation, *see* laxatives
contraceptives, oral, *see* oral contraceptives
controlled drugs 246
convulsions, *see* epilepsy
copper sulphate 569 (table)
coronary angiography/surgery 306–7
coronary heart disease, lipid
　　metabolism 454–5
coronary insufficiency, acute 307
corticosteroids 664–8; *see also*
　　glucocorticoids; mineralocorticoids
　Addison's disease 428–9
　adrenal adenoma, after removal of 430
　adverse effects 666–7
　　aseptic necrosis 491 (table)
　　in eyes (local application) 667
　　of inhalation 359, 667
　　non-thrombocytopenic purpura 142
　　osteoporosis 491 (table)
　　in skin (local application) 667
　anaphylactic shock 606
　angio-oedema 605
　blood dyscrasias 475
　in breast milk 151 (table)
　bronchial asthma 89, 355, 358
　cancer chemotherapy 592 (fig.)
　cerebral oedema,
　　meningitis-induced 496
　chronic active hepatitis 390
　Crohn's disease 382
　Dressler's syndrome 314
　giant cell (temporal) arteritis 538 (table)
　glomerulonephritis 408–10
　gout, acute 489
　in hepatic disease 137, 138, 387 (table)
　hypercalcaemia 440
　inhalation 89
　interactions 164 (table), 168 (table),
　　170 (table), 400, 667
　　with sulphonylureas 447 (table)
　intra-articular 482
　pericarditis 314
　polymyalgia rheumatica 538 (table)
　porphyria not precipitated by 130 (table)
　potencies, relative 666
　in pregnancy 148 (table)
　rebound phenomena 144, 491 (table)
　receptors 5, 61
　relative potencies 666
　rheumatoid arthritis 485–6
　status asthmaticus 358
　steroid-receptor complex 61
　thyrotoxic crisis 436
　tuberculosis
　　genito-urinary 413

　meningeal 497
　ulcerative colitis 381 (table), 381–2
　urticaria 605
　ureteric stricture, tubercular 413
　withdrawal
　　functional recovery after 78 (fig.)
　　muscular disorders induced by
　　　491 (table)
　withdrawal syndrome 78
corticotrophin, *see* adrenocorticotrophic
　　hormone
corticotrophins 668
cortisol, *see* hydrocortisone
cortisone 664–7
　ACTH deficiency 425
　Addison's disease 428–9
CosalgesicⓇ 578, 716
co-trifamole 755
co-trimazine 755
co-trimoxazole 669–70
　acute pyelonephritis 411
　adverse effects 670
　　pseudomembranous colitis 380
　cholera 380
　chronic airways obstruction 351–2
　in coeliac disease 19
　cystitis 411
　dialysis, effect of 421 (table)
　as first choice antibiotic 269 (table)
　gonorrhoea 424
　meningitis 495 (table), 496
　pneumonia 350 (table)
　in pregnancy 148 (table), 184 (table), 413
　prostatitis 412
　in renal failure 272, 406 (table)
　Salmonella gastroenteritis 379
　sensitivities of organisms 270 (table)
　shigellosis 378
　status asthmaticus 358
　typhoid fever 379
　urinary tract infection 411
　　in pregnancy 413
　　recurrent 412
cough suppressants 349–50
coumarins, *see also* warfarin
　interactions 164 (table), 170 (table),
　　171 (table)
　myocardial infarction, prevention of 315
　resistance to 129
counterfeit incorporation mechanism 73
cranial nerve VIII damage 64
Cremophor ELⓇ 547
crescendo angina 307
Crohn's disease 382, 391
cromoglycate (cromolyn, disodium
　　cromoglycate) 355, 359, 670
　allergic disorders 600 (table), 601 (fig.),
　　602
　allergic rhinitis (hay fever) 604

Clinical pharmacology 2–256; Drug therapy 258–612; Pharmacopoeia 614–781

bronchial asthma 88, 355, 359
powder 13
'spinhaler' 89
cryptococcosis, meningeal 285 (table),
  465 (table)
CSF, *see* cerebrospinal fluid
CSM, *see* Committee on Safety of Medicines
  (UK) 153–5, 202–3
curare compounds, *see also* neuromuscular
  blocking agents, depolarizing
  sensitivity to, in myasthenia gravis 513
Cushing's disease 429, 431
Cushing's syndrome 300, 429–31
cutaneous vasculitis 142
cyanide, poisoning by 565 (table), 580,
  585 (table), 588 (table)
cyanocobalamin 772
cyclic acetic acids 479 (table)
Cyclimorph® 715
cyclizine 637, 638
  acute myocardial infarction, vomiting
    in 311
  drug-induced vomiting 311, 536
  migraine 508 (table)
  in pregnancy 150
  vertigo 516 (table)
cyclo-oxygenase 479–80, 535
cyclopenthiazide 296, 394 (table), 761
cyclopentolate 616
cyclophosphamide 591 (table), 670–1
  adverse effects 671
    bladder cancer 146
    haemorrhagic cystitis 597 (table), 671
    male fertility impaired 147
    non-lymphocytic leukaemia 146
    respiratory disorder 363 (table)
  carcinoma of prostate 416
  dialysis, effect of 421 (table)
  glomerulonephritis 408, 409, 410
  immune suppression 600 (table), 610,
    611
  metabolism site 23
  non-Hodgkin's lymphomas 468
  Wegener's granulomatosis 410
cyclopropane 73, 548
cycloserine 361 (table), 362
cyclosporin A 600 (table), 611–12
cystinuria 414
cystitis 410, 411
cytarabine (ara-C, cytosine
    arabinoside) 591, 671–2
  counterfeit incorporation mechanism 73
  mechanism of action 592 (figs.)
  metabolism, site of 23
  myelogenous leukaemia, acute 466
cytochrome P450 163–4
cytosine arabinoside see cytarabine
cytotoxic drugs 589–99; *see also* individual
    names; cancer chemotherapy

adverse effects 595–7
  female infertility 147
  hyperuricaemia/gout 491
  pancytopenia 472 (table)
antibiotics 591 (table)
in breast milk 151 (table)
combination chemotherapy 594
counterfeit incorporation mechanism 73
immune suppression 600
monitoring therapy with 107–8, 594
in pregnancy 148 (table)
sites and mechanisms of action 590–4
toxic:therapeutic ratio 135
cytotoxic (Type II) reactions 140, 602–3

dactinomycin, *see* actinomycin D
danazol 373 (table), 375
dantrolene 131, 514, 515, 672
dapsone 673
  acetylation 122
  haemolysis induced by
    in G6PD deficiency 128 (table)
    in glutathione reductase deficiency 128
  mechanism of action 280
  methaemoglobin
    formation/reduction 128
  thrombocytopenia induced by
    473 (table)
daunorubicin 466
DC cardioversion 321, 322, 323, 326, 327–8
Debendox® 156
debrisoquine 619
  adverse effects 619
  hydroxylation, polymorphic 123, 124 (fig.)
  hypertension 92, 292 (table), 295, 299
  interactions 163, 171, (table), 619
  in pregnancy 187
decarboxylase inhibitors 166, 199, 696–7;
    see also benserazide; carbidopa
  Parkinsonism 499–500
Declaration of Helsinki (1964) 222
decongestants 604–5
deep vein thrombosis, after myocardial
    infarction 311
deferoxamine, *see* desferrioxamine
delirium tremens 77, 144, 560–1
demeclocycline (demethylchlor-
    tetracycline) 428, 758
De-Nol® 373
dependence, *see* drug dependence/abuse
depot administration 28
deprenyl, *see* selegiline
depression 525–8
  failure to respond to therapy 98
  prophylaxis 528–9
dermatophyte infections 284 (table)
desferrioxamine (deferoxamine) 673–4
  iron poisoning 569 (table), 582,
    584 (table), 588 (table)

Clinical pharmacology 2–256; Drug therapy 258–612; Pharmacopoeia 614–781

intrahepatic cholestasis   384 (table)
in breast milk   151 (table)
Campylobacter enteritis   380
as first choice antibiotic   269 (table)
half-time   33 (table)
in hepatic disease   272
infective endocarditis, pre-surgery
    338 (table)
non-gonococcal urethritis   424
pneumonia   350 (table)
ribosomal function inhibition   74
sensitivities of organisms   270 (table)
stability in saline/dextrose   160 (table)
syphilis   423
Escherichia coli   268 (table), 269 (table),
    270 (table)
meningitis   465 (table)
urinary tract infection   266
esophageal, *see* oesophageal
estrogens, *see* oestrogens
ethacrynic acid   394 (table)
adverse effects   400 (table)
    hyperuricaemia/gout   491
interactions   170 (table), 274 (table)
transport block in renal failure   399
ethambutol   276, 679
adverse effects   679
CSF penetration   271 (table)
dialysis, effect of   421 (table)
genito-urinary tuberculosis   413
half-time   33 (table)
pulmonary tuberculosis   360–2
in renal failure   48 (table, n.), 272
tuberculous meningitis   497
ethanol, *see* alcohol
ether   73, 548
ethinyloestradiol   744
combined with levonorgestrel   746, 747
combined with norethisterone   14.
    746 (table)
gonadotrophin deficiency   426
ethionamide   361 (table), 362
liver damage   384 (table)
ethosuximide   679
adverse effects   679
pancytopenia   472 (table)
porphyria precipitation   130 (table)
systemic lupus erythematosus-like
    syndrome   142, 143 (table),
    491 (table)
dosage/therapeutic plasma concentration
    ranges   504 (table)
epilepsy   502 (table), 503 (table)
ethyl alcohol, *see* alcohol
ethylene glycol, poisoning by   588 (table)
ethyloestrenol, *see* sex hormones, male
ethynodiol, *see* sex hormones, female
etomidate   544 (table), 547
eucainamide   325

eucalyptol   130 (table)
Eugynon-30®   746 (table)
Eugynon-50®   746 (table)
excretion of drugs   25–7
renal   25–7
    mechanisms of   26–7
exfoliative dermatitis   142
expectorants   350
extraction ratio, hepatic   53–4

faecal impaction   376
faecal softeners and lubricants   373 (table),
    374–5
Fansidar®   281
favism   128
fazadinium, *see* neuromuscular blocking
    agents, depolarizing
fecal, *see* faecal
female sex hormones, *see* sex hormones,
    female
fenbufen   479 (table)
fenclofenac   479 (table), 639
fenoprofen   479 (table), 481, 639
fenoterol   354
fentanyl   544
feprazone   479 (table)
ferrous salts   72, 460 (table), 693–4
absorption impaired by eggs   19
adverse effects   694
combined with folic acid   14, 460 (table)
interactions   694
monitoring therapy with   108
fertility impairment   147
fetal drug toxicity   147–50, 182–3
fever due to drugs   141
fibrinolytic drugs, *see* streptokinase;
    urokinase
first-order kinetics   29–30, 50
first-pass effect   12
first-pass metabolism   19–20, 95 (fig.)
fixed eruptions   142
flavoxate   415
contra-indications   415
flecainide   325
flucloxacillin   723, 725
adverse effects   725–6
as first choice antibiotic   268 (table)
infective endocarditis   340 (table)
interactions   726
pneumonia   350 (table)
sensitivities of organisms   270 (table)
stability in saline/dextrose   160 (table)
flucytosine   284 (table)
combined with amphotericin B, fungal
    meningitis   495 (table)
bone marrow suppression induced
    by   284
systemic mycoses   285 (table)

Clinical pharmacology 2–256; Drug therapy 258–612; Pharmacopoeia 614–781

gonadal steroids, *see* sex hormones
gonadorelin (GnRH), *see* gonadotrophins
gonadotrophins 742–4
  deficiency 425
gonococcal conjunctivitis 424
gonorrhoea 268 (table), 270 (table), 423–4
Goodpasture's syndrome 409
gout 486–91
  acute 486–7, 488–9
  blood uric acid, monitoring of 107
  drugs causing 491
  long-term 487, 489–90
  pathophysiology 487 (fig.)
  sites and mechanisms of action of
    drugs 487 (fig.)
  threatened attacks of 489
G6PD, *see* glucose-6-phosphate
  dehydrogenase
graded responses to drugs 80–4
Gramoxone® 579
granulocytopenia, *see* agranulocytosis
'grey syndrome' 25, 175, 184 (table)
griseofulvin 284 (table), 684
  absorption improved by fat 19
  adverse effects 684
  interactions 159, 164 (table), 170 (table),
    684
  porphyria precipitated by 130 (table), 273
  superficial mycoses 284 (table)
growth hormone (GH) deficiency 426
guanethidine 619
  adverse effects 619
  eye drops 436
  hypertension 92, 292 (table), 295, 299
  interactions 163, 171 (table), 619
  porphyria not precipitated by 130 (table)
Gynovlar-21® 746 (table)

haemodialysis, *see* dialysis
haemolytic anaemia, drug-induced 140,
  143, 383, 473 (table)
haemolytic anaemia, auto-immune
  607 (table)
haemoperfusion, charcoal 575
Haemophilus influenzae 266, 268 (table),
  269 (table), 270 (table)
Haemophilus influenzae meningitis 175,
  465 (table)
half-time (half-life) 32–9, 50
  drug accumulation rate in multiple
    dosing 34–7
  drug elimination time 32–4
  loading dose/maintenance dose
    relationship 37–9
  prolonged by reduced clearance 35–6,
    37 (fig.)
  of specific drugs 33 (table); *see also*
    specific drugs in the Pharmacopoeia
  uses of 32–9

haloperidol 519, 647–8
  adverse effects 70, 79, 647–8
  apparent volume of distribution
    40 (table)
  in breast milk 151 (table)
  dopamine receptor inhibition 64, 70
  elderly patients 182
  half-time 33 (table)
  interactions 648
  mania 70, 528
  poisoning 581
  schizophrenia 67, 70, 530–1
halothane 73, 544 (table), 549–50
  liver damage induced by 153,
    384, 385 (table), 548, 550
  malignant hyperthermia induced by 131
H_1 antagonists, *see* antihistamines
hashish, *see* cannabis
hay fever (acute allergic rhinitis) 601,
  604–5
HCG, *see* gonadotrophins
head and neck cancer 590 (table)
heart, *see* cardiac
hemo-, *see* haemo-
heparin 685
  acute myocardial infarction 309, 311
  adverse effects 685
    osteoporosis 491 (table)
  in breast milk 151 (table)
  contra-indications 343 (table)
  glomerulonephritis 409, 410
  half-time 33 (table)
  ileofemoral/other vein thrombosis 345–6
  non-ketotic hyperglycaemia 445
  placenta not crossed by 182–3
  in pregnancy 187
  pre-surgery 342
  protein binding 21 (table)
  pulmonary embolism 345–6
  toxic:therapeutic ratio 135
  unstable angina 307
  in venous thromboembolic disease 341–7
hepatic disorders, *see* liver *and* hepatic etc.
  below
hepatic encephalopathy 138, 387 (table),
  388, 388–9
hepatic extraction ratio 53–4
hepatitis, chronic active 390, 611
hepatitis B, immunization 286 (table),
  287 (table)
hepatolenticular degeneration (Wilson's
  disease) 498, 772
hepatotoxic drugs 383–6, 387 (table)
hereditary angio-oedema 139, 605
heroin, *see* diamorphine
Herpes simplex 277, 278 (table)
Herpes zoster 277, 278 (table)
histamine (H_1)-receptor antagonists, *see*
  antihistamines

Clinical pharmacology 2–256; Drug therapy 258–612; Pharmacopoeia 614–781

mefruside   292 (table), 394 (table)
megaloblastic anaemia   463 (table)
melanoma, malignant   590 (table)
melphalan   591 (table), 703–4
  adverse effects   146, 704
  interactions   704
  multiple myeloma   470
membrane reactive immunity (cytotoxic
    reaction)   140, 602–3
meninges, antibiotic penetration of   270
meningitis   268–9 (table), 495
  diagnosis   267
  tuberculous   496–7
meningococcus *see Neisseria meningitidis*
menotrophin *see* gonadotrophins
mepacrine
  haemolytic anaemia induced by
    in G6PD deficiency   128 (table)
    in glutathione reductase deficiency   128
  methaemoglobin
    formation/reduction   128
  thrombocytopenia induced by   473 (table)
meperidine *see* pethidine
mepivacaine   551, 552
meprobamate
  charcoal haemoperfusion   575
  dialysis, effect of   421 (table)
  adverse effects
    pancytopenia   472 (table)
    porphyria precipitation   130 (table)
    purpura, non-thrombocytopenic   142
    thrombocytopenia   473 (table)
mepyramine   70, 638
6-mercaptopurine   591 (table), 640–1
  adverse effects   641
    intrahepatic cholestasis   384 (table)
  interactions   165 (table), 165–6,
    170 (table), 641
  lymphoblastic leukaemia, acute 466–7, 598
  mechanism of action   592 (figs.)
mercury, poisoning by   588 (table)
mesna   671
mesterolone   749, 750
mestranol   748
  combined with norethisterone
    746 (table)
metabolism of drugs   23–5
  first-pass   19–20
metaraminol   606
metformin   441 (table), 447, 643
methadone   713, 716–17
  opiate dependence   715–16
  pain   541
  porphyria not precipitated by   130 (table)
  terminal malignant disease   542
methaemoglobin reductase
    deficiency   128–9
methanol, poisoning by   421 (table, n.),
    582, 588 (table)

methaqualone   421 (table), 575
methchloroethamine *see* mustine
methicillin   406 (table)
methimazole   652; *see also* carbimazole
  intrahepatic cholestasis induced by
    384 (table)
  mechanism of action   433
  in pregnancy   436
  in thyroid disease   137, 434, 437
methionine   578
methohexitone   544 (table), 546–7
methotrexate   591 (table), 597 (table),
    704–5
  adverse effects   363 (table), 384 (table),
    463 (table), 597 (table), 704
  bone marrow toxicity, reversal of   596,   704
  dialysis, effect of   421 (table)
  immune suppression   600 (table), 610
  interactions   165 (table), 166 (table), 167,
    170 (table), 705
  intrathecal   467, 595, 598
  lymphoblastic leukaemia, acute   466–7,
    598
  mechanism of action   592 (figs.)
  monitoring therapy with   107
  plasma drug concentrations   111 (table)
  in pregnancy   148 (table)
  psoriasis   611
  in renal failure   48 (table, n.)
  toxic:therapeutic ratio   135
methoxyflurane   73, 544 (table)
  liver damage   384 (table)
  malignant hyperthermia induced by   131
  phaeochromocytoma removal   431
methyl alcohol, *see* methanol
methylcellulose   373 (table)
  eye drops   436
methylclothiazide   394 (table)
α-methyldopa   705
  α-adrenergic activity   64
  adverse effects   705
    haemolytic anaemia   473 (table), 603
    hyperprolactinaemia   427 (table)
    liver damage   384 (table)
    porphyria precipitation   130 (table)
    thrombocytopenia   473 (table)
  agonist effect of α-methylnoradrenaline
  aromatic amino acid decarboxylation,
    inhibition of   64
  in breast milk   151 (table)
  dialysis, effect of   421 (table)
  combined with hydrochlorothiazide   15
  hypertension   92, 290 (table), 292 (table),
    293 (fig.), 295
  in pregnancy   300
  renal   299
  severe   298
  levodopa conversion to dopamine,
    inhibition of   64

Clinical pharmacology 2–256; Drug therapy 258–612; Pharmacopoeia 614–781

Clinical pharmacology 2–256; Drug therapy 258–612; Pharmacopoeia 614–781

Norimin® 746 (table)
Norinyl® 746 (table)
Norlestrin® 746 (table)
Norpace® 243
nortriptyline 763
    adverse effects 764
    in breast milk 151 (table)
    dialysis, effect of 421 (table)
    dose–response relationship 526
    hepatic extraction ratio 55 (table)
    interactions 171 (table), 764
    inverted U curve 111, 112 (fig.), 526
    monoamine reuptake, effect on
        521 (table)
    plasma concentrations 526
novobiocin
    bilirubin displacement 174
    in pregnancy 149 (table), 149–50
Nu-K® 732
nursing drug round 240
nystatin 74, 720–1
    in neutropenia 474–5
    superficial mycoses 284 (table)

oedema
    cardiac failure 328–36
    chronic liver disease 388–9
    diuretics, monitoring of 103
oesophageal reflux
    antacids 365
    carbenoxolone 372–3
    histamine (H₂) antagonists 371–2
oesophageal varices, bleeding 390
oestradiol, *see* oestrogens
oestriol, *see* oestrogens
oestrogens 591 (table), 744–9
    adverse effects 748–9
        gallstones 385 (table), 391–2
        hyperprolactinaemia 427 (table)
        intrahepatic cholestasis 385 (table)
        liver tumours 146, 384 (table)
    hypertension, effect on 290 (table)
    interactions 168 (table), 400, 749
    mechanisms of action 744–5
    parenteral 747
    pellet implants 28
    combined with progestogens 745–6,
        746–7; *see also* oral contraceptives
        adverse effects 748–9
        gonadotrophin deficiency 426
    thyroid funtion test interference
        437 (table)
    topical 747
    uses 745–7
oestrone, *see* oestrogens
Office of Population Censuses and Surveys
    (UK) 105, 156
oleandomycin 262 (table)
omnopon 543

Oncovin® 468
'on-off' phenomenon 500
opiate analgesics 713–16; *see also*
        individual names
    acute myocardial infarction 309, 310–11,
        312
    adverse effects 715–16
        hepatic 387 (table), 716
        respiratory 716
    angina pectoris 307
    arteriolar/venous dilatation 336 (table)
    cough suppressants 349–50
    dependence 556–8
        treatment 558, 715–6
    interactions 167, 168 (table), 716
    opioid receptors 534
    porphyria not precipitated by 130 (table)
    withdrawal syndrome 77, 556
oral contraceptives 745–7
    adverse effects 748–9
        amenorrhoea 749
        erythema nodosum 142
        gallstones 386, 749
        hypertension 290 (table)
        migraine 507, 510, 749
        pulmonary embolism 363 (table)
        thromboembolism 748
        tumours 363 (table), 748–9
    in breast milk 151 (table)
    interactions 164 (table), 171 (table),
        274 (table), 749
    thyroid function test interference
        437 (table)
    toxic:therapeutic ratio 135
oral hypoglycaemic drugs 447; *see also*
        individual names
    in breast milk 151 (table)
    hypoglycaemia induced by 448,
        588 (table)
    interactions 168 (table), 447 (table), 643,
        757
    in pregnancy 185
    toxic:therapeutic ratio 135
oral liquid solutions, bioavailability of 10
organophosphorus insecticides, poisoning
        by 581, 588 (table)
Orlest-21® 746 (table)
orphenadrine 617
    interactions 164 (table), 170 (table), 617
    Parkinsonism 498
    thyroid function test interference
        437 (table)
Ortho-novin® 746 (table)
osmotic diuretics 73
osmotic laxatives 373 (table), 375
osteomalacia 439
    anticonvulsant-induced 439
    of pregnancy 439
osteomyelitis, staphylococcal 268 (table), 271

Clinical pharmacology 2–256; Drug therapy 258–612; Pharmacopoeia 614–781

inert 193–4
mechanism of action 195–6
response to in pain 195 (fig.), 533
uses and abuses of 193–4
placental transfer of drugs 147, 182–3
plasma drug concentrations 17–18, 108–20
against time, plot interpretation 31–47
apparent volume of distribution
calculation 39–42, 51–2
clearance calculation 42–7, 52–5
half-time (half-life) calculation 32–9,
50–1
criteria for usefulness of routine
measurement 108–10
indications for measurement 111–13
compliance 190
individualizing therapy 112–13
toxicity suspected 112–13
measurement of proven/not proven
value 110–11
measurement of, in monitoring therapy
with specific drugs
aminoglycoside antibiotics 115 (table),
118–20, 633
anti-epileptic drugs 114–16
aspirin (salicylate) 115 (table), 575–6,
741
carbamazepine 115 (table), 116, 651
digitoxin 115 (table), 117, 653
digoxin 115 (table), 116–17, 653
lithium 115 (table), 117–18, 702
paracetamol 115 (table), 576–7
phenytoin 114–16, 731
theophylline 115 (table), 120, 781
plasma concentration *v.* time curves
during different dosage
regimens 34–9
steady-state concentrations 34–8, 113
timing of blood sample for correct
interpretation 113–14
plasmapheresis 409, 471, 511, 513, 514
plasma volume expanders 566
plasmids 265
platelet aggregation, reduction of 61, 315
platinum, *see* cisplatin
pneumococcal pneumonia
antibiotics 268 (table), 350–1
pathophysiology 85–6
pneumococcal infection, acute
bronchitis 266
pneumococcus, *see Streptococcus
pneumoniae*
poliomyelitis immunization 286 (table),
287 (table)
polyarteritis nodosa 142, 611
glomerulonephritis 410
polycythaemia rubra vera 464–5
polymixin B, interaction 168
polymyalgia rheumatica 610

polythiazide 394 (table)
population therapy 104–5
porphyria 129–31
drugs precipitating/not precipitating
130 (tables), 273
portal hypertension 388
positive inotropic drugs, *see* β-adrenoceptor
agonists; amrinone; cardiac
glycosides; dopamine; xanthine
derivatives
post-herpetic neuralgia 536
post-marketing
assessment/surveillance 151–7,
201–2
potassium canrenoate 394 (table); *see also*
canrenone; spironolactone
potassium citrate 414
potassium depletion, *see also* hypokalaemia
anti-arrhythmic drugs, reduced efficacy
of 97, 317, 701, 736, 738
cardiac glycosides, increased effect
of 117, 653
drugs causing 387 (table)
potassium hydroxide, poisoning by
588 (table)
potassium iodide 435; *see also* Lugol's
iodine
potassium perchlorate 433 (fig.),
472 (table)
potassium permanganate 569 (table)
potassium-sparing diuretics see diuretics,
potassium-sparing; amiloride;
canrenone; spironolactone;
triamterene
actions on renal tubule 395 (table)
potassium in treating hypokalaemia
(potassium chloride) 396–9, 401–2,
732–4
adverse effects 733–4
hyperkalaemia 401
oesophageal ulceration 401
digitalis-induced arrhythmias
316 (table), 326
digitalis poisoning 581
formulations of 231–2, 401, 732–3
i.v. administration 404, 733
diabetes mellitus 441–2
in renal failure 416, 420
practolol 622–4
β-adrenoceptor antagonism 70
adverse effects 153, 623
angina pectoris 70
hypertension 70
in hyperthyroidism 437
interactions 623–4
supraventricular tachycardia 323
tricyclic antidepressant poisoning 578
pralidoxime, organophosphorus
poisoning 581

Clinical pharmacology 2–256; Drug therapy 258–612; Pharmacopoeia 614–781

prazepam, half-time   524 (table, n.)
prazosin   734
  combined with β-adrenoceptor
      antagonists   297
  arteriolar/venous dilatation   336 (table)
  hypertension   92, 292 (table), 293 (fig.),
      295, 297–8
    in renal failure   407
    severe   298
  in pregnancy   187
  in renal failure   420
prednisolone   664–7
  administration time   234
  adverse effects   608, 666–7
  allergic rhinitis (hay fever)   604
  anaphylactic shock   606
  angio-oedema   605
  Dressler's syndrome   314
  enema   20
  glomerulonephritis   409–10
  Hodgkin's lymphoma   598
  hypercalcaemia   440
  interactions   667
  Jarisch–Herxheimer reaction   423
  lymphoblastic leukaemia, acute   466, 598
  lymphocytic leukaemia, chronic   467
  multiple myeloma   470
  myasthenia gravis   513–14
  non-Hodgkin's lymphomas   468
  oral therapy   608
  polymyalgia rheumatica   610
  temporal (giant cell) arteritis   610
  tuberculous meningitis   497
  ulcerative colitis   381 (table), 381, 382
  urticaria   605
prednisone combined with
      phenylbutazone   14–15
pre-eclampsia (toxaemia of
      pregnancy)   186, 300
pregnancy, drug therapy   182–7
  adverse effects on fetus and
      neonate   147–50, 182–3
  anaemia   184, 696–4
  antibiotic therapy   184–5
  anticoagulation   187, 776
  diabetes mellitus   185–6, 452
  drugs to avoid   148–50, 184 (table)
  epilepsy   187, 505
  hypertension
    chronic   186–7, 300
    pre-eclamptic   186, 300
  hyperthyroidism   185, 435–6
  maternal pharmacokinetics   183–4
  placental transfer of drugs   147, 182–3
  practical problems   184–7
  protein binding   22
  urinary tract infection   184–5, 412, 413
  vaccines   288, 289
  vomiting   370

pre-infarction angina   307
prescribing principles   227–37
  benefit:risk ratio   227, 236–7
  dosage regimens   232–4
    clearance, use of in calculating   46–7
    nomograms as guidelines   234–5
    renal impairment, adjustments
      in   417–9
    timing   234
    volume of distribution, use of in
      planning   41–2
  drug, choice of   228–30
  drug therapy indicated/not
      indicated   227, 267, 291–2, 322
  duration of treatment   235–6
  formulation, choice of   231–2
  route of administration, choice of   230–1
prescription form FP10 (UK)   241 (fig.)
Prescription Pricing Authority (UK)   155,
      157
prescription writing   238–47
  abbreviations   247
  controlled drugs   246
  proprietary names *v.* approved
      names   242–6
  sources of information about   251
preventing disease in the population   104–5
Priadel®   96, 702
prilocaine   551, 552
primaquine   280–1
  haemolysis induced by
    in G6PD deficiency   128 (table)
    in glutathione reductase deficiency   128
  methaemoglobin
    formation/reduction   128
primidone   502 (table), 503 (table), 726–7
  dialysis, effect of   412 (table)
  dosage/therapeutic plasma concentration
      range   504 (table)
  epilepsy   502 (table), 503 (table)
  pancytopenia induced by   472 (table)
Primotestan Depot®   750
Prinzmetal angina   303
probenecid   71, 735
  active tubular secretion of penicillin
      inhibited by   27
  adverse effects   735
  gout   487, 489
  haemolysis induced by
    in G6PD deficiency   128 (table)
    in glutathione reductase deficiency   128
  hyperuricaemia   490
  interactions   159, 167, 170 (table), 735
  methaemoglobin
      formation/reduction   128
  combined with penicillin
    in infective endocarditis   340
    in gonorrhoea   423
    in renal failure   416 (table)

Clinical pharmacology 2–256; Drug therapy 258–612; Pharmacopoeia 614–781

Clinical pharmacology 2–256; Drug therapy 258–612; Pharmacopoeia 614–781